July 22–24, 2013
Montréal, Québec, Canada

I0131991

**Association for
Computing Machinery**

Advancing Computing as a Science & Profession

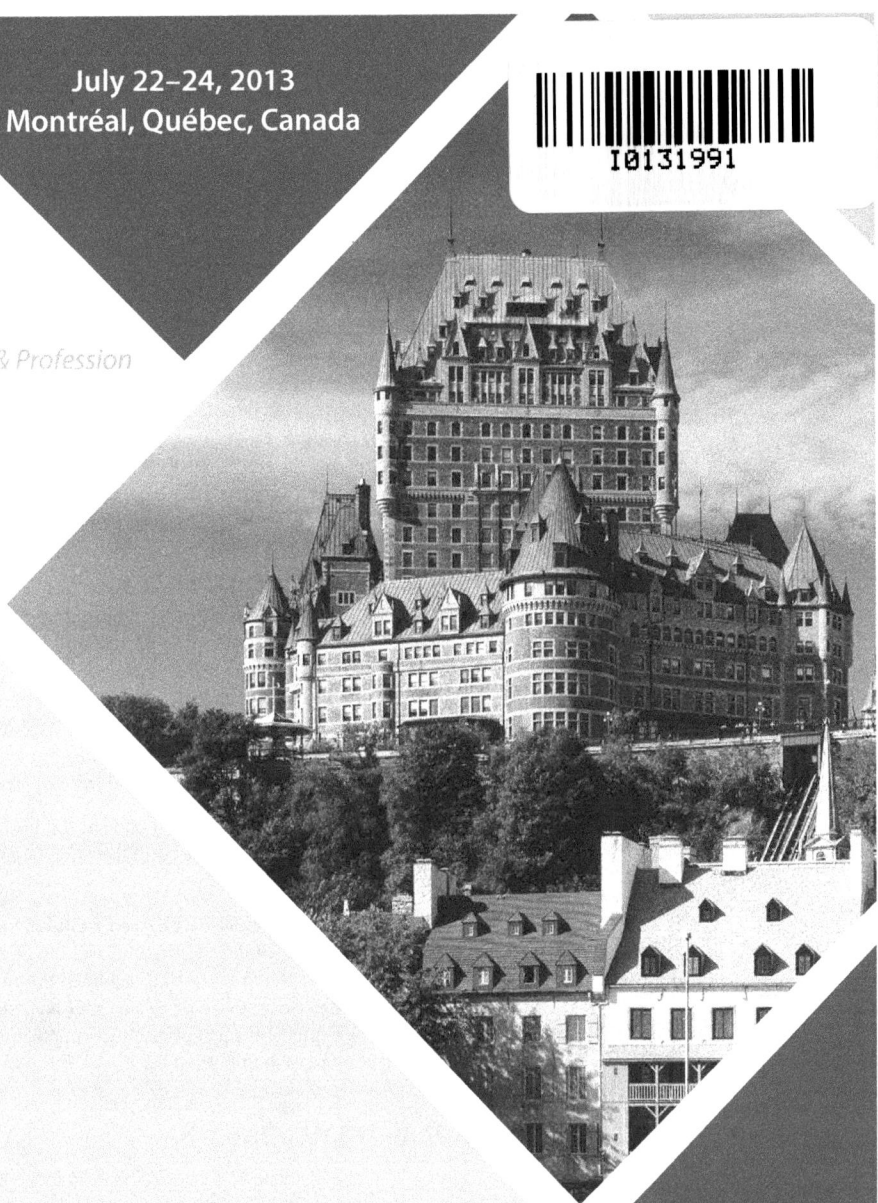

PODC'13

Proceedings of the 2013 ACM Symposium on
Principles of Distributed Computing

Sponsored by:
ACM SIGOPS and ACM SIGACT

Supported by:
Akamai, IBM, Microsoft Research, and Oracle Labs

Association for Computing Machinery

Advancing Computing as a Science & Profession

The Association for Computing Machinery
2 Penn Plaza, Suite 701
New York, New York 10121-0701

Notice to Past Authors of ACM-Published Articles

ISBN: 978-1-4503-2065-8

ACM Order Number : 536130

Additional copies may be ordered prepaid from:

ACM Order Department
PO Box 30777
New York, NY 10087-0777, USA

Phone: 1-800-342-6626 (USA and Canada)
+1-212-626-0500 (Global)
Fax: +1-212-944-1318
E-mail: acmhelp@acm.org
Hours of Operation: 8:30 am – 4:30 pm ET

Printed in the USA

PODC'13 Chair's Welcome

It is our great pleasure to welcome you to the *2013 ACM Symposium on Principles of Distributed Computing – PODC'13.* This year's symposium continues its tradition of being the premier forum for presentation of research on all aspects of distributed computing, including the theory, design, implementation and applications of distributed algorithms, systems and networks. During the years PODC has been the stage where many landmark results that have increased our understanding of this exciting and, in the Internet era, fundamental research endeavor have been presented. In the best tradition of theoretical discovery, the insights that have been provided have not only elucidated fundamental conceptual issues but also found their way in the real world of systems and applications.

The call for papers attracted 145 regular submissions and 15 brief announcement only submissions. The Program Committee accepted 37 papers and 17 brief announcements that cover a wide variety of topics. Every submitted paper was read and evaluated by Program Committee members assisted by external reviewers. The final decisions regarding acceptance or rejection of each paper were made during the electronic Program Committee meeting held during April 2008. Revised and expanded versions of a few best selected papers will be considered for publication in a special issue of the journal Distributed Computing and in JACM.

The Program Committee has selected Shiri Chechik as the recipient of this year best paper award for her paper: Compact Routing Schemes with Improved Stretch. The program committee decided to share the best student paper award between two papers: Fast Byzantine Agreement, by Nicolas Braud-Santoni, Rachid Guerraoui and Florian Huc, and Upper Bound on the Complexity of Solving Hard Renaming, by Hagit Attiya, Armando Castaneda, Maurice Herlihy and Ami Paz.

Three keynote talks will be given by Nancy Lynch, Michael Merritt and Marc Snir. Nancy Lynch will give a keynote talk as this year's ACM Athena Lecturer, an honor the ACM awards each year to a preeminent woman researcher for her fundamental contributions to computer science. Finally, this year we will celebrate the 60th birthday of Yehuda Afek.

Putting together *PODC'13* was a team effort. We first thank the authors for providing the content of the program. We are grateful to the Program Committee and the sub-reviewers, who worked very hard in reviewing papers and providing feedback for authors. The help of the Steering Committee and of the Conference Committee was timely and invaluable. Finally, we thank our sponsors, ACM SIGOPS, and ACM SIGACT and our generous corporate supporters, IBM, Microsoft Research, Oracle labs, and Akamai.

We hope that you will find this program interesting and thought-provoking and that the symposium will provide you with a valuable opportunity to share ideas with other researchers from institutions around the world.

Gadi Taubenfeld
PODC'13 Program Chair

Table of Contents

Session 4: Distributed Algorithms and Their Complexity

Session Chair: Philipp Woelfel *(University of Calgary)*

Session 5: Brief Announcements

Session Chair: Phillip Gibbons *(Intel Research - Pittsburgh)*

Session 6: Distributed Algorithms and Their Complexity

Session Chair: Fabian Kuhn *(University of Freiburg)*

Session 7: Fault Tolerance in Distributed Systems

Session Chair: Chryssis Georgiou *(University of Cyprus)*

Session 8: Renaming and Mutual Exclusion

Session Chair: Eric Ruppert *(York University)*

Session 9: Social and Peer to Peer Networks and Mobile Robots

Session Chair: Darek Kowalski *(University of Liverpool)*

Session 10: Byzantine Agreement and Self-Stabilization

Session Chair: Danny Hendler *(University of Liverpool)*

Session 11: Shared and Transactional Memory

Session Chair: Panagiota Fatourou *(FORTH ICS & University of Crete)*

Session 12: Radio and Wireless Networks

Session Chair: Luis Rodrigues *(INESC-ID, IST)*

Session 13: Sensor Network, Graph Algorithms and System Security

Session Chair: Seth Gilbert *(National University of Singapore)*

Author Index

PODC 2013 Symposium Organization

General Chair: Panagiota Fatourou *(FORTH ICS & University of Crete, Greece)*

Program Chair: Gadi Taubenfeld *(IDC, Israel)*

Organizing Chairs: Lata Narayanan *(Concordia University, Canada)*
Jarda Opatrny *(Concordia University, Canada)*

Publicity Chairs: Mark Tuttle *(Intel, USA)*
Christoph Lenzen *(Massachusettts Institute of Technology, USA)*

Treasurer Chair: Magnus Halldorsson *(Reykjavik University, Iceland)*

Steering Committee Chair: Alexander Shvartsman *(University of Connecticut, USA)*

Steering Committee: Panagiota Fatourou *(FORTH ICS & University of Crete, Greece)*
Pierre Fraigniaud *(CNRS & University Paris Diderot, France)*
Magnus Halldorsson *(Reykjavik University, Iceland)*
Alessandro Panconesi *(Sapienza University, Italy)*
Gadi Taubenfeld *(IDC, Israel)*
Nitin Vaidya *(University of Illinois, USA)*

Program Committee: James Anderson *(University of North Carolina at Chapel Hill, USA)*
James Aspnes *(Yale University, USA)*
Roberto Baldoni *(Sapienza University, Italy)*
Carole Delporte-Gallet *(University Paris Diderot, France)*
Keren Censor-Hillel *(Massachusetts Institute of Technology, USA)*
Shlomi Dolev *(Ben Gurion University, Israel)*
Panagiota Fatourou *(FORTH ICS & University of Crete, Greece)*
Antonio Fernandez Anta *(Inst. IMDEA Networks, Spain)*
Cyril Gavoille *(University of Bordeaux, France)*
Chryssis Georgiou *(University of Cyprus, Cyprus)*
Phil Gibbons *(Intel Research-Pittsburgh, USA)*
Seth Gilbert *(National University of Singapore, Singapore)*
Tim Harris *(Oracle Labs-Cambridge, UK)*
Danny Hendler *(Ben Gurion University, Israel)*
Prasad Jayanti *(Dartmouth College, USA)*
Flavio Junqueira *(Yahoo! Research, Spain)*
Amos Korman *(CNRS & University Paris Diderot, France)*
Dariusz Kowalski *(University of Liverpool, UK)*
Fabian Kuhn *(University of Freiburg, Germany)*
Sergio Rajsbaum *(UNAM, Mexico)*

Additional reviewers (continued):

Aniket Kate	Maria Potop-Butucaru
Iordanis Kerenedis	Ravi Prakash
Valerie King	Kirk Pruhs
Marek Klonowski	Leonardo Querzoni
Hirotada Kobayashi	Danny Raz
Eleftherios Kosmas	Adi Rosen
Danny Krizanc	George Saad
Petr Kuznetsov	Jared Saia
Michael Segal	Agustin Santos
João Leitão	Nuno Santos
Christoph Lenzen	Thomas Sauerwald
Du Li	Nicolas Schabanel
Cong Liu	Michael Schapira
Brendan Lucier	Christian Scheideler
Nuno Machado	Vincenzo Sciancalepore
Russell Martin	Andres Sevilla
Fabien Mathieu	Mordechai Shalom
Yves Metivier	Shantanu Sharma
Alessia Milani	Riccardo Silvestri
Neeraj Mital	Chengzheng Sun
Pascal Molli	Christopher Thraves
Mac Mollison	Corentin Travers
Oscar Morales	Gilles Tredan
Richard Mortier	Frédéric Tronel
Yoram Moses	Nitin Vaidya
Miguel Mosteiro	Damien Vergnaud
Mikhail Nesterenko	Kshitiz Verma
Calvin Newport	Laurent Viennot
Nicolas Nicolaou	Xavier Vilaça
Ilkka Norros	Rolf Wanka
Aditya Parameswaran	Bryan Ward
Merav Parter	Josef Widder
Boaz Patt-Shamir	Andreas Wiese
Andrzej Pelc	Zhou Yipeng
Franck Petit	Foivos Zakkak
Anna Philippou	Elli Zavou
David Pike	

PODC 2013 Sponsors and Supporters

Sponsors:
 **SIGOPS** **SIGACT**

Supporters:

Microsoft **Research**   Oracle Labs

Distributed Computing: An Empirical Approach

Michael Merritt
AT&T Labs Research
Florham Park, NJ
mischu@research.att.com

ABSTRACT

Michael Merritt is Executive Director of the Cross-Layer Analytics and Design Research Department, responsible for applied research directed at application, network, and infrastructure design and performance with particular emphasis on interactions that cross layers of abstraction and technology. Michael has published over thirty-five research articles, co-authored a book on database concurrency control, holds five patents, and served for many years as an area editor of Distributed Computing and the Journal of the ACM. He is a recognized expert in distributed computing, computer security, and network traffic analysis. He has taught at Georgia Tech, MIT, Stevens Institute of Technology, and Columbia University.

Categories and Subject Descriptors:

C.2.4 [Computer-Communication Networks]: Distributed Systems - *operating systems*

Keywords: Cross-layer interactions, empirical approach

Athena Lecture: Distributed Computing Theory for Wireless Networks and Mobile Systems

Nancy A. Lynch
Massachusetts Institute of Technology
Department of Electrical Engineering and Computer Science
32 Vassar Street
02139 Cambridge, USA
lynch@csail.mit.edu

ABSTRACT

Modern distributed computer systems are based on platforms that change dynamically. Many of these platforms utilize wireless communication, and many involve mobile nodes. These systems must handle complications like changing sets of participants, changing connectivity, and message collisions with resulting losses. Consequently, designing and analyzing algorithms for these systems is very hard.

What I would like to see is a *comprehensive theory* for dynamic distributed systems, and particularly for wireless networks and mobile systems. Such a theory would start with plausible physical network models. It would allow us to design and analyze low-level communication protocols, algorithms for data-oriented and control-oriented applications, and everything in between. The theory would identify key problems and sub-problems, and would include algorithms, algorithm design principles, ways of composing algorithms to build more elaborate algorithms, abstraction layers, lower bound theorems, impossibility results, and theorems comparing the power of different platforms. And all of this should rest on a common concurrency theory foundation.

Most of this talk will be devoted to a high-level overview of my research group's work in the past few years on theory for dynamic systems, especially wireless networks and mobile systems. I will first describe our work on algorithms for networks with reliable communication channels—algorithms for managing data, communicating, computing functions, and coordinating robots—and then our work on algorithms for wireless networks with channels that exhibit message collisions and losses. Although this work provides many pieces for the needed theory, a great deal of work is still needed. I will close by describing what remains to be done.

Categories and Subject Descriptors

F.2.m [**Analysis of Algorithms and Problem Complexity**]: Miscellaneous

General Terms

Algorithms, Theory

Keywords

distributed algorithms; dynamic systems; mobile systems; wireless networks

Biography

Nancy Lynch is the NEC Professor of Software Science and Engineering in the Department of Electrical Engineering and Computer Science at MIT. She heads the Theory of Distributed Systems research group in MIT's Computer Science and Artificial Intelligence Laboratory. She is also currently a Fellow at the Radcliffe Institute for Advanced Study.

Lynch received her B.S. degree in mathematics from Brooklyn College in 1968, and her PhD in mathematics from MIT in 1972. She has written numerous research articles about distributed algorithms and impossibility results, and about formal modeling and verification of distributed systems. Her best-known research contribution is the "FLP" impossibility result for distributed consensus in the presence of process failures, developed with Fischer and Paterson in 1982. Other well-known research contributions include the I/O automata mathematical system modeling frameworks, with Tuttle, Vaandrager, Segala, and Kaynar. Her recent work is focused on algorithms for mobile ad hoc networks.

Lynch has written books on "Atomic Transactions" (with Merritt, Weihl, and Fekete), on "Distributed Algorithms", and on "The Theory of Timed I/O Automata" (with Kaynar, Segala, and Vaandrager). She is an ACM Fellow, and a member of both the National Academy of Engineering and the American Academy of Arts and Sciences. With co-authors, she won the Dijkstra Prize in 2001 and again in 2007. She was co-winner of the first (2006) van Wijngaarden prize, and was awarded the 2007 Knuth Prize, and the 2010 IEEE Emanuel Piore award, as well as the 2012-2013 Athena award. Lynch has supervised over 27 PhD students and over 50 Masters students, as well as numerous postdoctoral research associates.

PODC'13, July 22–24, 2013, Montréal, Québec, Canada.
ACM 978-1-4503-2065-8/13/07.

Programming Models for Extreme-Scale Computing

Marc Snir
Argonne National Laboratory
Argonne, Illinois
snir@anl.gov

ABSTRACT
The first version of the MPI standard was released in November 1993. At the time, many of the authors of this standard, myself included, viewed MPI as a temporary solution, to be used until it is replaced by a good programming language for distributed memory systems. Almost twenty years later, MPI is the main programming model for High-Performance Computing, and practically all HPC applications use MPI, which is now in its third generation; nobody expects MPI to disappear in the coming decade. The talk will discuss some plausible reasons for this situation, and the implications for research on new programming models for Extreme-Scale Computing.

Categories and Subject Descriptors:
D.3.3 [Programming Languages]: Language Constructs and Features – *concurrent programming structures*

Keywords:
Extreme-scale computing, High-performance computing, Parallel Programming

Permission to make digital or hard copies of part or all of this work for personal or classroom use is granted without fee provided that copies are not made or distributed for profit or commercial advantage and that copies bear this notice and the full citation on the first page. Copyrights for third-party components of this work must be honored. For all other uses, contact the Owner/Author(s).

PODC'13, July 22–24, 2013, Montréal, Québec, Canada.
ACM 978-1-4503-2065-8/13/07.

On Deterministic Abortable Objects

(Extended Abstract)

Vassos Hadzilacos and Sam Toueg
Department of Computer Science
University of Toronto
{vassos,sam}@cs.toronto.edu

ABSTRACT

We define *deterministic abortable (DA) objects*, which guarantee that operations complete normally if executed solo, but may abort if executed concurrently with other operations. An operation that aborts has no effect on the object. This simple and attractive behavior is reminiscent of transactional memory, database transactions, and abortable mutual exclusion — techniques in which a process can, under contention, "bail out" of the computation without leaving a trace.

It is well-known that ordinary objects can be placed in a consensus hierarchy, based on their ability to implement n-Consensus (an object that allows up to n processes to agree on a value): an object is at level n if, together with registers, it can implement n-Consensus but not $(n+1)$-Consensus. We show that DA objects can be placed in an analogous hierarchy, called the DAC hierarchy, based on their ability to implement n-DAC, the DA counterpart of n-Consensus. We explore the similarities and differences between these two hierarchies.

It was previously known that 2-DAC is just as powerful as 2-Consensus, so the two hierarchies coincide at level 2. We show, however, that they diverge at higher levels. First, we show that ∞-DAC (which is at level ∞ of the DAC hierarchy) can not implement even 3-Consensus (which is at level 3 of the consensus hierarchy). Then we show that, for each n, n-Consensus cannot implement $(n+1)$-DAC. Finally, we show that, in general, there is no simple correspondence between the level of an object in one hierarchy and its counterpart in the other: We exhibit an ordinary object at level ∞ of the consensus hierarchy, whose DA counterpart is at level 1 in the DAC hierarchy.

Categories and Subject Descriptors

D.1.3 [**Programming Techniques**]: Concurrent Programming — *Distributed programming*; F.2.2 [**Analysis of Algorithms and Problem Complexity**]: Nonnumerical Algorithms and Problems

Keywords

shared memory, shared objects, synchronization, fault tolerance, wait freedom, consensus

1. INTRODUCTION

Motivation and related work. Linearizable wait-free shared objects [8] constitute a significant paradigm in distributed computing. Each object has a type that describes how the object behaves when accessed sequentially. When accessed concurrently, such objects behave as if they were accessed sequentially (linearizability), and they guarantee a response regardless of whether other concurrent operations are executed by processes that are fast, slow, or even crashed (wait freedom). Thus, linearizable wait-free objects provide the programmer with a powerful and convenient abstraction for building asynchronous shared-memory distributed systems that tolerate process crashes. Furthermore, they stand on a solid and well-studied theoretical foundation.

Unfortunately, in general, linearizable wait-free objects are difficult to implement efficiently. For this reason, considerable research effort has been placed on devising related concepts that present the user with weaker (though still useful) semantics but are easier to implement. One weakening of linearizable wait-free objects, proposed by Herlihy *et al.*, is to replace the wait freedom requirement by the weaker property of obstruction freedom [9]. In obstruction-free objects, an operation is required to return a response only if it runs solo (i.e., without other operations on the object executing concurrently) for sufficiently long [5]. This weakening makes obstruction-free objects easier to implement than wait-free ones in the following sense: in contrast to wait-free objects, *all* obstruction-free objects can be implemented using only shared registers.

The disadvantage of obstruction-free objects is that two concurrent operations may continually interfere with each other's execution and *never return a response*. If this happens, the caller has no opportunity to take remedial action such as wait for a while or attempt a different computation to achieve its goal. Attiya *et al.* [4] and Aguilera *et al.* [3] proposed enhancements to obstruction-free objects aimed at rectifying this disadvantage. These approaches ensure that control is eventually returned to the caller of an operation, even in the event of continual interference, while preserving the property that all objects can be implemented using only registers. Unfortunately, however, an operation that is interfered with may return control in a state where the caller of this operation does not know whether its operation actually took effect or not;[1] moreover, under continual interference from other operations, the caller may

---

[1] In [4], the operation is considered "'paused", and the caller of the paused operation is required to resume and complete it before it can do anything else; in [3], the caller has a choice: it can abandon the current operation and execute another one, perhaps on another

never be able to find out the fate of its operation. This is clearly undesirable.

Attiya *et al.* noted that an ideal enhancement to obstruction-free objects should always return control, and do so in a state where the caller always knows whether the operation it applied has taken effect or not. They proved, however, that this ideal is not compatible with the goal that all such objects be implementable using only registers, and they did not consider these objects further [4]. (We describe their result in more detail later in this section.)

In this paper we study the class of objects that display this ideal behaviour: When executed solo, an operation takes effect and returns a normal response; when executed concurrently, an operation either takes effect and returns a normal response, or it does not take effect and returns the special response "abort", denoted $\perp$. This is reminiscent of the attractive behavior of *transactional memory* [10]: a transaction that is concurrent with other ones may abort, and the caller of an aborted transaction knows that it did not take effect. We call such objects *deterministic abortable (DA)* objects.

By the result of Attiya *et al.* mentioned above, DA objects cannot be implemented using only registers. But what primitives are needed to implement them? How does each ordinary object, i.e., an object that does not abort, compare to its DA counterpart? What is the relative power of different DA objects in terms of their ability to implement other DA objects? Do DA objects form a hierarchy, analogous to the consensus hirerarchy [8] of ordinary objects? If so, how do these two hierarchies relate to each other? We now explain these questions in more detail and describe our answers for them.

To do so, we first need to recall some facts about ordinary objects. With an object of type n-Consensus, each of n processes can *propose* a value, and the object's response to every propose operation is the first proposed value. The type n-Consensus plays an important role in Herlihy's theory of ordinary linearizable wait-free objects because of the universality property it possesses: Using n-Consensus objects and registers it is possible to implement an object of any type shared by n processes [8]. Herlihy showed that ordinary types form a hierarchy, called the *consensus hierarchy*. A type T is at level n of this hierarchy, if objects of type T and registers can implement n-Consensus, but not $(n + 1)$-Consensus. Type T is at level ∞ of the hierarchy, if objects of type T and registers can implement n-Consensus for every n.

Our results. For each ordinary type T, we define its deterministic abortable counterpart, T^{da}. Objects of type T^{da} behave like objects of type T when accessed sequentially; when accessed concurrently, they may return a normal response (like T objects), which indicates that the applied operation took effect, or the special value "abort", denoted $\perp$, which indicates that the applied operation did not take effect. As with the objects defined in [9, 4, 3], we also require that a crash-interrupted operation on a DA object may interfere with other operations on this object and cause them to abort only for a finite period of time (so a process crash cannot render a DA object unusable forever).

To study the power of DA types, a natural question is whether they also form a strict hierarchy, analogous to Herlihy's consensus hierarchy for ordinary types. To answer this question, consider the DA counterpart of the n-Consensus type, which we call n-DAC. Intuitively, with an object of type n-DAC, up to n processes can *propose* a value, but a propose operation that is concurrent with other propose operations may now abort, i.e., return $\perp$, in which case it has no effect effect on the n-DAC object; if a propose operation does not abort, it behaves as in n-Consensus, and returns

———

object, or it may try to determine whether the interfered operation took effect using a special operation called "query".

the first value proposed by a non-aborted operation. It turns out that n-DAC is universal for DA types and n processes in the following sense: n-DAC objects and registers can implement an object of *any* DA type T^{da} shared by n processes (Theorem 9). Furthermore, n-DACs and registers cannot implement $(n + 1)$-DACs (Corollary 6). Thus, DA types indeed form a strict hierarchy, which we call the DAC hierarchy.

What is the relation, if any, between the DAC hierarchy (of deterministic abortable types) and Herlihy's consensus hierarchy (for ordinary types)? Attiya *et al.*, proved that a 2-DAC object and registers can implement a 2-Consensus object, and therefore *2-DAC is equivalent to 2-Consensus*. This raises the possibility that n-DAC is equivalent to n-Consensus for every n. If this holds, the DAC hierarchy and the consensus hierarchy would effectively coincide and there would be little reason to study DA types further.

We prove that, for all $n > 2$, n-DAC is *strictly weaker* than n-Consensus: n-DAC objects and registers cannot implement n-Consensus (Corollary 2). So the case of $n = 2$ where the DAC hierarchy and the consensus hierarchy coincide, is a singularity.

Given that the DAC hierarchy and the consensus hierarchy are different, a natural question is whether the DAC hierarchy is entirely contained in some finite portion of the consensus hierarchy. For example, *a priori* it is possible that 2-Consensus and registers can implement m-DAC objects *for every* m.[2] This would be good news for the implementor of DA objects, as it would imply a universal construction for DA objects based on Test-and-Set, a simple primitive that is equivalent to 2-Consensus [8] and is widely available in multiprocessor systems. So, more generally, the question is whether for some fixed n, n-Consensus and registers can implement m-DAC for every m.

We prove that this is not the case. In fact we prove that, for every n, n-Consensus and registers cannot even implement $(n + 1)$-DAC (Theorem 5).[3] It is well known that n-Consensus and registers cannot implement $(n + 1)$-Consensus [8, 12]. Since $(n + 1)$-DAC is strictly weaker than $(n + 1)$-Consensus, our impossibility result is stronger, and the proof is correspondingly harder.

So the DAC hierarchy is not subsumed within any finite portion of Herlihy's consensus hierarchy. The two hierarchies are indeed distinct and, in some sense, parallel domains that happen to meet briefly at level 2. This still leaves the possibility that there is a simple correspondence between the level of an ordinary type T in the consensus hierarchy and the level of its DA counterpart T^{da} in the DAC hierarchy, as we now explain.

In many instances, the DA counterpart of an ordinary type at level n of the consensus hierarchy is also at level n of the DAC hierarchy. For example, as we show in Section 6, the DA counterpart of n-Consensus (which is at level n of the consensus hierarchy), namely n-DAC, is at level n of the DAC hierarchy; the DA counterpart of Compare-and-Swap (which is at level ∞ of the consensus hierarchy [8]) is at level ∞ of the DAC hierarchy; and the DA counterparts of Test-and-Set, Fetch-and-Add and Stack (all of which are at level 2 of the consensus hierarchy [8]) are at level 2 of the DAC hierarchy.

Are the above facts instances of a general phenomenon? That is, is it true that for every n, if a type T is at level n of the consensus

———

[2]Indeed, in the full paper we show that 2-Consensus and registers can implement *all "one-shot" DA objects shared by m processes*, for every m. (A one-shot object can be accessed at most once by each process).

[3]A corollary of this is that the DAC hierarchy is strict: If n-Consensus objects and registers cannot implement $(n + 1)$-DACs then n-DACs (which are strictly weaker than n-Consensus objects) and registers can't either.

hierarchy, then its deterministic abortable counterpart T^{da} is also at level n of the DAC hierarchy? We show that this is not true: We exhibit a particular type, called *sticky register*, that is at level ∞ of Herlihy's consensus hierarchy but whose DA counterpart is only at level 1 of the DAC hierarchy.

Another contribution of this paper is to extend the applicability of the well-known bivalency technique for proving impossibility results [6, 13] to shared objects that can *not* be defined solely in terms of their sequential specification (e.g., objects that may abort if, and only if, they are accessed concurrently). With ordinary objects, the bivalency technique does not have to contend with concurrency: it generates algorithm executions where operations are applied to the underlying shared objects sequentially, as if every operation was atomic (and so interference due to concurrency simply does not exist). With shared objects whose behavior depends specifically on concurrency, such as abortable objects, this technique must be extended to deal *explicitly* with concurrent accesses. As we describe in Sections 3 and 6, this extension is not trivial, and, to the best of our knowledge, it is novel.

2. MODEL

Our model of computation is based on the model in Aguilera *et al.* [3], and we only summarize it informally here; a more detailed description of the model will be presented in the full paper. We consider a set Π of asynchronous processes and a set of objects $\mathcal{O}$. Processes in Π interact with objects in $\mathcal{O}$ by invoking operations on the objects and receiving corresponding responses from them. Each object has a number of ports through which processes apply their operations to, and receive responses from, the object.

Steps and histories. Each process $p \in \Pi$ executes *steps*, which are of three kinds: the invocation by p of an operation op on port i of an object $O \in \mathcal{O}$, denoted $(\text{INV}, p, op, i, O)$; the receipt by p of a response res from port i of an object $O \in \mathcal{O}$, denoted $(\text{RES}, p, res, i, O)$; or the crash of p, denoted (CRASH, p). (Crash steps are used to define the non-triviality requirement.)

A *history* H is a sequence of invocation, response, and crash steps that satisfies the following properties:

(a) For each process p, port i, and object O, the subsequence of H involving the steps of p on port i of O (i.e., steps of the form $(-, p, -, i, O)$) consists of zero or more consecutive pairs of invocation and response steps (the two steps of each pair are called *matching*), possibly followed by an invocation step.

(b) For each process p, no step of p follows (CRASH, p).

Let H be a history. An *operation execution opx* in H is either a pair consisting of an invocation of an operation and its matching response in H, in which case we say that opx is *complete* in H; or an invocation in H that has no matching response in H. Two operation executions are *concurrent* in H if neither one has a response step that precedes the invocation step of the other in H. H is *complete* if all the operation executions in H are complete. H is *wait-free* if all the operation executions invoked by processes that do not crash in H are complete.

For each process p, $H|p$ denotes the subsequence of H consisting of the steps of process p. For each object O, $H|O$ denotes the subsequence of H consisting of the steps on object O and the crash step of each process that crashes in H and has at least one step on O. H is a *p-solo* history if it consists of steps of process p only; and it is a *p-free* history if it contains no step of process p. H is a *history of object O* if $H = H|O$ — i.e., all invocation and response steps of H involve O.

Object types. Let $n \in \mathbb{Z}^+ \cup \{\infty\}$. An *object type* T is specified by a tuple (OP, RES, Q, n, δ), where OP is a set of operations, RES is a set of responses, Q is a set of states, $n \in \mathbb{Z}^+ \cup \{\infty\}$ is the

number of ports of T, and $\delta \subseteq Q \times OP \times [1..n] \times Q \times RES$ is a state transition relation. A tuple (s, op, i, s', res) in δ means that if type T is in state s when operation $op \in OP$ is invoked in its i-th port, then T can change its state to s' and return the response res. We assume that δ is total, i.e., for every $s \in Q$, $op \in O$, and $i \in [1..n]$, there is an $s' \in Q$ and a $res \in RES$ such that $(s, op, i, s', res) \in \delta$.

For each type $T = (OP, RES, Q, n, \delta)$, we define the *deterministic abortable (DA) counterpart* of T, as the type $T^{da} = (OP, RES^{da}, Q, n, \delta^{da})$ where $RES^{da} = RES \cup \{\bot\}$ for some $\bot \notin RES$, and, for every tuple (s, op, i, s', res) in δ, the state transition δ^{da} contains the following two tuples: (s, op, i, s', res) and $(s, op, i, s, \bot)$. These two tuples of δ^{da} correspond to op completing normally, and op aborting without taking effect. We say that T^{da} is a *deterministic abortable type*.

For each $n \in \mathbb{Z}^+ \cup \{\infty\}$, the n-Consensus type allows up to n processes to agree on a value proposed by one of them. Formally, n-*Consensus* is the type (OP, RES, Q, n, δ), where $OP = \{\text{PROP}(v) : v \in \mathbb{N}\}$, $RES = \mathbb{N}$, $Q = \mathbb{N} \cup \{\Lambda\}$, $n \in \mathbb{Z}^+ \cup \{\infty\}$, and $\delta = \{(\Lambda, \text{PROP}(v), i, v, v) : \forall v \in \mathbb{N}, i \in [1..n]\} \cup \{(u, \text{PROP}(v), i, u, u) : \forall u, v \in \mathbb{N}, i \in [1..n]\}$. The DA counterpart of n-Consensus is called n-DAC.

Object behaviour. Objects should be linearizable with respect to their types [11] and non-trivial [3]. Informally, a history H of an object O is *linearizable with respect to a type T (initialized to a state σ of T)*, if every operation execution in H appears to take effect instantaneously, at some point during the operation's execution interval, according to type T (initialized to σ) [11]. Informally, a history H of an object O is *non-trivial* if every operation execution that returns $\bot$ in H is concurrent with some other operation execution in H, and an operation that remains incomplete due to a crash does not cause infinitely many other operations to return $\bot$.

An object allows processes to access it concurrently by applying operations to *different* ports; the object's behaviour is unpredictable if processes apply operations concurrently to the same port. This leads us to the following definition: A history H is *legal* if for each object O and each port i of O, $H|O$ contains a response step from port i between any two invocation steps on port i.

Algorithm behaviour. Processes execute *algorithms* that use objects of certain types to *solve problems* (e.g., the n-Consensus and k-DAC problems defined in Sections 3 and 4) or to *implement objects* of different types (as we explain later in this section). The objects that an algorithm uses are called *base objects*. In an algorithm execution, each process accesses the base objects as prescribed by the algorithm.

Let $\mathcal{A}$ be an algorithm that uses base objects $O_1, O_2, \ldots$. The *history H of an execution E of $\mathcal{A}$* is the sequence of all the invocation and response steps on the objects $O_1, O_2, \ldots$ and all the crash steps that occur in E, in the order in which they occur in E.

We assume that algorithms ensure that processes access objects legally, i.e., they do not access the *same object port concurrently*. More precisely, consider an algorithm $\mathcal{A}$ that uses a sequence of base objects $O_1, O_2, \ldots$ of types $T_1, T_2, \ldots$ initialized to states $\sigma_1, \sigma_2, \ldots$, respectively. Algorithm $\mathcal{A}$ is *legal* if, for every execution E of $\mathcal{A}$, the history H of E has following property: for every finite prefix H' of H, if, for all base objects O_j the history $H'|O_j$ is linearizable with respect to T_j initialized to σ_j and nontrivial, then for all base objects O_j, $H'|O_j$ is a legal history. This property says that *if* all the base objects of the algorithm behaved correctly up to a given point of an execution, *then*, up to that point in the execution, no two processes access the same object port concurrently. Henceforth, we consider only legal algorithms.

Fair executions. Intuitively, the execution of an algorithm is fair if the scheduler does not prevent processes from taking their next step. More precisely, the execution E of an algorithm is *fair* if the following holds: If a process p takes only a finite number of steps in E, then either p completed its execution of the algorithm, or the last step of p in E is a crash or an invocation of an operation on a base object. (If the last step of process p is an invocation on a base object O_j, then p is "stuck" not because the scheduler is preventing it from taking a step but because O_j is not responding.) Henceforth, we consider only fair executions of algorithms.

Object implementations. An *implementation* I of a *target object* O from a sequence of *base objects* $O_1, O_2, \ldots$ is an algorithm given by a sequence of procedures $P_{op,i}$ that define how the operation op applied by any process to port i of O should be carried out in terms of operations applied to the ports of objects $O_1, O_2, \ldots$. In an execution E of implementation I, each process applies operations to the ports of the target object O, and carries out each operation op applied to port i of O by accessing base objects $O_1, O_2, \ldots$ as prescribed by the procedure $P_{op,i}$. The *history H of an execution E of I* is the sequence of all the invocation and response steps on the target object O and the base objects $O_1, O_2, \ldots$, and all the crash steps that occur in E, in the order in which they occur in E.

Let I be an implementation of object O from objects $O_1, O_2, \ldots$. We say that *I is an implementation of type T initialized to state σ from types $T_1, T_2, \ldots$ initialized to states $\sigma_1, \sigma_2, \ldots$* if, for every fair execution E of I, the history H of E has the following property: if (a) $H|O$ is a legal history, and (b) for every base object O_j, $H|O_j$ is linearizable with respect to T_j initialized to σ_j, non-trivial, and wait-free, then $H|O$ is linearizable with respect to T initialized to σ, non-trivial, and wait-free. We say that *T can be implemented from a set of types $\mathcal{T}$* if, for each state σ of T, there is a sequence of types $T_1, T_2, \ldots$ each of which belongs to $\mathcal{T}$, states $\sigma_1, \sigma_2, \ldots$ of $T_1, T_2, \ldots$, and an implementation I_σ such that I_σ is an implementation of T initialized to σ from $T_1, T_2, \ldots$ initialized to $\sigma_1, \sigma_2, \ldots$.

3. ∞-DAC IS WEAKER THAN 3-CONSENSUS

In this section we prove the following result:

Theorem 1 *3-Consensus cannot be implemented from ∞-DACs and registers.*

Trivially, for every $n \geq 1$, ∞-DAC implements n-DAC and, if $n > 2$, n-Consensus implements 3-Consensus. Thus, for every $n > 2$, n-Consensus is strictly stronger than its DA counterpart:

Corollary 2 *For every $n > 2$, n-Consensus cannot be implemented from n-DACs and registers.*

This is in sharp contrast to the situation when $n = 2$: As Attiya *et al.* showed, 2-Consensus *can* be implemented from registers and 2-DACs [4].

We now recall the n-Consensus *problem* (not to be confused with the n-Consensus *type*). In this problem, each of n processes has a binary input and is supposed to reach an irrevocable decision. We say that an algorithm $\mathcal{A}$ solves the *Consensus problem for n processes* (n-*Consensus problem* for short) if every fair execution of the algorithm satisfies the following properties.

- **Agreement:** If processes p decides v and process p' decides v', then $v = v'$.
- **Validity:** If a process decides v then some process's input is v.
- **Termination:** Every process that does not crash decides.

Given an object of type 3-Consensus, it is easy to solve the 3-Consensus problem. Thus, to prove Theorem 1 it suffices to show the following result.

Theorem 3 *There is no algorithm that solves the 3-Consensus problem using ∞-DACs and registers.*

For the remainder of this section, we abbreviate ∞-DAC as DAC.

We prove Theorem 3 using the bivalency technique introduced by Fischer *et al.* [6]. As we alluded in Section 1 we must address some challenges, which we now discuss. We assume, for contradiction, that there is an algorithm that solves n-Consensus using DACs and registers. We then prove that this algorithm must have a "delicate moment", in which the outcome of the decision — whether it is 0 or 1 — depends on whether some process p takes a step before or after some other process q. We then examine all the possible combinations of steps that p and q could be taking in this "delicate moment" and exclude every possibility.

In all other bivalency proofs we are familiar with, it suffices to consider executions in which the assumed algorithm accesses all base objects atomically. This simplifies the task considerably: There is no need to consider combinations of steps for p and q in which a base object is accessed concurrently. More importantly, we do not have to worry about the state of a base object when it is accessed concurrently. This is significant because the only information we have about the state of an object is derived from its type, which specifies the object's state only when the object is accessed atomically.

In our proof, however, the base objects are DACs and registers. We cannot require base objects to be accessed atomically because, without concurrent operations, DACs would effectively turn into Consensus objects, and the theorem would no longer hold: the n-Consensus problem can certainly be solved using Consensus objects! We are therefore forced to consider executions of the assumed algorithm in which the base objects are accessed concurrently. For our proof it suffices to consider executions in which the registers are accessed atomically and only the DACs can be accessed concurrently. Furthermore, it suffices to consider executions in which operations that access a DAC concurrently always return $\bot$. (As we will see in Section 6, it is not always possible to consider only such executions.) These restrictions strengthen the result: It is impossible to solve n-Consensus from DACs and registers *even* if we assume that the registers are accessed atomically and that DACs that are accessed concurrently necessarily return $\bot$. The main motivation for making these restrictions, however, is not to strengthen the result but to simplify the proof. There are fewer combinations of steps to consider, and less information that the state of DACs needs to record.

We now sketch the main ideas of the proof of Theorem 3. The detailed proof will be presented in the full paper. Suppose, for contradiction, that there is an algorithm $\mathcal{A}$ that solves the 3-Consensus problem using DACs and registers. An *event* e is a history that consists of (a) two matching steps on a register R, i.e., $e = (\text{INV}, p, -, i, R)(\text{RES}, p, -, i, R)$, or (b) an invocation on a DAC D, i.e., $e = (\text{INV}, -, -, -, D)$, or (c) a response from a DAC D, i.e., $e = (\text{RES}, -, -, -, D)$. Case (a) embodies the restriction that registers are accessed atomically. We now use the term "history" to refer specifically to sequences of such events.

A configuration represents the global state at some point of an execution of $\mathcal{A}$. Formally, a *configuration* C of $\mathcal{A}$ maps each process p to a state of p, each register R used by $\mathcal{A}$ to the present value stored in R, and each DAC D used by $\mathcal{A}$ to a pair (v, B), where $v \in \mathbb{N} \cup \{\Lambda\}$, and B is a function that maps each port i to a value in the set $\mathbb{N} \cup \{\varnothing, \kappa\}$. The first component v of D's state indicates that D is still "fresh" if $v = \Lambda$ or that its value has been set to $v \in \mathbb{N}$ by a PROP(v) operation. The function B records the "concurrency status" of each port of D:

- $B(i) = \varnothing$ means that D has responded to every operation applied to port i.
- $B(i) = u$, where $u \in \mathbb{N}$, means that some process has invoked PROP(u) on port i of D and has not received the corresponding response; furthermore, this incomplete operation has not been concurrent with any other operation on D.
- $B(i) = \kappa$ means that some process has invoked a PROP operation on port i of D and has not received the corresponding response; furthermore, this incomplete operation has been concurrent with some other operation on D.

An event e by process p that accesses object X (a DAC or a register) is *applicable* to configuration C if (a) e is the kind of event that $\mathcal{A}$ specifies that p should perform when it is in state $C(p)$, and (b) the response contained in e, if any, is the appropriate one when the state of X is $C(X)$. An event e that is applicable to a configuration C changes C to a new configuration, denoted $e(C)$. We must define how e changes C to $e(C)$, and what is the appropriate response (if any) contained in e. If e is an event on a register, the definitions of the appropriate response in e and of configuration $e(C)$ are obvious, but if e is an event on a DAC object X, these definitions are more complex because they must deal with non-atomic operations, as we now explain.

Suppose $e = (\text{RES}, p, res, i, X)$ is applicable to C. To determine the appropriate response res we must consider the state (v, B) of the DAC X in configuration C. (Note that in this case, $B(i) \neq \varnothing$.) If $B(i) = \kappa$ then $res = \bot$ (because it is a response to an operation that encountered concurrency at some point in the past); if $B(i) = u \in \mathbb{N}$ and $v = \Lambda$, then $res = u$ (because p proposed u, the operation did not encounter concurrency, and the DAC is still fresh); and if $B(i) = u \in \mathbb{N}$ and $v \neq \Lambda$, then $res = v$ (because p's operation did not encounter concurrency, but the DAC is not fresh, and its value is v). Note that with this definition an operation that encounters concurrency always returns $\bot$.

The event $e = (\text{RES}, p, res, i, X)$ changes the state of the DAC X from (v, B) in C to (v', B') in $e(C)$ as follows. If p's operation was never concurrent with any other operation, and the DAC was still fresh in C, then p sets the value of the DAC to its own proposal; otherwise, the value of the DAC remains unchanged (i.e, if $B(i) = u \in \mathbb{N}$ and $v = \Lambda$, then $v' = u$; otherwise, $v' = v$). The event e also marks the port i as unused and leaves all other ports unchanged (i.e., $B'(i) = \varnothing$ and $B'(j) = B(j)$ for all $j \neq i$).

Now suppose $e = (\text{INV}, p, \text{PROP}(u), i, X)$ is applicable to C. The event e changes the state of the DAC X from (v, B) in C to (v', B') in $e(C)$ as follows. The value of the DAC does not change (i.e., $v' = v$), but the concurrency status changes: If e is currently the only active operation on X, port i is marked with the value u that is being proposed (i.e., if for all j, $B(j) = \varnothing$, then $B'(i) = u$), and all other ports are left unchanged (i.e., $B'(j) = B(j)$ for all $j \neq i$). If, on the other hand, there are other active operations on X, then port i and all the other ports with active operations are marked as being concurrent (i.e., if for some j, $B(j) \neq \varnothing$, then $B'(i) = \kappa$ and $B'(j) = \kappa$ for all j such that $B(j) \neq \varnothing$), and all other ports are left unchanged (i.e., for all $j \neq i$, if $B(j) = \varnothing$ then $B'(j) = B(j)$).

The notion of applicability is extended from single events to histories in a standard way. If $H = e_1 e_2 \ldots e_k$ is applicable to configuration C, then $H(C)$ denotes the configuration that results when we successively apply the events of H in sequence, starting with configuration C. Let H be a history applicable to some initial con-

figuration of $\mathcal{A}$. The way we defined how events change configurations ensures that, for any base object X used by $\mathcal{A}$, $H|X$ is linearizable with respect to the type of X initialized to the state specified by $\mathcal{A}$. But if H is infinite, it is *not* necessarily the case that $H|X$ is nontrivial: If a process crashes in H after invoking a PROP operation on DAC X, by our definition of how a DAC behaves, X will return $\bot$ to all subsequent PROP operations! Thus, a crash-interrupted operation in H can cause an infinite number of aborts, contrary to the non-triviality requirement. We must take care to avoid such histories in our proof.

A configuration C' is *reachable* from configuration C if there is a finite history H applicable to C such that $H(C) = C'$. The "valence" of a configuration C is defined in the standard way [6]: For $v \in \{0, 1\}$, C is v-*valent* if there is no configuration C' such that C' is reachable from C and some process decides $\bar{v} = 1 - v$ in C'; C is *univalent* if it is 0-valent or 1-valent; and C is *bivalent* if it is not univalent.

Using arguments that are standard in bivalency proofs we can show the following:

Lemma 4 *There is a configuration C reachable from an initial configuration of $\mathcal{A}$, processes p and q, and events e_p and e'_p of p and e_q of q such that e_p and $e_q e'_p$ are applicable to C, $e_p(C)$ is 0-valent and $e_q e'_p(C)$ is 1-valent.*

Next, again using standard arguments, we can prove that in the configuration C of Lemma 4, p and q are about to access the same object X, and that X is not a register. It remains to argue that X is not a DAC either. Suppose, for contradiction, that X is a DAC. It is easy to show that if both e_p and e_q are invocations on X or both are responses from X, then e_p and e_q "commute" at C. That is, $e'_p = e_p$, $e_p e_q$ and $e_q e_p$ are both applicable to C, and $e_p e_q(C) = e_q e_p(C)$ — contradicting that $e_p(C)$ and $e_q e'_p(C)$ have different valences.

The interesting case is when e_p is an invocation on X and e_q is a response from X. (It turns out that the case when e_p is a response and e_q is an invocation is similar, with the roles of p and q reversed.) So, let $e_p = (\text{INV}, p, \text{PROP}(u), -, X)$ and $e_q = (\text{RES}, q, v, -, X)$, for some $u \in \mathbb{N}$ and $v \in \mathbb{N} \cup \{\bot\}$. Recall that e'_p is the event of p applicable to $e_q(C)$, and let e'_q be the event of q applicable to $e_p(C)$. Because processes are deterministic, we have that $e'_p = e_p$ and e'_q is a response step from X. Let $C_0 = e_p e'_q(C)$ and $C_1 = e_q e_p(C)$, and let r be the third process (other than p or q). We have: (1) C_0 is 0-valent and C_1 is 1-valent, and (2) C_0 and C_1 differ only in the states of process q and object X.

The basic idea behind the proof in this case is as follows: By (2), processes p and r cannot distinguish between C_0 and C_1; and by (1) they must distinguish between these two configurations before they can decide. Since X is the only object that is in a different state in C_0 than in C_1, starting from either of these configurations, before p and r can decide, they must access X and receive a response from it. But since both processes must access X, we can arrange for them to apply their operations on X concurrently, causing both operations to abort. This won't allow p and r to distinguish the two scenarios. So, they must access X again, and we can arrange that they do so concurrently again. We can repeat this forever, and prevent them from ever being able to decide.

There are significant hurdles to overcome for this idea to be turned into a proof: To argue that, starting from C_0 and C_1, r must receive a response from X before it can decide, *we cannot simply consider an infinite r-solo history applicable to C_0 (or C_1) and appeal to the Termination property.* This is because the last step of p before reaching C_0 and C_1 is an invocation on X, and so this incomplete operation will be concurrent with all subsequent operations of r and could cause an infinite number of r's operations on X to abort in that infinite r-solo history, contrary to the non-triviality requirement. $\mathcal{A}$ is not required to satisfy the Termination (or any other) property, however, unless the base objects behave properly — in particular, unless they are non-trivial. As noted earlier, special care must be taken to ensure that the histories involved in the proof satisfy non-triviality. The proof presented in the full paper handles these issues.

4. N-CONSENSUS IS WEAKER THAN $(N + 1)$-DAC

In this section we prove the following result:

Theorem 5 *For every* $n \geq 1$, $(n+1)$-*DAC cannot be implemented from* n-*Consensus and registers.*[4]

By Corollary 2, $(n + 1)$-DAC is strictly weaker than $(n + 1)$-Consensus. Therefore, Theorem 5 is stronger than the well-known result that $(n + 1)$-Consensus cannot be implemented from n-Consensus and registers.

Trivially, for every $n \geq 1$, n-Consensus implements n-DAC and so, as a corollary of Theorem 5 we have that the DAC hierarchy is strict:

Corollary 6 *For every* $n \geq 1$, $(n + 1)$-*DAC cannot be implemented from* n-*DACs and registers.*

As in the case of Theorem 1, it is more convenient to prove that n-Consensus and registers cannot solve a certain *problem* related to the type $(n + 1)$-DAC, rather than proving that they cannot implement that type. Finding the right formulation for this problem is the key to our proof. The desired problem must be (a) weak enough to be solvable using $(n + 1)$-DAC objects but (b) strong enough that it is not solvable using n-Consensus objects and registers. The natural choice for a bivalency proof, which in this case would be the $(n + 1)$-Consensus problem, satisfies (b) but not (a). So we must find a problem that is weaker than the $(n + 1)$-Consensus problem but not so weak that it can be solved using n-Consensus objects and registers.

Let Π be a set of k processes, and let p be a distinguished process in Π. Every process starts with a binary input and is supposed to decide irrevocably on a binary value; in addition, p can irrevocably abort instead of deciding. We say that an algorithm $\mathcal{A}$ for the processes in Π solves the *DAC problem for k processes* (k-*DAC problem* for short) if every fair execution of the algorithm satisfies the Agreement, Validity, Termination, and Nontriviality properties stated below.

- **Agreement:** If a process q decides v and a process q' decides v', then $v = v'$.
- **Validity:** If a process decides v, then v is the input of some process that does not abort.
- **Termination:** (a) If the distinguished process p does not crash, then p decides or aborts.
  (b) If a process $q \neq p$ does not crash and eventually executes solo (i.e., not interleaved with steps of other processes), then q decides.
- **Nontriviality:** If p aborts, then some process $q \neq p$ took at least one step.

---
[4]The special case $n = 1$ of this theorem follows from results of [4]. Here we prove the result for all $n \geq 1$.

We can think of the k-DAC problem as a weakening of the k-Consensus problem. As in k-Consensus, every process has a binary input value and is supposed to decide on one of the input values so that no two processes decide different values. In k-Consensus, every process that does not crash is required to decide (intuitively, processes are wait-free). In *obstruction-free* [9] k-Consensus, processes are required to reach a decision only if they do not crash and eventually execute *solo* (intuitively, processes are obstruction free). In the k-DAC problem, we require only the distinguished process p to be wait free; all other processes need only be obstruction free. Furthermore, p is not always required to decide: if it does not execute solo from the start, it is allowed to abort instead. But if p aborts, and it is the only process to have proposed a value v, then no process can decide v.

Looked at from this perspective, the k-DAC problem seems quite weak. It is known that if all processes are allowed to be obstruction free, consensus can be solved using only registers [9]. Here we allow all but one of the processes to be obstruction free; moreover, the only process required to be wait free has the option to abort instead of deciding, if it does not execute solo from the start. Despite its apparent weakness, the $(n + 1)$-DAC problem cannot be solved using n-Consensus objects and registers. In the full paper we prove this by adapting a bivalency argument to the very weak termination requirements of the $(n + 1)$-DAC problem.

Theorem 7 *For all* $n \geq 1$, *there is no algorithm that solves the* $(n + 1)$-*DAC problem using* n-*Consensus objects and registers.*

It is easy to see that the $(n + 1)$-DAC problem can be solved using an $(n + 1)$-DAC object D. Process p applies the operation PROP(u_p) to D, where u_p is its input value; if D returns $\bot$ then p aborts, otherwise p decides the value returned by D. Every other process $q \neq p$ repeatedly applies PROP(u_q) to D, where u_q is its input value, until D returns a non-$\bot$ value; if and when this happens, q decides that value. So we have:

Observation 8 *For all* $n \geq 0$, *there is an algorithm that solves the* $(n + 1)$-*DAC problem using an* $(n + 1)$-*DAC object.*

Theorem 7 and Observation 8 immediately imply Theorem 5.

5. UNIVERSAL CONSTRUCTION

Given any ordinary type T with n ports, it is easy to implement its DA counterpart T^{da} using n-DACs and registers. This universal construction of DA types is a simplification of Herlihy's *wait-free universal construction* [8] which implements any type T with n ports, using n-Consensus and registers.[5]

In Herlihy's universal construction of an ordinary object O of type T, the n processes sharing O maintain a list that represents the sequence of operations that were applied to O, in the order in which these operations were linearized. In particular, the k-th cell c in the list includes the following fields:

- $c.seq$, the sequence number of this cell in the list, i.e., k;
- $c.opn$, the k-th operation that was applied to O;
- $c.state$, the state of O after that operation;
- $c.res$, the response of O to that operation; and
- $c.next$, a pointer to the next cell in the list.

---
[5]In fact, this universal construction is very similar to the *non-blocking* version of Herlihy's universal construction, where slow processes may fail to complete their operations, but at least one process is guaranteed to complete its operations.

The first four of these fields are registers; the last one, i.e., the pointer to the next cell in the list, is an n-Consensus object. In addition to this list, each process p maintains a pointer, $head[p]$, to the last cell of the list that is knows about. Each entry of array $head$ is a register.

Initially, the list contains a single cell c_0 with $c_0.seq$ set to 0, $c_0.state$ set to the initial state of O, and $c_0.next$ set to the fresh state Λ of n-Consensus. The values of the other fields are immaterial. All elements of array $head$ point to c_0.

Roughly speaking, to apply an operation op, a process p proceeds as follows:

(1) It obtains a fresh cell, denoted $mycell$, to represent the operation op it is about to apply.

(2) It finds the cell c presently at the end of the list. Process p does this by scanning array $head$ and picking the cell with the maximum sequence number.

(3) It then fills the fields of $mycell$ with values appropriate for $mycell$ to become the successor of c in the list. Specifically, it sets $mycell.seq$ to $c.seq + 1$, $mycell.opn$ to op, and $mycell.state$ and $mycell.res$ to values determined by the state transition relation of type T.

(4) Finally, process p tries to thread $mycell$ after c, i.e., at what it believes is the end of the list. To do so, p must "win" the n-Consensus object in $c.next$ by applying PROP($mycell$) to it.

What if p fails to win the n-Consensus object in $c.next$ — i.e., if the PROP($mycell$) operation it applies to $c.next$ returns a value different from $mycell$? Of course, p could try to repeat steps (2)–(4), but it could find itself in exactly the same situation after retrying. Thus, with the above simple scheme, a slow process p may repeatedly (and forever) fail to append its own cell to the list. To prevent this from happening, Herlihy's universal construction incorporates a clever "helping" mechanism, not described here, whereby fast processes thread the operations of slow ones, so that every operation is threaded within a bounded number of steps of the process that invoked that operation.

To modify Herlihy's universal construction into one that uses n-DACs to implement any DA type, we use n-DACs instead of n-Consensus objects for the $next$ fields of the cells in the list, and we remove the helping mechanism: If a process p fails to thread its cell containing op at the end of the list, op just aborts and returns $\bot$.

In Figure 1, we present pseudo-code for the universal construction of DA types from n-DACs and registers: Given any type T with n ports, this algorithm implements an object O of type T^{da}, the DA counterpart of T, shared by n processes, using n-DACs and registers. The figure shows the pseudo-code executed by process p to apply operation op on port i of O. We assume that we are given the state transition relation of type T in the form of a function APPLY$_T(s, i, op)$, where s is a state, i is a port, and op is an operation of T, which returns a pair (s', res) such that (s, op, i, s', res) is in the state transition relation of type T — that is, s' is a possible new state and res is the associated response when operation op is applied to port i of an object of type T that is in state s.

In lines 1–7, process p obtains a fresh cell $mycell$, determines the cell c that it believes is currently at the end of the list, and prepares $mycell$ for threading after c.[6] In line 8, p attempts to thread $mycell$ at the end of the list by applying the operation PROP($mycell$) to its port of the n-DAC object in $c.next$;[7] the response of that opera-

---

[6]The fields opn and res that record, respectively, the operation that the cell represents and the response of that operation, are only used by the helping mechanism in Herlihy's construction; they are not needed for our purposes.

[7]Since n is the number of processes sharing O, each process has its own port in the n-DAC in the $next$ field of each cell.

CODE EXECUTED BY PROCESS p TO APPLY OPERATION op
ON PORT i OF A DA OBJECT OF TYPE T^{da}:

```
1   mycell := GETNEWCELL
2   for q := 1 to n do
3       if head[p].seq < head[q].seq then head[p] := head[q]
4   c := head[p]
5   mycell.seq := c.seq + 1
6   (newstate, response) := APPLY_T(c.state, i, op)
7   mycell.state := newstate
8   d := c.next : PROP(mycell)
9   if d = ⊥ then return ⊥
10  else
11      head[p] := d
12      if d = mycell then return response
13      else return ⊥
```

Figure 1: Universal construction: implementing an arbitrary deterministic abortable type T^{da} with n ports from n-DACs and registers.

tion is stored in d. If $d = mycell$, then p succeeded in appending $mycell$ to the list. Thus, op completes successfully: the state of the implemented object effectively becomes $newstate$ and op returns $response$ (line 12), consistent with the state transition function of T. If, on the other hand, $d \neq mycell$, then p failed to append $mycell$ to the list and so op itself aborts (lines 9 and 13). If $d \neq \bot$, p updates $head[p]$ to d (line 11).

This universal construction implements objects with the semantics we have defined for DA objects:

(1) An operation that aborts does not take effect.

(2) An operation that aborts is concurrent with another operation on the same object.

(3) An operation that remains incomplete due to a crash of a process cannot cause infinitely many operations to abort.

Property (1) holds because the cell representing an operation that aborts is not threaded to the list. To see why property (2) holds, we argue the contrapositive. Suppose a process p applies operation op to O and op is not concurrent with any other operation on O (this implies that no process q crashed while accessing O). We must show that op does not abort. Let c be the cell at the end of the list when p invokes op. At that time, the process q that appended c to the list had already updated $head[q]$ to point to c in line 11 (because op is not concurrent with any operation, and in particular with the operation that inserted c), and no element of $head$ points to a cell with sequence number higher than that of c (because c is the last cell in the list at that time). So after p completes the for loop of lines 2–3, $head[p]$ points to cell c, and p tries to thread its own cell immediately after c. Since no other process tries to thread a cell concurrently with op, process p wins $c.next$ and does not abort.

Finally, to see why property (3) holds, note that there are two ways that the crash of a process q can cause an operation on O invoked after q's crash to abort:

(a) *Process q crashed while proposing its cell to $c.next$.* Since $c.next$ is an n-DAC object, it satisfies the non-triviality property, and so the crash of q can cause only a finite number of operations applied to $c.next$ to abort. Therefore, in this case, the crash of q can cause only a finite number of operations on O (which attempt to thread their cell after c) to abort.

(b) *Process q crashed after successfully proposing its cell to $c.next$ and before updating $head[q]$ to point to its cell.* Thus, a process p that invokes an operation on O after q's crash will miss the new end of the list and will also apply its PROP operation to $c.next$, which is already won by q. After losing $c.next$, however, p updates c to point to the cell that q appended to the list (line 11). Consequently, p can abort *at most once* because of q's failure to update $head[q]$ after winning $c.next$. So, in this case, the crash of q can cause at most $n-1$ operations on O to abort: more precisely, for each process $p \neq q$, it can cause at most one operation of p on O to abort.

As a result of this universal construction, we have the following result:

Theorem 9 *For every $n \in \mathbb{Z}^+ \cup \{\infty\}$, every deterministic abortable type T^{da} with n ports can be implemented from n-DACs and registers.*

6. THE DAC HIERARCHY

We now explain why results in the previous sections imply that the DA types can be arranged in a hierarchy analogous to Herlihy's consensus hierarchy for ordinary types [8], and we compare these two hierarchies.

Recall that, for each $n \in \mathbb{Z}^+ \cup \{\infty\}$, the consensus hierarchy has a "level" n, which is a set of ordinary types. Type T is at level $n \in \mathbb{Z}^+$ of the consensus hierarchy if T and registers can implement n-Consensus but cannot implement $(n+1)$-Consensus; T is at level ∞ if T and registers can implement n-Consensus for all $n \in \mathbb{Z}^+$. For each n, the level of n-Consensus is obviously at least n, and, by a standard bivalency argument, it is no more than n; thus n-Consensus is at level n of the consensus hierarchy.

The *DAC hierarchy* is defined similarly. A DA type T^{da} is at level $n \in \mathbb{Z}^+$ of the DAC hierarchy if T^{da} and registers can implement n-DAC but cannot implement $(n+1)$-DAC; T^{da} is at level ∞ if T^{da} and registers can implement n-DAC for all $n \in \mathbb{Z}^+$. For each n, the level of n-DAC is obviously at least n, and, by Corollary 6, it is no more than n; so, n-DAC is at level n of the DAC hierarchy. Therefore, every level of the DAC hierarchy is nonempty.

Let T^{da}_n be any type at level $n \in \mathbb{Z}^+ \cup \{\infty\}$ of the DAC hierarchy. By definition, T^{da}_n (together with registers) implements n-DAC, so, by Theorem 9, it can implement every DA type with n ports. Thus, T^{da}_n *is universal for DA types with n ports.* Moreover, if $n \neq \infty$, T^{da}_n cannot implement $(n+1)$-DAC, and therefore it cannot implement any DA type at level $n+1$ of the DAC hierarchy.

The above properties of the DAC hierarchy are analogous to those of the consensus hierarchy. We now discuss some similarities and differences between these two hierarchies. As mentioned in Section 1, Attiya *et al.* showed that 2-Consensus can be implemented from 2-DAC and registers. Thus, 2-Consensus and 2-DAC are equivalent, and the two hierarchies effectively coincide at level 2. Since 2-Consensus is universal for ordinary types with 2 ports, the result by Attiya *et al.* immediately implies:

Observation 10 *Every type T^{da}_2 at level 2 of the DAC hierarchy (together with registers) can implement every ordinary type T with two ports of the consensus hierarchy.*

For $n > 2$, however, n-DAC does not implement n-Consensus (Corollary 2), and so the two hierarchies diverge at levels higher than 2. Lemma 11 below compares these two hierarchies at levels $n > 2$. In the following, we say that *type T is strictly weaker than type T'* if T can be implemented by T' and registers, but T' cannot be implemented by T and registers.

Lemma 11 *For $n > 2$, every DA type T^{da}_n with n ports at level n of the DAC hierarchy is strictly weaker than every ordinary type T at level n of the consensus hierarchy.*

PROOF. The lemma follows from the two claims below.
CLAIM 1: T^{da}_n *can be implemented by T and registers.* Since T is at level n of the consensus hierarchy, T and registers can implement n-Consensus, so they can implement n-DAC. By Theorem 9, n-DAC and registers can implement every DA type with n ports, including T^{da}_n. Thus T and registers can implement T^{da}_n.
CLAIM 2: T *cannot be implemented by T^{da}_n and registers.* Suppose, for contradiction, that T^{da}_n and registers can implement T. By Theorem 9, n-DAC and registers can implement T^{da}_n, so they can implement T. Since T is at level n of the consensus hierarchy, T implements n-Consensus. Thus n-DAC and registers can implement n-Consensus (for $n > 2$) — a contradiction to Corollary 2. □

By Theorem 5, for every level $n \in \mathbb{Z}^+$, there is a DA type, namely, $(n+1)$-DAC, that cannot be implemented using n-Consensus and registers. Thus, the DAC hierarchy is *not* subsumed within some finite portion of the consensus hierarchy.

In summary: (a) the two hierarchies are "parallel" structures that coincide at level 2; (b) at each level $n > 2$, the DA types with n ports in the DAC hierarchy are strictly weaker than the types at the corresponding level of the consensus hierarchy; and (c) the DAC hierarchy is not subsumed within some finite portion of the consensus hierarchy.

Another natural question about the two hierarchies is whether the level of an ordinary type T in the consensus hierarchy and the level of its DA counterpart T^{da} in the DAC hierarchy are related, and if so how. As noted above, n-Consensus is at level n of the consensus hierarchy and its DA counterpart, n-DAC, is also at level n of the DAC hierarchy. A similar phenomenon holds for several other well-known types. For example, Herlihy proved that the type Compare-And-Swap is at level ∞ of the consensus hierarchy by giving a simple implementation of ∞-Consensus from Compare-And-Swap [8]. A straightforward adaptation of this implementations shows that the DA counterpart of Compare-And-Swap is also at level ∞ of the DAC hierarchy.

Furthermore, Herlihy showed that a number of well-known types, including Test-And-Set, Fetch-And-Add, and Stack are at level 2 of the consensus hierarchy; we show that the DA counterparts of these types are also at level 2 of the DAC hierarchy.

Theorem 12 *The DA counterparts of types Test-And-Set, Fetch-And-Add, and Stack are at level 2 of the DAC hierarchy.*

PROOF SKETCH. Let T be any one of the (ordinary) types mentioned in the theorem. Herlihy gave an implementation of 2-Consensus from T and registers [8]. A simple modification of his implementation shows that T^{da} (the DA counterpart of T) and registers implement 2-DAC: The modification consists of replacing T with T^{da}, and having the PROP(v) operation on 2-DAC return $\bot$ if any of the operations on base objects of type T^{da} returns $\bot$. Thus, T^{da} is at least at level 2 of the DAC hierarchy.

To show that T^{da} is not at a level $n > 2$ in the DAC hierarchy, suppose, for contradiction, that it is. This implies that T^{da} and registers can implement 3-DAC. Afek *et al.* proved that 2-Consensus and registers can implement each of the types T under consideration [2, 1], so they can also implement their DA counterparts T^{da}. Since T^{da} and registers can implement 3-DAC, it follows that 2-Consensus and registers can implement 3-DAC, contradicting Theorem 5. □

Since for several types T, the level of T in the consensus hierarchy is the same as the level of its DA counterpart T^{da} in the DAC hierarchy, one might be tempted to formulate the following:

Conjecture 13 *For every ordinary type T, if T is at level n of the consensus hierarchy, then its DA counterpart T^{da} is also at level n of the DAC hierarchy.*

We now prove that this is, in fact, false. To do so, we exhibit an ordinary type, called *sticky register with n-ports*. For each $n \in \mathbb{Z}^+ \cup \{\infty\}$, this type is at level n of the consensus hierarchy, but its DA counterpart is at level 1 of the DAC hierarchy. Informally, a sticky register with n ports has operations READ and S-WRITE(v), for each $v \in \mathbb{N}$ (S-WRITE stands for "sticky-write"). Its set of states is $\mathbb{N} \cup \{\Lambda\}$, and its transition relation is as follows:

(1) S-WRITE(v) changes the state to v if the present state is Λ, and leaves the state unchanged otherwise. The operation always returns OK.

(2) READ has no effect on the state and returns the present state.

Deterministic abortable sticky register (DASR) is the DA counterpart of a sticky register.

Theorem 14 *For each $n \in \mathbb{Z}^+ \cup \{\infty\}$, sticky register with n ports is at level n of the consensus hierarchy, but its DA counterpart is at level 1 of the DAC hierarchy.*

It is easy to see that a sticky register with n ports can implement n-Consensus. To apply PROP(v) on port i, we apply S-WRITE(v) to the sticky register. We then apply READ to the sticky register and return the response of that operation as the response of PROP(v).

In the full paper we prove that DASR is at level 1 of the DAC hierarchy using a bivalency argument. Note that for this result we must contend with base objects that are deterministic abortable. Thus, we must consider histories in which base objects are accessed concurrently, as in Section 3. In this case, it turns out that we can assume that accesses to registers as well as write operations on DASRs are atomic; only read operations on DASRs need to be concurrent. Unlike the results of Section 3, however, we cannot restrict our attention to histories in which concurrent read operations on DASRs always return $\bot$. We must allow both the possibility of aborting and the possibility of normal completion for concurrent reads on DASRs. This is necessary and not merely a requirement for the sake of our particular proof: If concurrent read operations on DASRs were guaranteed to return $\bot$, then DASRs would be perfect "concurrency detectors" and could be used to solve consensus between two processes.

7. CONCLUSION

Deterministic abortable objects have a simple and attractive behavior: if a process tries to execute an operation and there is no interference, the operation succeeds, but if the operation is interfered with, the operation can be safely aborted without leaving any trace. This behavior is reminiscent of the semantics of transactional memory [10], database transactions [7], and abortable mutual exclusion [14] — three techniques that have been widely studied in theory and in practice.

Despite their attractive semantics, however, DA objects have received little attention. This may be because the previously known result about them, namely that 2-DACs can implement 2-Consensus, suggests that they are as powerful as ordinary objects. As we have shown, this is not true in general: the two kinds of objects have quite different properties. DA objects are, in some sense, strictly weaker than ordinary objects (e.g., ∞-DAC cannot implement even 3-Consensus), but they are not too weak (e.g., n-Consensus cannot implement even $(n + 1)$-DAC). We believe that DA objects are interesting and potentially useful, and we hope that our work will provide a basis for their further study.

Acknowledgements

We are grateful to Marcos Aguilera for fruitful discussions, and for an idea that led to the proof of Theorem 7. We thank the anonymous referees for their comments. This work was supported in part by grants from NSERC.

8. REFERENCES

[1] Y. Afek, E. Gafni, and A. Morrison. Common2 extended to stacks and unbounded concurrency. *Distributed Computing*, 20(4):239–252, 2007.

[2] Y. Afek, E. Weisberger, and H. Weisman. A completeness theorem for a class of synchronization objects (extended abstract). In *PODC '93: Proceedings of the 12th Annual ACM Symposium on Principles of Distributed Computing*, pages 159–170, 1993.

[3] M. Aguilera, S. Frolund, V. Hadzilacos, S. Horn, and S. Toueg. Abortable and query-abortable objects and their efficient implementation. In *PODC '07: Proceedings of the 26th Annual ACM Symposium on Principles of Distributed Computing*, pages 23–32, 2007.

[4] H. Attiya, R. Guerraoui, and P. Kouznetsov. Computing with reads and writes in the absence of step contention. In *DISC '05: Proceedings of the 19th International Symposium on Distributed Computing*, pages 122–136, 2005.

[5] F. Fich, M. Herlihy, and N. Shavit. On the space complexity of randomized synchronization. *J. ACM*, 45(5):843–862, 1998.

[6] M. Fischer, N. Lynch, and M. Paterson. Impossibility of distributed consensus with one faulty process. *J. ACM*, 32(2):374–382, 1985.

[7] J. Gray. Notes on data base operating systems. In *Advanced Course: Operating Systems*, pages 393–481. Lecture Notes in Computer Science 60, Springer-Verlag, 1978.

[8] M. Herlihy. Wait-free synchronization. *ACM Trans. Program. Lang. Syst.*, 13(1):124–149, 1991.

[9] M. Herlihy, V. Luchangco, and M. Moir. Obstruction-free synchronization: Double-ended queues as an example. In *ICDCS '03: Proceedings of the 23rd International Conference on Distributed Computing Systems*, pages 522–529, 2003.

[10] M. Herlihy and J. E. B. Moss. Transactional memory: Architectural support for lock-free data structures. In *Proceedings of the 20th Annual International Symposium on Computer Architecture*, pages 289–300, 1993.

[11] M. Herlihy and J. M. Wing. Linearizability: A correctness condition for concurrent objects. *ACM Trans. Program. Lang. Syst.*, 12(3):463–492, 1990.

[12] P. Jayanti and S. Toueg. Some results on the impossibility, universality, and decidability of consensus. In *WDAG '92: Proceedings of the 6th International Workshop on Distributed Algorithms*, pages 69–84, 1992.

[13] M. Loui and H. Abu-Amara. Memory requirements for agreement among unreliable asynchronous processes. In *Advances in Computing Research*, volume 4, pages 163–183. JAI Press Inc., 1987.

[14] M. Scott and W. Scherer. Scalable queue-based spin locks with timeout. In *PPoPP '01: Proceedings of the 8th ACM SIGPLAN Symposium on Principles and Practices of Parallel Programming*, pages 44–52, 2001.

Pragmatic Primitives for Non-blocking Data Structures

Trevor Brown
University of Toronto

Faith Ellen
University of Toronto

Eric Ruppert
York University

ABSTRACT

We define a new set of primitive operations that greatly simplify the implementation of non-blocking data structures in asynchronous shared-memory systems. The new operations operate on a set of Data-records, each of which contains multiple fields. The operations are generalizations of the well-known load-link (LL) and store-conditional (SC) operations called LLX and SCX. The LLX operation takes a snapshot of one Data-record. An SCX operation by a process p succeeds only if no Data-record in a specified set has been changed since p last performed an LLX on it. If successful, the SCX atomically updates one specific field of a Data-record in the set and prevents any future changes to some specified subset of those Data-records. We provide a provably correct implementation of these new primitives from single-word compare-and-swap. As a simple example, we show how to implement a non-blocking multiset data structure in a straightforward way using LLX and SCX.

Categories and Subject Descriptors

E.1 [**Data**]: Data Structures—*Distributed data structures*

Keywords

load-link/store-conditional; non-blocking; multiset

1. INTRODUCTION

Building a library of concurrent data structures is an essential way to simplify the difficult task of developing concurrent software. There are many lock-based data structures, but locks are not fault-tolerant and are susceptible to problems such as deadlock [11]. It is often preferable to use hardware synchronization primitives like compare-and-swap (CAS) instead of locks. However, the difficulty of this task has inhibited the development of *non-blocking* data structures. These are data structures which guarantee that some operation will eventually complete even if some processes crash.

Our goal is to facilitate the implementation of high-performance, provably correct, non-blocking data structures on any system that supports a hardware CAS instruction. We introduce three new operations, *load-link-extended* (LLX), *validate-extended* (VLX) and *store-conditional-extended* (SCX), which are natural generalizations of the well known *load-link* (LL), *validate* (VL) and *store-conditional* (SC) operations. We provide a practical implementation of our new operations from CAS. Complete proofs of correctness appear in [7]. We also show how these operations make the implementation of non-blocking data structures and their proofs of correctness substantially less difficult, as compared to using LL, VL, SC, and CAS directly.

LLX, SCX and VLX operate on *Data-records*. Any number of types of Data-records can be defined, each type containing a fixed number of *mutable* fields (which can be updated), and a fixed number of *immutable* fields (which cannot). Each Data-record can represent a natural unit of a data structure, such as a node of a tree or a table entry. A successful LLX operation returns a snapshot of the mutable fields of one Data-record. (The immutable fields can be read directly, since they never change.) An SCX operation by a process p is used to atomically store a value in one mutable field of one Data-record *and finalize* a set of Data-records, meaning that those Data-records cannot undergo any further changes. The SCX succeeds only if each Data-record in a specified set has not changed since p last performed an LLX on it. A successful VLX on a set of Data-records simply assures the caller that each of these Data-records has not changed since the caller last performed an LLX on it. A more formal specification of the behaviour of these operations is given in Section 3.

Early on, researchers recognized that operations accessing multiple locations atomically make the design of non-blocking data structures much easier [5, 13, 17]. Our new primitives do this in three ways. First, they operate on Data-records, rather than individual words, to allow the data structure designer to think at a higher level of abstraction. Second, and more importantly, a VLX or SCX can depend upon multiple LLXs. Finally, the effect of an SCX can apply to multiple Data-records, modifying one and finalizing others.

The precise specification of our operations was chosen to balance ease of use and efficient implementability. They are more restricted than multi-word CAS [13], multi-word RMW [1], or transactional memory [17]. On the other hand, the ability to finalize Data-records makes SCX more general than k-compare-single-swap [15], which can only change one word. We found that atomically changing one pointer and finalizing a collection of Data-records provides just enough power to implement numerous pointer-based data structures in which operations replace a small portion of the data structure. To demonstrate the usefulness of our new operations, in Section 5, we give an implementation of a simple, linearizable, non-blocking multiset based on an ordered, singly-linked list.

Our implementation of LLX, VLX, and SCX is designed for an asynchronous system where processes may crash. We assume shared memory locations can be accessed by single-word CAS, read and write instructions. We assume a safe garbage collector (as in the Java environment) that will not reallocate a memory location if any process can reach it by following pointers. This allows records to be reused.

Our implementation has some desirable performance properties. A VLX on k Data-records only requires reading k words of memory. If SCXs being performed concurrently depend on LLXs of disjoint sets of Data-records, they all succeed. If an SCX encounters no contention with any other SCX and finalizes f Data-records, then a total of $k+1$ CAS steps and $f+2$ writes are used for the SCX and the k LLXs on which it depends. We also prove progress properties that suffice for building non-blocking data structures using LLX and SCX.

2. RELATED WORK

Transactional memory [12, 17] is a general approach to simplifying the design of concurrent algorithms by providing atomic access to multiple objects. It allows a block of code designated as a transaction to be executed atomically, with respect to other transactions. Our LLX/VLX/SCX primitives may be viewed as implementing a restricted kind of transaction, in which each transaction can perform any number of reads followed by a single write and then finalize any number of words. It is possible to implement general transactional memory in a non-blocking manner (e.g., [11, 17]). However, at present, implementations of transactional memory in software incur significant overhead, so there is still a need for more specialized techniques for designing shared data structures that combine ease of use and efficiency.

Most shared-memory systems provide CAS operations in hardware. However, LL and SC operations have often been seen as more convenient primitives for building algorithms. Anderson and Moir gave the first wait-free implementation of small LL/SC objects from CAS using $O(1)$ steps per operation [3]. See [14] for a survey of other implementations that use less space or handle larger LL/SC objects.

Many non-blocking implementations of primitives that access multiple objects use the *cooperative technique*, first described by Turek, Shasha and Prakash [19] and Barnes [5]. Instead of using locks that give a process exclusive access to a part of the data structure, this approach gives exclusive access to *operations*. If the process performing an operation that holds a lock is slow, other processes can *help* complete the operation and release the lock.

The cooperative technique was also used recently for a wait-free universal construction [8] and to obtain non-blocking binary search trees [10] and Patricia tries [16]. The approach used here is similar.

Israeli and Rappoport [13] used a version of the cooperative technique to implement multi-word CAS from single-word CAS (and sketched how this could be used to implement multi-word SC operations). However, their approach applies single-word CAS to very large words. The most efficient implementation of k-word CAS [18] first uses single-word CAS to replace each of the k words with a pointer to a record containing information about the operation, and then uses single-word CAS to replace each of these pointers with the desired new value and update the status field of the record. In the absence of contention, this takes $2k+1$ CAS steps. In contrast, in our implementation, an SCX that depends on LLXs of k Data-records performs $k+1$ single-word CAS steps when there is no contention, no matter how many words each record contains. So, our weaker primitives can be significantly more efficient than multi-word CAS or multi-word RMW [1, 4], which is even more general.

If k Data-records are removed from a data structure by a multi-word CAS, then the multi-word CAS must depend on every mutable field of these records to prevent another process from concurrently updating any of them. It is possible to use k-word CAS to apply to k Data-records instead of k words with indirection: Every Data-record is represented by a single word containing a pointer to the contents of the record. To change any fields of the Data-record, a process swings the pointer to a new copy of its contents containing the updated values. However, the extra level of indirection affects all reads, slowing them down considerably.

Luchangco, Moir and Shavit [15] defined the k-compare-single-swap (KCSS) primitive, which atomically tests whether k specified memory locations contain specified values and, if all tests succeed, writes a value to one of the locations. They provided an *obstruction-free* implementation of KCSS, meaning that a process performing a KCSS is guaranteed to terminate if it runs alone. They implemented KCSS using an obstruction-free implementation of LL/SC from CAS. Specifically, to try to update location v using KCSS, a process performs $LL(v)$, followed by two collects of the other $k-1$ memory locations. If v has its specified value, both collects return their specified values, and the contents of these memory locations do not change between the two collects, the process performs SC to change the value of v. Unbounded version numbers are used both in their implementation of LL/SC and to avoid the ABA problem between the two collects.

Our LLX and SCX primitives can be viewed as multi-Data-record-LL and single-Data-record-SC primitives, with the additional power to finalize Data-records. We shall see that this extra ability is extremely useful for implementing pointer-based data structures. In addition, our implementation of LLX and SCX allows us to develop shared data structures that satisfy the non-blocking progress condition, which is stronger than obstruction-freedom.

3. THE PRIMITIVES

Our primitives operate on a collection of Data-records of various user-defined types. Each type of Data-record has a fixed number of mutable fields (each fitting into a single word), and a fixed number of immutable fields (each of which can be large). Each field is given a value when the Data-record is created. Fields can contain pointers that refer to other Data-records. Data-records are accessed using LLX, SCX and VLX, and reads of individual mutable or immutable fields of a Data-record. Reads of mutable fields are permitted because a snapshot of a Data-record's fields is sometimes excessive, and it is sometimes sufficient (and more efficient) to use reads instead of LLXs.

An implementation of LL and SC from CAS has to ensure that, between when a process performs LL and when it next performs SC on the same word, the value of the word has not changed. Because the value of the word could change and then change back to a previous value, it is not sufficient to check that the word has the same value when the LL and the SC are performed. This is known as the ABA problem. It also arises for implementations of LLX and SCX from CAS. A general technique to overcome this problem is described in Section 4.1. However, if the data structure designer can guarantee that the ABA problem will not arise (because each SCX never attempts to store a value into a field that previously contained that value), our implementation can be used in a more efficient manner.

Before giving the precise specifications of the behaviour of LLX and SCX, we describe how to use them, with the implementation of a multiset as a running example. The multiset abstract data type supports three operations: GET(key), which returns the number of occurrences of key in the multiset, INSERT($key, count$), which inserts $count$ occurrences of key into the multiset, and DELETE($key, count$), which deletes $count$ occurrences of key from the multiset and returns TRUE, provided there are at least $count$ occurrences of key in the multiset. Otherwise, it simply returns FALSE.

Suppose we would like to implement a multiset using a sorted, singly-linked list. We represent each node in the list by a Data-record with an immutable field key, which contains a key in the multiset, and mutable fields: $count$, which records the number of times key appears in the multiset, and $next$, which points to the next node in the list. The first and last elements of the list are sentinel nodes with count 0 and with special keys $-\infty$ and ∞, respectively, which never occur in the multiset.

Figure 5 shows how updates to the list are handled. Insertion behaves differently depending on whether the key is already present. Likewise, deletion behaves differently depending on whether it removes all copies of the key. For example, consider the operation DELETE($d, 2$) depicted in Figure 5(c). This operation removes node r by changing $p.next$ to point to a new copy of $rnext$. A new copy is used to avoid the ABA problem, since $p.next$ may have pointed to $rnext$ in the past. To perform the DELETE($d, 2$), a process first invokes LLXs on p, r, and $rnext$. Second, it creates a copy $rnext'$ of $rnext$. Finally, it performs an SCX that depends on these three LLXs. This SCX attempts to change $p.next$ to point to $rnext'$. This SCX will succeed only if none of p, r or $rnext$ have changed since the aforementioned LLXs. Once r and $rnext$ are removed from the list, we want subsequent invocations of LLX and SCX to be able to detect this, so that we can avoid, for example, erroneously inserting a key into a deleted part of the list. Thus, we specify in our invocation of SCX that r and $rnext$ should be *finalized* if the SCX succeeds. Once a Data-record is finalized, it can never be changed again.

LLX takes (a pointer to) a Data-record r as its argument. Ordinarily, it returns either a snapshot of r's mutable fields or FINALIZED. If an LLX(r) is concurrent with an SCX involving r, it is also allowed to fail and return FAIL. SCX takes four arguments: a sequence V of (pointers to) Data-records upon which the SCX depends, a subsequence R of V containing (pointers to) the Data-records to be fi-

nalized, a mutable field fld of a Data-record in V to be modified, and a value new to store in this field. VLX takes a sequence V of (pointers to) Data-records as its only argument. Each SCX and VLX and returns a Boolean value.

For example, in Figure 5(c), the DELETE($d, 2$) operation invokes SCX(V, R, fld, new), where $V = \langle p, r, rnext \rangle$, $R = \langle r, rnext \rangle$, fld is the next pointer of p, and new points to the node $rnext'$.

A terminating LLX is called *successful* if it returns a snapshot or FINALIZED, and *unsuccessful* if it returns FAIL. A terminating SCX or VLX is called *successful* if it returns TRUE, and *unsuccessful* if it returns FALSE. Our operations are wait-free, but an operation may not terminate if the process performing it fails, in which case the operation is neither successful nor unsuccessful. We say an invocation I of LLX(r) by a process p is *linked to* an invocation I' of SCX(V, R, fld, new) or VLX(V) by process p if r is in V, I returns a snapshot, and between I and I', process p performs no invocation of LLX(r) or SCX(V', R', fld', new') and no unsuccessful invocation of VLX(V'), for any V' that contains r. Before invoking VLX(V) or SCX(V, R, fld, new), a process must *set up* the operation by performing an LLX(r) linked to the invocation for each r in V.

3.1 Correctness Properties

An implementation of LLX, SCX and VLX is *correct* if, for every execution, there is a linearization of all successful LLXs, all successful SCXs, a subset of the non-terminating SCXs, all successful VLXs, and all reads, such that the following conditions are satisfied.

C1: Each read of a field f of a Data-record r returns the last value stored in f by an SCX linearized before the read (or f's initial value, if no such SCX has modified f).

C2: Each linearized LLX(r) that does not return FINALIZED returns the last value stored in each mutable field f of r by an SCX linearized before the LLX (or f's initial value, if no such SCX has modified f).

C3: Each linearized LLX(r) returns FINALIZED if and only if it is linearized after an SCX(V, R, fld, new) with r in R.

C4: For each linearized invocation I of SCX(V, R, fld, new) or VLX(V), and for each r in V, no SCX(V', R', fld', new') with r in V' is linearized between the LLX(r) linked to I and I.

The first three properties assert that successful reads and LLXs return correct answers. The last property says that an invocation of SCX or VLX does not succeed when it should not. However, an SCX can fail if it is concurrent with another SCX that accesses some Data-record in common. LL/SC also exhibits analogous failures in real systems. Our progress properties limit the situations in which this can occur.

3.2 Progress Properties

In our implementation, LLX, SCX and VLX are technically wait-free, but this is only because they may fail. So, we must state progress properties in terms of *successful* operations. The first progress property guarantees that LLXs on finalized Data-records succeed.

P1: Each terminating LLX(r) returns FINALIZED if it begins after the end of a successful SCX(V, R, fld, new)

with r in R or after another LLX(r) has returned FI-NALIZED.

The next progress property guarantees non-blocking progress of invocations of our primitives.

P2: If operations are performed infinitely often, then operations succeed infinitely often.

However, this progress property leaves open the possibility that only LLXs succeed. So, we want an additional progress property:

P3: If SCX and VLX operations are performed infinitely often, then SCX or VLX operations succeed infinitely often.

Finally, the following progress property ensures that *update* operations that are built using SCX can be made non-blocking.

P4: If SCX operations are performed infinitely often, then SCX operations succeed infinitely often.

When the progress properties defined here are used to prove that an application built from the primitives is non-blocking, there is an important, but subtle point: an SCX can be invoked only after it has been properly set up by a sequence of LLXs. However, if processes repeatedly perform LLX on Data-records that have been finalized, they may never be able to invoke an SCX. One way to prevent this from happening is to have each process keep track of the Data-records it knows are finalized. However, in many natural applications, for example, the multiset implementation in Section 5, explicit bookkeeping can be avoided. In addition, to ensure that changes to a data structure can continue to occur, there must always be at least one non-finalized Data-record. For example, in our multiset, *head* is never finalized and, if a node is reachable from *head* by following *next* pointers, then it is not finalized.

Our implementation of LLX, SCX and VLX in Section 4 actually satisfies stronger progress properties than the ones described above. For example, a VLX(V) or SCX(V, R, fld, new) is guaranteed to succeed if there is no concurrent SCX(V', R', fld', new') such that V and V' have one or more elements in common. However, for the purposes of the specification of the primitives, we decided to give progress guarantees that are sufficient to prove that algorithms that use the primitives are non-blocking, but weak enough that it may be possible to design other, even more efficient implementations of the primitives. For example, our specification would allow some spurious failures of the type that occur in common implementations of ordinary LL/SC operations (as long as there is some guarantee that not all operations can fail spuriously).

4. IMPLEMENTATION OF PRIMITIVES

The shared data structure used to implement LLX, SCX and VLX consists of a set of Data-records and a set of SCX-records. (See Figure 1.) Each Data-record contains user-defined mutable and immutable fields. It also contains a *marked* bit, which is used to finalize the Data-record, and an *info* field. The marked bit is initially FALSE and only ever changes from FALSE to TRUE. The *info* field points to an SCX-record that describes the last SCX that accessed the Data-record. Initially, it points to a *dummy* SCX-record. When an SCX accesses a Data-record, it changes the *info* field of the Data-record to point to its SCX-record. While this SCX is active, the *info* field acts as a kind of lock on the Data-record, granting exclusive access to this SCX, rather

type Data-record
 ▷ User-defined fields
 $m_1, \ldots, m_y$ ▷ mutable fields
 $i_1, \ldots, i_z$ ▷ immutable fields
 ▷ Fields used by LLX/SCX algorithm
 info   ▷ pointer to an SCX-record
 marked   ▷ Boolean

type SCX-record
 V ▷ sequence of Data-records
 R ▷ subsequence of V to be finalized
 fld   ▷ pointer to a field of a Data-record in V
 new   ▷ value to be written into the field *fld*
 old   ▷ value previously read from the field *fld*
 state   ▷ one of {InProgress, Committed, Aborted}
 allFrozen ▷ Boolean
 infoFields ▷ sequence of pointers, one read from the
   ▷ *info* field of each element of V

Figure 1: Type definitions for shared objects used to implement LLX, SCX, and VLX.

than to a process. (To avoid confusion, we call this *freezing*, rather than locking, a Data-record.) We ensure that an SCX S does not change a Data-record for its own purposes while it is frozen for another SCX S'. Instead, S uses the information in the SCX-record of S' to help S' complete (successfully or unsuccessfully), so that the Data-record can be unfrozen. This cooperative approach is used to ensure progress.

An SCX-record contains enough information to allow any process to complete an SCX operation that is in progress. V, R, fld and *new* store the arguments of the SCX operation that created the SCX-record. Recall that R is a subsequence of V and *fld* points to a mutable field f of some Data-record r' in V. The value that was read from f by the LLX(r') linked to the SCX is stored in *old*. The SCX-record has one of three states, InProgress, Committed or Aborted, which is stored in its *state* field. This field is initially InProgress. The SCX-record of each SCX that terminates is eventually set to Committed or Aborted, depending on whether or not it successfully makes its desired update. The dummy SCX-record always has *state* = Aborted. The *allFrozen* bit, which is initially FALSE, gets set to TRUE after all Data-records in V have been frozen for the SCX. The values of *state* and *allFrozen* change in accordance with the diagram in Figure 2. The steps in the algorithm that cause these changes are also indicated. The *infoFields* field stores, for each r in V, the value of r's *info* field that was read by the LLX(r) linked to the SCX.

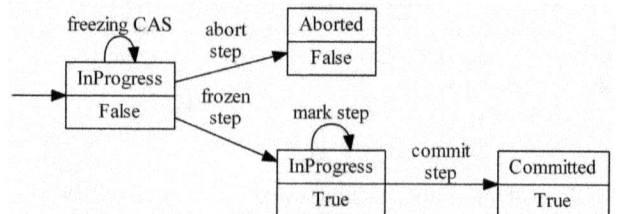

Figure 2: Possible [*state*, *allFrozen*] field transitions of an SCX-record.

We say that a Data-record r is *marked* when $r.marked =$ TRUE. A Data-record r is *frozen* for an SCX-record U if $r.info$ points to U and either $U.state$ is InProgress, or $U.state$ is Committed and r is marked. While a Data-record r is frozen for an SCX-record U, a mutable field f of r can be changed only if f is the field pointed to by $U.fld$ (and it can only be changed by a process helping the SCX that created U). Once a Data-record r is marked and $r.info.state$ becomes Committed, r will never be modified again in any way. Figure 3 shows how a Data-record can change between frozen and unfrozen. The three bold boxes represent frozen Data-records. The other two boxes represent Data-records that are not frozen. A Data-record r can only become frozen when $r.info$ is changed (to point to a new SCX-record whose state is InProgress). This is represented by the grey edges. The black edges represent changes to $r.info.state$ or $r.marked$. A frozen Data-record r can only become unfrozen when $r.info.state$ is changed.

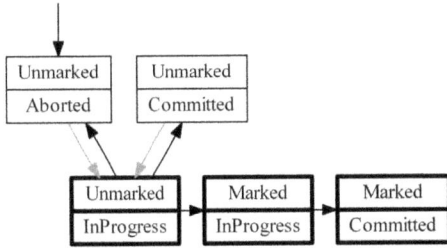

Figure 3: Possible transitions for the *marked* field of a Data-record and the *state* of the SCX-record pointed to by the *info* field of the Data-record.

4.1 Constraints

For the sake of efficiency, we have designed our implementation of LLX, VLX and SCX to work only if the primitives are used in a way that satisfies certain constraints, described in this section. We also describe general (but somewhat inefficient) ways to ensure these constraints are satisfied. However, there are often quite natural ways to ensure the constraints are satisfied without resorting to the extra work required by the general solutions.

Since our implementation of LLX, SCX and VLX uses helping to guarantee progress, each CAS of an SCX might be repeatedly performed by several helpers, possibly after the SCX itself has terminated. To avoid difficulties, we must show there is no ABA problem in the fields affected by these CAS steps.

The *info* field of a Data-record r is modified by CAS steps that attempt to freeze r for an SCX. All such steps performed by processes helping one invocation of SCX try to CAS the *info* field of r from the same old value to the same new value, and that new value is a pointer to a newly created SCX-record. Because the SCX-record is allocated a location that has never been used before, the ABA problem will not arise in the *info* field. (This approach is compatible with safe garbage collection schemes that only reuse an old address once no process can reach it by following pointers.)

A similar approach could be used to avoid the ABA problem in a mutable field of a Data-record: the new value could be placed inside a wrapper object that is allocated a new location in memory. (This is referred to as Solution 3 of the

ABA problem in [9].) However, the extra level of indirection slows down accesses to fields.

To avoid the ABA problem, it suffices to prove the following constraint is satisfied.

- **Constraint**: For every invocation S of SCX(V, R, fld, new), new is not the initial value of fld and no invocation of SCX(V', R', fld, new) was linearized before the LLX(r) linked to S was linearized, where r is the Data-record that contains fld.

The multiset in Section 5 provides an example of a simple, more efficient way to ensure that this constraint is always satisfied.

To ensure property P4, we put a constraint on the way SCX is used. Our implementation of SCX(V, R, fld, new) does something akin to acquiring locks on each Data-record in V. Livelock could occur if different invocations of SCX do not process Data-records in the same order. To prevent this, we could define a way of ordering all Data-records (for example, by their locations in memory) and each sequence passed to an invocation of SCX could be sorted using this ordering. However, this could be expensive. Moreover, to prove our progress properties, we do not require that *all* SCXs order their sequences V consistently. It suffices that, if all the Data-records stop changing, then the sequences passed to later invocations of SCX are all consistent with some total order. This property is often easy to satisfy in a natural way. More precisely, use of our implementation of SCX requires adherence to the following constraint.

- **Constraint**: Consider each execution that contains a configuration C after which the value of no field of any Data-record changes. There must be a total order on all Data-records created during this execution such that, if Data-record r_1 appears before Data-record r_2 in the sequence V passed to an invocation of SCX whose linked LLXs begin after C, then $r_1 < r_2$.

For example, if one was using LLX and SCX to implement an *unsorted* singly-linked list, this constraint would be satisfied if the nodes in each sequence V occur in the order they are encountered by following next pointers from the beginning of the list, *even if* some operations could reorder the nodes in the list. While the list is changing, such a sequence may have repeated elements and might not be consistent with any total order.

4.2 Detailed Algorithm Description and Sketch of Proofs

Pseudocode for our implementation of LLX, VLX and SCX appears in Figure 4. If x contains a pointer to a record, then $x.y := v$ assigns the value v to field y of this record, $\&x.y$ denotes the address of this field and all other occurrences of $x.y$ denote the value stored in this field.

THEOREM 1. *The algorithms in Figure 4 satisfy properties C1 to C4 and P1 to P4 in every execution where the constraints of Section 4.1 are satisfied.*

The detailed proof of correctness [7] is quite involved, so we only sketch the main ideas here.

An LLX(r) returns a snapshot, FAIL, or FINALIZED. At a high level, it works as follows. If the LLX determines that r is not frozen and r's *info* field does not change while the LLX reads the mutable fields of r, the LLX returns the values read as a snapshot. Otherwise, the LLX helps the SCX that last froze r, if it is frozen, and returns FAIL or

```
1   LLX(r) by process p
2   ▷ Precondition: r ≠ NIL.
3     marked₁ := r.marked                                                    ▷ order of lines 3–6 matters
4     rinfo := r.info
5     state := rinfo.state
6     marked₂ := r.marked
7     if state = Aborted or (state = Committed and not marked₂) then         ▷ if r was not frozen at line 5
8       read r.m₁, ..., r.m_y and record the values in local variables m₁, ..., m_y
9       if r.info = rinfo then                                               ▷ if r.info points to the same
10        store ⟨r, rinfo, ⟨m₁, ..., m_y⟩⟩ in p's local table                ▷ SCX-record as on line 4
11        return ⟨m₁, ..., m_y⟩

12    if (rinfo.state = Committed or (rinfo.state = InProgress and HELP(rinfo))) and marked₁ then
13      return FINALIZED
14    else
15      if r.info.state = InProgress then HELP(r.info)
16      return FAIL
```

```
17  SCX(V, R, fld, new) by process p
18  ▷ Preconditions: (1) for each r in V, p has performed an invocation I_r of LLX(r) linked to this SCX
                     (2) new is not the initial value of fld
                     (3) for each r in V, no SCX(V', R', fld, new) was linearized before I_r was linearized
19    Let infoFields be a pointer to a newly created table in shared memory containing,
          for each r in V, a copy of r's info value in p's local table of LLX results
20    Let old be the value for fld stored in p's local table of LLX results
21    return HELP(pointer to new SCX-record(V, R, fld, new, old, InProgress, FALSE, infoFields))
```

```
22  HELP(scxPtr)
23    ▷ Freeze all Data-records in scxPtr.V to protect their mutable fields from being changed by other SCXs
24    for each r in scxPtr.V enumerated in order do
25      Let rinfo be the pointer indexed by r in scxPtr.infoFields
26      if not CAS(r.info, rinfo, scxPtr) then                              ▷ freezing CAS
27        if r.info ≠ scxPtr then
28          ▷ Could not freeze r because it is frozen for another SCX
29          if scxPtr.allFrozen = TRUE then                                 ▷ frozen check step
30            ▷ the SCX has already completed successfully
31            return TRUE
32          else
33            ▷ Atomically unfreeze all nodes frozen for this SCX
34            scxPtr.state := Aborted                                       ▷ abort step
35            return FALSE

36    ▷ Finished freezing Data-records (Assert: state ∈ {InProgress, Committed})
37    scxPtr.allFrozen := TRUE                                              ▷ frozen step
38    for each r in scxPtr.R do r.marked := TRUE                            ▷ mark step
39    CAS(scxPtr.fld, scxPtr.old, scxPtr.new)                               ▷ update CAS

40    ▷ Finalize all r in R, and unfreeze all r in V that are not in R
41    scxPtr.state := Committed                                            ▷ commit step
42    return TRUE
```

```
43  VLX(V) by process p
44  ▷ Precondition: for each Data-record r in V, p has performed an LLX(r) linked to this VLX
45    for each r in V do
46      Let rinfo be the info field for r stored in p's local table of LLX results
47      if rinfo ≠ r.info then return FALSE        ▷ r changed since LLX(r) read info
48    return TRUE              ▷ At some point during the loop, all r in V were unchanged
```

Figure 4: Pseudocode for LLX, SCX and VLX.

FINALIZED. If the LLX returns FAIL, it is not linearized. We now discuss in more detail how LLX operates and is linearized in the other two cases.

First, suppose the LLX(r) returns a snapshot at line 11. Then, the test at line 7 evaluates to TRUE. So, either $state =$ Aborted, which means r is not frozen at line 5, or $state =$ Committed and $marked_2 =$ FALSE. This also means r is not frozen at line 5, since $r.marked$ cannot change from TRUE to FALSE. The LLX reads r's mutable fields (line 8) and rereads $r.info$ at line 9, finding it the same as on line 4. In Section 4.1, we explained why this implies that $r.info$ did not change between lines 4 and 9. Since r is not frozen at line 5, we know from Figure 3 that r is unfrozen at all times between line 5 and 9. We prove that mutable fields can change only while r is frozen, so the values read by line 8 constitute a snapshot of r's mutable fields. Thus, we can linearize the LLX at line 9.

Now, suppose the LLX(r) returns FINALIZED. Then, the test on line 12 evaluated to TRUE. In particular, r was already marked when line 3 was performed. If $rinfo.state =$ InProgress when line 12 was performed, HELP($rinfo$) was called and returned TRUE. Below, we argue that $rinfo.state$ was changed to Committed before the return occurred. By Figure 3(a), the $state$ of an SCX-record never changes after it is set to Committed. So, after line 12, $rinfo.state =$ Committed and, thus, r has been finalized. Hence, the LLX can be linearized at line 13.

When a process performs an SCX, it first creates a new SCX-record and then invokes HELP (line 21). The HELP routine performs the real work of the SCX. It is also used by a process to help other processes complete their SCXs (successfully or unsuccessfully). The values in an SCX-record's old and $infoFields$ come from a table in the local memory of the process that invokes the SCX, which stores the results of the last LLX it performed on each Data-record. (In practice, the memory required for this table could be greatly reduced when a process knows which of these values are needed for future SCXs.)

Consider an invocation of HELP(U) by process p to carry out the work of the invocation S of SCX(V, R, fld, new) that is described by the SCX-record U. First, p attempts to freeze each r in V by performing a *freezing CAS* to store a pointer to U in $r.info$ (line 26). Process p uses the value read from $r.info$ by the LLX(r) linked to S as the old value for this CAS and, hence, it will succeed only if r has not been frozen for any other SCX since then. If p's freezing CAS fails, it checks whether some other helper has successfully frozen the Data-record with a pointer to U (line 27).

If every r in V is successfully frozen, p performs a *frozen step* to set $U.allFrozen$ to TRUE (line 37). After this frozen step, the SCX is guaranteed not to fail, meaning that no process will perform an abort step while helping this SCX. Then, for each r in R, p performs a *mark step* to set $r.marked$ to TRUE (line 38) and, from Figure 3, r remains frozen from then on. Next, p performs an *update CAS*, storing new in the field pointed to by fld (line 39), if successful. We prove that, among all the update CAS steps on fld performed by the helpers of U, only the first can succeed. Finally, p unfreezes all r in V that are not in R by performing a *commit step* that changes $U.state$ to Committed (line 41).

Now suppose that, when p performs line 27, it finds that some Data-record r in V is already frozen for another invocation S' of SCX. If $U.allFrozen$ is FALSE at line 29, then

we can prove that no helper of S will ever reach line 37, so p can abort S. To do so, it unfreezes each r in V that it has frozen by performing an *abort step*, which changes $U.state$ to Aborted (line 34), and then returns FALSE (line 35) to indicate that S has been aborted. If $U.allFrozen$ is TRUE at line 29, it means that each element of V, including r, was successfully frozen by some helper of S and then, later, a process froze r for S'. Since S cannot be aborted after $U.allFrozen$ was set to TRUE, its state must have changed from InProgress to Committed before r was frozen for another SCX-record. Therefore, S was successfully completed and p can return TRUE at line 31.

We linearize an invocation of SCX at the first update CAS performed by one of its helpers. We prove that this update CAS always succeeds. Thus, all SCXs that return TRUE are linearized, as well as possibly some non-terminating SCXs. The first update CAS of SCX(V, R, fld, new) modifies the value of fld, so a read(fld) that occurs immediately after the update CAS will return the value of new. Hence, the linearization point of an SCX must occur at its first update CAS. There is one subtle issue about this linearization point: If an LLX(r) is linearized between the update CAS and commit step of an SCX that finalizes r, it might not return FINALIZED, violating condition C3. However, this cannot happen, because, before the LLX is linearized on line 13, the LLX either sees that the commit step has been performed or helps the SCX perform its commit step.

An invocation I of VLX(V) is executed by a process p after p has performed an invocation of LLX(r) linked to I, for each r in V. VLX(V) simply checks, for each r in V, that the $info$ field of r is the same as when it was read by p's last LLX(r) and, if so, VLX(V) returns TRUE. In this case, we prove that each Data-record in V does not change between the linked LLX and the time its $info$ field is reread. Thus, the VLX can be linearized at the first time it executes line 47. Otherwise, the VLX returns FALSE to indicate that the LLX results may not constitute a snapshot.

We remark that our use of the cooperative method avoids costly recursive helping. If, while p is helping S, it cannot freeze all of S's Data-records because one of them is already frozen for a third SCX, then p will simply perform an abort step, which unfreezes all Data-records that S has frozen.

We briefly sketch why the progress properties described in Section 3.2 are satisfied. It follows easily from the code that an invocation of LLX(r) returns FINALIZED if it begins after the end of an SCX that finalized r or another LLX sees that r is finalized. To prove the progress properties P2, P3 and P4, we consider two cases.

First, consider an execution where only a finite number of SCXs are invoked. Then, only finitely many SCX-records are created. Each process calls HELP(U) if it sees that $U.state =$ InProgress, which it can do at most once for each SCX-record U. Since every CAS is performed inside the HELP routine, there is some point after which no process performs a CAS, calls HELP, or sees a SCX-record whose $state$ is InProgress. A VLX can fail only when an $info$ field is modified by a concurrent operation and an LLX can only fail for the same reason or when it sees a SCX-record whose $state$ is InProgress. Therefore, all LLXs and VLXs that begin after this point will succeed, establishing P2 and P3. Moreover, P4 is vacuously satisfied in this case.

Now, consider an execution where infinitely many SCXs are invoked. To derive a contradiction, suppose only finitely

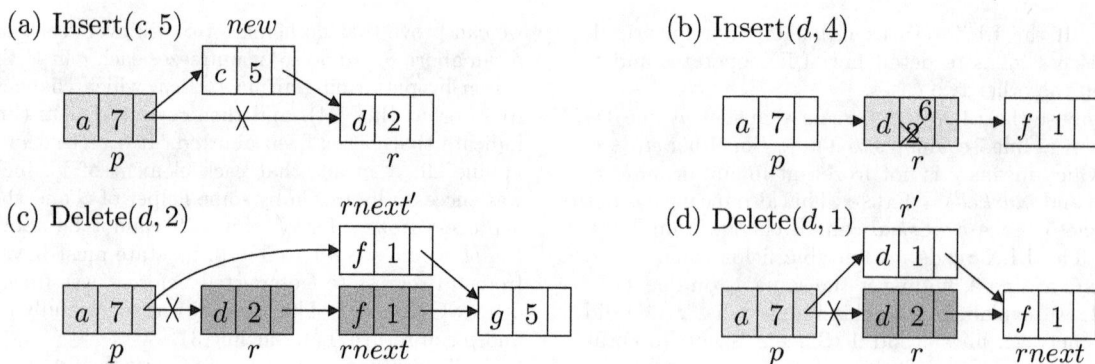

Figure 5: Using SCX to update a multiset. LLXs of all shaded nodes are linked to the SCX. Darkly shaded nodes are finalized by the SCX. Where a field has changed, the old value is crossed out.

many SCXs succeed. Then, there is a time after which no more SCXs succeed. The constraint on the sequences passed to invocations of SCXs ensures that all SCXs whose linked LLXs begin after this time will attempt to freeze their sequences of Data-records in a consistent order. Thus, one of these SCXs will succeed in freezing all of the Data-records that were passed to it and will successfully complete. This is a contradiction. Thus, infinitely many of the SCXs do succeed, establishing properties P2, P3 and P4.

4.3 Additional Properties

Our implementation of SCX satisfies some additional properties, which are helpful for designing certain kinds of non-blocking data structures so that query operations can run efficiently. Consider a pointer-based data structure with a fixed set of Data-records called *entry points*. An operation on the data structure starts at an entry point and follows pointers to visit other Data-records. (For example, in our multiset example, the head of the linked list is the sole entry point for the data structure.) We say that a Data-record is *in the data structure* if it can be reached by following pointers from an entry point, and a Data-record r is *removed from the data structure* by an SCX if r is in the data structure immediately prior to the linearization point of the SCX and is not in the data structure immediately afterwards.

If the data structure is designed so that a Data-record is finalized when (and only when) it is removed from the data structure, then we have the following additional properties.

PROPOSITION 2. *Suppose each linearized* SCX(V, R, fld, new) *removes precisely the Data-records in R from the data structure.*

- *If* LLX(r) *returns a value different from* FAIL *or* FINALIZED*, r is in the data structure just before the LLX is linearized.*
- *If an* SCX(V, R, fld, new) *is linearized and new is (a pointer to) a Data-record, then this Data-record is in the data structure just after the SCX is linearized.*
- *If an operation reaches a Data-record r by following pointers read from other Data-records, starting from an entry point, then r was in the data structure at some earlier time during the operation.*

The first two properties are straightforward to prove. The last property is proved by induction on the Data-records reached. For the base case, entry points are always reachable. For the induction step, consider the time when an

operation reads a pointer to r from another Data-record r' that the operation reached earlier. By the induction hypothesis, there was an earlier time t during the operation when r' was in the data structure. If r' already contained a pointer to r at t, then r was also in the data structure at that time. Otherwise, an SCX wrote a pointer to r in r' after t, and just after that update occurred, r' and r were in the data structure (by the second part of the proposition).

The last property is a particularly useful one for linearizing query operations. It means that operations that search through a data structure can use simple reads of pointers instead of the more expensive LLX operations. Even though the Data-record that such a search operation reaches may have been removed from the data structure by the time it is reached, the lemma guarantees that there *was* a time during the search when the Data-record was in the data structure. For example, we use this property to linearize searches in our multiset algorithm in Section 5.

5. AN EXAMPLE: MULTISET

We now give a detailed description of the implementation of a multiset using LLX and SCX. We assume that keys stored in the multiset are drawn from a totally ordered set and $-\infty < k < \infty$ for every key k in the multiset. As described in Section 3, we use a singly-linked list of nodes, sorted by key. To avoid special cases, it always has a sentinel node, *head*, with key $-\infty$ at its beginning and a sentinel node, *tail*, with key ∞ at its end. The definition of Node, the Data-record used to represent a node, and the pseudocode are presented in Figure 6.

SEARCH(key) traverses the list, starting from *head*, by reading *next* pointers until reaching the first node r whose key is at least *key*. This node and the preceding node p are returned. GET(key) performs SEARCH(key), outputs r's count if r's key matches *key*, and outputs 0, otherwise.

An invocation I of INSERT$(key, count)$ starts by calling SEARCH(key). Using the nodes p and r that are returned, it updates the data structure. It decides whether *key* is already in the multiset (by checking whether $r.key = key$) and, if so, it invokes LLX(r) followed by an SCX linked to r to increase $r.count$ by *count*, as depicted in Figure 5(b). Otherwise, I performs the update depicted in Figure 5(a): It invokes LLX(p), checks that p still points to r, creates a node, *new*, and invokes an SCX linked to p to insert *new* between p

```
type Node                                    14  INSERT(key, count)        ▷ Precondition: count > 0
    ▷ Fields from sequential data structure  15    while TRUE do
    key       ▷ key (immutable)              16      ⟨r, p⟩ := SEARCH(key)
    count     ▷ occurrences of key (mutable) 17      if key = r.key then
    next      ▷ next pointer (mutable)        18        localr := LLX(r)
    ▷ Fields defined by LLX/SCX algorithm     19        if localr ∉ {FAIL, FINALIZED} then
    info      ▷ a pointer to an SCX-record    20          if SCX(⟨r⟩, ⟨⟩, &r.count, localr.count + count) then return
    marked    ▷ a Boolean value               21      else
                                              22        localp := LLX(p)
shared Node tail := new Node(∞, 0, NIL)       23        if localp ∉ {FAIL, FINALIZED} and r = localp.next then
shared Node head := new Node(−∞, 0, tail)     24          if SCX(⟨p⟩, ⟨⟩, &p.next, new Node(key, count, r)) then return


 1  GET(key)                                  26  DELETE(key, count)         ▷ Precondition: count > 0
 2    ⟨r, −⟩ := SEARCH(key)                    27    while TRUE do
 3    if key = r.key then                      28      ⟨r, p⟩ := SEARCH(key)
 4      return r.count                         29      localp := LLX(p)
 5    else return 0                            30      localr := LLX(r)
                                               31      if localp, localr ∉ {FAIL, FINALIZED} and r = localp.next then
 6  SEARCH(key)                                32        if key ≠ r.key or localr.count < count then return FALSE
 7    ▷ Postcondition: p and r point to        33        else if localr.count > count then
         Nodes with p.key < key ≤ r.key.       34          if SCX(⟨p⟩, ⟨r⟩, &p.next, new
 8    p := head                                             Node(r.key, localr.count − count, localr.next)) then
 9    r := p.next                                          return TRUE
10    while key > r.key do                     35        else  ▷ assert: localr.count = count
11      p := r                                  36          if LLX(localr.next) ∉ {FAIL, FINALIZED} then
12      r := r.next                             37            if SCX(⟨p, r, localr.next⟩, ⟨r, localr.next⟩,
13    return ⟨r, p⟩                                            &p.next, new copy of localr.next) then return TRUE
```

Figure 6: Pseudocode for a multiset, implemented with a singly linked list.

and r. If p no longer points to r, the LLX returns FAIL or FINALIZED, or the SCX returns FALSE, then I restarts.

An invocation I of DELETE($key, count$) also begins by calling SEARCH(key). It invokes LLX on the nodes p and r and then checks that p still points to r. If r does not contain at least $count$ copies of key, then I returns FALSE. If r contains exactly $count$ copies, then I performs the update depicted in Figure 5(c) to remove node r from the list. To do so, it invokes LLX on the node, $rnext$, that $r.next$ points to, makes a copy $rnext'$ of $rnext$, and invokes an SCX linked to p, r and $rnext$ to change $p.next$ to point to $rnext'$. This SCX also finalizes the nodes r and $rnext$, which are thereby removed from the data structure. The node $rnext$ is replaced by a copy to avoid the ABA problem in $p.next$. If r contains more than $count$ copies, then I replaces r by a new copy r' with an appropriately reduced count using an SCX linked to p and r, as shown in Figure 5(d). This SCX finalizes r. If an LLX returns FAIL or FINALIZED, or the SCX returns FALSE then I restarts.

A detailed proof of correctness appears in [7]. It begins by showing that this multiset implementation satisfies some basic properties.

INVARIANT 3. *The following are true at all times.*
- *head always points to a node.*
- *If a node has key ∞, then its next pointer is NIL.*
- *If a node's key is not ∞, then its next pointer points to some node with a strictly larger key.*

It follows that the data structure is always a sorted list.

We prove the following lemma by considering the SCXs performed by update operations shown in Figure 5.

LEMMA 4. *The Data-records removed from the data structure by a linearized invocation of SCX(V, R, fld, new) are exactly the Data-records in R.*

This lemma allows us to apply Proposition 2 to prove that there is a time during each SEARCH when the nodes r and p that it returns are both in the list and $p.next = r$.

Each GET and each DELETE that returns FALSE is linearized at the linearization point of the SEARCH it performs. Every other INSERT or DELETE is linearized at its successful SCX. Linearizability of all operations then follows from the next invariant.

LEMMA 5. *At every time t, the multiset of keys in the data structure is equal to the multiset of keys that would result from the atomic execution of the sequence of operations linearized up to time t.*

To prove the algorithm is non-blocking, suppose there is some infinite execution in which only finitely many operations terminate. Then, eventually, no more INSERT or DELETE operations perform a successful SCX, so there is a time after which the pointers that form the linked list stop changing. This implies that all calls to the SEARCH subroutine must terminate. Since a GET operation merely calls SEARCH, all GET operations must also terminate. Thus, there is some collection of INSERT and DELETE operations that take steps forever without terminating. We show that each such operation sets up and performs an SCX infinitely often. For any INSERT or DELETE operation, consider any iteration of the loop that begins after the last successful SCX changes the list. By Lemma 4 and Proposition 2, the nodes p and r reached by the SEARCH in that iteration were in the data structure at some time during the SEARCH and, hence, throughout the SEARCH. So when the INSERT or DELETE performs LLXs on p or r, they cannot return FINALIZED. Moreover, they must succeed infinitely often by property P2, and this allows the INSERT or DELETE to perform an SCX infinitely often. By property P4, SCXs will succeed infinitely often, a contradiction.

Thus, we have the following theorem.

THEOREM 6. *The algorithms in Figure 6 implement a non-blocking, linearizable multiset.*

6. CONCLUSION

The LLX, SCX and VLX primitives we introduce in this paper can also be used to produce practical, non-blocking implementations of a wide variety of tree-based data structures. In [6], we describe a general method for obtaining such implementations and use it to design a provably correct, non-blocking implementation of a chromatic tree, which is a relaxed variant of a red-black tree. Furthermore, we provide an experimental performance analysis, comparing our Java implementation of the chromatic search tree to leading concurrent implementations of dictionaries. This demonstrates that our primitives enable efficient non-blocking implementations of more complicated data structures to be built (and added to standard libraries), together with manageable proofs of their correctness.

Our implementation of LLX, SCX and VLX relies on the existence of efficient garbage collection, which is provided in managed languages such as Java and C#. However, in other languages, such as C++, memory management is an issue. This can be addressed, for example, by the new, efficient memory reclamation method of Aghazadeh, Golab and Woelfel [2].

Acknowledgements.

Funding was provided by the Natural Sciences and Engineering Research Council of Canada.

7. REFERENCES

[1] Y. Afek, M. Merritt, G. Taubenfeld, and D. Touitou. Disentangling multi-object operations. In *Proc. 16th ACM Symposium on Principles of Distributed Computing*, pages 111–120, 1997.

[2] Z. Aghazadeh, W. Golab, and P. Woelfel. Brief announcement: Resettable objects and efficient memory reclamation for concurrent algorithms. In *Proc. 32nd ACM Symposium on Principles of Distributed Computing*, 2013.

[3] J. H. Anderson and M. Moir. Universal constructions for multi-object operations. In *Proc. 14th Annual ACM Symposium on Principles of Distributed Computing*, pages 184–193, 1995.

[4] H. Attiya and E. Hillel. Highly concurrent multi-word synchronization. *Theoretical Computer Science*, 412(12–14):1243–1262, Mar. 2011.

[5] G. Barnes. A method for implementing lock-free data structures. In *Proc. 5th ACM Symposium on Parallel Algorithms and Architectures*, pages 261–270, 1993.

[6] T. Brown, F. Ellen, and E. Ruppert. A general technique for non-blocking trees. Manuscript available from http://www.cs.utoronto.ca/~tabrown.

[7] T. Brown, F. Ellen, and E. Ruppert. Pragmatic primitives for non-blocking data structures. Manuscript available from http://www.cs.utoronto.ca/~tabrown.

[8] P. Chuong, F. Ellen, and V. Ramachandran. A universal construction for wait-free transaction friendly data structures. In *Proc. 22nd ACM Symposium on Parallelism in Algorithms and Architectures*, pages 335–344, 2010.

[9] D. Dechev, P. Pirkelbauer, and B. Stroustrup. Understanding and effectively preventing the ABA problem in descriptor-based lock-free designs. In *Proc. 13th IEEE Symposium on Object/Component/Service-Oriented Real-Time Distributed Computing*, pages 185–192, 2010.

[10] F. Ellen, P. Fatourou, E. Ruppert, and F. van Breugel. Non-blocking binary search trees. In *Proc. 29th ACM Symposium on Principles of Distributed Computing*, pages 131–140, 2010. Full version available as Technical Report CSE-2010-04, York University.

[11] K. Fraser and T. Harris. Concurrent programming without locks. *ACM Trans. Comput. Syst.*, 25(2), May 2007.

[12] M. Herlihy and J. E. B. Moss. Transactional memory: Architectural support for lock-free data structures. In *Proc. 20th Annual International Symposium on Computer Architecture*, pages 289–300, 1993.

[13] A. Israeli and L. Rappoport. Disjoint-access-parallel implementations of strong shared memory primitives. In *Proc. 13th ACM Symposium on Principles of Distributed Computing*, pages 151–160, 1994.

[14] P. Jayanti and S. Petrovic. Efficiently implementing a large number of LL/SC objects. In *Proc. 9th International Conference on Principles of Distributed Systems*, volume 3974 of *LNCS*, pages 17–31, 2005.

[15] V. Luchangco, M. Moir, and N. Shavit. Nonblocking k-compare-single-swap. *Theory of Computing Systems*, 44(1):39–66, Jan. 2009.

[16] N. Shafiei. Non-blocking Patricia tries with replace operations. In *Proc. 33rd International Conference on Distributed Computing Systems*, 2013. To appear.

[17] N. Shavit and D. Touitou. Software transactional memory. *Distributed Computing*, 10(2):99–116, Feb. 1997.

[18] H. Sundell. Wait-free multi-word compare-and-swap using greedy helping and grabbing. *International Journal of Parallel Programming*, 39(6):694–716, Dec. 2011.

[19] J. Turek, D. Shasha, and S. Prakash. Locking without blocking: Making lock based concurrent data structure algorithms nonblocking. In *Proc. 11th ACM Symposium on Principles of Database Systems*, pages 212–222, 1992.

The SkipTrie: Low-Depth Concurrent Search without Rebalancing

Rotem Oshman[*]
University of Toronto
rotem@cs.toronto.edu

Nir Shavit[†]
MIT
shanir@csail.mit.edu

ABSTRACT

To date, all concurrent search structures that can support predecessor queries have had depth logarithmic in m, the number of elements. This paper introduces the *SkipTrie*, a new concurrent search structure supporting predecessor queries in amortized expected $O(\log \log u + c)$ steps, insertions and deletions in $O(c \log \log u)$, and using $O(m)$ space, where u is the size of the key space and c is the contention during the recent past. The SkipTrie is a probabilistically-balanced version of a y-fast trie consisting of a very shallow skiplist from which randomly chosen elements are inserted into a hash-table based x-fast trie. By inserting keys into the x-fast-trie probabilistically, we eliminate the need for rebalancing, and can provide a lock-free linearizable implementation. To the best of our knowledge, our proof of the amortized expected performance of the SkipTrie is the first such proof for a tree-based data structure.

Categories and Subject Descriptors

E.1 [**Data**]: Data Structures—*distributed data structures*

Keywords

concurrent data structures, predecessor queries, amortized analysis

1. INTRODUCTION

In recent years multicore software research has focused on delivering improved search performance through the development of highly concurrent search structures [11, 14, 7, 16, 5, 4]. Although efficient hash tables can deliver expected constant search time for membership queries [11, 19, 12, 9,

[*]This work was supported in part by DARPA Grant FA8750-11-2-0225 and by a grant from Sun Microsystems.

[†]This work was supported in part by NSF grant CCF-1217921, DoE ASCR grant ER26116/DE-SC0008923, and by grants from the Oracle and Intel corporations.

13], all concurrent search structures that support predecessor queries have had depth and search time that is logarithmic in m, the number of keys in the set (without accounting for the cost of contention, which is typically not analyzed). This contrasts with the sequential world, in which van Emde Boas Trees [21], x-fast tries and y-fast tries [22] are known to support predecessor queries in $O(\log \log \mathbf{u})$ time, where $\mathbf{u}$ is the size of the key universe. This is, in many natural cases, a significant performance gap: for example, with $m = 2^{20}$ and $\mathbf{u} = 2^{32}$, $\log m = 20$ while $\log \log \mathbf{u} = 5$. Though one can lower this depth somewhat by increasing internal node fanout [5, 16], in the concurrent case the resulting algorithms involve complex synchronization, and their performance has never been analyzed.

This paper aims to bridge the gap between the sequential and the concurrent world by presenting the *SkipTrie*,[1] a new probabilistically-balanced data structure which supports efficient insertions, deletions and predecessor queries. We give a lock-free and linearizable implementation of the SkipTrie from CAS and DCSS instructions (see below for the reasoning behind our choice of primitives), and we analyze its expected amortized step complexity: we show that if $c(op)$ is the maximum interval contention of any operation that overlaps with op (that is, the maximum number of operations that overlap with any operation op' that itself overlaps with op), each SkipTrie operation op completes in expected amortized $O(\log \log \mathbf{u} + c(op))$ steps. We can also tighten the bound and replace the term $c(op)$ by the *point contention* of op—that is, the maximum number of operations that run concurrently at any point during the execution of op—by introducing more "helping" during searches.

The SkipTrie can be thought of as a y-fast trie [22] whose deterministic load balancing scheme has been replaced by a probabilistic one, negating the need for some of the complex operations on trees that the y-fast trie uses. Let us begin by recalling the construction of the x-fast trie and the y-fast trie from [22].

Willard's x-fast trie and y-fast trie. Given a set of integer keys $S \subseteq [\mathbf{u}]$, each represented using $\log \mathbf{u}$ bits, an *x-fast trie* over S is a hash table containing all the prefixes of keys in S, together with a sorted doubly-linked list over the keys in S. We think of the prefixes in the hash table as forming

[1]The name "SkipTrie" has been previously used in the context of P2P algorithms to describe an unrelated algorithm [15] that involves a traditional trie and a distributed skipgraph. We nevertheless decided to use it, as we believe it is the most fitting name for our construction.

a *prefix tree*, where the children of each prefix p are $p \cdot 0$ and $p \cdot 1$ (if there are keys in S starting with $p0$ and $p1$, respectively). If a particular prefix p has no left child (i.e., there is no key in S beginning with $p \cdot 0$), then in the hash table entry corresponding to p we store a pointer to the largest key beginning with $p \cdot 1$; symmetrically, if p has no right child $p \cdot 1$, then in the entry for p we store a pointer to the smallest key beginning with $p \cdot 0$. (Note that a prefix is only stored in the hash table if it is the prefix of some key in S, so there is always either a left child or a right child or both.)

To find the predecessor of a key x in S, we first look for the longest common prefix of x with any element in S, using binary search on the length of the prefix: we start with the top half of x (the first $\log \mathbf{u}/2$ bits), and query the hash table to check if there is some key that starts with these bits. If yes, we check if there is a key starting with the first $3 \log \mathbf{u}/4$ bits of x; if not, we check for the first $\log \mathbf{u}/4$ bits of x. After $O(\log \log \mathbf{u})$ such queries we have found the longest common prefix p of x with any element in the set S. This prefix cannot have both left and right children, as then it would not be the *longest* common prefix. Instead it has a pointer down into the doubly linked list of keys; we follow this pointer. If p has no left child, then we know that x begins with $p \cdot 0$, and the pointer leads us to the predecessor of x, which is the smallest key beginning with $p \cdot 1$; we are done. If instead p has no right child, then x begins with $p \cdot 1$, and the pointer leads us to the successor of x, which is the largest key beginning with $p \cdot 0$. In this case we take one step back in the doubly-linked list of leaves to find the predecessor of x.

The x-fast trie supports predecessor queries in $O(\log \log \mathbf{u})$ steps, but it has two disadvantages: (1) insertions and deletions require $O(\log \mathbf{u})$ steps, as every prefix of the key must be examined and potentially modified; and (2) the space required for the hash table is $O(|S| \cdot \log \mathbf{u})$, because the depth of the prefix tree is $\log \mathbf{u}$. To remedy both concerns, Willard introduced the *y-fast trie*. The idea is to split the keys in S into "buckets" of $O(\log \mathbf{u})$ consecutive keys, and insert only the smallest key from every bucket into an x-fast trie. Inside each bucket the keys are stored in a balanced binary search tree, whose depth is $O(\log \log \mathbf{u})$.

The cost of predecessor queries remains the same: first we find the correct bucket by searching through the x-fast trie in $O(\log \log \mathbf{u})$; then we search for the exact predecessor by searching inside the bucket's search tree, requiring another $O(\log \log \mathbf{u})$ steps.

As we insert and remove elements from the y-fast trie, a bucket may grow too large or too small, and we may need to split it into two sub-buckets or merge it with an adjacent bucket, to preserve a bucket size of, say, between $\log \mathbf{u}$ and $4 \log \mathbf{u}$ elements (the constants are arbitrary). To split a bucket, we must split its search tree into two balanced sub-trees, remove the old representative of the bucket from the x-fast trie, and insert the representatives of the new buckets. This requires $O(\log \mathbf{u})$ steps, but it is only performed "once in every $O(\log \mathbf{u})$ insertions", because there is a slack of $O(\log \mathbf{u})$ in the allowed bucket size. Therefore the amortized cost is $O(1)$. Similarly, to merge a bucket with an adjacent bucket, we must merge the balanced search-trees, remove the old representatives and insert the new one; we may also need to split the merged bucket if it is too large. All of this

requires $O(\log \mathbf{u})$ steps but is again performed only once in every $O(\log \mathbf{u})$ operations, for an amortized cost of $O(1)$.

The y-fast trie has an amortized cost of $O(\log \log \mathbf{u})$ for all operations (the search for the predecessor dominates the cost), and its size is $O(m)$. However, this only holds true if we continuously move the elements among the collection of binary trees, so that each tree always has about $\log \mathbf{u}$ elements. This kind of rebalancing—moving items between binary trees, into and out of the x-fast trie, and finally rebalances the trees—is quite easy in a sequential setting, but can prove to be a nightmare in a concurrent one. It is more complex than simply implementing a balanced lock-free binary search tree, of which no completely proven implementation is known to date [7]. One might instead use a balanced B+ tree, for which there is a known lock-free construction [3]; but this construction is quite complicated, and furthermore, the cost it incurs due to contention has not been analyzed. Instead we suggest a more lightweight, probabilistic solution, which does not incur the overhead of merging and splitting buckets.

The SkipTrie. The main idea of the SkipTrie is to replace the y-fast trie's balanced binary trees with a very shallow, truncated skiplist [18] of depth $\log \log \mathbf{u}$. Each key inserted into the SkipTrie is first inserted into the skiplist; initially it rises in the usual manner, starting at the bottom level and tossing a fair coin to determine at each level whether to continue on to the next level. If a key rises to the top of the truncated skiplist (i.e., to height $\log \log \mathbf{u}$), we insert it into the x-fast trie (see Fig. 1). We do not store any skiplist levels above $\log \log \mathbf{u}$. The nodes at the top level of the skiplist are also linked backwards, forming a doubly-linked list. The effect is a probabilistic version of the y-fast trie: when a key x rises to the top of the skiplist and is inserted into the x-fast trie, we can think of this as splitting the bucket to which x belongs into two sub-buckets, one for the keys smaller than x and one for the keys at least as large as x. The probability that a given node will rise to level $\log \log \mathbf{u}$ is $2^{-\log \log \mathbf{u}} = 1/\log \mathbf{u}$, and therefore in expectation the number of keys between any two top-level keys is $O(\log \mathbf{u})$. Thus we achieve in a much simpler manner the balancing among buckets required for the y-fast trie. In our version, we never have to rebalance, or take keys in and out of the x-fast trie to make sure they are "well spaced-out."

To find the predecessor of x in the SkipTrie, a thread first traverses the x-fast trie to find the predecessor of x among the top-level skiplist elements, and then traverses the skiplist to find the actual predecessor of x. Finding the right top-level skiplist element takes $O(\log \log \mathbf{u})$ steps, and searching the skiplist takes an expected $O(\log \log \mathbf{u})$ additional steps, for a total of $O(\log \log \mathbf{u})$. To delete a key, we first delete it from the skiplist, and if it was a top-level node, we also remove it from the x-fast trie. As with the y-fast trie, inserting or removing a key from the x-fast trie requires $O(\log \mathbf{u})$ steps, but the amortized cost is $O(1)$, because in expectation only one in every $O(\log \mathbf{u})$ keys rises into the x-fast trie. Finally, the expected size of the SkipTrie is $O(m)$, where m is the number of keys: the skiplist's size is well-known to be $O(m)$ (in our case it is even smaller, because it is truncated), and an x-fast trie over an expected $O(m/\log \mathbf{u})$ keys requires $O(m)$ space in expectation.

So how do we design a concurrent SkipTrie? Our data structure is the composition of a concurrent hash table, a

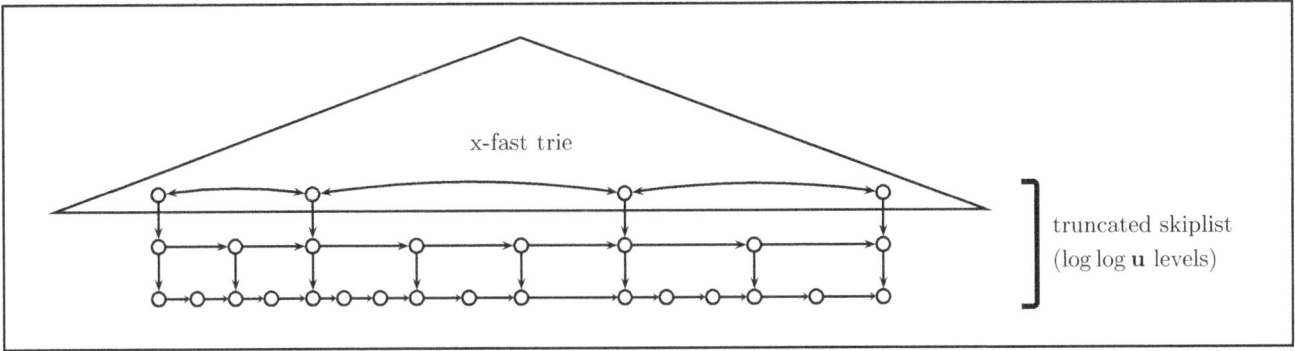

Figure 1: Illustration of a SkipTrie. The bottom is a truncated skiplist comprising $\log \log \mathbf{u}$ levels. Top-level skiplist nodes are linked in a doubly-linked list and inserted into an x-fast trie.

concurrent skiplist, a doubly-linked list (or two singly-linked lists sorted in opposite directions), and a concurrent implementation of an x-fast trie. For the hash table we use Split-Ordered Hashing [19], a resizable lock-free hash table that supports all operations in expected $O(1)$ steps. The other components we construct and analyze in this paper: although lock-free versions exist in the literature (e.g.,[8, 11, 14]), their step complexity has not been analyzed, and it appears that the penalty these implementations take for contention is too high for our desired amortized bounds. In terms of the construction itself, the most novel part is the x-fast trie, which to our knowledge has never been implemented concurrently before; in this extended abstract we focus on the x-fast trie and give only a quick sketch of the skiplist implementation. In addition, for lack of space, we give a high-level description of the analysis.

On the choice of atomic primitives. Our implementation of the SkipTrie uses single-word compare-and-swap (CAS) and double-wide double-compare-single-swap (DCSS) operations. A DCSS(X, old_X, new_X, Y, old_Y) instruction sets the value of X to new_X, conditioned on the current values of X and Y being old_X and old_Y, respectively. We use DCSS to avoid swinging list and trie pointers to nodes that are marked for deletion: we condition the DCSS on the target of the pointer being unmarked, so that we can rest assured that once a node has been marked and physically deleted, it will never become reachable again.

Although DCSS is not supported as a hardware primitive, we believe that given current trends in hardware and software transactional memory, it is quite reasonable to use lightweight transactions to implement a DCSS; indeed, support for hardware transactional memory is available in Intel's new Haswell microarchitecture, and the specialized STM of [6] sometimes outperforms hardware atomic primitives for very short transactions. Our implementation requires DCSS only for its amortized performance guarantee; we prove that even if some or all DCSS instructions are replaced with CAS (by dropping the second guard), the implementation remains linearizable and lock-free. In particular, after attempting the DCSS some fixed number of times and aborting, it is permissible to fall back to CAS.

We believe that our explicit use of DCSS captures some design patterns that are implicit in, e.g., [8], and other lock-free data structures built from CAS alone; these data structures

often "need" a DCSS, so they implement it from CAS, in a way that essentially amounts to a pessimistic transaction. We believe that on modern architecture it is preferable to use an actual DCSS (i.e., a short transaction) for this type of operation, as this allows for an optimistic implementation (as well as the pessimistic one if desired). Using DCSS also reduces the amount of "helping", which we view as an advantage (see below).

The disadvantage to using non-pessimistic transactional memory is that transactions may abort spuriously, while our analysis assumes the usual semantics of a DCSS, with no spurious aborts. However, a reasonable interpretation, at least for hardware transactional memory with very short transactions, is that spurious aborts occur only with very low probability, so their cumulative expected effect is small. Moreover, because our implementation remains correct even if DCSS is replaced with CAS, we can place a limit on the number of times a DCSS spuriously aborts, after which we fall back

Addressing the cost of contention. In order to bound the step complexity of operations as a function of the contention, we show that each step taken by an operation op can be *charged* to some operation op' that is part of the "contention" on op'. For example, if op traverses across a deleted node u, this step will be charged to the operation op' that deleted node u; we must then show that op and op' contend with each other, and also that op' is only charged a constant number of times by op.

The literature defines several measures for the amount of contention on an operation op. Among them are *interval contention* [1], which is the number of operations that overlap with op, and the *point contention* [2], which counts the maximum number of operations that run concurrently at any point during op. However, we believe that attempting to bound the step complexity as a function of the interval or point contention may be too pessimistic a design philosophy, as it spends significant effort addressing situations that are unlikely to arise in practice; it requires every operation to eagerly help operations in its vicinity to complete. This creates extra write contention.

Let us illustrate this idea using the doubly-linked list that will be presented in Section 3. The list maintains both `next` and `prev` pointers in each node, but since we do not use a double-compare-and-swap (DCAS), we cannot update both

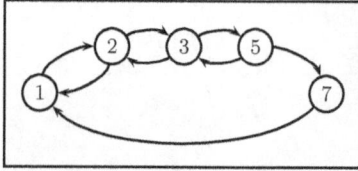

Figure 2: The doubly-linked list from the example in Section 1

pointers at the same time. Therefore, when inserting a new node, we first update the **next** pointer of its predecessor (this is the linearization point of an insert), and then we update the **prev** pointer of its successor. There is a short interval during which the **next** pointer of the predecessor already points to the new node, but the **prev** pointer of the successor points behind it.

Suppose that the list contains nodes 1 and 7, and we begin to insert node 5 (see Fig. 2). (We abuse notation slightly by using a number $i \in \mathbb{N}$ to refer to both the key i and the node that stores key i.) After linking node 5 in the *forward* direction, but before updating the **prev** pointer of node 7, the thread inserting node 5 is preempted. Then other threads insert nodes 2 and 3 into the list. We now have a gap of 3 nodes in the backwards direction: the **prev** pointer of node 7 still points to node 1, but in the forward direction we have nodes 2, 3 and 5 between nodes 1 and 7.

If a predecessor query Q searching for 6 begins at node 7 (e.g., because it has found node 7 by searching the x-fast trie), it will step back to node 1, then forward across nodes 2, 3, and 5. We must account for the three extra steps taken by Q. Note that the insertion of node 5 is not yet complete when Q begins its search, so stepping across node 5 can be charged to the point contention of Q. But what about nodes 2 and 3? The operations inserting them are done by the time Q begins. We cannot charge these steps to the point or interval contention of Q. There are two solutions:

(1) Prevent this situation from arising, by requiring inserts to "help" other inserts. If we wish to charge the extra steps to the interval or point contention of Q, the operations **insert**(2) and **insert**(3) *must not be allowed to complete* until the list has been repaired. This can be achieved by adding a flag, u.**ready**, which indicates whether the **prev** pointer of u's successor has been set to u. In order to set u.**ready** to 1, a thread must first ensure that u.**next**.**ready** = 1 (helping u.**next** if necessary), then it must set u.**next**.**prev** to point back to u, and only then can it set u.**ready** to 1. Because of the transitive nature of helping, we may have chains of **insert**s helping each other; however, there can be no deadlock, because nodes only help their successors.

If we use this solution, then in our example, when **insert**(5) is preempted, the **ready** flag of node 5 will not be set. Hence, **insert**(3) will help **insert**(5) by trying to set 7.**prev** to node 5. In turn, if **insert**(2) and **insert**(3) proceed in lockstep, then **insert**(2) will observe that **insert**(3) needs its help; it will help node 3 by helping node 5. As a result we will have **insert**(2), **insert**(3) and **insert**(5) all contending on 7.**prev**.

If our search query, starting from node 7 and searching for node 6, encounters the scenario depicted in Fig. 2, we can

now charge **insert**(2) and **insert**(3) for the extra steps, because these operations cannot have completed when the query begins. However, in order to avoid the potential extra *reads* by search queries that may or may not happen, we have created extra *write* contention by eagerly helping other operations complete. This pattern is common; for example, in the singly-linked list of [8], search queries must help clean the data structures by removing marked nodes that they come across, even though there is already a pending delete operation that will remove the marked node before it completes. This creates extra write contention on the base objects accessed by the pending delete, and is likely to slow its progress. We believe that such eager helping is not, in fact, helpful.[2]

The alternative is the following:

(2) Forgo eager helping, and instead relax our guarantee on the step complexity. This is the choice we make in the current paper. We observe that the "damage" caused by **insert**(2) and **insert**(3) is transient, and will be repaired as soon as **insert**(5) completes, setting 7.**prev** to node 5. In practice, it is unlikely that long gaps will form in the list.[3] Furthermore, the temporary gap in the list affects only *searches*, causing them to make extra reads; it does not create extra writes for any operation. Thus we allow the scenario depicted in Fig. 2, and similar scenarios. We allow operations to ignore temporary local obstacles that they come across as they traverse the list, as long as it is guaranteed that *some* operation will correct the problem before it completes.

To account for "transient" inconsistencies in the data structure, which are incurred during a recent operation and will be eliminated when the operation completes, we use the following definition:

DEFINITION 1.1 (OVERLAPPING-INTERVAL CONTENTION). *The* overlapping-interval contention $c_{OI}(op)$ *of an operation* op *is the maximum interval contention of an operation* op' *that overlaps with* op.

In our example above, the overlapping-interval contention of the query Q is at least the interval contention of **insert**(5), because these two operations overlap. In turn, the interval contention of **insert**(5) is at least 3, because, in addition to **insert**(5) itself, the operations **insert**(2) and **insert**(3) overlap with **insert**(5). Therefore we can charge the extra steps taken by Q to its overlapping-interval contention.

We remark that in our data structure, the overlapping-interval contention is only used to account for *reads*, never *writes*. The number of extra *write* steps performed by an operation op is bounded by the point contention of op.

Organization. The remainder of the paper is organized as follows. In Section 2 we sketch our new skiplist and its amortized analysis; for lack of space, we give only a brief overview. In Section 3 we give the construction of the doubly-linked list of the SkipTrie, and in Section 4 we construct the x-fast

---

[2]In Hebrew and Danish, the appropriate phrase is "a bear's help", referring to the tale of a man whose pet bear saw a fly on the man's nose and swatted him to death to get rid of it.

[3]For use-cases where many inserts or deletes with successive keys are frequent, it seems that approaches like flat combining are better suited in the first place.

trie and sketch the proof of its linearizability and amortized step complexity.

Notation and definitions. We use $p \preceq p'$ to denote the fact that p is a prefix of p', and $p \prec p'$ to denote a proper prefix. When referring to a trie node representing a prefix p, the 0-*subtree* (resp. 1-*subtree*) of p is the set of trie nodes representing prefixes or keys p' such that $p0 \preceq p'$ (resp. $p1 \preceq p'$). The *direction of a key x under a prefix $p \prec x$* is the bit d such that x belongs to the d-subtree of p.

We let p_i denote the i-th bit of p, and $p_{[i,\ldots,j]}$ denote bits i through j of p (inclusive), and we use $\mathsf{lcp}(x,y)$ to denote the longest common prefix of x and y.

2. AN EFFICIENT LOCK-FREE CONCURRENT SKIPLIST: A BRIEF OVERVIEW

For lack of space, we give only a brief overview of our skiplist construction. Our skiplist is constructed along similar lines as Lea's skiplist [14], and uses the idea of *back links* from [8, 20, 17]. It achieves an expected amortized cost of $O(\log\log \mathbf{u} + c_I)$, where c_I is the interval contention. If we also have traversals "help" inserts and deletes by raising and lowering towers of nodes they come across, we can tighten the bound and replace c_I with the point contention c_P.

The skiplist consists of $\log\log \mathbf{u}$ levels, each of which is itself a sorted linked list. We use the logical deletion scheme from [10], storing each node's `next` pointer together with its `marked` bit in one word. In addition, a list node contains a pointer `back` pointing backwards in the list, which allows operations to recover if the node is deleted "from under their feet"; a Boolean flag, `stop`, which is set to 1 when an operation begins deleting the node's tower in order to stop inserts from raising the tower further; and a pointer `down`, which points to the corresponding tower node on the level below.

A key procedure of the skiplist implementation is the search procedure, $\mathtt{listSearch}(x, \mathtt{start})$, which takes a node `start` on some level ℓ with $\mathtt{start.key} < x$, and returns a pair $(\mathtt{left}, \mathtt{right})$ of nodes on level ℓ such that $\mathtt{left.key} < x \leq \mathtt{right.key}$, and moreover, at some point during the invocation, `left` and `right` were both unmarked, and we had $\mathtt{left.next} = \mathtt{right}$. A similar function is used in the linked lists of [10] and [8]. This function also performs cleanup if necessary: if a marked node prevents it from finding an unmarked pair of nodes $(\mathtt{left}, \mathtt{right})$ as required (e.g., because there is a marked node between `left` and `right`), then $\mathtt{listSearch}$ will unlink the node. We use $\mathtt{listSearch}$ whenever we need to find the predecessor of a key x on a given level.

A traversal of the skiplist to find the predecessor of a key x begins at the top level, $\mathtt{TOP}$, from some node $\mathtt{start_{TOP}}$ that has $\mathtt{start_{TOP}.key} < x$. When we descend to level ℓ, we make a call to $\mathtt{listSearch}(x, \mathtt{start}_\ell)$, where $\mathtt{start}_\ell$ is the point from which we began the traversal on level ℓ, to obtain a pair $(\mathtt{left}_\ell, \mathtt{right}_\ell)$ bracketing the key x. Then we set $\mathtt{start}_{\ell-1} \leftarrow \mathtt{left}_\ell.\mathtt{down}$ and descend to the next level, where we call $\mathtt{listSearch}(x, \mathtt{start}_{\ell-1})$. Eventually we reach level 0; if $\mathtt{right}_0.\mathtt{key} = x$ then we return $\mathtt{right}_0$, and otherwise we return $\mathtt{left}_0$.

To insert a new key x, we first descend down the skiplist and locate the predecessor of x on every level. We choose a height $H(x) \sim Geom(1/2)$ for x. We first create a new node for x and insert it on the bottom level; this node is called

the *root*. Then we move up and insert x into every level up to $\min\{H(x), \mathtt{TOP}\}$. Each insertion is conditioned on the `stop` flag of the root remaining unset. To delete a key x, we find the root node of the tower corresponding to x, and set its `stop` flag. Then we delete x's tower nodes top-down, starting at the highest level on which x has been inserted.

Perhaps the most interesting feature of our skiplist is the analysis of its expected amortized step complexity. There are two key ideas:

1. How many times can an insert or delete operation "interfere" with other operations? If an insert or delete op causes a CAS or DCSS performed by another operation op' to fail, then op is charged for the extra step by op'. As two inserts go up the skiplist in parallel, or as two deletes go down, they may interfere with each other at most once on every level, because one successful CAS or DCSS is all that is necessary for an operation to move on from its current level.[4] However, they *can* interfere with each other on multiple levels. This might seem to lead to an amortized cost of $O(c_{OI} \cdot \log\log \mathbf{u})$ instead of $O(\log\log \mathbf{u} + c_{OI})$, as we may end up charging each operation once per level. However, we are saved by observing that an operation operation working on key x only "interferes" on levels $h \leq H(x)$, and $H(x)$ is geometrically distributed. Thus, in expectation, each operation only interferes with others on a constant number of levels, and the cost of contention is linear in expectation.

2. How can we bound the expected amortized cost of a skiplist traversal? We modify the beautiful analysis due to Pugh in [18], where he argues as follows: consider the traversal *in reverse order*, from the node found on the bottom level back to the top. Each time we make a "left" step in the inverted traversal, this corresponds to a node that made it to the current level, but did not ascend to the next level—otherwise we would have found it there, and we would not have needed to move to it on the level below. The probability of this is $1/2$, and the expected number of "left" steps between "up" steps is 2. Therefore, in expectation, the total number of "left" steps in the traversal is on the order of the height of the skiplist.

In our case, in addition to "left" and "up" (i.e., reversed "right" and "down") steps, we also have the following types of reversed steps:

- "Right" (reversed "left"): the current node in the traversal was marked, and we had to backtrack using its `back` pointer. We charge this step to the operation that marked the node. We show that the operation overlaps with the traversal, so this is permitted, and that we never step back over this node again.
- "Cleanup": the traversal stays in place, but CAS-es a marked node out of the list. This is again charged to the operation that marked the node.
- "Left that should have been up": we move to a node u on level ℓ, but the "true" height $H(u)$ chosen for u is greater than ℓ. Pugh's analysis does not account for this case, because it concerns only the "true" heights chosen for the nodes. In our case, we can show that since u's "true" height is greater than ℓ, we were "sup-

---

[4]Unless the CAS or DCSS is performed in order to "help" some other operation, but then the other operation will be charged instead.

posed" to find it before descending to level ℓ, and the reason we did not is that either u's tower is currently being raised by an insert, that had not reached level $\ell + 1$ when we descended to level ℓ, or u's tower is being lowered by a delete that had already removed the tower node from level $\ell + 1$ but has not yet reached level ℓ. We charge the inserting or deleting operation. Note that because traversals do not "help" inserts or deletes, we may charge the insert or delete once for every traversal that it overlaps with; this is why our bound is stated in terms of the interval contention rather than the point contention. To get the bound down to the point contention, traversals must help raise or lower towers, so that this situation is avoided.

The only steps that are not accounted for by charging other operations are the steps that Pugh's original analysis covers. Thus the expected amortized step complexity is $O(\log \log \mathbf{u} + c_I)$.

3. THE DOUBLY-LINKED LIST

Our doubly-linked list is built on top of the skiplist sketched in Section 2. We add to each top-level skiplist node a pointer, prev, which points to a node with a strictly smaller key. For linearizability we rely only on the forward direction of the list; the prev pointers are used only as "guides".

To insert a key into the list we call topleveLinsert, a procedure whose code is omitted here. In topleveInsert we create a new node, u, and insert it into the skiplist. If node u has reached the top level of the skiplist, we call fixPrev to set node u's prev pointer. Inside fixPrev, we locate node u's predecessor v in the list by calling listSearch with u's key, and then we attempt to set u.prev to v, provided that v remains unmarked and has v.next $= u$. If our attempt fails, we re-try, until we either succeed in setting u.prev or node u becomes marked. Upon success we set u.ready $\leftarrow 1$ to indicate that we have finished inserting node u into the doubly-linked list.

To delete a node u from the top level of the skiplist, we first ensure that u has been completely inserted (i.e., its prev pointer has been set), and if not, we finish inserting u by calling fixPrev. Then we delete it from all levels of the skiplist (top-down), which ensures that no next pointer points to u on any level. Finally, we remove u from the backwards direction on the top level by finding its successor v on the top level, and calling fixPrev to adjust v.prev so that it will no longer point back to u. If v became marked in the process, we find the new successor of u and try again. This ensures a type of local consistency for the doubly-linked list: the operation deleting u cannot complete until it has "observed" (inside fixPrev) a pair of unmarked nodes w, z that bracket u's key (w.key $< u$.key $\leq z$.key) and have w.next $= z$ and z.prev $= w$.

The key property of the top-level prev pointers is the following (addressing the scenario we described in Section 1 and Fig. 2):

LEMMA 3.1. *Suppose that u is an unmarked top-level node with u.prev $= v$, and there is a chain of nodes $u_0, \ldots, u_k$ such that $k > 1$, $u_0 = v$, $u_k = u$ and for each $i = 0, \ldots, k-1$ we have u_i.next $= u_{i+1}$, then the operation op inserting node u_{k-1} is still active, and furthermore, if $k > 2$, the operations that inserted nodes $u_1, \ldots, u_{k-2}$ overlap with op.*

Lemma 3.1 allows us to account for extraneous forward-steps

in the list: it shows that if, after following the prev pointer of some node u, we must step forward across a chain of nodes $u_0, \ldots, u_k$, then the extra steps to cross nodes $u_1, \ldots, u_{k-1}$ are covered under the interval contention of the operation inserting node u_{k-1}, and this operation is still active.

In addition to the lemma, we also rely on the fact that prev pointers are never set to marked nodes (this is a condition of the DCSS in fixPrev). Thus, if we follow a pointer u.prev and reach a marked node v, we know that v was marked after u.prev was updated for the last time. We will see in Section 4.2 that we only need to follow u.prev if node u was inserted during the current operation. Therefore we can conclude that crossing the marked node, v, is covered under the overlapping-interval contention of the current operation.

4. A LOCK-FREE CONCURRENT IMPLEMENTATION OF AN X-FAST TRIE

In this section we describe our lock-free implementation of an x-fast trie, and sketch its proof of linearizability and the analysis of its expected amortized performance.

In a sequential x-fast trie, only *unary nodes*, which are missing either a 0-subtree or a 1-subtree, store pointers into the linked list of keys. This is sufficient, because a binary search for the longest common prefix can never end at a binary node—if a prefix has both 0-children and 1-children, it is not the longest common prefix with any key. However, in a concurrent implementation it is useful to store pointers into the linked list even in binary nodes: suppose that a predecessor query Q looking for the predecessor of x looks up a prefix $p \prec x$ and sees that it exists in the trie, but the node representing it is binary and therefore stores no pointer into the linked list. Immediately afterwards, delete operations remove all the 0-children of p. Because Q found p in the trie, its future lookups will all be for longer prefixes p', where $p \cdot 0 \preceq p'$. But because all 0-children of p were deleted, these lookups will all fail, leaving Q "stuck" with no pointer into the linked list. The only possible recovery is to try to backtrack up the trie or to re-start the search, but these solutions are too expensive. Instead, we store in each trie node two pointers, to the largest child in the 0-subtree and the smallest child in the 1-subtree. This ensures that a query always holds a pointer to a top-level skiplist node, and indeed to a node that is not too far from its destination (and is updated to closer and closer nodes as the search progresses).

The data structure. The concurrent x-fast trie consists of a hash table prefixes, mapping prefixes to tree nodes representing them. A tree node n has a single field, n.pointers, which stores two pointers n.pointers$[0]$, n.pointers$[1]$ to the largest element in the 0-subtree and the smallest element in the 1-tree, respectively. Recall that "underneath" the x-fast trie we store all keys in a skiplist; the nodes pointed to by n.pointers$[d]$ for $d \in \{0, 1\}$ are top-level skiplist nodes. A value of n.pointers$[d] = $ null indicates that node n has no children in its d-subtree (except possibly new children currently being inserted).

Our goal is to ensure that n.pointers$[0]$ always points to the largest node in the 0-subtree that has been completely inserted (and not deleted yet), and symmetrically for n.pointers$[1]$; and furthermore, that if the deletion of top-

```
1   (left, right) ← listSearch(node.key, pred)
2   while !node.marked do
3   │   node_prev ← node.prev
4   │   if DCSS(node.prev, node_prev, left, left.succ, (node, 0)) then return
5   └   (left, right) ← listSearch(node.key, pred)
6   node.ready ← 1
```
Algorithm 1: fixPrev(pred, node)

```
1   if !node.ready then
2   │   fixPrev(pred, node)
3   skiplistDelete(pred, node)
4   repeat
5   │   (left, right) ← listSearch(node.key, right)
6   │   fixPrev(left, right)
7   until !right.marked
```
Algorithm 2: toplevelDelete(pred, node)

level skiplist node u has completed, then it is not pointed to by any trie node. In a sense, we can think of each trie node as a linearizable pair of pointers, reflecting all insert and delete operations that have already "crossed" the level of the trie node.

The hash table. As mentioned in Section 1, we use Split-Ordered Hashing [19] to implement the **prefixes** hash table. We require one additional method, compareAndDelete(p, n), which takes a prefix p and a trie node n, and removes p from **prefixes** iff the entry corresponding to p contains node n. This is easily achieved in the hash table of [19] by simply checking that p's entry corresponds to n before marking it.

4.1 X-Fast Trie Operations

Predecessor queries. For convenience, we divide our predecessor query into three procedures.

To find the predecessor of a key x, we first find its longest common prefix in the x-fast-trie using the LowestAncestor function, which performs a binary search on prefix length to locate the lowest ancestor of x in the tree; this is the node representing the longest common prefix that x has with any key in the trie. During the binary search, the query always remembers the "best" pointer into the linked list it has seen so far— the node whose key is closest to x. After log log $\mathbf{u}$ steps, LowestAncestor finishes its binary search and returns the "best" pointer into the doubly-linked list (i.e., the top level of the skiplist) encountered during the search.

The node returned by LowestAncestor may be marked for deletion, and its key may be greater than x. Therefore, inside the procedure xFastTriePred, we traverse back pointers (if the node is marked) or prev pointers (if the node is unmarked) until we reach a top-level skiplist node whose key is no greater than x. Finally, we call skiplistPred to find the true predecessor of x among all the keys in the SkipTrie.

```
1   curr ← LowestAncestor(key)
2   while curr.key > key do
3   │   if curr.marked then curr ← curr.back
4   └   else curr ← curr.prev
5   return curr
```
Algorithm 4: xFastTriePred(key)

```
1   return skiplistPred(key, xFastTriePred(key))
```
Algorithm 5: predecessor(key)

Insert operations. To insert a new key x, we first insert it into the skiplist; this is the linearization point of a successful insert, as after this point all searches will find x (until it is deleted). Then, if x reached the top level of the skiplist, we insert the prefixes of x into the trie as follows: for each prefix $p \preceq x$ from the bottom up (i.e., longer prefixes first), we look up the tree node corresponding to p in the **prefixes** hash table. If no such node is found, we create a new tree node pointing down to x and try to insert it into **prefixes**. Upon success, we return; upon failure, we start the current level over.

If a node is found but its **pointers** field is (null, null), we know that it is slated for deletion from **prefixes**; we help the deleting operation by deleting the node from **prefixes** ourselves. Then we start the current level over.

Finally, suppose that a tree node **n** is found in the hash table, and it has n.pointers $\neq$ (null, null). Let d be the direction of x's subtree under p, that is, $d \in \{0, 1\}$ satisfies $p \cdot d \preceq x$. If $d = 0$, then n.pointers$[d]$ should point to the largest key in **n**'s subtree and if $d = 1$ then n.pointers$[d]$ should point to the smallest key in **n**'s subtree. Thus, if $d = 0$ and n.pointers$[d]$.key $\geq x$, or if $d = 1$ and n.pointers$[d]$.key $\leq x$, then x is adequately represented in **n**, and we do not need to change anything; otherwise we try to swing the respective pointer n.pointers$[d]$ to point down to x, conditioned on x remaining unmarked.

Delete operations. To delete a key x, we first locate its predecessor **pred** among all top-level skiplist nodes, then try to delete x from the skiplist by calling either skiplistDelete, if the node is not a top-level node, or toplevelDelete if it is a top-level node. If we succeed, and if x was a top-level skiplist node, then we need to update x's prefixes in the trie so that they do not point down to the node u we just deleted. We go over the prefixes top-down (in increasing length), and for each prefix $p \prec x$, we check if **prefixes** contain an entry for p; if not, we move on to the next level. If it does contain an entry **n** for p, but n.pointers does not point down to u, we also move on. Finally, if n.pointers$[d] = u$ (where d is the direction of u under p, that is, $p \cdot d \preceq x$), then we

```
1   common_prefix ← ε
2   start ← 0 // The index of the first bit in the search window
3   size ← log u/2 // The size of the search window
4   ancestor ← prefixes.lookup(ε).pointers[key₀] // The lowest ancestor found so far
5   while size > 0 do
6   │   query ← common_prefix · (key[start,start+size−1])
7   │   direction ← key_{start+1}
8   │   query_node ← prefixes.lookup(query)
9   │   if query_node ≠ null then
10  │   │   candidate ← query_node.pointers[direction]
11  │   │   if candidate ≠ null and query ⪯ candidate.key then
12  │   │   │   if |key − candidate.key| ≤ |key − ancestor.key| then
13  │   │   │   │   ancestor ← candidate
14  │   │   │   common_prefix ← query
15  │   │   │   start ← start + size
16  │   size ← size/2
17  return ancestor
```

Algorithm 3: LowestAncestor(key)

```
1   pred ← xFastTriePred(key); if pred.key = key then return false
2   node ← toplevelInsert(key, pred)
3   if node = null then return false // key was already present
4   if node.orig_height ≠ TOP then return true // A non-top-level node was created
    // Insert into the prefix tree
5   for i = log u − 1, . . . , 0 do
6   │   p ← key[0,...,i]; direction ← key_{i+1}
7   │   while !node.marked do
8   │   │   tn ← prefixes.lookup(p)
9   │   │   if tn = null then // Create an entry for prefix p
10  │   │   │   tn ← new treeNode()
11  │   │   │   tn.pointers[direction] ← node
12  │   │   │   if prefixes.insert(p, tn) then break
13  │   │   else if tn.pointers = (null, null) then // The entry for p is in the process of being deleted; help delete it
14  │   │   │   prefixes.compareAndDelete(p, tn)
15  │   │   else
16  │   │   │   curr ← tn.pointers[direction]
17  │   │   │   if curr ≠ null and [(direction = 0 and curr.key ≥ key) or (direction = 1 and curr.key ≤ key)] then break
18  │   │   │   node_next = node.next
19  │   │   │   if DCSS(tn.pointers[direction], curr, node, node.succ, (node_next, 0)) then break
20  return true
```

Algorithm 6: insert(key)

call listSearch to find a pair of nodes (left, right) that
"bracket" key x on the top level of the skiplist: these nodes
satisfy left.next = right and left.key < x ≤ right.key,
and both of them are unmarked. If $d = 0$, then we swing
n.pointers[d] backwards to point to left, and if $d = 1$ we
swing n.pointers[d] forward to point to right. In both
cases we condition the switch on the new target, left or
right, remaining unmarked and adjacent to right or left
(respectively) on the top level of the skiplist.

4.2 Analysis of the Trie

Because prefixes is a linearizable hash table, our analysis treats it as an atomic object. For convenience we let
prefixes[p] denote the value currently associated with p in
the hash table (or null if there is none); that is, the result of
prefixes.lookup[p]. We also abuse notation slightly by using insert(u) and delete(u) to refer to an operation in the
SkipTrie whose top-level skiplist node is u (i.e., an insert
that created node u, or a delete that marked node u).

Linearizability of the trie is very easy to show: all we
have to show is that for each prefix p and direction d, if
prefixes[p] ≠ null and prefixes[p].pointers[d] ≠ null,
then prefixes[p].pointers[d] points to some node that was
reachable in the top level of the skiplist at some point in
time. This holds even if CAS is used instead of DCSS. The
properties of the doubly-linked list and the skiplist, which
are themselves linearizable, then guarantee that we will find
the predecessor of x.

For the amortized step complexity, we define the notion
of an operation *crossing* a certain level, which is informally
when its changes "take effect" on that level. We say that
insert(u) *crosses level ℓ* when one of the following occurs
inside the ℓ-th iteration of the for-loop: (1) a new node
for prefix p is successfully inserted into prefixes in line 12,
(2) the condition in line 17 evaluates to **true**, or (3) a successful DCSS occurs in line 19. We say that delete(u) *crosses
level ℓ* when one of the following occurs inside the ℓ-th iteration of the for-loop: (1) we set tn to null in line 8, or (2) we

```
1    pred ← pedecessor(key − 1);
2    (left, node) ← listSearch(key, pred)
3    if node.orig_height ≠ TOP then  return skiplistDelete(left, node)
4    if !toplevelDelete(left, node) then  return false
5    for i = 0, . . . , log u − 1 do
6    |    p ← key[0,...,i]
7    |    direction ← key_{i+1}
8    |    tn ← prefixes.lookup(p)
9    |    if tn = null then  continue
10   |    curr ← tn.pointers[direction]
11   |    while curr ≠ node do
12   |    |    (left, right) ← listSearch(key, left)
13   |    |    if direction = 0 then
14   |    |    |    DCSS(pointers[direction], curr, left, left.succ, (right, 0))
15   |    |    else
16   |    |    |    makeDone(left, right)
17   |    |    |    DCSS(pointers[direction], curr, right, (right.prev, right.marked), (left, 0))
18   |    |    curr ← tn.pointers[direction]
19   |    if !(p ⪯ curr.key) then // the sub-tree corresponding to p · direction has become empty
20   |    |    CAS(tn.pointers[direction], curr, null)
21   |    if tn.pointers = (null, null) then // the entire sub-tree corresponding to p has become empty
22   |    |    prefixes.compareAndDelete(p, tn)
23   return true
```

Algorithm 7: delete(key)

set curr to a value different from node in line 10 or line 18. We can show that once an operation has crossed a certain level, its effects on that level are persistent. For insert(u), this means that the trie points to a node "at least as good as u", and for delete(u), this means that u will never be reachable from the trie.

LEMMA 4.1. *Suppose that* insert(u) *has crossed level ℓ and u is unmarked. Let p be the length-ℓ prefix of u.key, and let $d \in \{0, 1\}$ be such that $p \cdot d \preceq u$.key. Then*

(a) prefixes$[p] \neq$ null *and* prefixes$[p]$.pointers$[d] \neq$ null, *and*

(b) If $d = 0$ then prefixes$[p]$.pointers$[d]$.key $\geq u$.key, *and if $d = 1$ then* prefixes$[p]$.pointers$[d]$.key $\leq u$.key.

If delete(u) *has crossed level ℓ, then either* prefixes$[p] =$ null, *or* prefixes$[p]$.pointers$[d] \neq u$.key.

When $Q =$ predecessor(x) finishes the binary search in the trie and lands in the top level of the skiplist, it may have to traverse prev pointers, back pointers of deleted nodes, and next pointers of unmarked nodes that stand between Q and its destination, the predecessor of x on the top level. We call the length of this top-level traversal *the list cost of* Q. To account for this cost, we calculate the *charge* that Q picks up as it searches through the tree: every time Q queries some level and "misses" an insert or delete that has not yet crossed that level, that operation pays Q one budget unit, which Q can then consume to traverse through the doubly-linked list.

More formally, we represent Q's binary search through the trie as a complete binary tree, where each node a is labeled with a search query $q(a) \in \{0, 1\}^*$. The root is labeled with the first query $x_{[0,...,\log u/2]}$ performed by the search. For an inner node a, the left child of a is labeled with the query performed if $q(a)$ is not found in the hash table, and the right child of a is labeled with the query performed if

$q(a)$ *is* found. For example, the root's children are labeled $x_{[0,...,\log u/4]}$ and $x_{[0,...,3 \log u/4]}$ respectively.

The leaves of the tree correspond to the result of the binary search; for a sequential trie, this is the longest common prefix of x with any key in the trie. In the concurrent trie this is no longer true, due to concurrent insertions and deletions: the contents of the prefixes hash table does not accurately reflect keys which are currently being inserted or removed. However, we can show that the search behaves properly with respect to keys which are *not* currently being inserted or removed.

Suppose that inside Q, LowestAncestor(x) eventually returns a node u with u.key $= y$. The path Q follows through its binary search tree is the path from the root to lcp(x, y), as y is the key returned. For a key $z \neq y$, define the *critical point for z* in Q's binary search tree to be the highest node where the path from the root to lcp(x, y) diverges from the path to lcp(x, z). Then using Lemma 4.1 we can show:

LEMMA 4.2. *If v is an unmarked node with v.key $= z$ such that $|z - x| < |y - x|$ and $\text{sign}(z - x) = \text{sign}(y - x)$ (that is, y and z are "on the same side" of x), and a is the critical point for z in Q's binary search tree, then when Q queried $q(a)$, the operation that inserted v had not yet crossed level $|q(a)|$.*

Thus, on a very high level, for any unmarked node v that is closer to the target node (i.e., closer to the predecessor of x on the top level of the skiplist) than the node returned by LowestAncestor, we can charge the operation that was not yet done inserting v when Q passed the critical point for v.key. In particular, when we follow prev pointers, the nodes we cross were inserted during Q. For marked nodes that are traversed, we show that we can charge the operation that marked them, and this is covered under the overlapping-interval contention. And finally, if, after moving backwards following prev pointers, we went "too far back" and must make extra forward steps, then Lemma 3.1 shows that all nodes we cross are either newly-inserted nodes or are covered under the overlapping-interval contention of Q. Therefore Q is adequately compensated for its list cost, and we can show that its expected amortized step complexity, considering just the x-fast trie (i.e., the binary search and the traversal in the top level of the skiplist), is $O(\log \log \mathbf{u} + c_{OI})$.

The remainder of the proof consists of "assigning the blame" for each DCSS instruction and hash-table operation executed by `insert` and `delete`. To cross a level, each operation needs to perform only one successful DCSS or hash-table operation. Every *failed* DCSS instruction or operation on `prefixes` is charged to the operation that caused it to fail, by executing some successful DCSS or operation on `prefixes`. The various trie operations can charge each other at most once per level, for a total amortized cost of at most $O(c_P \cdot \log \mathbf{u})$ when considering the x-fast trie by itself. However, because in expectation only one in every $\log \mathbf{u}$ SkipTrie operation must insert or delete from the x-fast trie, the expected amortized cost of SkipTrie insertions and deletions in the x-fast trie is only $O(c_P + \log \log \mathbf{u})$. Thus, the dominant cost is the cost of predecessor queries. (Note that $c_P \leq c_I \leq c_{OI}$ for any operation.)

Because expected amortized step complexity is compositional, we can combine our analysis of the various components of the SkipTrie to obtain the following bounds:

THEOREM 4.3. *The SkipTrie is a linearizable, lock-free data structure supporting* `insert`, `delete` *and* `predecessor` *queries in expected amortized* $O(\log \log \mathbf{u} + c_{OI})$, *where* c_{OI} *is the overlapping-interval contention of the operation.*

5. REFERENCES

[1] Yehuda Afek, Gideon Stupp, and Dan Touitou. Long lived adaptive splitter and applications. *Distrib. Comput.*, 15(2):67–86, April 2002.

[2] Hagit Attiya and Arie Fouren. Algorithms adapting to point contention. *J. ACM*, 50(4):444–468, July 2003.

[3] Anastasia Braginsky and Erez Petrank. A lock-free b+tree. In *Proceedings of the 24th ACM Symposium on Parallelism in Algorithms and Architectures, SPAA '12, Pittsburgh, PA, USA, June 25-27, 2012*, pages 58–67, 2012.

[4] Nathan G. Bronson, Jared Casper, Hassan Chafi, and Kunle Olukotun. A practical concurrent binary search tree. *SIGPLAN Not.*, 45:257–268, January 2010.

[5] R. Brown. Calendar queues: A fast priority queue implementation for the simulation event set problem. *Communications of the ACM*, 31(10):1220–1227, 1988.

[6] Aleksandar Dragojević and Tim Harris. Stm in the small: trading generality for performance in software transactional memory. In *Proceedings of the 7th ACM european conference on Computer Systems*, EuroSys '12, pages 1–14, 2012.

[7] Faith Ellen, Panagiota Fatourou, Eric Ruppert, and Franck van Breugel. Non-blocking binary search trees. In *Proceedings of the 29th ACM SIGACT-SIGOPS symposium on Principles of distributed computing*, PODC '10, pages 131–140, New York, NY, USA, 2010. ACM.

[8] M. Fomitchev and E. Ruppert. Lock-free linked lists and skip lists. In *PODC '04: Proceedings of the twenty-third annual ACM symposium on Principles of distributed computing*, pages 50–59, New York, NY, USA, 2004. ACM Press.

[9] Hui Gao, Jan Friso Groote, and Wim H. Hesselink. Almost wait-free resizable hashtable. In *IPDPS*, 2004.

[10] T. Harris. A pragmatic implementation of non-blocking linked-lists. In *Proceedings of the 15th International Conference on Distributed Computing*, DISC '01, pages 300–314, 2001.

[11] Maurice Herlihy and Nir Shavit. *The Art of Multiprocessor Programming*. Morgan Kaufmann, NY, USA, 2008.

[12] Maurice Herlihy, Nir Shavit, and Moran Tzafrir. Hopscotch hashing. In *Proceedings of the 22nd international symposium on Distributed Computing*, DISC '08, pages 350–364, Berlin, Heidelberg, 2008. Springer-Verlag.

[13] D. Lea. Concurrent hash map in JSR166 concurrency utilities. http://gee.cs.oswego.edu/dl/concurrency-interest/index.html.

[14] D. Lea. Concurrent skiplist map. in java.util.concurrent. http://gee.cs.oswego.edu/dl/concurrency-interest/index.html.

[15] Li Meifang, Zhu Hongkai, Shen Derong, Nie Tiezheng, Kou Yue, and Yu Ge. Pampoo: an efficient skip-trie based query processing framework for p2p systems. In *Proceedings of the 7th international conference on Advanced parallel processing technologies*, APPT'07, pages 190–198, Berlin, Heidelberg, 2007. Springer-Verlag.

[16] Aleksandar Prokopec, Nathan G. Bronson, Phil Bagwell, and Martin Odersky. Concurrent tries with efficient non-blocking snapshots. In *Proceedings of Principles and Practice of Parallel Programming*, New Orleans, USA, 2012.

[17] W. Pugh. Concurrent maintenance of skip lists. Technical Report CS-TR-2222.1, Institute for Advanced Computer Studies, Department of Computer Science, University of Maryland, 1989.

[18] W. Pugh. Skip lists: a probabilistic alternative to balanced trees. *ACM Transactions on Database Systems*, 33(6):668–676, 1990.

[19] O. Shalev and N. Shavit. Split-ordered lists: Lock-free extensible hash tables. In *The 22nd Annual ACM Symposium on Principles of Distributed Computing*, pages 102–111. ACM Press, 2003.

[20] John D. Valois. Lock-free linked lists using compare-and-swap. In *Proceedings of the fourteenth annual ACM symposium on Principles of distributed computing*, PODC '95, pages 214–222, 1995.

[21] P. van Emde Boas. Preserving order in a forest in less than logarithmic time. In *Proceedings of the 16th Annual Symposium on Foundations of Computer Science*, pages 75–84, Washington, DC, USA, 1975. IEEE Computer Society.

[22] Dan E. Willard. Log-logarithmic worst-case range queries are possible in space theta(n). *Inf. Process. Lett.*, 17(2):81–84, 1983.

Compact Routing Schemes with Improved Stretch

Shiri Chechik
Microsoft Research Silicon Valley
Mountain View CA, USA
shiri.chechik@gmail.com

ABSTRACT

We consider the problem of compact routing in weighted general undirected graphs, in which the goal is to construct local routing tables that allow information to be sent on short paths in the network. In this paper the first improvement to the work of Thorup and Zwick [SPAA'01] is presented. Specifically, we construct an improved routing scheme obtaining for every k routing tables of size $\tilde{O}\left(n^{1/k}\log D\right)$, and stretch $(4-\alpha)k-\beta$ for some absolute constants $\alpha,\beta > 0$, where D is the normalized diameter. This provides a positive answer to a main open question in this area as to the existence of a routing scheme with stretch $c \cdot k$ for some constant $c < 4$.

Categories and Subject Descriptors: F.2.2 Analysis of Algorithms and Problem Complexity: Nonnumerical Algorithms and Problems

Keywords: compact routing, stretch factor, name independent routing

1. INTRODUCTION

Routing is perhaps one of the most fundamental problems in the area of distributed networking. The goal in this problem is to construct a distributed mechanism that allows any node in the network to send packages of data to any other node efficiently. As in all distributed algorithms, a routing scheme runs locally on every node of the network allowing it to forward arriving data while utilizing local information that is stored at the node itself. This local information is commonly referred to as the routing table of the node.

Formally, a routing scheme is comprised of two phases, the preprocessing phase and the routing phase. In the first phase, the preprocessing phase, each node is assigned a routing table and a small size label (poly-logarithmic in the size of the network) that are stored locally at the node. In the second phase, the routing phase, the routing scheme allows any node to send information to any other node in a distributed manner. Specifically, the scheme allows every node,

Permission to make digital or hard copies of all or part of this work for personal or classroom use is granted without fee provided that copies are not made or distributed for profit or commercial advantage and that copies bear this notice and the full citation on the first page. Copyrights for components of this work owned by others than ACM must be honored. Abstracting with credit is permitted. To copy otherwise, or republish, to post on servers or to redistribute to lists, requires prior specific permission and/or a fee. Request permissions from permissions@acm.org.
PODC'13, July 22–24, 2013, Montréal, Québec, Canada.
Copyright 2013 ACM 978-1-4503-2065-8/13/07 ...$15.00.

upon receiving a message, to decide whether this message reached its final destination or to which of the node's neighbors this message should be sent next. In order to make such decisions, the node may use its own routing table and the header of the message that contains the label of the final destination and perhaps some additional information.

The stretch of a routing scheme is defined as the worst case ratio between the length of the path obtained by the routing scheme and the length of the shortest path between the source node and the destination node.

There are usually two key concerns in designing routing schemes. The first concern is to minimize the stretch of the routing scheme, and the second concern is to minimize the size of the routing tables. Much of the work on designing routing schemes focuses on the tradeoff between these two concerns.

An extreme case is when the designer is allowed to store linear size memory at the nodes. In this case it is possible to store a complete routing table at all nodes, i.e., for every node s and every destination t store the port of the neighbour of s on the shortest path from s to t. Using these routing tables it is possible to route messages on shortest path, namely, having a stretch of 1. The clear drawback of this solution is that we need routing tables of size $\Omega(n)$. In a large network, having routing tables of size $\Omega(n)$ can be too costly.

In many cases it would be desirable to store much smaller routing tables at the price of larger stretch. We say that a routing scheme is compact if the size of the routing tables is sub-linear in the number of nodes.

Many papers deal with the tradeoff between the size of the routing tables and the stretch (e.g. [16, 5, 6, 15, 7, 8, 13]). The first tradeoff was presented by Peleg and Upfal [16]. Their paper considered unweighted graph and achieved a bound on the total size of the routing tables. A tradeoff for weighted graphs with a guarentee on the maximum table size was later presented by Awerbuch *et al.* [5]. This paper presented a routing scheme that uses table size of $\tilde{O}(n^{1/k})$ with stretch $O(k^2 9^k)$. A better tradeoff was later obtained by Awerbuch and Peleg [6]. Efficient schemes for specific values of k were presented in [7, 8].

The best known tradeoff was achieved by Thorup and Zwick [17]. They showed a routing scheme that uses routing tables of size $\tilde{O}(n^{1/k})$, a stretch of $4k-5$ and labels size of $O(k \log n)$. This routing scheme assumes that the port numbers can be assigned by the routing process. In the case of fixed port model, namely, the port numbers are part of the input of the preprocessing phase, their labels size increases to $O(k \log^2 n)$. In addition, they showed that if a handshaking is allowed, namely the source node and the target node can communicate before the routing phase starts and agree on an $o(\log^2 n)$ bit header that is attached to the header of all messages, then the stretch can be reduced to $2k - 1$. However, in many cases, it would be desirable to avoid the use of handshaking, especially if the source wishes to send only a single message to the destination. In that case the overhead of establishing a handshake could be as high as sending the original message. Thorup and Zwick's scheme [17] of stretch of $2k - 1$ established using a handshake is essentially optimal assuming the girth conjecture of Erdős [9]. Erdős [9] conjectured that for every $k > 1$ there are graphs with $\Omega(n^{1+1/k})$ number of edges whose girth is at least $2k + 1$. If the conjecture is true, namely, there exists such a graph G, then any routing scheme of stretch less than $2k-1$ requires a total memory of at least $\Omega(n^{1+1/k})$ on some subgraphs of G. Namely, relying on this conjecture it is impossible to achieve a routing scheme that uses $O(n^{1/k})$ routing tables with less than $2k - 1$ stretch with or without handshaking. For further lower bounds see [16, 10, 12, 18, 14]. A main open problem in the area of compact routing schemes is on the gap between the stretch $4k - 5$ and $2k - 1$ in the case of no handshaking. In this paper, we give the first evidence that the asymptotically optimal stretch is less than $4k$ (for the case of routing tables of size $\tilde{O}(n^{1/k})$ and no handshaking). This is the first improvement to the stretch-space tradeoff of routing scheme since the result of Thorup and Zwick [SPAA'01].

A closely related variant is that of name independent routing scheme. In this variant the addresses of the nodes are fixed, namely, they are part of the input network and cannot be changed by the routing scheme. The problem of name independent routing was extensively studied. The first trade-off was presented by Awerbuch *et al.* [4]. They presented a compact name independent routing scheme with stretch that is exponential in k. This was followed by a series of improvements [6, 5, 3, 2, 1]. In [1], Abraham *et al.* presented a name independent routing scheme that uses $\tilde{O}(n^{1/k} \log D)$ with $O(k)$ stretch, where D is the normalized diameter.

All of our sizes, unless mentioned otherwise, are measured in the number of words, where a word is a storage unit large enough to contain any distance or an ID of a node.
Our contributions: We present the first improvement on the work of Thorup and Zwick [SPAA'01] by constructing a compact routing scheme in weighted general undirected graphs that uses tables of size $\tilde{O}(n^{1/k})$ and has stretch $c \cdot k$ for some absolute constant $c < 4$, thus, obtaining improved results for every $k \geq 4$. Specifically, for $k = 4$ we improve the 11 stretch of Thorup and Zwick to ≈ 10.52. In order to obtain this improved result we prove several structural properties on the Thorup and Zwick construction which might be of independent interest.
Paper Organization: Section 2 contains preliminaries and notations. In Section 3 we present the general framework used in the paper. In order to simplify presentation, we start by focusing on the case where $k = 4$ in Section 4. Section 5 contains the case of general k. For simplicity, we start by describing the scheme for unweighted graphs and later (in Section B) describe the modifications needed in order to handle weighted graphs.

2. PRELIMINARIES AND NOTATION

Let us introduce some notations that will be used throughout the text. For a graph G, denote by $V(G)$ and $E(G)$ respectively the sets of vertices and edges of G. Consider a rooted tree T and a node $v \in V(T)$. Denote by $r(T)$ the root of the tree T. Let $\mathbf{parent}(v, T)$ be the parent of v in the tree T or null in the case where v is the root of T. Let $\mathbf{childs}(v, T)$ be the set of children of v in the tree T. Let $\deg(v, T) = |\mathbf{childs}(v, T)|$, namely, the number of children of v in the tree T. Let $\mathbf{radius}(T)$ be the longest path from $r(T)$ to some node in T.

3. GENERAL FRAMEWORK

An essential ingredient in our routing scheme is a procedure for routing on rooted subtrees of the graph. Given a tree T, the procedure assigns every node v in T a label $L(v, T)$ and a routing table $A(v, T)$. Using the label $L(t, T)$ of some node t and the routing tables $A(v, T)$, it is possible to route to t from any node in T on their shortest (only) path in T. Thorup and Zwick presented a routing scheme on trees that uses $(1 + o(1)) \log n$ label size and these labels are the only information stored at the nodes. In the case of fixed port model, namely, the port numbers are not allowed to be changed, their labels size increases to $O(\log^2 n)$. A similar scheme was presented by Fraigniaud and Gavoille [11].

Our scheme is strongly based on Thorup-Zwick construction (with some new ideas). For completeness we now outline the compact routing scheme of Thorup and Zwick. For a given positive integer k, construct the sets $V = A_0 \supseteq A_1 \supseteq \cdots \supseteq A_{k-1} \supseteq A_k = \emptyset$ as follows. Each A_i for $1 \leq i \leq k - 1$ is obtained by sampling the nodes in A_{i-1} independently at random with probability $(n/ \ln n)^{-1/k}$. The pivot $p_i(v)$ is defined to be the closest node to v in A_i (break ties arbitrarily).

The bunch $B(v)$ of v is defined as follows. A node $w \in A_i \setminus A_{i+1}$ is added to $B(v)$ if $\mathbf{dist}(v, w) \leq \mathbf{dist}(v, A_{i+1})$. Namely,

$$B(v) = \bigcup_{i=0}^{k-1} \{w \in A_i \setminus A_{i+1} \mid \mathbf{dist}(v, w) < \mathbf{dist}(v, A_{i+1})\}.$$

Note that $\mathbf{dist}(v, A_k) = \infty$ and thus $A_{k-1} \subseteq B(v)$.

For a node $w \in A_i \setminus A_{i+1}$, the cluster $C(w)$ is defined as follows $C(w) = \{v \in V \mid \mathbf{dist}(w, v) \leq \mathbf{dist}(v, A_{i+1})\}$. Or in other words, the cluster of a node w is the set of nodes v such that $w \in B(v)$.

For every node $w \in V$, let $T(w)$ be the shortest path tree rooted at w spanning $C(w)$. For every node $w \in V$, invoke the routing scheme on trees on $T(w)$ and store the label $L(v, T(w))$ at the routing table $A_{TZ}(v)$ of v. The label $L_{TZ}(v)$ of v is the concatenation of $L(v, T(p_i(v)))$ for $1 \leq i \leq k - 1$. This completes the construction of the routing tables and the labels.

It was shown in [17] that for every node v, $|B(v)| = O(n^{1/k} \log n)$, namely there are st most $O(n^{1/k} \log n)$ nodes w such that $v \in C(w)$. We get that $|A_{TZ}(v)| = O(n^{1/k} \log^3 n)$. The size of the label $L_{TZ}(v)$ is $O(k \log^2 n)$ (we have to use the fixed port model since the trees may overlap).

The routing process is done as follows. Assume some node s wants to send a message to some node t given the label $L_{TZ}(t)$. The node s finds the first index i such that $p_i(t) \in B(s)$, or in other words that $s \in T(p_i(t))$ and then it routes the message to t on the tree $T(p_i(t))$ using $L(t, T(p_i(t)))$ ($\subseteq L_{TZ}(t)$).

Thorup and Zwick showed that the above scheme gives a stretch of $4k - 3$. The proof of the stretch was based on the following claim. Let i be the first index such that $p_i(t) \in B(s)$ and let $d = \mathbf{dist}(s, t)$. For every $j \leq i$, $\mathbf{dist}(t, p_j(t)) \leq 2jd$ and $\mathbf{dist}(s, p_j(s)) \leq (2j - 1)d$.

Note that the algorithm routes the message from s to t on $T(p_i(t))$ and that $\mathbf{dist}(s, p_i(t)) + \mathbf{dist}(t, p_i(t)) \leq \mathbf{dist}(s, t) + \mathbf{dist}(t, p_i(t)) + \mathbf{dist}(t, p_i(t)) \leq d + 4(k-1)d = (4k-3)d$. We thus get a stretch of $4k - 3$.

Thorup and Zwick also showed that by using a slightly different sampling procedure it is possible to reduce the stretch to $4k - 5$. The new sampling procedure guarantees that $|C(w)| \leq O(n^{1/k})$ for every $w \in A_0 \setminus A_1$. The algorithm stores the set $C(w)$ and the labels $L(v, T(w))$ for every $v \in C(w)$ in the table $A_{TZ}(w)$. In the routing process, the algorithm checks if $s \in A_0 \setminus A_1$ and $t \in C(s)$, if so it routes the message to t in $T(s)$. If $t \notin C(s)$ then by definition $\mathbf{dist}(t, p_1(t)) \leq \mathbf{dist}(s, t)$, (rather than $\mathbf{dist}(t, p_1(t)) \leq 2\mathbf{dist}(s, t)$). This saves up 2 to the total stretch, resulting with a stretch of $4k - 5$.

In our scheme we need the following stronger property. For every $w \in A_{\ell-1} \setminus A_\ell$: $|C(w)| \leq O(n^{\ell/k})$ for $\ell \leq r$ for some integer r. We thus employ this sampling procedure for every index i and slightly change the sampling probability used in [17].

We construct the sets A_i as follows, $A_0 = V, A_k = \emptyset$ and for each $1 \leq i \leq k - 1$, $A_i = \mathbf{center}(G, A_{i-1}, n^{1-i/k}/\log n)$.

Procedure $\mathbf{center}$ operates on a given graph G, set of nodes A' and a size s. It operates as follows. Initially set $A \leftarrow \emptyset$ and $W \leftarrow A'$. While $W \neq \emptyset$ do the following. Let $B' = sample(W, s)$, namely, B' is obtained by sampling every node in W independently at random with probability $s/|W|$, or $B' = W$ if $|W| \leq s$. Set $A \leftarrow A \cup B'$. Let $C_A(w) \leftarrow \{v \in V \mid \mathbf{dist}(w, v) < \mathbf{dist}(A, v)\}$, for every $w \in A'$. Set $W \leftarrow \{w \in A' \mid |C(w)| > 4n/s\}$. See Procedure 1 for the formal code.

The following lemma is crucial in our analysis. (The proof is deferred to the appendix.)

LEMMA 3.1. *For every node* $w \in A_i \setminus A_{i+1}$: $|C(w)| = O(n^{(i+1)/k})$. *In addition, for every node* $v \in V$: $|B(v)| = O(n^{1/k} \log n)$.

4. WARM-UP: THE CASE $K = 4$

In this section we present our routing scheme for the case $k = 4$.

An important ingredient in our routing algorithm is a procedure for name-independent routing on trees inspired from [2]. We present a name-independent routing scheme for a given tree T that is schematically done a follows. For a given tree T, distribute the labels $L(v, T)$ for every node $v \in V(T)$ among a subset of the nodes and design a search mechanism such that given $\mathbf{key}(v)$ can find in a distributed manner $L(v, T)$, where $\mathbf{key}(v)$ is a unique identifier of the node v in $[1..n]$.

Let us start with describing our search mechanism. We will later see how to use this mechanism in our routing scheme. The search mechanism presented here is designed specifically for the case of $k = 4$, in the case where $k > 4$ we need to use a more complicated search tree as will be described later on. We show the following lemma.

LEMMA 4.1. *Consider a tree* T *of depth* d', *a set of nodes* $\mathbf{core}(T) \subseteq V(T)$ *such that* $r(T) \in \mathbf{core}(T)$, $|\mathbf{core}(T)| \geq \lceil |V(T)|/n^{1/k} \rceil$ *and* $|V(T)| \leq n^{2/k}$. *One can construct a search scheme with the following properties.*
(1) The scheme stores $O(n^{1/k} \log^2 n)$ *information* $\mathbf{ST}(v, T)$ *at every node* $v \in \mathbf{core}(T)$.
(2) Given a key $\mathbf{key}$ *the algorithm can find* $L(\mathbf{key}, T)$ *(or decides that* $\mathbf{key} \notin V(T)$) *in a distributed manner by traveling on a path from the root* $r(T)$ *of length at most* $\mathbf{radius}(T)$.

Proof: The proof is by construction. Let $\mathcal{K} = \{\mathbf{key}(v) \mid v \in V(T)\}$. First, the algorithm distributes the keys $\mathcal{K}$ such that every node in $\mathbf{core}(T)$ stores $O(n^{1/k})$ keys and their matching labels. The algorithm assigns each node $v \in \mathbf{core}(T)$ an interval $I(v) = [n_1, n_2]$, the node v stores the labels of the keys in $\mathcal{K}$ in the range $[n_1, n_2]$. This is done as follows. Order the nodes at $\mathbf{core}(T)$ by some order. The algorithm stores at the first node in $\mathbf{core}(T)$ the first $n^{1/k}$ keys and their matching labels (the keys with the smallest IDs). The algorithm then assigns to the next node in $\mathbf{core}(T)$ the next $n^{1/k}$ keys and so on.

Recall that $|V(T)| \leq n^{2/k}$, we get that the algorithm assigns keys to at most $n^{1/k}$ nodes in $\mathbf{core}(T)$, let $\hat{\mathbf{core}}(T)$ be this set of nodes. Notice also that the algorithm cannot run out of nodes in $\mathbf{core}(T)$ as $|\mathbf{core}(T)| \geq \lceil |V(T)|/n^{1/k} \rceil$.

Consider a node $v \in \mathbf{core}(T)$, Let n_1 be the smallest key assigned to v and n_2 be the largest key assigned to v, the interval $I(v, T)$ of v is $[n_1, n_2]$. Note that all keys in the interval $I(v, T)$ are assigned to v. The node v stores the keys assigned to it and their matching labels. In addition, the root $r(T)$ stores the labels of the set $\hat{\mathbf{core}}(T)$ and their matching intervals.

This completes the construction of our search mechanism. We now turn to describe the search algorithm for a given key $\mathbf{key}$. We assume that the search algorithms starts at the root $r(T)$. Namely, the algorithm first routes the message to the root and only then it invokes the search algorithm. The root $r(T)$ checks which of the nodes in $\mathbf{core}(T)$ stores the label $L(\mathbf{key}, T)$, namely, the node z whose interval contains $\mathbf{key}$. The root $r(T)$ attaches to the header of the message the label $L(z, T)$ and routes the message to the node z using $L(z, T)$. The node z either stores the label $L(\mathbf{key}, T)$ or determines that $\mathbf{key}$ does not exist in T. One can see that the path obtained by this search mechanism is of length at most $\mathbf{radius}(T)$ (until reaching the node in T containing $L(\mathbf{key}, T)$ or deciding that $\mathbf{key} \notin V(T)$). We thus get that property (2) is satisfied. In addition, it is not hard to verify that property (1) is satisfied by construction. ∎

Constructing the labels and routing tables:

We now turn to describe the construction of the labels and routing tables in our routing scheme.

The first step of our algorithm is to assign every node $v \in V$ a unique identifier $\mathbf{key}(v)$ in the range $[1..n]$. Next, construct Thorup-Zwick routing tables and labels. The label $L(v)$ is defined as follows. Add the key $\mathbf{key}(v)$ to the label $L(v)$. Next, add to $L(v)$ the label $L_{TZ}(v)$ assigned to v by the Thorup-Zwick construction. In addition, add to $L(v)$ the distances $\mathbf{dist}(v, P_i(v))$ for every $1 \leq i \leq k - 1$.

It is not hard to verify that the asymptotic sizes of the labels $L(v)$ and $L_{TZ}(v)$ are the same.

The routing table $A(v)$ of the node v is constructed as follows. First, add to the routing table $A(v)$ the routing ta-

```
Algorithm center(G(V, E), A', s)

A ← ∅; W ← A'
while W ≠ ∅; do:
{
    A ← A ∪ sample(W, s)
    C_A(w) ← {v ∈ V | dist(w, v) < dist(A, v)}, for every w ∈ A';
    W ← {w ∈ A' | |C(w)| > 4n/s}
}
return A;
```

Figure 1: Choosing a set of centers with small size clusters.

ble $A_{TZ}(v)$ assigned to v by the Thorup-Zwick construction. In addition, we enhance the routing tables with additional information. We now describe the additional information stored at the nodes.

For every node $w \in V$, let $T(w)$ be the shortest path tree rooted at w spanning $C(w)$. For every node $w \in A_1 \setminus A_2$ and every distance $d' = (1+\epsilon)^j$ for $1 \leq j \leq \log D(w)$, where $D(w) = \mathbf{radius}(T(w))$, do the following.

The core $\mathbf{core}(w, d')$ is obtained by sampling every node $v \in T(w)$ independently at random with probability $4 \log n / n^{1/k}$. Let $T(w, d')$ be the tree $T(w)$ trimmed at distance d', i.e., the tree that is obtained by deleting all nodes from $T(w)$ that are at distance greater than d' from w. Let $C(w, d')$ be set of nodes in $T(w, d')$, i.e., all nodes v in $C(w)$ such that $\mathbf{dist}(v, w) \leq d'$.

For every node $w \in V$, and every distance $d' = (1+\epsilon)^j$ construct the search mechanism of Lemma 4.1 on $T(w, d')$ and $\mathbf{core}(w, d') \cup \{w\}$. Add to the routing tables $A(v)$ the information $\mathbf{ST}(v, T(w, d'))$ of the search mechanism for every $v \in \mathbf{core}(w, d') \cup \{w\}$.

This completes the construction of our labels and routing tables.

Let us now analyze the size of the routing tables.

By Chernoff bounds we show the following.

LEMMA 4.2. *With high probability the following two events occur. 1. For every node $w \in A_1 \setminus A_2$: $|\mathbf{core}(w, d')| \geq \lceil |C(w)| / n^{1/k} \rceil$. 2. For every node $v \in V$, there are at most $O(\log^2 n)$ nodes w and distances $d' = (1+\epsilon)^j$ for $1 \leq j \leq \log D(w)$ such that $v \in \mathbf{core}(w, d')$.*

Proof: The expected size μ_1 of $\mathbf{core}(w, d')$ is
$\mu_1 = (4 \log n |V(T)|) / n^{1/k}$

Recall that by Chernoff's bound, we have for a binomial random variable X such that $E[X] = \mu$, $Pr[X < (1+\delta)\mu] \leq exp(\mu\delta^2/2)$. We thus get that $Pr[|\mathbf{core}(w, d')| \leq (\log n |V(T)|) / n^{1/k}] \leq exp(\mu) < 1/n^2$. The first part follows.

To see the second part, recall that a node v belongs to $O(n^{1/k} \log n)$ clusters. For each cluster, the algorithm considers $O(\log n)$ distances d'. The probability that a node v belongs to $\mathbf{core}(w, d')$ is $4 \log n / n^{1/k}$. Thus the expected number μ_2 of nodes w and distances d' such that $v \in \mathbf{core}(w, d')$ is $O(\log^2 n)$. By applying Chernoff bound we get that with high probability there are at most $O(\log^2 n)$ nodes w and distances d' such that $v \in \mathbf{core}(w, d')$. ∎

We thus conclude the following.

LEMMA 4.3. *For every node v the expected size of the routing table $A(v)$ is $O(n^{1/k} \log^4 n)$.*

Proof: Recall that there are two main parts in the routing table $A(v)$. The first part is the routing table $A_{TZ}(v)$ of Thorup-Zwick scheme and the second part is the information $\mathbf{ST}(v, T(w, d'))$ of the search mechanism for every w and d' such that $v \in \mathbf{core}(w, d') \cup \{w\}$. It was shown in [17] that the size of $A_{TZ}(v)$ is $O(n^{1/k} \log^3 n)$. We left with bounding the size of the second part. By Lemma 4.2 there are $O(\log^2 n)$ sets $\mathbf{core}(w, d')$ such that $v \in \mathbf{core}(w, d')$. By Lemma 4.1 for each such set the size of $\mathbf{ST}(v, T(w, d'))$ is $O(n^{1/k} \log^2 n)$. The lemma follows. ∎

The routing phase: We now describe the routing phase for the case $k = 4$.

For a node v let $\Delta_j(v) = \mathbf{dist}(v, p_{j+1}(v)) - \mathbf{dist}(v, p_j(v))$. Let k' be the minimal index such that $p_{k'-1}(t) \in B(s)$, or 1 in case either $t \in B(s)$ or $s \in B(t)$.
Let $M = \max\{\Delta_j(s)/2, \Delta_j(t)/2 \mid 1 \leq j \leq k'-2\} \cup \{\Delta_0(s), \Delta_0(t)\} \cup \{\mathbf{dist}(s, p_{j+1}(s)) - \mathbf{dist}(t, p_j(t)) \mid 1 \leq j \leq k'-2\}$. Note that the information needed to calculate k' and M can be extracted during the routing process from the label $L(t)$ and the routing table $A(S)$.

The routing phase is done as follows.

First check if $s \in A_0 \setminus A_1$ and $s \in B(t)$, if so route the message to t on $T(s)$ using $L(t, T(s))$. Note that, this information can be extracted from s's routing table. If $s \in B(t)$ then by definition $t \in C(s)$ and recall that $s \in A_0 \setminus A_1$ stores the set $C(s)$ and the labels $L(x, T(s))$ for every $x \in C(s)$ (as part of the Thorup-Zwick routing $A_{TZ}(s)$).

Otherwise, check if either $p_1(t) \in B(s)$ or $p_2(t) \in B(s)$. If so route the message to t on $T(p_i(t))$ where $i \in \{1, 2\}$ is the minimal index such that $p_i(t) \in B(s)$

In all other cases, check if $\Delta_1(t) \leq c \cdot M$ (for some parameter $1 < c < 2$ to be fixed later on). If so, invoke the standard Thorup-Zwick routing algorithm. Otherwise do the following. Let $d' = (1+\epsilon)^i$ for some index i be the minimal distance such that $d' \geq (1+c) \cdot M$.

Check using the search mechanism if $p_1(s) \in B(t)$. This is done by routing the message from s to $p_1(s)$ in $T(p_1(s))$. Then search for the key $\mathbf{key}(t)$ in the tree $T(p_1(s), d')$, if the key exists in $T(p_1(s), d')$ then route the message to t and quit. Otherwise if the $\mathbf{key}(t)$ was not found, return the message to s and invoke the standard Thorup-Zwick routing algorithm. This completes the description of the routing process.

We now turn to analyze the stretch of our routing scheme.

Let $d = \mathbf{dist}(s, t)$. By Thorup-Zwick analysis, either both $\Delta_0(s) \leq d$ and $\Delta_0(t) \leq d$, or we can route the message on the exact shortest path from s to t. To see this, note that if $\Delta_0(s) > d$, then $t \in B(s)$ and the message can be routed from s to t on $T(t)$ using the label $L(t, T(t))$, where the label $L(t, T(t))$ can be extracted from t's label. Similarly, if $\Delta_0(t) > d$, then $s \in B(t)$ or in other words, $t \in C(s)$ and the message can be routed from s to t in $T(s)$ using $L(t, T(s))$. The label $L(t, T(s))$ can be extracted from s's routing table. So assume this is not the case, namely, $k' > 1$. We now show that M is a lower bound on the distance from s to t.

LEMMA 4.4. *If $k' > 1$ then $\mathbf{dist}(s, t) \geq M$.*

Proof: By the definition of k' and the assumption that $k' > 0$, we have $t \notin B(s)$ and $s \notin B(t)$. By the definition of $B(s)$ and $B(t)$, we have
$\mathbf{dist}(s, t) \geq \mathbf{dist}(s, p_1(s)) = \Delta_0(s)$ and
$\mathbf{dist}(s, t) \geq \mathbf{dist}(t, p_1(t)) = \Delta_0(t)$.
We now turn to show that
$\mathbf{dist}(s, t) \geq \max\{\Delta_j(s)/2, \Delta_j(t)/2 \mid 1 \leq j \leq k' - 2\}$. Note that for every j such that $p_j(t) \notin B(s)$, we have
$\mathbf{dist}(s, p_{j+1}(s)) \leq d + \mathbf{dist}(t, p_j(t))$. Hence
$\mathbf{dist}(t, p_{j+1}(t)) \leq d + \mathbf{dist}(s, p_{j+1}(s)) \leq 2d + \mathbf{dist}(t, p_j(t))$.
Hence, $d = \mathbf{dist}(s, t) \geq (\mathbf{dist}(t, p_{j+1}(t)) - \mathbf{dist}(t, p_j(t)))/2$
$= \Delta_j(t)/2$. In addition, we have
$\mathbf{dist}(t, p_j(t)) \leq d + \mathbf{dist}(s, p_j(s))$. Hence, $\mathbf{dist}(s, p_{j+1}(s)) \leq d + \mathbf{dist}(t, p_j(t)) \leq$
$d + d + \mathbf{dist}(s, p_j(s))$. We get that $d = \mathbf{dist}(s, t) \geq (\mathbf{dist}(s, p_{j+1}(s)) - \mathbf{dist}(s, p_j(s)))/2 = \Delta_j(s)/2$.
We are left to show that $\mathbf{dist}(s, t) \geq \max\{p_{j+1}(s) - p_j(t) \mid 1 \leq j \leq k'\}$. Consider $1 \leq j \leq k'$, notice that by the definition of k', $p_j(t) \notin B(s)$. We get that $\mathbf{dist}(s, p_{j+1}(s)) \leq \mathbf{dist}(s, t) + \mathbf{dist}(t, p_j(t))$. Hence, $\mathbf{dist}(s, t) \geq p_{j+1}(s) - p_j(t)$, as required. ∎

Lemma 4.4 gives us a good starting point. We already have a lower bound on $\mathbf{dist}(s, t)$. Notice that in the worst case, where Thorup-Zwick analysis gives a stretch of $4k - 5$ is when $\Delta_j(s)$ and $\Delta_j(t)$ are roughly $2M$ for any $j > 0$, and M is slightly smaller than $\mathbf{dist}(s, t)$.

We now turn to bound the stretch of our routing process.

LEMMA 4.5. *The stretch of our routing process is at most $\max\{7 + 2c, 9, 15/c + 2 + 2\epsilon(1/c + 1)\}$.*

Proof: First, notice that in one of the following three cases the stretch of the routing process is at most 7 (instead of 11) and we are done. 1. $s \in A_0 \setminus A_1$ and $s \in B(t)$. 2. $p_1(t) \in B(s)$. 3. $p_2(t) \in B(s)$. In the above mentioned cases, by following Thorup-Zwick analysis, one can show that the stretch of the routing process is at most 7.

So assume this is not the case. Recall that by Lemma 4.4, we have
$d = \mathbf{dist}(s, t) \geq \max\{\Delta_j(s)/2, \Delta_j(t)/2 \mid 1 \leq j \leq k' - 2\} \cup \{\Delta_0(s), \Delta_0(t)\} \cup \{\mathbf{dist}(s, p_{j+1}(s)) - \mathbf{dist}(t, p_j(t)) \mid 1 \leq j \leq k' - 2\}$.
Consider first the case where $\Delta_1(t) \leq c \cdot M$. Recall that in this case the algorithm routes the message to t on $T(p_3(t))$. Thus the length of path obtained by the routing scheme in this case is $\mathbf{dist}(s, p_3(t)) + \mathbf{dist}(t, p_3(t))$. Notice that in this case we have $\mathbf{dist}(t, p_2(t)) \leq \Delta_0(t) + \Delta_1(t) \leq M + c \cdot M = (1 + c)M \leq (1 + c)\mathbf{dist}(s, t)$. We thus get, $\mathbf{dist}(t, p_3(t)) \leq \Delta_0(t) + \Delta_1(t) + \Delta_2(t) \leq (1 + c)M + 2M \leq (3 + c)\mathbf{dist}(s, t)$. In addition, $\mathbf{dist}(s, p_3(t)) \leq \mathbf{dist}(s, t) + \mathbf{dist}(s, p_3(t)) \leq (4 + c)\mathbf{dist}(s, t)$. We get that $\mathbf{dist}(s, p_3(t)) + \mathbf{dist}(t, p_3(t)) \leq (7 + 2c)\mathbf{dist}(s, t)$. Hence, the stretch in this case is $7 + 2c$.

Finally, consider the case where $\Delta_1(t) > c \cdot M$. Let $d' = (1 + \epsilon)^i$ be the minimal distance such that $d' \geq (1 + c) \cdot M$ for some index i.

The algorithm searches for $\mathbf{key}(t)$ in the tree $T(p_1(s), d')$. Recall that $\mathbf{dist}(s, p_1(s)) \leq M$. Hence the algorithm traverses a path of at most M until reaching $p_1(s)$, it then finds $L(t, T(p_1(s), d'))$ or decides that $t \notin T(p_1(s), d')$ by traveling on a path of length at most d'. We now need to consider two subcases. The first subcase is when $t \in T(p_1(s), d')$. In that case the algorithm routes the message to t in $T(p_1(s), d')$. Note that the overall path in this case is at most $M + d' + d' + \mathbf{dist}(p_1(s), t) \leq 3\mathbf{dist}(s, t) + 2(1 + \epsilon)(1 + c) \cdot M \leq 9\mathbf{dist}(s, t)$.

The last case is when $t \notin T(p_1(s), d')$. Note that this could happen only if $\mathbf{dist}(s, t) \geq cM$.

In this case the algorithm reaches the root $p_1(t)$, tries to find $\mathbf{key}(t)$ in $T(p_1(s), d')$ fails, returns the message to s and then invoke the standard Thorup-Zwick algorithm. The total path traveled by the algorithm in this case is $M + 2d' + M + 11M$. Since $\mathbf{dist}(s, t) \geq cM$, we get that the stretch is $(2d' + 13M)/\mathbf{dist}(s, t) \leq (2d' + 13M)/(cM) \leq (2(1 + \epsilon)(1 + c)M + 13M)/(cM) == 15/c + 2 + 2\epsilon(1/c + 1)$. ∎

By setting $c = (\sqrt{145} - 5)/4$ and taking ϵ to be small enough, we get a stretch of roughly 10.52 instead of the stretch 11 obtained by Thorup-Zwick's routing scheme.

5. THE GENERAL CASE $K > 4$

For simplicity, we present the construction for unweighted graphs, we later (in Section B) explain the modifications needed to handle weighted graphs.

Let us start with a general overview of our routing scheme for general k. As in the case of $k = 4$, we start by constructing Thorup-Zwick routing tables and labels. Each node stores the routing table and the label assigned to it by the the Thorup-Zwick scheme. As in the case of $k = 4$, we construct a name-independent routing mechanism on the trees $T(w)$, by storing additional information at the nodes of $T(w)$, while keeping the tables size $\tilde{O}(n^{1/k})$.

Roughly speaking, the routing phase is done as follows. The source node s checks if the target node t satisfies $\mathbf{dist}(p_r(t), t) \leq c \cdot r \cdot M$ (for some parameters r and $1 < c < 2$ to be fixed later on). If so, the node s invokes the standard Thorup-Zwick routing algorithm. Otherwise an attempt is made to route the message to t on the tree $T(p_j(s))$ for some $j \leq r$. This is done by first searching for the label $L(t, T(p_j(s)))$ using the search mechanism constructed for $T(p_j(s))$. If $t \in T(p_j(s))$ then the label $L(t, T(p_j(s)))$ is found using the search algorithm and the message is then routed to t using $L(t, T(p_j(s)))$, otherwise the message is bounced back to s and s invokes the standard Thorup-Zwick routing algorithm.

Recall that in the Thorup-Zwick analysis we have $\mathbf{dist}(p_r(t), t) \leq (2 \cdot r - 1) \cdot M$, thus if $\mathbf{dist}(p_r(t), t) \leq c \cdot r \cdot M$ for small enough c then following Thorup-Zwick analysis we get a better stretch. Otherwise, there must be an index j such that $\Delta_j(t) > c \cdot M$ and the algorithm tries to route the message to t on $T(p_j(s))$ using the search mechanism. If $t \in T(p_j(s))$ then the algorithm finds $L(t, T(p_j(s)))$ and the message is routed to t on $T(p_j(s))$. Otherwise, the algorithm invokes the standard Thorup-Zwick routing algorithm. The detour for searching the label $L(t, T(p_j(s)))$ and returning back to s appears to be a waste in the case where $t \notin T(p_j(s))$, however, we show that the only case that $t \notin T(p_j(s))$ is when $\mathbf{dist}(s,t) \geq c \cdot M$. In this particular case we can actually show that the Thrup-Zwick algorithm gives a much better stretch. Hence, even combined with the path traveled by the search algorithm, overall we still get a smaller stretch than in the general case of the Thrup-Zwick analysis.

The search mechanism we use in this section is slightly different than the one we presented for the case of $k = 4$. In the general case, we are given a tree $T(w)$ such that $|T(w)| \leq n^{r/k}$ and $\mathbf{radius}(T(w)) \leq r\rho$ for some distance ρ and the goal is to design a search mechanism that finds the label $L(t, T(w))$ by traveling on a short path, where by a short path we mean $O(\mathbf{radius}(T))$ length. The main difficulty with the previous search mechanism is that in the general case, the node s cannot store a complete map that indicates which node in $T(w)$ contains the label of t (as otherwise we will have to violate the constraint that every node stores $\tilde{O}(n^{1/k})$ information). In fact, it is possible to show that if $|T(w)| > n^{r/k}$, then in the worst case the algorithm must visit at least r different nodes in order to find $L(t, T(w))$. Naively, we could partition the set of nodes $V(T(w))$ into $n^{1/k}$ sets and pick $n^{1/k}$ nodes $\mathbf{helpers}(w)$ in $T(w)$ and assign each such node with one of these sets. We could partition $V(T(w))$ into sets in such a way that each such set S corresponds to a continuous interval I. The node w would store a map between these intervals and the corresponding nodes $\mathbf{helpers}(w)$. The size of each such set is $|V(T(w))|/n^{1/k}$. We could continue this process partitioning these sets into smaller sets until we have sets of size $O(n^{1/k})$ that a single node can store. Using this search mechanism, it is possible to find the label $L(t, T(w))$ by vising r nodes in $T(w)$. However, note that naively these r nodes could be far away from one other (distance $2\mathbf{radius}(T(w))$), so naively this process could yield a path of length $O(r \cdot \mathbf{radius}(T(w)))$. We thus pick the nodes of $\mathbf{core}(T(w))$ in a more careful way, in order to reduce the maximum length of the path traveled by the search process to $O(\mathbf{radius}(T(w)))$ rather than $O(r \cdot \mathbf{radius}(T(w)))$. We pick the nodes $\mathbf{core}(T(w))$ in such a way that for every node $v \in T(v)$, $|\mathbf{core}(T) \cap \mathbf{childs}(v,T)| \geq \log n \lceil |\mathbf{childs}(v,T)|/n^{1/k} \rceil$. At every node $v \in \mathbf{core}(T(w))$ our search mechanism stores $O(\min\{\mathbf{deg}(\mathbf{parent}(v,T)), n^{1/k}\})$ information. We later show that we can pick $\mathbf{core}(T(w))$ in a way that maintain the requirement that every node stores at most $\tilde{O}(n^{1/k})$ information in total.

More precisely, we show the following search scheme (the proof is deferred to the appendix).

LEMMA 5.1. *Consider a tree T of depth d', a set of nodes $\mathbf{core}(T) \subseteq V(T)$ such that $r(T) \in \mathbf{core}(T)$, and that for every $v \in T(v)$,* $|\mathbf{core}(T) \cap \mathbf{childs}(v,T)| \geq \lceil |\mathbf{childs}(v,T)|/n^{1/k} \rceil$. *One can construct a search mechanism with the following properties.*
1. The search mechanism stores $O(s(v,T) \log^2 n)$ data size at every node $v \in \mathbf{core}(T)$ and at most $O(\log^2 n)$ data at the rest of the nodes of T, where $s(v,T) = \min\{\mathbf{deg}(\mathbf{parent}(v,T)), n^{1/k}\}$. Let $\mathbf{ST}(v,T)$ be the data stored at a node $v \in V(T)$.
2. Given a key $\mathbf{key}$, the algorithm can find $L(\mathbf{key}, T)$ (or decides that $\mathbf{key} \notin V(T)$) from $r(T)$ in a distributed manner, by traveling on a path of length at most $3\mathbf{radius}(T) +$

$2(\mathbf{ind}(T)-1)$, *where $\mathbf{ind}(T)$ is the minimal index such that* $|V(T)| \leq n^{\mathbf{ind}(T)/k}$.

Constructing the labels and routing tables:

We now describe the construction of the labels and routing tables of our routing scheme. First, construct Thorup-Zwick routing tables and labels.

The label $L(v)$ is defined as follows (similarly as in the case where $k = 4$). Add the key $\mathbf{key}(v)$ to the label $L(v)$. Next, add to $L(v)$ the label $L_{TZ}(v)$ assigned to v by the Thorup-Zwick construction. In addition, add to $L(v)$ the distances $\mathbf{dist}(v, P_i(v))$ for every $1 \leq i \leq k-1$.

The routing table $A(v)$ of the node v is constructed as follows. First, add to the routing table $A(v)$, the routing table $A_{TZ}(v)$ assigned to v by the Thorup-Zwick construction. In addition, we enhance the routing tables with the following additional information.

For every node $w \in V$ and distance $d' = (1+\epsilon)^j$ for $1 \leq j \leq \log n$ do the following. The core $\mathbf{core}(w, d')$ is obtained by sampling every node $v \in T(w)$ independently at random with probability
$\min(1, 4\log n/\mathbf{deg}(\mathbf{parent}(v,w)))$ when
$\mathbf{deg}(\mathbf{parent}(v,w)) < n^{1/k}$ and with probability $4\log n/n^{1/k}$ otherwise.

For every node $w \in V$, and every distance $d' = (1+\epsilon)^j$ construct the search mechanism of Lemma 5.1 on $T(w, d')$ and $\mathbf{core}(w, d') \cup \{w\}$. Add to the routing tables $A(v)$ the information $\mathbf{ST}(v, T(w, d'))$ of the search mechanism for every $v \in T(w, d')$.

This completes the construction of our labels and routing tables.

We now turn to analyze the size of the routing tables.

By Chernoff bounds we show the following two lemmas.

LEMMA 5.2. *With high probability for every node $w \in V$, distance d' and node $v \in T(w, d')$,*
$|\mathbf{childs}(v,w) \cap \mathbf{core}(w, d')| \geq \lceil |\mathbf{childs}(v,w)|/n^{1/k} \rceil$.

LEMMA 5.3. *With high probability for every node v, $|A(v)| = \tilde{O}(n^{1/k})$.*

Proof: Recall that $|B(v)| \leq O(n^{1/k} \log n)$, namely, there are at most $O(n^{1/k} \log n)$ nodes w such that $v \in C(w)$. Consider such a node w and distance $d' = (1+\epsilon)^j$ for some $1 \leq j \leq \log n$. Let $p(v,w,d')$ be the probability that $v \in \mathbf{core}(w, d')$, where $p(v,w,d')$ is $\min(1, 4\log n/\mathbf{deg}(\mathbf{parent}(v,w)))$ if $\mathbf{deg}(\mathbf{parent}(v,w)) < 1/n^{1/k}$ and $4\log n/n^{1/k}$ otherwise. Recall that by Lemma 5.1 the size of $\mathbf{ST}(v, T(w, d'))$ is $O(s(v,T) \log^2 n)$ if $v \in \mathbf{core}(T)$ and $O(\log^2 n)$ otherwise, where $s(v,T) = \min\{\mathbf{deg}(\mathbf{parent}(v,T)), n^{1/k}\}$.

We get that the expected size of $\mathbf{ST}(v, T(w, d'))$ is $O(\log^2 n s(v,T) \cdot p(v,w,d') + \log^2 n) = O(\log^2 n)$.

There are $O(n^{1/k} \log^2 n)$ nodes w such that $v \in C(w)$, for each such w the algorithm considers $\log n$ different distances d'. Hence, the expected size of $A(v)$ is $O(n^{1/k} \log^4 n)$. By applying Chernoff bound we can show that with high probability, the size of $A(v)$ is roughly its expectation, i.e., $O(n^{1/k} \log^4 n)$. ■

The routing phase: The routing phase is done as follows.

Let k' be the minimal index such that $p_{k'-1}(t) \in B(s)$, or 1 in case either $t \in B(s)$ or $s \in B(t)$.

Let $M = \max\{\Delta_j(s)/2, \Delta_j(t)/2 \mid 1 \leq j \leq k'-2\} \cup \{\Delta_0(s), \Delta_0(t)\} \cup \{\mathbf{dist}(s, p_{j+1}(s)) - \mathbf{dist}(t, p_j(t)) \mid 1 \leq j \leq k'-2\}$. Recall that by Lemma 4.4, we have $\mathbf{dist}(s,t) \geq M$.

We now present the routing process. The source node s checks if there exists an index $j \leq r$ such that $\mathbf{dist}(p_{j+1}(t), t) - \mathbf{dist}(p_{j-1}(t), t) \geq 2cM$ (for some integer $r < k$ and number $1 < c < 2$ to be fixed later on). If no such index exists, s invokes the standard Thorup-Zwick routing algorithm, otherwise do the following.

Let $d' = (1+\epsilon)^i$ be the minimal distance such that $d' \geq 2M + (j-2)cM + (2c-1)M$ for some index i .

The node s tries to find $L(t, T(p_j(s)))$ using the search mechanism constructed on $T(p_j(s), d')$. If the algorithm finds $L(t, T(p_j(s)))$ then the message is routed to t using $L(t, T(p_j(s)))$. Otherwise, the message is bounced back to s and the standard Thorup-Zwick routing algorithm is invoked.

This conclude the routing process.

The following lemma bound the stretch of our routing scheme.

LEMMA 5.4. *The maximum stretch obtained by our routing process is at most* $\max\{4k - 1 - 4r - 2c + 2rc, (1+\epsilon)(6 + 6rc)/(2c - 1) + (4k - 4r + 2rc - 2c + 2)/(2c - 1) + 2(r - 1)/M((2c-1)), (1+\epsilon)6(1 + rc) + 2(r - 1)/M\}$.

We need to consider few cases.

The simplest case is when there is no index $j \leq r$ such that $\mathbf{dist}(p_r(t), t) - \mathbf{dist}(p_{r-2}(t), t) \geq 2cM$. In this case the algorithm invokes the standard Thorup-Zwick algorithm. Note that in this case we have $\mathbf{dist}(t, p_r(t)) \leq M + (r-1)cM$, whereas in Thorup-Zwick analysis they have $\mathbf{dist}(t, p_r(t)) \leq M + 2(r-1)M$. This saves $2(r-1)(2-c)$ in the final stretch. So the total stretch is $4k - 5 - 2(r-1)(2-c) = 4k - 1 - 4r - 2c + 2rc$.

Consider now the case where there exists an index $j \leq r$ such that $\mathbf{dist}(p_r(t), t) - \mathbf{dist}(p_{r-2}(t), t) \geq 2cM$. Let $d' = (1+\epsilon)^i$ for some index i be the minimal distance such that $d' \geq 2M + (j-2)cM + (2c-1)M$.

There are two subcases. The first subcase is when $t \in T(p_j(s), d')$ and the second when $t \notin T(p_j(s), d')$. Consider the first subcase. In that case the algorithm routes the message to t in $T(p_j(s), d')$. The node s tries to find $L(t, T(p_j(s)))$ using the search mechanism constructed on $T(p_j(s), d')$. The algorithm traveled to $p_j(s)$ and from $p_j(s)$ it tried to find $L(t, T(p_j(s)))$ using the search mechanism. By Lemma C.1 the path traveled by the search mechanism from $p_j(s)$ until finding $L(t, T(p_j(s)))$ or deciding that $t \notin T(p_j(s))$ is $3d' + 2(j-1)$. Note that the overall path in this case is at most $6d' + 2(j-1) \leq (1+\epsilon)6(2M + (j-2)cM + (2c-1)M) + 2(j-1)$. The stretch in this case is at most $(1+\epsilon)6(1 + jc) + 2(j-1)/M$.

Consider now the subcase where $t \notin T(p_j(s), d')$. Note that this could happen only if $\mathbf{dist}(s, t) \geq (2c-1)M$. The total path traveled by the algorithm in this case is $6d' + 2(j-1) + (M + (j-1)cM + (k-j)2M) \leq (1+\epsilon)6(2M + (j-2)cM + (2c-1)M) + 2(j-1) + 2(M + (j-1)cM + (k-j)2M) \leq (1+\epsilon)M(6 + 6jc) + M(4k - 4j + 2jc - 2c + 2) + 2(j-1)$.

We know however that in this case $\mathbf{dist}(s, t) \geq (2c-1)M$. Hence the stretch in this case is at most $(1+\epsilon)(6+6jc)/(2c-1) + (4k - 4j + 2jc - 2c + 2)/(2c-1) + 2(j-1)/M((2c-1))$. ∎

By minimizing over r and c, one can show that the stretch obtained by Lemma 5.4 is less than $3.68 \cdot k$.

Graphs of bounded degree: We note that it is possible to further decrease the stretch in the case of bounded degree

graphs. In the case of bounded degree graphs, one can construct a more efficient search mechanism while maintaining the required constraints on the tables size. By using these better search mechanism we can further decrease the stretch to roughly $3.58k$ (details deferred to the full version).

6. CONCLUSIONS

In this paper we provide the first improvement to the work of Thorup and Zwick[SPAA'01], presenting a compact routing scheme for weighted general undirected graphs which uses tables of size $\tilde{O}\left(n^{1/k}\right)$ and has stretch $c \cdot k$ for some absolute constant $c < 4$, for every $k \geq 4$. We note that it is possible to obtain an improved guarantee for the stretch by a more careful analysis of our routing scheme. However, it seems unlikely that our scheme might allow the stretch to go as low as $2k$ since the algorithm must "detour" in order to find the $tŠs$ label in the tree $T(p_i(s))$ for some i. The main question that still remains unresolved is to prove or disprove the existence of a compact routing scheme that utilizes tables of size $\tilde{O}\left(n^{1/k}\right)$ and has stretch of $2k$ without the use of a handshake.

Acknowledgement: I'm extremely grateful to Ittai Abraham for very helpful discussions.

7. REFERENCES

[1] I. Abraham, C. Gavoille, and D. Malkhi. Routing with improved communication-space trade-off. In *Proc. 18th Annual Conference on Distributed Computing (DISC)*, 305–319, 2004.

[2] I. Abraham, C. Gavoille, D. Malkhi, N. Nisan, and M. Thorup. Compact name-independent routing with minimum stretch. In *Proc. 16th Annual ACM Symposium on Parallel Algorithms and Architecture (SPAA)*, 20Ü-24, 2004.

[3] M. Arias, L. Cowen, K. Laing, R. Rajaraman, and O. Taka, Compact routing with name independence. In *Proc. 15th Annual ACM Symposium on Parallel Algorithms and Architectures (SPAA)*, 184Ü-192, 2003.

[4] B. Awerbuch, A. Bar-Noy, N. Linial, and D. Peleg. Compact distributed data structures for adaptive routing. In *Proc. 21st ACM Symp. on Theory of Computing (STOC)*, 479Ü-489, 1989.

[5] B. Awerbuch, A. Bar-Noy, N. Linial, and D. Peleg. Improved routing strategies with succinct tables. In *J. Algorithms*, 11(3):307–341, 1990.

[6] B. Awerbuch and D. Peleg. Sparse partitions. In *Proc. 31st IEEE Symp. on Foundations of Computer Science (FOCS)*, 503–513, 1990.

[7] L.J. Cowen. Compact routing with minimum stretch. *J. Alg.*, 38:170–183, 2001.

[8] T. Eilam, C. Gavoille, and D. Peleg. Compact routing schemes with low stretch factor. In *J. Algorithms*, 46:97–114, 2003.

[9] P. Erdős. Extremal problems in graph theory. In *Theory of graphs and its applications*, pages 29Ü-36, 1964.

[10] P. Fraigniaud and C. Gavoille. Memory requirement for universal routing schemes. In *Proc. 14th ACM Symp. on Principles of Distributed Computing (PODC)*, 223–230, 1995.

[11] P. Fraigniaud and C. Gavoille. Routing in Trees. In *28th Int'l Coll. on Automata, Languages and Programming (ICALP)*, 757–772, 2001.

[12] C. Gavoille and M. Gengler. Space-efficiency for routing schemes of stretch factor three. In *J. Parallel Distrib. Comput.*, 61:679–687, 2001.

[13] C. Gavoille and D. Peleg. Compact and localized distributed data structures. In *Distributed Computing*, 16:111–120, 2003.

[14] C. Gavoille and C. Sommer. Sparse spanners vs. compact routing. In *Proc. 23th ACM Symp. on Parallel Algorithms and Architectures (SPAA)*, 225–234, 2011.

[15] D. Peleg. Distributed computing: a locality-sensitive approach. In *SIAM*, 2000.

[16] D. Peleg and E. Upfal. A trade-off between space and efficiency for routing tables. In *J. ACM*, 36(3):510–530, 1989.

[17] M. Thorup and U. Zwick. Compact routing schemes. In *Proc. 13th ACM Symp. on Parallel Algorithms and Architectures (SPAA)*, 1–10, 2001.

[18] M. Thorup and U. Zwick. Approximate distance oracles. In *J. ACM*, 52, 1–24, 2005.

APPENDIX

A. SOME PROOFS

Proof of Lemma 3.1:

The proof of Lemma 3.1 is strongly based on Lemma 3.2 and Theorem 3.1 from [17]. We state the lemmas here for completeness.

Let $B_A(v) = \{w \in V \mid \mathbf{dist}(w,v) < \mathbf{dist}(A,v)\}$ and $C_A(w) = \{v \in V \mid \mathbf{dist}(w,v) < \mathbf{dist}(A,v)\}$.

LEMMA A.1. *Let $W \subseteq V$, $1 \leq s \leq n$ and let $A' \leftarrow$ sample(W,s), namely A' is obtained by sampling every node in W independently at random with probability $s/|W|$, or $A' = W$ if $|W| \leq s$. Then, for every $v \in V$, we have $E[B_{A'}(v) \cap W] \leq |W|/s$.*

THEOREM A.2. *The expected size of the set A returned by algorithm* **center** *is at most $2s \log n$. In addition, for every $w \in A'$, $C_A(w) \leq 4n/s$.*

By Theorem A.2, we get that $|A_i| = O(n^{1-i/k})$ for $1 \leq i \leq k-1$.

Consider a node $w \in A_i \setminus A_{i+1}$. By Theorem A.2, $C(w) = C_{A_{i+1}}(w) \leq 4n/(n^{1-i+1/k}/\log n) = 4n/(n^{1-(i+1)/k}/\log n) = O(\log n \cdot n^{(i+1)/k})$.

We are left to show that $|B(v)| = O(n^{1/k} \log n)$ for every $v \in V$.

Let $\hat{A}$ be the set A after the first iteration of procedure **center** when invoked on the input $(G, A_{i-1}, n^{1-i/k}/\log n)$.

Note that $\hat{A} \subseteq A_i$. In addition, notice that for every two sets S_1 and S_2 such that $S_1 \subseteq S_2$: $B_{S_2}(v) \subseteq B_{S_1}(v)$. In particular, $B_{A_i}(v) \subseteq B_{\hat{A}}(v)$. We thus have by Lemma A.1, $E[B(v) \cap A_{i-1}] = E[B_{A_i}(v) \cap A_{i-1}] \leq E[B_{\hat{A}}(v) \cap A_{i-1}] \leq |A_{i-1}|/(n^{1-i/k}/\log n) = O(n^{1/k} \log n)$.

B. WEIGHTED GRAPHS

Let us explain the modifications needed to handle weighted graphs. The only place in the proof where we use the fact that the graph is unweighted is in the construction of the search mechanism. Recall that in our search mechanism, the set of intervals of the children of some node $v \in V(T)$ is stored in one of the children **helper**(v) of v (in the case where the degree is smaller than $n^{1/k}$). Notice that the weight of the edge $(v, \mathbf{helper}(v))$ may be large and thus may increase our stretch by a lot. The high level idea is to partition the children of every node v into $\log D$ sets such that the edges leading from v to the nodes in the same set is roughly of the same weight (up to $1 + \epsilon$ factor), where D is the diameter of the graph. Each such set is handled separately, where the keys assign to each set are consecutive, namely belong to one continuous interval. The node v stores the intervals of these $\log D$ sets and thus in the search process, the node v knows in each interval out of the $\log D$ intervals to search for the key. This increases the length of the path obtained by the search algorithm by at most a factor of $1 + \epsilon$ and the size of the routing tables by at most a factor of $\log D$.

C. THE SEARCH MECHANISM

In this section we prove Lemma 5.1.

Our search mechanism is operated on given tree T, and set of core nodes $\mathbf{core}(T) \subseteq V(T)$. Every node v in $V(T)$ has a unique key $\mathbf{key}(v)$ in $[1..n]$. The set $\mathbf{core}(T)$ satisfies the following property. For every $v \in T(v)$, $|\mathbf{core}(T) \cap \mathbf{childs}(v,T)| \geq \log n \lceil |\mathbf{childs}(v,T)|/n^{1/k}\rceil$. In addition, the root $r(T)$ of the tree belongs to $\mathbf{core}(T)$.

The goal is to design a search mechanism such that later in the routing phase it would be possible to find the label $L(v,T)$ given $\mathbf{key}(v)$ from any node in T by traveling on a "short" path. Our search scheme stores at every node $v \in \mathbf{core}(T)$ at most $O(s(v,T) \log n)$ data where $s(v,T) = \min\{\mathbf{deg}(\mathbf{parent}(v,T)), n^{1/k}\}$ and at most $O(\log n)$ data at the rest of the nodes.

Let $\mathbf{ST}(v,T)$ for some node $v \in V(T)$ be the data stored at the node v by our search mechanism. We then show that using the data stored at the nodes of the tree, it is possible to find the label of a given key (or decide that this key is not in $T(v)$) from the root $r(T)$ of T in a distributed manner on path of length at most $3\mathbf{radius}(T) + 2(\mathbf{ind}(T) - 1)$, where $\mathbf{ind}(T)$ is the minimal index such that $|V(T)| \leq n^{\mathbf{ind}(T)/k}$.

Let us now describe our search algorithm. Let $\mathcal{K} = \{\mathbf{key}(v) \mid v \in V(T)\}$. First the algorithm distributes the keys $\mathcal{K}$ such that every node stores the matching labels of $O(1)$ keys as follows. For a node $v \in T$, let $T[v]$ be the subtree of v in T.

The algorithm assigns each node v an interval $I(v) = [n_1, n_2]$, the subtree $T[v]$ contains the labels of the keys in $\mathcal{K}$ in the range $[n_1, n_2]$. The root of the tree $r(T)$ corresponds to the interval $[1..n]$.

Order the children z of $r(T)$ by $|T[z]|$ in non-increasing order. Let $z_1, ..., z_\ell$ be the children of $r(T)$ by that order. The algorithm stores at $r(T)$ the first key and its matching label (the key with the smallest ID). The algorithm then assigns to z_1 the next $|T[z_1]|$ keys and to z_2 the next $|T[z_2]|$ keys and so on. Let n_i^1 be the smallest key assigned to z_i and n_i^2 be the largest key assigned to z_i, the interval of z_i is $[n_i^1, n_i^2]$. The algorithm continues with this process recursively until all keys are assigned.

For a node $v \in V(T)$, let $I(v)$ be its corresponding interval. Consider a consecutive set of children $S = \{z_{j_1}...z_{j_2}\}$. Let $I(z_{j_1}) = [n_1^l, n_1^h]$ and $I(z_{j_2}) = [n_2^l, n_2^h]$. Let $I[S] = [n_1^l, n_2^h]$. Note that all keys in $[n_1^l, n_2^h]$ are stored at one of nodes in S.

We now enhance the nodes with additional information that will enable them to find the right label of a given key later in the routing process with the desired stretch.

Ideally we would like to store in each node the intervals of its children. If we could that, later in the routing process every node in the tree knows exactly to which child to forward the message in order to find the desired key. This way the key could be found from the root $r(T)$ by traveling over a path of at most $\mathbf{radius}(T)$ length. However this could result in storing too much information for some nodes. Therefore, in order to store at the nodes the desired amount of information, we use the children of the nodes to store some of this information.

Consider a node $v \in V(T)$. Let $w_1, ..., w_\ell$ be the set of children of v. Let $\mathbf{core}(v) = \mathbf{core}(T) \cap \mathbf{childs}(v, T)$. Let $\hat{I}(v)$ be the set of intervals of v's children together with the port leading from v to the child containing the relevant interval. If $|\mathbf{childs}(v, T)| \leq n^{1/k}$ then pick one node $\mathbf{helper}(v)$ in $\mathbf{core}(v)$ and store $\hat{I}(v)$ at $\mathbf{helper}(v)$. The node v stores the port leading to $\mathbf{helper}(v)$.

If $|\mathbf{childs}(v, T)| > n^{1/k}$ then we cannot store $\hat{I}(v)$ at a single node without violating the requirement that every node stores $\tilde{O}(n^{1/k})$ data.

Hence in this case we use techniques from [1]. It was shown in [1] that it is possible to store $O(n^{1/k})$ data at $\lceil |\mathbf{childs}(v, T)|/n^{1/k} \rceil$ children of v (in our case in $\mathbf{core}(T)$) such that it is possible to find the right child z of v such that $\mathbf{key} \in I(v)$ while traveling to at most j children of v and in addition, $|T[z]| \leq |T[v]|/n^{(j-1)/k}$. The general idea is to partition the children w_j of v into $n^{1/k}$ sets and pick $n^{1/k}$ children of v in $\mathbf{core}(T)$ and assign each such child with one of the sets. Each child continue partitioning its sets and pick other helper children of v that would be responsible for these sets, this process continue until the sets are of size at most $n^{1/k}$ and then the node just store the relevant intervals and matching children of v. This process give preference to nodes with larger subtrees. This increases the total length traveled by the search mechanism by at most $(\mathbf{ind}(T) - 1)$, since each time the algorithm traveled to j children (instead of 1 in the case where $\deg(v, T) \leq n^{1/k}$) of v in order to find the child z such that $\mathbf{key} \in I(z)$, the size of subtree of z decreases by at least $n^{(j-1)/k}$. Thus, our searching process might traveled to at most $\mathbf{ind}(T) - 1$ extra children and thus the total path traveled by the algorithm increases by $2(\mathbf{ind}(T) - 1)$ (the factor of 2 comes from the fact that the algorithm needs to travel to the child and back). For more details about this process we deferred the reader to [1] or to the full version of this paper.

This completes the construction of the search tree. Let us now turn to the searching phase. In the searching phase, the root $r(T)$ wants to find the label of some key or to discover that this key does not exist in $\mathcal{K}$. The algorithm checks if the label of the key is stored in $r(T)$. If not, the algorithm seek the child w of $r(T)$ such that $key \in I(w)$. The node $r(T)$ checks if it contains a reference to interval that contain key, if so travel to the relevant child.

Otherwise (in the case where $\deg(r(T), T) > n^{1/k}$), the algorithm finds the child z of $r(T)$ such that $\mathbf{key} \in I(z)$ using the method presented in [1]. This process continues recursively until finding the node u that contain $L(\mathbf{key}, T)$ or decides that $\mathbf{key} \notin V(T)$.

LEMMA C.1. *The path traversed by the algorithm until finding $L(t, T)$ or deciding that $t \notin V(T)$ is $3\mathbf{radius}(T) + 2(\mathbf{ind}(T) - 1)$.*

Proof: Consider first the case where the degree of all nodes in T is $O(n^1/k)$. In that case notice that in each step the algorithm travel to the to one child before traveling to the child z such that $\mathbf{key} \in I(z)$. Therefore the path traversed by the algorithm is at most $3\mathbf{radius}(T_1)$ (for every edge $e = (u, v)$ the algorithm traveled to a child z of u, then traveled back to u and continues to v, hence for each edge the algorithm traveled a path of 3). In the case where we have larger degrees recall that we use the method of [1] and as mentioned above the total increase of the length traveled by the search algorithm is $2(\mathbf{ind}(T) - 1)$. ∎

Optimal Deterministic Routing and Sorting on the Congested Clique

Christoph Lenzen
Massachusetts Institute of Technology
32 Vassar Street
02139 Cambridge, USA
clenzen@csail.mit.edu

ABSTRACT

Consider a clique of n nodes, where in each synchronous round each pair of nodes can exchange $\mathcal{O}(\log n)$ bits. We provide deterministic constant-time solutions for two problems in this model. The first is a routing problem where each node is source and destination of n messages of size $\mathcal{O}(\log n)$. The second is a sorting problem where each node i is given n keys of size $\mathcal{O}(\log n)$ and needs to receive the ith batch of n keys according to the global order of the keys. The latter result also implies deterministic constant-round solutions for related problems such as selection or determining modes.

Categories and Subject Descriptors

F.2.2 [**Analysis of Algorithms and Problem Complexity**]: Nonnumerical Algorithms and Problems—*routing and layout, sorting and searching*; C.2.4 [**Computer Communication Networks**]: Distributed Systems

General Terms

Algorithms, Performance, Theory

Keywords

CONGEST model; upper bounds; bulk-synchronous communication

1. INTRODUCTION & RELATED WORK

Arguably, one of the most fundamental questions in distributed computing is what amount of communication is required to solve a given task. For systems where communication is dominating the "cost"—be it the time to communicate information, the money to purchase or rent the required infrastructure, or any other measure derived from a notion of communication complexity—exploring the imposed limitations may lead to more efficient solutions.

Clearly, in such systems it does not make sense to make the complete input available to all nodes, as this would be too expensive; typically, the same is true for the output. For this reason, one assumes that each node is given a part of the input, and each node needs to compute a corresponding part of the output. For graph theoretic questions, the local input comprises the neighborhood of the node in the respective graph, potentially augmented by weights for its incident edges or similar information that is part of the problem specification. The local output then e.g. consists of indication of membership in a set forming the global solution (a dominating set, independent set, vertex cover, etc.), a value between 0 and 1 (for the fractional versions), a color, etc. For verification problems, one is satisfied if for a valid solution all nodes output "yes" and at least one node outputs "no" for an invalid solution.

Since the advent of distributed computing, a main research focus has been the *locality* of such computational problems. Obviously, one cannot compute, or even verify, a spanning tree in less than D synchronous communication rounds, where D is the diameter of the graph, as it is impossible to ensure that a subgraph is acyclic without knowing it completely. Formally, the respective lower bound argues that there are instances for which no node can reliably distinguish between a tree and a non-tree since only the local graph topology (and the parts of the prospective solution) up to distance R can affect the information available to a node after R rounds. More subtle such *indistinguishability* results apply to problems that *can* be solved in $o(D)$ time (see e.g. [6, 8, 11]).

This type of argument breaks down in systems where all nodes can communicate directly or within a few number of rounds. However, this does not necessitate the existence of efficient solutions, as due to limited bandwidth usually one has to be selective in what information to actually communicate. This renders otherwise trivial tasks much harder, giving rise to strong lower bounds. For instance, there are n-node graphs of constant diameter on which finding or verifying a spanning tree and many related problems require $\tilde{\Omega}(\sqrt{n})$ rounds if messages contain a number of bits that is polylogarithmic in n [3, 14, 15]; approximating the diameter up to factor $3/2-\varepsilon$ or determining it exactly cannot be done in $\tilde{o}(\sqrt{n})$ and $\tilde{o}(n)$ rounds, respectively [4]. These and similar lower bounds consider specific graphs whose topology prohibits to communicate efficiently. While the diameters of these graphs are low, necessitating a certain connectivity, the edges ensuring this property are few. Hence, it is impossible to transmit a linear amount of bits between some nodes of the graph quickly, which forms the basis of the above impossibility results.

This poses the question whether non-trivial lower bounds also hold in the case where the communication graph is well-connected. After all, there are many networks that do not feature small cuts, some due to natural expansion properties, others by design. Also, e.g. in overlay networks, the underlying network structure might be hidden entirely and algorithms may effectively operate in a fully connected system, albeit facing bandwidth limitations. Furthermore, while for scalability reasons full connectivity may not be applicable on a system-wide level, it could prove useful to connect multiple cliques that are not too large by a sparser high-level topology.

These considerations motivate to study distributed algorithms for a fully connected system of n nodes subject to a bandwidth limitation of $\mathcal{O}(\log n)$ bits per round and edge, which is the topic of the present paper. Note that such a system is very powerful in terms of communication, as each node can send and receive $\Theta(n \log n)$ bits in each round, summing up to a total of $\Theta(n^2 \log n)$ bits per round. Consequently, it is not too surprising that, to the best of our knowledge, so far no negative results for this model have been published. On the positive side, a minimum spanning tree can be constructed in $\mathcal{O}(\log \log n)$ rounds [9], and, given to each node the neighbors of a corresponding node in some graph as input, it can be decided within $\mathcal{O}(n^{1/3}/\log n)$ rounds whether the input graph contains a triangle [2]. These bounds are deterministic; constant-round randomized algorithms have been devised for the routing [7] and sorting [12] tasks that we solve deterministically in this work. The randomized solutions are about 2 times as fast, but there is no indication that the best deterministic algorithms are slower than the best randomized algorithms.

Contribution

We show that the following closely related problems can be deterministically solved, within a constant number of communication rounds in a fully connected system where messages are of size $\mathcal{O}(\log n)$.

Routing: Each node is source and destination of (up to) n messages of size $\mathcal{O}(\log n)$. Initially only the sources know destinations and contents of their messages. Each node needs to learn all messages it is the destination of. (Section 3)

Sorting: Each node is given (up to) n comparable keys of size $\mathcal{O}(\log n)$. Node i needs to learn about the keys with indices $(i-1)n+1, \ldots, in$ in a global enumeration of the keys that respects their order. Alternatively, we can require that nodes need to learn the indices of their keys in the total order of the union of all keys (i.e., all duplicate keys get the same index). Note that this implies constant-round solutions for related problems like selection or determining modes. (Section 4)

We note that the randomized algorithms from previous work are structurally very different from the presented deterministic solutions. They rely on near-uniformity of load distributions obtained by choosing intermediate destinations uniformly and independently at random, in order to achieve bandwidth-efficient communication. In contrast, the presented approach achieves this in a style that has the flavor of a recursive sorting algorithm (with a single level of recursion).

While our results are no lower bounds for well-connected systems under the CONGEST model, they shed some light

on why it is hard to prove impossibilities in this setting: Even without randomization, the overhead required for coordinating the efforts of the nodes is constant. In particular, any potential lower bound for the considered model must, up to constant factors, also apply in a system where each node can in each round send and receive $\Theta(n \log n)$ bits to and from arbitrary nodes in the system, with no further constraints on communication.

We note that due to this observation, our results on sorting can equally well be followed as corollaries of our routing result and Goodrich's sorting algorithm for a bulk-synchronous model [5]. However, the derived algorithm is more involved and requires at least an order of magnitude more rounds.

Since for such fundamental tasks as routing and sorting the amount of local computations and memory may be of concern, we show in Section 5 how our algorithms can be adapted to require $\mathcal{O}(n \log n)$ computational steps and memory bits per node. Trivially, these bounds are near-optimal with respect to computations and optimal with respect to memory (if the size of the messages that are to be exchanged between the nodes is $\Theta(\log n)$).

To complete the picture, in Section 6 we vary the parameters of bandwidth, message/key size, and number of messages/keys per node. Our techniques are sufficient to obtain asymptotically optimal results for almost the entire range of parameters. For keys of size $o(\log n)$, we show that in fact a huge number of keys can be sorted quickly; this is the special case for which our bounds might not be asymptotically tight.

2. MODEL

In brief, we assume a fully connected system of n nodes under the congestion model. The nodes have unique identifiers 1 to n that are known to all other nodes. Computation proceeds in synchronous rounds, where in each round, each node performs arbitrary, finite computations,[1] sends a message to each other node, and receives the messages sent by other nodes. Messages are of size $\mathcal{O}(\log n)$, i.e., in each message nodes may encode a constant number of integer numbers that are polynomially bounded in n.[2] To simplify the presentation, nodes treat also themselves as receivers, i.e., node $i \in \{1, \ldots, n\}$ will send messages to itself like to any other node $j \neq i$.

These model assumptions correspond to the congestion model on the complete graph $K_n = (V, \binom{V}{2})$ on the node set $V = \{1, \ldots, n\}$ (cf. [13]). We stress that in a given round, a node may send different messages along each of its edges and thus can convey a total of $\Theta(n \log n)$ bits of information. As our results demonstrate, this makes the considered model much stronger than one where in any given round a node must broadcast the same $\Theta(\log n)$ bits to all other nodes.

When measuring the complexity of the computations performed by the nodes, we assume that basic arithmetic operations on $\mathcal{O}(\log n)$-sized values are a single computational step.

---

[1] Our algorithms will perform polynomial computations with small exponent only.

[2] We will not discuss this constraint when presenting our algorithms and only reason in a few places why messages are not too large; mostly, this should be obvious from the context.

3. ROUTING

In this section, we derive a deterministic solution to the following task introduced in [7].

PROBLEM 3.1 (INFORMATION DISTRIBUTION TASK).
Each node $i \in V$ is given a set of n messages of size $\mathcal{O}(\log n)$

$$\mathcal{S}_i = \{m_i^1, \ldots, m_i^n\}$$

with destinations $d(m_i^j) \in V$, $j \in \{1, \ldots, n\}$. Messages are globally lexicographically ordered by their source i, their destination $d(m_i^j)$, and j. For simplicity, each such message explicitly contains these values, in particular making them distinguishable. The goal is to deliver all messages to their destinations, minimizing the total number of rounds. By

$$\mathcal{R}_k := \left\{ m_i^j \in \bigcup_{i \in V} \mathcal{S}_i \,\middle|\, d(m_i^j) = k \right\}$$

we denote the set of messages a node $k \in V$ shall receive. We require that $|\mathcal{R}_k| = n$ for all $k \in V$, i.e., also the number of messages a single node needs to receive is n.

We remark that it is trivial to relax the requirement that each node needs to send and receive *exactly* n messages; this assumption is made to simplify the presentation. If each node sends/receives at most n messages, our techniques can be applied without change, and instances with more than n sent/received messages per node can be split up into smaller ones.

3.1 Basic Communication Primitives

Let us first establish some basic communication patterns our algorithms will employ. We will utilize the following classical result.

THEOREM 3.2 (KOENIG'S LINE COLORING THM.).
Every d-regular bipartite multigraph is a disjoint union of d perfect matchings.

PROOF. See e.g. Theorem 1.4.18 in [10]. □

We remark that such an optimal coloring can be computed efficiently [1].[3]

Using this theorem, we can solve Problem 3.1 efficiently provided that it is known a priori to all nodes what the sources and destinations of messages are, an observation already made in [2]. We will however need a more general statement applying to subsets of nodes that want to communicate among themselves. To this end, we first formulate a generalization of the result from [2].

COROLLARY 3.3. *We are given a subset $W \subseteq V$ and a bulk of messages such that the following holds.*
1. *The source and destination of each message is in W.*
2. *The source and destination of each message is known in advance to all nodes in W, and each source knows the contents of the messages to send.*
3. *Each node is the source of $f|W|$ messages, where $f := \lfloor n/|W| \rfloor$.*
4. *Each node is the destination of $f|W|$ messages.*

Then a routing scheme to deliver all messages in 2 rounds can be found efficiently. The routing scheme makes use of edges with at least one endpoint in W only.

PROOF. Consider the bipartite multigraph $G = (S \,\dot\cup\, R, E)$ with $|S| = |R| = |W|$, where $S = \{1_s, \ldots, |W|_s\}$ and $R = \{1_r, \ldots, |W|_r\}$ represent the nodes in their roles as senders and receivers, respectively, and each input message at some node i that is destined for some node j induces an edge from i_s to j_r.

By Theorem 3.2, we can color the edge set of G with $m := f|W| \leq n$ colors such that no two edges with the same color have a node in common. Moreover, as all nodes are aware of the source and destination of each message, they can deterministically and locally compute the same such coloring, without the need to communicate. Now, in the first communication round, each node sends its (unique) message of color $c \in \{1, \ldots, m\}$ to node c. As each node holds exactly one message of each color, at most one message is sent over each edge, i.e., by the assumptions of the corollary this step can indeed be performed in one round. Observe that this rule ensures that each node will receive exactly one message of each color in the first round. Hence, because the coloring also guarantees that each node is the destination of exactly one message of each color, it follows for each $i, j \in \{1, \ldots, n\}$ that node i receives exactly f messages that need to be delivered to node j in the first round. Therefore all messages can be delivered by directly sending them to their destinations in the second round. □

We stress that we can apply this result concurrently to multiple disjoint sets W, provided that each of them satisfies the prerequisites of the corollary: since in each routing step, each edge has at least one endpoint in W, there will never be an edge which needs to convey more than one message in each direction. This is vital for the success of our algorithms.

An observation that will prove crucial for our further reasoning is that for subsets of size at most $\sqrt{n}$, the amount of information that needs to be exchanged in order to establish common knowledge on the sources and destinations of messages becomes sufficiently small to be handled. Since this information itself consists, for each node, of $|W|$ numbers that need to be communicated to $|W| \leq n/|W|$ nodes—with sources and destination known a priori!—we can solve the problem for *unknown* sources and destinations by applying the previous corollary twice.

COROLLARY 3.4. *We are given a subset $W \subseteq V$, where $|W| \leq \sqrt{n}$, and a bulk of messages such that the following holds.*
1. *The source and destination of each message is in W.*
2. *Each source knows the contents of the messages to send.*
3. *Each node is the source of $f|W|$ messages, where $f := \lfloor n/|W| \rfloor$.*
4. *Each node is the destination of $f|W|$ messages.*
Then a routing scheme to deliver all messages in 4 rounds can be found efficiently. The routing scheme makes use of edges with at least one endpoint in W only.

PROOF. Each node in W announces the number of messages it holds for each node in W to all nodes in W. This requires each node in W to send and receive $|W|^2 \leq f|W|$ messages. As sources and destinations of these helper messages are known in advance, by Corollary 3.3 we can perform

---

[3] Also, a simple greedy coloring of the line graph results in at most $2d - 1$ (imperfect) matchings, which is sufficient for our purposes. This will be used in Section 5 to reduce the amount of computations performed by the algorithm.

this preprocessing in 2 rounds. The information received establishes the preconditions of Corollary 3.3 for the original set of messages, therefore the nodes now can deliver all messages in another two rounds. □

3.2 Solving the Information Distribution Task

Equipped with the results from the previous section, we are ready to tackle Problem 3.1. In the pseudocode of our algorithms, we will use a number of conventions to allow for a straightforward presentation. When we state that a message is *moved* to another node, this means that the receiving node will store a copy and serve as the source of the message in subsequent rounds of the algorithm, whereas the original source may "forget" about the message. A step where messages are moved is thus an actual routing step of the algorithm; all other steps serve to prepare the routing steps. The current source of a message *holds* it. Moreover, we will partition the node set into subsets of size $\sqrt{n}$, where for simplicity we assume that $\sqrt{n}$ is integer. We will discuss the general case in the main theorem. We will frequently refer to these subsets, where W will invariably denote any of the sets in its role as source, while W' will denote any of the sets in its role as receiver (both with respect to the current step of the algorithm). Finally, we stress that statements about moving and sending of messages in the pseudocode do not imply that the algorithm does so by direct communication between sending and receiving nodes. Instead, we will discuss fast solutions to the respective (much simpler) routing problems in our proofs establishing that the described strategies can be implemented with small running times.

This being said, let us turn our attention to Problem 3.1. The high-level strategy of our solution is given in Algorithm 1.

Algorithm 1: High-level strategy for solving Problem 3.1.

---

1. Partition the nodes into the disjoint subsets $\{(i-1)\sqrt{n}+1,\ldots,i\sqrt{n}\}$ for $i \in \{1,\ldots,\sqrt{n}\}$.
2. Move the messages such that each such subset W holds exactly $|W||W'| = n$ messages for each subset W'.
3. For each pair of subsets W, W', move all messages destined to nodes in W' within W such that each node in W holds exactly $|W'| = \sqrt{n}$ messages with destinations in W'.
4. For each pair of subsets W, W', move all messages destined to nodes in W' from W to W'.
5. For each W, move all messages within W to their destinations.

Clearly, following this strategy will deliver all messages to their destinations. In order to prove that it can be deterministically executed in a constant number of rounds, we now show that all individual steps can be performed in a constant number of rounds. Obviously, the first step requires no communication. We leave aside Step 2 for now and turn to Step 3.

COROLLARY 3.5. *Step 3 of Algorithm 1 can be implemented in 4 rounds.*

PROOF. The proof is analogous to Corollary 3.4. First, each node in W announces to each other node in W the number of messages it holds for each set W'. By Corol-

lary 3.3, this step can be completed in 2 rounds, for all sets W in parallel.

With this information, the nodes in W can deterministically compute (intermediate) destinations for each message in W such that the resulting distribution of messages meets the condition imposed by Step 3. Applying Corollary 3.3 once more, this redistribution can be performed in another 2 rounds, again for all sets W concurrently. □

Trivially, Step 4 can be executed in a single round by each node in W sending exactly one of the messages with destination in W' it holds to each node in W'. According to Corollary 3.4, Step 5 can be performed in 4 rounds.

Regarding Step 2, we follow similar ideas. Algorithm 2 breaks our approach to this step down into smaller pieces.

Algorithm 2: Step 2 of Algorithm 1 in more detail.

---

1. Each subset W computes, for each set W', the number of messages its constituents hold in total for nodes in W'. The results are announced to all nodes.
2. All nodes locally compute a pattern according to which the messages are to be moved between the sets. It satisfies that from each set W to each set W', n messages need to be sent, and that in the resulting configuration, each subset W holds exactly $|W||W'| = n$ messages for each subset W'.
3. All nodes in subset W announce to all other nodes in W the number of messages they need to move to each set W' according to the previous step.
4. All nodes in W compute a pattern for moving messages within W so that the resulting distribution permits to realize the exchange computed in Step 2 in a single round (i.e., each node in W must hold exactly $|W'| = \sqrt{n}$ messages with (intermediate) destinations in W').
5. The redistribution within the sets according to Step 4 is executed.
6. The redistribution among the sets computed in Step 2 is executed.

We now show that following the sequence given in Algorithm 2, Step 2 of Algorithm 1 requires a constant number of communication rounds only.

LEMMA 3.6. *Step 2 of Algorithm 1 can be implemented in 7 rounds.*

PROOF. We will show for each of the six steps of Algorithm 2 that it can be performed in a constant number of rounds and that the information available to the nodes is sufficient to deterministically compute message exchange patterns the involved nodes agree upon.

Clearly, Step 1 can be executed in two rounds. Each node in W simply sends the number of messages with destinations in the ith set W' it holds, where $i \in \{1,\ldots,\sqrt{n}\}$, to the ith node in W. The ith node in W sums up the received values and announces the result to all nodes.

Regarding Step 2, consider the following bipartite graph $G = (S \dot\cup R, E)$. The sets S and R are of size $\sqrt{n}$ and represent the subsets W in their role as senders and receivers, respectively. For each message held by a node in the ith set W with destination in the jth set W', we add an edge from $i \in S$ to $j \in R$. Note that after Step 1, each node can locally construct this graph. As each node needs to send and receive n messages, G is of uniform degree $n^{3/2}$. By Theorem 3.2, we can color the edge set of G with $n^{3/2}$ colors so that no two edges of the same color share a node. We require that a message of color $c \in \{1, \ldots, n^{3/2}\}$ is sent to the $(c \bmod \sqrt{n})^{th}$ set. Hence, the requirement that exactly n messages need to be sent from any set W to any set W' is met. By requiring that each node uses the same deterministic algorithm to color the edge set of G, we make sure that the exchange patterns computed by the nodes agree.

Note that a subtlety here is that nodes cannot yet determine the precise color of the messages they hold, as they do not know the numbers of messages to sets W' held by other nodes in W and therefore also not the index of their messages according to the global order of the messages. However, each node has sufficient knowledge to compute the number of messages it holds with destination in set W' (for each W'), as this number is determined by the total numbers of messages that need to be exchanged between each pair W and W' and the node index only. This permits to perform Step 3 and then complete Step 2 based on the received information.[4]

As observed before, Step 3 can be executed quickly: Each node in W needs to announce $\sqrt{n}$ numbers to all other nodes in W, which by Corollary 3.3 can be done in 2 rounds. Now the nodes are capable of computing the color of each of their messages according to the assignment from Step 2.

With the information gathered in Step 3, it is now feasible to perform Step 4. This can be seen by applying Theorem 3.2 again, for each set W to the bipartite multigraph $G = (W \dot\cup R, E)$, where R represents the $\sqrt{n}$ subsets W' in their receiving role with respect to the pattern computed in Step 2, and each edge corresponds to a message held by a node in W with destination in some W'. The nodes can locally compute this graph due to the information they received in Steps 2 and 3. As G has degree n, we obtain an edge-coloring with n colors. Each node in W will move a message of color $i \in \{1, \ldots, n\}$ to the $(i \bmod \sqrt{n})^{th}$ node in W, implying that each node will receive for each W' exactly $\sqrt{n}$ messages with destination in W'.

Since the exchange pattern computed in Step 4 is, for each W, known to all nodes in W, by Corollary 3.3 we can perform Step 5 for all sets in parallel in 2 rounds. Finally, Step 6 requires a single round only, since we achieved that each node holds for each W' exactly $\sqrt{n}$ messages with destination in W' (according to the pattern computed in Step 2), and thus can send exactly one of them to each of the nodes in W' directly.

Summing up the number of rounds required for each of the steps, we see that $2 + 0 + 2 + 0 + 2 + 1 = 7$ rounds are required in total, completing the proof. $\square$

Overall, we have shown that each step of Algorithm 1 can be executed in a constant number of rounds if $\sqrt{n}$ is integer. It is not hard to generalize this result to arbitrary values of n without incurring larger running times.

THEOREM 3.7. *Problem 3.1 can be solved deterministically within* 16 *rounds.*

PROOF. If $\sqrt{n}$ is integer, the result immediately follows from Lemma 3.6, Corollary 3.5, and Corollary 3.4, taking

---

into account that the fourth step of the high-level strategy requires one round.

If $\sqrt{n}$ is not integer, consider the following three sets of nodes:

$$
\begin{aligned}
V_1 &:= \{1, \ldots, \lfloor\sqrt{n}\rfloor^2\}, \\
V_2 &:= \{n - \lfloor\sqrt{n}\rfloor^2 + 1, \ldots, n\}, \text{ and} \\
V_3 &:= \{1, \ldots, n - \lfloor\sqrt{n}\rfloor^2\} \cup \{\lfloor\sqrt{n}\rfloor^2 + 1, \ldots, n\}.
\end{aligned}
$$

V_1 and V_2 satisfy that $|V_1| = |V_2| = \lfloor\sqrt{n}\rfloor^2$. Hence, we can apply the result for an integer root to the subsets of messages for which either both sender and receiver are in V_1 or, symmetrically, in V_2. Doing so in parallel will increase the message size by a factor of at most 2. Note that for messages where sender and receiver are in $V_1 \cap V_2$ we can simply delete them from the input of one of the two instances of the algorithm that run concurrently, and adding empty "dummy" messages, we see that it is irrelevant that nodes may send or receive less than n messages in the individual instances.

Regarding V_3, denote for each node $i \in V_3$ by $S_i \subseteq \mathcal{S}_i$ the subset of messages for which i and the respective receiver are neither both in V_1 nor both in V_2. In other words, for each message in S_i either $i \in V_1 \cap V_3$ and the receiver is in $V_2 \cap V_3$ or vice versa. Each node $i \in V_3$ moves the jth message in S_i to node j (one round). No node will receive more than $|V_2 \cap V_3| = |V_1 \cap V_3|$ messages with destinations in $V_1 \cap V_3$, as there are no more than this number of nodes sending such messages. Likewise, at most $|V_2 \cap V_3|$ messages for nodes in $V_2 \cap V_3$ are received. Hence, in the subsequent round, all nodes can move the messages they received for nodes in $V_1 \cap V_3$ to nodes in $V_1 \cap V_3$, and the ones received for nodes in $V_2 \cap V_3$ to nodes in $V_2 \cap V_3$ (one round). Finally, we apply Corollary 3.4 to each of the two sets to see that the messages $\bigcup_{i \in V_3} S_i$ can be delivered within 4 rounds. Overall, this procedure requires 6 rounds, and running it in parallel with the two instances dealing with other messages will not increase message size beyond $\mathcal{O}(\log n)$. The statement of the theorem follows. $\square$

4. SORTING

In this section, we present a deterministic sorting algorithm. The problem formulation is essentially equivalent to the one in [12].

PROBLEM 4.1 (SORTING). *Each node is given n keys of size $\mathcal{O}(\log n)$ (i.e., a key fits into a message). We assume w.l.o.g. that all keys are different.[5] Node i needs to learn the keys with indices $i(n-1) + 1, \ldots, in$ according the total order of all keys.*

4.1 Sorting Fewer Keys with Fewer Nodes

Again, we assume for simplicity that $\sqrt{n}$ is integer and deal with the general case later on. Our algorithm will utilize a subroutine that can sort up to $2n^{3/2}$ keys within a subset $W \subset V$ of $\sqrt{n}$ nodes, communicating along edges with at least one endpoint in the respective subset of nodes. The latter condition ensures that we can run the routine in parallel for disjoint subsets W. We assume that each of the nodes in W initially holds $2n$ keys. The pseudocode of our approach is given in Algorithm 3.

---

[4]Formally, this can be seen as a deferred completion of Step 2.

[5]Otherwise we order the keys lexicographically by key, node whose input contains the key, and a local enumeration of

---
Algorithm 3: Sorting $2n^{3/2}$ keys with $|W| = \sqrt{n}$ nodes. Each node in W has $2n$ input keys and learns their indices in the total order of all $2n^{3/2}$ keys.

---

1. Each node in W locally sorts its keys and selects every $(2\sqrt{n})^{th}$ key according to this order (i.e., a key of local index i is selected if $i \bmod 2\sqrt{n} = 0$).
2. Each node in W announces the selected keys to all other nodes in W.
3. Each node in W locally sorts the union of the received keys and selects every $\sqrt{n}^{th}$ key according to this order. We call such a key *delimiter*.
4. Each node $i \in W$ splits its original input into $\sqrt{n}$ subsets, where the jth subset $K_{i,j}$ contains all keys that are larger than the $(j-1)^{th}$ delimiter (for $j = 1$ this condition does not apply) and smaller or equal to the jth delimiter.
5. Each node $i \in W$ announces for each j $|K_{i,j}|$ to all nodes in W.
6. Each node $i \in W$ sends $K_{i,j}$ to the jth node in W.
7. Each node in W locally sorts the received keys. The sorted sequence now consists of the concatenation of the sorted sequences in the order of the node identifiers.
8. Keys are redistributed such that each node receives $2n$ keys and the order is maintained.

Let us start out with the correctness of the proposed scheme.

LEMMA 4.2. *When executing Algorithm 3, the nodes in W are indeed capable of computing their input keys' indices in the order on the union of the input keys of the nodes in W.*

PROOF. Observe that because all nodes use the same input in Step 3, they compute the same set of delimiters. The set of all keys is the union $\bigcup_{j=1}^{\sqrt{n}} \bigcup_{i \in W} K_{i,j}$, and the sets $K_{i,j}$ are disjoint. As the $K_{i,j}$ are defined by comparison with the delimiters, we know that all keys in $K_{i,j}$ are larger than keys in $K_{i',j'}$ for all $i' \in W$ and $j' < j$, and smaller than keys in $K_{i',j'}$ for all $i' \in W$ and $j' > j$. Since in Step 7 the received keys are locally sorted and Step 8 maintains the resulting order, correctness follows. $\square$

Before turning to the running time of the algorithm, we show that the partitioning of the keys by the delimiters is well-balanced.

LEMMA 4.3. *When executing Algorithm 3, for each $j \in \{1, \ldots, \sqrt{n}\}$ it holds that*
$$\left| \bigcup_{i \in W} K_{i,j} \right| < 4n.$$

PROOF. Due to the choice of the delimiters, $\bigcup_{i \in W} K_{i,j}$ contains exactly $\sqrt{n}$ of the keys selected in Step 1 of the algorithm. Denote by d_i the number of such selected keys in $K_{i,j}$. As in Step 1 each node selects every $(2\sqrt{n})^{th}$ of its keys and the set $K_{i,j}$ is a contiguous subset of the ordered sequence of input keys at w, we have that $|K_{i,j}| < 2\sqrt{n}(d_i +$

---

identical keys at each node.

---

1). It follows that
$$
\begin{aligned}
\left| \bigcup_{i \in W} K_{i,j} \right| &= \sum_{i \in W} |K_{i,j}| \\
&< 2\sqrt{n} \sum_{i \in W} (d_i + 1) \\
&= 2\sqrt{n}(\sqrt{n} + |W|) = 4n.
\end{aligned}
$$

$\square$

We are now in the position to complete our analysis of the subroutine.

LEMMA 4.4. *Given a subset $W \subseteq V$ of size $\sqrt{n}$ such that each $w \in W$ holds $2n$ keys, each node in W can learn about the indices of its keys in the total order of all keys held by nodes in W within 10 rounds. Furthermore, only edges with at least one endpoint in W are used for this purpose.*

PROOF. By Lemma 4.2, Algorithm 3 is correct. Hence, it remains to show that it can be implemented with 10 rounds of communication, using no edges with both endpoints outside W.

Steps 1, 3, 4, and 7 involve local computations only. Since $|W| = \sqrt{n}$ and each node selects exactly $\sqrt{n}$ keys it needs to announce to all other nodes, according to Corollary 3.3 Step 2 can be performed in 2 rounds. The same holds true for Step 5, as again each node needs to announce $|W| = \sqrt{n}$ values to each other node in W. In Step 6, each node sends its $2n$ input keys and, by Lemma 4.3, receives at most $4n$ keys. By bundling a constant number of keys in each message, nodes need to send and receive at most $n = |W| \cdot n / |W|$ messages. Hence, Corollary 3.4 states that this step can be completed in 4 rounds. Regarding Step 8, observe that due to Step 5 each node knows how many keys each other node holds at the beginning of the step. Again bundling a constant number of keys into each message, we thus can apply Corollary 3.3 to complete Step 8 in 2 rounds. In total, we thus require $0 + 2 + 0 + 0 + 2 + 4 + 2 = 10$ communication rounds.

As we invoked Corollaries 3.3 and 3.4 in order to define the communication pattern, it immediately follows from the corollaries that all communication is on edges with at least one endpoint in W. $\square$

4.2 Sorting All Keys

With this subroutine at hand, we can move on to Problem 4.1. Our solution follows the same pattern as Algorithm 3, where the subroutine in combination with Theorem 3.7 enables that sets of size $\sqrt{n}$ can take over the function nodes had in Algorithm 3. This increases the processing power by factor $\sqrt{n}$, which is sufficient to deal with all n^2 keys. Algorithm 4 shows the high-level structure of our solution.

The techniques and results from the previous sections are sufficient to derive our second main theorem without further delay.

THEOREM 4.5. *Problem 4.1 can be solved in 37 rounds.*

PROOF. We discuss the special case of $\sqrt{n} \in \mathbb{N}$ first, to which we can apply Algorithm 4. Correctness of the algorithm follows analogously to Lemma 4.2. Steps 1 and 5 require local computations only. Step 2 involves one round

---
Algorithm 4: Solving Problem 4.1.
---

1. Each node locally sorts its input and selects every $\sqrt{n}^{th}$ key (i.e., the index in the local order modulo $\sqrt{n}$ equals 0).
2. Each node transmits its ith selected key to node i.
3. Using Algorithm 3, nodes $1, \ldots, \sqrt{n}$ sort the in total $n^{3/2}$ keys they received (i.e., determine the respective indices in the induced order).
4. Out of the sorted subsequence, every n^{th} key is selected as *delimiter* and announced to all nodes (i.e., there is a total of $\sqrt{n}$ delimiters).
5. Each node $i \in V$ splits its original input into $\sqrt{n}$ subsets, where the jth subset $K_{i,j}$ contains all keys that are larger than the $(j-1)^{th}$ delimiter (for $j = 1$ this condition does not apply) and smaller or equal to the jth delimiter.
6. The nodes are partitioned into $\sqrt{n}$ disjoint sets W of size $\sqrt{n}$. Each node $i \in V$ sends $K_{i,j}$ to the jth set W (i.e., each node in W receives either $\lfloor |K_{i,j}|/|W| \rfloor$ or $\lceil |K_{i,j}|/|W| \rceil$ keys, and each key is sent to exactly one node).
7. Using Algorithm 3, the sets W sort the received keys.
8. Keys are redistributed such that each node receives n keys and the order is maintained.
---

of communication. Step 3 calls Algorithm 3, which according to Lemma 4.4 consumes 10 rounds. However, we can skip the last step of the algorithm and instead directly execute Step 4. This takes merely 2 rounds, since there are $\sqrt{n}$ nodes each of which needs to announce at most $2\sqrt{n}$ values to all nodes and we can bundle two values in one message. Regarding Step 6, observe that, analogously to Lemma 4.3, we have for each $j \in \{1, \ldots, \sqrt{n}\}$ that

$$\left| \bigcup_{i \in V} K_{i,j} \right| = \sum_{i \in V} |K_{i,j}| < \sqrt{n}(n + |V|) = 2n^{3/2}.$$

Hence, each node needs to send at most n keys and receive at most $2n$ keys. Bundling up to two keys in each message, nodes need to send and receive at most n messages. Therefore, by Theorem 3.7, Step 6 can be completed within 16 rounds. Step 7 again calls Algorithm 3, this time in parallel for all sets W. Nonetheless, by Lemma 4.4 this requires 10 rounds only because the edges used for communication are disjoint. Also here, we can skip the last step of the subroutine and directly move on to Step 8. Again, Corollary 3.3 implies that this step can be completed in 2 rounds. Overall, the algorithm runs for $0 + 1 + 8 + 2 + 0 + 16 + 8 + 2 = 37$ rounds.

With respect to non-integer values of $\sqrt{n}$, observe that we can increase message size by any constant factor to accommodate more keys in each message. This way we can work with subsets of size $\lfloor \sqrt{n} \rfloor$ and similarly select keys and delimiters in Steps 1 and 4 such that the adapted algorithm can be completed in 37 rounds as well. □

We conclude this section with a corollary stating that the slightly modified task of determining each input key's position in a global enumeration of the *different* keys that are present in the system can also be solved efficiently. Note that this implies constant-round solutions for determining modes and selection as well.

COROLLARY 4.6. *Consider the variant of Problem 4.1 in which each node is required to determine the index of its input keys in the total order of the union of all input keys. This task can be solved deterministically in a constant number of rounds.*

PROOF. After applying the sorting algorithm, each node announces (i) its smallest and largest key, (ii) how many copies of each of these two keys it holds, and (iii) the number of distinct keys it holds to all other nodes. This takes one round, and from this information all nodes can compute the indices in the non-repetitive sorted sequence for their keys. Applying Theorem 3.7, we can inform the nodes whose input the keys were of these values in a constant number of rounds. □

5. COMPUTATIONS AND MEMORY

Examining Algorithms 1 and 2 and how we implemented their various steps, it is not hard to see that all computations that do not use the technique of constructing some bipartite multigraph and coloring its edges merely require $\mathcal{O}(n)$ computational steps (and thus, as all values are of size $\mathcal{O}(\log n)$, also $\mathcal{O}(n \log n)$ memory). Leaving the work and memory requirements of local sorting operations aside, the same applies to Algorithms 3 and 4. Assuming that an appropriate sorting algorithm is employed, the remaining question is how efficiently we can implement the steps that do involve coloring.

The best known algorithm to color a bipartite multigraph $H = (V, E)$ of maximum degree Δ with Δ colors requires $\mathcal{O}(|E| \log \Delta)$ computational steps [1]. Ensuring that $|E| \in \mathcal{O}(n)$ in all cases where we appeal to the procedure will thus result in a complexity of $\mathcal{O}(n \log n)$. Unfortunately, this bound does not hold for the presented algorithms. More precisely, Step 3 of Algorithm 1 and Steps 2 and 4 of Algorithm 2 violate this condition. Let us demonstrate first how this issue can be resolved for Step 3 of Algorithm 1.

LEMMA 5.1. *Steps 3 and 4 of Algorithm 1 can be executed in 3 rounds such that each node performs $\mathcal{O}(n)$ steps of local computation.*

PROOF. Each node locally orders the messages it holds according to their destination sets W'; using bucketsort, this can be done using $\mathcal{O}(n)$ computational steps. According to this order, it moves its messages to the nodes in W following a round-robin pattern. In order to achieve this in 2 rounds, it first sends to each other node in the system one of the messages; in the second round, these nodes forward these messages to nodes in W. Since an appropriate communication pattern can be fixed independently of the specific distribution of messages, no extra computations are required.

Observe that in the resulting distribution of messages, no node in W holds more than $2\sqrt{n}$ messages for each set W': For every full $\sqrt{n}$ messages some node in W holds for set W', every node in W gets exactly one message destined for W', plus possible one residual message for each node in W that does not hold an integer multiple of $\sqrt{n}$ messages for W'. Hence, moving at most two messages across each edge in a single round, Step 4 can be completed in one round. □

Note that we save two rounds for Step 3 in comparison to

Corollary 5.2, but at the expense of doubling the message size in Step 4.

The same argument applies to Step 4 of Algorithm 2.

COROLLARY 5.2. *Steps 3 to 5 of Algorithm 2 can be executed in 2 rounds, where each node performs $\mathcal{O}(n)$ steps of local computation.*

Step 2 of Algorithm 2 requires a different approach still relying on our coloring construction.

LEMMA 5.3. *A variant of Algorithm 2 can execute Step 2 of Algorithm 1 in 5 rounds using $\mathcal{O}(n \log n)$ steps of local computation and memory bits at each node.*

PROOF. As mentioned before, the critical issue is that Steps 2 and 4 of Algorithm 2 rely on bipartite graphs with too many edges. Corollary 5.2 applies to Step 4, so we need to deal with Step 2 only.

To reduce the number edges in the graph, we group messages from W to W' into sets of size n. Note that not all respective numbers are integer multiples of n, and we need to avoid "incomplete" sets of smaller size as otherwise the number of edges still might be too large. This is easily resolved by dealing with such "residual" messages by directly sending them to their destinations: Each set will hold less than n such messages for each destination set W' and therefore can deliver these messages using its n edges to set W'.[6]

It follows that the considered bipartite multigraph will have $\mathcal{O}(n)$ edges and maximum degree $\sqrt{n}$. It remains to argue why all steps can be performed with $\mathcal{O}(n \log n)$ steps and memory at each node. This is obvious for Step 1 and Step 6 and follows from Corollary 5.2 for Steps 3 to 5. Regarding Step 2, observe that the bipartite graph considered can be constructed in $\mathcal{O}(n)$ steps since this requires adding $\sqrt{n}$ integers for each of the $\sqrt{n}$ destination sets (and determining the integer parts of dividing the results by n). Applying the algorithm from [1] then colors the edges within $\mathcal{O}(n \log n)$ steps. Regarding memory, observe that all other steps require $\mathcal{O}(n)$ computational steps and thus trivially satisfy the memory bound. The algorithm from [1] computes the coloring by a recursive divide and conquer strategy; clearly, an appropriate implementation thus will not require more than $\mathcal{O}(n \log n)$ memory either. □

We conclude that there is an implementation of our scheme that is simultaneously efficient with respect to running time, message size, local computations, and memory consumption.

THEOREM 5.4. *Problem 3.1 can be solved deterministically within 12 rounds, where each node performs $\mathcal{O}(n \log n)$ steps of computation using $\mathcal{O}(n \log n)$ memory bits.*

This result immediately transfers to Problem 4.1.

COROLLARY 5.5. *Problem 4.1 and its variant discussed in Corollary 4.6 can be solved in a constant number of rounds, where each node performs $\mathcal{O}(n \log n)$ steps of computation using $\mathcal{O}(n \log n)$ memory bits.*

---

[6] The nodes account for such messages as well when performing the redistribution of messages within W in Steps 3 to 5.

6. VARYING MESSAGE AND KEY SIZE

In this section, we discuss scenarios where the number and size of messages and keys for Problems 3.1 and 4.1 vary. This also motivates to reconsider the bound on the number bits that nodes can exchange in each round: For message/key size of $\Theta(\log n)$, communicating $B \in \mathcal{O}(\log n)$ bits over each edge in each round was shown to be sufficient, and for smaller B the number of rounds clearly must increase accordingly.[7] We will see that most ranges for these parameters can be handled asymptotically optimally by the presented techniques. For the remaining cases, we will give solutions in this section. We remark that one can easily verify that the techniques we propose in the sequel are also efficient with respect to local computations and memory requirements.

6.1 Large Messages or Keys

If messages or keys contain $\omega(\log n)$ bits and B is not sufficiently large to communicate a single value in one message, splitting these values into multiple messages is a viable option. For instance, with bandwidth $B \in \Theta(\log n)$, a key of size $\Theta(\log^2 n)$ would be split into $\Theta(\log n)$ separate messages permitting the receiver to reconstruct the key from the individual messages. This simple argument shows that in fact not the total number of messages (or keys) is decisive for the more general versions of Problems 3.1 and 4.1, but the number of bits that need to be sent and received by each node. If this number is in $\Omega(n \log n)$, the presented techniques are asymptotically optimal.

6.2 Small Messages

If we assume that in Problem 4.1 the size of messages is bounded by $M \in o(\log n)$, we may hope that we can solve the problem in a constant number of rounds even if we merely transmit $B \in \mathcal{O}(M)$ bits along each edge. With the additional assumption that nodes can identify the sender of a message even if the identifier is not included, this can be achieved if sources and destinations of messages are known in advance: We apply Corollary 3.3 and observe that because the communication pattern is known to all nodes, knowing the sender of a message is sufficient to perform the communication and infer the original source of each message at the destination.

On the other hand, if sources/destinations are unknown, consider inputs where $\Omega(n^2)$ messages cannot be sent directly from their sources to their destinations (i.e., using the respective source-receiver edge) within a constant number of rounds. Each of these messages needs to be forwarded in a way preserving their destination, i.e., at least one of the forwarding nodes must learn about the destination of the message (otherwise correct delivery cannot be guaranteed). Explicitly encoding these values for $\Omega(n^2)$ messages requires $\Omega(n^2 \log n)$ bits. Implicit encoding can be done by means of the round number or relations between the communication partners' identifiers. However, encoding bits by introducing constraints reduces (at least for worst-case inputs) the number of messages that can be sent by a node accordingly. These considerations show that in case of Problem 3.1, small messages do not simplify the task.

---

[7] Formally proving a lower bound is trivial in both cases, as nodes need to communicate their n messages to deliver all messages or their n keys to enable determining the correct indices of all keys, respectively.

6.3 Small Keys

The situation is different for Problem 4.1. Note that we need to drop the assumption that all keys can be distinguished, as this would necessitate key size $\Omega(\log n)$. In contrast, if keys can be encoded with $o(\log n)$ bits, there are merely $n^{o(1)}$ different keys. Hence, we can statically assign disjoint sets of $\log^2 n$ nodes to each key κ (for simplicity we assume that $\log n$ is integer). In the first round, each node binary encodes the number of copies it holds of κ and sends the ith bit to $\log n$ of these nodes. The jth of the $\log n$ receiving nodes of bit i counts the number of nodes which sent it a 1, encodes this number binary, and transmits the jth bit to all nodes. With this information, all nodes are capable of computing the total number of copies of κ in the system.

In order to assign an order to the different copies of κ in the system (if desired), in the second round we can require that in addition the jth node dealing with bit i sends to node $k \in \{1, \ldots, n\}$ the jth bit of an encoding of the number of nodes $k' \in \{1, \ldots, k-1\}$ that sent a 1 in the first round. This way, node k can also compute the number of copies of κ held by nodes $k' < k$, which is sufficient to order the keys as intended.

It is noteworthy that this technique can actually be used to order a much larger total number of keys, since we "used" very few of the nodes. If we have $K \leq n/\log^2 n$ different keys, we can assign $m := \lfloor n/K \rfloor$ nodes to each key. This permits to handle any binary encoding of up to $\lfloor \sqrt{m} \rfloor$ many bits in the above manner, potentially allowing for huge numbers of keys. At the same time, messages contain merely 2 bits (or a single bit, if we accept 3 rounds of communication). More generally, each node can be concurrently responsible for B bits, improving the power of the approach further for non-constant values of B.

7. CONCLUSIONS

We showed that in a clique with a bandwidth restriction of $\mathcal{O}(\log n)$ bits per link and round, asymptotically optimal deterministic solutions to routing and sorting can be found. In particular, this entails that a clique in the CONGEST model is, up to constant factors, equivalent to an n-node system with bulk-synchronous communication of bandwidth $\mathcal{O}(n \log n)$. We hope that this observation may serve in future work addressing lower and upper bounds in this model.

The precise time bounds that can be achieved for the routing and sorting problem in our model remain open. Straightforward indistinguishability arguments show that neither randomized nor deterministic algorithms can solve either problem in 2 rounds, since it is impossible to guarantee that all nodes make consistent communication decisions without exchanging *some* information first. However, this simple line of reasoning cannot yield stronger results, as in principle each piece of information can be communicated to each node in the first round, and it is hard to believe that 3-round solutions are possible. Hence, proving non-trivial lower bounds on these problems may provide new techniques and insights that could enhance our understanding of the limitations of the CONGEST model in well-connected topologies.

Acknowledgements

The author would like to thank Shiri Chechic, Quentin Godfroy, Merav Parter, and Jukka Suomela for valuable discussions, and the anonymous reviewers for their helpful comments. This material is based upon work supported by the National Science Foundation under Grant Nos. CCF-AF-0937274, CNS-1035199, 0939370-CCF and CCF-1217506, the AFOSR under Contract No. AFOSR Award number FA9550-13-1-0042, the Swiss National Science Foundation (SNSF), the Swiss Society of Friends of the Weizmann Institute of Science, and the German Research Foundation (DFG, reference number Le 3107/1-1).

8. REFERENCES

[1] R. Cole, K. Ost, and S. Schirra. Edge-Coloring Bipartite Multigraphs in $\mathcal{O}(|E| \log \Delta)$ Time. *Combinatorica*, 21:5–12, 2001.

[2] D. Dolev, C. Lenzen, and S. Peled. "Tri, Tri again": Finding Triangles and Small Subgraphs in a Distributed Setting. In *Proc. 26th Symposium on Distributed Computing (DISC)*, pages 195–209, 2012.

[3] M. Elkin. An Unconditional Lower Bound on the Time-Approximation Tradeoff for the Minimum Spanning Tree Problem. *SIAM Journal on Computing*, 36(2):463–501, 2006.

[4] S. Frischknecht, S. Holzer, and R. Wattenhofer. Networks Cannot Compute Their Diameter in Sublinear Time. In *Proc. 23rd Symposium on Discrete Algorithms (SODA)*, pages 1150–1162, 2012.

[5] M. T. Goodrich. Communication-Efficient Parallel Sorting. *SIAM Journal on Computing*, 29(2):416–432, Oct. 1999.

[6] F. Kuhn, T. Moscibroda, and R. Wattenhofer. Local Computation: Lower and Upper Bounds. *Computing Research Repository*, abs/1011.5470, 2010.

[7] C. Lenzen and R. Wattenhofer. Tight Bounds for Parallel Randomized Load Balancing. In *Proc. 43rd Symposium on Theory of Computing (STOC)*, pages 11–20, 2011.

[8] N. Linial. Locality in Distributed Graph Algorithms. *SIAM Journal on Computing*, 21(1):193–201, 1992.

[9] Z. Lotker, B. Patt-Shamir, and D. Peleg. Distributed MST for Constant Diameter Graphs. *Distributed Computing*, 18(6):453–460, 2006.

[10] L. Lovász and M. D. Plummer. *Matching Theory*. American Mathematical Society, 2009. Reprint with corrections.

[11] M. Naor. A Lower Bound on Probabilistic Algorithms for Distributive Ring Coloring. *SIAM Journal on Discrete Mathematics*, 4(3):409–412, 1991.

[12] B. Patt-Shamir and M. Teplitsky. The Round Complexity of Distributed Sorting: Extended Abstract. In *Proc. 30th Symposium on Principles of Distributed Computing (PODC)*, pages 249–256, 2011.

[13] D. Peleg. *Distributed Computing: A Locality-Sensitive Approach*. Society for Industrial and Applied Mathematics, 2000.

[14] D. Peleg and V. Rubinovich. Near-tight Lower Bound on the Time Complexity of Distributed MST Construction. *SIAM Journal on Computing*, 30:1427–1442, 2000.

[15] A. D. Sarma, S. Holzer, L. Kor, A. Korman, D. Nanongkai, G. Pandurangan, D. Peleg, and R. Wattenhofer. Distributed Verification and Hardness of Distributed Approximation. *SIAM Journal on Computation*, 41(5):1235–1265, 2012.

Brief Announcement: Fair Maximal Independent Sets in Trees*

Jeremy T. Fineman
Georgetown University
Washington, DC
jf474@georgetown.edu

Calvin Newport
Georgetown University
Washington, DC
cn248@georgetown.edu

Tonghe Wang
Georgetown University
Washington, DC
tw473@georgetown.edu

ABSTRACT

Finding a maximal independent set (MIS) is a classic problem in graph theory that has been widely study in the context of distributed algorithms. Standard distributed MIS solutions focus on time complexity. Here we focus on a novel attribute, *fairness*, where we consider an MIS algorithm *fair* if all nodes have similar probabilities of joining the set. In many contexts, fairness is important because a node's election to the MIS can have an impact on the resources it consumes. This paper addresses fairness by providing a provably fair and efficient distributed MIS algorithm for unrooted trees. The algorithm runs in $O(\log n)$ time and guarantees a correct MIS such that each node enters the set with probability at least $1/4 - \epsilon$, for arbitrarily small ϵ.

Categories and Subject Descriptors

G.2.2 [**Discrete Mathematics**]: Graph Theory—*graph algorithms, trees*; F.2.2 [**Analysis of Algorithms and Problem Complexity**]: Nonnumerical Algorithms and Problems—*computations on discrete structures*

Keywords

maximal independent set; fairness; symmetry breaking

1. INTRODUCTION

In graph theory, a ***maximal independent set (MIS)*** of an undirected graph $G = (V, E)$ is a subset of nodes $I \subseteq V$ such that every node in $V \setminus I$ neighbors a node in I, and no two nodes from I neighbor each other. In distributed and parallel algorithms, an MIS provides an important symmetry breaking function, and they are therefore used as building blocks for many higher level applications.

*This research is supported in part by a Ford Motor Company University Research Program grant and NSF CCF-1218188.

This short paper focuses on a novel attribute of distributed MIS solutions: *their fairness*. In practice, whether a node is selected to join the MIS might have a significant impact on the amount of work the node has to perform in the higher-level application using the structure. Because work consumes resources, the probability with which nodes join the MIS in a given graph matters. We argue, therefore, that the fairness of an MIS algorithm can be just as important as its time complexity. This paper is the first (to the best of our knowledge) to initiate the study of this property.

Formally, for a given MIS algorithm $\mathcal{A}$, graph $G = (V, E)$, and node $u \in V$, let $P_{\mathcal{A},G}(u)$ describe the probability that u joins the MIS when we execute $\mathcal{A}$ in G. A *fair* algorithm would yield similar values of P for all nodes, regardless of the underlying graph G. In practice, this property might not be easily achieved with an efficient distributed algorithm. Consider, for example, the $O(\log n)$-time distributed MIS protocol by Luby [5]—one of the most well-cited and used distributed MIS algorithms. Call this algorithm $\mathcal{L}$ and let G be a star graph over $V = \{u_1, u_2, ..., u_n\}$ centered on u_1. It is not hard to show that $P_{\mathcal{L},G}(u_i) = \Theta(n \cdot P_{\mathcal{L},G}(u_1))$, for any $i > 1$—indicating a major gap in the probability of joining the MIS, depending on a node's graph location. Similar gaps in probability occur for Luby's algorithm—and those with similar logic—in many other graphs with large differences in node degrees.

It is not difficult to create a *centralized* algorithm $\mathcal{A}'$ that guarantees $P_{\mathcal{A}',G}(u) = P_{\mathcal{A}',G}(v) \; \forall u, v \in V$, for any $G \in \mathcal{B}$, where $\mathcal{B}$ is the class of bipartite graphs (e.g., our SLOW-FAIRMIS algorithm described below). The real challenge is to find an efficient *distributed* algorithm that can approximate this guarantee. In this paper, we tackle this challenge for $\mathcal{T} \subset \mathcal{B}$, where $\mathcal{T}$ is the class of unrooted trees. In more detail, we describe a distributed MIS algorithm FASTFAIR-MIS that when run on a graph $G \in \mathcal{T}$, guarantees a correct MIS such that $P_{\text{FASTFAIRMIS},G}(u) \geq 1/4 - \epsilon$, for every node u and an arbitrarily small factor ϵ. It terminates in $O(\log n)$ rounds (the same time complexity guarantee as most distributed MIS solutions, including the solution in [5]). If fairness is ignored, there are faster known algorithms for restricted graph classes, including an $O(\sqrt{\log n \log \log n})$ algorithm for trees [4] (which nearly matches an $\Omega(\sqrt{\log n})$ lower bound [3]), and $o(\log n)$-time algorithms for low-degree graphs (e.g., [1]). We also note that in concurrent work, Harris et al. [2] study a different non-efficiency property of distributed MIS solutions: the average degree of the MIS nodes in the graph. This complementary study supports our argument that distributed symmetry breaking is interesting beyond just the time complexity perspective.

2. ALGORITHM

We assume the synchronous network model. Fix some graph $G = (V, E)$, where $G \in \mathcal{T}$ and $n = |V|$ describes the number of nodes. Without losing generality, assume that each node is assigned a unique identifier. Each node knows its own ID and its immediate neighbors' IDs, as well as n. It has no other *a priori* topology information. In the following, for $U \subseteq V$, we use $G(U)$ to refer to the subgraph of G induced by vertex set U, which comprises the vertices U and the edges of G whose endpoints are both in U. We use $N(u)$, for node u, to describe the neighbors of u in G, and use $D(G) = \max_{u,v \in V} d_G(u, v)$ to describe the diameter of G, where $d_G(u, v)$ describes the length of the shortest path from u to v.

Algorithm Overview.

Figure 1 describes FASTFAIRMIS, a distributed algorithm that generates a fair MIS in unrooted trees in $O(\log n)$ time. This algorithm uses, as a subroutine, SLOWFAIRMIS, a distributed algorithm that can generate an perfectly fair MIS in unrooted trees in $O(D(G))$ time, where G is the tree in which it is executed. At a high level these two algorithms work together as follows: FASTFAIRMIS starts by having nodes partition the original tree G, in a distributed manner, into components of smaller size. The nodes then execute SLOWFAIRMIS in each of these resulting components, covering them with a fair MIS. Next, a careful *stitching* process (Stages 2–3) is used to resolve MIS conflicts between neighboring components in a local manner. We will prove that our initial partition breaks G into components with diameter $O(\log n)$, with high probability, allowing SLOWFAIRMIS to be executed efficiently. We will also prove that the stitching step only reduces the fairness of the algorithm by a small constant factor.

The SLOWFAIRMIS Algorithm.

The algorithm takes a single parameter, $\widehat{D}$, which is an estimated upper bound on the diameter of the tree in which it is executed. The algorithm starts by having each node run a basic flood-based leader election algorithm for $\widehat{D}$ rounds: each node in each round broadcasts the largest id it has received so far, adopt this as its leader at the end of $\widehat{D}$ rounds. After the election concludes, the leader u (or, potentially multiple leaders if $\widehat{D}$ is an underestimate), selects a bit b_u with uniform randomness. It then initiates a breadth first search, beginning at itself, terminating after $\widehat{D}$ rounds, even if some nodes have not been reached. The search message includes the current depth of the search (u considers itself at level 0) and b_u. Each node (including u), that learns it is in some level i, joins to the MIS if $i + b_u \equiv 0 \pmod 2$. It is straightforward to show:

LEMMA 1. *Assume SLOWFAIRMIS is called by every node in unrooted tree $G = (V, E)$ during the same round with the same parameter $\widehat{D}$. Let $I(G)$ be the nodes that join the MIS. If $\widehat{D} \geq D(G)$, then: (a) $I(G)$ is a correct MIS for G; and (b) $\forall u \in V : P_{\text{SLOWFAIRMIS},G}(u) = 1/2$.*

PROOF. If $\widehat{D} \geq D(G)$, then the leader election correctly elects a single leader and the breadth-first search reaches all

Stage 1: Cut ($\forall v \in V$)
Cooperate with each neighbor $u \in N(v)$ to set $\quad (u, v).cut = 1$ with probability $\frac{1}{2}$.
Call SLOWFAIRMIS with $\widehat{D} = \gamma$, ignoring edges with $cut = 1$.
if v joined MIS, then add v to $\mathcal{I}$.
Stage 2: Resolve ($\forall v \in \mathcal{I}$)
Call SLOWFAIRMIS with $\widehat{D} = \gamma$.
if v joined MIS, then keep v in $\mathcal{I}$;
else remove v from $\mathcal{I}$.
Stage 3: Maximal ($\forall v \ s.t. \ (N_G(v) \cup \{v\}) \cap \mathcal{I} = \emptyset$)
Call SLOWFAIRMIS with $\widehat{D} = \gamma$.
if v joined MIS, then add v to $\mathcal{I}$.
Stage 4: Fix ($\forall v \in V$)
if $v \in \mathcal{I}$ and $N_G(v) \cap \mathcal{I} \neq \emptyset$, then remove v from $\mathcal{I}$.
if $v \in \mathcal{I}$, then v outputs "in MIS" and terminates;
elseif $N_G(v) \cap \mathcal{I} \neq \emptyset$, then v outputs "not in MIS" and terminates ;
else Call LUBYMIS and mimic output.

Figure 1: The four stages of the FastFairMIS algorithm. In the above, $\gamma = \Theta(\log n)$ and each stage runs for a fixed number of rounds (i.e., nodes not participating in a stage still wait the fixed number of rounds before proceeding to the next stage). The set notation next to each stage name indicates the nodes that execute that stage.

nodes. Because G is a tree, it is easy to see that (a) holds. To show (b), fix some node $v \in T$. Let u be the leader in G. Depending on the parity of $d_T(u, v)$, one value for b_u will put v in $I(G)$ and one will keep v out of $I(G)$. The fairness follows from the fact that b_u is chosen with uniform probability. □

The FASTFAIRMIS Algorithm.

We now describe our main result, the FASTFAIRMIS algorithm. This algorithm consists of the four *stages* described in Figure 1. Notice, not all nodes participate in each stage. The first three stages, however, each run for a fixed number of rounds (the $\Theta(\log n)$ time required by the call to SLOWFAIRMIS, plus the constant number of extra rounds needed for local communication, when relevant), so non-participants simply wait that number of rounds before proceeding to the next stage. This ensures all nodes start each of these stages during the same round.

Stage 1 divides the tree into components by cutting edges and attempts to create a fair MIS $\mathcal{I}$ in each. If it completes, this stage has all nodes covered, but there might be MIS conflicts between neighbors in distinct components. Stage 2 resolves these conflicts by running SLOWFAIRMIS only on "MIS" nodes (those in $\mathcal{I}$), causing some nodes to drop out of $\mathcal{I}$. If Stages 1 and 2 are successful, then $\mathcal{I}$ is now an independent set, but not necessarily maximal. Stage 3 restores maximality by running SLOWFAIRMIS on uncovered nodes. The resulting MIS stitches safely with the existing IS $\mathcal{I}$.

We will prove that in each stage, the components calling SLOWFAIRMIS have diameters no larger than the estimate passed to the algorithm, ensuring that it executes successfully. Assuming this occurs, the algorithm will end with $\mathcal{I}$ describing a valid MIS. We are left only to prove that $P_{\text{FASTFAIRMIS},G} > 1/4$ for every node. With low probability, however, we might arrive at Stage 4 with an invalid MIS due to SLOWFAIRMIS failing to compete on a large diameter component in a previous stage. To correct for this possibility, at the start of Stage 4, we remove all independence violations leaving $\mathcal{I}$. All uncovered nodes then run a standard MIS algorithm (in the current write up, we use the MIS algorithm of Luby [5], which we call LUBYMIS in Figure 1). The resulting MIS will stitch together with the earlier independent set, but we make no guarantee about its fairness. In other words, LUBYMIS is only ever called as a fallback in the low probability event that one of the previous three stages failed. The impact on fairness of this low probability event shows up in the small $\epsilon < 1/n$ factor present in our final fairness bound of $1/4 - \epsilon$.

THEOREM 2. *For any unrooted tree $T = (V, E)$, the* FAST-FAIRMIS *algorithm, when executed in T, constructs a correct MIS such that $P_{\text{FASTFAIRMIS},G}(u) \geq 1/4 - \epsilon$, for every $u \in V$ and some $\epsilon < 1/n$. It terminates in $O(\log n)$ rounds, with probability at least $1 - 1/n$.*

PROOF (SKETCH). We have three properties to prove: the time complexity, correctness, and fairness of FASTFAIRMIS. In the following, let G_1 be the subgraph of T that results when we remove edges with $cut = 1$. Let $\{G_1(V_1^j)\}_{j=1}^{\omega_1}$ be the $\omega_1 \geq 1$ resulting components in G_1. To distinguish the value of our set $\mathcal{I}$ at the end of each stage, we use the notation $\mathcal{I}_1, \mathcal{I}_2, \mathcal{I}_3$ to describe $\mathcal{I}$ at the end of Stages 1, 2 and 3, respectively.

Time Complexity & Fairness. Time complexity follows directly from the fixed-length of Stages 1 to 3 and the $O(\log n)$ bound on LUBYMIS proved in [5]. For correctness, we note that Stage 4 starts by removing any independence violations, then ensures maximality by running LUBYMIS on the remaining uncovered nodes. To prove fairness below, however, it is important that we also prove that $\mathcal{I}_3$ is a correct MIS under the assumption that Stages 1 to 3 have successful calls to SLOWFAIRMIS. To do so, we first argue that $\mathcal{I}_2$ is an independent set on T. Consider any $u \neq v$. If u and v are from the same component $G_1(V_1^1)$, then by assumption they cannot both be in $\mathcal{I}_1$. Because Stage 2 only removes nodes from $\mathcal{I}$, this independence remains in $\mathcal{I}_2$. On the other hand, if $u \in G_1(V_1^i)$ and $v \in G_1(V_1^j)$ for $i \neq j$, and $(u, v) \in E$, then both u and v called SLOWFAIRMIS in Stage 2. By assumption, they cannot both remain in $\mathcal{I}$. We next argue that given this independence on $\mathcal{I}_2$, the call to SLOW-FAIRMIS by uncovered in Stage 3 will provide maximality and provide a correct MIS.

Fairness. As argued above, if Stages 1 to 3 are successful, $\mathcal{I}_3$ is our final MIS. Under this assumption of success, the probability that u is in the MIS is greater than $Pr\{u \in \mathcal{I}_1\} - Pr\{u \in \mathcal{I}_1 \setminus \mathcal{I}_2\} = 1/2 - 1/4 = 1/4$ (we can ignore stage 3 in this calculation as it can only increase the join probability). For our final fairness, we need subtract a factor ϵ, which captures the probability that Stages 1 to 3 fail. We are left to bound $\epsilon < 1/n$. To do so, we note that for both Stages 1 and 2, a given path of length ℓ is included in a component with probability $2^{-\ell}$. If we set $\gamma = c \log n$ for a sufficiently large constant c, a union bound over the polynomially-many paths in T shows that $Pr\{\text{Length of any path} \geq \gamma\} \leq 1/n^2$. For Stage 3, we note that for a path $u_1, u_2, ..., u_\ell$ of length ℓ and consisting of nodes uncovered by $\mathcal{I}_2$, each u_i was never previously in $\mathcal{I}$ (if it was, it would be covered in this stage), and, therefore, each u_i has a neighbor v_i that was in $\mathcal{I}_1$ but not $\mathcal{I}_2$. Furthermore, because T is a tree, for v_i, v_j, $i \neq j$, v_i and v_j are in different components in Stage 2 and therefore their outcomes in Stage 2 are independent.

Because SLOWFAIRMIS is fair, $Pr\{v_i \notin \mathcal{I}_2\} = 1/2$. The same argument as above shows for that sufficiently large γ, are Stage 3 components are sufficiently small also with probability $\leq 1/n^2$. A final union bound gives us the needed $\epsilon < 1/n$. $\square$

3. CONCLUSION

The fairness of an MIS algorithms is a new property that bounds the difference in join probabilities for nodes constructing an MIS in a given graph. We call an MIS algorithm fair with respect to a graph class if this difference is bounded by a constant for all pairs of nodes in all graphs in the class. We note that existing algorithms, such as Luby's [5], are unfair in many graphs, and then present a new solution, FASTMIS: a distributed MIS algorithm that is provably fair and runs in $O(\log n)$ time in unrooted trees. Identifying new upper and lower bounds for other common graph classes remains interesting future work.

4. REFERENCES

[1] L. Barenboim, M. Elkin, S. Pettie, and J. Schneider. The locality of distributed symmetry breaking. In *Proceedings of the 2012 IEEE 53rd Annual Symposium on Foundations of Computer Science*, FOCS '12, pages 321–330, Washington, DC, USA, 2012. IEEE Computer Society.

[2] D. G. Harris, E. Morsy, G. Pandurang, P. Robinson, and A. Srinivasan. Efficient Computation of Balanced Structures. In *Proceedings of the International Colloquium on Automata, Languages and Programming*, 2013.

[3] F. Kuhn, T. Moscibroda, and R. Wattenhofer. Local computation: Lower and upper bounds. *CoRR*, abs/1011.5470, 2010.

[4] C. Lenzen and R. Wattenhofer. MIS on trees. In *Proceedings of the 30th annual ACM SIGACT-SIGOPS symposium on Principles of distributed computing*, PODC '11, pages 41–48, New York, NY, USA, 2011. ACM.

[5] M. Luby. A simple parallel algorithm for the maximal independent set problem. *SIAM J. Comput.*, 15(4):1036–1055, Nov. 1986.

Brief Announcement: Threshold Load Balancing in Networks*

Martin Hoefer
Max-Planck-Institut für Informatik
Saarland University, Saarbrücken, Germany
mhoefer@mpi-inf.mpg.de

Thomas Sauerwald
Max-Planck-Institut für Informatik
Saarland University, Saarbrücken, Germany
sauerwal@mpi-inf.mpg.de

ABSTRACT

We study probabilistic protocols for concurrent threshold-based load balancing in networks. There are n resources or machines represented by nodes in an undirected graph and $m \gg n$ users that try to find an acceptable resource by moving along the edges of the graph. Users accept a resource if the load is below a *threshold*. Such thresholds have an intuitive meaning, e.g., as deadlines in a machine scheduling scenario, and they allow the design of protocols under strong locality constraints. When migration is partly controlled by resources and partly by users, our protocols obtain rapid convergence to a balanced state, in which all users are satisfied. We show that convergence is achieved in a number of rounds that is only logarithmic in m and polynomial in structural properties of the graph. Even when migration is fully controlled by users, we obtain similar results for convergence to approximately balanced states.

Categories and Subject Descriptors

F.2.2 [**Analysis of Algorithms and Problem Complexity**]: Nonnumerical Algorithms and Problems

Keywords

Load Balancing; Distributed Protocols; Random Walks

1. INTRODUCTION

Load balancing is a fundamental requirement of many distributed systems. The locality of information and communication inherent in many applications like multicore computer systems or wireless networks often render centralized optimization impossible. Instead, these cases require distributed load balancing algorithms that respect locality constraints, but nonetheless rapidly achieve balanced conditions. A successful approach to this problem are load balancing protocols, in which tasks are concurrently migrated in a distributed fashion. A variety of such protocols have been studied in the past, but they usually rely on machines to make migration decisions. Being a fundamental resource allocation problem the interpretation of "load" and "machine" can greatly vary (e.g., in wireless networks it can mean "interference" and "channel", respectively), and in many cases machine-controlled reallocation represent an unreasonable means of centralized control. Protocols that avoid this feature have been popular in the area of algorithmic game theory. Here tasks are controlled by (selfish) users that follow a protocol to migrate their task to a less populated machine, see [9]. While having distributed control, these protocols usually require strong forms of global knowledge, e.g., the number of underloaded/overloaded machines [6], or load differences among machines in the system [2,3].

An interesting approach are threshold-based load balancing protocols initially studied in [7], in which reallocation decisions are based on an acceptance threshold. In the simplest variant, there is a uniform threshold T and each user is satisfied if the machine it is currently assigned to has a number of assigned users below T. Otherwise, the user is dissatisfied and decides to migrate to another machine chosen uniformly at random. The great advantage of threshold-based protocols is that they can be implemented using only the information about the currently allocated machine and *without having to obtain non-local information* about other machines, the current load or migration pattern in the system, etc. Successful balancing obviously also depends on a suitable threshold T.

While threshold load balancing protocols are attractive, their behavior is not well-understood in many standard load balancing scenarios. In particular, previous works [1,7] have only addressed the case when every machine is available to every user throughout the whole balancing process (i.e., when a "complete network" exists among resources). In this paper, we advance the understanding of these protocols in scenarios with locality restrictions to user migration. In particular, we assume that there is an undirected graph $G = (V, E)$ and each vertex $v \in V$ is a *machine* or *resource*. Users can access machines only *depending on their location*, i.e., a user on machine $v \in V$ can only move to neighboring machines in G.

Contribution. We study protocols for threshold load balancing with resource-controlled and user-controlled migration. We assume thresholds are *feasible*, i.e., they allow a *balanced state* in which all users are satisfied and consider

*Supported by DFG through Cluster of Excellence MMCI and grant Ho 3831/3-1.

the expected convergence time to such a state. Our protocols achieve rapid convergence in a number of rounds only logarithmic in the number m of users and a polynomial depending on the graph structure. Hence, even in this very decentralized setting, efficient load balancing is possible.

In our first model, user migration is partly controlled by resources, i.e., we allow each dissatisfied resource to pick the users that should move. Each of the picked users then moves to an adjacent resource that it chooses uniformly at random. For *user-independent thresholds*, where for every resource v all users have the same threshold T_v, the protocol converges in $\mathcal{O}(\mathsf{H}(G) \cdot \log(m))$ rounds, where $\mathsf{H}(G)$ is the maximum hitting time between any pair of nodes in G. If thresholds are arbitrary but satisfy an *above average* property, the same holds and additionally the number of rounds is roughly in the order of $\mathcal{O}(\mathsf{MIX}(G) \cdot \log(m) + \mathsf{H}(G) \cdot \log(n))$. This is a much better bound as the mixing time $\mathsf{MIX}(G)$ of a random walk is significantly smaller than $\mathsf{H}(G)$ for many graphs G. This bound is shown to be essentially tight, as there are graphs G, above average thresholds, and initial allocations for which the protocol needs $\Omega(\mathsf{MIX}(G) \cdot \log(m))$ rounds to reach a balanced state.

Further, we consider a protocol that is fully user-controlled for the case of user-independent thresholds. In this case, each dissatisfied user independently at random decides to migrate to an adjacent resource with a probability depending on the locally observed loads and its intrinsic thresholds. When our aim is to balance approximately, we can establish similar bounds of $\mathcal{O}(\mathsf{H}(G) \cdot \log(m))$ and $\mathcal{O}(\mathsf{MIX}(G) \cdot \log(m))$ for the cases of arbitrary and above average user-independent thresholds, respectively.

Related Work. In algorithmic game theory several protocols for user-controlled selfish load balancing games have been proposed, using which a set of selfish users can reach a Nash equilibrium in a distributed and concurrent fashion. However, with the exception of [3] the protocols were studied only for the complete network. There are two approaches that yield convergence time of $O(\log \log m + \operatorname{poly}(n))$, but either the number of underloaded/overloaded resources must be known [6], or users must be able to inspect load differences among resources in the system [2]. The latter is also necessary in [3], where the protocol from [2] is extended to arbitrary networks and convergence times of $O(\log(m) \cdot \operatorname{poly}(n))$ are shown.

Our threshold protocols that avoid this problem were proposed and analyzed for the complete network in [1], in which convergence in $O(\log(m))$ rounds is shown for both resource- and user-controlled cases and user-independent and above average thresholds. We remark that there is an interpretation of our scenario as selfish load balancing game by assuming that each user experiences a private cost of 1 whenever the load on their allocated resource exceeds the threshold and 0 otherwise. In this way, our protocols can be interpreted to converge to Nash equilibria (i.e., the balanced states) of the game. For the case of resource-controlled migration, we assume that user thresholds are common knowledge. It is an interesting open problem to derive protocols for users private thresholds.

Load balancing with resource-controlled protocols has also received much interest in the distributed computing literature in recent years. The most prominent approaches are diffusion and dimension-exchange models [8], and the vast

majority of the literature concentrates on the case of $m = n$ users. For this case, a wide variety of different bounds for general graphs and special topologies are known. However, in these models even the number of users that migrate from one resource to a specific (adjacent) resource is steered by the two resources.

2. MODEL

Definition and Potential. There are n *machines* or *resources*, which are nodes in a graph $G = (V, E)$, and a set $[m]$ of m users. Each user has a unit-size task. It allocates the task to a resource and possibly moves along edges of the graph to find a resource with acceptable load. In particular, user i has a *threshold* T_v^i for each resource $v \in V$. A *state* is an assignment $a = (a_1, \ldots, a_m) \in V^m$ of users to resources. We let $x_v = |\{i \mid a_i = v\}|$ denote the *load* on resource v, and we call x the *profile* of state a. If i is assigned to v and $x_v \leq T_v^i$, then i is happy with its choice. Otherwise, it is dissatisfied and motivated to leave. We consider distributed load balancing protocols to steer migration of dissatisfied users. We call a set of thresholds *user-independent* if $T_v^i = T_v$ for all $i \in [m]$ and $v \in V$. We call thresholds *resource-independent* if $T_v^i = T^i$ for all $i \in [m]$ and $v \in V$. Finally, we define the *average* as $\overline{T} = \lceil m/n \rceil$, and call a set of thresholds *above average* if $T_v^i > \overline{T}$ for all $i \in [m]$ and $v \in V$. For thresholds that are not user-independent (i.e., resource-independent or arbitrary) we will throughout make the assumption that they are above average. We call a state *balanced* if $x_v \leq T_v^i$ for all resources v and all users i assigned to v. A set of thresholds T_v^i is called *feasible* if it allows a balanced state. Many of our proofs are based on a potential function argument. We define a *potential* $\Phi(x) = \sum_{v \in V} \Phi_v(x)$ as follows. Consider the users assigned to resource v ranked in non-increasing order of T_v^i. Let $k \in \{1, \ldots, x_v\}$ be the last position in the ranking at which there is a user i such that $k \leq T_v^i$. If there is no such position, we let $k = 0$. The contribution to the potential is $\Phi_v(x) = x_v - k$. Observe that if thresholds are user-independent, $\Phi_v(x) = \max\{x_v - T_v, 0\}$.

Random Walks. For an undirected, connected graph G, let Δ, d, and δ be the maximum, average, and minimum degree of G, respectively. For a node $v \in V$, $d(v)$ is the degree of node v. If a user is continuously dissatisfied, its movements will form a random walk. The transition matrix of the random walk is the $n \times n$-matrix $\mathbf{P}$ which is defined by $P_{u,v} := \frac{1}{d(u)}$ for $\{u, v\} \in E$ and $P_{u,v} := 0$ otherwise. Hence, the random walk moves in each step to a randomly chosen neighbor. Let $\mathbf{P}^t$ be the t-th power of $\mathbf{P}$. Then $P_{u,v}^t$ is the probability that a random walk starting from u is located at node v at step t. We denote by $\lambda_1 \geq \lambda_2 \geq \ldots \geq \lambda_n$ the n eigenvalues of $\mathbf{P}$. We now define

$$\mu := 1 - \max_{2 \leq i \leq n} \{|\lambda_i| : |\lambda_i| < 1\}.$$

(this definition differs slightly from the one of the spectral gap which is $1 - \max_{2 \leq i \leq n} |\lambda_i|$.) We further denote the stationary distribution of the random walk by the vector π with $\pi_i = d(i)/(2m)$, where m is the number of edges in G. For connected graphs, this distribution is the unique vector that satisfies $\pi \cdot \mathbf{P} = \pi$. We define the *mixing time* to be $\mathsf{MIX}(G) := 4 \log n / \mu$. It is a well-known fact that $1/\mu$ is always at most polynomial in n, for instance, using the conductance we have $\mathsf{MIX}(G) \leq 4n^4 \log n$. We denote the *hitting time* by $\mathsf{H}(u, v)$ which is the expected time for a random walk to reach v when starting from u ($\mathsf{H}(u, u) = 0$). We define the maximum hitting time as $\mathsf{H}(G) := \max_{u,v \in V} \mathsf{H}(u, v)$.

3. CONVERGENCE TIMES

Resource-Controlled Migration. We first consider a protocol with migration being partly resource- and partly user-controlled. In each round, every resource v decides which of its assigned users to evacuate. The evacuation choice of the resource is done in accordance with the definition of the potential. Users currently assigned to v are ordered in non-increasing order of T_v^i. Let k be the last position in the ranking at which there is a user i with $k \leq T_v^i$. All users ranked after i are assigned to leave the resource. Each user that is assigned to leave picks a neighboring resource uniformly at random and moves to this resource. All movements are concurrent, and there is no coordination between resources. A round ends when all users have moved and each resource has updated its sorted list of currently allocated users. Note that this protocol tries to accommodate as many users as possible on the resource and assigns exactly $\Phi_v(x)$ many users to leave.

For our analysis, we split a single round into two phases – a *removal phase*, where resources remove the users to be evacuated and an *arrival phase*, where users arrive on their new resources. Note that in one round of the resource-controlled protocol the *potential $\Phi(x)$ does not increase*. This insight allows us to view migrating users as random walks. We assume a token is given in the arrival phase from a migrating user to the user it causes to migrate in the next round. The number of tokens in the system for state a with load profile x is exactly $\Phi(x)$, and each token performs a random walk over G. If a user causes no other user to migrate in the next round, the token is removed and the random walk is stopped.

Theorem 3.1. *For feasible user-independent or above average thresholds, the protocol converges to a balanced state in an expected number of $\mathcal{O}(\mathsf{H}(G) \cdot \ln(m))$ rounds.*

Theorem 3.2. *For above average thresholds the protocol converges to a balanced state in an expected number of rounds of*

$$\mathcal{O}\left(\left(\frac{1}{\varepsilon_{\min}} \cdot \frac{d}{\delta} \cdot \mathsf{MIX}(G) \cdot \ln(m) \right) + \left(\mathsf{H}(G) \cdot \ln(n) \right) \right) .$$

The following theorem shows that the bound in the previous theorem is essentially tight for our protocol. There is a class of graphs and starting states such that the convergence time of our protocol is characterized by the problem of moving a large number of users over a relatively sparse cut. This allows us to establish a lower bound using the mixing time. The lower bound of the theorem holds for every mixing time in $\Omega(n)$ and $O(n^2)$.

Theorem 3.3. *There is a class of graphs such that for above average thresholds the protocol converges to a balanced state in an expected number of $\Omega(\mathsf{MIX}(G) \cdot \ln(m))$ rounds.*

User-Controlled Migration. Let us now consider a fully distributed protocol for the case of user-independent thresholds. In our protocol, in each round every user located on resource v decides to migrate away from v with a probability $p_v(x) = \alpha \cdot (\Phi_v(x)/T_v)$. If a user decides to migrate, it

moves to a neighboring resource of v chosen uniformly at random. This approach has the advantage that resources do not have to sort and control movements of users. One challenge of the user-controlled migration is that expected potential value can increase in the next round. This makes the analysis harder than for resource-controlled migration or user-controlled migration on complete graphs, as in both cases the (expected) potential is non-increasing.

When more than $\Phi_v(x)$ users migrate from v in a round, this leads to creation of new random walks. We term each random walk created in this manner *excess (random) walk*. In contrast, we refer to *ordinary random walks*.

In the following two theorems we assume $\alpha = 1/(2e)$ and extend Theorems 3.1 and 3.2 to the scenario of user-controlled migration. The idea is to bound the increase due to excess random walks and show that the potential (i.e., the number of random walks) still drops by a constant factor as long as the potential is sufficiently large.

Theorem 3.4. *For feasible user-independent thresholds after $\mathcal{O}(\mathsf{H}(G) \cdot \log m)$ rounds in expectation we reach a state with profile x where $\Phi(x) = \mathcal{O}(n \cdot \mathsf{H}(G))$.*

Theorem 3.5. *For user-independent thresholds with $T_v \geq (1 + \varepsilon_{\min}) \cdot \overline{T}$, after*

$$\mathcal{O}\left(\frac{1}{\varepsilon_{\min}} \cdot \frac{d}{\delta} \cdot \mathsf{MIX}(G) \cdot \log(m) \right)$$

rounds in expectation we reach a state with profile x where $\Phi(x) = \mathcal{O}\left(n \cdot \frac{1}{\varepsilon_{\min}} \cdot \frac{d}{\delta} \cdot \mathsf{MIX}(G) \right)$.

4. REFERENCES

[1] H. Ackermann, S. Fischer, M. Hoefer, M. Schöngens. Distributed algorithms for QoS load balancing. *Distrib. Comput.*, 23(5–6):321–330, 2011.

[2] P. Berenbrink, T. Friedetzky, L. Goldberg, P. Goldberg, Z. Hu, R. Martin. Distributed delfish load balancing. *SIAM J. Comput.*, 37(4):1163–1181, 2007.

[3] P. Berenbrink, M. Hoefer, T. Sauerwald. Distributed selfish load balancing on networks. In *Proc. SODA*, pp. 1487–1497, 2011.

[4] R. Elsässer, B. Monien, S. Schamberger. Distributing unit size workload packages in heterogeneous networks. *J. Graph Alg. Appl.*, 10(1):51–68, 2006.

[5] R. Elsässer, T. Sauerwald. Discrete Load Balancing is (Almost) as Easy as Continuous Load Balancing. In *Proc. PODC*, pp. 346–354, 2010.

[6] E. Even-Dar, Y. Mansour. Fast convergence of selfish rerouting. In *Proc. SODA*, pp. 772–781, 2005.

[7] S. Fischer, P. Mähönen, M. Schöngens, B. Vöcking. Load balancing for dynamic spectrum assignment with local information for secondary users. In *Proc. DySPAN*, 2008.

[8] Y. Rabani, A. Sinclair, R. Wanka. Local divergence of Markov chains and the analysis of iterative load balancing schemes. In *Proc. FOCS*, pp. 694–705, 1998.

[9] B. Vöcking. Selfish load balancing. In N. Nisan et al., eds., *Algorithmic Game Theory*, chapter 20. Cambridge Univ. Press, 2007.

Fast Byzantine Agreement

Nicolas Braud-Santoni[*]
EPFL, Switzerland
nicolas.braud-
santoni@ens-cachan.fr

Rachid Guerraoui
EPFL, Switzerland
rachid.guerraoui@epfl.ch

Florian Huc
EPFL, Switzerland
florian.huc@gmail.com

ABSTRACT

This paper presents the first probabilistic Byzantine Agreement algorithm whose communication and time complexities are poly-logarithmic. So far, the most effective probabilistic Byzantine Agreement algorithm had communication complexity $\tilde{O}\left(\sqrt{n}\right)$ and time complexity $\tilde{O}(1)$. Our algorithm is based on a novel, unbalanced, almost everywhere to everywhere Agreement protocol which is interesting in its own right.

Categories and Subject Descriptors

C.2.4 [**Computer-Communication Networks**]: Distributed Systems

Keywords

Byzantine Agreement, randomized algorithm

1. INTRODUCTION

The Byzantine Agreement problem.

Given a system of size n in which a Byzantine adversary controls at most t nodes (referred thereafter as *Byzantine nodes*), the Byzantine Agreement problem [LSP82] is about having all non-Byzantine nodes (or *correct* nodes) reach an agreement. The constraints imposed on the agreement are that all the correct nodes have to agree on a single output, which the adversary cannot impose to be *bad*.

Here *bad* can be subject to various interpretations:

- when the output is a single bit, it is required to be the input of one of the correct nodes;

- when the output is a string of $O(\log n)$ random bits, the adversary should not be able to bias *too many* bits of the output[1].

Like [PR10, BOPV06, BO83, Rab83], we consider the latter case.

---

[*]On leave from ENS de Cachan, Brittany campus, France.
[1]Here, "too many" will be made precise later on.

Deterministic setting.

Lamport, Shostak and Pease [LSP82, PSL80] have shown that the Byzantine Agreement problem cannot be solved without transferable authentication (or some other form of non-equivocation) when $n \leq 3t$. Furthermore, they gave a solution whose time complexity is $t + 1$. Later, Fischer and Lynch, in [FL82], proved that $t + 1$ is a lower bound on the time complexity in the worst case, while a lower bound on message complexity of $\Omega\left(n^2\right)$ was given in [DR85].

The result of [LSP82, PSL80] was improved in [GM98], in which the authors proposed an algorithm using $t + 1$ steps, and whose computation and message complexities are polynomial. The case where *transferable signatures* are available was considered in [DR85]; under this condition, algorithms to solve the Byzantine Agreement problem exist without any restriction on the number of Byzantine nodes t [LSP82, PSL80]. The authors also proposed an algorithm using $O\left(n + t^2\right)$ messages, and an optimality proof.

Randomized algorithms.

To circumvent these lower bounds on time and communication complexities, randomization is crucial. Randomized Byzantine Agreement algorithms with constant expected time complexity were first proposed in [Rab83, DPPU86]. In [PR10], an algorithm with constant expected time complexity and $\tilde{O}\left(n^2\right)$ communication[2] complexity was proposed, under the assumption that communication channels are *private*. This algorithm works for asynchronous systems, but tolerates only $t < n/4$ malicious nodes.

In [HKK08], the authors proved an $\Omega\left(\sqrt[3]{n}\right)$ lower bound on both message (for at least one node) and time complexities for Byzantine Agreement algorithms in synchronous systems, under some restrictive assumptions.

Almost-everywhere agreement.

A relaxed version of the Byzantine Agreement problem, namely the *almost-everywhere Byzantine Agreement* problem, was introduced by Dwork *et al.* in [DPPU86]. This problem is a relaxation of the classical Byzantine Agreement problem, in the sense that it only requires that all but an $O\left(\log^{-1} n\right)$ fraction of the nodes agree on a common output.

This problem was first efficiently solved in [KSSV06], in which the authors proposed an algorithm whose message and computation complexity are poly-logarithmic in n for each node, and so is the number of rounds required. Later, an efficient *almost-everywhere reduction* (construction of Byzantine Agreement from *almost-everywhere Byzantine Agreement*) was proposed in [KS09, KLST11], using $\tilde{O}\left(\sqrt{n}\right)$ bits per node and poly-logarithmic time. This yields an algorithm for Byzantine Agreement with the same complexity, which, up to our knowl-

---

[2]$\tilde{O}$ is the same as O up to a poly-logarithmic factor.

edge, was the most efficient Byzantine Agreement protocol in terms of communication complexity until the present paper.

Our contribution.

We propose a new *almost-everywhere to everywhere* algorithm with amortized communication complexity $\tilde{O}(1)$ per node, denoted **AER**. Its time complexity is constant for synchronous executions, with non-rushing Byzantine nodes (defined in Section 2.1), and $O\left(\frac{\log n}{\log\log n}\right)$ for asynchronous ones. Composed with an *almost-everywhere agreement protocol* (along the lines of [KSSV06]), this yields the most effective protocol for Byzantine Agreement to date, using poly-logarithmic communication and time; this novel protocol is denoted **BA**.

The high-level idea underlying **AER** is the following: each node starts with a candidate string. The hypothesis is that more than half of the nodes are both correct and have the same candidate string, *i.e.* the correct one. Each node starts to diffuse its candidate string during a first phase (called push phase, Section 3.1.1). Then in a second phase (pull phase, Section 3.1.2), the bogus strings are discarded so that each node keeps only the correct string. The originality of our protocol, compared to previous ones, is that we relax load-balancing and we introduce new sampler properties so as to reduce communication complexity.

Comparison with existing protocols.

The complexity of push-pull protocols[3], like [KLST11], is dictated by the complexity of the first phase and the size of the candidate lists it produces.

To yield a more efficient protocol (in communication), we propose a solution to limit the total number of candidate strings in the whole system, and a way to diffuse them at a lower cost. Moreover, we introduce a way for each node to filter push requests. However, a Byzantine adversary can seize control of several *Input Quorums*[4], associated to a few nodes, and force these nodes to verify an *almost-linear* number of strings: as such, **AER** is not *load-balanced*.

AER has additional properties that are quite distinctive:

- this algorithm remains *correct and efficient* under asynchrony;

- unlike many randomized protocols, success is guaranteed when there is no Byzantine fault;

- against a *non-rushing* adversary, the algorithm terminates in *constant* expected time.

BA is, up to our knowledge, the first Byzantine Agreement protocol with poly-logarithmic complexity in both time and communication. Figure 1 compares with the state of the art, under various models:

S(N)R synchronous model, with (non-)*rushing* adversary;
APC asynchronous model, with *private communication channels*.

Roadmap.

We introduce our model and some background notions in Section 2. Section 3 describes our protocol and Section 4 describes its analysis. We discuss some future work in Section 5.

---

[3]Push-pull protocols are defined more precisely in Section 2.3
[4]Quorums are defined in Section 2.2

Figure 1: Comparison with other protocols

(a) « almost-everywhere to everywhere »

	[KLST11]	**AER**	**AER**
Model	SR	SNR	Async
Time	$O\left(\log^2 n\right)$	$O(1)$	$O\left(\frac{\log n}{\log\log n}\right)$
Bits	$\tilde{O}\left(\sqrt{n}\right)$	$O\left(\log^2 n\right)$	$O\left(\log^2 n\right)$
Load-Balanced	Yes	No	No

(b) Byzantine Agreement

	[BOPV06]	[KLST11]	**BA**	[PR10]	[KS13]
Model	SR	SR	SR	APC	Async
Time	$O(\log n)$	Polylog	Polylog	$O(1)$	$\tilde{O}\left(n^{2.5}\right)$
Bits	$n^{O(\log n)}$	$\tilde{O}\left(\sqrt{n}\right)$	Polylog	$\Omega\left(n^2\log n\right)$	?
n	$4t+1$	$3t+1$	$3t+1$	$4t+1$	$500t$

2. PRELIMINARIES

2.1 Model

We consider the model of Lamport, Shostak & Peace's original Byzantine Agreement paper [LSP82], further used in [KS09, KLST11]: a fully-connected network of n nodes with an adversary controlling t nodes.

Unlike these papers, we assume the network to be asynchronous, except in Lemma 8 and Lemma 9. We also require that each node possesses a *private* random number generator.

An event is said to occur *with high probability* (*w.h.p.*) iff it occurs with probability greater than $1 - O\left(n^{-3}\right)$.

Network.

The network is *fully-connected*, and communication channels are authenticated - the identity of the sender is known to the recipient; *transferable authentication* is not required, nor any weaker form of *non-equivocation*. However, we require the network to be *reliable*: a message sent (to a non-faulty node) will be eventually delivered. In the synchronous case, we also assume that a message sent during round r will be delivered during round $r + 1$.

Adversary.

A node controlled by the adversary is called *Byzantine* and can deviate arbitrarily from the algorithm. Furthermore, the adversary has full knowledge of the network and can coordinate the nodes it controls.

In particular, the actions of Byzantine nodes can depend on any messages sent, especially those sent by correct nodes. Two variations are considered:

- A *rushing* adversary knows the messages sent by the correct nodes at a given time step before choosing which messages to send.
- A non-rushing adversary chooses the messages it sends at a given time step independently of the messages sent by the correct nodes during the same time step.

The results we present assume some arbitrary $\varepsilon > 0$ is fixed, and $(3 + \varepsilon) \cdot t < n$; however other bounds on t are used and mentioned for related work. It is also assumed that $1/2 + \varepsilon$ fraction of the nodes are both correct and know a common string g_{string}, taken with uniform probability. This is equivalent to the assumption that all but a $1/4$ fraction of the correct nodes know g_{string}. Such an assumption can be ensured by the use of the protocol presented in [KSSV06], as mentioned in the introduction.

Finally, as in [LSP82], we consider a non-adaptive adversary: corrupt nodes are chosen before the algorithm is executed.

Complexity.

We consider two metrics for the complexity of the algorithm:

- Time complexity is the number of steps taken before all correct nodes return an agreement value.
- Communication complexity is the total number of exchanged bits (in worst case) divided by the number of nodes. This is called *amortized*[5] complexity, and is the same as *worst case* complexity for *load-balanced* algorithms.

Furthermore, we use the $\tilde{O}$ notation, which is the same as O, up to a poly-logarithmic factor.

2.2 Samplers

Like [KLST11, KKK$^+$, CD89], our work relies on the notion of *samplers*. The intuition is as follows:

- if nodes choose deterministically the nodes they contact, either there are a linear number of them (thus $\Omega(n)$ communication complexity) or there are few enough for the adversary to corrupt a majority;
- if uniformly-random sets (called *quorums*) are chosen, the byzantine nodes can follow the algorithm, but contact many disjoint sets, which would then need communicate amongst *quorums*: again, this yields unreasonably high *worst-case* complexity.

Samplers are a middle ground, in the sense that the choice of *quorums* is directed by both deterministically-known information (like the identity of a node), and random sources (either a local RNG[6] or g_{string}, which is known *almost-everywhere*).

Definitions.

First, we introduce some notations:

- $[n]$ denotes the set of integers from 1 to n.
- $[n]^d$ is the set of size d strings, with elements in $[n]$.
- $\mathscr{D}$ is the *agreement domain*, of cardinal $D = n^c$.
- $\mathscr{R}$ is the domain of *random labels*, used in our algorithm. Its cardinal, R, is polynomial.

DEFINITION 1 ([KLST11]). *A function* $\mathbb{S}: X \to Y$ *is a* (θ, δ)-*sampler if for any set* $S \subseteq Y$ *at most a* δ *fraction of the inputs* x *have* $\frac{|\mathbb{S}(x) \cap S|}{|S|} > \frac{|S|}{n} + \theta$.

We define $H(i, x) = \mathbb{S}(i \cdot n + x)$ for $i \in \mathscr{D}$ and $x \in [n]$:
The separation in two variables will be used to define *push quorums* and *pull quorums* (Sections 3.1.1 and 3.1.2).

Furthermore, we denote by $H^{-1}(i, x)$ the set of nodes y such that $x \in H(i, y)$. A node x is said to be *overloaded* by H (for some constant a) if there is a $i \in \mathscr{D}$ such that $\left| H^{-1}(i, x) \right| > a \cdot d$

Lemmata.

The following lemma is about the existence of samplers:

LEMMA 1 ([KLST11]). *For every constant* c, *for* $s = n$, $\delta = D^{-1}$ *and any* $\theta > 0$, *there is a* (θ, δ)-*sampler* $H: \mathscr{D} \times [n] \to [s]^d$ *with* $d = O\left(\frac{\log(1/\delta)}{\theta^2}\right)$ *such that for all* $i \in \mathscr{D}$, *no* $x \in [n]$ *is overloaded.*

We further use the following lemma:

---

[5]Note that the amortization is over the set of nodes, not time. However, *average* complexity would refer to averaging over possible (random) runs of the algorithm.
[6]Random Number Generator, assumed uniformly-random and private

LEMMA 2 (SECTION 4.1). *For* $\mathscr{R}$ *with cardinality polynomial in* n, *there exists* $d = O(\log n)$ *such that there is a mapping* $J: [n] \times \mathscr{R} \to [n]^d$ *such that for any subset of* $[n]$ *of size* $(1/2 + \varepsilon) \cdot n$, *whose elements are called* good *nodes, we have:*

1. *At most* n *elements of* $[n] \times \mathscr{R}$ *are mapped to a set containing a minority of* good *nodes.*

2. *For any* $L \subset [n] \times \mathscr{R}$, *s.t.* $\forall x \in [n], |L \cap (\{x\} \times \mathscr{R})| \leq 1$ *and* $|L| = O\left(\frac{n}{\log n}\right)$, *with* $L^{\perp} = \{y \mid \exists r \in \mathscr{R} \text{ s.t. } (y, r) \in L\}$:

$$\sum_{(x,r) \in L} \left| J(x, r) \setminus L^{\perp} \right| > \frac{2d |L|}{3}$$

Property 1 comes from [KLST11], and forbids the Byzantine adversary from corrupting too many potential quorums. Property 2 is a novel property that prevents the Byzantine adversary from "cornering" a set of nodes and isolate it from the rest of the network. It is used in Algorithms 2 and 3.

2.3 Pulls and Pushes

In our context, it is convenient to model communication as *pushes* and *pulls*, two ways according to which a node x can get information.

A push occurs when x receives information from other nodes without asking for it, whereas in a pull, x sends a request to one or more other nodes, and receives information as a consequence. Notice that nodes may ignore pushes and pull requests. Pushes have the advantage of requiring less communication. On the other hand, a node receiving a push has not selected the sender, enabling Byzantine nodes to flood the network.

In this work, we design filters according to which push requests are accepted, preventing the Byzantine nodes from harming **AER**:

- When pull requests are initiated by x, it yields some guarantees on the nodes to which pull requests are addressed.
  Here, they are selected randomly, ensuring *w.h.p.* (with high probability) a majority of correct nodes.
- As in [KS09], *pull requests* are filtered to prevent Byzantine nodes from triggering too many replies (poor worst case complexity).

3. ALMOST EVERYWHERE TO EVERYWHERE

The almost-everywhere to everywhere problem [KS09] consists of propagating a piece g_{string} of information that is detained by many nodes to all nodes of the system.

The main contribution of this paper is an algorithm which solves this problem *w.h.p.* with amortized communication complexity $\tilde{O}(1)$ under the hypothesis that g_{string} is $c \log n$ bits long for some large enough constant c, and that $2/3 + \varepsilon$ of its bits are uniformly random.

Together with the algorithm presented in [KSSV06], **AER** yields a Byzantine Agreement protocol, noted **BA**, with amortized complexity $\tilde{O}(1)$.

3.1 Overview of our protocol

Preconditions.

AER enables all the nodes to agree on a common string called g_{string}, under two assumptions. First, all nodes must share three sampling functions: I, H and J:

- I defines the Push Quorums used to diffuse candidate strings. Lemma 1 yields a (θ, δ)-sampler $I: \mathscr{D} \times [n] \to [n]^d$ for $\theta =$

$O(1)$, $\delta = n^{-c}$ and $d = O(\log n)$ such that no $x \in [n]$ is overloaded;
- H define Pull Quorums with the same properties;
- J generates Poll Lists during the pull phase.
  It has the properties described in Lemma 2.

Secondly, each node x knows a candidate s_x:

- s_x can be equal to g_{string}, random, set to a default value, or even chosen by the adversary.
- However, more than half of the nodes must be correct and know g_{string}, *i.e.* they have $s_x = g_{\text{string}}$. Under the assumption that $t < (1/3 - \varepsilon) \cdot n$, it is equivalent to assume that $3/4$ of the correct nodes know g_{string}.
- g_{string} is $c \log n$ bits long for some large enough constant c, and $2/3 + \varepsilon$ of its bits were chosen uniformly at random.

The protocol.

AER proceeds in two phases:

Push This first phase consists of several *pushes* which provide each node x with a list L_x of at most $O(n)$ candidates for g_{string}, containing g_{string} *w.h.p.* This phase has a message complexity of $\tilde{O}(n)$, and the sum of the sizes of the lists is $O(n)$, amortizing to $O(1)$ per node.

Pull Each node x sends a *pull* query to a set of sample nodes to verify each candidate $s \in L_x$, to find g_{string}. We will show how to answer the pull queries, so as to identify g_{string} without having high worst case complexity.

3.1.1 Push

To each pair of string s and node x, the sampler I assigns a set of $O(\log n)$ nodes. x may receive pushes for s from nodes in $I(s, x)$: the Push Quorum of x according to s. If more than half of the nodes of $I(s, x)$ push for s, s is added to x's candidates list, L_x.

Since nodes do not react to the reception of messages by sending messages, this phase is *impervious to flooding*: the adversary cannot increase the communication complexity of this phase by sending many candidate strings to all nodes.

However, flooding may increase the number of candidate strings for each node. The filter defined by I prevents this: Lemma 4 states that the sum of the size of the candidate list is $O(n)$, while Lemma 3 implies that the number of messages sent during the first phase by *any good node* is $\tilde{O}(1)$.

In Figure 2a, a node x adds a string s_1 to its list of candidate strings (which originally contains only s_x, its initial candidate string), and ignores another string s_2. Indeed x receives s_1 from more than half of the nodes of $I(x, s_1)$, while it receives s_2 from less than half of the nodes of $I(x, s_2)$.

3.1.2 Pull

Checking a string s involves simultaneously a *Poll List* $J(x, r_x)$ (where r_x is taken at random) which is deemed *authoritative*, and *Pull Quorums* of the form $H(\cdot, s)$. They can be seen as proxies, used to *forward and filter* x's pull requests, so as to prevent it from flooding the network.

In Figure 2b, a node x performs a pull request to verify a string $s \in L_x$. An arrow to a quorum represents a message sent to all the nodes of the quorum, and similarly, an arrow from a quorum means that all the correct nodes of the quorum send the message.

Algorithm 1: Sending *pull* requests

Data: L_x, list of candidates for node x
has_decided, a boolean denoting whether x has decided or not
Result: String agreed upon, *w.h.p.*
Bit complexity: $O(|L_x| \cdot \log n)$ messages, of $O(\log n)$ size
Time complexity: 1 if all messages are sent in a single round.
$\qquad\qquad |L_x|$ otherwise

for $s \in L_x$ **do**
$\quad r_{x,s} \leftarrow UniformRand()$
$\quad$ Send Poll $(s, r_{x,s})$ to all nodes in $J(x, r_{x,s})$
$\quad$ Send Pull $(s, r_{x,s})$ to all nodes in $H(s, x)$
Upon event $\langle Unicast.deliver \mid w[Answer(s)] \rangle$ **do**
$\quad$ **if** $w \in J(x, r_{x,s})$ *and* w *hasn't sent another Answer(s) message yet* **then**
$\quad\quad count_s$ ++
$\quad\quad$ **if** $count_s > 1/2 |J(x, r_{x,s})|$ **then**
$\quad\quad\quad has\_decided \leftarrow true$
$\quad\quad\quad s_{\text{this}} \leftarrow s$
$\quad\quad\quad$ **return** s

Sending queries.

As formalized in Algorithm 1, each node x verifies each string $s \in L_x$ by polling a set of nodes:

- x chooses a random string $r_{x,s}$ to define the Poll List $J(x, r_{x,s})$. A different random string is used *for each candidate string*.
- x sends a pull request (containing $r_{x,s}$) to the Poll List $J(x, r_{x,s})$ and its Pull Quorum $H(s, x)$.

Answering.

This second part corresponds to Algorithms 2 and 3.

- A node $y \in H(s, x)$ forwards a request received from x iff s is its initial candidate string (s_y). The request is forwarded to the nodes in $J(x, r_x)$ through their Pull Quorums.
- A node z in the Pull Quorum of $w \in J(x, r_x)$ ($z \in H(s, w)$) forwards the request to w iff $s = s_z$ and z received the request from more than half of the nodes of $H(s, x)$.
- Finally, a node $w \in J(x, r_x)$ replies to a pull request from x if:
  1. the pull request was received from a majority of $H(s, w)$;
  2. either it one of its pull requests was answered (thus w knows g_{string} *w.h.p.*), and s_w was changed accordingly;
  3. or it currently has received less than $\log^2 n$ pull requests.

If x receives answers from a majority of nodes in $J(x, r_x)$, s is deemed to be the global string.

4. ANALYSIS OF AER

In this section, we prove that **AER** brings all correct nodes to agree on g_{string} *w.h.p.*, with poly-logarithmic time and space complexity; but first, we must prove Lemma 2.

4.1 Proof of Lemma 2

In this section, we use graph theoretic considerations in order to prove Lemma 2:

LEMMA 2. *For $\mathcal{R}$ with cardinality polynomial in n, there exists $d = O(\log n)$ such that there is a mapping $J : [n] \times \mathcal{R} \to [n]^d$ such that*

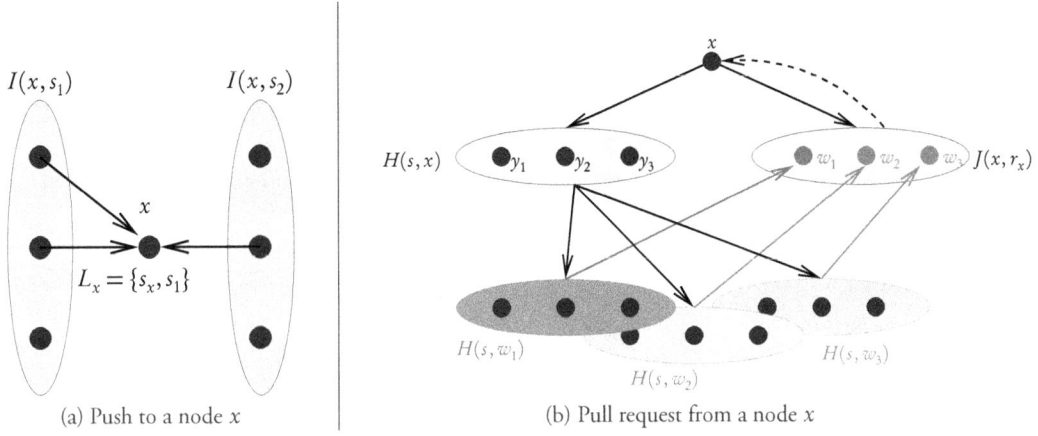

Figure 2: Push and Pull phases of **AER**

Algorithm 2: Routing *pull* requests

Data: The current node (called this) believes g_{string} to be s_{this}

$FwCount_{s,x}$ and $Fw_2Count_{s,x}$, sets of counters, initialized at 0

Upon event $\langle Unicast.deliver \mid x\,[Pull(s,r)] \rangle$ **do**

    if $s = s_{\text{this}}$ and $this \in H(s,x)$ **then**

        // Keep track of senders to prevent flooding

        for $w \in J(x,r)$ **do**

            Send $Fw_1(x,s,r,w)$ to $H(s,w)$

Upon event $\langle Unicast.deliver \mid y\,[Fw_1(x,s,r,w)] \rangle$ **do**

    if $this \in H(s,w)$, $y \in H(s,x)$, $s = s_{\text{this}}$ and $w \in J(x,r)$ **then**

        $FwCount_{s,x}{+}{+}$

        if $FwCount_{s,x} > {}^1\!/2\,|H(s,x)|$ **then**

            Send $Fw_2(x,s,r)$ to w

            $FwCount_{s,x} \leftarrow -\infty$ // Forward only once

---

for any subset of $[n]$ *of size* $(1/2 + \varepsilon) \cdot n$, *whose elements are called* good nodes, *we have:*

1. *At most n elements of* $[n] \times \mathscr{R}$ *are mapped to a set containing a minority of* good *nodes.*

2. *For any* $L \subset [n] \times \mathscr{R}$, *s.t.* $\forall x \in [n], |L \cap (\{x\} \times \mathscr{R})| \leq 1$ *and* $|L| = O\left(\frac{n}{\log n}\right)$, *with* $L^{\perp} = \{y \mid \exists r \in \mathscr{R} \text{ s.t. } (y,r) \in L\}$:

$$\sum_{(x,r) \in L} \left| J(x,r) \setminus L^{\perp} \right| > \frac{2d\,|L|}{3}$$

Henceforth, these properties will be called Properties 1 and 2. In [KLST11], Lemma 4 state that Property 1 happen with probability at least $1/2$.

In the following subsection, we show that Property 2 holds *w.h.p.* It follows that, for all n big enough, there is a digraph satisfying both properties; this proves Lemma 2.

We use a graph-based formulation adapted from [Zuc97], which is a powerful tool for proving the existence of a family of samplers.

Algorithm 3: Answering *pull* requests

Data: The current node (called this) believes g_{string} to be s_{this}

$Count_s$, set of counters, initialized at 0

$Polled$, set of pairs (n,s) corresponding to received poll requests

Upon event $\langle Unicast.deliver \mid z\,[Fw_2(x,s,r)] \rangle$ **do**

    if $Count_s > \log^2 n$ **then**

        Wait for has_decided

    if $this \in J(x,r)$, $z \in H(s,this)$ and $s = s_{\text{this}}$ **then**

        $Fw_2Count_{s,x}{+}{+}$

        if $Fw_2Count_{s,x} > {}^1\!/2\,|H(s,this)|$ and $(x,s) \in Polled$

        then

            $Count_s{+}{+}$

            Send $Answer(s)$ to x

            $Fw_2Count_{s,x} \leftarrow -\infty$ // Forward once

Upon event $\langle Unicast.deliver \mid x\,[Poll(s,r)] \rangle$ **do**

    if $this \in J(x,r)$ **then**

        $Polled \leftarrow Polled \cup \{(x,s)\}$

        if $Fw_2Count_{s,x} > {}^1\!/2\,|H(s,this)|$ **then**

            // Necessary in the asynchronous case

            $Count_s{+}{+}$

            Send $Answer(s)$ to x

            $Fw_2Count_{s,x} \leftarrow -\infty$ // Forward once

---

4.1.1 Graph-theoretic formulation

Model.

We consider *random digraphs* on vertex set $V = [n] \cup ([n] \times \mathscr{R})$. We call $\mathscr{R}$ the set of labels. We call a vertex of $[n] \times \mathscr{R}$ a *labeled vertex*, and a vertex from $[n]$ an *unlabeled one*.

We use ∂L, a notion similar to the *border* of a subgraph, defined as follow.

For $L \subseteq [n] \times \mathscr{R}$ such that $\forall x \in [n], |L \cap (\{x\} \times \mathscr{R})| \leq 1$:

$$\partial L = E_G \cap \left(L \times \left([n] \setminus L^{\perp} \right) \right).$$

In other words, ∂L is the set of edges from the labeled vertices in L to the unlabeled vertices in $[n] \setminus L^{\perp}$. Given this, we use a metric

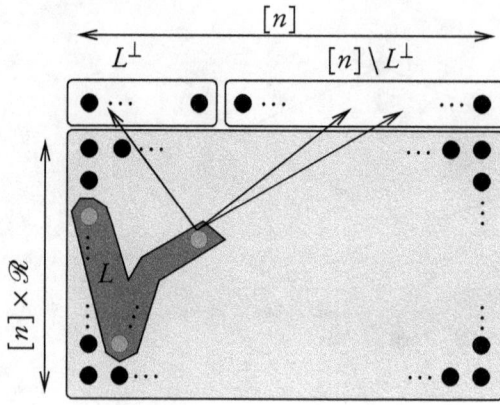

Figure 3: Our digraph model

closely related to the *isoperimetric number* [Bol88]:

$$i_\alpha = \min\left\{ \left.\frac{|\partial L|}{|L|}\ \right|\ 1 \le |L| \le \alpha n \right\}$$

The digraph G we consider (which is illustrated in the following figure) is taken uniformly such that:

1. The vertices of G in $[n] \times \mathscr{R}$ have exactly d out-neighbors (counting with multiplicity) in $[n]$ for $d = \log n$.

2. $E \subseteq ([n] \times \mathscr{R}) \times [n]$: a vertex (labeled with a point in $\mathscr{R}$) is connected to unlabeled vertices.

3. E is uniformly random; it implies that edges are chosen independently.

Let $P(u, s)$ be the probability that there is a set $L \subset [n] \times \mathscr{R}$ with $|L| = u$ and $\forall x \in [n], |L \cap (\{x\} \times \mathscr{R})| \le 1$ such that $|\partial L| = s$.

Result.

$P(u, s) = o(2^{-n})$ for $0 < u \le \frac{n}{\log n}$ and $s < 2/3 \cdot d \cdot u$; hence, G satisfies Property 2 with probability $1 - o(n^2 2^{-n})$.

4.1.2 Proof

Since edges are taken uniformly, we can fix the set $L \subset [n] \times \mathscr{R}$ and have:

$$P(u, s) \le \binom{n}{u} \cdot \mathbb{P}[|\partial U| = s|P]$$

Enumeration.

We consider u vertices with d edges, which makes $n^{d \cdot u}$ possibilities for the edges.

There are $R^u \cdot \binom{d \cdot u}{s}(n - u)^s u^{du-s}$ sets E such that our property holds:

- We must choose u labels with values in $\mathscr{R}$: there are R^u possibilities.

- We must choose s edges (amongst the $d \cdot u$ in U) that will be in ∂U.

- These s edges go to vertices in $[n] \setminus L^\perp$: there are $(n - u)^s$ possibilities.

- The remaining vertices are connected to nodes in P: u^{du-s} possibilities.

Upper bound on the probability.

This yields the exact value of $\mathbb{P}[|\partial L| = s]$:

$$\mathbb{P}[|\partial L| = s] = \frac{R^u \cdot \binom{d \cdot u}{s}(n - u)^s u^{du-s}}{n^{d \cdot u}}$$

We can now upper-bound $P(u, s)$:

$$
\begin{aligned}
P(u, s) &\le \binom{n}{u} \cdot \frac{R^u \cdot \binom{d \cdot u}{s}(n - u)^s u^{du-s}}{n^{d \cdot u}} \\[4pt]
&\le \binom{n}{u}\binom{du}{s} \cdot R^u \cdot \left(\frac{u}{n}\right)^{du} \cdot \left(\frac{n}{u} - 1\right)^s \\[4pt]
&\le \left(\frac{ne}{u}\right)^u R^u \cdot \left(\frac{u}{n}\right)^{du} \cdot \left(\frac{due}{s}\right)^s \left(\frac{n}{u} - 1\right)^s \\[4pt]
&\qquad \text{using inequality } \binom{n}{x} \le \left(\frac{n \cdot e}{x}\right)^x \\[4pt]
&\le \left(\frac{neR}{u}\right)^u \cdot \left(\frac{u}{n}\right)^{du} \cdot \left(\frac{d(n - u)e}{s}\right)^s \\[4pt]
&\le \left(\frac{neR}{u}\right)^u \cdot (\log n)^{\frac{-dn}{\log n}} \cdot \left(\frac{dne}{s}\right)^s \text{ since } 0 < u \le \frac{n}{\log n} \\[4pt]
&\le \left(\frac{neR}{u}\right)^u \cdot \log^{-n} n \cdot \left(\frac{dne}{s}\right)^s \text{ because } d = \log n \\[4pt]
&\le (eR\log n)^{\frac{n}{\log n}} \cdot \log^{-n} n \cdot (3/2 \cdot d\,e)^{2/3 \cdot n} \\[4pt]
&\qquad \text{because } \left(\frac{\alpha}{x}\right)^x \text{ increases until } \frac{\alpha}{e} \text{ and } s \le 2/3 \cdot d \cdot u \\[4pt]
&\le \left[\frac{(eR\log n)^{\frac{1}{\log n}} \cdot (3/2 \cdot e)^{2/3}}{\sqrt[3]{\log n}}\right]^n \\[4pt]
&\le \left[\frac{O(1)}{\sqrt[3]{\log n}}\right]^n \text{ because } (R\log n)^{\frac{1}{\log n}} \text{ is bounded} \\[4pt]
P(u, s) &= o\left(2^{-n}\right) \qquad\qquad\qquad\qquad\qquad \square
\end{aligned}
$$

4.2 Push phase

LEMMA 3. *The communication complexity of the Push is $O(s \log n)$ on each node ($s = O(\log n)$ being the size of g_{string}).*

PROOF. By the definition of I (Lemma 1), no node is overloaded. Hence, each correct node y sends its candidate string to $O(\log n)$ nodes, namely the nodes x such that $y \in I(s_y, x)$.

Therefore, during the Push, the number of messages sent *by any correct nodes* is $O(\log n)$, each containing a string having the same size as g_{string}. $\square$

LEMMA 4. *The sum of the sizes of the candidates list of the correct nodes is $O(n)$.*

PROOF. A node y accepts a candidate string s iff more than half of the nodes of $I(s, y)$ sent it. By assumption, $1/2 + \varepsilon$ fraction of the nodes are both correct and have g_{string} as initial string. Therefore, since I is a sampler, at most $O(n)$ quorums have a majority of nodes sending a string different from g_{string}. These quorums inject at most $O(n)$ wrong strings (in total) to the lists of candidate strings of the correct nodes. Therefore the sum of the size of the candidates list is $O(n)$. $\square$

LEMMA 5. *There is a constant c such that, when g_{string} is $c \log n$ bits long, and $2/3 + \varepsilon$ of the bits are uniformly random, w.h.p. each node of the system has g_{string} in its candidate list at the end of the Push phase.*

PROOF. Looking at the Input Quorums, since I is a sampler, whatever are the nodes corrupted by the adversary and the knowledgeable nodes, at most $O(n)$ of the quorums do not have a correct and knowledgeable majority. If a node x does not have g_{string} in its candidate list L_x, it means that $I(g_{string}, x)$ does not have a correct and knowledgeable majority; we call such an Input Quorum *bad*. It is sufficient to prove that the probability of $I(g_{string}, x)$ to be bad is negligible.

g_{string} has length $c \log n$ for some constant c (that we choose thereafter), and the Byzantine nodes generate a $1/3 - \varepsilon$ fraction of its bits. Among all the choices, $O(n^c)$ of them lead to good Input Quorums for all of the nodes of the network, and $O(n)$ lead to at least one bad Input Quorum.

The probability for a chosen string to match a specific string leading to a bad Input Quorums is upper bounded by $2^{-2/3 \cdot c \log n}$. By the union bound over the n such strings, we get that the probability to choose one of them is less than $n^{-c'}$ for some constant $0 < c' < 2/3c$.

From this, we conclude that each correct node has g_{string} in its candidate list with probability greater than $1 - n^{-c'}$. □

4.3 Pull phase

It now remains to analyze the pull phase.

LEMMA 6. *Any polling request (for g_{string}) is answered in $O\left(\frac{\log n}{\log \log n}\right)$ time steps.*

PROOF. A node receives a message from a correct node in its poll list iff it is not overloaded or if it has already received an answer from a majority of nodes in its pull request.

Now, notice that to overload a node x whose original string g_{string}, the adversary must have $O\left(\log^2 n\right)$ of its nodes to send a pull request to x. This pull request will be considered by x iff it is for g_{string}. Therefore, the adversary must send $O\left(\log^2 n\right)$ pull requests corresponding to g_{string}. But then, *w.h.p.*, the quorum associated to g_{string} are all correct, which implies that the adversary can send pull requests at most once for each node it controls, as otherwise the pull requests will not be forwarded by the associated quorums. Therefore, the adversary can overload $O\left(\frac{n}{\log n}\right)$ nodes with request associated to g_{string} (each node can send $O(\log n)$ requests, and a node is overloaded if it receives more than $\log^2 n$ requests).

The adversary can also overload a node x whose original string is $s \neq g_{string}$ and that was chosen by the adversary. But to overload such a node, the adversary need to corrupt the quorum $H(x, s)$ and $H(a, s)$ for $\log^2 n$ nodes a controlled by the adversary, as otherwise the pull requests would not be forwarded. Therefore, in this case also, the adversary can overload at most $O\left(\frac{n}{\log n}\right)$ nodes.

The adversary knows[7] the nodes to which pull requests are addressed, before choosing its own pull requests. Therefore, it can overload all the nodes x' to which a given node x has sent pull requests. It can further overload all the nodes to which all x' have sent their pull requests and so on.

From the properties of J, we know that each set L of at most $\frac{n}{\log n}$ nodes send at least $2/3 \cdot d |L|$ pull requests to nodes outside L. This implies that by overloading $\frac{n}{\log n}$ nodes, the adversary can at most overload a sequence of length $O\left(\frac{\log n}{\log \log n}\right)$ in such a way. There-

---

[7]In the asynchronous (or synchronous rushing) model; the case of the (less general) synchronous model with non-rushing adversary is addressed in Lemma 8.

fore, in $O\left(\frac{\log n}{\log \log n}\right)$ steps, each node receives answer from its pull requests. □

LEMMA 7. *Any node decides on g_{string} w.h.p.*

PROOF. There are two ways for a node not to decide on g_{string}:

1. its poll request for g_{string} isn't answered;

2. a poll request for another string s was answered first.

Lemma 6 ensures that, *w.h.p.*, 1. does not happen.

Assuming x decides on s, then $J(x, r_x)$ is composed in majority of nodes that are either Byzantine or that decided on s. Taking the first node to decide on s, the sample $J(x, r_x)$ must be composed mostly of Byzantine nodes. *W.h.p.* this doesn't happen, because r_x is uniformly random, J is a sampler, and the adversary chose the Byzantine nodes before r_x was chosen. □

LEMMA 8. *Any polling request (for g_{string}) is answered in $O(1)$ time steps w.h.p., if the adversary is non rushing.*

PROOF. If the adversary is not rushing, it does not know which nodes a correct node address its pull requests to. Therefore, *w.h.p.*, each correct node pulls a majority of nodes that are both correct and not overloaded. It follows that *w.h.p.* each correct node receives an answer in a constant number of steps. □

4.4 Result

From this we obtain the following two lemmata:

LEMMA 9. *For n nodes in a synchronous full information message passing model with a non-adaptive non-rushing Byzantine adversary which controls less than a $1/3 - \varepsilon$ fraction of the nodes, if more than $3/4$ of the correct nodes know a string g_{string} (random enough), there is an algorithm such that w.h.p.:*

- *At the end of the algorithm, each correct node knows g_{string}.*

- *The algorithm takes $O(1)$ rounds and $\tilde{O}(n)$ messages are exchanged in total.*

LEMMA 10. *For n nodes in a asynchronous full information message passing model with a non-adaptive Byzantine adversary which controls less than a $1/3 - \varepsilon$ fraction of the nodes, if more than $3/4$ of the correct nodes know a string g_{string} (random enough), there is an algorithm such that w.h.p.:*

- *At the end of the algorithm, each correct node knows g_{string}.*

- *The algorithm takes $O\left(\frac{\log n}{\log \log n}\right)$ rounds and $\tilde{O}(n)$ messages are exchanged in total.*

Note that, to obtain an amortized communication complexity of $\tilde{O}(1)$, the condition that the algorithm is load-balanced was relaxed.

5. CONCLUSION

We propose an asynchronous *almost-everywhere to everywhere agreement* protocol with poly-logarithmic complexity, which yields the first poly-logarithmic algorithm for Byzantine Agreement. Future work could focus on *almost-everywhere Agreement*, for which no efficient asynchronous protocol is known. Another interesting and challenging question is to find the best complexity that is achievable by a load-balanced algorithm in the general case, and - more generally - characterize the trade-off between load-balancing and communication complexity.

6. REFERENCES

[BO83]   M. Ben-Or. Another advantage of free choice (extended abstract): Completely asynchronous agreement protocols. In *Proceedings of the second annual ACM symposium on Principles of distributed computing (PODC'83)*, pages 27--30. ACM, 1983.

[Bol88]   B. Bollobas. The isoperimetric number of random regular graphs. *European Journal of Combinatorics*, pages 241--244, 1988.

[BOPV06]   M. Ben-Or, E. Pavlov, and V. Vaikuntanathan. Byzantine agreement in the full-information model in $o(\log n)$ rounds. In *Proceedings of the thirty-eighth annual ACM symposium on Theory of computing*, pages 179--186. ACM, 2006.

[CD89]   B. Chor and C. Dwork. Randomization in byzantine agreement. *Advances in COmputing Research 5: Randomness and Computation*, pages 443--497, 1989.

[DPPU86]   C. Dwork, D. Peleg, N. Pippenger, and E. Upfal. Fault tolerance in networks of bounded degree. In *Proceedings of the eighteenth annual ACM symposium on Theory of computing (STOC'86)*, pages 370--379. ACM, 1986.

[DR85]   D. Dolev and R. Reischuk. Bounds on information exchange for byzantine agreement. *Journal of the ACM*, 32(1):191--204, 1985.

[FL82]   M.J. Fischer and N.A. Lynch. A lower bound for the time to assure interactive consistency. *Information Processing Letters*, 14(4):183--186, 1982.

[GM98]   J.A. Garay and Y. Moses. Fully polynomial byzantine agreement for n> 3t processors in t+ 1 rounds. *SIAM J. Comput.*, 27(1):247--290, 1998.

[HKK08]   D. Holtby, B.M. Kapron, and V. King. Lower bound for scalable byzantine agreement. *Distributed Computing*, 21(4):239--248, 2008.

[KKK+]   B. Kapron, D. Kempe, V. King, J. Saia, and V. Sanwalani. Fast asynchronous byzantine agreement and leader election with full information.

[KLST11]   V. King, S. Lonargan, J. Saia, and A. Trehan. Load balanced scalable byzantine agreement through quorum building, with full information. *Distributed Computing and Networking*, pages 203--214, 2011.

[KS09]   V. King and J. Saia. From almost everywhere to everywhere: Byzantine agreement with $\tilde{o}(n^{3/2})$ bits. *Distributed Computing*, pages 464--478, 2009.

[KS13]   V. King and J. Saia. Byzantine agreement in polynomial expected time. In *45th Symposium on the Theory of Computing (STOC'13)*, 2013.

[KSSV06]   V. King, J. Saia, V. Sanwalani, and E. Vee. Towards secure and scalable computation in peer-to-peer networks. In *47th Annual IEEE Symposium on on the Foundations of Computer Science (FOCS'06)*, pages 87--98, 2006.

[LSP82]   L. Lamport, R. Shostak, and M. Pease. The Byzantine Generals Problem. *ACM Transactions on Programming Languages and Systems*, 4(3):382--401, July 1982.

[PR10]   Arpita Patra and C. Pandu Rangan. Brief announcement: communication efficient asynchronous byzantine agreement. In *Proceedings of the 29th ACM symposium on Principles of distributed computing (PODC'10)*, pages 243--244, 2010.

[PSL80]   M. Pease, R. Shostak, and L. Lamport. Reaching agreement in the presence of faults. *Journal of the ACM*, 27(2):228--234, 1980.

[Rab83]   M.O. Rabin. Randomized byzantine generals. In *24th Annual Symposium on Foundations of Computer Science (FOCS'83)*, pages 403--409. IEEE, 1983.

[Zuc97]   D. Zuckerman. Randomness-optimal oblivious sampling. *Random Struct. Algorithms*, pages 345--367, 1997.

Byzantine Vector Consensus in Complete Graphs [*]

Nitin H. Vaidya
Department of Electrical and Computer
Engineering
University of Illinois at Urbana-Champaign
Urbana, Illinois, U.S.A.
nhv@illinois.edu

Vijay K. Garg
Department of Electrical and Computer
Engineering
University of Texas at Austin
Austin, Texas, U.S.A.
garg@ece.utexas.edu

ABSTRACT

Consider a network of n processes, each of which has a d-dimensional vector of reals as its *input*. Each process can communicate directly with all the processes in the system; thus the communication network is a *complete graph*. All the communication channels are reliable and FIFO (first-in-first-out).

- We prove that in a synchronous system, $n \geq \max(3f + 1, (d+1)f+1)$ is necessary and sufficient for achieving Byzantine vector consensus.

- In an asynchronous system, it is known that *exact* consensus is impossible in presence of faulty processes. For an asynchronous system, we prove that $n \geq (d+2)f + 1$ is necessary and sufficient to achieve *approximate* Byzantine vector consensus.

Our sufficiency proofs are constructive. We prove sufficiency by providing explicit algorithms that solve exact BVC in synchronous systems, and approximate BVC in asynchronous systems.

Categories and Subject Descriptors

C.2.4 [**Distributed Systems**]: Distributed applications

General Terms

Algorithms, Theory

Keywords

Byzantine consensus, vector inputs, asynchronous and synchronous systems

[*]This research is supported in part by National Science Foundation awards CNS-1059540 and CNS-1115808 and the Cullen Trust for Higher Education. Any opinions, findings, and conclusions or recommendations expressed here are those of the authors and do not necessarily reflect the views of the funding agencies or the U.S. government.

1. INTRODUCTION

This paper addresses *Byzantine vector consensus* (BVC), wherein the input at each process is a d-dimensional vector of reals, and each process is expected to decide on a *decision vector* that is in the *convex hull* of the input vectors at the non-faulty processes. The system consists of n processes in $\mathcal{P} = \{p_1, p_2, \cdots, p_n\}$. We assume $n > 1$, since consensus is trivial for $n = 1$. At most f processes may be Byzantine faulty, and may behave arbitrarily [13]. All processes can communicate with each other directly on *reliable FIFO* (first-in first-out) channels. Thus, the communication network is a *complete graph*. The input *vector* at each process may also be viewed as a *point* in the d-dimensional Euclidean space $\mathbf{R}^d$, where $d > 0$ is a finite integer. Due to this correspondence, we use the terms *point* and *vector* interchangeably. Similarly, we interchangeably refer to the d *elements* of a vector as *coordinates*. We consider two versions of the Byzantine vector consensus (BVC) problem, *Exact BVC* and *Approximate BVC*. Mendes and Herlihy have independently obtained similar results for *approximate* BVC [15].

Exact BVC

Exact Byzantine vector consensus must satisfy the following three conditions.

- *Agreement*: The decision (or output) vector at all the non-faulty processes must be identical.

- *Validity*: The decision vector at each non-faulty process must be in the convex hull of the input vectors at the non-faulty processes.

- *Termination*: Each non-faulty process must terminate within a finite amount of time.

The traditional consensus problem [14, 11] is obtained when $d = 1$; we refer to this as *scalar* consensus. $n \geq 3f+1$ is known to be necessary and sufficient for achieving Byzantine *scalar* consensus in complete graphs [13, 14]. We observe that simply performing *scalar* consensus on each dimension of the input vectors independently does not solve the *vector* consensus problem. In particular, even if validity condition for *scalar consensus* is satisfied for each dimension of the vector separately, the above *validity* condition of vector consensus may not necessarily be satisfied. For instance, suppose that there are four processes, with one faulty process. Processes p_1, p_2 and p_3 are non-faulty, and have the following 3-dimensional input vectors, respectively: $\mathbf{x}_1 = [\frac{2}{3}, \frac{1}{6}, \frac{1}{6}]$, $\mathbf{x}_2 = [\frac{1}{6}, \frac{2}{3}, \frac{1}{6}]$, $\mathbf{x}_3 = [\frac{1}{6}, \frac{1}{6}, \frac{2}{3}]$. Process p_4 is faulty. If we perform Byzantine *scalar* consensus on each dimension of the vector separately, then the processes may possibly agree on the decision vector $[\frac{1}{6}, \frac{1}{6}, \frac{1}{6}]$, each element of which satisfies *scalar* validity condition *along each dimension* separately; however, this decision vector *does not* satisfy the validity condition for BVC because it is *not* in the convex hull of input vectors of non-faulty processes. In this example, since every non-faulty process has a probability vector as its input vector, BVC validity condition requires that the decision vector should also be a probability vector. In general, for many optimization problems [4], the set of feasible solutions is a convex set in Euclidean space. Assuming that every non-faulty process proposes a feasible solution, BVC guarantees that the vector decided is also a feasible solution. Using scalar consensus along each dimension is not sufficient to provide this guarantee.

Approximate BVC

In an *asynchronous* system, processes may take steps at arbitrary relative speeds, and there is no fixed upper bound on message delays. Fischer, Lynch and Paterson [10] proved that exact consensus is impossible in asynchronous systems in the presence of even a single crash failure. As a way to circumvent this impossibility result, Dolev et al. [5] introduced the notion of *approximate* consensus, and proved the correctness of an algorithm for approximate Byzantine *scalar* consensus in asynchronous systems when $n \geq 5f + 1$. Subsequently, Abraham, Amit and Dolev [1] established that approximate Byzantine *scalar* consensus is possible in asynchronous systems if $n \geq 3f + 1$. Other algorithms for approximate consensus have also been proposed (e.g., [3, 9]). We extend the notion of approximate consensus to *vector* consensus. *Approximate BVC* must satisfy the following conditions:

- *ϵ-Agreement*: For $1 \leq l \leq d$, the l-th elements of the decision vectors at any two non-faulty processes must be within ϵ of each other, where $\epsilon > 0$ is a pre-defined constant.

- *Validity*: The decision vector at each non-faulty process must be in the convex hull of the input vectors at the non-faulty processes.

- *Termination*: Each non-faulty process must terminate within a finite amount of time.

The main contribution of this paper is to establish the following bounds for *complete graphs*.

- In a synchronous system, $n \geq \max(3f+1, (d+1)f+1)$ is necessary and sufficient for *Exact BVC* in presence of up to f Byzantine faulty processes. (Theorems 1 and 3).

- In an asynchronous system, $n \geq (d+2)f+1$ is necessary and sufficient for *Approximate BVC* in presence of up to f Byzantine faulty processes. (Theorems 4 and 5).

Observe that the two bounds above are different when $d > 1$, unlike the case of $d = 1$ (i.e., scalar consensus). When $d = 1$, in a complete graph, $3f + 1$ processes are sufficient for exact consensus in synchronous systems, as well as approximate consensus in asynchronous systems [1]. For $d > 1$, the lower bound for asynchronous systems is larger by f compared to the bound for synchronous systems.

In prior literature, the term *vector consensus* has also been used to refer to another form of consensus, wherein the input at each process is a *scalar*, but the agreement is on a vector containing these scalars [7, 18]. Thus, our results are for a different notion of consensus.

Many notations introduced throughout the paper are also summarized in Appendix A. We use operator $|.|$ to obtain the size of a *multiset* or a *set*. We use operator $\|.\|$ to obtain the absolute value of a scalar.

2. SYNCHRONOUS SYSTEMS

In this section, we derive necessary and sufficient conditions for exact BVC in a synchronous system with up to f faulty processes. The discussion in the rest of this paper assumes that the network is a *complete graph*, even if this is not stated explicitly in all the results.

2.1 Necessary Condition for Exact BVC

THEOREM 1. $n \geq \max(3f + 1, (d+1)f + 1)$ *is necessary for Exact BVC in a synchronous system.*

PROOF. From [13, 14], we know that, for $d = 1$ (i.e., scalar consensus), $n \geq 3f + 1$ is a necessary condition for achieving exact Byzantine consensus in presence of up to f faults. If we were to restrict the d-dimensional input vectors to have identical d elements, then the problem of vector consensus reduces to scalar consensus. Therefore, $n \geq 3f+1$ is also a necessary condition for *Exact BVC* for arbitrary d. Now we prove that $n \geq (d+1)f + 1$ is also a necessary condition. Since the state of two processes may be identical, in the discussion below, we use a *multiset* to represent the collection of the states of a subset of processes.

First consider the case when $f = 1$, i.e., at most one process may be faulty. Since none of the non-faulty processes know which process, if any, is faulty, as elaborated in Appendix B, the decision vector must be in the convex hull of each multiset containing the input vectors of $n - 1$ of the processes (there are n such multisets).

Thus, this intersection must be non-empty, for all possible input vectors at the n processes. (Appendix B provides further clarification.) We now show that the intersection may be empty when $n = d + 1$; thus, $n = d + 1$ is not sufficient for $f = 1$.

Suppose that $n = d + 1$. Consider the following set of input vectors. The input vector of process p_i, where $1 \leq i \leq d$, is a vector whose i-th element is 1, and the remaining elements are 0. The input vector at process p_{d+1} is the all-0 vector (i.e., the vector with all elements 0). Note that the d input vectors at $p_1, \cdots, p_d$ form the standard basis for the d-dimensional vector space. Also, none of the $d + 1$ input vectors can be represented as a convex combination of the remaining d input vectors. For $1 \leq i \leq d + 1$, let Q_i denote the convex hull of the inputs at the $n - 1 = d$ processes in $\mathcal{P} - \{p_i\}$. We now argue that $\cap_{i=1}^{d+1} Q_i$ is empty.

For $1 \leq i \leq d$, observe that for all the points in Q_i, the i-th coordinate is 0. Thus, any point that belongs to the intersection $\cap_{i=1}^{d} Q_i$ must have all its coordinates 0. That is, only the all-0 vector belongs to $\cap_{i=1}^{d} Q_i$. Now consider Q_{d+1}, which is the convex hull of the inputs at the first d processes. Due to the choice of the inputs at the first d processes, the origin (i.e., the all-0 vector) does not belong to Q_{d+1}. From the earlier observation on $\cap_{i=1}^{d} Q_i$, it follows that $\cap_{i=1}^{d+1} Q_i = \emptyset$. Therefore, the *Exact BVC* problem for $f = 1$ cannot be solved with $n = d + 1$. Thus, $n = d + 1$ is not sufficient. It should be easy to see that $n \leq d + 1$ is also not sufficient. Thus, $n \geq d + 2$ is a necessary condition for $f = 1$.

Now consider the case of $f > 1$. Using the commonly used simulation approach [13], we can prove that $(d + 1)f$ processes are not sufficient. In this approach, f *simulated processes* are implemented by a single process. If a correct algorithm were to exist for tolerating f faults among $(d+1)f$ processes, then we can obtain a correct algorithm to tolerate a single failure among $d + 1$ processes, contradicting our result above. Thus, $n \geq (d + 1)f + 1$ is necessary for $f \geq 1$. (For $f = 0$, the necessary condition holds trivially.) □

2.2 Sufficient Condition for Exact BVC

We now present an algorithm for Exact BVC in a synchronous system, and prove its correctness in a complete graph with $n \geq \max(3f + 1, (d + 1)f + 1)$. The algorithm uses function $\Gamma(Y)$ defined below, where Y is a multiset of points. $\mathcal{H}(T)$ denotes the convex hull of a multiset T.

$$\Gamma(Y) = \cap_{T \subseteq Y, |T| = |Y| - f} \mathcal{H}(T). \quad (1)$$

The intersection above is over the convex hulls of all subsets of Y of size $|Y| - f$.

Exact BVC algorithm for $n \geq \max(3f+1, (d+1)f+1)$:

---

1. Each process uses a scalar *Byzantine broadcast* algorithm (such as [13, 6]) to broadcast each element of its input vector to all the other processes (each element is a scalar). The *Byzantine broadcast* algorithm allows a designated sender to broadcast a scalar value to the other processes, while satisfying the following properties when $n \geq 3f + 1$: (i) all the non-faulty processes decide on an identical scalar value, and (ii) if the sender is non-faulty, then the value decided by the non-faulty processes is the sender's proposed (scalar) value. Thus, non-faulty processes can agree on the d elements of the input vector at each of the n processes.

   At the end of the this step, each non-faulty process would have received an *identical* multiset S containing n vectors, such that the vector corresponding to each non-faulty process is identical to the input vector at that process.

2. Each process chooses as its *decision* vector a point in $\Gamma(S)$; all non-faulty processes choose the point identically using a deterministic function. We will soon show that $\Gamma(S)$ is non-empty.

When n is larger than the lower bound, complexity of the above algorithm may be improved by first performing consensus among $\max(3f + 1, (d + 1)f + 1)$ of the processes, with the remaining processes choosing majority vote on the

decision vectors received from any $2f + 1$ of these processes as their own decision.

We now prove that the above Exact BVC algorithm is correct. Later, we show how the *decision vector* can be found in Step 2 using linear programming. The proof of correctness of the above algorithm uses the following celebrated theorem by Tverberg [19]:

THEOREM 2. (Tverberg's Theorem [19]) *For any integer $f \geq 1$, and for every multiset Y containing at least $(d + 1)f + 1$ points in $\mathbf{R}^d$, there exists a partition $Y_1, \cdots, Y_{f+1}$ of Y into $f + 1$ non-empty multisets such that $\cap_{l=1}^{f+1} \mathcal{H}(Y_l) \neq \emptyset$.*

The points in multiset Y above are not necessarily distinct [19]; thus, the same point may occur multiple times in Y. The partition in Theorem 2 is called a *Tverberg partition*, and the points in $\cap_{l=1}^{f+1} \mathcal{H}(Y_l)$ in Theorem 2 are called *Tverberg points*. Figure 1 illustrates a Tverberg partition of a set of 7 vertices in 2-dimensions. The 7 vertices are at the corners of a heptagon. Thus, $n = 7$ here, and $d = 2$. Let $f = 2$. Then, $n = (d + 1)f + 1$, and Tverberg's Theorem (Theorem 2) implies the presence of a Tverberg partition consisting of $f + 1 = 3$ subsets. Figure 1 shows the convex hulls of the three subsets in the Tverberg partition: one convex hull is a triangle, and the other two convex hulls are each a line segment. In this example, the three convex hulls intersect in exactly one point. Thus, there is just one Tverberg point. In general, there can be multiple Tverberg points.

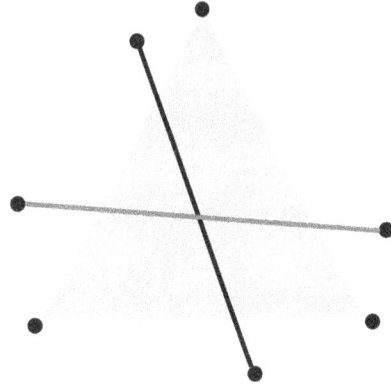

Figure 1: Illustration of a Tverberg partition (inspired by an illustration authored by David Eppstein [8]).

The lemma below is used to prove the correctness of the above algorithm, as well as the algorithm presented later in Section 3.

LEMMA 1. *For any multiset Y containing at least $(d + 1)f + 1$ points in $\mathbf{R}^d$, $\Gamma(Y) \neq \emptyset$.*

PROOF. Consider a Tverberg partition of Y into $f+1$ non-empty subsets $Y_1, \cdots, Y_{f+1}$, such that the set of Tverberg points $\cap_{l=1}^{f+1} \mathcal{H}(Y_l) \neq \emptyset$. Since $|Y| \geq (d+1)f+1$, by Theorem 2, such a partition exists. By (1) we have

$$\Gamma(Y) = \cap_{T \subseteq Y, |T| = |Y| - f} \mathcal{H}(T). \quad (2)$$

Consider any T in (2). Since $|T| = |Y| - f$ and there are $f + 1$ subsets in the Tverberg partition of Y, T excludes elements from at most f of these subsets. Thus, T contains at least one subset from the partition. Therefore, for **each** T, $\cap_{l=1}^{f+1} \mathcal{H}(Y_l) \subseteq \mathcal{H}(T)$. Hence, from (2), it follows that $\cap_{l=1}^{f+1} \mathcal{H}(Y_l) \subseteq \Gamma(Y)$. Also, because $\cap_{l=1}^{f+1} \mathcal{H}(Y_l) \neq \emptyset$, it now follows that $\Gamma(Y) \neq \emptyset$. $\quad\square$

We can now prove the correctness of our Exact BVC algorithm.

THEOREM 3. $n \geq \max(3f + 1, (d + 1)f + 1)$ *is sufficient for achieving Exact BVC in a synchronous system.*

PROOF. We prove that the above *Exact BVC* algorithm is correct when $n \geq \max(3f+1, (d+1)f+1)$. The *termination* condition holds because the *Byzantine broadcast* algorithm used in Step 1 terminates in finite time. Since $|S| = n \geq (d+1)f+1$, by Lemma 1, $\Gamma(S) \neq \emptyset$. By (1) we have

$$\Gamma(S) = \cap_{T \subseteq S, |T|=|S|-f} \mathcal{H}(T). \tag{3}$$

At least one of the multisets T in (3), say T^*, must contain the inputs of *only* non-faulty processes, because $|T| = |S| - f = n - f$, and there are at most f faulty processes. By definition of $\Gamma(S)$, $\Gamma(S) \subseteq \mathcal{H}(T^*)$. Then, from the definition of T^*, and the fact that the decision vector is chosen from $\Gamma(S)$, the *validity* condition follows.

Agreement condition holds because all the non-faulty processes have identical S, and pick as their decision vector a point in $\Gamma(S)$ using a deterministic function in Step 2. $\quad\square$

We now show how Step 2 of the Exact BVC algorithm can be implemented using linear programming. The input to the linear program is $S = \{\mathbf{s}_i : 1 \leq i \leq n\}$, a multiset of d-dimensional vectors. Our goal is to find a vector $\mathbf{z} \in \Gamma(S)$; or equivalently, find a vector $\mathbf{z}$ that can be expressed as a convex combination of vectors in T for all choices $T \subseteq S$ such that $|T| = n - f$. The linear program uses the following $d + \binom{n}{n-f}(n-f)$ variables.

- $\mathbf{z}_1, ..\mathbf{z}_d$: variables for d elements of vector $\mathbf{z}$.

- $\alpha_{T,i}$: coefficients such that $\mathbf{z}$ can be written as convex combination of vectors in T. We include here only those $n - f$ indices i for which $\mathbf{s}_i \in T$.

For every T, the linear constraints are as follows.

- $\mathbf{z} = \sum_{\mathbf{s}_i \in T} \alpha_{T,i} \mathbf{s}_i$ ($\mathbf{z}$ is a linear combination of $\mathbf{s}_i \in T$)

- $\sum_{\mathbf{s}_i \in T} \alpha_{T,i} = 1$ (The sum of all coefficients for a particular T is 1)

- $\alpha_{T,i} \geq 0$ for all $\mathbf{s}_i \in T$.

For every T, we get $d+1+n-f$ linear constraints, yielding a total of $\binom{n}{n-f}(d+1+n-f)$ constraints in $d + \binom{n}{n-f}(n-f)$ variables. Hence, for any *fixed* f, a point in $\Gamma(S)$ can be found in polynomial time by solving a linear program with the number of variables and constraints that are polynomial in n and d (but not in f). However, when f grows with n, the computational complexity is high. Observe that we are interested in any feasible vector $\mathbf{z}$ that satisfies above linear constraints and any deterministic optimization objective function can be used in the linear program.

We note here that the above Exact BVC algorithm remains correct if the non-faulty processes identically choose *any point* in $\Gamma(S)$ as the decision vector. In particular, as

seen in the proof of Lemma 1, all the Tverberg points are contained in $\Gamma(S)$, therefore, one of the Tverberg points for multiset S may be chosen as the decision vector. It turns out that, for arbitrary d, currently there is no known algorithm with polynomial complexity to compute a Tverberg point for a given multiset [2, 16, 17]. However, in some restricted cases, efficient algorithms are known (e.g., [12]).

3. ASYNCHRONOUS SYSTEMS

We develop a tight necessary and sufficient condition for *approximate* asynchronous BVC.

3.1 Necessary Condition for Approximate Asynchronous BVC

THEOREM 4. $n \geq (d + 2)f + 1$ *is necessary for approximate BVC in an asynchronous system.*

PROOF. We first consider the case of $f = 1$. Suppose that a correct algorithm exists for $n = d + 2$. Denote by $\mathbf{x}_k$ the input vector at each process p_k. Now consider a process p_i, where $1 \leq i \leq d+1$. Since a correct algorithm must tolerate one failure, process p_i must terminate in all executions in which process p_{d+2} does not take any steps. Suppose that all the processes are non-faulty, but process p_{d+2} does not take any steps until all the other processes terminate. At the time when process p_i terminates $(1 \leq i \leq d+1)$, it cannot distinguish between the following $d + 1$ scenarios:

- Process p_{d+2} has crashed: In this case, to satisfy the *validity* condition, the decision of process p_i must be in the convex hull of the inputs of processes $p_1, \cdots, p_{d+1}$. That is, the decision vector must be in the convex hull of X_i^{d+2} defined below.

  $$X_i^{d+2} = \{\mathbf{x}_k : 1 \leq k \leq d+1\} \tag{4}$$

  $\mathbf{x}_{d+2}$ is not included above, because until process p_i terminates, p_{d+2} does not take any steps (so p_i cannot learn any information about $\mathbf{x}_{d+2}$).

- Process p_j $(j \neq i, 1 \leq j \leq d+1)$ is faulty, and process p_{d+2} is slow, and hence p_{d+2} has not taken any steps yet: Recall that we are considering p_i at the time when it terminates. Since process p_{d+2} has not taken any steps yet, process p_i cannot have any information about the input at p_{d+2}. Also, in this scenario p_j may be faulty, therefore, process p_i cannot trust the correctness of the input at p_j. Thus, to satisfy the validity condition, the decision of process p_i must be in the convex hull of X_i^j defined below.

  $$X_i^j = \{\mathbf{x}_k : k \neq j \text{ and } 1 \leq k \leq d+1\} \tag{5}$$

The decision vector of process p_i must be valid independent of which of the above $d+1$ scenarios actually occurred. Therefore, observing that $\mathcal{H}(X_i^{d+2}) \supseteq \mathcal{H}(X_i^j)$, where $j \neq i$, we conclude that the decision vector must be in

$$\cap_{j \neq i, 1 \leq j \leq d+1} \mathcal{H}(X_i^j) \tag{6}$$

Recall that $\epsilon > 0$ is the parameter of the ϵ-agreement condition in Section 1. For $1 \leq i \leq d$, suppose that the i-th element of input vector $\mathbf{x}_i$ is 2ϵ, and the remaining $d - 1$ elements are 0. Also suppose that $\mathbf{x}_{d+1}$ and $\mathbf{x}_{d+2}$ are both equal to the all-0 vector.

Let us consider process p_{d+1}. In this case, $\mathcal{H}(X_{d+1}^j)$ for $j \leq d$ only contains vectors whose j-th element is 0. Thus, the intersection of all the convex hulls in (6) only contains the all-0 vector, which, in fact, equals $\mathbf{x}_{d+1}$. Thus, the decision vector of process p_{d+1} must be equal to $\mathbf{x}_{d+1}$. We can similarly show that for each p_i, $1 \leq i \leq d + 1$, the intersection in (6) only contains vector $\mathbf{x}_i$, and therefore, the decision vector of process p_i must be equal to its input $\mathbf{x}_i$. The input vectors at each pair of processes in $p_1, \cdots, p_{d+1}$ differ by 2ϵ in at least one element. This implies that the ϵ-agreement condition is not satisfied. Therefore, $n = d + 2$ is not sufficient for $f = 1$. It should be easy to see that $n \leq d + 2$ is also not sufficient.

For the case when $f > 1$, by using a *simulation* similar to the proof of Theorem 1, we can now show that $n \leq (d+2)f$ is not sufficient. Thus, $n \geq (d+2)f+1$ is necessary for $f \geq 1$. (For $f = 0$, the necessary condition holds trivially.) $\square$

3.2 Sufficient Condition for Approximate Asynchronous BVC

We will prove that $n \geq (d + 2)f + 1$ is sufficient by proving the correctness of an algorithm presented in this section. Mendes and Herlihy have also independently obtained the above necessary condition for approximate BVC, and developed a different algorithm [15].

The algorithm presented below executes in asynchronous rounds. Each process p_i maintains a local state $\mathbf{v}_i$, which is a d-dimensional vector. We will refer to the value of $\mathbf{v}_i$ at the *end* of the t-th round performed by process p_i as $\mathbf{v}_i[t]$. Thus, $\mathbf{v}_i[t-1]$ is the value of $\mathbf{v}_i$ at the *start* of the t-th round of process p_i. The initial value of $\mathbf{v}_i$, namely $\mathbf{v}_i[0]$, is equal to p_i's *input* vector, denoted as $\mathbf{x}_i$. The messages sent by each process anytime during its t-th round are tagged by the round number t. This allows a process p_i in its round t to determine, despite the asynchrony, whether a message received from another process p_j was sent by p_j in p_j's round t.

The proposed algorithm is obtained by suitably modifying a *scalar* consensus algorithm presented by Abraham, Amit and Dolev [1] to achieve asynchronous approximate Byzantine scalar consensus among $3f + 1$ processes. We will refer to the algorithm in [1] as the AAD algorithm. We first present a brief overview of the AAD algorithm, and describe its properties. We adopt our notation above when describing the AAD algorithm (the notation differs from [1]). One key difference is that, in our proposed algorithm $\mathbf{v}_i[t]$ is a vector, whereas in AAD description below, it is considered a scalar. The AAD algorithm may be viewed as consisting of three components:

1. *AAD component #1:* In each round t, the AAD algorithm requires each process to communicate its state $\mathbf{v}_i[t-1]$ to other processes using a mechanism that achieves the properties described next. AAD ensures that each non-faulty process p_i in its round t obtains a set $B_i[t]$ containing at least $n - f$ tuples of the form $(p_j, \mathbf{w}_j, t)$, such that the following properties hold:

   - (Property 1) For any two non-faulty processes p_i and p_j:
   $$|B_i[t] \cap B_j[t]| \geq n - f \qquad (7)$$
   That is, p_i and p_j learn at least $n - f$ identical tuples.

   - (Property 2) If $(p_l, \mathbf{w}_l, t)$ and $(p_k, \mathbf{w}_k, t)$ are both in $B_i[t]$, then $p_l \neq p_k$. That is, $B_i[t]$ contains at most one tuple for each process.

   - (Property 3) If p_k is non-faulty, and $(p_k, \mathbf{w}_k, t) \in B_i[t]$, then $\mathbf{w}_k = \mathbf{v}_k[t-1]$. That is, for any non-faulty process p_k, $B_i[t]$ may only contain the tuple $(p_k, \mathbf{v}_k[t-1], t)$. (However, it is possible that, corresponding to some non-faulty process, $B_i[t]$ does not contain a tuple at all.)

2. *AAD component #2:* Process p_i, having obtained set $B_i[t]$ above, computes its new state $\mathbf{v}_i[t]$ as a function of the tuples in $B_i[t]$. The primary difference between our proposed algorithm and AAD is in this step. The computation of $\mathbf{v}_i[t]$ in AAD is designed to be correct for scalar inputs (and scalar decision), whereas our approach applies to d-dimensional vectors.

3. *AAD component #3:* AAD includes a sub-algorithm that allows the non-faulty processes to determine when to terminate their computation. Initially, the processes cooperate to estimate a quantity δ as a function of the input values at various processes. Different non-faulty processes may estimate different values for δ, since the estimate is affected by the behavior of faulty processes and message delays. Each process then uses $1 + \lceil \log_2 \frac{\delta}{\epsilon} \rceil$ as the threshold on the minimum number of rounds necessary for the non-faulty processes to converge within ϵ of each other. The base of the logarithm above is 2, because the range of the values at the non-faulty processes is shown to shrink by a factor of $\frac{1}{2}$ after each asynchronous round of AAD [1]. Subsequently, when the processes reach respective thresholds on the rounds, they exchange additional messages. After an adequate number of processes announce that they have reached their threshold, all the non-faulty processes may terminate.

It turns out that the Properties 1, 2 and 3 hold even if *Component #1* of AAD is used with $\mathbf{v}_i[t]$ as a *vector*. We exploit these properties in our algorithm below. The proposed algorithm below uses a function Φ, which takes a set, say set B, containing tuples of the form $(p_k, \mathbf{w}_k, t)$, and returns a multiset containing the points (i.e., $\mathbf{w}_k$). Formally,

$$\Phi(B) = \{\mathbf{w}_k : (p_k, \mathbf{w}_k, t) \in B\} \qquad (8)$$

A mechanism similar to that in AAD may potentially be used to achieve termination for the approximate BVC algorithm below as well. The main difference from AAD would be in the manner in which the threshold on the number of rounds necessary is computed. However, for brevity, we simplify our algorithm by assuming that there exists an upper bound U and a lower bound ν on the values of the d elements in the inputs vectors at non-faulty processes, and that these bounds are known *a priori*. Thus, all the elements in each input vector will be $\leq U$ and $\geq \nu$. This assumption holds in many practical systems, because the input vector elements represent quantities that are constrained. For instance, if the input vectors are probability vectors, then $U = 1$ and $\nu = 0$. If the input vectors represent locations in 3-dimensional space occupied by mobile robots, then U and ν are determined by the boundary of the region in which the robots are allowed to operate. The advantage of the AAD-like solution over our simple approach is that, depending on the actual inputs, the algorithm may potentially terminate sooner, and the AAD mechanism prevents faulty processes from causing the non-faulty processes to run longer than necessary. However, the simple static approach for termination presently suffices to prove the correctness of our approximate BVC algorithm, as shown later.

Asynchronous Approximate BVC algorithm
for $n \geq (d+2)f + 1$:

---

1. In the t-th round, each non-faulty process uses the mechanism in *Component #1* of the AAD algorithm to obtain a set $B_i[t]$ containing at least $n - f$ tuples, such that $B_i[t]$ satisfies properties 1, 2, and 3 described earlier for AAD. While these properties were proved in [1] for scalar states, the correctness of the properties also holds when $\mathbf{v}_i$ is a vector.

2. In the t-th round, after obtaining set $B_i[t]$, process p_i computes its new state $\mathbf{v}_i[t]$ as follows. Form a multiset Z_i using the steps below:

   - Initialize Z_i as empty.
   - For each $C \subseteq B_i[t]$ such that $|C| = n - f \geq (d+1)f + 1$, add to Z_i one deterministically chosen point from $\Gamma(\Phi(C))$. Since $|\Phi(C)| = |C| \geq (d+1)f + 1$, by Lemma 1, $\Gamma(\Phi(C))$ is non-empty.

   Note that $|Z_i| = \binom{|B_i[t]|}{n-f} \leq \binom{n}{n-f}$. Calculate

   $$\mathbf{v}_i[t] = \frac{\sum_{\mathbf{z} \in Z_i} \mathbf{z}}{|Z_i|} \qquad (9)$$

3. Each non-faulty process terminates after $1 + \lceil \log_{1/(1-\gamma)} \frac{U - \nu}{\epsilon} \rceil$ rounds, where γ ($0 < \gamma < 1$) is a constant defined later in (11). Recall that ϵ is the parameter of the ϵ-agreement condition.

THEOREM 5. *$n \geq (d+2)f + 1$ is sufficient for approximate BVC in an asynchronous system.*

PROOF. Without loss of generality, suppose that m processes $p_1, p_2, \cdots p_m$ are non-faulty, where $m \geq n - f$, and the remaining $n - m$ processes are faulty. In the proof, we will often omit the round index $[t]$ in $B_i[t]$, since the index should be clear from the context. In this proof, we consider the steps taken by the non-faulty processes in their respective t-th rounds, where $t > 0$. We now define a *valid* point. The definition is used later in the proof.

DEFINITION 1. *A point $\mathbf{r}$ is said to be* valid *if there exists a representation of $\mathbf{r}$ as a convex combination of $\mathbf{v}_k[t-1]$, $1 \leq k \leq m$. That is, there exist constants β_k, such that $0 \leq \beta_k \leq 1$ and $\sum_{1 \leq k \leq m} \beta_k = 1$, and*

$$\mathbf{r} = \sum_{1 \leq k \leq m} \beta_k \mathbf{v}_k[t-1] \qquad (10)$$

*β_k is said to be the **weight** of $\mathbf{v}_k[t-1]$ in the above convex combination.*

In general, there may exist multiple such convex combination representations of a *valid* point $\mathbf{r}$. Observe that at least one of the weights in any such convex combination must be $\geq \frac{1}{m} \geq \frac{1}{n}$.

For the convenience of the readers, we break up the rest of this proof into three parts.

Part I:.

At a non-faulty process p_i, consider any $C \subseteq B_i$ such that $|C| = n - f$ (as in Step 2 of the algorithm). Since $|\Phi(C)| = |C| = n - f \geq (d+1)f + 1$, by Lemma 1, $\Gamma(\Phi(C)) \neq \emptyset$. So Z_i will contain a point from $\Gamma(\Phi(C))$ for each C.

Now, $C \subseteq B_i$, $|\Phi(C)| = n - f$, and there are at most f faulty processes. Then Property 3 of B_i implies that at least one $(n - 2f)$-size subset of $\Phi(C)$ must also be a subset of $\{\mathbf{v}_1[t-1], \mathbf{v}_2[t-1], \cdots, \mathbf{v}_m[t-1]\}$, i.e., contain only the state of non-faulty processes. Therefore, all the points in $\Gamma(\Phi(C))$ must be *valid* (due to (1) and Definition 1). This observation is true for each set C enumerated in Step 2. Therefore, all the points in Z_i computed in Step 2 must be valid. (Recall that we assume processes $p_1, \cdots, p_m$ are non-faulty.)

Part II:.

Consider any two non-faulty processes p_i and p_j.

- *Observation 1:* As argued in Part I, all the points in Z_i are valid. Therefore, all the points in Z_i can be expressed as convex combinations of the state of non-faulty processes, i.e., $\{\mathbf{v}_1[t-1], \cdots, \mathbf{v}_m[t-1]\}$. Similar observation holds for all the points in Z_j too.

- *Observation 2:* By Property 1 of B_i and B_j,

  $$|B_i \cap B_j| \geq n - f.$$

  (As noted earlier, we omit the round index $[t]$ when discussing the sets $B_i[t]$ and $B_j[t]$ here.) Therefore, there exists a set $C_{ij} \subseteq B_i \cap B_j$ such that $|C_{ij}| = n - f$. Therefore, Z_i and Z_j both contain one identical point from $\Gamma(\Phi(C_{ij}))$. Suppose that this point is named $\mathbf{z}_{ij}$. As shown in Part I above, $\mathbf{z}_{ij}$ must be *valid*. Therefore, there exists a convex combination representation of $\mathbf{z}_{ij}$ in terms of the states $\{\mathbf{v}_1[t-1], \mathbf{v}_2[t-1], \cdots, \mathbf{v}_m[t-1]\}$ of non-faulty processes. Choose any one such convex combination. There must exist a non-faulty process, say $p_{g(i,j)}$, such that the weight associated with $\mathbf{v}_{g(i,j)}[t-1]$ in the convex combination for $\mathbf{z}_{ij}$ is $\geq \frac{1}{m} \geq \frac{1}{n}$. Note that, to simplify the notation, the notation $g(i, j)$ does not make the round index t explicit. However, it should be noted that $g(i, j)$ for processes p_i and p_j can be different in different rounds. We can now make the next observation.

- *Observation 3:* Recall from (9) that $\mathbf{v}_i[t]$ is computed as the average of the points in Z_i, and $|Z_i| = \binom{|B_i|}{n-f} \leq \binom{n}{n-f}$. By *Observations 1*, all the points in Z_i are valid, and by *Observation 2*, $\mathbf{z}_{ij} \in Z_i$. These observations together imply that $\mathbf{v}_i[t]$ is also valid, and *there exists a representation of $\mathbf{v}_i[t]$ as a convex combination of $\{\mathbf{v}_1[t-1], \cdots, \mathbf{v}_m[t-1]\}$, wherein the weight of $\mathbf{v}_{g(i,j)}[t-1]$ is $\geq \frac{1}{n\binom{|B_i|}{n-f}} \geq \frac{1}{n\binom{n}{n-f}}$*. Similarly, we can show that *there exists a representation of $\mathbf{v}_j[t]$ as a convex combination of $\{\mathbf{v}_1[t-1], \cdots, \mathbf{v}_m[t-1]\}$, wherein the weight of $\mathbf{v}_{g(i,j)}[t-1]$ is $\geq \frac{1}{n\binom{n}{n-f}}$*. Define

  $$\gamma = \frac{1}{n\binom{n}{n-f}} \qquad (11)$$

Consensus is trivial for $n = 1$, so we consider finite $n > 1$. Therefore, $0 < \gamma < 1$.

Part III:.

Observation 3 above implies that for any $\tau > 0$, $\mathbf{v}_i[\tau]$ is a convex combination of $\{\mathbf{v}_1[\tau-1], \cdots, \mathbf{v}_m[\tau-1]\}$. Applying this observation for $\tau = 1, 2, \cdots, t$, we can conclude that $\mathbf{v}_i[t]$ is a convex combination of $\{\mathbf{v}_1[0], \cdots, \mathbf{v}_m[0]\}$, implying that the proposed algorithm satisfies the **validity** condition for approximate consensus. (Recall that $\mathbf{v}_k[0]$ equals process p_k's input vector.)

Let $\mathbf{v}_{il}[t]$ denote the l-th element of the vector state $\mathbf{v}_i[t]$ of process p_i. Define $\Omega_l[t] = \max_{1 \le k \le m} \mathbf{v}_{kl}[t]$, the maximum value of l-th element of the vector state of non-faulty processes. Define $\mu_l[t] = \min_{1 \le k \le m} \mathbf{v}_{kl}[t]$, the minimum value of l-th element of the vector state of non-faulty processes. Appendix C proves, using *Observations 1* and *3* above, that for $1 \le l \le d$,

$$\Omega_l[t] - \mu_l[t] \le (1-\gamma)(\Omega_l[t-1] - \mu_l[t-1]), \quad (12)$$

By repeated application of (12) we get

$$\Omega_l[t] - \mu_l[t] \le (1-\gamma)^t (\Omega_l[0] - \mu_l[0]) \quad (13)$$

Therefore, for a given $\epsilon > 0$, if

$$t > \log_{1/(1-\gamma)} \frac{\Omega_l[0] - \mu_l[0]}{\epsilon}, \quad (14)$$

then

$$\Omega_l[t] - \mu_l[t] < \epsilon. \quad (15)$$

Since (14) and (15) hold for $1 \le l \le d$, and $U \ge \Omega_l[0]$ and $\nu \le \mu_l[0]$ for $1 \le l \le d$, if each non-faulty process terminates after $1 + \lceil \log_{1/(1-\gamma)} \frac{U-\nu}{\epsilon} \rceil$ rounds, ϵ-agreement is ensured. As shown previously, validity condition is satisfied as well. Thus, the proposed algorithm is correct, and $n \ge (d+2)f + 1$ is sufficient for approximate consensus in asynchronous systems. $\quad \square$

4. SUMMARY

This paper addresses Byzantine vector consensus (BVC) wherein the input at each process, and its decision, is a vector. We derive tight necessary and sufficient bounds on the number of processes required for *Exact BVC* in synchronous systems, and *Approximate BVC* in asynchronous systems.

Acknowledgments:.

Nitin Vaidya acknowledges Eli Gafni for suggesting the problem, Lewis Tseng for feedback, and Jennifer Welch for answering queries on distributed computing. Vijay Garg acknowledges John Bridgman and Constantine Caramanis for discussions on the problem.

5. REFERENCES

[1] I. Abraham, Y. Amit, and D. Dolev. Optimal resilience asynchronous approximate agreement. In *OPODIS*, 2004.

[2] P. Agarwal, M. Sharir, and E. Welzl. Algorithms for center and Tverberg points. In *Proceedings of the twentieth annual symposium on Computational geometry*, pages 61–67. ACM, 2004.

[3] M. Ben-Or, D. Dolev, and E. Hoch. Simple gradecast based algorithms. *arXiv preprint arXiv:1007.1049*, 2010.

[4] S. Boyd and L. Vandenberghe. *Convex optimization*. Cambridge university press, 2004.

[5] D. Dolev, N. A. Lynch, S. S. Pinter, E. W. Stark, and W. E. Weihl. Reaching approximate agreement in the presence of faults. *J. ACM*, 33:499–516, May 1986.

[6] D. Dolev, R. Reischuk, and H. Strong. Early stopping in byzantine agreement. *Journal of the ACM (JACM)*, 37(4):720–741, 1990.

[7] A. Doudou and A. Schiper. Muteness detector for consensus with Byzantine processes. In *ACM PODC*, 1998.

[8] D. Eppstein. A Tverberg partition of the seven points of a regular heptagon into three subsets with intersecting convex hulls, 2010. Available from http://commons.wikimedia.org/wiki/File:Tverberg_heptagon.svg.

[9] A. D. Fekete. Asymptotically optimal algorithms for approximate agreement. In *Proceedings of the fifth annual ACM symposium on Principles of distributed computing*, PODC '86, pages 73–87, New York, NY, USA, 1986. ACM.

[10] M. J. Fischer, N. A. Lynch, and M. S. Paterson. Impossibility of distributed consensus with one faulty process. *J. ACM*, 32:374–382, April 1985.

[11] J. Garay and Y. Moses. Fully polynomial byzantine agreement for processors in rounds. *SIAM Journal on Computing*, 27(1):247–290, 1998.

[12] S. Jadhav and A. Mukhopadhyay. Computing a centerpoint of a finite planar set of points in linear time. *Discrete & Computational Geometry*, 1994.

[13] L. Lamport, R. Shostak, and M. Pease. The Byzantine generals problem. *ACM Trans. Prog. Lang. Syst.*, 4(3):382–401, July 1982.

[14] N. A. Lynch. *Distributed algorithms*. Morgan Kaufmann Publishers, 1995.

[15] H. Mendes and M. Herlihy. Multidimensional approximate agreement in byzantine asynchronous systems. In *45th ACM Symposium on the Theory of Computing (STOC)*, June 2013.

[16] G. Miller and D. Sheehy. Approximate centerpoints with proofs. *Computational Geometry*, 43(8):647–654, 2010.

[17] W. Mulzer and D. Werner. Approximating Tverberg points in linear time for any fixed dimension. In *Proceedings of the 2012 symposuim on Computational Geometry*, pages 303–310. ACM, 2012.

[18] N. Neves, M. Correia, and P. Verissimo. Solving vector consensus with a wormhole. *IEEE Trans. on Parallel and Distributed Systems*, December 2005.

[19] M. A. Perles and M. Sigron. A generalization of Tverberg's theorem, 2007. CoRR, http://arxiv.org/abs/0710.4668.

APPENDIX

A. NOTATIONS

This appendix summarizes some of the notations and terminology introduced in the paper.

- n = number of processes.
- $\mathcal{P} = \{p_1, p_2, \cdots, p_n\}$ is the set of processes in the system.
- f = maximum number of Byzantine faulty processes.

- d = dimension of the input vector as well as decision vector at each process.

- $\mathbf{x}_i$ = d-dimensional input vector at process p_i. The vector is equivalently viewed as a point in the Euclidean space $\mathbf{R}^d$.

- $\mathcal{H}(Y)$ denotes the convex hull of the points in multiset Y.

- m : The proof of Theorem 5 assumes, without loss of generality, that for $m \geq n - f$, processes $p_1, \cdots, p_m$ are non-faulty, and the remaining $n - m$ processes are faulty.

- $\Gamma(.)$ is defined in (1).

- $\Phi(.)$ is defined in (8).

- $\mathbf{v}_i[t]$ is the state of process p_i at the end of its t-th round of the asynchronous BVC algorithm, $t > 0$. Thus, $\mathbf{v}_i[t-1]$ is the state of process p_i at the start of its t-th round, $t > 0$. $\mathbf{v}_i[0]$ for process p_i equals its input $\mathbf{x}_i$.

- $\mathbf{v}_{il}[t]$ is the l-th element of $\mathbf{v}_i[t]$, where $1 \leq l \leq d$.

- $B_i[t]$ defined in Section 3.2, is a set of tuples of the form $(p_j, \mathbf{w}_j, t)$, obtained by process p_i in Step 1 of the approximate consensus algorithm.

- *Weight* in a convex combination is defined in Definition 1

- $\gamma = \frac{1}{n\binom{n}{n-f}}$, as defined in (11). Note that $0 < \gamma < 1$ for finite $n > 1$.

- $\Omega_l[t] = \max_{1 \leq k \leq m} \mathbf{v}_{kl}[t]$

- $\mu_l[t] = \min_{1 \leq k \leq m} \mathbf{v}_{kl}[t]$

- $\rho_l[t] = \Omega_l[t] - \mu_l[t]$

- $|Y|$ denotes the size of a *multiset* Y.

- $\| a \|$ is the absolute value of a real number a.

B.   CLARIFICATION FOR THE PROOF OF THEOREM 1

In the proof of Theorem 1, when considering the case of $f = 1$, we claimed the following:

> Since none of the non-faulty processes know which process, if any, is faulty, as elaborated in Appendix B, the decision vector must be in the convex hull of each multiset containing the input vectors of $n - 1$ of the processes (there are n such multisets). Thus, this intersection must be non-empty, for all possible input vectors at the n processes.

Now we provide an explanation for the above claim.

Suppose that the input at process p_i is $\mathbf{x}_i$, $1 \leq i \leq n$. All the processes are non-faulty, but the processes do not know this fact. The decision vector chosen by the processes must satisfy the *agreement* and *validity* conditions both.

- With $f = 1$, any one process may potentially be faulty. In particular, process p_i $(1 \leq i \leq n)$ may possibly be faulty. Therefore, the input $\mathbf{x}_i$ of process p_i cannot be trusted by other processes. Then to ensure *validity*, the decision vector chosen by any other process p_j $(j \neq i)$ must be in the convex hull of the inputs at the processes in $\mathcal{P} - \{p_i\}$ (i.e., all processes except p_i). Thus, the decision vector of process p_j $(j \neq i)$ must be in the convex hull of the points in multiset X^i below.

$$X^i = \{\mathbf{x}_k \ : \ k \neq i, \ 1 \leq k \leq n\}.$$

- To ensure *agreement*, the decision vector chosen by all the processes must be identical. Therefore, the decision vector must be in the intersection of the convex hulls of all the multisets X^i $(1 \leq i \leq n)$ defined above. Thus, we conclude that the decision vector must be in the intersection below, where $\mathcal{H}(X^i)$ denotes the *convex hull* of the points in multiset X^i, and Q_i denotes $\mathcal{H}(X^i)$.

$$\cap_{i=1}^{n} \mathcal{H}(X^i) \ = \ \cap_{i=1}^{n} Q_i \qquad (16)$$

If the intersection in (16) is empty, then there is no decision vector that satisfies *validity* and *agreement* conditions both. Therefore, the intersection must be non-empty.

As shown in the proof of Theorem 1, if n is not large enough, then the intersection in (16) may be empty.

C.   PROOF OF CLAIM IN PART III

$\mathbf{v}_{il}[t]$ denotes the l-th element of the vector state $\mathbf{v}_i[t]$ of process p_i, $1 \leq l \leq d$. Processes $p_1, \cdots, p_m$ are non-faulty, and processes $p_{m+1}, \cdots, p_n$ are faulty, where $m \geq n - f$. Recall that, for $1 \leq l \leq d$,

$$\Omega_l[t] \ = \ \max_{1 \leq k \leq m} \mathbf{v}_{kl}[t] \qquad (17)$$

$$\mu_l[t] \ = \ \min_{1 \leq k \leq m} \mathbf{v}_{kl}[t] \qquad (18)$$

Define $\qquad\qquad\qquad\qquad\qquad\qquad\qquad (19)$

$$\rho_l[t] \ = \ \Omega_l[t] - \mu_l[t] \qquad (20)$$

Equivalently,

$$\rho_l[t] \ = \ \max_{1 \leq i,j \leq m} \| \mathbf{v}_{il}[t] - \mathbf{v}_{jl}[t] \| \qquad (21)$$

where $\| . \|$ operator yields the absolute value of the scalar parameter.

Consider any two non-faulty processes p_i, p_j (thus, $1 \leq i, j \leq m$). Consider $1 \leq l \leq d$. Then

$$\mu_l[t-1] \ \leq \ \mathbf{v}_{il}[t-1] \ \leq \ \Omega_l[t-1] \qquad (22)$$

$$\mu_l[t-1] \ \leq \ \mathbf{v}_{jl}[t-1] \ \leq \ \Omega_l[t-1] \qquad (23)$$

Observations 1 and *3* in Part III of the proof of Theorem 5, and the definition of γ, imply the existence of constants α_k's and β_k's such that:

$$\mathbf{v}_i[t] \ = \ \sum_{k=1}^{m} \alpha_k \mathbf{v}_k[t-1] \quad \text{where} \qquad (24)$$

$$\alpha_k \geq 0 \text{ for } 1 \leq k \leq m, \text{ and } \sum_{k=1}^{m} \alpha_k = 1 \qquad (25)$$

$$\alpha_{g(i,j)} \geq \gamma \qquad (26)$$

$$\mathbf{v}_j[t] \ = \ \sum_{k=1}^{m} \beta_k \mathbf{v}_k[t-1] \quad \text{where} \qquad (27)$$

$$\beta_k \geq 0 \text{ for } 1 \leq k \leq m, \text{ and } \sum_{k=1}^{m} \beta_k = 1 \qquad (28)$$

$$\beta_{g(i,j)} \geq \gamma \qquad (29)$$

In the following, let us abbreviate $g(i,j)$ simply as g. Thus, $\alpha_{g(i,j)}$ is same as α_g, and $\beta_{g(i,j)}$ is same as β_g. From

(24) and (27), focussing on just the operations on l-th elements, we obtain

$$\mathbf{v}_{il}[t] \ = \ \sum_{k=1}^{m} \alpha_k \, \mathbf{v}_{kl}[t-1]$$

$$\leq \ \alpha_g \, \mathbf{v}_{gl}[t-1] \ + \ (1-\alpha_g)\, \Omega_l[t-1] \qquad (30)$$
$$\text{because } \mathbf{v}_{kl}[t-1] \leq \Omega_l[t-1],\ \forall k$$

$$\leq \ \gamma \, \mathbf{v}_{gl}[t-1] \ + $$
$$(\alpha_g - \gamma)\mathbf{v}_{gl}[t-1] \ + \ (1-\alpha_g)\, \Omega_l[t-1]$$

$$\leq \ \gamma \, \mathbf{v}_{gl}[t-1] \ + $$
$$(\alpha_g - \gamma)\Omega_l[t-1] \ + \ (1-\alpha_g)\, \Omega_l[t-1]$$
$$\text{because } \mathbf{v}_{gl}[t-1] \leq \Omega_l[t-1] \text{ and } \alpha_g \geq \gamma$$

$$\leq \ \gamma \, \mathbf{v}_{gl}[t-1] \ + \ (1-\gamma)\, \Omega_l[t-1] \qquad (31)$$

$$\mathbf{v}_{jl}[t] \ = \ \sum_{k=1}^{m} \beta_k \, \mathbf{v}_{kl}[t-1]$$

$$\geq \ \beta_g \, \mathbf{v}_{gl}[t-1] \ + \ (1-\beta_g)\, \mu_l[t-1]$$
$$\text{because } \mathbf{v}_{kl}[t-1] \geq \mu_l[t-1],\ \forall k$$

$$\geq \ \gamma \, \mathbf{v}_{gl}[t-1] \ + $$
$$(\beta_g - \gamma)\mathbf{v}_{gl}[t-1] \ + \ (1-\beta_g)\, \mu_l[t-1]$$

$$\geq \ \gamma \, \mathbf{v}_{gl}[t-1] \ + $$
$$(\beta_g - \gamma)\mu_l[t-1] \ + \ (1-\beta_g)\, \mu_l[t-1]$$
$$\text{because } \mathbf{v}_{gl}[t-1] \geq \mu_l[t-1], \text{ and } \beta_g \geq \gamma$$

$$\geq \ \gamma \, \mathbf{v}_{gl}[t-1] \ + \ (1-\gamma)\, \mu_l[t-1] \qquad (32)$$

Subtracting (32) from (31), we get

$$\mathbf{v}_{il}[t] - \mathbf{v}_{jl}[t] \ \leq \ (1-\gamma)\,(\Omega_l[t-1] - \mu_l[t-1]) \quad (33)$$

By swapping the role of p_i and p_j above, we can also show that

$$\mathbf{v}_{jl}[t] \ - \ \mathbf{v}_{il}[t] \ \leq \ (1-\gamma)\,(\Omega_l[t-1] - \mu_l[t-1]) \quad (34)$$

Putting (33) and (34) together, we obtain

$$\| \, \mathbf{v}_{il}[t] - \mathbf{v}_{jl}[t] \, \| \ \leq \ (1-\gamma)\,(\Omega_l[t-1] - \mu_l[t-1])$$
$$\text{because } \Omega_l[t-1] \geq \mu_l[t-1]$$
$$\leq \ (1-\gamma)\, \rho_l[t-1]$$
$$\text{by the definition of } \rho_l[t-1]$$

Because the previous inequality holds for all $1 \leq i, j \leq m$, we get

$$\max_{1 \leq i, j \leq m} \| \, \mathbf{v}_{il}[t] - \mathbf{v}_{jl}[t] \, \| \ \leq \ (1-\gamma)\rho_l[t-1]$$
$$\Rightarrow \ \rho_l[t] \ \leq \ (1-\gamma)\,\rho_l[t-1] \quad \text{by (21)}$$
$$\Rightarrow \ \Omega_l[t] - \mu_l[t] \ \leq \ (1-\gamma)\,(\Omega_l[t-1] - \mu_l[t-1])$$

This proves (12).

Fast Byzantine Agreement in Dynamic Networks

John Augustine
Dept. of Comp. Sci. & Engg.,
Indian Inst. of Tech. Madras,
Chennai, TN, 600036, India.
augustine@cse.iitm.ac.in.

Gopal Pandurangan[*][†]
Div. of Mathematical Sciences,
Nanyang Technological Univ.,
Singapore 637371.
gopalpandurangan@gmail.com.

Peter Robinson[‡]
Div. of Mathematical Sciences,
Nanyang Technological Univ.,
Singapore 637371.
peter.robinson@ntu.edu.sg.

ABSTRACT

We study Byzantine agreement in dynamic networks where topology can change from round to round and nodes can also experience heavy *churn* (i.e., nodes can join and leave the network continuously over time). Our main contributions are randomized distributed algorithms that achieve *almost-everywhere Byzantine agreement* with high probability even under a large number of adaptively chosen Byzantine nodes and continuous adversarial churn in a number of rounds that is polylogarithmic in n (where n is the stable network size). We show that our algorithms are essentially optimal (up to polylogarithmic factors) with respect to the amount of Byzantine nodes and churn rate that they can tolerate by showing a lower bound. In particular, we present the following results:

1. An $O(\log^3 n)$ round randomized algorithm to achieve almost-everywhere Byzantine agreement with high probability under a presence of up to $O(\sqrt{n}/\text{polylog}(n))$ Byzantine nodes and up to a churn of $O(\sqrt{n}/\text{polylog}(n))$ nodes per round. We assume that the Byzantine nodes have knowledge about the entire state of network at every round (including random choices made by all the nodes) and can behave arbitrarily. We also assume that an adversary controls the churn — it has complete knowledge and control of what nodes join and leave and at what time and has unlimited computational power (but is oblivious to the topology changes from round to round). Our algorithm requires only polylogarithmic in n bits to be processed and sent (per round) by each node.

2. We also present an $O(\log^3 n)$ round randomized algorithm

that has same guarantees as the above algorithm, but works even when the connectivity of the network is controlled by an adaptive adversary (that can choose the topology based on the current states of the nodes). However, this algorithm requires up to polynomial in n bits to be processed and sent (per round) by each node.

3. We show that the above bounds are essentially the best possible, if one wants fast (i.e., polylogarithmic run time) algorithms, by showing that any (randomized) algorithm to achieve agreement in a dynamic network controlled by an adversary that can churn up to $\Theta(\sqrt{n \log n})$ nodes per round should take at least a *polynomial* number of rounds.

Our algorithms are the first-known, fully distributed, Byzantine agreement algorithms in highly dynamic networks. We view our results as a step towards understanding the possibilities and limitations of highly dynamic networks that are subject to malicious behavior by a large number of nodes.

Categories and Subject Descriptors

F.2.2 [**Theory of Computation**]: [Analysis of Algorithms and Problem Complexity—Nonnumerical Algorithms and Problems]

Keywords

Byzantine agreement; dynamic network; distributed algorithm; randomized algorithm; expander graph.

1. INTRODUCTION

Motivated by the need for robust and secure distributed computation in distributed large-scale (sparse) networks such as peer-to-peer (P2P) and overlay networks, we study the fundamental Byzantine agreement problem in dynamic networks. The Byzantine agreement problem in dynamic networks is challenging because the goal is to guarantee Byzantine *almost-everywhere* agreement, i.e., most nodes[1] should reach agreement, despite the adversarial network dynamism and the presence of Byzantine nodes. In fact, Byzantine agreement has been a challenging problem even in static networks. Indeed, until recently, almost all the work known in the literature (see e.g., [15, 19, 20, 21, 34]) have addressed the Byzantine almost-everywhere agreement problem only in static networks. Unfortunately, these approaches do not work for dynamic networks with changing topology.

Such approaches in static networks fail in dynamic networks where both nodes and edges can change by a large amount in every round. For example, Upfal [34] showed how one can achieve

[*]Research supported in part by the following grants: Nanyang Technological University grant M58110000, Singapore Ministry of Education (MOE) Academic Research Fund (AcRF) Tier 2 grant MOE2010-T2-2-082, and a grant from the US-Israel Binational Science Foundation (BSF).

[†]Also affiliated with the Department of Computer Science, Brown University, Box 1910, Providence, RI 02912, USA.

[‡]Research supported in part by the following grants: Nanyang Technological University grant M58110000, Singapore Ministry of Education (MOE) Academic Research Fund (AcRF) Tier 2 grant MOE2010-T2-2-082.

[1]In sparse, bounded-degree networks, an adversary can always isolate some number of non-faulty nodes, hence almost-everywhere is the best one can hope for in such networks [15].

almost-everywhere agreement under up to a linear number — up to εn, for a sufficiently small $\varepsilon > 0$ — of Byzantine faults in a bounded-degree expander network (n is the network size). The algorithm required $O(\log n)$ rounds and polynomial (in n) number of messages; however, the local computation required by each processor is exponential. Furthermore, the algorithm requires knowledge of the global topology, since at the start, nodes need to have this information hardcoded.

The work of King et al. [22] is important in the context of dynamic (especially, P2P) networks, as it was the first to study scalable (polylogarithmic communication and number of rounds) algorithms for distributed agreement and leader election that are tolerant to Byzantine faults. However, as pointed out by the authors, their algorithm works only for static networks. Similar to Upfal's algorithm, the nodes require hardcoded information on the network topology to begin with and thus the algorithm does not work when the topology changes. In fact, this work ([22]) raised the open question of whether one can design Byzantine agreement protocols that can work in highly dynamic networks with a large churn rate.

1.1 Our Main Results

We study Byzantine agreement in dynamic networks where topology can change from round to round and nodes can also experience heavy *churn* (i.e., nodes can join and leave the network continuously over time). Our goal is to design fast distributed algorithms (running in a small number of rounds) that guarantee, despite a relatively large number of byzantine nodes and high node churn, that almost all nodes reach byzantine agreement.

Before we state our results, we briefly describe the key ingredients of our model here. (Our model is described in detail in Section 2.) We consider a dynamic network as a sparse bounded degree expander graph whose topology — both nodes and edges — can change arbitrarily from round to round and is controlled by an adversary. However, we assume that the total number of nodes in the network is stable. The number of node changes *per round* is called the *churn rate* or *churn limit*. We consider a churn rate of up to some $O(\sqrt{n}/\text{polylog}(n))$, where n is the stable network size. (As we show later, this is essentially the largest possible churn rate if one requires "fast" algorithms.) Furthermore, we assume that a large number of nodes can be *Byzantine*. We allow up to $O(\sqrt{n}/\text{polylog}(n))$ Byzantine nodes in any round (again, this is the best possible if one requires "fast" algorithms). Byzantine nodes are "adaptive", in the sense that they know the entire states of all nodes at the beginning of every round and thus can take the current state of the computation into account when determining their next action. In each round, the *adversary* can observe the current state of all the nodes and then choose some $O(\sqrt{n}/\text{polylog}(n))$ nodes that are replaced by new nodes.

Note that our model is quite general in the sense that we only assume that the topology is an expander graph at every step; no other special properties are assumed. Indeed, expanders have been used extensively to model dynamic (especially P2P) networks[2] in which the expander property is preserved under insertions and deletions of nodes (e.g., [26, 30]). Since we do not make assumptions on how the topology is preserved, our model is applicable to all such expander-based networks. (We note that various prior works on dynamic network models make similar assumptions on preservation of topological properties like connectivity, expansion etc. at every

step under dynamic *edge* insertions/deletions — cf. Section 1.3. The issue of how such properties are preserved are abstracted away from the model, which allows us to focus on the dynamism. Indeed, this abstraction has been a feature of most dynamic models as can be seen in the survey by Casteigts *et al.* [11].)

We study Byzantine almost-everywhere agreement in our model. By "almost-everywhere", we mean that almost all nodes, except possibly $O(\sqrt{n}/\text{polylog}(n))$ nodes should reach agreement on a common value. (This agreed value must be the input value of some node.)

Our main contributions are randomized distributed algorithms that guarantee *almost-everywhere Byzantine agreement* with high probability even under a large number of Byzantine nodes and continuous adversarial churn in a polylogarithmic number of rounds. We show that our algorithms are essentially optimal (up to polylogarithmic factors) with respect to the amount of Byzantine nodes and churn rate they can tolerate by showing a lower bound. In particular, we present the following results:

1. (cf. Section 3) An $O(\log^3 n)$ round randomized algorithm that achieves almost-everywhere Byzantine agreement with high probability under a presence of up to $O(\sqrt{n}/\text{polylog}(n))$ Byzantine nodes and up to a churn of $O(\sqrt{n}/\text{polylog}(n))$ nodes per round. We assume that the Byzantine nodes have knowledge about the entire state of network at every round (including random choices made by all the nodes). We also assume that an adversary controls the churn — it has complete knowledge and control of what nodes join and leave and at what time and has unlimited computational power (but is *oblivious* to the topology changes from round to round). Our algorithm requires only polylogarithmic in n bits to be processed and sent (per round) by each node.

2. (cf. Section 4) We also present an $O(\log^3 n)$ round randomized algorithm that has same guarantees as the above algorithm, but works even when the churn and network topology are controlled by an adaptive adversary (that can choose the topology based on the current states of the nodes). However, this algorithm requires up to polynomial in n bits to be processed and sent (per round) by each node. It also requires assuming that a node can contact other nodes directly if it knows their IDs.

3. (cf. Section 5) We show that the above bounds are essentially the best possible, if one wants fast (i.e., polylogarithmic run time) algorithms, by showing that any (randomized) algorithm to achieve agreement in a dynamic network in which churn is controlled by an adaptive adversary that can churn up to $\Theta(\sqrt{n \log n})$ nodes per round should take at least a *polynomial* number of rounds. The proof of the lower bound result relies neither on the nature of the connectivity nor on the presence of Byzantine nodes. Therefore, the lower bound applies to both cases mentioned above and additionally proves the tightness of the algorithm provided in [4] for reaching almost everywhere agreement under an adaptive adversary.

To the best of our knowledge, our algorithms are the first-known, fully-distributed, Byzantine agreement algorithms that work under highly dynamic settings. We view our results as a step towards understanding the possibilities and limitations of highly dynamic networks that are subject to malicious behavior by a large number of nodes. Our algorithms are localized (do not require any global topological knowledge), simple, and easy to implement. These algorithms can serve as building blocks for implementing other nontrivial distributed computing tasks in dynamic networks.

Due to lack of space, some proofs are in the full paper [3].

---

[2]Expander graphs have been used extensively as candidates to solve the Byzantine agreement and related problems in bounded degree graphs even in static settings (e.g., see [15, 19, 20, 21, 34]). Here we show that similar expansion properties are beneficial in the more challenging setting of dynamic networks.

1.2 Technical Contributions

The main technical challenge that we have to overcome is designing and analyzing distributed algorithms with the presence of Byzantine nodes in networks where both nodes and edges can change by a large amount. We derive techniques for doing fast distributed computation in such networks. The main technical tool that we use is random walks. Flooding techniques proved useful in solving the agreement problem under high churn but without Byzantine nodes [4], but they are not useful in the presence of Byzantine nodes because they can send a lot of (useless) messages along with those of good nodes. On the other hand, if good nodes use random walks (which are lightweight and local) in their information spreading protocol, the Byzantine nodes are no longer able to flood the network very much.

We show how random walks can be used in a dynamic network with Byzantine nodes and high adversarial node churn. The basic idea is simple: use random walks to sample tokens (approximately) uniformly at random. All nodes generate tokens (which contain the source node's id) and send those tokens via random walks continuously over time. These random walks, once they "mix" (i.e., reach close to the stationary distribution), reach essentially "random" destinations in the network. Thus the destination nodes receive a steady stream of tokens from essentially random nodes, thereby allowing them to sample nodes uniformly from the network. While this is easy to establish in a static network, it is no longer true in a dynamic network with Byzantine nodes and adversarial churn — these can cause many random walks to be lost and also introduce bias. We show a technical result that "most" random walks do mix (despite byzantine nodes and large adversarial churn) and have the usual desirable properties as in a static network. For solving Byzantine agreement, we then use a majority rule to progress towards agreement. A technical difficulty is dealing with random samples that are only approximately uniform and not identically distributed.

We note that the random walk technique assumes that the external adversary that controls the topology is oblivious to the random walks. In other words, we assume that the edge changes are fixed by the adversary in advance before the algorithm starts. However, the adversary can still monitor the entire network in each round and fully controls the node churn. We also show how to achieve Byzantine agreement even under an adversary that controls the connectivity from round to round. Random walk techniques do not work in this case, but we show how to adapt information spreading techniques developed in [4] to achieve Byzantine agreement. For this case, we additionally assume that nodes can directly contact any other node if it knows the ID of that node[3]. We use this "overlay" link as a verification mechanism to authenticate the message sent by correct nodes.

Our lower bound proof builds on well-established ideas used in several consensus lower bound proofs [2]. We use coin flipping games which were first studied by Ben-Or and Linial [9]. Subsequently, these coin flipping games have been used several times to prove lower bounds on running time of distributed consensus algorithms; see Aspnes [1] along with the references therein. Our proof structure is similar to the work by Ben-Or and Bar-Joseph [8], which in turn builds on [17, 14, 1, 9]. We remark that the lower bound holds under an adaptive adversarial churn of $\tilde{O}(\sqrt{n})$ nodes per round even without any Byzantine nodes. Therefore, it establishes the tightness of results in this paper as well as the $O(\text{polylog}(n))$ round algorithm for almost everywhere agree-

ment (given in [4]) for an adaptive adversary that can churn at most $O(\sqrt{n})$ nodes per round.

1.3 Other Related Work

Distributed Agreement. The distributed agreement problem is important in a wide range of applications, such as database management, fault-tolerant analysis of aggregate data, and coordinated control of multiple agents or peers. There is a long line of research on various versions of the problem with many important results (see e.g., [2, 27] and the references therein). The relaxation of achieving agreement "almost everywhere" was introduced by [15] in the context of fault-tolerance in networks of bounded degree where all but $O(t)$ nodes achieve agreement despite $t = O(\frac{n}{\log n})$ faults. This result was improved by [34], which showed how to guarantee almost everywhere agreement in the presence of a linear fraction of faulty nodes. Both the work of [15, 34] crucially use expander graphs to show their results. We also refer to the related results of Berman and Garay on the butterfly network [10].

Byzantine Agreement. There has been significant work in designing peer-to-peer networks that are provably robust to a large number of Byzantine faults [16, 18, 28, 32]. These focus only on robustly enabling storage and retrieval of data items. The problem of achieving almost-everywhere agreement among nodes in P2P networks (modeled as an expander graph) is considered by King et al. in [22] in the context of the leader election problem; essentially, [22] is a sparse (expander) network implementation of the full information protocol of [21]. More specifically, [22] assumes that the adversary corrupts a constant fraction $b < 1/3$ of the processes that are under its control throughout the run of the algorithm. The protocol of [22] guarantees that with constant probability an uncorrupted leader will be elected and that a $1 - O(\frac{1}{\log n})$ fraction of the uncorrupted processes know this leader. We note that the algorithm of [22] does not work for dynamic networks. The work of [4] addresses the agreement problem in a dynamic P2P network under an adversarial churn model where the churn rates can be very large, up to linear in the number of nodes in the network. (It also crucially makes use of expander graphs.) However, their algorithms and techniques will not work under the presence of Byzantine nodes; even one malicious node can foil their algorithms.

Dynamic Networks. To address highly unpredictable network dynamics, strong adversarial dynamic models have been studied by [5, 12, 29, 24]; also see the recent survey of [11] and the references therein. The works of [24, 5, 12] study a model in which the communication graph can change completely from one round to another, with the only constraint being that the network is *connected at each round* ([24] and [12] also consider a stronger model where the constraint is that the network should be an expander or should have some specific expansion in each round). The model has also been applied to agreement problems in dynamic networks; various versions of coordinated consensus (where all nodes must agree) have been considered in [24].

We note that the model of [23] allows only edge changes from round to round while the nodes remain fixed. In this work, we consider a dynamic network model where both nodes and edges can change by a large amount (this model was introduced in [4]). Therefore the model we consider is more general than the model of [23], as it is additionally applicable to dynamic settings with node churn; however, we note our algorithms also apply to the edge-changing expander model of [23]. An important aspect of our algorithms is that they will work and terminate correctly even when the network keeps continually changing. We note that there has been

---

[3]This is a typical assumption in P2P and overlay networks.

considerable prior work in dynamic P2P networks (see [30] and the references therein) but these do not assume that the network keeps continually changing over time.

Fault-Tolerance. In most work on fault-tolerant agreement problems the adversary a priori commits to a fixed set of faulty nodes. In contrast, [13] considers an adversary that can corrupt the state of some (possibly changing) set of $O(\sqrt{n})$ nodes in every round. The median rule of [13] provides an elegant way to ensure that most nodes stabilize on a common output value within $O(\log n)$ rounds, assuming a complete communication graph. The median rule, however, only guarantees that this agreement lasts for some polynomial number of rounds, whereas we are able to retain agreement ad infinitum.

In the context of maintaining properties in P2P networks, Kuhn et al. consider in [25] that up to $O(\log n)$ nodes can crash or join per constant number of time steps. Despite this amount of churn, it is shown in [25] how to maintain a low peer degree and bounded network diameter in P2P systems by using the hypercube and pancake topologies. Scheideler and Schmid show in [33] how to maintain a distributed heap that allows join and leave operations and, in addition, is resistent to Sybil attacks. A robust distributed implementation of a distributed hash table (DHT) in a P2P network is given by [6], which can withstand two important kind of attacks: adaptive join-leave attacks and adaptive insert/lookup attacks by up to εn adverserial peers. The work of [31] gives a self-healing distributed algorithm to maintain an expander under adversarial insertions and deletions.

2. PRELIMINARIES

Dynamic Network Model. We consider a synchronous dynamic network with Byzantine nodes represented by a graph with a dynamically changing topology (both nodes and edges change) whose nodes execute a distributed algorithm and whose edges represent connectivity in the network. The computation is structured into synchronous rounds, i.e., we assume that nodes run at the same processing speed and any message that is sent by some node u to its neighbors in some round $r \geqslant 1$ will be received by the end of r. The dynamic network is represented by a sequence of graphs $\mathcal{G} = (G^0, G^1, \ldots)$ where each $G^r = (V^r, E^r)$. Nodes might be subjected to churn, which means that in each round, up to $\varepsilon C(n)$ nodes $(C(n) \in O(\sqrt{n}/\log^{k'} n)$, the constant k' will be fixed in the analysis) can be replaced by new nodes, for a fixed small constant $\varepsilon > 0$. We require that, for all $r \geqslant 0$, $|V^r \setminus V^{r+1}| = |V^{r+1} \setminus V^r| \leqslant \varepsilon C(n)$. Furthermore, we allow the edges to change arbitrarily in each round, but the underlying graph is a D-regular expander graph where D is a constant. (our algorithms can be extended to work with non-constant D as well; the regularity assumption can also be relaxed as long as the degrees are within a constant factor of each other).

Up to $B(n) \in O(\sqrt{n}/\log^k n)$ nodes (k is a constant that will be fixed in the analysis) can be *Byzantine* and deviate arbitrarily from the given protocol. We say that a node u is *correct* if u is not a Byzantine node and use V_{corr} to denote the set of correct nodes in the network. Byzantine nodes are "adaptive", in the sense that they know the entire states of all nodes at the beginning of every round and thus can take the current state of the computation into account when determining their next action. This setting is commonly referred to as the *full information model*. We consider the usual assumption that Byzantine nodes cannot fake their identity, i.e., if a Byzantine node w sends a message to nodes u and v, then both u and v can identify w as the same sender of the message.

Note that this does not stop Byzantine nodes from forwarding fake messages on behalf of other nodes as we do not assume any authentication service. We assume, without loss of generality, that the adversary only subjects correct nodes to churn, i.e., Byzantine nodes remain in the network permanently. (Our algorithms can be easily extended to the case, when Byzantine nodes are subject to churn as well).

We assume that if a node u enters the network at some later round r, then u knows the number of rounds that have passed since the start of the computation. Any information about the network at large is only learned through the messages that u receives. Furthermore, node u has no a priori knowledge about who its neighbors will be in the future.

In every round, the *churn adversary* determines which nodes are being replaced by new nodes, whereas the rewiring of the connection links between nodes is under the control of the *connectivity adversary*. We now describe the sequence of events that occur in each round $r \geqslant 1$. Firstly, the churn adversary observes the state of all nodes in V^{r-1} and then chooses up to $\varepsilon C(n)$ nodes to be replaced by correct nodes, yielding the set V^r.

Next, the connectivity adversary determines the new edge set E^r such that the graph $G^r = (V^r, E^r)$ is a D-regular non-bipartite expander graph. We distinguish two kinds of connectivity adversaries:

The topology-adaptive adversary can observe the entire state of the network in every round r (including all the random choices made until round $r - 1$), and then chooses the edges E^r of G^r.

The topology-oblivious adversary on the other hand, must choose E^r obliviously to the set of nodes in the network and their current state including random choices. In other words, the topology-oblivious adversary treats the nodes in the graph as black boxes when rewiring the edges.

At this point, we emphasize that Byzantine nodes and the churn adversary are always adaptive and are unaffected by whether the connectivity adversary is topology-adaptive or topology-oblivious. In particular, the adversary in our model is strictly more powerful than the *oblivious adversary* (e.g. [4]) that needs to determine the entire sequence of graphs in advance.

After the adversaries have made their moves, the algorithm operates on the graph $G^r = (V^r, E^r)$ in round r. Each correct node u becomes aware of its current neighbors in G^r, can perform local computation and is able to reliably exchange messages with its neighbors according to the edges in E^r.

Almost Everywhere (AE) Byzantine Agreement. We now define the AE BYZANTINE AGREEMENT problem. Each correct node $v \in V^0$ has an associated input value from $\mathcal{V} = \{0, 1\}$ and is equipped with a special decision variable DEC_u (initialized to a neutral state denoted by $\perp$). Nodes that are not initially in the network have an arbitrary input value. We say that a node u *decides on* VAL when u assigns $\text{VAL} \in \mathcal{V}$ to its DEC_u. Note that this decision is irrevocable, i.e., every node can decide at most once in a run of an algorithm. As long as $\text{DEC}_u = \perp$, we say that u is *undecided*. AE BYZANTINE AGREEMENT requires that a large fraction of the correct nodes come to a stable agreement on one of input values in $\mathcal{V}$. More precisely, *an algorithm solves* AE BYZANTINE AGREEMENT *in R rounds*, if it exhibits the following characteristics in every run.

Almost Everywhere Agreement: We say *the network has reached almost everywhere agreement by round R on the decision value* VAL* if at least $n - O(C(n) + B(n))$ correct nodes in V^R have decided on the same value $\text{VAL}^* \in \mathcal{V}$.

Validity: If all correct nodes start with $\text{VAL} \in \mathcal{V}$, then VAL is the only admissible decision value for all but $O(B(n) + C(n))$ nodes.

3. TOPOLOGY-OBLIVIOUS ADVERSARY

In this section we show how to use random walks to achieve almost-everywhere agreement in a highly dynamic network despite the presence of Byzantine nodes without using non-scalable techniques like flooding messages of size polynomial in n. Instead, our approach works in the CONGEST model of communication where all correct nodes are restricted to send $O(\log n)$ messages of $O(\log n)$ bits over each link in any round. Note that we do not assume *any* restriction on the message sizes sent by Byzantine nodes.

Our agreement algorithm consists of two separate parts: First, we show how to provide almost uniform sampling via random walks to a large set of nodes despite the presence of Byzantine nodes and churn (cf. Theorem 1). The main technical difficulty with this approach is to show that the Byzantine nodes and *adaptively* chosen churn nodes cannot bias the outcome of most random walks. We then use a majority rule to converge to an agreement. More specifically, each (correct) node attempts to update its output value by using the majority of two of its received samples (if possible) and its current output value. We show that within $O(\log^3 n)$ rounds almost all nodes will converge to a common output value and thus achieve almost everywhere agreement in $O(\text{polylog}(n))$ rounds (cf. Theorem 2).

3.1 Sampling in a Dynamic Network with Byzantine Nodes

We describe a distributed random walk implementation which proceeds by token passing. When a node u initiates a random walk it generates a token with its id, a counter initialized to the length of the walk, and some possibly attached information of $O(\log n)$ size. This token is then forwarded to a (current) neighbor of u chosen uniformly at random, which in turn forwards the token and so forth, whereas the counter is decreased by 1 in each step until it reaches 0, which marks the final destination of this walk. Since Byzantine nodes can deviate arbitrarily from this protocol, nodes only forward tokens that are *legit*, which means that they adhere to above described data format. In particular, a correct node ignores all received tokens whose counter violates the initial counter value according to the algorithm. Our agreement algorithm requires nodes to initiate $h \log n$ random walks simultaneously, for a fixed constant h. During the run of the algorithm, a node u might receive a large number of tokens (possibly generated by Byzantine nodes). Nevertheless, node u only forwards at most $h \log n$ tokens in each step in order to ensure (whp) passage of random walks that matter to us. More precisely, the random walks that arrive at a node u are placed in a FIFO buffer according to the order of their arrival. In every round, node u sends out at most $h \log n$ top elements in the buffer.

We say that a node is *affected* if it is connected to a Byzantine node at some point; otherwise we call it *unaffected*. If a random walk only ever visits unaffected correct nodes up to (but excluding) round t, we say that the walk is *good until round t* and becomes *bad from round $t + 1$ on*. A walk that always visits unaffected correct nodes is simply called *good*.

The next lemma motivates us to focus only on Byzantine nodes throughout the main analysis of this section, since any network with a sufficiently large number of Byzantine nodes can simulate the effect that churn has when running the token forwarding algorithm.

LEMMA 1. *Let $\mathcal{H} = (H^0, H^1, \dots)$ be a dynamic n-node expander network and suppose that at most $\varepsilon_1 \sqrt{n}/\log^k n$ are Byzan-*

tine and up to $\varepsilon_2 \sqrt{n}/\log^{k+3} n$ nodes are subjected to churn in any round. Let $\mathcal{G} = (G^0, G^1, \dots)$ be a dynamic n-node expander network where the topology is dynamic, but there is no churn, $V(G^0) = V(H^0)$, and suppose that at most $(\varepsilon_1 + \varepsilon_2)\sqrt{n}/\log^k n$ nodes are Byzantine in $\mathcal{G}$. For any run α of the token-forwarding algorithm on network $\mathcal{H}$, there is a run β on network $\mathcal{G}$ where all correct nodes receive the exact same sequence of tokens as in α during the first $\Theta(\log^3 n)$ rounds.

The next lemma shows that since our network is a regular expander, the random walk tokens that are injected by Byzantine nodes cannot (significantly) slow down the tokens of most correct nodes:

LEMMA 2. *Consider a dynamic network $\mathcal{G}$ of D-regular non-bipartite expander graphs determined by a topology-oblivious adversary and suppose that at most $\sqrt{n}/\log^k n$ nodes are Byzantine. If each correct node s starts $h \log n$ random walks of length $\tau = $ M $\log n$, for some sufficiently large constant $M > 0$, then, with high probability, there exists a set S of size $\geq n - O(\sqrt{n}/\log^{k-2} n)$, such that every token ρ that originated from a node $s \in S$ and only reached unaffected nodes, can complete τ steps in τ^2 rounds. Moreover, ρ remains no longer than τ rounds at the same node.*

PROOF. Since correct nodes ignore all non-legit tokens, we can restrict our attention to the case where Byzantine nodes only generate legit tokens. The token forwarding algorithm implies that, during a single round, a correct node forwards at most $h \log n$ tokens, no matter how many tokens it currently buffers. (Recall that we assume that a node can send up to $O(h \log n)$ tokens over each link per round.) Considering that all graphs in $\mathcal{G}$ are D-regular, the expected number of tokens received by any unaffected node is $\leq h \log n$. Over τ^2 rounds, each Byzantine node can be connected to at most $D \log^2 n$ distinct correct nodes (which become affected). Hence, at least $n - (D+1)\sqrt{n}/\log^{k-2} n$ nodes remain unaffected until round τ^2 and initially generate $h \log n$ tokens each; let S denote this set. By applying a standard Chernoff bound, it follows that with probability $\geq 1 - n^{-4}$, each node in S receives at most $2h \log n$ tokens in a round r. Taking a union bound over τ^2 rounds and all unaffected nodes, the same is true at every node in S during rounds $[1, \tau^2]$ with probability $\geq 1 - n^{-2}$.

According to our token forwarding algorithm, tokens are forwarded using a FIFO policy. Moreover, each node forwards up to $h \log n$ tokens per round and thus it follows that any token arriving at a node u in round i, can be delayed for at most i additional rounds. It follows that, after $\tau^2 \in O(\log^2 n)$ rounds, all good tokens have taken τ steps with high probability. $\square$

Now that Lemma 2 ensures that most random walk tokens will take sufficiently many steps within some polylogarithmic number of rounds, we are ready to present our main technical result that characterizes random walk sampling in a dynamic byzantine network: it shows that there is a large set of nodes that have access to well-mixed random walk tokens. We assume that correct nodes generate new tokens every τ^2 rounds.

THEOREM 1 (DYNAMIC SAMPLING). *Let $T = \tau^2$ and consider a dynamic n-node expander network $\mathcal{G}$ under a topology-oblivious adversary, and suppose that at most $O(\sqrt{n}/\log^k n)$ nodes are Byzantine. There exists a set of nodes CORE of size $\geq n - O(\sqrt{n}/\log^{k-4} n)$ such that, in every interval $[iT, (i+1)T]$ for $0 \leq i \leq \Theta(\log n)$, $\Theta(\log n)$ random walk tokens terminate at all except at most $O(\sqrt{n}/\log^{k-6} n)$ nodes in CORE, and each token has probability in $[\frac{1}{n} - \frac{1}{n^3}, \frac{1}{n} + \frac{1}{n^3}]$ to have originated at any particular node in CORE.*

PROOF SKETCH. We first, we describe the set CORE and bound its size: Let B' denote the set of Byzantine nodes together with the set of nodes that are affected at some point during $[1, T \log n]$ rounds. Since a Byzantine node can be connected to at most $O(\log^3 n)$ distinct nodes during $[1, T \log n]$, it follows therefore that $|B'| \in O(\sqrt{n}/\log^{k-3} n)$. We know from [7] that, upon removing set B' from an n-node network with constant expansion, there is a subgraph of size $n - O(|B'|)$ in the remainder graph that itself nevertheless has constant expansion. We apply this result to every round $r \in [1, T \log^2 n]$ and denote the resulting expander subgraph by H^r. Let S^{iT} be the set of nodes, such that good tokens originating from S in round iT can complete τ steps in T rounds. By virtue of Lemma 2, we know that S^{iT} has size $\geqslant n - O(\sqrt{n}/\log^{k-2} n)$, and, by taking a union bound, the set $S = \bigcap_{i=1}^{\Theta(\log n)} S^{iT}$ has size $\geqslant n - O(\sqrt{n}/\log^{k-3} n)$. We define CORE $= S \cap \bigcap_{r=1}^{T \log n} V(H^r)$ and observe that we get $|\text{CORE}| \geqslant n - O(\sqrt{n}/\log^{k-4} n)$ with high probability.

Next, we bound the number of tokens that are received by nodes in CORE in any particular interval $[iT, (i+1)T]$: Recall that nodes in CORE are never adjacent to Byzantine nodes. Thus, any token that is sent across a link of the cut $(\text{CORE}, V \setminus \text{CORE})$ was sent by a correct node. From Lemma 2, we know that (w.h.p.) at most $O(\log^2 n)$ tokens are sent across any edge during $[iT, (i+1)T]$. The size of the cut $(V, V \setminus \text{CORE})$ in any round r is bounded by $D(n - |\text{CORE}|)$ and thus at most $O(\sqrt{n}/\log^{k-6} n)$ walks originating from outside CORE reach nodes in CORE and vice versa. Recalling that the number of generated tokens inside CORE in round iT is $|\text{CORE}| h \log n$, at least $n \log n - O(\sqrt{n}/\log^{k-6} n)$ walks remain among nodes in CORE. From Lemma 2 we know that the expected number of tokens that terminate at any node $u \in \text{CORE} \subset S^{iT}$ is $h \log n$. Applying a standard Chernoff bound it follows that at most $2h \log n$ tokens terminate at u with high probability. This shows that each of at least $n - \sqrt{n}/\log^{k-6} n$ nodes in CORE are the final destination of $\Theta(\log n)$ tokens originating from within CORE by round $(i+1)T$.

Finally, we show that the origins of these tokens that terminate among nodes in CORE are almost uniformly distributed on CORE: For the sake of our analysis, we consider a (virtual) dynamic network $\bar{\mathcal{G}} = (\bar{G}^0, \bar{G}^1, \dots)$ that consists of the same correct nodes as $\mathcal{G}$, with the difference that we replace Byzantine nodes by correct nodes and assume that $E(\bar{G}^r) = E(G^r)$, for all rounds r. In contrast to the actual network $\mathcal{G}$, we assume that edges in the virtual network $\bar{\mathcal{G}}$ have infinite bandwidth. We use the notation $\bar{v}_j$ to refer to the node in $\bar{\mathcal{G}}$ that corresponds to $v_j \in \mathcal{G}$. Recall that $\bar{\mathcal{G}}$ is a sequence of D-regular expander networks determined by the topology-*oblivious* adversary. Consider the *reversed dynamic network* given by reversing the order of the graphs of $\bar{\mathcal{G}}$, i.e., $(\bar{G}^r, \bar{G}^{r-1}, \dots, \bar{G}^0)$. Due to D-regularity, the probability of a random walk token to move from some node $\bar{v}$ to $\bar{u}$, is the same as the probability as a token moving from $\bar{u}$ to $\bar{v}$ in a random walk on this reversed dynamic network. It follows from [12] that, after taking τ steps, a random walk originates from any particular node in $\bar{\mathcal{G}}$ with probability in $[\frac{1}{n} - \frac{1}{n^3}, \frac{1}{n} + \frac{1}{n^3}]$. Note that the above remains true even if we delay the token at every visiting node for some number of rounds, as long as the token makes τ steps in total.

Returning to our network $\mathcal{G}$, consider a token ρ (generated in round iT) and suppose that ρ terminated at some node v_τ by round $(i+1)T$. We define $(v_\tau, \dots, v_0)$ to be the sequence of tokens visisted by ρ (in reverse), where $v_i \in \text{CORE}$. Let $(r_\tau, \dots, r_0)$ denote the sequence of rounds such that ρ is forwarded from v_j to v_{j+1} in round r_j, for $0 \leqslant j \leqslant \tau$. In the remainder of the proof, we show that v_0 is almost uniformly distributed among the nodes in CORE. Consider a token $\bar{\rho}$ that terminated at node $\bar{v}_\tau$ in the virtual

network $\bar{\mathcal{G}}$, and suppose that the random sources of $\bar{v}_j \in \bar{\mathcal{G}}$ and $v_j \in \mathcal{G}$ are coupled, for $0 \leqslant j \leqslant \tau$. In round iT, node $\bar{v}_0$ holds $\bar{\rho}$ and, due to the coupling of the random sources, $\bar{v}_0$ forwards $\bar{\rho}$ to the neighbor $\bar{v}_1$ (corresponding to v_1) in round r_0. Node $\bar{v}_1$ in turn delays $\bar{\rho}$ until round r_1 and then forwards $\bar{\rho}$ to neighbor $\bar{v}_2$ and so forth. Hence, $\bar{\rho}$ takes the exact same sequence of steps in $\bar{\mathcal{G}}$ as it does in $\mathcal{G}$. By the above property of reversability of random walks on $\bar{\mathcal{G}}$, it follows that $\bar{\rho}$ is almost uniformly distributed among CORE, and thus the probability of ρ having originated from any particular node in CORE is in $[\frac{1}{n} - \frac{1}{n^3}, \frac{1}{n} + \frac{1}{n^3}]$. □

3.2 AE Byzantine Agreement Algorithm

Theorem 1, shows the existence (w.h.p.) of a large set of correct nodes CORE where all but $O(\sqrt{n}/\log^{k-6})$ nodes can sample almost uniformly among this set. As we will see in our analysis, our agreement algorithm takes $T_1 = O(\log^3 n)$ rounds to reach agreement among a large subset of CORE with high probability.

Our algorithm proceeds in phases that are spaced $T = \tau^2 \in O(\log^2 n)$ rounds apart, during which each correct node u updates its *output value* EST_u. Initially, EST_u is initialized to the input value assigned by the adversary. At the beginning of a phase each node generates $h \log n$ random walk tokens and attaches its current value of EST_u to the token. We call the round ending a phase i the *checkpoint* i; note that the first checkpoint occurs in round T. In each checkpoint, every correct node u picks 2 arbitrary samples y_1 and y_2 among all samples that it received in this round (if possible) and sets EST_u to the majority value of DEC_u, y_1, and y_2.

Let $\mathbf{0}^r$ (resp. $\mathbf{1}^r$) denote the set of nodes in CORE that have an output value of 0 (resp. 1) at the end of checkpoint round r. Define the *imbalance*

$$\Delta^r \triangleq (\max(|\mathbf{0}^r|, |\mathbf{1}^r|) - \min(|\mathbf{0}^r|, |\mathbf{1}^r|))/2.$$

We omit the superscript r if it is clear from the context. In the proof of the following lemma, we use the Lyapunov Condition and the central limit theorem, to show that our agreement algorithm has a constant probability of swaying the decision one way.

LEMMA 3. *Consider any checkpoint r, and let $c > 0$ be any constant. For any $\Delta^r \geqslant 0$ it holds that with constant probability $\Delta^{r+1} \geqslant c\sqrt{n}$.*

THEOREM 2. *Consider a dynamic n-node expander network $\mathcal{G}$ under a topology-oblivious adversary. Suppose furthermore that at most $O(\sqrt{n}/\log^k n)$ are Byzantine and up to $O(\sqrt{n}/\log^{k+3} n)$ nodes are subjected to churn in any round. There is an algorithm that achieves AE BYZANTINE AGREEMENT in $O(\log^3 n)$ rounds with high probability.*

PROOF SKETCH. By Lemma 1, we can focus on the case where there is no churn but $O(\sqrt{n}/\log^k n)$ Byzantine nodes. If the initial imbalance is small, then we can apply Lemma 3 to show that with constant probability we get an imbalance of $\Omega(\sqrt{n})$. In the full paper [3], we show that this is sufficient to further increase this imbalance over the next $O(\log n)$ checkpoints. In other words, after some $T_d \in O(\log^3 n)$ rounds, all but $O(\sqrt{n}/\log^{k-6} n)$ nodes in CORE are using a common output value with high probability.

Thus we instruct every node to decide in round T_d on its current output, which shows almost everywhere agreement. □

4. TOPOLOGY-ADAPTIVE ADVERSARY

Recall that the topology-adaptive connectivity adversary can observe the entire state of the network in every round r (including all the random choices made until round $r - 1$), and then chooses the edges E^r of G^r. To counter this rather powerful adversary, we assume that a node u can communicate directly with any node v using a *direct link* if u knows the id of v[4]. Initially however, a correct node has only local knowledge and does not know any information about the network at large. Thus it can communicate only with its current neighbors. We assume that the stable network size n is common knowledge among the nodes in the network.

4.1 Dynamic Distance and Influence Set

We consider the notions of dynamic distance and influence sets that are related to similar notions introduced in [4]. To prevail against the powerful topology-adaptive adversary we use message flooding to disseminate and gather information. We begin with some fundamental definitions.

Informally, the dynamic distance from node u to node v is the number of rounds required for a message at u to reach v without passing through a Byzantine node. We now formally define the notion of *dynamic distance* of a node v from u starting at round r, denoted by $\mathrm{DD}_r(u \to v)$. When the subscript r is omitted, we may assume that $r = 1$. Suppose that node u joins the network in round r_u and, from round $\max(r_u, r)$ onward, u initiates a message m for flooding whose terminating condition is: $\langle$ HAS REACHED $v \rangle$. If u is churned out before r, then $\mathrm{DD}_r(u \to v)$ is undefined. We define $\mathrm{DD}_r(u \to v) = \Delta r$ if the first of those flooded messages reaches v in round $r + \Delta r$ without passing through any Byzantine node. Note that this definition allows $\mathrm{DD}_r(u \to v)$ to be infinite under two scenarios. Firstly, node v may be churned out before any copy of m reaches v. Secondly, at each round, v can be shielded by churn nodes or Byzantine nodes that absorb or corrupt the flooded messages.

The *influence set* of a node u after R rounds starting at round r is defined as $\mathrm{INFLUENCE}_r(u, R) \triangleq \{v \in V_{\mathrm{corr}}^{r+R} : \mathrm{DD}_r(u \to v) \leqslant R\}$, where V_{corr}^{r+R} denotes the set of correct nodes in round $r + R$. Note that we require $\mathrm{INFLUENCE}_r(u, R)$ to be a subset of V^{r+R}. Intuitively, we want the influence set of u (in this dynamic setting) to capture the correct nodes *currently* in the network that were influenced by u. Note however that the influence set of a node u is meaningful even after u is churned out. When considering only a single node u, the adversary can easily prevent the influence set of this node from ever reaching any significant size by simply shielding u with Byzantine nodes or subjecting the neighbors of u to churn in every round. This motivates us to define the influence set of any set of nodes $U \subseteq V_{\mathrm{corr}}^r$ as

$$\mathrm{INFLUENCE}_r(U, R) \triangleq \cup_{u \in U} \mathrm{INFLUENCE}_r(u, R).$$

We say that a node $u \in V_{\mathrm{corr}}^r$ is *suppressed for* R rounds if $|\mathrm{INFLUENCE}_r(u, R)| < n - \beta\sqrt{n}$ where $\beta > \varepsilon$ is a sufficiently large constant depending on the expansion of $\mathcal{G}$ (cf. [4]). Otherwise we say that u is *unsuppressed*. With this notion in mind, we define the *influence time* $T_{\mathrm{infl}}(n)$ to denote the minimal number of rounds, such that, for any round r, there exists a set $V^* \subseteq V_{\mathrm{corr}}^r$ of at least $n - \beta\sqrt{n}$ unsuppressed nodes such that $|\mathrm{INFLUENCE}_r(V^*, T_{\mathrm{infl}}(n))| > n - \beta\sqrt{n}$. Note that the presence of a Byzantine node v has the same effect regarding influence sets of nodes in V_{corr} as subjecting a (correct) node v to churn in *every* round. Thus the following result regarding the influence time, which is shown in Lemma 3.4 in [4] for the case where the adversary can only subject nodes to churn, holds analogously in the case where we have Byzantine nodes:

---

[4]This is a typical assumption in the context of P2P networks, where a node can establish communication with another node if it knows the other node's IP address.

LEMMA 4. *Suppose that up to $\varepsilon\sqrt{n}/\log^2 n$ nodes can be subjected to churn in any round and there are at most $\varepsilon\sqrt{n}$ Byzantine nodes controlled by an adaptive adversary. Then the influence time $T_{\mathrm{infl}}(n)$ is $O(\log^2 n)$.*

4.2 Support Estimation

A crucial technique that is used by our agreement algorithm is measuring the "support" of a specific input value at any specific point in time. In more detail, suppose that we have $\mathcal{R}$ nodes colored red in V^0. $\mathcal{R}$ is also called the *support* of red nodes. We want the nodes in the network to estimate $\mathcal{R}$ under a topology-adaptive adversary, which chooses $\mathcal{R}$ nodes in V^0 that are colored red. The support estimation problem can be solved efficiently in the absence of Byzantine nodes if the churn itself is chosen obliviously (cf. [4]). In the presence of Byzantine nodes and in absence of any authentication service, however, we essentially need to resort to full information exchange to obtain an accurate estimate.

We defer the full description of our support estimation procedure and its analysis to the full paper [3]. In the proof of Theorem 3, we leverage the fact that a node can *directly* communicate with any other node that is known to it. This is necessary to ensure that Byzantine nodes cannot bias the outcome of the support estimation by generating fake counts on behalf of non-existing nodes.

THEOREM 3. *There is a support estimation algorithm that terminates in $O(T_{\mathrm{infl}}(n))$ rounds and at least $n - \beta\sqrt{n}$ nodes reach an accurate estimate of $\mathcal{R}$ that is bounded by $\delta \in O(\sqrt{n})$. Furthermore, these nodes are aware that their estimate is accurate, while the remaining nodes are aware that their estimate is inaccurate.*

4.3 AE Byzantine Agreement

Our agreement algorithm is based on a variant of the "stable agreement" algorithm of [4] that we have extended to handle Byzantine nodes. We now present an overview of the algorithm and defer the details and its pseudo code to the full paper [3]. Initially, every node u sets its current value (on which it eventually decides) to the input value assigned by the adversary. Computation takes place in so called *checkpoint* rounds, which are spaced $\Theta(\log^2 n)$ rounds apart. (Note that we assume access to a synchronous clock, thus every node knows when the checkpoints take place.) In each checkpoint, every correct node initiates support estimation to determine the number of nodes that currently have a value of 0 (resp. 1), the outcome of which will be available in the next checkpoint. According to Theorem 3, the estimate will be accurate within an error range of $O(\sqrt{n})$ for all but $O(\sqrt{n})$ nodes. If the support estimation reveals the number of 0s and 1s to be in a so called "middle region", i.e., within a range of $O(\sqrt{n})$ of $n/2$, then nodes update their current value with the outcome of an unbiased coin flip. Note that this cannot violate validity, since Theorem 3 guarantees that this only happens if both input values (0 and 1) were present in the network initially. We show that the coin flipping sways the current proportion of input values by $c\sqrt{n}$ one way or the other, with constant probability. For a sufficiently large constant c, this "jump" out of the middle region is large enough to guarantee that most nodes will accurately estimate support of the dominating value to be above the middle region in all future checkpoints. Once this large imbalance is reached, nodes simply reinforce the support estimation by deterministically changing their output value to the outcome of the support estimation. It follows that after $O(\log n)$ checkpoints, i.e., $O(\log^3 n)$ rounds, a sufficiently large imbalance is achieved with high probability and all but $O(\sqrt{n})$ nodes will agree on the dominating value.

THEOREM 4. *There exists an algorithm that achieves* AE BYZANTINE AGREEMENT *in* $O(\log^3 n)$ *rounds (with high probability) against a topology-adaptive adversary that controls up to* $O(\sqrt{n})$ *Byzantine nodes and can subject* $O(\frac{\sqrt{n}}{\log^2 n})$ *nodes to churn per round.*

5. A TIGHT LOWER BOUND

Our primary interest in this paper is to understand what can and cannot be done in polylog n rounds. With this in mind we prove an $\Omega(\sqrt{n})$ lower bound on the expected termination time of any randomized algorithm for agreement even when the only adversary's behavior is limited to churning $\tilde{O}(\sqrt{n})$ nodes per round. In particular, we stress that this lower bound does not require the adversary to exploit the power of byzantine nodes. Moreover, this lower bound holds even when the topology is fixed, which implies that our algorithms for both topology-oblivious and topology-adaptive models are tight up to polylogarithmic factors.

Let $\mathcal{I}$ be the set of all legal strategies. Thus, each $I \in \mathcal{I}$ consists of a sequence of graphs $(G^0, G^1, \ldots,)$ with each vertex in G^0 assigned a bit value and the node churn bounded from above by at most $8\sqrt{n \log n} + 1$. We assume that the topology remains fixed but to keep with the expander graph assumption made in the rest of the paper, we assume that the topology of the graph is a D-regular non-bipartite expander. The adversary initially commits to G^0 along with input bits for each $v \in V^0$. Each round $r \geq 1$ starts with G^{r-1}. The adaptive adversary knows the state of each $v \in V^{r-1}$ at the start of round r and can observe all the the random numbers that are generated. Thus, it is aware of all the computations performed in v (and therefore the messages it intends to send) in round r. Prior to any communication, the adaptive adversary churns out up to $8\sqrt{n \log n} + 1$ nodes and replaces them with in an equal number of new nodes after which the network graph becomes $G^r = (V^r, E^r)$. Nodes now communicate with their neighbors in G^r.

For the purpose of proving the lower bound on the running time of our algorithm, we focus on the *clean* version of the almost everywhere agreement problem in which we require all nodes that decide to be in agreement with each other. Thus, while there can be $O(C(n))$ undecided nodes, no node is allowed to decide wrongly. We subsequently show how this lower bound on the clean version of the almost everywhere agreement problem can be extended to the *unclean* version of the problem where some of the $O(C(n))$ nodes that are not in agreement with the rest of the nodes may decide on the wrong value.

We define the state of the network at any time as the graph of the nodes in the network at that time along with the state of each node. Consider a dynamic network that has reached a state S at the start of a round r. At this point an adversarial strategy is a sequence of graphs $(G^r, G^{r+1}, \ldots)$. We define $\mathcal{I}(S)$ to be the set of adversarial strategies given that the network has reached a particular state S. Considering the space of future random bits, for each $I \in \mathcal{I}(S)$, we can define $\Pr(I) \triangleq \Pr[\text{the network agrees on 1 under strategy I}]$. In particular, we will be interested in the strategies that maximize or minimize the probability of agreeing on 1, hence, we define $\max(S) = \max_{I \in \mathcal{I}(S)} \Pr(I)$; we define $\min(S)$ similarly.

Suppose we are at the start of round r and the network is in state S. We classify S based on the description in Table 1. Notice that the rows in Table 1 exhaustively classify S.

In addition to the classification of states defined in Table 1, we also define two phases that the network can enter. We say that the network is under a *mildly 1-valent* phase in round r if (i) at some round $k < r$, the adversary started implementing a strategy ψ such

Table 1: Classification of states under an algorithm $\mathcal{A}$.

Classification of S	$\min(S)$	$\max(S)$
null valent	$\geq 1/\sqrt{n} - r/n$	$\leq 1 - 1/\sqrt{n} + r/n$
0-valent	$< 1/\sqrt{n} - r/n$	$\leq 1 - 1/\sqrt{n} + r/n$
1-valent	$\geq 1/\sqrt{n} - r/n$	$> 1 - 1/\sqrt{n} + r/n$
bivalent	$< 1/\sqrt{n} - r/n$	$> 1 - 1\sqrt{n} + r/n$

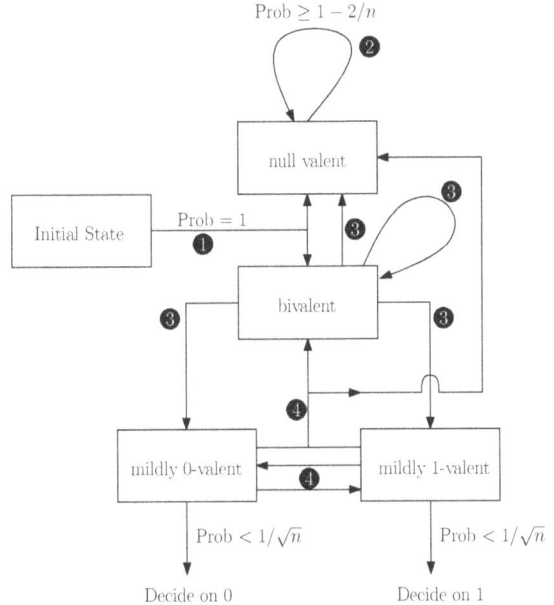

Figure 1: Proof structure.

that $\Pr(\psi) \leq 1/\sqrt{n}$, (ii) the adversary continued to implement ψ until round r and (iii) the network has remained 1-valent. We can of course define a *mildly 0-valent* phase of the network in a similar manner.

The following lemma establishes the basis for our inductive argument. It is marked ❶ in Figure 1. Its proof uses the standard technique of enumerating initial states and showing how two slightly different initial states that have different valencies can, with small amount of churn, lead to the same subsequent state.

LEMMA 5. *Given an algorithm $\mathcal{A}$ that solves consensus, there exists an initial state that is either null valent or bivalent.*

With Lemma 5 ensuring a non univalent starting point, we now begin the inductive step our argument. The next lemma shows that if the network enters a null valent state, then with high probability, it remains null valent. It is marked ❷ in Figure 1. While we defer the proof of the following lemma to the full version of the paper [3], we remark that the proof of the following lemma uses the notion of coin flipping games, which have been employed before in establishing lower bounds on agreement protocols in networks with adaptive faults (see [1, 8]).

LEMMA 6. *Let S be a null valent state at the start of round r under an algorithm $\mathcal{A}$ that solves consensus. There is an adaptive adversarial strategy with churn limited to $8\sqrt{n \log n}$ that will ensure that, with probability $1 - 2/n$, the network will move to another null valent state at the start of round $r + 1$.*

In the following lemma, we show that the adversary can ensure that the only univalent states that the network enters are the mildly univalent states. The transitions mentioned in the following Lemma 7 are marked ❸ in Figure 1.

81

LEMMA 7. *Let S be a bivalent state at the start of round r under an algorithm $\mathcal{A}$ that solves consensus. There is an adaptive adversarial strategy with churn limited to $8\sqrt{n\log n}$ that will ensure that at the end or round r, the network will be in one of the following states: (i) null valent, (ii) bivalent, (iii) mildly 1-valent, or (iv) mildly 0-valent.*

PROOF. Recall that the adaptive adversary can observe the state of each node. In particular, the adaptive adversary observes all the coin tosses made by each of the nodes in the network. Being computationally unbounded, the adversary can simulate various combinations of churn that respect the churn limit of $8\sqrt{n\log n}$. The adversary chooses a combination of churn that leads to either a null valent or bivalent state if it exists. Thus, we can limit our concern to the case where all combinations of churn lead to univalent states at the end of round r. We assume without loss of generality that not churning out any node moves the network to a 1-valent state. We then focus on the adversarial strategy $\min(S)$. If under this strategy, the network becomes 1-valent at the end of round r, then, we continue under $\min(S)$. Otherwise, the network state will become 0-valent at the end of round r under $\min(S)$. We show that this is not possible by showing that a non-univalent state can be attained as follows. Let C be the set of nodes churned out at round r according to $\min(S)$. We pick an arbitrary permutation $(c_1, c_2, \ldots)$ of C and consider what happens. Given our assumption that the state is 1-valent at the end of round r when no node is churned out, we can find an i such that churning out $C_1 = (c_1, c_2, \ldots, c_i)$ keeps the network 1-valent at the end of round r, but churning out $C_2 = (c_1, c_2, \ldots, c_i, c_{i+1})$ moves the network to a 0-valent state at the end of round r. However, if we churn out c_{i+1} at the start of round $r + 1$, does the network remain 0-valent? The problem is that the network cannot distinguish between whether it reached the state via churning out C_1 or C_2. Thus, the state achieved by churning out C_1 (or C_2) cannot be univalent. □

LEMMA 8. *Consider a dynamic network that is currently in a mildly 1-valent (resp., 0-valent) state at the start of some round r. An adaptive adversary can ensure that at the start of round $r+1$ the network either (i) remains mildly 1-valent (resp., mildly 0-valent), (ii) becomes mildly 0-valent (reps., mildly 1-valent), or (iii) non-univalent. (The transitions mentioned in this lemma are marked ❹ in Figure 1.)*

PROOF. If there is a strategy for the adversary to move the network to a non-univalent state, it will do so. So for this proof we focus on the case where there is no such non-univalent strategy.

By the definition of mildly 1-valent state, we know that at some round $k < r$, the adversary chose a strategy ψ such $\Pr(\psi) \leq 1/\sqrt{(n)}$ at the time ψ was chosen. Furthermore, the adversary has stuck with ψ since that round k. Thus, if the adversary continues with ψ, at the start of round $r + 1$, the network can either remain mildly 1-valent or become 0-valent. We need to show that if it were to become 0-valent, the adaptive adversary has another strategy to move the network to a mildly 0-valent state. Since the network was mildly 1-valent at the start of round r, there was a strategy ϕ at the start of round r such that $\Pr(\phi) \geq 1 - 1/\sqrt{n}$. After the adversary observes the coin tosses in round r, it checks to see if the network has entered a 0-valent state. If yes, it continues with ϕ and we can observe that we have entered a mildly 0-valent state. Can the network enters a 1-valent state by applying ϕ? Then, as in the proof of Lemma 7, we can check the state by stopping the nodes one-by-one in ϕ. There will be a switch from 0-valency to 1-valency which can be used to show that we can reach a bivalent state, which contradicts our earlier assumption that the adversary cannot move the

network to a non-univalent state. Thus, we continue to be mildly univalent, except, now we are mildly 0-valent. □

The upshot of Lemma 8 is that when the network enters a mildly 1-valent phase, there is only a probability of at most $1/\sqrt{n}$ that it will stay in that phase and decide on a 1. In other words, with probability at least $1 - 1/\sqrt{n}$, the network will move to becoming mildly 0-valent (or non-univalent, which is only better from the adversarial point of view). Thus, we can conclude that the expected number of steps for any algorithm to achieve almost everywhere agreement in the clean sense is at least $\sqrt{n}$. Furthermore, it is quite easy to apply Theorem 1 to adapt an algorithm for the unclean version of almost everywhere agreement to get an algorithm for the clean version. This adaptation incurs a multiplicative factor overhead in running time that is only polylogarithmic in n. Thus we get

THEOREM 5. *The expected number of steps for any algorithm to achieve almost everywhere agreement (either in the clean sense or the unclean sense) in a dynamic network that is controlled by an adaptive adversary that can churn at most $8\sqrt{n\log n} + 1$ nodes per round is at least $\sqrt{n}$.*

6. CONCLUSION

We presented distributed algorithms for Byzantine agreement problem in dynamic networks with churn. Our algorithms are essentially optimal with respect to the amount of churn and Byzantine nodes in this setting. As a next step, it might be worthwhile to investigate whether our techniques can serve as useful building blocks for tackling other important tasks like aggregation or leader election in highly dynamic networks.

7. REFERENCES

[1] James Aspnes. Lower bounds for distributed coin-flipping and randomized consensus. In *STOC '97*, p. 559–568, New York, NY, USA, 1997. ACM.

[2] Hagit Attiya and Jennifer Welch. *Distributed Computing: Fundamentals, Simulations and Advanced Topics (2nd edition)*. John Wiley Interscience, March 2004.

[3] John Augustine, Gopal Pandurangan, and Peter Robinson. Fast Byzantine Agreement in Dynamic Networks. (to appear in arXiv), 2013.

[4] John Augustine, Gopal Pandurangan, Peter Robinson, and Eli Upfal. Towards robust and efficient computation in dynamic peer-to-peer networks. In *ACM-SIAM*, SODA 2012, p. 551–569. SIAM.

[5] Chen Avin, Michal Koucký, and Zvi Lotker. How to explore a fast-changing world (cover time of a simple random walk on evolving graphs). In *ICALP*, p. 121–132, 2008.

[6] Baruch Awerbuch and Christian Scheideler. Towards a scalable and robust dht. *Theory Comput. Syst.*, 45(2):234–260, 2009.

[7] Amitabha Bagchi, Ankur Bhargava, Amitabh Chaudhary, David Eppstein, and Christian Scheideler. The effect of faults on network expansion. *Theory Comput. Syst.*, 39(6):903–928, 2006.

[8] Ziv Bar-Joseph and Michael Ben-Or. A tight lower bound for randomized synchronous consensus. In *PODC '98*, p. 193–199, New York, NY, USA, 1998. ACM.

[9] M. Ben-Or and N. Linial. Collective coin flipping. In Silvio Micali, editor, *Advances in Computing Research 5: Randomness and Computation*, volume 5, p. 91–115. JAI Press, 1989.

[10] Piotr Berman and Juan A. Garay. Fast consensus in networks of bounded degree. *Distributed Computing*, 7(2):67–73, 1993.

[11] Arnaud Casteigts, Paola Flocchini, Walter Quattrociocchi, and Nicola Santoro. Time-varying graphs and dynamic networks. *CoRR*, abs/1012.0009, 2010. Short version in ADHOC-NOW 2011.

[12] A. Das Sarma, A. Molla, and G. Pandurangan. Fast distributed computation in dynamic networks via random walks. In *DISC*, 2012.

[13] Benjamin Doerr, Leslie Ann Goldberg, Lorenz Minder, Thomas Sauerwald, and Christian Scheideler. Stabilizing consensus with the power of two choices. In *SPAA*, p. 149–158, 2011.

[14] Danny Dolev and H. Raymond Strong. Authenticated algorithms for byzantine agreement. *SIAM J. Comput.*, 12(4):656–666, 1983.

[15] Cynthia Dwork, David Peleg, Nicholas Pippenger, and Eli Upfal. Fault tolerance in networks of bounded degree. *SIAM J. Comput.*, 17(5):975–988, 1988.

[16] Amos Fiat and Jared Saia. Censorship resistant peer-to-peer content addressable networks. In *SODA*, p. 94–103, 2002.

[17] Michael J. Fischer and Nancy A. Lynch. A lower bound for the time to assure interactive consistency. *Inf. Process. Lett.*, 14(4):183–186, 1982.

[18] Kirsten Hildrum and John Kubiatowicz. Asymptotically efficient approaches to fault-tolerance in peer-to-peer networks. In *DISC*, volume 2848 of *LNCS*, p. 321–336. Springer, 2003.

[19] Bruce M. Kapron, David Kempe, Valerie King, Jared Saia, and Vishal Sanwalani. Fast asynchronous byzantine agreement and leader election with full information. *ACM Transactions on Algorithms*, 6(4), 2010.

[20] Valerie King and Jared Saia. Breaking the $O(n^2)$ bit barrier: scalable Byzantine agreement with an adaptive adversary. In *PODC*, p. 420–429, 2010.

[21] Valerie King, Jared Saia, Vishal Sanwalani, and Erik Vee. Scalable leader election. In *SODA*, p. 990–999, 2006.

[22] Valerie King, Jared Saia, Vishal Sanwalani, and Erik Vee. Towards secure and scalable computation in peer-to-peer networks. In *FOCS*, p. 87–98, 2006.

[23] Fabian Kuhn, Nancy Lynch, and Rotem Oshman. Distributed computation in dynamic networks. In *ACM STOC*, p. 513–522, 2010.

[24] Fabian Kuhn, Rotem Oshman, and Yoram Moses. Coordinated consensus in dynamic networks. In *PODC*, p. 1–10, 2011.

[25] Fabian Kuhn, Stefan Schmid, and Roger Wattenhofer. Towards worst-case churn resistant peer-to-peer systems. *Distributed Computing*, 22(4):249–267, 2010.

[26] C. Law and K.-Y. Siu. Distributed construction of random expander networks. In *INFOCOM 2003*, volume 3, p. 2133 – 2143 vol.3, march-3 april 2003.

[27] Nancy Lynch. *Distributed Algorithms*. Morgan Kaufman Publishers, Inc., San Francisco, USA, 1996.

[28] Moni Naor and Udi Wieder. A simple fault tolerant distributed hash table. In *IPTPS*, p. 88–97, 2003.

[29] Regina O'Dell and Roger Wattenhofer. Information dissemination in highly dynamic graphs. In *DIALM-POMC*, p. 104–110, 2005.

[30] Gopal Pandurangan, Prabhakar Raghavan, and Eli Upfal. Building low-diameter p2p networks. In *FOCS*, p. 492–499, 2001.

[31] Gopal Pandurangan, Peter Robinson, and Amitabh Trehan. DEX: Self healing Expanders. Manuscript, 2013.

[32] Christian Scheideler. How to spread adversarial nodes?: rotate! In *STOC*, p. 704–713, 2005.

[33] Christian Scheideler and Stefan Schmid. A distributed and oblivious heap. In *Automata, Languages and Programming*, volume 5556 of *LNCS*, p. 571–582. Springer, 2009.

[34] Eli Upfal. Tolerating a linear number of faults in networks of bounded degree. *Inf. Comput.*, 115(2):312–320, 1994.

Synchronous Byzantine Agreement
with Nearly a Cubic Number of Communication Bits

Dariusz R. Kowalski[*]
Department of Computer Science
University of Liverpool
Liverpool L69 3BX, UK
D.Kowalski@liverpool.ac.uk

Achour Mostéfaoui[†]
LINA/Dept. d'Informatique
University of Nantes
France
achour.mostefaoui@univ-nantes.fr

ABSTRACT

This paper studies the problem of Byzantine consensus in a synchronous message-passing system of n processes. The first deterministic algorithm, and also the simplest in its principles, was the Exponential Information Gathering protocol (EIG) proposed by Pease, Shostak and Lamport in [19]. The algorithm requires processes to send exponentially long messages. Many follow-up works reduced the cost of the algorithm. However, they had to either lower the maximum number of faulty processes t from the optimal range $t < n/3$ to some smaller range of t [4, 11, 18], or increase the maximum worst-case number of rounds needed for termination (the lower bound being $t + 1$) [3, 9, 20].

Garay and Moses [13] were the first and only who solved the problem by using a polynomial number of communication bits, for the whole optimal range $t < n/3$ of the number of Byzantine processes and within the optimal number $(t+1)$ of communication rounds. Their solution, though very complex and sophisticated, requires processes to send $O(n^9)$ bits in total.

In this work, we present much simpler solution that also holds for the whole optimal range $t < n/3$ and the optimal number $t + 1$ of communication rounds, and at the same time lowers the number of exchanged communication bits to $O(n^3 \log n)$. For achieving such an improvement, processes no more exchange relayed proposed values, but information on suspicions "who suspects who", the size of which is quadratic in n in the worst case.

Categories and Subject Descriptors

C.2.4 [**Computer-Communication Networks**]: Distributed Systems; C.4 [**Computer Systems Organization**]: Per-

formance of Systems—*Fault tolerance*; D.4.1 [**Operating Systems**]: Process Management—*concurrency, multiprocessing, synchronization*; F.2 [**Analysis of Algorithms and Problem Complexity**]: Miscellaneous

General Terms

Algorithms, Reliability, Theory

Keywords

Agreement problem, Byzantine process, Consensus, Synchronous distributed system, Message-passing model, Round-based protocol, EIG.

1. INTRODUCTION

The Consensus problem is considered as a fundamental problem in fault-tolerant distributed systems. In case processes can exhibit a malicious behavior, the obtained variant of consensus is often called Byzantine Agreement. In order to assure perfect reliability, deterministic solutions are of utmost importance for this problem, and this is also the focus of this paper; for recent advances and references to the area of randomized solutions we refer the reader to the work by King and Saia [15] and by Aspnes [1].

The first and the simplest designed deterministic algorithm for the synchronous distributed computing model is the exponential information gathering protocol (from now on called EIG protocol) based on a tree construction proposed by Bar-Noy, Dolev, Dwork and Strong [3] as a simple reformulation of the original protocol proposed by Pease, Shostak and Lamport in 1980 [19]. The algorithm requires processes to send exponentially long messages and performs exponentially many local computation steps, in terms of the number n of processes. Many researchers have since tried to reduce the cost of the solution, However most of them either lowered the maximal range of the tolerated number of faulty processes t from $t < n/3$ (the upper bound) to some smaller values [11, 18, 4] or increased the maximum number of rounds needed in the worst case to terminate (the lower bound being $t + 1$) [3, 9, 20]. For such a purpose, they developed a series of techniques to exploit the redundancy encountered in the tree structure of the EIG protocol, sacrificing the optimum fault-tolerance or the minimum number of communication rounds. [3, 7] propose a trade-off between the number of rounds and the bit complexity for any constant d they increase the number of rounds to $t + t/d$ while decreasing the bit complexity to $O(n^d)$. Similarly, [4] pro-

[*]The work of this author was supported by the Polish National Science Centre grant DEC-2012/06/M/ST6/00459.

[†]The work of this author was supported by the ANR French Research Council [grant number ANR-11-BS02-014].

poses a trade-off between the resilence of the protocol and the bit complexity for any constant ϵ the ration of faulty processes is increased to $(3+\epsilon)t$ while the bit complexity is lowered to $poly(n) \cdot O(2^{1/\epsilon})$.

Garay and Moses [13] were the first and only who solved the problem with polynomial number of communication bits and polynomial local computation cost, still meeting both the bound of $t < n/3$ on the number of Byzantine processes and the number of $t + 1$ communication rounds. Their solution is very complex, and both polynomials are actually large — according to our estimates they are both $O(n^9)$ — thus leaving a huge space for improvement. The only known lower bound $\Omega(nt)$ on the number of communication bits was proved by Dolev and Reischuk [10]; this bound becomes $\Omega(n^2)$ for linear number of Byzantine processes. The bound $t < n/3$ on the number of Byzantine processes necessary for reaching consensus was given by Lamport, Shostak and Pease [16]. Fisher and Lynch [12] proved the lower bound $(t+1)$ on the number of communication rounds, which holds even for milder process failures such as crashes. The interested reader can find in [14] the history of the improvements introduced from the initial protocol in 1980 [19] to the polynomial one in 1998 [14] (the full version of [13]). We are not aware of any improvements since then.

The table below taken from [13] gives an overview of the most important improvment over time concerning the consensus problem. Other improvments occured but they consider randomization; King and Saia [15] reduced the bit complexity to sub-quadratic.

Protocol	n	rounds	comm. bits
PSL 1980 [19]	$3t+1$	$t+1$	$\exp(n)$
DFFLS,TPS 1982 [9, 20]	$3t+1$	$> 2t$	$poly(n)$
C 1985 [7]	$4t+1$	$t+t/d$	$O(n^d)$
BD,DRS 1986 [2, 11]	$\Omega(t^2)$	$t+1$	$poly(n)$
BDDS 1987 [3]	$3t+1$	$t+t/d$	$O(n^d)$
MW 1988 [18]	$6t+1$	$t+1$	$poly(n)$
BGP 1989 [5]	$4t+1$	$t+1$	$poly(n)$
BG 1991 [4]	$(3+\epsilon)t$	$t+1$	$poly(n)O(2^{1/\epsilon})$
GM 1993 [13]	$3t+1$	$t+1$	$O(n^9)$
This paper	$3t+1$	$t+1$	$O(n^3 \log n)$

Our result.

In this work, we present a solution that is simpler yet more efficient in terms of communication complexity than the best known deterministic solution by Garay and Moses [14]. In particular, it matches the two bounds: $t < n/3$ on the number of tolerated Byzantine processes, and $t+1$ on the number of communication rounds, while the total number of communication bits $O(n^3 \log n)$ sent by non-Byzantine processes is close by factor $O(n \log n)$ to the lower bound $\Omega(n^2)$ on the total number of communication bits. In order to achieve this, the processes do not exchange the values they received in the previous rounds, but instead, they exchange a "digest" on the information they received. Based on these digests, they locally maintain information of "who suspects who" during each round. Thanks to this technique, the size of the exchanged information much reduced compared to former works, and the crucial part of the analysis shows that this very limited information is still sufficient to "mimic" the evaluation procedure done by the original EIG protocol "in spirit". It needs to be said that the evaluation made by our algorithms, based on very limited information exchange,

might be slightly different than the evaluation made by the original EIG algorithm executed against the same adversarial schedule, but similar mechanisms guarantee agreement and validity of the final evaluation throughout correct nodes.

EIG protocol vs. our approach.

The EIG protocol works in two phases. During the first phase, processes exchange messages during $t + 1$ communication rounds. At each round each process forwards all the information it received in the previous round to all processes. This protocol can be seen as the fully informed protocol, and hence it results in super-exponential communication complexity (understood as the number of exchanged bits). The collected information is stored in tree-like data structures, to which we refer as *evaluation trees*. At the end of round $t+1$, the second phase (local computation on the local trees) is started. It consists of a bottom-up computation on each of the collected trees (one per process), where a resolved value is associated to each node of the tree structure by applying a resolution function to the children of this node. The decision value of the process is the resolved value associated with the set of roots of the trees. The polynomial protocol by Garay and Moses [13] uses the same tree structures, though parts of the trees are cut using sophisticated techniques. One of the introduced techniques consists in detecting cheating processes (Byzantine processes) in a given round in order to prevent them from cheating in subsequent rounds.

Our protocol is similar to the EIG protocol in its way of proceeding, as processes exchange information during $(t+1)$ rounds and store the information they receive in local data structures. The fundamental difference is in the nature of the stored data. Instead of storing proposed values and then arrays of received values, arrays of arrays of received values, etc., the processes exchange only a relatively small digest of received information. More precisely, each process manages an array of process ids of size n, where it stores the ids of processes it itself suspects to be Byzantine. At the end of each round this information is updated and the new array is sent to all processes in the next round. Moreover, in order to detect cheating processes, a classical confirmation mechanism is used. All information broadcast by a process during a round is echoed by each receiving process to all other processes (the same mechanism is used for the consistent broadcast of Bracha and Toueg [6]). A message sent at a round r is confirmed at some process p_i at the end of round $r+1$ and its sender in consequently not suspected if the same copy is relayed to p_i by at least $(n-t)$ processes during round $r + 1$. Conversely, if the message of some process is not confirmed in the next round, the sender is suspected. The fact that processes exchange suspicion arrays prevents the size of the exchanged information from exponential growth. To ease the presentation of our algorithm, we assume that the suspicion information is stored in a data structure similar to the EIG tree, although the size of the information sent by each correct process during each round is only quadratic in the number n of processes.[1]

In the remainder, we proceed as follows. In Section 2 we introduce the model and the consensus problem in more de-

---

[1]This suggests that the bit complexity of the algorithm is $O(n^4)$, as each of the n processes sends up to n^2 bits during each of the $t < n/3$ rounds of the algorithm; however we will show later in Section 6 that this amount of information can be reduced to $O(n^3 \log n)$.

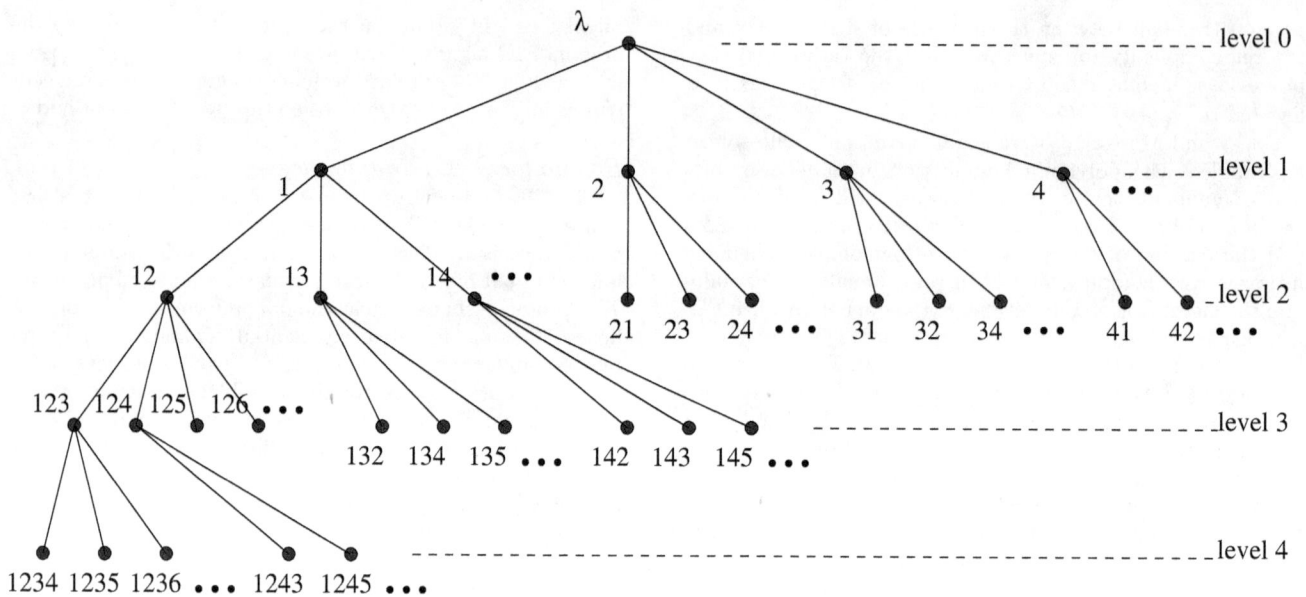

Figure 1: An EIG tree

2. BYZANTINE AGREEMENT AND COMPUTATION MODEL

In this paper, we consider the classical Byzantine distributed synchronous message-passing model. The system is composed of a set Π of n synchronous processes, with ids in $\{1, \ldots, n\}$, which communicate through a reliable synchronous point to point channels (there is an a priori known bound on both message transfer delays and local computation of processes). Moreover, up to t processes can exhibit a *Byzantine* behavior, which means that such a process can behave in an arbitrary manner. This is the most severe process failure model: a Byzantine process can crash, fail to send or receive messages, send arbitrary messages, start in an arbitrary state, send different values to different processes, perform arbitrary state transitions, etc. A process that exhibits a Byzantine behavior during an execution is called *faulty*. Otherwise, it is called *correct*.

In the *Byzantine Agreement* problem, also called *Consensus*, each process p_i proposes an initial value v_i (this can be any value). Contrarily to many previous works including the only polynomial solution of Garay and Moses [14] that restrict the set of proposable values to $\{0, 1\}$ (called binary consensus, only two different values are proposable), we consider multivalued consensus.

The goal for each (correct) process is to decide on a value. A Byzantine agreement protocol has to satisfy the following three properties:

In this paper we consider deterministic synchronous round-based algorithms. Moreover, we do not use authentica-

tion (public key asymmetric cryptography to sign messages). During a round, each correct process may send to all processes, including itself, a unique message whose content is specified by the executed algorithm, and all messages are received within the same round. Then each process performs some local computation before starting a new round, or it decides and terminates.

The efficiency of algorithms is measured by the number of communication rounds (optimally $t + 1$), and the number of bits sent in messages by correct processes (for which the known lower bound is $\Omega(n^2)$). Fault tolerance of algorithms is measured by the number of Byzantine processes that can be tolerated — ideally any number $t < n/3$.

3. THE EIG TREE STRUCTURE

The exponential information gathering tree (EIG tree) is a data structure used to recording the information received by a given process along the successive rounds of an n-process round-based distributed computation. This structure is costly to maintain, as its number of nodes is exponential in the number n of processes. The trees we consider have (at the end of the $t + 1$ rounds of the execution) exactly $t + 2$ levels (from 0 to $t + 1$).[2] A node of level ℓ has exactly $n - \ell$ children and has a label that consists of an ℓ element string of process ids (a process id appears at most once in a given label). The root of this tree is labeled with an empty string λ. The set of labels of the EIG tree is the set of all possible strings of size at most $t + 1$, hence the size of the tree. Figure 1 presents an example of an EIG tree associated with some process p_i. We consider in this example a number of processes n greater than 5 but we cannot represent the whole tree. One can see that starting from level 1, and for

---

[2]Sometimes an EIG tree was presented as a collection of n trees, each of $t + 1$ levels ranging from 1 to $t + 1$; these trees correspond to the n subtrees of our single EIG tree, each rooted in a distinct node at level 1. Both these approaches are equivalent.

the sake of clarity, many nodes are not represented and are replaced by $(\cdots)$.

During the execution of the original EIG protocol, each node x of the tree is used to store two values: $val(x)$ and $newval(x)$. The value of $val(x)$ of a node x on level ℓ is assigned during round ℓ. It is the ℓ-th hand report of some initial value (i.e., received through the chain of processes represented by the ids constituting the label of node x). The value $newval(x)$ of a node x is assigned during the decision procedure after the $t + 1$ rounds.

4. THE MAIN ALGORITHM

The proposed protocol proceeds in $t+1$ synchronous rounds, similarly to the EIG protocol. During a round r, each process sends a same message to all other processes (sending phase), next it waits for the messages sent to it (reception phase), and then it does local computation on both received and locally stored data. The fundamental difference between our solution and the EIG algorithm, as mentioned earlier, is in the nature of the stored and sent data. In other words, we use the same EIG tree structure that is decorated in a different way. Instead of storing the proposed values and then the arrays of received values, the arrays of arrays of received values, etc., kept in the exponential size EIG tree structure, the processes maintain and exchange only a digest of received information. More precisely, during the first two rounds, processes exchange proposed values (similarly to the EIG protocol). Then, starting from the third round, each process informs the other processes which processes it is sure are Byzantine.

To ease the presentation of our algorithm, we say that a correct process p_c received a default value $\perp$, which cannot be proposed to the consensus, from a Byzantine process p_b, when process p_c received no value, or it received a non well-formed message, or if it has itself suspected p_b as being Byzantine in a previous round.

The two basic ideas that underlie and distinguish the proposed approach from previous works are: the exchange of suspicion information (except for the first two rounds) instead of the proposed values or the whole history of messages, and the use of the echo mechanism (here, called a confirmation mechanism) introduced by Bracha and Toueg [6] for asynchronous systems. A message can be safely delivered (we say here that it is *confirmed*) if it has been echoed by at least $(n - t)$ different processes. Bracha and Toueg proved that this mechanism ensures that if a correct process confirms a value from a given process at some round, no other correct process can confirm a different value from the same process at the same round (either it confirms the same value or no value at all). Moreover, values broadcast by correct processes are always confirmed (safely delivered) by at least all correct processes. They proved that in order to implement this mechanism, it is necessary to have $t < n/3$.

During a round r, $r \geq 3$, each process broadcasts a message that contains two parts. The first part is the data that the process wants to disseminate, called *main information* or *main part* of a message, and the second part consists of the main information the process has received from each process in the previous round. This second part is called the *proof* by Bracha and Toueg [6]; we call it the *echo*, due to its nature, and it will serve to confirm the main information of the previous round. A main information received from a given process p_j at round r is *confirmed* to a process p_i at

round $r + 1$ if it has been echoed to p_i (i.e., forwarded in the echo part of messages at round $r + 1$) by at least $(n - t)$ different processes.

In the algorithm description below, we only specify the behavior of correct processes, as Byzantine processes, due to their malicious nature, are not bounded by the rules of the algorithm.

4.1 Principles of the Algorithm

Each process maintains two data structures: an EIG tree to store received values, and a set byz (initialized to $\emptyset$) to store the ids of the processes it suspects to be Byzantine (it suspects by itself, not as reported by some other process). Similarly to the original EIG protocol, each node of the EIG tree with label x can store values (noted $val(x)$ and $newval(x)$ in the original EIG protocol). In the present paper, each node stores *three*: values $val(x)$ and $cval(x)$, representing respectively the main part and the echo part of messages, and $newval(x)$ assigned to node x in the decision procedure at the end of round $t + 1$. $newval(x)$ can be seen as a correction of $val(x)$. The values $val(x)$ and $cval(x)$ are collected during the different rounds, and $newval(x)$ is set during the extraction of the decision value after the $t + 1$ rounds. In the presentation of the algorithm, when we say that we *decorate node x*, we mean that the variables $val(x)$ and $cval(x)$ associated with the node labeled x are set to some values (except of nodes x on level 1, for which $cval(x)$ is not defined).

The following algorithm describes the execution of the protocol from the point of view of a correct process p_i and shows how this process manages its two data structures: the EIG tree and the set byz_i.

Round 1. Each process sends its initial value to all other processes; this is the main part of the message and there are no echoes in this round. The values received by process p_i are used to decorate the nodes of *level 1* of the EIG tree maintained by p_i. As explained above, if p_i has not received a message, or received a non well-formed message from a given process p_x, it decorates the node labeled x with the value $\perp$, i.e., $val(x) \leftarrow \perp$. If it received a proposable value v, it sets $val(x)$ to v. The variable $cval(x)$ is not used for nodes x on level 1.

Round 2. Each process p_i sends an empty main part and echoes the messages (i.e., initial values) it received in the first round. Thus, each message is a sequence of up to n initial values. The values received by p_i (up to $n(n - 1)$ values) are used to decorate the nodes of level 2 of the EIG tree maintained by p_i. Node $x = jk$ is decorated by the value v, i.e., $cval(x) \leftarrow v$, if p_k reports that it received v from p_j at level 1; $cval(x)$ is set to $\perp$ if no valid value is reported. The variable $val(x)$ will be set during the next round. Moreover, during the computation phase of round 2 (after the confirmation checking of the messages sent during the first round), a correct process p_i adds to its set byz_i of suspected Byzantine processes any process p_b whose initial value (the one it received directly from p_b at round 1) is not confirmed at round 2.

Round 3. Each process p_i attaches its local set byz_i of Byzantine processes as the main part of its message (the "digest"), and echoes the arrays of initial values it received during round 2 (i.e., up to n arrays of n values each).

Here we can see a difference from the original EIG protocol. During a round r, $3 \leq r \leq t+1$, a correct process not only decorates the nodes of level r but also possibly the nodes from level $r-1$ to level $t+1$. Indeed, the confirmation mechanism needs two rounds to detect Byzantine behaviors and once we uncovered a Byzantine process, of course we never rely on what she says. For example, if p_j behaved in a Byzantine way (e.g., sending different values to different correct processes) during round 1, it will be suspected by at least one correct process p_k at the latest at the end of round 2 (using the confirmation mechanism). Then, p_k sends the information "p_k suspects p_j" to the other processes at round 3. We will see below how the variables $val(x)$ and $cval(x)$ associated with the different nodes x are set. Finally, p_i enriches its list of Byzantine processes using the confirmation mechanism applied to the messages received in the previous round and echoed in this round.

Round r, $4 \leq r \leq t+1$. Starting from round 4, rounds are the same as for round 3, except that the messages sent by the different processes include the list of Byzantine processes as the main part of the message, and echo the lists received during the previous round in the echo part (the proposed values are no more sent). We will define below how the variables $val(x)$ and $cval(x)$ associated with the different nodes x are set in these rounds.

Once the $t+1$ rounds are terminated, the EIG tree is decorated as follow. Recall that we already showed how to define $val(v)$ for any node x on level 1 of the tree, and also the values $cval(x)$ for nodes on level 2. In the following, we decorate the EIG tree with two values $\top$ and $\bot$. The value $\top$ means "do not suspect" whereas the value $\bot$ means "suspect". For example, when $val(x)$ of some node $x = yjk$ is set to $\top$, this means that p_k reported that it suspects p_j, and when $cval(x)$ of some node $x = yjk\ell$ is set to $\top$, this means that p_ℓ reported that p_k does not suspect p_j (this is a second-hand information — an echo).

- For each node x from a level greater than 1 and at most t, $x = yk\ell$ where y is a string (possibly empty) of ids and k, ℓ are ids of two other processes not listed in y: p_i sets $val(x)$ to $\top$ if p_ℓ never reported to p_i by round t that it suspects p_k; otherwise, $val(x)$ is set to $\bot$.

- For each node x from a level greater than 2, $x = yjk\ell$ where y is a string (possibly empty) of ids and j, k are ids of two other processes not listed in y: p_i sets $cval(x)$ to $\top$ if p_ℓ never reported by round $t+1$ to p_i that p_k reported that it suspects p_j (this value is reported in the second-hand information included in the echo part of the message received by p_i from p_ℓ); otherwise, $cval(x)$ is set to $\bot$.

- One can note that for the nodes of level $t+1$ (i.e., the leaves of the EIG tree), the variable $val(x)$ is set to no value, so for each leaf node x, $x = yk\ell$ where y is a string (possibly empty) of ids and k, ℓ are ids of two

other processes not listed in y: p_i sets $val(x)$ to $\top$ if p_ℓ did not report to p_i that it suspects p_k; otherwise, $val(x)$ is set to $\bot$.

Remark 1: Note that, except for the third round, the echoes are not themselves echoed. This however does not influence the later evaluation and decision making, since similarly to the EIG protocol, there is high redundancy in the received information and some of it can be skipped, as pointed out in many previous works including [13]. Moreover, from round to round, the number of nodes in subsequent levels of the constructed EIG tree grows, whereas the new available information (main part of received messages) remains quadratic. This means that all the collected information can be stored in arrays instead of the EIG tree structure. The tree is however used to ease the presentation of the decision making and its analysis.

4.2 Extracting the final decision value

As for the EIG protocol, the decision making consists in assigning new values to the nodes of the EIG tree of each correct process, starting from the leaves (bottom-up evaluation). Let x be a node of the tree and $val(x)$ and $cval(x)$ be the values with which node x is decorated. The evaluation mechanism of the nodes consists in assigning a new value $newval(x)$ to each node x, the new value of the root being the decision value. Let us consider the EIG tree of a correct process p_i.

- When x is a leaf, $newval(x) \leftarrow val(x)$. This will be one of $\top$ or $\bot$.

- When x is an internal node on level l ranging from t down to 1, $newval(x)$ is set to a value v (this is a value equal to $\top$ or $\bot$ for levels greater or equal than 2, and for level 1 it is either a proposed value or $\bot$ if no valid value is received) if there are $(n - t - l)$ children of x the new values of which are set to $\top$ and among them there is a strict majority with the variable $cval$ set to v. More formally:
  (i) Let $T = \{y \mid y$ child of $x \wedge newval(y) = \top\}$.
  (ii) $newval(x) \leftarrow v$ if a strict majority of the $cval$ of the children of x that belong to T are set to a same value v.

- When $x = \lambda$, $newval(x) \leftarrow v$ if a strict majority of the new values of its children (these are either proposed values or the default value $\bot$ if no valid value has been computed) are set to a same non-$\bot$ value v; otherwise it is set to a default value v_0.

The intuition that is behind the values $val(x)$, $cval(x)$ and $newval(x)$ of a node x of a given level l is the following. For the nodes of level 1 and level 2, $val(x)$ is a proposed value as in the original EIG protocol. For the other levels $l, 1 < l \leq t$, let us consider that $x = yjk$. $val(x)$ is set to $\top$ if p_k reported that it does not suspect p_j. $cval(x)$ is the echo received from p_k of the value $val(yj)$ (if both p_j and $_k$ are correct $cval(x) = val(yj)$).

The values $newval$ are a correction of val during the execution of the decision making procedure according to what the child nodes of x reported as an echo of $val(x)$. $newval(x)$ is the information whether p_i considers that p_k suspects p_j or not. $val(x)$ is the suspicion information reported by p_k and $newval(x)$ is the information "computed" by p_i (using the echoes and the suspicion information of the lower levels) on whether p_k suspects p_j or not. Then the values *newval* of this level are used as a mask to re-apply the confirmation mechanism. Only the echoes $cval(xjk)$ of the processes p_k that do not suspect process p_y ($newval(xjk)$ evaluated to $\top$) are considered for the confirmation mechanism of the value $val(xj)$ of node xj (xj is the parent node of node xjk). For a node x of level 1, $newval(x)$ does not contain an information about suspicions as there is only one process id in the label x; it is indeed the corrected value of the original value received by p_i from p_j.

Let us note that whereas in the original EIG protocol only the values associated to the leaves of the tree are used to compute the decision value, i.e., $newval(x)$ for each non-leaf node is a function of the new values assigned to its child nodes, in our protocol the value $newval(x)$ depends on both *newval* and *cval* values associated with its child nodes.

5. CORRECTNESS PROOF

The correctness proof is tailored along the analysis of the (original) EIG protocol as proposed by Bar-Noy et al. [3] and described in the book by Lynch [17]. Although the steps of both analysis are similar, due to the use of the concept of EIG trees, the proofs often rely on different arguments — more subtle in case of our protocol, as it uses only a small amount of exchanged information. The proof of termination is obvious, therefore in the remainder we focus on validity and agreement.

LEMMA 1. *Each message sent by a correct process at round r is confirmed by at least all correct processes at round $r+1$. Said otherwise, a correct process p_i never suspects a correct process p_j and thus always relays correctly the messages of p_j.*

PROOF. The confirmation mechanism says that an information sent by a process p_j in the main part of a message is confirmed if it is echoed by at least $(n - t)$ different processes; otherwise, the sender is necessarily Byzantine (assuming $t < n/3$). If a correct process p_i sends a message at some round r, it will send the very same message m to all processes and at least all correct processes ($n - t$ processes) will echo the main part of m to all processes at round $r+1$. Consequently at the end of round $r+1$ all correct processes will receive at least $n - t$ echos related to message m broadcast at round r by p_i. □

Notation: As each process maintains its own EIG tree structure, there are n nodes labeled x, one for each process of the system. Thus, $val(x)_i$ is used to refer to the value that is associated with the node labeled x of the EIG tree maintained by process p_i.

LEMMA 2. *After $t+1$ rounds of the proposed protocol, the following holds. If p_i, p_j and p_k are correct processes, with $i \neq j$, then $val(x)_i = val(x)_j$ for every label x ending in k. Similarly, $cval(x)_i = cval(x)_j$ if x belongs to a level greater than 1 (otherwise, it is not set).*

PROOF. The proof of this lemma follows directly from the fact that a correct process sends the same messages to all processes including itself, and that $val(x)_i$ and $cval(x)_i$ are either proposed values or suspicion information reported to p_i by p_k. □

Lemma 3 extends the previous one to new values.

LEMMA 3. *After $t + 1$ rounds of the proposed protocol, the following holds. Suppose that x is a label ending with the index of a correct process. Then there is a value v such that $val(x)_i = newval(x)_i = v$ for all correct processes p_i.*

PROOF. The proof is by induction on the length of the tree labels from $t+1$ down to 1.

Base case: the leaves x of the tree (of length $t+1$). From Lemma 2, $val(x)_i$ is the same (call this value v) for all correct processes p_i. And by definition of new values, $newval(x)_i = val(x)_i$ for all correct processes p_i.

Induction: Let us consider a label x of length $\ell, 1 \leq \ell \leq t$ ending with the index of a correct process p_j ($x = yj$). By Lemma 2 all correct processes p_i have the same $val(x)_i$ (call it v). By the proposed algorithm, for any node labeled xk (k being the id of a correct process), $cval(xk)_i = val(x)_i = v$ as $cval(xk)_i$ is the echo of $val(x)_i$ sent by process p_k.

Moreover, by Lemma 1, no correct process suspects a correct process. Consequently, for any node labeled xk (k being the id of a correct process), $val(xk)_i = \top$. By the induction hypothesis, $newval(xk)_i = \top$. Let us now show that a strict majority of the children of node x are correct processes. Indeed, x has $n - \ell$ children. As there are at most t Byzantine processes, we are sure that at least $(n - t - l)$ child nodes xk of x end with the id k of a correct process. As $\ell \leq t$ we have $(n - t - l) \geq (n - 2t) > t$ because $n > 3t$. To sum up, for all child nodes xk of x (p_k being a correct process), we have $newval(xk)_i = \top$ and $cval(xk)_i = val(x)_i$ and these child processes are a strict majority. Consequently, by the decision making procedure of the proposed algorithm, $newval(x)_i$ is set to $val(x)_i$ proving the lemma. (Although for $\ell = 1$ or 2, the values of *val* and *cval* are proposed values, the same reasoning holds.) □

THEOREM 1. *(Validity) If all correct processes begin with the same initial value v, then the only possible decision value for correct processes is v.*

PROOF. If all correct processes propose the same value v, then $val(j)_i = v$ for any pair p_i, p_j of correct processes. By Lemma 3 $newval(j)_i = v$ for any pair p_i, p_j of correct processes. The majority rule used by the decision procedure implies that $newval(\lambda)_i = v$ for all correct processes p_i. □

In order to prove the agreement property of the protocol, we reuse the definition of path covering set similarly to the EIG protocol. A subset C of the nodes of an EIG tree is a *path covering* if every path from the root to a leaf of the tree contains at least one node in C. Moreover a node x is said to be common for a given execution of the protocol (recall that each process has its own version of the tree) if $newval(x)_i$ is the same for all correct processes p_i. A given path covering is said to be common for an execution if all of its nodes are common in that execution.

The proof of the next Lemma is exactly the same as for the original EIG protocol, however we include it here for completeness.

LEMMA 4. *([17]) After $t + 1$ rounds of the proposed protocol, there exists a path covering that is common in this execution.*

PROOF. We prove that the set C of all the nodes whose labels are of the form xi where p_i is a correct process is a common path covering. First, by Lemma 3 all these nodes are common as they end with a correct process id. Second, as each path from the root to a leaf has exactly $t+1$ non-root nodes and no process id appears more than once, consequently there is at least one node whose label ends with the id of a correct process since there are at most t Byzantine processes. □

LEMMA 5. *After $t+1$ rounds of the proposed protocol, the following holds. If there is a common path covering of the sub-tree rooted at a node labeled x, then either x is common or one of its ancestors is common.*

PROOF. The proof is by induction on the length of the tree labels from $t+1$ down to 1.

Base case: The leaves x of the tree (of length $t+1$). The only node of the common path covering is x itself, which is common by definition of a common path covering.

Induction: Assume the lemma is true for labels greater then l, where $0 \leq l \leq t$, if any. Let x be a node label of size l and C a common path covering rooted at x. If $x \in C$ or if x ends with the id of a correct process then the lemma holds by, respectively, the definition of C and Lemma 3. If x has a correct ancestor then the lemma also holds. So let us consider the case where x is composed of the ids of Byzantine processes. By the definition of a common path covering, any child $x\ell$ of x is a common path covering and, moreover, by the induction hypothesis, ℓ is common. According to the decision making procedure (the computing of $newval(x)$), there are three cases to consider:

- x belongs to level $l = t$. As the process ids that compose a node x of level $l = t$ are all Byzantine (see above), consequently all its child nodes end with the id j of correct processes and these nodes are common by the induction hypothesis. On the other side, for each child node xj, $cval(xj)$ is a value reported by a correct process p_j. By Lemma 1, correct processes report correctly messages and thus, as the decision making procedure is deterministic and correct processes have the same data concerning x, all correct processes will compute the same $newval(x)$ and x is common.

- x belongs to level $l \leq t - 1$. Suppose $x = yj$, for some node y and process p_j. Let us consider the set of process ids $top\_set = \{k \mid xk$ is a child node of $x \wedge newval(xk) = \top\}$. This set contains process ids k such that the child node of x the label of which terminates with the id k has a newval set to $\top$. This set is the same for all the EIG trees maintained by the different correct processes by the induction hypothesis. If $\mid top\_set \mid < (n-t-l)$ then by the decision making procedure, any correct process p_i sets $newval(x)$ to the same value $\bot$ and the lemma follows.

  If $\mid top\_set \mid \geq (n-t-l)$ then at least $(n-t-l)-(t-l) = n-2t > t+1$ of the processes represented in top_set are correct (recall that the number of Byzantine processes whose ids are in top_set is at most $t-l$ as x is composed of the ids of l Byzantine processes). This means that among the processes represented in the set top_set there is a strict majority of correct processes. Moreover, this majority of such correct processes p_k do not suspect process p_j (recall that $x = yj$) by the definition of the set top_set and by Lemma 3 applied to node

xk. If they do not suspect p_j this means that they reported the same value $cval(xk)$. Indeed, if two correct processes report different values from some process, it is necessary that at most one of these processes can confirm the value it reported and the second one will suspect the sender (by the confirmation mechanism). Hence, the value $cval(xk)$ is a strict majority among the processes of top_set, and consequently this same value is assigned to $newval(x)$ and x is common.

- $x = \lambda$ (level $l = 0$). By the definition of $newval(x)$ and the induction hypothesis, x is common. In more details, suppose to the contrary that λ is not common. Then, by inductive hypothesis, each of its children y consisting of a unique process id would be common, which means that it has the same $newval(y)_k$ across correct processes p_k. Consequently, by the definition of $newval(\lambda)$ and by the fact that the number of children of λ consisting of a correct process id is at least $n - t > t$, the $newval(\lambda)_i$ are the same across correct processes p_i. This means that λ is common, violating our contradictory assumption.

□

THEOREM 2. *(Agreement) The proposed protocol ensures the agreement property of consensus.*

PROOF. After $t+1$ rounds of the algorithm, by lemmas 4 and 5 and the fact that the node λ has no ancestor, λ is common. Agreement follows as $newval(\lambda)$ is the decision value. □

6. COMPLEXITY ANALYSIS AND IMPROVEMENT

If we consider binary consensus (only two possible value can be proposed), the main algorithm, as described in Section 4, achieves $O(n^3)$ communication complexity, in terms of the number of bits sent by any correct process. Each process sends, respectively, $O(1)$, $O(n)$ and $O(n^2)$ bits during the first three rounds, and then $O(n^2)$ bits in each subsequent round: a list of suspected processes and the echoes of the lists received in the previous round (n^2 bits at most). For the maximal value of t (which is $O(n)$), the communication bit complexity of this protocol is $O(n^3)$ per process, and thus $O(n^4)$ for all correct processes in total.

In the case of multivalued consensus, the proposed value of each process is taken from a set V of proposable values, the size of which is k. The bit complexity of the first three rounds becomes $O(n^2) \log_2 k$ per process, where the factor $\log_2 k$ comes from the size of the binary representation of a proposed value. The complexity of the subsequent rounds of the algorithm does not depend on k, as processes only exchange suspicion information, namely, $O(n^3)$ bits per process. The total bit complexity is thus $O(\max(n^4, n^3 \log k))$. If $\log_2 k = O(n)$, the bit complexity of the algorithm is $O(n^4)$.

However, similarly to the floodset protocol for solving the consensus problem in crash-prone synchronous systems, our protocol can be modified to use only an incremental dissemination of the suspicions (instead of sending the whole list of suspected processes all the time). Indeed, once a process suspects another process it will suspect it until the end of the execution and there is no need to resend this information at each round. Namely, each suspicion is sent only once, that is, in the first time where it is discovered. A correct process can suspect at most t processes. Obviously, if a suspicion is sent only once, the echo is also sent only once by correct processes. A Byzantine process can be suspected by possibly all the other processes. Due to the relay, we can say that during the execution of the protocol each process sends t suspicions and relays $(n-1)t$ suspicions. Each relay of a suspicion needs two process ids, i.e., who suspects who. That is, the protocol needs $O(nt \log n)$ bits per process, where the factor $\log_2 n$ comes from the size of the binary representation of a process id. Moreover, each process sends respectively $O(1)$, $O(n)$ and $O(n^2)$ bits during the first three rounds, which are special rounds. Finally, the property of well-formed messages requires from each process to send its id, of logarithmic size, to each process in every round; this contributes another $O(t \log n)$ to the bit communication complexity per each process. For the maximal value of t, which is $O(n)$, the bit communication complexity of the modified protocol is $O(n^2 \log n)$ per process, therefore $O(n^3 \log n)$ in total for binary consensus.

Again, if we consider that the proposed values are taken from a set V of size k then the complexity of the algorithm becomes $O(n^3 \log(\max(n, k)))$.

Acknowledgments

We would like to thank Nancy Lynch for suggesting this research direction when Achour Mostefaoui spent three months visiting her group. We are also thankful to Yoram Moses for all the discussions and valuable remarks. Finally we would like to thank the anonymous reviewers whose comments helped to improve this paper.

7. REFERENCES

[1] Aspnes J., Faster randomized consensus with an oblivious adversary. *Proc. 31st ACM Symposium on Principles of Distributed Computing (PODC 2012)*, pp. 1-8, 2012.

[2] Bar-Noy A., Dolev D., Families of Consensus Algorithms. *Proc. 3rd Aegean Workshop on Computing (AWOC 1988)*, pp. 380-390 1988.

[3] Bar-Noy A., Dolev D., Dwork C., and Strong H.R., Shifting Gears: Changing Algorithms on the Fly To Expedite Byzantine Agreement. *Proc. 6th ACM Symposium on Principles of Distributed Computing (PODC 1987)*, pp. 42-51 1987.

[4] Berman P., Garay J., Efficient Distributed Consensus with $n = (3 + \epsilon)t$ Processors. *5th International Workshop on Distributed Algorithms (WDAG'91)*, Delphi, Greece, LNCS 579 Springer, pp. 129-142, 1991.

[5] Berman P., Garay J., Perry K., Towards Optimal Distributed Consensus (Extended Abstract). *Proc. 30th IEEE Symposium on Foundations of Computer Science (FOCS 1989)*, pp. 410-415 1989. FOCS 1989: 410-415.

[6] Bracha G. and Toueg S., Resilient Consensus Protocols. *Proc. 2nd ACM Symposium on Principles of Distributed Computing (PODC 1983)*, ACM Press, Montreal.

[7] Coan B., A Communication-Efficient Canonical Form for Fault-Tolerant Distributed Protocols. *Proc. 5th ACM Symposium on Principles of Distributed Computing (PODC 1986)*, pp. 63-72, 1986.

[8] Chlebus B.S., Kowalski D.R., and Strojnowski M., Fast Scalable Deterministic Consensus for Crash Failures. *Proc. 28th ACM Symposium on Principles of Distributed Computing (PODC 2009)*, pp. 111-120, 2009.

[9] Dolev D., Fischer M., Fowler R., Lynch N., Strong R., An Efficient Algorithm for Byzantine Agreement without Authentication. *Information and Control*, vol 52(3):257-274, 1982.

[10] Dolev D. and Reischuk R., Bounds on Information Exchange for Byzantine Agreement. *Journal of the ACM* 32(1): 191-204, 1985.

[11] Dolev D., Reischuk R., Strong R., Early Stopping in Byzantine Agreement. *Journal of the ACM*, vol 37(4):720-741, 1990.

[12] Fisher M. and Lynch N., A lower Bound for the Time to Assure Interactive Consistency. *Information Processing Letters*, 14: 183-186, 1982.

[13] Garay J.A. and Moses Y., Fully polynomial Byzantine agreement in $t + 1$ rounds. *Proc. 25th ACM Symposium on Theory of Computing (STOC 1993)*, ACM Press, pp. 31-41, 1993.

[14] Garay J.A. and Moses Y., Fully Polynomial Byzantine Agreement for $n > 3t$ Processors in $t + 1$ Rounds. *SIAM Journal on Computing*, vol 27(1):247-290, 1998.

[15] King V. and Saia J., Breaking the $O(n^2)$ Bit Barrier: Scalable Byzantine Agreement with an Adaptive Adversary. *Proc. 29th ACM Symposium on Principles of Distributed Computing (PODC 2010)*, pp. 420-429, 2010.

[16] Lamport L., Shostak R., and Pease M., The Byzantine Generals Problem. *ACM Transactions on Programming Languages and Systems*, 4: 382-401, 1982.

[17] Lynch N.A., Distributed Algorithms. *Morgan Kaufmann*, 1996.

[18] Moses Y., Waarts O., Coordinated Traversal: $(t + 1)$-Round Byzantine Agreement in Polynomial Time. *29th IEEE Symposium on Foundations of Computer Science (FOCS'88)*, pp. 246-255, 1988.

[19] Pease L., Shostak R., and Lamport L., Reaching Agreement in Presence of Faults. *Journal of the ACM*, 27(2):228-234, 1980.

[20] Toueg S., Perry K., Srikanth T., Fast Distributed Agreement. *SIAM Journal of Computing*, vol 16(3):445-457, 1987.

How to Meet Asynchronously at Polynomial Cost

Yoann Dieudonné
MIS, Université de Picardie
Jules Verne
Amiens, FRANCE
yoann.dieudonne@u-
picardie.fr

Andrzej Pelc[*]
Département d'informatique
Université du Québec en
Outaouais
Gatineau, Québec J8X 3X7,
Canada
pelc@uqo.ca

Vincent Villain
MIS, Université de Picardie
Jules Verne
Amiens, FRANCE
vincent.villain@u-
picardie.fr

ABSTRACT

Two mobile agents starting at different nodes of an unknown network have to meet. This task is known in the literature as *rendezvous*. Each agent has a different label which is a positive integer known to it, but unknown to the other agent. Agents move in an asynchronous way: the speed of agents may vary and is controlled by an adversary. The cost of a rendezvous algorithm is the total number of edge traversals by both agents until their meeting. The only previous deterministic algorithm solving this problem has cost exponential in the size of the graph and in the larger label. In this paper we present a deterministic rendezvous algorithm with cost *polynomial* in the size of the graph and in the *length* of the *smaller* label. Hence we decrease the cost exponentially in the size of the graph and doubly exponentially in the labels of agents.

As an application of our rendezvous algorithm we solve several fundamental problems involving teams of unknown size larger than 1 of labeled agents moving asynchronously in unknown networks. Among them are the following problems: **team size**, in which every agent has to find the total number of agents, **leader election**, in which all agents have to output the label of a single agent, **perfect renaming** in which all agents have to adopt new different labels from the set $\{1, \ldots, k\}$, where k is the number of agents, and **gossiping**, in which each agent has initially a piece of information (value) and all agents have to output all the values. Using our rendezvous algorithm we solve all these problems at cost polynomial in the size of the graph and in the smallest length of all labels of participating agents.

Categories and Subject Descriptors

F.2 [**ANALYSIS OF ALGORITHMS AND PROBLEM COMPLEXITY**]: General

---

[*]Partially supported by NSERC discovery grant and by the Research Chair in Distributed Computing at the Université du Québec en Outaouais.

General Terms

Algorithms, Theory

Keywords

asynchronous mobile agents, network, rendezvous, deterministic algorithm, leader election, renaming, gossiping

1. INTRODUCTION

The background. Two mobile agents, starting at different nodes of a network, possibly at different times, have to meet. This basic task, known as *rendezvous*, has been thoroughly studied in the literature. It even has applications in human and animal interaction, e.g., when agents are people that have to meet in a city whose streets form a network, or migratory birds have to gather at one destination flying in from different places. In computer science applications, mobile agents usually represent software agents in computer networks, or mobile robots, if the network is a labyrinth or is composed of corridors in a building. The reason to meet may be to exchange data previously collected by the agents, or to coordinate some future task, such as network maintenance or finding a map of the network.

In this paper we consider the rendezvous problem under a very weak scenario which assumes little knowledge and control power of the agents. This makes our solutions more widely applicable, but significantly increases the difficulty of meeting. More specifically, agents do not have any a priori information about the network, they do not know its topology or any bounds on parameters such as the diameter or the size. We seek rendezvous algorithms that do not rely on the knowledge of node labels, and can work in anonymous networks as well (cf. [5]). The importance of designing such algorithms is motivated by the fact that, even when nodes are equipped with distinct labels, agents may be unable to perceive them because of limited sensory capabilities, or nodes may refuse to reveal their labels, e.g., due to security or privacy reasons. Note that if nodes had distinct labels that can be perceived by the agents, then agents might explore the network and meet in the smallest node, hence rendezvous would reduce to exploration. Agents have distinct labels, which are positive integers and each agent knows its own label, but not the label of the other agent. The label of the agent is the only a priori initial input to its algorithm. During navigation agents gain knowledge of the visited part of the network: when an agent enters a node, it learns the port number by which it enters and the degree of the node. The main difficulty of the scenario is the asynchronous way in which agents move: the speed of the agents may vary, may be different for each of them, and is totally controlled by an adversary. This feature of the model is also what makes it more realistic than the synchronous scenario: in practical applications the speed of agents depends on various factors that are beyond their control, such as congestion in different parts of the network or mechanical characteristics in the case of mobile robots. Notice that in the asynchronous scenario we cannot require that agents meet in a node: the adversary can prevent this even in the two-node graph. Thus, similarly as in previous papers on asynchronous rendezvous [10, 16, 18, 19, 28], we allow the meeting either in a node or inside an edge. The cost of a rendezvous algorithm is the total number of edge traversals by both agents until their meeting.

Our results. The main result of this paper is a deterministic rendezvous algorithm, working in arbitrary unknown networks and whose cost is polynomial in the size of the network and in the *length* of the *smaller* label (i.e. in the logarithm of this label). The only previous algorithm solving the asynchronous rendezvous problem [18] is exponential in the size of the network and in the larger label. Hence we decrease the cost exponentially in the size of the network and doubly exponentially in the labels of agents.

As an application of our rendezvous algorithm we solve several fundamental problems involving teams of unknown size larger than 1 of labeled agents moving asynchronously in unknown networks. Among them are the following problems: `team size`, in which every agent has to find the total number of agents, `leader election`, in which all agents have to output the label of a single agent, `perfect renaming` in which all agents have to adopt new different labels from the set $\{1, \ldots, k\}$, where k is the number of agents, and `gossiping`, in which each agent has initially a piece of information (value) and all agents have to output all the values. Using our rendezvous algorithm we solve all these problems at cost (total number of edge traversals by all agents) polynomial in the size of the graph and in the smallest length of all labels of participating agents. To the best of our knowledge this is the first solution of these problems for asynchronous mobile agents, even regardless of the cost.

Several omitted proofs will appear in the journal version of the paper.

The model. The network is modeled as a finite undirected connected graph, referred to hereafter as a graph. Nodes are unlabeled, but edges incident to a node v have distinct labels in $\{0, \ldots, d-1\}$, where d is the degree of v. Thus every undirected edge $\{u, v\}$ has two labels, which are called its *port numbers* at u and at v. Port numbering is *local*, i.e., there is no relation between port numbers at u and at v. Note that in the absence of port numbers, edges incident to a node would be undistinguishable for agents and thus gathering would be often impossible, as the adversary could prevent an agent from taking some edge incident to the current node.

In order to avoid crossings of non-incident edges, we consider an embedding of the underlying graph in the three-dimensional Euclidean space, with nodes of the graph being points of the space and edges being pairwise disjoint line segments joining them. Agents are modeled as points moving inside this embedding. (This embedding is only for the clarity of presentation; in fact crossings of non-incident edges would make rendezvous simpler, as agents traversing distinct edges could sometimes meet accidentally at the crossing point.)

There are two agents that start from different nodes of the graph and traverse its edges. They cannot mark visited nodes or traversed edges in any way. Agents have distinct labels which are strictly positive integers. Each agent knows only its own label which is an initial input to its deterministic algorithm. Agents do not know the topology of the graph or any bound on its size. They can, however, acquire knowledge about the network: When an agent enters a node, it learns its degree and the port of entry. We assume that the memory of the agents is unbounded: from the computational point of view they are modeled as Turing machines.

Agents navigate in the graph in an asynchronous way which is formalized by an adversarial model used in [10, 16, 18, 19, 28] and described below. Two important notions used to specify movements of agents are the *route* of the agent and its *walk*. Intuitively, the agent chooses the route *where* it moves and the adversary describes the walk on this route, deciding *how* the agent moves. More precisely, these notions are defined as follows. The adversary initially places an agent at some node of the graph. The route is chosen by the agent and is defined as follows. The agent chooses one of the available ports at the current node. After getting to the other end of the corresponding edge, the agent chooses one of the available ports at this node or decides to stay at this node. It does so on the basis of all information currently available to it. The resulting route of the agent is the corresponding sequence of edges $(\{v_0, v_1\}, \{v_1, v_2\}, \ldots)$, which is a (not necessarily simple) path in the graph.

We now describe the walk f of an agent on its route. Let $R = (e_1, e_2, \ldots)$ be the route of an agent. Let $e_i = \{v_{i-1}, v_i\}$. Let $(t_0, t_1, t_2, \ldots)$, where $t_0 = 0$, be an increasing sequence of reals, chosen by the adversary, that represent points in time. Let $f_i : [t_i, t_{i+1}] \rightarrow [v_i, v_{i+1}]$ be any continuous function, chosen by the adversary, such that $f_i(t_i) = v_i$ and $f_i(t_{i+1}) = v_{i+1}$. For any $t \in [t_i, t_{i+1}]$, we define $f(t) = f_i(t)$. The interpretation of the walk f is as follows: at time t the agent is at the point $f(t)$ of its route. This general definition of the walk and the fact that (as opposed to the route) it is designed by the adversary, are a way to formalize the asynchronous characteristics of the process. The movement of the agent can be at arbitrary speed, the adversary may sometimes stop the agent or move it back and forth, as long as the walk in each edge of the route is continuous and covers all of it. This definition makes the adversary very powerful, and consequently agents have little control on how they move. This makes a meeting between agents hard to achieve. Agents with routes R_1 and R_2 and with walks f_1 and f_2 meet at time t, if points $f_1(t)$ and $f_2(t)$ are identical. A meeting is guaranteed for routes R_1 and R_2, if the agents using these routes meet at some time t, regardless of the walks chosen by the adversary.

Related work. In most papers on rendezvous a synchronous scenario was assumed, in which agents navigate in the graph in synchronous rounds. An extensive survey of randomized rendezvous in various scenarios can be found in [5], cf. also [3, 4, 6, 7]. Deterministic rendezvous in networks has been surveyed in [33]. Several authors considered the geometric scenario (rendezvous in an interval of the real line, see, e.g., [11], or in the plane, see, e.g., [8, 9]). Rendezvous of more than two agents, often called gathering, has been studied, e.g., in [21, 22, 32, 37]. In [21] agents were anonymous, while in [37] the authors considered gathering many agents with unique labels. Gathering many labeled agents in the presence of Byzantine agents was studied in [22]. The problem was also studied in the context of multiple robot systems, cf. [14, 23], and fault tolerant gathering of robots in the plane was studied, e.g., in [2, 15].

For the deterministic setting a lot of effort has been dedicated to the study of the feasibility of rendezvous, and to the time required to achieve this task, when feasible. For instance, deterministic rendezvous with agents equipped with tokens used to mark nodes was considered, e.g., in [31]. Deterministic rendezvous of two agents that cannot mark nodes but have unique labels was discussed in [20, 29, 36]. These papers are concerned with the time of synchronous rendezvous in arbitrary graphs. In [20] the authors show a rendezvous algorithm polynomial in the size of the graph, in the length of the shorter label and in the delay between the starting time of the agents. In [29, 36] rendezvous time is polynomial in the first two of these parameters and independent of the delay.

Memory required by two anonymous agents to achieve deterministic rendezvous has been studied in [25, 26] for trees and in [17] for general graphs. Memory needed for randomized rendezvous in the ring is discussed, e.g., in [30].

Asynchronous rendezvous of two agents in a network has been studied in [10, 16, 18, 19, 28]. The model used in the present paper has been introduced in [19]. In this paper the authors investigated the cost of rendezvous in the infinite line and in the ring. They also proposed a rendezvous algorithm for an arbitrary graph with a known upper bound on the size of the graph. This assumption was subsequently removed in [18], but both in [19] and in [18] the cost of rendezvous was exponential in the size of the graph and in the larger label. In [28] asynchronous rendezvous was studied for anonymous agents and the cost was again exponential. The only asynchronous rendezvous algorithms at polynomial cost were presented in [10, 16], but in these papers authors restricted attention to infinite multidimensional grids and they used the powerful assumption that each agent knows its starting coordinates. (The cost in this case is polynomial in the initial distance).

A different asynchronous scenario was studied in [13, 23] for the plane. In these papers the authors assumed that agents are memoryless, but they can observe the environment and make navigation decisions based on these observations.

The four problems that we solve in the context of asynchronous mobile agents as an application of our rendezvous algorithm, are widely researched tasks in distributed computing, under many scenarios. Counting the number of agents is a basic task, cf. [27], as many mobile agents algorithms depend on this knowledge. Leader election, cf. [34], is a fundamental problem in distributed computing. Renaming was introduced in [1] and further studied by many authors. Gossiping, also called all-to-all communication, is one of the basic primitives in network algorithms, cf. [24].

2. PRELIMINARIES

Throughout the paper, the number of nodes of a graph is called its size. In this section we recall two procedures known from the literature, that will be used as building blocks in our algorithms. The aim of both of them is graph exploration, i.e., visiting all nodes and traversing all edges of the graph by a single agent. The first procedure, based on universal exploration sequences (UXS), is a corollary of the result of Reingold [35]. Given any positive integer n, it allows the agent to traverse all edges of any graph of size at most n, starting from any node of this graph, using $P(n)$ edge traversals, where P is some polynomial. (The original procedure of Reingold only visits all nodes, but it can be transformed to traverse all edges by visiting all neighbors of each visited node before going to the next node.) After entering a node of degree d by some port p, the agent can compute the port q by which it has to exit; more precisely $q = (p + x_i) \mod d$, where x_i is the corresponding term of the UXS.

A *trajectory* is a sequence of nodes of a graph, in which each node is adjacent to the preceding one. (Hence it is a sequence of nodes visited following a route.) Given any starting node v, we denote by $R(n, v)$ the trajectory obtained by Reingold's procedure. The procedure can be applied in any graph starting at any node, giving some trajectory. We say that the agent *follows* a trajectory if it executes the above procedure used to construct it. This trajectory will be called *integral*, if the corresponding route covers all edges of the graph. By definition, the trajectory $R(n, v)$ is integral if it is obtained by Reingold's procedure applied in any graph of size at most n starting at any node v.

The second procedure [12] is performed by an agent using a fixed token placed at the starting node of the agent. (It is well known that a terminating exploration even of all anonymous rings of unknown size by a single agent without a token is impossible.) In our applications the roles of the token and of the exploring agent will be played by agents. The procedure works at cost polynomial in the size of the graph. Moreover, at the end of it the agent is with the token and has a complete map of the graph with all port numbers marked. We call this procedure EST, for *exploration with a stationary token*. We denote by $T(EST(n))$ the maximum number of edge traversals in an execution of the procedure EST in a graph of size at most n.

For a positive integer x, by $|x|$ we denote the length of its binary representation, called the length of x. Hence $|x| = \lceil \log x \rceil$. All logarithms are with base 2. For two agents, we say that the agent with larger (smaller) label is larger (resp. smaller). For any trajectory $T = (v_0, \ldots, v_r)$, we denote by $\overline{T}$ the reverse trajectory $(v_r, \ldots, v_0)$. For two trajectories $T_1 = (v_0, \ldots, v_r)$ and $T_2 = (v_r, v_{r+1}, \ldots, v_s)$ we denote by $T_1 T_2$ the trajectory $(v_0, \ldots, v_r, v_{r+1}, \ldots, v_s)$. For any trajectory $T = (v_0, \ldots, v_r)$, for which $v_r = v_0$ and for any positive integer x, we define T^x to be $TT \ldots T$, with x copies of T. For any trajectory T we define $|T|$ to be the number of nodes in T.

3. THE RENDEZVOUS ALGORITHM

In this section we describe and analyze our rendezvous algorithm working at polynomial cost. Its high-level idea is based on the following observation. If one agent follows an integral trajectory during some time interval, then it must either meet the other agent or this other agent must perform at least one complete edge traversal during this time interval, i.e., it must make *progress*. A naive use of this observation leads to the following simple algorithm: an agent with label L starting at node v of a graph of size n follows the trajectory $R(n, v)^{(P(n)+1)^L}$ and stops. Indeed, in this case the number of integral trajectories $R(n, v)$ performed by the larger agent is larger than the number of edges traversed by the smaller agent and consequently, if they have not met before, the larger agent must meet the smaller one after the smaller agent stops, because the larger agent will still perform at least one entire trajectory afterwards. However, this simple algorithm has two major drawbacks. First, it requires knowledge of n (or of an upper bound on it) and second, it is exponential in L, while we want an algorithm *polylogarithmic* in L. Hence the above observation has to be used in a much more subtle way. Our algorithm constructs a trajectory for each agent, polynomial in the size of the graph and polylogarithmic in the shorter label, i.e., polynomial in its length, which has the following *synchronization* property that holds in a graph of arbitrary unknown size. When one of the agents has already followed some part of its trajectory, it has either met the other agent, or this other agent must have completed some other related part of its trajectory. (In a way, if the meeting has not yet occurred, the other agent has been "pushed" to execute some part of its route.) The trajectories are designed in such a way that, unless a meeting has already occurred, the agents are forced to follow in the same time interval such parts of their trajectories that meeting is inevitable. A design satisfying this synchronization property is difficult due to the arbitrary behavior of the adversary and is the main technical challenge of the paper.

3.1 Formulation of the algorithm

We first define several trajectories based on trajectories $R(k, v)$. Each trajectory is defined using a starting node v and a parameter k. Notice that, similarly as the basic trajectory $R(k, v)$, each of these trajectories (of increasing complexity) can be defined in any graph, starting from any node v.

DEFINITION 3.1. *The trajectory $X(k, v)$ is the sequence of nodes $R(k, v)\overline{R(k, v)}$.*

DEFINITION 3.2. *The trajectory $Q(k, v)$ is the sequence of nodes $X(1, v)X(2, v)\ldots X(k, v)$.*

DEFINITION 3.3. *Let $R(k, v_1) = (v_1, v_2, \ldots v_s)$. Let $Y'(k, v_1) = Q(k, v_1)(v_1, v_2)Q(k, v_2)(v_2, v_3)Q(k, v_3)\ldots(v_{s-1}, v_s)Q(k, v_s)$. We define the trajectory $Y(k, v_1)$ as $Y'(k, v_1)\overline{Y'(k, v_1)}$.*

DEFINITION 3.4. *The trajectory $Z(k, v)$ is the sequence of nodes $Y(1, v)Y(2, v)\ldots Y(k, v)$.*

DEFINITION 3.5. *Let $R(k, v_1) = (v_1, v_2, \ldots v_s)$. Let $A'(k, v_1) = Z(k, v_1)(v_1, v_2)Z(k, v_2)(v_2, v_3)Z(k, v_3)\ldots(v_{s-1}, v_s)Z(k, v_s)$. We define the trajectory $A(k, v_1)$ as $A'(k, v_1)\overline{A'(k, v_1)}$.*

DEFINITION 3.6. *The trajectory $B(k, v)$ is the sequence of nodes $Y(k, v)^{2|A(4k)|}$.*

DEFINITION 3.7. *The trajectory $K(k, v)$ is the sequence of nodes $X(k, v)^{2(|B(4k)|+|A(8k)|)}$.*

DEFINITION 3.8. *The trajectory $\Omega(k, v)$ is the sequence of nodes $X(k, v)^{(2k-1)|K(k)|}$.*

If the node v is clear from the context, we will sometimes omit it, thus writing $X(k)$ instead of $X(k, v)$, etc.

Using the above defined trajectories we describe Algorithm RV-asynch-poly executed by an agent with label L in an arbitrary graph. The agent first modifies its label. If $x = (c_1 \ldots c_r)$ is the binary representation of L, define the *modified label* of the agent to be the sequence $M(x) = (c_1 c_1 c_2 c_2 \ldots c_r c_r 01)$. Note that, for any x and y, the sequence $M(x)$ is never a prefix of $M(y)$. Also, $M(x) \neq M(y)$ for $x \neq y$.

Algorithm RV-asynch-poly.
Let x be the binary representation of the label L of the agent and let $M(x) = (b_1 b_2 \ldots b_s)$. Let v be the starting node of the agent.
Execute until rendezvous.
$i = 1$; $k = 1$;
repeat
    while $i \leq min(k, s)$ **do**
        if $b_i = 1$ **then** follow the trajectory $B(2k, v)^2$
        else follow the trajectory $A(4k, v)^2$
        if $min(k, s) > i$ **then** follow the trajectory $K(k, v)$
        else follow the trajectory $\Omega(k, v)$
        $i := i + 1$
    $i := 1$
    $k := k + 1$

3.2 Proof of correctness and cost analysis

We will use the following terminology refering to parts of the trajectory constructed by Algorithm RV-asynch-poly. The part before the start of $\Omega(1, v)$ is called the *first piece* and is denoted $\mathcal{T}(1)$, the part between the end of $\Omega(1, v)$ and the beginning of $\Omega(2, v)$ is called the *second piece* and is denoted $\mathcal{T}(2)$, etc. In general, the part between the end of $\Omega(i - 1, v)$ and the beginning of $\Omega(i, v)$ is called the *ith piece* and is denoted $\mathcal{T}(i)$. The trajectory $\Omega(r, v)$ between pieces $\mathcal{T}(r)$ and $\mathcal{T}(r + 1)$, is called the *rth fence*.

Inside each piece, the trajectory $B(2k, v)^2$ and the trajectory $A(4k, v)^2$ are called *segments*. Each of the two trajectories $B(2k, v)$ in the segment $B(2k, v)^2$ and each of the two trajectories $A(4k, v)$ in the segment $A(4k, v)^2$ are called *atoms*. We denote by $S_i(k)$ the segment in the kth piece corresponding to the bit b_i in $M(x)$. Each trajectory $K(k, v)$ is called a *border*. We denote by $K_{j,j+1}(k)$ the border between the segment $S_j(k)$ and the segment $S_{j+1}(k)$.

The following three lemmas establish various synchronization properties concerning the execution of the algorithm by the agents. They show that, unless agents have already met before, if one agent executes some part of Algorithm RV-asynch-poly, then the other agent must execute some other related part of it. These lemmas show the interplay of pieces, fences, segments, atoms and borders that are followed by each of the agents: these trajectories are the milestones of synchronization. In all lemmas we suppose that agents a and b execute Algorithm RV-asynch-poly in a graph of size n, and we let l to be the length of the smaller of their modified labels.

LEMMA 3.1. *Suppose that agents a and b operate in a graph G. Let v be a node of G and let m be a positive integer. If in some time interval I agent b keeps repeating the trajectory $X(m, v)$ and agent a follows at least one entire* trajectory $X(m,v)$, then the agents must meet during time interval I. The lemma remains true when X is replaced by Y.

LEMMA 3.2. *Let b be the first agent to complete its $(2(n+l))$th fence. If the agents have not met before, then during the time segment in which agent b follows its $(2(n+l))$th fence, agent a follows a trajectory included in $r\Omega_a(j)s$, for some fixed j satisfying $n+l+1 \leq j \leq 2(n+l)$, where r is the last atom of its jth piece $\mathcal{T}_a(j)$, $\Omega_a(j)$ is its jth fence, and s is the first atom of its $(j+1)$th piece $\mathcal{T}_a(j+1)$. This j will be called the index of agent a.*

LEMMA 3.3. *Let b be the first agent to complete its $(2(n+l))$th fence. Let t be the first time at which an agent finishes its $(2(n+l)+1)$th piece. If the agents do not meet by time t, then the following properties hold, for j denoting the index of agent a.*

- **Property 1.** *Let t' be the time when agent a completes a segment $S_i(j+1)$, if this segment exists. Let t'' be the time when agent b completes the border $K_{i,i+1}(2(n+l)+1)$, if this border exists. Then $t' < t''$.*

- **Property 2.** *Let t' be the time when agent b completes a segment $S_i(2(n+l)+1)$, if this segment exists. Let t'' be the time when agent a completes the border $K_{i,i+1}(j+1)$, if this border exists. Then $t' < t''$.*

- **Property 3.** *Let t' be the time when agent a completes a border $K_{i,i+1}(j+1)$, if this border exists. Let t'' be the time when agent b completes the first atom of the segment $S_{i+1}(2(n+l)+1)$, if this segment exists. Then $t' < t''$.*

- **Property 4.** *Let t' be the time when agent b completes a border $K_{i,i+1}(2(n+l)+1)$, if this border exists. Let t'' be the time when agent a completes the first atom of the segment $S_{i+1}(j+1)$, if this segment exists. Then $t' < t''$.*

THEOREM 3.1. *There exists a polynomial $\Pi(x,y)$, non decreasing in each variable, such that if two agents with labels L_1 and L_2 execute Algorithm RV-asynch-poly in a graph of size n, then their meeting is guaranteed by the time one of them performs $\Pi(n, \min(|L_1|, |L_2|))$ edge traversals.*

PROOF. Let $m = \min(|L_1|, |L_2|)$. Let a be the agent with label L_1 and let b be the agent with label L_2. Let M_a be the modified label of agent a and let M_b be the modified label of agent b. Let l be the length of the shorter of labels M_a, M_b. Hence $l = 2m + 2$. As observed before, the modified label of one agent cannot be a prefix of the modified label of the other. Hence there exists an integer $l \geq \lambda > 1$, such that the λth bit of M_a is different from the λth bit of M_b. Let t be the first time at which an agent finishes its $(2(n+l)+1)$th piece. By Lemma 3.3, if the agents have not met by time t, then one of them cannot have completed the first atom of $S_\lambda(k_1)$ as long as the other agent has not completed $K_{\lambda-1,\lambda}(k_2)$ (i.e. started $S_\lambda(k_2)$), for some $2(n+l)+1 \geq k_1, k_2 \geq n+l+2$. (Since $k_1, k_2 \geq n+l+2$ and $l \geq \lambda > 1$, these objects must exist.)

First suppose that the λth bit of M_a is 1. There are two possible cases.

• agent a follows the entire trajectory $B(2(j+1))$ while b is following $S_\lambda(2(n+l)+1) = A(8(n+l)+4)^2$.

Since $j \geq n+l+1$, by Definition 3.6 the trajectory $B(2(j+1))$ contains $2|A(8j+8)| \geq 2|A(8(n+l+1)+8)|$ integral trajectories $Y(2(j+1))$. Moreover, according to Algorithm RV-asynch-poly, the number of nodes in $S_\lambda(2(n+l)+1)$ is $2|A(8(n+l)+4)|$. So, the trajectory $B(2(j+1))$ contains more integral trajectories $Y(2(j+1))$ than there are nodes in $S_\lambda(2(n+l)+1)$, hence there is a meeting.

• agent b follows the entire trajectory $A(4(2(n+l)+1))$ while agent a is following $S_\lambda(j+1) = B(2(j+1))^2$.

The trajectory $S_\lambda(j+1)$ consists of repetitions of $Y(2(j+1), v)$ for some node v. Since by Lemma 3.2, $j \leq 2(n+l)$, the trajectory $A(4(2(n+l)+1))$, contains $Y(2(j+1), u)$ for every node u of the graph, which implies a meeting by Lemma 3.1.

Next suppose that the λth bit of M_a is 0. There are two possible cases.

• agent a follows the entire trajectory $A(4(j+1))$ while agent b is following $S_\lambda(2(n+l)+1) = B(2(2(n+l)+1))^2$.

The trajectory $S_\lambda(2(n+l)+1)$ consists of repetitions of $Y(4(n+l)+2)$ for some node v. Since by Lemma 3.2, $j \geq n+l+1$, the trajectory $A(4(j+1))$, contains $Y(4(n+l)+2, u)$ for every node u of the graph, which implies a meeting by Lemma 3.1.

• agent b follows the entire trajectory $B(2(2(n+l)+1))$ while agent a is following $S_\lambda(j+1) = A(4(j+1))^2$.

By Definition 3.6 the trajectory $B(2(2(n+l)+1))$ contains $2|A(16(n+l)+8)|$ integral trajectories $Y(2(2(n+l)+1))$. Moreover, since $j \leq 2(n+l)$, the number of nodes in $S_\lambda(j+1)$ is $2|A(4(j+1))|$ i.e., at most $2|A(8(n+l)+4)|$. So, the number of integral trajectories $Y(2(2(n+l)+1))$ in $B(2(2(n+l)+1))$ is larger than the number of nodes in $S_\lambda(j+1)$, hence there is a meeting.

Hence in all cases agents meet by the time when the first of the agents completes its $(2(n+l)+1)$th piece. Now the proof can be completed by the following estimates which are a consequence of the formulation of the algorithm and of the definitions of respective trajectories. (Recall that P is the polynomial describing the number of edge traversals in the trajectory obtained by Reingold's procedure.)

For any v, $|X(k,v)| \leq X_k^* = 2P(k)+1$. For any v, $|Q(k,v)| \leq Q_k^* = \sum_{i=1}^{k} X_i^*$.

For any v, $|Y(k,v)| \leq Y_k^* = 2P(k) \cdot Q_k^*$. For any v, $|Z(k,v)| \leq Z_k^* = \sum_{i=1}^{k} Y_i^*$.

For any v, $|A(k,v)| \leq A_k^* = 2P(k) \cdot Z_k^*$. For any v, $|B(k,v)| \leq B_k^* = 2A_{8k}^* \cdot Y_k^*$.

For any v, $|K(k,v)| \leq K_k^* = 2B_{8k}^* \cdot X_k^*$. For any v, $|\Omega(k,v)| \leq \Omega_k^* = (2k-1)K_k^* \cdot X_k^*$.

For every integer $k > 0$, let T_k^* denote the number of nodes in a piece in iteration k of the repeat loop in Algorithm RV-asynch-poly. Let $N = 2(n+l)+1$. Recall that $l = 2m+2$. We have $T_k^* \leq N(2A_{4k}^* + 2B_{2k}^* + K_k^*)$. For any agent, the length of the trajectory it follows by the time it completes the $(2(n+l)+1)$th piece is at most $\sum_{k=1}^{N}(T_k^* + \Omega_k^*)$. Let $\Pi(n,m) = \sum_{k=1}^{N}(T_k^* + \Omega_k^*)$. It follows from the above discussion that agents must meet by the time one of them performs $\Pi(n,m)$ edge traversals. Since T_k^* and Ω_k^* are polynomials in k, while N and l are polynomials in n and m, the function $\Pi(n,m)$ is a polynomial. Since the polynomial $P(k)$ is non-decreasing, Π is non-decreasing in each variable. This completes the proof. $\square$

4. APPLICATIONS: SOLVING PROBLEMS FOR MULTIPLE ASYNCHRONOUS AGENTS

In this section we apply our polynomial-cost rendezvous algorithm for asynchronous agents to solve four basic distributed problems involving multiple asynchronous agents in unknown networks. Agents solve these problems by exchanging information during their meetings. The scenario for all the problems is the following. There is a team of $k > 1$ agents having distinct integer labels, located at different nodes of an unknown network. The adversary wakes up some of the agents at possibly different times. A dormant agent is also woken up by an agent that visits its starting node, if such an agent exists. As before, each agent knows a priori only its own label. Agents do not know the size of the team and, as before, have no a priori knowledge concerning the network. The assumptions concerning the movements of agents remain unchanged. We only need to add a provision in the model specifying what happens when agents meet. (For rendezvous, this was the end of the process.) This addition is very simple. When (two or more) agents meet, they notice this fact and can exchange all previously acquired information. However, if the meeting is inside an edge, they continue the walk prescribed by the adversary until reaching the other end of the current edge. New knowledge acquired at the meeting can then influence the choice of the subsequent part of the routes constructed by each of the agents. It should be noted that the possibility of exchanging all current information at a meeting is formulated only for simplicity. In fact, during a meeting, our algorithm prescribes the exchange of only at most k labels of other agents that the meeting agents have already heard of, their initial values in the case of the gossiping problem, and a constant number of control bits.

We now specify the four problems that we want to solve:
- team size: every agent has to output the total number k of agents;
- leader election: all agents have to output the label of a single agent, called the leader;
- perfect renaming: all agents have to adopt new different labels from the set $\{1,\ldots,k\}$, where k is the number of agents;
- gossiping: each agent has initially a piece of information (value) and all agents have to output all the values; thus agents have to exchange all their initial information.

The cost of a solution of each of the above problems is the total number of edge traversals by all agents until they output the solution. Using our rendezvous algorithm we solve all these problems at cost polynomial in the size of the graph and in the smallest length of all labels of participating agents.

Let us first note that accomplishing all the above tasks is a consequence of solving the following problem: at some point each agent acquires the labels of all the agents *and is aware* of this fact. We call this more general problem Strong Global Learning (SGL), where the word "strong" emphasizes awareness of the agents that learning is accomplished.[1] Indeed, if each agent gets the labels of all the agents *and is aware* of

it, then each agent can count all agents, thus solving team size, each agent can output the smallest label as that of the leader, thus solving leader election, each agent can adopt the new label i if its original label was ith in increasing order among all labels, thus solving perfect renaming, and each agent can output all initial values, thus solving gossiping, if we append in the algorithm for SGL the initial value to the label of each agent.

Hence it is enough to give an algorithm for the SGL problem, working at cost polynomial in the size of the graph and in the smallest length of all labels of participating agents. This is the aim of the present section. Notice that this automatically solves all distributed problems that depend only on acquiring by all agents the knowledge of all labels and *being aware of this fact*. (The above four problems are in this class.) We stress this latter requirement, because it is of crucial importance. Note, for example, that none of the above four problems can be solved even if agents eventually learn all labels but are never aware of the fact that no other agents are in the network. This detection requirement is non-trivial to achieve: recall that agents have no a priori bound on the size of the graph or on the size of the team.

We now describe Algorithm SGL solving the SGL problem at cost polynomial in the size of the graph and in the smallest length of all labels of participating agents. In this description we will use procedure RV-ASYNCH-POLY(L) to denote Algorithm RV-asynch-poly as executed by an agent with label L. For technical reasons, an agent with label L will execute RV-ASYNCH-POLY(L') for L' different from L, i.e., an agent will mimic the execution of Algorithm RV-asynch-poly by an agent with a label different from its own.

Algorithm SGL

For ease of presentation we will define three states in which an agent can be. These states are *traveller*, *explorer* and *token*. Transitions between states depend on the history of the agent, and more specifically on comparing the labels exchanged during meetings.

The high-level idea of the algorithm is the following. An agent a with label L wakes up in state *traveller* and executes procedure RV-ASYNCH-POLY($L+1$) until the first meeting when it meets either other agents in state *traveller* or in state *token*. Then, depending on the comparison of labels of the agents it meets, it transits either to state *token* or to state *explorer*. In the first case it terminates its current move and stays idle. In the second case it simulates procedure *EST* learning the map of the graph and in particular its size n. Then it executes procedure RV-ASYNCH-POLY(1) until it performed $\Pi(n, 1)$ edge traversals. Now it has met all agents in state *traveller*. At this point two consecutive DFS traversals of the already known graph permit it to learn all labels of participating agents and to convey this knowledge to all agents in state *token*. All other agents will in turn get this knowledge from these agents.

Below we specify what an agent a with label L does in each state and how it transits from state to state. Each agent has a set variable W, called its *bag*, initialized to $\{L\}$, where L is its label. At each point of the execution of the algorithm the value of the bag is the set of labels of agents that a has been informed about. More precisely, during any meeting of a with agents whose current values of their bags

---

[1] Notice that the assumption that the number k of agents is larger than 1 is necessary. For a single agent neither SGL nor any of the above mentioned problems can be solved. Indeed, for example in an oriented ring of unknown size (ports 0,1 at all nodes in the clockwise direction), a single agent cannot realize that it is alone.

are $W_1, W_2, \ldots, W_i$, respectively, agent a sets the value of its bag W to $W \cup W_1 \cup W_2 \cup \cdots \cup W_i$. Notice that since each bag can be only incremented, the number of updates of each bag is at most $k - 1$, where k is the number of agents.

State *traveller.*

The agent a wakes up in this state and starts executing procedure RV-ASYNCH-POLY($L + 1$) until the first meeting. Suppose the first meeting is with a set Z of agents. If Z contains an agent in state *token*, then let b be the smallest agent in this state in set Z. Agent a transits to state *explorer* and considers b as its token. If Z does not contain any agent in state *token* but contains agents in state *traveller*, then let c be the smallest agent in this state in set Z. If a is smaller than c, then a transits to state *token* and all agents in state *traveller* from Z transit to state *explorer* considering a as their token. If a is larger than c, then a and all agents in state *traveller* from Z except c transit to state *explorer* and they consider c (which transits to state *token*) as their token. Finally, if Z consists only of agents in state *explorer*, then agent a ignores this meeting and continues executing procedure RV-ASYNCH-POLY($L + 1$) until the next meeting.

State *token.*

In this state the agent a completes the traversal of the current edge and remains idle at its extremity forever. As soon as it gets the information (from some agent in state *explorer*) that its current bag contains all labels of participating agents, agent a outputs the value of its bag.

State *explorer.*

When agent a transits to this state, it has just met an agent b in state *token* (or which has just transited to state *token*), that a considers as its token. Actions of a are divided into two phases.

Phase 1. If the meeting was at a node, agent a performs the procedure *EST* with the token at this node. If the meeting was inside an edge e, agent a simulates procedure *EST* in a graph G' differing from the real graph by adding a node w of degree 2 inside edge e and treating the agent b as the token residing at w. During the simulation, when a subsequently meets b, this can happen either inside edge e or in one of the extremities u, v of e. In the first case agent a behaves as if the meeting of the token were in w. In particular, if all meetings with b during the simulation of *EST* are inside e, agent a acts as follows after each meeting. It finishes the traversal of e going, say to u and then either simulates the next move by going to v if the simulated move is from w to v or by doing nothing, if the simulated move is from w to u. If some meeting with b during the simulation is at one of the extremities, a aborts the simulation and launches *EST* in the real graph with the token at this node. (In this case agent b playing the role of the token will stay idle forever at the node.) After completing Phase 1 agent a learns the complete map of the graph, and in particular its size n.

Phase 2. Knowing the size n of the graph, agent a executes procedure RV-ASYNCH-POLY(1) until it performed $\Pi(n, 1)$ edge traversals. (Note that $|1| = 1$.) We will show that at this point it met all agents that were either still dormant or were in state *traveller*. The labels of all remaining agents are in the union of bags of all agents currently in state *token*. Agent a performs two consecutive DFS traversals of the graph (whose map is already known to it), traversing all of its edges. After the first DFS traversal agent a has in its bag the labels of all participating agents. During the second

DFS traversal, all these labels are transmitted to all agents in state *token*, together with the information that this is the set of all labels. After completing the second traversal agent a outputs the value of its bag.

THEOREM 4.1. *Upon completion of Algorithm SGL, each agent outputs the set of labels of all participating agents. The total cost of the algorithm is polynomial in the size of the graph and in the smallest length of all labels of participating agents.*

5. CONCLUSION

We presented an algorithm for asynchronous rendezvous of agents in arbitrary finite connected graphs, working at cost polynomial in the size of the graph and in the length of the smaller label. In [18], where the exponential-cost solution was first proposed, the authors stated the following question:

Does there exist a deterministic asynchronous rendezvous algorithm, working for all connected finite unknown graphs, with complexity polynomial in the labels of the agents and in the size of the graph?

Our result gives a strong positive answer to this problem: our algorithm is polynomial in the *logarithm* of the smaller label and in the size of the graph.

In this paper we did not make any attempt at optimizing the cost of our rendezvous algorithm, the only concern was to keep it polynomial. Cost optimization seems to be a very challenging problem. Even finding the optimal cost of exploration of unknown graphs of known size is still open, and this is a much simpler problem, as it is equivalent to rendezvous of two agents one of which is inert.

We also applied our rendezvous algorithm to solve four fundamental distributed problems in the context of multiple asynchronous mobile agents. The cost of all solutions is polynomial in the size of the graph and in the length of the smallest of all labels.

6. REFERENCES

[1] H. Attiya, A. Bar-Noy, D. Dolev, D. Koller, D. Peleg and R. Reischuk, Renaming in an asynchronous environment, Journal of the ACM 37 (1990), 524-548.

[2] N. Agmon and D. Peleg, Fault-tolerant gathering algorithms for autonomous mobile robots, SIAM J. Comput. 36 (2006), 56-82.

[3] S. Alpern, The rendezvous search problem, SIAM J. on Control and Optimization 33 (1995), 673-683.

[4] S. Alpern, Rendezvous search on labelled networks, Naval Research Logistics 49 (2002), 256-274.

[5] S. Alpern and S. Gal, The theory of search games and rendezvous. Int. Series in Operations research and Management Science, Kluwer Academic Publisher, 2002.

[6] J. Alpern, V. Baston, and S. Essegaier, Rendezvous search on a graph, Journal of Applied Probability 36 (1999), 223-231.

[7] E. Anderson and R. Weber, The rendezvous problem on discrete locations, Journal of Applied Probability 28 (1990), 839-851.

[8] E. Anderson and S. Fekete, Asymmetric rendezvous on the plane, Proc. 14th Annual ACM Symp. on Computational Geometry (1998), 365-373.

[9] E. Anderson and S. Fekete, Two-dimensional rendezvous search, Operations Research 49 (2001), 107-118.

[10] E. Bampas, J. Czyzowicz, L. Gasieniec, D. Ilcinkas, A. Labourel, Almost optimal asynchronous rendezvous in infinite multidimensional grids, *Proc. 24th International Symposium on Distributed Computing (DISC 2010), LNCS 6343*, 297-311.

[11] V. Baston and S. Gal, Rendezvous search when marks are left at the starting points, Naval Research Logistics 48 (2001), 722-731.

[12] J. Chalopin, S. Das, A. Kosowski, Constructing a map of an anonymous graph: Applications of universal sequences, Proc. 14th International Conference on Principles of Distributed Systems (OPODIS 2010), 119-134.

[13] M. Cieliebak, P. Flocchini, G. Prencipe, N. Santoro, Solving the robots gathering problem, Proc. 30th International Colloquium on Automata, Languages and Programming (ICALP 2003), 1181-1196.

[14] R. Cohen and D. Peleg, Convergence properties of the gravitational algorithm in asynchronous robot systems, SIAM J. Comput. 34 (2005), 1516-1528.

[15] R. Cohen and D. Peleg, Convergence of autonomous mobile robots with inaccurate sensors and movements, SIAM J. Comput. 38 (2008), 276-302.

[16] A. Collins, J. Czyzowicz, L. Gasieniec, A. Labourel, Tell me where I am so I can meet you sooner. *Proc. 37th International Colloquium on Automata, Languages and Programming (ICALP 2010)*, 502-514.

[17] J. Czyzowicz, A. Kosowski and A. Pelc, How to meet when you forget: Log-space rendezvous in arbitrary graphs, *Distributed Computing*, 25, 165-178 (2012)

[18] J. Czyzowicz, A. Labourel, A. Pelc, How to meet asynchronously (almost) everywhere, ACM Transactions on Algorithms 8 (2012), article 37.

[19] G. De Marco, L. Gargano, E. Kranakis, D. Krizanc, A. Pelc, U. Vaccaro, Asynchronous deterministic rendezvous in graphs, *Theoretical Computer Science*, 355, 315-326 (2006)

[20] A. Dessmark, P. Fraigniaud, D. Kowalski, A. Pelc. Deterministic rendezvous in graphs. Algorithmica 46 (2006), 69-96.

[21] Y. Dieudonné, A. Pelc, Anonymous Meeting in Networks, Proc. 24rd Annual ACM-SIAM Symposium on Discrete Algorithms (SODA 2013), 737-747.

[22] Y. Dieudonné, A. Pelc, D. Peleg, Gathering despite mischief, Proc. 23rd Annual ACM-SIAM Symposium on Discrete Algorithms (SODA 2012), 527-540.

[23] P. Flocchini, G. Prencipe, N. Santoro, P. Widmayer, Gathering of asynchronous oblivious robots with limited visibility, Proc. 18th Annual Symposium on Theoretical Aspects of Computer Science (STACS 2001), Springer LNCS 2010, 247-258.

[24] P. Fraigniaud, E. Lazard, Methods and problems of communication in usual networks. Discrete Applied Mathematics 53 (1994), 79-133.

[25] P. Fraigniaud, A. Pelc, Deterministic rendezvous in trees with little memory, Proc. 22nd International Symposium on Distributed Computing (DISC 2008), LNCS 5218, 242-256.

[26] P. Fraigniaud, A. Pelc, Delays induce an exponential memory gap for rendezvous in trees, Proc. 22nd Ann. ACM Symposium on Parallel Algorithms and Architectures (SPAA 2010), 224-232.

[27] P. Fraigniaud, A. Pelc, Decidability classes for mobile agents computing, Proc. 10th Latin American Theoretical Informatics Symposium (LATIN 2012), LNCS 7256, 362-374.

[28] S. Guilbault, A. Pelc, Asynchronous rendezvous of anonymous agents in arbitrary graphs, *Proc. 15th International Conference on Principles of Distributed Systems (OPODIS 2011), LNCS 7109*, 162-173.

[29] D. Kowalski, A. Malinowski, How to meet in anonymous network, in 13th Int. Colloquium on Structural Information and Comm. Complexity, (SIROCCO 2006), Springer LNCS 4056, 44-58.

[30] E. Kranakis, D. Krizanc, and P. Morin, Randomized rendez-vous with limited memory, Proc. 8th Latin American Theoretical Informatics (LATIN 2008), Springer LNCS 4957, 605-616.

[31] E. Kranakis, D. Krizanc, N. Santoro and C. Sawchuk, Mobile agent rendezvous in a ring, Proc. 23rd Int. Conference on Distributed Computing Systems (ICDCS 2003), IEEE, 592-599.

[32] W. Lim and S. Alpern, Minimax rendezvous on the line, SIAM J. on Control and Optimization 34 (1996), 1650-1665.

[33] A. Pelc, Deterministic rendezvous in networks: A comprehensive survey, Networks 59 (2012), 331-347.

[34] N.L. Lynch, Distributed algorithms, Morgan Kaufmann Publ. Inc., San Francisco, USA, 1996.

[35] O. Reingold, Undirected connectivity in log-space, Journal of the ACM 55 (2008).

[36] A. Ta-Shma and U. Zwick. Deterministic rendezvous, treasure hunts and strongly universal exploration sequences. *Proc. 18th ACM-SIAM Symposium on Discrete Algorithms (SODA 2007)*, 599-608.

[37] X. Yu and M. Yung, Agent rendezvous: a dynamic symmetry-breaking problem, Proc. International Colloquium on Automata, Languages, and Programming (ICALP 1996), Springer LNCS 1099, 610-621.

On the Complexity of Universal Leader Election

Shay Kutten[*]
Faculty of IE&M,
Technion, Haifa 32000.
kutten@ie.technion.ac.il

Gopal Pandurangan[† ‡]
Div. of Mathematical Sciences,
Nanyang Technological Univ.,
Singapore 637371.
gopalpandurangan@gmail.com

David Peleg[§]
Dept. of Computer Science,
The Weizmann Institute,
Rehovot, Israel.
david.peleg@weizmann.ac.il

Peter Robinson[¶]
Div. of Mathematical Sciences,
Nanyang Technological Univ.,
Singapore 637371.
peter.robinson@ntu.edu.sg

Amitabh Trehan[*]
Faculty of IE&M,
Technion, Haifa 32000.
amitabh.trehaan@gmail.com

ABSTRACT

Electing a leader is a fundamental task in distributed computing. In its *implicit* version, only the leader must know who is the elected leader. This paper focuses on studying the message and time complexity of *randomized* implicit leader election in synchronous distributed networks. Surprisingly, the most "obvious" complexity bounds have not been proven for randomized algorithms. The "obvious" lower bounds of $\Omega(m)$ messages (m is the number of edges in the network) and $\Omega(D)$ time (D is the network diameter) are non-trivial to show for randomized (Monte Carlo) algorithms. (Recent results that show that even $\Omega(n)$ (n is the number of nodes in the network) is *not* a lower bound on the messages in complete networks, make the above bounds somewhat less obvious). To the best of our knowledge, these basic lower

[*]Research supported in part by the Israel Science Foundation and by the Technion TASP center.

[†]Research supported in part by the following grants: Nanyang Technological University grant M58110000, Singapore Ministry of Education (MOE) Academic Research Fund (AcRF) Tier 2 grant MOE2010-T2-2-082, MOE AcRF Tier 1 grant MOE2012-T1-001-094, and a grant from the US-Israel Binational Science Foundation (BSF).

[‡]Also affiliated with the Department of Computer Science, Brown University, Box 1910, Providence, RI 02912, USA.

[§]Supported in part by the Israel Science Foundation (grant 894/09), the United States-Israel Binational Science Foundation (grant 2008348), the Israel Ministry of Science and Technology (infrastructures grant), and the Citi Foundation.

[¶]Research supported in part by the following grants: Nanyang Technological University grant M58110000, Singapore Ministry of Education (MOE) Academic Research Fund (AcRF) Tier 2 grant MOE2010-T2-2-082.

bounds have not been established even for deterministic algorithms (except for the limited case of comparison algorithms, where it was also required that some nodes may not wake up spontaneously, and that D and n were not known).

We establish these fundamental lower bounds in this paper for the general case, even for randomized Monte Carlo algorithms. Our lower bounds are universal in the sense that they hold for all universal algorithms (such algorithms should work for all graphs), apply to every D, m, and n, and hold even if D, m, and n are known, all the nodes wake up simultaneously, and the algorithms can make any use of node's identities. To show that these bounds are tight, we present an $O(m)$ messages algorithm. An $O(D)$ time algorithm is known. A slight adaptation of our lower bound technique gives rise to an $\Omega(m)$ message lower bound for randomized broadcast algorithms.

An interesting fundamental problem is whether *both* upper bounds (messages and time) can be reached *simultaneously* in the randomized setting for all graphs. (The answer is known to be negative in the deterministic setting). We answer this problem partially by presenting a randomized algorithm that matches both complexities in some cases. This already separates (for some cases) randomized algorithms from deterministic ones. As first steps towards the general case, we present several universal leader election algorithms with bounds that trade-off messages versus time. We view our results as a step towards understanding the complexity of universal leader election in distributed networks.

Categories and Subject Descriptors

F.2.2 [**Theory of Computation**]: [Analysis of Algorithms and Problem Complexity—Nonnumerical Algorithms and Problems]

Keywords

Leader election; lower bound; distributed algorithm.

1. INTRODUCTION

Leader election is a fundamental and classical problem in distributed computing. Due to shortage of space, we rely on the reader's familiarity with its long history and many theoretical implications. Previous work is too rich to survey here, see, e.g., [3, 14, 19, 20]. Still, let us stress that this long-studied task is relevant today more than ever, with its practical applications to the emerging area of large scale and resource-constrained networks such as peer-to-peer networks (e.g., that of Akamai [16]), ad hoc and sensor networks (e.g., [9, 21]). For example, minimizing messages and time for basic tasks such as leader election can help in minimizing energy consumption in ad hoc and sensor networks. Hence, it is desirable to achieve fast, low cost and scalable leader election. This is one of the reasons why this paper concentrates on randomized algorithms, that have been shown to reduce complexity dramatically in various contexts. (In fact, it was recently shown that the randomized message complexity of leader election in complete graphs is sublinear, $O(\sqrt{n} \log^{3/2} n)$[12].) Interestingly, although the leader election task is so well studied, some basic theoretical questions concerning its complexity have not been answered yet, especially (but not only) for the randomized case.

Informally, the leader election task requires a group of processors in a distributed network to elect a unique leader among themselves, i.e., exactly one processor must output the decision that it is the leader, say, by changing a special *status* component of its state to the value *leader*, with all the other nodes changing their *status* component to the value *non-leader*. These nodes need not be aware of the identity of the leader. This *implicit* version of leader election is rather standard (cf. [14]), and is sufficient in many applications, e.g., its original application for token generation in a token ring environment [13]. (In the *explicit* variant, every node must also know the identity of the unique leader.) This paper *focuses on implicit leader election*, although our algorithms apply to the explicit version as well.

The study of leader election algorithms is usually concerned with both message and time complexity. Both may appear to be very well understood. For example, Awerbuch [4] presented a deterministic algorithm (that takes $O(n)$ rounds and uses $O(m + n \log n)$ messages) that was claimed to be optimal both in terms of time complexity and in terms of message complexity. As demonstrated in [17], the time in Awerbuch's algorithm may be optimal only existentially, that is, only in the case that $n = O(D)$, where n is the number of nodes, and D the diameter of the graph. Moreover, these claims of optimality rely on the tacit assumption that D and m (the number of edges) are lower bounds on the time and the number of messages required for leader election, respectively. Surprisingly, even for deterministic algorithms, the only proof we are aware of for a lower bound of $\Omega(m)$ on the message complexity of leader election is for the rather limited case where (a) the algorithms are only *comparison* algorithms (that may not manipulate the actual value of node's identities, but only compare identities with each other), (b) spontaneous wakeup of the nodes is not guaranteed, and (c) network parameters (such as n) are not known to the nodes. This limited case admits a very short and elegant proof, cf. [20]. Unfortunately, that proof fails completely if one of the assumptions is removed[1]. (As a by

product of our results for randomized algorithms, we get rid of all these special assumptions for deterministic algorithms too.) For the time complexity of leader election, the situation is even less stable, and the lower bound of D seems to be folklore, cf. [5, 20].)

Let us assume for a moment that the above lower bounds were indeed "obvious" (though not formally proven for the general case) for deterministic algorithms. Are they indeed that obvious for randomized ones? The work of [12] demonstrated that, for randomized algorithms, the "obvious" lower bound of $\Omega(n)$ messages for a complete graph (as well as other classes of graphs with sufficiently small mixing times such as expanders and hypercubes) does not hold. Specifically, it presented an algorithm that executes in $O(1)$ time and uses only $O(\sqrt{n} \log^{3/2} n)$ messages to elect a leader in a complete graph (and similarly for other families of high-expansion graphs). Consequently, it would appear that the obvious lower bounds on time and messages must be revisited, especially for randomized algorithms.

This paper concerns *universal* leader election algorithms, namely, algorithms that work for all graphs. The unconditional randomized lower bounds of $\Omega(m)$ messages and $\Omega(D)$ time shown in this paper (cf. Table 1) subsume the above deterministic bounds in a general way. These bounds apply to a large class of graphs for (essentially) every given m, D, and n. They hold even for non-comparison algorithms and even if nodes have knowledge of these parameters. They also hold for synchronous networks, and even if all the nodes wake up simultaneously. Finally, they hold not only for the $\mathcal{CONGEST}$ model [18] (where sending a message of $O(\log n)$ bits takes one unit of time) but also for the $\mathcal{LOCAL}$ model (where the number of bits in a message is allowed to be arbitrary).

We note that the universal lower bounds of $\Omega(m)$ and $\Omega(D)$ do not follow from currently known results. There are several known lower bounds for *deterministic* leader election algorithms in cycles (e.g., [7]) and complete graphs (e.g., [11, 2]), which also imply bounds for (deterministic) *universal* algorithms. These results alone do not, however, imply that a universal algorithm cannot do significantly better in other classes of networks. For example, the deterministic lower bound of $\Omega(n \log n)$ messages in ring graphs (cf. [7, 20]) does not imply a lower bound of $\Omega(m)$ messages (even for deterministic algorithms) in general graphs. Moreover, it does not even imply the necessity of $\Omega(n \log n)$ messages for every graph, since there exist graphs with n nodes where the number of messages required is smaller (e.g., a star graph). It may even be possible to design a universal election algorithm that will use only $O(n)$ messages when executed on a star graph.

Compared to deterministic algorithms, lower bounds (and their proofs) for randomized algorithms, particularly Monte Carlo ones, are more delicate. For example, consider the following simple algorithm (which assumes the nodes know n): "Each node elects itself as leader with probability $1/n$." The probability of this algorithm resulting in exactly one leader is $\binom{n}{1} \frac{1}{n} (1 - 1/n)^{n-1} \approx 1/e \approx 0.368$. Hence there exists a randomized algorithm that elects a leader in one

---

[1]Interestingly, even in the *explicit* deterministic variant, an "obvious" lower bound of $\Omega(m)$ messages was *not* known. Indeed, the explicit version seems to require a broadcast of the leader's name. Still, the known lower bound of $\Omega(m)$ on deterministic broadcast was shown only for the case where the nodes do not wake up simultaneously [5]. Hence in the general case, it was not known that conveying the leader's

identity to every node consumes $\Omega(m)$ messages. As opposed to the number of edges, still for the explicit variant, $\Omega(n)$ (the number of *nodes*) and $\Omega(D)$ do seem to be known lower bounds on the messages and time. Nevertheless, $\Omega(D)$ time is not obvious for the implicit variant studied here.

time unit, without sending any messages, and succeeds with constant (albeit small) probability! In contrast, as proved later in the paper, if the success probability is required to be a somewhat larger constant, then the time lower bound becomes $\Omega(D)$ and the message lower bound becomes $\Omega(m)$.

To the best of our knowledge, previous work on time complexity bounds for leader election in general networks is scarce. In a recent work[8], the authors study *deterministic* algorithms for variants of leader election in *anonymous* networks called *weak* (resp., *strong*) leader election, which require the algorithm to elect a leader in the given network if possible. It is shown in [8] that $D + \lambda$ is a lower bound in this setting, where λ is a *symmetry* parameter, which is the smallest depth at which the views of the nodes become distinguishable.

Over two decades ago, the following basic open problem was raised in [17]: Is it possible to design a universal algorithm for leader election that is *simultaneously both time and message optimal*? In view of the lower bounds in this paper, this question can be reformulated as follows: Is there an $O(D)$ time and $O(m)$ messages universal leader election algorithm? The answer is negative if we restrict ourselves to deterministic algorithms, since it is known that for a cycle any $O(n)$ time deterministic algorithm requires at least $\Omega(n \log n)$ messages (even when nodes know n) [7]. However, the problem still stands for randomized algorithms. We provide a partial answer for this problem by presenting a randomized algorithm that matches both complexities for $m \geqslant n^{1+\varepsilon}$ (for any fixed constant $\varepsilon > 0$), assuming n is known. This already separates randomized algorithms from deterministic ones. Another such case (for every m) when both lower bounds can be matched is when n and D are known. As first steps for the more general case, we present several universal leader election algorithms with bounds that trade-off messages versus time. In particular, to also show that our lower bounds are tight, we present a simple deterministic algorithm that uses $O(m)$ messages. An $O(D)$ time algorithm is already known [17].

1.1 Our Results

This paper presents lower and upper bounds for universal leader election algorithms in synchronous arbitrary networks. Our results on leader election are summarized in Table 1. The formal statements of our algorithms and their full proofs are in the full paper. The tight bounds are the lower ones – Theorem 3.13 and Theorem 3.1, as demonstrated by Theorem 4.1 (and [17]). Corollary 3.12 shows that a slight adaptation of our lower bound technique implies an $\Omega(m)$ message lower bound for solving the broadcast problem. Note that Theorem 4.3.(B) presents a case where one can match *both* lower bounds simultaneously with a constant (though close to 1) probability. Corollary 4.4 shows a case where both bounds can be matched with high success probability[2] (but with a constraint on m). Corollary 4.5 demonstrates a case with probability 1, but with an extra assumption (knowledge of D). The other results in the table may be of interest by themselves. They were obtained on the way to reaching the above results, or in trying to get close to a tight upper bound for the general case.

---

[2]Throughout, "with high probability (w.h.p.)" means with probability at least $1 - 1/n$.

2. PRELIMINARIES

We consider a system of n nodes, represented as an undirected connected (not necessarily complete) graph $G = (V, E)$. Each node u runs an instance of a distributed algorithm and has a unique identifier $\mathtt{ID}_u$ of $O(\log n)$ bits chosen by an adversary from an arbitrary set of integers Z of size n^4 (the nodes themselves may not have knowledge of n, nor of Z). The lower bounds hold even when nodes have unique identities (IDs). However, for some of the algorithms, we do not assume that the nodes have unique identities (IDs). Hence, the randomized algorithms in this paper also work for anonymous networks. To make the lower bounds more general, we assume that all nodes wake up simultaneously at the beginning of the execution.

The computation advances in synchronous rounds, where in every round, nodes can send messages, receive messages that were sent in the same round by neighbors in G, and perform some local computation. Our algorithms work in the $\mathcal{CONGEST}$ model [18], where in each round a node can send at most one message of size $O(\log n)$ bits on a single edge. In contrast, our lower bounds apply even in the $\mathcal{LOCAL}$ model [18], where there is no restriction on message size.

For randomized (Las Vegas and Monte Carlo) algorithms, we also assume that every node has access to the outcome of unbiased private coin flips. Messages are the only means of communication; in particular, nodes cannot access the coin flips of other nodes, and do not share any memory. The classical leader election literature distinguishes between the *simultaneous wakeup model* where all nodes are awake initially and start executing the algorithm simultaneously, and the *adversarial wakeup model* where the nodes are awoken at arbitrary points in time, with the restriction that nodes wake upon receiving a message and at least one node is initially awake. Our lower bounds hold even if the nodes are initially awake. In contrast, the analysis of some of the algorithms holds even for the case of adversarial wakeup.

Initially, each node is given a port numbering where each port is connected to an incident edge leading to a neighbor. However, the node has no knowledge of the neighbor at the other endpoint of edge. Recall that our lower bounds hold even if the nodes know some of the graph parameters, such as n, D, and m. Some of our algorithms work without this assumption. However, other algorithms rely on the assumption that the nodes know one or more of these parameters (cf. Table 1).

2.1 Leader Election (LE)

We now define the leader election problem formally. Every node u has a special variable $\mathtt{status}_u$ that can be set to a value in $\{\perp, \text{NON-ELECTED}, \text{ELECTED}\}$; initially $\mathtt{status}_u = \perp$. An *algorithm A solves leader election in T rounds* if, from round T on, *exactly one* node has its status set to ELECTED while all other nodes are in state NON-ELECTED.

We say that A is a *universal* leader election algorithm, with error probability ε, if for any choice of n and m, the probability that A succeeds is at least $1 - \varepsilon$ on any network of n nodes and m edges, and any ID assignment chosen from any integer set of large polynomial (in n) size; for our lower bounds we assume that $|Z| \geqslant n^4$. In particular, if A is a deterministic algorithm or a randomized Las Vegas algorithm, then A is universal if and only if it achieves leader election on every network under all ID assignments.

	TIME	MESSAGES	KNOWLEDGE	SUCCESS PROBABILITY
Lower Bounds:				
Theorem 3.13	–	$\Omega(m)^\dagger$	n, m, D	$\geqslant 53/56$
Theorem 3.1	$\Omega(D)^*$	–	n, m, D	$\geqslant 15/16 + \varepsilon$ ††
Randomized Algorithms:				
Theorem 4.3	$O(D)$	$O(m \min(\log f(n), D))^{\dagger, \#}$	n	$\geqslant 1 - 1/e^{\Theta(f(n))}$
Theorem 4.3.(A)	$O(D)$	$O(m \min(\log \log n, D))^\dagger$	n	$\geqslant 1 - n^{-1}$
Theorem 4.3.(B)	$O(D)$	$O(m)^\dagger$	n	$\geqslant 1 - \varepsilon$ ††
Corollary 4.4	$O(D)$	$O(m)^\dagger$, if $m \geqslant n^{1+\varepsilon}$ ††	n	$\geqslant 1 - n^{-1}$
Corollary 4.2	$O(D)$	$O(m \min(\log n, D))^\$$	–	$\geqslant 1 - n^{-1}$
Corollary 4.5	$O(D)^\dagger$	$O(m)^\dagger$	n, D	1
Theorem 4.6	$O(D \log n)^\$$	$O(m + n \log n)^\$$	n	$\geqslant 1 - n^{-1}$
Deterministic Algorithms:				
Theorem 4.7	$O(D \log n)$	$O(m \log n)$	–	
Theorem 4.1	arbitrary	$O(m)$	–	

$\$$ with high probability. † in expectation. * with constant probability. $^\#$ for any $f(n) \in \Omega(1)$. †† for any fixed constant $\varepsilon > 0$.

Table 1: Upper and lower bounds for universal leader election algorithms.

3. RANDOMIZED LOWER BOUNDS

As mentioned earlier, to the best of our knowledge, lower bounds for randomized (especially Monte Carlo) algorithms have not been studied. Here we present two basic lower bounds that apply to randomized algorithms, including Monte Carlo algorithms with (suitably large) *constant* success probability: an $\Omega(m)$ bound on the number of messages and an $\Omega(D)$ bound on the time. Our message lower bound applies to any m and n, i.e., we show that given any n and m, there exists a graph with $\Theta(n)$ nodes and $\Theta(m)$ edges, where the lower bound holds. Our time lower bound states that for every n and D ($2 < D < n$), there exists a graph with $\Theta(n)$ nodes and $\Theta(D)$ diameter for which the time needed is $\Omega(D)$, even with constant success probability. Also, these lower bounds hold even if the nodes have knowledge of the global parameters n, D and m. Our lower bounds apply to all algorithms (and not just comparison-based ones) and hold even if the all nodes wake up simultaneously.

Our message lower bound is proved by first showing a lower bound for a related problem referred to as *"bridge crossing (BC)"*. In the bridge crossing problem, it is required that at least one message is sent across a "bridge" edge connecting two specific subgraphs. We then show conditions under which any universal leader election algorithm must solve BC. We first show a lower bound of the expected message complexity of deterministic algorithms for BC and LE, and then use Yao's lemma (cf. Lemma 3.2) to show that it applies also to the expected message complexity of randomized algorithms on the worst-case input. The proof involves constructing a suitable graph that ensures that a knowledge of n, m, D, and identity assignment will be useless to any algorithm; it also involves a counting argument to lower bound the number of messages sent.

Our $\Omega(D)$ time lower bound is proven directly for Monte Carlo algorithms by a probabilistic argument. We show that for a suitably constructed graph of a given size and diameter, any Monte Carlo algorithm that needs to succeed with a suitably large constant probability must communicate over a distance of $\Omega(D)$ edges. Otherwise, there might not be a unique leader.

3.1 Message Complexity Lower Bound

THEOREM 3.1. *Let R be a universal leader election algorithm that succeeds with probability at least $1 - \beta$, for some constant $\beta \leqslant 3/56$. For every sufficiently large n and $n \leqslant m \leqslant \binom{n}{2}$, there exists a (connected) graph G of n nodes and $\Theta(m)$ edges, such that the expected number of messages used by R on G is $\Omega(m)$. The above holds even if n, m and D are known to the algorithm and all nodes wake up simultaneously.*

For simplicity, we first describe the proof assuming the nodes do not know the diameter D. At the end of the proof, we explain why this proof fails for weaker algorithms, which are guaranteed to work correctly only when the nodes know D, and then outline the modifications necessary to allow the proof to handle this harder case as well.

The proof is based on constructing a graph family referred to as *dumbbell graphs*. Given R, n and m, pick one specific 2-connected graph G_0 of n nodes and m edges, and a range $Z = [1, n^4]$ of ID's. This G_0 has many instantiations, obtained by fixing the node ID assignment and the port number mapping. An ID assignment is a function $\varphi : V(G_0) \mapsto Z$. A port mapping for node v is a mapping $P_v : [1, deg_v] \mapsto \Gamma(v)$ (namely, v's neighbors). A port mapping for the graph G_0 is $P = \langle P_{v_1}, \ldots, P_{v_n} \rangle$. Every choice of φ and P yields a concrete graph $G_{\varphi, P}$. Denote the set of id's of this graph by $ID(G_{\varphi, P}) = \{\varphi(v) \mid v \in V(G_0)\}$. Let $\mathcal{G}$ be the collection of concrete graphs $G_{\varphi, P}$ obtained from G_0. For a graph $G \in \mathcal{G}$, and an edge e of G_0, the "open graph" $G[e]$ is obtained by erasing e and leaving the two ports that were attached to it empty. Let $\mathcal{G}^{open}$ be the collection of open graphs obtained from G_0.

For two open graphs $G'[e']$ and $G''[e'']$ with disjoint sets of ID's, $ID(G'[e']) \cap ID(G''[e'']) = \emptyset$, let $Dumbbell(G'[e'], G''[e''])$ be the graph obtained by taking one copy of each of these graphs, and connecting their open ports. Hence a dumbbell graph is composed of two open graphs plus two connecting edges, referred to as *bridges*. Moreover, we say that $G'[e']$ *participates on the left* and $G''[e'']$ *participates on the right* in $Dumbbell(G'[e'], G''[e''])$. (Strictly speaking, there could be two such graphs, but let us consider only one of them.

For concreteness, if $e' = (v', w')$ and $e'' = (v'', w'')$ where $ID(v') < ID(w')$ and $ID(v'') < ID(w'')$, then the graph $Dumbbell(G'[e'], G''[e''])$ contains the bridge edges (v', v'') and (w', w''). Create a collection $\mathcal{I}$ of inputs for our problem consisting of all the dumbbell graphs

$$\mathcal{I} = \{Dumbbell(G'[e'], G''[e'']) \mid G'[e'], G''[e''] \in \mathcal{G}^{open},$$
$$ID(G'[e']) \cap ID(G''[e'']) = \emptyset\}.$$

Partition the collection of inputs $\mathcal{I}$ into classes as follows: for every two graphs $G', G'' \in \mathcal{G}$, define the class $\mathcal{C}(G', G'') = \{Dumbbell(G'[e'], G''[e'']) \mid e', e'' \in E(G_0)\}$, consisting of the m^2 dumbbell graphs constructed from G' and G''. Finally, create a uniform distribution Ψ on $\mathcal{I}$.

We now give a high level overview of the main ideas of the proof of Theorem 3.1. First, we would like to prove that every deterministic algorithm D that achieves LE on every graph in collection $\mathcal{I}$, has expected message complexity $\Omega(m)$ on Ψ. Yao's minimax principle (cf. Lemma 3.2) then implies that the randomized algorithm R has expected message complexity $\Omega(m)$ on some graph G^* of $\mathcal{I}$. Since every graph in the collection $\mathcal{I}$ has $2m$ edges, this implies a lower bound of $\Omega(m)$ for R.

To prove this, we define an intermediate problem on the input collection $\mathcal{I}$, called *bridge crossing* (BC). An algorithm for this problem is required to send a message on one of the two bridge edges connecting the two open graphs (from either direction). More precisely, any algorithm solving BC is allowed to start simultaneously at all nodes, and succeeds if during its execution, a message has crossed one of the two connecting bridge edges. (Note that in our model, the nodes are unaware of their neighbors' identities, and in particular, the four nodes incident to the two bridge edges are unaware of this fact.)

LEMMA 3.2 (MINIMAX PRINCIPLE, PROP. 2.6 IN [15]). *Consider a finite collection of inputs $\mathcal{I}$ and a distribution Ψ on it. Let X be the minimum expected cost of any deterministic algorithm that succeeds on at least a $1 - 2\beta$ fraction of the graphs in the collection $\mathcal{I}$, for some positive constant β. Then $X/2$ lower bounds the expected cost of any randomized algorithm R on the worst-case graph of $\mathcal{I}$ that succeeds with probability at least $1 - \beta$.*

Basic counting yields the following:

FACT 3.3. *Let the node degrees in G_0 be $d_1, \ldots, d_n$, where $d_i = deg(v_i, G_0)$ for $1 \leqslant i \leqslant n$.*

(a) *The number of different possible port assignments is $K = \prod_{i=1}^{n} d_i!$.*

(b) *The number of different possible ID assignments is $\binom{n^4}{n}$.*

(c) *The number of graphs in the collection $\mathcal{G}$ is $g = K \cdot \binom{n^4}{n}$.*

(d) *The number of graphs in the collection $\mathcal{G}^{open}$ is $g^{open} = g \cdot m$.*

(e) *The number of graphs in each class $\mathcal{C}(G', G'')$ is m^2.*

(f) *For every graph $G' \in \mathcal{G}$, the number of graphs $G'' \in \mathcal{G}$ ID disjoint from G' is $\tilde{g} = K \cdot \binom{n^4 - n}{n}$.*

(g) *The number of classes $\mathcal{C}(G', G'')$ in the input collection $\mathcal{I}$ is $\tilde{h} = g \cdot \tilde{g}$.*

(h) *The number of dumbbell graphs in the input collection $\mathcal{I}$ is $\tilde{d} = \tilde{h} \cdot m^2$.*

Also, straightforward calculations yield the following.

LEMMA 3.4. $\tilde{g} \geqslant (1 - 1/n)g$.

LEMMA 3.5. *For every deterministic algorithm A and for every two disjoint graphs $G', G'' \in \mathcal{G}$, if A achieves BC on at least εm^2 graphs in the class $\mathcal{C}(G', G'')$, for constant $0 < \varepsilon \leqslant 1$, then the expected message complexity of A on inputs taken from $\mathcal{C}(G', G'')$ with a uniform distribution is $\varepsilon^2 m/8 = \Omega(m)$.*

PROOF. Consider two disjoint graphs $G', G'' \in \mathcal{G}$ and an algorithm A satisfying the premise of the lemma. Perform the following experiment. Run the code of algorithm A on the nodes of the $2n$-node graph G'^2 composed of two (disconnected) copies of G'. Denote this execution by $EX(G')$. (Of course, since G' is not a dumbbell graph, this is not a legal input for A, so there are no guarantees on the output or even termination of this execution.) The algorithm will send some messages, and then possibly halt. For each edge e (interpreted as a directed edge), identify the first time $t(e)$ in which a message was sent over e (in this direction) in this execution. Order the (directed) edges in increasing order of $t(e)$, getting the list $\hat{E}' = (e'_1, \ldots, e'_{k'})$. (Edges on which no messages were sent are not included in this list, so $k' \leqslant 2m$.) Run a similar experiment $EX(G'')$ on G'', getting a list $\hat{E}'' = (e''_1, \ldots, e''_{k''})$.

Now consider the m^2 executions $EX(Dumbbell(G'[e'], G''[e'']))$ of A on the dumbbell graphs in the class $\mathcal{C}(G', G'')$. In at least εm^2 of these executions, the algorithm A succeeds, so (at least) one message crosses one bridge in one direction. Without loss of generality, in at least $\varepsilon m^2/2$ of these executions, the first crossing message was sent from G' to G''.

Partition the dumbbell graphs in the class $\mathcal{C}(G', G'')$ into subclasses $C_0, C_1, \ldots, C_{k'}$, where the subclass C_i for $1 \leqslant i \leqslant k'$ contains all the dumbbell graphs $Dumbbell(G'[e'], G''[e''])$ in which $e' = e'_i$ and in execution $EX(Dumbbell(G'[e'], G''[e'']))$, the first crossing message went over the edge e'_i from $G'[e']$ to $G''[e'']$. The subclass C_0 contains all the remaining graphs of the class $\mathcal{C}(G', G'')$.

Consider an execution $EX(Dumbbell(G'[e'], G''[e'']))$ in which BC was achieved, and assuming that the first crossing message was sent in round t from G' to G'', say, over port p that in the original G' was used for e'. A crucial observation is that the part of this execution restricted to $G'[e']$ is identical to the execution $EX(G')$ up to and including round t. Similarly, the part of this execution restricted to $G''[e'']$ is identical to the execution $EX(G'')$ up to and including round t. This implies that e' must occur in the list $\hat{E}'$ in some position, as e'_j. In particular, it follows that the subclass C_0 contains only dumbbell graphs in which the first crossing message went from $G''[e'']$ to $G'[e']$ plus all the dumbbell graph in which no message crossed. In addition, it follows that $|C_0| \leqslant (1 - \varepsilon)m^2/2$ and $\sum_{i=1}^{k'} |C_i| \geqslant \varepsilon m^2/2$. Moreover, in the execution $EX(Dumbbell(G'[e'], G''[e'']))$, algorithm A must have sent at least one message on each of the edges e'_i for $1 \leqslant i \leqslant j$, i.e., A must have sent at least j messages.

We define $\ell_j = |C_j|$ to be the number of executions $EX(Dumbbell(G'[e'], G''[e'']))$ in which the first crossing message was sent from G' to G'' over the edge e'_j. This requires, in particular, that $e' = e'_j$. As there are exactly m dumbbell graphs $Dumbbell(G'[e'_j], G''[e''])$, it follows that $\ell_j \leqslant m$. Let $B = \sum_{j=1}^{k'} \ell_j$. By assumption, $B \geqslant \varepsilon m^2/2$. Let Q be the total number of messages sent by A in all these executions. Then $Q \geqslant \sum_{j=1}^{k'} \ell_j \cdot j$. To lower bound Q, note that this last sum is minimized if the first B/m summands are $\ell_i = m$, for

$i = 1, \ldots, B/m$, and the remaining summands are 0. Hence

$$Q \geqslant \sum_{j=1}^{B/m} m \cdot j \geqslant \frac{m}{2} \cdot \frac{B}{m} \cdot \left(\frac{B}{m} + 1\right) \geqslant B^2/(2m) \geqslant \varepsilon^2 m^3/8.$$

Therefore the expected cost incurred by A over the class $\mathcal{C}(G', G'')$ is at least $\varepsilon^2 m/8 = \Omega(m)$. $\square$

LEMMA 3.6. *Every deterministic algorithm A that achieves BC on at least $1/4$ of the dumbbell graphs in the collection $\mathcal{I}$ has expected message complexity $\Omega(m)$ on Ψ.*

PROOF. Consider an algorithm A as in the lemma. Let z denote the number of dumbbell graphs in the collection $\mathcal{I}$ on which algorithm A achieves BC. By the assumption of the lemma, $z \geqslant \tilde{d}/4$. Let X denote the set of pairs of disjoint graphs (G', G'') such that algorithm A achieves BC on at least $m^2/8$ of the m^2 dumbbell graphs $Dumbbell(G'[e'], G''[e''])$ in the class $\mathcal{C}(G', G'')$. Let Y denote the set of remaining pairs (such that A achieves BC on fewer than $m^2/8$ of the dumbbell graphs in $\mathcal{C}(G', G'')$). Let $x = |X|$ and $y = |Y|$. Note that $x + y = \tilde{h}$.

CLAIM 3.7. $x \geqslant \tilde{h}/8$.

PROOF. Observe that z, the number of dumbbell graphs in $\mathcal{I}$ on which algorithm A achieves BC, cannot exceed $xm^2 + ym^2/8$, hence

$$xm^2 + ym^2/8 \geqslant z \geqslant \tilde{d}/4 = \tilde{h}m^2/4.$$

Hence assuming, to the contrary, that $x < \tilde{h}/8$, implies that

$$\frac{\tilde{h}}{8} \cdot m^2 + \frac{7\tilde{h}}{8} \cdot \frac{m^2}{8} > xm^2 + ym^2/8 \geqslant \frac{\tilde{h}m^2}{4},$$

or $15/64 > 1/4$, contradiction. $\square$

By Lemma 3.5, for every pair of disjoint graphs $(G', G'') \in X$, the expected message complexity of A on inputs taken from $\mathcal{C}(G', G'')$ with a uniform distribution is at least $m/2^7$. Hence the total number of messages sent by the algorithm when executed over all inputs from $\mathcal{C}(G', G'')$ is at least, $(xm^2) \cdot m/2^7 + (ym^2) \cdot 0$. The first summand stands for the xm^2 graphs in the x classes of X, and the second summand stands for the graphs in the classes of Y. By Claim 3.7, this is at least $(\tilde{h}/2^3) \cdot (m^3/2^7) = \tilde{d}m/2^{10}$, hence the expected message complexity of algorithm A over all disjoint graph pairs in $\mathcal{I}$ (with a uniform distribution) is at least $m/2^{10} = \Omega(m)$.

LEMMA 3.8. *Let ε and $\delta \geqslant 1/4$ be positive constants such that $7\varepsilon + \delta \leqslant 1$. If a deterministic universal LE algorithm A solves LE on at least a $1 - \varepsilon$ fraction of the input graphs in $\mathcal{I}$, then A achieves BC on at least a δ fraction of the graphs in $\mathcal{I}$.*

PROOF. Denote by $\mathcal{I}^{LE}$ (respectively, $\mathcal{I}^{BC}$) the set of input dumbbell graphs on which algorithm A achieves LE (resp., BC). Let $\mathcal{I}^* = \mathcal{I}^{LE} \setminus \mathcal{I}^{BC}$. By the assumption of the lemma, $|\mathcal{I}^{LE}| \geqslant (1 - \varepsilon)\tilde{d}$. Assume, towards contradiction, that $|\mathcal{I}^{BC}| < \delta\tilde{d}$. Then

$$|\mathcal{I}^*| > (1 - \varepsilon - \delta)\tilde{d}. \tag{1}$$

Let W denote the set of open graphs $G'[e']$ that participate on the left in dumbbell graphs in $\mathcal{I}^*$. Formally,

$$W = \{G'[e'] \in \mathcal{G}^{open} \mid \exists G''[e''] \text{ s.t. } (G'[e'], G''[e'']) \in \mathcal{I}^*\}.$$

Let $Z = \mathcal{G} \setminus W$. Note that $|W| + |Z| = gm$. Observe that

$$(1 - \varepsilon - \delta)g\tilde{g}m^2 = (1 - \varepsilon - \delta)\tilde{d} < |\mathcal{I}^*| \leqslant |W|\tilde{g}m. \tag{2}$$

The last inequality follows from the fact that we can combine $G'[e'] \in W$ to form a dumbbell with any $G''[e'']$ of the $\tilde{g}$ disjoint graphs where e'' can be any one of m edges.

OBSERVATION 3.9. $|W| > (1 - \varepsilon - \delta)gm$.

COROLLARY 3.10. $|Z| < (\varepsilon + \delta)gm$.

Consider an execution of algorithm A on a dumbbell graph $(G'[e'], G''[e'']) \in \mathcal{I}^*$. Necessarily, in one of the two graphs, all nodes ended in state NON-ELECTED, and in the other graph, exactly one node ended in state ELECTED and all the others in state NON-ELECTED. Suppose all nodes in $G'[e']$ ended in state NON-ELECTED. Then for every other dumbbell graph $(G'[e'], G'''[e''']) \in \mathcal{I}^*$ or $(G'''[e'''], G'[e']) \in \mathcal{I}^*$ in which $G'[e']$ participates, the run on $G'[e']$ will behave the same as in the run on $(G'[e'], G''[e''])$, so all nodes in $G'[e']$ will end in state NON-ELECTED.

This observation implies that the open graphs in W can be partitioned into two sets:
- the set W_{NE} of graphs $G'[e'] \in W$ for which in executions on dumbbell graphs belonging to $\mathcal{I}^*$, all nodes in $G'[e']$ end in state NON-ELECTED, and
- the set W_E of graphs $G'[e'] \in W$ for which in executions on dumbbell graphs belonging to $\mathcal{I}^*$, exactly one node ends in state ELECTED and all other nodes end in state NON-ELECTED.

For every open graph $G'[e'] \in W_{NE}$, let

$$\Gamma(G'[e']) = \{G''[e''] \in \mathcal{G}^{open} \mid G'[e'] \text{ and } G''[e''] \text{ are disjoint}\}.$$

Also let

$$\begin{aligned} \Gamma_{NE}(G'[e']) &= W_{NE} \cap \Gamma(G'[e']), \\ \Gamma_E(G'[e']) &= W_E \cap \Gamma(G'[e']), \\ \Gamma_Z(G'[e']) &= Z \cap \Gamma(G'[e']). \end{aligned}$$

Denote the sizes of these sets by $\gamma(G'[e'])$, $\gamma_{NE}(G'[e'])$, $\gamma_E(G'[e'])$, and $\gamma_Z(G'[e'])$, respectively. Note that

$$\gamma_{NE}(G'[e']) + \gamma_E(G'[e']) + \gamma_Z(G'[e']) = \gamma(G'[e']) = \tilde{g}m. \tag{3}$$

We separate the analysis into two cases.

Case 1: $|W_{NE}| > |W|/2$: By Obs. 3.9, $|W_{NE}| > (1 - \varepsilon - \delta)gm/2$. By the assumption of Case 1, $\gamma_E(G'[e']) \leqslant |W_E| \leqslant |W|/2 \leqslant gm/2$. By Cor. 3.10, $\gamma_Z(G'[e']) \leqslant |Z| < (\varepsilon + \delta)gm$. Combining the last two facts with Eq. (3) and Lemma 3.4, implies that

$$\begin{aligned} \gamma_{NE}(G'[e']) &= \tilde{g}m - (\gamma_E(G'[e']) + \gamma_Z(G'[e'])) \\ &\geqslant (1 - 1/n)gm - gm/2 = (1/2 - 1/n)gm. \end{aligned}$$

Our key observation is that every pair of open graphs from W_{NE} forms a dumbbell graph on which algorithm A fails to solve LE, since no node will end in state ELECTED. This allows us to lower bound the number X of dumbbell graphs on which agorithm A fails to solve leader election: summing over all graphs in W_{NE}, we get that

$$\begin{aligned} X &\geqslant \sum_{G'[e'] \in W_{NE}} \gamma_{NE}(G'[e']) \geqslant |W_{NE}| \cdot (1/2 - 1/n)gm \\ &> ((1 - \varepsilon - \delta)gm/2) \cdot ((1/2 - 1/n)gm) \\ &\geqslant (1 - \varepsilon - \delta)\tilde{d}/6. \end{aligned}$$

On the other hand, recall that we have assumed that $|\mathcal{I}^{LE}| \geqslant (1-\varepsilon)\tilde{d}$, so $X \leqslant \varepsilon\tilde{d}$. It follows that $(1-\varepsilon-\delta)\tilde{d}/6 < \varepsilon\tilde{d}$. Rearranging, we get that $7\varepsilon + \delta > 1$, contradicting the assumption of the lemma.

Case 2: $|W_E| > |W|/2$: A similar contradiction is derived, based on the observation that every pair of open graphs from W_E forms a dumbbell graph on which algorithm A fails to solve LE.

This completes the proof of Lemma 3.8. $\square$

Combining Lemmas 3.6 and 3.8 allows us to use a reduction of BC to LE to show the claimed result for a universal randomized algorithm R that achieves LE with probability at least $1-\beta$: Suppose that A is a universal deterministic leader election algorithm that achieves LE on at least a $1-2\beta$ fraction of the dumbbell graphs in $\mathcal{I}$. By Lemma 3.8, we know that A achieves BC on at least a $\delta \geqslant 1/4$ fraction of the dumbbell graphs in $\mathcal{I}$. Applying Lemma 3.6 yields that A must have an expected message complexity of $\Omega(m)$ on distribution Ψ, which shows the theorem for deterministic algorithms. By a simple application of Yao's minimax principle (cf. Lemma 3.2), it follows that the $\Omega(m)$ bound for deterministic algorithms is a lower bound for the expected message complexity of R (under the worst case input), thereby completing the proof of Theorem 3.1.

At this point, let us explain why the above proof fails for weaker algorithms, which are guaranteed to work correctly only when the nodes know D. The problem occurs in the proof of Lemma 3.5. In that proof, we run an experiment where we execute algorithm A (which is now assumed to work correctly only when the nodes are given the diameter $\mathrm{Diam}(G)$ as part of their inputs) on an "illegal" graph G'^2 composed of two (disconnected) copies of G'. We then argue that the execution on the dumbbell graphs serving as the "real" inputs will behave the same as on the illegal graph G'^2 (so long as there was no bridge crossing). But this claim no longer holds when the nodes get the diameter D as part of their input, since the diameter of the dumbbell graph is different from that of the illegal graph G'^2 (which is infinite), so a node v will see a different input in the two execution.

To fix this problem, a natural idea would be to "feed" the nodes participating in the experiment on the illegal graph G'^2 a "fake" input on the diameter, i.e., set the input variable $DIAM_v$ at each node v to D', where D' is the diameter of the dumbbell graph. (Again, as this input is illegal, it is not guaranteed that the algorithm will generate a meaningful output, but still, the execution will behave the same as in the "real" execution on the dumbbell graph.)

A technical difficulty that prevents us from using this idea directly is that there are many dumbbell graphs for a given pair G', G'', and they have different diameters. This means that no *single* experiment (run with a specific value of D fed to the nodes) will be similar to *all* executions on all dumbbell graphs.

Hence to overcome this difficulty, it is necessary to pick G_0 and construct the collection of input graphs for the algorithm so that no matter which graphs G' and G'' are chosen, and which edges e' and e'' are crossed-over, the diameter of the resulting dumbbell graph is always the same. The observation that assists us in achieving this property is that we are free to select the graph G_0, so long as we adhere to the requirements that its size is n nodes and $\Theta(m)$ edges. So let us pick G_0 to have the following structure. Let κ be

the largest integer such that $\binom{\kappa}{2} + \kappa \leqslant m$. Let G_0^1 be the complete graph on κ nodes, with $m_1 = \binom{\kappa}{2}$ edges. Let G_0^2 be a path of $n-\kappa$ nodes, $(b_1, \ldots, b_{n-\kappa})$. Combine the two graphs into G_0 by adding κ edges connecting b_1 to every node in G_0^1. It is straightforward to verify that the resulting graph G_0 satisfies the size requirements.

Next, we modify the proof by limiting the ways in which we create open graphs from G_0. Specifically, we will consider only open graphs obtained by disconnecting an edge e' in the clique G_0^1. That is, the resulting family of open graphs will contain only graphs $(G'[e'])$ for $e' \in E(G_0^1)$.

The key observation is that no matter which two edges e' and e'' of G_0^1 we choose to disconnect in G' and G'' respectively, the resulting dumbbell graph $Dumbbell(G'[e'], G''[e''])$ will always have the same diameter, $D = 2n - 2\kappa + 1$ (which is the distance between the two endpoints $b_{n-\kappa}$ of the two graphs $G'[e']$ and $G''[e'']$).

One can verify that with this change, the rest of the proof goes through, with m_1 replacing m in the intermediate claims. In particular, the number of graphs in each class $\mathcal{C}(G', G'')$ becomes m_1^2, and so on. We end up proving that any deterministic leader election algorithm uses an average of $\Omega(m_1)$ messages on the collection $\mathcal{I}$ of inputs. Those messages are sent over the edges of the κ-clique (we cannot prove that there will be any messages sent over the edges of the paths G_0^2 in either side of the dumbbell graphs). Yet as $m_1 = \Omega(m)$, this suffices to establish the desired lower bound of $\Omega(m)$ on the expected message complexity of R on the worst case input.

3.2 A Message Lower Bound for Broadcast

We can leverage our lower bound technique to show an analogous bound for the *broadcast problem* [5], where a single node must convey a message to all other nodes. In fact, we can show a lower bound of $\Omega(m)$ messages even for the weaker *majority broadcast* problem, where the message of a single node needs to reach $> n/2$ nodes.

Consider the same collection of dumbbell graphs $\mathcal{I}$ as in Lemma 3.6. If a deterministic algorithm B successfully broadcasts in some execution on a graph $G \in \mathcal{I}$, then B also achieves bridge crossing in G. The following is immediate from Lemma 3.6:

LEMMA 3.11. *Suppose that there is an algorithm B that achieves broadcast on at least $1/4$ of the graphs in $\mathcal{I}$. Then B has expected message complexity of $\Omega(m)$ on Ψ.*

By a direct application of Lemma 3.2, we get a lower bound for randomized algorithms:

COROLLARY 3.12. *Let R' be an algorithm that successfully broadcasts a message from a source node to a majority of nodes with probability at least $1 - \beta$, for some constant $\beta \leqslant 3/8$. For every sufficiently large n and $n \leqslant m \leqslant \binom{n}{2}$, there exists a (connected) graph G of n nodes and $\Theta(m)$ edges, such that the expected number of messages used by R' on G is $\Omega(m)$. The above holds even if n, m and D are known to the algorithm and all nodes wake up simultaneously.*

3.3 Time Complexity Lower Bound

THEOREM 3.13. *Consider a universal leader election algorithm R that succeeds with probability $1 - \beta$, where $\beta < 1/16$ in the anonymous setting and $\beta < 1/16 - \varepsilon$, if nodes*

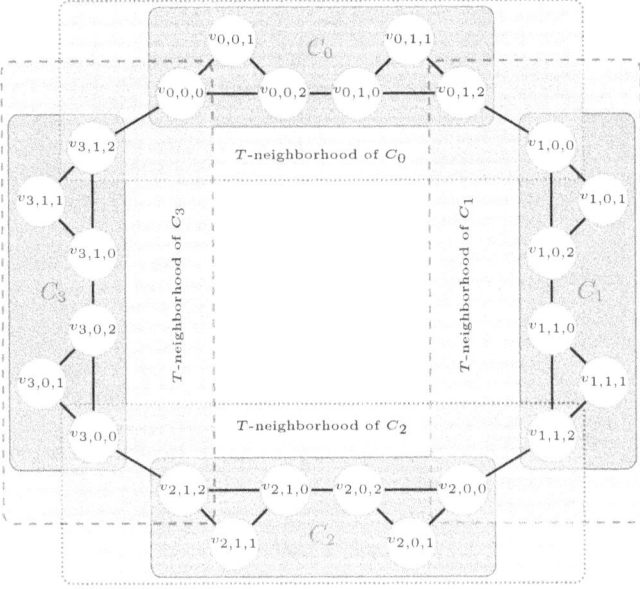

Figure 1: The Clique-Cycle Construction of Theorem 3.13 for $D' = 8$ and $n' = 24$. The blue dotted rectangles form H_Z and the red dashed rectangles correspond to $H_{Z'}$.

have unique ids, for any constant $\varepsilon > 0$. Then, for every n and every nondecreasing function $D(n)$ with $2 < D(n) < n$, there exists a graph of $n' \in \Theta(n)$ nodes and diameter $D' \in \Theta(D(n))$ where R takes $\Omega(D')$ rounds with constant probability. This is true even if all nodes know n' and D', and wake up simultaneously.

PROOF. For a given n and $D(n)$, we construct the following lower bound graph G: Let $D' = 4\lceil(D(n)/4)\rceil$ and let $n' = \gamma(n)D' \in \Theta(n)$, where $\gamma(n) > 0$ is the smallest integer such that $\gamma(n)D' \geq n$. The graph G contains D' cliques, each of size $\gamma(n)$. Partition the cliques into 4 subgraphs $C_0, \ldots, C_3$ referred to as *arcs*, each containing $D'/4$ cliques. Let $c_{i,j}$ denote the j-th clique in the i-th arc and let $v_{i,j,k}$ be the k-th node in $c_{i,j}$, for $0 \leq i \leq 3$, $0 \leq j \leq D'/4 - 1$, and $0 \leq k \leq \gamma(n) - 1$. The graph G is a cycle C formed by the D' cliques connected the following way: For every i (adhering to the range defined above) and every $j \leq D'/4 - 2$, the edge $(v_{i,j,\gamma(n)-1}, v_{i,j+1,0})$ connects the clique $c_{i,j}$ to the clique $c_{i,j+1}$ within the same arc C_i. The connections between arcs C_i and $C_{i+1 \bmod 4}$ are given by the edges $(v_{i,D'/4-1,\gamma(n)-1}, v_{(i+1 \bmod 4),0,0})$. See Figure 1 for an example.

We first consider the anonymous case, where each node starts in the same initial state. Let T be the random variable denoting the running time of the assumed algorithm R and suppose that the event $T \in o(D')$ happens with probability δ. Consider the two sets of nodes formed by non-adjacent arcs $Z = (C_0, C_2)$ and $Z' = (C_1, C_3)$. Let $\phi : V(G) \to V(G)$ be a mapping such that $\phi(v_{i,j,k}) = v_{(i+1 \bmod 4),j,k}$. Let H_Z be the subgraph consisting of Z and its T-neighborhood and define $H_{Z'}$ analogously. By the definition of the adjacencies of C, it follows that the subgraph induced by $\phi(H_Z)$ is isomorphic to H_Z'.

Let *configuration* $\mathcal{C} = \langle\sigma_1, \ldots, \sigma_\ell\rangle$ denote a vector where each entry σ_i denotes a *potential local state* of a node. For

a set of nodes $S = \{u_1, \ldots, u_\ell\}$, we say that S *realizes* σ *in round* r, if node u_i is in state σ_i in round r; let $E(\mathcal{C}, S, r)$ denote the event that this happens. The following claim shows that the mapping ϕ induces equi-probable realizations of any local states σ, for any pair of nodes v and $\phi(v)$. Note, however, that Claim 3.14 does *not* imply that events $E(\sigma, v, r)$ and $E(\sigma, \phi(v), r)$ are stochastically independent. The proof of the next claim follows by a symmetry argument and is deferred to the full paper:

CLAIM 3.14. *For any round r and any configuration $\mathcal{C}$, we have* $\mathbb{P}[E(\mathcal{C}, Z, r) \mid T \in o(D')] = \mathbb{P}[E(\mathcal{C}, Z', r) \mid T \in o(D')]$.

Note that we do not claim independence of the events $E(\mathcal{C}, Z, r)$ and $E(\mathcal{C}, Z', r)$. Let L (resp., L') be the event that one node in Z (resp., Z') becomes leader and let L_i be the event that there is one leader elected in arc C_i. It holds that $\mathbb{P}[L \mid T \in o(D')] = \mathbb{P}[L' \mid T \in o(D')]$; let q denote this probability. If the algorithm terminates in $T = o(D) = o(D')$ rounds, then there is no causal influence between C_0 and C_2, which means that $E(\mathcal{C}, C_0, r)$ and $E(\mathcal{C}, C_2, r)$ are stochastically independent (as opposed to events $E(\mathcal{C}, Z, r)$ and $E(\mathcal{C}, Z', r)$ above!) for any configuration $\mathcal{C}$ and round $r \leq T$. In particular, this includes all configurations that satisfy L_i. Let $p = \mathbb{P}[L_0 \mid T \in o(D')]$; again due to symmetry, we know that $\mathbb{P}[L_0 \mid T \in o(D')] = \cdots = \mathbb{P}[L_3 \mid T \in o(D')]$, and due to independence of L_0 and L_2, $q = 2p(1 - p)$. Let One be the event that the algorithm elects 1 leader. We know that

$$\mathbb{P}[One \mid T \in o(D')] = \frac{\mathbb{P}[One]}{\mathbb{P}[T \in o(D')]}$$
$$- \frac{\mathbb{P}[One \mid T \in \Omega(D')]\mathbb{P}[T \in \Omega(D')]}{\mathbb{P}[T \in o(D')]}$$
$$\geq (1 - \beta - (1 - \delta))/\delta = 1 - \frac{\beta}{\delta},$$

and clearly

$$\mathbb{P}[One \mid T \in o(D')] \leq \mathbb{P}[L \mid T \in o(D')] + \mathbb{P}[L' \mid T \in o(D')]$$
$$= 2q.$$

Thus $q \geq \frac{1}{2}(1 - \beta/\delta)$, which means that $p \geq \frac{1}{2}(1 - \sqrt{\beta/\delta})$. We know that $\beta = \mathbb{P}[error] \geq p^2$ and thus $\frac{1}{4}(1 - \sqrt{\beta/\delta})^2 \leq \beta$. Note that since $\beta < 1/16$, this inequality requires $\delta < 1/4$ and therefore $T \in \Omega(D')$ with constant probability. This completes the proof for the anonymous case.

Finally, for the non-anonymous case we show a reduction to the anonymous case. Now suppose that R is an algorithm designed for a setting where each node has a unique id and again assume that R takes only $o(D)$ rounds with probability $1 - \delta$, for some fixed constant δ. Consider algorithm R' that extends algorithm R by causing each node to choose an id uniformly at random from $[1, n^4]$ initially. This id is then used as input for algorithm R (instead of the id assigned in an non-anonymous network in which R is guaranteed to work). The event U, where all chosen ids are unique, occurs with probability at least $1 - n^{-2}$. By definition of R', we have $\mathbb{P}[R' \text{ succeeds} \mid U] = \mathbb{P}[R \text{ succeeds}]$ and, from the anonymous case, we know that $\mathbb{P}[R' \text{ succeeds}] \leq 15/16$. It follows that $\mathbb{P}[R' \text{ succeeds} \mid U] \leq (15/16)/\mathbb{P}[U] \leq 15/16(1 - n^{-2})$ for sufficiently large n. This shows that algorithm R succeeds with probability at most $15/16 + \varepsilon$, for any constant $\varepsilon > 0$. □

4. MATCHING (OR APPROACHING) THE LOWER BOUNDS

The purpose of algorithms in this paper is twofold: (1) to show the tightness of the message lower bound (the tightness of the time lower bound follows from [17]), and (2) addressing the fundamental question: can both lower bounds $O(D)$ time and $O(m)$ messages be matched or approached simultaneously? For goal (1) above, we show that there exists a deterministic universal algorithm that is optimal in the number of messages, i.e., an $O(m)$ algorithm. However, this algorithm takes arbitrary (albeit finite) time (which depends exponentially on the size of the smallest ID). This algorithm is a generalization of the one presented by Fredrickson and Lynch for rings [7].

THEOREM 4.1. *There is a deterministic leader election algorithm that uses $O(m)$ messages.*

We now briefly highlight the techniques behind the universal algorithms for goal (2), and point at their new parts (compared to previous work). We defer the full description of the algorithms to the full paper. (Our algorithms work in the $\mathcal{CONGEST}$ model).

4.1 Matching (sometimes) both lower bounds simultaneously

As mentioned earlier (cf. Section 1), only randomized algorithms have the hope of matching both lower bounds simultaneously. We start with the *least element lists (Least-El list)* algorithm of [10]. It can be used to elect a unique leader (with probability 1) in $O(D)$ time and $O(m \min(\log n, D))$ messages [10]. The main idea was to use random IDs. Each node simply floods its ID and the largest ID wins. If the IDs are chosen randomly, it can be shown that the number of messages that every node v has to forward is bounded by $O(\log n)deg(v)$, where $deg(v)$ is v's degree; this yields the desired message bound. However, in previous work, the resulting algorithm needed to know n, the number of nodes.

In the current paper, we show, first, that a standard trick can be used to get rid of this assumption, by showing that nodes can get an estimate of n (up to a constant factor) in $O(m \min(\log n, D))$ messages and $O(D)$ time: Each node u flips an unbiased coin until the outcome is heads; let X_u denote the random variable that contain the number of times that X_u is flipped. Then, nodes exchange their respective values of X_u whereas each node only forwards the highest value of X_u (once) that it has seen so far. This shows that a node can see at most D (currently) highest values. We observe that X_u is geometrically distributed and denote its global maximum by $\bar{X}$. For any u, $\mathbb{P}[X_u \geqslant 2\log_2 n] = 1/2^{2\log_2 n}$, and by taking a union bound, $\mathbb{P}[\bar{X} \geqslant 2\log_2 n] \leqslant 1/n$. Furthermore,

$$\mathbb{P}[\bar{X} < \log_2 n - \log_2(\log n)] = 1 - (1 - 1/2^{\log_2 n - \log_2(\log n)})^n$$
$$\approx 1 - \exp(-n/2^{\log_2 n - \log_2(\log n)}).$$

It follows that each node forwards at most $O(\log n)$ distinct values (w.h.p.) and thus the total number of messages is $O(m \min(\log n, D))$ with high probability.

COROLLARY 4.2. *Consider a network of n nodes, m edges, and diameter D, and assume that nodes do not have knowledge of n. There is a randomized algorithm that achieves leader election with high probability, takes $O(D)$ time and* has a message complexity of $O(m \min(\log n, D))$ with high probability.

This, however, is still away from our upper bound goal to see whether it is possible to match both lower bounds. Hence, we reached another improvement to the Least-El list algorithm of [10]. That is, we show that if, instead of allowing every node to be a candidate, only $\log n$ nodes are allowed to be candidates, then the (expected) message complexity can be improved to $O(m \log \log n)$ with the same time bound. (Note that the candidates are chosen randomly and do not have any a priori knowledge of each other.) This yields a Monte-Carlo algorithm that succeeds with high probability. More generally, we show it is possible to obtain a trade-off between the success probability and the number of messages. In particular, we get an $O(m)$ messages, $O(D)$ time algorithm with large constant success probability (for any large pre-specified constant).

THEOREM 4.3. *Consider a network of n nodes, m edges, and diameter D and assume that each node knows n. Let $f(n) \leqslant n$ be any function such that $f(n) \in \Omega(1)$. There is a randomized leader election algorithm A that terminates in $O(D)$ rounds, has an expected message complexity of $O(m \cdot \min(\log f(n), D))$ and succeeds with probability $1 - 1/e^{\Theta(f(n))}$. This implies the following:*
(A) There is an algorithm that takes $O(D)$ time, has an expected message complexity of $O(m \cdot \min(\log \log n, D))$ and succeeds with high probability.
(B) For any small constant $\varepsilon > 0$, there is an algorithm that takes $O(D)$ time, sends $O(m)$ messages and succeeds with probability at least $1 - \varepsilon$.

This matches our lower bounds of time and messages for the case when the success probability is constant. However, the above improvement requires nodes to have knowledge of n.

We also managed to match both lower bounds simultaneously, for graphs that are "somewhat dense," i.e., with $m > n^{1+\varepsilon}$ for any fixed constant $\varepsilon > 0$ (known to the algorithm). This is done by combining a randomized spanner algorithm due to [6] and the above Least-El list algorithm to achieve leader election with *high* probability.

COROLLARY 4.4. *Consider a network of n nodes, m edges, and diameter D and assume that each node knows n. Let $\varepsilon > 0$ be a fixed constant. If $m \geqslant n^{1+\varepsilon}$, then there is a randomized algorithm that achieves leader election with high probability, takes $O(D)$ time and has an expected message complexity of $O(m)$.*

Finally, we show in Corollary 4.5 that if nodes have knowledge of both n and D, then one can obtain a randomized Las Vegas algorithm with expected time complexity $O(D)$ and expected message complexity $O(m)$.

COROLLARY 4.5. *Consider a network of n nodes, m edges, and diameter D, and assume that nodes have knowledge of n and D. There is a randomized algorithm that achieves leader election with probability 1, has an expected time complexity of $O(D)$ and an expected message complexity of $O(m)$.*

4.2 Approaching both lower bounds simultaneously

The Least-El list based algorithms above indeed match both lower bounds sometimes. However, at some other times their message complexity is higher than m by a multiplicative factor that may be larger than a constant. For completeness, we also present a randomized algorithm with a better message complexity in the worst case, although at some small time penalty:

THEOREM 4.6. *Consider any network of n nodes, m edges, and diameter D, and assume that each node has knowledge of n. There is an algorithm that elects a unique leader (w.h.p.) in $O(D \log n)$ rounds and uses $O(m + n \log n)$ messages.*

This Monte-Carlo algorithm (the "clustering algorithm") is not based on the Least-El list approach, used by the other randomized algorithms above. In this algorithm (which also relies on prior knowledge of n), about $\log n$ nodes choose to be candidates and grow clusters till they essentially meet. The trick then is to first sparsify this graph and reduce the number of edges to about $\min(m, n + \log^2 n)$. However, this sparsification increases the diameter of the residual graph to $O(D \log n)$. One can then apply the Least-El list algorithm to the residual graph to obtain an overall bound of $O(D \log n)$ time and $O(m + n \log n)$ messages.

Finally, as mentioned, in the deterministic case, it is impossible to match both lower bounds simultaneously. Hence, [1] posed that goal of reaching $O(m + n \log n)$ messages and $O(D)$ simultaneously. They presented a sketch of an elegant deterministic algorithm that "grows kingdoms"; a leader candidate's kingdoms keep growing (by building BFS trees) till only one kingdom is left. Unfortunately, one can show counter examples to the hope that this algorithm doubles the diameters of winning kingdoms every round. We present a modified variant of the algorithm of [1]. The modification ensures that the (upper bound on the) number of kingdoms is reduced by a constant factor in every phase. Our algorithm requires no knowledge of n or any other parameter (it does however require unique identities, which is necessary.) This yields a $O(D \log n)$ time and $O(m \log n)$ messages deterministic algorithm. It is an open question whether the running time can be improved to $O(D)$ (with the same number of messages) in the deterministic case.

THEOREM 4.7. *Consider any network of n nodes, m edges, and diameter D. There is a deterministic algorithm that elects a unique leader in $O(D \log n)$ time while using $O(m \log n)$ messages.*

5. CONCLUSION

We studied the role played by randomization in universal leader election. Some open questions on randomized leader election are raised by our work: (1) Can we find tight (universal) upper and lower bounds for general graphs with and without knowledge of n? (2) Can we show the following conjecture: Any algorithm (even randomized Monte Carlo with high success probability) without knowledge of global parameters (e.g. n, D, m) that finishes in $O(D)$ rounds, needs at least $\Omega(m \log D)$ messages (in expectation or with high probability).

6. REFERENCES

[1] H. Abu-Amara and A. Kanevsky. On the complexities of leader election algorithms. In *ICCI*, 202–206, 1993.

[2] Y. Afek and E. Gafni. Time and message bounds for election in synchronous and asynchronous complete networks. *SIAM Journal on Computing*, 20(2):376–394, 1991.

[3] Hagit Attiya and Jennifer Welch. *Distributed Computing. (2nd ed.).* John Wiley Interscience, 2004.

[4] B. Awerbuch. Optimal distributed algorithms for minimum weight spanning tree, counting, leader election, and related problems. In STOC '87, pages 230–240, New York, USA, 1987. ACM.

[5] Baruch Awerbuch, Oded Goldreich, Ronen Vainish, and David Peleg. A trade-off between information and communication in broadcast protocols. *J. ACM*, 37(2):238–256, April 1990.

[6] Surender Baswana and Sandeep Sen. A simple and linear time randomized algorithm for computing sparse spanners in weighted graphs. *Random Struct. Algorithms*, 30(4):532–563, 2007.

[7] Greg N. Frederickson and Nancy A. Lynch. Electing a leader in a synchronous ring. *Journal of the ACM*, 34(1):98–115, 1987.

[8] Emanuele G. Fusco and Andrzej Pelc. Knowledge, level of symmetry, and time of leader election. In *ESA*, pages 479–490, 2012.

[9] Saurabh Ganeriwal, Ram Kumar, and Mani B. Srivastava. Timing-sync protocol for sensor networks. In *SenSys*, pages 138–149, 2003, New York, USA, 2003. ACM.

[10] Maleq Khan, Fabian Kuhn, Dahlia Malkhi, Gopal Pandurangan, and Kunal Talwar. Efficient distributed approximation algorithms via probabilistic tree embeddings. *Distributed Computing*, 25(3):189–205, 2012.

[11] E. Korach, S. Moran, and S. Zaks. Optimal lower bounds for some distributed algorithms for a complete network of processors. *Theoretical Computer Science*, 64(1):125 – 132, 1989.

[12] Shay Kutten, Gopal Pandurangan, David Peleg, Peter Robinson, and Amitabh Trehan. Sublinear bounds for randomized leader election. In *ICDCN'13*, pages 348–362, 2013.

[13] Gérard Le Lann. Distributed systems - towards a formal approach. In *IFIP Congress*, p. 155–160, 1977.

[14] Nancy Lynch. *Distributed Algorithms.* Morgan Kaufman Publishers, Inc., San Francisco, USA, 1996.

[15] Rajeev Motwani and Prabhakar Raghavan. *Randomized Algorithms.* Cambridge Univ. Press, 1995.

[16] Erik Nygren, Ramesh K. Sitaraman, and Jennifer Sun. The Akamai network: a platform for high-performance internet applications. *SIGOPS Oper. Syst. Rev.*, 44(3):2–19, August 2010.

[17] David Peleg. Time-optimal leader election in general networks. *Journal of Parallel and Distributed Computing*, 8(1):96 – 99, 1990.

[18] David Peleg. *Distributed Computing: A Locality-Sensitive Approach.* SIAM, Philadelphia, 2000.

[19] Nicola Santoro. *Design and Analysis of Distributed Algorithms (Wiley Series on Parallel and Distributed Computing).* Wiley-Interscience, 2006.

[20] Gerard Tel. *Introduction to distributed algorithms.* Cambridge University Press, New York, USA, 1994.

[21] Yong Yao and Johannes Gehrke. The cougar approach to in-network query processing in sensor networks. *SIGMOD Rec.*, 31(3):9–18, 2002.

Brief Announcement: A Simple Stretch 2 Distance Oracle*

Rachit Agarwal   P. Brighten Godfrey

University of Illinois at Urbana-Champaign, IL, USA
{agarwa16, pbg}@illinois.edu

ABSTRACT

We present a distance oracle that, for weighted graphs with n vertices and m edges, is of size $8n^{4/3}m^{1/3}\log^{2/3}n$ and returns stretch-2 distances in constant time. Our oracle achieves bounds identical to the constant-time stretch-2 oracle of Pǎtraşcu and Roditty, but admits significantly simpler construction and proofs.

Categories and Subject Descriptors

E.1 [**Data Structures**]: Graphs and Networks; G.2.2 [**Discrete Mathematics**]: Graph Theory—*graph algorithms*

General Terms

ALgorithms, Theory

Keywords

Approximate distance oracles, distance queries

1. INTRODUCTION

A distance oracle is a compact representation of the all-pairs shortest path matrix of a graph. To achieve a compact (that is, subquadratic in number of vertices) representation, we allow approximation measured in terms of *stretch*. A stretch-c oracle returns, for any pair of vertices at distance d, a distance estimate of at most $c \cdot d$; corresponding path can be retrieved in constant time per hop. Distance oracles have a wide range of applications including compact routing [1,5,9] and quickly computing paths on large networks [1,3,10]. For general weighted graphs, Thorup and Zwick [10] designed an oracle of size $O(n^{3/2})$ that returns distances of stretch 3 in constant time. Furthermore, they showed that this oracle is optimal in the worst case — there exist graphs for which any oracle that returns distances of stretch 3 requires space $\Omega(n^{3/2})$ and that returns distances of stretch less than 3 requires space $\Omega(n^2)$.

---

*This work was supported by National Science Foundation grant CNS 1017069.

However, the graphs that constitute the hard cases for stretch less than 3 are extremely dense, while essentially all real-world graphs are sparse. For oracles that improve upon the Thorup-Zwick oracle by exploiting graph sparsity, new upper bounds [1, 2, 4–7] and lower bounds [8] have recently been derived. In particular, Pǎtraşcu and Roditty [6] designed a constant-time stretch-2 oracle of size $O(n^{4/3}m^{1/3})$ for weighted graphs; their construction was extended for larger stretch values for unweighted [1] and for weighted graphs [7]. In fact, a more general space-stretch-time trade-off can be achieved [2,4,5] by exploiting graph sparsity; this further reduces the space requirements for stretch 2 and larger [5] and even allows computing distances of stretch less than 2 [2,4].

A particularly interesting result among the aforementioned is that of Pǎtraşcu and Roditty [6] — a stretch-2 constant-time oracle of size $O(n^{4/3}m^{1/3})$. However, their construction uses substantially more complex techniques than oracles for dense graphs and oracles with super-constant query time. For weighted graphs, their algorithm for constructing the oracle is particularly complex — it first samples a set of edges A and a set of vertices B (each with a different probability); it then constructs partial shortest path trees around each vertex in B with a stopping criteria that depends on edges in set A. Finally, the algorithm constructs partial shortest path trees around each remaining vertex with a new stopping criteria that depends on edges in set A, vertices in set B and the edges explored while constructing partial shortest path trees around vertices in set B.

We present a new constant-time stretch-2 oracle for *weighted* graphs that admits significantly simpler construction and proofs. Our algorithm requires sampling a set A of vertices and constructing partial shortest path trees around each vertex using a single stopping criteria that depends only on vertices in set A:

THEOREM 1. *Given a weighted undirected graph with n vertices and m edges with non-negative edge weights, there exists a distance oracle of expected size $8n^{4/3}m^{1/3}\log^{2/3}n$ that returns a stretch-2 distance in constant time.*

Our construction uses the notion of balls used in [10] and of vicinities used in [2, 4, 5]. We say that a pair of vertices have a ball-vicinity intersection if the ball of one vertex has a non-empty intersection with the vicinity of the other vertex. To bound the space requirements, we exploit graph sparsity to prove a non-trivial upper bound on the number of vertex pairs with ball-vicinity intersection; this requires a special ball construction algorithm previously used in design of compact routing schemes [9]. Furthermore, to bound the stretch, we show that for any pair of vertices with non-intersecting ball-vicinity, a stretch-2 distance can be computed by storing a small amount of information per vertex in the graph.

2. PRELIMINARIES

We assume that $G = (V, E)$ is a weighted undirected graph with n vertices and m edges with non-negative edge weights. Let $d(s, t)$ denote the shortest distance between a pair of vertices $s, t \in V$. For any subset of vertices $V' \subset V$, we denote by $N(V')$ the set of neighbors of vertices in V'. Given a vertex v and a subset of vertices $L \subset V$, we let the **nearest vertex in set** L, denoted by $\ell(v)$, be the vertex $a \in L$ that minimizes $d(v, a)$, ties broken arbitrarily. The **ball radius** of v, denoted by r_v, is the distance between v and $\ell(v)$.

Balls and Vicinities, Inverse-balls and Inverse-Vicinities. We will also need the following definitions:

- **Ball of a vertex** $B(v)$: the set of vertices $w \in V$ for which $d(v, w) < r_v$;

- **Inverse-Ball of a vertex** $\bar{B}(v)$: the set of vertices that contain v in their ball;

- **Vicinity of a vertex** $B^+(v)$: the set of vertices in $B(v) \cup N(B(v))$;

- **Inverse-vicinity of a vertex** $\bar{B}^+(v)$: the set of vertices that contain v in their vicinity.

Our construction of balls, vicinities, inverse-balls and inverse-vicinities will use the following result:

LEMMA 2. [2,9] *For any weighted undirected graph and for any $1 \leq \alpha \leq n$, there exists a subset of vertices L of expected size $8n \log n / \alpha$ such that $|\bar{B}(v)| \leq \alpha$ and $|\bar{B}^+(v)| \leq \alpha \deg(v)$ for each vertex v in the graph.*

The first part of the lemma that shows the existence of a set L to bound the size of the inverse-ball of each vertex is due to Thorup and Zwick [9]; for sake of completeness, the algorithm for constructing such a set L is informally described in Appendix A. It is easy to verify that the set of vertices in the inverse-vicinity of any vertex v is given by $\bar{B}^+(v) = \bigcup_{w \in N(v)} \bar{B}(w)$; this leads to the bound on the size of the inverse-vicinity of each vertex (using the same set L). We emphasize that the above lemma bounds the size of set L in expectation, while the size of inverse-ball and inverse-vicinity for any vertex is bounded deterministically.

3. DISTANCE ORACLE

Our construction of the oracle begins by creating a set L of vertices using the result of Lemma 2 (the value of α will be specified later). The oracle stores, for each $v \in V$:

- a hash table storing the exact distance to each vertex in L;

- the nearest vertex $\ell(v)$ and the ball radius r_v; and

- a hash table storing the exact distance to each vertex in the set $S_v = \{w : B(v) \cap B^+(w) \neq \emptyset\}$, that is, to each vertex w whose vicinity intersects with the ball of v.

Query algorithm. When queried for the distance between vertices $s, t \in V$, the algorithm returns the exact distance if $s \in S_t$ or if $t \in S_s$. Else, the algorithm returns $d(s, \ell(s)) + d(t, \ell(s))$ if $r_s \leq r_t$ and $d(t, \ell(t)) + d(s, \ell(t))$ otherwise.

3.1 Proof of Theorem 1

The proof borrows two ideas from [2]. The first is used to bound the size of the oracle — intuitively, if each vertex has a small size inverse-ball (or equivalently, is contained in a few balls) as guaranteed by Lemma 2, then the number of vertex pairs with ball-vicinity intersection is also small, thereby bounding $\sum_v |S_v|$. The second is used to bound the stretch — any pair of vertices s, t with non-intersecting ball-vicinity must be rather far away and either the path $s \rightsquigarrow \ell(s) \rightsquigarrow t$ or the path $t \rightsquigarrow \ell(t) \rightsquigarrow s$ must be a stretch-2 path.

LEMMA 3. *Let $G = (V, E)$ be a weighted undirected graph with n vertices and m edges. For any fixed $1 \leq \alpha \leq n$, if the oracle is constructed as above, then: $\sum_{v \in V} |S_v| \leq 2\alpha^2 m$.*

Proof: For any vertex $w \in V$, let $\gamma(w)$ be the number of vertex pairs whose ball-vicinity intersection contains w; that is, $\gamma(w) = |\{(u, v) : w \in B(u) \cap B^+(v)\}|$. Then, by definition, we get that $\sum_{v \in V} |S_v| \leq \sum_{w \in V} \gamma(w)$. Recall, using Lemma 2, each vertex w (deterministically) belongs to at most α balls and at most $\alpha \deg(w)$ vicinities. Hence, the number of ball-vicinity intersections that can occur at w is bounded by $\gamma(w) \leq \alpha^2 \deg(w)$. Hence, $\sum_{v \in V} |S_v| \leq \sum_{w \in V} \gamma(w) \leq 2\alpha^2 m$. □

LEMMA 4. [2] *Let $G = (V, E)$ be a weighted undirected graph. For any pair of vertices $s, t \in V$, if $B(s) \cap B^+(t) = \emptyset$, then the shortest distance is lower bounded as $d(s, t) \geq r_s + r_t$.*

Proof: Let $P = (s, x_1, x_2, \ldots, t)$ be the shortest path between s and t. Let $i_0 = \max\{i | x_i \in P \cap B(s)\}$, $w = x_{i_0}$ and $w' = x_{i_0+1}$. Since $w' \notin B(s)$, we get that $d(s, w') \geq r_s$. Since $B(s) \cap B^+(t) = \emptyset$, we have that $w \notin B^+(t)$ and hence, $w' \notin B(t)$ leading to the fact that $d(t, w') \geq r_t$. Finally, w' being on the shortest path between s and t, we have that $d(s, t) = d(s, w') + d(t, w') \geq r_s + r_t$. □

Proof of Theorem 1. We first bound the size of the oracle. Using Lemma 2, the expected size of set L is $8n \log n / \alpha$; and, using Lemma 3, the size of set $\sum_{v \in V} |S_v|$ is bounded by $2\alpha^2 m$. Hence, the oracle's size is bounded by $8n^2 \log n / \alpha + 2\alpha^2 m$; this expression is minimized for $\alpha = 2n^{2/3} m^{-1/3} \log^{1/3}(n)$, leading to the desired bound.

Next, we show that the query algorithm returns a distance of at most $2d(s, t)$. If $B(s) \cap B^+(t) \neq \emptyset$, the algorithm returns the exact distance. For the case when $B(s) \cap B^+(t) = \emptyset$, assume, without loss of generality, that $r_s \leq r_t$. Then, using Lemma 4, $d(s, t) \geq 2r_s$; or equivalently, $2r_s \leq d(s, t)$. The distance returned by the query algorithm is $d(s, \ell(s)) + d(t, \ell(s))$, which using triangle inequality, is at most $2d(s, \ell(s)) + d(s, t) = 2r_s + d(s, t) \leq 2d(s, t)$, as claimed. □

For the special case of unweighted graphs, it is possible to reduce the space requirements at the cost of a small additive stretch. Pătraşcu and Roditty [6] designed a constant time oracle of size $O(n^{5/3})$ for unweighted graphs that, for any pair of vertices at distance d, returns a path of length at most $2d + 1$. Using ideas similar to above, we get a simplified construction for the case of unweighted graphs as well (see Appendix B).

4. REFERENCES

[1] I. Abraham and C. Gavoille. On approximate distance labels and routing schemes with affine stretch. In *International Symposium on Distributed Computing (DISC)*, pages 404–415, 2011.

[2] R. Agarwal. Distance oracles with super-constant query time, Technical report, 2013.

[3] R. Agarwal, M. Caesar, P. B. Godfrey, and B. Y. Zhao. Shortest paths in less than a millisecond. In *ACM SIGCOMM Workshop on Online Social Networks (WOSN)*, 2012.

[4] R. Agarwal and P. B. Godfrey. Distance oracles for stretch less than 2. In *ACM-SIAM Symposium on Discrete Algorithms (SODA)*, 2013.

[5] R. Agarwal, P. B. Godfrey, and S. Har-Peled. Approximate distance queries and compact routing in sparse graphs. In *Proc. IEEE Conference on Computer Communications (INFOCOM)*, pages 1754–1762, 2011.

[6] M. Pătraşcu and L. Roditty. Distance oracles beyond the Thorup-Zwick bound. In *Proc. IEEE Annual Symposium on Foundations of Computer Science (FOCS)*, pages 815–823, 2010.

[7] M. Pătraşcu, L. Roditty, and M. Thorup. A new infinity of distance oracles for sparse graphs. In *IEEE Symposium on Foundations of Computer Science (FOCS)*, 2012.

[8] C. Sommer, E. Verbin, and W. Yu. Distance oracles for sparse graphs. In *Proc. IEEE Annual Symposium on Foundations of Computer Science (FOCS)*, pages 703–712, 2009.

[9] M. Thorup and U. Zwick. Compact routing schemes. In *Proc. ACM Symposium on Parallel Algorithms and Architectures (SPAA)*, pages 1–10, 2001.

[10] M. Thorup and U. Zwick. Approximate distance oracles. *Journal of the ACM*, 52(1):1–24, January 2005.

APPENDIX

A. INFORMAL PROOF OF LEMMA 2

Fix some $1 \le \alpha \le n$. The algorithm maintains two set of vertices — a set L that constitutes the final output of the algorithm and another set W that contains all vertices that have inverse-ball of size more than α. The set L is initialized to an empty set and W is initialized to the vertex set V. The algorithm runs in multiple iterations; in each iteration, it uniform randomly samples $4n/\alpha$ vertices from W, inserts them to set L; re-computes the inverse-ball of each vertex and updates W to all vertices that still contains more than α vertices in their inverse-ball. The algorithm terminates when W contains $4n/\alpha$ or fewer vertices; in this case, all vertices in W are inserted in set L.

The main idea behind the proof of correctness is as follows. Clearly, by construction, each vertex has inverse-ball of size at most α. The main challenge is to bound the size of set L. It is shown in [9] that the expected number of iterations performed by the algorithm before termination is at most $2 \log n$; since $4n/\alpha$ vertices are added to L in each iteration, the size of the set L output by the algorithm is at most $8n \log n/\alpha$.

B. UNWEIGHTED GRAPHS

A stretch-(c, c') oracle for unweighted graphs returns, for any pair of vertices at distance d, a path of length at most $c \cdot d + c'$. Pătraşcu and Roditty [6] designed a constant-time stretch-$(2, 1)$ oracle of size $O(n^{5/3})$ for general unweighted graphs. Using ideas similar to those for weighted graphs, we get a simpler construction for the case of unweighted graphs as well:

THEOREM 5. *Given a unweighted undirected graph with n vertices and m edges, there exists a distance oracle of expected size $4n^{5/3} \log^{2/3} n$ that returns a stretch-$(2, 1)$ distance in constant time.*

Abraham and Gavoille [1] presented a similar construction and further generalized it for larger stretch values. Due to the focus on small stretch values, our exposition is slightly simpler than their. The construction and proofs for the following oracle is similar to that for weighted graphs with the only difference that it now suffices to consider ball-ball intersections rather than ball-vicinity intersections.

B.1 Distance oracle

Our construction of the oracle begins by creating a set L of vertices using the result of Lemma 2 (the value of α will be specified later). The oracle stores, for each $v \in V$:

- a hash table storing the exact distance to each vertex in L;
- the nearest vertex $\ell(v)$ and the ball radius r_v; and
- a hash table storing the exact distance to each vertex in the set $S_v = \{w \,:\, B(v) \cap B(w) \ne \emptyset\}$, that is, to each vertex w whose ball intersects with the ball of v.

Query algorithm. When queried for the distance between vertices $s, t \in V$, the algorithm returns the exact distance if $s \in S_t$ or if $t \in S_s$. Else, the algorithm returns $d(s, \ell(s)) + d(t, \ell(s))$ if $r_s \le r_t$ and $d(t, \ell(t)) + d(s, \ell(t))$ otherwise.

B.2 Proof of Theorem 5

As with the proof of Theorem 1, this proof uses two ideas. The first is used to bound the oracle's size — we show that if each vertex has a small size inverse-ball (or equivalently, is contained in a few balls) as guaranteed by Lemma 2, then the number of vertex pairs with ball-ball intersection is also small, thereby bounding $\sum_v |S_v|$. Second, we show that any pair of vertices s, t with non-intersecting ball-ball must be rather far away and either the path $s \leadsto \ell(s) \leadsto t$ or the path $t \leadsto \ell(t) \leadsto s$ must be a stretch-$(2, 1)$ path.

LEMMA 6. *Let $G = (V, E)$ be a unweighted undirected graph with n vertices. For any fixed $1 \le \alpha \le n$, if the oracle is constructed as above, then:* $\sum_{v \in V} |S_v| \le \alpha^2 n$.

Proof: For any vertex $w \in V$, let $\gamma(w)$ be the number of vertex pairs whose ball-ball intersection contains w; that is, $\gamma(w) = |\{(u, v) \,:\, w \in B(u) \cap B(v)\}|$. Then, by definition, we get that $\sum_{v \in V} |S_v| \le \sum_{w \in V} \gamma(w)$. Recall, using Lemma 2, each vertex w (deterministically) belongs to at most α balls. Hence, the number of ball-ball intersections that can occur at w is bounded by α^2; consequently, we have that for any vertex $w \in V$, $\gamma(w) \le \alpha^2$. Hence, $\sum_{v \in V} |S_v| \le \sum_{w \in V} \gamma(w) \le \alpha^2 n$. $\square$

Proof of Theorem 5. We first bound the size of the oracle. Using Lemma 2, the expected size of set L is $8n \log n/\alpha$; and, using Lemma 6, the size of set $\sum_{v \in V} |S_v|$ is bounded by $\alpha^2 n$. Hence, the size of the oracle is bounded by $8n^2 \log n/\alpha + \alpha^2 n$; this expression is minimized for $\alpha = 2n^{1/3} \log^{1/3}(n)$, leading to the desired bound.

Next, we show that the query algorithm returns a distance of at most $2d(s, t) + 1$. If $B(s) \cap B(t) \ne \emptyset$, the algorithm returns the exact distance. For the case when $B(s) \cap B(t) = \emptyset$, assume, without loss of generality, that $r_s \le r_t$. Let $P = (s, x_1, x_2, \ldots, t)$ be the shortest path between s and t. Let $i_0 = \max\{i | x_i \in P \cap B(s)\}$, $w = x_{i_0}$ and $w' = x_{i_0+1}$. Since $w' \notin B(s)$, we get that $d(s, w') \ge r_s$. Since $B(s) \cap B(t) = \emptyset$, we have that $w \notin B(t)$ and hence, $d(t, w) \ge r_t$. Finally, w' being on the shortest path between s and t, we have that $d(s, t) = d(s, w') + d(t, w') = d(s, w') + d(t, w) - 1 \ge r_s + r_t - 1 \ge 2r_s - 1$; or equivalently, $2r_s \le d(s, t) + 1$. The distance returned by the query algorithm is $d(s, \ell(s)) + d(t, \ell(s))$, which using triangle inequality, is at most $2d(s, \ell(s)) + d(s, t) = 2r_s + d(s, t) \le 2d(s, t) + 1$, as claimed. $\square$

Brief Announcement: Pareto Optimal Solutions to Consensus and Set Consensus

Armando Castañeda[*]
Department of Computer
Science, Technion
armando@cs.technion.ac.il

Yannai A. Gonczarowski[†]
Center for the Study of
Rationality and Institute of
Mathematics, Hebrew
University of Jerusalem
yannai@gonch.name

Yoram Moses[‡]
Department of Electrical
Engineering, Technion
moses@ee.technion.ac.il

ABSTRACT

A protocol P is *Pareto-optimal* if no protocol Q can decide as fast as P for all adversaries, while allowing at least one process to decide strictly earlier, in at least one instance. Pareto optimal protocols cannot be improved upon. We present the first Pareto-optimal solutions to consensus and k-set consensus for synchronous message-passing with crashes failures. Our k-set consensus protocol strictly dominates all known solutions, and our results expose errors in [1,7,8,12]. Our proofs of Pareto optimality are completely constructive, and are devoid of any topological arguments or reductions.

Categories and Subject Descriptors

C.2.4 [**Computer-Communication Networks**]: Distributed Systems-Distributed applications; D.4.5 [**Operating Systems**]: Reliability-Fault-tolerance; D.4.7 [**Operating Systems**]: Organization and Design-Distributed systems

Keywords

Consensus, k-set consensus, optimality, knowledge.

1. INTRODUCTION

The very first consensus protocols were ***worst-case*** optimal [13] (decisions are always taken no later than the known

[*]Supported in part at the Technion by an Aly Kaufman Fellowship.

[†]Supported in part by an ISF grant, by the Google Inter-university center for Electronic Markets and Auctions, and by the European Research Council under the European Community's Seventh Framework Programme (FP7/2007-2013) / ERC grant agreement no. [249159].

[‡]The Israel Polak academic chair at Technion; this work was supported in part by the ISF grant 1520/11.

worst-case lower bound), deciding in exactly $t+1$ rounds in all runs [4, 17], where t is an upper bound on the number of failing processes. It was soon realised that these can be strictly improved upon by ***early stopping*** protocols [3], which are also worst-case optimal, but can often decide much faster than the original ones. Following [11], this paper studies protocols that cannot be strictly improved upon, and are thus optimal in a much stronger sense.

An ***adversary*** is a tuple $\alpha = (\vec{v}, \mathsf{F})$, where $\vec{v}$ is a vector of input values from a domain V and F is a failure pattern. A *context* is a set of adversaries. W.l.o.g., we consider only full-information protocols (fip's). For a protocol P and an adversary $\alpha = (\vec{v}, \mathsf{F})$, we use $P[\alpha]$ to denote the run of P with inputs $\vec{v}$ and failure pattern F. We say that a protocol Q ***dominates*** a protocol P in context γ, denoted by $Q \preceq_\gamma P$ if, for every adversary $\alpha \in \gamma$ and every process i, if i decides in $P[\alpha]$ at time m_i, then i decides in $Q[\alpha]$ at some time $m_i' \leq m_i$. Q ***strictly dominates*** P if $Q \preceq_\gamma P$ and $P \npreceq_\gamma Q$. Here we consider the synchronous message-passing model with n processes and $t < n$ crash failures.

The early-stopping consensus protocols of [3] strictly dominate the protocols of [17], which always decided at time $t+1$. Nevertheless, these early stopping protocols may not be optimal solutions to consensus. A protocol P is an ***all-case optimal*** solution to a decision task T if P solves T and it dominates every protocol P' that solves T [13]. All-case optimal solutions to the *simultaneous* variant of consensus, in which all decisions are required to occur at the same time were presented in [5]. For the standard *eventual* variant of consensus, in which decisions are not required to occur simultaneously, no all-case optimal solution exists [15]. Consequently, Halpern, Moses and Waarts [12] initiated the study of a notion of optimality that is achievable by eventual consensus protocols:

DEFINITION 1. *A protocol P is a **Pareto-optimal** solution to a decision task T in a context γ if P solves T in γ and no protocol Q solving T in γ strictly dominates P.*

In other words, for all protocols Q that solve T, if there exist an adversary α and process i s.t. i decides in $Q[\alpha]$ strictly earlier than in $P[\alpha]$, there must exist some adversary β and process j s.t. j decides in $P[\beta]$ strictly earlier than in $Q[\beta]$.

Halpern, Moses and Waarts logically characterised Pareto optimality, and presented a simple and efficient consensus protocol $P0_{\text{opt}}$ that they claimed was Pareto optimal.

We present Pareto-optimal protocols for consensus and k-set consensus. A new knowledge-based analysis [6,10] allows a simpler and more intuitive approach to Pareto optimality than that used in [12]. Our contributions are:

1. A Pareto-optimal consensus protocol, which strictly dominates the $P0_{\text{opt}}$ protocol from [12], proving that $P0_{\text{opt}}$ is, in fact, *not* Pareto optimal.

2. A Pareto-optimal protocol for k-set consensus, which strictly dominates all published solutions for k-set consensus in the synchronous model [2,7–9,16].

3. For a run with f failures, our protocols decide in at most $f + 1$ and $\lfloor \frac{f}{k} \rfloor + 1$ rounds, respectively, contradicting lower bound proofs in [1,8] and possibly [7], and answering an open problem from [8]. This emphasises the subtlety of topology-based lower bounds [8] and of reduction-based ones [1,7]. Notably, our proofs of Pareto optimality are completely constructive, devoid of any topological arguments or reductions.

2. PARETO-OPTIMAL CONSENSUS AND SET CONSENSUS

A **node** is a pair $\langle i, m \rangle$ referring to i's state at time m. $\langle j, \ell \rangle$ is **seen** by $\langle i, m \rangle$ (in a given run r) if there exists a message chain from j at time ℓ to i at time m. $\langle j, \ell \rangle$ is **hidden** from $\langle i, m \rangle$ (in r) if (a) i does not know that j has failed before time ℓ, and (b) $\langle j, \ell \rangle$ is not seen by $\langle i, m \rangle$. A **hidden path** w.r.t. $\langle i, m \rangle$ in run r is a sequence of processes $j_0, \ldots, j_{m-1}, j_m$ s.t. $\langle j_\ell, \ell \rangle$ is hidden from $\langle i, m \rangle$, for all ℓ.

Our construction of Pareto optimal protocols is assisted and guided by a knowledge-based analysis, in the spirit of [6, 10]. We consider the truth of facts at *points* (r, m)—time m in run r, with respect to a set of runs R (which we call a **system**). The systems we are interested in have the form $R_P = R(P, \gamma)$ where P is a protocol and γ is the t-resilient synchronous message-passing model with inputs in $\mathtt{V} = \{0, 1\}$. We write $(R, r, m) \models A$ to state that fact A holds, or is satisfied, at (r, m) in the system R. We write $K_i A$ to denote that **process i knows** A, and define: $(R, r, m) \models K_i A$ iff $(R, r', m) \models A$ for all $r' \in R$ s.t. i has the same local state at (r, m) and (r', m).

A Pareto-optimal consensus protocol.

The definition of consensus implies that $\exists v$ (the fact "*some process started with v*") is a precondition for deciding v. Thus, the Knowledge of Preconditions Theorem [14] implies:

LEMMA 1. $K_i \exists v$ *is a precondition for i deciding on v, for every value v in any consensus protocol.*

While $K_i \exists v$ is a necessary condition for deciding v, if $K_i \exists 0$ is used as a sufficient condition for decide_0 then $K_i \exists 1$ cannot

be sufficient for decide_1, since this may prevent agreement: Everyone would decide on their own value at time 0. The following is a consensus protocol in which decisions on 0 are performed as soon as possible:

Protocol P_0 (for an undecided process i at time m):

> **if** $K_i \exists 0$ **then** decide_0
> **if** $m = t + 1$ and $\neg K_i \exists 0$ **then** decide_1

The following lemma provides a key step to designing a Pareto-optimal consensus protocol that dominates P_0:

LEMMA 2. *If $Q \preceq P_0$ solves consensus, then every active process i decides 0 in Q when $K_i \exists 0$ first holds.*

In consensus, a precondition for deciding 1 in run r is that no correct process **ever** decides 0. By Lemma 2, in any consensus protocol that dominates P_0 processes decide 0 as soon as they know $\exists 0$. It follows that a precondition for deciding 1 in such a protocol is that no correct process will *ever* know $\exists 0$ (denoted by $\mathsf{never\text{-}known}(\exists 0)$). Indeed, by the Knowledge of Preconditions Theorem [14], a process deciding 1 must know this fact. This is equivalent to knowing that no active process *currently knows* $\exists 0$.

LEMMA 3. *The following are equivalent at time m:*
(i) $K_i(\mathsf{never\text{-}known}(\exists 0))$, *and*
(ii) $\neg K_i \exists 0$ **&** *there is no hidden path w.r.t.* $\langle i, m \rangle$.

I.e., as long as there is a hidden path w.r.t. $\langle i, m \rangle$, process i considers it possible that some process currently knows $\exists 0$. Once such a path is excluded, the process can safely decide 1. This leads to a Pareto-optimal (fip) protocol in which decisions on 0 occur as soon as possible, and on 1 as soon as a process knows that 0 will never be decided on:

Protocol OPT_0 (for an undecided process i at time m):

> **if** $K_i \exists 0$ **then** decide_0
> **elseif** no hidden path w.r.t. $\langle i, m \rangle$ exists **then** decide_1

THEOREM 1. OPT_0 *is a Pareto optimal consensus protocol; in every execution, all processes decide in OPT_0 by time $f + 1$ at the latest, where f is the number of processes that actually fail in the execution.*

Both OPT_0 and the protocol $P0_{\text{opt}}$ from [12] decide 0 when $\exists 0$ is known, but they differ in the rule for deciding 1. In $P0_{\text{opt}}$ a process decides 1 following a round in which it has not discovered a new failure. This condition implies the nonexistence of a hidden path, but is strictly weaker than it. E.g., in a run in which all initial nodes are seen at $\langle i, 2 \rangle$ but process i has seen one failure in each of the first two rounds, i decides in OPT_0 but does not decide in $P0_{\text{opt}}$.

COROLLARY 1. *Protocol $P0_{\text{opt}}$ [12] is not Pareto optimal.*

A Pareto-optimal k-set consensus protocol.

OPT_0 can readily be extended to cover the case in which $\mathtt{V} = \{0, \ldots, d\}$ for $d > 1$. The rule for 0 is unchanged, and if no hidden path exists a process can decide on the minimal value it has seen. Thus, a process decides v when it knows $\exists v$ and that correct processes will never see a smaller value. We call this protocol $\mathrm{OPT}_{\min}$.

For k-set consensus the input domain is $V = \{0, .., d\}$, $d \geq k$, and it is required that the correct processes decide on at most k distinct values (thus 1-set consensus is consensus).

We present a k-set consensus protocol $\textsc{Opt}_{\min\text{-}k}$ that generalizes $\textsc{Opt}_{\min}$, in which every process decides on a ***low*** value (i.e. a value in $\{0, \ldots, k-1\}$) as soon as possible, and decides on a ***high*** (i.e. non-low) value w as soon as it knows that no k values smaller than w will be decided on. In every run, let $V\langle i, m \rangle$ denote the set of all values v s.t. $K_i \exists v$ holds at m. Process i is called ***low*** at time m if $V\langle i, m \rangle$ contains a low value, otherwise it is ***high***. We call $v \in V$ ***minimal*** in r if it is a minimal value of some set $V\langle i, m \rangle$ in r. Finally, the ***hidden capacity*** $\mathsf{HC}(i, m)$ of $\langle i, m \rangle$ (in r) is the number c of pairwise node-disjoint hidden paths w.r.t. $\langle i, m \rangle$.

Our Pareto-optimal k-set consensus protocol is the fip with the following single decision rule:

Protocol $\textsc{Opt}_{\min\text{-}k}$ (for an undecided process i at time m):

> **if** $\langle i, m \rangle$ is low or $\mathsf{HC}(i, m) < k$ **then** $\text{decide}_{\min V\langle i, m \rangle}$

Hidden capacity plays an analogous role to hidden paths. We note that it is possible both to implement fip's for crash failures and to compute $\mathsf{HC}(i, m)$ efficiently. Our correctness proof for $\textsc{Opt}_{\min\text{-}k}$ is based on a generalization of Lemma 3:

LEMMA 4. *In the crash model, if $\langle i, m \rangle$ is a high node with minimal value v, then K_i(fewer than k values smaller than v will ever be minimal values) is equivalent to $\mathsf{HC}(i, m) < k$.*

To show that $\textsc{Opt}_{\min\text{-}k}$ is Pareto optimal, one additionally needs an analogue of Lemma 2. Unfortunately, while in every protocol dominating $\textsc{Opt}_{\min\text{-}k}$ every process must decide when it becomes low, it is no longer true, due to the relaxed k-set agreement condition, that every such process must decide on its minimal value. Nonetheless, we show that under certain conditions, a low process knowing exactly one low value must decide on it. Establishing this analogue of Lemma 2 is the main technical challenge in our proof. Notably, this proof is constructive, and does not employ topological arguments, reductions or simulations. Fortunately, this analogue of Lemma 2, despite the added conditions it requires, allows us to prove the following, showing that no k-set consensus protocol strictly dominates $\textsc{Opt}_{\min\text{-}k}$:

COROLLARY 2. *Let P be a k-set consensus protocol, in which an undecided low process decides immediately. Then no high process with hidden capacity $\geq k$ can decide in P.*

Using Lemma 4 and Corollary 2, we can prove:

THEOREM 2.

(i) $\textsc{Opt}_{\min\text{-}k}$ is a Pareto optimal k-set consensus protocol.

(ii) In every execution, all processes decide in $\textsc{Opt}_{\min\text{-}k}$ by time $\lfloor \frac{f}{k} \rfloor + 1$ at the latest, where f is the number of processes that actually fail in the execution.

Discussion. Interestingly, all known k-set consensus protocols in the synchronous crash model [2,7,9,16] are ***strictly dominated*** by $\textsc{Opt}_{\min\text{-}k}$. Moreover, as pointed out by an anonymous referee, its properties contradict the published lower bounds in [1,8] and possibly [7] (whose model is slightly

nonstandard). Although $\textsc{Opt}_{\min\text{-}k}$ decides in $\lfloor \frac{f}{k} \rfloor + 1$ rounds, since f is not known in advance it would be able to stop only in $\min\{\lfloor \frac{t}{k} \rfloor + 1, \lfloor \frac{f}{k} \rfloor + 2\}$ rounds. In the case of consensus, this is perfectly consistent with [3], who mention in passing that decision by time $f + 1$ is possible. However, [1, 7, 8] claim to prove explicitly that no k-set consensus protocol can always decide by time $\lfloor \frac{f}{k} \rfloor + 1$ (also contradicting [3] and $\textsc{Opt}_0$ even when $k = 1$). In fact, [8] pose as an open question whether decision is *ever* possible before time $\lfloor \frac{f}{k} \rfloor + 2$. Both of our Pareto-optimal protocols $\textsc{Opt}_0$ and $\textsc{Opt}_{\min\text{-}k}$ contradict these stated lower bounds, and provide a negative answer to this open problem. Moreover, they are not only optimal in a worst-case sense; they are truly unbeatable in the sense that no protocol can strictly improve upon them. These are the first such protocols.

3. REFERENCES

[1] D. Alistarh, S. Gilbert, R. Guerraoui, and C. Travers. Of choices, failures and asynchrony: The many faces of set agreement. *Algorithmica*, 62(1-2):595–629, 2012.

[2] S. Chaudhuri, M. Herlihy, N. A. Lynch, and M. R. Tuttle. Tight bounds for k-set agreement. *J. ACM*, 47(5):912–943, 2000.

[3] D. Dolev, R. Reischuk, and H. R. Strong. Early stopping in Byzantine agreement. *J. of the ACM*, 34(7):720–741, 1990.

[4] D. Dolev and H. R. Strong. Requirements for agreement in a distributed system. In H. J. Schneider, editor, *Distributed Data Bases*, pages 115–129. North-Holland, Amsterdam, 1982.

[5] C. Dwork and Y. Moses. Knowledge and common knowledge in a Byzantine environment: crash failures. *Information and Computation*, 88(2):156–186, 1990.

[6] R. Fagin, J. Y. Halpern, Y. Moses, and M. Y. Vardi. *Reasoning about Knowledge*. MIT Press, 2003.

[7] E. Gafni, R. Guerraoui, and B. Pochon. The complexity of early deciding set agreement. *SIAM J. Comput.*, 40(1):63–78, 2011.

[8] R. Guerraoui, M. Herlihy, and B. Pochon. A topological treatment of early-deciding set-agreement. *Theor. Comput. Sci.*, 410(6-7):570–580, 2009.

[9] R. Guerraoui and B. Pochon. The complexity of early deciding set agreement: How can topology help? *Electr. Notes Theor. Comput. Sci.*, 230:71–78, 2009.

[10] J. Y. Halpern and Y. Moses. Knowledge and common knowledge in a distributed environment. *J. of the ACM*, 37(3):549–587, 1990.

[11] J. Y. Halpern, Y. Moses, and O. Waarts. A characterization of eventual Byzantine agreement. In *Proc. 9th ACM Symp. on Principles of Distributed Computing*, pages 333–346, 1990.

[12] J. Y. Halpern, Y. Moses, and O. Waarts. A characterization of eventual byzantine agreement. *SIAM J. Comput.*, 31(3):838–865, 2001.

[13] M. Herlihy, Y. Moses, and M. R. Tuttle. Transforming worst-case optimal solutions for simultaneous tasks into all-case optimal solutions. In *PODC*, pages 231–238, 2011.

[14] Y. Moses. *Knowledge and Distributed Coordination*. Morgan Claypool. in preparation.

[15] Y. Moses and M. R. Tuttle. Programming simultaneous actions using common knowledge. *Algorithmica*, 3:121–169, 1988.

[16] P. Raipin Parvédy, M. Raynal, and C. Travers. Early-stopping k-set agreement in synchronous systems prone to any number of process crashes. In *PaCT*, pages 49–58, 2005.

[17] M. Pease, R. Shostak, and L. Lamport. Reaching agreement in the presence of faults. *J. of the ACM*, 27(2):228–234, 1980.

Brief Announcement:
Self-Stabilizing Resource Discovery Algorithm*

Seda Davtyan
Computer Science & Engineering
University of Connecticut
seda@engr.uconn.edu

Kishori M. Konwar
Immunology and Microbiology
University of British Columbia
kishori@interchange.ubc.ca

Alexander A. Shvartsman
Computer Science & Engineering
University of Connecticut
aas@cse.uconn.edu

ABSTRACT

Distributed cooperative computing in networks involves marshaling collections of network nodes possessing the necessary computational resources. Before the willing nodes can act in a concerted way they must first discover one another. This is the general setting of the Resource Discovery Problem (RDP). This paper presents a self-stabilizing algorithm that solves RDP in a deterministic synchronous setting. The solution approach is formulated in terms of evolving *knowledge graphs*, where vertices represent the participating network nodes, and edges represent one node's knowledge about another. Ideally, the diameter of such a graph is one, i.e., each node knows all others. The algorithm works in rounds as it evolves the knowledge graph with the goal of reducing its diameter. This is accomplished by nodes sharing their knowledge through gossip messages. We prove that the algorithm is *self-stabilizing*, i.e., it tolerates arbitrary perturbations in the nodes' local states and is guaranteed to solve the problem once such failures subside. The algorithm has stabilization time of $O(D)$, and it takes at most $4D + 4$ complete round to stabilize, where D is the diameter of the initial knowledge graph, and the corresponding message complexity is $O(|V| \cdot D)$, where V is the set of participating nodes.

Categories and Subject Descriptors: F.2.0 [Theory of Computation]: ANALYSIS OF ALGORITHMS AND PROBLEM COMPLEXITY – *General*

Keywords: Resource Discovery; Self-Stabilization; Distributed Cooperation; Fault-Tolerance

1. INTRODUCTION

A large collection of networked computers may need to cooperate in implementing a distributed system, for example, to provide a shared data service, or to perform a set of tasks. The necessary first step in such settings is to discover the relevant computational resources in the network. This step is formalized as the Resource Discovery Problem, where each

---

*This work is supported in part by the NSF award 1017232.

willing resource must find all other resources willing to collaborate. This problem was introduced by Harchol-Balter, Leighton, and Lewin [5]. Kutten, Peleg, and Vishkin [6] gave an efficient deterministic algorithm for the problem. However it does not have strong fault-tolerance properties and does not deal with dynamic situations, thus its guarantees do not hold in the presence of failures. Additionally, it assumes that certain knowledge of the nodes is non-decreasing.

Our goal is to design algorithms that can deal with transient failures, and in particular we are interested in *self-stabilizing* solutions, cf. [3]. Here the algorithm must be able to bring a system into a legitimate state in spite of arbitrary state corruptions, and once failures subside, such a legitimate state is reached in a finite time. For additional details we refer the reader to [2].

2. THE PROBLEM AND SYSTEM MODEL

We consider the Resource Discovery Problem (RDP) in deterministic synchronous settings. Let there be a universe of processes, with unique identifiers from a well-ordered set U. Let $V \subseteq U$ be the set of processes chosen by the environment to participate in the computation. We let v_0 stand for $\min\{v : v \in V\}$. The set V, its cardinality, and v_0 are unknown to the processes, but each process v in V is aware of one other process in V: each v has a constant $nb_v \in V$, where $v \neq nb_v$, representing the knowledge of v of some other process (a neighbor). This induces a directed graph.

DEFINITION 1. *Given the set V and nb_v for all $v \in V$, we define the **connectivity graph** as the directed graph $G = (V, E)$, where $E = \{(u, v) : nb_u = v\}$.*

We assume that the connectivity graph is at least *weakly-connected*, representing the setting where each process has the knowledge of at least one other process (as in the original formulation in [5]). We assume that each process v has three local variables, $prt_v \in V$, $C_v \in 2^V$ and K_v, where $prt_v = u$ means that v considers u to be its *parent*, $u \in C_v$ means that v considers u to be its *child*, with C_v being the set of all children of v, and finally $u \in K_v$ means that v knows u. We now define the *Resource Discovery Problem*.

DEFINITION 2. *Given the weakly-connected graph G, the **Resource Discovery Problem** (RDP) is to establish and maintain the following invariant on configurations:*
$(\exists v \in V : (C_v = V) \wedge (\forall u \in V : prt_u = v)) \wedge (\forall u \in V : K_u = V)$, *that is, (1) there exists a node $v \in V$ such that $C_v = V$, and (2) for every node $u \in V$ we have $prt_u = v$, and (3) for every node $u \in V$ we have $K_u = V$.*

For convenience we let G^u be the undirected graph induced by G, called the *initial knowledge graph*. Let D be the diameter of G^u and $dist(u, v)$ be the length of the shortest path from node u to v in G^u.

The nodes communicate using point-to-point messages. Sending (multicasting) messages requires that the sending node has the identifiers of the destination nodes (arbitrary broadcast is not allowed). The communication is synchronous in the sense that there is a known upper bound d on message delays. If a node expects a message from another node and the message is sent, then it is delivered within d time units. Nodes have access to synchronous timers that can be used to implement message time-outs. Local computation takes negligible time relative to d. We do not assume that all nodes begin participating in the computation simultaneously; instead we allow the nodes to join the computation at arbitrary times. At a high level, the computation is structured in terms of synchronous rounds, however the activities within each round are not synchronized across the nodes.

The nodes are subject to arbitrary perturbations to their local (volatile) states and arbitrary crash and restart events that occur in matched pairs. The static code of each node, its constants, and the clock are incorruptible. All other variables are subject to corruption. Here a corrupted variable may contain a value that is syntactically *indistinguishable* from a valid value. This is in contrast with some works in self-stabilization, where failures cause erasures of variable values, making such failures easily detectable, cf. [4]. Other works, e.g., [7], assume that any node identifier must represent an actual node in the system. Finally, we also allow the adversary to corrupt messages in transit.

We denote a transition from configuration σ_i to σ_{i+1} by $\sigma_i \xrightarrow{\tau} \sigma_{i+1}$ and we let $\sigma \xrightarrow{*}{\tau} \sigma'$ stand for the fact that σ' can be reached from σ by zero or more transitions.

Self-stabilization is the ability of a system to recover from transient failures following their cessation. The impact of a failure is that the transition from configuration σ to configuration σ' may not obey the transition function τ, that is, a failure may cause $\sigma' \neq \tau(\sigma)$. Thus we assume that the local state of any node can be corrupted, and in particular, that a system can start in any configuration. In designing solutions resilient to transient failures we will use self-stabilization techniques, formalized in terms of closure and convergence properties (cf. [1]).

DEFINITION 3. *(**Self-stabilization**) Let problem P be to establish and maintain invariant $\psi()$, given as a predicate on configurations. System $S = (\Sigma, A, \tau)$ is a self-stabilizing solution for problem P, if the following two conditions hold:*
Closure: $\forall \sigma \in \Sigma, \forall a \in A : \psi(\sigma) \implies \psi(\tau(\sigma, a))$,
i.e., τ maintains the invariant.
Convergence: $\forall \sigma \in \Sigma : \exists \sigma' \in \Sigma : \sigma \xrightarrow{*}{\tau} \sigma' \land \psi(\sigma')$,
i.e., $\psi()$ can be established in the absence of failures.

Measures of efficiency. We assess the efficiency of the algorithm in terms of *stabilization time* and *stabilization message complexity*. The stabilization time is measured in terms of the worst case number of rounds following the cessation of perturbations needed to establish the resource discovery invariant. The stabilization message complexity is measured in terms of the worst case number of point-to-point messages sent among the *participants* to establish the resource discovery invariant following the cessation of perturbations.

Data-types:
U, the set of node identifiers M, the set of messages

Constants: **Derived Constants:**
$nb : U$
$t : real > 0$ $\widehat{N} = \{i\} \cup \{nb\}$

Signature:
   Input: Internal:
     $\mathsf{mrecv}(m, u)_i$, $m \in M$, $u \in U$ $\mathsf{restart}_i$
     join_i reset_i
     $\mathsf{perturb}_i$ $\mathsf{end\text{-}round}_i$
   Output:
     $\mathsf{msend}(m, I)_i$, $m \in M$, $I \subset U$

State:
$active : bool$ $R : 2^U$
$phase : \{\mathsf{gossip}, \mathsf{confirm}\}$ $Dest : 2^U$
$clock : real$ $C : 2^U$
$prt : U$ $New\_C : 2^U$
$pp : U$ $Nbrs : 2^U$
$do\_msend : bool$ $K : 2^U$
                         $ProP : 2^U$

Figure 1: Signature and state of RD_i at node i in V

3. ALGORITHM RDS

The algorithm has an iterative structure, where each iteration consists of two synchronous rounds. The first round is referred to as the gossip phase and the second round as the confirm phase. In both phases nodes propagate information to other nodes, while in the confirm phase the nodes additionally validate the identities of the nodes to whom the information was propagated in the gossip phase.

The behavior of each node $i \in V$ is specified as a timed I/O automaton, called RD_i. The specification is given in Figure 1 that defines constants, signature, and state variables, and Figure 2 that defines the transitions and the trajectory. The full system, called RDS, is the composition of automata RD_i for $i \in V$, the multicast implementation, and the $Channel_{i,j}$ automata for $i, j \in V$ (not specified here).

The main variables are $active_i$, C_i, K_i, $Nbrs_i$, and prt_i. Boolean $active_i$ indicates whether node i is active or not, set C_i contains the children of node i, set K_i contains its siblings in the evolving knowledge graph, set $Nbrs_i$ contains the identifiers of the nodes that i considers to be neighbors in G^u, and prt_i is the identifier of the node that node i considers to be its parent. The remaining variables are used for control: $phase_i$, pp_i, New_C_i, do_msend_i, R_i, and $Dest_i$.

The environment may activate node i by using input action join_i, and it may disable and/or corrupt the state of node i by means of input action $\mathsf{perturb}_i$, where HAVOC assigns arbitrary values to the state variables, modeling a transient failure. If HAVOC sets $active$ to $false$, the action models a crash of the node. Internal action $\mathsf{restart}_i$ is always enabled, modeling the assumption that each node $i \in V$ is eventually active. Nodes gossip by sending and receiving messages through actions msend_i and mrecv_i.

Variable $clock$ represents the time of the synchronous system. Recall that failures cannot change the synchronous nature of the system, and thus this is the only variable that is not affected by transient failures. The constant t is used to control the duration of rounds (t is readily obtained from the structure of the algorithm and from the knowledge of the worst case message delivery delay d). The trajectory specification says that time "stops" when $clock \% t = 0$ for

Transitions:

Input join$_i$
    Effect:
        $active \leftarrow true$
Output msend$(\langle N, p, ch \rangle, I)_i$
    Precondition:
        $active \land do\_msend$
        $\langle N, p, ch \rangle = \langle \widehat{N}, prt, C \rangle$
        $I = Dest$
    Effect:
        $do\_msend \leftarrow false$
Input mrecv$(\langle N, p, ch \rangle, s)_i$
    Effect:
        if $active$ then
            $R \leftarrow R \cup \{s\}$
            if $phase = $ gossip then
                if $i \in N$ then
                    $Nbrs \leftarrow Nbrs \cup \{s\}$
                if $p = i$ then
                    $New\_C \leftarrow New\_C \cup \{s\}$
            if $phase = $ confirm then
                if $p \leq prt$ then
                    $ProP \leftarrow ProP \cup \{p\}$
                if $prt = s$ then
                    $K \leftarrow ch$

Input perturb$_i$
    Effect:
        HAVOC
Internal end-round$_i$
    Precondition:
        $active$
        $clock \% t = 0$
        $clock \% 2t = t \lor prt \in R$
    Effect:
        if $clock \% 2t = 0$ then
            $prt \leftarrow \min \{u : u \in R \cup \widehat{N}\}$
            $R \leftarrow \emptyset$
            $pp \leftarrow \min\{u : u \in ProP \cup \widehat{N}\}$
            $ProP \leftarrow \emptyset$
            $New\_C \leftarrow \emptyset$
            $Nbrs \leftarrow \widehat{N}$
            $Dest \leftarrow \{prt\} \cup \{pp\} \cup Nbrs \cup C$
            $phase \leftarrow $ gossip
        else /* start confirm phase */
            $C \leftarrow New\_C$
            $Dest \leftarrow R \cup Nbrs$
            $phase \leftarrow $ confirm
        $do\_msend \leftarrow true$
        $clock \leftarrow clock + \epsilon$

Internal restart$_i$
    Effect:
        $active \leftarrow true$
Internal reset$_i$
    Precondition:
        $active \land clock \% 2t = 0 \land prt \notin R$
    Effect:
        $prt \leftarrow pp \leftarrow \min\{u : u \in \widehat{N}\}$
        $R \leftarrow \emptyset$
        $ProP \leftarrow \emptyset$
        $C \leftarrow New\_C \leftarrow \emptyset$
        $Nbrs \leftarrow \widehat{N}$
        $Dest \leftarrow \{prt\} \cup \{pp\} \cup Nbrs \cup C$
        $phase \leftarrow $ gossip
        $do\_msend \leftarrow true$
        $clock \leftarrow clock + \epsilon$

Trajectories
    stop when
        $active \land clock \% t = 0$
    evolve
        $d(clock) = 1$

Figure 2: Transitions of RD_i at node i for $i \in V$

an active node. The value of *clock* is used to determine whether an active node is in the gossip or confirm phase.

A round ends with either action end-round$_i$ or action reset$_i$. Action end-round$_i$ is enabled every t time units (specified by $clock \% t = 0$ in the code) at the conclusion of each round if the node's state suggests that its parent is active (this does not mean that perturbations did not occur). Action reset$_i$ is enabled every $2t$ time units (when $clock \% 2t = 0$) and the parent does not respond during the iteration. In this case the node gives up, resets its state and starts anew.

4. ALGORITHM ANALYSIS

Our analysis shows that algorithm *RDS* satisfies the *Closure* and *Convergence* properties of Definition 3. In the analysis we let A denote the set of all actions of the algorithm, excluding actions join and perturb.

THEOREM 1. **(Closure)** *Consider any execution prefix of RDS consisting of complete iterations, where σ is the final configuration. If σ is legitimate, then any extension of the execution by up to one complete iteration using only the actions from A results in $\sigma \xrightarrow{*}_{\tau} \sigma'$, where σ' is a legitimate configuration.*

We prove the following convergence property.

THEOREM 2. **(Convergence)** *Consider an execution prefix of RDS that ends with configuration σ. Any fair extension of the execution of a sufficient length that uses only the actions from A reaches a configuration σ_l in at most $2D + 2$ complete iterations, such that σ_l is a legitimate configuration.*

Finally we reason about the efficiency of the algorithm.

THEOREM 3. *Any execution prefix of RDS ending in an arbitrary configuration can be infinitely extended to solve the resource discovery problem. The stabilization time of the algorithm is $O(D)$, taking at most $4D + 4$ complete rounds to stabilize. The stabilization message complexity is $O(|V| \cdot D)$.*

Recall that an important goal of the algorithm is to manage the overall communication complexity in the presence of perturbations. To limit the number of messages sent to bogus destinations, the algorithm refreshes the states of the nodes in each iteration. The convergence of the algorithm in $O(D)$ rounds is largely due the fact that it does not aggregate knowledge across multiple iterations.

Lastly we note that if the initial knowledge graph is not connected, or if permanent crashes disconnect the graph, then our algorithm solves the problem for each (weakly) connected component. Our follow up work will focus on improving efficiency and stronger adversarial behaviors.

5. REFERENCES

[1] Anish Arora and Mohamed G. Gouda. Closure and convergence: A foundation of fault-tolerant computing. *IEEE Trans. Software Eng.*, 19(11):1015–1027, 1993.

[2] S. Davtyan, K.M. Konwar, and A.A. Shvartsman. Self-stabilizing resource discovery algorithm. http://engr.uconn.edu/~sad06005/TR/DKS13.pdf, 2013.

[3] E. W. Dijkstra. A belated proof of self-stabilization. *Distributed Computing*, 1(1), 1986.

[4] S. Dolev and T. Herman. Superstabilizing protocols for dynamic distributed systems. *Chicago Journal of Theoretical Computer Science*, 1997.

[5] M. Harchol-Balter, F. T. Leighton, and D. Lewin. Resource discovery in distributed networks. In *Proceedings of the 18th Symposium on Principles of Distributed Computing*, pages 229–237, 1999.

[6] S. Kutten, D. Peleg, and U. Vishkin. Deterministic resource discovery in distributed networks. In *Proceedings of the 13th ACM Symposium on Parallel Algorithms and Architectures*, pages 77–83, 2001.

[7] R.M. Nor, M. Nesterenko, and C. Scheideler. Corona: A stabilizing deterministic message-passing skip list. In *Proc. of 13th Int-l Symp. on Stabilization, Safety, and Security of Distributed Systems*, pages 356–370, 2011.

Brief Announcement: Parameterized Model Checking of Fault-tolerant Distributed Algorithms by Abstraction *

Annu John
TU Wien
john@forsyte.at

Igor Konnov
TU Wien
konnov@forsyte.at

Ulrich Schmid
TU Wien
s@ecs.tuwien.ac.at

Helmut Veith
TU Wien
veith@forsyte.at

Josef Widder
TU Wien
widder@forsyte.at

ABSTRACT

We introduce an automated method for parameterized verification of fault-tolerant distributed algorithms. It rests on a novel parametric interval abstraction (PIA) technique, which works for systems with multiple parameters, for instance, where n and t are parameters describing the system size and the bound on the number of faulty processes, respectively. The PIA technique allows to map typical threshold-range intervals like $[1, t + 1)$ and $[t + 1, n - t)$ to values from a finite abstract domain. Applying PIA to both the local states of the processes and the global system state, the parameterized verification problem can be reduced to finite-state model checking. We demonstrate the practical feasibility of our method by verifying several variants of the well-known consistent broadcasting algorithm by Srikanth and Toueg for different fault models. To the best of our knowledge, this is the first successful automated parameterized verification of a Byzantine fault-tolerant distributed algorithm for message-passing systems.

Categories and Subject Descriptors: C.2.4 [Computer-Communication Networks]: Distributed Systems; D.2.4 [Software Engineering]: Software/Program Verification—Model checking; F.3.1 [Theory of Computation]: Specifying and Verifying and Reasoning about Programs.

General Terms: Algorithms, Theory, Verification.

Keywords: parameterized model checking, fault-tolerance, Byzantine faults, abstraction.

Introduction. Model checking was introduced [2, 15] thirty years ago as a technique to automatically verify specifications of finite state systems. Originally, the idea was to use (exhaustive) state space exploration of the given system implementation in order to either show the correctness of the system or find an incorrect execution (a counterexample). Today, however, basically all research in model checking deals with *infinite* systems, in one sense or another.

Parameterized model checking considers concurrent or distributed systems that are composed of an unknown number n of processes. As n, and hence the system state space, is not a priori bounded, finite state model checking techniques cannot be directly applied. Nevertheless, state-of-the-art parameterized model checking techniques nowadays allow the verification of safety properties of mutual exclusion algorithms and cache coherence protocols for arbitrarily many processes, cf. [7] for an overview.

However, no existing parameterized model checking technique is applicable to fault-tolerant distributed algorithms: Besides the problem of incorporating faults (which requires an exhaustive specification of *incorrect* behaviors), fault-tolerant distributed algorithms are typically only correct under conditions such as "at most t among $n > 3t$ processes may be faulty". The latter makes it imperative to handle multiple parameters such as n, t, and the number f of faulty processes in a run of the algorithm, as well as resilience conditions such as $n > 3t \land f \le t$. In the context of fault-tolerant distributed algorithms, model checking was hence limited to verifying small system instances. For instance, the authors of [18, 17, 11, 9] fixed the number n of processes a priori to some small value, say, $n = 4$ to 10, and used model checking for ruling out errors in these particular system instances. Although it is tempting to verify a "large enough" model and assume that this implies the algorithm's correctness in the general case, this is not necessarily true.

In our recent work [7], announced here, we introduce a parameterized model checking technique, which allows to verify homogeneous fault-tolerant distributed algorithms that contain threshold-guarded commands such as

```
if received <m> from n-t distinct processes
then action(m);
```

which are used to achieve fault tolerance in distributed algorithms. Typical numbers used for thresholds are $n/2$ (for majority [3, 14]), $t + 1$ (to wait for a message from at least one correct process [16, 3]), or $n - t$ (to wait for at least $t + 1$ messages from correct processes provided $n > 3t$ in the Byzantine case [16, 3]). Note carefully that the system size and the code of every individual process of the algorithm are parameterized here.

---

*A full version of this paper can be found at arXiv [7]. Supported by the Austrian National Research Network S11403 and S11405 (RiSE) of the Austrian Science Fund (FWF), and by the Vienna Science and Technology Fund (WWTF) grant PROSEED, ICT12-059, and VRG11-005.

PODC'13, July 22–24, 2013, Montréal, Québec, Canada.
ACM 978-1-4503-2065-8/13/07.

The primary technique we employ is *abstraction*: We define parameterized abstraction mappings that, for each n, t, and f, map the concrete system instance — defined via n, t, and f — to a single abstract finite state system. Since this is done in a way that preserves the behaviors of all concrete system instances, finite model checking of the abstract system can be used to verify the distributed algorithm for all concrete values of the parameters (possibly after some refinement steps to circumvent spurious counterexamples).

Our abstraction proceeds in two steps. Both steps are based on *parametric interval abstraction* (PIA), a new generalization of interval abstraction where the interval borders are functions of parameters rather than constants. For instance, for a distributed algorithm containing the thresholds $t + 1$ and $n - t$, we introduce an abstract PIA domain containing four totally ordered *abstract values*, corresponding to the parametric intervals $[0, 1)$ and $[1, t + 1)$ and $[t + 1, n - t)$ and $[n - t; \infty)$. Note carefully that the abstract values are the same for any choice of concrete parameter values. Concrete values v in a system instance with fixed values for n and t are just mapped to the abstract value that corresponds to the interval v belongs to. In more detail, using PIA, we obtain a finite-state model checking problem in two steps:

Step 1: PIA data abstraction. Intuitively, instead of tracking concrete numbers of messages sent and received, for each process we record only to which parametric intervals these numbers belong. Hence, threshold guards are abstracted to expressions over (finitely many) abstract values. Thus, we abstract away unbounded variables and parameters from the process code to obtain a (still parameterized) system, where the replicated processes themselves are finite-state and *independent* of the parameters.

Step 2: PIA counter abstraction. For the homogeneous (fully symmetric) distributed systems we consider, instead of representing the system state as an array — indexed by processes — of local process states, one can think of the system state as an array — indexed by local states — of the number of processes that are in the corresponding local state. In the latter case, an element of the array is called a *counter*. Again, instead of tracking concrete counter values, we only maintain counters that are abstracted to the PIA domain. As Step 1 guarantees that we need only finitely many counters, Step 2 of the PIA counter abstraction finally yields a finite-state system.

In the case of hand-written proofs, the presentation of the computational model and the algorithm is not of central concern, as long as there is an unambiguous understanding of the used terms. Automatic verification, on the contrary, requires to encode all necessary terms in the input language of the model checker. Obvious candidates for the input language are TLA [10] and IOA [12]. However, for our abstraction method, a new variant of control flow automata (CFA) [5] is more natural, and the ways to express nondeterminism in our CFA variant are particularly suitable to model the influence of faults and uncertain message delays. In [8], we describe in detail how fault-tolerant message passing algorithms are specified using CFAs. As the CFA formalism is rather low-level compared to the way distributed algorithms are typically stated in the literature, interfaces to higher-level languages are subject to future work.

To show the feasibility of our approach, we have implemented the PIA abstractions and the refinement loop in OCaml as a prototype tool BYMC. It uses YICES to con-

---

Algorithm 1 Core logic of the algorithm from [16].

Code for processes i if it is correct:
Variables
1: $v_i \in \{\text{FALSE}, \text{TRUE}\}$
2: $\text{accept}_i \in \{\text{FALSE}, \text{TRUE}\} \leftarrow \text{FALSE}$

Rules
3: **if** v_i **and** not sent $\langle$echo$\rangle$ before **then**
4:     *send* $\langle$echo$\rangle$ to all;
5: **if** *received* $\langle$echo$\rangle$ from at least $t + 1$ *distinct* processes **and** not sent $\langle$echo$\rangle$ before **then**
6:     *send* $\langle$echo$\rangle$ to all;
7: **if** *received* $\langle$echo$\rangle$ from at least $n - t$ *distinct* processes **then**
8:     $\text{accept}_i \leftarrow \text{TRUE}$;

---

struct the abstract system, and SPIN [6] to model check this system, which is finite state. For the experiments summarized in Table 1, we primarily used variants of the Byzantine fault-tolerant consistent broadcasting algorithm CB by Srikanth and Toueg [16]; e.g., the pseudo code of the Byzantine case is given in Algorithm 1. We focused on the core functionality (the threshold guards), and replaced the initialization phase, which originally is initiated by a (possibly Byzantine faulty) broadcaster, by non-deterministic initialization of the v_i variable. In addition we verified the folklore reliable broadcast algorithm RBC ("send to all, then deliver"). The safety and liveness specifications considered for CB are unforgeability U ("no spurious delivery"), correctness C ("delivery for correct sender"), and relay R ("agreement on delivery") as defined in [16]. We provided several variants of CB, for different fault models and resilience conditions: (BYZ) for t Byzantine faults and $n > 3t$, (SYM) for t symmetric (identical Byzantine) faults and $n > 2t$, (OMIT) for t send omission faults and $n > 2t$, and (CLEAN) for t clean crash faults and $n > t$. The RBC algorithm tolerates crash faults, and was checked for the trivial resilience condition $n \geq t \geq f$; in addition to the above specifications, it also involves the property agreement A as defined in [4].

Our experiments were conducted on a 3.3GHz Intel® Core™ 4GB machine; some results are summarized in Table 1. The column "Refinements" shows the number of refinement steps applied to circumvent spurious counterexamples; "Spin Time" refers to the SPIN running time after the last refinement step. To demonstrate that our approach indeed works, we checked CB under both legal and illegal conditions: (A) the above mentioned legal resilience conditions such as $n > 3t \wedge f \leq t$ in the Byzantine case; (B) $f \leq t + 1$ (illegal); (C) $n \geq 3t$ instead of $n > 3t$ (illegal); (D) $n \geq 2t$ instead of $n > 2t$ (illegal). Note that (B) captures the case where more faults occur than expected by the algorithm designer, while (C) and (D) capture the cases where the algorithms were designed by assuming wrong resilience conditions.

Currently, we are exploring our method, and considering suitable extensions to it, in order to cover other fault-tolerant distributed algorithms, such as fast Byzantine consensus [13], condition-based consensus [14], and other broadcasting implementations [1]. Major verification challenges result from, e.g., unique process ids and non-homogeneous algorithms, the need for a compositional reasoning to handle multiple instances of an algorithm used at each process, and the treatment of synchrony and time.

$M \models \varphi$?	Res. Cond.	Spin Time	Spin Memory	Spin States	Spin Depth	Refinements	Total Time
$Byz \models U$	(A)	2.3 s	82 MB	483k	9154	0	4 s
$Byz \models C$	(A)	3.5 s	104 MB	970k	20626	10	32 s
$Byz \models R$	(A)	6.3 s	107 MB	1327k	20844	10	24 s
$Sym \models U$	(A)	0.1 s	67 MB	19k	897	0	1 s
$Sym \models C$	(A)	0.1 s	67 MB	19k	1113	2	3 s
$Sym \models R$	(A)	0.3 s	69 MB	87k	2047	12	16 s
$Omt \models U$	(A)	0.1 s	66 MB	4k	487	0	1 s
$Omt \models C$	(A)	0.1 s	66 MB	7k	747	5	6 s
$Omt \models R$	(A)	0.1 s	66 MB	8k	704	5	10 s
$Cln \models U$	(A)	0.3 s	67 MB	30k	1371	0	2 s
$Cln \models C$	(A)	0.4 s	67 MB	35k	1707	4	8 s
$Cln \models R$	(A)	1.1 s	67 MB	51k	2162	13	31 s
$RBC \models U$	—	0.1 s	66 MB	0.8k	232	0	1 s
$RBC \models A$	—	0.1 s	66 MB	1.7k	333	0	1 s
$RBC \models R$	—	0.1 s	66 MB	1.2k	259	0	1 s
$RBC \not\models C$	—	0.1 s	66 MB	0.8k	232	0	1 s
$Byz \not\models U$	(B)	5.2 s	101 MB	1093k	17685	9	56 s
$Byz \not\models C$	(B)	3.7 s	102 MB	980k	19772	11	52 s
$Byz \not\models R$	(B)	0.4 s	67 MB	59k	6194	10	17 s
$Byz \models U$	(C)	3.4 s	87 MB	655k	10385	0	5 s
$Byz \models C$	(C)	3.9 s	101 MB	963k	20651	9	32 s
$Byz \not\models R$	(C)	2.1 s	91 MB	797k	14172	30	78 s
$Sym \not\models U$	(B)	0.1 s	67 MB	19k	947	0	2 s
$Sym \not\models C$	(B)	0.1 s	67 MB	18k	1175	2	4 s
$Sym \models R$	(B)	0.2 s	67 MB	42k	1681	8	12 s
$Omt \models U$	(D)	0.1 s	66 MB	5k	487	0	1 s
$Omt \not\models C$	(D)	0.1 s	66 MB	5k	487	0	2 s
$Omt \not\models R$	(D)	0.1 s	66 MB	0.1k	401	0	2 s

Table 1: Experimental data on abstraction of algorithms tolerant to faults

1. REFERENCES

[1] G. Bracha and S. Toueg. Asynchronous consensus and broadcast protocols. *JACM*, 32(4):824–840, Oct. 1985.

[2] E. M. Clarke and E. A. Emerson. Design and synthesis of synchronization skeletons using branching-time temporal logic. In *Logic of Programs*, volume 131 of *LNCS*, pages 52–71, 1981.

[3] C. Dwork, N. Lynch, and L. Stockmeyer. Consensus in the presence of partial synchrony. *JACM*, 35(2):288–323, 1988.

[4] D. Fisman, O. Kupferman, and Y. Lustig. On verifying fault tolerance of distributed protocols. In *TACAS*, volume 4963 of *LNCS*, pages 315–331. Springer, 2008.

[5] T. A. Henzinger, R. Jhala, R. Majumdar, and G. Sutre. Lazy abstraction. In *POPL*, pages 58–70. ACM, 2002.

[6] G. Holzmann. *The SPIN Model Checker*. Addison-Wesley, 2003.

[7] A. John, I. Konnov, U. Schmid, H. Veith, and J. Widder. Counter attack on Byzantine generals: Parameterized model checking of fault-tolerant distributed algorithms. *arXiv CoRR*, abs/1210.3846, 2012.

[8] A. John, I. Konnov, U. Schmid, H. Veith, and J. Widder. Starting a dialog between model checking and fault-tolerant distributed algorithms. *arXiv CoRR*, abs/1210.3839, 2012.

[9] A. John, I. Konnov, U. Schmid, H. Veith, and J. Widder. Towards modeling and model checking fault-tolerant distributed algorithms. In *SPIN*, LNCS, 2013. (to appear).

[10] L. Lamport. *Specifying Systems, The TLA+ Language and Tools for Hardware and Software Engineers*. Addison-Wesley, 2002.

[11] L. Lamport. Byzantizing Paxos by refinement. In *DISC*, volume 6950 of *LNCS*, pages 211–224. Springer, 2011.

[12] N. Lynch and M. Tuttle. An introduction to input/output automata. Technical Report MIT/LCS/TM-373, Laboratory for Computer Science, MIT, 1989.

[13] J.-P. Martin and L. Alvisi. Fast Byzantine consensus. *IEEE Trans. Dependable Sec. Comput.*, 3(3):202–215, 2006.

[14] A. Mostéfaoui, E. Mourgaya, P. R. Parvédy, and M. Raynal. Evaluating the condition-based approach to solve consensus. In *DSN*, pages 541–550. IEEE Computer Society, 2003.

[15] J. Queille and J. Sifakis. Specification and verification of concurrent systems in cesar. In *International Symposium on Programming*, volume 137 of *LNCS*, pages 337–351. Springer, 1982.

[16] T. Srikanth and S. Toueg. Simulating authenticated broadcasts to derive simple fault-tolerant algorithms. *Dist. Comp.*, 2:80–94, 1987.

[17] W. Steiner, J. M. Rushby, M. Sorea, and H. Pfeifer. Model checking a fault-tolerant startup algorithm: From design exploration to exhaustive fault simulation. In *DSN*, pages 189–198, 2004.

[18] T. Tsuchiya and A. Schiper. Verification of consensus algorithms using satisfiability solving. *Dist. Comp.*, 23(5–6):341–358, 2011.

Brief Announcement: On Minimum Interaction Time for Continuous Distributed Interactive Computing

Lu Zhang
zh0007lu@ntu.edu.sg

Xueyan Tang
asxytang@ntu.edu.sg

Bingsheng He
bshe@ntu.edu.sg

School of Computer Engineering
Nanyang Techonological University
Singapore 639798

ABSTRACT

In this paper, we study the interaction times of continuous distributed interactive computing in which the application states change due to not only user-initiated operations but also time passing. We formulate the Minimum Interaction Time problem as a combinatorial problem of how the clients are assigned to the servers and the simulation time settings of the servers. We also outline two approaches to approximate the problem.

Categories and Subject Descriptors

C.2.4 [**Computer-Communication Networks**]: Distributed Systems—*Distributed applications*; G.1.6 [**Numerical Analysis**]: Optimization—*Constrained optimization*

Keywords

Distributed interactive computing; interactivity; consistency

1. INTRODUCTION

Recent years have witnessed rapid development of distributed interactive computing in many areas. In large-scale distributed interactive computing, the application state (such as the virtual worlds in multiplayer online games) is typically maintained across a group of geographically distributed servers [5]. Each participant, known as a client, is assigned to one server and connects to it for sending user-initiated operations. When the application state changes, state updates are delivered to the clients by their assigned servers to reflect the changes. In this way, Distributed Interactive Applications (DIAs) enable participants at different locations to interact with each other in real time.

Interactivity is of crucial importance to DIAs for supporting graceful interactions among participants. The interactivity performance can be characterized by the duration from the time when a client issues an operation to the time when the effect of the operation is presented to others

[3]. This duration is known as the *interaction time* between clients. Since the clients interact with one another through their assigned servers, the interaction time between any pair of clients must include not only the network latencies between the clients and their assigned servers, but also the network latency between their assigned servers. These latencies are directly affected by how the clients are assigned to the servers [7]. In addition to network latencies, the interaction time is also influenced by the need for consistency maintenance in DIAs. Consistency means that shared common views of the application state must be created among all clients and it is a fundamental requirement for supporting meaningful interactions [1].

In this paper, we study the interaction times of DIAs. We focus on continuous DIAs in which the application state changes due to not only user-initiated operations but also time passing. In continuous DIAs, the progress of the application state is normally measured along a synthetic timescale known as the *simulation time* (for example, the time elapsed in the virtual game world). To ensure consistency among the application states at the servers, each user operation must be executed by all servers at the same simulation time [4]. As a result, maintaining consistency in continuous DIAs often entails artificial synchronization delays in the interactions among clients. The amount of synchronization delays is dependent on the simulation time settings of the clients and servers.

We formulate the Minimum Interaction Time (MIT) problem for continuous DIAs as a combinatorial optimization problem that includes two sets of variables: the client assignment and the simulation time offsets among servers. We also outline two approaches to approximate the MIT problem: by fixing the client assignment and by fixing the simulation time offsets among servers. In an earlier work [6], we studied some client assignment heuristics for continuous DIAs under a special case of operation execution. This paper generalizes the study by conducting in-depth theoretical analysis of consistency-constrained simulation time settings and achievable interactivity.

2. PROBLEM FORMULATION

A DIA can be modeled by a network consisting of a set of nodes V. A distance $d(u, v)$ is associated with each pair of nodes $(u, v) \in V \times V$, representing the network latency of the routing path between nodes u and v. Denote by $S \subseteq V$ the set of servers and $C \subseteq V$ the set of clients in the network. Each client is assigned to a server for sending user

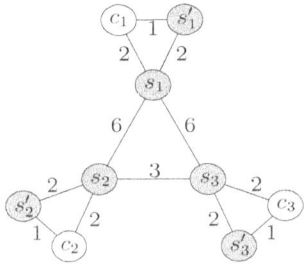

Figure 1: An example network in a DIA.

operations and receiving state updates. For each client $c \in C$, we denote by $s_A(c) \in S$ the server that c is assigned to in a client assignment A.

Each server and client has an associated simulation time to characterize its view of the application state. To provide realistic real-time interaction experiences, the simulation times of all the servers and clients should advance at the same rate as that of the wall-clock time, but they do not have to be synchronized. For each client $c \in C$, we denote by $\delta_c \in \mathbb{R}$ the offset of c's simulation time relative to the wall-clock time (a positive offset means that c's simulation time is ahead of the wall-clock time). Similarly, for each server $s \in S$, we denote by $\delta_s \in \mathbb{R}$ the offset of s's simulation time relative to the wall-clock time.

When a client issues an operation, the effect of the operation is presented to other clients through the following process. First, the client sends the operation to its assigned server. Then, the server forwards the operation to all the other servers. On receiving the operation, each server executes the operation, possibly after some synchronization delay, to compute the new state of the application. Finally, each server delivers the resultant state update to all the clients assigned to it. Since clients inherit the application state from their assigned servers, in order for all clients to always see identical states at the same simulation time, the application states at all the servers must be identical at any simulation time. This in turn requires each user operation to be executed by all servers at the same simulation time, since the state of a continuous DIA changes due to both user operations and time passing. Given a client assignment A and the simulation time offsets of servers $\Delta = \{\delta_s \mid s \in S\}$, our analysis shows that the lowest achievable average interaction time between all pairs of clients that satisfies the above consistency constraint is $D(A, \Delta) =$

$$\frac{1}{|C|}\left(2 \cdot \sum_{i=1}^{|C|} d(c_i, s_A(c_i)) + \sum_{i=1}^{|C|} \max_{s \in S}\left\{d(s_A(c_i), s) + \delta_s\right\} - \sum_{i=1}^{|C|} \delta_{s_A(c_i)}\right),$$

where $|C|$ is the number of clients. Therefore, we define the Minimum Interaction Time (MIT) problem as follows:

Definition 1. Given a set of servers S and a set of clients C in a network, and the distance $d(u, v)$ between each pair of nodes $u, v \in C \cup S$, the MIT problem is to find a client assignment A and the simulation time offsets of servers Δ that minimize the average interaction time, i.e., to find

$$\min_{A, \Delta} D(A, \Delta).$$

We present an example to illustrate how A and Δ affect the average interaction time. In the network shown

in Figure 1, there are three clients c_1, c_2, c_3 and six servers $s_1, s_2, s_3, s'_1, s'_2, s'_3$. A natural configuration is to assign each client c_i to server s'_i (i.e., the nearest server), and synchronize the simulation times of the assigned servers of all the clients, as shown in Figure 2(a), where each client and server is marked with its simulation time offset.[1] Note that the simulation time of each client must lag behind the simulation time of its server due to the network latency of delivering state updates. Suppose that client c_1 issues an operation at simulation time t. As shown in Figure 2(b), the operation first reaches server s'_1 at simulation time $t + 2$, and is then delivered to the other two servers at simulation time $t + 12$. Thus, the operation can be executed by all the three servers at the same simulation time $t + 12$ at the earliest, and finally, all the clients receive and present the resultant state updates at simulation time $t + 12$. Therefore, the interaction time from client c_1 to all the clients is 12. Figure 2(c) shows that the interaction time from client c_2 (or c_3) to all the clients is also 12. Consequently, the average interaction time under this configuration is 12.

We can improve the interactivity by tuning the simulation time offsets Δ. Figure 3(a) shows a simulation time setting that reduces the average interaction time to 11. Alternatively, we can also improve the interactivity by tuning the client assignment A. Figure 3(b) shows a client assignment that leads to the average interaction time of 10. The optimal solution to the MIT problem is to tune both A and Δ together as shown in Figure 3(c), which gives the best achievable average interaction time of 9.

3. RESULTS

As seen above, the MIT problem is a combinatorial optimization problem with two sets of variables: the client assignment and the simulation time offsets of servers. We can show that the MIT problem is NP-complete. We consider approximating the MIT problem by fixing the client assignment and/or the simulation time offsets. An intuitive and easy-to-implement strategy for client assignment is to assign each client to its nearest server, i.e., the server with the shortest network latency to it. This is known as the *nearest-server assignment* and is widely used in many applications [2]. On the other hand, a simple and straightforward setting of simulation times is to synchronize the simulation times of the servers. Denote such simulation time setting by Δ_0 and denote the nearest-server assignment by N. If N and Δ_0 are employed together, the resultant interaction time $D(N, \Delta_0)$ can be arbitrarily worse than the minimum interaction time $\min_{A,\Delta} D(A, \Delta)$. Interestingly, however, constant approximation factors can be achieved by *either* fixing the client assignment at N or fixing the simulation time offsets at Δ_0.

(1) Approximating MIT Problem by Fixing Client Assignment. When the client assignment is fixed, we have the following results about finding the simulation time offsets of servers that minimize the interaction time, i.e., finding $\min_\Delta D(A, \Delta)$.

Definition 2. A *perfect selection* from a $n \times n$ matrix is to select n elements from the matrix, so that there is exactly one element selected in each row and in each column. A

---

[1]The simulation times of the servers not assigned any client are not really restricted by the consistency constraint. They can be set to lag behind the wall clock time by an arbitrarily large amount and are not marked in the figure.

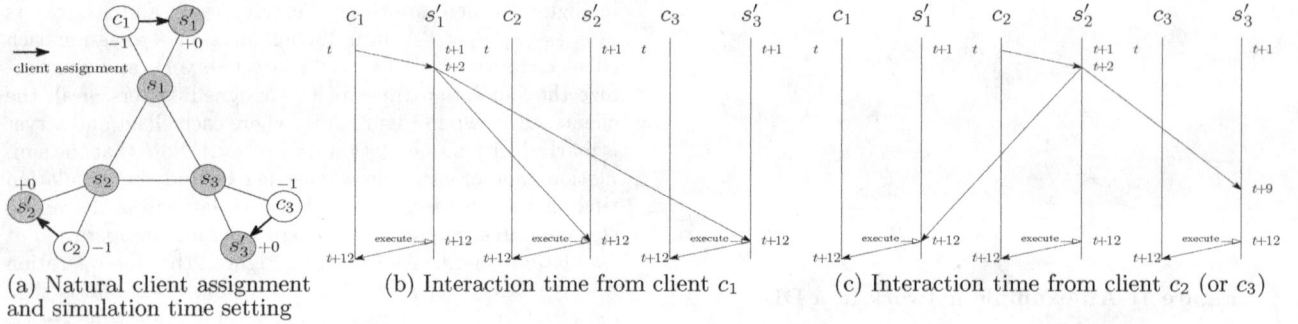

(a) Natural client assignment and simulation time setting

(b) Interaction time from client c_1

(c) Interaction time from client c_2 (or c_3)

Figure 2: A natural configuration.

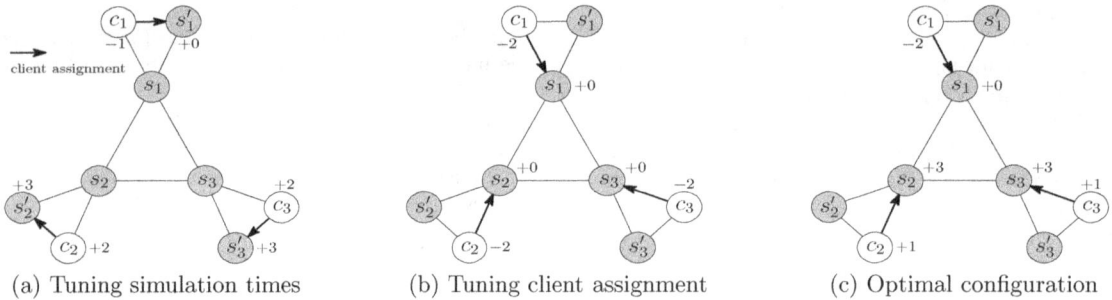

(a) Tuning simulation times

(b) Tuning client assignment

(c) Optimal configuration

Figure 3: Improved configurations.

maximum perfect selection is a perfect selection that has the largest sum of the selected elements among all perfect selections from the matrix.

Definition 3. Given a matrix $\mathbf{Q}$, define $\mathbb{S}(\mathbf{Q})$ as the sum of the elements in a maximum perfect selection from $\mathbf{Q}$.

THEOREM 1. *Given a client assignment A, let $\mathbf{Q}_A$ be a $|C| \times |C|$ matrix of $d(s_A(c_i), s_A(c_j))$ $(i, j = 1, 2, \cdots, |C|)$. Then,*

$$\min_{\Delta} D(A, \Delta) = \frac{1}{|C|} \Big(2 \cdot \sum_{i=1}^{|C|} d(c_i, s_A(c_i)) + \mathbb{S}(\mathbf{Q}_A) \Big).$$

We have developed a $O(|C|^2|S|)$ algorithm to compute $\min_{\Delta} D(A, \Delta)$, where $|C|$ is the number of clients and $|S|$ is the number of servers. For networks with the triangle inequality, it can be shown that the minimum achievable interaction time under the nearest-server assignment is within 3 times of the optimal solution to the MIT problem.

THEOREM 2. $\min_{\Delta} D(N, \Delta) \leq 3 \cdot \min_{A, \Delta} D(A, \Delta)$.

(2) Approximating MIT Problem by Fixing Simulation Time Offsets. Finding $\min_A D(A, \Delta)$ is also an NP-complete problem. For networks with the triangle inequality, our analysis shows that this approach can approximate the MIT problem within a factor of 2 if the simulation times of all servers are synchronized.

THEOREM 3. $\min_A D(A, \Delta_0) \leq 2 \cdot \min_{A, \Delta} D(A, \Delta)$.

4. ACKNOWLEDGMENTS

This work is supported by an Inter-disciplinary Strategic Competitive Fund of Nanyang Technological University 2011 for "C3: Cloud-Assisted Green Computing at NTU Campus".

5. REFERENCES

[1] D. Delaney, T. Ward, and S. McLoone. On consistency and network latency in distributed interactive applications: A survey-Part I. *Presence: Teleoperators & Virtual Environments*, 15(2):218–234, 2006.

[2] C. Ding, Y. Chen, T. Xu, and X. Fu. CloudGPS: A scalable and ISP-friendly server selection scheme in cloud computing environments. In *Proceedings of IEEE/ACM IWQoS 2012*, 2012.

[3] C. Jay, M. Glencross, and R. Hubbold. Modeling the effects of delayed haptic and visual feedback in a collaborative virtual environment. *ACM Transactions on Computer-Human Interaction*, 14(2), 2007.

[4] M. Mauve, J. Vogel, V. Hilt, and W. Effelsberg. Local-lag and timewarp: Providing consistency for replicated continuous applications. *IEEE Transactions on Multimedia*, 6(1):47–57, 2004.

[5] F. Safaei, P. Boustead, C. Nguyen, J. Brun, and M. Dowlatshahi. Latency-driven distribution: infrastructure needs of participatory entertainment applications. *IEEE Communications Magazine*, 43(5):106–112, 2005.

[6] L. Zhang and X. Tang. The client assignment problem for continuous distributed interactive applications. In *Proceedings of IEEE ICDCS 2011*, pages 203–214, 2011.

[7] L. Zhang and X. Tang. Optimizing client assignment for enhancing interactivity in distribute interactive applications. *IEEE/ACM Transactions on Networking*, 20(6):1707–1720, 2012.

Brief Announcement: Deterministic Self-Stabilizing Leader Election with O(loglog n)-bits

Lélia Blin
Université d'Evry Val d'Essonne, France.
LIP6-CNRS UMR 7606.
lelia.blin@lip6.fr

Sébastien Tixeuil
UPMC Sorbonne Universités,France.
LIP6-CNRS UMR 7606.
Institut Universitaire de France.
sebastien.tixeuil@lip6.fr

ABSTRACT

This paper focuses on *compact* deterministic self-stabilizing solutions for the leader election problem. Self-stabilization is a versatile approach to withstand any kind of transient failures. Leader election is a fundamental building block in distributed computing, enabling to distinguish a unique node, in order to, *e.g.*, execute particular actions. When the protocol is required to be *silent* (i.e., when communication content remains fixed from some point in time during any execution), there exists a lower bound of $\Omega(\log n)$ bits of memory per node participating to the leader election (where n denotes the number of nodes in the system). This lower bound holds even in rings.

We present a new deterministic (non-silent) self-stabilizing protocol for n-node rings that uses only $O(\log \log n)$ memory bits per node, and stabilizes in $O(n \log^2 n)$ time. Our protocol has several attractive features that make it suitable for practical purposes. First, the communication model matches the one that is expected by existing compilers for real networks. Second, the size of the ring (or any upper bound for this size) needs not to be known by any node. Third, the node identifiers can be of various sizes. Finally, no synchrony assumption besides a weak fair scheduler is assumed. Therefore, our result shows that, perhaps surprisingly, trading silence for exponential improvement in term of memory space does not come at a high cost regarding stabilization time, neither it does regarding minimal assumptions about the framework for our algorithm.

Categories and Subject Descriptors: C.2.4 [Distributed Systems]: Distributed applications

General Terms: Algorithms, Reliability

Keywords: Self-stabilization, Memory space, Complexity, Leader Election

1. INTRODUCTION

This paper is targeting the issue of designing efficient self-stabilization algorithms for the leader election problem. *Self-stabilization* [11, 12, 27] is a general paradigm to pro-vide forward recovery capabilities to distributed systems and networks. Intuitively, a protocol is self-stabilizing if it is able to recover from any transient failure, without external intervention. *Leader election* is one of the fundamental building blocks of distributed computing, as it permits to distinguish a single node in the system, and thus to perform specific actions using that node. Leader election is especially important in the context of self-stabilization as many protocols for various problems assume that a single leader exists in the system, even when faults occur. Hence, a self-stabilizing leader election mechanism permits to run such protocols in networks where no leader is a priori given, by using simple composition techniques [12].

Most of the literature in self-stabilization is dedicated to improving efficiency after failures occur, including minimizing the stabilization time, i.e., the maximum amount of time one has to wait before recovering from a failure. While stabilization time is meaningful to evaluate the efficiency of an algorithm in the presence of failures, it does not necessarily capture the overhead of self-stabilization when there are no faults [1], or after stabilization. Another important criterium to evaluate this overhead is the *memory space* used by each node. This criterium is motivated by two practical reasons. First, self-stabilizing protocols require that *some* communications carry on forever (in order to be able to detect distributed inconsistencies due to transient failures [6, 10]). So, minimizing the memory space used by each node enable to minimize the amount of information that is exchanged between nodes. Indeed, protocols are typically written in the state model, where the state of each node is available for reading to every neighbor, and all existing stabilization-preserving compilers [25, 8, 3, 26] expect this communication model. Second, minimizing memory space enables to significantly reduce the cost of redundancy when mixing self-stabilization and replication, in order to increase the probability of masking or containing transient faults [18, 17, 9]. For instance, duplicating every bit three times at each node permits to withstand one randomly flipped bit. More generally, decreasing the memory space allows the designer to duplicate this memory many times, in order to tolerate many random bit-flips.

A foundational result regarding memory space in the context of self-stabilization is due to Dolev *et al.* [13]. It states that, n-node networks, $\Omega(\log n)$ bits of memory are required for solving global tasks such as leader election. Importantly, this bound holds even for the ring. A key component of this lower bound is that it holds only whenever the protocol is assumed to be *silent*. (Recall that a protocol is silent if each

PODC'13, July 22–24, 2013, Montréal, Québec, Canada.
ACM 978-1-4503-2065-8/13/07.

of its executions reaches a point in time beyond which the registers containing the information available at each node do *not* change). The lower bound can be extended to *non-silent* protocols, but only for specific cases. For instance, it holds in anonymous (uniform) unidirectional rings of prime size [16, 7]. As a matter of fact, most deterministic self-stabilizing leader election protocols [2, 14, 4] use at least $\Omega(\log n)$ bits of memory per node. Indeed, either these protocols directly compare node identifiers (and thus communicate node identifiers to neighbors), or they compute some variant of a hop-count distance to the elected node (and this distance can be as large as $\Omega(n)$ to be accurate).

A few previous works [24, 21, 5, 22] managed to break the $\Omega(\log n)$ bits lower bound for the memory space of self-stabilizing leader election algorithms. Nevertheless, the corresponding algorithms exhibit shortcomings that hinder their relevance to practical applications. For instance, the algorithms by Mayer *et al.* [24], by Itkis and Levin [21], and by Awerbuch and Ostrovstky [5] use a constant number of bits per node only. However, these algorithms guarantee *probabilistic* self-stabilization only (in the Las Vegas sense). In particular, the stabilization time is only *expected* to be polynomial in the size of the network, and all three algorithms make use of a source of random bits at each node. Moreover, these algorithms are designed for a communication model that is more powerful than the classical state model used in this paper. (The state model is the model used in most available compilers for actual networks [25, 8, 3, 26]). More specifically, Mayer *et al.* [24] use the message passing model, and Awerbuch and Ostrovsky [5] use the link-register model, where communications between neighboring nodes are carried out through dedicated registers. Finally, Itkis and Levin [21] use the state model augmented with reciprocal pointer to neighbors. In this model, not only a node u is able to distinguish a particular neighbor v (which can be done using local labeling), but also this distinguished neighbor v is aware that it has been selected by u. Implementing this mutual interaction between neighbors typically requires distance-two coloring, link coloring, or two-hops communication. All these techniques are impacting the memory space requirement significantly [23]. It is also important to note that, the communication models in [5, 21, 24] allow nodes to send different information to different neighbors, while this capability is beyond the power of the classical state model. The ability to send different messages to different neighbors is a strong assumption in the context of self-stabilization. It allows to construct a "path of information" that is consistent between nodes. This path is typically used to distribute the storage of information along a path, in order to reduce the information stored at each node. However, this assumption prevents the user from taking advantage of the existing compilers. So implementing the protocols in [5, 21, 24] to actual networks requires to rewrite all the codes from scratch.

To our knowledge, the only *deterministic* self-stabilizing leader election protocol using sub-logarithmic memory space in the classical model is due to Itkis *et al.* [22]. Their elegant algorithm uses only a constant number of bits per node, and stabilizes in $O(n^2)$ time in n-node rings. However, the algorithm relies on several restricting assumptions. First, the algorithm works properly only if the size of the ring is *prime*. Second, it assumes that, at any time, a *single* node is scheduled for execution, that is, it assumes a *central* scheduler [15]. Such a scheduler is far less practical that the clas-sical *distributed* scheduler, which allows any set of processes to be scheduled concurrently for execution. Third, the algorithm in [22] assumes that the ring is *oriented*. That is, every node is supposed to possess a consistent notion of left and right. This orientation permits to mimic the behavior of reciprocal pointer to neighbors mentioned above. Extending the algorithm by Itkis *et al.* [22] to more practical settings, i.e., to non-oriented rings of arbitrary size, to the use of a distributed scheduler, etc, is not trivial if one wants to preserve a sub-logarithmic memory space at each node. For example, the existing transformers enabling to enhance protocols designed for the central scheduler in order to operate under the distributed scheduler require $\Theta(\log n)$ memory at each node [15]. Similarly, self-stabilizing ring-orientation protocols exist, but those which preserve sub-logarithmic memory space either works only in rings of odd size for deterministic guarantees [19], or just provide probabilistic guarantees [20]. Moreover, in both cases, the stabilization time is $O(n^2)$, which is pretty big.

To make a long story short, all existing self-stabilizing leader election algorithm designed in a practical communication model, and for rings of arbitrary size, without a priori orientation, use $\Omega(\log n)$ bits of memory per node. Breaking this bound, without introducing any kind of restriction on the settings, requires, beside being non-silent, a completely new approach.

Our results..

In this paper, we present a deterministic (non-silent) self-stabilizing leader election algorithm that operates under the distributed scheduler in non-anonymous undirected rings of arbitrary size. Our algorithm is non-silent to circumvent the lower bound $\Omega(\log n)$ bits of memory per node in [13]. It uses only $O(\log \log n)$ bits of memory per node, and stabilizes in $O(n \log^2 n)$ time.

Unlike the algorithms in [24, 21, 5], our algorithm is deterministic, and designed to run under the classical state-sharing communication model, which allows it to be implemented by using actual compilers [25, 8, 3, 26]. Unlike [22], the size of the ring is arbitrary, the ring is not assumed to be oriented, and the scheduler is distributed. Moreover the stabilization time of our algorithm is smaller than the one in [22]. Similarly to [24, 21, 5], our algorithm uses a technique to distribute the information among nearby nodes along a sub-path of the ring. However, our algorithm does not rely on powerful communication models such as the ones used in [24, 21, 5]. Those powerful communication models make easy the construction and management of such sub-paths. The use of the classical state-sharing model makes the construction and management of the sub-paths much more difficult. It is achieved by the use of novel information distribution and gathering techniques.

Besides the use of a sub-logarithmic memory space, and beside a quasi-linear stabilization time, our algorithm possesses several attractive features. First, the size (or any value upper bound for this size) need not to be known to any node. Second, the node identifiers (or identities) can be of various sizes (to model, e.g., Internet networks running different versions of IP). Third, no synchrony assumption besides weak fairness is assumed (a node that is continuously enabled for execution is eventually scheduled for execution).

At a high level, our algorithm is essentially based on two techniques. One consists in electing the leader by comparing the identities of the nodes, bitwise, which requires special care, especially when the node identities can be of various sizes. The second technique consists in maintaining and merging trees based on a parenthood relation, and verifying the absence of cycles in the 1-factor induced by this parenthood relation. This verification is performed using small memory space by grouping the nodes in hyper-nodes of appropriate size. Each hyper-node handles an integer encoding a distance to a root. The bits of this distance are distributed among the nodes of the hyper-nodes to preserve a small memory per node. Difficulties arise when one needs to perform arithmetic operations on these distributed bits, especially in the context in which nodes are unaware of the size of the ring. The precise design of our algorithm requires overcoming many other difficulties due to the need of maintaining correct information in an environment subject to arbitrary faults.

To sum up, our result shows that, perhaps surprisingly, trading silence for exponential improvement in term of memory space does not come at a high cost regarding stabilization time, neither it does regarding minimal assumptions about the communication framework.

2. REFERENCES

[1] Jordan Adamek, Mikhail Nesterenko, and Sébastien Tixeuil. Using abstract simulation for performance evaluation of stabilizing algorithms: The case of propagation of information with feedback. In *Proceedings of the International Conference on Stabilization, Safety, and Security in Distributed Systems (SSS 2012)*, Lecture Notes in Computer Science (LNCS), Toronto, Canada, October 2012. Springer Berlin / Heidelberg.

[2] Anish Arora and Mohamed G. Gouda. Distributed reset. *IEEE Trans. Computers*, 43(9):1026–1038, 1994.

[3] Mahesh Arumugam and Sandeep S. Kulkarni. Prose: A programming tool for rapid prototyping of sensor networks. In Stephen Hailes, Sabrina Sicari, and George Roussos, editors, *S-CUBE*, volume 24 of *Lecture Notes of the Institute for Computer Sciences, Social Informatics and Telecommunications Engineering*, pages 158–173. Springer, 2009.

[4] Baruch Awerbuch, Shay Kutten, Yishay Mansour, Boaz Patt-Shamir, and George Varghese. A time-optimal self-stabilizing synchronizer using a phase clock. *IEEE Trans. Dependable Sec. Comput.*, 4(3):180–190, 2007.

[5] Baruch Awerbuch and Rafail Ostrovsky. Memory-efficient and self-stabilizing network {RESET} (extended abstract). In James H. Anderson, David Peleg, and Elizabeth Borowsky, editors, *PODC*, pages 254–263. ACM, 1994.

[6] Joffroy Beauquier, Sylvie Delaët, Shlomi Dolev, and Sébastien Tixeuil. Transient fault detectors. *Distributed Computing*, 20(1):39–51, June 2007.

[7] Joffroy Beauquier, Maria Gradinariu, and Colette Johnen. Randomized self-stabilizing and space optimal leader election under arbitrary scheduler on rings. *Distributed Computing*, 20(1):75–93, January 2007.

[8] Andrew R. Dalton, William P. McCartney, Kajari Ghosh Dastidar, Jason O. Hallstrom, Nigamanth Sridhar, Ted Herman, William Leal, Anish Arora, and Mohamed G. Gouda. Desal alpha: An implementation of the dynamic embedded sensor-actuator language. In *ICCCN*, pages 541–547. IEEE, 2008.

[9] Sylvie Delaët, Shlomi Dolev, and Olivier Peres. Safe and eventually safe: Comparing self-stabilizing and non-stabilizing algorithms on a common ground. In Tarek F. Abdelzaher, Michel Raynal, and Nicola Santoro, editors, *OPODIS*, volume 5923 of *Lecture Notes in Computer Science*, pages 315–329. Springer, 2009.

[10] Stéphane Devismes, Toshimitsu Masuzawa, and Sébastien Tixeuil. Communication efficiency in self-stabilizing silent protocols. In *Proceedings of the IEEE International Conference on Distributed Computing Systems (ICDCS 2009)*, pages 474–481, Montreal, Canada, June 2009. IEEE Press.

[11] Edsger W. Dijkstra. Self-stabilizing systems in spite of distributed control. *Commun. ACM*, 17(11):643–644, 1974.

[12] Shlomi. Dolev. *Self-stabilization*. MIT Press, March 2000.

[13] Shlomi Dolev, Mohamed G. Gouda, and Marco Schneider. Memory requirements for silent stabilization. *Acta Inf.*, 36(6):447–462, 1999.

[14] Shlomi Dolev and Ted Herman. Superstabilizing protocols for dynamic distributed systems. *Chicago J. Theor. Comput. Sci.*, 1997, 1997.

[15] Swan Dubois and Sébastien Tixeuil. A taxonomy of daemons in self-stabilization. Technical Report 1110.0334, ArXiv eprint, October 2011.

[16] Faith E. Fich and Colette Johnen. A space optimal, deterministic, self-stabilizing, leader election algorithm for unidirectional rings. In Jennifer L. Welch, editor, *DISC*, volume 2180 of *Lecture Notes in Computer Science*, pages 224–239. Springer, 2001.

[17] Mohamed G. Gouda, Jorge Arturo Cobb, and Chin-Tser Huang. Fault masking in tri-redundant systems. In Ajoy Kumar Datta and Maria Gradinariu, editors, *SSS*, volume 4280 of *Lecture Notes in Computer Science*, pages 304–313. Springer, 2006.

[18] Ted Herman and Sriram V. Pemmaraju. Error-detecting codes and fault-containing self-stabilization. *Inf. Process. Lett.*, 73(1-2):41–46, 2000.

[19] Jaap-Henk Hoepman. Self-stabilizing ring-orientation using constant space. *Inf. Comput.*, 144(1):18–39, 1998.

[20] Amos Israeli and Marc Jalfon. Uniform self-stabilizing ring orientation. *Inf. Comput.*, 104(2):175–196, 1993.

[21] Gene Itkis and Leonid A. Levin. Fast and lean self-stabilizing asynchronous protocols. In *FOCS*, pages 226–239. IEEE Computer Society, 1994.

[22] Gene Itkis, Chengdian Lin, and Janos Simon. Deterministic, constant space, self-stabilizing leader election on uniform rings. In Jean-Michel Hélary and Michel Raynal, editors, *WDAG*, volume 972 of *Lecture Notes in Computer Science*, pages 288–302. Springer, 1995.

[23] Toshimitsu Masuzawa and Sébastien Tixeuil. On bootstrapping topology knowledge in anonymous networks. *ACM Transactions on Adaptive and Autonomous Systems (TAAS)*, 4(1), January 2009.

[24] Alain J. Mayer, Yoram Ofek, Rafail Ostrovsky, and Moti Yung. Self-stabilizing symmetry breaking in constant-space (extended abstract). In S. Rao Kosaraju, Mike Fellows, Avi Wigderson, and John A. Ellis, editors, *STOC*, pages 667–678. ACM, 1992.

[25] Tommy M. McGuire and Mohamed G. Gouda. *The Austin Protocol Compiler*, volume 13 of *Advances in Information Security*. Springer, 2005.

[26] Young ri Choi and Mohamed G. Gouda. A state-based model of sensor protocols. *Theor. Comput. Sci.*, 458:61–75, 2012.

[27] Sébastien Tixeuil. *Algorithms and Theory of Computation Handbook, Second Edition*, chapter Self-stabilizing Algorithms, pages 26.1–26.45. Chapman & Hall/CRC Applied Algorithms and Data Structures. CRC Press, Taylor & Francis Group, November 2009.

Brief Announcement: Scalable Anonymous Communication with Byzantine Adversary*

Josh Karlin
Google Inc.
5 Cambridge Center
Cambridge, MA 02142
jkarlin@google.com

Joud Khoury
Raytheon BBN Technologies
10 Moulton St
Cambridge, MA 02138
jkhoury@bbn.com

Jared Saia
University of New Mexico
Computer Science Dept.
Albuquerque, NM 87131
saia@cs.unm.edu

Mahdi Zamani
University of New Mexico
Computer Science Dept.
Albuquerque, NM 87131
zamani@cs.unm.edu

ABSTRACT

We describe an algorithm for fully-anonymous broadcast in large-scale networks. The protocol is similar to the dining cryptographers networks (DC-NETS) in that both are based on secure multi-party computation (MPC) techniques. However, we address the weaknesses of DC-NETS, which are poor scalability and vulnerability to jamming attacks. When compared to the state-of-the-art, our protocol reduces the total bit complexity from $O(n^2)$ to $\tilde{O}(n)$ per anonymous message sent in a network of size n at the expense of an increase in total latency from $O(1)$ to $\text{polylog}(n)$. Our protocol can tolerate up to $1/3$ dishonest parties, which are controlled by a static computationally-unbounded Byzantine adversary.

Categories and Subject Descriptors

C.2.0 [**Computer-Communication Networks**]: General—*Security and protection*; C.2.2 [**Computer-Communication Networks**]: Network Protocols—*Applications*

General Terms

Algorithms, Design, Security

Keywords

Anonymity; Multi-Party Computation; Byzantine Resilience

1. Introduction

An anonymity system attempts to obscure the relation between sent messages and their intended receivers, their

---

*A full version of this paper is available at
http://cs.unm.edu/~zamani/papers/podc13-full.pdf

PODC'13, July 22–24, 2013, Montréal, Québec, Canada.
ACM 978-1-4503-2065-8/13/07.

true senders, or both (also called *fully-anonymous*). In an age where government and financial entities are increasingly engaged in sophisticated cyber-warfare, we choose to protect against the Byzantine adversary, who is able to launch both passive (*e.g.* eavesdropping, non-participation) and active attacks (*e.g.* jamming, message dropping, corruption, and forging).

Mix networks (MIX-NETS) and Dining Cryptographers networks (DC-NETS) are two widely-accepted architectures for providing sender and receiver anonymity, both of which were originally proposed by Chaum [1, 2]. MIX-NETS are cryptographic in nature, require semi-trusted infrastructure nodes, and are known to be vulnerable to traffic analysis and to active adversaries [5].

DC-NETS [2, 4, 6], on the other hand, provide a provably-secure anonymous broadcast protocol among a group of parties without requiring trusted third-parties. DC-NETS prevent an adversary from tracing any message to its actual sender by using secure Multi-Party Computation (MPC) protocols. However, DC-NETS face several challenges. First, a reservation mechanism is required to schedule which party is broadcasting without compromising the anonymity of the sender. Second, DC-NETS are susceptible to jamming attacks, where the adversary renders the channel useless by continuously transmitting in every round. Third, typical DC-NETS are not scalable given that the bit complexity required to anonymously broadcast a single bit within a group of size n is $\Omega(n^2)$ per anonymous message sent.

State-of-the-art approaches that address some of these challenges include [4, 6]. The majority of these methods are cryptographic in nature, and scale poorly with network size, rendering them impractical for large networks. We are not aware of any provably-secure, fully-anonymous, DC-NETS-based protocols that scale better than $\Theta(n^2)$ bits per anonymous bit sent.

In this paper, we use a recent scalable MPC algorithm [3] to provide full anonymity at a total bit complexity of $\tilde{O}(n)$ per anonymous message and a total latency of $\tilde{O}(n)^1$. Our

---

[1] The synchrony assumption is due to [3]. We are currently working to adapt the synchronous construction of [3] to an asynchronous setting, which can be simply used as a basis for an asynchronous version of the current paper.

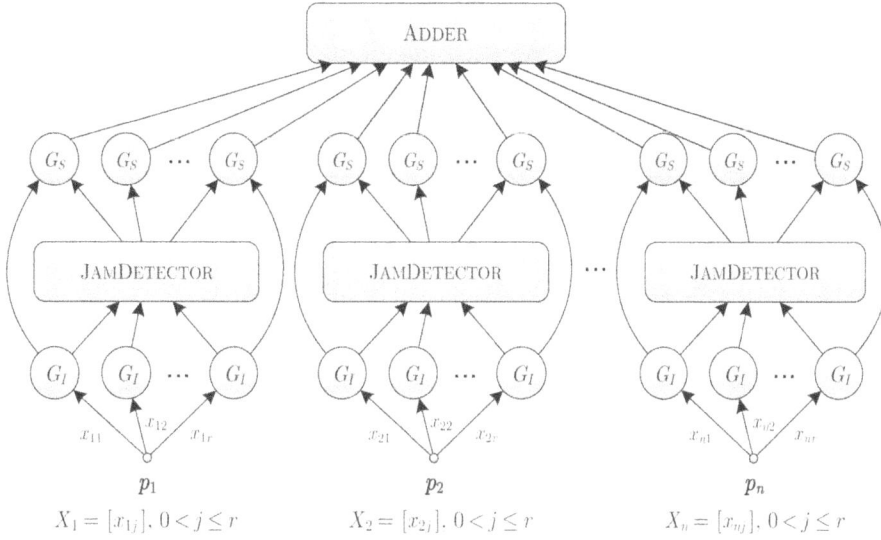

Figure 1: Our circuit for n parties showing JamDetector and Adder subcirciuts as black-boxes.

protocols do not require the presence of any trusted third-party.

2. Our Results

Our main result is as follows.

THEOREM 1. *Assume there are n parties in a fully connected network with private channels, up to $t < n/3$ of which are controlled by an adversary, and each party has a constant-size message to broadcast. If all honest parties follow our protocol, then with high probability:*

1. *Each honest party broadcasts its message to all other honest parties with probability $1/k$, where $k > 1$ is a constant,*

2. *The communication is fully-anonymous.*

3. *Each party sends $\tilde{O}(n)$ bits and performs $\tilde{O}(n)$ computations. The latency of the protocol is $\mathsf{polylog}(n)$.*

3. Our Approach

Assume n parties $p_1, ..., p_n$, where for $1 \leq i \leq n$, party p_i has a message m_i to broadcast to the network anonymously. Party p_i chooses a number $l \in [1, r]$ uniformly at random and forms a vector $X_i = [x_{ij}]$, where $x_{il} = m_i$ and $x_{ij} = 0$ (for all $1 \leq j \leq r$ and $j \neq l$). For some constant $k > 1$, each of the $r = kn$ positions in X_i is referred to as a *slot*. For simplicity, we assume r is an integer power of two. The parties then run the MPC algorithm of [3] to compute a function $f(X_1, X_2, ..., X_n)$ such that every party learns the vector addition $\sum_{i=1}^{n} X_i$ and none of the parties can send more than one non-zero input. In the following, we explain the circuit that computes function f.

Our Circuit Figure 1 shows the circuit, which consists of two major subcircuits: JamDetector that detects jamming inputs and Adder that computes the component-wise addition. We now describe each part of the circuit in detail.

- **Input gates:** In Figure 1, gates labeled G_I are called *input gates* and compute the identity function $G_I(x_{ij}) = x_{ij}$. Input gates are necessary for ensuring consistency

among all inputs a party sends during the protocol execution.

- **Jam detector:** Each party is associated with exactly one JamDetector subcircuit. The subcircuit has r inputs and r outputs: all outputs are set to zero if no jamming is detected for the corresponding party otherwise all outputs are set to a non-zero value. Figure 2 depicts a circuit for $n = 2$ and $r = 4$ showing the subcircuit in detail. Each JamDetector consists of three types of gates, defined in the following on the field $\mathbb{F}$:

$$G_1(y) = \begin{cases} 0, & \text{if } y = 0 \\ 1 & \text{otherwise} \end{cases} \qquad G_3(y) = \begin{cases} 0, & \text{if } y = 0, 1 \\ -1 & \text{otherwise} \end{cases}$$

$$G_2(y_1, y_2) = \begin{cases} 0, & \text{if } y_1 + y_2 = 0 \\ 1, & \text{if } y_1 + y_2 = 1 \\ 2 & \text{otherwise} \end{cases}$$

Each JamDetector contains a perfect binary tree consisting of only G_2 gates over r leaf nodes, consisting of only G_2 gates. This tree is connected from its root gate to an inverted perfect binary tree of only G_3 gates over $r/2$ leaf nodes, consisting of only G_3 gates.

- **Selector gates:** Gates labeled G_S in Figure 1 and Figure 2 are called *selector gates*. Each of these gates acts like a selector function: if the first input (which is an output of a JamDetector subcircuit) is zero, it simply outputs the second input otherwise it outputs zero. The selector gate is defined as follows:

$$G_S(y_1, y_2) = \begin{cases} y_2, & \text{if } y_1 = 0 \\ 0 & \text{otherwise} \end{cases}$$

where y_1 is the output of corresponding G_3 and y_2 is the output of corresponding input gate.

- **Adder:** There is one Adder subcircuit, which is a simple sum circuit and consists of r perfect binary trees each of which has n leaf nodes. The j-th binary tree sums up the outputs of all the j-th selector gates from all parties.

129

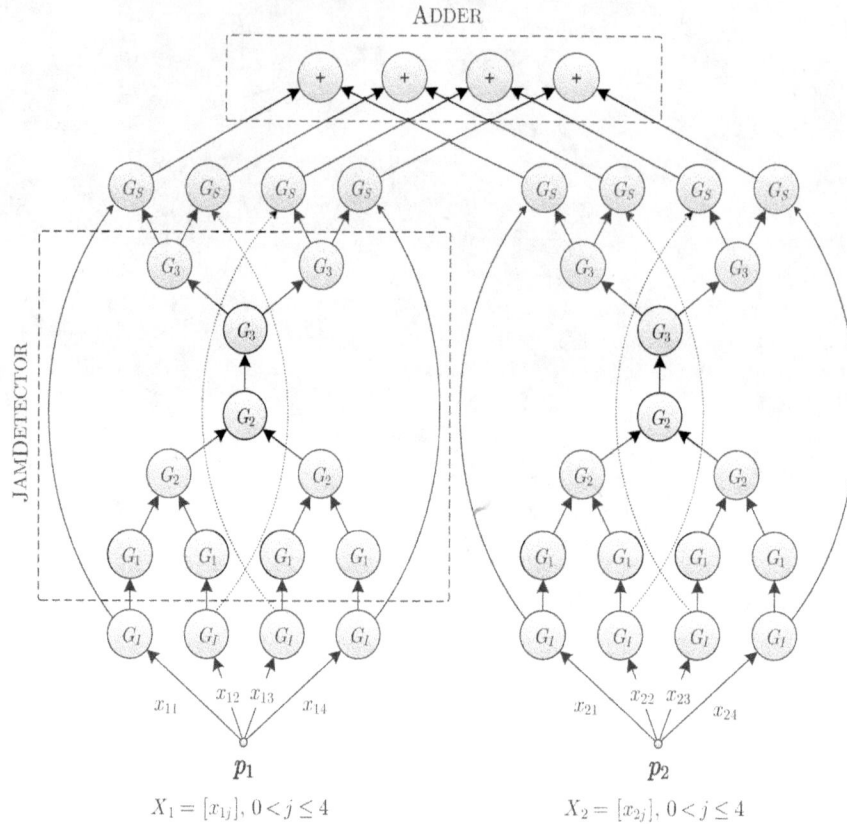

Figure 2: Our circuit for $n = 2$ and $r = 4$. The figure shows the JamDetector subcircuit in detail.

Circuit Computation Using the MPC algorithm of [3], the inputs of all parties are sent up the circuit simultaneously. The JamDetector subcircuit filters out any jamming inputs and sends the rest of them up to Adder. The Adder subcircuit computes the sum of all non-jamming inputs and finally, the result is sent down to every party via the output propagation algorithm described in [3]. The MPC algorithm ensures that (1) the output of the circuit is computed correctly and is reliably sent to all parties; and (2) no party learns any information about the inputs or outputs of intermediate gates, except what can be learned from their own input and the final output of the circuit.

4. Conclusion

We described an efficient Byzantine-resilient protocol for fully-anonymous broadcast communication in large-scale networks. Unlike DC-Nets, our protocol guarantees jamming-resistant communication at a small latency cost. Several open problems remain including the following. First, it may be possible to decrease message cost significantly in practice by using threshold cryptography to speed up Byzantine agreement that is used repeatedly in MPC algorithms for simulating a reliable broadcast channel. Second, we are interested in the average cost of our protocol when multiple broadcasts occur and thus, it may be possible to blacklist parties that exhibit adversarial behavior. We hope to create an algorithm that achieves average resource costs per anonymous message sent that is significantly better than our algorithm for a single shot communication.

5. Acknowledgments

This research was supported by IARPA under agreement number W911NF-11-2-0051. The authors would like to thank Mahnush Movahedi for making a valuable contribution to the discussions and for her supportive comments.

6. References

[1] D. Chaum. Untraceable electronic mail, return addresses, and digital pseudonyms. *Commun. ACM*, 24(2):84–90, Feb. 1981.

[2] D. Chaum. The dining cryptographers problem: Unconditional sender and recipient untraceability. *Journal of Cryptology*, 1:65–75, 1988.

[3] V. Dani, V. King, M. Movahedi, and J. Saia. Brief announcement: breaking the o(nm) bit barrier, secure multiparty computation with a static adversary. In *Proc. of the 2012 ACM Symposium on Principles of Distributed Computing*, PODC '12, pages 227–228, New York, NY, USA, 2012. ACM. Full version available at http://arxiv.org/abs/1203.0289.

[4] P. Golle and A. Juels. Dining cryptographers revisited. In *EUROCRYPT '04*, May 2004.

[5] A. Pfitzmann and M. Waidner. Networks without user observability design options. In *EUROCRYPT '85*, pages 245–253, New York, NY, USA, 1986.

[6] L. von Ahn, A. Bortz, and N. J. Hopper. *k*-anonymous message transmission. In *Proc. of the 10th ACM conference on computer and communications security*, CCS '03, pages 122–130, New York, NY, USA, 2003.

Brief Announcement: Brokerage and Closure in a Strategic Model of Social Capital

Samuel D. Johnson
Department of Computer Science
University of California, Davis
samjohnson@ucdavis.edu

Raissa M. D'Souza
Department of Computer Science
University of California, Davis
raissa@cse.ucdavis.edu

ABSTRACT

This paper introduces a model of strategic network formation grounded in two disparate modes of acquiring social capital – brokerage and closure – through the unification of a dual-level view of interactions between individuals and between groups of individuals referred to as *structural autonomy*. After motivating and introducing the model, we establish the existence of equilibrium and propose interesting open questions and extensions to the basic model for future research.

Categories and Subject Descriptors

F.2.2 [**Theory of Computation**]: Analysis of Algorithms and Problem Complexity—*Nonnumerical Algorithms and Problems*; G.2.2 [**Mathematics of Computing**]: Discrete Mathematics—*graph theory, network problems*

Keywords

game theoretic models, network design

1. INTRODUCTION

This paper introduces a model of strategic network formation grounded in two disparate modes of acquiring social capital – brokerage and closure – referred to as *structural autonomy* [3]. Structural autonomy considers a dual-level view of individual and collective action, calling on individuals to cooperate within groups, and then for the groups themselves to compete against one another. Examples of such environments are prevalent in many social settings, from the internal cooperation among producers and external structure of the markets in which the producers are situated [5], to the cooperation among guild (team) members who collaborate to accomplish quests in massively multiplayer online role-playing games [14].

There are examples in the literature of network formation games where agents seek to maximize brokerage [6, 13] or closure [1], independently, but ours appears to be the first

to involve agents pursuing both brokerage and closure simultaneously. This model, the STRUCTURAL AUTONOMY CONNECTIONS (SAC) game is formally defined in Section 2, and the existence of equilibrium is established in 2.1. Open problems and extensions to the basic SAC model are discussed in Section 3 as suggestions for future research. The remainder of Section 1 is devoted to a brief review of the necessary background on social capital, brokerage, closure, and structural autonomy.

1.1 Social Capital via Brokerage and Closure

Social capital accounts for the value that one gains from their relationship with society, often considered in terms of one's location in a social network. By introducing this notion of value, Coleman [7] brought social structure into the rational action paradigm, an area that had previously been dominated by a premise of extreme individualism. Coleman argued that *closure*, where an individual is connected to others who are themselves connected to one another, serves as one source of social capital. Through closure, mechanisms such as reputation, trust, and the establishment of norms and shared vision are enabled. Coleman [7] gives an example where the lack of closure in the social networks around high school students and their families is correlated to high school dropout rates, highlighting the ability of closure to act as an enforcement mechanism for social norms and reputation.

Another source of social capital is proposed by Burt's theory of *structural holes* (*cf.*, [2, 3]). This theory is based on the idea that individuals create value by filling "holes" in their social network, acting as a broker between two (or more) otherwise disconnected groups. The social capital afforded to such hole-spanning individuals, called *brokers*, can be described as a *vision advantage*, since exposure to diverse groups, each with their own sets of expertise, puts the broker "at risk of having good ideas" [3]. The brokerage advantage exists insofar that the lack of alternate means of connectivity (across the structural hole) provides the broker with sole access and control over the bridge they provide.

It should be clear that closure and brokerage operate on opposite ends of the same space – where closure thrives on the interconnectedness of third-parties, brokerage deteriorates. The *network constraint* [3] characterizes this space, and is defined for an individual $i \in N$ in a network $G = (N, E)$ as:

$$C_i(G) = \sum_{j \in N \setminus \{i\}} \left(p_{ij}(G) + \sum_{q \in N \setminus \{i,j\}} p_{iq}(G) p_{qj}(G) \right)^2 . \quad (1)$$

PODC'13, July 22–24, 2013, Montréal, Québec, Canada.
ACM 978-1-4503-2065-8/13/07.

Here $p_{ij}(G)$ is the proportion of time and energy that i invests in maintaining their link with j. We will make the assumption that i invests uniformly across their links, so $p_{ij}(G)$ equals the inverse of i's degree in G. Intuitively, the network constraint provides a summary index measuring the extent to which an individual's resources are constrained by their direct and indirect network relationships. Buskens and van de Rijt [6] show that (1) evaluates to a value in the range $[0, 9/8]$. Here, we will make use of a 0/1 *network constraint*, denoted by $\mathcal{C}_i(G) = \max\{C_i(G), 1\}$, to force the constraint to a value in the range $[0, 1]$. Also, we will use $\mathcal{C}(G) = \frac{1}{|N|}\mathcal{C}_i(G)$ to denote the average (normalized) network constraint among all agents N in G.

1.2 Structural Autonomy

Structural autonomy is defined with a dual-level view of individuals and their connections in a network. We assume that group *membership* is given, so that each agent knows who is and is not on their *team*, but nothing is assumed about how these groups are organized – internally or externally.

Let $\mathcal{N} = (N_1, N_2, \ldots, N_m)$ be a partition of N agents into m groups. Given a network $G = (N, E)$ and a partition $\mathcal{N}$, let $\mathcal{G} = (\mathcal{N}, \mathcal{E})$ be the *inter-group network* (or simply the *group network*) induced by collapsing the groups into single nodes. An edge $\{N_i, N_j\}$ is present in $\mathcal{E}$ if there exist a pair of individuals $i \in N_i$ and $j \in N_j$ such that $\{i, j\} \in E$. Burt [3] relates the performance of a group N_i to its structural autonomy, which is a non-linear combination of the closure among individuals within N_i and the brokerage beyond N_i; *i.e.*, Structural Autonomy $= \alpha$Closure$^\beta$Brokerage$^\gamma$. Here, we will use the normalized network constraint as a basis for both closure and brokerage, and define the structural autonomy of a group $N_i \in \mathcal{N}$ in a graph $G = (N, E)$ as

$$\Pi_{N_i}(G) = \alpha \mathcal{C}(G_{N_i})^\beta (1 - \mathcal{C}_{N_i}(\mathcal{G}))^\gamma, \qquad (2)$$

where G_{N_i} is the *intra-group network* induced by the subgraph of G consisting only of vertices in N_i, $\mathcal{G}$ is the inter-group network induced by the partitioning $\mathcal{N}$, and α, β, γ are constants. With the β and γ terms assuming values greater than one, the structural autonomy decreases more rapidly with reductions from higher levels of intra-group closure, $\mathcal{C}(G_{N_i})$, or inter-group brokerage, $(1 - \mathcal{C}_{N_i}(\mathcal{G}))$ than from lower levels.[1] Throughout the remainder of this paper, we will simply assume that $\alpha = 1$.

2. MODEL

In this section we formally present the STRUCTURAL AUTONOMY CONNECTIONS (SAC) network formation game. A SAC instance is described by a partitioning $\mathcal{N} = (N_1, \ldots, N_m)$ over a set of agents N, where each group N_i is composed of n individual agents (and therefore, $|N| = mn$). The strategy space for each agent i is defined to be $S_i = \mathcal{P}(N \setminus \{i\})$, the power set of all other agents, which represents the set of all possible sets of links that agent i could form. Edge formation is *bilateral*, so a joint strategy profile $s = (s_1, \ldots, s_{mn})$ specifies an undirected graph $G_s = (N, E_s)$ with edges $E_s = \{\{i, j\} : j \in s_i \land i \in s_j\}$.

As a notational tool, we will use $\tau(i)$ to denote the group (or *team*) that agent i belongs to. This way, given an arbitrary agent $i \in N$, we can identify their group by $N_{\tau(i)} = \{j : \tau(j) = \tau(i)\}$.

Agents' strategy choices are motived by a utility function that is defined at the group level. Thus, each agent selects a strategy so as to maximize the utility of their respective group. Using a modified definition of structural autonomy as the starting point (see Equation (4) below), we define the utility for an agent i given a joint strategy profile $s = (s_1, \ldots, s_{mn})$ by

$$u_i(s) = \frac{1}{n}\bar{\Pi}_{N_{\tau(i)}}(G_s). \qquad (3)$$

This utility function can be interpreted as splitting the gains that the group acquires through structural autonomy evenly among its n members – *i.e.*, the *equal split* rule (*cf.*, [11]).

From the definition of network constraint given in Equation (1), it would seem that isolated nodes experience the lowest network constraint possible (*i.e.*, zero). In empirical studies, isolates are usually discarded [4, Appendix B]. However, in our strategic model, we cannot simply throw them out; so instead we penalize isolates in order to incentivize them to build links. Since our definition of structural autonomy, Equation (2), simultaneously "rewards" a high network constraint (in the closure term, $\mathcal{C}(G_{N_i})^\beta$) and a low network constraint (in the brokerage term, $(1 - \mathcal{C}_{N_i}(\mathcal{G}))^\gamma$), we will have to choose our penalty carefully so that it incentivizes isolates to connect (thus increasing brokerage) but does not incentivize connected agents to disconnect (thereby decreasing closure).[2] Our solution to this dilemma is to modify our definition of structural autonomy to incorporate penalties for brokerage isolates while leaving the network constraint definition alone;

$$\bar{\Pi}_{N_i}(G) = \begin{cases} 0 & \text{if } N_i \text{ is isolated in } \mathcal{G} \\ \Pi_{N_i}(G) & \text{otherwise.} \end{cases} \qquad (4)$$

2.1 Existence of Equilibrium

In settings with bilateral edge formation, *pairwise stability* [11] is a commonly used solution concept, and is the one that we employ for the SAC model. A network G_s is pairwise stable if:[3]

1. $\forall \{i, j\} \in G_s$, $u_i(G_s) \geq u_i(G_s - \{i, j\})$ and $u_j(G_s) > u_j(G - \{i, j\})$, and

2. $\forall \{i, j\} \notin G_s$, if $u_i(G_s + \{i, j\}) > u_i(G_s)$ then $u_j(G_s + \{i, j\}) < u_j(G_s)$.

Pairwise stability stipulates that a network is stable so long as no two agents can benefit by building a link between themselves and no individual agent would be better off by severing one of their existing connections.

Theorem 2 establishes the existence of pairwise stable equilibrium for the SAC model – an important first step

---

[1]In Burt's work [5, 3], structural autonomy is formulated slightly differently than Equation (2). See [3, Chapter 3.3.3] for details.

[2]For example, if we penalize isolates by giving them a network constraint of 1 in the hope of incentivizing the formation of brokerage links in the inter-group network, we would find that this "penalty" would simultaneously incentivize all the individuals in each group N_i to isolate themselves from their fellow group members in G_{N_i}.

[3]Given a graph $G = (N, E)$, the shorthand $G + \{i, j\}$ refers to the graph $G' = (N, E')$ obtained from G where $E' = E \cup \{i, j\}$. $G - \{i, j\}$ is similarly defined.

attesting to its validity and applicability. Our construction relies upon the following result of Buskens and van de Rijt [6] as well as a couple of properties regarding trees and the network constraint (the proofs of which are omitted).

THEOREM 1 ([6]). *All multipartite inter-group networks are pairwise stable if the parts are of equal size and each has more than a single agent.*

LEMMA 1. *The average network constraint for a tree with l leaves and maximum degree d is at most*

$$\frac{n - l - dl}{nd}.$$

COROLLARY 1. *Among tree networks, the average network constraint is maximized in a star topology.*

COROLLARY 2. *As $n \to \infty$, the average network constraint of an n-node star approaches 1.*

THEOREM 2. *For every SAC instance with $n \geq 5$ agents per group there exists at least one pairwise stable outcome.*

PROOF SKETCH. Consider the following construction: For each group $N_i \in \mathcal{N}$ build a star among the n agents in N_i. Next, build edges $\{i, j\}$ between nodes $i \in N_i$ and $j \in N_j$ so that the resulting inter-group graph $\mathcal{G}$ is a balanced multipartite network.

By Corollary 2, the intra-group star networks achieve the maximum amount of closure, and by Theorem 1, the inter-group brokerage network is pairwise stable. □

3. FUTURE RESEARCH

We believe that the SAC model of strategic network formation gives rise to a wealth of interesting questions and quantities that can be the subject of future research. In this section we highlight a handful of those that we find most interesting.

Open problems concerning the basic SAC model (as presented in Section 2) involve investigating the structures of equilibrium strategies to determine: (i) the variety of intra- and inter-group network topologies that are supported in equilibrium; (ii) how different values of β and γ effect equilibrium structures, and whether values can be determined that mirror observed social structures (like the above mentioned massively multiplayer online role-playing games); (iii) the range of utility values realized in equilibrium; and (iv) whether there exists an appropriate definition of *social value* function in the SAC model, and if so, what is the *Price of Anarchy* and *Price of Stability* given this function? Another interesting problem is to determine the effect that the addition of supplemental edges will have on an equilibrium networks.

An interesting extension to the basic SAC model is to incorporate elements of a *coalition game* and require that, instead of agents evenly splitting the value afforded by their groups structural autonomy (as is the case with the utility function given in Equation (3)), the agents within a group must choose how to allocate the group's value among themselves (*cf.*, [10, 11]). This extension opens a rich array of research possibilities. For example, will brokerage agents demand higher payoffs than those who do not contribute any inter-group edges? Under what conditions can an agent with only closure ties demand a larger allocation than an agent with brokerage ties? To what extent can inequality exist (*cf.*, [9]) and can it lead to groups splitting apart (*cf.*, [12])?

More generally, since many complex social and technical networks are in fact interacting networks-of-networks, the authors believe that an examination of such networks in a strategic, game theoretic setting is of fundamental interest, especially as multiple scales of analysis are needed (*cf.*, [8]).

4. ACKNOWLEDGMENTS

We gratefully acknowledge financial support from the Army Research Laboratory award W911NF-09-2-0053 and the Defense Threat Reduction Agency award HDTRA1-10-1-0088.

5. REFERENCES

[1] M. J. Burger and V. Buskens. Social context and network formation: An experimental study. *Social Networks*, 31(1):63–75, January 2009.

[2] R. S. Burt. Autonomy in a social topology. *American Journal of Sociology*, 85(4):892–925, January 1980.

[3] R. S. Burt. *Brokerage and Closure: An Introduction to Social Capital*. Oxford University Press, Great Clarendon Street, Oxford OX2 6DP, 2005.

[4] R. S. Burt. *Neighbor Networks: Competitive Advantage Local and Personal*. Oxford University Press, Oxford, 2010.

[5] R. S. Burt, M. Guilarte, H. J. Raider, and Y. Yasuda. Competition, contingency, and the external structure of markets. In P. Ingram and B. S. Silverman, editors, *Advances in Strategic Management*, volume 19, pages 167–217. Emerald Group Publishing Limited, 2002.

[6] V. Buskens and A. van de Rijt. Dynamics of networks if everyone strives for structural holes. *American Journal of Sociology*, 114(2):371–407, September 2008.

[7] J. S. Coleman. Social capital in the creation of human capital. *American Journal of Sociology*, 94:S95–S120, 1988.

[8] R. M. D'Souza. Complex networks: A winning strategy. *Nature Physics*, 9:212–213, April 2013.

[9] R. M. D'Souza and S. D. Johnson. Inequality and network formation games. arXiv:1303.1434, March 2013.

[10] M. O. Jackson. Allocation rules for network games. *Games and Economic Behavior*, 51(1):128–154, April 2005.

[11] M. O. Jackson and A. Wolinsky. A strategic model of social and economic networks. *Journal of Economic Theory*, 71(1):44–74, 1996.

[12] W. Kets, G. Iyengar, R. Sethi, and S. Bowles. Inequality and network structure. *Games and Economic Behavior*, 73(1):215–226, September 2011.

[13] J. Kleinberg, S. Suri, Éva Tardos, and T. Wexler. Strategic network formation with structural holes. In *EC '08: Proceedings of the 9th ACM conference on Electronic commerce*, pages 284–293, New York, NY, USA, 2008. ACM.

[14] C. Shen, P. Monge, and D. Williams. Virtual brokerage and closure: Network structure and social capital in a massively multiplayer online game. *Communication Research*, August 2012.

Brief Announcement: Techniques for Programmatically Troubleshooting Distributed Systems

Sam Whitlock
International Computer
Science Institute (ICSI)
1947 Center St.
Berkeley, CA 94704
samw@icsi.berkeley.edu

Colin Scott
University of California
Berkeley
387 Soda Hall
Berkeley, CA 94720-1776
cs@cs.berkeley.edu

Scott Shenker
ICSI & University of California
Berkeley
387 Soda Hall
Berkeley, CA 94720-1776
shenker@icsi.berkeley.edu

ABSTRACT

The distributed systems research community has developed many provably correct algorithms and abstractions that are in wide use. However, practical implementations of distributed systems often contain many bugs, and practitioners spend much of their time troubleshooting these bugs. In this paper we present an algorithm, retrospective causal inference, to ease the burden of troubleshooting. We end by enumerating several open research problems related to the troubleshooting process.

Categories and Subject Descriptors

D.2.5 [**Software Engineering**]: Testing and Debugging—*distributed debugging, debugging aids, tracing*

General Terms

Algorithms, Theory

Keywords

troubleshooting; automation; tools

1. INTRODUCTION

Despite a wealth of abstractions and provably correct algorithms developed by the distributed systems research community, practical implementations of even simple distributed systems often contain bugs. Finding and fixing the causes of these bugs is a time-consuming task. For example, a 2006 survey found that software developers at Microsoft spend 49% of their time troubleshooting bugs [1]. The same study found that 70% of the reported concurrency bugs take days to months to fix, and 74% of respondents considered bug reproducibility hard or very hard.

The *de facto* method for troubleshooting is painstaking manual analysis of runtime logs. Such manual troubleshooting is hindered by the large number of inputs to distributed systems; troubleshooters find little immediate use from traces containing many inputs prior to a fault, since they are forced to manually filter extraneous

```
procedure REPLAY(subsequence)
  for eᵢ in subsequence
    if eᵢ is an internal event
      and eᵢ is not marked absent :
        then  Δ ← |eᵢ.time − eᵢ₋₁.time| + ε
              wait up to Δ seconds for eᵢ
              if eᵢ did not occur :
                then mark eᵢ as absent
    else if eᵢ is an input :
        then  if a successor of eᵢ occurred :
                comment: waited too long
                then return REPLAY(subsequence)
              else inject eᵢ

comment: See Figure 2 for invocation
```

Figure 1: `Replay` **is responsible for replaying subsequences of events chosen by delta debugging (Figure 2) and determining if the bug reappears.**

inputs before they can start fruitfully examining the source of the errant behavior. It is no surprise that when asked to describe their ideal tool, most practitioners said "automated troubleshooting" [9].

We have developed an algorithm, retrospective causal inference, as a step towards automated troubleshooting. Given a trace of causally-ordered events that leads to a bug, retrospective causal inference finds a locally minimal subsequence of the trace that is sufficient for reproducing the bug. This smaller set of events provides developers a better understanding of how the bug in their code was triggered.

We have applied retrospective causal inference [4] to one type of distributed system: control software for software-defined networks. Our initial experiments have been highly promising: of five bugs discovered in a five day investigation, retrospective causal inference reduced the size of the input trace to 18 events in the worst case and 2 events in the best case. In this brief announcement we describe retrospective causal inferenceand enumerate several open research problems related to the troubleshooting process.

2. APPROACH

One well-known method for finding event traces that lead to bugs is symbolic execution [3]: given source code as input, symbolic execution builds a model of the distributed state machine. With a model of the distributed state machine in hand, finding and minimizing errant event traces is fairly straightforward. Unfortunately, building this model from source code involves enumerating an exponential number of code paths. Although formal methods can, in theory, locate and minimize errant behavior, it quickly becomes an impractical option for real systems.

2.1 Minimized Event Sequences

Practitioners instead typically rely on execution logs to help them debug their distributed systems. Execution logs represent a particular subpath through the distributed state machine (where each event in the log represents a state transition) that is known to trigger a bug.[1]

Execution logs can be quite large, and it is time-consuming to analyze them by hand. It is not apparent from the logs which events are relevant and which are extraneous, leaving the developers to use their judgment about which code paths led to the errant behavior.

Deterministic replay systems allow troubleshooters to reproduce system executions, but merely replaying the execution does not immediately aid in deducing which transitions were causally related to the bug and which were not. Practitioners need a small sequence of transitions that triggers the bug. By examining each of the state transitions in such a sequence, they can get a better understanding of the code path that contains the root cause. Thus, given a bug-inducing execution log, it would be highly desirable to automatically find the *minimal causal sequence* (MCS): a subsequence of the trace that leads the state machine to a bug state, and has the additional property that if any of the transitions are removed from the sequence, the bug state is not reached. Finding minimal causal sequences is the goal of our work.

2.2 Replay, Pruning, and the Functional Equivalence of Events

The software engineering community has explored several search algorithms [6,8] for minimizing test cases. We focus on a particular algorithm suited to our goal: delta debugging [8]. Given a single input (*e.g.* an HTML page) for a non-distributed program (*e.g.* Firefox), delta debugging repeatedly runs the program on subsets of the input until it finds a minimal subset (*e.g.* a single tag) that is sufficient for triggering a known bug.

Delta debugging has not yet been applied to distributed systems. Doing so is complicated because the inputs to distributed systems are spread across time and across multiple processes, rather than being injected at a single point in time into a single process. This substantially complicates the task of testing whether a subsequence chosen by delta debugging contains the minimal causal sequence.

Elsewhere, we describe a system for replaying event subsequences chosen by delta debugging [4]. Here we focus on the algorithmic challenges posed by our system. When we replay a subsequence chosen by delta debugging, we must ensure that causality is maintained. Specifically, to reliably reproduce the original bug we need to inject each input event e at exactly the point when all other events, both internal to the system (such as messages sent between nodes or internal state changes) and external to the system (such as node crashes that we inject), that precede it in the happens-before relation ($\{i \mid i \rightarrow e\}$) from the original execution have occurred [5].

At first glance, it seems that allowing delta debugging to alter the history of the log will prevent us from being able to maintain causality during replay; if we diverge at all from the original event

trace we may find ourselves on a different path through the state machine, unable to reason about the original happens-before constraints. Consider for example that the sequence numbers of the messages passed throughout the system may change if we prune a single event at the beginning of the trace. Once on a diverged path, it is unclear whether the original bug will still be triggered.

Our approach to coping with divergence has been to apply heuristics to allow us to maintain causality as best we can. First, we explicitly disallow delta debugging from subdividing the trace in a way that leaves an invalid input sequence. We accomplish this by telling delta debugging to only remove atomic groups of inputs. For example, if we prune a controller failure event, we make sure to prune the controller's subsequent recovery event. This approach currently depends on our domain knowledge of the semantics of input events.

Next we need to cope with the fact that the syntax of internal events may change subtly after pruning inputs. We observe that many events are *functionally equivalent*, in the sense that they have the same effect on the state of the system with respect to triggering the bug (despite syntactic differences). For example, it is unlikely that the code responsible for incrementing the sequence number of messages is related to a buggy replication algorithm, meaning that we can often safely ignore the sequence numbers of messages. By disregarding irrelevant state, we draw an equivalence relation between the events across divergent runs, allowing us to compare executions generated by different subsequences of the original event trace. In this way we can maintain causality of events in the same equivalence classes.[2]

When comparing a pruned execution history to the original, there are two other subtleties we need to consider: some events from the original execution may be absent, and other events may be entirely new. We cope with absent events by timing out after some duration if they do not occur. We currently allow new events—internal events that are not functionally equivalent to any events observed in the original trace—to simply occur, and do not use them to dictate the timing of external events.

2.3 Retrospective Causal Inference

We have developed an algorithm, retrospective causal inference, that combines these heuristics to find minimal causal subsequences of event traces. We show pseudocode for retrospective causal inference in Figure 2. Using our replay system [4], we have found and minimized several buggy traces in open source distributed systems.

3. OPEN PROBLEMS

The algorithm we described in the previous section has worked well in practice, but it leaves open some questions that, if addressed, may yield a more principled approach to troubleshooting distributed systems.

How should new events be handled? New events ultimately leave open multiple possibilities for where we should inject the next input. Consider the following case: if i_2 and i_3 are internal events observed during replay that are both in the same equivalence class as a single event i_1 from the original run, we could inject the next input after i_2 or after i_3.

Exploring both possibilities would incur exponential runtime. Our approach to dealing with new events, ignoring them, is a heuristic. We believe that there may be more principled approaches that are still tractable for large real-world systems.

---

[1]We have shown elsewhere [4] how these event traces can be obtained.

[2]Incidentally, ignoring extraneous message fields is similar to how practitioners examine event logs by hand: they intuitively disregard certain information they deem to be irrelevant.

Figure 2: Delta Debugging Algorithm From [7]

Input: $T_\mathbf{x}$ s.t. $T_\mathbf{x}$ is a trace and $Replay(T_\mathbf{x}) = \mathbf{X}$. Output: $T'_\mathbf{x} = ddmin(T_\mathbf{x})$ s.t. $T'_\mathbf{x} \subseteq T_\mathbf{x}$, $Replay(T'_\mathbf{x}) = \mathbf{X}$, and $T'_\mathbf{x}$ is minimal.

$$ddmin(T_\mathbf{x}) = ddmin_2(T_\mathbf{x}, \emptyset) \quad \text{where}$$

$$ddmin_2(T'_\mathbf{x}, R) = \begin{cases} T'_\mathbf{x} & \text{if } |T'_\mathbf{x}| = 1 \text{ ("base case")} \\ ddmin_2(T_1, R) & \text{else if } Replay(T_1 \cup R) = \mathbf{X} \text{ ("in } T_1\text{")} \\ ddmin_2(T_2, R) & \text{else if } Replay(T_2 \cup R) = \mathbf{X} \text{ ("in } T_2\text{")} \\ ddmin_2(T_1, T_2 \cup R) \cup ddmin_2(T_2, T_1 \cup R) & \text{otherwise ("interference")} \end{cases}$$

where $Replay(T)$ denotes the state of the system after executing the trace T, $\mathbf{X}$ denotes a correctness violation, $T_1 \subset T'_\mathbf{x}$, $T_2 \subset T'_\mathbf{x}$, $T_1 \cup T_2 = T'_\mathbf{x}$, $T_1 \cap T_2 = \emptyset$, and $|T_1| \approx |T_2| \approx |T'_\mathbf{x}|/2$ hold.

Is there a better definition of functional equivalence? Our current definition of functional equivalence is based on guess-work and domain knowledge: we intuitively disregard certain pieces of information in each internal event because we know that they typically do not determine whether the bug appears. We believe that formulating functional equivalence in terms of knowledge states of the distributed system [2] will yield a more principled approach. If retrospective causal inference has insight into what pieces of knowledge the nodes of a distributed system act upon, it can make stronger statements about what parts of each message or internal state change are capable of affecting the actions of a given node. By comparing the internal events across runs based on what pieces of information actually affect the end state, we can draw stronger functional equivalencies between events.

What types of systems are most amenable to troubleshooting? Suppose you are troubleshooting a bug in a system that takes a small number of inputs and performs a long series of computations after receiving the inputs. If you prune a single input event, every successive intermediate state, including the final state, diverges from the states in the original execution. In this scenario, the minimal causal sequence will often be the original event sequence in its entirety, and the minimization provided by retrospective causal inference would have no value.

We conjecture that retrospective causal inference operates best on systems that have 'quiescent' state machines, where each input event only triggers a small number of internal state transitions. We successfully tested retrospective causal inference on control-plane systems (software-defined network controllers), which tend to have this property. It is unclear whether other systems would be equally amenable to retrospective causal inference.

What types of bugs does this technique perform poorly well on? Even with a MCS in hand, troubleshooters need to match the MCS to the errant code path that ultimately triggers the bug. Retrospective causal inference helps by making the execution trace easy to understand, but the programmer may not easily be able to match the sequence to a code path. Consider for example a bug that is triggered the 27th time the letter 'a' appears in the sequence of events. There are many different event subsequences that can trigger such a bug. Due to the difficulty of distributed replay, it is very possible that retrospective causal inference will return different bug-triggering sequences on successive invocations. It would require a great deal of insight for a practitioner to deduce a pattern they all share.

We are not certain what types of bugs retrospective causal inference is most useful for. In our experience, bugs that are triggered without prior complicated event sequences provide short, insightful MCSes. For example, if a system does not support a particular type of input event (*e.g.* virtual machine migration), then the first occur-

rence of such an event in any sequence of input events will trigger the bug; in such a case, retrospective causal inference will return the single event.

4. CONCLUSION

Developers of distributed systems must be mindful of the minute details of computer systems. The troubleshooting tools available for single-process systems are rarely applicable to distributed systems, leaving practitioners with few viable troubleshooting options when they observe errant behavior in their distributed systems. Developers consequently spend much more of their time and effort troubleshooting bugs. We believe that a principled approach to automated troubleshooting is possible, and we have taken a first step here by presenting an algorithm for automatically minimizing errant event traces. We hope that the distributed systems community will further investigate the theoretical issues behind systematic troubleshooting.

5. REFERENCES

[1] P. Godefroid and N. Nagappan. Concurrency at Microsoft - An Exploratory Survey. CAV '08.

[2] J. Y. Halpern and Y. Moses. Knowledge and Common Knowledge in a Distributed Environment. JACM '90.

[3] J. C. King. Symbolic Execution and Program Testing. CACM '76.

[4] C. Scott, A. Wundsam, S. Whitlock, A. Or, E. Huang, K. Zarifis, and S. Shenker. How Did We Get Into This Mess? Isolating Fault-Inducing Inputs to SDN Control Software. Technical Report UCB/EECS-2013-8, University of California, Berkeley, '13.

[5] G. Tel. *Introduction to Distributed Algorithms*. Thm. 2.21. Cambridge University Press, 2000.

[6] A. Whitaker, R. Cox, and S. Gribble. Configuration Debugging as Search: Finding the Needle in the Haystack. SOSP '04.

[7] A. Zeller. Yesterday, my program worked. Today, it does not. Why? ESEC/FSE '99.

[8] A. Zeller and R. Hildebrandt. Simplifying and Isolating Failure-Inducing Input. IEEE TSE '02.

[9] H. Zeng, P. Kazemian, G. Varghese, and N. McKeown. A Survey on Network Troubleshooting. Technical Report TR12-HPNG-061012, Stanford University '12.

Stone Age Distributed Computing
(Extended Abstract)

Yuval Emek
Distributed Computing Group
ETH Zurich, Switzerland
yemek@ethz.ch

Roger Wattenhofer[*]
Distributed Computing Group
ETH Zurich, Switzerland
wattenhofer@ethz.ch

ABSTRACT

A new model that depicts a network of randomized finite state machines operating in an asynchronous environment is introduced. This model, that can be viewed as a hybrid of the message passing model and cellular automata is suitable for applying the distributed computing lens to the study of networks of sub-microprocessor devices, e.g., biological cellular networks and man-made nano-networks. Although the computation and communication capabilities of each individual device in the new model are, by design, much weaker than those of an abstract computer, we show that some of the most important and extensively studied distributed computing problems can still be solved efficiently.

Categories and Subject Descriptors

F.1.1 [**Computation by Abstract Devices**]: Models of computation

Keywords

Cellular automata, efficient algorithms, finite state machines, message passing

1. INTRODUCTION

Due to the major role that the Internet plays today, models targeted at understanding the fundamental properties of networks focus mainly on "Internet-capable" devices. Indeed, the standard network model in distributed computing is the so called *message passing* model, where nodes may exchange large messages with their neighbors, and perform arbitrary local computations. Recently, there is a trend to study distributed computing aspects in networks of sub-microprocessor devices, e.g., networks of biological cells [3, 16] or nano-scale mechanical devices [4]. However, the suitability of the message passing model to these types of networks is far from being certain: Do tiny bio/nano nodes

"compute" and/or "communicate" essentially the same as a computer? Since such nodes will be fundamentally more limited than silicon-based devices, we believe that there is a need for a network model, where nodes are by design below the computation and communication capabilities of Turing machines.

Networked finite state machines. In this paper, we introduce a new model, referred to as *networked finite state machines (nFSM)*, that depicts a network of randomized finite state machines (a.k.a. automata) progressing in asynchronous steps (refer to Section 2 for a formal description). Under the nFSM model, nodes communicate by transmitting messages belonging to some finite communication alphabet Σ such that a message $\sigma \in \Sigma$ transmitted by node u is delivered to its neighbors (the same σ to all neighbors) in an asynchronous fashion. Each neighbor v of u has a port corresponding to u in which the last message delivered from u is stored.

The access of node v to its ports is limited: In each step of v's execution, the next state and the message transmitted by v at this step are determined by v's current state and by the current number $\sharp(\sigma)$ of appearances of each letter $\sigma \in \Sigma$ in v's ports. The crux of the model is that $\sharp(\sigma)$ is calculated according to the *one-two-many*[1] principle: the node can only count up to some predetermined *bounding parameter* $b \in \mathbb{Z}_{>0}$ and any value of $\sharp(\sigma)$ larger than b cannot be distinguished from b.

The nFSM model satisfies the following *model requirements*, that we believe, make it more applicable to the study of general networks consisting of weaker devices such as those mentioned above:

(M1) The model is applicable to arbitrary network topologies.

(M2) All nodes run the same protocol executed by a (randomized) FSM.

(M3) The network operates in a fully asynchronous environment with adversarial node activation and message delivery delays.

(M4) All features of the FSM (specifically, the state set Q, message alphabet Σ, and bounding parameter b) are of constant size independent of any parameter of the network (including the degree of the node executing the FSM).

The last requirement is perhaps the most interesting one

---

[*]Part of this work was done while the author was in Microsoft Research, Redmond, WA.

---

[1]The one-two-many theory states that some small isolated cultures (e.g., the Piraha tribe of the Amazon [26]) did not develop a counting system that goes beyond 2. This is reflected in their languages that include words for "1", "2", and "many" that stands for any number larger than 2.

as it implies that a node cannot perform any calculation that involves variables beyond some predetermined constant. This comes in contrast to many distributed algorithms operating under the message passing model that strongly rely on the ability of a node to perform such calculations (e.g., count up to some parameter of the network or a function thereof).

Results. Our investigation of the new nFSM model begins by observing that the computational power of a network operating under this model is not stronger than (and in some sense equivalent to) that of a randomized Turing machine with linear space bound (due to space limitations, this part is deferred to the full version). Since the computational power of a network operating under the message passing model is trivially equivalent to that of a (general) Turing machine, there exist distributed problems that can be solved by a message passing algorithm in constant time but cannot be solved by an nFSM algorithm at all. Nevertheless, as the main technical contribution of this paper, we show that some of the most important problems in distributed computing admit efficient (namely, with polylogarithmic run-time) nFSM algorithms. Specifically, problems such as maximal independent set, node coloring, and maximal matching that have been extensively studied since the early 1980s, always assuming a network of some sort of abstract computers, can in fact be solved, and fast, when each device is nothing but a FSM.

Applicability to biological cellular networks. Regardless of the theoretical interest in implementing efficient algorithms using weaker assumptions, we believe that our new model and results should be appealing to anyone interested in understanding the computational aspects of biological cellular networks. A basic dogma in biology (see, e.g., [41]) states that all cells communicate and that they do so by emitting special kinds of ligand molecules (e.g. the DSL family of proteins) that bind in a reversible, non-covalent, fashion to designated receptors (e.g. the NOTCH family of transmembrane receptors) in neighboring cells. These, in turn, release some intracellular signaling proteins that penetrate the nucleus to modify gene expression (determining the cell's actions).

Translated to the language of the nFSM model, the different types of ligand molecules correspond to the different letters in the communication alphabet, where an emission of a ligand corresponds to transmitting a letter. The effect that the ligands-receptors binding has on the concentration level of the signaling proteins in the nucleus corresponds to the manner in which a node in our model interprets the content of its ports. (The one-two-many counting is the discrete analogue of the ability to distinguish between different concentration levels, considering the fact that once the concentration exceeds some threshold, a further increase cannot be detected.) Using an FSM as the underlying computational model of the individual node seems to be the right choice especially in the biological setting as demonstrated by Benenson et al. [17] who showed that essentially all FSMs can be implemented by enzymes found in cells' nuclei. One may wonder if the specific problems studied in the current paper have any relevance to biology. Indeed, Afek et al. [3] discovered that a biological process that occurs during the development of the nervous system of the Drosophila melanogaster is in fact equivalent to solving the MIS problem.

Related work and comparison to other models. As mentioned above, the message passing model is the gold standard when it comes to understanding distributed network algorithms [32, 40]. Several variants exist for this model, differing mainly in the bounds imposed on the message size (e.g., the *congest* and *local* models [44]) and the level of synchronization. Indeed, most theoretical literature dealing with distributed network algorithms relies on one of these variants. Our nFSM model adopts the concept of an asynchronous message-based communication scheme from the message passing literature.

As the traditional message passing model allows for sending different messages to different neighbors in each round of the execution, it was too powerful for many settings. In particular, with the proliferation of wireless networks, more restrictive message passing models appeared such as the *radio network* model [20]. Over the years, several variants of the radio network model were introduced, the most extreme one in terms of its weak communication capabilities is the *beeping* model [24, 22], where in each round a node can either beep or stay silent, and can only distinguish between the case in which no node in its neighborhood beeps and the case in which at least one node beeps. Efficient algorithms and lower bounds for the MIS problem under the beeping model were developed by Afek et al. [3, 2]. Note that the beeping model resembles our nFSM model in the sense that the "beeping rule" can be viewed as counting under the one-two-many principle with bounding parameter $b = 1$. However, it is much stronger in other perspectives: (i) the beeping model assumes synchronous communication and does not seem to have a natural asynchronous variant; and (ii) the local computation is performed by a Turing machine whose memory is allowed to grow with time and with the network size (this is crucial for the algorithms of Afek et al. [3, 2]). In that regard, the beeping model is still too strong to capture the behavior of biological cellular networks.

Our nFSM model is also closely related to (and inspired by) the extensively studied *cellular automaton* model [47, 25, 48] that captures a network of FSMs, arranged in a grid topology (some other highly regular topologies were also considered), where the transition of each node depends on its current state and the states of its neighbors. Still, the nFSM model differs from the cellular automaton model in many aspects. In particular, the latter model is not applicable to non-regular network topologies and although a small fraction of the cellular automata literature is dedicated to cellular automata with asynchronous node activation [38, 39] (see also [1]), these do not support asynchronous message delivery. As such, cellular automata do not seem to provide a good abstraction for the sub-microprocessor networks we would like to focus on. Moreover, the main goal of our work is to study to what extent can such networks compute solutions quickly, a goal that lies outside the typical interest of the cellular automata community.

Another model that resembles the nFSM model is that of *communicating automata* [18]. This model also assumes that each node in the network operates an FSM in an asynchronous manner, however the steps of the FSMs are message driven: for each state q of node v and for each message m that node v may receive from an adjacent node u while residing in state q, the transition function of v should have an entry characterized by the 3-tuple (q, u, m) that determines its next move. Consequently, different nodes would typically operate different FSMs and the size of the FSM operated by node v inherently depends on the degree of v and thus, the communicating automata model is still too strong to faithfully represent biological cellular networks.

The *population protocols* model, introduced by Angluin et al. [6] (see also [8, 37]), depicts a network of finite state machines communicating through pairwise rendezvous controlled by a fair adversarial scheduler. While in the full version we reveal some interesting connections between the nFSM model and population protocols, there are two conceptual differences between these models: First, population protocols are only required to *eventually converge* to a correct output and are allowed to return arbitrary (wrong) outputs beforehand. This provides population protocols with the power to solve, e.g., the consensus problem in arbitrary networks, in contrast to nFSM protocols that should irrevocably return a correct output (see Section 2) and therefore, cannot solve this problem (cf. [23]). Second, while the focus of the current paper is mainly on run-time complexity, there is an inherent problem with establishing run-time bounds for population protocols due to the nature of the adversarial scheduler that can delay the execution for arbitrarily long periods. Indeed, the population protocols literature is typically concerned with what can be computed, rather than how fast. An exception is the probabilistic variant of the model [7, 19], where interactions are selected randomly, rather than adversarially, but this variant is no longer fully asynchronous (in the adversarial sense). On top of that, the rendezvous based communication does not seem to fit the communication mechanisms in most biological cellular networks.

2. MODEL

Throughout, we assume a network represented by a finite undirected graph $G = (V, E)$. Under the *networked finite state machines (nFSM)* model, each node $v \in V$ runs a protocol depicted by the 8-tuple

$$\Pi = \langle Q, Q_I, Q_O, \Sigma, \sigma_0, b, \lambda, \delta \rangle , \qquad (1)$$

where

- Q is a finite set of *states*;
- $Q_I \subseteq Q$ is the subset of *input states*;
- $Q_O \subseteq Q$ is the subset of *output states*;
- Σ is a finite *communication alphabet*;
- $\sigma_0 \in \Sigma$ is the *initial letter*;
- $b \in \mathbb{Z}_{>0}$ is a *bounding parameter*; let $B = \{0, 1, \ldots, b-1, {}^{\geq}b\}$ be a set of $b + 1$ distinguishable symbols;
- $\lambda : Q \to \Sigma$ assigns a *query letter* $\sigma \in \Sigma$ to every state $q \in Q$; and
- $\delta : Q \times B \to 2^{Q \times (\Sigma \cup \{\varepsilon\})}$ is the *transition function*.

It is important to point out that protocol Π is oblivious to the graph G. In fact, the number of states in Q, the size of the alphabet Σ, and the bounding parameter b are all assumed to be universal constants, independent of any parameter of the graph G. In particular, the protocol executed by node $v \in V$ does not depend on the degree of v in G. We now turn to describe the semantics of the nFSM model.

Communication. Node v communicates with its adjacent nodes in G by *transmitting* messages. A transmitted message consists of a single letter $\sigma \in \Sigma$ and it is assumed that this letter is delivered to all neighbors u of v. Each neighbor u has a *port* $\psi_u(v)$ (a different port for every adjacent node v) in which the last message σ received from v is stored. At the beginning of the execution, all ports store the initial letter σ_0. It will be convenient to consider the case in which v does not transmit any message (and hence does not affect the corresponding ports at the adjacent nodes) as a transmission of the special *empty symbol* ε.

Execution. The execution of node v progresses in discrete *steps* indexed by the positive integers. In each step $t \in \mathbb{Z}_{>0}$, node v resides in some state $q \in Q$. Let $\lambda(q) = \sigma \in \Sigma$ be the query letter that λ assigns to state q and let $\sharp(\sigma)$ be the number of appearances of σ in v's ports in step t. Then, the pair (q', σ') of state $q' \in Q$ in which v resides in step $t + 1$ and message $\sigma' \in \Sigma \cup \{\varepsilon\}$ transmitted by v in step t (recall that ε indicates that no message is transmitted) is chosen *uniformly at random*[2] (and independently of all other random choices) among the pairs in

$$\delta \left(q, \beta_b \left(\sharp(\sigma) \right) \right) \subseteq Q \times (\Sigma \cup \{\varepsilon\}) ,$$

where $\beta_b : \mathbb{Z}_{\geq 0} \to B$ is defined as

$$\beta_b(x) = \begin{cases} x & \text{if } 0 \leq x \leq b-1 ; \\ {}^{\geq}b & \text{otherwise} . \end{cases}$$

Informally, this can be thought of as if v queries its ports for appearances of σ and "observes" the exact value of $\sharp(\sigma)$ as long as it is smaller than the bounding parameter b; otherwise, v merely "observes" that $\sharp(\sigma) \geq b$ which is indicated by the symbol ${}^{\geq}b$.

Input and output. Initially (in step 1), each node resides in one of the input states of Q_I. The choice of the initial state of node $v \in V$ reflects the input passed to v at the beginning of the execution. This allows our model to cope with distributed problems in which different nodes get different input symbols. When dealing with problems in which the nodes do not get any initial input (such as the graph theoretic problems addressed in this paper), we shall assume that Q_I contains a single state referred to as the *initial* state.

The output states Q_O are mapped to the possible output values of the problem. For each possible output value o, it is required that the subset $P_o \subseteq Q_O$ of output states mapped to o form a *sink* with respect to the transition function δ in the sense that a node v that moves to a P_o-state will remain in P_o indefinitely, in which case the output of v is determined (irrevocably) to be o. We say that the (global) execution of the protocol is in an *output configuration* if all nodes reside in output states of Q_O.

Asynchrony. The nodes are assumed to operate in an *asynchronous* environment. This asynchrony has two facets: First, for the sake of convenience, we assume that the actual application of the transition function in each step $t \in \mathbb{Z}_{>0}$ of node $v \in V$ is instantaneous (namely, lasts zero time) and occurs at the end of the step;[3] the length of step t of node v, denoted $L_{v,t}$, is defined as the time difference between the application of the transition function in step $t - 1$ and that of step t. It is assumed that $L_{v,t}$ is finite, but apart from that, we do not make any other assumptions on this length, that is, the step length $L_{v,t}$ is determined by the adversary independently of all other step lengths $L_{v',t'}$. In particular,

---

[2] The protocol is deterministic if the images under δ are always singleton subsets of $Q \times (\Sigma \cup \{\varepsilon\})$.

[3] This assumption can be lifted at the cost of a more complicated definition of the adversarial policy described soon.

we do not assume any synchronization between the steps of different nodes whatsoever.

The second facet of the asynchronous environment is that a message transmitted by node v in step t (if such a message is transmitted) is assumed to reach the port $\psi_u(v)$ of an adjacent node u after a finite time delay, denoted $D_{v,t,u}$. We assume that if v transmits message $\sigma_1 \in \Sigma$ in step t_1 and message $\sigma_2 \in \Sigma$ in step $t_2 > t_1$, then σ_1 reaches u before σ_2 does. Apart from this "FIFO" assumption, we do not make any other assumptions on the delays $D_{v,t,u}$. In particular, this means that under certain circumstances, the adversary may overwrite message σ_1 with message σ_2 in port $\psi_u(v)$ of u so that u will never "know" that message σ_1 was transmitted.[4]

Consequently, a *policy* of the adversary is captured by: (1) the length $L_{v,t}$ of step t of node v for every $v \in V$ and $t \in \mathbb{Z}_{>0}$; and (2) the delay $D_{v,t,u}$ of the delivery of the transmission of node v in step t to an adjacent node u for every $v \in V$, $t \in \mathbb{Z}_{>0}$, and $u \in N(v)$.[5] Assuming that the adversary is oblivious to the random coin tosses of the nodes, an adversarial policy is depicted by infinite sequences of $L_{v,t}$ and $D_{v,t,u}$ parameters.

For further information on asynchronous environments, we refer the reader to one of the standard textbooks [34, 40].

Correctness and run-time measures. A protocol Π for problem P is said to be *correct* under the nFSM model if for every instance of P and for every adversarial policy, Π reaches an output configuration w.p. 1, and for every output configuration reached by Π w.p. > 0, the output of the nodes is a valid solution to P.[6] Given a correct protocol Π, the complexity measure that interests us in the current paper is the *run-time* of Π defined as the (possibly fractional) number of *time units* that pass from the beginning of the execution until an output configuration is reached, where a time unit is defined[7] to be the maximum among all step length parameters $L_{v,t}$ and delivery delay parameters $D_{v,t,u}$ in the adversarial policy (cf. [9, 40]). Following the standard procedure in this regard, we say that the run-time of a correct protocol Π for problem P is $f(n)$ if for every n-node instance of P and for every adversarial policy, the run-time of Π is at most $f(n)$ in expectation and w.h.p. The protocol is said to be *efficient* if its run-time is polylogarithmic in the size of the network (cf. [32]).

2.1 Multi-letter queries

According to the model as presented thus far, each state $q \in Q$ is associated with a single query letter $\sigma = \lambda(q)$ and the application of the transition function when node v resides in state q is determined by $\beta_b(\sharp(\sigma))$, namely the num-

---

[4]Often, much stronger assumptions are made in the literature. For example, a common assumption for asynchronous environments is that the port of node u corresponding to the adjacent node v is implemented by a buffer so that messages cannot be "lost". We do not make any such assumption for our nFSM model.

[5]We use the standard notation $N(v)$ for the *neighborhood* of node v in G, namely, the subset of nodes adjacent to v.

[6]Throughout, w.p. and w.h.p. abbreviate "with probability" and "with high probability", respectively.

[7]Note that time units are defined solely for the purpose of the analysis. Under an asynchronous environment, the nodes have no notion of time and in particular, they cannot measure a single time unit.

ber of appearances of the letter σ in the ports of v counted up to the bounding parameter b. However, in many applications, the transition of node v residing in state q depends on multiple-letters. This motivates the introduction of the *multi-letter query* feature that replaces an nFSM protocol as described in (1) by the 7-tuple

$$\Pi = \langle Q, Q_I, Q_O, \Sigma, \sigma_0, b, \delta \rangle \,,$$

where Q, Q_I, Q_O, Σ, σ_0, and b are defined (and play the same role) as in (1), and the domain of the transition function δ is extended so that

$$\delta : Q \times B^\Sigma \to 2^{Q \times (\Sigma \cup \{\varepsilon\})} \,.$$

The semantics of the nFSM model when augmented with the multi-letter query feature is as follows. Suppose that in step $t \in \mathbb{Z}_{>0}$, node v resides in state $q \in Q$ and the number of appearances of σ in v's ports in step t is $\sharp(\sigma)$ for every letter $\sigma \in \Sigma$. Then, the pair (q', σ') of state $q' \in Q$ in which v resides in step $t+1$ and message $\sigma' \in \Sigma \cup \{\varepsilon\}$ transmitted by v in step t is chosen uniformly at random among the pairs in

$$\delta \left(q, \langle \beta_b(\sharp(\sigma)) \rangle_{\sigma \in \Sigma} \right) \subseteq Q \times (\Sigma \cup \{\varepsilon\}) \,,$$

where $\langle \beta_b(\sharp(\sigma)) \rangle_{\sigma \in \Sigma}$ denotes the vector mapping $\beta_b(\sharp(\sigma))$ to each $\sigma \in \Sigma$. One may wonder if the nFSM model augmented with the multi-letter query feature is strictly stronger than the nFSM model without that feature; in Section 3, we show that this is not the case.

3. CONVENIENT TRANSFORMATIONS

In this section, we show that the nFSM protocol designer may, in fact, assume a slightly more "user-friendly" environment than the one described in Section 2. This is based on the design of black-box *compilers* transforming a protocol that makes strong assumptions on the environment into one that does not make any such assumptions.

As described in Section 2, the nFSM model assumes an asynchronous environment. Nevertheless, it will be convenient to extend the nFSM model to *synchronous* environments. One natural such extension augments the model described in Section 2 with the following two *synchronization properties* that should hold for every two adjacent nodes $u, v \in V$ and for every $t \in \mathbb{Z}_{>0}$:

(S1) when node u is in step t, node v is in step $t-1$, t, or $t+1$; and

(S2) at the end of step $t+1$ of u, port $\psi_u(v)$ stores the message transmitted by v in step t of v's execution (or the last message transmitted by v prior to step t if v does not transmit any message in step t).

An environment in which properties (S1) and (S2) are guaranteed to hold is called a *locally synchronous* environment. Local-only communication can never achieve global synchrony, however, research in the message passing model has shown that local synchrony is often sufficient to provide efficient algorithms [9, 11, 10]. To distinguish a protocol assumed to operate in a locally synchronous environment from those making no such assumptions, we shall often refer to the execution steps of the former as *rounds* (cf. fully synchronized protocols).

THEOREM 1. *Every nFSM protocol $\Pi = \langle Q, Q_I, Q_O, \Sigma, \sigma_0, b, \lambda, \delta \rangle$ designed to operate in a locally synchronous environment can be simulated in an* *asynchronous environment by a protocol $\widehat{\Pi}$ with the same bounding parameter b at the cost of a constant multiplicative run-time overhead.*

The procedure in charge of the simulation promised in Theorem 1 (whose proof is deferred to the full version) is referred to as a *synchronizer* [9].

Now that we may assume a synchronous environment, it is easy to show that by augmenting the nFSM model with the multi-letter query feature introduced in Section 2.1, one does not (asymptotically) enhance the power of the model. Indeed, at the cost of increasing the number of states and the run-time by constant factors, we can subdivide each round into $|\Sigma|$ subrounds, dedicating each subround to a different letter in Σ, so that at the end of the round, the state of v reflects $\beta_b(\sharp(\sigma))$ for every $\sigma \in \Sigma$.

THEOREM 2. *Every nFSM protocol with the multi-letter query feature can be simulated by an nFSM protocol without this feature and the same bounding parameter b at the cost of a constant multiplicative run-time overhead.*

4. EFFICIENT ALGORITHMS

As stated earlier, the main technical contribution of this paper is cast in the development of efficient nFSM algorithms for some of the most important and extensively studied problems in distributed computing. These problems include maximal independent set, maximal 2-hop independent set, node coloring of bounded degree graphs with $\Delta + 1$ colors, node 2-hop coloring of bounded degree graphs with $\Delta^2 + 1$ colors, node coloring of (undirected) trees with 3 colors, and maximal matching (where we use a small unavoidable modification of the model). The maximal independent set problem is treated in Section 4.1; due to space limitation, the treatment of all other problems is deferred to the full version.

4.1 Maximal independent set

Given a graph $G = (V, E)$, the *maximal independent set (MIS)* problem asks for a node subset $U \subseteq V$ which is independent in the sense that $(U \times U) \cap E = \emptyset$, and maximal in the sense that $U' \subseteq V$ is not independent for every $U' \supset U$. The challenge of designing a fast distributed MIS algorithm was first posed by Valiant in the early 1980s [46]. Distributed MIS algorithms with logarithmic run-time operating in the message passing model were subsequently presented by Luby [33] and independently, by Alon et al. [5].[8] Luby's algorithm has since become a specimen of distributed algorithms; in the last 25 years, researchers have tried to improve it, if only e.g., with an improved bit complexity [36], on special graph classes [42, 31, 14], or in a weaker communication model [2]. An $\Omega(\sqrt{\log n})$ lower bound on the run-time of any distributed MIS algorithm operating in the message passing model was established by Kuhn et al. [30]. Our goal in this section is to establish the following theorem.

THEOREM 3. *There exists an nFSM protocol with bounding parameter $b = 1$ that computes an MIS for any n-node graph in time $O(\log^2 n)$.*

---

[8]The focus of [33] and [5] was actually on the PRAM model, but their algorithms can be adapted to the message passing model.

Outline of the key technical ideas. The protocol promised by Theorem 3 is inspired by the existing message passing MIS algorithms. Common to all these algorithms is that they are based on the concept of grouping consecutive rounds into *phases*, where in each phase, nodes compete against their neighbors over the right to join the MIS. Existing implementations of such competitions require at least one of the following three capabilities: (1) performing calculations that involve super-constant variables; (2) communicating with each neighbor independently; or (3) sending messages of a logarithmic size. The first two capabilities are clearly out of the question for an nFSM protocol. The third one is also not supported by the nFSM model, but perhaps one can divide a message with a logarithmic number of bits over logarithmically many rounds, sending $O(1)$ bits per round (cf. Algorithm B in [36])?

This naive attempt results in super-constant long phases, while no FSM can count the rounds in such phases — a task essential for deciding if the current phase is over and the next one should begin. Furthermore, to guarantee fair competition, the phases must be aligned across the network, thus ruling out the possibility to start node v's phase i before phase $i-1$ of some node $u \neq v$ is finished. In fact, an efficient algorithm that requires $\omega(1)$ long aligned phases cannot be implemented under the nFSM model. So, how can we decide if node v joins the MIS using constant size messages without the ability to maintain long aligned phases?

This issue is resolved by relaxing the requirements that the phases are aligned and of a predetermined length, introducing a feature referred to as a *tournament*. Our tournaments are only "softly" aligned and their lengths are determined probabilistically, in a manner that can be maintained under the nFSM model. Nevertheless, they enable a fair competition between neighboring nodes, as desired.

The protocol. Employing Theorems 1 and 2, we assume a locally synchronous environment and use multiple-letter queries. The state set of the protocol is $Q = \{\text{WIN}, \text{LOSE}, \text{DOWN}_1, \text{DOWN}_2, \text{UP}_0, \text{UP}_1, \text{UP}_2\}$, with $Q_I = \{\text{DOWN}_1\}$ (the initial state of all nodes) and $Q_O = \{\text{WIN}, \text{LOSE}\}$, where WIN (respectively, LOSE) indicates membership (resp., non-membership) in the MIS output by the protocol. The states in $Q_A = Q - Q_O$ are called the *active* states and a node in an active state is referred to as an *active* node. We take the communication alphabet Σ to be identical to the state set Q, where the letter transmissions are designed so that node v transmits letter q whenever it moves to state q from some state $q' \neq q$; no letter is transmitted in a round at which v remains in the same state. Letter DOWN_1 is the initial letter stored in all ports at the beginning of the execution. The bounding parameter is set to $b = 1$.

A schematic description of the transition function is provided in Figure 1; its logic is as follows. Each state $q \in Q_A$ has a subset $D(q) \subseteq Q_A - \{q\}$ of *delaying states*: node v remains in the current state q if and only if (at least) one of its neighbors is in some state in $D(q)$. This is implemented by querying on the letters (corresponding to the states) in $D(q)$, staying in state q as long as at least one of these letters is found in the ports. Specifically, state DOWN_1 is delayed by state DOWN_2, which is delayed by all three UP states. State UP_j, $j = 0, 1, 2$, is delayed by state $\text{UP}_{j-1 \bmod 3}$, where state UP_0 is also delayed by state DOWN_1.

States WIN and LOSE are sinks. Assuming that an active node v does not find any delaying letter in its ports, the

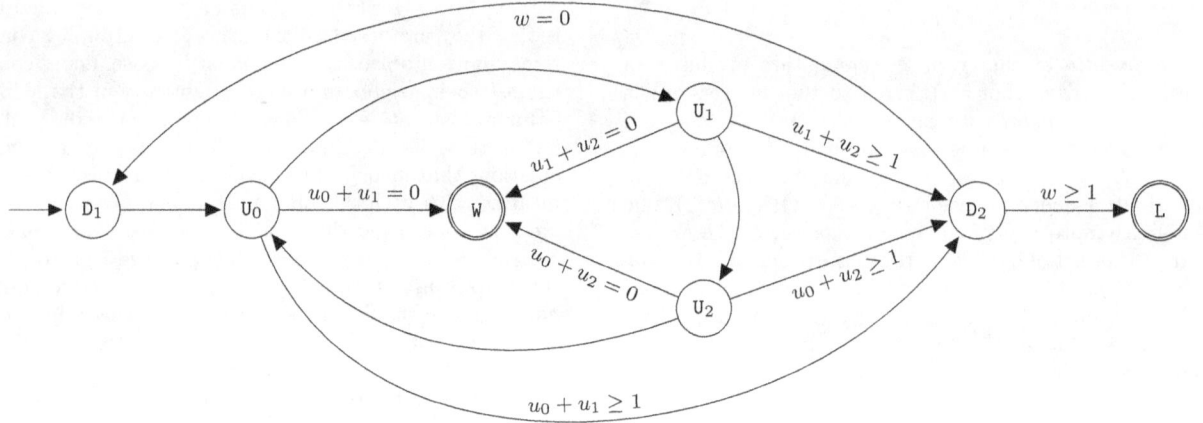

Figure 1: The transition function of the MIS protocol with state names abbreviated by their first (capital) letter. The node stays in state q (a.k.a. *delayed*) as long as letter q' appears (at least once) in its ports for any state q' such that a $q' \to q$ transition is defined (for clarity, this is omitted from the figure). Assuming that the node is not delayed, each transition specified in the figure is associated with a condition on the number of appearances of the query letters in the ports (depicted by the corresponding lower-case letter) so that the transition is followed only if the condition is satisfied (an empty condition is satisfied by all port configurations); if some port configuration satisfies several transition conditions, then one of them is chosen uniformly at random.

logic of the UP and DOWN states is as follows. From state DOWN$_1$, v moves to state UP$_0$. From state DOWN$_2$, v moves to state DOWN$_1$ if $\sharp(\text{WIN}) = 0$, that is, if it does not find any WIN letter in its ports; otherwise, it moves to state LOSE. When in state UP$_j$, v tosses a fair coin and proceeds as follows: if the coin turns head, then v moves to state UP$_{j+1 \bmod 3}$; if the coin turns tail, then v moves to state WIN if $\sharp(\text{UP}_j) = \sharp(\text{UP}_{j+1 \bmod 3}) = 0$ (note that $\sharp(\text{UP}_{j-1 \bmod 3})$ must be 0 as $\text{UP}_{j-1 \bmod 3} \in D(\text{UP}_j)$); and to state DOWN$_2$ otherwise. This completes the description of our nFSM protocol for the MIS problem.

Turns and tournaments. Our protocol is designed so that an active node v traverses the DOWN and UP states in a (double-)circular fashion: an inner loop of the UP states (moving from state UP$_j$ to state UP$_{j+1 \bmod 3}$) nested within an outer loop consisting of the DOWN states and the inner loop. Of course, v may spend more than one round at each state $q \in Q_A$ (delayed by adjacent nodes in states $D(q)$); we refer to a maximal contiguous sequence of rounds that v spends in the same state $q \in Q_A$ as a q-*turn*, or simply as a *turn* if the actual state q is irrelevant. A maximal contiguous sequence of turns that starts at a DOWN$_1$-turn and does not include any other DOWN$_1$-turn (i.e., a single iteration of the outer loop) is referred to as a *tournament*. We index the tournaments and the turns within a tournament by the positive integers. Note that by definition, every tournament i of v starts with a DOWN$_1$-turn, followed by a non-empty sequence of UP-turns; tournament i can end with an UP-turn from which v moves to state WIN, with a DOWN$_2$-turn from which v moves to state LOSE, or with a DOWN$_2$-turn from which v moves to

DOWN$_1$ starting tournament $i + 1$. The following observation is established by induction on the rounds.

OBSERVATION 1. *Consider some active node $v \in V$ in turn $j \in \mathbb{Z}_{>0}$ of tournament $i \in \mathbb{Z}_{>0}$ and some active node $u \in N(v)$.*

- *If this is a DOWN$_1$-turn of v ($j = 1$), then u is in either (a) the last (DOWN$_2$-)turn of tournament $i-1$; (b) turn 1 of tournament i; or (c) turn 2 of tournament i.*
- *If this is an UP-turn of v ($j \geq 2$), then u is in either (a) turn $j - 1$ of tournament i; (b) turn j of tournament i; (c) turn $j + 1$ of tournament i; or (d) the last (DOWN$_2$-)turn $j' \leq j+1$ of tournament i.*
- *If this is a DOWN$_2$-turn of v (the last turn of this tournament), then u is in either (a) an UP-turn $j' \geq j - 1$ of tournament i; (b) the last (DOWN$_2$-)turn of tournament i; or (c) turn 1 of tournament $i + 1$.*

Given some $U \subseteq V$ and $i, j \in \mathbb{Z}_{>0}$, let $T^U(i,j)$ denote the first time at which every node $v \in U$ satisfies either
(1) v is inactive;
(2) v is in tournament $i' > i$;
(3) v is in the last (DOWN$_2$-)turn of tournament i; or
(4) v is in turn $j' \geq j$ of tournament i.
Note that $T^U(i,j)$ is well defined even if some node $v \in U$ does not reach turn j of tournament i. Employing Observation 1, the delaying states feature guarantees that

$$T^{\{v\}}(i, j+1) \ \leq \ T^{N(v) \cup \{v\}}(i, j) + 1 \qquad (2)$$

for every $v \in V$ and $i, j \in \mathbb{Z}_{>0}$. Since $T^U(i,j) \leq T^V(i,j)$ for every $U \subseteq V$, we can apply inequality (2) to each node

$v \in V$, concluding that

$$T^V(i, j+1) \leq T^V(i, j) + 1,$$

which immediately implies that

$$T^V(i, k+1) \leq T^V(i, 1) + k. \qquad (3)$$

Moreover, if no node in V goes beyond turn j of tournament i, then

$$T^V(i+1, 1) = T^V(i, j+1) \leq T^V(i, j) + 1. \qquad (4)$$

The virtual graph G_i. Let V_i be the set of nodes for which tournament i exists and let $G_i = (V_i, E_i)$ be the subgraph induced on G by V_i, where $E_i = E \cap (V_i \times V_i)$. Given some node $v \in V_i$, let $N_i(v) = \{u \in V_i \mid (u, v) \in E_i\}$ be the neighborhood of node v in G_i and let $d_i(v) = |N_i(v)|$ be its degree. Note that the graph G_i is virtual in the sense that it is defined solely for the sake of the analysis: we do not assume that there exists some time at which the graph induced by any meaningful subset of the nodes (say, the nodes in tournament i) agrees with G_i.

Given some node $v \in V_i$, let $X^v(i)$ denote the number of UP-turns in tournament i of v and recall that the total number of turns in this tournament is at most $X^v(i) + 2$, accounting for the DOWN$_1$ turn in the beginning of the tournament and the DOWN$_2$-turn in its end. The logic of the UP states implies that $X^v(i)$ is a Geom$(1/2)$-random variable, namely, it obeys the geometric distribution with parameter $1/2$. The key observation now is that conditioned on G_i, the random variables $X^v(i)$, $v \in V_i$, are independent. Moreover, the graph G_{i+1} is fully determined by the random variables $X^v(i)$, $v \in V_i$. Since the maximum of (at most) n independent Geom$(1/2)$-random variables is $O(\log n)$ w.h.p., inequalities (3) and (4) yield the following observation.

OBSERVATION 2. *For every $i \in \mathbb{Z}_{>0}$, $T^V(i, 1)$ is finite w.p. 1 and*

$$T^V(i+1, 1) \leq T^V(i, 1) + O(\log n)$$

w.h.p.

Our protocol is designed so that node v moves to an output state (WIN or LOSE) in the end of each tournament w.p. > 0. Moreover, the logic of state DOWN$_2$ guarantees that if node v moves to state WIN in the end of tournament i, then all its active neighbors move to state LOSE in the end of their respective tournaments i. The correctness of our protocol now follows from Observation 2: the protocol reaches an output configuration w.p. 1 and every output configuration reflects an MIS. It remains to bound the run-time of our protocol; the following lemma plays a major role in this task.

LEMMA 1. *There exist two constants $0 < p, c < 1$ such that $|E_{i+1}| \leq c|E_i|$ w.p. $\geq p$.*

We will soon prove Lemma 1, but first, let us explain why it suffices for the completion of our analysis. Define the random variable $Y = \min\{i \in \mathbb{Z}_{>0} : |E_i| = 0\}$. Lemma 1 implies that Y is stochastically dominated by a random variable that obeys distribution $O(\log n) + \text{NB}(O(\log n), 1-p)$, namely, a fixed term of $O(\log n)$ plus the negative binomial distribution with parameters $O(\log n)$ and $1-p$, hence $Y = O(\log n)$ in expectation and w.h.p. Since the nodes

in $V - V_i$ are all in an output state (and will remain in that state), and since the logic of the UP states implies that a degree-0 node in G_i will move to state WIN in the end of tournament i (w.p. 1) and thus, will not be included in V_{i+1}, we can employ Observation 2 to conclude that the run-time of our protocol is indeed $O(\log^2 n)$.

The remainder of this section is dedicated to establishing Lemma 1. The proof technique we use for that purpose resembles (a hybrid of) the techniques used in [5] and [36] for the analysis of their MIS algorithms. We say that node $v \in V_i$ is *good* in G_i if

$$|\{u \in N_i(v) \mid d_i(u) \leq d_i(v)\}| \geq d_i(v)/3,$$

i.e., if at least third of v's neighbors in G_i have degrees smaller or equal to that of v. The following lemma is established in [5].

LEMMA 2 ([5]). *More than half of the edges in E_i are incident on good nodes in G_i.*

Disjoint winning events. Consider some good node v in G_i with $d = d_i(v) > 0$ and let $\widehat{N}_i(v) = \{u \in N_i(v) \mid d_i(u) \leq d\}$. Recall that the definition of a good node implies that $|\widehat{N}_i(v)| \geq d/3$. We say that node $u \in \widehat{N}_i(v)$ *wins* v in tournament i if

$$X^u(i) > \max\left\{X^w(i) \mid w \in N_i(u) \cup \widehat{N}_i(v) - \{u\}\right\}$$

and denote this event by $A_i(u, v)$. The main observation now is that if u wins v in tournament i, then in the end of their respective tournaments i, u moves to state WIN and v moves to state LOSE. Moreover, the events $A_i(u, v)$ and $A_i(w, v)$ are disjoint for every $u, w \in \widehat{N}_i(v)$, $u \neq w$.

Fix some node $u \in \widehat{N}_i(v)$. Let $u_1, \ldots, u_k$ be the nodes in $N_i(u) \cup \widehat{N}_i(v)$, where $0 < k \leq 2d$ by the definition of a good node. Let $B_i(u, v)$ denote the event that the maximum of $\{X^{u_\ell}(i) \mid 1 \leq \ell \leq k\}$ is attained at a single $1 \leq \ell \leq k$. Since $X^{u_1}(i), \ldots, X^{u_k}(i)$ are independent random variables that obey distribution Geom$(1/2)$, it follows that $\mathbb{P}(B_i(u, v)) \geq 2/3$ and therefore,

$$\mathbb{P}(A_i(u, v)) = \mathbb{P}(A_i(u, v) \mid B_i(u, v)) \cdot \mathbb{P}(B_i(u, v)) \geq \frac{1}{k} \cdot \frac{2}{3}.$$

Given that v is good in G_i and recalling the disjointness of the $A_i(u, v)$ events, the last inequality implies that

$$\mathbb{P}(v \notin V_{i+1}) \geq \mathbb{P}\left(\bigvee_{u \in \widehat{N}_i(v)} A_i(u, v)\right)$$

$$= \sum_{u \in \widehat{N}_i(v)} \mathbb{P}(A_i(u, v)) \geq \frac{d}{3} \cdot \frac{1}{2d} \cdot \frac{2}{3} = \frac{1}{9}.$$

Combined with Lemma 2, we conclude that $\mathbb{E}[|E_{i+1}|] < \frac{17}{18}|E_i|$. Lemma 1 now follows by Markov's inequality, thus establishing Theorem 3.

4.2 Node coloring

Given a graph $G = (V, E)$, the *coloring* problem asks for an assignment of colors to the nodes such that no two neighboring nodes have the same color. A coloring using at most k colors is called a *k-coloring*. The smallest number of colors needed to color graph G is referred to as the *chromatic number* of G, denoted by $\chi(G)$. In general, $\chi(G)$ is difficult to compute even in a centralized model [15]. As such, the distributed computing community is generally satisfied already with a $(\Delta + 1)$-, $O(\Delta)$- or even $\Delta^{O(1)}$-coloring, where $\Delta = \Delta(G)$ is the largest degree in the graph G, with possibly $\Delta(G) \gg \chi(G)$ [21, 32, 45, 12, 29, 35, 13, 43]. As the output of each node under the nFSM model is taken from a predetermined constant size set, we cannot hope to solve these problems for general graphs. Instead, we observe that the following simple nFSM protocol colors any *bounded degree* graph in logarithmic time: As long as node v is still uncolored, it picks an available color c uniformly at random, where initially, the set of available colors is $\{1, \ldots, d+1\}$ for some constant $d \geq \Delta$. Then, v proposes color c to its neighbors and colors itself (irrevocably) with c if none of its neighbors proposed c in the previous round.

THEOREM 4. *Given some constant d, there exists an nFSM protocol with bounding parameter $b = 1$ that $(d+1)$-colors any n-node graph satisfying $\Delta \leq d$ in time $O(\log n)$.*

As Δ may grow quickly with n even for relatively simple graph classes, we turn our attention to a natural graph class that features a small chromatic number regardless of Δ: trees. Any tree T has a chromatic number $\chi(T) = 2$. Unfortunately, it is easy to show that in general, the task of 2-coloring trees requires run-time proportional to the diameter of the tree even under the message passing model, and hence cannot be achieved by an efficient distributed algorithm. The situation improves dramatically once 3 colors are allowed; indeed, Cole and Vishkin [21] presented a distributed algorithm that 3-colors directed paths, and in fact, any directed tree (directed in the sense that each node knows the port leading to its unique parent), in time $O(\log^* n)$. Linial [32] showed that this is asymptotically optimal.

Since it is not clear how to represent directed trees in the nFSM model, we focus on undirected trees. A lower bound result of Kothapalli et al. [28] shows that under the *anonymous* (namely, the nodes are not assumed to have unique identifiers) message passing model, 3-coloring undirected trees requires $\Omega(\log n)$ time as long as the size of each message is $O(1)$. We show that this lower bound is tight under the nFSM model (proof deferred to the full version).

THEOREM 5. *There exists an nFSM protocol with bounding parameter $b = 3$ that 3-colors any n-node (undirected) tree in time $O(\log n)$.*

4.3 The square graph

Consider some graph $G = (V, E)$, node $v \in V$, and positive integer k. We define the k-*hop neighborhood* of v in G, denoted by $N^k(v)$, as the set of all nodes $u \in V$, $u \neq v$, at distance at most k from v. The kth *power* of G, denoted by G^k, is the graph obtained from G by extending its edge set so that v is adjacent to all nodes in $N^k(v)$ for every $v \in V$. The second power G^2 of G is called the *square* of G. The proof of Lemma 3 is deferred to the full version.

LEMMA 3. *For every nFSM protocol Π with bounding parameter $b = 1$, there exists an nFSM protocol Π^2 with bounding parameter $b = 2$ such that for every graph G, the execution of Π^2 on G simulates the execution of Π on G^2 with a constant multiplicative run-time overhead.*

A node subset $U \subseteq V$ is a k-*hop independent set* of the graph $G = (V, E)$ if $v \in U$ implies that $u \notin U$ for every $u \in N^k(v) - \{v\}$; the *maximal k-hop independent set*

(MkIS) problem asks for a k-hop independent set $U \subseteq V$ which is maximal in the sense that $U' \subseteq V$ is not a k-hop independent set for any $U' \supset U$. Likewise, the k-*hop coloring* problem asks for an assignment of colors to the nodes such that the color of v differs from the color of u for every $u \in N^k(v) - \{v\}$. Cast in this terminology, the MIS and coloring problems are special cases of the MkIS set and k-hop coloring problems, respectively, for $k = 1$. It is shown in [23] that the MkIS and k-hop coloring problems cannot be solved for $k \geq 3$ by a distributed algorithm even under the much stronger anonymous message passing model. In contrast, the $k = 2$ case is resolved positively by plugging Theorems 3 and 4 into Lemma 3.

COROLLARY 1. *Given some constant d, there exists an nFSM protocol with bounding parameter $b = 2$ that computes a 2-hop coloring with $(d^2 + 1)$ colors for any n-node graph satisfying $\Delta \leq d$ in time $O(\log n)$.*

COROLLARY 2. *There exists an nFSM protocol with bounding parameter $b = 2$ that computes an M2IS for any n-node graph in time $O(\log^2 n)$.*

Corollary 1 essentially provides us with the power to implement independent communication along each edge in bounded degree graphs: Given a 2-hop coloring c, we can append the pair $(c(u), c(v))$ to a message originated at node u whose destination is node $v \in N(u)$. This way, node v can detect that the message was sent by u, whereas any node $w \in N(u) - \{v\}$ can ignore it.

Simulating population protocols. Corollary 2 also has an interesting implication that takes us back to the comparison between the nFSM model and the population protocols model (see Section 1) as it allows us to simulate the rendezvous based communication of any population protocol (in arbitrary interaction graphs). To explain how this is done, we need to introduce the notion of an *oriented matching* consisting of a set $M = \{(x_1, y_1), \ldots, (x_k, y_k)\}$ of ordered node pairs satisfying (1) $(x_i, y_i) \in E$ for every $1 \leq i \leq k$; and (2) $(x_i, y_j) \notin E$ for every $1 \leq i, j \leq k$, $i \neq j$. We refer to the nodes $x_1, \ldots, x_k$ as *leaders* and to the nodes $y_1, \ldots, y_k$ as *subordinates*.

Based on the M2IS protocol promised in Corollary 2, we present in the full version an nFSM protocol that computes an oriented matching M; specifically, upon termination of this protocol, each node knows if it is a leader, a subordinate, or neither. Moreover, for every edge $e \in E$ in each one of its two possible orientations, it holds that M is a singleton $M = \{e\}$ w.p. > 0. By the definition of an oriented matching, each leader x_i (respectively, subordinate y_i) can now safely communicate with its subordinate y_i (resp., leader x_i) without risking interference from other leaders (resp., subordinates). Therefore, we can apply the rule of the simulated population protocol to each (x_i, y_i) pair and update x_i and y_i's states under this simulated protocol accordingly. With an appropriate node delaying mechanism (see, e.g., Section 4.1), this process can be repeated indefinitely, thus yielding a schedule that must be fair (cf. [8]) due to the probabilistic guarantees of M.

LEMMA 4. *The model obtained from nFSM by relaxing the correctness requirement to an eventually converging correctness is at least as strong, in terms of its computational power, as the population protocols model (with the same interaction graph).*

4.4 Maximal matching

Given a graph $G = (V, E)$, an edge subset $M \subseteq E$ is called a *matching* if every node $v \in V$ is incident on at most one edge in M. The *maximal matching (MM)* problem asks for a matching which is maximal in the sense that $M' \subseteq E$ is not a matching for every $M' \supset M$. A message passing MM algorithm with logarithmic run-time was developed by Israeli and Itai [27], whereas the $\Omega(\sqrt{\log n})$ lower bound of [30] applies to the MM problem as well.

We would like to design an nFSM protocol for the MM problem. However, the nFSM model as defined in Section 2 is not expressive enough for this problem: in a complete bipartite graph with n nodes in each side for example, the number of maximal matchings is $n!$, while an nFSM protocol with c output states can only specify $c^{2n} \ll n!$ different (global) outputs. In other words, the nFSM model is geared towards problems whose output is specified by labeling the graph's nodes, whereas the output in the MM problem requires assigning (binary) labels to the graph's edges.

This obstacle is tackled by slightly extending the nFSM model in a manner that enhances it with the power to cope with edge labeling problems such as MM without violating model requirements (M1)–(M4) (see Section 1). To that end, we augment the 8-tuple $\Pi = \langle Q, Q_I, Q_O, \Sigma, \sigma_0, b, \lambda, \delta \rangle$ introduced in Section 2 with a finite *internal alphabet* Γ and with a *port transition function*

$$\eta : Q \times \Gamma \times \Sigma \to 2^\Gamma .$$

We also change the function $\lambda : Q \to \Sigma$ to $\lambda : Q \to \Gamma$ and the initial letter $\sigma_0 \in \Sigma$ to $\gamma_0 \in \Gamma$.

The new semantics is as follows. While the communication alphabet Σ is still used for message transmission, each port now contains some letter of the internal alphabet Γ, hence the function λ now maps Q to a query letter in Γ. Given some node $v \in V$ and port $\psi_v(u)$ corresponding to neighbor u of v, the port transition function η takes the current state $q \in Q$ of v, the letter $\gamma \in \Gamma$ currently stored in $\psi_v(u)$, and the new letter $\sigma \in \Sigma$ delivered to v from u, and returns some letter $\gamma' \in \Gamma$ chosen uniformly at random from $\eta(q, \gamma, \sigma) \subseteq \Gamma$; the letter γ' is then stored in $\psi_v(u)$ (replacing γ). This can be viewed as a FSM that controls the letters stored in each one of v's ports (the same FSM for all ports).

Using this *extended nFSM* model, we can now specify edge labels through the ports of the nodes residing in output states. In particular, an MM protocol can specify its output matching M as follows. The protocol designer designates some letter $\gamma_{out} \in \Gamma$ for the purpose of outputting M. Node $v \in V$ residing in an output state may have at most one port $\Psi_v(u)$ storing the letter γ_{out} in which case it is guaranteed that port $\Psi_u(v)$ also stores γ_{out}, thus marking that $(u, v) \in M$. Note that this cannot be achieved under the (non extended) nFSM model, where, by definition, if $\psi_v(u)$ stores the letter $\sigma \in \Sigma$ at the end of the execution, then $\psi_w(u)$ also stores σ for every $w \in N(u)$. The proof of the following theorem is deferred to the full version.

THEOREM 6. *There exists an extended nFSM protocol with bounding parameter $b = 2$ that computes an MM for any n-node graph in time $O(\log^2 n)$.*

5. CONCLUSIONS

Motivated by networks of sub-microprocessor devices, we introduce the new nFSM model that depicts a network of randomized finite state machines whose communication relies on aggregating the messages from all neighbors according to the one-two-many scheme. Although each individual node in this model is, by design, much weaker than the the nodes under the standard message passing model, we show that the collaborative power of the network's nodes is still sufficiently strong to allow efficient algorithms for some of the most important distributed computing problems.

Given the dynamic nature of many biological cellular networks, it would be very interesting to extend the nFSM model to networks that may undergo failures and/or dynamic insertions. Among the open questions that fascinate us in that regard are: What problems can be solved efficiently in such dynamic scenarios? Is is still possible to locally synchronize the nFSM model in the face of dynamic changes?

6. ACKNOWLEDGMENTS

We would like to thank Jasmin Smula for her help with various parts of this paper.

7. REFERENCES

[1] H. Abelson, D. Allen, D. Coore, C. Hanson, G. Homsy, T. F. Knight, Jr., R. Nagpal, E. Rauch, G. J. Sussman, and R. Weiss. Amorphous computing. *Commun. ACM*, 43(5):74–82, May 2000.

[2] Y. Afek, N. Alon, Z. Bar-Joseph, A. Cornejo, B. Haeupler, and F. Kuhn. Beeping a maximal independent set. In *DISC*, pages 32–50, 2011.

[3] Y. Afek, N. Alon, O. Barad, E. Hornstein, N. Barkai, and Z. Bar-Joseph. A Biological Solution to a Fundamental Distributed Computing Problem. *Science*, 331(6014):183–185, Jan. 2011.

[4] I. F. Akyildiz, J. M. Jornet, and M. Pierobon. Nanonetworks: a new frontier in communications. *Commun. ACM*, 54(11):84–89, Nov. 2011.

[5] N. Alon, L. Babai, and A. Itai. A fast and simple randomized parallel algorithm for the maximal independent set problem. *J. Algorithms*, 7:567–583, December 1986.

[6] D. Angluin, J. Aspnes, Z. Diamadi, M. J. Fischer, and R. Peralta. Computation in networks of passively mobile finite-state sensors. *Distributed Computing*, pages 235–253, mar 2006.

[7] D. Angluin, J. Aspnes, and D. Eisenstat. Fast computation by population protocols with a leader. *Distributed Computing*, 21(3):183–199, sep 2008.

[8] J. Aspnes and E. Ruppert. An introduction to population protocols. In B. Garbinato, H. Miranda, and L. Rodrigues, editors, *Middleware for Network Eccentric and Mobile Applications*, pages 97–120. Springer-Verlag, 2009.

[9] B. Awerbuch. Complexity of network synchronization. *J. ACM*, 32(4):804–823, 1985.

[10] B. Awerbuch, B. Patt-Shamir, D. Peleg, and M. E. Saks. Adapting to asynchronous dynamic networks (extended abstract). In *STOC*, pages 557–570, 1992.

[11] B. Awerbuch and D. Peleg. Network synchronization with polylogarithmic overhead. In *FOCS*, pages 514–522, 1990.

[12] L. Barenboim and M. Elkin. Distributed (delta+1)-coloring in linear (in delta) time. In *STOC*, pages 111–120, 2009.

[13] L. Barenboim and M. Elkin. Deterministic distributed vertex coloring in polylogarithmic time. *J. ACM*, 58(5):23, 2011.

[14] L. Barenboim, M. Elkin, S. Pettie, and J. Schneider. The locality of distributed symmetry breaking. *CoRR*, abs/1202.1983, 2012.

[15] M. Bellare, O. Goldreich, and M. Sudan. Free bits, pcps, and nonapproximability-towards tight results. *SIAM J. Comput.*, 27(3):804–915, 1998.

[16] Y. Benenson. Biomolecular computing systems: principles, progress and potential. *Nat Rev Genet*, 13(7):455–468, July 2012.

[17] Y. Benenson, T. Paz-Elizur, R. Adar, E. Keinan, Z. Livneh, and E. Shapiro. Programmable and autonomous computing machine made of biomolecules. *Nature*, 414(6862):430–434, Nov. 2001.

[18] D. Brand and P. Zafiropulo. On communicating finite-state machines. *J. ACM*, 30:323–342, April 1983.

[19] I. Chatzigiannakis and P. G. Spirakis. The dynamics of probabilistic population protocols. In *DISC*, DISC '08, pages 498–499, Berlin, Heidelberg, 2008. Springer-Verlag.

[20] I. Chlamtac and S. Kutten. On Broadcasting in Radio Networks–Problem Analysis and Protocol Design. *Communications, IEEE Transactions on [legacy, pre - 1988]*, 33(12):1240–1246, 1985.

[21] R. Cole and U. Vishkin. Deterministic coin tossing with applications to optimal parallel list ranking. *Inf. Control*, 70(1):32–53, July 1986.

[22] A. Cornejo and F. Kuhn. Deploying wireless networks with beeps. In *DISC*, pages 148–162, 2010.

[23] Y. Emek, J. Seidel, and R. Wattenhofer. Distributed computability: Anonymity, revocability, and randomization. A manuscript.

[24] R. Flury and R. Wattenhofer. Slotted Programming for Sensor Networks. In *IPSN*, April 2010.

[25] M. Gardner. The fantastic combinations of John Conway's new solitaire game 'life'. *Scientific American*, 223(4):120–123, 1970.

[26] P. Gordon. Numerical Cognition Without Words: Evidence from Amazonia. *Science*, 306(5695):496–499, Oct. 2004.

[27] A. Israeli and A. Itai. A fast and simple randomized parallel algorithm for maximal matching. *Inf. Process. Lett.*, 22(2):77–80, 1986.

[28] K. Kothapalli, C. Scheideler, M. Onus, and C. Schindelhauer. Distributed Coloring in $\tilde{O}(\sqrt{\log n})$ Bit Rounds. In *IPDPS*, 2006.

[29] F. Kuhn. Weak graph colorings: distributed algorithms and applications. In *SPAA*, pages 138–144, New York, NY, USA, 2009. ACM.

[30] F. Kuhn, T. Moscibroda, and R. Wattenhofer. What cannot be computed locally! In *PODC*, pages 300–309, 2004.

[31] C. Lenzen and R. Wattenhofer. MIS on trees. In *PODC*, pages 41–48, New York, NY, USA, 2011.

[32] N. Linial. Locality in distributed graph algorithms. *SIAM J. Comput.*, 21:193–201, Feb. 1992.

[33] M. Luby. A simple parallel algorithm for the maximal independent set problem. *SIAM J. Comput.*, 15:1036–1055, November 1986.

[34] N. A. Lynch. *Distributed Algorithms*. Morgan Kaufmann, 1st edition, 1996.

[35] Y. Métivier, J. M. Robson, N. Saheb-Djahromi, and A. Zemmari. About randomised distributed graph colouring and graph partition algorithms. *Inf. Comput.*, 208(11):1296–1304, Nov. 2010.

[36] Y. Métivier, J. M. Robson, N. Saheb-Djahromi, and A. Zemmari. An optimal bit complexity randomised distributed MIS algorithm. *Distributed Computing*, 23(5-6):331–340, Jan. 2011.

[37] O. Michail, I. Chatzigiannakis, and P. G. Spirakis. *New Models for Population Protocols*. Synthesis Lectures on Distributed Computing Theory. Morgan & Claypool Publishers, 2011.

[38] K. Nakamura. Asynchronous cellular automata and their computational ability. *Syst Comput Controls*, 5(5):58–66, 1974.

[39] C. L. Nehaniv. Asynchronous automata networks can emulate any synchronous automata network. *Journal of Algebra*, pages 1–21, Dec. 2003.

[40] D. Peleg. *Distributed computing: a locality-sensitive approach*. Society for Industrial and Applied Mathematics, Philadelphia, PA, USA, 2000.

[41] D. Sadava. *Life: The Science of Biology*. Sinauer Associates, 2011.

[42] J. Schneider and R. Wattenhofer. An optimal maximal independent set algorithm for bounded-independence graphs. *Distributed Computing*, 22(5-6):349–361, 2010.

[43] J. Schneider and R. Wattenhofer. Distributed Coloring Depending on the Chromatic Number or the Neighborhood Growth. In *SIROCCO*, June 2011.

[44] J. Suomela. Survey of local algorithms. *To appear in ACM Computing Surveys*, 2012. http://www.cs.helsinki.fi/u/josuomel/doc/local-survey.pdf.

[45] M. Szegedy and S. Vishwanathan. Locality based graph coloring. In *STOC*, pages 201–207, 1993.

[46] L. G. Valiant. Parallel computation. In *7th IBM Symp. on Math. Foundations of Computer Science*, 1982.

[47] J. von Neumann. *Theory of Self-Reproducing Automata*. University of Illinois Press, Champaign, IL, USA, 1966.

[48] S. Wolfram. *A new kind of science*. Wolfram Media, Champaign, Illinois, 2002.

Feedback from Nature: an Optimal Distributed Algorithm for Maximal Independent Set Selection

Alex Scott
Mathematical Institute
University of Oxford, UK
scott@maths.ox.ac.uk

Peter Jeavons
Dept. of Computer Science
University of Oxford, UK
peter.jeavons@cs.ox.ac.uk

Lei Xu
Dept. of Computer Science
University of Oxford, UK
lei.xu@cs.ox.ac.uk

ABSTRACT

Maximal Independent Set selection is a fundamental problem in distributed computing. A novel probabilistic algorithm for this problem has recently been proposed by Afek et al, inspired by the study of the way that developing cells in the fly become specialised. The algorithm they propose is simple and robust, but not as efficient as previous approaches: the expected time complexity is $O(\log^2 n)$. Here we first show that the approach of Afek et al cannot achieve better efficiency than this across all networks, no matter how the global probability values are chosen.

However, we then propose a new algorithm that incorporates another important feature of the biological system: the probability value at each node is adapted using local feedback from neighbouring nodes. Our new algorithm retains all the advantages of simplicity and robustness, but also achieves the optimal efficiency of $O(\log n)$ expected time. The new algorithm also has only a constant message complexity per node.

Categories and Subject Descriptors

F.2.2 [**Analysis of Algorithms and Problem Complexity**]: Nonnumerical Algorithms and Problems—*Computations on discrete structures*; G.2.2 [**Discrete mathematics**]: Graph Theory—*Graph Algorithms*

General Terms

Algorithms, Theory, Performance

Keywords

beeping model; expected complexity; feedback; intercellular signalling; MIS; message complexity; randomised algorithms

1. INTRODUCTION

One of the most fundamental problems in distributed computing is to choose a set of local leaders in a network of connected processors so that every processor is either a leader or connected to a leader, and no two leaders are connected to each other. This problem is known as the maximal independent set (MIS) selection problem and has been extensively studied [16, 15, 3, 13, 14, 19, 18].

Different maximal independent sets for the same network can vary greatly in size. In contrast to the MIS selection problem, the related problem of finding a *maximum size* independent set (MaxIS) is notoriously hard. It is equivalent to finding a maximum clique in the complementary network, and is therefore **NP**-hard [12] (and hard to approximate [10]). However, computing an arbitrary MIS (not necessarily of the maximum possible size) using a centralised sequential algorithm is trivial: simply scan the nodes in arbitrary order. If a node u does not violate independence, add u to the MIS. If u violates independence, discard it. Hence the real challenge is to compute such an MIS efficiently in a distributed way with no centralised control. Here we present a new distributed approach to this problem which achieves optimal efficiency.

Afek *et al.* have recently pointed out the similarity between the MIS selection problem and neural precursor selection during the development of the nervous system of the fruit fly *Drosophila* [2]. During development, certain cells in the pre-neural clusters of the fly specialise to become sensory organ precursor (SOP) cells, which later develop into cells attached to small bristles (microchaetes) on the fly that are used to sense the environment. During the first stage of this developmental process each cell either becomes an SOP or a neighbour of an SOP, and no two SOPs are neighbours. These observed conditions are identical to the formal requirements in the maximal independent set selection problem (see Figure 1).

Afek *et al.* also pointed out that the method used by the fly to select the SOPs appears to be rather different from standard known algorithms for choosing an MIS [16, 3, 18]. These algorithms rely on arithmetic calculations and precise numerical comparisons, and generally require explicit information about the number of active neighbours that each node in the network currently has. They also generally rely on exchanging complex messages representing precise numerical information. By contrast, the cells of the fly appear to solve the problem without clear central control using only simple local interactions between certain membrane-bound proteins, notably the proteins Notch and Delta [6, 7, 8].

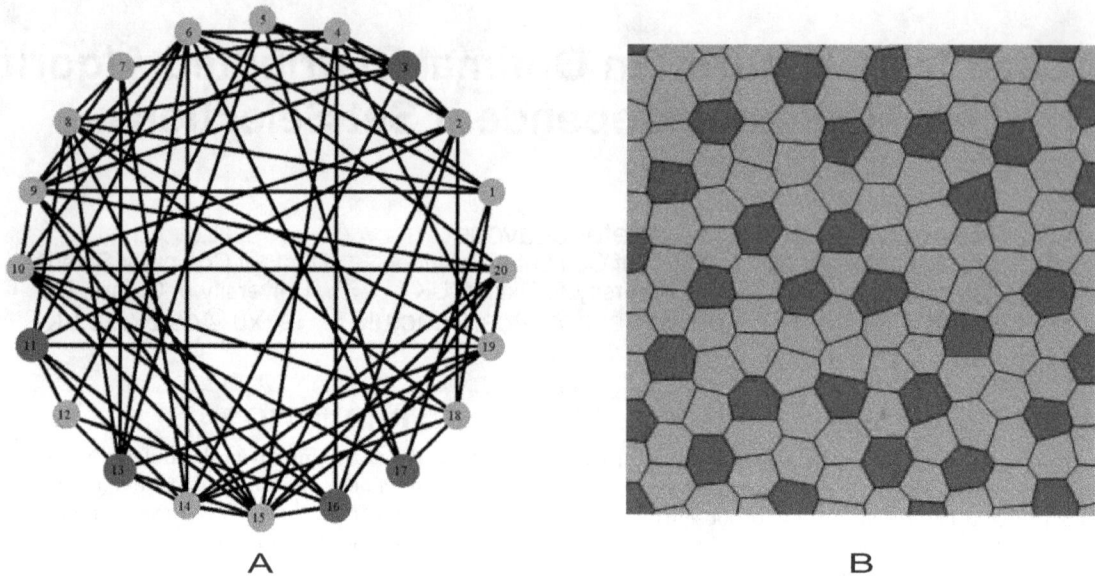

Figure 1: (A) An MIS selected from a random undirected graph with 20 nodes. The set of vertices $v_3, v_{11}, v_{13}, v_{16}, v_{17}$ is an MIS because no two nodes in this set are adjacent, and no further node of the graph can be added to this set without violating this property. (B) The selection of SOP cells in the fly appears to be formally similar to an MIS selection proble: each cell either becomes an SOP or a neighbour of an SOP, and no two SOPs are neighbours.

Afek *et al.* compared statistics derived from the observed SOP selection times with several in silico models for stochastic accumulation of Notch and Delta. They finally constructed a consistent model with stochastic rate change that did not require knowledge about the number of active neighbours and used only single-bit (threshold) communication. Based on this stochastic rate change model, they proposed a new general-purpose distributed algorithm for solving the MIS selection problem in an arbitrary network [2].

The algorithm proposed by Afek *et al.* is fully synchronous and operates over discrete time steps. At each step, each node may choose, with a certain probability (that varies over time), to signal to all its neighbours that it wishes to join the independent set. If a node chooses to issue this signal, and none of its neighbours choose to do so in the same time step, then it successfully joins the independent set, and becomes inactive, along with all its immediate neighbours. However if any of these neighbouring nodes issue the same signal at the same time step, then the cell does not succeed in joining the independent set at that step. This process is repeated until all nodes eventually become inactive. This algorithm is remarkably simple: it requires no knowledge about the number of active neighbours and uses only one-bit messages. The computation at each individual node can be described by a simple automaton, as shown in Figure 2.

As originally presented [2], the algorithm uses a sequence of gradually increasing global probability values calculated from the total number of nodes of the graph and its maximum degree. The algorithm was further refined by Afek *et al.* in a later paper [1]. In the later version the probability values are chosen according to a fixed pattern, so that individual nodes require no knowledge about the size of the graph or its maximum degree.

However, in both versions the new approach they propose has a major drawback: the expected number of time steps required is $O(\log^2 n)$. This makes the algorithm usable, but not as fast as previous algorithms. The most well-known distributed algorithm for maximal independent set selection is the elegant randomized algorithm of [3, 16], generally known as Luby's algorithm, which has an expected running time which is $O(\log n)$. Several other previous algorithms have also achieved an upper bound of $O(\log n)$ on the expected number of steps required to compute a maximal independent set, and this has been shown to be the best possible bound for all networks when using 1-bit messages [18].

To investigate the running time in practice, we implemented the refined version of the algorithm, described in [1], where the probabilities are chosen by repeatedly sweeping across a wider and wider range of different values. Following the scheme specified in [1], we divide the computation into *phases*, numbered $1, 2, 3, \ldots$. Each phase k consists of $k + 1$ time steps. The value of the probability p varies as follows: during each phase k the value of p is 1 initially, and gets halved after each successive time step in phase k. Thus, the value of p during the computation will take the following values in successive time steps: $\underline{1}, \underline{1}, \frac{1}{2}, \underline{1}, \frac{1}{2}, \frac{1}{4}, \underline{1}, \frac{1}{2}, \frac{1}{4}, \frac{1}{8}, \underline{1}, \frac{1}{2}, \frac{1}{4}, \frac{1}{8}, \frac{1}{16}, \ldots$ (where the underlinings indicate the phases). We ran this version of the algorithm on random networks with different numbers of nodes, where each edge is present with probability $1/2$. We found that the mean number of time steps required to complete the algorithm and choose a maximal independent set in these networks was close to the exact value of $\log^2 n$, where n is the number of nodes (and the logarithm is to base 2). These experimental results are shown as the upper line of data points in Figure 4.

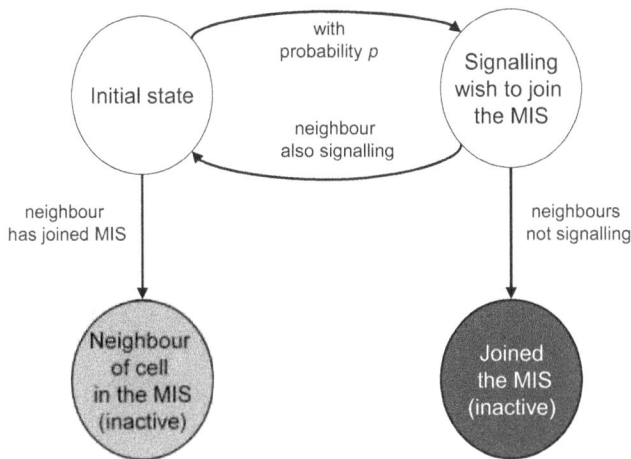

Figure 2: Abstract state-based description of the process at each node. At each step a node may signal that it wishes to join the independent set by moving to the state at the top right with probability p (which varies with time). It then responds to the signals from neighbouring cells.

2. RESULTS

In this paper we investigate whether the simple algorithmic approach proposed by Afek *et al.* can be improved to make it competitive with the most efficient standard approaches in the number of steps required. Our first analytical result gives a negative answer to this question by showing that computing a maximal independent set using this algorithmic approach will require more than some constant multiple of $\log^2 n$ time steps on some families of networks with n nodes *whatever sequence of global probability values is used* (see Theorem 1).

Does this mean that the simple mechanism used by biological cells for "fine-grained" pattern formation has an inherently lower efficiency compared with carefully engineered algorithms such as Luby's algorithm? To answer that question we looked more closely at the mechanism of "fine-grained" pattern formation during cell development.

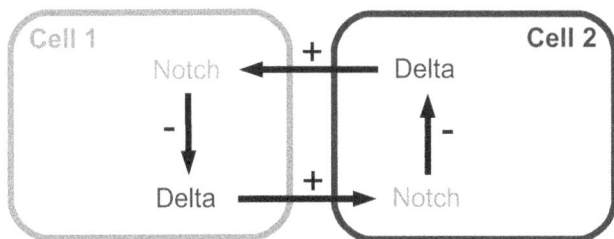

Figure 3: Notch-Delta signalling constructs a positive feedback loop to amplify small differences between cells. Any increase in the concentration of Delta in cell 2 leads to increased activation of Notch in cell 1, which then leads to a decreased activation of Delta in cell 1. This feedback loop leads to mutually exclusive signalling states in the two cells.

The Notch-Delta signalling pathway provides a communication channel between neighbouring cells during development. It is thought to play a critical role in the formation of "fine-grained" patterns in the development of many organisms [21, 9], helping to generate distinct cell fates among groups of initially equivalent neighbouring cells. In particular, many studies have shown that Notch-Delta signalling regulates the selection of *Drosophila* neural precursors from groups of equipotent proneural cells in a way which resembles the MIS selection problem [5, 4, 21]. The transmembrane protein Delta has been shown to have two activities: Delta in one cell can bind to, and transactivate, the transmembrane protein Notch in its neighbouring cells [5]; Delta and Notch in the same cell mutually inactivate each other [11, 17]. The interaction of the transmembrane proteins Notch and Delta constitutes a positive feedback mechanism which generates an ultrasensitive switch between two mutually exclusive signalling states: *sending* (high Delta/low Notch) and *receiving* (high Notch/low Delta). A slight excess of Delta production in one cell can generate a strong signalling bias in one direction: the cell becomes a sender and its neighbours become receivers [21]. At the multicellular level, this lateral inhibition mechanism can break the symmetry among cells and amplify small differences between neighbouring cells, thus facilitating pattern formation (see Figure 3).

It is clear that the cells participating in this developmental process do not act autonomously - they continuously adjust their behaviour based on the signals they receive from the cells around them. We abstracted from the positive feedback mechanism of Notch-Delta signalling to construct the distributed algorithm described in Figure 5. It uses similar processing at each node to the algorithm of Afek et al, but each node now has its own independently updated probability value. These values all start at $1/2$, but are decreased by a fixed factor whenever one or more neighbouring cells signal that they wish to join the independent set. They are also increased by the same factor (up to a maximum of $1/2$) whenever no neighbouring cell issues such a signal.

Our main result shows that choosing the probabilities in this way, using a simple local feedback mechanism, gives an algorithm whose expected time to compute a maximal independent set is only $O(\log n)$ (see Corollary 5). Hence this new simple algorithm performs as well as all previous algorithms for this problem, and, indeed, as well as the theoretical optimal performance.

To illustrate this result we implemented the new algorithm with the probability p at each node varying as follows: p is initially set to $1/2$. At any time step where there is a signal from at least one neighbouring cell the value of p is halved. At all other time steps it is doubled (up to a maximum of $1/2$). We then ran this new algorithm on random networks with different numbers of nodes, where each edge is present with probability $1/2$. We found that the mean number of rounds required to complete the algorithm and choose a maximal independent set in these networks was now close to $2.5 \log n$, where n is the number of nodes (and the logarithm is again to base 2). These experimental results are shown as the lower line of data points in Figure 4.

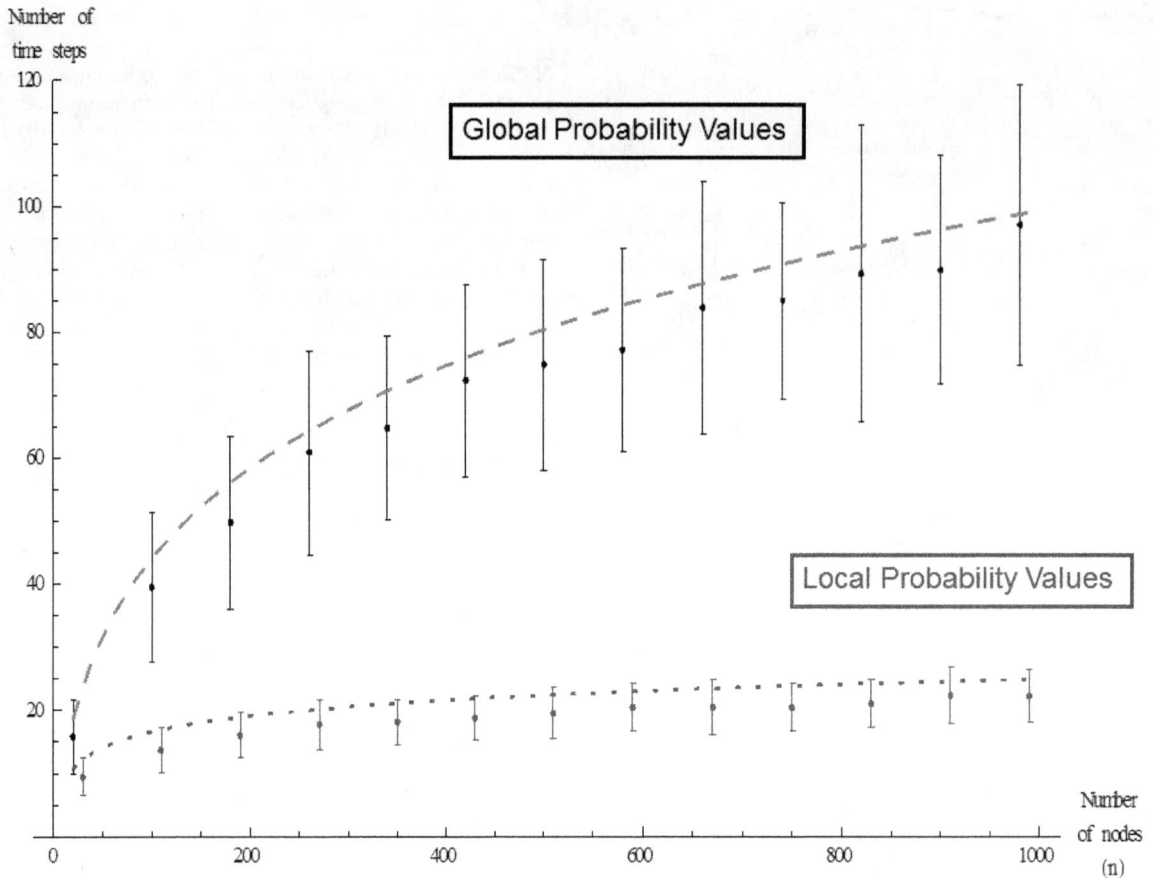

Figure 4: Actual performance of the computation of the MIS on random networks where each edge is present with probability $1/2$. The upper points (black) show the mean number of time steps taken by the algorithm over 100 trials with global sweeping probabilities as specified in [1]. The lower points (blue) the same for locally chosen probabilities with feedback as proposed here. Error bars indicate standard deviations over 100 trials in each case. The upper dashed line shows the value of $\log^2 n$ and the lower dotted line shows the value of $2.5 \log n$ for comparison (all logarithms to base 2).

```
 1. Set local value of p = 1/2;
 2. while active, at each time step do

 3.     FIRST EXCHANGE:
 4.     With probability p,
            start signalling to all neighbours;
 5.     if any neighbour is signalling then
 6.         Stop signalling (if started);
 7.         p ← p/2
 8.     else
 9.         p ← min{2p, 1/2}

10.     SECOND EXCHANGE:
11.     if signalling then
12.         Join the MIS;
13.         Terminate (become inactive)
14.     else if any neighbour signalling then
15.         Terminate (become inactive)
```

Figure 5: The new algorithm we propose with local probabilities at each node

3. LOWER BOUND FOR GLOBALLY CHOSEN PROBABILITY VALUES

Following [1], we refer to the signalling at each node as "beeping". At each time step, each node chooses to beep with a certain probability, and this beep is immediately heard by each of its neighbours.

In this section we consider the class of algorithms described in [2] where each node runs through a preset sequence $p_1, p_2, \ldots$ of probabilities for beeping. We assume that all nodes beep with probability p_i in the ith time step. Our first result gives an explicit family of graphs with $O(n)$ vertices, for which *any* such algorithm takes at least a fixed multiple of $\log^2 n$ steps. (We generally omit floors and ceilings for clarity.)

THEOREM 1. *There is a constant $a > 0$ such that the following holds. Let G be the graph consisting of $n^{1/3}$ disjoint copies of the complete graph K_d, for each $d = 1, \ldots, n^{1/3}$. Let $T = a \log^2 n$ and let $p_1, \ldots, p_T$ be any sequence of probabilities. Then with high probability, the algorithm using the probability sequence $p_1, \ldots, p_T$ does not terminate within T steps.*

PROOF. Fix d, and consider a copy K of K_d. The probability that some vertex of K is added to the independent set at the ith step is the probability that exactly one vertex of K beeps, and so equals

$$dp_i(1 - p_i)^{d-1} \leq dp_i \exp(-(d-1)p_i). \quad (1)$$

Note that the function xe^{-x} is bounded on $[0, \infty)$, and has maximum $1/e$ (at $x = 1$). So for $d > 2$,

$$dp_i \exp(-(d-1)p_i) = \frac{d}{d-1} \cdot (d-1)p_i \exp(-(d-1)p_i) \leq \frac{3}{2e}.$$

Also, for $x \in [0, 3/2e]$, we have $1 - x \geq \exp(-2x)$. So, by inequality 1, the probability that all the vertices of K are still active after T steps is at least

$$\prod_{i=1}^{T} \left(1 - dp_i e^{-(d-1)p_i}\right) \geq \prod_{i=1}^{T} \exp(-2dp_i e^{-(d-1)p_i})$$

$$= \exp\left(-\sum_{i=1}^{T} 2dp_i e^{-(d-1)p_i}\right)$$

$$\geq \exp\left(-\sum_{i=1}^{T} 6dp_i e^{-dp_i}\right).$$

The last inequality follows from the fact that $e^{p_i} \leq e \leq 3$.

Hence if $\sum_{i=1}^{T} 6dp_i e^{-dp_i} < \frac{1}{4} \log n$ then the nodes of K remain active with probability at least $n^{-1/4}$. In that case the probability that the nodes in all the copies of K_d become inactive is at most

$$(1 - n^{-1/4})^{n^{1/3}} \leq \exp(-n^{1/12}),$$

and so with high probability (i.e, tending to 1 as $n \to \infty$) the algorithm fails to terminate.

It follows that we may assume that $\sum_{i=1}^{T} 6dp_i e^{-dp_i} > \frac{1}{4} \log n$ for every choice of $d \geq 3$. We will show that this implies $T = \Omega(\log^2 n)$.

Let us choose d at random. We define a probability distribution for d by

$$\mathbb{P}[d = r] = \frac{c}{r \log n},$$

for $r = 3, \ldots, n^{1/3}$ (where c is a normalizing constant: note that $c = \Theta(1)$, as $\sum_{i=1}^{n^{1/3}} 1/r = \Theta(\log n)$). Then, for any $p \in [0, 1]$,

$$\mathbb{E}[dpe^{-dp}] = \sum_{r=3}^{n^{1/3}} \frac{c}{r \log n} rpe^{-rp} \leq \frac{c}{\log n} \sum_{r=0}^{\infty} pe^{-rp}.$$

But $\sum_{r=0}^{\infty} pe^{-rp} = p/(1 - e^{-p}) < 2$, as $p \in [0, 1]$; so we have $\mathbb{E}[dpe^{-dp}] < 2c/\log n$. By linearity of expectation, choosing a random d, we have

$$\mathbb{E}\left[\sum_{i=1}^{T} 6dp_i e^{-dp_i}\right] < 12cT/\log n.$$

Hence there is some value of d for which

$$\sum_{i=1}^{T} 6dp_i e^{-dp_i} < 12cT/\log n.$$

By the argument above, this quantity must be at least $\frac{1}{4} \log n$, and so we must have $T = \Omega(\log^2 n)$. $\square$

4. UPPER BOUND FOR LOCALLY CHOSEN PROBABILITY VALUES

In this section we consider the new class of algorithms described in Figure 5, where each node maintains its own independent probability value which varies over time.

Definition 1. We define the following distributed algorithm for computing a maximal independent set in an arbitrary graph.

At each time step t, there is an integer $n(v, t)$ attached to each vertex v, and v beeps with probability $2^{-n(t,v)}$. We set $n(0, v) = 1$ for every v.

At each time step, we update according to the following local rules:

- If v beeps and no neighbour of v beeps, then v is added to the independent set and becomes inactive (along with its neighbours).

- If some neighbour w of v beeps, and no neighbour of w beeps, then v becomes inactive (as w is added to the independent set).

- If v does not beep and no neighbour of v beeps, we set $n(t + 1, v) = \max\{n(t, v) - 1, 1\}$.

- If some neighbour of v beeps, but no neighbour is added to the independent set, we set $n(t + 1, v) = n(t, v) + 1$.

It follows from the analysis of [2] that if this algorithm terminates (i.e., all nodes become inactive) then it correctly identifies an MIS. The only question is the number of time steps required.

Note that, unlike Luby's algorithm [3, 16], it is not true that at every time step we can expect at least some constant fraction of the edges to be incident to nodes that become inactive at that step. For example, in a complete graph nodes will only become inactive when exactly one node beeps. The probability of this happening at the first step is only $n/2^n$, so at the first step the expected number of edges that are incident to nodes that become inactive is only $n^3/2^{n+1}$. Hence we must carry out a more detailed analysis over a sequence of time steps.

THEOREM 2. *There is a constant K_0 such that the following holds: For any graph G with n vertices, and any $k \geq 1$, the algorithm in Definition 1 terminates in at most $K_0(k+1)\log n$ steps, with probability at least $1 - \epsilon$, where ϵ is $O(1/n^k)$.*

Before beginning the proof of Theorem 2, it will be useful to define some notation and record a few simple facts.

Let us define a measure $\mu_t(\cdot)$ on $V = V(G)$ by setting

$$\mu_t(v) = \mathbb{P}[v \text{ beeps at time } t] = 2^{-n(t,v)}.$$

(By convention, we set $\mu_t(v) = 0$ if v is inactive at time t; this simplifies notation, while allowing us to ignore the contribution of inactive vertices.) For any $S \subseteq V$ we write $\mu_t(S)$ for $\sum_{v \in S} \mu_t(v)$.

We will frequently use the following inequality, which holds for $\delta \in [0, 1]$:

$$1 - \delta \leq \exp(-\delta) \leq 1 - \delta/2. \qquad (2)$$

We will also need the following Chernoff-type inequality: if X is a sum of Bernoulli random variables, and $\mathbb{E}X = \mu$, then for every $\delta > 0$,

$$\mathbb{P}[X > \mu + \delta] \leq \exp(-\delta^2/(2\mu + 2\delta/3)).$$

In particular,

$$\mathbb{P}[X > 2\mu] \leq \exp(-\mu/3). \qquad (3)$$

We will also need the following simple bounds.

PROPOSITION 3. *For any set S of vertices,*

$$\exp(-2\mu_t(S)) \leq \mathbb{P}[\text{no vertex in } S \text{ beeps at time } t]$$
$$\leq \exp(-\mu_t(S)).$$

PROOF. By inequality (2), the probability that no vertex in S beeps at time t is

$$\prod_{v \in S}(1 - \mu_t(v)) \leq \prod_{v \in S} \exp(-\mu_t(v)) = \exp(-\mu_t(S)).$$

On the other hand,

$$\prod_{v \in S}(1 - \mu_t(v)) \geq \prod_{v \in S} \exp(-2\mu_t(v)) = \exp(-2\mu_t(S)),$$

where the last inequality used (2) and the fact that $\mu_t(x) \leq 1/2$ for every x and t. $\square$

The set of vertices adjacent to a given vertex x will be called the set of *neighbours* of x, and denoted $\Gamma(x)$. We will say that a vertex x at time t is λ-*light* if $\mu_t(\Gamma(x)) \leq \lambda$, that is, if the total weight of its neighbours is not too large (and so it is not too likely to hear a beep at time t). Otherwise we say that x is λ-*heavy*. Note that a fixed vertex may move back and forth between being heavy and light over time.

Our first result shows that a light vertex is quite likely to be added to the independent set if it beeps.

LEMMA 4. *Let S be a set of λ-light vertices at time t. Then the probability that some vertex in S is added to the independent set at time t is at least $e^{-2\lambda}(1 - e^{-\mu_t(S)})$.*

PROOF. Let us order the vertices of S as $s_1, \ldots, s_r$. Then the probability that some vertex of S is added to the independent set at time t is at least the probability that the earliest vertex of S that beeps is added to the independent set. For $i = 1, \ldots, r$, define events E_i and F_i by

$$E_i = (s_i \text{ beeps}; s_1, \ldots, s_{i-1} \text{ do not beep})$$

$$F_i = (\text{no neighbour of } s_i \text{ beeps}).$$

The events $E_i \cap F_i$ are pairwise disjoint, so the probability that the earliest vertex of S that beeps is added to the independent set is

$$\mathbb{P}[\bigcup_{i=1}^{r}(E_i \cap F_i)] = \sum_{i=1}^{r} \mathbb{P}[E_i \cap F_i] = \sum_{i=1}^{r} \mathbb{P}[E_i]\mathbb{P}[F_i|E_i].$$

It is easily seen that $\mathbb{P}[F_i|E_i] \geq \mathbb{P}[F_i]$, and so by Proposition 3 we have

$$\mathbb{P}[F_i|E_i] \geq \mathbb{P}[F_i] \geq \exp(-2\mu_t(\Gamma(s_i))) \geq \exp(-2\lambda),$$

as s_i is λ-light, and so

$$\sum_{i=1}^{r} \mathbb{P}[E_i]\mathbb{P}[F_i|E_i] \geq \exp(-2\lambda)\sum_{i=1}^{r} \mathbb{P}[E_i].$$

But $\sum_{i=1}^{r} \mathbb{P}[E_i]$ is simply the probability that some vertex in S beeps, and so by Proposition 3 is at least $1 - \exp(-\mu_t(S))$. Thus the probability that some vertex of S is added to the independent set at time t is at least

$$\exp(-2\lambda)\sum_{i=1}^{r} \mathbb{P}[E_i] \geq e^{-2\lambda}(1 - e^{-\mu_t(S)}).$$

$\square$

PROOF OF THEOREM 2. Fix a vertex v. Let $K_0 = 10^{11}$ and set $K = K_0(k+1)$. Let $\alpha = 10^{-3}$, $\beta = 1/50$ and $\lambda = 7$.

We shall show that, with failure probability $O(1/n^{k+1})$, v becomes inactive within $K\log n = (k+1) \cdot K_0 \log n$ steps. Taking a union bound over all n choices of v, it follows that with failure probability $O(1/n^k)$ every vertex becomes inactive and the algorithm terminates within $K\log n$ steps, which proves the theorem.

For $t \geq 1$, let

$$L_t = L_t(v) = \{x \in \Gamma(v) : \mu_t(\Gamma(x)) \leq \lambda\}$$
$$H_t = H_t(v) = \{x \in \Gamma(v) : \mu_t(\Gamma(x)) > \lambda\}.$$

Thus $L_t(v) \cup H_t(v)$ partitions the neighbourhood of v into light and heavy vertices. We will follow the behaviour of $\mu_t(L_t)$ and $\mu_t(H_t)$ over time.

The idea of the argument is roughly as follows: if $\mu_t(L_t)$ is large at many time steps, then by Lemma 4 it is very likely that some neighbour of v will be added to the independent set on one of these occasions, leading to v becoming inactive. If this does not happen, then $\mu_t(L_t)$ will be small most of the time, and we can concentrate on H_t. Now vertices that are heavy at time t are likely to hear beeps and so drop in weight (as their beeping probability drops); it will follow that with high probability $\mu_{t+1}(H_t)$ is a constant factor smaller than $\mu_t(H_t)$ most of the time. Now we look at the evolution of $\mu_t(\Gamma(v))$: it may be large and increasing for some small fraction of the time, but mostly it is either shrinking or else it is already small. It will follow that most of the time $\mu_t(\Gamma(v))$ is small. But then most of the time v will not hear beeps. Since this also implies that $\mu_t(v)$ will be large most of the time, it is very likely that v will beep and not hear any beeps, and so get added to the independent set.

At each time step t, we consider the following four possible events:

(E1) $\mu_t(L_t) \geq \alpha$ ['$\Gamma(v)$ has a significant weight of light neighbours']

(E2) $\mu_t(L_t) < \alpha$ and $\mu_t(\Gamma(v)) \leq \beta$ ['v is very light']

(E3) $\mu_t(L_t) < \alpha$, $\mu_t(\Gamma(v)) > \beta$ and $\mu_{t+1}(\Gamma(v)) \leq \frac{1}{\sqrt{2}}\mu_t(\Gamma(v))$ ['the neighbourhood of v shrinks significantly in weight during step t']

(E4) $\mu_t(L_t) < \alpha$, $\mu_t(\Gamma(v)) > \beta$ and $\mu_{t+1}(\Gamma(v)) > \frac{1}{\sqrt{2}}\mu_t(\Gamma(v))$ ['the neighbourhood of v does not shrink significantly in weight during step t (and may grow)']

Exactly one of these events must occur at each time step. Note that we know whether (E1) or (E2) occur at the beginning of the time step; if neither occurs, then we must look at the beeps to determine which of (E3) and (E4) occurs.

We organize the proof as a series of claims.

CLAIM 1. *With failure probability $O(1/n^{k+1})$, (E1) occurs at most $(K\log n)/40$ times in the first $K\log n$ time steps.*

Each time that (E1) occurs, it follows from Lemma 4 that some vertex of L_t is added to the independent set (and so v becomes inactive and the process at v terminates) with probability at least $e^{-2\lambda}(1 - e^{-\mu_t(L_t)}) \geq e^{-2\lambda}(1 - e^{-\alpha})$. Let $c_1 = e^{-2\lambda}(1 - e^{-\alpha})$: the probability that (E1) occurs $(K\log n)/40$ times without v becoming inactive is at most $(1 - c_1)^{(K\log n)/40} \leq \exp(-(c_1 K_0/40)(k + 1)\log n)$. By our choice of K_0, we have $K_0 > 40/c_1$, so this probability is less than $\exp(-(k+1)\log n) = n^{-(k+1)}$. This proves the claim.

The bad event for us will be (E4), so let us bound the probability that (E4) occurs.

CLAIM 2. *At each time step t, the probability that (E4) occurs is at most $1/80$.*

If (E4) can occur, then we must have $\mu_t(L_t) < \alpha$ and $\mu_t(\Gamma(v)) > \beta$. If $x \in H_t$ then the probability that no neighbour of x beeps at time t is at most $\exp(-\mu_t(\Gamma(x)) \leq \exp(-\lambda)$. Let H_t^0 be the set of vertices in H_t that do not hear a beep at time t, and let $H_t^1 = H_t \setminus H_t^0$. Then $\mathbb{E}[\mu_t(H_t^0)] \leq \exp(-\lambda)\mu_t(H_t)$, and so by Markov's inequality

$$\mathbb{P}[\mu_t(H_t^0) \geq 80\exp(-\lambda)\mu_t(H_t)] \leq 1/80. \qquad (4)$$

Now all vertices in H_t^1 must halve their weight at the next time step, while vertices in L_t and H_t^0 may either halve or double their weight (additionally, some weights may get set to 0 if vertices become inactive). So

$$\mu_{t+1}(\Gamma(v)) \leq \frac{1}{2}\mu_t(H_t^1) + 2\mu_t(H_t^0) + 2\mu_t(L_t)$$
$$= \frac{1}{2}\mu_t(\Gamma(v)) + \frac{3}{2}\mu_t(H_t^0) + \frac{3}{2}\mu_t(L_t)$$

It follows from (4) that, with probability at least $79/80$,

$$\mu_{t+1}(\Gamma(v)) \leq \frac{1}{2}\mu_t(\Gamma(v)) + \frac{3}{2}80e^{-\lambda}\mu_t(H_t) + \frac{3}{2}\mu_t(L_t)$$
$$< \frac{1}{\sqrt{2}}\mu_t(\Gamma(v)),$$

where the final inequality follows from our choices of α, β and λ, as $\mu_t(L_t) < \alpha$ and $\mu_t(\Gamma(v)) > \beta$. Thus the probability that (E4) occurs is at most $1/80$. This proves the claim.

CLAIM 3. *With failure probability $O(1/n^{k+1})$, (E4) occurs at most $(K\log n)/40$ times in the first $K\log n$ time steps.*

At each step, the probability of (E4) depends on the past history of the process. However, by Claim 2, it is always at most $1/80$, and so we can couple occurrences of (E4) with a sequence of independent events each occurring with probability $1/80$. It follows that the number of occurrences of (E4) in the first $K\log n$ time steps is stochastically dominated by a binomial random variable X with parameters $K\log n$ and $1/80$. The probability that (E4) occurs more than $(K\log n)/40$ times is therefore, by (3), at most

$$\mathbb{P}[X > 2\mathbb{E}X] \leq \exp(-\mathbb{E}X/3) \leq \exp(-(K\log n)/240)$$

which is $O(n^{-(k+1)})$, proving the claim.

From Claim 1 and Claim 3, we conclude that with failure probability $O(n^{-(k+1)})$, (E1) and (E4) altogether occur at most $K(\log n)/20$ times in the first $K\log n$ time steps. We next show that, with small failure probability, $\mu_t(\Gamma(v))$ is small most of the time.

CLAIM 4. *With failure probability $O(1/n^{k+1})$, $\mu_t(\Gamma(v)) > 2\beta$ for at most $(K\log n)/6$ time steps in the first $K\log n$ time steps.*

Let T be the set of times $t \geq 1$ at which $\mu_t(\Gamma(v)) > 2\beta$. We decompose T into (maximal) intervals of integers, say as $T_1 \cup \cdots \cup T_r$. Let $T_i = [s_i, t_i]$ be one of these intervals. We colour each integer $t \in T_i$ red if (E1) or (E4) occurred at the previous step, and *blue* if (E3) occurred (note that (E2) cannot occur, as $\mu_{t-1}(\Gamma(v)) \geq \mu_t(\Gamma(v))/2 > \beta$). Let r_i be the number of red elements and b_i the number of blue elements. We have $\mu_t(\Gamma(v)) \leq \mu_{t-1}(\Gamma(v))/\sqrt{2}$ at blue steps, and $\mu_t(\Gamma(v)) \leq 2\mu_{t-1}(\Gamma(v))$ otherwise. So

$$\mu_{t_i}(\Gamma(v)) \leq \mu_{s_i-1}(\Gamma(v)) \cdot 2^{r_i}/\sqrt{2}^{b_i} \leq \mu_{s_i-1}(\Gamma(v)) \cdot 2^{r_i - \frac{1}{2}b_i}.$$

Since $\mu_{t_i}(\Gamma(v)) > 2\beta$ it follows that

$$r_i > \frac{1}{2}b_i + \log_2 2\beta - \log_2(\mu_{s_i-1}(\Gamma(v))).$$

However, $\mu_{s_i-1}(\Gamma(v)) \leq 2\beta$ in all cases where $s_i > 1$, and $\mu_0(\Gamma(v)) < \frac{1}{2}n$. Summing over i, we see that the total number of red elements in T is greater than half the total number of blue elements in T plus $\log_2 2\beta$ minus $\log_2 \frac{1}{2}n$. But red steps correspond to events (E1) and (E4), which altogether occur at most $(K\log n)/20$ times in the first $K\log n$ time steps, so the total number of elements in T is less than $(K\log n)/6$. This proves the claim.

CLAIM 5. *With failure probability $O(1/n^{k+1})$, v hears a beep at most $(K\log n)/3$ times among the first $K\log n$ time steps*

From the previous claim, we may assume that $\mu_t(\Gamma(v)) < 2\beta$ for at least $(5/6)K\log n$ steps out of the first $K\log n$

153

time steps. If $\mu_t(\Gamma(v)) < 2\beta$, it follows from Proposition 3 that the probability that v hears no beeps is at least

$$\exp(-2\mu_t(\Gamma(v))) \geq \exp(-4\beta) \geq 1 - 4\beta,$$

and so v hears a beep with probability at most $4\beta < 1/12$. Then (3) implies that with failure probability $O(n^{-(k+1)})$ there are at most $(K \log n)/6$ steps among the first $K \log n$ at which $\mu_t(\Gamma(v)) < 2\beta$ and v hears a beep. Since there are at most $(K \log n)/6$ steps at which $\mu_t(\Gamma(v)) \geq 2\beta$, it follows that, with failure probability $O(n^{-(k+1)})$, v hears beeps at most $(K \log n)/3$ times among the first $K \log n$ time steps, proving the claim.

CLAIM 6. *With failure probability $O(1/n^{k+1})$, either v becomes inactive or $\mu_t(v) = \mu_{t+1}(v) = 1/2$ at least $(K \log n)/3$ times in the first $K \log n$ time steps.*

Suppose that $\mu_{t+1}(v) = \mu_t(v)/2$ on a occasions, $\mu_{t+1}(v) = 2\mu_t(v)$ on b occasions and $\mu_{t+1}(v) = \mu_t(v) = 1/2$ on c occasions. We know that $a \leq (K \log n)/3$, by the previous claim, and $b \leq a$ (as $\mu_0(v) = 1/2$, and $\mu_t(v)$ is bounded above by $1/2$), so either v becomes inactive in the first $K \log n$ time steps, or else we must have $c \geq (K \log n)/3$.

We can now complete the proof of Theorem 2. If $\mu_t(v) = 1/2$ and v hears no beeps at time t then v becomes inactive with probability $1/2$. The probability that v remains active for at least $(K \log n)/3$ such steps is at most $(1/2)^{(K \log n)/3} = O(n^{-(k+1)})$. On the other hand, by the claim above, with failure probability $O(1/n^{k+1})$, either v becomes inactive or there are at least $K(\log n)/3$ steps in the first $K \log n$ at which $\mu_t(v) = \mu_{t+1}(v) = 1/2$, and so in particular $\mu_t(v) = 1/2$ and v hears no beeps. We conclude that v becomes inactive with failure probability $O(n^{-(k+1)})$. $\square$

COROLLARY 5. *The expected number of steps taken by the algorithm in Definition 1 on any graph with n nodes is $O(\log n)$.*

PROOF. Let T be the total number of steps taken by the algorithm and let $T' = \lceil T/(K_0 \log n) \rceil$, where K_0 is the constant identified in Theorem 2.

By Theorem 2, we have that, for any $k \geq 1$, $\mathbb{P}[T' > k+1] \leq c/n^k$ for some constant c. Hence $\mathbb{P}[T' = k+2] \leq c/n^k$, so $\mathbb{E}[T'] \leq 1 + 2 + \sum_{i=3}^{\infty} ic/n^{i-2} = c'$, for some constant c'. Hence $\mathbb{E}[T]$ is $O(\log n)$. $\square$

Theorem 2 and Corollary 5 establish upper bounds on the running time that are logarithmic in the number of nodes. Our simulations show that in practice the constants are rather low, leading to an efficient practical algorithm (see, for example, Figure 4).

5. BIT COMPLEXITY

We have shown that the expected number of time steps to complete the execution of the randomised algorithm defined in Section 4 grows at most logarithmically with the number of nodes. Another important resource to be considered in any distributed algorithm is the total number of messages sent (the message complexity), and their total size (in bits), which is sometimes referred to as the bit complexity. In this section we will show that the expected number of times that each node beeps is bounded by a constant. Hence the expected bit complexity per channel for this algorithm *does not increase at all* with the number of nodes.

THEOREM 6. *The expected total number of beeps emitted by any node executing the algorithm in Definition 1 is $O(1)$.*

PROOF. Let v be a node executing the algorithm in Definition 1, and consider the whole sequence of time steps until v becomes inactive. At each step, the probability that v beeps is $2^{-n(v,t)}$, which we will denote by p_t. The initial value of p_t is $\frac{1}{2}$.

Consider first the subsequence of steps where v hears a beep from its neighbours, halves its own probability of beeping, and reaches a value p_t that is its lowest value so far. The expected number of times that v beeps during this subsequence of steps is $\frac{1}{2} + \frac{1}{4} + \frac{1}{8} + \cdots \leq 1$.

At all other time steps, one of the following 3 things happens:

Case 1 v hears no beep from its neighbours, and so doubles its probability of beeping (from p_t to $2p_t$)

Case 2 v hears a beep from its neighbours, and so halves its probability of beeping (from p_t to $\frac{1}{2}p_t$)

Case 3 v hears no beep from its neighbours, and so leaves its probability unchanged at the maximum value of $\frac{1}{2}$.

Now we consider how many times v beeps during these steps.

If v beeps at any step where Case 3 holds, then it becomes inactive, so the total number of beeps at such steps is at most one.

For each step t where Case 1 holds, and the probability increases from p_t to $2p_t$, we look for a corresponding step $t' > t$ when the probability next drops back to p_t. (If there is no such step, because v becomes inactive before the probability returns to p_t, then we simply add a dummy step t' to the end of the sequence.) Note that each step where Case 2 holds is now paired with an earlier step where Case 1 holds.

Now consider the pairs (t, t'), and define B_t to be the event that v beeps at either time t or time t' (or both). The total number of times that v beeps at steps where Case 1 or Case 2 holds is at most twice the number of times that events of the form B_t occur.

If B_t occurs, then the probability that v beeps at time t is $p_t/(p_t(1-2p_t) + 2p_t(1-p_t) + 2p_t^2) > \frac{1}{3}$. However, if v beeps at time t, then it is added to the independent set, and becomes inactive. Hence the expected number of events B_t that occur before v becomes inactive is less than 3.

We have shown that the expected number of times that v beeps is less than $1 + 1 + 2 \times 3$, which proves the result. $\square$

Our simulations show that in practice the mean number of times that each node beeps is very low and does not increase with the size of the graph. For example, for random graphs with edge probability $\frac{1}{2}$, and for rectangular grid graphs it is around 1.1 (see Figure 6).

Afek *et al.* do not discuss the expected number of beeps at each node in their algorithm with sweeping global probabilities [1]. Our experimental results for this algorithm on random graphs with edge probability $\frac{1}{2}$ are shown in Figure 6, and appear to increase with the size of the network. However, when the initial global probabilities are calculated from the overall network size, and gradually increased, as described in [2], the mean number of beeps at each node does appear to be bounded by a constant. This is consistent with the claim made in [2] that the message complexity for this version of the algorithm is optimal.

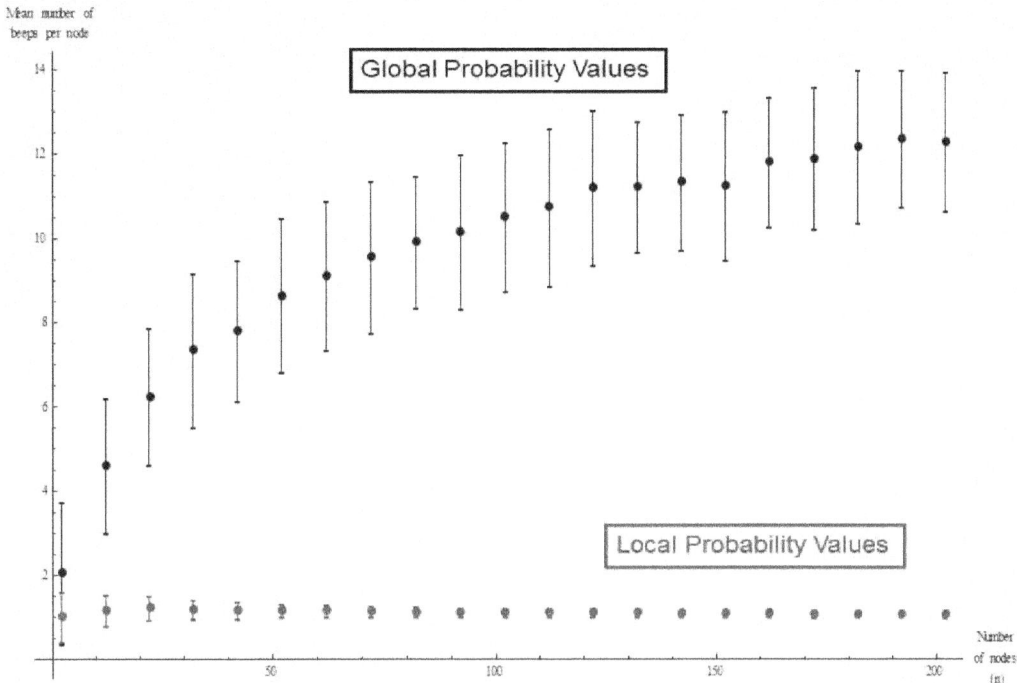

Figure 6: **Actual performance of the computation of the MIS on random networks where each edge is present with probability 1/2. The upper points (black) show the mean number of beeps at each node over 200 trials with global sweeping probabilities as specified in [1]. The lower points (blue) the same for locally chosen probabilities with feedback as proposed here. Error bars indicate standard deviations over 200 trials in each case.**

6. CONCLUSION

In conclusion, we have constructed a simple randomised algorithmic solution to a fundamental distributed computing problem – the maximal independent set selection problem, inspired by the intercellular signalling mechanism used for "fine-grained" pattern formation in many biological organisms. Our algorithm has optimal expected time complexity, and optimal expected message complexity. To achieve this good performance it is necessary to exploit local feedback - we have shown analytically that it cannot be made so time efficient if the processors do not adapt their probability of signalling to their local environment.

Our algorithm uses simple identical processors and one-bit messages, and its expected running time grows only logarithmically with the number of nodes, and is therefore much lower than the time required by a centralised sequential algorithm. Moreover, the individual processors need no information about the global properties of the network, such as its size, and do not need to identify which neighbours sent which message. These features make the algorithm useful for many applications, such as ad hoc sensor networks and wireless communication systems. Selecting a maximal independent set can also be used as a fundamental building block in algorithms for many other problems in distributed computing.

We also note that the algorithm we have proposed here is highly robust, in the sense that it retains its good performance even when various features are changed. For example, the probabilities at each node do not need to increase

and decrease by a precise factor - the analysis we have given here can be adapted to a wide range of different values for these factors, which may vary between nodes and over time. Similarly, the initial values for the probabilities at each node may be different from $\frac{1}{2}$, and may vary from node to node, without any significant impact on performance (as long as sufficiently many of them are bounded away from zero). This robustness is likely to be a key feature of the algorithm in any biological context.

The relationship between "fine-grained" pattern formation and the maximal independent set selection problem that we have investigated here is therefore a strikingly successful example of the increasing convergence between systems biology and computational thinking [20].

7. REFERENCES

[1] Y. Afek, N. Alon, Z. Bar-Joseph, A. Cornejo, B. Haeupler, and F. Kuhn. Beeping a maximal independent set. In *Proceedings of the 25th international conference on Distributed Computing*, DISC'11, pages 32–50, Berlin, Heidelberg, 2011. Springer-Verlag.

[2] Y. Afek, N. Alon, O. Barad, E. Hornstein, N. Barkai, and Z. Bar-Joseph. A biological solution to a fundamental distributed computing problem. *Science*, 331(6014):183–185, 2011.

[3] N. Alon, L. Babai, and A. Itai. A fast and simple randomized parallel algorithm for the maximal independent set problem. *Journal of Algorithms*, 7:567–583, December 1986.

[4] O. Barad, E. Hornstein, and N. Barkai. Robust selection of sensory organ precursors by the Notch-Delta pathway. *Current Opinion in Cell Biology*, 23(6):663 – 667, 2011.

[5] O. Barad, D. Rosin, E. Hornstein, and N. Barkai. Error minimization in lateral inhibition circuits. *Science Signaling*, 3(129):ra51, 2010.

[6] S. J. Bray. Notch signalling: a simple pathway becomes complex. *Nature reviews. Molecular cell biology*, 7(9):678–689, Sept. 2006.

[7] J. R. Collier, N. A. M. Monk, P. K. Maini, and J. H. Lewis. Pattern formation by lateral inhibition with feedback: a mathematical model of Delta-Notch intercellular signalling. *Journal of Theoretical Biology*, 183(4):429–446, 1996.

[8] R. Ghosh and C. J. Tomlin. Lateral inhibition through Delta-Notch signaling: a piecewise affine hybrid model. In *Proceedings of the 4th International Workshop on Hybrid Systems: Computation and Control*, HSCC '01, pages 232–246, London, UK, 2001. Springer-Verlag.

[9] K. G. Guruharsha, M. W. Kankel, and S. Artavanis-Tsakonas. The Notch signalling system: recent insights into the complexity of a conserved pathway. *Nature Reviews. Genetics*, 13(9):654–666, Sept. 2012.

[10] J. Håstad. Clique is hard to approximate within $n^{1-\epsilon}$. *Acta Mathematica*, 48:105–142, 1999.

[11] T. L. Jacobsen, K. Brennan, A. M. Arias, and M. A. T. Muskavitch. Cis-interactions between Delta and Notch modulate neurogenic signalling in Drosophila. *Development*, 125(22):4531–40, 1998.

[12] R. M. Karp. Reducibility among combinatorial problems. In R. E. Miller and J. W. Thatcher, editors, *Complexity of Computer Computations*, The IBM Research Symposia Series, pages 85–103. Plenum Press, New York, 1972.

[13] F. Kuhn, T. Moscibroda, T. Nieberg, and R. Wattenhofer. Fast deterministic distributed maximal independent set computation on growth-bounded graphs. In P. Fraigniaud, editor, *Distributed Computing: 19th International Conference, DISC 2005*, volume 3724 of *Lecture Notes in Computer Science*, pages 273–283, Berlin, November 2005. Springer-Verlag.

[14] F. Kuhn, T. Moscibroda, and R. Wattenhofer. The price of being near-sighted. In *Proceedings of the 17th annual ACM-SIAM Symposium on Discrete Algorithms*, SODA '06, pages 980–989, New York, NY, USA, 2006.

[15] N. Linial. Locality in distributed graph algorithms. *SIAM Journal on Computing*, 21(1):193–201, Feb. 1992.

[16] M. Luby. A simple parallel algorithm for the maximal independent set problem. In *Proceedings of the seventeenth annual ACM Symposium on Theory of Computing*, STOC '85, pages 1–10, New York, NY, USA, 1985.

[17] M. Matsuda and A. B. Chitnis. Interaction with Notch determines endocytosis of specific Delta ligands in zebrafish neural tissue. *Development*, 136(2):197–206, 2009.

[18] Y. Métivier, J. M. Robson, N. Saheb-Djahromi, and A. Zemmari. An optimal bit complexity randomized distributed MIS algorithm. *Distributed Computing*, 23:331–340, 2011.

[19] T. Moscibroda and R. Wattenhofer. Maximal independent sets in radio networks. In *Proceedings of the 24th annual ACM Symposium on Principles of Distributed Computing*, PODC '05, pages 148–157, New York, NY, USA, 2005.

[20] S. Navlakha and Z. Bar-Joseph. Algorithms in nature: the convergence of systems biology and computational thinking. *Molecular Systems Biology*, 7(1), Nov. 2011.

[21] D. Sprinzak, A. Lakhanpal, L. LeBon, L. A. Santat, M. E. Fontes, G. A. Anderson, J. Garcia-Ojalvo, and M. B. Elowitz. Cis-interactions between Notch and Delta generate mutually exclusive signalling states. *Nature*, 465(7294):86–90, Apr. 2010.

What Can Be Decided Locally Without Identifiers?

Pierre Fraigniaud
CNRS and University Paris Diderot
pierre.fraigniaud@
liafa.univ-paris-diderot.fr

Amos Korman
CNRS and University Paris Diderot
amos.korman@
liafa.univ-paris-diderot.fr

Mika Göös
Department of Computer Science
University of Toronto
mika.goos@mail.utoronto.ca

Jukka Suomela
Helsinki Institute for Information Technology HIIT
Department of Computer Science
University of Helsinki
jukka.suomela@cs.helsinki.fi

ABSTRACT

Do unique node identifiers help in deciding whether a network G has a prescribed property $\mathcal{P}$? We study this question in the context of *distributed local decision*, where the objective is to decide whether G has property $\mathcal{P}$ by having each node run a constant-time distributed decision algorithm. In a *yes*-instance all nodes should output *yes*, while in a *no*-instance at least one node should output *no*.

Recently, Fraigniaud et al. (OPODIS 2012) gave several conditions under which identifiers are not needed, and they conjectured that identifiers are not needed in any decision problem. In the present work, we disprove the conjecture. More than that, we analyse two critical variations of the underlying model of distributed computing:

(**B**): the size of the identifiers is *bounded* by a function of the size of the input network,

(¬**B**): the identifiers are *unbounded*,

(**C**): the nodes run a *computable* algorithm,

(¬**C**): the nodes can compute any, possibly *uncomputable* function.

While it is easy to see that under (¬**B**, ¬**C**) identifiers are not needed, we show that under all other combinations there are properties that can be decided locally if and only if identifiers are present.

Categories and Subject Descriptors

C.2.4 [**Computer-Communication Networks**]: Distributed Systems; F.1.2 [**Computation by Abstract Devices**]: Modes of Computation

Keywords

distributed complexity, local decision, identifiers, computability theory

1. INTRODUCTION

In this work we ask and answer a simple question: *Do we need unique node identifiers when locally deciding a graph property?* While this question is a natural one, our answers are somewhat artificial—but only necessarily so.

Local Decision

A property of graphs $\mathcal{P}$ is *locally decidable* if there is a distributed algorithm A (in the usual $\mathcal{LOCAL}$ model; see Section 1.2) with a constant running time $t = O(1)$ that when run on a graph G can decide whether $G \in \mathcal{P}$ in the following sense:

- if $G \in \mathcal{P}$, then A outputs *yes* on every node of G, and
- if $G \notin \mathcal{P}$, then A outputs *no* on at least one node of G.

Here, the output of A on a node $v \in V(G)$ can only depend on the information that is available to within t steps of v in G. This includes not only the radius-t neighbourhood topology around v, but also—as is often assumed—numerical identifiers $\mathrm{Id}(u)$ for each node u in the neighbourhood. The assignment $\mathrm{Id} : V(G) \to \mathbb{N}$ is one-to-one.

Do We Need Identifiers?

Recently, Fraigniaud et al. [2] asked if it makes any difference in this context to have A's output depend on the identifiers $\mathrm{Id}(v)$. After all, whether G has the property $\mathcal{P}$ does not depend on how the nodes of G are labelled with identifiers, and moreover, the usual challenge of *local symmetry breaking* does not arise in the context of decision problems.

They conjectured that for any local algorithm A that decides a property $\mathcal{P}$ there is an equivalent *Id-oblivious* local algorithm A^* that decides $\mathcal{P}$ and that does not use identifiers in the sense that the output of A^* on a node $v \in V(G)$ does not change if we reassign the identifiers, i.e., $A^*(G, \mathrm{Id}, v) = A^*(G, \mathrm{Id}', v)$ for any two assignments $\mathrm{Id}, \mathrm{Id}' : V(G) \to \mathbb{N}$.

In this work, we disprove the conjecture. We show that there are graph properties whose local decision requires the output of a constant-time algorithm to depend on the identifier assignment—if the details of the underlying model of distributed computation are set up in a particular way.

Assumptions

To understand what our question entails on a technical level, we need to make explicit two critical assumptions about the model of computing.

Size of identifiers. It is commonly assumed that the identifiers are given as $O(\log n)$-bit labels in a graph with n nodes. It is debatable whether it is natural to require bounded identifiers in our case of constant-time algorithms; in any case, we consider both alternatives:

(**B**) The size of identifiers is *bounded* by a function of n.
(¬**B**) The size of identifiers is *unbounded*.

Note that, since a local algorithm operates on a graph component-wise, there is no distinction between (**B**) and (¬**B**) if we allow all disconnected graphs as input: in either case there will be no bound on $\mathrm{Id}(v)$ as a function of the size of v's component. Thus, in what follows, we will assume that the input graph is connected. We will show that whether identifiers help in local decision depends on which of the assumptions (**B**) or (¬**B**) we adopt.

Computability. Second, should we restrict the power of local computations? We have two alternatives:

(**C**) The nodes run a *computable* algorithm.
(¬**C**) The nodes can compute any function, possibly *uncomputable*.

For many questions in distributed computing, the distinction between (**C**) and (¬**C**) is inconsequential. However, we will show that whether identifiers help in local decision depends on which of the assumptions (**C**) or (¬**C**) we adopt.

Id-Oblivious Simulation

Our results are best motivated by the observation that identifiers are not needed under (¬**B**, ¬**C**). Indeed, if A is a t-time algorithm deciding a property $\mathcal{P}$, we can simulate A by an Id-oblivious t-time algorithm A^*.

> Id-oblivious simulation A^*: For each local neighbourhood (G', v), $G' \subseteq G$, algorithm A^* checks whether there is a local assignment $\mathrm{Id}' : V(G') \to \mathbb{N}$ that makes the output $A(G', \mathrm{Id}', v)$ be *no*. If such an assignment exists, we let A^* output *no* on v, too; otherwise, we let A^* output *yes* on v.

We first note that, even though A^* is well-defined, it is not obvious how to compute it, since finding out whether Id' exists might involve an exhaustive search over an infinite domain. For example, even if A was computable to start with, our A^* is now deciding, a priori, a *computably enumerable* predicate. However, under (¬**C**), this is not a problem.

To see that A^* correctly decides $\mathcal{P}$, we note that A^* outputs *no* on some node in G, if and only if there is some global assignment $\mathrm{Id} : V(G) \to \mathbb{N}$ (i.e., extension of Id') that makes A output *no* on some node. The identifiers in the assignment Id may be very large, but under (¬**B**) this is not a problem. Thus, (G, Id) is a valid input for A, and the correctness of A^* now follows from that of A.

Our main result in this work is showing that there is no general Id-oblivious simulation in case one of the assumptions (**B**) or (**C**) is imposed.

1.1 Our Results

We show that identifiers are necessary in local decision under (**B**), and under (**C**).

THEOREM 1. *Assume* (**B**) *or* (**C**). *There is a locally decidable property $\mathcal{P}$ that cannot be decided with an Id-oblivious local algorithm.*

In particular, this separates the classes LD and LD* that were previously conjectured to be equal under (¬**B**, **C**) by Fraigniaud et al. [2]. Here, LD is the class of locally decidable properties, and LD* $\subseteq$ LD is the class of properties decidable with an Id-oblivious local algorithm.

We prove the separation LD* $\neq$ LD assuming (**B**, ¬**C**) in Section 2, and again assuming (**C**) in Section 3. For the latter, more involved separation, we end up using ideas from classical (sequential) computability theory. The use of these techniques should not come as a surprise given that LD* $=$ LD under (¬**B**, ¬**C**) as discussed above. We collect the relationships between LD* and LD in the following table:

	(**C**)	(¬**C**)	
(**B**)	$\neq$	$\neq$	$\rightarrow$ Section 2
(¬**B**)	$\neq$	$=$	

$\hookrightarrow$ Section 3

Finally, we note that the property $\mathcal{P}$ that witnesses LD $\neq$ LD* under (**C**) becomes decidable with an Id-oblivious algorithm if we allow *randomness*.

COROLLARY 1. *Property $\mathcal{P}$ can be decided (w.h.p.) with an Id-oblivious randomised local algorithm.*

Randomised local decision was previously studied by Fraigniaud et al. [3, 4]. The corollary above indicates, in particular, that in the Id-oblivious model, the threshold result [4, Theorem 3.3] that pertains to so-called hereditary properties (see Section 1.3) does not hold in general.

1.2 Local Decision in the $\mathcal{LOCAL}$ Model

A *labelled graph* is a pair $(G, \boldsymbol{x})$, where $G = (V(G), E(G))$ is a simple undirected graph and function $\boldsymbol{x}$ associates a *label* or a *local input*, denoted $\boldsymbol{x}(v)$, with each node $v \in V(G)$.

A *labelled graph property* is a collection $\mathcal{P}$ of labelled graphs that is closed under graph isomorphism. That is, if $(G, \boldsymbol{x}) \in \mathcal{P}$, and $(G', \boldsymbol{x}')$ is isomorphic to $(G, \boldsymbol{x})$, then $(G', \boldsymbol{x}') \in \mathcal{P}$. Examples of labelled graph properties include the following:

- "proper 3-colouring": $(G, \boldsymbol{x}) \in \mathcal{P}$ if $\boldsymbol{x}$ is a proper 3-colouring of G,

- "maximal independent set": $(G, \boldsymbol{x}) \in \mathcal{P}$ if the nodes with $\boldsymbol{x}(v) = 1$ form a maximal independent set in G,

- "planar graphs": $(G, \boldsymbol{x}) \in \mathcal{P}$ if G is a planar graph (and $\boldsymbol{x}$ is arbitrary).

In particular, all graph properties can be interpreted as labelled graph properties. If $\mathcal{P}$ is a property, we say that any pair $(G, \boldsymbol{x}) \in \mathcal{P}$ is a *yes-instance* and any pair $(G, \boldsymbol{x}) \notin \mathcal{P}$ is a *no-instance*.

An *input* is a triple $(G, \boldsymbol{x}, \mathrm{Id})$, where $(G, \boldsymbol{x})$ is a labelled graph and $\mathrm{Id} : V(G) \to \mathbb{N}$ is a one-to-one function. We say that $\mathrm{Id}(v)$ is the *unique identifier* of node $v \in V(G)$.

Local Algorithms

Let $B(v, t) \subseteq V(G)$ consist of the nodes that are within distance t from v in graph G. We write $(G, \boldsymbol{x}, \mathrm{Id}) \restriction B(v, t)$ for the restriction of the structure $(G, \boldsymbol{x}, \mathrm{Id})$ to $B(v, t)$. In other words, this is the radius-t neighbourhood of node v in graph G.

We will now formally define what we mean by a local algorithm and its local horizon. For our purposes, a local algorithm is easiest to define as a function that maps local neighbourhoods to local outputs. To this end, let A be a function that associates a *local output*

$$A(G, \boldsymbol{x}, \mathrm{Id}, v) \in \{yes, no\}$$

with each node $v \in V$ for any input $(G, \boldsymbol{x}, \mathrm{Id})$. We say that A is a *local algorithm* with local horizon t if

$$A(G, \boldsymbol{x}, \mathrm{Id}, v) = A(G', \boldsymbol{x}', \mathrm{Id}', v)$$

whenever $(G, \boldsymbol{x}, \mathrm{Id}) \restriction B(v, t) = (G', \boldsymbol{x}', \mathrm{Id}') \restriction B(v, t)$. That is, in a local algorithm the local output of node v depends only on the information that is available in the radius-t neighbourhood of node v.

Moreover, we say that local algorithm A is *Id-oblivious* if

$$A(G, \boldsymbol{x}, \mathrm{Id}, v) = A(G, \boldsymbol{x}, \mathrm{Id}', v)$$

for any two assignments $\mathrm{Id}, \mathrm{Id}' : V(G) \to \mathbb{N}$. That is, renumbering the identifiers does not change the output of an Id-oblivious algorithm. Indeed, we may write the output simply as $A(G, \boldsymbol{x}, v)$.

While in the above description we have specified a local algorithm as a mapping from local neighbourhoods to local outputs, we could equally well specify a local algorithm from the perspective of networked state machines that exchange messages with each other: graph G is the structure of the network, each node is a computer, each edge is a communication link, all nodes run the same algorithm, and a node $v \in V(G)$ initially knows only $\boldsymbol{x}(v)$ and $\mathrm{Id}(v)$. In essence, a local algorithm with local horizon t is equivalent to a distributed algorithm that runs in $t \pm 1$ synchronous communication rounds in the $\mathcal{LOCAL}$ model [16, 20].

Assumptions

Under assumption (**B**), we require that there is a function f such that $\mathrm{Id}(v) < f(|V(G)|)$ for any input $(G, \boldsymbol{x}, \mathrm{Id})$.

Under assumption (**C**), we require that local algorithm A is a computable function of the local neighbourhood. Put otherwise, we require that there is a Turing machine M_A such that for any input $(G, \boldsymbol{x}, \mathrm{Id})$ and any node $v \in G$, given a string that encodes node v and the local neighbourhood $(G, \boldsymbol{x}, \mathrm{Id}) \restriction B(v, t)$, machine M_A halts and outputs $A(G, \boldsymbol{x}, \mathrm{Id}, v)$.

Local Decision

Local algorithm A *decides* a property $\mathcal{P}$ if the following holds for any input $(G, \boldsymbol{x}, \mathrm{Id})$:

- if $(G, \boldsymbol{x}) \in \mathcal{P}$, then $A(G, \boldsymbol{x}, \mathrm{Id}, v) = yes$ for every node $v \in V(G)$,

- if $(G, \boldsymbol{x}) \notin \mathcal{P}$, then $A(G, \boldsymbol{x}, \mathrm{Id}, v) = no$ for at least one node $v \in V(G)$.

If there is a local algorithm that decides $\mathcal{P}$, we say that $\mathcal{P}$ is in class LD. If there is an Id-oblivious local algorithm that decides $\mathcal{P}$, we say that $\mathcal{P}$ is in class LD*.

Promise Problems

While our constructions do not make use of promise problems, we will refer to them in some introductory examples. If we say that we have *promise* $\mathcal{P}'$, then we are only interested in inputs $(G, \boldsymbol{x}, \mathrm{Id})$ with $(G, \boldsymbol{x}) \in \mathcal{P}'$.

In particular, if $(G, \boldsymbol{x}, \mathrm{Id})$ is an input that violates the promise, we do not put any requirements on $A(G, \boldsymbol{x}, \mathrm{Id}, v)$. Even if we work under assumption (**C**), we do not require that machine M_A halts for inputs that violate the promise. Put otherwise, A can be a partial function, undefined for inputs that violate the promise.

1.3 Related Work

The question of how to locally decide (or verify) properties has been gaining attention in recent years [1, 2, 4, 9, 11–14]. While the original focus was on the $\mathcal{LOCAL}$ model [4], recent work has taken the first steps towards a computational complexity theory in various other contexts of distributed computing [5–7].

Local Decision

Fraigniaud et al. [4] define three classes of decision problem: LD, NLD and BPLD. Class NLD is a nondeterministic version of LD, and class BPLD is a randomised version of LD. Informally, classes LD, NLD and BPLD are distributed analogues of classes P, NP and BPP.

One of the main results of the paper [4] pertains to *hereditary* properties—in essence, these are graph properties that are closed under vertex deletion. It is shown that for hereditary properties there exists a sharp threshold for randomisation, above which randomisation does not help.

Identifiers and Local Decision

More recently, Fraigniaud et al. [2] defined the *Id-oblivious* model, and the corresponding class LD*, aiming to better understand the role of identities in local decision. They also conjectured that LD* = LD. Informally, the conjecture states that for constant time computations, identities do not play any role except for allowing nodes to identify their local neighbourhoods.

Several positive evidences were given supporting this conjecture [2]. Specifically, it is shown that LD* = LD holds for hereditary properties and for graph problems defined on paths, with a finite set of input values. Moreover, it was shown that equality holds in the non-deterministic setting, i.e., NLD* = NLD.

Identifiers and Local Construction

The role of identifiers is different in local algorithms that need to *construct* a solution. From the perspective of construction tasks, it is easy to see that the usual $\mathcal{LOCAL}$ model is much stronger than the Id-oblivious model: there are many tasks that are trivial in $\mathcal{LOCAL}$ and impossible to solve with an Id-oblivious algorithm (examples: finding an orientation of the edges; 2-colouring a 1-regular graph).

Therefore to ask meaningful questions related to the role of unique identifiers in construction tasks, we usually compare the $\mathcal{LOCAL}$ model with models that retain some symmetry-breaking information. Two such models are OI, *order-invariant algorithms*, and PO, *port numbering and orientation*. Informally, we can characterise the models as follows (see, e.g., Göös et al. [8] for more details).

- In the OI model [18], the output of an algorithm is not allowed to change if we reassign the identifier while preserving their relative order.

- In the PO model [17], there is an ordering on the incident edges, and all edges carry an orientation.

Note that the OI model is stronger than the Id-oblivious model: in the Id-oblivious model, $A^*(G, \mathrm{Id}, v) = A^*(G, \mathrm{Id}', v)$ for *any* two assignments $\mathrm{Id}, \mathrm{Id}': V(G) \to \mathbb{N}$, while in the OI model, we only require this for assignments that satisfy $\mathrm{Id}(u) < \mathrm{Id}(v) \iff \mathrm{Id}'(u) < \mathrm{Id}'(v)$. This difference makes the OI model much stronger.

Indeed, it turns out that from the perspective of strictly local algorithms, for many graph problems models $\mathcal{LOCAL}$ and OI are equally strong: Naor and Stockmeyer [18] prove that for problems whose *decision* version can be solved locally, *construction* is possible in $\mathcal{LOCAL}$ if and only if it is possible in OI. More recently, Göös et al. [8] show that there is also a general class of *optimisation* problems for which $\mathcal{LOCAL}$, OI and PO are equally expressive.

The results of Naor and Stockmeyer [18] and Göös et al. [8] focus on bounded-degree graphs. They also make a subtle technical assumption: each node produces a local output from a constant-size set. This is necessary: Hasemann et al. [10] give an example of a natural problem that violates this assumption—and separates $\mathcal{LOCAL}$ and OI.

Bounds on n

It turns out that in decision problems, unique identifiers are helpful for one reason, and for one reason only: obtaining an estimate on n, the number of nodes. Indeed, by prior work we already know that $\mathsf{LD}^* = \mathsf{LD}$ holds assuming that every node knows an upper bound on the total number of nodes in the input graph [2].

Of course we can interpret a decision problem as a very special kind of construction problem, and therefore the present work also shows that some construction problems can exploit numerical identifiers to learn about n. However, this is a highly atypical example. For classical graph problems this information does not help a local algorithm—the identifiers are typically used for local symmetry breaking and their numerical magnitude is inconsequential.

However, if we step outside the field of strictly local algorithms, it is common to *assume* that all nodes know the same upper bound on n. This is a convenient assumption that often simplifies algorithm design. Korman et al. [15] show that in many cases it is merely a convenience—the knowledge of an upper bound on n is not essential.

2. SEPARATION UNDER BOUNDED IDENTIFIERS

In this section we work under assumption $(\mathbf{B}, \neg\mathbf{C})$ and exhibit a locally decidable property $\mathcal{P}$ that cannot be decided with an Id-oblivious local algorithm.

Let $f \colon \mathbb{N} \to \mathbb{N}$ be such that $\mathrm{Id}(v) < f(n)$ for all $v \in V(G)$, where G is a connected input graph. The reason identifiers are useful is that they leak information about n. For example, if a node is given an identifier i, it can deduce that $n > f^{-1}(i)$, where we denote by $f^{-1}(i)$ the smallest j such that $f(j) \geq i$.

Promise Problem

As an illustration, we first describe a simple promise problem in $\mathsf{LD} \smallsetminus \mathsf{LD}^*$.

> Promise problem: The instances are labelled graphs (G, r), where G is an n-cycle and $r \in \mathbb{N}$ is a constant input label. We promise that either $n = r$ or $n = f(r)$.

We have a *yes*-instance if $n = r$ and a *no*-instance if $n = f(r)$.

Note that r-cycles and $f(r)$-cycles cannot be told apart by an Id-oblivious algorithm as they are locally indistinguishable topology-wise when r is large. However, we can solve the problem using identifiers: the $f(r)$-cycles can be rejected, because there is a node with identifier at least $f(r)$, which is too large to be found in the r-cycle. (We can exploit assumption $(\neg\mathbf{C})$ here if f is uncomputable.)

It is not much harder to design a promise-free example in $\mathsf{LD} \smallsetminus \mathsf{LD}^*$—we do this next.

Promise-Free Problem

Define $R(r) := f(2^{r+1} + 1)$. The key idea is that

- if the instance is a complete depth-r binary tree, all identifiers are smaller than $R(r)$,

- if the instance is a complete depth-$R(r)$ binary tree, there is an identifier at least $R(r)$.

Intuitively, we can use identifiers to accept "small" instances and reject "large" instances. The nontrivial part is to make sure that we can also reject instances that are neither small nor large.

A *layered depth-k tree* is a complete binary tree of depth k where, in addition, nodes at each level are connected by a path in the natural order; see Figure 1. Denote by T_r the labelled graph consisting of a layered depth-$R(r)$ tree. Each node of T_r is labelled with (r, x, y), where the coordinates (x, y) indicate the position of the node in the binary tree.

Write $H \leq_r T_r$ if a labelled graph H is an induced subgraph of the labelled graph T_r, and the topology of H is a layered depth-r tree. Call $u \in V(H)$ a *border node* if u has a neighbour in $V(T_r) \smallsetminus V(H)$. We define H^+ to be H together with a new node (*pivot node*) that is adjacent to all the border nodes of H; see Figure 1. We collect $\mathcal{H}_r := \{H^+ : H \leq_r T_r\}$. We are now ready to define

$$\mathcal{P} := \bigcup_{r \geq 0} \mathcal{H}_r, \qquad \mathcal{P}' := \mathcal{P} \cup \{T_r : r \geq 0\}.$$

We will refer to labelled graphs in $\mathcal{P}$ as "small" instances and graphs in $\mathcal{P}' \smallsetminus \mathcal{P}$ as "large" instances. Of course instances of $\mathcal{P}$ are only small in comparison with the parameter r that is encoded in the labelling of the graph; we have arbitrarily large graphs in both $\mathcal{P}$ and $\mathcal{P}'$.

We will next show that the construction satisfies the following properties:

- $\mathcal{P}' \in \mathsf{LD}^*$, that is, even if we do not have access to unique identifiers, we can verify that the input is *either* small *or* large. Hence we do not need to rely on a promise—we can locally verify it.

- $\mathcal{P} \in \mathsf{LD}$, that is, we can reject large instances with the help of identifiers,

- $\mathcal{P} \notin \mathsf{LD}^*$, that is, we cannot distinguish between small and large instances with Id-oblivious algorithms.

$(\mathcal{P}' \in \mathsf{LD}^*)$: The overall structure of a layered depth-$R(r)$ tree is straightforward to verify locally with the help of coordinates; we can also easily check that all nodes agree on the value of r. We can verify that the coordinates satisfy $0 \leq x < 2^y$ and $0 \leq y \leq R(r)$, there is no parent iff $y = 0$, there are no children iff $y = R(r)$, etc.

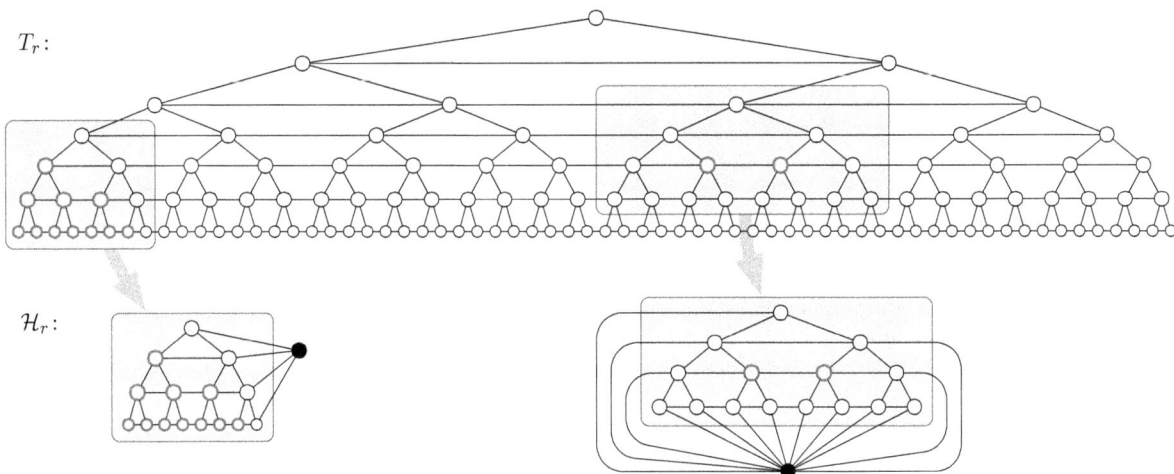

Figure 1: Graph T_r is a layered tree of depth $R(r) \gg r$. Each graph $H^+ \in \mathcal{H}_r$ is a layered tree of depth r, augmented with a single pivot node (black). The nodes that are far from the boundary (highlighted) have local neighbourhoods that are indistinguishable from the local neighbourhood of the same node in T_r.

The non-trivial part is the case of a pivot node. The crucial property is that a pivot node sees *all* border nodes of a small instance. Therefore a pivot node can verify that the size of the border (as well as the coordinates of the border nodes) agree with the definition of a small instance.

In essence, if we encounter a pivot node, we must have a small instance: if we fix the structure near the border nodes, and then complete it so that it is locally consistent with the structure of a layered tree, we will arrive at a labelled graph in $\mathcal{P}$. On the other hand, if we never encounter a pivot node, we must have a large instance.

($\mathcal{P} \notin \mathsf{LD}^*$): Suppose for contradiction that A^* is a t-time Id-oblivious algorithm that decides $\mathcal{P}$. For a large enough $r \gg t$, we have that each t-neighbourhood in T_r is already found in one of the *yes*-instances in $\mathcal{H}_r$. But because A^* accepts all of $\mathcal{H}_r$, it must also accept the *no*-instance T_r, which is a contradiction.

($\mathcal{P} \in \mathsf{LD}$): The only difficulty in locally deciding $\mathcal{P}$ is to be able to reject T_r while accepting all graphs in $\mathcal{H}_r$. But there is a node in T_r with an identifier at least $R(r)$, which is too large to be found in the graphs $\mathcal{H}_r$.

3. SEPARATION UNDER COMPUTABILITY

In this section we assume that all local algorithms are computable (**C**). We will exhibit a locally decidable property $\mathcal{P}$ that cannot be decided by an Id-oblivious local algorithm.

Promise Problem

Again, to illustrate our approach, we first describe a simple promise problem that separates LD^* and LD.

> Promise problem $\mathcal{R}$: The instances are labelled graphs (G, M) such that G is an n-cycle; the constant input label M is a Turing machine; and if M halts in exactly s steps (when started on a blank tape) then we promise that $n \geq s$.
>
> We have a *yes*-instance if M runs forever and a *no*-instance if M halts.

($\mathcal{R} \in \mathsf{LD}$): The problem $\mathcal{R}$ is locally decidable using identifiers. Indeed, a node with identifier i first simulates M for i steps. Then, if M stops within this many steps, we output *no*; otherwise we output *yes*. For correctness, note that our promise implies that for every *no*-instance (G, M) where M halts, there will be some node v with identifier at least as large as M's run-time, and v will be able to reject (G, M).

($\mathcal{R} \notin \mathsf{LD}^*$): On the other hand, it is easy to see that any Id-oblivious algorithm for $\mathcal{R}$ has to solve the halting problem without the additional knowledge of M's run-time, which is an uncomputable task.

In this section, our goal is to construct a promise-free version of this decision problem.

3.1 Overview

The computationally difficult part in our decision problem $\mathcal{P}$ will be to determine whether a given Turing machine M halts and outputs 0 (when started on a blank tape).

To make $\mathcal{P}$ easy for an algorithm using identifiers, we will require that the instance G contains a grid-like locally checkable execution table of M. This way—as in the promise problem example—there will be some node v that has an identifier larger than M's run-time. The node v can then locally simulate M to discover its output.

To make $\mathcal{P}$ hard for an Id-oblivious algorithm, we need to obfuscate the structure of G so that its local topology does not reveal any useful information about the execution of M. In particular, even if M halts, no local neighbourhood of G should certify this fact. This way, an Id-oblivious algorithm is left with trying to find out M's output without any additional means. More formally, such an algorithm would need to separate the languages

$$L_i := \{M : M \text{ outputs } i\}, \qquad i = 0, 1,$$

which is known to be impossible for a computable function:

LEMMA 1 (E.G. [19, P. 65]). *The languages L_0 and L_1 are computably inseparable, i.e., there is no computable set R such that $L_0 \subseteq R$ and $L_1 \cap R = \varnothing$.* $\square$

Implementation

For a pair (M, r), where M halts and $r \in \mathbb{N}$ is a locality parameter, we will construct a graph $G(M, r)$ satisfying the following properties.

(P1) The execution table of M is contained in $G(M, r)$.

(P2) It is locally decidable (even in LD^*) whether an instance is of the form $G(M, r)$.

(P3) The r-neighbourhoods of $G(M, r)$ reveal only computable information about M. More formally, there is an algorithm B that halts on all inputs (N, r), where N is any Turing machine, and outputs a finite set of r-neighbourhoods $B(N, r)$ such that

$$N \text{ halts} \implies$$
$$B(N, r) = \{ \ r\text{-neighbourhoods of } G(N, r) \ \}.$$

Note, especially, that B halts even if N does not!

Suppose for a moment that we have a construction satisfying (P1–P3). We can now define

$$\mathcal{P} := \{G(M, r) : M \text{ outputs } 0\}.$$

THEOREM 2. $\mathcal{P} \in \mathsf{LD} \smallsetminus \mathsf{LD}^*$ under (**C**).

PROOF. ($\mathcal{P} \in \mathsf{LD}$): Given (G, Id) as input, a node $v \in V(G)$ computes in two stages. First, v performs its local test according to (P2) to see if $G = G(M, r)$ for some (M, r). If this test fails, v outputs *no*. Otherwise v proceeds to the second stage where v locally simulates M for $\mathrm{Id}(v)$ steps. If the simulation finishes and M outputs something other than 0, then v outputs *no*; otherwise v outputs *yes*.

For correctness, we need only note that in case all nodes pass the first stage, we have that $G = G(M, r)$, and thus, by (P1), there will be some node v with so large an identifier that v will finish the simulation of M in the second stage and discover M's true output.

($\mathcal{P} \notin \mathsf{LD}^*$): For the sake of contradiction, suppose that an Id-oblivious algorithm A^* with run-time t decides $\mathcal{P}$. We show how A^* can be exploited to separate the languages L_0 and L_1.

> **Separation algorithm** R: Given a Turing machine N we first compute $B(N, t)$. Then, we run A^* on all the t-neighbourhoods in $B(N, t)$. We accept N precisely if A^* accepts all of $B(N, t)$.

First, note that, by (P3), our algorithm R halts on every input N. Moreover, suppose that N halts. Then R accepts N iff A^* accepts every t-neighbourhood of $G(N, r)$ iff A^* accepts $G(N, r)$ iff $G(N, r) \in \mathcal{P}$ iff N outputs 0. But this contradicts Lemma 1. $\square$

Indeed, it remains to give the details of a construction satisfying (P1–P3).

3.2 Construction of $G(M, r)$

Let M be a Turing machine that halts. Each node in the graph $G = G(M, r)$ will have (M, r) as part of their input labelling. The graph G will consist of two parts:

- the *execution table* T of M, and
- a certain *fragment collection* $\mathcal{C}$.

See Figure 2.

Execution Table

Let s be the running time of M. The execution table T of M will be represented, as per usual, as a labelled square grid graph on nodes $[s+1] \times [s+1]$, where two nodes are adjacent if their Euclidean distance is 1. We think of the edges of T as being oriented from top to bottom and from left to right. Such an orientation can be locally supplied by labelling (x, y) with $(x \bmod 3, y \bmod 3)$.

Labels for execution. The i-th row of T corresponds to the configuration of M before the i-th step of the execution: the nodes are labelled with tape cell contents, and the read-write head of the machine is owned by exactly one node per row; this node also records the state of the machine. The first row contains just blank symbols, and the computation starts with the head on the leftmost node, which we call the *pivot node*.

The exact details of this labelling scheme are not important. Any reasonable scheme will do. We only require that the size of the labels is bounded by a computable function of M. For example, we cannot allow the nodes on the i-th row to hold the number i in their labels, since, intuitively, this would leak information about M's run-time to an Id-oblivious algorithm. (More precisely, this would mess up our construction of $\mathcal{C}$ below.)

Local decidability. It is well known that valid executions of a Turing machine can be checked locally—at least once we somehow know that the instance is really a labelled square grid and not, e.g., a torus-like graph that locally looks like a grid. To make T locally checkable, we need to augment it with some special structure; we take care of this technicality in the appendix.

Fragment Collection

The purpose of the fragment collection $\mathcal{C}$ is to ensure property (P3).

Intuition. If we had $G = T$, an Id-oblivious algorithm could decide whether M outputs 0 simply by checking if there was a local neighbourhood in $G = T$ where M is in a halting state with output 0.

To prevent this from happening, we add superfluous table fragments to G. In fact, we will let G contain all syntactically possible execution table fragments. This way, the answer to the question "Does there exists a local neighbourhood in G where M is in such-and-such a state" will always be *yes*. In effect, when an Id-oblivious algorithm is exploring G locally, it learns nothing about the execution of M that it could not compute by itself.

Construction. Let F be a $3r \times 3r$ grid graph. Consider labelling F in all possible ways that satisfy the local consistency rules of T. That is, we put no limitations on how the boundary nodes are labelled, as long as

- the (mod 3)-labels give a consistent orientation, and
- every 2×2 sub-table of F is consistent with the transition function of M.

We let $\mathcal{C} = \mathcal{C}(M, r)$ consist of these labelled versions of F.

The important property here is that every r-neighbourhood in T (including those near a boundary of T) is found already in some labelled fragment in $\mathcal{C}$.

Efficiency. The construction of $\mathcal{C}$ is purely syntactic: for any machine N (that does not necessarily halt), we can efficiently generate $\mathcal{C}(N, r)$ by a simple enumeration of all

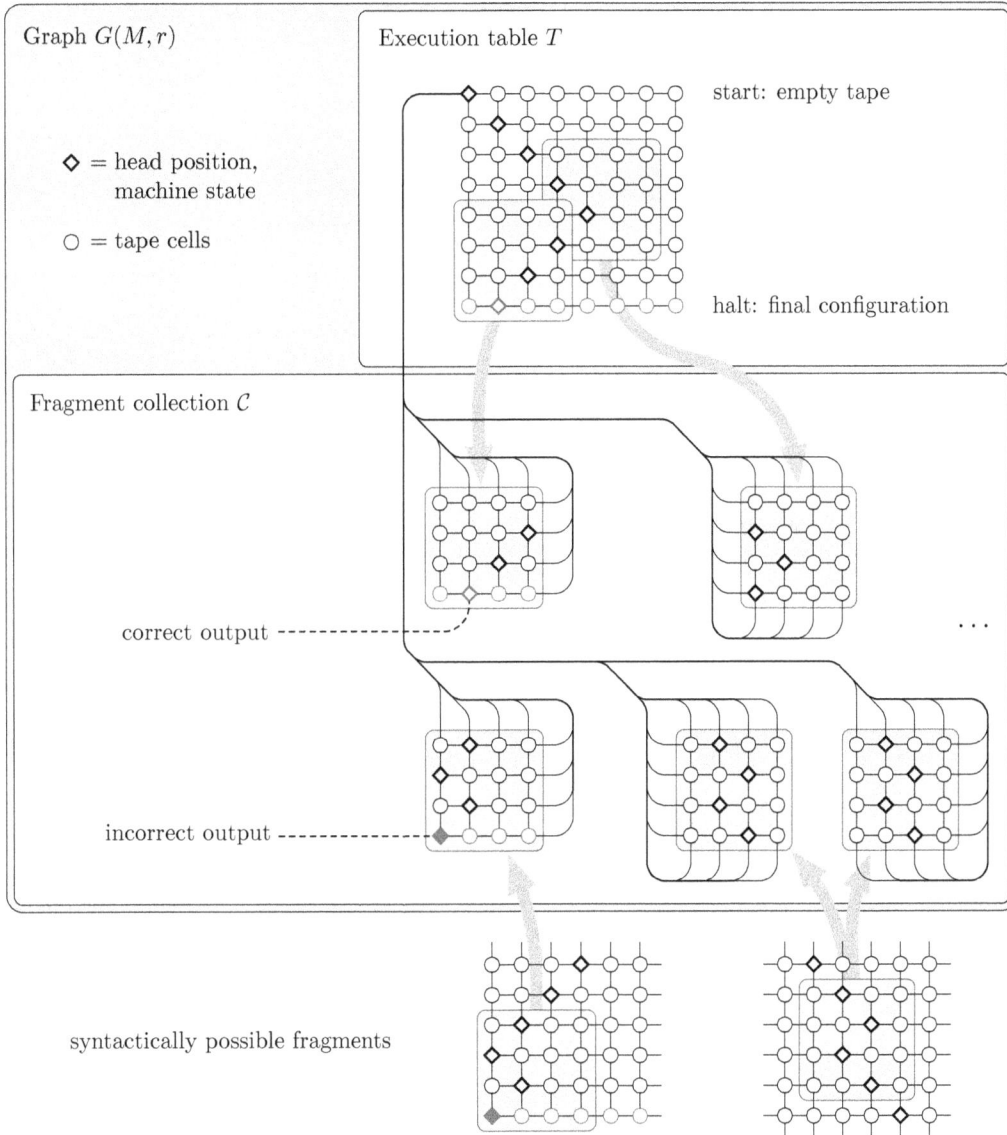

Figure 2: Construction of graph $G(M,r)$.

possible labellings, as our labelling scheme uses bounded labels. We record this observation.

LEMMA 2. *There is an algorithm that on input (N,r) outputs the finite collection $\mathcal{C}(N,r)$.* □

Putting G Together

To construct G we glue together T and the fragments $\mathcal{C}$. Details follow.

Natural borders. Consider the leftmost column of nodes C in a labelled fragment $F \in \mathcal{C}$. We call C a *natural border* if C could, in principle, appear on the leftmost column of an execution table of M, i.e., if the machine head never moves to, or appears from, the left of C. We say that the rightmost column is *natural* under analogous circumstances. The bottom row is *natural* if it does not contain the machine head in a non-halting state. The top row is never natural.

Here is a technical point: we need the non-natural borders to always form a connected subgraph of F. The only situation

where this is currently violated is when precisely the top and bottom rows of F are non-natural, but this is easily fixed by replacing F with two of its variants where the left and right borders are interpreted non-natural in turn. We now gain the following property, which becomes useful when proving that G is locally decidable.

> **Border property**: Given a subgraph induced on the non-natural borders of a fragment $F \in \mathcal{C}$, the local transition rules of M reconstruct F uniquely.

Construction. The graph G consists of (i) the table T, (ii) the fragments $\mathcal{C}$, and also (iii) new edges that connect each node of a non-natural border in $\mathcal{C}$ to the pivot node of T.

This completes the description of G. We leave the straightforward but tedious details of checking that G is locally decidable to the appendix.

Efficiency. Finally, for the purposes of (P3), we note that our construction of $G(M,r)$ is highly explicit in the sense that the set of r-neighbourhoods of $G(M, r)$ can be computed even without the knowledge of M halting.

> **Neighbourhood generator B:** On input (N, r), where N does not necessarily halt, we first compute $\mathcal{C} = \mathcal{C}(N, r)$ using Lemma 2. Then, we begin constructing the (possibly infinite) computation table T of N for some $4r$ rows, each of width $4r$; call the resulting table fragment $T_{4r} \subseteq T$. We then glue $\mathcal{C}$ to the pivot of T_{4r} as described above to obtain a graph G_{4r}. Finally, we output the set of r-neighbourhoods in G_{4r} that do not contain nodes from the bottom row of T_{4r}.

The correctness of B follows from the observation that, if N halts, every r-neighbourhood in $G(N, r)$ is already found in G_{4r}. This establishes property (P3) and completes our proof.

3.3 Randomisation Helps an Id-Oblivious Algorithm

To conclude this section, we point to another application of our property $\mathcal{P}$, this time in the setting of *randomised* local decision. Namely, we observe that $\mathcal{P}$ can be decided by an Id-oblivious algorithm if and only if we allow randomness.

A *randomised* local algorithm has access to an unbounded string of random bits. For $p, q \in (0, 1]$, we say that a randomised local algorithm A is a (p, q)-*decider* for $\mathcal{P}$ if the following holds for any input $(G, \boldsymbol{x}, \mathrm{Id})$:

- if $(G, \boldsymbol{x}) \in \mathcal{P}$, then $A(G, \boldsymbol{x}, \mathrm{Id}, v) = yes$ for all $v \in V(G)$ with probability at least p,

- if $(G, \boldsymbol{x}) \notin \mathcal{P}$, then $A(G, \boldsymbol{x}, \mathrm{Id}, v) = no$ for at least one $v \in V(G)$ with probability at least q.

The power of randomness is still lacking a full characterisation in the context of local decision [3, 4].

Randomised Id-oblivious Decider for $\mathcal{P}$

Even though an Id-oblivious algorithm cannot use randomness to generate a fresh set of globally unique identifiers without any knowledge of n, we can still generate a few large numbers with high probability. This suffices for deciding $\mathcal{P}$ without identifiers, since, in addition to (P2), we only need some node v to obtain a number $n_v \geq n$ so that v can finish simulating M in n_v steps.

To this end, we let a node v toss a coin repeatedly until a head occurs, say after ℓ_v tosses. We set $n_v := 4^{\ell_v}$. The probability that no node has $n_v \geq n$ is then

$$\Pr[\forall v \colon n_v < n] \leq (1 - 1/\sqrt{n})^n = o(1).$$

That is, with probability at least $1 - o(1)$ we can reject an instance $G(M, r)$ where M halts with output other than 0. Hence, we obtain an Id-oblivious $(1, 1 - o(1))$-decider for $\mathcal{P}$. This proves Corollary 1.

4. ACKNOWLEDGEMENTS

We thank the anonymous reviewers for their helpful feedback. This work was supported in part by the ANR project DISPLEXITY, and the INRIA project GANG, the Academy of Finland, Grants 132380 and 252018, and by the Research Funds of the University of Helsinki.

5. REFERENCES

[1] A. Das Sarma, S. Holzer, L. Kor, A. Korman, D. Nanongkai, G. Pandurangan, D. Peleg, and R. Wattenhofer. Distributed verification and hardness of distributed approximation. *SIAM Journal on Computing*, 41(5):1235–1265, 2012.

[2] P. Fraigniaud, M. M. Halldorsson, and A. Korman. On the impact of identifiers on local decision. In *Proc. 16th Conference on Principles of Distributed Systems (OPODIS 2012)*, volume 7702 of *LNCS*, pages 224–238, Berlin, 2012. Springer.

[3] P. Fraigniaud, A. Korman, M. Parter, and D. Peleg. Randomized distributed decision. In *Proc. 26th Symposium on Distributed Computing (DISC 2012)*, volume 7611 of *LNCS*, pages 371–385, Berlin, 2012. Springer.

[4] P. Fraigniaud, A. Korman, and D. Peleg. Local distributed decision. In *Proc. 52nd Symposium on Foundations of Computer Science (FOCS 2011)*, Los Alamitos, 2011. IEEE Computer Society Press.

[5] P. Fraigniaud and A. Pelc. Decidability classes for mobile agents computing. In *Proc. 10th Latin American Symposium on Theoretical Informatics (LATIN 2012)*, volume 7256 of *LNCS*, pages 362–374, Berlin, 2012. Springer.

[6] P. Fraigniaud, S. Rajsbaum, and C. Travers. Locality and checkability in wait-free computing. In *Proc. 25th Symposium on Distributed Computing (DISC 2011)*, volume 6950 of *LNCS*, pages 333–347, Berlin, 2011. Springer.

[7] P. Fraigniaud, S. Rajsbaum, and C. Travers. Universal distributed checkers and orientation-detection tasks. Submitted, 2012.

[8] M. Göös, J. Hirvonen, and J. Suomela. Lower bounds for local approximation. In *Proc. 31st Symposium on Principles of Distributed Computing (PODC 2012)*, pages 175–184, New York, 2012. ACM Press.

[9] M. Göös and J. Suomela. Locally checkable proofs. In *Proc. 30th Symposium on Principles of Distributed Computing (PODC 2011)*, pages 159–168, New York, 2011. ACM Press.

[10] H. Hasemann, J. Hirvonen, J. Rybicki, and J. Suomela. Deterministic local algorithms, unique identifiers, and fractional graph colouring. In *Proc. 19th Colloquium on Structural Information and Communication Complexity (SIROCCO 2012)*, volume 7355 of *LNCS*, pages 48–60, Berlin, 2012. Springer.

[11] L. Kor, A. Korman, and D. Peleg. Tight bounds for distributed MST verification. In *Proc. 28th Symposium on Theoretical Aspects of Computer Science (STACS 2011)*, volume 9 of *LIPIcs*, pages 69–80, Dagstuhl, 2011. Schloss Dagstuhl.

[12] A. Korman and S. Kutten. Distributed verification of minimum spanning trees. *Distributed Computing*, 20(4):253–266, 2007.

[13] A. Korman, S. Kutten, and T. Masuzawa. Fast and compact self stabilizing verification, computation, and fault detection of an MST. In *Proc. 30th Symposium on Principles of Distributed Computing (PODC 2011)*, pages 311–320, New York, 2011. ACM Press.

[14] A. Korman, S. Kutten, and D. Peleg. Proof labeling schemes. *Distributed Computing*, 22(4):215–233, 2010.

[15] A. Korman, J.-S. Sereni, and L. Viennot. Toward more localized local algorithms: removing assumptions concerning global knowledge. In *Proc. 30th Symposium on Principles of Distributed Computing (PODC 2011)*, pages 49–58, New York, 2011. ACM Press.

[16] N. Linial. Locality in distributed graph algorithms. *SIAM Journal on Computing*, 21(1):193–201, 1992.

[17] A. Mayer, M. Naor, and L. Stockmeyer. Local computations on static and dynamic graphs. In *Proc. 3rd Israel Symposium on the Theory of Computing and Systems (ISTCS 1995)*, pages 268–278, Piscataway, 1995. IEEE.

[18] M. Naor and L. Stockmeyer. What can be computed locally? *SIAM Journal on Computing*, 24(6):1259–1277, 1995.

[19] C. H. Papadimitriou. *Computational Complexity*. Addison-Wesley Publishing Company, 1994.

[20] D. Peleg. *Distributed Computing: A Locality-Sensitive Approach*. SIAM Monographs on Discrete Mathematics and Applications. SIAM, Philadelphia, 2000.

APPENDIX

In this appendix we present the details that were skipped in Section 3.2.

Pyramidal Execution Table

We describe how to augment the execution table T of M so that it becomes locally checkable. For clarity of exposition, we assume that $s + 1$ is a power of 2, say $s + 1 = 2^h$ for some h—this assumption is easy to remove by modifying the following constructions slightly.

Denote the node set of T by $[2^h] \times [2^h] \times \{0\}$. We use an idea from Section 2: we attach a pyramid-shaped *layered quadtree* on top of T. That is, let $T^\triangle$ be the graph that is arranged in layers $z = 0, 1, \ldots, h$ such that T makes up the 0-th level; the z-th level contains a square grid on nodes $[2^{h-z}] \times [2^{h-z}] \times \{z\}$; and each node (x, y, z) on level $z \leq h-1$ is connected to $(\lceil x/2 \rceil, \lceil y/2 \rceil, z+1)$ on level $z+1$; see Figure 3. The new nodes $V(T^\triangle) \setminus V(T)$ do not receive labels, except, of course, the universal label (M, r).

Pyramidal Fragments

Since our construction is now going to use the pyramidal $T^\triangle$ instead of T, we need to adjust our definition of the table fragments $\mathcal{C}$ accordingly. Analogously, we consider the pyramidal versions the fragments in $\mathcal{C}$:

$$\mathcal{C}^\triangle := \{F^\triangle : F \in \mathcal{C}\}.$$

However, since attaching a pyramid on top of a fragment decreases shortest-path distances between nodes, we need to use larger fragments than in Section 3.2. To fool an r-time algorithm, it is sufficient that the pyramids $F^\triangle$ have height $3r$ (i.e., grid-size is $2^{3r} \times 2^{3r}$). This way we recover the critical property: each r-neighbourhood that could syntactically arise in $T^\triangle$ can already be found in $\mathcal{C}^\triangle$.

The graph $G(M, r)$ is then defined similarly as in Section 3.2: we glue the fragments $\mathcal{C}^\triangle$ to the pivot of $T^\triangle$ by their non-natural borders.

Note also that in verifying the property (P3) we now need the neighbourhood generator B to first construct a sub-table $T_R \subseteq T$ containing some $R = 2^{4r}$ initial rows and columns, and then glue $\mathcal{C}^\triangle$ and $T_R^\triangle$ together.

$G(M, r)$ Is Locally Decidable

Suppose we are given an instance G; we argue how to locally decide (even in LD^*) whether $G = G(M, r)$ for some (M, r).

1. All nodes first make sure they are given the same pair (M, r) as part of their local input.

2. Each node in G should then belong to a layered quadtree. By design, the structure of a quadtree is such that the nodes can locally tell apart adjacent layers and recognise the inter-layer edges. In particular, each pyramid has a unique top node, which fixes its global structure.

   If the general quadtree structure is consistent, we can ignore all but the bottommost layer of each pyramid, and be convinced that G consists of square grids that are connected together by some inter-grid edges.

3. The labelling inside each grid should follow the local execution rules of M. Also, we should have a consistent orientation on each grid.

4. The border nodes of a grid can collectively verify that the grid is either *fragment-like* (all nodes in the topmost row are incident to inter-grid edges) or a full execution table (the top-left node is the only node incident to inter-grid edges).

5. All top-left grid corners should see at least one *pivot candidate* v that is part of a full execution table. But we can impose that any such v is globally unique:

   - First, v's own execution table, call it T, cannot have any other nodes with outgoing inter-grid edges assuming that all nodes in T pass steps 3 and 4.
   - Second, consider the grids $\mathcal{C}$ that adjoin v. Node v can check that each grid in $\mathcal{C}$ has fragment-like non-natural borders. In particular, we can check that the non-natural borders form a connected subgraph in each grid—if the bottom row of a grid is non-natural, it is sufficient to verify that one of the side borders is also non-natural. But then, exploiting the *Border property* from Section 3.2, v can figure out the exact structure of $\mathcal{C}$ provided the nodes in $\mathcal{C}$ have passed step 3. It follows that there are no inter-grid edges unseen by v.

   This establishes the uniqueness of v.

6. Finally, v can check that $\mathcal{C} = \mathcal{C}(M, r)$ using Lemma 2.

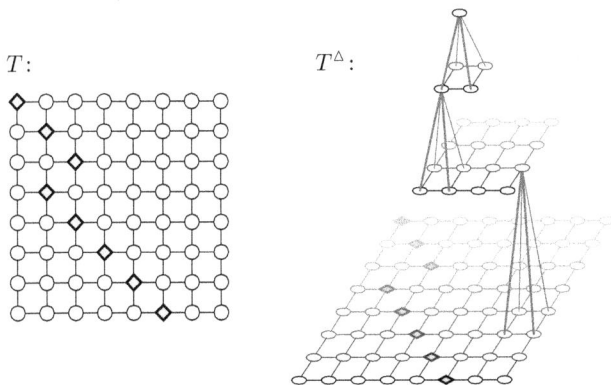

Figure 3: Table T and pyramid $T^\triangle$.

Synchrony Weakened by Message Adversaries vs Asynchrony Restricted by Failure Detectors

Michel Raynal
Institut Universitaire de France
& IRISA, Campus de Beaulieu
35042 Rennes Cedex, France
raynal@irisa.fr

Julien Stainer
IRISA, Université de Rennes
Campus de Beaulieu
35042 Rennes Cedex, France
julien.stainer@irisa.fr

ABSTRACT

A message adversary is a daemon that suppresses messages in round-based message-passing synchronous systems in which no process crashes. A property imposed on a message adversary defines a subset of messages that cannot be eliminated by the adversary. It has recently been shown that when a message adversary is constrained by a property denoted TOUR (for tournament), the corresponding synchronous system and the asynchronous crash-prone read/write system have the same computability power for task solvability.

This paper introduces new message adversary properties (denoted SOURCE and QUORUM), and shows that the synchronous round-based systems whose adversaries are constrained by these properties are characterizations of classical asynchronous crash-prone systems (1) in which processes communicate through atomic read/write registers or point-to-point message-passing, and (2) enriched with failure detectors such as Ω and Σ. Hence these properties characterize maximal adversaries, in the sense that they define strongest message adversaries equating classical asynchronous crash-prone systems. They consequently provide strong relations linking round-based synchrony weakened by message adversaries with asynchrony restricted with failure detectors. This not only enriches our understanding of the synchrony/asynchrony duality, but also allows for the establishment of a meaningful hierarchy of property-constrained message adversaries.

Categories ands Subject Descriptors

D.1.3 [**Programming techniques**]: *Concurrent Programming*
F.1.1 [**Computation by Abstract Devices**]: Models of Computation, *automata, relations among models*

Keywords: Asynchronous system, Distributed computability, Failure detector, Message adversary, Message-passing model, Model equivalence, Ω, Process crash, Quorum, Read/write model, Round, Σ, Simulation, Source, Synchronous system, Task, Tournament, Wait-freedom.

1. INTRODUCTION

Message adversaries for synchronous message-passing systems. In a round-based message-passing synchronous system, processes communicate by exchanging messages at every round, and the synchrony assumption provided by the model guarantees that the messages sent at the beginning a round are received by their destination processes by the end of the corresponding round. Assuming that no process is faulty, the notion of a *message adversary* has been introduced in [22] (where it is called *mobile transmission failures*) to model messages losses and study their impact on the computability power of synchronous systems [22, 23].

Interestingly, the notion of constraining message deliveries has also been investigated in asynchronous systems, with distinct names, and in different contexts. As an example, asynchronous message patterns which allow failure detectors to be implemented despite asynchrony have been investigated in [10, 16]. The view of failure detectors as schedulers which encapsulate fairness assumptions can also be related to this approach [7, 17]. Recently, assumptions on message deliveries and message exchange patterns have been used to define new asynchronous computation models and study their computability power [6, 13, 18, 24]. The general idea, which underlies these works, consists in capturing the "weakest pattern of information exchange" that allows a family of problems to be solved despite failures.

Notation. The notation $\mathcal{SMP}_n[adv : AD]$ is used to denote a round-based synchronous system made up of n sequential processes whose communications are under the control of the adversary AD. While, in every round, each process sends a message to each other process, the power of the adversary AD consists in suppressing some of these messages (which are consequently never received).

According to their power, several classes of adversaries can be defined. $\mathcal{SMP}_n[adv : \emptyset]$ denotes a synchronous system in which the adversary has no power (it can suppress no message), while $\mathcal{SMP}_n[adv : \infty]$ denotes the synchronous system in which the adversary can suppress all messages. It is easy to see that, from a message adversary and computability point of view, $\mathcal{SMP}_n[adv : \emptyset]$ is the most powerful crash-free synchronous system model, while $\mathcal{SMP}_n[adv : \infty]$ is the weakest. More generally, the weaker the message adversary AD, the more powerful the system.

Asynchrony from synchrony. Informally, a *task* is a one-shot distributed computing problem where each process has a private input, and each process has to compute a local output such that each output may depend on the input values of the participating processes. The most famous and studied task is the consensus task.

Afek and Gafni addressed recently task solvability in synchronous message-passing systems weakened by message adversaries [1][1]. Let $\mathcal{ARW}_{n,n-1}[fd : \emptyset]$ denote the asynchronous read/write model where up to $(n-1)$ processes may crash ("$fd : \emptyset$" stands for "no failure detector", see below; this is the classical read/write wait-free model [11]). Afek and Gafni's main results are the following ones.

- Their first result concerns the adversary TOUR (for tournament) whose behavior is the following one. For each pair of processes p_i and p_j, and in each synchronous round, TOUR is allowed to suppress either the message sent by p_i to p_j or the message sent by p_j to p_i, but not both. The important result attached to TOUR is that $\mathcal{SMP}_n[adv : \text{TOUR}]$ and $\mathcal{ARW}_{n,n-1}[fd : \emptyset]$ have the same computability power for read/write wait-free solvable tasks.

- In addition to TOUR, two more adversaries, denoted TP and PAIRS, are described and it is shown that the three adversary-based distributed synchronous models $\mathcal{SMP}_n[adv : \text{TOUR}]$, $\mathcal{SMP}_n[adv : \text{TP}]$, and $\mathcal{SMP}_n[adv : \text{PAIRS}]$ are equivalent for task solvability. Moreover, $\mathcal{SMP}_n[adv : \text{PAIRS}]$ is used to show that, from a topology point of view, the protocol complex of PAIRS is a subdivided complex. This means that the message adversary PAIRS (and consequently also TOUR and TP) captures, in a very simple way, Herlihy and Shavit's condition equating the read/write wait-free model with a complex subdivision [12].

Failure detectors for asynchronous crash-prone systems. Informally, a failure detector is a device that provides each process p_i with information on failures [4]. According to the quality and the type of information they provide, several classes of failure detectors can be defined (see [19] for an introductory survey).

The failure detectors denoted Ω and Σ are among the most important failure detectors. This is due to the following reasons: (1) Ω is the weakest failure detector that allows consensus to be solved in $\mathcal{ARW}_{n,n-1}[fd : \emptyset]$ [5, 15]; (2) Σ is the weakest failure detector that allows an atomic register to be implemented on top of $\mathcal{AMP}_{n,n-1}[fd : \emptyset]$ [8], where $\mathcal{AMP}_{n,n-1}[fd : \emptyset]$ denotes the classical asynchronous message-passing system where up to $(n-1)$ processes may crash and every message is eventually received. "Weakest" means that any failure detector that allows to solve consensus (resp., implement a register) provides at least as much information on failures as the one provided by Ω (resp., Σ). Finally, the pair (Σ, Ω) is the weakest failure detector that allows consensus to be solved in $\mathcal{AMP}_{n,n-1}[fd : \emptyset]$ [5, 8].

Let FD denote a failure detector. $\mathcal{ARW}_{n,n-1}[fd : \text{FD}]$ denotes the asynchronous read/write model where up to $(n-1)$ processes may crash, augmented with FD. Similarly, $\mathcal{AMP}_{n,n-1}[fd : \text{FD}]$ denotes $\mathcal{AMP}_{n,n-1}[fd : \emptyset]$ augmented with FD.

Content of the paper. Following Afek and Gafni's seminal approach, the aim of the paper is to better understand and extend the message adversary approach, and capture its relations with asynchrony restricted by failure detectors. Considering the reliable synchronous round-based message-passing model ($\mathcal{SMP}_n[adv : \emptyset]$) as core model, the paper has the following contributions. Those concern (1) the crash-prone asynchronous read/write model, and (2) the crash-prone message-passing model, both enriched with failure detectors. These contributions are described in the hierarchy depicted in Figure 1. $A \simeq_M B$ means that the computing model A

can be simulated in the model B and vice-versa. $A \simeq_T B$ means that any task that can be solved in the model A, can be solved in the model B and vice-versa. An arrow from A to B means that the model A is stronger than the model B, but not vice-versa. These arrows follow from known results (e.g., $\mathcal{ARW}_{n,n-1}[fd : \Omega]$ is stronger than both $\mathcal{ARW}_{n,n-1}[fd : \emptyset]$ and $\mathcal{AMP}_{n,n-1}[fd : \Omega]$). Let us observe that, as they are failure-free, the system models $\mathcal{SMP}_n[adv : \emptyset]$, $\mathcal{ARW}_{n,0}[fd : \emptyset]$, and $\mathcal{AMP}_{n,0}[fd : \emptyset]$, are computationally equivalent (first line of the figure).

- Starting from the fact that the property TOUR (for tournament) captures the constraint on message delivery such that $\mathcal{SMP}_n[adv : \text{TOUR}] \simeq_T \mathcal{ARW}_{n,n-1}[fd : \emptyset]$, Section 3 focuses on the properties of a message adversary which allow to enrich $\mathcal{SMP}_n[adv : \text{TOUR}]$ to obtain $\mathcal{ARW}_{n,n-1}[fd : \Omega]$. To that end (1) it presents a new message delivery property, denoted SOURCE, and (2) shows that $\mathcal{SMP}_n[adv : \text{SOURCE}, \text{TOUR}]$ and $\mathcal{ARW}_{n,n-1}[fd : \Omega]$ are equivalent for task solvability. It follows that SOURCE is a minimal requirement that has to be added to $\mathcal{SMP}_n[adv : \text{TOUR}]$ in order to proceed from the model $\mathcal{SMP}_n[adv : \text{TOUR}]$ to the model $\mathcal{ARW}_{n,n-1}[fd : \Omega]$.

- Then Section 4 shows that, by weakening $\mathcal{SMP}_n[adv : \text{SOURCE}, \text{TOUR}]$ into $\mathcal{SMP}_n[adv : \text{SOURCE}]$, the resulting synchronous message-passing system is such that we have $\mathcal{SMP}_n[adv : \text{SOURCE}] \simeq_T \mathcal{AMP}_{n,n-1}[fd : \Omega]$. It follows that SOURCE captures the weakest property on message delivery that an adversary AD has to satisfy so that any task solvable in $\mathcal{AMP}_{n,n-1}[fd : \Omega]$ can be solved in $\mathcal{SMP}_n[adv : \text{AD}]$.[2] Said differently, when considering tasks solvability in crash-prone asynchronous systems enriched with Ω, what allows going from "message-passing" communication to "read/write" communication is characterized by the property TOUR from a message adversary point of view in a synchronous system (vertical arrow on the right of Figure 1).

- Then Section 5 focuses on a new message delivery property denoted QUORUM, and shows that a message adversary constrained by this property captures in $\mathcal{SMP}_n[adv : \emptyset]$ the same computability power (from a task point of view) as the one added by the failure detector Σ to $\mathcal{AMP}_{n,n-1}[fd : \emptyset]$. To that end, it shows that $\mathcal{SMP}_n[adv : \text{QUORUM}] \simeq_T \mathcal{AMP}_{n,n-1}[fd : \Sigma]$.

- Finally, as a consequence of the previous results, Section 6 shows that the properties SOURCE + QUORUM characterize the pair of failure detectors $\Sigma + \Omega$, i.e., $\mathcal{SMP}_n[adv : \text{SOURCE}, \text{QUORUM}] \simeq_T \mathcal{AMP}_{n,n-1}[fd : \Sigma, \Omega]$.

As indicated, the paper provides message adversary-based characterizations of failure detectors for both read/write and message-passing crash-prone asynchronous systems. The aim of these results is to enrich our understanding of both message adversaries used to weaken communication in synchronous systems and failure detectors used to enrich asynchronous crash-prone systems. They complement the results of [1] and exhibit strong intimate relations linking synchrony, message losses, and round-based model, on the one side, with asynchrony, process crashes, and failure detectors, on the other side. Interestingly, this seems to show that $\mathcal{SMP}_n[adv : \emptyset]$ (basic reliable synchronous round-based model)

---

[1] A close approach focused only on consensus is presented in [3].

[2] As shown in [1] with the properties TOUR, TP, and PAIRS, several properties can be equivalent (i.e., each one can be implemented in $\mathcal{SMP}_n[adv : \emptyset]$ under the control of an adversary constrained by any other one). Hence, if a property P is the "weakest", so are the properties equivalent to P.

$$\mathcal{SMP}_n[adv:\emptyset] \simeq_M \mathcal{AMP}_{n,0}[fd:\emptyset] \simeq_M \mathcal{ARW}_{n,0}[fd:\emptyset]$$

Section 6
$$\mathcal{SMP}_n[adv:\text{SOURCE, QUORUM}] \simeq_T \mathcal{AMP}_{n,n-1}[fd:\Sigma,\Omega]$$

$$\mathcal{SMP}_n[adv:\text{QUORUM}] \simeq_T \mathcal{AMP}_{n,n-1}[fd:\Sigma] \qquad \mathcal{SMP}_n[adv:\text{SOURCE, TOUR}] \simeq_T \mathcal{ARW}_{n,n-1}[fd:\Omega]$$
Section 5 Section 3

$$\mathcal{SMP}_n[adv:\text{TOUR}] \simeq_T \mathcal{ARW}_{n,n-1}[fd:\emptyset] \qquad \mathcal{SMP}_n[adv:\text{SOURCE}] \simeq_T \mathcal{AMP}_{n,n-1}[fd:\Omega]$$
[1] Section 4

$$\mathcal{SMP}_n[adv:\infty] \simeq_T \mathcal{AMP}_{n,n-1}[fd:\emptyset] \qquad \text{Section 2}$$

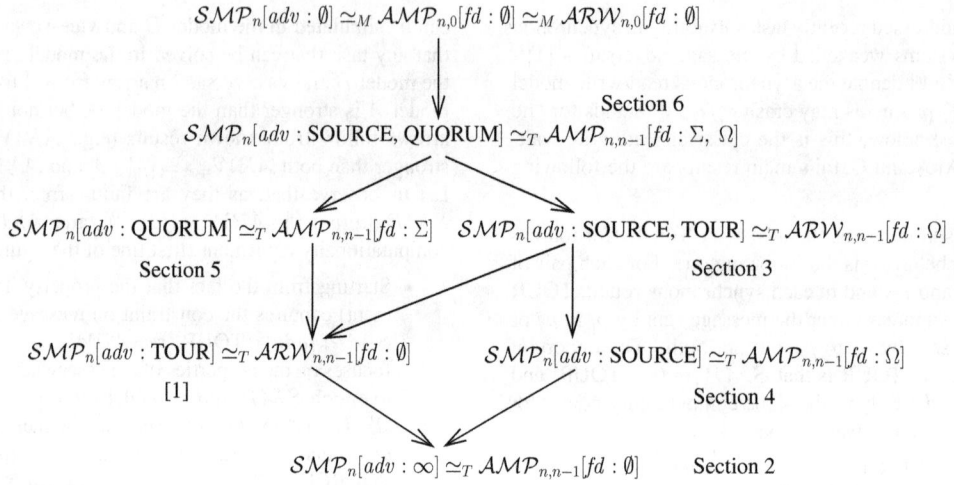

Figure 1: A message adversary hierarchy based on task equivalence and failure detectors

and the notion of a message adversary are central in the quest for a universal model of distributed computing.

Roadmap. The paper is composed of 7 sections. Section 2 presents base models, message adversaries, and failure detectors. Section 3 introduces the property SOURCE on message deliveries, and show that it characterizes the failure detector Ω in read/write systems. Section 4 shows that, taken alone, the property SOURCE characterizes the failure detector Ω in asynchronous message-passing systems. Section 5 and Section 6 introduce the property QUORUM and show that it characterizes the failure detector Σ. Finally, Section 7 concludes the paper. Due to page limitation, all missing proofs can be found in [21].

2. MODELS, MESSAGE ADVERSARIES, FAILURE DETECTORS, TASKS

2.1 Base Computation Models

The base computation models relevant to this paper have been presented in the introduction. They are (1) the reliable round-based synchronous model $\mathcal{SMP}_n[adv:\emptyset]$ possibly weakened with a message adversary AD, and (b) the crash-prone asynchronous models $\mathcal{ARW}_{n,n-1}[fd:\emptyset]$ (basic *read/write wait-free* model [11]) and $\mathcal{AMP}_{n,n-1}[fd:\emptyset]$, both possibly enriched with a failure detector FD.

2.2 Message Adversary, Message Graphs, and Dynamic Graphs in Synchronous Systems

Message adversary. Given a run of a synchronous system, a message adversary suppresses messages sent by processes. A property associated with a message adversary restricts its power by specifying messages which cannot be suppressed. A message adversary is consequently defined by a set of properties which constrain its behavior.

Message graphs associated with the rounds of a synchronous system. Given a message adversary AD, and a round r of a run of a synchronous system, let $\mathcal{G}^r$ be the directed graph (as defined in [1]), whose vertices are the process identities, and such that there is an edge from i to j iff the adversary AD does not suppress the

message sent by p_i to p_j at round r. We consider the following definition associated with each graph $\mathcal{G}^r$.

- $i \xrightarrow{r} j$ means that the directed edge (i,j) belongs to $\mathcal{G}^r$ (at round r, the message from p_i to p_j is not removed by the adversary).

The property TOUR. As indicated in the introduction, the property TOUR [1] restricts the behavior of a message adversary as follows. For any r, and any pair of processes (p_i, p_j), $\mathcal{G}^r$ contains the directed edge (i,j) or the directed edge (j,i) or both. This means that, at every round, the adversary cannot suppress both the messages sent to each other by two processes. Hence, the graphs $\mathcal{G}^r$ associated with the rounds r of a run in $\mathcal{SMP}_n[adv:\text{TOUR}]$ are such that:

$$\forall r \geq 1 : \forall (i,j) : (i \xrightarrow{r} j) \vee (j \xrightarrow{r} i).$$

Strongly/weakly correct processes in a synchronous run. The aim of this section is to introduce the notion of a *strongly correct* process which captures the processes whose an infinite number of messages are received (directly or indirectly) by any other process [20]. Such a notion is defined as follows.

- $i \overset{\geq r}{\rightsquigarrow} j$ means that there is a directed path starting from p_i and leading to p_j in a dynamically defined sequence of message graphs starting at a round $\geq r$. More formally,
$$\exists k \geq 0, \, \exists r_1 < \cdots < r_k, \, \exists \lambda_0, \lambda_1, \ldots, \lambda_k \in \{1, \ldots, n\} :$$
$$(r_1 \geq r) \wedge (\lambda_0 = i \wedge \lambda_k = j)$$
$$\wedge (\forall m \in \{1, \ldots, k\} : \lambda_{m-1} \xrightarrow{r_m} \lambda_m).$$

- $i \overset{\infty}{\rightsquigarrow} j \overset{def}{=} (\forall r > 0 : i \overset{\geq r}{\rightsquigarrow} j)$. Hence, $i \overset{\infty}{\rightsquigarrow} j$ means that, whatever r, there is eventually a directed path starting at p_i at a round $\geq r$ and finishing at p_j in the dynamically defined sequence of message graphs.

- $(i \overset{\infty}{\leftrightsquigarrow} j) \Leftrightarrow (i \overset{\infty}{\rightsquigarrow} j \wedge j \overset{\infty}{\rightsquigarrow} i)$. Assuming each process always receive its own messages, this relation is reflexive, symmetric, and transitive. Hence, it is an equivalence relation.

- Let G be the graph whose vertices are $\{1, \ldots, n\}$ and directed edges are defined by the relation $\overset{\infty}{\leftrightsquigarrow}$; let $SC(G)$ be the graph of its strongly connected components. If $SC(G)$ has a single

168

vertex X with no input edge, the processes in X are called *strongly correct* processes, while the processes in $\{1, ..., n\} \setminus X$ are called *weakly correct*. If $SC(G)$ has several vertices with no input edge, all processes are weakly correct.

Let $\mathcal{SC}$ denote the (possibly empty) set of strongly correct processes in a synchronous round-based system under the control of a message adversary.

2.3 Failure Detectors in Asynchr. Systems

While a message adversary weakens a synchronous round-based system (made up of reliable processes) by suppressing messages, a failure detector enriches an asynchronous system where no message is lost but where processes may suffer crash failures. Informally, a failure detector is a device that provides each process p_i with a read-only local variable xx_i containing (possibly unreliable) information on process crashes [4]. This paper considers two failure detectors. Let τ denote any time instant; xx_i^τ denotes the value of xx_i at time τ. This time notion, which is used in the definition of a failure detector, is not accessible to the processes. The identity of a process p_i is i. Given a run, a process that crashes is said to be *faulty* in that run, otherwise it is *correct*. Let $\mathcal{C}$ denote the sets of identities of the correct processes.

- Ω is called an *eventual leader* failure detector [5]. In the system models $\mathcal{ARW}_{n,n-1}[fd : \Omega]$ or $\mathcal{AMP}_{n,n-1}[fd : \Omega]$, each process p_i is endowed with a local variable $xx_i = leader_i$ that always contains a (possibly changing) process identity. Moreover, there is an unknown but finite time τ and a process identity $\ell \in \mathcal{C}$ such that $\forall \tau' \geq \tau : (i \in \mathcal{C}) \Rightarrow (leader_i^{\tau'} = \ell)$.

- Σ is called a *quorum* failure detector [8]. In the system model $\mathcal{AMP}_{n,n-1}[fd : \Sigma]$, each process p_i is endowed with a local variable $xx_i = qr_i$ that always contains a non-empty set of process identities and is such that (1) $\forall \tau, \tau', \forall i, j: qr_i^\tau \cap qr_j^{\tau'} \neq \emptyset$ (intersection property), and (2) $\forall i \in \mathcal{C} : \exists \tau : \forall \tau' \geq \tau : qr_i^{\tau'} \subseteq \mathcal{C}$ (liveness property).

2.4 Tasks

A task is a one-shot computation problem specified in terms of an input/output relation Δ. Each process starts with a private input value and must eventually compute a private output value, which is a function of of the inputs of the participating processes. From an external observer point of view, an input vector $I[1..n]$ specifies the input value $I[i] = v_i$ of each process p_i. Similarly, an output vector $O[1..n]$ specifies a result value $O[j]$ for each process p_j.

A task is defined by a set of input vectors and a relation Δ which describes which output vectors are correct for each input vector I. More precisely, for each valid input vector I, the values computed by the processes must be such that there is an output vector $O \in \Delta(I)$ such that, for each j, $O[j]$ is the value computed by p_j; moreover, if no value is computed by p_j, it is because p_j has crashed during the computation. (A formal introduction to tasks can be found in [12].)

THEOREM 1. *A task T can be solved in $\mathcal{SMP}_n[adv : \infty]$ iff it can be solved in $\mathcal{AMP}_{n,n-1}[fd : \emptyset]$.*

3. THE PAIR SOURCE + TOUR CAPTURES EXACTLY Ω IN $\mathcal{ARW}_{n,n-1}[fd : \emptyset]$

This section shows that the computing models $\mathcal{SMP}_n[adv : \text{SOURCE, TOUR}]$ and $\mathcal{ARW}_{n,n-1}[fd : \Omega]$ have the same computational power for tasks.

3.1 The Property SOURCE

This property is defined as follows:
$$\exists s \in \{1, \ldots, n\} : \exists r_0 \geq 1 :$$
$$\forall r \geq r_0 : \forall i \in \{1, \ldots, n\} : (s \xrightarrow{r} i).$$
This statement means that, in each run of $\mathcal{SMP}_n[adv : \text{SOURCE}]$, there are a process p_s and a round r_0, such that, at every round $r \geq r_0$, the adversary does not suppress the message sent by p_s to the other processes.

3.2 From the Read/Write Model $\mathcal{ARW}_{n,n-1}[fd : \Omega]$ to $\mathcal{SMP}_n[adv : \text{SOURCE, TOUR}]$

This section presents a simulation of the synchronous model $\mathcal{SMP}_n[adv : \text{SOURCE, TOUR}]$ on top of $\mathcal{ARW}_{n,n-1}[fd : \Omega]$ such that, any task that can be solved in $\mathcal{ARW}_{n,n-1}[fd : \Omega]$ can be solved in $\mathcal{SMP}_n[adv : \text{SOURCE, TOUR}]$.

Global and local variables of the simulation. The simulation uses a shared 3-dimensional array MEM where $MEM[i][r][j]$ is an atomic read/write register written by p_i and read by p_j. This register contains the message sent by p_i to p_j in round r of the simulation of $\mathcal{SMP}_n[adv : \text{SOURCE, TOUR}]$; $\bot$ is a default value used to indicate that no message has yet been written or the corresponding message has been suppressed by the adversary. The local variable r_i simulates the current round number of $\mathcal{SMP}_n[adv : \text{SOURCE, TOUR}]$, while ls_state_i represents the local simulation state. The local variable $msgs\_to\_send_i[1..n]$ contains the messages that p_i will send to each other process during the next simulated round ($msgs\_to\_send_i[j]$ contains the message for p_j). $leader_i$ is the read-only local variable containing the current local output of Ω.

The simulation is locally defined by the function simulate(). It takes as input parameters the current local state of the simulation and the messages received from the other processes at the current round. It modifies accordingly the local simulation state and computes the messages that will be sent to the other processes during the next round.

Simulation algorithm. The local simulation algorithm is described in Figure 2. The local simulator of process p_i first proceeds to the next round (line 5) and waits until its current leader has sent it a message (predicate $MEM[leader_i][r_i][i] \neq \bot$) or it is its own leader (lines 6-8). When this occurs, the simulator writes in $MEM[i][r_i]$ the messages sent by p_i at the current round (line 9). Then, p_i consumes messages (line 10), and uses them to modify its local simulation state and compute the message it will send during the next round (line 11).

LEMMA 1. *If a task can be solved in the synchronous model $\mathcal{SMP}_n[adv : \text{SOURCE, TOUR}]$, it can be solved in the enriched read/write model $\mathcal{ARW}_{n,n-1}[fd : \Omega]$.*

3.3 From $\mathcal{SMP}_n[adv : \text{SOURCE, TOUR}]$ to the Read/Write Model $\mathcal{ARW}_{n,n-1}[fd : \Omega]$

This section presents a simulation of $\mathcal{ARW}_{n,n-1}[fd : \Omega]$ on top of $\mathcal{SMP}_n[adv : \text{SOURCE, TOUR}]$ such that, any task that can be solved in $\mathcal{SMP}_n[adv : \text{SOURCE, TOUR}]$ can be solved in $\mathcal{ARW}_{n,n-1}[fd : \Omega]$. This simulation has the same structure as the simulation of $\mathcal{ARW}_{n,n-1}[fd : \emptyset]$ on top of $\mathcal{SMP}_n[adv : \emptyset]$ described in [1]. Basically, it adds to it the management of the local variables $missed_i$ (defined below) from which Ω is extracted.

Global and local variables of the simulation. The shared memory of $\mathcal{ARW}_{n,n-1}[fd : \Omega]$ is made up of an array of single-

Figure 2: From the enriched read/write model $\mathcal{ARW}_{n,n-1}[fd : \Omega]$ **to** $\mathcal{SMP}_n[adv : \textbf{SOURCE, TOUR}]$

writer/multi-reader atomic registers $MEM[1..n]$ such that only p_i can write $MEM[i]$. The simulation associates a sequence number with each read or write operation of a simulated process p_i. To simplify notations, a read of $MEM[\ell]$ by p_i is denoted $read_i(\ell)$ and a write of v into $MEM[i]$ is denoted $write_i(v)$.

As in the previous simulation, the procedure simulate() is used to locally simulate the behavior of p_i from its current step until its next invocation of a communication operation (i.e., a read or a write of the simulated shared memory). The simulation stops just before this invocation. It takes as input parameters the current local state of p_i (ls_state_i) and the last value read from the shared memory by p_i. This value, saved in $read\_value_i$ (and initialized to $\bot$), is meaningless if the operation is a write. The local variable $next\_op_i$ contains p_i's next read or write operation to be simulated.

The local variable $view_i$ contains all the read/write operations issued by the processes and known by p_i. Such an operation is represented by a triple $(j, seq\_nb, next\_op)$. The simulation algorithm is a full information algorithm and consequently the set $view_i$ increases forever.

The local variable $informed_i$ contains the set of processes which, to p_i knowledge, know the last read/write operation it is currently simulating. Finally, the set $missed_i$ (from which Ω is built) contains pairs (k, r) whose meaning is the following:
$((k, r) \in missed_i) \Rightarrow$ there is at least one process that, during round r of the simulation, has not received and delivered the message sent by (the simulator of) p_k during that round.

Simulation algorithm. The simulation algorithm is described in Figure 3. When it starts a new round, the simulator of p_i sends its control local state, i.e., the triple $(i, view_i, missed_i)$ to each other process (line 5). Then (lines 6-10), it considers all the messages it has received during the current round r, and updates accordingly rec_msg_i and $missed_i$.

Lines 11-12 locally implement Ω (see below). The local variable $informed_i$ is then updated to take into account what has been learnt from the messages just received. Let us notice (line 13) that it follows from TOUR that $(j \notin rec\_from_i) \Rightarrow p_j$ has received p_i's round r message.

Then (the simulator of) p_i executes rounds in $\mathcal{SMP}_n[adv : \textbf{SOURCE, TOUR}]$ until it learns that (the simulators of) all the processes know its last read/write operation (line 15). Then, it invokes simulate($ls\_state_i, read\_value_i$) (line 16). If its (simulated) shared memory operation is a read, the value $read\_value_i$ is the value obtained by this read operation. Otherwise (the simulated

operation is a write of p_i), $read\_value_i$ is useless. As already indicated, the invocation of simulate($ls\_state_i, read\_value_i$) simulates then the behavior of p_i until its next read/write operation.

If the operation at which the local simulation stopped is a read of $MEM[\ell]$ (line 17), the local simulator computes, and deposits in $read\_value_i$, the value that will be associated with this read (line 18-22). If p_ℓ has not issued a write, $read\_value_i$ is set to the default value $\bot$ (line 19). Otherwise, $read\_value_i$ is set to the last value written by p_ℓ (line 18-21). Then, whatever the next operation (read or write) of p_i, the local simulator associates a sequence number with it and adds the triple $(i, seq\_nb_i, next\_op_i)$ to $view_i$ (line 24-25). Moreover, as its scope is the simulation of $next\_op_i$, the set $informed_i$ is reset to $\{i\}$.

As previously indicated, the current value (kept in ℓd_i) of the read-only variable $leader_i$, which locally implements Ω, is computed from the set $missed_i$ at lines 11-12. The simulator of p_i (1) computes, for each p_j, the set of rounds at which at least one simulator has not received the round r message sent by p_j's simulator (these are messages suppressed by the adversary); then (2) it associates with each p_j the cardinality of the previous set; and finally, (3) it considers the process p_ℓ for which the adversary has suppressed the less messages (if there are several such processes, ties are solved by using the total order on process identities).

LEMMA 2. *If a task can be solved in* $\mathcal{ARW}_{n,n-1}[fd : \Omega]$, *it can be solved in* $\mathcal{SMP}_n[adv : \textbf{SOURCE, TOUR}]$.

3.4 The Pair of Adversaries SOURCE + TOUR Captures Exactly Ω in the Read/Write Model $\mathcal{ARW}_{n,n-1}[fd : \emptyset]$

THEOREM 2. *A task can be solved in the synchronous model* $\mathcal{SMP}_n[adv : \textbf{SOURCE, TOUR}]$ *iff it can be solved in the enriched read/write model* $\mathcal{ARW}_{n,n-1}[fd : \Omega]$.

Proof The proof follows immediately from Lemma 1 and Lemma 2.
$\square_{Theorem\ 2}$

Remark. Let us remark that it is not possible to conclude from the previous theorem and the fact that Ω is the weakest failure detector to solve consensus in $\mathcal{ARW}_{n,n-1}[fd : \emptyset]$, that the property SOURCE + TOUR defines a weakest message adversary AD allowing consensus to be solved in $\mathcal{SMP}_n[adv : \text{AD}]$. It remains possible that a property AD weaker than SOURCE + TOUR allows consensus to be solved in $\mathcal{SMP}_n[adv : \text{AD}]$. Said differently nothing allows us to claim that the "granularity" on the properties which can be defined to constrain message adversaries is the same as the "granularity" on the information on failures provided by failure detectors. (The approach investigated in [3] is a step in that direction.)

4. SOURCE CAPTURES EXACTLY THE FAILURE DETECTOR Ω IN $\mathcal{AMP}_{n,n-1}[fd : \emptyset]$

4.1 From $\mathcal{AMP}_{n,n-1}[fd : \Omega]$ to $\mathcal{SMP}_n[adv : \textbf{SOURCE}]$

The algorithm described in Figure 5 presents a simulation (for tasks) of $\mathcal{SMP}_n[adv : \textbf{SOURCE}]$ on top of $\mathcal{AMP}_{n,n-1}[fd : \Omega]$. Its principles are close to the ones of the simulation of Figure 2. The algorithm ensures that the eventual leader p_ℓ satisfies the property SOURCE. Hence, there are strongly correct processes and the eventual leader is one of them. The aim of the simulation algorithm is then to eventually withdraw all the messages except the ones from the leader.

```
initialization:
(1)   ls_state_i ← initial state of the local simulated algorithm; read_value_i ← ⊥;
(2)   (next_op_i, ls_state_i) ← simulate(ls_state_i, read_value_i);
(3)   seq_nb_i ← 1; informed_i ← {i}; missed_i ← ∅;
(4)   view_i ← {(i, seq_nb_i, next_op_i)}.

round r = 1, 2, · · · do:
(5)   send(i, view_i, missed_i) to each other process;
(6)   rec_msgs_i ← set of triples (j, view_j, missed_j) received during this round;
(7)   view_i ← view_i ∪ (⋃_{(j,view_j,missed_j)∈rec_msgs_i} view_j);
(8)   missed_i ← missed_i ∪ (⋃_{(j,view_j,missed_j)∈rec_msgs_i} missed_j);
(9)   rec_from_i ← {j ∈ {1,...,n} : ∃(j, view_j, missed_j) ∈ rec_msgs_i} ∪ {i};
(10)  missed_i ← missed_i ∪ {(k, r) : k ∈ {1,...,n} \ rec_from_i};
(11)  min_missed_i ← min{|{r' : (j, r') ∈ missed_i}|, j ∈ {1,...,n}};
(12)  ℓd_i ← min{j : |{r' : (j, r') ∈ missed_i}| = min_missed_i};
(13)  informed_i ← informed_i ∪ ({1,...,n} \ rec_from_i)
(14)              ∪ {j ∈ rec_from_i : (i, seq_nq_i, next_op_i) ∈ view_j};
(15)  if (informed_i = {1,...,n}) then
(16)     (next_op_i, ls_state_i) ← simulate(ls_state_i, read_value_i);
(17)     if (next_op_i = read_i(ℓ)) then
(18)        if (∄(ℓ, −, write_ℓ(−)) ∈ view_i)
(19)        then read_value_i ← ⊥
(20)        else max_snℓ_i ← max{sn_ℓ, (ℓ, sn_ℓ, write_ℓ(−)) ∈ view_i};
(21)             read_value_i ← v_ℓ : (ℓ, max_snℓ_i, write_ℓ(v_ℓ)) ∈ view_i
(22)        end if
(23)     end if;
(24)     seq_nb_i ← seq_nb_i + 1; informed_i ← {i};
(25)     view_i ← view_i ∪ {(i, seq_nb_i, next_op_i)}
(26)  end if.

when leader_i is read: return (ℓd_i).
```

Figure 3: Simulation of $\mathcal{ARW}_{n,n-1}[fd : \Omega]$ in $\mathcal{SMP}_n[adv : \textbf{SOURCE, TOUR}]$

Local variables of the simulation. As in the previous simulations, r_i is the locally simulated round number; $msgs\_to\_send_i[j]$ (initialized to $\bot$) contains the next simulated message to be sent to p_j; $rec\_msg_i[r]$ contains the simulated messages received at round r; $sim\_rec\_msgs_i[x]$ contains the message received from the process p_x currently considered as the leader by p_i; $leader_i$ is the read-only variable provided by Ω.

```
(1)   r_i ← 0; sim_rec_msgs_i[1,...,n] ← [⊥,...,⊥];
(2)   (msgs_to_send_i[1,...,n], ls_state_i)
              ← simulate(sim_rec_msgs_i);
(3)   for each r > 0
              do rec_msgs_i[r][1,...,n] ← [⊥,...,⊥] end for;
(4)   repeat forever
(5)      r ← r_i + 1;
(6)      for each j ∈ {1,...,n}
              do send(r_i, msgs_to_send_i[j]) to p_j end for;
(7)      repeat cur_ℓd_i ← leader_i
(8)        until (cur_ℓd_i = i ∨ rec_msgs_i[r_i][cur_ℓd_i] ≠ ⊥)
(9)      end repeat;
(10)     sim_rec_msgs_i[cur_ℓd_i] ← rec_msgs_i[r_i][cur_ℓd_i];
(11)     (msgs_to_send_i[1,...,n], ls_state_i)
              ← simulate(sim_rec_msgs_i);
(12)     sim_rec_msgs_i[1,...,n] ← [⊥,...,⊥]
(13)  end repeat.

when (r, m) received from p_j: rec_msgs_i[r][j] ← m.
```

Figure 5: From $\mathcal{AMP}_{n,n-1}[fd : \Omega]$ to $\mathcal{SMP}_n[adv : \textbf{SOURCE}]$

Simulation algorithm. The procedure simulate() takes as input parameter the simulated messages received by p_i at the current round, and simulates the local algorithm until the next sending of messages by p_i. This procedure returns the simulated messages to be sent at the beginning of the next round.

After the initialization stage (lines 1-3), the local simulator of p_i enters a loop whose each body execution simulates a round of the synchronous system. It first sends the messages that p_i has to send at the current round (line 6). Then it waits until it has received a message from its current leader or it is its own leader (lines 7-9). When this occurs, it retrieves the message sent by its current leader (line 10) and invokes the procedure simulate() with this message as input parameter, before proceeding to the simulation of the next synchronous round.

LEMMA 3. *If a task can be solved in $\mathcal{SMP}_n[adv : \text{SOURCE}]$, it can be solved in $\mathcal{AMP}_{n,n-1}[fd : \Omega]$.*

Proof The simulator concerned by this lemma is the one described in Figure 5. Let us first show that no correct process remains blocked forever in the loop lines of 7-9. Indeed, there is a finite time τ after which an eventual leader (say p_ℓ) is elected by Ω at each process. It then follows from the first part of the predicate of line 8 that p_ℓ cannot remain blocked at line 8, and consequently executes rounds forever. Moreover, as its messages are eventually received at each round by all correct processes, it follows that there is a time after which the second part of the predicate of line 8 is always satisfied by these processes. Consequently, none of them can remain blocked forever at line 8.

```
initialization:
(1)   ls_state_i ← initial state of the local simulated algorithm;
(2)   msgs_to_rec_i ← ∅; msgs_received_i ← ∅;
(3)   (msgs_to_send_i, ls_state_i) ← simulate(ls_state_i, msgs_to_rec_i);
(4)   view_i ← msgs_to_send_i; missed_i ← ∅; ℓd_i ← i.

round r = 1, 2, ··· do:
(5)   send(i, view_i, missed_i) to each other process;
(6)   rec_msgs_i ← set of triples (j, view_j, missed_j) received during this round;
(7)   view_i ← view_i ∪ (⋃_(j,view_j,missed_j)∈rec_msgs_i view_j);
(8)   missed_i ← missed_i ∪ (⋃_(j,view_j,missed_j)∈rec_msgs_i missed_j);
(9)   rec_from_i ← {j ∈ {1,...,n} : ∃(j, view_j, missed_j) ∈ rec_msgs_i} ∪ {i};
(10)  missed_i ← missed_i ∪ {(k,r) : k ∈ {1,...,n} \ rec_from_i};
(11)  min_missed_i ← min{|{r' : (j,r') ∈ missed_i}|, j ∈ {1,...,n}};
(12)  ℓd_i ← min{j : |{r' : (j,r') ∈ missed_i}| = min_missed_i};
(13)  if (ℓd_i ∈ rec_from_i) then
(14)     let view_ℓd_i be such that (ℓd_i, view_ℓd_i, missed_ℓd_i) ∈ rec_msgs_i;
(15)     msgs_to_rec_i ← msgs_to_rec_i ∪ {(ℓd_i, i, m) : (ℓd_i, i, m) ∈ view_ℓd_i};
(16)     if (msgs_to_send_i ⊆ view_ℓd_i) then
(17)        (msgs_to_send_i, ls_state_i) ← simulate(ls_state_i, msgs_to_rec_i \ msgs_received_i);
(18)        msgs_received_i ← msgs_to_rec_i; view_i ← view_i ∪ msgs_to_send_i
(19)     end if
(20)  end if.

when leader_i is read: return (ℓd_i).
```

Figure 4: Simulation of $\mathcal{AMP}_{n,n-1}[fd : \Omega]$ in $\mathcal{SMP}_n[adv : \textbf{SOURCE}]$

The previous reasoning shows also that the eventual leader elected by Ω behaves as a source, and consequently the property SOURCE is satisfied in the simulated synchronous system.   □_Lemma 3

4.2   From $\mathcal{SMP}_n[adv : \textbf{SOURCE}]$ to $\mathcal{AMP}_{n,n-1}[fd : \Omega]$

The simulation algorithm is described in Figure 4. It is similar to the algorithm of Figure 3 (which simulates $\mathcal{ARW}_{n,n-1}[fd : \Omega]$ on top of $\mathcal{SMP}_n[adv : \textbf{SOURCE, TOUR}]$).

Local variables of the simulation. The local variables ls_state_i, $view_i$, rec_from_i, and $missed_i$ have the same meaning as in Figure 3. The local variable denoted $msgs\_to\_rec_i$ contains messages to be consumed by the simulated process (it corresponds to $read\_value_i$ in Figure 3). The variable $msgs\_to\_send_i$ contains the messages to be sent in the next simulation round (it corresponds to $next\_op_i$ in Figure 3). The variable $msgs\_received_i$ is a new variable containing the messages already received by the simulated process p_i. Finally, $ℓd_i$ is the local variable containing the current local value of Ω built by the algorithm.

Simulation algorithm. As in the simulation of Figure 3, lines 1-4 are an initialization stage. Similarly to previous simulations, the procedure simulate() locally simulates the process p_i. It takes messages to be consumed by p_i as input parameter and returns the next set of messages to be sent.

The simulation algorithm is a full information algorithm. During each simulation round r, the simulator of p_i first sends its control local state to each other process, and waits for the same information from them (lines 5-6). Then, according to the messages it has received during the current round, it updates $view_i$, $missed_i$, and rec_from_i (lines 7-10). As in Figure 3, it also computes the identity $ℓd_i$ of its current candidate to be the eventual leader (lines 11-12).

If a simulation message has been received from the process $p_{ℓd_i}$, the simulator of p_i strives to make p_i progress. It considers the last message sent by $p_{ℓd_i}$ to p_i (triple $(ℓd_i, i, m)$), and adds it to the set $msgs\_to\_rec_i$ (lines 14-15). Then, if the messages p_i has to send are known by its current leader $p_{ℓd_i}$ (line 16), the procedure simulate() is invoked to make p_i progress (line 17), and the local control variables $msgs\_received_i$ and $view_i$ are updated accordingly (line 18).

LEMMA 4. *If a task can be solved in $\mathcal{AMP}_{n,n-1}[fd : \Omega]$, it can be solved in $\mathcal{SMP}_n[adv : \textbf{SOURCE}]$.*

Proof The simulator concerned by this lemma is the one described in Figure 4. Preliminary definition on simulators in $\mathcal{SMP}_n[adv : \textbf{SOURCE}]$.

Let S be the set of processes which satisfy the property SOURCE. As, by assumption there at least one source, we have $S \neq \emptyset$. Moreover, due the definition of the set $\mathcal{SC}$ of strongly correct simulators we have $S \subseteq \mathcal{SC}$. Let S' be the set of processes which, albeit they are not necessarily source, appear as sources to all processes of $\mathcal{SC}$. Hence we have $S \subseteq S' \subseteq \mathcal{SC}$, and $S' \neq \emptyset$.

The variables $leader_i$ implement Ω.

According to the definition of $\mathcal{SC}$, there is a round r_0 after which no more message from a weakly correct simulator is received (directly or indirectly) by a strongly correct simulator. Let $r_1 = \max\{r_s, s \in S'\}$ where r_s is the first round after which no message sent by p_s to a strongly correct simulator is eliminated. As, after r_1, each strongly correct simulator receives at every round a message from each simulator in S', it follows that none of them adds a pair $(s, r), r \geq r_1, s \in S'$ in its variable $missed_i$ at line 10. After $r_2 = \max\{r_0, r_1\}$, the only pairs $(s, r), s \in S'$ $(r < r_1)$ that are added by a strongly correct simulator in its variable $missed_i$ are those that have been added by other strongly correct simulators at line 8 or line 11 before r_2. Since strongly correct simulators are infinitely often able to transmit (directly or not) messages to each other, there is a round $r_3 \geq r_2$ such that any strongly correct simulator p_i has received (directly or not) during a round $rj \geq r_2$ the information contained in the variable $missed_j$ from each other strongly correct simulator p_j. After r_3, for any $s \in S'$, the number of pairs (s, r) in the variables $missed_i$ of all strongly correct simulators p_i is the same and does not increase anymore.

For each simulator p_i, $i \notin S'$, there is an infinite number of rounds r such that p_i's message is not received during round r by at least one of the strongly correct simulator p_j, and accordingly, this simulator adds a pair (i, r) to its variable $missed_j$ during round r at line 10. As the strongly correct simulators communicate (directly or not) infinitely often with each other, all of them eventually add this pair to their variable $missed$ during r (at line 10) or later (at line 8). Consequently, for each such simulator p_i, $i \notin S'$, the number of pairs (i, r) in the variable $missed_j$ of every strongly simulator p_j increases forever.

It follows from the previous discussion that the minimal number of rounds missed by a simulator (as calculated at line 12, and using simulator identity to do tie-breaking) eventually becomes and remains the same at each strongly correct simulator. Let ℓd denote this simulator identity. As it is the identity that is eventually always returned when $leader_i$ is read by any simulated process p_i whose simulator is strongly correct, the unicity eventual property of Ω is ensured for these processes. The next paragraph shows that the set of strongly correct simulators corresponds exactly to the set of correct simulated processes. As $p_{\ell d}$ is strongly correct, the elected process is a correct process, which concludes the proof of Ω.

Correct and faulty (simulated) processes in $\mathcal{AMP}_{n,n-1}[fd : \Omega]$. It follows from the previous paragraphs that each strongly correct simulator p_i is always eventually able to transmit (directly or not) a new message m to $p_{\ell d}$, and then eventually receive (directly) a message from $p_{\ell d}$ containing m. Hence the conditions of line 13 and line 16 are fulfilled an infinite number of times and, consequently, the corresponding simulator can always issue enough steps (line 17) to progress in the simulated code.

Hence, the correct simulated processes and the faulty simulated processes are the ones simulated by the strongly correct and weakly correct simulators, respectively.

Linearization of communication operations.
Let us consider a simulated process p_i that sends a message m to a simulated process p_j. This operation is disseminated to each simulator by p_i's simulator at line 5. Then a simulator considers this simulated message m only at line 17 when the second input parameter of its invocation of simulate() contains the message m. (Let us observe, that this message m arrives at a simulator p_k from its current leader ℓd_k, lines 13 and 16).

Let τ_1 be the time of the first invocation of simulate() by a simulator such that m belongs to the second input parameter of this invocation, where $\tau_1 = \infty$ if there is no such invocation. Let τ_2 be the time at which the simulator of p_i starts the execution of simulate() (line 17) after it has disseminated m, where $\tau_2 = \infty$ if there is no such invocation.

The send of m is linearized at time $\min(\tau_1, \tau_2)$ (let us notice that the simulation of p_i does not progress between the sending of m by p_i and its linearization point). If $\min(\tau_1, \tau_2) = \infty$, the send of m is linearized after the receiver p_j has computed its result.

The reception of m is linearized at the time of the invocation by p_j of simulate() whose second input parameter contains the message m, or after p_j has computed its result if there is no such invocation. $\square_{Lemma\ 4}$

4.3 The Message Adversary SOURCE Captures Exactly Ω in $\mathcal{AMP}_{n,n-1}[fd : \emptyset]$

THEOREM 3. *A task can be solved in $\mathcal{AMP}_{n,n-1}[fd : \Omega]$ iff it can be solved in $\mathcal{SMP}_n[adv : \text{SOURCE}]$.*

Proof The proof follows directly from Lemma 3 and Lemma 4.
$\square_{Theorem\ 3}$

5. THE ADVERSARY QUORUM CAPTURES EXACTLY Σ IN $\mathcal{AMP}_{n,n-1}[fd : \emptyset]$

This section shows that the computing models $\mathcal{SMP}_n[adv : \text{QUORUM}]$ and $\mathcal{AMP}_{n,n-1}[fd : \Sigma]$ have the same computational power for tasks.

5.1 The Property QUORUM

Let us remember that $\mathcal{SC}$ is the set of strongly correct processes in the considered synchronous message-passing system (processes whose an infinite number of messages are received by each other process). The property QUORUM is defined as follows:

$$\left[\forall i, j : \forall r_i, r_j : (\{k : k \xrightarrow{r_i} i\} \cap \{k : k \xrightarrow{r_j} j\} \neq \emptyset) \right]$$
$$\wedge (\mathcal{SC} \neq \emptyset).$$

This property is a statement of Σ suited to the context of round-based synchronous message-passing systems prone to message adversaries. Given any pair of processes p_i and p_j, its first part states that, whatever the synchronous rounds r_i and r_j executed by p_i and p_j, respectively, there is a process p_k whose messages to p_i at round r_i and to p_j at round r_j are not eliminated by the adversary (intersection property). The second part states that there is at least one process whose messages are infinitely often received by each other process (liveness property). Theorem 4 will show that this formulation of Σ is correct for the equivalence of $\mathcal{AMP}_{n,n-1}[fd : \Sigma]$ and $\mathcal{SMP}_n[adv : \text{QUORUM}]$ for task solvability.

```
(1)   r_i ← 0; sim_rec_msgs_i[1, . . . , n] ← [⊥, . . . , ⊥];
(2)   (msgs_to_send_i[1, . . . , n], ls_state_i)
            ← simulate(sim_rec_msgs_i);
(3)   for each r > 0
            do rec_msgs_i[r][1, . . . , n] ← [⊥, . . . , ⊥] end for;
(4)   repeat forever
(5)       r ← r_i + 1;
(6)       for each j ∈ {1, . . . , n}
              do send(r_i, msgs_to_send_i[j]) to p_j end for;
(7)       repeat cur_qr_i ← qr_i
(8)           until (∀j ∈ cur_qr_i \ {i} : rec_msgs_i[r_i][j] ≠ ⊥)
(9)       end repeat;
(10)      for each j ∈ cur_qr_i
              do sim_rec_msgs_i[j] ← rec_msgs_i[r_i][j] end for;
(11)      (msgs_to_send_i[1, . . . , n], ls_state_i)
                ← simulate(sim_rec_msgs_i);
(12)      sim_rec_msgs_i[1, . . . , n] ← [⊥, . . . , ⊥]
(13)  end repeat.

when (r, m) received from p_j:   rec_msgs_i[r][j] ← m.
```

Figure 6: From asynchronous $\mathcal{AMP}_{n,n-1}[fd : \Sigma]$ to synchronous $\mathcal{SMP}_n[adv : \text{QUORUM}]$

5.2 From Asynchronous $\mathcal{AMP}_{n,n-1}[fd : \Sigma]$ to Synchronous $\mathcal{SMP}_n[adv : \text{QUORUM}]$

The simulation from $\mathcal{AMP}_{n,n-1}[fd : \Sigma]$ to $\mathcal{SMP}_n[adv : \text{QUORUM}]$ is described in Figure 6. It has the same local variables as, and is very close to, the one of Figure 5. In addition to the

```
initialization:
(1)    ls_state_i ← initial state of the local simulated algorithm;
(2)    msgs_to_rec_i ← ∅; msgs_received_i ← ∅;
(3)    (msgs_to_send_i, ls_state_i) ← simulate(ls_state_i, msgs_to_rec_i);
(4)    view_i ← msgs_to_send_i; rec_from_i ← {1, ..., n}.

round r = 1, 2, ··· do:
(5)    send(i, view_i) to each other process;
(6)    rec_msgs_i ← set of pairs (j, view_j) received during this round;
(7)    view_i ← view_i ∪ (⋃_(j,view_j)∈rec_msgs_i view_j);
(8)    rec_from_i ← {j ∈ {1, ..., n} : ∃(j, view_j) ∈ rec_msgs_i} ∪ {i};
(9)    if (msgs_to_send_i ∈ ⋂_(j,view_j)∈rec_msgs_i view_j) then
(10)       msgs_to_rec_i ← msgs_to_rec_i ∪ {(j, i, m) : (j, view_j) ∈ rec_msgs_i ∧ (j, i, m) ∈ view_j};
(11)       (msgs_to_send_i, ls_state_i) ← simulate(ls_state_i, msgs_to_rec_i \ msgs_received_i);
(12)       msgs_received_i ← msgs_to_rec_i; view_i ← view_i ∪ msgs_to_send_i
(13) end if.

when qr_i is read:  return(rec_from_i).
```

Figure 7: Simulation of $\mathcal{AMP}_{n,n-1}[fd : \Sigma]$ in $\mathcal{SMP}_n[adv : \textbf{QUORUM}]$

local output of the failure detector Σ, which is denoted qr_i, the only modifications are the lines 7-10 which differ in both algorithms.

The simulator of p_i waits until it has received a message from each process that appears in its current quorum qr_i (lines 7-9). It then invokes the procedure simulate() with these messages as input (line 10).

The principle of this simulation is the following: after some time, the simulated message adversary suppresses all the messages sent by processes that do not belong to a quorum, but is prevented from suppressing the messages sent by processes belonging to quorums.

LEMMA 5. *If a task can be solved in $\mathcal{SMP}_n[adv : \textbf{QUORUM}]$, it can be solved in $\mathcal{AMP}_{n,n-1}[fd : \Sigma]$.*

5.3 From Synchronous $\mathcal{SMP}_n[adv : \textbf{QUORUM}]$ to Asynchronous $\mathcal{AMP}_{n,n-1}[fd : \Sigma]$

This simulation algorithm is described in Figure 7. It is very close to the simulation of $\mathcal{AMP}_{n,n-1}[fd : \Omega]$ on top of the model $\mathcal{SMP}_n[adv : \textbf{SOURCE}]$ presented in Figure 4. It has the same local variables, except the variable $missed_i$ which is now useless. The value returned when qr_i is read by a simulated process p_i is now the current value of the set rec_from_i.

The only other difference appears at lines 9-10. The simulation of the simulated process p_i (invocation of the procedure simulate() at lines 11) is now constrained by the predicate of line 9 which states that the messages that p_i wants to send (the messages saved in $msg\_to\_send_i$) must be known by at all the simulators defining the current quorum of p_i (set rec_from_i). When this is satisfied, the set of messages to be received by p_i in the next invocation of simulate() is redefined (line 11) to include the last simulated messages sent to p_i by processes p_j such that $j \in rec\_from_i$.

LEMMA 6. *If a task can be solved in $\mathcal{AMP}_{n,n-1}[fd : \Sigma]$, it can be solved in $\mathcal{SMP}_n[adv : \textbf{QUORUM}]$.*

5.4 The Message Adversary QUORUM Captures Exactly Σ in $\mathcal{AMP}_{n,n-1}[fd : \emptyset]$

THEOREM 4. *A task can be solved in the synchronous model $\mathcal{SMP}_n[adv : \textbf{QUORUM}]$ iff it can be solved in the message-passing model $\mathcal{AMP}_{n,n-1}[fd : \Sigma]$.*

Proof Follows immediately from Lemmas 5 and 6. $\square_{Theorem\ 4}$

6. THE PAIR OF MESSAGE ADVERSARIES (SOURCE, QUORUM) CAPTURES EXACTLY THE PAIR (Σ, Ω) IN $\mathcal{AMP}_{n,n-1}[fd : \emptyset]$

Let us notice that the properties SOURCE and QUORUM are independent of one another in the sense that none of them can be obtained from the other. It follows that the power provided by SOURCE and the power provided by QUORUM can be added. More specifically, we have the following:

- A merge of the simulation of $\mathcal{SMP}_n[adv : \text{SOURCE}]$ in $\mathcal{AMP}_{n,n-1}[fd : \Omega]$ (Figure 5) with the simulation of the model $\mathcal{SMP}_n[adv : \text{QUORUM}]$ in $\mathcal{AMP}_{n,n-1}[fd : \Sigma]$ (Figure 6) provides a simulation of the model $\mathcal{SMP}_n[adv : \text{SOURCE}, \text{QUORUM}]$ in $\mathcal{AMP}_{n,n-1}[fd : \Sigma, \Omega]$. The difference between this simulation and the one of Figure 5 (or Figure 6) is at lines 7-10 which becomes

```
(7)   repeat cur_ld_i ← leader_i; cur_qr_i ← qr_i until
(8)      [(∀j ∈ cur_qr_i \ {i} : rec_msgs_i[r_i][j] ≠ ⊥)
             ∧ (cur_ld_i = i ∨ rec_msgs_i[r_i][cur_ld_i] ≠ ⊥)]
(9)   end repeat;
(10)  for each j ∈ cur_qr_i ∪ cur_ld_i
         do sim_rec_msgs_i[j] ← rec_msgs_i[r_i][j] end for.
```

The proof is the same as in Lemma 5 augmented by the fact that the eventual leader elected by Ω verifies the property SOURCE as shown in Lemma 3.

- Similarly, adding the management of $missed_i$ and the procedure to query Ω (as done at lines 8-11 of Figure 4) to the simulation of $\mathcal{AMP}_{n,n-1}[fd : \Sigma]$ in $\mathcal{SMP}_n[adv : \text{QUORUM}]$ (Figure 7) provides a simulation of the asynchronous model $\mathcal{AMP}_{n,n-1}[fd : \Sigma, \Omega]$ in synchronous $\mathcal{SMP}_n[adv : \text{SOURCE}, \text{QUORUM}]$.

The linearization points and the proof of the properties of Σ are the same as in Lemma 6, while the proof of the properties of Ω follows the one of Lemma 4. Let us finally notice that it follows directly from the properties SOURCE and QUORUM that a process verifying the SOURCE property appears eventually in all the simulated quorums.

Theorem 5 then follows:

THEOREM 5. *A task can be solved in the synchronous model $\mathcal{SMP}_n[adv : \text{SOURCE}, \text{QUORUM}]$ iff it can be solved in in the enriched message-passing model $\mathcal{AMP}_{n,n-1}[fd : \Sigma, \Omega]$.*

174

7. CONCLUSION

Considering crash-free synchronous round-based systems, message adversaries have been designed as daemons that suppress messages. Failure detectors have been introduced to enrich crash-prone asynchronous (read/write or message-passing) systems. A previous work [1] has shown that, from a task solvability point of view, the message adversaries constrained by a property denoted TOUR (for tournament) characterizes the well-known wait-free read/write model.

Considering task solvability, this paper has introduced relations linking failures detectors and message adversaries. More precisely, it has introduced two new properties, denoted SOURCE and QUORUM, which are restrictions on message adversaries, and has shown that

- The synchronous message adversaries SOURCE+TOUR characterizes the asynchronous wait-free read/write model enriched with Ω,

- The synchronous message adversary SOURCE characterizes the asynchronous Ω-enriched crash-prone message-passing model,

- The synchronous message adversary QUORUM characterizes the asynchronous crash-prone message-passing model enriched with Σ,

- The synchronous message adversaries SOURCE+QUORUM characterizes the asynchronous crash-prone message-passing model enriched with the pair (Σ, Ω).

Hence, when considering task solvability, these characterizations state properties' defining the strongest message adversaries for synchronous round-based message-passing systems equating classical asynchronous crash-prone systems. Interestingly, this allows for the establishment of a hierarchy on message adversaries (e.g., $\mathcal{SMP}_n[adv : \text{QUORUM}]$ is stronger than $\mathcal{SMP}_n[adv : \text{TOUR}]$ as shown on the left of Figure 1; this follows from the fact that the computability power of Σ is strictly stronger than read/write registers).

In our understanding of the foundations of distributed computing, a lot of issues remain still open. As examples, here are two interesting message adversary-related problems. Which is the weakest message adversary AD such that consensus can be solved in $\mathcal{SMP}_n[adv : \text{AD}]$? (The only thing we know is that the synchronous model $\mathcal{SMP}_n[adv : \text{CONS}]$ is weaker than or equivalent to synchronous model $\mathcal{SMP}_n[adv : \text{SOURCE, TOUR}]$ and strictly stronger than $\mathcal{SMP}_n[adv : \text{TOUR}]$). Is the addition of the constraint $|\mathcal{SC}| \geq n - t$ to an adversary sufficient to characterize t-resilient asynchronous crash-prone read/write or message-passing systems?

Acknowledgments

This work has been partially supported by the French ANR project DISPLEXITY devoted to computability and complexity in distributed computing. Special thanks to D. Imbs and S. Rajsbaum for discussions on distributed computing models, and to the referees for their constructive comments.

8. REFERENCES

[1] Afek Y. and Gafni E., Asynchrony from synchrony. *Proc. Int'l Conference on Distributed Computing and Networking (ICDCN'13)*, Springer LNCS 7730, pp. 225-239, 2013.

[2] Afek Y., Gafni E, and Linial N., A king in two tournaments. *Unpublished report*, 3 pages, March 2012. http://www.cs.huji.ac.il/ nati/PAPERS/king_tournaments.pdf.

[3] Biely M., Robinson P., and Schmid U., Agreement in directed dynamic networks. *Proc. 19th Int'l Colloqium on Structural Information and Communication Complexity (SIROCCO'12)*, Springer LNCS 7355, pp 73-84, 2012.

[4] Chandra T. and Toueg S., Unreliable failure detectors for reliable distributed systems. *Journal of the ACM*, 43(2):225-267, 1996.

[5] Chandra T., Hadzilacos V. and Toueg S., The weakest failure detector for solving consensus. *Journal of the ACM*, 43(4):685-722, 1996.

[6] Charron-Bost B. and Schiper A., The *heard-of* model: computing in distributed systems with benign faults. *Distributed Computing*, 22(1):49-71, 2009.

[7] Cornejo A., Rajsbaum S., Raynal M., Travers C., Failure Detectors as Schedulers (Brief Announcement). *Proc. 26th ACM Symposium on Principles of Distributed Computing (PODC)*, ACM Press, pp. 308-309, 2007.

[8] Delporte-Gallet C., Fauconnier H., and Guerraoui R., Tight failure detection bounds on atomic object implementations. *Journal of the ACM*, 57(4), Article 22, 2010.

[9] Delporte-Gallet C., Fauconnier H., and Toueg S., The minimum information about failures for solving non-local tasks in message-passing systems. *Distributed Computing*, 24(5):255-269, 2011.

[10] Fernández Anta A. and Raynal M., From an asynchronous intermittent rotating star to an eventual leader. *IEEE Transactions on Parallel Distributed Systems*, 21(9):1290-1303, 2010.

[11] Herlihy M.P., Wait-free synchronization. *ACM Transactions on Programming Languages and Systems*, 13(1):124-149, 1991.

[12] Herlihy M.P. and Shavit N., The topological structure of asynchronous computability. *Journal ACM*, 46(6):858-923, 1999.

[13] Kuhn F., Lynch N.A., and Oshman R., Distributed computation in dynamic networks. *Proc. 42nd ACM Symposium on Theory of Computing (STOC'10)*, ACM press, pp. 513-522, 2010.

[14] Landau H.G., On dominance relations and the structure of animal societies, III: The condition for score structure. *Bulletin of Mathematical Biophysics*, 15(2):143-148, 1953.

[15] Lo W.-K. and Hadzilacos V., Using failure detectors to solve consensus in asynchronous shared-memory systems. *Proc. 8th Int'l Workshop on Distributed Algorithms (WDAG'94)*, Springer LNCS 857, pp. 280-295, 1994.

[16] Mourgaya E., Mostéfaoui A., and Raynal M., Asynchronous implementation of failure detectors. *Proc. Int'l IEEE Conference on Dependable Systems and Networks (DSN 2003)*, IEEE Press, pp. 351-360, 2003.

[17] Pike S.M., Sastry S. and Welch J.L., Failure detectors encapsulate fairness. *Distributed Computing*, 25(4): 313-333, 2012.

[18] Rajsbaum S., Raynal M., Travers C., The iterated restricted immediate snapshot model. *Proc. 14th Annual Int'l Conference on Computing and Combinatorics (COCOON 2008)*, Springer LNCS 5092, pp. 487-497, 2008.

[19] Raynal M., Failure detectors for asynchronous distributed systems: an introduction. *Wiley Encyclopedia of Computer Science and Engineering*, 2:1181-1191, 2009.

[20] Raynal M. and Stainer J., Increasing the power of the iterated immediate snapshot model with failure detectors. *Proc. 19th Int'l Colloquium on Structural Information and Communication Complexity (SIROCCO'12)*, Springer LNCS 7355, pp. 231-242, 2012.

[21] Raynal M. and Stainer J., Round-based synchrony weakened by message adversaries *vs* asynchrony enriched with failure detectors. *Tech Report 8235*, IRISA, Université de Rennes (F), 19 pages, 2012. (http://hal.inria.fr/hal-00787978/)

[22] Santoro N. and Widmayer P., Time is not a healer. *Proc. 6th Annual Symposium on Theoretical Aspects of Computer Science (STACS'89)*, Springer LNCS 349, pp. 304-316, 1989.

[23] Santoro N. and Widmayer P., Agreement in synchronous networks with ubiquitous faults. *Theoretical Computer Science*, 384(2-3): 232-249, 2007.

[24] Schmid U., Weiss B., and Keidar I., Impossibility results and lower bounds for consensus under link failures. *SIAM Journal of Computing*, 38(5): 1912-1951, 2009.

Highly Dynamic Distributed Computing with Byzantine Failures

Rachid Guerraoui
Lab. de Programmation
Distribuée
EPFL, Switzerland
rachid.guerraoui@epfl.ch

Florian Huc
Lab. de Programmation
Distribuée
EPFL, Switzerland
florian.huc@gmail.com

Anne-Marie Kermarrec
INRIA Rennes
Bretagne-Atlantique
France
anne-marie.kermarrec.@inria.fr

ABSTRACT

This paper shows for the first time that distributed computing can be both reliable and efficient in an environment that is both highly dynamic and hostile. More specifically, we show how to maintain clusters of size $O(\log N)$, each containing more than two thirds of honest nodes with high probability, within a system whose size can vary *polynomially* with respect to its initial size. Furthermore, the communication cost induced by each node arrival or departure is polylogarithmic with respect to N, the maximal size of the system. Our clustering can be achieved despite the presence of a Byzantine adversary controlling a fraction $\tau \leq \frac{1}{3} - \epsilon$ of the nodes, for some fixed constant $\epsilon > 0$, independent of N. So far, such a clustering could only be performed for systems whose size can vary constantly and it was not clear whether that was at all possible for polynomial variances.

Categories and Subject Descriptors

F.2.2 [**Theory of Computation**]: Analysis of algorithms and problem complexity—*Nonnumerical Algorithms and Problems*

Keywords: Byzantine failures ; random walks ; dynamic networks

1. INTRODUCTION

Distributed computing can be achieved reliably in a system where at most one third of the processes are controlled by an adversary. Typically, assuming some synchrony, the seminal agreement problem [25] can be solved and used to emulate a single highly available process. This is a basic building block to achieve distributed computations in a reliable manner. Yet, with a large number of nodes, this technique is very expensive. One way to reduce the complexity consists in clustering the nodes within smaller subsets, picked randomly, so that each cluster contains two

third of correct nodes whp, e.g., as proposed in [11]. In short, instead of reducing a system of many processes into a system of one reliable process that performs the computation, the idea here is to reduce it to a system of several reliable processes, each corresponding to one of the clusters. These processes share the load of the computations reducing thereby their complexity.

So far, clustering techniques mainly assumed a static distributed system: the number n of processes is assumed to be fixed a priori and processes do not join or leave the system [14] (a few can typically fail). Some approaches have explored dynamic settings, but in a limited fashion: the number of processes n is assumed to only vary by a constant factor [6, 7, 12, 31]. Yet, whether this is at all possible to go beyond has been considered an open question so far [18, 19].

This paper answers the question positively. We show, for the first time, that it is possible to perform distributed computing reliably and efficiently in a system which size can vary in a *polynomial* manner. At the heart of this result lies a new technique to partition nodes in a dynamic number of clusters, which involves a radical departure from previous schemes that assume a static number of clusters [6, 7, 12, 31]. Indeed, tolerating an increase in the number of nodes from n to n^2 (and more generally from $n^{1/y}$ to n^z for some constants $y, z > 1$), with a static number of clusters, yields a significant increase in the number of nodes within each cluster, leading to a high-complexity computation, in the vein of a single cluster approach. However, handling dynamic clusters is not trivial. For instance, using classical De Brujin graphs for clustering [6] in a dynamic setting requires a good estimation of the number of nodes. In turn, this potentially requires techniques with high complexity, e.g., typically $\tilde{O}(n^{3/2})$ [24].

Our clustering approach achieves a polylogarithmic complexity by using random walks on expander graphs with small degrees. To ensure that each cluster contains two thirds of correct nodes with high probability, we exchange nodes between clusters whenever new nodes join or leave the system. The nodes that are candidate to the exchange are selected using continuous random walks [1]. These provide a uniformly chosen sample even if the underlying graph is not regular. To ensure that a walk ends up fast on a node picked quasi uniformly, we connect clusters through small degree expanders [20].

The distributed construction of this expander requires specific care in regulating the choice of edges. Although several expanders could be used, our approach relies on OVER, a technique (Over-Valued Erdös Rèiny graph) from Erdös Rèiny random graphs to preserve a small degree and a good expansion coefficient. OVER is described in the long version of this paper [16] for space reasons. This technique tolerates more crashes than [3, 15, 26] and yields a different degree than [2]. In the rest of the paper, we present NOW (Neighbors On Watch), a protocol maintaining the cluster partition in Section 3 and analyze it in Section 4. We review the related work in Section 5 and conclude in Section 6.

2. MODEL AND BACKGROUND

System assumptions.

In short, our network model is the one of [7] with the difference that we allow the size of the system to vary *polynomially*. More specifically, we consider a dynamic synchronous network with a discrete time variable t_i. Each node can send messages to any node it knows through a private channel; in this sense the network is reconfigurable as connections between nodes can be added or removed. We do not assume that each node knows all other nodes in the network (except during the initialization phase in which the global structure of the network is computed once). Instead, each node knows polylog(N) nodes and only knows an upper bound on the current size of the network. We also assume that, initially, the number of nodes is n_{t_0} for some $\sqrt{N} \leq n_{t_0} \leq N$, and the current number of nodes n in the network remains between $\sqrt{N}$ and N (this can be relaxed to $N^{1/y} \leq n \leq N^z$ for all constants $y, z > 1$). The size of the network can increase or decrease at any time. For simplicity of presentation, we assume (as in [7, 26]) that when a node joins or leaves, the actions relative to previous joins and leaves are over. This corresponds to a time step.ÈIJ* Moreover, nodes do not need to take any specific action when leaving the network. Instead, we assume a mechanism enabling a node to detect if one of its neighbors has crashed or left the network.

Adversary model.

Our adversary is that of [7] with the difference that in our case it controls a fraction $\tau \leq \frac{1}{3} - \epsilon$ (for some constant $\epsilon > 0$) nodes, from the beginning (vs. $\tau \leq \frac{1}{2} - \epsilon$ after some initialization phase; note that using cryptographic tools, we could also assume $\tau \leq \frac{1}{2} - \epsilon$ by leveraging broadcast algorithms [13].).

NOW tolerates a static Byzantine (sometimes called *active*) adversary controlling a fraction $\tau \leq \frac{1}{3} - \epsilon$ (for some constant $\epsilon > 0$) of the nodes, having a full knowledge of the network at any time, as in [7, 18], i.e it knows the position of any node at any time. A typical objective for the adversary is to gain the lead in one (or more) of the clusters. At the beginning of the protocol, the adversary can choose a fraction τ of the nodes to corrupt. We assume that, at initialization, the honest nodes form a connected component, that the adversary cannot split it into disjoint parts, that each node controlled by the adversary is adjacent to at least one honest node, and that no honest node

---

9*However, the analysis can be generalized to several parallel join and leave operations.

leaves or joins the network until the initialization is over. Also, nodes' identities cannot be forged. Moreover during the execution of the protocol, each time a node joins the network, the adversary can choose to corrupt it or not, as in [6, 7]. However, the adversary cannot decide to corrupt nodes at a later time (in this sense the adversary is static and not adaptive). Furthermore, the adversary can induce churn as in [6, 7] by join-leave attacks or by forcing honest nodes to leave the system (e.g., through a DOS attack). The size of the network can vary polynomially and each node is assigned a unique identifier.

Background on OVER: expander graph.

Our clustering technique, which we call NOW (Neighbors On Watch) and that maintains a cluster partition is based on a protocol to distributively maintain an expander overlay. Although various expanders (e.g. [2]) could be used, we assume that NOW relies on OVER. For space reasons, the detailed description of OVER is deferred to the long version of the paper [16]. In OVER, the graph vertices represent the clusters of nodes maintained by NOW, hence they can be considered as honest since each vertex is composed of more than two thirds of honest nodes whp. We further assume that each vertex leaving the overlay graph is chosen at random (this assumption will be ensured in Section 3.3).

OVER ensures that, starting from a random graph drawn from the Erdös-Rényi model, whp, at any time during a sequence of vertex additions and removals polynomial in N, the resulting graph has a large isoperimetric constant and a low degree (ensuring properties 1 and 2). We use the notation $\widehat{G}^R$ where the $\hat{}$ relates to the fact that we consider an overlay, and the ^{R} that it is an instance of a random graph. The evolution of the graph is represented by a sequence $\widehat{G}^R_{t_0}, \ldots, \widehat{G}^R_{t_i}, \ldots$. n_{t_i} denotes the number of vertices of $\widehat{G}^R_{t_i}$.

PROPERTY 1. *Whp, at any time t after a number of time steps polynomial in n, $\widehat{G}^R_t = (\hat{V}^R_t, \hat{E}^R_t)$ has an isoperimetric constant $I(\widehat{G}^R_t) \geq \log^{1+\alpha} N/2$, where:*
$$I(\widehat{G}^R_t) = \inf_{S \subset \hat{V}^R_t : |S| \leq n_t/2} E(S, \bar{S})/|S|.$$

PROPERTY 2 (MAXIMUM DEGREE OF $\widehat{G}^R$). *Whp, at any time t after a number of time steps polynomial in n, $\widehat{G}^R_t$ has maximal degree at most $c \log^{1+\alpha} N$ for a large enough constant c and an arbitrarily small (pre-)chosen constant α.*

Those properties enable to achieve short random walks leading to pick nodes uniformly at random. Note that OVER enables to tolerate simultaneous failures as long as the targets are picked uniformly at random. NOW together with OVER can also tolerate the failures of nodes chosen by the adversary as long as one failure per round is assumed.

Notations.

We use the time step as a subscript to indicate the instant at which a variable is considered (e.g., n_{t_i} is the number of nodes at time t_i, $\#C_{t_i}$ is the number of clusters, and $|C_j|_{t_i}$ the size of C_j). We may omit the index of the time step when there is no ambiguity (e.g., n stands for the current number of nodes in the network). The *communication cost* is the number of messages[†] exchanged, and the *round complexity*, is the number of communication rounds (i.e. the number of successive messages) required by a protocol to terminate. Notice that a time step is composed of several communication rounds, but we will prove that they are polylog(N). Given a graph $G = (V, E)$, and a vertex $v \in G$, we denote by d_v its degree. Similarly, for a given cluster C, d_C denotes the number of clusters adjacent to C.

3. NOW: OVERLAY OF CLUSTERS

NOW (Neighbors On Watch) maintains both an overlay of clusters and the partition of the nodes into clusters. NOW relies on the fact that the overlay is guaranteed to have a low maximum degree and good expansion properties. This is provided by the protocol OVER that we present in the long version of the paper [16] but could also be ensured by other protocols which differ either in the number of failures they can provide [3, 15, 26] or their degree (e.g., 4 in [2] instead of $\log^{1+\alpha} N$ in OVER for some arbitrarily small constant $\alpha > 0$)). NOW further ensures that each cluster contains more than two thirds of honest nodes whp. The clusters have size $O(\log N)$ and are used to inhibit the behavior of the Byzantine nodes. NOW relies on two phases: *initialization* and *maintenance*. In a nutshell, the initialization phase generates the initial overlay, while the maintenance phase ensures that after a polynomially long sequence of leave and join operations, the required properties still hold. The overlay $\widehat{G}^R$ is first constructed during the initialization phase of NOW, and recursively maintained by OVER as described in [16].

3.1 Preliminaries

A node of a cluster C is linked to all the other nodes of C and knows their identities. An edge between two clusters C_i and C_j in $\widehat{G}^R$ means that all nodes of C_i are linked to all nodes of C_j and know their identities (and *vice-versa*). A node only needs to know the identities of the nodes in its cluster and the neighboring ones. The initialization phase (Section 3.2) is itself divided into two sub-phases. First, a discovery algorithm is run in order for the nodes to acquire a global knowledge of the network. Afterwards, a Byzantine agreement algorithm [19] is used to construct an initial overlay of clusters. The maintenance phase ensures that each cluster contains more than two thirds of honest nodes whp when nodes join or leave and preserves the properties of the overlay.

Random number generation.

We assume the existence of randNum, a distributed random number generation protocol, enabling the nodes of a cluster to agree on a common integer chosen uniformly at random from the interval $(0, r)$. randNum is secure as long as the Byzantine nodes are less than two thirds in the cluster and is presented the long version of the paper [16].

Cluster random choice.

Furthermore, we assume the existence of a function called randC1 (Algorithm in [16]), to randomly select a cluster. To achieve the random selection (randC1), we perform a biased CTRW [‡] on $\widehat{G}^R$, the overlay. We bias our CTRW such that a cluster is chosen according to the distribution $(|C_i|/n)$. With clusters of size $O(\log N)$, this primitive has an expected communication cost of $O(\log^5 N)$. Indeed, the expected number of clusters visited during the walk is $O(\log^3 N)$ (whp, we do $O(\log n)$ CTRW each of length $O(\log^2 n)$) and at each cluster a random integer from the range $(0, O(\log^{1+\alpha} N))$ is generated at a cost of $O(\log^2 N)$. The expected round complexity of this primitive is $O(\log^4 N)$.

Node shuffling.

In order to avoid an adversary to focus on one cluster and gradually pollute it with Byzantine nodes, shuffling nodes between clusters is necessary upon nodes arrival and departure. The shuffling is implemented by the algorithm called exchange and detailed in [16]. Basically some clusters exchange their nodes with nodes chosen at random from other clusters. For each node x to be exchanged from cluster C (x is determined by the protocol exchange), a cluster is chosen at random using randC1. The chosen cluster, C', is informed that it will receive x. The cluster C' chooses one of its nodes (using the primitive randNum) to send in replacement of x. During an exchange, if C is adjacent to another cluster, the nodes of this cluster are informed of the new composition of C. This step is fundamental since a node from a neighboring cluster accepts a message from C if and only if at least half plus one of the nodes of C send it. The new nodes of C are informed by the former nodes of this cluster of the local structure of the overlay (i.e., the neighboring clusters of C in the overlay). The expected communication cost and round complexity of exchange are $O(\log^6 N)$ and $O(\log^4 N)$.

3.2 NOW: Initialization Phase

Network Discovery.

The protocol starts by running an algorithm that informs each node of the identifiers of all other nodes. The global knowledge of the nodes in the network is needed only at initialization. Note that this computation is performed while the size of the network is still "small" in practice. Afterwards, it is possible to use standard off-the-shelf Byzantine agreement algorithms to construct an initial partition forming the vertices of the overlay $\widehat{G}^R$. This algorithm (Provided in [16]) terminates after a number of communication rounds at most the diameter of the graph considering only the edges adjacent to at least one honest node. When the algorithm terminates, it is guaranteed that all

---

9[†]We consider messages of identical size. Hence the communication cost is proportional to the number of bits sent.

9[‡]A vertex C_i of $\widehat{G}^R$ is a cluster in G. A biased CTRW from C_i is a sequence of CTRW as follows: the nodes of C_i choose collaboratively the next cluster C_j and decrease the duration of the CTRW using randNum which goes on similarly. When the remaining duration is negative or null, a random number between 0 and 1 is chosen. If it is smaller than $|C_i|/\max_C |C|$, the biased CTRW ends, otherwise a CTRW starts again. A node of a cluster C_j pursues the random walk if and only if it receives an identical message from at least half plus one of the nodes of the neighboring cluster from which the CTRW comes.

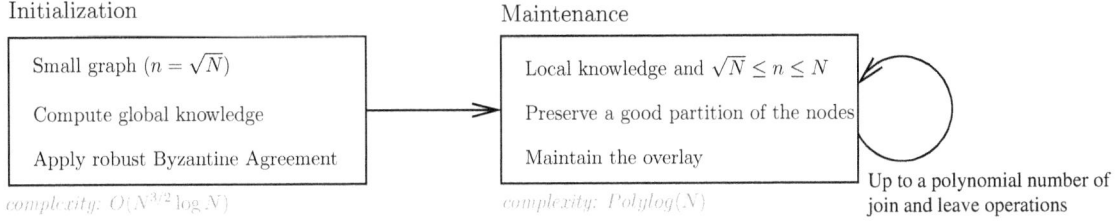

Figure 1: Overview of NOW.

honest nodes know the identities of all nodes in the network. Its communication cost is $O(n \times e)$ where $e = |E|$ (see [16] for the theorem and details).

Clusterization.

Once all the honest nodes know the identities of all the nodes in the network, any Byzantine agreement protocol can be used, such as [19] whose complexity is $\tilde{O}(n\sqrt{n})$. This protocol works in the presence of a static Byzantine adversary controlling less than $1/3 - \epsilon$ of the nodes for some positive constant ϵ. A representative cluster of logarithmic size containing more than two thirds of honest nodes is selected. Afterwards, we use the nodes of this representative cluster to randomly partition the network into $\#C$ clusters, $\{C_1, \ldots, C_{\#C}\}$, each of size $k \log N$, for some constant k. The constant k is a security parameter of the protocol that is chosen *a priori* depending on the requirements of the application considered: the higher k, the less chances the adversary has to control more than a third of the nodes of one of the clusters. Choosing the partition at random ensures that whp, there is more than two thirds of honest nodes in each cluster. This can be proved using standard Chernoff bound and union bound arguments. To obtain a random partition, it is sufficient for the representative cluster to order the nodes at random by calling the primitive `randNum`. Once the random ordering has been computed, the partition is obtained by taking for each cluster $k \log N$ successive nodes. Afterwards, $\widehat{G}_{t_0}^R$ is initiated on top of this partition: for each pair of clusters, the representative cluster determines with probability $p = \log^{1+\alpha} N / \sqrt{N}$ whether or not they will be linked by an edge in $\widehat{G}_{t_0}^R$. Finally, the representative cluster tells each node x the cluster it belongs to, the identities of the other nodes in this cluster, and the adjacent clusters as well as their composition (i.e., the identities of the nodes). The node x is "linked" to all these nodes and can for efficiency purposes forget the identifier of any other node that it may know. It is fundamental for the security of our protocol that each cluster contains more than two thirds of honest nodes. Indeed, a node receiving a message from all the nodes of a particular cluster considers this message valid if and only if, it receives the same message from more than half of the nodes of this cluster. Using this rule for inter-cluster communication, together with the condition that each cluster has more than two thirds of honest nodes, is sufficient to ensure the correctness of the protocol.

3.3 NOW: Maintenance Phase

While the initialization phase of NOW ensures the desired properties for both the overlay and the clusters, maintaining these properties under high dynamics is challenging. In this section, we describe how to preserve the property that each cluster is composed of an honest majority in the presence of nodes join and leave operations. Shuffling the network is crucial at this point as mentioned in [6, 7, 31] to avoid the adversary to control a majority of nodes in a cluster after a few steps by using a very simple strategy: the adversary chooses a specific cluster and keeps adding and removing the Byzantine nodes until they fall into that cluster. Similarly, it is crucial to introduce dynamics with shuffling if nodes are forced to leave the network by the adversary. The shuffling is generated upon *Join* and *Leave* operations. Complementary, the *Split* and *Merge* operations ensure that the clusters remain of size $\Omega(\log N)$, and that the required properties of $\widehat{G}^R$ (i.e., expansion and low maximum degree) are preserved.

The NOW following operations are invoked by the nodes upon joining, or leaving the network, or simultaneously by all the nodes of a cluster involved in a split or a merge operation.

Join.

This operation (as well as the leave operation), initiated by a node joining the network, is inspired by [6, 7, 31]. When a node x joins the network, we assume that it gets in contact with a cluster of the overlay. This cluster chooses another cluster using `randCl` in which x is inserted. The chosen cluster proceeds by inserting x and uses `exchange` for all of its nodes. This operation has a communication cost of polylog(N).

Split.

This operation is initiated simultaneously by all nodes of a cluster C if after a join operation, the size of this cluster is larger than $lk \log N$ for some fixed parameter l (l is a constant greater than $\sqrt{2}$ which influences the number of split and merge operations). Then C has to be split in two, the old and the new clusters. To this end, the nodes of C generate a random partition of C. The old cluster keeps its neighbors in $\widehat{G}^R$, whereas the new cluster is added to the overlay using `Add` as described in [16]. This procedure has a communication cost of polylog(N) and a $O(\log^4 N)$ round complexity. Recall that each node knows the exact composition of its cluster, therefore a split operation can be easily achieved.

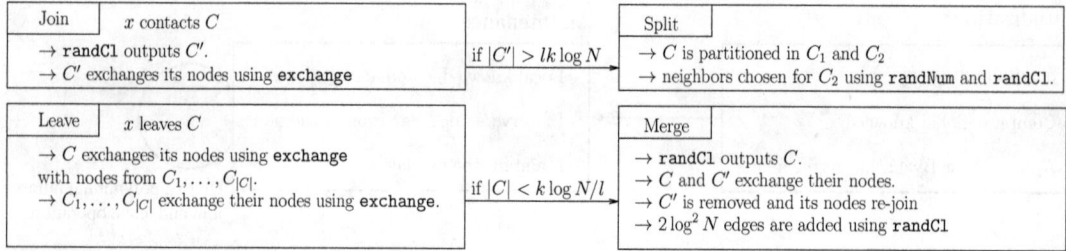

Join	x contacts C
→ randCl outputs C'.	
→ C' exchanges its nodes using exchange	

if $|C'| > lk \log N$

Split	
→ C is partitioned in C_1 and C_2	
→ neighbors chosen for C_2 using randNum and randCl.	

Leave	x leaves C
→ C exchanges its nodes using exchange with nodes from $C_1, \ldots, C_{|C|}$.	
→ $C_1, \ldots, C_{|C|}$ exchange their nodes using exchange.	

if $|C| < k \log N/l$

Merge	
→ randCl outputs C.	
→ C and C' exchange their nodes.	
→ C' is removed and its nodes re-join	
→ $2 \log^2 N$ edges are added using randCl	

Figure 2: Maintenance of the overlay. Each operation has a $\mathrm{polylog}(N)$ complexity.

Algorithm 1 Join operation.

9

Require: Node x contacting cluster C to join the network.
Ensure: The preservation of the properties of the overlay and of the clusters.

Nodes of C choose a cluster C' using randCl.
All nodes of C' add x to their local view of C'.
All nodes of C' send a message to all the nodes from the neighboring clusters informing that x is added to C'.
All nodes of C' send their neighborhood to x using the path used to find C' in randCl.

if $|C'| > kl \log n$ **then**

  Nodes of C' compute a partition of C' into two parts of roughly the same size using randCl: C_1 and C_2.
  Nodes of C_1 keep their neighborhood.
  Nodes of C_1 and C_2 send a message informing that C' is replaced by C_1 to the neighbors of C_1.
  Nodes of C_2 are given a new neighborhood using Add(C_2) (Algorithm of OVER [16]).

end if

Algorithm 2 Leave operation.

9

Require: Node x from a cluster C leaving the network.
Ensure: The preservation of the properties of the overlay and the clusters.

Nodes of C remove x from their view.
Nodes of C send a message to their neighbors informing them to remove x from their view.
A node that is a neighbor of C receiving a message to remove $x \in C$ from more than half of the nodes of C removes it from its view.
C exchanges its nodes using exchange.
A cluster exchanging one or more of its nodes with C execute the exchange procedure.

if $|C'| < k \log n/l$ **then**

  Nodes of C inform all their neighbors that C is removed.
  Nodes of C execute Remove(C_1) ([16]) of OVER.
  A node that is a neighbor of C receiving a message that C is removed from more than half of the nodes of C removes it from its view.
  Nodes of C execute Algorithm 1 as to rejoin the network.

end if

Leave.

This operation occurs when a node from a cluster C leaves the network or when the other nodes of C detect its absence. C exchanges all its nodes using the primitive exchange. Then, a cluster receiving one or more nodes from C execute exchange for all of its nodes. This process has a communication cost of $\mathrm{polylog}(N)$ and a $O(\log^4 N)$ round complexity.

Merge.

This operation is initiated simultaneously by all nodes of a cluster C containing less than $\frac{k \log N}{l}$ users (for the same fixed parameter l described previously). In this situation, a cluster, chosen at random in order to ensure Properties 1 and 2, has to be removed. This is achieved using the primitive randCl. Nodes in C proceed as if they were joining the network while the nodes from the chosen cluster C' become members of C. In $\widehat{G}^R$, C' is removed by using the operation Remove described in [16].

4. NOW: ANALYSIS

In this section, we prove that after a polynomial sequence of join and leave operations (some of them inducing some splitting and merging of clusters), each cluster contains more than two thirds of honest nodes as long as the fraction of Byzantine nodes τ controlled by the adversary is smaller than $1/3 - \epsilon$ (for some constant $\epsilon > 0$ independent of n).

The results are proved under the assumption that the random choices of nodes are perfectly uniform (i.e, the small bias induced by the random walk is ignored). This assumption is justifed by the fact that we consider a mixing time after which the distance from the desired distribution is $O(n^{-c})$ for some arbitrarily large constant c. More specifically, we describe the output of a CTRW using two random variables X and Y. X indicates whether or not the output of the CTRW has the desired distribution and is defined as follows: we consider the probability distribution $\mathcal{D}$ of the endpoints of a CTRW, and set p_v as the probability node v is hit. Set $p_{min} = \min_v(p_v)$. The binary random variable X has value 1 with probability $n \times p_{min}$ and 0 otherwise. Y is equal to node v with probability $(p_v - p_{min})/(\sum_w (p_w - p_{min}))$. We can reproduce $\mathcal{D}$ by first evaluating X. Then, if $X = 1$, the endpoint is picked according to the desired distribution. Else, the endpoint is picked according to Y. We have $P(X = 0) \leq n \times \max(p_v - p_{min}) = O(n^{-c+1})$, which means that the probability of the endpoint not to be picked as desired is $O(n^{-c+1})$. Conditional to that, in the following we assume that the random choices made using a CTRW are as desired, i.e $(|C|/n)$ for each cluster C where $|C|$ is its size.

4.1 Status of a cluster after `exchange`

At each time step, we assume that either a join or leave operation takes place or nothing occurs. These operations may in turn induce the splitting or merging of clusters. A split operation is done directly at the time it occurs, whereas, when a cluster executes a merge operation, we consider that its nodes re-join the network in subsequent time steps inducing normal join operations. Given a cluster C, p_t^C is the proportion of Byzantine nodes in C at time t.

LEMMA 1 (2/3 OF HONEST NODES IN A CLUSTER). *If a cluster C has exchanged all its nodes at time step t, we have $P(p_t^C > \tau(1+\epsilon)) \leq n^{-\gamma}$, for any positive constant γ, as long as the security parameter k is large enough.*

PROOF. When a cluster C exchanges one of its nodes with another cluster, this cluster is first selected at random according to the probability distribution $(|C|_{t_i}/n)$, and then a node is chosen out of it uniformly at random. In this scenario, the probability of performing an exchange with a Byzantine node is τ.

Using standard Chernoff bound arguments, we can derive the following result on the number X of Byzantine nodes among $|C|_{t_i}$ nodes: $P(X > (1+\epsilon)\tau|C|_{t_i}) \leq e^{-\epsilon^2 \tau |C|_{t_i}/3}$. Therefore as $|C|_{t_i} \geq (k \log N)/l$, we have $P(X > (1+\epsilon)\tau|C|_{t_i}) \leq N^{-\gamma}$ when k is sufficiently large for some constant γ. □

This lemma is a consequence of the Chernoff bound arguments [17] and implies that to obtain more than two thirds of honest nodes in a cluster whp, it is sufficient that $\tau + \epsilon < 1/3$, which is true by assumption on τ.

REMARK 1 (INCREASING THE ROBUSTNESS). *One can tolerate a fraction of Byzantine nodes up to $1/2 - \epsilon$, but then we need to use cryptographic tools to allow for broadcast and Byzantine agreement.*

4.2 Evolution of the divergence

To summarize, we have seen that each time a cluster exchanges all of its nodes, as long as $\tau(1+\epsilon) < 1/3$, we obtain more than two thirds of honest nodes whp in the resulting cluster. We now proceed by proving that in between two exchanges, this property also holds. To realize this, we focus on a specific cluster C and consider a sequence of s join and leave operations.

We first prove that if the cluster has less than a $\tau(1+\epsilon/2)$ fraction of Byzantine nodes, then after it has exchanged $O(\log N)$ of its nodes, it does not have more than a $\tau(1+\epsilon)$ fraction of Byzantine nodes. Then, we prove that if it has between a $\tau(1 + \epsilon/2)$ and $\tau(1 + \epsilon)$ fraction of Byzantine nodes, then after it has exchanged $O(\log N)$ of its nodes, it has less than a $\tau(1 + \epsilon/2)$ fraction of Byzantine nodes whp.

LEMMA 2. *If a cluster C has less than $\tau(1 + \epsilon/2)|C|$ Byzantine nodes, then after $O(\log N)$ node exchanges with nodes chosen uniformly at random, the cluster does not contain more than $\tau(1+\epsilon)|C|$ Byzantine nodes whp.*

PROOF. A cluster C with a fraction p of Byzantine nodes has a probability at most $p(1-\tau)$ to have this fraction decreased by $1/|C|$, and at least $(1-p)\tau$ to have it increased by the same amount. If this fraction is at most $\tau(1+\epsilon/2)$,

we prove that it increases by ϵ with probability $o(1/N^\gamma)$, for γ being arbitrarily large depending on the chosen value of k.

The fraction of Byzantine nodes in the cluster is dominated by the martingale with starting state $\tau(1 + \epsilon/2)$, which increases or decreases by $1/|C|$ with probability τ. We now show that whp, this martingale will not exceed $\tau(1+\epsilon)$ after $O(\log N)$ steps (recall that $k \log N/l \leq |C| \leq kl \log N$).

For k large enough, let $T^{exchange}$ stands for the number of exchanges. It is $O(\log N)$ and hence there is a constant M such that $T \leq M \log N$. We can derived from Azuma-Hoeffding's inequality that:

$$Prob(p^C > \tau(1 + \epsilon/2)) < e^{-\epsilon^2/4 \sum_{i=1}^{T^{exchange}} 1/|C|^2}$$
$$\leq e^{-\epsilon(k/l)^2 \log^2 N/4(M \log N)}$$
$$= e^{-\epsilon(k/l)^2 \log(N)/4M} = n^{-\gamma}$$

□

Similarly, if a cluster has more than a $\tau(1+\epsilon/2)$ fraction of Byzantine nodes, we have that after $O(\log N)$ exchanges, the cluster has less than a $\tau(1+\epsilon/2)$ fraction of Byzantine nodes.

LEMMA 3. *Given a cluster C whose fraction of Byzantine nodes is between $\tau(1 + \epsilon)$ and $\tau(1 + \epsilon/2)$ (for some constant $\epsilon > 0$ independent of n), then whp, the fraction of Byzantine nodes in this cluster is less than $\tau(1 + \epsilon/2)$ after $O(\log N)$ exchanges with nodes chosen uniformly at random.*

PROOF. We use the same arguments for the previous theorem. Here, the fraction of Byzantine node will decrease of $1/|C|$ with probability at least $\tau(1+\epsilon/2)$ and will increase by $1/|C|$ with probability τ. Therefore, as we start from a fraction of at most $\tau(1 + \epsilon)$, whp, after $O(\log N)$ exchanges, the fraction of Byzantine nodes in this cluster is less than $\tau(1 + \epsilon/2)$. □

When we look at a sequence of s exchanges affecting a given cluster C, we can split this sequence in alternating sub-sequences to apply Lemmas 2 and 3. Some sequences might lead to a fraction of Byzantine nodes between $\tau(1 + \epsilon/2)$ and $\tau(1 + \epsilon)$, while the following one will lead to a fraction of Byzantine nodes bellow $\tau(1 + \epsilon/2)$ whp. Hence, for a sequence s whose length is polynomial, by the union bound, we obtain that is there is always (whp) more than two thirds of honest node in each cluster for an adequate k.

THEOREM 3. *Whp, after a number of steps polynomial in N, at each time step, all clusters are composed of more than two thirds of honest nodes.*

PROOF. Notice that to apply the previous lemmas, one has to ensure that the exchanged nodes are replaced by nodes chosen uniformly at random. This is ensured by our join and leave operations. This is clear for a join operation by the use of a biased CTRW to select the replacement node. For a leave operation, this is also clear for the cluster C from which the node leaves has its nodes exchanged with nodes selected uniformly at random. However, if we look at a cluster C' with which C has exchanged nodes, then the probability that C' receives a Byzantine node is not necessarily τ as it is equal the proportion of Byzantine nodes in C. This is why we enforce C' to exchange all its nodes.

Now, given a specific cluster, C we consider an alternating sequence of time steps $t_1, \ldots, t_i, \ldots$ when the fraction of nodes controlled by the adversary in C becomes larger or equal to $\tau(1 + \epsilon/2)$ and when it becomes smaller.

Consider i such that at t_i the fraction of nodes controlled by the adversary in C is less than $\tau(1 + \epsilon/2)$ (this is in particular true at the beginning). Then at t_{i+1}, it becomes greater or equal to $\tau(1 + \epsilon/2)$ and is less than $\tau(1+\epsilon)$. Lemma 3 ensures that time step t_{i+2} comes within $O(\log N)$ steps, and Lemma 2 ensures that between t_{i+1} and t_{i+2}, the adversary never controls more than a $\tau(1+\epsilon)$ fraction of nodes of the cluster.

By an union bound over all clusters, we have the announced result. $\square$

REMARK 2. *Considering an adversary controlling at most a fraction $1/r - \epsilon$ of the nodes for some constant $\epsilon > 0$ and $r \geq 2$ independent of n, it is possible to strengthen Theorem 3 to obtain that in all the clusters the adversary controls at most a fraction $1/r$ of the nodes.*

5. RELATED WORK

Several authors studied the impact of dynamics on distributed computations [9, 8]. In [10, 21, 22], the communication links of a dynamic network may be modified by the adversary under some connectivity restrictions. In [4], the authors study the scenario in which the adversary can force a large number of nodes of its choice to leave the network while other nodes naturally join the network at the same time. These join and leave operations impact the topology. Yet the size of the network is assumed to remain constant. The authors assume furthermore that the nodes are connected via an expander graph. Depending on whether the adversary has to decide in advance the identities of the nodes to be kicked-out of the network, the authors propose almost-everywhere agreement protocols tolerating at each time step a churn of, respectively $O(n)$ and $O(\sqrt{n})$. The two main differences with our work are that (1) all nodes are assumed to be honest (i.e., the adversary is only external) and (2) nodes are connected via an expander graph by assumption. In contrast, our protocol tolerates a Byzantine adversary controlling a constant fraction of the nodes of the network and dynamically maintains the expander graph.

Some protocols have been proposed to maintain P2P overlay networks. Some offer efficient routing strategies and tolerate crashes, e.g. CAN, Pastry or Tapestry [29, 30, 33]. Some are dedicated to asynchronous networks with concurrent joins and leaves [27]. However, none guarantees both that each node has a low degree and that the resulting overlay exhibits good expansion properties in the sense we require here. Protocols such as SHELL [32] organize peers into a heap structure resilient to large Sybil attacks, while the overlay presented in [23] is resilient to an adversary that can force several peers to crash and join in a arbitrary manner. In [23], the number of join and leave operations tolerated at each turn is proportional to the degree of the

nodes, which is optimal. However, the communication cost for maintaining the overlay is high as all the nodes of the network exchange messages at each step.

Other protocols considered unstructured overlays. The protocol of [26] builds an overlay corresponding to an expander graph obtained from the union of several random cycles. This protocol has been further extended and analyzed in [3, 15]. Maintaining unstructured overlays induces fewer message exchanges compared to structured overlays [23, 29, 30, 33] since only a polylogarithmic number of nodes are involved in the communication upon a join or a leave operation. Some of the previous constructions [3, 15] and [26] can be complemented by a recent protocol from Pandurangan and Trehan [28] which preserves the expansion properties of a graph upon adversarial node removals. Nevertheless, the healing procedure proposed does not ensure an absolute expansion factor as we do.

The closest to ours, from the model perspective (dynamic network), is the one developed by Awerbuch and Scheideler [5, 6, 7, 31]. They consider a synchronous network in which an adversary can force nodes to join and leave at each time step, with the constraint that the number of nodes in the network is always within a constant factor of the initial size. Their protocols further require that initially the network is exclusively composed of honest nodes and that the Byzantine ones join the network only after a particular initialization phase has taken place. Within this model, the authors propose a technique to maintain clusters of size $O(\log n)$ composed of a majority of honest ones. Our approach improves upon these previous works in several ways as we do not assume that initially the network is exclusively composed of honest nodes, we describe more precisely how to distributively perform all the operations, and, more importantly, we maintain a partition of the nodes when the size of the network varies polynomially.

6. CONCLUDING REMARKS

This paper answers positively the following question raised in [19]: "Can we [..] address problems of robustness in networks subject to churn? An idea is to assume that: 1) the number of processors fluctuates between n and $\sqrt{n}$ where n is the size of name space; 2) the processors do not know explicitly who is in the system at any time; and 3) that the number of bad processors in the system is always less than a $1/3$ fraction. In such a model, can we 1) do Byzantine agreement; and 2) maintain small (i.e. polylogorathimic size) quorums of mostly good processors?"

Our clustering protocol can be leveraged to implement efficient and robust algorithms for various problems such as broadcast, agreement, aggregation, and sampling in the context of highly dynamic networks. A broadcast algorithm using our technique would have for instance $\tilde{O}(n)$ message complexity as compared to $O(n^2)$ without the clustering. Similarly, a sampling algorithm relying on our protocol would have a polylog(n) message complexity per sample.

We currently seek schemes to alleviate the need of the assumption of synchronous nodes. Another objective is to devise a procedure for the initialization phase of NOW whose communication cost is $o(n_{t_0}^2)$ (as opposed to $O(n_{t_0}^3)$).

7. REFERENCES

[1] D. Aldous and J. Fill. Reversible markov chains and random walks on graphs. http://stat-www.berkeley.edu/users/aldous/RWG/book.html.

[2] J. Aspnes and U. Wieder. The expansion and mixing time of skip graphs with applications. *ACM Symposium on Parallelism in Algorithms and Architectures (SPAA'05)*, pages 126–134, 2005.

[3] J. Aspnes and Y. Yin. Distributed algorithms for maintaining dynamic expander graphs. Citeseer, 2008.

[4] J. Augustine, G. Pandurangan, P. Robinson, and E. Upfal. Towards robust and efficient computation in dynamic peer-to-peer networks. *Arxiv preprint*, arXiv:1108.0809, 2011.

[5] B. Awerbuch and C. Scheideler. Group spreading: A protocol for provably secure distributed name service. *Automata, Languages and Programming*, pages 187–210, 2004.

[6] B. Awerbuch and C. Scheideler. Towards scalable and robust overlay networks. In *Proceedings of the International Workshop on Peer-To-Peer Systems (IPTPS'07)*, 2007.

[7] B. Awerbuch and C. Scheideler. Towards a scalable and robust DHT. *Theory of Computing Systems*, 45(2):234–260, 2009.

[8] R. Baldoni, S. Bonomi, and A. S. Nezhad. An algorithm for implementing bft registers in distributed systems with bounded churn. In *SSS*, pages 32–46, 2011.

[9] R. Baldoni, S. Bonomi, and M. Raynal. An implementation in a churn prone environment. In *SIROCCO*, pages 15–29, 2009.

[10] H. Baumann, P. Crescenzi, and P. Fraigniaud. Parsimonious flooding in dynamic graphs. In *Proceedings of the 28th symposium on Principles of distributed computing (PODC'09)*, 2009.

[11] Z. Galil and M. Yung. Partitioned encryption and achieving simultaneity by partitioning. *Information Processing Letters*, 26(2):81 – 88, 1987.

[12] S. Gambs, R. Guerraoui, H. Harkous, F. Huc, and A.-M. Kermarrec. Scalable and secure polling in dynamic distributed networks. *SRDS*, 2012.

[13] J. Garay, J. Katz, R. Kumaresan, and H. Zhou. Adaptively secure broadcast, revisited. In *30th annual Symposium on Principles of Distributed Computing (PODC'11)*, 2011.

[14] A. Giurgiu, R. Guerraoui, K. Huguenin, and A. Kermarrec. Computing in social networks. *Stabilization, Safety, and Security of Distributed Systems*, pages 332–346, 2010.

[15] C. Gkantsidis, M. Mihail, and A. Saberi. Random walks in peer-to-peer networks. In *Proceedings of the 23rd Annual Joint Conference of the IEEE Computer and Communications Societies (INFOCOM'2004)*, volume 1, 2004.

[16] R. Guerraoui, F. Huc, and A.-M. Kermarrec. Highly dynamic distributed computing with byzantine failures. *Arxiv preprint*, arXiv:1202.3084, 2013.

[17] M. Habib, C. McDiarmid, J. Ramirez-Alfonsin, and B. Reed. *Probabilistic Methods for Algorithmic Discrete Mathematics*. Springer Verlag, Berlin, 1998.

[18] V. King, S. Lonargan, J. Saia, and A. Trehan. Load balanced scalable byzantine agreement through quorum building, with full information. *Distributed Computing and Networking*, pages 203–214, 2011.

[19] V. King and J. Saia. Scalable Byzantine Computation. *ACM SIGACT News*, 41(3), 2010.

[20] M. Krebs and A. Shaheen. *Expander Families and Cayley Graphs: A Beginner's Guide*. Oxford University Press, USA, 2011.

[21] F. Kuhn, N. Lynch, and R. Oshman. Distributed computation in dynamic networks. In *Proceedings of the 42nd symposium on Theory of computing (STOC'10)*, pages 513–522, 2010.

[22] F. Kuhn, Y. Moses, and R. Oshman. Coordinated consensus in dynamic networks. In *Proceedings of the 30th annual symposium on Principles of distributed computing (PODC'11)*, pages 1–10, 2011.

[23] F. Kuhn, S. Schmid, and R. Wattenhofer. Towards worst-case churn resistant peer-to-peer systems. *Distributed Computing*, 22(4):249–267, 2010.

[24] K. L., E. Liberty, and O. Somekh. Estimating sizes of social networks via biased sampling. In *Proceedings of the 20th international conference on World wide web*, pages 597–606. ACM, 2011.

[25] L. Lamport, R. Shostak, and M. Pease. The Byzantine Generals Problem. *ACM Transactions on Programming Languages and Systems (TOPLAS'82)*, 4(3):382–401, July 1982.

[26] C. Law and K. Siu. Distributed construction of random expander graphs. In *Proceedings of 22nd Annual Joint Conference of the IEEE Computer and Communications Societies (INFOCOM'2003)*, pages 2133–2143, 2003.

[27] X. Li, J. Misra, and C. Plaxton. Active and concurrent topology maintenance. *Distributed Computing*, pages 320–334, 2004.

[28] G. Pandurangan and A. Trehan. Xheal: localized self-healing using expanders. In *Proceedings of the 30th annual symposium on Principles of distributed computing (PODC'11)*, pages 301–310, 2011.

[29] S. Ratnasamy, P. Francis, M. Handley, R. Karp, and S. Shenker. A scalable content-addressable network. In *Conference on Applications, technologies, architectures, and protocols for computer communications*, pages 161–172, 2001.

[30] A. Rowstron and P. Druschel. Pastry: Scalable, decentralized object location, and routing for large-scale peer-to-peer systems. In *Proceedings of Middleware'01*, pages 329–350, 2001.

[31] C. Scheideler. How to spread adversarial nodes? Rotate! *Proceedings of the 37th annual symposium on Theory of computing (STOC'05)*, page 704, 2005.

[32] C. Scheideler and S. Schmid. A distributed and oblivious heap. *Automata, Languages and Programming*, pages 571–582, 2009.

[33] B. Zhao, L. Huang, J. Stribling, S. Rhea, A. Joseph, and J. Kubiatowicz. Tapestry: A resilient global-scale overlay for service deployment. *IEEE Journal on Selected Areas in Communications*, 22(1):41–53, 2004.

Brief Announcement: Constructing Fault-Tolerant Overlay Networks for Topic-based Publish/Subscribe [*]

Chen Chen
University of Toronto
chenchen@eecg.toronto.edu

Roman Vitenberg
University of Oslo, Norway
romanvi@ifi.uio.no

Hans-Arno Jacobsen
University of Toronto
jacobsen@eecg.toronto.edu

ABSTRACT

We incorporate fault tolerance in designing reliable and scalable overlay networks to support topic-based pub/sub communication. We propose the MinAvg-kTCO problem parameterized by k: use the minimum number of edges to create a *k-topic-connected overlay* ($kTCO$) for pub/sub systems, i.e., for each topic the sub-overlay induced by nodes interested in the topic is k-connected.

We prove the NP-completeness of MinAvg-kTCO and show a lower-bound for the hardness of its approximation. With regard to MinAvg-2TCO, we present GM2, the first polynomial time algorithm with an approximation ratio. With regards to MinAvg-kTCO, where $k \geq 2$, we propose a simple and efficient heuristic algorithm, namely HararyPT, that aligns nodes across different sub-overlays.

We experimentally demonstrate the scalability of GM2 and HararyPT under representative pub/sub workloads.

Categories and Subject Descriptors

C.2.1 [**Computer-Communication Networks**]: Network Architecture and Design—*network topology*; G.2.2 [**Discrete Mathematics**]: Graph Theory—*network problems*

General Terms

Algorithms, Theory, Experimentation

Keywords

Overlay networks, reliability, publish/subscribe

1. INTRODUCTION

Publish/Subscribe (pub/sub) systems constitute an attractive choice as the communication paradigm and messaging substrate for building large-scale distributed systems. In the topic-based pub/sub model, a publisher associates its

---

[*]A full version of this paper is available in [2].

publication message with a specific topic, and subscribers register their interest in a subset of all topics.

A distributed topic-based pub/sub system is often organized as an application-level overlay of brokers (e.g., simply referred to as nodes) connected in a federated or in a peer-to-peer manner. The overlay infrastructure directly impacts the pub/sub system's performance and scalability, e.g., the message routing cost. Constructing a high-quality broker overlay is a fundamental problem that has received attention both in industry and academia [4, 1].

Gregory Chockler *et al.* define a *topic-connected overlay* (TCO), as an overlay, where all pub/sub nodes interested in the same topic are organized in a connected dissemination sub-overlay [4]. A TCO ensures that nodes not interested in a topic never need to contribute to disseminating information on that topic. Publication routing atop TCOs saves bandwidth and computational resources otherwise wasted on forwarding messages of no interest to the node. A TCO also results in more efficient routing protocols, a simpler matching engine, and smaller forwarding tables.

Unfortunately, topic-connectivity per se does not address critical reliability requirements for the pub/sub overlay. In particular, there is no guarantee that topic-connectivity is preserved under even a single node crash. That is, all the desirable properties about TCOs are fragile and easily break in a dynamic environment. The root cause for this lies in the definition of TCO and TCO-related problems [4, 1]. These definitions make an implicit assumption that the pub/sub overlay is reliable and robust, i.e., nodes and links in the network are fault-free.

In order to address this shortcoming, we propose the problem of constructing a k-topic-connected overlay ($kTCO$): topic-connectivity still holds as long as fewer than k nodes fail simultaneously on the same topic (see Def. 1 in §3). The extension from TCO to $kTCO$ captures the overlay's resilience to churn by introducing a safety factor, k. This safety factor is important from an engineering perspective because pub/sub systems are dynamic in nature. Node churn may occur due to administrative maintenance or inevitable failures, such as hardware faults, misconfigurations, or software bugs. In practice, the set of active machines in a data center shows non-negligible variations over time.

Advocates for TCO-structured pub/sub overlays might argue that $kTCO$ is not necessary. In principle, the TCO can always be reconstructed in the presence of churn. However, this is impractical and wasteful since state-of-the-art algorithms suffer from a high computational complexity [4, 1]. On the other hand, a few pub/sub systems (e.g., [3]) have explored the problem of dynamically maintaining the *TCO*. Basically, these approaches constantly make incremental adjustments to the overlay in presence of churn. However, the overlays they produced are not as optimal in terms of the node degree as the centralized algorithms for *TCO* construction, as corroborated by experimental studies. Besides, approaches for incremental overlay maintenance can be applied to *kTCO* as well to produce even more reliable solutions.

Furthermore, *kTCO* can lead to better performance. First, *kTCO* indicates that *k* disjoint data paths exist from end to end for each topic. Thus, we can harvest network intelligence in the routing protocols on top of *kTCO* by steering the traffic among multiple alternate paths in a more optimized and secure manner. Second, we reduce the diameters of the overlay, as we improve its connectivity (see §6). With lower diameters, message delays are likely to be diminished because fewer hops are needed for message delivery.

Nevertheless, these merits of *kTCO* come at a price – additional links are required. However, it is also imperative for a pub/sub overlay network to have low node degrees. This is because it costs a lot of resources to maintain adjacent links for a high-degree node (i.e., monitor links and neighbors [4]). For a typical pub/sub system, each link would also have to accommodate a number of protocols, service components, message queues, and so on. While overlay designs for different applications might be principally different, they all strive to maintain bounded node degrees, e.g., DHTs, wireless networks, and survivable network designs.

In this paper, we formally study the fundamental trade-offs between attaining the *kTCO* property while preserving low node degrees. Our main contributions are as follows:

1. We propose the MinAvg-*k*TCO problem of devising *kTCO* with the minimum number of links (see Problem 1 in §3). We formally prove the hardness of MinAvg-*k*TCO in §3.

2. We design two algorithms for MinAvg-*k*TCO. First, with regards to MinAvg-*2*TCO, we present GM*2*, the first polynomial time approximation algorithm in §4. Second, with regards to MinAvg-*k*TCO, where $k \geq 2$, we propose a simple and efficient heuristic algorithm, namely HararyPT, that aligns nodes across different sub-overlays (see §5).

3. We validate GM*2* and HararyPT with comprehensive experiments under characteristic pub/sub workloads in §6. GM*2* outputs a *2TCO*, whose average node degree is around 1.5 times that of the *1TCO* produced by the state-of-the-art algorithm. GM*2* also improves the topic diameters by 50%.

2. BACKGROUND

Let $I(V, T, Int)$ represent an input instance, where V is the set of nodes, T is the set of topics, and Int is the interest function such that $Int : V \times T \rightarrow \{true, false\}$. Since the domain of the interest function is a Cartesian product, we also refer to this function as an interest matrix. Given an interest function Int, we say that a node v is interested in some topic t if and only if $Int(v, t) = true$. We also say that node v subscribes to topic t.

We denote a *topic-based pub/sub overlay network* (TPSO) as $TPSO(V, T, Int, E)$. A $TPSO(V, T, Int, E)$ can be illustrated as an undirected graph $G = (V, E)$ over the node set V with the edge set $E \subseteq V \times V$. Given $TPSO(V, T, Int, E)$, the sub-overlay *induced* by $t \in T$ is a subgraph $G^{(t)} = (V^{(t)}, E^{(t)})$ such that $V^{(t)} = \{v \in V | Int(v, t)\}$ and $E^{(t)} = \{(v, w) \in E | v \in V^{(t)} \wedge w \in V^{(t)}\}$. A *topic-connected compo-*

nent (*TC-component*) on topic $t \in T$, is a maximal connected subgraph in $G^{(t)}$. A *TPSO* is called *topic-connected* if for each topic $t \in T$, $G^{(t)}$ has at most one *TC-component*. We denote the *topic-connected overlay* as $TCO(V, T, Int, E)$.

3. THE MINAVG-*k*TCO PROBLEM

The definition of a *k*-connected graph can be directly applied to the sub-overlay induced by a topic $t \in T$. We call a $TCO(V, T, Int, E)$ *k*-**connected for topic** $t \in T$ if $G^{(t)} = (V^{(t)}, E^{(t)})$ is *k*-connected, i.e., $|V^{(t)}| > k$ and $G^{(t)} - X = (V^{(t)} - X, E^{(t)} \backslash \{e(v, w) | \text{either } v \in X \text{ or } w \in X\})$ is connected for every $X \subseteq V^{(t)}$ with $|X| < k$.

We want to extend the definition of *k*-connectivity to a *TPSO* considering all topics in T. However, given a parameter k, $|V^{(t)}|$ might be smaller than k for some topic $t \in T$; in these cases, "*k*-connectivity" is not defined in classic graph theory, but we need to adopt a convention for *TPSO*. Intuitively, for a fixed k, a *k*-topic-connected overlay should have the property that the *TPSO* can still provide pub/sub service (for all topics) as long as fewer than k nodes fail simultaneously on the same topic $t \in T$. If $|V^{(t)}| < k$, the removal of $(k - 1)$ nodes on t implies that there are no subscribers to t any more, and thus the overlay no longer serves t. To ensure the pub/sub service continues with topic t under other cases, we need to make sure $G^{(t)}$ has no separate set, i.e., $G^{(t)}$ is a complete graph. With this convention, we formally give Def. 1 and Problem 1.

DEFINITION 1. *A $TCO(V, T, Int, E)$ is k-**topic-connected** if for any $t \in T$, $G^{(t)} = (V^{(t)}, E^{(t)})$ is either (1) k-connected or (2) a clique if $|V^{(t)}| \leq k$. We denote a k-**topic-connected** **overlay** by $kTCO(V, T, Int, E)$ (or kTCO).*

PROBLEM 1. *The **MinAvg-k*TCO*(V, T, Int) problem parameterized by an integer k is defined as: Given a set of nodes V, a set of topics T, and the interest function Int, construct a kTCO that has the least possible total number of edges, i.e., the minimum average node degree.*

For brevity, we often omit "parameterized by k" and just refer to the problem as MinAvg-*k*TCO.

THEOREM 1. *Given any positive integer k, MinAvg-k*TCO* is NP-complete and can not be approximated in polynomial time within a factor of $O(\log |V|)$ unless $\mathrm{P} = \mathrm{NP}$.*

4. GM*2* ALGORITHM TO BUILD *2*TCO

Alg. 1 The GM*2* algorithm for *2TCO*

GM*2*(V, T, Int)

Input: V, T, Int
Output: $2TCO(V, T, Int, E_{\mathsf{GM2}})$
1: $E_{\mathsf{GM2}} \leftarrow \emptyset$, $E_{pot} \leftarrow V \times V$
2: **while** $TPSO(V, T, Int, E_{\mathsf{GM2}})$ is not *2TCO* **do**
3:     **for all** $e = (v, w) \in E_{pot}$ **do**
4:         $estimate(e, E_{\mathsf{GM2}}) \leftarrow |\{t \in T | Int(v, t) \wedge Int(w, t) \wedge$ no *TC-block* in $G^{(t)}$ contains both v and $w\}|$
5:     $e \leftarrow$ find e s.t. $estimate(e, E_{\mathsf{GM2}})$ is max among E_{pot}
6:     $E_{\mathsf{GM2}} \leftarrow E_{\mathsf{GM2}} \cup \{e\}$, $E_{pot} \leftarrow E_{pot} - \{e\}$
7: **return** $2TCO(V, T, Int, E_{\mathsf{GM2}})$

For the MinAvg-*2*TCO problem, we devise Greedy Merge for the *2TCO* algorithm, GM*2* for short.

Given a $TPSO(V, T, Int, E)$, the *2-topic-connected component* on topic $t \in T$, is a maximal 2-connected subgraph induced on topic t (i.e., it is not contained in any larger 2-connected subgraph induced on t). We also call it *topic-connected block*, *TC-block* for short.

As specified in Alg. 1, GM2 starts with $TPSO(V, T, Int, E)$ where $E = \emptyset$. The algorithm carefully adds an edge to E iteration by iteration until $TPSO(V, T, Int, E)$ contains at most one *TC-block* for each $t \in T$.

We denote by P_i the set of edges added to the overlay after the i-th iteration of GM2. Line 4 of Alg. 1 defines the *estimate* of e's contribution on topic t: $estimate^{(t)}(e(v, w), P_i) =$

$$\begin{cases} 0, \text{ if some block in } \left(V^{(t)}, P_i^{(t)} \right) \text{ contains both } v \text{ and } w \\ 1, \text{ otherwise} \end{cases}$$

The overall *edge estimate* is defined as

$$estimate(e, P_i) = \sum_{t \in T} estimate^{(t)}(e, P_i) \; .$$

LEMMA 1. *Alg. 1 takes time $O(|V|^4|T|)$ to output a 2TCO.*

LEMMA 2. *The approximation ratio of Alg. 1 is $O(U + \ln |V||T|)$, where $U = \max\{|V^{(t)}|, t \in T\}$.*

5. HARARYPT TO BUILD κTCO

With regard to MinAvg-kTCO, we design the Harary-Per-Topic Algorithm (HararyPT), as specified in Alg. 2.

Alg. 2 Harary-Per-Topic for $kTCO$

HararyPT$(I(V, T, Int), k)$
Input: $I(V, T, Int), k$
Output: $kTCO(V, T, Int, E_{\text{HPT}})$
1: $\mathbb{V} \leftarrow$ get an arbitrary sequence for V
2: **for all** $t \in T$ **do**
3: $\quad E^{(t)} \leftarrow \texttt{buildHarary}(k, \mathbb{V}^{(t)})$
4: $E_{\text{HPT}} \leftarrow \bigcup_{t \in T} E^{(t)}$
5: **return** $kTCO(V, T, Int, E_{\text{HPT}})$

HararyPT stems from graph theory about Harary graphs. Function $\texttt{buildHarary}(k, \mathbb{V}^{(t)})$ (Line 3 of Alg. 2) represents the standard procedure to construct the k-connected Harary graph for a given sequence of nodes $\mathbb{V}^{(t)}$.

In order to promote edge sharing across different sub-overlays, Alg. 2 first obtains a node sequence for all the nodes in Line 1. Then Alg. 2 adopts the same linear ordering for all Harary constructions across all topics (Lines 2-3). By sharing the determined node sequence, these Harary graphs are likely to share a lot of edges, especially when the workloads are highly correlated. As a consequence, the output $kTCO$ tends to have a low node degree.

6. EVALUATION

We implemented GM2, HararyPT, and other auxiliary algorithms in Java. We use GM as a baseline, because it produces a $1TCO$ with the lowest average node degree among all known polynomial-time algorithms [4]. We also develop the *Cycle-Per-Topic* algorithm (CyclePT) that mimics the common practice of building a separate overlay for each topic independently (usually a tree but we use a cycle that has the same average node degree and achieves $2TCO$).

We set $|V| \in [100, 1\,000]$, $|T| = 200$, and each node has a fixed subscription size of 30. Each topic $t \in T$ is associated

with probability $p(t)$, $\sum_{t \in T} p(t)=1$, and each node $v \in V$ subscribes to t with a probability $p(t)$. The value of $p(t)$ is distributed according to either an exponential, a Zipfian, or a uniform distribution, which we call Expo, Zipf, or Unif, for short. These distributions are representative of actual workloads used in industrial pub/sub systems today [3].

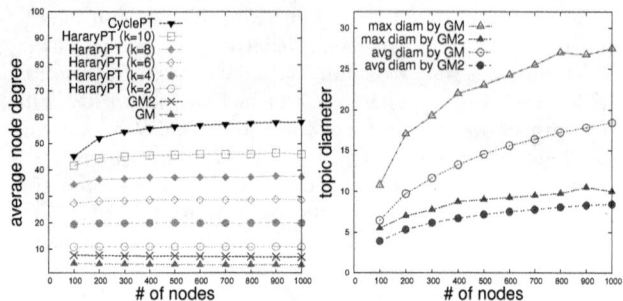

Figure 1: Node degree – Expo   Figure 2: Topic diameter – Unif

Fig. 1 compares the average node degrees in the output overlays produced by different algorithms under Expo. For a specific algorithm $\mathcal{A}$, we denote by $\bar{d}_{\mathcal{A}}$ the average node degree produced by $\mathcal{A}$. We focus on GM2 in Fig. 1. First, $\bar{d}_{\text{GM2}}$ and $\bar{d}_{\text{GM}}$ are quite close: $\bar{d}_{\text{GM2}}$ is smaller than $1.65 \cdot \bar{d}_{\text{GM}}$, on average. Second, $\bar{d}_{\text{CyclePT}}$ is about 5 times higher than $\bar{d}_{\text{GM2}}$ and tends to increase with the number of nodes, while $\bar{d}_{\text{GM2}}$ and $\bar{d}_{\text{GM}}$ decrease as the number of nodes scales up. The decrease of $\bar{d}_{\text{GM2}}$ and $\bar{d}_{\text{GM}}$ lies in the fact that increasing the number of nodes leads to higher chances for both GM2 and GM to find neighbors with more interest overlap, thus reducing overall number of neighbors needed.

Fig. 1 also shows that HararyPT significantly reduces unnecessary redundancy as compared to CyclePT. With fewer edges than $2TCO$s produced by CyclePT, HararyPT can achieve $12TCO$ under Expo.

We also look at *topic diameters* in the output overlays. Given $2TCO(V, T, Int, E)$, the topic diameter for $t \in T$ is $diam^{(t)} = diam(G^{(t)})$, where $diam(G^{(t)})$ is the maximum shortest distance between any two nodes in $G^{(t)} = (V^{(t)}, E^{(t)})$. We denote the maximum and average topic diameter across all topics as $Diam$ and $\overline{diam}$, respectively. Fig. 2 shows that GM2 significantly outperforms GM in terms of both $Diam$ and $\overline{diam}$. Under Unif, $Diam_{\text{GM2}}$ is $0.40 \cdot Diam_{\text{GM}}$, and $\overline{diam}_{\text{GM2}}$ is $0.50 \cdot \overline{diam}_{\text{GM}}$, on average. Besides, the gaps of $(Diam_{\text{GM}} - Diam_{\text{GM2}})$ and $(\overline{diam}_{\text{GM}} - \overline{diam}_{\text{GM2}})$ grow as the input instances scale up.

7. REFERENCES

[1] C. Chen, R. Vitenberg, and H.-A. Jacobsen. A generalized algorithm for publish/subscribe overlay design and its fast implementation. In *DISC*, 2012.

[2] C. Chen, R. Vitenberg, and H.-A. Jacobsen. Constructing fault-tolerant overlay networks for topic-based pub/sub. Technical report, U. of Toronto & U. of Oslo, 2013. http://msrg.org/papers/TR-kTCO.

[3] G. Chockler, R. Melamed, Y. Tock, and R. Vitenberg. Spidercast: A scalable interest-aware overlay for topic-based pub/sub communication. In *DEBS'07*.

[4] G. Chockler, R. Melamed, Y. Tock, and R. Vitenberg. Constructing scalable overlays for pub-sub with many topics: Problems, algorithms, and evaluation. In *PODC*, 2007.

Brief Announcement: Byzantine Agreement with a Strong Adversary in Polynomial Expected Time

Valerie King[*]
Dept. of Computer Science, University of Victoria
P.O. Box 3055
Victoria, BC, Canada V8W 3P6
val@cs.uvic.ca

Jared Saia[†]
Dept. of Computer Science, University of New
Mexico
Albuquerque, NM 87131-1386
saia@cs.unm.edu

ABSTRACT

In a paper appearing in STOC 2013, we considered Byzantine agreement in the classic asynchronous message-passing model. The adversary is *adaptive*: it can determine which processors to corrupt and what strategy these processors should use as the algorithm proceeds. Communication is *asynchronous*: the scheduling of the delivery of messages is set by the adversary, so that the delays are unpredictable to the algorithm. Finally, the adversary has *full information*: it knows the states of all processors at any time, and is assumed to be computationally unbounded. Such an adversary is also known as "strong". We presented the first known polynomial expected time algorithm to solve asynchronous Byzantine Agreement when the adversary controls a constant fraction of processors. This is the first improvement in running time for this problem since Ben-Or's exponential expected time solution in 1983.

Categories and Subject Descriptors

F.2.2 [**Theory of Computation**]: Analysis of Algorithms and Problem Complexity—*Nonnumerical Algorithms and Problems*

Keywords

Byzantine Agreement, Distributed Computing, Randomized Algorithms, Consensus

1. INTRODUCTION

How can we build a reliable system our of unreliable parts? Byzantine agreement is fundamental to addressing this question. The Byzantine agreement problem is to devise an algorithm so that n agents, each with an private input can agree

[*]This research was partially supported by an NSERC grant

[†]This research was partially supported by NSF CAREER Award 0644058, NSF CCR-0313160, and an AFOSR MURI grant.

PODC'13, July 22–24, 2013, Montréal, Québec, Canada.
ACM 978-1-4503-2065-8/13/07.

on a single common output that is equal to some agent's input. For example, if all processors start with 1, they must all decide on 1. The processors should successfully terminate despite the presence of $t = \theta(n)$ bad processors. An adversary controls the behavior of the bad processors which can deviate from the algorithm in arbitrary ways. Byzantine agreement is one of the most fundamental problems in distributed computing. Studied for over 30 years, it is referenced in thousands of papers.

In a paper presented at STOC 2013, we considered Byzantine agreement in the challenging classic asynchronous model. The adversary is *adaptive*: it can determine which processors to corrupt and what strategy these processors should use as the algorithm proceeds. Communication is *asynchronous*: the scheduling of the delivery of messages is set by the adversary, so that the delays are unpredictable to the algorithm. Finally, the adversary has *full information*: it knows the states of all processors at any time, and is assumed to be computationally unbounded. Such an adversary is also known as "strong" [3].

The major constraint on the adversary is that it cannot predict future coinflips, and we assume that each processor has its own fair coin and may at any time flip the coin and decide what to do next based on the outcome of the flip.

Time in this model is defined to be the maximum length of any chain of messages (see [8, 3]). In particular, all computation by individual processors is assumed to be instantaneous, and sending a message over the network is counted as taking 1 unit of time.

The only previously known results for this classic model are the works of Ben-Or (1983) [5] and Bracha (1984) [4]. Ben-Or gave a Byzantine agreement algorithm tolerating $t < n/5$. Bracha improved this tolerance to $t < n/3$. Unfortunately, both of these algorithms run in exponential expected time if $t = \Theta(n)$. As recently as 2006, Ben-Or, Pavlov and Vaikuntanathan [6] wrote:

"In the case of an asynchronous network, achieving even a polynomial-rounds BA protocol is open. We note that the best known asynchronous BA protocols [5, 4] have exponential expected round-complexity"

We presented the first algorithm for this problem to achieve better than exponential expected run time. Our main result is the following.

THEOREM 1. *Let n be the number of processors. There is a $t = \Theta(n)$ such that Byzantine Agreement can be solved in expected time $O(n^{2.5})$ and expected polynomial bits of com-*

munication, in the asynchronous message passing model with an adaptive, full-information adversary that controls up to t processors.

Note that we leave open the problem of whether the computations required by each individual processor can be done in polynomial time.

2. TECHNICAL OVERVIEW

We start with Ben-Or's 1983 algorithm. In this algorithm, roughly speaking, the processors take the majority of each others' votes. When there is a sufficiently large majority of processors which agree on the same bit, the adversary cannot affect the outcome. When there is not a sufficiently large majority, some or all of the processors flip their coins. If the processors which flip their coins happen to all flip them to the same value and that value happens to agree with the value held by the processors which do not flip, the algorithm terminates successfully in the next round. Ben-Or's algorithm reduces Byzantine agreement to the problem of generating a mutually agreed upon coinflip. In this sense it is similar to Rabin's global coinflip algorithm [11], which however assumes the existence of a global coin.

We thus follow the technique in the consensus literature of reducing the agreement problem to the problem of producing a commonly agreed upon coinflip (see the survey [1]; we were particularly inspired by the result in [2] for producing consensus in a shared memory model). The consensus problem is equivalent to Byzantine agreement, except that processors taken over by the adversary suffer crash faults and thus no longer send out messages.

In the consensus problem, a prevalent technique for generating a common coin is to have the processors generate and send out many coinflips. If the bias of these coinflips is sufficiently high, then if each processor takes the majority value of the coinflips, 1) all processors will obtain the same value; and 2) that value will be an unbiased coinflip. It suffices to generate n^2 individual coinflips to ensure that with constant probability, the bias generated by these coinflips will exceed the $O(n)$ bias that the adversary can introduce through scheduling of messages and crash faults.

Unfortunately, in Byzantine agreement, the adversary can introduce $\Theta(nt) = \Theta(n^2)$ bias through adversarily determined "coinflips". Thus, we need a new technique for limiting adversarial bias. Our basic approach is for each processor to run Ben-Or's algorithm multiple times and, for each processor p to add processors with suspiciously large bias to its "suspect list" so that their coinflips are subsequently ignored by p.

In particular, over enough iterations of Ben-Or's algorithm, if no decision has occurred, there must be a group of t or fewer processors which have produced coinflips with a suspiciously high amount of bias. These highly biased coinflips must have been received by enough good processors to prevent a decision. We show that a good processor can use information about these coinflips to ensure that its suspect list has the following properties. First, if Ben-Or's fails over many iterations, eventually all bad processors will be added to the suspect list. Second, no more than t good processors are ever added to the suspect list.

When all bad processors are added to each good processor's suspect list, agreement is reached within an expected constant number of iterations of Ben-Or's algorithm. One technical challenge is to show that not too many good processors are added to the suspect list of any good processor.

3. RELATED WORK

Randomized algorithms for Byzantine agreement with resilience $t = \Theta(n)$ and constant expected time have been known for 25 years, under the assumption of private channels (so that the adversary cannot see messages passed between processors) [9], or cryptographic assumptions. Under these kind of assumptions, more recent work shows that optimal resilience can be achieved [7].

Byzantine agreement was also more recently shown to require only polylogarithmic time in the full information model if the adversary is *static*, meaning that the adversary must choose the faulty processors at the start, without knowing the random bits of the algorithm [10]. The technique is to elect a very small subset of processors which contain a less than 1/3 fraction of faulty processors; this subset then runs the exponential time algorithm on their inputs. Such a technique does not seem applicable when the adversary is adaptive and can decide to corrupt the elected set after it sees the result of the election.

4. CONCLUSION AND FUTURE WORK

We have described an algorithm to solve Byzantine agreement in polynomial expected time. Our algorithm works in the asynchronous message-passing model, when an adaptive and full-information adversary controls a constant fraction of the processors. Our algorithm is designed so that in order to thwart it, corrupted nodes must engage in statistically deviant behavior which is detectable by individual nodes. Essentially, this reduces the network communication problem to an individual computation problem. This suggests a new paradigm for secure distributed computing: the design of algorithms that force attackers into behavior that is statistically deviant and detectable.

Our result leaves much room for improvement, in terms of the resilience and expected time. First, we did not work hard at reducing the resilience which now stands at $n/500$. Can we increase this value? Second, it is not clear whether the expected time can be brought down to the known lower bound of $\tilde{\Omega}(n)$ or whether Byzantine agreement is intrinsically harder than consensus, in terms of time or step complexity. Finally, we believe that we can reduce the *computational* cost of our algorithm to polynomial time, and are actively working on this problem.

5. REFERENCES

[1] J. Aspnes. Randomized protocols for asynchronous consensus. *Journal of Distributed Computing*, 16:165–175, 2003.

[2] H. Attiya and K. Censor. Tight bounds for asynchronous randomized consensus. *Journal of the ACM*, 55(5), 2008.

[3] H. Attiya and J. Welch. *Distributed Computing: Fundamentals, Simulations and Advanced Topics (2nd edition)*, page 14. John Wiley Interscience, March 2004.

[4] M. Bellare and P. Rogaway. Random oracles are practical: a paradigm for designing efficient protocols.

In *ACM Conference on Computer and Communications Security*, pages 62–73, 1993.

[5] M. Ben-Or. Another advantage of free choice (Extended Abstract): Completely asynchronous agreement protocols. In *Principles of Distributed Computing (PODC)*, pages 27–30, 1983.

[6] M. Ben-Or, E. Pavlov, and V. Vaikuntanathan. Byzantine agreement in the full-information model in o (log n) rounds. In *Proceedings of the ACM Symposium on Theory of Computing (STOC)*, 2006.

[7] R. Canetti and T. Rabin. Fast asynchronous Byzantine agreement with optimal resilience. In *ACM Symposium on Theory of Computing (STOC)*, 1993.

[8] B. Chor and C. Dwork. Randomization in Byzantine agreement. *Advances in Computing Research*, 5:443–498, 1989.

[9] P. Feldman and S. Micali. Byzantine agreement in constant expected time (and trusting no one). In *Foundations of Computer Science (FOCS)*, pages 267–276, 1985.

[10] B. Kapron, D. Kempe, V. King, J. Saia, and V. Sanwalani. Scalable algorithms for byzantine agreement and leader election with full information. *ACM Transactions on Algorithms(TALG)*, 2009.

[11] M. Rabin. Randomized Byzantine generals. In *Foundations of Computer Science (FOCS)*, pages 403–409, 1983.

Upper Bound on the Complexity of Solving Hard Renaming*

(Extended Abstract)

Hagit Attiya
Technion
hagit@cs.technion.ac.il

Armando Castañeda
Technion
armando@cs.technion.ac.il

Maurice Herlihy
Brown
herlihy@cs.brown.edu

Ami Paz
Technion
amipaz@cs.technion.ac.il

ABSTRACT

The M-renaming task requires $n+1$ processes, each starting with a unique input name (from an arbitrary large range), to coordinate the choice of new output names from a range of size M. This paper presents the first upper bound on the complexity of *hard renaming*, i.e., $2n$-renaming, when $n+1$ is not a prime power. It is known that $2n$-renaming can be solved if and only if $n+1$ is not a prime power; however, the previous proof of the "if" part was non-constructive, involving an approximation theorem; in particular, it did not yield a concrete upper bound on the complexity of the resulting protocol.

Categories and Subject Descriptors

F.1.2 [**Computation By Abstract Devices**]: Modes of Computation—*Parallelism and concurrency*; F.2.2 [**Analysis of Algorithms and Problem Complexity**]: Nonnumerical Algorithms and Problems

General Terms

Algorithms, Theory

Keywords

Combinatorial topology, distributed systems, shared memory, wait-free computation, renaming, symmetry breaking

*Attiya, Castañeda and Paz are supported in part by Yad-HaNadiv fundation and the Israel Science Foundation (grant number 1227/10).
Castañeda is also supported by an Aly Kaufman Fellowship.
Herlihy is supported by NSF 000830491

1. INTRODUCTION

In the *renaming* task [1], there are $n+1$ processes[1], each with a unique *input name* taken from a namespace of size N, which can be arbitrarily large. The processes must coordinate so that each process chooses a unique *output name* taken from a namespace of size M, where typically $M \ll N$. The protocol must be *symmetric*: processes may compare input names for order, but may not apply any other operations to those names. Processes communicate by reading and writing a shared memory, and scheduling is *asynchronous*: there is no bound on their relative speeds, and any proper subset may fail by halting at any moment.

Attiya et al. [1] give an $(n+1)$-process protocol for $M = 2n + 1$ names. The case where $M = 2n$, sometimes called *hard renaming*, remained open until Herlihy and Shavit [9] gave a proof that there is no wait-free read-write protocol for hard renaming. Castañeda and Rajsbaum [6], however, found a mistake in that proof, so that the impossibility claim is valid only when $n+1$ is a prime power (cf. [2]). Castañeda and Rajsbaum [4] (see also [2]) showed that for other values of n, there does exist a wait-free $(n + 1)$-process hard renaming protocol, but their construction was existential. In particular, that construction did not shed any light on the complexity of any such protocol.

This paper gives the first constructive analysis of hard renaming, yielding an explicit upper bound on the complexity of hard renaming protocols. The construction is expressed in the language of elementary combinatorial topology, a formalism that has proved useful for analyzing renaming [4–6,9] and related tasks.

Instead of focusing directly on hard renaming, we will look at a simpler task. In the *weak symmetry-breaking* (WSB) task [8], each process starts with its input name and every non-faulty process decides on a binary output value. If all $n + 1$ processes decide, then at least one decides 0 and at least one decides 1. A symmetric protocol that implements WSB yields a symmetric protocol for hard renaming [8], and vice versa, so the two tasks are equivalent.

We consider a model in which the computation proceeds in a sequence of asynchronous rounds (iterations). In each iteration, a process writes its current state to a new mem-

---

[1]Choosing $n+1$ processes rather than n simplifies the topological notation but slightly complicates the computing notation. Choosing n processes makes the opposite trade-off. We choose $n + 1$ for compatibility with prior work.

ory and takes an *immediate snapshot* [3] of that memory, yielding a kind of instantaneous view of the entire memory.[2] After the processes have completed enough rounds, each process chooses a binary value and halts.

Iterated immediate snapshots have a natural interpretation in terms of the elementary structures of combinatorial topology. Each process state can be identified with a *vertex*, and each system state with a *simplex*, the higher-dimensional generalization of an edge or a triangle. The collection of all possible system states forms a *simplicial complex*, the higher-dimensional generalization of a graph.

Think of the processes as starting out on the vertices of a simplex representing the initial system state (e.g., three processes on the corners of a triangle). An immediate snapshot protocol has the effect of *subdividing* the original simplex into smaller simplexes, one for each possible interleaving. Because these smaller simplexes fit together in a regular way, they are called a *subdivision* of the original simplex.

A single-round execution moves the processes from the vertices of the original simplex to the vertices of a smaller simplex within the new subdivision. Iterating this process produces finer and finer subdivisions of the original simplex. After some number of iterations, each process, having arrived at vertex in the latest subdivision, chooses its binary decision value. We can think of this decision as placing a zero or one pebble on each vertex, resulting in a *zero-one* coloring of the final subdivided simplex. As explained later, this coloring must satisfy certain simple combinatorial properties. It turns out that the algorithmic question whether a WSB protocol exists is equivalent to the purely combinatorial question whether there exists a subdivision of the right kind induced by iterated immediate snapshots that has the right kind of zero-one coloring. If so, then the protocol's *round complexity* is just the number of repeated immediate snapshots needed to construct that subdivision.

We are now ready to explain this paper's technical contribution. In prior work, Castañeda and Rajsbaum [6] characterized when a WSB protocol exists. First, they constructed a different subdivision, together with a coloring, that, while not being right, was nevertheless "close" to being of the right kind. They then applied a sequence of local adjustments to both the subdivision and its coloring to produce a new subdivision, still not of the right kind, but endowed with a coloring of the right kind. Using a variant of the classical Simplicial Approximation Theorem of topology [9], they argued that a protocol that executes *sufficiently many* iterations of immediate snapshot can be mapped onto the constructed subdivision, resulting in both the right kind of subdivision and the right kind of coloring to yield a protocol. The nature of the proof, however, did not provide any bounds on how many rounds are sufficient for this approximation.

In this paper, we use a novel construction to produce a subdivision of the right kind, in the sense that we can bound the number of rounds needed to produce it, together with a coloring that is "close" to, but not exactly, of the right kind. Next, we apply a sequence of local adjustments to the subdivision and the coloring. Each adjustment changes the number of rounds in a precisely-characterized way. After the changes, we get both the right kind of subdivision and the right kind of coloring, along with an upper bound on the number rounds used by the corresponding protocol; this

bound is in $O(n^{q+3})$, where q is the largest prime power in the prime factorization of $n + 1$.

We see this explicit construction as a first step toward extending the topological formalism, previously focused on lower bounds and existence proofs, to encompass complexity and explicit protocol construction.

2. BASIC ELEMENTS OF COMBINATORIAL TOPOLOGY

A *simplicial complex* is a finite set V and a collection of subsets $\mathcal{K}$ of V closed under containment. An element of V is called a *vertex* of $\mathcal{K}$; each vertex has an associated *name*, name(v). A set in $\mathcal{K}$ is called a *simplex*; while different vertexes in V may posses the same name, we assume that the vertexes of a simplex have distinct names.[3] A (proper) subset of a simplex σ is called a *(proper) face*. The *dimension* of σ, dim σ, is $|\sigma| - 1$. The dimension of a complex $\mathcal{K}$, dim $\mathcal{K}$, is the maximal dimension of a simplex of $\mathcal{K}$. A *facet* of $\mathcal{K}$ is any of its simplexes that is not a proper face of any simplex; a complex $\mathcal{K}$ is *pure* if all its facets are with the same dimension, dim $\mathcal{K}$. We use "k-simplex" as shorthand for "k-dimensional simplex" and similarly for "k-face" and "k-complex". Given two complexes $\mathcal{K}$ and $\mathcal{L}$, we say $\mathcal{L}$ is a *subcomplex* of $\mathcal{K}$ if every simplex of $\mathcal{L}$ is a simplex of $\mathcal{K}$.

Given a simplex σ, $\mathsf{P}\,\sigma$, the powerset of σ, is the complex containing all faces of σ. Usually, we just write σ instead of $\mathsf{P}\,\sigma$. The *star* of a simplex $\sigma \in \mathcal{K}$, denoted $\mathsf{Star}(\sigma, \mathcal{K})$, is the subcomplex of $\mathcal{K}$ whose facets are the simplexes of $\mathcal{K}$ that contain σ.

A *coloring* of a complex $\mathcal{K}$ is a map from the vertices of $\mathcal{K}$ to a set of *colors*; if there are only two colors, we say that the coloring is *binary*, and it is denoted bin. For a simplex σ of $\mathcal{K}$, we denote bin(σ) = {bin(v) : $v \in \sigma$}; a simplex σ is *b-monochromatic* if bin(σ) = {b}.

In the rest of the paper, each vertex v is a pair (P_i, S_i), where $P_i = $ name(v) is the name of v, and S_i is the *state* of v. For a simplex σ, names(σ) = {name(v) : $v \in \sigma$}.

For disjoint complexes $\mathcal{K}$ and $\mathcal{L}$, their *join*, $\mathcal{K} * \mathcal{L}$, is the complex {$\sigma \cup \tau : \sigma \in \mathcal{K} \wedge \tau \in \mathcal{L}$}. A *vertex map* f carries vertices of $\mathcal{K}$ to vertices of $\mathcal{L}$; the map is *simplicial* if it carries simplexes of $\mathcal{K}$ to simplexes of $\mathcal{L}$; it is *name-preserving*, if for every vertex $v \in \mathcal{K}$, name(v) = name($f(v)$).

A pure n-complex $\mathcal{K}$ is an *n-manifold* if every $(n-1)$-simplex is a face of exactly one or two facets. A *boundary simplex* is an $(n-1)$-simplex that belongs to exactly one facet. The *boundary* of $\mathcal{K}$, Bd $\mathcal{K}$, is the $(n-1)$-dimensional subcomplex of $\mathcal{K}$ containing every boundary simplex and all its faces. The *dual graph* of a manifold $\mathcal{K}$ is the graph whose vertices correspond to the facets of $\mathcal{K}$, and there is an edge between two distinct vertices if their facets share a face of dimension $n - 1$.

An n-manifold $\mathcal{K}$ is *orientable* if its facets (its n-simplexes) can be partitioned into two disjoint classes, $+1$ and -1, such that every pair of distinct facets sharing an $(n-1)$-face are in distinct classes.[4] Such a partitioning is an *orientation* of $\mathcal{K}$. Suppose, in addition, that $\mathcal{K}$ has a binary

---

[2]This model is equivalent to the standard read-write model, incurring at most a quadratic multiplicative overhead [7].

[3]In the language of topology, this means that our definitions are specialized under the assumption that all simplexes and complexes are *chromatic*. For succinctness, this fact is omitted in the rest of the paper.

[4]We adopt here a simplified definition of orientability for chromatic manifolds.

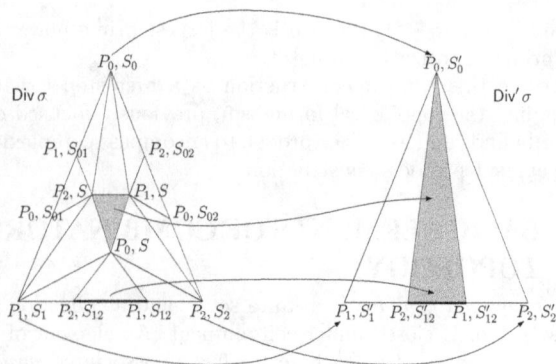

Figure 1: A name-preserving and color-preserving simplicial map.

coloring. A monochromatic n-simplex of $\mathcal{K}$ with orientation $\xi \in \{+1, -1\}$ is *counted by orientation* as ξ, if it is 0-monochromatic, and as $(-1)^n \xi$, if it is 1-monochromatic.

Informally, a *subdivision* of a simplex σ, $\mathsf{Div}\,\sigma$, is a complex constructed by subdividing each $\sigma' \subseteq \sigma$ into smaller simplexes.[5] A subdivision $\mathsf{Div}\,\sigma$ maps each $\sigma' \subseteq \sigma$ to the pure complex $\mathsf{Div}\,\sigma'$ of dimension $\dim \sigma'$ containing the simplexes that subdivide σ'. For all $\sigma', \sigma'' \subseteq \sigma$, $\mathsf{Div}\,\sigma' \cap \mathsf{Div}\,\sigma'' = \mathsf{Div}(\sigma' \cap \sigma'')$. We require that for every face σ' of σ, and every vertex $v \in \mathsf{Div}\,\sigma'$, $\mathsf{name}(v) \in \mathsf{names}(\sigma') \subseteq \mathsf{names}(\sigma)$.[6] For every simplex $\tau \in \mathsf{Div}\,\sigma$, its *carrier*, $\mathsf{Car}(\tau, \mathsf{Div})$, is the face $\sigma' \subseteq \sigma$ of smallest dimension such that $\tau \in \mathsf{Div}\,\sigma'$. For any subdivision $\mathsf{Div}\,\sigma$ and face σ' of σ, $\mathsf{Div}\,\sigma'$ is an orientable manifold [13, Sec. 65].

Figure 1 contains two subdivisions of a 2-simplex $\sigma = \{(P_0, T_0), (P_1, T_1), (P_2, T_2)\}$. For the subdivision $\mathsf{Div}'\,\sigma$ at the right, $\mathsf{Div}'\,\{(P_0, T_0)\} = (P_0, S_0')$ and $\mathsf{Div}'\,\{(P_1, T_1), (P_2, T_2)\}$ is the 1-complex containing the four vertices at the bottom.

Given two subdivisions $\mathsf{Div}\,\sigma$ and $\mathsf{Div}'\,\sigma$, a simplicial map ϕ from $\mathsf{Div}\,\sigma$ to $\mathsf{Div}'\,\sigma$ is *carrier-preserving* if for every $\tau \in \mathsf{Div}\,\sigma$, $\mathsf{Car}(\phi(\tau), \mathsf{Div}') \subseteq \mathsf{Car}(\tau, \mathsf{Div})$.

We shall be interested in name-preserving and carrier-preserving simplicial maps between subdivisions. For every name-preserving and carrier-preserving simplicial map $\phi : \mathsf{Div}\,\sigma \to \mathsf{Div}'\,\sigma$ and every face σ' of σ, ϕ maps each $\dim(\sigma')$-simplex of $\mathsf{Div}\,\sigma'$ to a $\dim(\sigma')$-simplex of $\mathsf{Div}'\,\sigma'$.

Figure 1 shows a name-preserving and carrier-preserving simplicial map $\phi : \mathsf{Div}\,\sigma \to \mathsf{Div}'\,\sigma$, which maps simplex $\{(P_1, S_{12}), (P_2, S_{12})\} \in \mathsf{Div}\,\{(P_1, T_1), (P_2, T_2)\}$ to simplex $\{(P_1, S_{12}'), (P_2, S_{12}')\} \in \mathsf{Div}'\,\{(P_1, T_1), (P_2, T_2)\}$; it maps the central 2-simplex in $\mathsf{Div}\,\sigma$ to the central 2-simplex in $\mathsf{Div}'\,\sigma$.

3. SUBDIVISIONS AND PROTOCOLS

In this section we define two subdivisions. The first is the well-known K-th *standard subdivision*; this is the right kind of subdivision mentioned in the introduction: it easily leads to a protocol based on iterated immediate snapshots, which solves WSB if there is an associated binary coloring of the right kind, without all-zero or all-one simplexes, as defined below. To construct a coloring of the right kind, however,

---

[5]The complete definition of subdivisions is more involved and can be found in standard texts [11, 13].

[6]Because all our complexes and simplexes are chromatic, the subdivisions we consider are also chromatic.

it is convenient to work with another subdivision, called the *extended cone*, which is introduced later in this section. Section 5 shows how to "lift" the coloring of an extended cone to a coloring of a standard subdivision, without violating its properties.

For the rest of the paper, fix an n-simplex
$$\sigma = \{(P_0, S_0), \ldots, (P_n, S_n)\}.$$

DEFINITION 1. *In the* standard subdivision *[9] of σ (Figure 2(a)),* $\mathsf{Std}\,\sigma$, *for each face $\sigma' \subseteq \sigma$, each vertex of $\mathsf{Std}\,\sigma'$ has the form (P_i, σ_i), where P_i is a process name in $\mathsf{names}(\sigma_i)$, and σ_i is a face of σ'. A set of vertices $\{(P_0, \sigma_0), \ldots, (P_k, \sigma_k)\}$ is a simplex of $\mathsf{Std}\,\sigma'$ if, for $0 \leq i, j \leq k$, (1) if $i \neq j$ then $P_i \neq P_j$, (2) $\sigma_i \subseteq \sigma_j$ or vice versa, and (3) if $P_i \in \mathsf{names}(\sigma_j)$, then $\sigma_i \subseteq \sigma_j$.*
Repeating this subdivision K times yields the K-th standard subdivision of σ, $\mathsf{Std}^K \sigma$.

It is known that if each process starts with an input described as a distinct vertex of an n-simplex σ, the sets of compatible process states after an immediate snapshot are exactly the simplexes of $\mathsf{Std}\,\sigma$ [3]. After K rounds of immediate snapshot, each process stops in a local state described as a distinct vertex of $\mathsf{Std}^K \sigma$, and each global state is a simplex of $\mathsf{Std}^K \sigma$. For each face $\sigma' \subseteq \sigma$, $\mathsf{Std}^K \sigma'$ contains all (and only) K round immediate snapshot executions in which the processes in σ' participate, and the rest crash without taking any computation step. A K-round iterated immediate snapshot protocol is therefore completely characterized by defining the decision output for each process' final state, i.e., an output coloring δ from the vertices of Std^K to an output set A, which in the case of WSB is $A = \{0, 1\}$.

To solve WSB, if all processes participate then both colors must be chosen, implying that $\mathsf{bin}(\tau) = \{0, 1\}$, for every n-simplex $\tau \in \mathsf{Std}^K \sigma$, i.e., τ is not monochromatic (because $\tau \in \mathsf{Std}^K \sigma$ corresponds to an execution in which all processes decide). We also want the resulting protocol to be symmetric, which means that for any two faces σ', σ'' of σ with the same dimension, the decisions of processes in executions in $\mathsf{Std}^K \sigma'$ and $\mathsf{Std}^K \sigma''$ are the same, modulo the relative order of process names in $\mathsf{names}(\sigma')$ and $\mathsf{names}(\sigma'')$. This captures the notion that processes can only apply comparison operations over its inputs (names). To ensure that the resulting protocol is symmetric, bin must satisfy a symmetry property formalized as follows.

Given two faces σ', σ'' of σ with the same dimension, let ord be the unique *ordering* bijection from $\mathsf{names}(\sigma')$ to $\mathsf{names}(\sigma'')$, i.e., for every $P, Q \in \mathsf{names}(\sigma')$, $P < Q$ if and only if $\mathsf{ord}(P) < \mathsf{ord}(Q)$. Let $\mathsf{Div}\,\sigma$ be a subdivision of σ; a simplicial bijection $\phi : \mathsf{Div}\,\sigma' \to \mathsf{Div}\,\sigma''$ is *order-preserving* if for every vertex $v \in \mathsf{Div}\,\sigma'$, $\mathsf{ord}(\mathsf{name}(v)) = \mathsf{name}(\phi(v))$. A coloring bin of $\mathsf{Div}\,\sigma$ is *symmetric* if, for every pair of proper faces σ', σ'' of σ with the same dimension, there is an order-preserving simplicial bijection $\phi : \mathsf{Div}\,\sigma' \to \mathsf{Div}\,\sigma''$ such that for every $v \in \mathsf{Div}\,\sigma'$, $\mathsf{bin}(v) = \mathsf{bin}(\phi(v))$.

Figure 3 shows a 2-dimensional subdivision with a symmetric binary coloring (white and black dots). For ease of notation, only names of vertexes are depicted. Observe that the binary coloring defines monochromatic 2-simplexes. In this dimension, it is impossible to have a symmetric binary coloring without monochromatic 2-simplexes [4].

The symmetry of the standard subdivision guarantees that for any two faces σ', σ'' of σ with the same dimension, there is an order-preserving simplicial bijection ϕ from $\mathsf{Div}\,\sigma'$ to

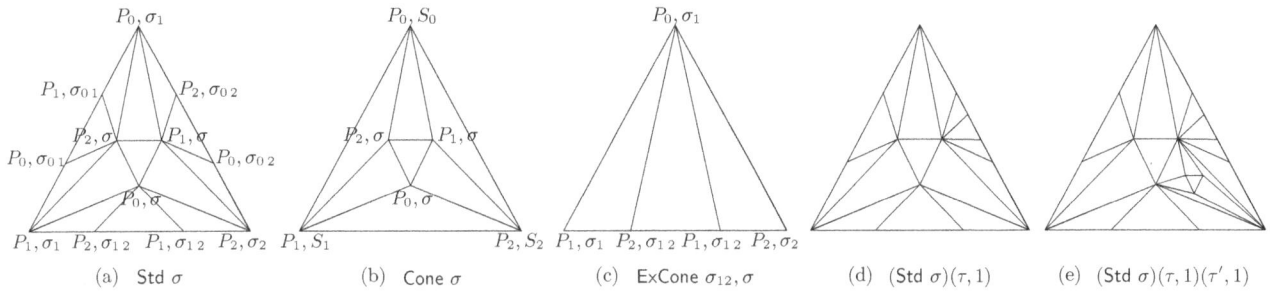

Figure 2: The standard subdivision (a) and a cone subdivision (b) of $\sigma = \{(P_0, S_0), (P_1, S_1), (P_2, S_2)\}$. If σ_{ij} is the face $\{(P_i, S_i), (P_j, S_j)\}$ of σ and σ_i is the face $\{(P_i, S_i)\}$, (c) is the first extended cone of σ_{12} over σ; (d) is obtained from a subdivision over $\mathsf{Std}\,\sigma$, by subdividing the simplex $\tau = \{(P_0, \sigma_{02}), (P_2, \sigma_{02})\}$ of $\mathsf{Std}\,\sigma$, and (e) is obtained by from a subdivision over (d), by subdividing $\tau' = \{(P_0, \sigma), (P_1, \sigma), (P_2, \sigma_2)\}$.

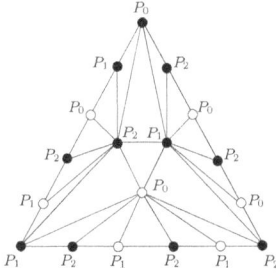

Figure 3: A symmetric binary coloring.

$\mathsf{Div}\,\sigma''$: for every $(P, S) \in \mathsf{Std}^K \sigma'$, $\phi(P, S) = (\mathsf{ord}(P), \mathsf{ord}(S))$, where $\mathsf{ord} : \mathsf{names}(\sigma') \to \mathsf{names}(\sigma'')$ is the ordering bijection and $\mathsf{ord}(S)$ is obtained by replacing every process name Q in S with $\mathsf{ord}(Q)$. To guarantee the resulting WSB protocol is symmetric, the coloring bin of $\mathsf{Std}^K \sigma$ has to be symmetric, i.e., $\mathsf{bin}(P, S) = \mathsf{bin}(\phi(P, S))$.

Thus, finding a symmetric coloring of $\mathsf{Std}^K \sigma$, without monochromatic simplexes, is sufficient for solving WSB with K immediate snapshot iterations, and hence hard renaming with $K + n$ immediate snapshot iterations [7, 8]. However, it is easier to construct this coloring by using the following type of subdivisions.

DEFINITION 2. *The cone [6] of σ, $\mathsf{Cone}\,\sigma$, is defined so that for each proper face σ' of σ, $\mathsf{Cone}\,\sigma'$ is the complex $\mathsf{P}\,\sigma'$ (Figure 2(b)). For σ itself, each vertex of $\mathsf{Cone}\,\sigma$ has the form (P_i, σ_i), where P_i is a process name in $\mathsf{names}(\sigma)$ and σ_i is either a vertex of σ or σ itself. A set of vertices $\{(P_0, \sigma_0), \dots, (P_k, \sigma_k)\}$ is a simplex of $\mathsf{Cone}\,\sigma$ if the P_i are distinct, and if $k = n$, then there is at least one $\sigma_i = \sigma$. $\mathsf{Cone}^K \sigma$, the K-th cone of σ, repeats this subdivision K times on n-simplexes.*

DEFINITION 3. *Consider a simplex τ (possibly not a face of σ) and its K-th cone $\mathsf{Cone}^K \tau$, for some $K \geq 1$. The K-th extended cone of τ over σ, $\mathsf{ExCone}^K(\tau, \sigma)$, is defined as follows. For every face $\rho \subseteq \sigma$, let $\rho = \sigma' \cup \tau'$, where $\tau' \subseteq \tau$ and $\sigma' \subseteq \sigma \setminus \tau$. Then, $\mathsf{ExCone}^K(\tau, \rho) = \sigma' * \mathsf{Cone}^K \tau'$. (See Figure 2(c).) When τ is understood from the context, we simply write $\mathsf{ExCone}^K \sigma$.*

Let $\mathcal{K}$ be a complex, τ be a simplex of $\mathcal{K}$ and $\ell \geq 1$ an integer. The complex $\mathcal{K}(\tau, \ell)$ is defined to be $\bigcup_{\sigma \in \mathcal{K}} \mathsf{ExCone}^\ell(\tau, \sigma)$. We say that $\mathcal{K}(\tau, \ell)$ is *obtained from a subdivision over $\mathcal{K}$.*

In Figure 2(d), $(\mathsf{Std}\,\sigma)(\tau, 1)$ is obtained by a subdivision of $(\mathsf{Std}\,\sigma)$: first taking the cone of $\tau = \{(P_0, \sigma_{02}), (P_2, \sigma_{02})\} \in \mathsf{Std}\,\sigma$ and then extending it over all simplexes of $\mathsf{Std}\,\sigma$ that contain τ. In Figure 2(e), $(\mathsf{Std}\,\sigma)(\tau, 1)(\tau', 1)$ is obtained from a cone subdivision over $(\mathsf{Std}\,\sigma)(\tau, 1)$, where $\tau' = \{(P_0, \sigma), (P_1, \sigma), (P_2, \sigma_2)\} \in \mathsf{Std}\,\sigma$; in this case there are no simplexes of $(\mathsf{Std}\,\sigma)(\tau, 1)$ on which to extend the first cone of τ' because τ' is a facet. Note that the order of the subdivisions does not affect the resulting subdivision, that is, $\mathcal{K}(\tau, 1)(\tau', 1) = \mathcal{K}(\tau', 1)(\tau, 1)$. This happens because neither τ is in $\mathsf{Star}(\tau', \mathsf{Std}\,\sigma)$, nor τ' is in $\mathsf{Star}(\tau, \mathsf{Std}\,\sigma)$.

In general, simplexes $\tau_1, \dots, \tau_j \in \mathcal{K}$ are *independent* if for every k and m, $1 \leq k \neq m \leq j$, $\tau_k \notin \mathsf{Star}(\tau_m, \mathcal{K})$. Let $\mathcal{K}(\tau_1, \tau_2, \dots, \tau_j, \ell)$ be the complex $\mathcal{K}(\tau_1, \ell)(\tau_2, \ell) \cdots (\tau_j, \ell)$. The next lemma shows that for independent simplexes $\tau_1, \dots, \tau_j \in \mathcal{K}$ and a permutation π of $\{1, \dots, j\}$,

$$\mathcal{K}(\tau_1, \tau_2, \dots, \tau_j, \ell) = \mathcal{K}(\tau_{\pi(1)}, \tau_{\pi(2)}, \dots, \tau_{\pi(j)}, \ell)$$

hence the subdivisions on independent simplexes in a complex can be applied simultaneously.

LEMMA 1. *Let $\mathcal{K}$ be a complex, $\tau_1, \dots, \tau_j \in \mathcal{K}$ be independent simplexes and $\ell \geq 1$ be an integer. For every permutation π of $\{1, \dots, j\}$,*

$$\mathcal{K}(\tau_1, \tau_2, \dots, \tau_j, \ell) = \mathcal{K}(\tau_{\pi(1)}, \tau_{\pi(2)}, \dots, \tau_{\pi(j)}, \ell).$$

Given a subdivision $\mathsf{Div}\,\sigma$ of σ, let $\tau_1, \dots, \tau_j$ be independent simplexes of $\mathsf{Div}\,\sigma$. For any $\ell \geq 1$, Div' is a function that maps faces of σ to subcomplexes of $\mathsf{Div}\,\sigma(\tau_1, \dots, \tau_j, \ell)$: for every face $\sigma' \subseteq \sigma$, $\mathsf{Div}'\,\sigma' = \mathsf{Div}\,\sigma'(\tau_1, \dots, \tau_j, \ell)$.

LEMMA 2. $\mathsf{Div}'\,\sigma$ *is a subdivision of σ.*

In Section 4 we use the process just described to get an n-dimensional subdivision $\mathsf{Div}\,\sigma$ with a symmetric binary coloring without monochromatic n-simplexes, provided $n + 1$ is not a prime power. Then, in Section 5 we construct a color-preserving and carrier-preserving simplicial map $\phi : \mathsf{Std}^K \sigma \to \mathsf{Div}\,\sigma$, for a K that is related with the number of subdivisions needed to obtain $\mathsf{Div}\,\sigma$. Finally, from ϕ we construct a symmetric binary coloring without monochromatic n-simplexes for Std^K, which implies a K round WSB protocol.

In other words, the subdivision $\mathsf{Div}\,\sigma$ and its symmetric binary coloring represent a set of decisions satisfying the WSB conditions, and the map $\phi : \mathsf{Std}^K \sigma \to \mathsf{Div}\,\sigma$, defines the processes' decisions at the end of a K-round protocol.

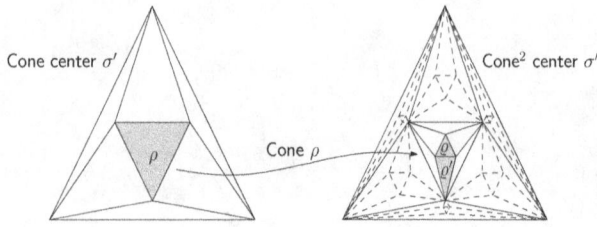

Figure 4: Obtaining monochromatic simplexes.

4. CONSTRUCTING SUBDIVISIONS WITH-OUT MONOCHROMATIC SIMPLEXES

We now construct a subdivision of an n-simplex σ together with a symmetric coloring bin without monochromatic n-simplexes, when $n+1$ is not a prime power. We first construct a subdivision $\mathsf{Div}_1\,\sigma$ and a symmetric coloring bin with an even number of monochromatic n-simplexes. We then adjust $\mathsf{Div}_1\,\sigma$ and bin to construct a subdivision $\mathsf{Div}_2\,\sigma$ with no monochromatic n-simplexes. Both subdivisions agree on $\mathsf{Bd}\,\sigma$, so the final coloring is symmetric.

4.1 First step

When $n+1$ is not a prime power, the binomial coefficients $\binom{n+1}{1},\ldots,\binom{n+1}{n}$ are relatively prime, implying that there is an integer solution $k_0,\ldots,k_{n-1}$ for the Diophantine equation

$$1 + \sum_{i=0}^{n-1} \binom{n+1}{i+1} k_i = 0\ .$$

Since $\binom{n+1}{1} = \binom{n+1}{n}$, we can choose $k_0 \in \{0,-1\}$ by choosing an appropriate value for k_{n-1}. Let

$$\ell = \max\left\{\lceil \log_{2^{i+1}-1}(|k_i|)\rceil : i = 1,\ldots,n-1\right\} + 2\ .$$

The Subdivision.

Consider an n-simplex σ; we start with the standard subdivision $\mathsf{Std}\,\sigma$. For every face $\sigma' \subseteq \sigma$, let $\mathsf{center}\,\sigma'$ denote the $\dim\sigma'$-simplex of $\mathsf{Std}\,\sigma'$ such that, for each vertex $(P_i, S_i) \in \mathsf{center}\,\sigma'$, $S_i = \sigma'$. For example, for the standard subdivision in Figure 2(a), $\mathsf{center}\,\sigma_{12} = \{(P_1, \sigma_{12}), (P_2, \sigma_{12})\}$ and $\mathsf{center}\,\sigma = \{(P_0, \sigma), (P_1, \sigma), (P_2, \sigma)\}$.

$\mathsf{Div}_1\,\sigma$ is obtained via one subdivision over $\mathsf{Std}\,\sigma$ as follows.

Let $\sigma_{i1},\ldots,\sigma_{i\binom{n+1}{i+1}}$, $i \in \{0,\ldots,n-1\}$, be all i-dimensional faces of σ, in an arbitrary order. For every $j \in \{1,\ldots,\binom{n+1}{i+1}\}$, consider the i-simplex $\mathsf{center}\,\sigma_{ij}$; these simplexes are independent.

For every face $\sigma' \subseteq \sigma$, we define $\mathsf{Div}_1\,\sigma'$ to be the complex

$$\mathsf{Std}\,\sigma'(\mathsf{center}\,\sigma_{01},..,\mathsf{center}\,\sigma_{ij},..,\mathsf{center}\,\sigma_{n-1\,n},\ell)$$

where $0 \le i \le n-1$ and $1 \le j \le \binom{n+1}{i+1}$. By Lemma 2, $\mathsf{Div}_1\,\sigma$ is a subdivision of σ. Moreover, for every pair of i-faces, $\sigma',\sigma'' \subset \sigma$, there is a unique order-preserving simplicial bijection $\phi : \mathsf{Div}_1\,\sigma' \to \mathsf{Div}_1\,\sigma''$.

The Binary Coloring.

We give a coloring to $\mathsf{Div}_1\,\sigma$, such that (1) $\mathsf{Div}_1\,\sigma$ has no 1-monochromatic n-simplexes, and (2) $\mathsf{Div}_1\,\sigma$ has an even number of 0-monochromatic n-simplexes, whose count, by

orientation, is zero. The initial coloring bin colors all vertexes of the n-dimensional simplex $\mathsf{center}\,\sigma$ of $\mathsf{Std}\,\sigma$ with 0; all other vertexes of $\mathsf{Div}_1\,\sigma$ are colored 1. By the next lemma, every n-simplex of $\mathsf{Div}_1\,\sigma$ contains a face of $\mathsf{center}\,\sigma$, ensuring that $\mathsf{Div}_1\,\sigma$ has no 1-monochromatic n-simplexes.

LEMMA 3. *Let $\mathsf{Div}_1\,\sigma$ be the subdivision obtained in the first step of the construction. Then, every n-simplex of $\mathsf{Div}_1\,\sigma$ contains a face of $\mathsf{center}\,\sigma$.*

PROOF. It can be seen that every n-simplex of $\mathsf{Std}\,\sigma$ contains a face of $\mathsf{center}\,\sigma$. Moreover, for every simplex $\tau = \mathsf{center}\,\sigma_{i,j}$ and n-simplex $\rho \in \mathsf{Std}\,\sigma$ with $\tau \subset \rho$, it can be proved that $\rho \setminus \tau$ is a face of $\mathsf{center}\,\sigma$. During the operation for obtaining $\mathsf{Div}_1\,\sigma$, τ is ℓ-coned and extended to all simplexes of $\mathsf{Std}\,\sigma$ containing τ. Thus, ρ is replaced in $\mathsf{Div}_1\,\sigma$ with all n-simplexes in $\mathsf{ExCone}^\ell(\tau,\rho) = (\rho \setminus \tau) * \mathsf{Cone}^\ell\,\tau$. Therefore, each n-simplex in $\mathsf{ExCone}^\ell(\tau,\rho)$ contains $\rho \setminus \tau$, hence a face of $\mathsf{center}\,\sigma$. $\square$

Consider an i-face $\sigma' \subset \sigma$, $i \in \{0,\ldots,n-1\}$. Below we describe how to recolor the interior vertices of $\mathsf{Div}_1\,\sigma'$ to get exactly $|k_i|$ 0-monochromatic i-simplexes, without changing the coloring of $\mathsf{Bd}\,\mathsf{Div}_1\,\sigma'$. Then, for every other i-face $\sigma'' \subset \sigma$, we replicate bin in the interior of σ'', using the unique order-preserving bijection $\phi : \mathsf{Div}_1\,\sigma' \to \mathsf{Div}_1\,\sigma''$, ensuring that bin remains symmetric.

For an integer k, let $\mathsf{sign}(k) = +1$ if $k \ge 0$, and -1, otherwise. For every $i \in \{0,\ldots,n-1\}$, for each i-face $\sigma' \subset \sigma$, the $|k_i|$ 0-monochromatic i-simplexes in $\mathsf{Div}_1\,\sigma'$ must satisfy the following orientability property. Let ρ be an i-simplex of $\mathsf{Div}_1\,\sigma'$; ρ is a face of a unique n-simplex $\tau \in \mathsf{Div}_1\,\sigma$ and $\tau \setminus \rho$ is a face of $\mathsf{center}\,\sigma$, hence, all vertices in $\tau \setminus \rho$ have color 0. Thus, if ρ is 0-monochromatic then τ is 0-monochromatic. The 0-monochromatic simplexes $\rho \in \mathsf{Div}_1\,\sigma'$ are chosen so that there exists a simple path in the dual graph of $\mathsf{Div}_1\,\sigma$ whose (1) initial n-simplex (graph node) contains ρ, and whose last n-simplex is $\mathsf{center}\,\sigma$ and (2) if $\mathsf{sign}(k_i) = -1$, then path's length is odd, otherwise it is even.[7] Such a path can be computed by running BFS in the dual graph.

As mentioned, because ρ is 0-monochromatic, so is τ. Orient $\mathsf{Div}_1\,\sigma$ so that $\mathsf{center}\,\sigma$ has $+1$ orientation. If $\mathsf{sign}(k_i) = -1$, then the length of the path is odd, hence it has an even number of simplexes and τ has -1 orientation (adjacent n-simplexes in the path have opposite orientations). Similarly, if $\mathsf{sign}(k_i) = +1$, then the length of the path is even, and τ has $+1$ orientation. Hence, τ is counted by orientation as $\mathsf{sign}(k_i)$. Therefore, the $|k_i|$ 0-monochromatic i-simplexes in $\mathsf{Div}_1\,\sigma'$ "induce" $|k_i|$ 0-monochromatic n-simplexes in $\mathsf{Div}_1\,\sigma$, each one of them counted as $\mathsf{sign}(k_i)$.

For the case $i = 0$, for each 0-face v of σ, $\mathsf{Div}\,v$ contains exactly one simplex, which induces one n-simplex, τ, in $\mathsf{Div}\,\sigma$. Since τ and $\mathsf{center}\,\sigma$ share an $(n-1)$-face, τ has -1 orientation and if it is counted as -1, if it is 0-monochromatic.

Therefore, we get $\binom{n+1}{i+1}|k_i|$ 0-monochromatic n-dimensional simplexes in all i-faces of σ, all counted as $\mathsf{sign}(k_i)$; the simplex $\mathsf{center}\,\sigma$ is counted as $+1$. Hence, the number of monochromatic n-simplexes of $\mathsf{Div}_1\,\sigma$, counting by orientation, is $1 + \sum_{i=0}^{n-1}\binom{n+1}{i+1}k_i$, which is zero by the choice of the k_i's.

It remains to show that we can obtain exactly $|k_i|$ 0-monochromatic i-simplexes in $\mathsf{Div}_1\,\sigma'$ with the appropriate

---

[7]Since $\mathsf{Div}_1\,\sigma$ is orientable, if there is path satisfying (1) and (2), then any path satisfying (1) necessarily satisfies (2).

194

SEA$(\mathcal{P})$
(01) **if** $|\mathcal{P}| = 2$ **then**
(02)   **do** $\mathcal{P}' \leftarrow \mathcal{P}(\mathcal{P}(0,1), 1)$ % subdivide the $(n-1)$-face $\mathcal{P}(0,1)$
(03)   **color** the new vertices in $\mathcal{P}'$ with 1
(04)   **exit**
(05) **else**
(06)   **let** $m \leftarrow 0$
(07)   **while** *true* **do**
(08)   **if** $\#0(\mathcal{P}(m+1, m+2)) \geq n+1-m$ **then**
(09)   **case A:**
(10)   **do** $\mathcal{P}' \leftarrow \mathcal{P}(\mathcal{P}(m, m+1), 1)$ % subdivide the $(n-1)$-face $\mathcal{P}(m, m+1)$
(11)   **color** some of the new vertices in $\mathcal{P}'$ with 0 to get two 0-monochromatic n-simplexes
(12)   **let** $\mathcal{P}_1 \leftarrow$ shortest path inside $\mathcal{P}$ matching $\mathcal{P}_{\text{init}}$ and a new 0-monochromatic n-simplex
(13)   **let** $\mathcal{P}_2 \leftarrow$ shortest path inside $\mathcal{P}$ matching a new 0-monochromatic n-simplex and $\mathcal{P}_{\text{last}}$
(14)   **if** $\mathcal{P}_1$ and $\mathcal{P}_2$ share an n-simplex **then**
(15)   **subdivide** the unique $(n-1)$-simplex of $\mathcal{P}_1$ that does not belong to $\text{Bd}\,\mathcal{P}_2$,
(16)   or vice versa, to get disjoint matching paths $\mathcal{P}_1', \mathcal{P}_2'$
(17)   **do** $\mathcal{P}_1 \leftarrow \mathcal{P}_1'$; $\mathcal{P}_2 \leftarrow \mathcal{P}_2'$
(18)   **case B:**
(19)   **do** $\mathcal{P}' \leftarrow \mathcal{P}(\mathcal{P}(m-1, m), 1)$ % subdivide the $(n-1)$-face $\mathcal{P}(m-1, m)$
(20)   **color** some of the new vertices in $\mathcal{P}'$ with 0 to get two 0-monochromatic n-simplexes
(21)   **let** $\mathcal{P}_1 \leftarrow$ shortest path inside $\mathcal{P}$ matching $\mathcal{P}_{\text{init}}$ and a new 0-monochromatic n-simplex
(22)   **let** $\mathcal{Q} \leftarrow$ shortest path inside $\mathcal{P}$ matching a new 0-monochromatic n-simplex and $\mathcal{P}_{\text{last}}$
(23)   **do** $\mathcal{Q}' \leftarrow \mathcal{Q}(\mathcal{Q}(m, m+1), 1)$ % subdivide the $(n-1)$-face $\mathcal{Q}(m, m+1)$
(24)   **color** some of the new vertices in $\mathcal{Q}'$ with 0 to get two 0-monochromatic n-simplexes
(25)   **let** $\mathcal{P}_2 \leftarrow$ shortest path inside $\mathcal{P}$ matching $\mathcal{Q}_{\text{init}}'$ and a new 0-monochromatic n-simplex
(26)   **let** $\mathcal{P}_3 \leftarrow$ shortest path inside $\mathcal{P}$ matching a new 0-monochromatic n-simplex and $\mathcal{Q}_{\text{last}}'$
(27)   **invoke SEA** with all paths $\mathcal{P}_i$, independently
(28)   **exit**
(29) $m \leftarrow m+1$

Figure 5: The simplex elimination algorithm.

sign, for each i-face $\sigma' \subset \sigma$, $i \in \{0, \dots, n-1\}$. First, for every 0-face v of σ, if $k_0 = -1$, then set $\text{bin}(v) = 0$. Consider now any i-face $\sigma' \subset \sigma$, for some $i \in \{1, \dots, n-1\}$. Recall that we construct $\text{Div}_1\,\sigma'$ by taking the subdivision Cone^ℓ center σ' and then extending it to all simplexes of $\text{Std}\,\sigma$ containing center σ'. The idea is to find distinct i-simplexes $\rho_1, \dots, \rho_{|k_i|}$ in Cone^ℓ center $\sigma' \subset \text{Div}_1\,\sigma$ such that, for every $1 \leq j \neq t \leq |k_i|$,

$$\text{Star}(\rho_j, \text{Cone}^\ell \text{ center } \sigma') \cap \text{Bd}\,\text{Cone}^\ell \text{ center } \sigma' = \emptyset$$

and

$$\text{Star}(\rho_j, \text{Cone}^\ell \text{ center } \sigma') \cap \text{Star}(\rho_t, \text{Cone}^\ell \text{ center } \sigma') = \emptyset.$$

When we change the coloring of each ρ_j from 1 to 0, the first condition guarantees that $\text{Bd}\,\text{Div}_1\,\sigma'$ remains the same, and the second condition guarantees that we get exactly one more 0-monochromatic i-simplex in $\text{Div}_1\,\sigma'$, i.e., ρ_j.

Consider, for example, $\ell = 2$ and $|k_i| = 1$, and the i-simplex, ρ, at the center of Cone center σ', which does not contain vertices of $\text{Bd}\,\text{Cone}$ center σ'. By the definition of the cone subdivision, $\text{Cone}\,\rho \subset \text{Cone}^2$ center σ'. We can adjust the value of bin on a simplex in $\text{Cone}\,\rho$ to obtain exactly one 0-monochromatic i-simplex in Cone^2 center σ'. According to $\text{sign}(k_i)$, we choose either the i-simplex ϱ at the center of $\text{Cone}\,\rho$, or any i-simplex ϱ' sharing an $(i-1)$-face with ϱ. The star subcomplexes of ϱ and ϱ' in $\text{Div}_1\,\sigma'$, respectively, do not intersect $\text{Bd}\,\text{Cone}^2$ center σ'. Figure 4 shows this construction in dimension 2. Thus, we can modify the coloring of the vertices of a simplex in Cone^2 center σ' and obtain exactly one 0-monochromatic i-simplex in $\text{Div}_1\,\sigma'$, which contains Cone^2 center σ'.

A straightforward calculation shows that $\text{Cone}^{\ell-2}$ center σ' contains $(2^{i+1}-1)^{\ell-2}$ simplexes of dimension i. As explained

above, for each i-dimensional simplex $\rho \in \text{Cone}^{\ell-2}$ center σ', it is possible to get one 0-monochromatic i-simplex in

$$\text{Cone}^2 \rho \subset \text{Cone}^\ell \text{ center } \sigma'.$$

Therefore, by modifying the coloring of Cone^ℓ center σ', we can get $(2^{i+1}-1)^{\ell-2}$ 0-monochromatic i-dimensional simplexes in Cone^ℓ center σ'. Thus, in $\text{Div}_1\,\sigma'$ we can get $|k_i|$ monochromatic i-simplexes since

$$\ell = \max\left\{ \lceil \log_{2^{i+1}-1}(|k_i|) \rceil : i = 1, \dots, n-1 \right\} + 2$$

which is the parameter we used for obtaining $\text{Div}_1\,\sigma$.

By replicating the coloring of $\text{Div}_1\,\sigma'$ in $\text{Div}_1\,\sigma''$, for every i-face $\sigma'' \subset \sigma$ distinct from σ', we get:

THEOREM 4. *Let $k_0, \dots, k_{n-1}$ be an integer solution to $1 + \sum_{i=0}^{n-1} \binom{n+1}{i+1} k_i = 0$ with $k_0 \in \{0, -1\}$. The first step of the construction produces a subdivision $\text{Div}_1\,\sigma$ with a symmetric binary coloring with zero monochromatic n-simplexes, counting by orientation.*

4.2 Second Step

To go from a subdivision with zero monochromatic simplexes counted by orientation to a subdivision without monochromatic simplexes, we show how to "cancel" pairs of monochromatic simplexes of opposite orientation. The *simplex elimination algorithm* (SEA), whose pseudocode appears in Figure 5, takes a path $\mathcal{P}$ of n-simplexes in $\text{Div}_1\,\sigma$ connecting two 0-monochromatic simplexes of opposite orientation, and subdivides that path, leaving its boundary unchanged, so that the new subdivision $\mathcal{P}'$ has no monochromatic n-simplexes. Each application of SEA yields a new subdivision $\text{Div}_1'\,\sigma$ with fewer monochromatic simplexes. After enough applications, we have constructed a subdivision $\text{Div}_2\,\sigma$ with no monochromatic n-simplexes, symmetric on the boundary.

Figure 6: A matching path of length 2.

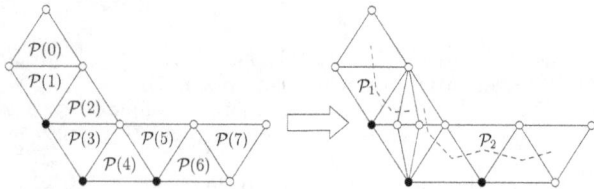

Figure 7: A matching path of length 8.

Consider an n-complex containing all n-simplexes in a simple path Q in the dual graph of $\mathsf{Div}_1 \sigma$ such that (1) the n-simplexes at its ends are 0-monochromatic with opposite orientations, and (2) no other n-simplexes in the path are monochromatic. The *length* of $\mathcal{P}$, $|\mathcal{P}|$, is the number of n-simplexes in $\mathcal{P}$; the definition of orientability implies that $|\mathcal{P}|$ is even. The n-simplexes of $\mathcal{P}$ are numbered from 0 to $|\mathcal{P}|-1$, with $\mathcal{P}(m)$ denoting the mth n-simplex. We say that $\mathcal{P}$ is a *matching path* from $\mathcal{P}_{\text{init}} = \mathcal{P}(0)$ to $\mathcal{P}_{\text{last}} = \mathcal{P}(|\mathcal{P}|-1)$. $\mathcal{P}(m,m+1)$ is the $(n-1)$-face shared between $\mathcal{P}(m)$ and $\mathcal{P}(m+1)$. For any $\tau \in \mathcal{P}$, $\#b(\tau)$ is the number of vertices of τ with color b.

If $\mathcal{P}$ contains two adjacent monochromatic simplexes, then SEA subdivides their shared $(n-1)$-face and sets the colors of all new vertices to 1, Lines 02 and 03. Figure 6 depicts an example in dimension 2 where white and black dots represent binary colors.

If $|\mathcal{P}| > 2$ then SEA looks for the *subdividing point* m of $\mathcal{P}$, which is identified in Line 08, i.e., the smallest integer such that $\#0(\mathcal{P}(m+1,m+2)) \geq n+1-m$. A useful property of m is that it bounds the length of $\mathcal{P}$: $|\mathcal{P}| \geq 2(m+1)$. There are two cases:

Case A: If $\#0(\mathcal{P}(m)) \neq \#0(\mathcal{P}(m+1))$ and $\#0(\mathcal{P}(m,m+1)) \neq n+1-m$, SEA subdivides $\mathcal{P}(m,m+1)$ and colors, roughly, m of the new vertices with 0 (and the rest with 1) to get two new 0-monochromatic n-simplexes (Lines 10 and 11). (See Figure 7 for an example in dimension 2.) Since at most m of the new vertices are colored 0, any shortest path from a new 0-monochromatic n-simplex to $\mathcal{P}(m-1)$ or $\mathcal{P}(m+2)$ has at most m simplexes. Then, the algorithm finds two paths $\mathcal{P}_1$ and $\mathcal{P}_2$ (Lines 12 and 13). The path $\mathcal{P}_1$ has length $2m$ because it contains $\mathcal{P}(0), \ldots, \mathcal{P}(m-1)$ and any shortest path from $\mathcal{P}(m-1)$ to a new 0-monochromatic n-simplex contains at most m simplexes; thus, $|\mathcal{P}_1| < |\mathcal{P}|$, since $|\mathcal{P}| \geq 2(m+1)$. A similar argument shows that $|\mathcal{P}_2| = |\mathcal{P}| - 2$. It is possible that $\mathcal{P}_1$ and $\mathcal{P}_2$ share an n-simplex in Line 14, and SEA subdivides one $(n-1)$-face (Line 15). Then, SEA invokes Line 27 with inputs $\mathcal{P}_1$ and $\mathcal{P}_2$.

Case B: For all other values of $\#0(\mathcal{P}(m))$ and $\#0(\mathcal{P}(m+1))$, a similar analysis implies that $|\mathcal{P}_1| = 2(m-1)$ and $|\mathcal{Q}| = |\mathcal{P}|$ in Line 22, then $|\mathcal{P}_2| = 2m$ and $|\mathcal{P}_3| = |\mathcal{Q}| - 2$ in Line 26.

After running SEA with $\mathcal{P}$, the resulting subdivision $\mathsf{Div}_1' \sigma$ with the coloring bin may still have 0-monochromatic n-sim-

plexes, but in total two fewer monochromatic simplexes than $\mathsf{Div}_1 \sigma$. Moreover, $\mathsf{Bd}\,\mathsf{Div}_1' \sigma = \mathsf{Bd}\,\mathsf{Div}_1 \sigma$ because SEA does not affect boundaries: it subdivides only shared $(n-1)$-faces and modifies the coloring bin only of vertices not in $\mathsf{Bd}\,\mathcal{P}$.

THEOREM 5. *Given a matching path $\mathcal{P}$ of $\mathsf{Div}_1 \sigma$, SEA produces a subdivision $\mathsf{Div}_1' \sigma$ with $\mathsf{Bd}\,\mathsf{Div}_1' \sigma = \mathsf{Bd}\,\mathsf{Div}_1 \sigma$ and a symmetric binary coloring with two fewer monochromatic n-simplexes than $\mathsf{Div}_1 \sigma$, and zero monochromatic n-simplexes, counting by orientation. For every n-simplex $\rho \in \mathsf{Div}_1 \sigma$, if $\rho \notin \mathcal{P}$, then $\rho \in \mathsf{Div}_1' \sigma$.*

Eliminating All Monochromatic Simplexes.

Let $\mathsf{Div}_1 \sigma$ be the subdivision produced in Section 4.1. To eliminate all monochromatic n-simplexes in $\mathsf{Div}_1 \sigma$, we first get any matching path $\mathcal{P}$, which can be computed by running BFS on the dual graph of $\mathsf{Div}_1 \sigma$. By Theorem 5, after running SEA on $\mathcal{P}$, we get a subdivision $\mathsf{Div}_1' \sigma$ with $\mathsf{Bd}\,\mathsf{Div}_1' \sigma = \mathsf{Bd}\,\mathsf{Div}_1 \sigma$ and two fewer monochromatic n-simplexes. Then, we repeat with subdivision $\mathsf{Div}' \sigma$.

THEOREM 6. *The second step produces a subdivision $\mathsf{Div}_2 \sigma$ with a symmetric binary coloring and no monochromatic n-simplexes.*

We stress that SEA works for with any n-dimensional subdivisions, $n \geq 2$: given subdivision $\mathsf{Div}\,\sigma$ with x monochromatic n-simplexes, counting by orientation, the process described above produces a subdivision with exactly $|x|$ monochromatic n-simplexes.

5. FROM SUBDIVISION TO PROTOCOL

So far, we have seen how to construct a subdivision with a symmetric binary coloring. That subdivision is an abstraction of the set of valid decisions for WSB. In this section, for any $\mathsf{Div}\,\sigma$ obtained from extended cone subdivisions, we show how to explicitly get a simplicial map $\mathsf{Std}^K \sigma \to \mathsf{Div}\,\sigma$, where K is on function of the number of operations used for obtaining $\mathsf{Div}\,\sigma$, which gives a K-round iterated immediate snapshot protocol. This result, whose proof is constructive, is our main technical contribution.

Let $\mathsf{Div}_0 \sigma, \ldots, \mathsf{Div}_m \sigma$ be a sequence of subdivisions of σ such that $\mathsf{Div}_0 \sigma = \mathsf{Std}\,\sigma$, i.e., the first standard subdivision, and for every $i \in \{1, \ldots, m\}$, $\mathsf{Div}_i \sigma$ is obtained by a subdivision of $\mathsf{Div}_{i-1} \sigma$; i.e., for some independent simplexes $\tau_{i,1}, \ldots, \tau_{i,j(i)} \in \mathsf{Div}_{i-1} \sigma$ and an integer $\ell_i \geq 1$,

$$\mathsf{Div}_i \sigma' = \mathsf{Div}_{i-1} \sigma'(\tau_{i,1}, \ldots, \tau_{i,j(i)}, \ell_i),$$

for every face $\sigma' \subseteq \sigma$ (see Section 2).

For an n-dimensional simplex $\rho \in \mathsf{Div}_i \sigma$, $i \in \{0, \ldots, m\}$, level ρ is an upper bound on the number of subdivisions that should be applied to σ until ρ appears. For every n-simplex $\rho \in \mathsf{Div}_0 \sigma$, level $\rho = 1$, since ρ is obtained by the first standard subdivision. For $i \in \{1, \ldots, m\}$, for every n-dimensional simplex $\rho \in \mathsf{Div}_i \sigma$ such that $\rho \notin \mathsf{Div}_{i-1} \sigma$ (i.e., ρ was created in the i-th subdivision),

level $\rho = \max \left\{ \text{level } \varrho : \varrho \in (\mathsf{Div}_{i-1} \setminus \mathsf{Div}_i \sigma) \wedge \dim \varrho = n \right\} + \ell_i$,

where ℓ_i is the integer used in the i-th subdivision. For $\mathsf{Div}_i \sigma$,

level $\mathsf{Div}_i \sigma = \max \left\{ \text{level } \rho : \rho \in \mathsf{Div}_i \sigma \wedge \dim \rho = n \right\}$.

Theorem 7 maps an iterated standard subdivision into an extended cone subdivision, while preserving the properties of the coloring associated with the latter subdivision.

THEOREM 7. *For every $i \in \{0, \ldots, m\}$, there exists a name-preserving and carrier-preserving simplicial map $\phi_i : \mathsf{Std}^{K(i)}\, \sigma \to \mathsf{Div}_i\, \sigma$, where $K(i) = \mathsf{level}\,\mathsf{Div}_i\, \sigma$. Moreover, ϕ_i preserves the symmetry properties of $\mathsf{Div}_i\, \sigma$.*

The proof of Theorem 7 inductively computes the simplicial map $\phi_i : \mathsf{Std}^{K(i)}\, \sigma \to \mathsf{Div}_i\, \sigma$. Since the K-th standard subdivision implies a K-round iterated immediate snapshot protocol, the proof shows how to explicitly get an iterated immediate snapshot protocol from any subdivision obtained throughout extended cone subdivisions. Moreover, it quantifies the round complexity of the resulting protocol.

PROOF. We proceed by induction on i. For $i = 0$, $\mathsf{Div}_0\, \sigma = \mathsf{Std}\,\sigma$ and every n-simplex of $\mathsf{Div}_0\, \sigma$ has level equal to 1, hence $K(0) = 1$. Clearly, there is a name-preserving and carrier-preserving simplicial map $\phi_0 : \mathsf{Std}\,\sigma \to \mathsf{Div}_0\,\sigma$; ϕ_0 is the identity simplicial map that maps every vertex to itself; ϕ_0 preserve any symmetry property of $\mathsf{Div}_0\,\sigma$.

For the rest of the proof, let $\mathsf{Std}^0 = \mathsf{P}$.

For some $i \geq 0$, suppose there is a name-preserving and carrier-preserving simplicial map $\phi_i : \mathsf{Std}^{K(i)}\, \sigma \to \mathsf{Div}_i\, \sigma$. Furthermore, assume that for every n-dimensional simplex $\rho \in \mathsf{Div}_i\, \sigma$, there is an n-complex $\mathcal{L} \subseteq \mathsf{Std}^{\mathsf{level}\,\rho}\,\sigma$ such that $\mathsf{Std}^{K(i)-\mathsf{level}\,\rho}\,\mathcal{L} = \phi_i^{-1}(\mathsf{P}\,\sigma)$. This means that ϕ_i "folds" a subcomplex of $\mathsf{Std}^{K(i)}\, \sigma$ on ρ, and that complex corresponds to the $\big(K(i) - \mathsf{level}\,\rho\big)$-th standard subdivision of a subcomplex of $\mathsf{Std}^{\mathsf{level}\,\rho}\,\sigma$. Note that this assumption holds in the base of the induction: first, for every n-simplex $\rho \in \mathsf{Div}_0\,\sigma$, $K(0) - \mathsf{level}\,\rho = 0$; second, for every $\rho' \in \mathsf{P}\,\rho$, $\phi_0^{-1}(\rho')$ contains exactly one $(\dim \rho')$-simplex, which is a face of the unique simplex in $\phi_0^{-1}(\rho)$, and hence $\phi_i^{-1}(\mathsf{P}\,\rho) = \mathsf{P}(\varrho) \subset \mathsf{Std}\,\sigma$, where $\varrho \in \phi_0^{-1}(\rho)$. Then, $\mathsf{Std}^0\,\mathsf{P}\,\varrho = \mathsf{P}\,\varrho = \phi_i^{-1}(\mathsf{P}\,\rho)$.

Let $\tau_1, \ldots, \tau_j$ be the independent simplexes of $\mathsf{Div}_i\,\sigma$ and ℓ be the integer used to obtain $\mathsf{Div}_{i+1}\,\sigma$ from $\mathsf{Div}_i\,\sigma$, namely $\mathsf{Div}_{i+1}\,\sigma = \mathsf{Div}_i\,\sigma(\tau_1, \ldots, \tau_j, \ell)$. To obtain ϕ_{i+1}, consider each n-dimensional simplex ρ of $\mathsf{Div}_i\,\sigma$; there are two cases, depending on whether ρ was affected by the $(i+1)$-th iteration.

Case A: ρ is not affected in the $(i+1)$-th iteration ($\rho \in \mathsf{Div}_{i+1}$). Let $\mathcal{L} \subseteq \mathsf{Std}^{\mathsf{level}\,\rho}\,\sigma$ such that $\mathsf{Std}^{K(i)-\mathsf{level}\,\rho}\,\mathcal{L} = \phi_i^{-1}(\mathsf{P}\,\rho)$. The existence of $\mathcal{L}$ is guaranteed by the induction hypothesis. Observe that $K(i) \leq K(i+1) \leq K(i) + \ell$. Let k be the integer such that $K(i+1) = K(i) + k$.

Consider any n-simplex $\varrho \in \mathcal{L}$. If $k \geq 1$, then it can be shown that there is a name-preserving and carrier-preserving simplicial map $\xi_\varrho : \mathsf{Std}^k\,\varrho \to \mathsf{P}\,\varrho$; and if $k = 0$, then obviously there is such a map $\xi_\varrho : \mathsf{Std}^0(\varrho) \to \mathsf{P}\,\varrho$ (recall that $\mathsf{Std}^0 = \mathsf{P}$). Also, clearly there is a (unique) name-preserving simplicial bijection $\zeta_\varrho : \mathsf{P}\,\varrho \to \mathsf{P}\,\rho$. Then, ϕ_{i+1} maps every simplex $\varrho' \in \mathsf{Std}^k\,\varrho \subset \mathsf{Std}^{K(i+1)}\,\sigma$ to $\zeta_\varrho \circ \xi_\varrho(\varrho') \in \mathsf{P}\,\rho \subset \mathsf{Div}_{i+1}\,\sigma$. By definition of ϕ_{i+1},

$$\mathsf{Std}^{K(i)-\mathsf{level}\,\rho+k}\,\mathcal{L} = \mathsf{Std}^{K(i+1)-\mathsf{level}\,\rho}\,\mathcal{L} = \phi_{i+1}^{-1}(\rho).$$

Case B: If ρ is affected in the $(i+1)$-th iteration ($\rho \notin \mathsf{Div}_{i+1}\,\sigma$), then ρ contains a simplex $\tau \in \{\tau_1, \ldots, \tau_j\}$, which is one of the simplexes used to obtain $\mathsf{Div}_{i+1}\,\sigma$ from $\mathsf{Div}_i\,\sigma$. Note that there cannot exist a $\tau' \in \{\tau_1, \ldots, \tau_j\}$ distinct from τ such that $\tau' \subseteq \rho$ because this would imply that $\rho \in$

$\mathsf{Star}(\tau', \mathsf{Div}_i\,\sigma)$, and hence τ and τ' would not be independent.

Let $\ell_{\max} = \max\{\mathsf{level}\,\varrho : \varrho \in (\mathsf{Div}_i\,\sigma \setminus \mathsf{Div}_{i+1}\,\sigma) \wedge \dim\rho = n\}$; hence $\mathsf{level}\,\rho \leq \ell_{\max}$. From the definition of level, it follows that, for every n-simplex $\gamma \in \mathsf{ExCone}^\ell(\tau, \rho)$ (which belongs also to $\mathsf{Div}_{i+1}\,\sigma$), $\mathsf{level}\,\gamma = \ell_{\max} + \ell$.

Let $\mathcal{L} \subseteq \mathsf{Std}^{\mathsf{level}\,\rho}\,\sigma$ such that $\mathsf{Std}^{K(i)-\mathsf{level}\,\rho}\,\mathcal{L} = \phi_i^{-1}(\mathsf{P}\,\rho)$. The existence of $\mathcal{L}$ is guaranteed by the induction hypothesis. Consider the complex $\mathsf{Std}^{\ell_{\max}-\mathsf{level}\,\rho}\,\mathcal{L}$. Note that

$$\mathsf{Std}^{\ell_{\max}-\mathsf{level}\,\rho}\,\mathcal{L} \subseteq \mathsf{Std}^{\ell_{\max}}\,\sigma.$$

For every n-dimensional simplex $\varrho \in \mathsf{Std}^{\ell_{\max}-\mathsf{level}\,\rho}\,\mathcal{L}$, ϕ_{i+1} will "fold" $\mathsf{Std}^{K(i+1)-\ell_{\max}}\,\varrho \subseteq \mathsf{Std}^{K(i+1)}\,\sigma$ on $\mathsf{ExCone}^\ell(\tau, \rho)$.

We show first that $K(i+1) - \ell_{\max} \geq \ell$. There are two cases. If $K(i) = K(i+1)$, then it must be that $K(i) - \ell_{\max} \geq \ell$, because otherwise $\ell_{max} + \ell > K(i)$, and hence $K(i+1) > K(i)$, since every n-simplex of $\mathsf{ExCone}^\ell(\tau, \rho)$ has level $\ell_{max} + \ell$. The fact that $K(i) = K(i+1)$ implies that $K(i+1) - \ell_{\max} \geq \ell$.

In the second case, if $K(i) < K(i+1)$, then it must be that $K(i) - \ell_{\max} < \ell$. Thus, we can write $K(i) - \ell_{\max} = \ell - \ell'$, for some $1 \leq \ell' \leq \ell$. In fact, due to the definition of $K(i+1)$, it follows that $K(i+1) = K(i) + \ell'$; thus, $K(i+1) - \ell_{\max} = K(i) + \ell' - \ell_{\max} = \ell' + (\ell - \ell') = \ell$.

Therefore, in both cases, we can write $K(i+1) = \ell_{\max} + \ell + h$, for some $h \geq 0$.

Now, for an n-simplex $\varrho \in \mathsf{Std}^{\ell_{\max}-\mathsf{level}\,\rho}\,\mathcal{L} \subseteq \mathsf{Std}^{\ell_{\max}}\,\sigma$, let τ' be the face of ϱ with $\mathsf{names}(\tau') = \mathsf{names}(\tau)$. The next lemma (whose proof will appear in the full version), guarantees the existence of a name-preserving and carrier-preserving simplicial map $\xi_\varrho : \mathsf{Std}^{\ell+h}\,\varrho \to \mathsf{ExCone}^{\ell+h}(\tau', \varrho)$.

LEMMA 8. *For every $K \geq 1$ and $h \geq 0$, there exists a name-preserving and carrier-preserving simplicial map $\phi : \mathsf{Std}^{K+h}\,\sigma \to \mathsf{ExCone}^{K+h}(\tau, \sigma)$ such that for every n-simplex $\rho \in \mathsf{ExCone}^{K+h}(\tau, \sigma)$, there is an n-complex $\mathcal{L} \subseteq \mathsf{Std}^K\,\sigma$ such that $\mathsf{Std}^h\,\mathcal{L} = \phi^{-1}(\mathsf{P}\,\rho)$.*

Clearly, there is a name-preserving simplicial bijection

$$\zeta_\varrho : \mathsf{ExCone}^{\ell+h}(\tau', \varrho) \to \mathsf{ExCone}^{\ell+h}(\tau, \rho).$$

Then, ϕ_{i+1} maps every simplex $\varrho' \in \mathsf{Std}^{\ell+h}\,\varrho \subset \mathsf{Std}^{K(i+1)}\,\sigma$ to

$$\zeta_\varrho \circ \xi_\varrho(\varrho') \in \mathsf{ExCone}^{\ell+h}(\tau, \rho) \subset \mathsf{Div}_{i+1}\,\sigma.$$

Consider now an n-simplex $\gamma \in \mathsf{ExCone}^{\ell+h}(\tau, \rho)$. As already explained, $\mathsf{level}(\gamma) = \ell_{\max} + \ell$. Since ζ_ϱ is a name-preserving simplicial bijection, $\zeta_\varrho^{-1}(\gamma)$ contains a unique n-simplex, say γ'. By Lemma 8, there is a $\mathcal{K} \subseteq \mathsf{Std}^\ell\,\varrho$ such that $\mathsf{Std}^h\,\mathcal{K} = \xi_\varrho^{-1}(\mathsf{P}\,\gamma')$. Observe that $\phi_{i+1}^{-1}(\mathsf{P}\,\gamma) = \xi_\varrho^{-1}(\mathsf{P}\,\gamma') = \mathsf{Std}^h\,\mathcal{K}$. We have noted above that $\varrho \in \mathsf{Std}^{\ell_{\max}}\,\sigma$, from which follows that $\mathcal{K} \subseteq \mathsf{Std}^{\ell_{\max}+\ell}\,\sigma$. Finally, note that $K(i+1) - \mathsf{level}(\gamma) = \ell_{\max} + \ell + h - (\ell_{\max} + \ell) = h$.

In both cases, the induction step follows. Finally, ϕ_{i+1} preserve any symmetry property of $\mathsf{Div}_{i+1}\,\sigma$ because ϕ_i preserves any symmetry property of $\mathsf{Div}_i\,\sigma$, by induction the hypothesis, and ϕ_{i+1} is extended from ϕ_i using the same construction in both cases. $\square$

Theorem 7 and the subdivision constructed in Section 4 give our main result: a WSB protocol with a bound on the number of rounds, when $n + 1$ is not a prime power.

THEOREM 9. *If $n + 1$ is not a power of a prime number, then there is an explicit read/write wait-free protocol solving $(n + 1)$-process WSB in $O(n^{q+3})$ iterations of immediate snapshot, where q is the largest prime power in the prime factorization of $n + 1$.*

PROOF. There is an integer solution $k_0, \dots, k_{n-1}$ of the equation $1 + \sum_{i=0}^{n-1} \binom{n+1}{i+1} k_i = 0$ such that $\max\{|k_i|\} < n^2$, and $k_i = 0$, for $i = 0, \dots, n - q - 1$ (see Lemma 12 in the appendix).

By Theorem 4, the first step of the construction in Section 3 produces a subdivision $\mathsf{Div}_1 \sigma$ with a symmetric coloring where the number of monochromatic n-simplexes is zero counting by orientation (but not zero). Recall that $\mathsf{Div}_1 \sigma$ is obtained from a single subdivision over $\mathsf{Std}\,\sigma$. This operation depends on

$$\ell = \max\left\{\lceil \log_{2^{i+1}-1}(|k_i|) \rceil : i = 1, \dots, n-1\right\} + 2.$$

Since $\mathsf{level}\,\mathsf{Std}\,\sigma = 1$, the definition of level implies that

$$\mathsf{level}\,\mathsf{Div}_1 \sigma = \max\left\{\lceil \log_{2^{i+1}-1}(|k_i|) \rceil : i = 1, \dots, n-1\right\} + 3.$$

Note that $q \leq \frac{n+1}{2}$, since $n + 1$ is not a prime power. Hence, every $i \in \{n - q, \dots, n - 1\}$ is in $\Theta(n)$, and

$$\log_{2^{\Theta(n)}}(n^2) = 2\frac{\log_2 n}{\log_2(2^{\Theta(n)})} = 2\frac{\log_2 n}{\Theta(n)} \in O(1).$$

Observe that the total number of monochromatic n-simplexes of $\mathsf{Div}_1 \sigma$ is

$$1 + \sum_{i=n-q}^{n-1} \binom{n+1}{i+1} |k_i| = 2r$$

for some integer r. We now bound r. Since $\binom{n+1}{i+1} \in O(n^{n-i})$, and $|k_i| < n^2$, it follows that $|k_i|\binom{n+1}{i+1} \in O(n^{n-i+2})$, and

$$1 + \sum_{i=n-q}^{n-1} \binom{n+1}{i+1} |k_i| \in O(n^{q+2}).$$

Therefore, $r \in O(n^{q+2})$.

By Theorem 4, $\mathsf{Div}_2 \sigma$ is a subdivision with a symmetric coloring without monochromatic n-simplexes, which is produced after r iterations of eliminating matching paths, starting from $\mathsf{Div}_1 \sigma$. For $j = 1, \dots, r$, let $\mathsf{Div}_{1,j} \sigma$ be the subdivision produced after j iterations, and $\mathsf{Div}_{1,0} \sigma$ be $\mathsf{Div}_1 \sigma$.

LEMMA 10. *For every $j = 0, \dots, r$,*

$$\mathsf{level}\,\mathsf{Div}_{1,j} \sigma \leq \mathsf{level}\,\mathsf{Div}_1 \sigma + 2j(n + 2).$$

PROOF. The base of the induction $j = 0$ is simple: $\mathsf{Div}_{1,j} = \mathsf{Div}_1 \sigma$. For the induction step, assume

$$\mathsf{level}\,\mathsf{Div}_{1,j} \sigma \leq \mathsf{level}\,\mathsf{Div}_1 \sigma + 2j(n + 2).$$

Consider the path $\mathcal{P}$ that is eliminated in the $(j + 1)$-st iteration and let $\mathsf{Div}'_{1,j} \sigma$ be the subdivision obtained from running SEA with $\mathcal{P}$. If $|\mathcal{P}| \leq 2(n + 1)$ the height of the recursion tree of SEA is at most $n + 1$. Also, in every invocation, SEA subdivides at most two $(n - 1)$-faces. From the fact that SEA only subdivides simplexes in $\mathcal{P}$, it follows that $\mathsf{level}\,\mathsf{Div}'_{1,j} \sigma \leq \mathsf{level}\,\mathcal{P} + 2(n + 1)$.

When $|\mathcal{P}| > 2(n + 1)$, the following claim shows that we can "chop" $\mathcal{P}$ using a constant number of subdivisions.

CLAIM 1. *For any matching path $\mathcal{P}$, at most two subdivisions are needed to produce non-intersecting matching paths of length at most $2(n + 1)$.*

To prove the claim, first we get

$$\mathcal{P}' = \mathcal{P}(\mathcal{P}(n, n + 1), \dots, \mathcal{P}(tn, t(n + 1)), 1)$$

where t is the largest integer such that $\mathcal{P}(tn, t(n + 1))$ is an n-face of $\mathcal{P}$ and $\mathcal{P}(t + 1)$ is not monochromatic. Then we modify the coloring of the new vertices to get $2t$ new 0-monochromatic n-simplexes, and hence get t matching paths. It may be the case that some paths are not disjoint, and thus one more subdivision is needed. Essentially, Case A of Figure 5 is executed in parallel in several parts of $\mathcal{P}$. After two subdivisions, $\mathcal{P}$ is "chopped" into short paths, from which the claim follows.

Thus, when SEA is invoked with a path $\mathcal{P}$ larger than $2(n + 1)$, a simple preprocessing stage chops $\mathcal{P}$ into paths of size at most $2(n+1)$, and then SEA is invoked with each one of these paths. Therefore, $\mathsf{level}\,\mathsf{Div}'_{1,j} \sigma \leq \mathsf{level}\,\mathcal{P} + 2(n + 2)$.

We have that $\mathsf{level}\,\mathsf{Div}'_{1,j} \sigma \leq \mathsf{level}\,\mathsf{Div}_{1,j} \sigma + 2(j+1)(n+2)$, because $\mathsf{level}\,\mathcal{P} \leq \mathsf{level}\,\mathsf{Div}_{1,j}$, and by the induction hypothesis, $\mathsf{level}\,\mathsf{Div}_{1,j} \sigma \leq \mathsf{Div}_1 \sigma + 2j(n+2)$. Lemma 10 follows. $\square$

Since $r \in O(n^{q+2})$ and $\mathsf{Div}_2 \sigma = \mathsf{Div}_{1,r}$, $\mathsf{level}\,\mathsf{Div}_2 \sigma \in O(n^{q+3})$.

Theorem 7 gives a name-preserving and carrier-preserving simplicial map $\delta : \mathsf{Std}^K \sigma \to \mathsf{Div}_2 \sigma$ with $K \in O(n^{q+3})$. Coloring each vertex $v \in \mathsf{Std}^K \sigma$ with $\mathsf{bin}(\delta(v))$ is symmetric and without monochromatic n-simplexes, giving a WSB protocol with $O(n^{q+3})$ rounds. $\square$

It is known [7,8] that a single instance of a WSB protocol allows to solve $2n$-renaming in the iterated model, with an $O(n)$ round additive overhead. Therefore, we get:

COROLLARY 11. *If $n + 1$ is not a power of a prime number, then there is an explicit read-write wait-free protocol solving $(n+1)$-process $2n$-renaming in $O(n^{q+3})$ rounds in the iterated model of computation, where q is the largest prime power in the prime factorization of $n + 1$.*

Improving the round complexity.

The number of rounds for solving WSB and hard renaming can be significantly improved by getting disjoint paths matching all monochromatic n-simplexes of the subdivision in the first step (disjoint in the sense that they do not share n-simplexes). If one is able to get those paths and the k_i's in the first step are small (Lemma 12 in the appendix), the round complexity of the resulting protocol would be $O(n)$. The idea is that SEA can be executed in parallel over all matching paths because for any distinct two of them, $\mathcal{P}, \mathcal{P}'$, any $(n - 1)$-simplexes $\tau \in \mathcal{P}$ and $\tau' \in \mathcal{P}'$ that do not belong to $\mathsf{Bd}\,\mathcal{P}$ and $\mathsf{Bd}\,\mathcal{P}'$, respectively, are independent, since $\mathcal{P}$ and $\mathcal{P}'$ are disjoint. Thus, any cone subdivision over them can be executed in parallel.

For example, for $n + 1 = 6$ processes and coefficients $k_0 = -1, k_1 = -1, k_2 = 1, k_3 = 0$ and $k_4 = 0$, we can get disjoint matching paths, and thus get a 6-process protocol that solves WSB in 17 rounds.

6. DISCUSSION

The proof of Theorem 7 gives a fully combinatorial and constructive proof of the sufficiency part of the Asynchronous

Computability Theorem [9], for specific subdivisions. The construction in Section 4 is similar to an earlier construction of Castañeda and Rajsbaum [6]. The differences are that in the earlier construction, the first step constructs the analog of $\mathrm{Div}_1\,\sigma$, and its binary coloring, inductively by dimension, without explicit bounds on the number of subdivisions needed. Here, $\mathrm{Div}_1\,\sigma$ is constructed in a single operation and its coloring is given in a concrete manner. The simplex elimination algorithm presented here is an improved version of the elimination algorithm in Castañeda and Rajsbaum [6]. In the algorithm presented here, every invocation produces paths shorter than the input path, at the cost of producing more sub-paths. The problem of finding disjoint sets of paths in a graph is known as the *disjoint path problem*, which is NP-complete [10]. (For our purposes, however, such paths are found off-line as part of the protocol design.)

Acknowledgements. We thank Ofir David for suggesting the technique used in the proof of Lemma 12 and the anonymous referees for helpful comments.

7. REFERENCES

[1] H. Attiya, A. Bar-Noy, D. Dolev, D. Peleg, and R. Reischuk. Renaming in an Asynchronous Environment. *J. ACM*, 1990.

[2] H. Attiya and A. Paz. Counting-based impossibility proofs for renaming and set agreement. DISC 2012, pages 356–370.

[3] E. Borowsky and E. Gafni. A Simple Algorithmically Reasoned Characterization of Wait-Free Computations (Extended Abstract). PODC 1997, pages 189–198.

[4] A. Castañeda and S. Rajsbaum. New combinatorial topology bounds for renaming: the lower bound. *Distributed Computing*, 22:287–301, 2010.

[5] A. Castañeda, S. Rajsbaum, and M. Raynal. The renaming problem in shared memory systems: An introduction. *Comput. Sci. Rev.*, 5(3):229–251, 2011.

[6] A. Castañeda and S. Rajsbaum. New combinatorial topology bounds for renaming: The upper bound. *J. ACM*, 59(1):3, 2012.

[7] E. Gafni and S. Rajsbaum. Distributed programming with tasks. OPODIS 2010, pages 205–218.

[8] E. Gafni, S. Rajsbaum, and M. Herlihy. Subconsensus Tasks: Renaming Is Weaker Than Set Agreement. DISC 2006, *Lecture Notes in Computer Science*, Vol. 4167, pages 329–338.

[9] M. Herlihy and N. Shavit. The topological structure of asynchronous computability. *J. ACM*, 46(6):858–923, 1999.

[10] R. M. Karp. On the computational complexity of combinatorial problems. *Networks*, 5:45–68, 1975.

[11] D. N. Kozlov. *Combinatorial Algebraic Topology*, volume 21 of *Algorithms and Computation in Mathematics*. Springer, 1 edition, Oct. 2007.

[12] E. Lucas. Théorie des fonctions numériques simplement périodiques. *American Journal of Mathematics*, 1(3):197–240, 1878.

[13] J. Munkres. *Elements of Algebraic Topology*. Prentice Hall, 2 edition, Jan. 1984.

APPENDIX

LEMMA 12. *If $n + 1$ is not a power of a prime number, then there is an integer solution $(k_0, \ldots, k_{n-1})$ to $1 + \sum_{i=0}^{n-1} \binom{n+1}{i+1} k_i = 0$ with $\max\{|k_i|\} < n^2$. Moreover, $k_i = 0$, for $i = 0, \ldots, n - q - 1$, where q is the largest prime power in the prime factorization of $n + 1$.*

PROOF. If $n + 1$ is not a prime power, the binomial coefficients $\binom{n+1}{n-q+1}, \ldots, \binom{n+1}{n}$ are relatively prime; this can be deduced, i.e., from Lucas' theorem [12]. Thus, an integer solution $(0, \ldots, 0, a_{n-q}, \ldots, a_{n-1})$ to the equation exists, and can be found using the extended Euclidean algorithm. Consider such a solution, and take all the coefficients modulo $n + 1$

$$a_i' = a_i \mod n + 1; \; 0 \le i \le n - 1.$$

We now build a new solution, $(k_0, \ldots, k_{n-1})$. Let $k_i = 0$, for $i = 0, \ldots, n - q - 1$. The first nonzero coefficient is

$$k_{n-q} = a_{n-q}'$$

and the rest of the coefficients are defined recursively, as follows.

For $n - q < t < n - 1$, assume $k_0, \ldots, k_{t-1}$ are already defined. Let $S_{t-1} = \sum_{i=0}^{t-1} k_i \binom{n+1}{i+1}$, and let

$$k_t = \min\left\{ k \equiv a_t' \pmod{n+1} \; \middle| \; S_{t-1} + k\binom{n+1}{t+1} > 0 \right\}.$$

Note that by this definition, for all t, $n - q < t < n - 1$, it holds that $S_t = S_{t-1} + k_t\binom{n+1}{t+1}$, and the choice of k_t guarantees $0 < S_t \le (n+1)\binom{n+1}{t+1}$. Also note that $1 + S_t + \sum_{i=t+1}^{n-1} a_i'\binom{n+1}{i+1} \equiv 0 \pmod{n+1}$ for every such t.

By the minimality of k_t and the inequality $S_{t-1} > 0$, it follows that $k_t \le a_t' \le n$. On the other hand, since $0 < S_t = S_{t-1} + k_t\binom{n+1}{t+1} \le (n+1)\binom{n+1}{t} + k_t\binom{n+1}{t+1}$ one has

$$k_t > -\frac{(n+1)\binom{n+1}{t}}{\binom{n+1}{t+1}} = -\frac{(n+1)(t+1)}{n+1-t} \ge -\frac{n^2+n}{2}.$$

Hence $|k_t| < n^2$.

Let the last coefficient be

$$k_{n-1} = -\frac{1 + S_{n-2}}{n+1},$$

which is an integer by the observation $1 + S_t + \sum_{i=t+1}^{n-1} a_i'\binom{n+1}{i+1} \equiv 0 \pmod{n+1}$ applied to $t = n - 2$. From $0 < S_{n-2} \le (n+1)\binom{n+1}{n-1}$, it also follows that $|k_{n-1}| \le \frac{1}{n+1} + \frac{(n+1)n}{2} < n^2$.

By the choice of k_{n-1},

$$1 + \sum_{i=0}^{n-1} \binom{n+1}{i+1} k_i = S_{n-2} + k_{n-1}\binom{n+1}{n} = 0,$$

hence $(k_0, \ldots, k_{n-1})$ is an integer solution to the equation satisfying $k_i = 0$ for $i = 0, \ldots, n - q - 1$, and $|k_i| < n^2$ for any value of i. $\square$

Randomized Loose Renaming in O(log log n) Time

[Extended Abstract]

Dan Alistarh[*]
Computer Science and
Artificial Intelligence Lab, MIT
alistarh@mit.edu

James Aspnes[†]
Dept. of Computer Science
Yale University
aspnes@cs.yale.edu

George Giakkoupis[‡]
INRIA Rennes – Bretagne
Atlantique
george.giakkoupis@inria.fr

Philipp Woelfel[§]
Dept. of Computer Science
University of Calgary
woelfel@ucalgary.ca

ABSTRACT

Renaming is a classic distributed coordination task in which a set of processes must pick distinct identifiers from a small namespace. In this paper, we consider the time complexity of this problem when the namespace is linear in the number of participants, a variant known as loose renaming. We give a non-adaptive algorithm with $O(\log \log n)$ (individual) step complexity, where n is a known upper bound on contention, and an adaptive algorithm with step complexity $O((\log \log k)^2)$, where k is the actual contention in the execution. We also present a variant of the adaptive algorithm which requires $O(k \log \log k)$ *total* process steps. All upper bounds hold with high probability against a strong adaptive adversary.

We complement the algorithms with an $\Omega(\log \log n)$ expected time lower bound on the complexity of randomized renaming using test-and-set operations and linear space. The result is based on a new coupling technique, and is the first to apply to non-adaptive randomized renaming. Since our algorithms use $O(n)$ test-and-set objects, our results provide matching bounds on the cost of loose renaming in this setting.

[*]This author was supported by the SNF Postdoctoral Fellows Program, NSF grant CCF-1217921, DoE ASCR grant ER26116/DE-SC0008923, and by grants from the Oracle and Intel corporations.

[†]Supported in part by NSF grant CCF-0916389.

[‡]This work was funded in part by INRIA Associate Team RADCON, and ERC Starting Grant GOSSPLE 204742.

[§]This research was undertaken, in part, thanks to funding from the Canada Research Chairs program and the HP Labs Innovation Research Program.

Categories and Subject Descriptors

E.1 [**Data Structures**]: Distributed Data Structures; F.2.2 [**Analysis of Algorithms and Problem Complexity**]: Nonnumerical Algorithms and Problems

Keywords

Distributed computing, shared memory, renaming, upper bounds, lower bounds

1. INTRODUCTION

The *renaming* problem [8] is a fundamental task in distributed computing. It can be seen as the dual of *consensus* [33]: if to reach consensus processes must *agree* on a single value, for renaming processes must *disagree* constructively by returning distinct identifiers from a small namespace. Considerable effort, e.g., [8, 9, 13, 17], went into analyzing the feasibility and complexity of renaming in asynchronous shared-memory and message-passing systems. From a theoretical perspective, the problem is known to have a rich structure, in particular given its connections to algebraic topology, e.g., [18, 19, 28]. On the other hand, renaming is known to be related to practical problems such as mutual exclusion [5], counting [4], or concurrent memory management [27].

A significant amount of research, e.g., [2, 10, 31], studied efficient renaming in asynchronous shared memory. Early work focused on *non-adaptive* renaming, where the maximum number of processes n is known, and each process must obtain a unique name from a target namespace of size m, where m is a function of n. If $m = n$, i.e., the namespace size is optimal, then renaming is *strong* (or *tight*); otherwise, renaming is *loose*. A stronger variant of the problem is *adaptive* renaming [1], where the size of the target namespace and the complexity of the algorithm must depend on the contention k in the current execution, as opposed to the number of processes in the system, n.

Randomization has proved a very useful tool for getting fast renaming algorithms. Intuitively, a process can simply pick a name at random, repeating the choice in case of a collision. If the space is large enough, then the expected number of collisions is small. Using a similar idea, Panconesi, Papatriantafilou, Tsigas and Vitányi [32] obtained a loose renaming algorithm with poly-logarithmic expected step complexity against a strong adversary. Further work, e.g., [4, 6, 20], resulted in algorithms for strong renaming and with logarithmic expected step complexity. Recently, [5] gave a lower bound of $\Omega(\log(k/c))$ expected process steps for adaptive renaming into a namespace of size ck, for any constant $c \geq 1$, extending an information-based technique of Jayanti [29]. This result suggested that the logarithmic complexity threshold is inherent for adaptive renaming, and that no asymptotic complexity gain can be obtained by relaxing the namespace size within constant factors.

In this paper, we contradict this intuition by presenting two renaming algorithms which achieve linear namespace size with *sub-logarithmic* step complexity. Our first algorithm, called ReBatching, uses $(1 + \epsilon)n$ names for any fixed constant $\epsilon > 0$, and all processes finish it in time $O(\log \log n)$, with high probability. The second algorithm is adaptive, and all processes obtain names of value $O(k)$ in $O((\log \log k)^2)$ steps, both with high probability, where k is the contention in the execution. We also give a more complex variant of this second algorithm with $O(\log \log k)$ *average* step complexity. The algorithms use test-and-set (TAS) operations and linear space.

Both our algorithms circumvent the logarithmic lower bound of [5], but in different ways. ReBatching is not affected by the bound since it is not adaptive, while the adaptive algorithm circumvents it since the ck namespace bound is ensured only with high probability, rather than with probability 1.

On the negative side, we prove a lower bound of $\Omega(\log \log n)$ expected worst-case steps for renaming algorithms which use only TAS primitives and linear space in n. Since both our algorithms verify these assumptions, they are time-optimal in this setting.

Our algorithms work against a strong adaptive adversary, which can examine the processes' entire state when deciding on scheduling and crashes. They improve exponentially on the best previously known algorithms [6, 32]. Our lower bound is the first to apply to non-adaptive randomized renaming, and exhibits a new trade-off between space and expected running time for this problem.

The intuition behind our algorithms is simple: processes share a sequence of indexed shared memory locations; a process obtains a name by performing a successful TAS on a location, returning the index of that location as its name. If unsuccessful, the process tries again. Thus, the key to obtaining a fast algorithm is to minimize the contention between process probes.

In this context, ReBatching allocates a set of $2n$ locations, split into disjoint batches $B_0, B_1, \ldots$ of decreasing length, such that batch B_i has approximately $n/2^i$ consecutive locations. Each process will perform a *constant* number of probes in each batch, until it first acquires a location. The key idea in the analysis is that, as the execution progresses to later batches, the number of processes surviving up to some batch B_ℓ is proportional to $O(n/2^{2^\ell})$, while the space available in the batch is $\Theta(n/2^\ell)$. This phenomenon perpetuates so that, when $\ell = \log \log n$, there are essentially no more processes competing.

The adaptive algorithm works as follows. Processes share a set of ReBatching objects $R_1, R_2, \ldots$, where object number i provides a distinct namespace of size $\Theta(2^i)$. Processes first "race" to obtain a unique name by accessing objects

R_{2^ℓ} for $\ell = 0, 1, \ldots$, until successful in some object. Since the names obtained may be super-linear in k, processes proceed to a second *search* phase, in which they "crunch" the namespace by essentially running by binary search on the ReBatching objects. The step complexity of the algorithm is $O((\log \log k)^2)$ and all processes obtain names of value $O(k)$, both with high probability. We also consider a more complex version, in which processes pipeline their steps in the ReBatching objects to amortize the complexity of the failed ReBatching calls. The resulting algorithm has total step complexity $O(k \log \log k)$ with high probability, and the same namespace guarantees as the simpler version.

Our lower bound considers algorithms using linear space and TAS operations, and proves that any such algorithm must cause some process to take $\Theta(\log \log n)$ steps with constant probability. We first reduce the problem to one where, to obtain a name, a process must *win* a TAS (i.e., change the value of that location). Even given this reduction, processes do learn new information from their unsuccessful probes, which can lead to complex correlations of future probes. To circumvent this issue, we construct an execution in which processes are carefully pruned in each round to ensure independence between the survivors. This reduces the problem to one where each process loses each trial with a fixed probability, independently of the actions of other processes. In turn, this will show that some processes must still take steps after $\Theta(\log \log n)$ rounds.

The main technical ingredient of the lower bound is a coupling gadget which guarantees that the number of processes accessing and leaving a location is a Poisson random variable, ensuring independence. The resulting worst-case execution is composed of layers in which each process takes steps in randomly permuted order. Such an execution can in fact be created by an *oblivious* adversary, so the lower bound works in this weaker adversarial model as well. Interestingly, both our algorithms match this time bound, and work even for an adaptive adversary.

Our work can be seen as part of a wider effort investigating sub-logarithmic-time algorithms for fundamental distributed tasks. Tight bounds of $\Theta(\log n/ \log \log n)$ are known for randomized mutual exclusion against a strong adversary [23, 25, 26]. Against a weak adversary, randomized algorithms with $O(\log \log n)$ complexity have been recently given for test-and-set [3, 22] and consensus [7], while Bender and Gilbert [14] provide a mutual exclusion algorithm with $O((\log \log n)^2)$ amortized expected RMR complexity. However, prior to our paper, no algorithms with $O(\log \log n)$ step complexity were known against a strong adversary for *any* non-trivial problem in asynchronous shared-memory.

2. MODEL AND PROBLEM STATEMENT

We assume the standard asynchronous shared memory model with n processes $p_1, \ldots, p_n$. Processes follow an algorithm, composed of *steps*. Without loss of generality, each step is comprised of local computations, and one shared memory step. Processes share registers, on which they can perform TAS operations. We say that a process *wins* a TAS if it successfully changes the value of the register and returns 0; otherwise, the process *loses* the TAS, returning 1. Any number of processes may fail by crashing. A failed process does not take further steps in the execution.

We consider randomized algorithms, in which processes' actions may depend on the outcomes of local random coin flips. We assume that each process starts with an initial name from an unbounded namespace, and that processes share a consistent indexing of the memory locations on which they perform shared-memory operations.

The order in which processes take steps and their crashes are controlled by an *adversary*. In this paper, we consider two standard types of adversarial schedulers. The *adaptive* (or *strong*) adversary is allowed to see the state of all processes (including the results of coin flips) when making its scheduling choices. The weaker *oblivious* adversary knows the algorithm, but not the results of coin flips when deciding the schedule.

The renaming problem [8] is defined as follows. Given a target namespace size $m \geq n$, each of the n processes must eventually return a unique name v_i between 1 and m. A correct algorithm must guarantee *termination, namespace size* and *uniqueness* in every execution. In the classic (non-adaptive) renaming problem [8], the parameters n and m are known by the processes.

The *adaptive* renaming problem [1], which we also consider in this paper, requires that the complexity of the protocol and the size of the resulting namespace should only depend on the number of participating processes k in the current execution. In this paper, we also relax the *namespace size* requirement to be probabilistic.

We focus on two complexity measures. The first is *(individual) step complexity*, i.e., the maximum number of steps that *any* process performs in an execution. The second measure is *total step complexity* (also known as *work*) which counts the *total* number of steps that *all* processes perform during the execution.

We say that an event occurs *with high probability (w.h.p.)* if its probability is at least $1 - 1/n^c$, where $c > 1$ is a constant. For adaptive algorithms, where the bound on n may not be known, we will express high probability as $1 - 1/k^c$, where k is the contention in the execution.

Test-and-Set vs. Read-Write. Previous work on this problem, e.g., [4,6,32], considered the read-write shared-memory model, implemented randomized TAS out of reads and writes, and then solved renaming on top of TAS. In this paper, we assume hardware TAS is given. Otherwise, we could implement randomized adaptive TAS which we could then use as part of our algorithms. This would increase our expected worst-case complexity by a multiplicative $O(\log \log k)$ factor.[1] On the other hand, if we only employ read-write registers, the high probability bounds for our algorithms become at least logarithmic, as logarithmic w.h.p. bounds are inherent even for two-process randomized TAS out of reads and writes [22].

3. RELATED WORK

Renaming was introduced in [8], and early work focused on its solvability in asynchronous crash-prone settings [8,13,17], showing that $(2n-1)$-renaming can be achieved in message-passing and read-write shared-memory. A namespace lower bound of $(2n-1)$ was shown by Herlihy and Shavit [28], highlighting deep connections with algebraic topology. Castañeda and Rajsbaum [18, 19] further characterized the

---

[1] This holds since each TAS is accessed by $O(\log k)$ processes in our algorithm, w.h.p. Also notice that the linearization issues pointed out in [24] are circumvented since we only require simple leader election algorithms to make our algorithms work, as opposed to fully linearizable TAS objects.

namespace size, while some of the results were recently re-derived by Attiya and Paz [11] using counting arguments. Significant effort went into obtaining efficient deterministic algorithms, e.g., [2, 10, 31]. We refer the reader to [16] for a survey of deterministic and long-lived solutions.

Panconesi et al. [32] were the first to use randomization, and gave an algorithm guaranteeing a namespace of size $(1+\epsilon)n$, with $O(M \log^2 n)$ expected running time, where M is the size of the initial namespace, and $\epsilon > 0$ is a constant. This cost can be reduced to $O(\text{polylog } n)$ if adaptive test-and-set [6, 22] is used. Eberly, Higham, and Warpechowska-Gruca [20] obtained strong long-lived randomized renaming with amortized step complexity $O(n \log n)$. Reference [6] gave an algorithm guaranteeing a namespace of size ck and running in time $O(\log^2 k)$, both with high probability in k. In [4], Alistarh, Aspnes, Censor-Hillel, Gilbert and Zadimoghaddam gave a strong adaptive algorithm with $O(\log k)$ step complexity, which is optimal for these namespace requirements [5]. All these references implement test-and-set out of read-write registers, while we assume that test-and-set is given in hardware. We discuss our results in the read-write model at the end of Section 2.

Reference [5] shows a linear time lower bound for deterministic implementations of renaming in a polynomial namespace in n, and a logarithmic lower bound on the expected step complexity of adaptive ck-renaming against a strong adversary, when the namespace size is guaranteed in every execution. Both our algorithms circumvent the second bound, as discussed in Section 1.

The idea of splitting the available space into several disjoint levels to minimize the number of collisions, used in the ReBatching algorithm, is similar to the multi-level hashing schemes by Broder and Karlin [15] and Fotakis, Pagh, Sanders and Spirakis [21]. However, we consider a concurrent setting with an adaptive adversary, and use different analysis techniques.

4. NON-ADAPTIVE ALGORITHM

We present the ReBatching algorithm (for *relaxed batching*), which solves renaming using a namespace of size $(1 + \epsilon)n$, and has step complexity $O(\log \log n)$ w.h.p.

The algorithm allocates a shared memory array of TAS objects of size $m = (1 + \epsilon)n$, for some constant $\epsilon > 0$ that is a parameter of the algorithm. The idea is that each shared TAS object is associated with a name, and a process needs to win the TAS operation in order to acquire that name. The key to the performance of the algorithm is to probe TAS objects in a random fashion, but in a way that minimizes the number of failed probes by each process. E.g., if processes do just uniform random probes among all objects, then with probability $1 - o(1)$ some process will have to do $\Omega(\log n)$ probes before it acquires a name.

The TAS objects are arranged into disjoint *batches* $B_0, \ldots, B_\kappa$, where $\kappa = \lceil \log \log n \rceil$, and $|B_i| = b_i$ with

$$b_i = \begin{cases} n, & \text{if } i = 0; \\ \lceil \epsilon n / 2^i \rceil, & \text{if } 1 \leq i \leq \kappa. \end{cases} \tag{1}$$

We assume that n is sufficiently large so that the total size of batches does not exceed $m = (1 + \epsilon)n$. (We have $\sum_i b_i \leq n + \sum_{1 \leq i \leq \kappa} (\epsilon n / 2^i + 1) = (1 + \epsilon)n - \epsilon n / 2^\kappa + \kappa$, and $\epsilon n / 2^\kappa$ is greater than $\kappa = \lceil \log \log n \rceil$ when n is greater than a sufficiently large constant.)

```
Class ReBatching(n, ε)
```
/* $m = \lceil(1+\epsilon)n\rceil$ */
shared: array $B[0 \ldots m-1]$ of TAS objects
/* **for each** $0 \le i \le \kappa = \lceil\log\log n\rceil$,
    $B_i = B[s_i..s_i + b_i - 1]$, **where** $s_i = \sum_{0 \le j < i} b_j$
    and b_i is given in (1)   */

Method GetName()
1 **for** $0 \le i \le \kappa$ **do**
2 | $u \leftarrow$ TryGetName(i)
3 | **if** $u \ne -1$ **return** u
4 **end**
   /* backup phase   */
5 **for** $0 \le u \le m-1$ **do**
6 | **if** $B[u]$.TAS() $= 0$ **return** u
7 **end**
8 **return** -1

Method TryGetName(i)
   /* t_i is defined in (2)   */
9   **for** $1 \le j \le t_i$ **do**
10 | choose $x \in \{0, \ldots, b_i - 1\}$ unif. at random
11 | **if** $B_i[x]$.TAS() $= 0$ **return** $s_i + x$
12 **end**
13 **return** -1

Figure 1: The ReBatching algorithm.

To acquire a name, a process accesses the batches in increasing order of their index i. For each batch B_i, the process calls TAS on (at most) t_i objects from that batch chosen independently and uniformly at random. The process stops as soon as it wins one TAS operation. The number t_i of probes by a process on batch B_i is

$$t_i = \begin{cases} \lceil 17 \ln(8e/\epsilon)/\epsilon \rceil, & \text{if } i = 0; \\ 1, & \text{if } 1 \le i \le \kappa - 1; \quad (2) \\ \beta, & \text{if } i = \kappa, \end{cases}$$

where $\beta \ge 1$ is a constant that can be tuned to achieve the desired high probability on the event that all processes acquire names by these probes. As a backup, processes that fail to win a TAS despite trying on all batches proceed to call TAS on *all* objects sequentially. Our analysis will show that this backup phase is executed with very low probability.

Pseudocode for the algorithm is given in Figure 1.

Analysis. The proof of correctness for the algorithm is straightforward, therefore we focus on the analysis of its running time. In the rest of this section we prove the following theorem.

THEOREM 4.1. *For any fixed $\epsilon > 0$, the* ReBatching *algorithm for a namespace of size $(1+\epsilon)n$ uses $O(n)$ TAS objects and achieves w.h.p. step complexity at most $\log\log n + O(1)$ and total step complexity $O(n)$ against an adaptive adversary. (Both bounds hold also in expectation.)*

For each $1 \le i \le \kappa + 1$, let n_i be the total number of processes that execute t_{i-1} probes on B_{i-1} but fail in all of them to acquire a name. I.e., their call TryGetName($i-1$) returns -1 (line 2 of the pseudocode), and thus they must then call TryGetName(i) if $i \le \kappa$, or run the backup phase if

$i = \kappa + 1$. We will show now that n_i drops roughly as $n/2^{2^i}$. Let

$$n_i^* = \begin{cases} \epsilon n / 2^{2^i + i + \delta}, & \text{if } 1 \le i \le \kappa - 1; \\ \log^2 n, & \text{if } i = \kappa, \end{cases}$$

where $\delta > 0$ is an arbitrary small constant; let also $n_{\kappa+1}^* = 0$. Recall that β is the number t_κ of probes on B_κ.

LEMMA 4.2. *With probability $1 - 1/n^{\beta - o(1)}$, we have that $n_i \le n_i^*$ for all $1 \le i \le \kappa + 1$.*

PROOF. We will bound the probability of the events

$$\mathcal{E}_i := \begin{cases} n_1 > n_1^*, & \text{if } i = 0; \\ (n_{i+1} > n_{i+1}^*) \wedge (n_i \le n_i^*), & \text{if } 1 \le i \le \kappa. \end{cases}$$

The lemma the follows by an application of the union bound.

We bound first the probability that $n_1 \ge n_1^*$, i.e., at least n_1^* processes fail in all their t_0 probes on B_0. We assume that for each of the n process, all the t_0 random choices of objects from B_0 that the process will probe are decided in advance (and revealed to the adaptive adversary). Of course the process may end up not probing all those objects, as it may win some TAS sooner or crash. Then, the event that n_1^* of the n processes fail in all their t_0 probes on B_0, occurs only if the following event occurs: There is a set P of n_1^* processes, and a set $L \subseteq B_0$ of n_1^* objects from B_0, such that no process from P chooses any object from L. The reason is that since the size of B_0 is $b_0 = n$, for each process that fails to win any TAS in B_0 there is a distinct object in B_0 that is not probed by any process. For a fixed pair of sets P and L, the probability that no process from P chooses any object from L is

$$\left(1 - \frac{|L|}{b_0}\right)^{t_0|P|} = \left(1 - \frac{n_1^*}{n}\right)^{t_0 n_1^*} \le e^{-t_0(n_1^*)^2/n} = e^{-t_0 \alpha^2 n},$$

where $\alpha := n_1^*/n = \epsilon/2^{3+\delta}$. Further, the number of possibilities to choose a set P of n_1^* out of n processes and a set L of n_1^* objects from B_0 is

$$\binom{n}{n_1^*}\binom{b_0}{n_1^*} = \binom{n}{n_1^*}^2 \le \left(\frac{en}{n_1^*}\right)^{2n_1^*} = \left(\frac{e}{\alpha}\right)^{2\alpha n} = e^{2\alpha n \ln(e/\alpha)}.$$

From the union bound then, the probability that there is at least one pair P, L such that no process from set P chooses any object from set L is bounded by the product $e^{-t_0 \alpha^2 n} \cdot e^{2\alpha n \ln(e/\alpha)} = e^{-\Omega(n)}$. Therefore, the same bound holds for the event that $n_1 \ge n_1^*$, and thus

$$\Pr(\mathcal{E}_0) \le \Pr(n_1 \ge n_1^*) = e^{-\Omega(n)}.$$

Next we bound the probability of event $\mathcal{E}_i = (n_i \le n_i^*) \wedge (n_{i+1} > n_{i+1}^*)$, for the case of $1 \le i \le \kappa - 1$. Recall that each process does at most $t_i = 1$ probe on B_i. Consider all processes that do a probe on B_i but fail to win the TAS operation, and let $p_1, p_2, \ldots$ be the list of those processes, in the order in which they finish their last TAS operation on B_{i-1}. W.l.o.g. we assume that a list $\ell_1, \ell_2, \ldots$ of objects from B_i is chosen in advanced, each object chosen independently and uniformly at random, and that process p_j probes object ℓ_j of B_i if it is scheduled to do such a probe. We can now relate n_{i+1} to the number of collisions in list $\ell_1, \ell_2, \ldots$; a *collision* occurs in position j if $\ell_j = \ell_{j'}$ for some $j' < j$. The total number of collisions in the first n_i positions is then an upper bound on the number n_{i+1} of processes that do an unsuccessful probe in B_i. Since the event $\mathcal{E}_i$ we are interested in holds only if $n_i \leq n_i^*$, we consider just the first n_i^* entries in the list, $\ell_1, \ldots, \ell_{n_i^*}$. The probability of a collision in position j is at most $(j-1)/b_i$, as at most $j-1$ out of the b_i objects in B_i have already been selected. Thus, if X_j is the indicator random variable of the event that there is a collision in position j, then

$$\Pr(X_j = 1 \mid \ell_1 \ldots \ell_{j-1}) \leq (j-1)/b_i. \qquad (3)$$

The expectation of the total number of collisions in the first n_i^* positions is then

$$\mathbf{E}\left[\sum_{j=1}^{n_i^*} X_j\right] \leq \sum_{j=1}^{n_i^*} \frac{j-1}{b_i} \leq \frac{(n_i^*)^2/2}{b_i} \leq \frac{(\epsilon n/2^{2^i+i+\delta})^2/2}{\epsilon n/2^i}$$

$$= \epsilon n/2^{2^{i+1}+i+1+2\delta} \leq n_{i+1}^*/2^\delta.$$

Further, because of the special type of dependence (3) between the X_j, a simple coupling argument gives that the above sum of X_j is dominated by the sum of n_i^* independent binary random variables Y_j with $\Pr(Y_j) = (j-1)/b_i$ (see e.g., [12, Lemma 3.1], for a similar result). It follows then from Chernoff bounds that

$$\Pr\left(\sum_{j=1}^{n_i^*} X_j > n_{i+1}^*\right) = e^{-\Omega(n_{i+1}^*)} = 1/n^{\omega(1)},$$

and this implies $\Pr(\mathcal{E}_i) = 1/n^{\omega(1)}$.

It remains to bound the probability of $\mathcal{E}_\kappa = (n_\kappa \leq n_\kappa^*) \wedge (n_{\kappa+1} > 0)$. As before we decide in advance the $t_\kappa = \beta$ random choices of objects from B_i to be probed by the j-th process that does an unsuccessful probe on $B_{\kappa-1}$; let L_j denote the multi-set of those choices. It suffice to consider just $L_1, \ldots, L_{n_\kappa^*}$, as $\mathcal{E}_\kappa$ occurs only if $n_\kappa \leq n_\kappa^*$. We have that $n_{\kappa+1} > 0$ holds only if there is some $j \leq n_\kappa^*$ for which $L_j \subseteq \bigcup_{j \neq j' \leq n_\kappa^*} L_{j'}$, i.e., for some j, each of the objects contained in L_j is contained also in at least one other $L_{j'}$. As $\left|\bigcup_{j \neq j' \leq n_\kappa^*} L_{j'}\right| \leq t_\kappa(n_\kappa^* - 1)$, the probability of the latter event is bounded by

$$n_\kappa^* \left(\frac{t_\kappa(n_\kappa^* - 1)}{b_\kappa}\right)^{t_\kappa} = 1/n^{\beta - o(1)},$$

and thus $\Pr(\mathcal{E}_\kappa) = 1/n^{\beta - o(1)}$.

To complete the proof of Lemma 4.2, we observe that the event we are interested in, that for all $1 \leq i \leq \kappa + 1$ it holds $n_i \leq n_i^*$, is equivalent to $\bigwedge_{i=0}^{\kappa} \overline{\mathcal{E}_i} = 1 - \bigvee_{i=0}^{\kappa} \mathcal{E}_i$. The lemma now follows from the bounds we have shown for $\Pr(\mathcal{E}_i)$ and the union bound. $\square$

From Lemma 4.2 it follows that with probability $1 - 1/n^{\beta - o(1)}$, no process reaches the backup phase, any process executes at most $t_0 + (\kappa - 1) \cdot 1 + \beta = \log \log n + O(1)$ probes on all batches, the total number of probes by all processes is at most $nt_0 + \sum_{1 \leq i \leq \kappa} n_i^* t_i = O(n)$. Therefore, w.h.p. the step complexity is at most $\log \log n + O(1)$ and the total step complexity $O(n)$. Further, each process executes $O(n)$ steps in the worst-case (i.e., when it has to enter the backup phase and probe all m locations), thus the worst-case step complexity is $O(n)$ and the worst-case total step complexity is $O(n^2)$. It follows that for $\beta \geq 2$ the expected step complexity is $\log \log n + O(1)$, and for $\beta \geq 3$ the expected

total step complexity is $O(n)$. This completes the proof of Theorem 4.1.

5. ADAPTIVE ALGORITHMS

Next we present two adaptive renaming algorithms. The first one has step complexity $O((\log \log k)^2)$ w.h.p., and the second has total step complexity $O(k \log \log k)$ w.h.p. In both algorithms, the largest name assigned to any process is $O(k)$ w.h.p.

Our algorithms don't need to know the number n of processes in the system, but if they don't then they require unbounded space. In fact, for ease of exposition we present our algorithms in such a way that they use an unbounded number of ReBatching objects $R_1, R_2, \ldots$, where R_i provides a namespace of size $O(2^i)$ and thus is constructed from $O(2^i)$ TAS objects. If n is known, it is straight forward to modify the algorithms so that they use only the first $2^{\log n + 1}$ TAS objects and thus $O(n)$ TAS objects in total are sufficient.

5.1 Adaptive ReBatching

We describe now the algorithm with step complexity $O((\log \log k)^2)$, which we call AdaptiveReBatching. The algorithm uses slightly modified ReBatching objects, in which the backup phase (lines 5–7 in Figure 1) is omitted, and thus a GetName call returns -1 if no name is acquired during any of the TryGetName calls (in line 2). A collection $R_1, R_2, \ldots$ of such ReBatching objects is used, where object R_i provides a namespace of size $m_i = (1 + \epsilon)n_i$ with $n_i = 2^i$. Precisely, the namespace of R_i is $\{s_i, \ldots, s_i + m_i - 1\}$, where $s_i = \sum_{1 \leq j < i} m_j$.

Each process p first tries to get a name by doubling the index of the ReBatching object it accesses after each unsuccessful trial. Precisely, p repeatedly calls R_{2^ℓ}.GetName for $\ell = 0, 1, \ldots$ until it succeeds in getting a name; let 2^{ℓ^*} be the index of the object from which p gets that name. Next, p tries to acquire a smaller name by doing a binary search on objects $R_{2^{\ell^*-1}+1}, \ldots, R_{2^{\ell^*}}$. Precisely, p initially sets $a \leftarrow 2^{\ell^*-1} + 1$ and $b \leftarrow 2^{\ell^*}$; while $a < b$, it sets $d \leftarrow \lfloor (a+b)/2 \rfloor$, and calls R_d.GetName; if the call returns a name then the value of b is updated setting $b \leftarrow d$, otherwise a's value is updated letting $a \leftarrow d + 1$. Once $a \geq b$, p stops and gets assigned the name it acquired from R_b.

THEOREM 5.1. *The* AdaptiveReBatching *algorithm has step complexity* $O((\log \log k)^2)$ *w.h.p., and the largest name it assigns to any process is* $O(k)$ *w.h.p.*

PROOF. From Theorem 4.1 and Lemma 4.2, we obtain that w.h.p. all GetName calls to objects R_i with index $i \geq \log k$ (and thus $n_i \geq k$) succeed in returning a name and complete in $O(\log \log n_i)$ steps. Precisely, for each $i \geq \log k$, all R_i.GetName calls succeed with probability $1 - 1/n_i^c$, for a constant $c > 0$, and thus by the union bound, all R_i.GetName calls for *all* $i \geq \log k$ succeed with probability at least $1 - \sum_{i \geq \log k} 1/n_i^c = 1 - O(1/k^c)$.

It follows that in the first part of the algorithm (in which processes access objects R_{2^ℓ} for $\ell = 1, 2, \ldots$), w.h.p. every process acquires a name from some object R_i with $i \leq 2^{\lceil \log \log k \rceil}$, after accessing at most $\lceil \log \log k \rceil + 1$ objects (namely, objects R_ℓ for $0 \leq \ell \leq \lceil \log \log k \rceil$), spending at most $\log \log k + O(1)$ steps on each of them. Thus, processes complete this part in $O((\log \log k)^2)$ steps w.h.p.

In the binary search part, a process searches among at most $2^{\lceil \log \log k \rceil}$ objects, thus it accesses at most $\log \log k +$

204

$O(1)$ of them, spending again at most $\log \log k + O(1)$ steps on each. Thus, this second part takes $O((\log \log k)^2)$ steps w.h.p., as well.

Finally, since w.h.p. all calls $R_i.\texttt{GetName}$ for $i \geq k$ return a name, binary search guarantees that every process will finally obtain a name from some object R_i with $n_i \leq 2^{\lceil \log k \rceil}$. Thus the largest name is w.h.p. at most $\sum_{0 \leq i \leq \lceil \log k \rceil} m_i \leq 4(1+\epsilon)k$. $\square$

5.2 Faster Adaptive ReBatching

The `AdaptiveReBatching` algorithm presented in the previous section has total step complexity $\Theta(k(\log \log k)^2)$. We propose now a variant of this algorithm, called `FastAdaptiveReBatching`, which reduces the total step complexity to $O(k \log \log k)$. Pseudocode for this algorithm is provided in Figure 2.

As before, we use a collection $R_1, R_2, \ldots$ of `ReBatching` objects, where object R_i, for $i \geq 1$, has parameter $n_i = 2^i$, but now we require that $\epsilon = 1$ and thus the namespace of R_i has size $2n_i = 2^{i+1}$. The general idea is the same as in the previous algorithm: A process searches for the smallest index i^*, such that it can acquire a name from R_{i^*} but not from R_{i^*-1} (implying that at least $\Omega(n_{i^*})$ processes participate). The difference to the previous algorithm is that when a process tries to get a name from object R_i, it executes only a constant number of probes on this object, by calling `TryGetName`, as opposed to $\Theta(\log \log n_i)$ many, when calling `GetName`. This may yield "false negative" results, so a process may have to revisit an object R_i again at a later point if it has not already obtained a name from some object R_j with index $j < i$. Therefore, a process keeps track of a lower bound a, and an upper bound b on i^*, as well as the total number t of times it has executed `TryGetName` on object R_a. The upper bound b is "hard" in the sense that the process has already obtained a name u from R_b. The lower bound a is "weak" meaning that it might still be possible for the process to find a name from some object R_i with $i < a$.

Processes try to find i^* and to acquire a name from R_{i^*} using a recursive method $\texttt{Search}(a, b, u, t)$. A call to this method requires that $a < b$, that u is a name the process has already acquired from R_b, and that the process has previously called $R_a.\texttt{TryGetName}(j)$ for $j = 0, \ldots, t-1$. The method guarantees to return a name u' from some object R_i, $a \leq i \leq b$, that the process has acquired (possibly $u' = u$ and $i = b$). Moreover, if $i > a$, then the process has called $\texttt{TryGetName}(j)$ on R_{i-1} for each $j = 0, \ldots, \kappa(i-1)$, where $\kappa(s) = \lceil \log(s) \rceil$ is the maximum batch index in R_s; thus, w.h.p. the number of processes participating is $\Omega(n_i)$, and so u' is not "too large". But if $i = a$, then no guarantees are provided by `Search` on the number of times the process has tried to find a name in R_{i-1}.

$\texttt{Search}(a, b, u, t)$ is implemented as follows. If $t > \kappa(a)$, the process can simply return u (in line 11) because it has already executed enough `TryGetName` calls on R_a (the implementation guarantees that $b = a + 1$ in this case). If $t \leq \kappa(a)$, the process executes $R_a.\texttt{TryGetName}(t)$, and if the call returns a name, the `Search` method can simply return that name (lines 12–13); in this case a can be used as a new upper bound. Otherwise, the process tries to improve the upper bound b: It chooses the median $d = \lceil (a+b)/2 \rceil$ of the indices $a+1, \ldots, b$ (line 14). If $d < b$, then the process uses d as its new lower bound and tries to obtain a new name u from $R_d, \ldots, R_b$ using a recursive call $\texttt{Search}(d, b, u, 0)$

Class `FastAdaptiveReBatching`

shared: $R_1, R_2, \ldots$, where R_i is a $\texttt{ReBatching}(n_i, \epsilon)$ object with $n_i = 2^i$ and $\epsilon = 1$
/* R_i's namespace is $\{2^{i+1}, \ldots, 2^{i+2} - 1\}$. */

Method `GetName()`

```
1  ℓ ← −1
2  repeat
3  |   ℓ ← ℓ + 1
4  |   u ← R_{2^ℓ}.TryGetName(0)
5  until u ≠ −1
6  while ℓ ≥ 1 and u ∈ R_{2^ℓ} do
7  |   u ← Search(2^{ℓ−1}, 2^ℓ, u, 1)
8  |   ℓ ← ℓ − 1
9  end
10 return u
```

Method `Search(a, b, u, t)`

```
   /* κ(i) = ⌈log(i)⌉                                 */
11 if t > κ(a) return u
12 u' ← R_a.TryGetName(t)
13 if u' ≠ −1 return u'
14 d ← ⌈(a + b)/2⌉
15 if d < b then u ← Search(d, b, u, 0)
16 if u ∈ R_d then u ← Search(a, d, u, t + 1)
17 return u
```

Figure 2: The `FastAdaptiveReBatching` algorithm.

(line 15). If that method returns a name from R_i for some $i > d$, then the ongoing `Search` can finish and return the name u in line 17: It is guaranteed that $\kappa(i-1)$ unsuccessful `TryGetName` calls on R_{i-1} have been performed. If the recursive `Search` call in line 15 returns a name from R_d, then d becomes the new upper bound and the process continues its recursive search by calling $\texttt{Search}(a, d, u, t+1)$ in line 16. Finally, in case $d = b$, and thus $b = a + 1$, the process simply calls $\texttt{Search}(a, b, u, t+1)$ in line 16, trying to either get a name from R_a, or confirmation that a is the right lower bound.

Using `Search` the renaming algorithm works as follows: A process first searches for an initial upper bound similarly to the previous algorithm, by executing `TryGetName(0)` on R_{2^ℓ} for each $\ell = 0, 1, \ldots$, until it finds a name (lines 1–5). Once it has found the first name u in R_{2^ℓ}, its upper bound is $a = 2^\ell$ and its lower bound is $b = 2^{\ell-1}$. Then the process calls the method $\texttt{Search}(2^{\ell-1}, 2^\ell, u, 1)$ in line 7. (The last parameter is 1 instead of 0, because $R_2^{\ell-1}$ has already been accessed once by the process.) If this call returns a name in R_i for some $i > 2^{\ell-1}$, then the process can finish and use that name—since it has executed $R_{i-1}.\texttt{TryGetName}(j)$ calls for $j = 1, \ldots, \kappa(i-1)$, we have w.h.p. that $\Omega(n_i)$ processes are participating. If the `Search` call returns a name in $R_{2^{\ell-1}}$, then the process has to consider smaller `ReBatching` objects, so it sets $\ell = \ell - 1$ and repeats the `Search` step with the smaller upper and lower bounds.

In the rest of this section we sketch a proof of the following theorem.

THEOREM 5.2. *The `FastAdaptiveReBatching` algorithm has total step complexity $O(k \log \log k)$ w.h.p., and the largest name it assigns to any process is $O(k)$ w.h.p.*

To facilitate the proof, we give an equivalent description of the algorithm in terms of the underlying binary search tree on objects $R_1, R_2, \ldots$ In this tree, for each index i that is a power of two, objects $R_1, \ldots, R_{i-1}$ form a perfect binary subtree, and each internal node R_j has the property that objects in its left (right) subtree have indices smaller (resp. greater) than j. (Thus, odd-indexed objects are the leaves, and each internal node's index is the average of its two children's indices.) In the following we will often say 'node i' instead of 'node R_i'. The FastAdaptiveReBatching algorithm can now be described in terms of the above tree as follows.

A process p starts from the leftmost leaf (node 1), and walks upwards (along the path $2^0, 2^1, \ldots$), calling TryGetName(0) on each node it visits, until it gets a name (lines 1–5). We will see that w.h.p. this happens after traversing at most $\log \log k + O(1)$ nodes, thus p acquires a name from some node $2^\ell = O(\log k)$. Next, p tries to get a smaller name by searching in the left subtree of node 2^ℓ (lines 6–9). In this search, p may visit the same node more than once, and each time it does it calls TryGetName(t), where t is the number of times it has visited the node before. Precisely, p visits first the root $2^{\ell-1}$ of the left subtree of node 2^ℓ, and for each node a that p visits:

• If the TryGetName call on node a (line 12) fails to return a name, then p proceeds to visit the right child d of a if a is an internal node (line 15); or if a is a leaf, p visits a again (line 16) until it finally gets a name (line 13) or has tried unsuccessfully on all batches of a (line 11).

• Suppose now that the TryGetName call on a (line 12) succeeds in acquiring a name. Standard binary search would move to the left child of a, or finish if a is a leaf. Here, however, p tries again on the most recently visited node a' from which p has not succeeded in acquiring a name yet (line 7 or 16). (Node a' can be found by following the upward path from a; a' is the first node to be reached through its right child.) If p succeeds in getting a name from a', then it repeats the above procedure with a' in place of a. Otherwise, it visits the left child of a; or if a is a leaf it keeps trying on a' until it gets a name or fails on all batches of a', as before.

The formal proof that the above description is equivalent to the FastAdaptiveReBatching algorithm is omitted due to space restrictions.

We first bound the index of the object from which a process gets a name in the first phase of the algorithm.

CLAIM 5.3. *W.h.p. in the loop in lines 1–5 every process gets a name from some object R_i with index $i \leq i_{max}$, where*

$$i_{max} := 2^{\lceil \log \log k \rceil + 2} < 8 \log k.$$

The claim holds because $n_{i_{max}} \geq k^4$, thus the probability that two fixed processes that access $R_{i_{max}}$ make the same random choice for their first probe is at most $1/n^4$. Taking the union bound over the at most k^2 pairs yields the claim.

Next we bound the total number of steps by processes before they obtain a *small* name, where a name is *small* if it comes from an object R_i with index $i \leq i_{min}$ for

$$i_{min} := \lceil \log k \rceil + 2.$$

For each index $i \geq i_{min}$ and batch j of R_i, we bound the number of processes accessing that batch. For simplicity, we assume that the number of probes per process on each batch is the same for all batches, and equal to $t_* := \max_j \{t_j\}$ (see Eq. (2)); thus $t_* = O(1)$.

Let $\mathcal{P}$ denote the path in the tree between nodes i_{max} and i_{min}. For each $i_{min} \leq i \leq i_{max}$, let h_i be the distance of node i from path $\mathcal{P}$. Further, for each $l \geq 0$, let $k_l = k/2^{2^l + l - 1}$.

CLAIM 5.4. *W.h.p. for all pairs i, j with $i_{min} \leq i \leq i_{max}$ and $0 \leq j \leq \lceil \log(i) \rceil$, we have that at most $k_{h_i + j}$ processes call R_i.TryGetName(j).*

The proof of Claim 5.4 is similar to that of Lemma 4.2, and relies on the following result.

CLAIM 5.5. *Let $i \geq i_{min}$, $0 \leq j \leq \lceil \log(i) \rceil$, and $l \geq j$. The probability that at most k_l processes call R_i.TryGetName(j) and more than k_{l+1} of these calls fail to return a name is bounded by $1/n_i^{t_* - o(1)}$.*

To prove Claim 5.5 we distinguish two cases. If $k_{l+1} = \omega(i)$, then we use the same collision-counting argument as in the proof of Lemma 4.2 (for batches 1 up to $\kappa - 1$). If $k_{l+1} = O(i)$, then we employ the argument used for the last batch in the proof of Lemma 4.2.

To show Claim 5.4, we use Claim 5.5 and the union bound to obtain w.h.p. for all pairs i, j with $i_{min} \leq i \leq i_{max}$ and $0 \leq j \leq \lceil \log(i) \rceil$, that either more than $k_{h_i + j}$ processes call R_i.TryGetName(j) or at most $k_{h_i + l + 1}$ of these calls fail to return a name. We complete the proof by showing that if the above event holds, then for every pair i, j at most $k_{h_i + l}$ processes call R_i.TryGetName(j). The proof of the last statement is by induction on $l = h_i + j$. In this induction, the more interesting case is when $j = 0$ and $h_i > 0$, and thus we must argue that no more than k_{h_i} processes call R_i.TryGetName(0): Consider the first node $r < i$ in the path P_i from i to $\mathcal{P}$; r the first node along P_i reached through its right child. From $\mathcal{P}$'s definition it follows that such a node r exists and $r \geq i_{min}$. The distance from i to r is $h_i - h_r$, and thus there are $h_i - h_r - 1$ nodes between them. Each node that accesses R_i must have previously successfully obtained names from those $h_i - h_r - 1$ nodes, and must have failed to get names from batches $0, \ldots, (h_i - h_r - 1)$ of R_r. Thus, the number of nodes that access i is bounded by the number of processes that failed to obtain a name by call R_r.TryGetName($h_i - h_r - 1$). The latter number is bounded by $k_{h_r + (h_i - h_r)} = k_{h_i}$, by the induction hypothesis and the event we assumed at the beginning.

From Claim 5.4 it follows that the number of steps by processes on objects $i \geq i_{min}$ is bound w.h.p. by the sum of all $k_{h_i + j}$; we show this to be $O(k \log \log k)$. Further we show a deterministic bound of $O(k \log \log k)$ on the steps by processes on objects R_i with $i < i_{min}$, before these processes acquire a small name. Thus, we have the following result.

LEMMA 5.6. *The total number of steps by all processes before they acquire a small name is $O(k \log \log k)$ w.h.p.*

It remains to bound the steps by processes *after* they have acquired a small name. As processes do not know k, they continue to search for even smaller names. We observe that no process does more than $O(\log \log k)$ *consecutive* failed TryGetName calls (on the same or different objects): After the first $O(\log \log k)$ of them the process reaches a leaf, and after $O(\log \log k)$ additional ones the process stops. Further, no more than $O(k)$ TryGetName calls can be successful on objects R_i with $i \leq i_{min}$, as they have $O(k)$ names in total. The next (deterministic) bound then follows.

LEMMA 5.7. *The total number of steps by processes after they acquire a small name is bounded by $O(k \log \log k)$.*

To complete the proof of Theorem 5.2, we argue that w.h.p. every process acquires a name from some object R_i with $i \leq \lceil \log k \rceil$. The reason is that a process returns a name from R_i only after it has tried and failed on all batches of R_{i-1}, and if $i > \lceil \log k \rceil$ this happens with probability polynomially small in k.

6. LOWER BOUND

Our lower bound shows that, under reasonable conditions, an oblivious adversary can force some process in any loose renaming algorithm using only TAS objects to take $\Omega(\log \log n)$ steps. For simplicity, the lower bound assumes a non-adaptive algorithm. Formally, we show:

THEOREM 6.1. *For any algorithm that assigns unique names to n processes using $s = O(n)$ TAS objects, where the initial namespace has size $M \geq n^2$ and the output namespace has size $m = O(n)$, there exists an oblivious adversary strategy that, with constant probability, forces at least one process to take $\Omega(\log \log n)$ steps.*

Proof Strategy. The proof starts with a sequence of reductions. We first reduce the problem of renaming using TAS to the problem of arranging for each process to win some TAS in a related model. We then show that every process wins a TAS only if it wins a TAS in a layered execution where each round of operations applies to locations in a new array of test-and-sets that replicates the collection used by the original algorithm.

Next, we construct an initial, independent Poisson distribution on the number of processes applying each sequence of probes. Even though processes learn information from losing test-and-sets in early rounds, by carefully pruning out processes we can restore independence between the pruned survivors. This reduces the problem to one where each class of processes loses with a fixed, independent probability in each round regardless of the actions of other processes. This is sufficient to show that some processes remain after $\Theta(\log \log n)$ rounds.

Preliminaries. We assume that processes are deterministic, and that the behavior of a process is fully determined by its initial name. We assume an oblivious adversary, so the lower bound extends to randomized algorithms by Yao's Principle [34].

The behavior of a process with a given initial name is a **type**, which specifies what operations it carries out. A type is a function from sequences of TAS return values (0 or 1) to operations $\text{TAS}(T[j])$ or $\textbf{return}(j)$, where $\text{TAS}(T[j])$ applies a TAS operation to $T[j]$, $1 \leq j \leq s$, and $\textbf{return}(j)$ returns the name j, $1 \leq j \leq m$. An algorithm is a (possibly random) assignment of types to processes. We will show a lower bound for any fixed assignment of types, and use Yao's Principle [34] to extend this to randomized algorithms.

An adversary controls the interleaving of operations in the system. The adversary is oblivious, which means that it chooses a schedule consisting of a sequence of process ids without regard to the types of the processes. At each step, the next process in the sequence carries out the operation selected by its type based on the outcome of previous operations; if this operation is $\textbf{return}(j)$, the process chooses name j and executes only no-ops if scheduled again.

Recall that a random variable X is **Poisson** with **rate** λ if $\Pr[X = k] = e^{-\lambda} \lambda^k / k!$; we indicate this by $X \sim \text{Pois}(\lambda)$. The rate λ also gives both the expectation and variance of X. Let $P_\lambda(n) = \sum_{k=0}^{n} e^{-\lambda} \lambda^k / k!$ be the cumulative distribution function $\Pr[X \leq n]$ for $X \sim \text{Pois}(\lambda)$.

Due to space limitations, the proofs of the technical claims have been deferred to the full version of this paper.

6.1 Reductions and Adversarial Execution

To simplify the lower bound argument, we constrain the interaction between processes through a sequence of reductions. The first eliminates the distinction between $\text{TAS}(T[j])$ and $\textbf{return}(s)$ operations; in the revised problem, a process acquires a name by *winning* a TAS object. (Recall that a process **wins** a TAS object if it is the first to access it.) In the reduced problem, $\textbf{return}(j)$ operations are replaced by $\text{TAS}(T[j])$ operations on a larger array in the code of each process (which is given by its *type*).

LEMMA 6.2. *For any renaming algorithm A on s TAS objects, with an output namespace of size m, there exists an algorithm A' on $s + m$ TAS objects, such that for any schedule σ involving n processes, if every process in σ chooses a unique name when running algorithm A, every process in σ wins some TAS object in algorithm A'.*

For the second reduction, we replace the single array T of TAS objects with a sequence of arrays T_ℓ, where each array T_ℓ is of the same length as T, and the ℓ-th TAS operation by a process is always applied to an object in T_ℓ. We also show that we can assume that any process leaves the protocol immediately if it wins a TAS.

LEMMA 6.3. *Let A be an algorithm in which processes carry out operations on an array of TAS objects $T[1] \ldots T[s]$. Let A' be a modified algorithm in which a process (a) leaves the protocol immediately as soon as it wins a TAS; and (b) carries out its ℓ-th TAS operation (if it has not already left) on $T_\ell[j]$, where j is the index yielded by its type in A assuming it loses its first $\ell - 1$ TAS operations. Then if A and A' are run with the same schedule σ, the set S' of processes that appear in σ but fail to win a TAS in A' is a subset of the corresponding set S of processes that appear in σ but do not win a TAS in A.*

The Execution. We now construct a layered schedule σ such that any algorithm takes $\Omega(\log \log n)$ layers with constant probability to reduce the number of remaining processes to a constant. Each layer of σ consists of a single step by each process instance. These steps are ordered by a random permutation that is chosen uniformly and independently for each layer. Since σ does not depend on the actions of the algorithm, it can be supplied by an oblivious adversary.

The main challenge is that, in such an execution, the number of processes that have not yet won a TAS, and thus must continue, may drop very fast as we proceed through layers. To lower bound the number of processes that continue, we use a Poisson approximation (see, e.g., [30, §5.4]) to make the initial number of processes accessing each TAS independent, and apply a coupling gadget to keep the surviving processes in each layer independent of each other. We cannot apply this directly to the original process, since, for example, if p and q both access the same TAS object $T_\ell[j]$, the fact that

207

p lost it may increase the conditional probability that q lost it as well. We *mark* a subset of survivors for each TAS such that the counts of marked processes are independent. Marking *does* require observing the execution of the algorithm, but it is only used in the analysis and does not affect the behavior of the algorithm or the adversary.

Precisely, for $i = 1 \ldots M$, let X_i^0 be independent Poisson random variables, where X_i^0 has rate λ_i^0. We interpret X_i^0 as the number of instances of process p_i that are included in the execution σ. If $X_i^0 > 1$, we are in trouble, but we ensure that the chance that this occurs is small by choosing small enough λ_i^0; the cost of infrequently generating a bad schedule will be compensated for by the useful properties of Poisson random variables that we exploit later in the proof.

We define *marked* processes to be the processes that do not win a TAS up to some point in the execution. Formally, for a layer ℓ and a process p_i, the variable X_i^ℓ indicates the number of *marked* instances of p_i. Initially, after 0 layers, all instances of all processes are marked. After $\ell \geq 1$ layers, which processes are marked is precisely determined by a procedure described in Section 6.2. Our goal is to obtain a lower bound on the number of such processes in each layer.

We will show that our marking procedure ensures that the X_i^ℓ are independent Poisson random variables, with rates that evolve predictably as a consequence of the probabilities that the various types assign to each TAS object $T_\ell[j]$. Then the total number of marked processes in each layer ℓ will also follow a Poisson distribution, with rate $\lambda^\ell = \sum_i \lambda_i^\ell$.

6.2 Execution Analysis

We start by carefully constructing a Poisson random variable Y with the property that, if we mark the last Y processes to access a TAS, then we get independent Poisson counts on the number of marked processes of each type.

LEMMA 6.4. *Fix an index set S, and let $X_i \sim \text{Pois}(\lambda_i)$ be independent random variables, for all $i \in S$. Let $Z = \sum_{i \in S} X_i \sim \text{Pois}(\lambda)$, where $\lambda = \sum_{i \in S} \lambda_i$. Let $Y \sim \text{Pois}(\gamma)$ be a random variable that is coupled with Z such that $Y \leq \max(0, Z - 1)$ always and Y is conditionally independent of the X_i conditioned on Z. Choose a permutation π of a string σ consisting of X_i instances of each i in S uniformly at random. Let X_i' for each i in S be the number of instances of i that occur in the last Y positions in π. Then the X_i' are independent Poisson random variables with $X_i' \leq X_1$, and $X_i' \sim \text{Pois}\left(\lambda_i \cdot \frac{\gamma}{\lambda}\right)$.*

We will now show that for every $Z \sim \text{Pois}(\lambda)$, there is a coupled random variable $Y \sim \text{Pois}(\min(\lambda^2/4, \lambda/4))$ with $Y \leq \max(0, X - 1)$ always. Since our construction of Y does not depend on the decomposition of Z into X_i, it can also be made to have the conditional independence property required by Lemma 6.4. To demonstrate the existence of the desired Y, we consider the cumulative distribution functions of Z and Y. We prove the following.

LEMMA 6.5. *For all $n \in \mathbb{N}$ and all $\lambda \geq 0$, $P_\lambda(n+1) \leq P_{\min(\lambda^2/4, \lambda/4)}(n)$.*

Marked processes. We now have the machinery we need to characterize how many processes are marked at each layer. We first describe the marking procedure precisely.

In layer ℓ, for each TAS object $T_\ell[j]$ there is a set of types S_j^ℓ that apply an operation to $T_\ell[j]$. Let $Z_j^\ell = \sum_{i \in S_j^\ell} X_i^\ell$ be the number of marked processes that access $T_\ell[j]$, and let $Y_j^\ell \leq \max(0, X - 1)$ be the coupled Poisson variable whose existence is implied by Lemma 6.5. Let the last Y_j^ℓ marked processes to access $T_\ell[j]$ keep their marks for the next round; note that because $Y_j^\ell < Z_j^\ell$ when Z_j^ℓ is nonzero, none of these processes can be the first to access T_j^ℓ. From Lemma 6.4, the counts $X_i^{\ell+1}$ of processes of each type that retain their marks are independent Poisson random variables, and the rate $\lambda_i^{\ell+1}$ of X_i^ℓ is equal to $\lambda_i^\ell \left(\mathbf{E}[Y_j^\ell] / \mathbf{E}[Z_j^\ell] \right)$ where type i accesses $T_\ell[j]$ in layer ℓ.

We now show that no matter how types choose TAS objects, the total expected number of marked processes does not drop too fast from layer ℓ to layer $\ell + 1$.

LEMMA 6.6. *Let s be the number of TAS objects in layer ℓ. If $\lambda^\ell \leq s/2$ then $\lambda^{\ell+1} \geq \frac{(\lambda^\ell)^2}{4s}$. If $\lambda^\ell > s/2$ then $\lambda^{\ell+1} \geq \frac{\lambda^\ell}{4}$.*

Final Argument. We now complete the proof of Theorem 6.1. Assume an algorithm A that assigns unique names from 1 to $m = O(n)$ to n processes out of an initial namespace of $M \geq n^2$ using $s = O(n)$ TAS objects. Note that m and s must both be at least n.

To build the adversarial execution, we choose $X_i^0 \sim \text{Pois}(n/2M)$ initial instances of each process i, so that $\lambda^0 = n/2$, and construct the rest of the layered execution σ with $s+m$ TAS objects per layer as described in the preceding sections.

Let $r^\ell = \lambda^\ell/(s+m)$ be the ratio between the total expected number of marked processes after ℓ layers and the number of TAS objects in each layer. For $\ell = 0$ this gives $r^0 = (n/2)/(s+m)$, which is both $\Omega(1)$ and bounded above by $1/4$. For $\ell \geq 1$, $r^\ell \leq r^0 \leq 1/4$, which implies $\lambda^\ell = (s+m)r^\ell \leq (s+m)/2$. Lemma 6.6 then shows that $r^{\ell+1} = \lambda^{\ell+1}/(s+m) \geq (\lambda^\ell)^2/4(s+m)^2 = ((s+m)r^\ell)^2/4(s+m)^2 = (r^\ell)^2/4$.

We solve the recurrence to get $r^\ell \geq (r^0)^{2^\ell}/4^{(2^\ell-1)} = 4(r^0/4)^{2^\ell}$. Choosing $\ell = \lfloor \lg \lg(s+m) + \lg \lg(4/r_0) \rfloor = \Omega(\log \log n)$ gives $r^\ell \geq 4(r^0/4)^{\lg(s+m)\lg(4/r_0)} = 4/(s+m)$. Hence the expected number of surviving processes at layer $\ell = \Omega(\log \log n)$ is $\lambda^\ell \geq 4$.

To complete the argument, we apply the union bound to all the ways in which the procedure generating the schedule may fail. First, our initial choice of processes might include more than n processes. Since $\mathbf{E}[X^0] = \lambda^0 = n/2$, this occurs with probability at most $1/2$. Second, our initial choice of processes might include two or more copies of the same process. For each type i, $\Pr[X_i^0 \geq 2] = 1 - e^{-\lambda_i^0}(1 + \lambda_i^0) \leq 1 - (1 - \lambda_i^0)(1 + \lambda_i^0) = (\lambda_i^0)^2 = (n/2M)^2$. Summing the bound over all M types gives a bound of $M(n/2M)^2 = n^2/4M \leq 1/4$ on the probability that any of these events occur. Finally, we must consider the possibility that there are no marked processes after round ℓ. This occurs with probability $e^{-\lambda^\ell} \leq e^{-4}$.

It follows that we get an execution with at least one marked process (and thus at least one process that has not yet acquired a name) after $\Omega(\log \log n)$ layers with probability at least $1 - 1/2 - 1/4 - e^{-4} \geq 0.23168 = \Omega(1)$. This concludes the proof of Theorem 6.1.

7. CONCLUSION AND FUTURE WORK

We presented sub-logarithmic randomized algorithms for loose renaming against a strong adversarial scheduler, and a lower bound suggesting that $\Omega(\log \log n)$ is an inherent threshold when using linear space. Our algorithms circumvent the classic logarithmic information-based lower bounds, e.g., [29], either by exploiting extra information about maximal contention n, or by allowing for error in the namespace size. Thus, a natural extension of our work would be to exploit these ideas for sub-logarithmic implementations of other concurrent data structures. Additional directions for future work would be to improve the individual step complexity for adaptive renaming, and to generalize the lower bound technique.

8. REFERENCES

[1] Y. Afek, H. Attiya, A. Fouren, G. Stupp, and D. Touitou. Long-lived renaming made adaptive. In *Proc. of 18th PODC*, pages 91–103, 1999.

[2] Y. Afek and M. Merritt. Fast, wait-free $(2k-1)$-renaming. In *Proc. of 18th PODC*, pages 105–112, 1999.

[3] D. Alistarh and J. Aspnes. Sub-logarithmic test-and-set against a weak adversary. In *Proc. of 25th DISC*, pages 97–109, 2011.

[4] D. Alistarh, J. Aspnes, K. Censor-Hillel, S. Gilbert, and M. Zadimoghaddam. Optimal-time adaptive strong renaming, with applications to counting. In *Proc. of 30th PODC*, pages 239–248, 2011.

[5] D. Alistarh, J. Aspnes, S. Gilbert, and R. Guerraoui. The complexity of renaming. In *Proc. of 52nd FOCS*, pages 718–727, 2011.

[6] D. Alistarh, H. Attiya, S. Gilbert, A. Giurgiu, and R. Guerraoui. Fast randomized test-and-set and renaming. In *Proc. of 24th DISC*, pages 94–108, 2010.

[7] J. Aspnes. Faster randomized consensus with an oblivious adversary. In *Proc. of 31st PODC*, pages 1–8, 2012.

[8] H. Attiya, A. Bar-Noy, D. Dolev, D. Peleg, and R. Reischuk. Renaming in an asynchronous environment. *J. of the ACM*, 37(3):524–548, 1990.

[9] H. Attiya and T. Djerassi-Shintel. Time bounds for decision problems in the presence of timing uncertainty and failures. *J. of Parallel Distrib. Comp.*, 61(8):1096–1109, 2001.

[10] H. Attiya and A. Fouren. Adaptive and efficient algorithms for lattice agreement and renaming. *SIAM J. on Comp.*, 31(2):642–664, 2001.

[11] H. Attiya and A. Paz. Counting-based impossibility proofs for renaming and set agreement. In *Proc. of 26th DISC*, pages 356–370, 2012.

[12] Y. Azar, A. Broder, A. Karlin, and E. Upfal. Balanced allocations. *SIAM J. on Comp.*, 29(1):180–200, 1999.

[13] A. Bar-Noy and D. Dolev. Shared-memory vs. message-passing in an asynchronous distributed environment. In *Proc. of 8th PODC*, pages 307–318, 1989.

[14] M. Bender and S. Gilbert. Mutual exclusion with $O(\log^2 \log n)$ amortized work. In *Proc. of 52nd FOCS*, pages 728–737, 2011.

[15] A. Broder and A. Karlin. Multilevel adaptive hashing. In *Proc. of 1st SODA*, pages 43–53, 1990.

[16] A. Brodsky, F. Ellen, and P. Woelfel. Fully-adaptive algorithms for long-lived renaming. *Distr. Comp.*, 24(2):119–134, 2011.

[17] J. Burns and G. Peterson. The ambiguity of choosing. In *Proc. of 8th PODC*, pages 145–157, 1989.

[18] A. Castañeda and S. Rajsbaum. New combinatorial topology bounds for renaming: the lower bound. *Distr. Comp.*, 22(5-6):287–301, 2010.

[19] A. Castañeda and S. Rajsbaum. New combinatorial topology bounds for renaming: The upper bound. *J. of the ACM*, 59(1):3, 2012.

[20] W. Eberly, L. Higham, and J. Warpechowska-Gruca. Long-lived, fast, waitfree renaming with optimal name space and high throughput. In *Proc. of 12th DISC*, pages 149–160, 1998.

[21] D. Fotakis, R. Pagh, P. Sanders, and P. G. Spirakis. Space efficient hash tables with worst case constant access time. *Theory of Comp. Syst.*, 38(2):229–248, 2005.

[22] G. Giakkoupis and P. Woelfel. On the time and space complexity of randomized test-and-set. In *Proc. of 31st PODC*, pages 19–28, 2012.

[23] G. Giakkoupis and P. Woelfel. A tight RMR lower bound for randomized mutual exclusion. In *Proc. of 44th ACM STOC*, pages 983–1002, 2012.

[24] W. Golab, L. Higham, and P. Woelfel. Linearizable implementations do not suffice for randomized distributed computation. In *Proceedings of the 43rd annual ACM symposium on Theory of computing*, STOC '11, pages 373–382, New York, NY, USA, 2011. ACM.

[25] D. Hendler and P. Woelfel. Adaptive randomized mutual exclusion in sub-logarithmic expected time. In *Proc. of 29th PODC*, pages 141–150, 2010.

[26] D. Hendler and P. Woelfel. Randomized mutual exclusion with sub-logarithmic RMR-complexity. *Distr. Comp.*, 24(1):3–19, 2011.

[27] M. Herlihy, V. Luchangco, and M. Moir. The repeat offender problem: A mechanism for supporting dynamic-sized, lock-free data structures. In *Proc. of 16th DISC*, pages 339–353, 2002.

[28] M. Herlihy and N. Shavit. The topological structure of asynchronous computability. *J. of the ACM*, 46(2):858–923, 1999.

[29] P. Jayanti. A time complexity lower bound for randomized implementations of some shared objects. In *Proc. of 17th PODC*, pages 201–210, 1998.

[30] M. Mitzenmacher and E. Upfal. *Probability and Computing: Randomized Algorithms and Probabilistic Analysis*. Cambridge University Press, 2005.

[31] M. Moir and J. H. Anderson. Wait-free algorithms for fast, long-lived renaming. *Sci. Comput. Program.*, 25(1):1–39, 1995.

[32] A. Panconesi, M. Papatriantafilou, P. Tsigas, and P. M. B. Vitányi. Randomized naming using wait-free shared variables. *Distr. Comp.*, 11(3):113–124, 1998.

[33] M. Pease, R. Shostak, and L. Lamport. Reaching agreement in the presence of faults. *J. of the ACM*, 27(2):228–234, 1980.

[34] A. C.-C. Yao. Probabilistic computations: Toward a unified measure of complexity. In *Proc. of 18th FOCS*, pages 222–227, 1977.

Byzantine Renaming in Synchronous Systems with $t < N$

Oksana Denysyuk
INESC-ID, Instituto Superior Técnico
Universidade Técnica de Lisboa, Portugal
oksana.denysyuk@ist.utl.pt

Luís Rodrigues
INESC-ID, Instituto Superior Técnico
Universidade Técnica de Lisboa, Portugal
ler@ist.utl.pt

ABSTRACT

In this paper we consider the fundamental problems of re-naming and order-preserving renaming [1] in a synchronous message passing system with Byzantine failures. We study the feasibility of solving these problems using randomized algorithms under both *non-rushing* and *rushing* adversaries. We first show that there is a randomized algorithm that solves renaming efficiently for *any* $t < N$ under the *non-rushing* adversary (N is the number of processes, and t is the maximum number of Byzantine processes). This result establishes a separation between randomized and determin-istic renaming, since it is known that there are no efficient deterministic algorithms for $t \geq N/3$. Our algorithm ter-minates in $\mathcal{O}(\log N)$ rounds w.h.p. We next consider the renaming problem in the harder setting with the *rushing* adversary. Interestingly, we show that in this setting the al-gorithm also works with $t = 1$ but fails for larger t. We then give an algorithm that works with any $t < N$ by relying on cryptographic commitment. Finally, we turn our attention to the problem of order-preserving renaming, which requires the new names to preserve the order of the initial identifiers. For this problem, we prove a tight $t < N/3$ bound that holds for both deterministic and randomized algorithms.

Categories and Subject Descriptors

F.2.2 [**Theory of Computation**]: Analysis of Algorithms and Problem Complexity—*Nonnumerical Algorithms and Prob-lems*

General Terms

Theory, Algorithms, Reliability

Keywords

Renaming problem; Byzantine failures; randomized algo-rithms; synchronous message passing model.

1. INTRODUCTION

This paper concerns the fundamental problems of *renam-ing* and *order-preserving renaming* defined by Attiya, Bar-Noy, Dolev, Peleg, and Reischuk [1]. The renaming prob-lem is informally described as follows: a set of N processes $\{p_1, \ldots, p_N\}$ with unique ids from a possibly unbounded namespace must pick new names from a smaller bounded range $[1, \ldots, M]$. The range of values to which new names belong is called the *target namespace*. If the size of the target namespace is equal to the number of processes, i.e. $M = N$, the renaming is called *tight*. The order-preserving variant of the renaming problem requires the new names to preserve the ordering of the original ids (i.e., if p_i and p_j are correct processes and p_i has a smaller id than p_j, then the new name of p_i must be smaller than the new name of p_j).

In this paper we consider a synchronous message-passing model where up to t processes may be Byzantine. In this model, renaming can be solved easily for any $t < N$ with very inefficient algorithms whose round complexity is pro-portional to the highest correct process id [21]. We are in-terested in *efficient* algorithms, that is, algorithms whose round complexity is bounded by a function of N (not by the highest id). It has been shown that no such algorithms exist if $t \geq N/3$ [21], but this impossibility concerns only *deterministic* algorithms.

We show that, with the help of randomization, renaming can be solved efficiently for any $t < N$. Therefore, our result implies that randomization is an important and necessary technique for solving renaming efficiently. To our knowl-edge, this is the first paper to study randomized solutions for renaming in this model.

When considering randomized algorithms, the literature considers two adversaries with different powers. With the *non-rushing* adversary, processes are forced to take steps si-multaneously at the beginning of each round. Therefore, Byzantine processes must choose messages to send in each round *before* learning the random choices made by the cor-rect processes in the same round. With the *rushing* ad-versary, Byzantine processes may execute each step after learning about the random choices of the correct processes. In [15], non-rushing and rushing adversaries are called si-multaneous and sequential, respectively. In this paper, we study renaming under both adversaries.

We first note that it is possible to solve renaming using a consensus algorithm to agree on a set of identifiers. It is also known that sometimes randomization can be used to solve consensus [3] when deterministic algorithms fail [12]. Thus, one might wonder whether we could obtain an efficient randomized renaming algorithm that tolerates $t < N$ Byzantine failures, as follows: first, obtain an efficient randomized consensus algorithm that tolerates $t < N$ Byzantine failures; then use this algorithm to solve renaming. Unfortunately, this approach would not work: it has been shown that with Byzantine failures and $t \geq N/3$, any randomized consensus algorithm fails with probability at least $1/3$ [15, 17]. This result holds even with the non-rushing adversary.

In seeking efficient algorithms for renaming, we first consider the weaker non-rushing adversary. We propose an algorithm based on a simple idea: each process randomly chooses a new id from the range $\{1, \ldots, N\}$ and applies tie-breaking rules to solve collisions. We show that this algorithm terminates in $\mathcal{O}(\log N)$ rounds w.h.p.

We next consider the more challenging *rushing* adversary. We show that our first algorithm can tolerate $t = 1$ Byzantine failure but the algorithm fails if $t > 1$. This is because, in each round, Byzantine processes can first observe the choice of a correct process and mimic it, causing infinitely many collisions. To tackle this problem, we use a cryptographic commitment primitive to force processes to commit to a choice without revealing their value; this technique prevents Byzantine processes from constantly mimicking the choices of correct processes. Using cryptographic commitment, we show how to extend the previous algorithm to work for any $t < N$.

To use cryptographic commitment, we must assume a polynomially bounded adversary, so that the adversary cannot break the cryptographic primitive. We believe our use of cryptography is sensible in the following two ways. First, we do not assume a primitive that needs a public key infrastructure (PKI). By contrast, primitives such as *digital signatures*, which are frequently used to cope with Byzantine processes, require a PKI. The problem is that a PKI implies that processes have the public key of all processes, but the public key serves as a unique process id; and if processes have knowledge of unique ids for each other, the renaming problem becomes trivial (e.g., each process sorts these ids, and then outputs as its new name the position of its id in this sorted order).

Second, even if the adversary breaks the cryptographic primitive by luck (by guessing the random seed used by a correct process to commit a value), the algorithm never violates the properties of the renaming problem, though termination may get delayed. Even in this case, termination is ensured with probability one. By contrast, certain algorithms that rely on cryptography will fail with non-zero probability when the adversary is lucky [9].

We then turn our attention to the order-preserving renaming problem [1]. This variant is interesting in settings where the original identifiers encode some additional information, such as their relative priority in accessing a shared resource. We prove that it is impossible to solve order-preserving renaming if $t \geq N/3$, even if one could use randomized algorithms. Thus, randomization does not help solving this problem, in contrast to the renaming problem. To our knowledge, this is the first result that separates the resiliency of renaming and order-preserving renaming algorithms. Interestingly, the impossibility applies to a target namespace of any size. The proof reduces the case of $N > 3$ to the case of $N = 3$. It then considers a candidate algorithm for the case $N = 3$ and shows that it must fail, by constructing an indistinguishability ring of executions that

violates the properties of order-preserving renaming. This technique was applied previously to the problem of consensus with Byzantine failures [11]. Here we extend it to order-preserving renaming, which is a weaker problem and hence harder to prove impossibility results for. In our proof, we construct a ring of size larger than the target namespace and use the following argument to establish a contradiction: roughly, we show that names must increase as we traverse the ring in one direction, but this exhausts the target namespace after going around the ring.

1.1 Summary of Contributions

Table 1 graphically presents our contributions, shown in gray, in the context of the known results[1].

In summary, we make the following contributions:

- We show that by using randomization, renaming can be solved in $\mathcal{O}(\log N)$ rounds w.h.p. for any $t < N$ under a non-rushing adversary.

- We show that renaming can be solved in $\mathcal{O}(\log N)$ rounds w.h.p. with $t = 1$, even under the rushing adversary.

- We show that renaming can be solved in $\mathcal{O}(\log N)$ rounds w.h.p. for any $t < N$ under a polynomially bounded rushing adversary, by using cryptographic commitment.

- All our algorithms solve tight renaming.

- We show that *order-preserving* renaming cannot be solved if $t \geq N/3$; this impossibility applies to both deterministic and randomized algorithms.

1.2 Paper Organization

The remainder of this paper is organized as follows. In Section 2, we formalize the system model and in Section 3 we state the problem definition. Section 4 is dedicated to related work. In Section 5 we present a randomized renaming algorithm that works under the non-rushing adversary. In Section 6, we first show that our algorithm tolerates one Byzantine process even under the rushing adversary, and then we extend the algorithm to work for any $t < N$. In Section 7, we prove the $t < N/3$ bound for the order-preserving variant in both deterministic and randomized settings. Finally, in Section 8, we present conclusions and outline directions for future work.

2. SYSTEM MODEL

We consider a synchronous round-based message-passing system of $N \geq 3$ processes $p_1, \ldots, p_N$, where N is known a priori. Each correct process has a unique identifier, originally known only to the process itself. Execution proceeds in rounds; in each round, a process can send messages to its neighbors, receive at most one message from each neighbor, and change state. In randomized algorithms, the process obtains a fixed-length string of private random bits before changing state. We consider a fully-connected network with

---

[1]Table 1 considers the case $N \geq 3$. If $N = 2$ then there is a simple deterministic algorithm that solves renaming and order-preserving renaming with $t < N$: in round 1, the two processes exchange their ids; at the end of round 1, each process decides on a new name that is the position of its id in a sorted pair of ids.

System Model			Renaming	Order-Preserving Renaming
Algorithm	Adversary	Resiliency		
Deterministic	n/a	$t < N/3$	$\mathcal{O}(\log N)$ [21]	$\mathcal{O}(\log N)$ [7]
	n/a	$N/3 \leq t < N$	unbounded [21]	impossible
Randomized	non-rushing	$t < N$	$\mathcal{O}(\log N)$ w.h.p	impossible
	rushing	$t = 1$	$\mathcal{O}(\log N)$ w.h.p	impossible for $N = 3$
	rushing, comp.bounded	$t < N$	$\mathcal{O}(\log N)$ w.h.p	

Table 1: Round complexity of our contributions (in gray) in the context of the known results for $N \geq 3$ [1].

bidirectional links between every pair of processes. The bidirectional links of each process are numbered $1, \ldots, N$; there is no global assignment of processes to link numbers, and different processes may have inconsistent link numberings. We denote by $link_i(p_j)$ the number at p_i of the bidirectional link to p_j. At each process, we assume that link number N is the self-loop, and that a process knows the number of the link from which it receives a message.

The system is subject to Byzantine failures of processes, as we explain next.

2.1 Power of the Adversary

Byzantine processes exhibit arbitrary behavior and are allowed to collude among themselves. We model the behavior of the Byzantine processes by an adversary that knows the protocol, can decide which processes to corrupt at any time during the execution, and has full control of the corrupted processes. We assume that the adversary does not have access to the private random bits of the correct processes, and we allow the adversary to corrupt at most t processes.

Additionally, we distinguish between rushing and non-rushing adversaries. The *non-rushing* adversary cannot decide the messages to be sent during a particular round based on the messages the corrupted processes receive during that same round. Under the *rushing* adversary, it is pessimistically assumed that the messages addressed to the Byzantine processes are always delivered immediately, and that the adversary has time to inspect the messages addressed to the corrupted processes before issuing its messages in the same round.

The adversary is allowed to eavesdrop the communication between the correct processes. However, the adversary is unable to send messages in the name of correct processes, or modify messages that the correct processes send.

2.2 Cryptographic Techniques

When we use cryptography in Section 6, we consider a computationally bounded adversary that is limited to computing polynomially bounded functions. We assume the availability of a cryptographic commitment scheme. Roughly speaking, such a scheme has two separate stages, commitment stage and revealing stage, with the following interface for each respective stage:

- COMMIT(*value*): a process generates a cryptographic commitment to a value, without revealing the value.

- REVEAL(*value*): a process reveals the value, which must match the previously announced commitment.

The properties of a commitment scheme can be informally stated as follows.

- *Hiding:* it is computationally hard for the receiver to know in the commitment stage the value to which the sender commits.

- *Binding:* it is computationally hard for the sender to commit more than one value and to reveal a value that it has not committed.

For a more formal treatment, we refer the reader to [14].

3. PROBLEM DEFINITION

The renaming problem can be precisely defined as follows. Each process has an *initial id* in some *original namespace*, and it must decide on a new name in some *target namespace* $\{1, \ldots, M\}$, where $M \geq N$ is a parameter of the problem, such that the following conditions must hold [1]:

- *Termination:* Each correct process eventually decides on a new name.

- *Validity:* If a correct process decides, it decides on a new name in $\{1, \ldots, M\}$.

- *Uniqueness:* No two correct processes decide on the same new name.

For randomized algorithms, the termination property is weakened to

- *Termination with probability 1:* With probability 1, every correct process eventually decides on a new name.

When $M = N$ the problem is called *tight* renaming. The stronger *order-preserving* variant of renaming is obtained by adding the following property:

- *Order-Preserving [1]:* New names of the correct processes preserve the order of the initial ids.

In general, algorithms can have unbounded running time. In this work we are interested in *efficient* algorithms, whose round complexity can be bounded by a function of N, the number of processes (this property is also known in the literature as *strong termination* [8]). For randomized algorithms, we require the *probabilistic* round complexity of an efficient algorithm to be bounded by a function of N.

4. RELATED WORK

Related work concerns other solutions and lower bounds for the renaming problem (Section 4.1), techniques from cryptography (Section 4.2), and the symmetry breaking problem (Section 4.3).

4.1 Renaming Problem

The renaming problem was originally introduced in [1] for the asynchronous message-passing model with crash failures. The authors presented renaming and order-preserving renaming algorithms for $t < N/2$. This bound was also shown to be optimal.

The first paper to address the renaming problem in synchronous message-passing systems prone to Byzantine failures is [21], which shows that renaming can be solved deterministically for any $t < N$ with the following algorithm: a process waits until the round corresponding to the value of its id, then picks an available name, and sends its decision to other processes. The remaining processes exclude the announced decision from the available names. Since all correct processes have different ids, no two correct processes decide in the same round, and hence they always choose distinct names. This algorithm, however, is not efficient because its running time depends on the values of original ids, which can be taken from an *unbounded* namespace. The same paper shows that the unbounded running time is required for deterministic renaming if $t \geq N/3$. It is also shown that a weaker renaming problem with a *bounded* original namespace can be solved in $\mathcal{O}(N \log \lceil N_{max}/N \rceil)$ rounds for $t < N$, where N_{max} is the size of the original namespace. The paper also presents a renaming algorithm for $t < N/3$ with round complexity of $\mathcal{O}(\log N)$. The algorithm is based on the crash-tolerant renaming algorithm introduced in [5] and the automatic crash-to-Byzantine translation techniques introduced in [2, 20] with modifications to avoid using process ids.

The order-preserving renaming problem in the same model was studied in [7], which proposes an algorithm for $t<N/3$ with $\mathcal{O}(\log N)$ round complexity. This algorithm is based on Byzantine-tolerant approximate agreement and works as follows. Processes exchange their ids, order the set of the received ids, and propose for each id a new name, which is the rank of that id in the ordered set. Then, processes run a coordinated Byzantine-tolerant approximate agreement on the rank of each id.

4.2 Cryptography

As mentioned earlier, the usual authentication-based approach to mitigate the power of the Byzantine processes cannot be applied in renaming, because the unique identities of processes are not known *a priori*. We circumvent this difficulty by using a cryptographic commitment primitive. The concept of commitment was first formally introduced in [19] but appeared earlier in [4, 10] and is central in cryptographic protocol design. Often described as the digital analogue of sealed envelopes, commitment schemes enable a party, known as the *sender*, to commit itself to a value (binding property) while keeping it secret from the *receiver* (hiding property).

Since it is impossible to have both binding and hiding properties against an unbounded adversary [14], the existing commitment protocols usually provide the following properties. In the *statistically-binding* commitment, e.g. [22], the binding property holds with overwhelming probability against the computationally bounded adversary. On the other hand, in the *statistically-hiding* commitment, e.g. [6], the hiding property holds with overwhelming probability against the computationally bounded adversary.

4.3 Randomized Symmetry Breaking

Finally, the randomization techniques used in this paper bear some similarities to the techniques employed in the symmetry breaking problem. A notable example is the work by Itai and Rodeh [16] that addresses symmetry breaking in anonymous rings. The paper presents a randomized ring leader election algorithm that works as follows. Each process randomly picks a value from a given range and sends it through the ring. The process that has picked the largest value becomes a leader. In case of a collision, the processes with the largest value repeat the algorithm until one process wins. Several other papers applied randomization techniques to the leader election problem, e.g. [13, 18]. To our knowledge, Byzantine failures were not considered in this line of research.

5. BYZANTINE RENAMING UNDER THE NON-RUSHING ADVERSARY

In this section we consider the non-rushing adversary and present an algorithm (Alg. 1) that solves renaming efficiently. In fact, the algorithm solves tight renaming, where $M = N$.

The algorithm is based on the following idea. A process chooses uniformly at random a name from $\{1, \ldots, N\}$ and exchanges its choice with all other processes. If no other process picks the same name, the process is done and informs all other processes. Otherwise, the process excludes names already chosen by other processes and then restarts. Since the adversary cannot inspect the random choices of the correct processes before issuing its messages, each process will eventually pick a unique name. All Byzantine processes can do is to repeatedly claim t distinct available names to increase the chance of collisions. For example, in the presence of $N - 1$ Byzantine processes, the correct process has a chance of $1/N$ of not colliding with the choices of the Byzantine processes. Hence, without additional rules, the expected decision time for a correct process could be linear in the size of the network.

To speed up the decision time, we use a tie breaking rule that allows processes to decide even in the case of collisions. Tie breaking is done by appointing in each phase a set of processes whose choices, in case of a collision, have priority over the choice of the given process. These sets are calculated in each phase as follows. In odd phases, the set consists of the undecided neighbors with ids lower than *myId* (the id of the current process); in even phases, the set consists of undecided neighbors with ids higher than *myId*. Roughly speaking, with this rule, in a given phase, a correct process competes with some fraction of undecided processes, and, in the following phase, competes with the remaining fraction of undecided processes. As we will show, this tie breaking rule reduces the decision time to a factor of $\log N$. Hence, the algorithm terminates in $\mathcal{O}(\log N)$ rounds w.h.p (i.e., with probability at least $\left(1 - \frac{1}{N^c}\right)$, where $c > 0$ is a constant).

We now describe the algorithm in detail. Each process p_i stores the following data structures:

- ids_i: an array that stores ids (not names) that p_i knows about, indexed by the link to which they are connected, i.e. $ids_i[j]$ stores the id of the neighbor connected to link j of p_i. Initially, $ids_i[j] = \bot$ for every j.

- $freenames_i$: the set of names that p_i believes to be free

Algorithm 1 Renaming with $t < N$

```
01  Initialization:
02      undecided := {1, ..., N};           // set of links to undecided neighbors
03      freenames := {1, ..., N};           // set of available names
04      foreach i ∈ {1, ..., N} do
05          ids[i] := ⊥;                    //array that stores old ids of all neighbors

06  In Phase 1 do
        // Phase 1 has a single round
07      send ⟨ID, myId⟩ to all links;
08      foreach i ∈ {1, ..., N} do
09          if ⟨ID, id⟩ has been received from link i then
10              ids[i] := id;
11      proceed to Phase 2;

12  In Phase φ > 1 do
        // Round 1
        // choose priority set for the current phase
13      if φ is odd then
14          plinks := {i ∈ undecided : ids[i] < myId};
15      else
16          plinks := {i ∈ undecided : ids[i] > myId};
17      myName := choose an element in freenames uniformly at random;
18      send ⟨PROPOSAL, myName⟩ to every link i such that i ∈ undecided \ plinks;
        // check for collisions
19      if ∃i ∈ plinks : ⟨PROPOSAL, name_i⟩ has been received from link i such that myName = name_i then
20          winner := false;
21      else
22          winner := true;

        //Round 2
23      if winner = true then
24          send ⟨DECIDED, myName⟩ to every link i such that i ∈ undecided;
25          return myName;
26      else
27          foreach i ∈ undecided do
28              if ⟨DECIDED, name_i⟩ has been received from link i then
29                  undecided := undecided \ {i};
30                  freenames := freenames \ {name_i};
31          proceed to Phase φ + 1;
```

(not selected by its neighbors). Initially, $freenames_i = \{1, \ldots, N\}$ (all possible names).

- $undecided_i$: the set of links to neighbors that p_i believes to not have decided yet. Initially, $undecided_i = \{1, \ldots, N\}$ (all links).

The purpose of the first phase of the algorithm is for processes to exchange their initial ids. Each process sends its own id to all links and stores the ids it receives from other links (Lines 07-10). The ids received in phase 1 are used in all subsequent phases.

The following phases are tournament phases, where processes compete for available names. There are two ways of winning a tournament: if there are no collisions on the name chosen by a process in the current phase (i.e., the process was the only one to make that choice) or, when collisions occur, by winning a tie breaking rule, which differs according to the phase number. The tie breaking rule updates $plinks$ in each phase as follows. In odd phases, $plinks$ includes undecided neighbors with ids lower than $myId$; in even phases, $plinks$ includes undecided neighbors with ids higher than $myId$ (Lines 13-16). In what follows, recall that $link_j(p_i)$ denotes the number at process p_j of the bidirectional link to p_i (see Section 2). The relevant property of the $plinks$ assignment is that, for any phase ϕ, when considering any two correct processes p_i and p_j, if $link_i(p_j) \in plinks_i$, then $link_j(p_i) \notin plinks_j$. Furthermore, if $link_i(p_j) \in plinks_i$ in ϕ, and p_i and p_j do not decide in ϕ, then $link_j(p_i) \in plinks_j$ in $\phi + 1$.

Each tournament phase has two rounds. In the first round, a correct process selects $plinks$, picks randomly a name from $freenames$, and sends the name to the undecided neighbors that do not belong to $plinks$ (Lines 17-18). There is no need to send the name to the neighbors in $plinks$ because if a collision occurs in this phase, they will ignore the choice of the given process. A process wins the tournament if it has not received the same name from any process in $plinks$. At the end of the first round, processes check if they have won the tournament (Lines 19-22).

In the second round, if a correct process has won the tournament, it sends a $\langle DECIDED, myName \rangle$ message to all undecided neighbors and terminates, returning variable $myName$ as its new name (Lines 23-25). Otherwise, if the process did not win, it collects $\langle DECIDED, name_i \rangle$ messages from its neighbors, removes these neighbors from $undecided$ (doing so excludes these neighbors from all succeeding tournaments), and removes the names elected by the decided processes from $freenames$ (Lines 26-30).

Each undecided process keeps executing consecutive tournament phases until it wins a name in one of the tournaments.

Analysis

In the following we prove the correctness of Alg. 1. Whenever needed to distinguish between local variables at distinct processes, we use subscript $_i$ to indicate the local variables of process p_i. Superscript $^\phi$ indicates the value of a variable in Round 1 of phase ϕ.

LEMMA 1. *For any phase $\phi > 0$ and any correct processes p_i and p_j, if p_i has not decided a new name before ϕ, then $link_j(p_i) \in undecided_j$ in Round 1 of ϕ.*

PROOF. Assume there exist correct undecided processes p_i and p_j such that $link_j(p_i) \notin undecided_j$ in Round 1 of ϕ. By the algorithm, the links to all neighbors are initially in $undecided_j$ (Line 02) and are excluded from the set only when a $\langle \text{DECIDED}, \cdot \rangle$ message is received from the corresponding neighbor (Lines 28-29). Thus, p_j must have previously received $\langle \text{DECIDED}, v_i \rangle$ from p_i. This, in turn, means that p_i sent $\langle \text{DECIDED}, v_i \rangle$ before ϕ (Lines 24-25). But by assumption p_i is undecided in Round 1 of ϕ—a contradiction. $\square$

The following lemma states that each correct process considers available at least as many names as there are processes participating in each tournament phase.

LEMMA 2. *For every correct process p_i, in Round 1 of any phase $\phi \geq 2$,*

$$|undecided_i| \leq |freenames_i|.$$

PROOF. By induction on the phase number.
Base case. By the algorithm, p_i starts with $|undecided_i| = |freenames_i| = N$ (Lines 02-03). Thus, in Round 1 of phase $\phi = 2$, $|undecided_i| = |freenames_i|$.
Induction step. Assume $|undecided_i| \leq |freenames_i|$ in Round 1 of phase ϕ. In Round 2 of the same phase, p_i only accepts $\langle \text{DECIDED}, . \rangle$ messages from the links in $undecided_i$ (Line 27-28). For each link $j \in undecided_i$, if $\langle \text{DECIDED}, v_j \rangle$ message has been received from j in the current phase, p_i removes j from $undecided_i$; and, if $v_j \in freenames_i$, p_i also removes v_j from $freenames_i$ (Lines 28-30). As a result, in Round 1 of phase $\phi + 1$, $|undecided_i| \leq |freenames_i|$. $\square$

The following lemma establishes the *uniqueness* property of the algorithm based on two following observations: in case of a collision, at most one correct process (with the smallest id in odd phases and with the largest id in even phases) wins the tie breaking; the winning process always announces its decision before returning.

LEMMA 3. *No two correct processes decide on the same name in Alg 1.*

PROOF. Assume, by contradiction, that there are two correct processes p_i and p_j that decide on the same name v in phases ϕ_i and ϕ_j respectively. We will distinguish two possible scenarios.
Case 1. $\phi_i \neq \phi_j$. Without loss of generality, assume $\phi_i < \phi_j$. By the algorithm, if p_i decided on v in ϕ_i, then p_i sent $\langle \text{DECIDED}, v \rangle$ in Round 2 of ϕ_i to all undecided neighbors before returning the new name (Lines 24-25). By Lemma 1, $link_j(p_i) \in undecided_j$ and $link_i(p_j) \in undecided_i$ in Round 1 of ϕ_i. Therefore, p_i sent v to p_j, and p_j excluded v from $freenames_j$ in Round 2 of ϕ_i (Lines 27-30). On the other hand, if p_j decided on v in phase ϕ_j, then p_j must have chosen v from $freenames_j$ in ϕ_j (Line 17), which contradicts the previous statement.
Case 2. $\phi_i = \phi_j = \phi$. Without loss of generality, assume that $id_i < id_j$ and ϕ is odd (for even values of ϕ the argument is symmetric). If both p_i and p_j decided on v in Round 2 of ϕ, then p_i and p_j were both undecided in Round 1 of ϕ.

Also, by Lemma 1, $link_j(p_i) \in undecided_j$ and $link_i(p_j) \in undecided_i$ in Round 1 of ϕ. Processes p_i and p_j randomly picked v from $freenames$ and sent v to their neighbors in $undecided \setminus plinks$ (Lines 17-18). By assumption, $id_i < id_j$; therefore, $link_j(p_i) \in undecided_j \setminus plinks_j$. Hence, p_i sent v to p_j in Round 2 (Line 18). Since $link_j(p_i) \in plinks_j$, p_j received v from p_i (Lines 19-20). But by assumption, p_j decided on v in Round 2, which is possible only if p_j had not received v from any link in $plinks_j$ in Round 1 (Lines 19-22)—a contradiction. $\square$

Complexity

In the following we calculate the round complexity of the algorithm. Recall that we consider the *non-rushing* adversary, whose behavior is independent from the random choices of the correct processes in the current round.

We now prove that each correct process decides w.h.p. after $O(\log N)$ rounds. To do so, we consider an arbitrary correct process p_0 and give an upper bound on the probability that p_0 has not decided after $\mathcal{O}(\log N)$ rounds.

Intuitively, the adversary can decrease the probability that p_0 decides in some phase by making certain Byzantine processes (those not in $plinks_0$) announce their decision in the previous phase. However, once a process decides, it is excluded from subsequent tournaments, and so the adversary can do this only a limited number of times. We will show that the adversary has to make a large fraction of processes to decide in order to decrease by a constant factor the probability that p_0 does not decide. Thus, in each phase, the adversary has to carefully balance the number of processes that it causes to decide and the probability that p_0 does not decide. We will show that, whatever the strategy of the adversary, after $\mathcal{O}(\log N)$ rounds, p_0 decides w.h.p.

LEMMA 4. *Under the non-rushing adversary, the probability that a correct process p_0 decides by round $12 \log N + 3$ is at least $1 - \frac{1}{N^2}$.*

PROOF. In the analysis, we assume without loss of generality that the adversary controls *all* processes other than p_0; if the probability lower bound holds in this case, then it also holds if the adversary can control a smaller number of processes. We say that a link ℓ decides at an epoch e (or at a round r) if p_0 receives a $\langle decided, \cdot \rangle$ message from link ℓ in epoch e (or round r). Intuitively, we are considering a p_0-centric view of the system since p_0 is the only correct process. We say that *link ℓ is undecided at epoch e (or round r)* if ℓ has not decided at epoch e (round r) or earlier.

Recall that the algorithm is organized in phases of two rounds each. We will further group two consecutive phases into an epoch $e \geq 1$: epoch e has phases $2e + 1$ and $2e + 2$. For convenience we also define epoch 0 as having just a single phase, phase 2.

In each epoch, we pick one phase to scrutinize more carefully; this is called the *chosen phase* of the epoch. For the other phase, we will use a trivial upper bound of 1 on the probability of non-termination. The chosen phase of epoch e is determined as follows. At the beginning of last round before epoch e,[2] consider the sets $pl1 = \{i \in undecided_0 : ids_0[i] < myId_0\}$; and $pl2 = \{i \in undecided_0 : ids_0[i] > myId_0\}$, where $undecided_0$, $ids_0[i]$, and $myId_0$ are variables of process p_0. If $|pl1| < |pl2|$ then we pick the first phase of epoch e as the chosen phase, otherwise we pick the second

---

[2]The last round before epoch e is when the adversary can make links decide before starting epoch e.

Algorithm 2 Renaming with the Use of Commitment

// In Alg 1 replace the lines

17   send ⟨PROPOSAL, $myName$⟩ to every link i such that $i \in undecided \setminus plinks$;

18   **if** $\exists i \in plinks :$ ⟨PROPOSAL, $name_i$⟩ has been received from link i such that $myName = name_i$ **then**

// by the following

17   COMMIT $(\phi, myName, myId)$ to every link i such that $i \in undecided \setminus plinks$;

     // Round 2

18a   REVEAL $(\phi, myName, myId)$ to every link i such that $i \in undecided \setminus plinks$;

18b   **if** $\exists i \in plinks :$ such that $(\phi, name_i, ids[i])$ has been revealed from link i **and** $myName = name_i$ **then**

---

phase. Intuitively, we want the phase with fewest priority links, where $pl1$ is the priority links of the first phase and $pl2$ is the priority links of the second phase (see Lines 13-16 of Alg.1). We let pl_e and npl_e be the priority links and non-priority links, respectively, of the chosen phase evaluated at the beginning of last round before epoch e. That is, $pl_e = pl1$, $npl_e = pl2$ if the chosen phase is the first phase, and $pl_e = pl2$, $npl_e = pl1$ if the chosen phase is the second phase.

For each epoch e, we define the following variables:

- N_e = the number of undecided links at the beginning of the last round before epoch e;

- $\gamma_e = |pl_e| / N_e$;

- $\alpha_e = \frac{|links\ in\ npl_e\ that\ decide\ before\ the\ chosen\ phase\ of\ e|}{N_e}$;

- $\bar{\alpha}_e = 1 - \alpha_e$;

- c_e = number of links in pl_e that decide before the chosen phase of epoch e.

We now bound the probability P_e that p_0 does not decide in the chosen phase of epoch e, as follows:

$$P_e \leq \frac{N_e \gamma_e - c_e}{N_e \bar{\alpha}_e - c_e} \leq \frac{N_e \gamma_e}{N_e \bar{\alpha}_e} \leq \frac{1}{2\bar{\alpha}_e} \qquad (1)$$

Here, the first inequality holds because the best strategy for the adversary to delay termination is to claim as many free names as it can (at most $N_e \gamma_e - c_e$, the number of priority links) over the total number of free names (at least $N_e \bar{\alpha}_e - c_e$, the number of undecided links). The second inequality holds because $(a-c)/(b-c) < a/b$ for any positive integers a, b, c such that $a < b$ and $c < b$. The third inequality holds because $\gamma_e \leq 1/2$ by definition of γ_e and of the chosen phase.

We can trivially upper bound by 1 the probability that p_0 does not decide in the non-chosen phase of epoch e. Thus, from (1), the probability that p_0 does not decide in epoch e is upper bounded by $\frac{1}{2\bar{\alpha}_e}$ as well. Therefore, the probability $\mathcal{P}_e$ that p_0 does not decide in any of epochs $1, \ldots, e$ is upper bounded by

$$\mathcal{P}_e \leq P_1 \times \cdots \times P_e \leq \frac{1}{2^e \bar{\alpha}_1 \ldots \bar{\alpha}_e} \qquad (2)$$

Note that $N_{e+1} \leq N_e \bar{\alpha}_e$ because at least $\alpha_e N_e$ links decide before the chosen phase of epoch $e+1$. Therefore,

$$N_{e+1} \leq N_1 \bar{\alpha}_1 \bar{\alpha}_2 \ldots \bar{\alpha}_e \qquad (3)$$

We do not know the values of $\bar{\alpha}_i$ because they depend on the strategy of the adversary. However, from (2) and (3), we can upper bound the product $\mathcal{P}_e N_{e+1}$:

$$\mathcal{P}_e N_{e+1} \leq N_1 / 2^e \leq N / 2^e \qquad (4)$$

For $e = 3 \log N$, we obtain $\mathcal{P}_e N_{e+1} \leq 1/N^2$. If p_0 has not decided by the end of epoch e then $1 \leq N_{e+1}$. Therefore, $\mathcal{P}_e \leq \mathcal{P}_e N_{e+1}$, and so $\mathcal{P}_e \leq 1/N^2$. Note that each epoch has two phases, and each phase has two rounds. Moreover, there are three initial rounds before epoch 1. Thus, there are $3 + 12 \log N$ rounds until the end of epoch e. Therefore, the probability that process p_0 has not decided by round $3 + 12 \log N$ is upper bounded by $1/N^2$. □

We now use Lemma 4 to calculate the overall round complexity of Alg. 1.

THEOREM 5. *Under the non-rushing adversary, all correct processes decide on a new name in $\mathcal{O}(\log N)$ communication rounds w.h.p.*

PROOF. By Lemma 4, the probability that a correct process decides in at most $12 \log N + 3$ rounds is at least $1 - \frac{1}{N^2}$. By taking a union bound, the probability that there exists at least one correct process that has not decided after $12 \log N + 3$ rounds is at most $\frac{1}{N}$. □

We now have all ingredients necessary to prove the correctness of Alg. 1.

THEOREM 6 (CORRECTNESS). *Under the non-rushing adversary, Alg. 1 implements tight renaming for any $t < N$.*

PROOF. *Validity* condition is satisfied by the algorithmic construction: processes propose new names from the set $\{1, \ldots, N\}$ and decide only on the values they have proposed. *Uniqueness* follows from Lemma 3. *Termination with probability* 1 follows from Theorem 5. □

6. RENAMING UNDER THE RUSHING ADVERSARY

In this section we consider the rushing adversary, which is allowed to inspect the messages from correct processes before having Byzantine processes send their own messages. As a result, in our algorithm, the Byzantine processes can echo the choices of each correct process causing infinitely many collisions. Surprisingly, even in this case, correct processes are still able to decide on new names in the presence of *one* Byzantine process.

6.1 Case of t=1

We now show that the algorithm of Section 5 works under the rushing adversary for $t = 1$. The *validity* property

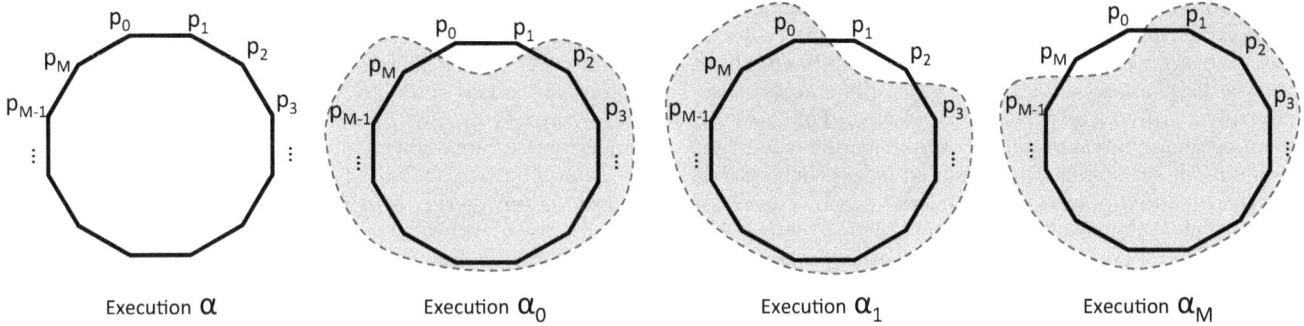

Figure 1: Indistinguishable executions for $N = 3$ and $t = 1$ (area in gray corresponds to a system simulated by a single Byzantine process).

follows from the algorithm construction. *Uniqueness* follows from Lemma 3.

It remains to show the *termination with probability 1*. Consider an execution of Alg. 1 with $t = 1$. For any $\phi \geq 2$, if a correct process has a link to the Byzantine process in the *plinks* set of phase ϕ, then this process will ignore the choice of the Byzantine process in $\phi + 1$. As a result, the Byzantine process can influence the outcome of a half of tournament phases, while in the remaining phases the correct process is competing only with the undecided correct neighbors.

THEOREM 7. *Under the rushing adversary with $t = 1$, Alg. 1 terminates in $\mathcal{O}(\log N)$ rounds w.h.p.*

PROOF. Let p_i be an undecided correct process. For any two consecutive phases there exists a phase, say ϕ, when the link to a Byzantine process $\notin plinks_i^{\phi}$. Therefore, the choice of the Byzantine process is ignored by p_i in every such ϕ (Line 19). Since by Lemma 2, in each phase there are as many free names as undecided processes, the expected decision time for p_i is at most double the decision time under the non-rushing adversary (see Lemma 4 and Theorem 5). □

6.2 General Case of t>1

If $t > 1$, two Byzantine processes can announce to a correct process p_i a smaller id and a larger id than p_i's identifier, and then generate collisions deterministically in each tournament phase. In this way, the correct processes are never able to decide. To prevent such behavior, we introduce in Alg. 1 a cryptographic commitment primitive. In the modified algorithm, depicted in Alg. 2, the random choices of processes are not announced immediately. Instead, the undecided processes first commit to their choices without revealing the actual values, and in a subsequent round reveal their choices. Thus, the adversary is required to commit the values of the corrupted processes without knowing the values committed by the correct processes (hiding property). Furthermore, the adversary is not able to modify its choices during the revealing stage (binding property). Therefore, the algorithm operates analogously to its non-rushing counterpart.

As noted before in the text, with small probability, the adversary is able to break the commitment. In this case, it will be able to reproduce the value of a correct process, causing a collision. However, since in different phases processes use independent instances of commitment, correct processes still decide with probability 1. Therefore, under the com-

putationally bounded adversary, with probability 1, Alg. 2 terminates correctly.

Commitment abstraction can be implemented in constant number of rounds, e.g. [22]. Hence, the total round complexity of Alg. 2 is logarithmic.

7. ORDER-PRESERVING RENAMING

In this section we study the order-preserving variant where the new names are required to preserve the order of the initial ids. We first establish the separation result for order-preserving renaming by showing that there is no deterministic algorithm with $N \leq 3t$ that implements order-preserving renaming. Our proof method is based on the indistinguishability argument widely used in the literature on Byzantine fault tolerance, e.g. [11, 17, 15].

We first give the impossibility proof for deterministic algorithms in the system with $N = 3$ and $t = 1$. In the proof, we consider the easiest case of order-preserving renaming from a *bounded* original namespace of size $M + 1$ into a target namespace of size M, for some arbitrary $M \geq N$. This implies *a fortiori* that the impossibility applies to namespaces of any size, as long as the original namespace is larger than the target namespace (otherwise the problem becomes trivial).

We take a candidate algorithm for the case $N = 3$ and construct an indistinguishability ring of executions, which violates the properties of order-preserving renaming. Namely, we construct a ring of size $M + 1$ and assign inputs in such a way that new names must increase as we traverse the ring in one direction, but this exhausts the target namespace after going around the ring.

THEOREM 8. *There is no deterministic algorithm that solves order-preserving renaming in a system with $N = 3$ and $t = 1$.*

PROOF. Assume by contradiction there exists an algorithm π that solves order-preserving renaming for $N = 3$ and $t = 1$ from the original namespace of size $M + 1$ into the target namespace of size M, for some $M \geq 3$. Without loss of generality we assume π is a full-information algorithm.

Consider a system with $M + 1$ processes $p_0, \ldots, p_M$. We consider an execution α of π in this system, where processes are arranged in a ring as depicted in Fig. 1, and process p_i has original id i. This is an execution with $M + 1 > N$ processes, even though algorithm π is designed for $N = 3$

processes, but we will argue this execution has some interesting properties. For every pair of adjacent processes in the ring, their view of the system is indistinguishable from the view in a 3-process system in which the two processes are connected to a corrupted third process. For instance, processes p_0 and p_1 cannot distinguish execution α from execution α_0 in Fig. 1 where both p_0 and p_1 are connected to a single corrupted process that simulates p_M and p_2. That is, the single Byzantine process sends to p_0 exactly what p_M sends to p_0 in α, and the same Byzantine process sends to p_1 exactly what p_2 sends to p_1 in α (in Fig. 1, the gray area in execution α_0 depicts the system simulated by a single Byzantine process). By assumption, in α_0 processes p_0 and p_1 decide on valid names in the correct order. Moreover, since p_0 and p_1 cannot distinguish execution α from execution α_0, they decide in α exactly on the same names as in α_0. Similarly, p_1 and p_2 cannot distinguish α from α_1 in Fig. 1, and so on for each pair of adjacent processes in the ring. Therefore, in α, each pair of adjacent processes decides on valid names in the correct order.

By the validity property, in α process p_0 decides on a new name v_0 such that $1 \leq v_0 \leq M$. By the order-preserving property, p_1 decides on name v_1 such that $1 \leq v_0 < v_1$. Applying the order-preserving property to the new names of all pairs of processes from p_0 to p_M, we see that process p_M decides on a new name v_M such that $1 \leq v_0 < v_1 < \ldots < v_{M-1} < v_M$. Thus, $v_M > M$. But by the validity property, $v_M \leq M$—a contradiction to the existence of algorithm π. □

Theorem 8 is generalized to the case of $t = \lceil N/3 \rceil$ by having three processes simulate the N-process system as described in [21]. More precisely, if there is an algorithm π for N processes and $t = \lceil N/3 \rceil$, we can use π to obtain an algorithm for three processes and $t = 1$, which contradicts Theorem 8. The algorithm for three processes works as follows. Each process simulates $\lceil N/3 \rceil$ or $\lfloor N/3 \rfloor$ processes running algorithm π, for a total of N simulated processes, where the simulated processes start with names that respect the id ordering of the three processes; each process then decides on the new name of any of the processes that it simulates.

Theorem 8 concerns deterministic algorithms. We now consider *randomized* algorithms. We use the indistinguishability argument to show that any randomized algorithm with $N = 3$ has a non-zero probability of error when running in the system depicted in Fig. 1. Again, we assume the easiest case of order-preserving renaming from the original namespace of size $M + 1$ into the target namespace of size M, for some arbitrary $M \geq N$. In our proof, we assume the non-rushing adversary, which is weaker than the rushing counterpart. Therefore, the impossibility holds under both adversaries.

THEOREM 9. *Under the non-rushing adversary, there is no randomized algorithm that solves order-preserving renaming in a system with $N = 3$ and $t = 1$.*

PROOF. Assume that there exists a (full information) randomized algorithm π' that solves order-preserving renaming for $N = 3$ and $t = 1$ from the original namespace of size $M + 1$ into the target namespace of size M, for some $M \geq 3$.

Consider a system composed by $M + 1$ processes $p_0, \ldots, p_M$ arranged in a ring as depicted in Fig. 1. We show that there exists a finite execution in the ring such that all $M + 1$ processes terminate. From that point, the proof proceeds as in

Theorem 8. The proof of the existence of such execution is slightly technical but follows from the termination with probability 1 of π'. The proof will construct increasingly larger executions in which, successively, processes $p_0, \ldots, p_M$ terminate, by arguing for each process p_i that it would terminate with probability 1 in a 3-process system.

More precisely, for each pair of processes p_i and p_{i+1} the execution in the ring is indistinguishable from an execution α_i where p_i and p_{i+1} is connected to a single Byzantine process that behaves exactly like p_{i-1} and p_{i+2} in α (the arithmetic of indices is done modulo $(M + 1)$). From the termination with probability 1 property of order-preserving renaming, (*) all correct processes in a 3-process system running π' with $t = 1$ terminate with probability 1. We now consider executions of π' in the ring of $M + 1$ processes. We first claim that there is a finite execution β_0 of π' in the ring such that p_0 and p_1 terminate. This follows from (*) and the fact that an execution in the ring is indistinguishable by p_0 and p_1 from an execution in a 3-process system. We now claim that we can extend execution β_0 such that p_2 also terminates. Indeed, β_0 is indistinguishable by p_1 and p_2 from an execution in a 3-process system. Since β_0 is finite, it occurs with positive probability $p_0 > 0$. If p_2 never terminates in any extensions of β_0, we can find a set of executions with probability $p_0 > 0$ where p_2 never terminates, contradicting (*). Therefore, in some extension of β_0, p_2 terminates. Let β_1 be the finite execution that combines β_0 and this extension until p_0, p_1, and p_2 terminate. We apply the same argument with execution β_1 and process p_3 to obtain a finite execution β_2 where $p_0, \ldots, p_3$ terminate. We continue this construction with all other processes, to obtain a finite execution β_{M-1} where all processes $p_0, \ldots, p_M$ terminate. □

Theorem 9 is generalized to the case of $t = \lceil N/3 \rceil$ by the simulation of [21] as previously described for the deterministic algorithm.

8. CONCLUSIONS

Our results contribute to a better understanding of fault tolerance and efficiency of renaming in different settings. Namely, we showed that with the use of randomization renaming can be solved efficiently for any $t < N$ under the *non-rushing* adversary. Our solution, presented in Alg. 1, terminates in $\mathcal{O}(\log N)$ rounds w.h.p., and works for any $t < N$. We also showed that Alg. 1 works for $t = 1$ under the *rushing* adversary. For the general case of $t > 1$, we strengthened our algorithm with a cryptographic commitment scheme. An open problem is whether it is possible to avoid the use of cryptography when $t > 1$.

We then considered the order-preserving renaming and proved a $t < N/3$ bound for both deterministic and randomized protocols. This result reveals a separation between the resiliency of renaming and order-preserving renaming. It would be interesting to find minimum assumptions on the power of the adversary necessary to solve order-preserving renaming with $t \geq N/3$.

Acknowledgments

The authors are thankful to Henrique Moniz for his helpful comments on this work.

This work was partially supported by Fundação para a Ciência e Tecnologia (FCT) via the INESC-ID multi-annual funding through the PIDDAC Program fund grant, under project PEst-OE/EEI/LA0021/2013, and via the project PEPITA (PTDC/EEI-SCR/2776/2012).

9. REFERENCES

[1] Hagit Attiya, Amotz Bar-Noy, Danny Dolev, David Peleg, and Rüdiger Reischuk. Renaming in an asynchronous environment. *J. ACM*, 37:524–548, July 1990.

[2] Rida A. Bazzi and Gil Neiger. Simplifying fault-tolerance: providing the abstraction of crash failures. *J. ACM*, 48:499–554, May 2001.

[3] Michael Ben-Or. Another advantage of free choice (extended abstract): Completely asynchronous agreement protocols. In *Proceedings of the second annual ACM symposium on Principles of distributed computing*, PODC '83, pages 27–30, New York, NY, USA, 1983. ACM.

[4] Manuel Blum. Coin flipping by telephone a protocol for solving impossible problems. *SIGACT News*, 15(1):23–27, January 1983.

[5] Soma Chaudhuri, Maurice Herlihy, and Mark R. Tuttle. Wait-free implementations in message-passing systems. *Theor. Comput. Sci.*, 220:211–245, June 1999.

[6] Ivan Damgård and Eiichiro Fujisaki. A statistically-hiding integer commitment scheme based on groups with hidden order. In *Proceedings of the 8th International Conference on the Theory and Application of Cryptology and Information Security: Advances in Cryptology*, ASIACRYPT '02, pages 125–142, London, UK, UK, 2002. Springer-Verlag.

[7] Oksana Denysyuk and Luís Rodrigues. Order-preserving renaming in synchronous systems with byzantine faults. In *Proceedings of the 33rd International Conference on Distributed Computing Systems*, ICDCS '13, page to appear. IEEE Computer Society, 2013.

[8] Edsger W. Dijkstra. On weak and strong termination. In *Selected Writings on Computing: A Personal Perspective*, pages 355–357. Springer-Verlag, 1982.

[9] Danny Dolev and H. Raymond Strong. Authenticated algorithms for byzantine agreement. *SIAM Journal on Computing*, 12(4):656–666, 1983.

[10] Shimon Even, Oded Goldreich, and Abraham Lempel. A randomized protocol for signing contracts. *Commun. ACM*, 28(6):637–647, June 1985.

[11] Michael J. Fischer, Nancy A. Lynch, and Michael Merritt. Easy impossibility proofs for distributed consensus problems. In *Proceedings of the fourth annual ACM symposium on Principles of distributed computing*, PODC '85, pages 59–70, New York, NY, USA, 1985. ACM.

[12] Michael J. Fischer, Nancy A. Lynch, and Michael S. Paterson. Impossibility of distributed consensus with one faulty process. *J. ACM*, 32:374–382, April 1985.

[13] Greg N. Frederickson and Nancy A. Lynch. Electing a leader in a synchronous ring. *J. ACM*, 34(1):98–115, January 1987.

[14] Oded Goldreich. *The Foundations of Cryptography - Volume 1, Basic Techniques*. Cambridge University Press, 2001.

[15] R. L. Graham and A. C. Yao. On the improbability of reaching byzantine agreements. In *Proceedings of the twenty-first annual ACM symposium on Theory of computing*, STOC '89, pages 467–478, New York, NY, USA, 1989. ACM.

[16] Alon Itai and Michael Rodeh. Symmetry breaking in distributive networks. *Foundations of Computer Science, IEEE Annual Symposium on*, 0:150–158, 1981.

[17] Anna Karlin and Andrew Chi-Chih Yao. Probabilistic lower bounds for byzantine agreement. *Manuscript*, 1986.

[18] Shay Kutten, Gopal Pandurangan, David Peleg, Peter Robinson, and Amitabh Trehan. Sublinear bounds for randomized leader election. In *Distributed Computing and Networking*, volume 7730 of *Lecture Notes in Computer Science*, pages 348–362. Springer Berlin Heidelberg, 2013.

[19] Moni Naor. Bit commitment using pseudo-randomness. In Gilles Brassard, editor, *Advances in Cryptology : CRYPTO '89 Proceedings*, volume 435 of *Lecture Notes in Computer Science*, pages 128–136. Springer New York, 1990.

[20] Gil Neiger and Sam Toueg. Automatically increasing the fault-tolerance of distributed systems. In *Proceedings of the seventh annual ACM Symposium on Principles of distributed computing*, PODC '88, pages 248–262, New York, NY, USA, 1988. ACM.

[21] Michael Okun, Amnon Barak, and Eli Gafni. Renaming in synchronous message passing systems with byzantine failures. *Distributed Computing*, 20:403–413, 2008.

[22] Rafael Pass and Alon Rosen. Concurrent non-malleable commitments. In *Proceedings of the 46th Annual IEEE Symposium on Foundations of Computer Science*, FOCS '05, pages 563–572, Washington, DC, USA, 2005. IEEE Computer Society.

An O(1)-Barriers Optimal RMRs
Mutual Exclusion Algorithm[*]

(Extended Abstract)

Hagit Attiya
Department of
Computer-Science
Technion
hagit@cs.technion.ac.il

Danny Hendler
Department of
Computer-Science & Telekom
Innovation Laboratories
Ben-Gurion University of the
Negev
hendlerd@cs.bgu.ac.il

Smadar Levy
Department of
Computer-Science
Ben-Gurion University of the
Negev
raykgold@bgu.ac.il

ABSTRACT

Mutual exclusion is a fundamental coordination problem. Over the last 20 years, shared-memory mutual exclusion research focuses on *local-spin* algorithms and uses the *remote memory references* (RMRs) metric.

To ensure the correctness of concurrent algorithms in general, and mutual exclusion algorithms in particular, it is often required to prohibit certain re-orderings of memory instructions that may compromise correctness, by inserting *memory barrier* instructions. Memory barriers incur non-negligible overhead and may significantly increase the algorithm's time complexity.

This paper presents the first read/write mutual exclusion algorithm with asymptotically optimal complexity under both the RMRs and barriers metrics: each passage through the critical section incurs $O(\log n)$ RMRs and a constant number of barriers. The algorithm works in the popular *Total Store Ordering* model.

Categories and Subject Descriptors

D.1.3 [**Programming Techniques**]: Concurrent Programming—*Concurrent programming*; F.1.2 [**Computation By Abstract Devices**]: Modes of Computation—*Parallelism and concurrency*

General Terms

Algorithms, Architecture

Keywords

Shared memory, mutual exclusion, total store ordering

---

[*]Partially supported by the Israel Science Foundation (grant number 1227/10)

1. INTRODUCTION

Concurrent algorithms and, in particular, mutual exclusion (mutex) algorithms, are almost always designed under the assumption that memory accesses are atomic, i.e. linearizable [11], or at least sequentially consistent [18]. In practice, however, modern compilers optimize code so as to issue certain instructions out of order, based on the memory model supported by the architecture. The memory model dictates which operation pairs can be reordered [1, Figure 8]. For example, the *total store ordering* (*TSO*) model [19] ensures that writes are not reordered, but it is possible to perform a read from address a before a write to address $b \neq a$ that is earlier in program order is performed. The TSO model is supported by several common architectures, including SPARC [19] and x86 [12].[1] This model is weaker than sequential consistency, and hence, also weaker than linearizability.

To ensure the correctness of a concurrent algorithm, it is possible to prohibit the reordering of memory instructions, by inserting a *barrier* (also called a *fence*) instruction between the memory instructions. Inserting a barrier incurs significant overhead, but it is unavoidable since it has been shown [3] that every mutex algorithm must ensure that there is *a read after a write to a different location*, unless strong atomic operations such as, e.g., *compare-and-swap* (CAS) are used (and these also incur significant overhead).

Over the last 20 years, shared-memory mutual exclusion research investigates the *remote memory references* (RMR) complexity of local-spin mutex algorithms; much of this work focuses on (deterministic) read/write mutual exclusion (see [6, 13, 14, 15, 26] for some examples).

There are such algorithms that incur only a logarithmic number of RMRs per *passage* (entry and corresponding exit of the critical section) [26], which is asymptotically optimal [4][2], but they require a logarithmic number of barriers as well. On the other hand, it is easily shown that the well-known Bakery mutex algorithm [17] requires only a constant number of barriers per passage. However, it incurs a linear number of RMRs, even in un-contended, solo, passages. So

---

[1]Owens et al. [22] prove Intel x86 is equivalent to Sparc TSO.
[2]The lower bound of [4] applies also to mutual exclusion algorithms that may use *comparison* primitives, such as CAS, in addition to reads and writes.

is there an inherent tradeoff between the RMR and barrier complexity of read/write mutual exclusion?

This paper shows that it is possible to win on both measures, by presenting a read/write mutual exclusion algorithm that combines optimal RMR complexity with a constant number of memory barriers, in the popular TSO model.

Local-spin mutex research considers both the *Distributed Shared Memory* (DSM) and the *Cache Coherent* (CC) system models. The prevailing DSM memory model is much weaker than TSO [7], however. We therefore consider the CC model in this work.

Mutex algorithms that incur $O(1)$ RMRs and memory barriers per passage can be devised if atomic operations such as swap and fetch-and-add are available. Two key such algorithms are the CLH lock [5, 20] and the MCS lock [21] Both these algorithms use the swap operation.

The rest of this paper is organized as follows. In Section 2, we provide required background, describe the high-level ideas underlying our algorithm and provide intuitions as to why it works under TSO. Section 3 presents a more precise model. Section 4 presents the algorithm in detail (using CAS) and Section 5 proves its correctness; Section 6 explains how to modify the algorithm so it uses only read and write operations. We conclude, in Section 6, with a short discussion of our results and directions for future research. The appendix present preliminary results of an experimental evaluation of our algorithm.

2. BACKGROUND AND OVERVIEW OF THE ALGORITHM

To understand the importance of the execution order of memory access instructions, consider the following simplified code for the *Bakery* mutex algorithm [17].

```
1: Choosing[i] = true
2: Num[i]=1 + max(Num[1],..., Num[n])
3: Choosing[i]=false
4: for (j = 1; j ≤ n; j++)
5:     while (Choosing[j]) nop
6:     while ((Num[j] ≠ 0) and ((Num[j], j) < (Num[i], i))) nop
Critical Section
7: Number[i]=0
```

Roughly, the key for showing the safety of the Bakery algorithm is that a process first announces its participation (by setting its number to a positive value) and then reads to verify that no other process holds a smaller number. However, when the architecture only guarantees total store ordering, the read of Line 6 may be performed early, before the writes of Lines 2 and 3 are visible to the other processes. Thus, it is possible that two processes will read zero from each other's entry of the Num array, and both will enter the critical section. This reordering of instructions can be excluded by inserting a barrier between Line 3 and Line 4. Adding two addition barriers (after Lines 1 and 7) ensures that the Bakery algorithm is correct under the TSO model.

Unfortunately, the Bakery algorithm incurs significant overhead, apparently because of high RMR complexity: a process needs to read the numbers of all potential contenders for the critical section. This produces $O(n)$ RMRs, where n is the number of processes.

Figure 1(a) shows the time taken by a single thread to perform 1M solo passages in the Bakery algorithm, as a function of n. (More information about the tests on which these graphs are based is provided in the appendix.) A second running thread caused the thread performing passages to incur RMRs. We tested performance with and without the algorithm's barriers[3]. Thus, per every x-axis value, there are 2 bars showing the time taken with (light bars) and without (dark bars) barriers. As shown by Figure 1(a), barriers account for a relatively small fraction of the time complexity of the Bakery algorithm. However, the algorithm's time complexity grows quickly with n.

The number of RMRs can be significantly reduced by employing a *tournament tree* mutex algorithm [26]. The algorithm uses a balanced binary tree with n nodes, each associated with a two-process mutual exclusion algorithm. A process starts at a dedicated (virtual) leaf and climbs up the tree, competing in a two-process mutex algorithm at each node, until it wins at the root and enters the critical section. This algorithm incurs $O(\log n)$ RMRs per passage through the critical section, which is optimal [4]. To ensure the correctness of the two-process mutex performed at the nodes on the path to the root, it is necessary to insert a barrier in the code of each internal node (see Figure 2(a)). This means that a process performs $\Theta(\log n)$ barriers on each passage to the critical section, leading to a significant overhead, as can be seen in Figure 1(b).

A balanced binary tree with n leaves is a key data structure also in our mutual exclusion algorithm; however, we use it for *collecting* a list of waiting processes, rather than as an arbitration mechanism. Entry to the critical section is guarded by two mechanisms: The first, which is expected to play the main role in lightly-contended situations, is a lock manipulated with *CAS* operations (we explain how the CAS can be replaced with reads and writes in Section 6). The second mechanism is a *promotion queue* of waiting processes, collected on the binary tree.

A process exiting the critical section goes down the path from the root to its leaf, collecting waiting processes (whose identifiers it reads from each path node and its child nodes) and adding them to the promotion queue. If the queue is not empty, the exiting process *promotes* one of the processes in the queue into the critical section. The promotion queue is manipulated only by processes exiting the critical section, that is, in exclusion.

A similar promotion mechanism has been used in prior mutex algorithms (e.g., [10]). The key novelty of our algorithm is the simple manner in which processes announce their wish to enter the critical section. A process wishing to enter the critical section writes its id in all nodes on the path from its leaf to the root and tries to grab the lock. If it fails, then it is ensured that some exiting process will find it and add it to the promotion queue; therefore, it can wait for its promotion, spinning on a dedicated variable (Figure 2(b)).

To understand where a barrier should be inserted, it is instrumental to think about the core argument in showing why a process p eventually enters the critical section, namely, the proof that a waiting process will eventually be enqueued to the promotion queue. For the current discussion alone, assume that the memory is sequentially consistent and that each process enters the critical section only once.

Consider the highest node v in which process p's id is not overwritten by another process (its own leaf, in the worst case); let u be its parent. We can argue, by induction, that

---

[3]Removing the barriers makes the algorithm incorrect in general but not in solo executions.

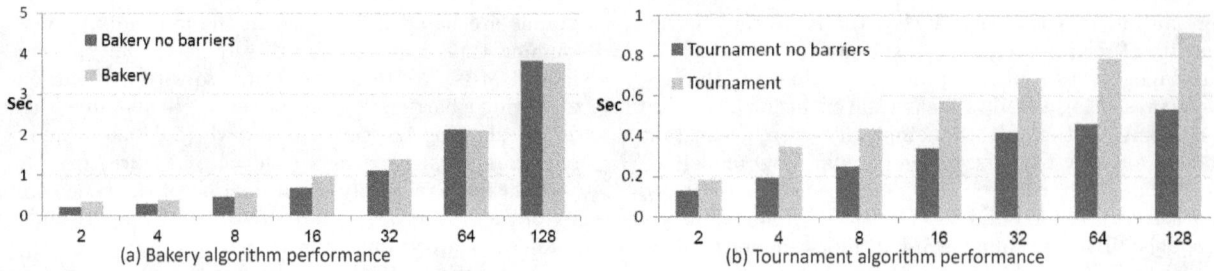

Figure 1: Time to perform 1M passages as a function of the number of threads supported in the Bakery (a) and Tournament tree (b) algorithms.

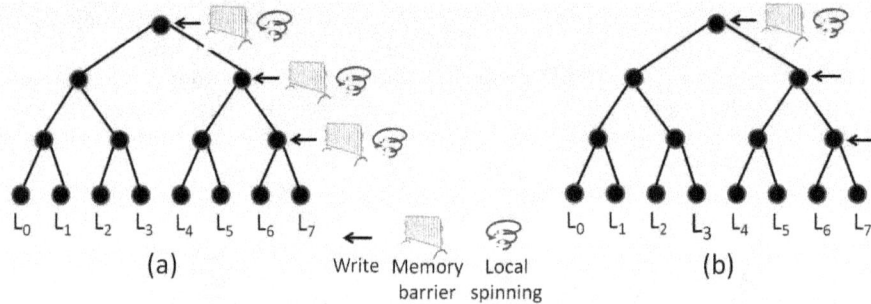

Figure 2: Entry section synchronization pattern in previous optimal-RMR algorithms (a) and in our algorithm (b).

q, the last process to overwrite p's id in u, eventually enters the critical section. The sequence of operations p and q perform (shown below) guarantees that q reads p from v and enqueues it.

```
p              q
write to v
write to u
               write to u      (overwrites p)
               enters CS
               exits CS
               reads p from v  (p not overwritten in v)
```

While this description assumes sequential consistency (by assuming all operations are ordered sequentially), it relies in fact on two orders: that the writes of p (to v and u) are executed in program order, and that the writes of p are executed before it fails to win the lock. TSO enforces the first ordering, and *a single* barrier is inserted to ensure the second ordering.

Thus, in our algorithm processes use a synchronization pattern fundamentally different than that used by previous optimal-RMR algorithms as they access the tree while performing their entry section. Previous optimal-RMR mutex algorithms used a synchronization pattern as in the tournament tree (Figure 2(a)). As a process climbs up the path from its leaf to a new node v in the course of the entry section, it performs the following operations. First, it has to write to node v. Then, it has to perform a memory barrier for ensuring the visibility of the write. Finally, it reads v and may need to locally spin until some condition is met.

In our algorithm, a process performing the entry section *only writes* to all non-root nodes along its path, as shown in Figure 2(b); it does not perform memory barrier operations on such nodes, nor does it busy wait on them or even read them. A process may need to perform the write-fence-read

sequence of operations only when it reaches the root node. A detailed description of the algorithm appears in Section 4.

3. SHARED-MEMORY SYSTEM WITH TOTAL STORE ORDERING (TSO)

We now present an operational model for the behavior of a shared-memory system with relaxed memory ordering, which is a simplified version of the model used by Park and Dill [23]. The model is tailored to describe TSO, but it can be extended to describe other memory models (see [16, 23, 25]).

There is a set of n processes, $p_1, \ldots, p_n$, each of which has its own abstract *store queue*. A process executes memory operations—read, write and compare-and-swap—in the order specified by its algorithm, called *program order*. Write operations may be delayed and executed after load operations following them in the program order, due to various implementation techniques or compiler optimizations. This is modeled by having write operations go to the store queue rather than directly to the shared memory.

A *configuration* describes the state of a system: It contains the local state of each process, including its location in its algorithm and the contents of its store queue. It also contains the value of each shared variable. In the *initial configuration*, all processes are in their initial state and their store queues are empty; all shared variables hold their initial values.

An *execution fragment* E is a sequence of steps, picked by an adversarial scheduler. The adversary picks a process for the next step, and then decides whether to let the process execute another step according to its algorithm or to *perform* the first write operation in the store queue (if any). If the adversary takes a write operation from the store buffer, then

222

it changes the value of the relevant shared variable to the parameter of the write. The write operation is *performed* at this step.

What happens when a process takes a step depends on the type of step:

1. A *write* operation is placed at the end of the store queue. The write operation is *issued* at this step.

2. A *read* operation returns the value of the variable, and the process changes its local state accordingly. If there are writes to this variable in the store queue, the value is read from the most recent write in the queue; otherwise, the value of the variable is read from the shared memory.[4] The read operation is performed at this step.

3. A *barrier* operation enforces the adversary to perform all the writes in the store queue (if any) in the order they were issued. The writes become visible and the queue is emptied. The barrier operation is performed at this step.

4. A *compare-and-swap* (*CAS*) operation atomically compares the value of the shared variable with its first parameter, and if they are equal, sets the value of the variable to its second parameter. The CAS operation is performed at this step. If there are writes to the variable in the store queue when the CAS is issued, then the adversary performs all these writes (and those preceding them in the buffer, if any) and removes them from the store queue before the CAS step is taken.

Note that in this model, writes become visible to all other processes at the same time (this means that the memory is *coherent*). An *execution* is an execution fragment that starts in the initial configuration.

We assume a *cache-coherent* (CC) system, in which each processor[5] maintains local copies of shared variables it reads inside its cache, whose consistency is ensured by a coherence protocol. At any given time, a variable is remote to a processor if the corresponding cache does not contain an up-to-date copy of the variable. A memory access to a remote variable is called a *remote memory reference* (RMR). Each write to a shared variable incurs an RMR.[6] A read by process p of a shared variable v incurs an RMR if (1) it is the first read of v by p, or (2) it is preceded by a write of another process to v that was performed after p's previous read of v.

4. THE ALGORITHM

We now provide a detailed description of our algorithm, whose pseudo-code is presented by Algorithm 1. Note that Algorithm 1 uses the CAS operation. In Section 6, we explain how it can be transformed to a read-write algorithm that maintains the properties we require.

The data structure underlying the algorithm is a binary tree with leaves $L_0, \ldots, L_{n-1}$ (statement **1**). Leaf L_p, for

---

[4] In our algorithm, a read accesses a variable that was previously written to by the same thread only after a barrier, so the first condition is never satisfied.

[5] The model assumes that distinct processes run on distinct processors.

[6] This is not necessarily the case in write-back CC systems. Any upper bound on the RMR complexity in our model holds also for the write-back model.

$p \in \{0, \ldots, n-1\}$, is statically assigned to process p. Tree nodes store integer values and are initialized to -1.

Our algorithm uses a *promotion* mechanism. This mechanism allows a process performing its exit section to facilitate the entry of other processes whose identifiers it reads along the path from the root to its leaf. Identifiers of promoted processes that did not yet enter the critical section are stored in a FIFO queue named *promQ* (statement **3**). Processes apply operations to *promQ* before they release the lock, hence its implementation is not required to support concurrent access.

Each process has an entry in the *inPromQ* array, indicating whether or not it is currently in the promotion queue. Process identifiers are enqueued to the promotion queue only on condition that they are not already in it. The *inPromQ* array is used for checking this condition by performing a single read operation.

The *apply* array is used by processes to apply for promotion (statement **5**). A promoted process busy-waits on its entry of the *signal* array until it is signalled to enter the critical section (statement **7**). The *lock* integer either stores the identifier of the process currently holding the lock, or -1 if the lock is free (statement **11**). It is manipulated using read, write and CAS operations.

The *exits* shared integer counts the number of critical section exits. It is required for preventing a possible scenario in which a process busy-waiting on *lock* incurs a non-constant number of RMRs if the lock owner releases and re-captures *lock* multiple times.

The Entry Section. To enter the critical section, process p first initializes its entry of the *signal* array and sets its entry of the *apply* array to apply for promotion (statements **17–18**). Process p then traverses up the path from L_p to the root, writing its identifier to each node along this path (statements **19–21**). After having completed this sequence of writes, p performs a single memory barrier to ensure that these writes become visible before it proceeds (statement **22**).

Process p then attempts to capture the lock using a CAS operation (statement **23**). (We note that, in some architectures, the execution of a CAS operation triggers the execution of a memory barrier. In such architectures, the memory barrier of statement **22** is not required.) If the CAS succeeds, then p enters the critical section. If the CAS fails, however, then the process that owns the lock when p's unsuccessful CAS is performed (henceforth denoted by r) may fail to observe p, in which case it will not promote it. This may happen if r has already begun its exit section and already read the nodes on the intersection of p's and r's paths to the root before p performed its memory barrier.

To overcome this potential race condition, p has to busy wait until either another complete execution of the exit section takes place since its CAS failed, the lock becomes free, or the lock is handed to it (statement **25**). (It is also possible that the CAS of statement **23** fails because the lock is handed to p before it performs the CAS.) Then, p attempts to capture the lock again (statement **26**). If it succeeds, it enters the critical section. If it fails, implying that either the lock was re-captured since p's CAS in statement **23** failed or that the lock was handed to p, then p awaits to be signalled (statement **27**). As we prove, this must eventually happen, and when it does, p enters the critical section.

Algorithm 1: mutual exclusion algorithm for process $p \in \{0, \ldots, n-1\}$

```
1  shared T: Binary tree with leaves L_0, ..., L_{n-1}
   /* Integer nodes initialized to -1 */
2
3  shared promQ: Queue of int init φ        /* Queue of
   processes to be promoted */
4
5  shared apply: array [0..n-1] of boolean init false
   /* Applying-for-promotion array */
6
7  shared signal: array [0..n-1] of boolean  /* Array for
   signalling promoted processes */
8
9  shared inPromQ: array [0..n-1] of boolean init false
   /* promQ membership array */
10
11 shared lock: int init -1      /* Lock, supporting read,
   write and CAS operations */
12
13 shared exits: int init 0        /* Number of CS exits,
   incremented on exit section */
14
15 local r: boolean, int next, e;
16 Procedure Entry(){
17    signal[p] ← false
18    apply[p] ← true
19    foreach node n on the path from L_p to the root do
20       |  n ← p
21    end
22    Barrier
23    if CAS(lock, -1, p) ≠ -1 then
24       |  e ← exits
25       |  await ((exits - e ≥ 2) ∨ lock ∈ {p, -1})
26       |  if CAS(lock, -1, p) ≠ -1 then
27       |  |  await (signal[p])
28       |  end
29    end
30 Procedure Exit(){
31    apply[p] ← false
32    exits ← exits+1
33    foreach node n on the path from the root to L_p's parent do
34       |  q_1 ← n, q_2 ← n.left, q_3 ← n.right
35       |  foreach q ∈ {q_1, q_2, q_3} \ {-1, p} do
36       |  |  if apply[q] ∧ ¬inPromQ[q] then
37       |  |  |  promQ.enqueue(q)
38       |  |  |  inPromQ[q] ← true
39       |  |  end
40       |  end
41    end
42    if promQ.isEmpty() then
43       |  lock ← -1
44    else
45       |  next ← Q.dequeue()
46       |  inPromQ[next] ← false
47       |  lock ← next
48       |  signal[next] ← true
49    end
50    Barrier
```

The Exit Section. To exit the critical section, process p first resets its entry of the *apply* array as it no longer requires promotion (statement **31**). Process p then descends down the path from the root to its leaf (statement **33**), reading the identifiers written at every internal node along this path and its child nodes (statement **34**). Process p promotes any process that applies for promotion whose identifier it reads,

by enqueueing it to the promotion queue if it is not already there (statements **35–40**).

After having descended to its leaf, p checks the promotion queue (statement **42**). If it is empty, then p releases the lock (statement **43**), otherwise p dequeues the first process from the promotion queue, resets its *inPromQ* entry, hands over the lock to it and signals it that is may now enter the critical section (statements **45–48**). Before exiting, p performs a memory barrier to ensure that the write operations it performed in its critical and exit sections are all visible (statement **50**).

5. CORRECTNESS AND COMPLEXITY PROOFS

In this section, we prove that our algorithm satisfies mutual exclusion and starvation freedom in TSO systems. Then we show that the algorithm provides $(\log n + 3)$-bounded waiting (formally defined later). This is followed by a proof that the algorithm has optimal RMR complexity and uses only a constant number of barriers.

A *passage* is the sequence of steps taken by a process as it performs the entry, critical and exit sections. For the purposes of the proofs in this section, statement **50**, where a process performs a memory barrier to ensure that its writes in the critical and exit sections are performed, is not considered part of the exit section.

A mutual exclusion algorithm provides k-*bounded waiting* if, in every execution, no process enters the critical section more than k times while another process is waiting in its its entry section.

The next theorem summarizes the properties of the algorithm.

THEOREM 1. *Algorithm 1 satisfies mutual exclusion, starvation-freedom and $(\log n + 3)$-bounded waiting under TSO. Each passage of the algorithm incurs $O(\log n)$ RMRs and a constant number of barriers.*

We start with a few definitions. For execution fragments E, F, we write $E \preceq F$ if E is a prefix of F. Let $pc(C, p)$ denote the value of p's program counter in configuration C, that is, the number of the next pseudocode statement that p will execute after configuration C. $C.v$ denotes the value of shared variable v in configuration C. Similarly, $pc(E, p)$ and $E.v$ denote the value of p's program counter and the value of shared variable v in the configuration reached after execution E.

DEFINITION 1. *We say that a passage starts when a process issues statement* **17**. *We say that a process completes its exit section and completes a passage when statement* **43** *or statement* **48** *are performed. We say that a process is in a passage in configuration C if there is a passage that p started in the execution leading to C but did not yet complete. Let p be a process in its entry section. We say that p is in the doorway if it did not yet perform statement* **23**; *otherwise, we say that p is in the waiting section. A process p owns the lock in configuration C if $C.lock = p$ holds.*

Invariant (d) of the following lemma immediately implies mutual exclusion.

LEMMA 2. *The following invariants hold in every reachable configuration C of the algorithm.*

(a) If p is in the critical section in C, then p owns the lock in C.

(b) If p is in the exit section in C and $pc(C, p) \neq 48$, then p owns the lock in C. If $pc(C, p) = 48$, then the lock owner is some process q, where q's identifier was dequeued by p in statement **45** of its current passage.

(c) $|\{r | (C.signal[r] = true) \wedge (17 < pc(C, r) < 49)\}| \leq 1$. If there is such a process r, then r owns the lock in C and no process $q \neq r$ is in the critical or exit sections in C.

(d) At most one process is in the critical or exit sections.

PROOF. All invariants clearly hold in the initial configuration. The only pseudo-code statements that may violate these invariants are the following.

1. Statements **23** and **26**, if the CAS is successful: this makes the executing process enter the critical section and, it is also the lock owner.

2. Statement **27**, if performed by process p when $signal[p] = true$ holds, as this makes p enter the critical section.

3. Statement **43**: the execution of this statement by process p changes the value of $lock$ and after its execution p is no longer the lock owner. Also, from Definition 1, after performing statement **43** p completes the exit section.

4. Statement **47**: the execution of this statement changes the identity of the lock owner.

5. Statement **48**: the execution of this statement sets an entry of the $signal$ array. Also, from Definition 1, after performing statement **48** p completes the exit section.

We call the above statements *i-statements* and prove the lemma by induction on the number of these statements that are performed in an execution. For the base case, consider an execution E in which no i-statements are performed. Since no successful CAS is performed in E, no process could have entered the CS from statement **23**. This also implies that no process could have been signalled in E, which implies in turn that Invariant (c) holds, since upon starting the entry section a process resets its entry of the $signal$ array (statement **17**). As no process was signalled in E, no process could have entered the CS from statement **27**, hence Invariants (a), (b) and (d) also hold.

We note that the first statement of the entry code by a process resets its entry of the $signal$ array and therefore cannot violate Invariant (c) (clearly it cannot violate Invariants (a), (b) or (d)).

For the induction step, assume the claim holds for any execution where some $k \geq 0$ i-statements are performed, and let $E = E'sE''$ be an execution where exactly $k + 1$ i-statements are performed, the last of which is s. Let C be the configuration after E'. The following cases exist.

1. Step s is the execution of a successful CAS in statement **23** or statement **26** by some process p. Process p is in the critical section in Cs and is the lock owner, thus Invariant (a) is not violated by s. Since the CAS is successful, $C.lock=-1$ holds and so no process is the lock owner in C. By the induction hypothesis, applied to Invariant (a), this implies that no process is in the

critical section in C. By the induction hypothesis, applied to Invariant (b), this also implies that there is no process in the exit section in C, hence Invariants (b) and (d) hold in Cs. Finally, since no process was signalled in s, Invariant (c) is not violated by s.

2. Step s is the execution of statement **27** by process p and $C.signal[p] = true$ holds. Process p is in the critical section in Cs. By the induction hypothesis, applied to Invariant (c), p is the lock owner in C hence also in Cs, so Invariant (a) holds in Cs. Also by the induction hypothesis, applied to Invariant (c), there is no process in the critical or exit sections in C, so both Invariants (b) and (d) hold in Cs. By the induction hypothesis, applied to Invariant (c), p is the only process whose entry of the $signal$ array is set in C, hence it is also the only such process in Cs, so Invariant (c) holds also in Cs.

3. Step s is the execution of statement **43** by some process p. By the induction hypothesis, applied to Invariant (d), p is the only process in the critical and exit sections in C, hence there is no process in the critical or exit sections in Cs, implying that Invariants (a), (b) and (d) hold in Cs. Invariant (c) also holds in Cs, since statement **43** does not set an entry of the $signal$ array.

4. Step s is the execution of statement **47** by some process p that hands over the lock to some process q. By the induction hypothesis, applied to Invariant (d), p is the only process in the critical or exit sections in C, hence, in Cs, there is no process in the critical section and p is the only process in the exit section, thus Invariants (a) and (d) hold in Cs. Since $pc(C, p) = 47$, it follows from the induction hypothesis, applied to Invariant (b) that p is the lock owner in C. Consequently, it follows from $pc(Cs, p) = 48$ that Invariant (b) also holds in Cs. Finally, since statement **47** does not set an entry of the $signal$ array and $17 < pc(C, p), pc(Cs, p) < 49$, Invariant (c) cannot be violated by the execution of s.

5. Step s is the execution of statement **48** by some process p. By the induction hypothesis, applied to Invariant (d), p is the only process in the critical and exit sections in C, thus there is no process in these sections in Cs and Invariants (a), (b) and (d) hold in Cs. Since p is in the exit section in C, it follows by the induction hypothesis, applied to Invariant (c) that p is the only process not in its remainder section that may have its entry of the $signal$ array set in C. Since $pc(C, p) = 48$, it follows from the induction hypothesis, applied to Invariant (b) that there is a process q, whose identifier is written in p's *next* variable in C, that holds the lock in C. Since p exits the critical section once having performed statement **47**, $\{r | (C.signal[r] = true) \wedge (17 < pc(C, r) < statement\ 49)\} = \{q\}$ and Invariant (c) holds in Cs.

$\square$

COROLLARY 3. *The algorithm satisfies mutual exclusion.*

We proceed to prove that the algorithm satisfies starvation freedom. Corollary 3 implies:

COROLLARY 4. *The promotion queue is accessed in a sequential manner.*

LEMMA 5. *Let q be a process that is enqueued by some process p to promQ in some point t of the execution, then (a) q is in its entry section in t, and (b) q eventually enters the critical section after t.*

PROOF. A process q sets its entry of the *apply* array in the beginning of its entry section (statement **18**) and resets it at the beginning of its exit section (statement **31**). Since p is in the exit section in t, it follows from Invariant (d) of Lemma 2 that q cannot be in its critical or exit sections, hence claim (a) holds.

By Corollary 4, operations on *promQ* are applied in a sequential manner. From statements **42–48**, process p eventually dequeues the oldest item in *promQ*, say process q', hands over the lock to it, and signals it. By claim (a), q' is in its entry section. Regardless of whether q' performs the CAS operations of statement **23** and statement **26** before or after the lock is handed over to it, these CAS operations will fail and q' is bound to reach statement **25** and will eventually enter the critical section. Proceeding inductively, all processes that precede q in *promQ* (if any) will eventually enter and exit the critical section. It follows that process q eventually enters the critical section. □

LEMMA 6. *Let p be a process that performs statement **23** and receives its own identifier p as the result of the CAS operation. Then p eventually enters the critical section.*

PROOF. Since $lock = p$ when p performs statement **23**, some process q hands the lock to p during its exit section and signals p. By Invariant (c) of Lemma 2, once p is signalled no other process enter the critical section before it, hence, $lock=p$ continues to hold as long as p is in its entry section. Thus, p eventually evaluates the second condition of statement **25** as true and fails the CAS of statement **26**. It follows that p eventually evaluates the condition of statement **27** as true and enters the critical section. □

DEFINITION 2. *Let p be a process and let $l \in \{0,\ldots,\log n\}$ be a tree level (the root is in level 0). We let n_p^l denote the node along the path from L_p to the root that is at level l, where the leaves are at level $\log n$. Let E be an execution. We let $l_p(E)$ denote the highest (smallest) level l such that $n_p^l = p$ holds after E.*

LEMMA 7. *The algorithm satisfies starvation freedom.*

PROOF. Assume, by way of contradiction, that there is an infinite execution EE' such that, at the end of E, a non-empty set S of *starved processes* are busy-waiting either at statement **25** or at statement **27** but none of them enter the critical section in the (infinite) execution fragment E'. The following claim states that there is a prefix of E' after which the values l_p are "stable" for every starved process p.

CLAIM 1. *There is a prefix E_1 of E' such that $\forall p \in S, \forall E_1 E_2 \preceq E' : l_p(EE_1E_2) = l_p(EE_1)$.*

PROOF. Let p be a starved process. First we note that $l_p(F)$ is well defined for all $E \preceq F \preceq EE'$, since $L_p = p$ always holds for every process in the waiting section. From the definitions of E and of starved processes, p does not issue a write during E'. It follows that l_p is non-decreasing during

E', that is, $F_1 \preceq F_2 \preceq E' \implies l_p(EF_1) \leq l_p(EF_2)$. Finally, since $l_p \in \{0,\ldots,\log n\}$, l_p may increase at most $\log n$ times during E' and the claim follows. □

We reach a contradiction by proving the following inductive claim.

CLAIM 2. *Let p be a process. If $l_p(EE_1) = k$, for $k \in \{0,\ldots,\log n\}$, then p is not starved in EE'.*

PROOF. We prove the claim by induction on $l_p(EE_1)$.

Base: for the base case, $l_p(EE_1) = 0$ so $n_p^{l_p}$ after EE_1 is the root. Consider process p's last execution of the doorway when it last wrote its identifer to the root node and then performed the barrier in statement **22**. Clearly, p's identifier is not overwritten in the root in the rest of the execution. From the definition of execution E and since p is starved, when p proceeded to perform the CAS of statement **23** during E, the CAS must have failed. Let t be the point in the execution when p performs this CAS. The preceding barrier performed by p in statement **22** guarantees that p's identifier is written at the root in t. If the lock owner at t is p, then by Lemma 6, p eventually enters the critical section. Assume otherwise, then some other process r holds the lock in t. We have the following possibilities:

1. Process r did not yet read the root node in statement **34** of its exit section. In this case, r is bound to read p's identifier in its exit section and to enqueue p to the promotion queue. By Lemma 5, p eventually enters the critical section.

2. Process r reads the root node in statement **34** of its exit section before t but, as it is still the lock owner in t, did not complete its passage. Eventually r exits the critical section. If process p executes statements **25–26** before the lock is re-captured, then the CAS of statement **26** succeeds and p enters the critical section. Otherwise, some process r' (possibly $r' = r$) enters the critical section after t. Hence, when r' performs its exit section, it reads p's identifier from the root node and promotes it if it was not promoted earlier, and by Lemma 5(b), p eventually enters the critical section.

Induction: Assume the claim holds for all levels l, $0 \leq l \leq k < \log n$, we prove that it holds also for level $k+1$. Let process p be a starved process such that $l_p(EE_1) = k+1$, so n_p^{k+1} is the highest node along the path from L_p to the root such that $n_p^{k+1} = p$ after EE_1.

Consider process p's last execution of the doorway when it last wrote its identifer to node n_p^{k+1} and let t denote the point in the execution when this write is performed. Clearly, p's identifier is not overwritten in n_p^{k+1} in the rest of the execution. After writing to n_p^{k+1}, p proceeds to write its identifier to higher nodes along the path to the root and then performs the barrier in statement **22**. Let t_1 be the point in the execution when p's next write to n_p^k is performed and let t_2 be the point when it performs statement **22**. By total store ordering, $t \leq t_1 \leq t_2$. From the definition of l_p, n_p^k is overwritten after t_1. Let $t' > t_1$ be the point when n_p^k is last written in EE_1 and let q be the process that issues this write operation. Since q is the last process to write to n_p^k in EE_1, $l_q(EE_1) \leq k$. It follows from the induction hypothesis that q is not starved and therefore q enters and exits the critical section after t'. Since $t' > t_1 \geq t$, q reads p's identifier in the course of its exit section in statements **35–40**. By Lemma 5(b), p eventually enters the critical section. □

Claim 2, capturing the informal argument presented in Section 2, implies Lemma 7.

Bounded Waiting. We now prove that our algorithm provides $O(\log n)$-bounded waiting.

LEMMA 8. *The algorithm provides* $(\log n + 3)$*-bounded waiting.*

The key to the proof is Lemma 9 below. Essentially, the lemma establishes that if a process p is "overtaken" $\log n + 2$ times by some other process q, then some process is bound to read L_p in the course of its exit section and promote p before q will enter the critical section once again.

We use the following notation in the proofs that follow. Let $\mathcal{P}$ be a passage by some process p. Then $c(\mathcal{P})$ is the point in the execution when p completes the doorway during $\mathcal{P}$ and $s(\mathcal{P})$ is the point when p either succeeds in its CAS operation on the lock or is enqueued by some other process to the promotion queue (in statement **37**) during $\mathcal{P}$. For $l \in \{0, \ldots, \log n\}$, let $t^l(\mathcal{P})$ be the point when p's write to n_p^l in the course of $\mathcal{P}$'s doorway is performed.

LEMMA 9. *Consider a passage $\mathcal{P}$ by process p in which it does not enter the critical section directly from statement **23**. The following holds for all $l \in \{0, \ldots, \log n\}$: if some process q enters the critical section $l + 2$ times during $(c(\mathcal{P}), s(\mathcal{P}))$, then some process reads node n_p^l during $(t^l(\mathcal{P}), s(\mathcal{P}))$ as it performs statement **34** during its exit section before the $(l + 2)$'th entry of q.*

PROOF. We prove the claim by induction on l.

Base: for the base case, $l = 0$ and n_p^0 is the root node. If p enters the critical section from statement **26** and no other process enters the critical section during $(c(\mathcal{P}), s(\mathcal{P}))$, then the claim clearly holds. Otherwise, let p' be the first process to enter the critical section at some point $t' \in (t^0(\mathcal{P}), s(\mathcal{P}))$. Clearly from the code, p' reads the root node in statement **34** in the course of its exit section. Assume it reads the root node at point t'' after t'. Then no process q enters the critical section twice during $(c(\mathcal{P}), t'')$ and $t'' \in (t^0(\mathcal{P}), s(\mathcal{P}))$ holds, which proves the claim.

Induction: Assume the claim holds for all $0 \leq l \leq m < \log n$, we prove it holds for $m + 1$. Assume there is a process q that enters the critical section $m + 3$ times during $(c(\mathcal{P}), s(\mathcal{P}))$. Let t' be the point in the execution when q enters the critical section for the $(m + 2)$'th time during $(c(\mathcal{P}), s(\mathcal{P}))$. By the induction hypothesis, there is a point $t'' \in (t^m(\mathcal{P}), s(\mathcal{P}))$, before t', when some process q' reads node n_p^m as it executes statement **34** in the course of its exit section.

Let r be the value read by q' in t''. Since $t'' < t' < s(\mathcal{P})$, $r \neq p$, as otherwise p would have been promoted by q' before t' hence before $s(\mathcal{P})$, contradicting the definition of $s(\mathcal{P})$. Since $t'' \in (t^m(\mathcal{P}), s(\mathcal{P}))$, it follows that r has a passage $\mathcal{R}$ whose doorway completes during $(t^m(\mathcal{P}), s(\mathcal{P}))$. By total store ordering, $t^{m+1}(\mathcal{P}) \leq t^m(\mathcal{P})$ hence r completes $\mathcal{R}$'s doorway during $(t^{m+1}(\mathcal{P}), s(\mathcal{P}))$.

The following possibilities exist:

1. r is in the entry section of $\mathcal{R}$ in t''. In this case, q' promotes r during its exit section before q enters the critical section for the $(m + 2)$'th time. Since q may appear in the promotion queue at most once, r will read n_p^{m+1} (say, at point t^*) during its exit section, before q enters the critical section for the $(m + 3)$'th time. Since q enters the critical section for the $(m + 3)$'th time before $s(\mathcal{P})$, it follows that $t^* \in (t^{m+1}, s(\mathcal{P}))$ holds, hence the claim holds for $m + 1$.

2. r already completed passage $\mathcal{R}$ before t''. This implies that r performed the exit section of $\mathcal{R}$ during $(t^{m+1}(\mathcal{P}), t'')$ and read n_p^{m+1} before q enters the critical section for the $(m+2)$'th time. The claim for $m+1$ follows.

□

Proof of Lemma 8: Let p a process that performs a passage $\mathcal{P}$. If p enters the critical section from statement **23**, then it shifts directly from the doorway to the critical section without waiting and the claim is not violated. Assume otherwise, then the conditions of Lemma 9 hold.

Assume that some process q enters the critical section $\log n + 3$ times during $(c(\mathcal{P}), s(\mathcal{P}))$ and let t' be the point in the execution when q enters for the $(\log n + 2)$'th time. By Lemma 9, there is a point execution t'', that follows $t^{\log n}(\mathcal{P})$ and precedes t', which in turn, precedes $s(\mathcal{P})$), in which some process q' reads L_p as it performs statement **34** during its exit section. Since $L_p = p \wedge apply[p] = true$ holds as long as p is waiting, q' promotes p in this passage. After p is promoted, q may enter the critical section at most once more—for the $(\log n + 2)$'th time—before p, since every process appears at most once in the promotion queue. This is a contradiction. □

RMR and Barrier Complexity

LEMMA 10. *A process performs a constant number of barriers and incurs $O(\log n)$ RMRs during a passage.*

PROOF. The first part of the lemma is clear from the pseudocode. To prove the second part, we only need to consider the number of RMRs incurred while a process p busy waits in statement **25** and statement **27**, since p traverses $O(\log n)$ nodes in its entry and exit sections. Since p reads variable *exits* before executing statement **25**, the first condition of this statement guarantees that p incurs at most 4 RMRs while executing it: at most twice when it reads variable *exits* and at most twice when it reads *lock*. As for statement **27**, since *signal[p]* is only reset by p, p cannot incur more than a single RMR in the course of busy waiting in this statement. □

All the variables used by our algorithms are of bounded size, with the exception of the *exits* variable. This variable is used to prevent a scenario in which a busy-waiting process incurs a non-constant number of RMRs while reading the same identifier from *lock* again and again and the proof of Lemma 10 above relies on its usage. We get the following from Lemma 8:

OBSERVATION 1. *Lemma 10 continues to hold if the* exits *variable supports $(n - 1)(\log n + 2) + 1$ values and is incremented modulo this value.*

6. A READ/WRITE IMPLEMENTATION

We now show that we can avoid CAS operations and transform the algorithm to an optimal-RMR, constant-barriers algorithm that uses only reads and writes.

Golab et al. [8, Theorem 42] establish that every mutual exclusion algorithm A that uses reads, writes, and *comparison* operations such as compare-and-swap, can be transformed to a mutual exclusion algorithm A' that uses only reads and writes and has the same RMR complexity up to a constant factor. However, we also require that the algorithm obtained by applying the transformation of [8] to Algorithm 1 will need only a constant number of barriers per passage.

The transformation of [8] for cache-coherent algorithms is based on an implementation of an $O(1)$ RMRs, locally-accessible and writable CAS object from reads and writes. This is a complex implementation composed of multiple implementation layers [8, Figure 1]. The bottom-most layer is an $O(1)$ RMRs implementation of *Leader Election* (LE) from reads and writes [9], and the implementations of the other layers appear in [8].

The proof of the following lemma is provided in the full paper. It establishes that *Read* operations on the simulated comparison object that do not incur RMRs perform no writes. *Read* operations that do incur RMRs, as well as *Write* or *ECAS* operations (see [8]) applied to the simulated object, perform a constant number of writes.

LEMMA 11. *Operations on a comparison object simulated by [8] perform at most a constant number of writes. Moreover, a Read operation on a simulated comparison object performs write operations only if the simulated Read operation incurs an RMR.*

THEOREM 12. *There is a read-write mutual exclusion algorithm for the TSO model that satisfies starvation-freedom and $(\log n + 3)$-bounded waiting, for which each passage incurs $O(\log n)$ RMRs and a constant number of barriers.*

PROOF. Let A' be the read-write algorithm obtained by applying the transformation of [8] to Algorithm 1. We show that A' retains the properties specified in Theorem 1. From [8, Theorem 42] and Theorem 1, A' satisfies mutual exclusion and starvation-freedom and has $O(\log n)$ RMR complexity. Since Algorithm 1 does not apply CAS operations in its doorway, $(\log n+3)$-bounded waiting is also retained.[7]

We now show that A' has constant barrier complexity. The only shared variable on which CAS operations are performed in Algorithm 1 is the *lock* variable. From Lemma 11, each CAS operation applied in Algorithm 1 to *lock* causes a constant number of write operations in A'. At most two CAS operations are applied to *lock* in every passage of Algorithm 1 (in statement **23** and statement **26**) and only a single Write operation (in statement **43** or statement **47**), hence their transformation causes at most a constant increase in the number of barriers required per passage.

By Lemma 11, every read operation of *lock* in Algorithm 1 that incurs an RMR adds a constant number of write operations per passage of A'. Since the *exits* variable is incremented on every exit of the critical section, a process may incur only a constant number of RMRs while busy-waiting on *lock* in statement **25**. It follows that the transformation only adds to A' a constant number of write operations per passage. Inserting a barrier after each of these write operations preserves the correctness of the transformation. □

We present the first mutual exclusion algorithm, using only reads and writes, that has optimal complexity under both the RMRs and barriers metrics. Each passage of the algorithm through the critical section incurs $O(\log n)$ RMRs and a constant number of barriers. This is also the first algorithm possessing such properties within the class of algorithms that may use comparison primitives such as CAS in addition to reads and writes.

It is easily seen that the progress guarantees of the new algorithm depend on TSO. Specifically, under *partial store ordering* (PSO), our algorithm does not guarantee deadlock-freedom, although mutual exclusion is not violated. Whether or not an algorithm with the same properties exists for PSO systems is an interesting open question. It is also unclear how *abortable* [13] or *adaptive* [2] mutex algorithms with the same properties may be constructed. We leave these questions for future work.

Acknowledgements.
We thank Dave Dice, Michael Kuperstein, Martin Vechev and Eran Yahav, for helpful discussions and the anonymous reviewers for their useful comments.

7. REFERENCES

[1] S. V. Adve and K. Gharachorloo. Shared memory consistency models: A tutorial. *IEEE Computer*, 29(12):66–76, 1996.

[2] J. H. Anderson and Y.-J. Kim. Adaptive mutual exclusion with local spinning. In *DISC*, pages 29–43, 2000.

[3] H. Attiya, R. Guerraoui, D. Hendler, P. Kuznetsov, M. M. Michael, and M. T. Vechev. Laws of order: expensive synchronization in concurrent algorithms cannot be eliminated. In *POPL*, pages 487–498, 2011.

[4] H. Attiya, D. Hendler, and P. Woelfel. Tight RMR lower bounds for mutual exclusion and other problems. In *STOC*, pages 217–226, 2008.

[5] T. Craig. Building FIFO and priority-queuing spin locks from atomic swap. Technical report, 1993.

[6] R. Danek and W. M. Golab. Closing the complexity gap between FCFS mutual exclusion and mutual exclusion. In *DISC*, pages 93–108, 2008.

[7] D. Dice. personal communication, May 2013.

[8] W. M. Golab, V. Hadzilacos, D. Hendler, and P. Woelfel. RMR-efficient implementations of comparison primitives using read and write operations. *Distributed Computing*, 25(2):109–162, 2012.

[9] W. M. Golab, D. Hendler, and P. Woelfel. An $O(1)$ rmrs leader election algorithm. *SIAM J. Comput.*, 39(7):2726–2760, 2010.

[10] D. Hendler and P. Woelfel. Randomized mutual exclusion with sub-logarithmic rmr-complexity. *Distributed Computing*, 24(1):3–19, 2011.

[11] M. P. Herlihy and J. M. Wing. Linearizability: a correctness condition for concurrent objects. *ACM Transactions on Programming Languages and Systems*, 12(3):463–492, 1990.

---

[7]As observed by [8], if the doorway code of algorithm A applies comparison primitives, then even if A satisfies k-bounded waiting, for any k, A' will not. This is because the implementations of [8, 9] are blocking but the doorway code is required to be wait-free.

[12] Intel Corporation. *Intel® 64 and IA-32 Architectures Software Developer's Manual.* Number 253669-033US. December 2009.

[13] P. Jayanti. Adaptive and efficient abortable mutual exclusion. In *PODC*, pages 295–304, 2003.

[14] P. Jayanti, S. Petrovic, and N. Narula. Read/write based fast-path transformation for FCFS mutual exclusion. In *SOFSEM*, pages 209–218, 2005.

[15] Y.-J. Kim and J. Anderson. A time complexity bound for adaptive mutual exclusion. In *DISC*, pages 1–15, 2001.

[16] M. Kuperstein, M. Vechev, and E. Yahav. Automatic inference of memory fences. In *FMCAD*, pages 111 –119, 2010.

[17] L. Lamport. A new solution of dijkstra's concurrent programming problem. *Commun. ACM*, 17(8):453–455, 1974.

[18] L. Lamport. How to make a correct multiprocess program execute correctly on a multiprocessor. *IEEE Trans. Computers*, 46(7):779–782, 1997.

[19] D. L.Weaver and T. Germond, editors. *The SPARC Architecture Manual.* Prentice Hall, 1994.

[20] P. Magnusson, A. Landin, and E. Hagersten. Queue locks on cache coherent multiprocessors. In *IPPS*, pages 165–171, 1994.

[21] J. M. Mellor-Crummey and M. L. Scott. Algorithms for scalable synchronization on shared-memory multiprocessors. *ACM Trans. Comput. Syst.*, 9(1):21–65, 1991.

[22] S. Owens, S. Sarkar, and P. Sewell. A better x86 memory model: x86-tso. In *Theorem Proving in Higher Order Logics*, pages 391–407, 2009.

[23] S. Park and D. Dill. An executable specification and verifier for relaxed memory order. *Computers, IEEE Transactions on*, 48(2):227 –235, 1999.

[24] G. L. Peterson. Myths about the mutual exclusion problem. *Inf. Process. Lett.*, 12(3):115–116, 1981.

[25] P. Sewell, S. Sarkar, S. Owens, F. Z. Nardelli, and M. O. Myreen. x86-tso: a rigorous and usable programmer's model for x86 multiprocessors. *Commun. ACM*, 53(7):89–97, 2010.

[26] J.-H. Yang and J. Anderson. A fast, scalable mutual exclusion algorithm. *Distributed Computing*, 9(1):51–60, 1995.

APPENDIX

A. EVALUATION

The empirical evaluation, based on which Figures 1 and 3 (below) were derived were conducted on a Sun Fire T200 machine with a single UltraSPARC T1 chip (1.2GHz), comprising 8 cores, each with 4 hyper threads, running the SunOS 5.11 operating system.

We tested 3 algorithms: the Bakery algorithm [17], a tournament-tree mutex algorithm implementing Peterson's 2-process mutex algorithm [24] in each internal node, and the new algorithm (using hardware CAS). All algorithms were implemented in C and compiled using Sun's CC compiler version 5.9 with the -O5 flag.[8]

We did not conduct a comprehensive evaluation of the new

---

[8]The code can be downloaded from

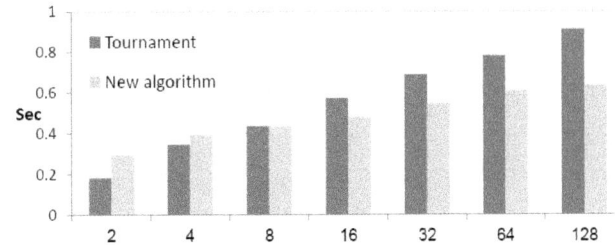

Figure 3: Time to perform 1M passages as a function of the number of threads supported.

algorithm under contended workloads. Rather, in order to empirically validate the significance of the barriers metric, we compared the time complexity of solo passages with and without memory barriers. We note that, although removing the barriers makes these algorithm incorrect in general, it causes no correctness issues in solo executions.

For each algorithm, we measured the time it took a single thread (henceforth thread 1) to complete 1M solo passages (with and without barriers) as a function of the number of threads supported by the algorithm. Each data point in Figures 1 and 3 is the average of 100 different runs.

In order to verify that the thread performing passages incurs RMRs, a second thread (henceforth thread 2), bound to a different core, was also running throughout the test and writing to variables read by thread 1 in order to invalidate the corresponding cache lines, thus causing thread 1 to incur L1 cache-misses when reading these variables.

The writes of thread 2 are such that thread 1 never has to wait for thread 2. These are the variables to which thread 2 repeatedly writes in the course of the test for each of the 3 algorithms.

Bakery: thread 2 writes 0 to its *choosing* flag, thus causing thread 1 to incur an RMR whenever reading this flag in its entry section.

Tournament: thread 2 writes 0 to the b flag variable in Peterson's algorithm corresponding to thread 1's rival in each node along its path to the root, thus causing thread 1 to incur an RMR on each such node in its entry section.

New algorithm: thread 2 writes -1 to all the internal nodes along thread 1'th path to the root, thus causing thread 1 to incur an RMR on each such node in its entry section.

Figure 3 compares the time it takes a thread to perform 1M solo passages when performing the tournament and the new algorithm (using hardware CAS). For trees of 2 and 3 levels ($n = 2$ or $n = 4$), solo passages of the tournament tree are faster, since the new algorithm has more overhead, especially in its exit section. For $n \geq 16$, however, solo passages of the new algorithm are faster and the gap increases with n, since the number of barriers in the tournament algorithm grows with n.

---

http://code.google.com/p/optimal-rmrs-constant-fences-mutex/.

Fair and Resilient Incentive Tree Mechanisms *

Yuezhou Lv
Tsinghua University
Beijing, China
lvyz11@tsinghua.edu.cn

Thomas Moscibroda
Microsoft Research Asia & Tsinghua University
Beijing, China
moscitho@microsoft.com

ABSTRACT

We study *Incentive Trees* for motivating the participation of people in crowdsourcing or human tasking systems. In an Incentive Tree, each participant is rewarded for contributing to the system, as well as for soliciting new participants into the system, who then themselves contribute to it and/or themselves solicit new participants. An Incentive Tree mechanism is an algorithm that determines how much reward each individual participant receives based on all the participants' contributions, as well as the structure of the solicitation tree. The sum of rewards paid by the mechanism to all participants is linear in the sum of their total contribution.

In this paper, we investigate the possibilities and limitations of Incentive Trees via an axiomatic approach by defining a set of desirable properties that an incentive tree mechanism should satisfy. We give a mutual incompatibility result showing that there is no incentive tree mechanism that simultaneously achieves all the properties. We then present two novel families of incentive tree mechanisms. The first family of mechanisms achieves all desirable properties, except that it fails to protect against a certain strong form of multi-identity attack; the second set of mechanisms achieves all properties, including the strong multi-identity protection, but fails to give participants the opportunity to achieve unbounded reward. Given the above impossibility result, these two mechanisms are effectively the best we can hope for. Finally, our model and results generalize recent studies on multi-level marketing mechanisms.

Categories and Subject Descriptors

J.4 [**Social and Behavioral Sciences**]: Economics

Keywords

multi-level marketing, incentive trees, reward mechanisms

*This work was supported in part by the National Basic Research Program of China Grant 2011CBA00300, 2011CBA00302, the National Natural Science Foundation of China Grant 61033001, 61061130540, and the Hi-Tech research and Development Program of China Grant 2006AA10Z216.

1. INTRODUCTION

There has recently been substantial interest in crowdsourcing and human-computation systems. These systems are based on mobilizing and utilizing people's work in order to quickly and efficiently achieve certain tasks. Commercial offerings such as Gigwalk [1] or Amazon's Mechanical Turk [2] allow users to submit tasks and recruit people to complete those tasks. Crowdsourcing is increasingly being used as the method of choice to obtain large-scale user data, such as environmental data, application traces, or to generate indoor-localization maps, e.g. [15, 14]. One key challenge in successfully deploying any such system is the question of how to incentivize people to actually perform tasks and contribute meaningfully. In fact, the same challenge is found in many other systems that rely on user contributions. For example, systems such as social forums, file-sharing services, public computing projects (e.g. SETI@Home), collaborative reference work, etc suffer from the well-known network-effect bootstrapping problem. These systems can become self-sustaining when the scale of the participation list exceeds a certain threshold, but below this threshold, they may not provide sufficient inherent benefit for users to participate in.

One common type of incentive mechanisms for raising user participation in such systems is *Incentive Trees*. Incentive Trees are tree-based mechanisms in which (i) each participant is rewarded for contributing to the system, and in addition, (ii) a participant that has already joined the system can make referrals, and thereby solicit new participants to also join the system and contribute to it. The mechanism incentivizes such solicitations by making a solicitor's reward depend on the contributions (and recursively also on their further solicitations, etc) made by such solicitees. Incentive Trees have been widely used in a variety of domains and under different names, e.g., in *referral trees*, *multi-level marketing* schemes, affiliate marketing or even in the form of the infamous illegal Pyramid Schemes. The question of how people can be incentivized using Incentive Trees to participate in crowdsourcing or network-effect systems is of significant interest and starting from the work on *Lottery Trees* in [9], and most prominently through the work by the MIT team on the Red Balloon Challenge [6] has recently attracted significant interest from the research community.

In this work, we study the foundations of *Incentive Trees*. An *Incentive Tree Mechanism* takes as input a weighted tree, where each node's weight denotes its contribution to the system, and the tree structure reflects the solicitation history. Based on this input, the mechanism then computes a reward for each node in the tree in such a way that the sum of rewards is linear in the sum of contributions. The question is, how should this reward function look like? Ideally, an Incentive Tree Mechanism is constructed such that every participant is optimally incentivized to both i) contribute to the system as much as possible, and ii) solicit as many new and itself highly-contributing and highly-solicitating participants as possible. As we will see, simultaneously achieving both *contribution and solicitation incentive* is challenging, especially if the mechanism should satisfy additional properties, such as fairness or robustness to strategic behavior.

In this paper, we take an axiomatic approach. We define a set of basic, desirable properties which ideally an incentive tree mechanism should satisfy. These include trivial properties such as the continuing solicitation and continuing contribution incentive properties, as well as more sophisticated properties that relate to the mechanisms resilience to strategic behavior. These are critically important. In web-based campaigns for example, resilience to multi-identity (Sybil [7]) attacks is key.[1]

Results: We study 8 properties of Incentive Trees, that have also been studied in earlier work on incentive trees and multi-level marketing; and suitably generalize these properties to our more general model. We present two novel families of incentive tree reward mechanisms, both of which are based on algorithmic techniques previously unused in the literature on multi-level marketing or incentive trees. The first family of mechanisms achieves all desirable properties, except that it fails to protect against a certain strong form of Sybil attack (technically, it satisfies all properties except UGSA). The second family of mechanisms does yield protection against the strong form of Sybil attack, but fails to give participants the opportunity to achieve unbounded reward (technically, it satisfies all properties except PO/URO). Both mechanisms are resilient to the well-known multi-identity attacks discussed above. Finally, we show that under some mild assumptions, these two mechanisms are essentially the best we can hope for. Specifically, we give an impossibility result showing that no reward scheme can simultaneously achieve UGSA and PO/URO, while maintaining the other properties. Thus, our results imply that that both of our mechanisms achieve a notion of optimality relative to the axiomatic properties we define in this paper: The mechanisms are optimal in the sense that they achieve a maximal mutually satisfiable subset of properties.

1.1 Related Work

The two works most related to ours are the ones by Douceur and Moscibroda on Lottery Trees [9], and the work by Emek et al. on multi-level marketing schemes [10]. The former work is aimed at motivating people to participate in networked systems and bootstrap systems that rely on the network effect. The paper addresses the following question: Assume some system organizer is willing to spend a fixed amount of money in order to incentivize people to do a specific type of work, how should the system be organized to maximize the resulting work? The authors propose *Lottery Trees*, formalize a set of desirable properties, prove impossibility results, and devise two non-trivial mechanisms one of which achieves near-optimality in terms of achieved desirable

properties. Our model differs from [9]: In our incentive tree model, the total amount of reward distributed to the participants *grows linearly* in the total contribution, whereas in [9], the total reward is a fixed, constant value. This difference significantly changes the achievable properties.

The work by Emek et al. [10] has initiated the algorithmic study on multi-level marketing mechanisms. It proposes mechanisms for a model in which users can purchase items (specifically, each user can purchase one item of a fixed unit price). Participants join the system by buying a product, and can then refer friends to also buy this product. The paper proves several properties of such unit-price multi-level marketing schemes and proposes mechanisms that achieve a subset of these properties. The incentive tree model we study in this paper can directly be translated into the multi-level marketing context. When viewed in this context, our work yields a substantially generalized version of the model in [10]: Participants correspond to buyers, and a participant's contribution corresponds to the amount of goods purchased. The difference is that whereas in [10], each buyer can only purchase a single item of unit price (i.e., each participant makes the same contribution to the system), in our model participants can make arbitrary contributions, i.e., each buyer can buy goods at arbitrary price. This generalized version of the problem yields a richer structure, and allows us to generalize the desirable properties in meaningful ways. The results in this paper directly apply to this generalized version of the multi-level marketing model.

In addition to these two works, there has recently been many other work on incentive systems [6]. For example, the Bitcoin system by Babaioff et al. [12] studies a problem similar to multi-level marketing. The paper uses a game-theoretic solution concept to study a problem in which agents are incentivized to forward sensitive information in such a way that the overall system performance is maximized. The work of Drucker and Fleischer [11] studies a multi-level marketing model with multi-items proving properties defined in [10]. Other related work such as [5] on query incentive networks, [4] on finding influential users in a social network, or [3] on the effects of social structure on behavior and norms, is only loosely related to our work. Finally, incentive mechanisms have also been used in mobile systems to recruit people [13] [14].

2. MODEL

In our model, participants can join a system and *contribute* to it (e.g. by doing work such as finding weather balloons, uploading crowd-sourced data, solving tasks, etc). For a participant u, we denote its contribution by $C(u)$, $C(u) \geq 0$. Participants can also *solicit* new participants. Such referrals induce a *referral forest* F. Each participant is a node $u \in F$, and there is a directed edge (u, v) between two participants u and v if v has joined the system in response to a solicitation by u. In other words, if u joins the system via a referral by v, it becomes a child-node of v in F. A new participant u who joins the system independently of any solicitation joins F as an independent node. For simplicity, we consider the equivalent *referral-tree* T, in which there is an imaginary root node r with contribution $C(r) = 0$, and all root-nodes in F are children of r. T is a weighted tree in which the weight of a node u is its contribution to the system $C(u)$. We denote by $C(T) = \sum_{u \in T} C(u)$ the total contribution in the system.

---

[1] In the commonly employed refer-a-friend programs, for example, it is often very easy to forge identities by creating new free email accounts, and then "referring oneself" in order to get extra reward.

A *reward mechanism* is a function that takes as input the weighted referral tree T, and computes for each $u \in T$ a non-negative real *reward*, denoted by $R(u)$. Following [10], we impose a *budget constraint* on this function: The system administrator is willing to spend no more than a certain fraction $\Phi \leq 1$ of the total accumulated contribution on rewarding participants. That is, the total reward $R(T) = \sum_{u \in T} R(u)$ paid to participants grows linearly in the total contribution, i.e., $R(T) \leq \Phi \cdot C(T)$. While in principle, any function satisfying these properties defines a possible reward mechanism, a well-functioning mechanism should maintain several desirable properties, which we define in Section 3.

Generalized Multi-Level Marketing When viewed in the context of multi-level marketing, our model generalizes the model of Emek et al. [10], allowing buyers to purchase not just a single item of unit price or multi-items, but purchase items at arbitrary prices. Buyers can purchase goods from a seller. For some buyer u, her contribution to the system $C(u)$ is the total *cost* of the goods purchased. The seller is willing to return a certain fraction of his total income in the form of rewards $R(u)$ to the buyers. Notice that in this context, the amount of money a buyer u effectively ends up paying for the goods is his *pay*, $Pay(u) = C(u) - R(u)$. And since a buyer's reward can potentially exceed his cost (if he accumulates many contributing descendants), we also consider the *profit* as $P(u) = R(u) - C(u)$.

Comparison to Existing Models: The two main parameters in our model are contribution and reward. Many existing models have restrictions on either or both parameters. The Pachira in [9], Geometric Mechanism in [10] as well as the winning strategy in the DARPA network challenge [6] demand the total reward to be fixed. In [6] [10] the contribution of each node is the same, while in [9], contributions are allowed to be variable. In previous multilevel marketing models [10] [11], the total reward is linear in the total contribution, but the contribution (payment) of each node is fixed. We generalize these models such that each participant can make different contributions of arbitrary size, and the total reward paid to participants is linear in the total system contribution.

Tree Notation: We use standard tree notation. T_u denotes the subtree rooted at node u. $p_T(u)$ denotes the parent of a node u in T. Finally, $dep_p(u)$ denotes the *depth* of u in T_p, i.e., the distance between u and p. To simplify notation, we define $dep_p(u) = -\infty$ if $u \notin T_p$.

3. DESIRABLE PROPERTIES

In this section, we define the set of desirable properties that an incentive tree mechanism should ideally satisfy. Several of these properties are inspired by related properties defined in [9] for lottery trees; others are taken from [10] and adjusted appropriately to the generalized model with arbitrary contributions.

3.1 Basic Properties

Continuing Contribution Incentive (CCI) [9]: A reward mechanism satisfies CCI if it provides a participant u with increasing reward in response to an increase of u's contribution. This encourages participants to continue contributing to the system (e.g., to continue purchasing goods from the seller). Formally, given a referral tree T. If a node $u \in T$ increases its contribution, $C'(u) > C(u)$, and the con-

tribution of all other nodes $v \in T \setminus \{u\}$ remains the same, $C'(v) = C(v)$, then the reward of u increases: $R'(u) > R(u)$.

Continuing Solicitation Incentive (CSI) [9]: A reward mechanism satisfies CSI if every participant always has an incentive to solicit new participants. This encourages ongoing solicitation and ensures continuing growth of the system. Let T_u and T'_u be the subtree rooted at u before and after a new participant has joined the system in u's subtree. Then, $R'(u) > R(u)$.

Reward Proportional to Contribution (ϕ-RPC) [9]: This property suggests that a reward mechanism should maintain some basic notion of fairness among the participants, the degree of which is determined by the parameter ϕ. We say that a reward mechanism satisfies ϕ-RPC for some $0 \leq \phi \leq 1$, if a participant u who contributes $C(u)$, should at least receive a reward of $R(u) \geq \phi C(u)$. In other words, every participant should receive at least a ϕ-fraction of his contribution to the system. Note that we assume $\phi \leq \Phi$ since otherwise no reward mechanism can satisfy the ϕ-RPC property.

Unbounded Reward Opportunity (URO) [10]: This property demands that there should be no limit to the reward a participant can potentially receive, even when his own contribution is fixed by constant. Formally, a reward mechanism satisfies URO if for every positive real R, $C(u)$ and positive integer k, there exists k trees $T_1, \cdots, T_k$ attached to u in the referral tree such that $R(u) \geq R$.

Profitable Opportunity (PO): The PO property is a weaker version of URO. It suggests that a buyer with any positive contribution has the opportunity to get positive profit (reward minus contribution). Formally, a reward mechanism satisfies PO if for every positive real $C(u)$ and positive integer k, there exists k trees $T_1, \cdots, T_k$ attached to u in the referral tree such that $R(u) \geq C(u)$. A mechanism that satisfies URO satisfies PO.

Subtree Locality (SL) [10]: This property demands that the reward paid to a participant u is determined uniquely by its subtree T_u, $R(u) = f(T_u)$. The property ensures that each user is credited only for actions (contributions and solicitations) performed by itself, or its descendants. Violation of this property can have undesirable consequences. For example, the reward of a user could increase or decrease without him having taken any action (no new purchases or newly solicited buyers in his subtree). Note that as an important special case, the SL property subsumes the so-called *Unprofitable Solicitor Bypassing (USB)* property defined in [9]. This property demands that for a new participant, it should not matter where in the tree he joins, such that a new participant has no incentive to join the system as a child of someone other than his solicitor.

3.2 Sybil-Attack Resilience Properties

It is desirable that a reward mechanism is robust against strategic behavior by participants. In particular, we seek mechanisms that are resilient against *multi-identity attacks*, commonly known as Sybil-Attacks [7]. A participant who is able to forge multiple identities (which is typically simple in web-based applications) should not be able to use this ability and "cheat" the mechanism for his own benefit. Previous work has defined two different notions of Sybil resilience.

Unprofitable Sybil Attack (USA) [9]: This property is taken directly from [9], and it captures the classic notion of Sybil resilience. The USA property imposes that no participant can increase his profit purely by pretending to have multiple identities: A mechanism satisfies USA if a participant with a given contribution cannot increase his reward by joining the system as a set of Sybil nodes instead of joining as a single node. In other words, a participant who makes a certain contribution to the system should never have a benefit of "splitting" himself and its contribution up and making these contributions as two or more identities, even if these "Sybil identities" join the tree as if referring themselves.

Unprofitable Generalized Sybil Attack (UGSA): This property is strictly stronger than USA. It is a generalization of the so-called *Profitable Sybil Attack* or *Split Proof* property as defined in [10] for the restricted single-item multi-level marketing model. The property demands that a participant can never increase his profit by joining the tree as multiple identities, even if by doing so, he increases his contributions, i.e., purchases additional goods.

We can formally define USA and UGSA as follows. Given a tree T_0. Let u be a participant that joins the tree. Let T_1' be the tree that results when u joins T as a single node. Alternatively, u can join the tree as a set of Sybil nodes $S_u = \{u_1, \ldots, u_k\}$, which can be arbitrarily connected in the referral tree. Let T_1'' be the tree that results when u joins T as the Sybil node set S_u. Let $J = v_1, v_2, \ldots$ be an arbitrary sequence of new participants joining the tree, and let $T_1', T_2', \ldots$ and $T_1'', T_2'', \ldots$ be a sequence of trees resulting from these joins. Notice that in the case u joins as a set of Sybil nodes, there can be many different such sequences because any new child solicited by u can join as a child of any of the Sybil nodes $u_1, \ldots, u_k$. Finally, let $R_i'(u), C_i'(u)$ be the reward and cost of u in T_i', and let $R_i''(u) = \sum_{j=1..k} R_i''(u_j), C_i''(u) = \sum_{j=1..k} C_i''(u_j)$ be the total reward and cost of u in T_i'', respectively. We say that a reward mechanism satisfies USA if for any $i > 0$, $R_i'(u) \geq R_i''(u)$, if $C_i'(u) = C_i''(u)$. We say that a reward mechanism satisfies UGSA if for any $i > 0$, $R_i'(u) - C_i'(u) \geq R_i''(u) - C_i''(u)$, if $C_i'(u) \leq C_i''(u)$. Notice that the UGSA property strictly subsumes the USA property by taking $C_i'(u) = C_i''(u)$.

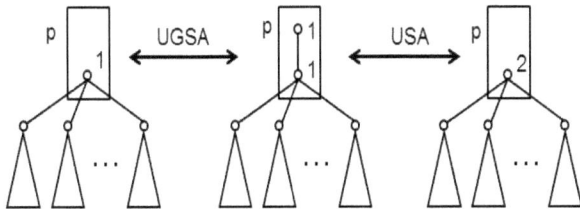

Figure 1: Participant p joining (left) as a single node with cost 1; (middle) as two Sybil nodes that refer one another, each with cost 1; and (right) as a single node with cost 2.

The difference between USA and UGSA is illustrated in Figure 1. USA requires that a participant who contributes a certain amount be unable to increase his reward by joining as multiple identities. Therefore, participant p in the right figure must receive at least as much reward as participant p in the middle figure. UGSA *additionally* demands that p's profit (=reward-cost) in the middle figure cannot exceed his profit in the left figure.

It is interesting to discuss the relative importance of these properties from the point of view of the system administra-

tor or the seller in a multi-level marketing context. USA is clearly a desirable property from his point of view because if USA is violated, he will simply pay too much reward for no additional contribution. The case of UGSA is much less clear. In particular, it is possible that UGSA is violated even though the seller does not actually lose money (i.e., if the contribution exceeds the reward). This is possible if the Sybil buyer p increases his contribution not at the cost of the system administrator, but at the cost of other participants in the system, for instance the parent of p. Practically speaking, we therefore believe that USA is a more fundamental and important property than UGSA. When discussing our TDRM mechanism (end of Section 4.3), we will give a concrete example of TDRM violating UGSA.

4. REWARD MECHANISMS

We start by briefly reviewing existing (multi-level marketing and incentive tree) algorithms and analyze which desirable properties they achieve. We then give an impossibility proof showing that there can be no reward mechanism that simultaneously satisfies URO and UGSA. As the main technical contribution of this paper, we then present two novel reward mechanisms, both of which achieve a maximal subset of mutually satisfiable properties. The mechanism in Section 4.3 achieves all properties except UGSA, and the mechanism in Section 4.4 achieves all properties except URO/PO.

4.1 Existing Incentive Tree Mechanisms

Geometric Mechanism: The simple geometric reward mechanism is commonly used, e.g. in [6]. The idea is that a certain fraction a of a node's contribution "bubbles-up" to its parent, a fraction a^2 bubbles up to its grand-parents, etc. Given two constants $0 < a < 1$ and $b \geq \phi$ such that $b \leq (1 - a)\Phi$, the reward of a participant u in the $(a, b) - geometric$ mechanism is defined as follows.

Algorithm 1: (a, b)-Geometric Mechanism
$$R(u) = \sum_{v \in T_u} a^{dep_u(v)} \cdot b \cdot C(v) \ ;$$

The condition $b \leq (1-a)\Phi$ is to ensure the budget constraint. Specifically, the total reward that a node u is responsible for is at most $b\frac{1}{1-a}C(u)$, which should be less than $\Phi C(u)$. The fairness property $\phi - RPC$ is satisfied if we also set $b \geq \phi$. It is easy to derive the following theorem.

THEOREM 4.1. *The $(a, b) - Geometric Mechanism$ with $\phi \leq b \leq (1 - a)\Phi$ achieves all desirable properties, except USA and UGSA.*

The reason why USA (and thus, UGSA) is violated is also easy to see. A node can increase his reward by splitting itself into multiple Sybil nodes that are linked to each other as a chain. Some of the "bubbled-up" reward is then handed to other Sybil nodes of u and the total sum of rewards accumulated by u is larger than if u joins as a single node.

Multi-Level Marketing Mechanisms derived from Incentive Tree Mechanisms: In [9], two incentive tree mechanisms are given (called *Luxor* and *Pachira*) for a model in which the total reward in the system is a fixed constant. Any such incentive tree mechanism A for the fixed total reward model can be transformed into an incentive tree mechanism $L - A$ in our model by simply multiplying the reward paid to a user u by a factor of $\Phi C(T)$ (assuming that the total reward is normalized to 1). Applying this transformation to Luxor and Pachira yields two mechanisms L-Luxor and L-Pachira. As it turns out, L-Luxor is very similar to the $(a, b) - GeometricMechanism$, and achieves the same properties. On the other hand, L-Pachira is interesting. For two parameters $0 \leq \beta \leq 1$ and $\delta > 0$, the $(\beta, \delta) - L - PachiraMechanism$ is defined as follows.

Algorithm 2: (β, δ)-L-Pachira Mechanism

Let u be a participant with k children $q_1, \dots, q_k$;

Define $\pi(x) = \beta x + (1 - \beta)x^{1+\delta}$;

$R(u) = \Phi \cdot C(T) \cdot \left[\pi(\frac{C(T_u)}{C(T)}) - \sum_{i=1}^{k} \pi(\frac{C(T_{q_i})}{C(T)}) \right]$;

It was shown in [9] that Pachira achieves USA, and the same proof carries over to L-Pachira as well. Moreover, $\phi - RPC$ can be satisfied by setting $\beta \geq \phi/\Phi$. Pachira does not satisfy the CSI property in the Incentive Tree model. But when transforming it into the multi-level marketing model, L-Pachira does achieve CSI, although the fact is not straightforward. On the other hand, it is easy to see that L-Pachira fails to satisfy the SL constraint, because of its dependency on the total system contribution $C(T)$.

THEOREM 4.2. *The $(\beta, \delta) - L - PachiraMechanism$ with $\beta \geq \phi/\Phi$ achieves all desirable properties, except SL and UGSA.*

Split-Proof Mechanism [10]: For the single-item multi-level marketing model studied in [10], Emek et al. give a mechanism that achieves several properties, including the single-item model equivalent of UGSA and URO. This algorithm is based on the idea of computing a deepest binary subtree of the referral tree and then computing the rewards based on that subtree. Unfortunately, this fails the basic CSI property because depending on the number of direct children it has, a node may no longer have an incentive to directly solicit additional children.

4.2 Impossibility Result

The subsequent constructions of our two new mechanisms are motivated by the following impossibility result, which suggests that *if a mechanism satisfies the SL property, then UGSA and PO (and thus URO) are mutually incompatible.* Since SL is a fundamental property, this result motivates our search for i) a mechanism that achieves all the properties except UGSA (Section 4.3) and ii) a mechanism that achieves all the properties except PO/URO (Section 4.4).

THEOREM 4.3. *There is no incentive tree mechanism that can simultaneously achieve SL, PO and UGSA.*

PROOF. We prove the theorem by contradiction. Suppose a mechanism A can achieve SL, PO and UGSA. In the following proof, all reward computations are done using mechanism A.

Consider a node v^* with $C(v^*) > 0$. According to **PO**, there exists a case in which v^* has one child tree, and yet v^*'s profit is positive, $P(v^*) = R(v^*) - C(v^*) > 0$. We denote the child tree as T^* and its root as u^*. Suppose the contribution of u^* is $C(u^*)$ and $T^* \setminus \{u^*\}$ forms a set of subtrees denoted as $T_1, \dots, T_k$. According to **SL**, $R(v^*)$ only depends on $C(v^*)$ and T^*. We compare two cases. The first case is exactly as described above (Fig. 2 (left)). The profit of u^* is

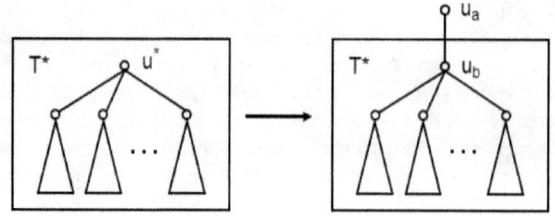

Figure 2: Illustration of notation used in the proof.

$P(u^*) = R(u^*) - C(u^*)$. In the second case (Fig. 2 (right)), node u^* launches a (generalized) Sybil attack by joining the referral tree as two nodes u_a and u_b with $C(u_a) = C(v^*)$ and $C(u_b) = C(u^*)$. Notice that the Sybil attack is generalized (i.e., of the USGA-type), since the total contribution of u_a and u_b exceeds the contribution of u^*. Further notice that in the second case, the root of v^*'s descendant tree is u_a; u_a is u_b's parent; and u_b is the parent of $T_1, \dots, T_k$, i.e., we keep every node in T^* unchanged except u^*.

According to **SL**, it must hold that u_a has the same reward as v^* (with T^* attached to it), and for the same reason, u_b must have the same reward as u^*. Specifically, it holds that $R(u_a) = R(v^*)$ and $R(u_b) = R(u^*)$. The total profit of u^*'s two Sybil nodes u_a and u_b is thus $P'(u^*) = R(u_a) + R(u_b) - C(u_a) - C(u_b) = (R(v^*) - C(v^*)) + (R(u^*) - C(u^*)) > P(u^*)$. This implies that u^* can get more profit by contributing more, which violates **UGSA**. □

4.3 Satisfying All But UGSA: Topology-Dependent Reward Mechanisms (TDRM)

We construct the mechanism in two steps. We first give an intermediate mechanism which manages to satisfy USA, but does not satisfy budget constraint. This preliminary form of the mechanism could be turned into a feasible reward mechanism that satisfies the budget constraint, but doing so would violate Subtree Locality (SL). We then show how we can eliminate the shortcomings of this preliminary mechanism in such a way that both budget constraint and SL are satisfied.

As we discussed in the previous section, the reason why the simple Geometric Mechanism fails the USA property is that it is beneficial for a node to split up and accumulate its own "bubbled up" rewards. This can be avoided by *changing the linear dependency of a node's reward on its own and other node's contribution to a dependency that is of quadratic nature*. Specifically, when computing the reward of a participant u, we multiply u's contribution with the contribution of every node in u's subtree, *including itself*. In this way, even though u could still accumulate "bubbled-up" rewards from its own Sybil nodes, we can show that it is always beneficial for u to focus its total contribution in a single node. The resulting mechanism works as follows.

Algorithm 3: Preliminary Version of TDRM – Not a correct reward mechanism

---

$R(u) = C(u) \cdot \sum_{v \in T_u} a^{dep_u(v)} \cdot b \cdot C(v)$;

The problem is that while the structure of this quadratic geometric reward mechanism is such that it achieves USA, it is not in fact a feasible mechanism: It fails the budget constraint. On the positive, its structure is such that it does achieve USA. To see why, consider a node u. Suppose u can benefit from splitting itself into a set of Sybil nodes $u_1, \ldots, u_k$, such that $C(u) = \sum_{i=1..k} C(u_i)$. We can re-write the reward of u if it remains a single node as

$$R(u) = C(u)^2 + C(u) \sum_{v \in T_u \setminus u} a^{dep_u(v)} \cdot b \cdot C(v).$$

If it splits itself into Sybil nodes, its new reward is at most

$$
\begin{aligned}
R'(u) \ \leq \ & [C(u_1) + \ldots + C(u_k)] \cdot \sum_{v \in T_u \setminus u} a^{dep_u(v)} \cdot b \cdot C(v) \\
& + (C(u_1) + \ldots + C(u_k))^2
\end{aligned}
$$

because the distance between any descendant $v \in T_u$ to any of the Sybil nodes u_i is at least as big as the original distance between u and v in T. Comparing the two expressions, it can be seen that splitting u into multiple nodes $u_1, \ldots, u_k$ does neither increase the first summand (because of the quadratic term), nor the second.

The fundamental problem with this approach is that in order to stay within budget, we would need to scale down the rewards $R(u)$ that are distributed to the participants. However, the amount by which we would need to scale would depend on a global property of the referral tree, for example $C(T)$. Thus, such a scaling would fundamentally violate the SL property. In order to overcome this problem, we would like to constrain the reward a node can obtain. This will allow us to meet the budget constraint by scaling each node's reward by a constant factor, independent of $C(T)$. This could easily be achieved if there was a constant upper bound μ on the contribution $C(u)$ of every node $u \in T$. However, since our model allows a participant to potentially have an unlimited contribution, our mechanism simulates such an upper bound μ by splitting each participant with contribution exceeding μ into a set of nodes, each with contribution at most μ. The mechanism then computes the rewards in the resulting *Reward Computation Tree* (RCT), which may differ from the referral tree. In fact, one user can correspond to multiple nodes in the RCT. A participant's final reward is the sum of the rewards of his corresponding nodes in the RCT.

The effect of computing the rewards in the Reward Computation Tree in this way is that for participants with very large contribution, the algorithm effectively *linearizes* this node's reward with regard to its contribution. In the process, we need to be careful about not violating the USA property. Specifically, in order to make sure that this linearization does not thwart the USA-achieving structure of the quadratic reward computation, the mechanism must be careful about the way it splits participants with large contribution. In particular, our mechanism ensures that for any such split, it is the best possible split for such a participant. In other words, even though the splitting effectively reduces the reward of very large contributors (compared to the preliminary quadratic TDRM mechanism), participants can nevertheless *not benefit from a Sybil attack, because they are already given the best possible split.*

The TDRM mechanism works as follows. Given four parameters $\lambda < \Phi - \phi$, $\mu > 0$, a and b, such that $a + b < 1$, TDRM first transforms the referral tree T into a reward computation tree T', and then computes the rewards on T'. We denote by $C(u)$ and $C'(u)$ the contributions of a node u in T and T', respectively. For a participant $u \in T$, we de-

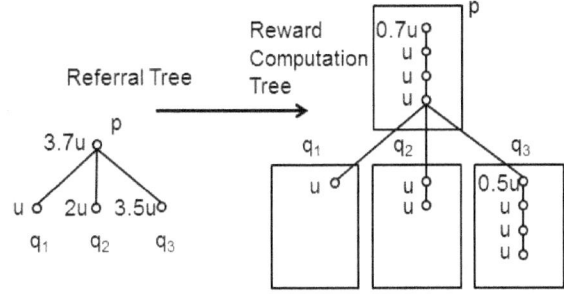

Figure 3: Transformation of a referral tree T into a reward computation tree T' by TDRM.

fine a chain CH_u of length N_u in T' as a sequence of nodes $m_1^u, \ldots, m_{N_u}^u$, such that m_i^u is the parent node of m_{i+1}^u, for all $i = 1 \ldots N_u - 1$. We call m_1^u and $m_{N_u}^u$ the head and the tail of the chain, respectively.

Algorithm 4: TDRM Mechanism

Transformation of T into T':
for $u \in T$ **do**
$\quad N_u = \lceil C(u)/\mu \rceil$;
$\quad$ Create a chain CH_u of length N_u in T', such that
$\quad C'(m_i^u) = \begin{cases} C(u) - (N_u - 1)\mu & \text{, if } i = 1 \\ \mu & \text{, if } i > 1 \end{cases}$;
end
for *Every directed edge* $(u, v) \in T$ **do**
$\quad$ Create a directed edge $(m_{N_u}^u, m_1^v)$ in T';
end
for $w \in T'$ **do**
$\quad R'(w) = \frac{\lambda}{\mu} C(w) \sum_{x \in T'_w} a^{dep_w(x)} b \cdot C(x) + \phi C(w)$;
$\quad$ – *Reward Calculation in T'*
end
for $u \in T$ **do**
$\quad R(u) = \sum_{v \in CH_u} R'(v)$;
$\quad$ – *Reward Calculation in T*
end

Figure 3 gives an example of how the mechanism transforms the referral tree T (left) into a corresponding reward computation tree T' (right). After this transformation, TDRM first computes the rewards for each node in T' according a function similar to the one given in the preliminary TDRM mechanism. Finally, the reward of a participant $u \in T$ is computed as the sum of all the nodes in the corresponding chain CH_u in T'. It remains to show that the mechanism meets the budget constraint – we do this in the next section. With this, we can prove the following key theorem.

THEOREM 4.4. *The TDRM mechanism with parameters* $\lambda < \Phi - \phi$, $b < 1 - a$, and $\mu > 0$ *achieves all desirable properties except UGSA.*

PROOF. It will be convenient to use the following definition. Let S_A, S_B be two subsets of T'. We define

$$B(S_A, S_B) = \sum_{u \in S_A} \sum_{v \in S_B} \frac{\lambda}{\mu} b \cdot C(u) C(v) a^{dep_u(v)}.$$

Intuitively, $B(S_A, S_B)$ is the sum of the rewards accumulated by nodes in S_A through nodes in S_B. Using this definition, we can reformulate the reward function $R(u)$ for $u \in T$ as $R(u) = B(CH_u, T'_{m_1^u}) + \phi C(u)$.

Budget Constraint: We start by proving that the mechanism meets the budget constraint. First, observe that the total rewards in the referral tree is equivalent to the total rewards in the reward computation tree. Then, in the reward computation tree T', it holds that

$$\sum_{u \in T'} R(u) = \sum_{u \in T'} [C(u) \cdot \frac{\lambda}{\mu} \sum_{v \in T'} a^{dep_u(v)} \cdot bC(v) + \phi C(u)]$$

$$< \sum_{v \in T'} [\lambda \cdot C(v) \sum_{i=0}^{\infty} a^i b] + \sum_{u \in T'} \phi C(u)$$

$$< (\lambda + \phi) \sum_{u \in T'} C(u).$$

By the constraint imposed on λ, this last expression is at most $\Phi \sum_{u \in T'} C(u)$, which is the budget.

We now prove the desirable properties one by one.

CCI: Consider a participant u, who increases his contribution from $C(u)$ to $C^*(u) = C(u) + \epsilon$. Let $R^*(u)$ and $CH_u^* = \{m_1^{*u}, \ldots, m_{N_u^*}^{*u}\}$ denote the new reward and the new corresponding chain, respectively. There are two cases depending on whether u's contribution increase leads to a change of its corresponding chain CH_u^* in the RCT, or not. We consider the two cases independently.

First, if $N_u^* = N_u$, then only the head-node m_1^{u}'s contribution increases in T': $C(m_1^{*u}) = C(m_1^u) + \epsilon$. We can get $R^*(u) > R(u)$.

Second, if $N_u^* > N_u$, then we only need to consider the sub-chain in CH_u^* with N_u nodes from the leaf node up. As each node of the sub-chain has contribution μ, we get that $R^*(u) > R(u)$.

ϕ-RPC: By the definition of the $R(u)$, it holds that $R(u) = B(CH_u, T_{m_1^u}) + \phi C(u) > \phi C(u)$.

CSI: The property holds because by the definition of $R(u)$, the reward of a participant u is strictly increasing when a new node v attaches to u.

SL: The property holds because by the definition of $R(u)$, the reward of a participant u is independent of any node outside of T_u.

URO: Consider a participant u, whose contribution is $C(u) = s\mu + \epsilon$, for some integer s and $0 < \epsilon \le \mu$, and suppose u has k children in the referral tree, namely there are k trees attached to u. Here s can be any non-negative integer and k can be any positive integer. We denote one of u's children as v and the corresponding subtree as T_v. Suppose v has ℓ children with contribution μ. It holds that $R(u)$ is at least $R'(m_{N_u}^u)$ in the reward computation tree. Calculating the value of $R'(m_{N_u}^u)$ using the definition, it can be shown that $R'(m_{N_u}^u) \ge \ell \cdot a^2 b\lambda\epsilon$. As ℓ can become arbitrarily large, the reward of $R(u)$ can increase to infinity.

USA: At the heart of our proof is that TDRM satisfies USA. To do so, we define an $\epsilon - chain$ as a chain in the reward computation tree of which only the head node can have contribution less than μ.

USA states that no participant can increase his reward by pretending to have multiple identities. Consider a participant u that joins the referral tree as j Sybil nodes ($j \ge 1$), $v_1, v_2, \ldots, v_j$, with total contribution $C(u)$. Further assume that u has s children, $q_1, \ldots, q_s$. Suppose $v_1, v_2, \ldots, v_j$ are transformed into k nodes $u_1, \ldots, u_k$ in the reward computation tree. By definition, it holds that $C(u) = \sum_{i=1}^k C(u_i)$ and $C(u_i) \le \mu, i = 1, \ldots, k$. For $q_1, \ldots, q_s$, we denote the subtrees rooted at $q_1, \ldots, q_s$ in the reward computation tree

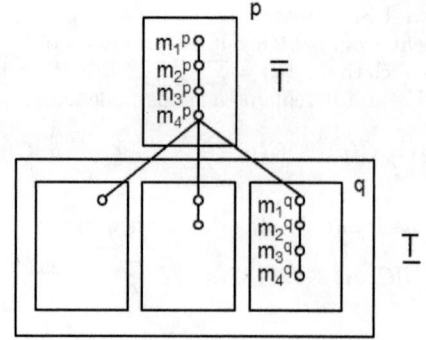

Figure 4: Illustration of notation used in the proof.

as $T_1, \ldots, T_s$. We define a *partition* as any configuration of nodes $u_1, \ldots, u_k$, subtrees $T_1, \ldots, T_s$, and contributions $C(u_i)$, $(i = 1, \ldots, k)$ in the reward computation tree that can feasibly result from node u joining the referral tree as a set of multiple Sybil nodes.

Our proof idea is the following: Consider the set of optimal partitions for u in the reward computation tree (partitions maximizing $R(u)$). We show that at least one optimal partition has the structure of a single $\epsilon - chain$ in the RCT. In other words, we show that u's best possible Sybil attack is to join in such a way that the resulting structure in the RCT is an $\epsilon - chain$. However, since the *TDRM mechanism transforms u into an $\epsilon - chain$ in the RCT even if u joins as a single node*, it follows that u has no benefit of joining the referral tree as multiple Sybil identities. The mechanism itself will give u the best possible split, thus giving u no incentive to split itself.

We formally prove this intuition by a sequel of structural lemmas. The lemmas describe the properties of a reward-maximizing partition $u_1, \ldots, u_k, T_1, \ldots, T_s$ in the RCT, ultimately showing that the optimal such partition is an $\epsilon - chain$. As a first step, notice that because we have proven SL in TDRM, we consider only $u_1, \ldots, u_k, T_1, \ldots, T_s$ in the RCT. All other nodes are irrelevant for u's reward. The first lemma shows that $u_1, \ldots, u_k, T_1, \ldots, T_s$ forms a tree. Here notice that according to the soliciting sequence, u_i can not be a child of T_j ($i = 1, 2, \ldots, k$, $j = 1, 2, \ldots, s$).

LEMMA 4.5. *If $R(u)$ is maximized, $u_1, \ldots, u_k, T_1, \ldots, T_s$ forms a tree.*

PROOF. We prove the lemma by contradiction. Suppose $R(u)$ is maximized and $u_1, \ldots, u_k, T_1, \ldots, T_s$ forms a forest F with more than one tree. We pick any two trees T_α, T_β in F with roots α and β. As u is the parent of $q_1, \ldots, q_s$, it holds that $T_1, \ldots, T_s$ will be attached as subtrees to $u_1, \ldots, u_k$. Thus, $\alpha, \beta \in \{u_1, \ldots, u_k\}$. Now, assume that we attach T_β to α, thereby making it one tree. The attachment does not change the reward accumulated by nodes in T_β, but it strictly increases the rewards accumulated by α (due to the CSI property). This contradicts the assumption that $R(u)$ is maximized. $\square$

Thus if $R(u)$ is maximized, $u_1, \ldots, u_k, T_1, \ldots, T_s$ forms a tree. We denote this tree as T_u, and define $\overline{T_u}$ as the tree induced by $u_1, \ldots, u_k$, and $\underline{T_u}$ as the forest induced by $T_1, \ldots, T_s$. With these definitions, we can write $R(u)$ as

$$R(u) = B(\overline{T_u}, \overline{T_u}) + B(\overline{T_u}, \underline{T_u}) + \phi C(u).$$

Before continuing the proof, we distinguish different parts of $R(u)$: The *inner reward* $R^i(u) = B(\overline{T_u}, \overline{T_u})$ which is the part of reward purely coming from u's own contribution, and the *external reward* $R^e(u) = B(\overline{T_u}, \underline{T_u})$ which is the part of reward coming from u's descendants. Then we can rewrite $R(u)$ as $R(u) = R^i(u) + R^e(u) + \phi C(u)$. According to our assumption that u has a fixed contribution, the third term $\phi C(u)$ is a constant and does not influence u's decision.

As mentioned before, we need to prove that the best partition of u, maximizing the reward, is an ϵ–chain. Concretely, as $R(u) = R^i(u) + R^e(u) + \phi C(u)$, we show that u can maximize $R^i(u)$ and $R^e(u)$, respectively, if $\overline{T_u}$ is an $\epsilon-chain$. Our next step is to prove u's partition as an $\epsilon-chain$ will maximize $R^i(u)$. We transform the topology of $\overline{T_u}$ step by step. The lemma below shows that if u wants to maximize his inner reward $R^i(u)$ at most one node in $\overline{T_u}$ can have contribution less than μ.

LEMMA 4.6. *If $R^i(u)$ is maximized, there can be at most one node $v \in \overline{T_u}$ with contribution $C(v) < \mu$.*

PROOF. We prove the lemma by contradiction. Suppose there is more than one node with contribution less than μ. We denote two such nodes as x, y, i.e., $x, y \in \overline{T_u}$ with $C(x) < \mu$ and $C(y) < \mu$. Let $S_u = \overline{T_u} \setminus \{x, y\}$, and let P_x, P_y be the set of ancestors of x, y in the reward computation tree. The inner reward of u is $R^i(u) = B(\overline{T_u}, \overline{T_u})$ $= B(\{x,y\}, S_u) + B(S_u, S_u) + B(\{x,y\}, \{x,y\}) + B(S_u, \{x,y\})$.
To simplify the calculation, we define a function $\gamma_p(S) = \sum_{v \in S} \frac{b\lambda}{\mu} C(v) \max\{a^{dep_p(v)}, a^{dep_v(p)}\}$ for any node p in $\overline{T_u}$. According to the definition of $B(\cdot)$, it can be shown that

$$B(\{x,y\}, S_u) = B(x, S_u) + B(y, S_u)$$
$$= C(x)\gamma_x(T_x \setminus \{x,y\}) + C(y)\gamma_y(T_y \setminus \{x,y\}),$$
$$B(S_u, \{x,y\}) = B(S_u, x) + B(S_u, y)$$
$$= C(x)\gamma_x(P_x \setminus \{x,y\}) + C(y)\gamma_y(P_y \setminus \{x,y\}),$$
$$B(\{x,y\}, \{x,y\})$$
$$= \frac{b\lambda}{\mu}[(a^{dep_x(y)} + a^{dep_y(x)})C(x)C(y) + C(x)^2 + C(y)^2].$$

Expanding $R^i(u)$ and combining the above bounds, we get
$$R^i(u) = C(x)\gamma_x((P_x \cup T_x) \setminus \{x,y\})$$
$$+ C(y)\gamma_y((P_y \cup T_y) \setminus \{x,y\}))$$
$$+ \frac{b\lambda}{\mu}[(a^{dep_x(y)} + a^{dep_y(x)})C(x)C(y) + C(x)^2 + C(y)^2]$$
$$+ B(S_u, S_u). \qquad (1)$$

Without loss of generality, suppose $\gamma_x((P_x \cup T_x) \setminus \{x,y\}) \geq \gamma_y((P_y \cup T_y) \setminus \{x,y\})$. Then, consider two cases:
a) If $C(x) + C(y) > \mu$, we can change $C(x)$ to μ and $C(y)$ to $C(x) + C(y) - \mu$.
b) If $C(x) + C(y) \leq \mu$, we can change $C(x)$ to $C(x) + C(y)$ and $C(y)$ to 0.
In both cases, the change does not have an impact on the total contribution, but it increases $R^i(u)$. Specifically, the sum of the first two expressions in (1) will increase due to the change. Then, using the fact that if for two reals A and B with $A > B, 0 < t < \frac{A-B}{2}, k < 2$ and $S_1 = A^2 + B^2 + kAB$ and $S_2 = (A-t)^2 + (B+t)^2 + k(A-t)(B+t)$, it holds that $S_1 > S_2$, it follows that the third expression in (1) also increases. Meanwhile, the forth expression is unchanged. This leads to a contradiction because it means that this hypothetic partition does not maximize the inner reward. □

Next, we characterize the *location* of the at most one node in $\overline{T_u}$ that has contribution less than μ. Due to space limitations, we omit full proofs, and instead sketch the main proof ideas.

LEMMA 4.7. *If $R^i(u)$ is maximized, $\overline{T_u}$ is an $\epsilon - chain$ or a chain in which only the leaf node has contribution less than μ.*

Proof Sketch. According to Lemma 4.6, if $R^i(u)$ is maximized, there is at most one node with contribution less than μ in $\overline{T_u}$. We call it $\epsilon - node$ and suppose its contribution is $\epsilon (< \mu)$. (Here we need to pay attention that the $\epsilon - node$ has contribution strictly less than μ.) We can prove the lemma by case analysis and contradiction.
a) Suppose $\overline{T_u}$ is not a chain. We distinguish three subcases.
a1) Suppose in $\overline{T_u}$, there is an $\epsilon - node$ and the $\epsilon - node$ is not a leaf node. We denote the $\epsilon - node$ as x with $C(x) = \epsilon$, and denote the leaf node which is a descendent of x as y with $C(y) = \mu$. If we change $C(x)$ to μ and $C(y)$ to ϵ, $R^i(u)$ increases which contradicts the assumption.
a2) Suppose in $\overline{T_u}$, there is an $\epsilon - node$ and the $\epsilon - node$ is a leaf node. In this case, $\overline{T_u}$ has at least two leaf nodes. At least one leaf node denoted as x has contribution μ. Then we can delete x, add a new node y with contribution $C(y) = \mu$ and make the remaining tree $\overline{T_u} \setminus \{x\}$ attached as a subtree to y. $R^i(u)$ will increase.
a3) Suppose in $\overline{T_u}$, there is no $\epsilon - node$. The proof method is the same as that in a2).
b) Suppose $\overline{T_u}$ is a chain and there is an $\epsilon - node$ which is neither the root nor the leaf of the chain. We denote the $\epsilon - node$ as x and the leaf of the chain as y. We can increase $R^i(u)$ by changing $C(x)$ to μ and changing $C(y)$ to ϵ which contradicts the assumption. □

Thus we have shown that an $\epsilon - chain$ in the reward computation tree maximizes $R^i(u)$. We will now prove that u's partition as an $\epsilon - chain$ also maximizes his external reward $R^e(u)$. The next lemma shows it is better to root each tree in $\underline{T_u}$ to one leaf node in $\overline{T_u}$.

LEMMA 4.8. *or any given topology $\overline{T_u}$, suppose $u_1, u_2, ..., u_k$ are the nodes in $\overline{T_u}$. There exists a partition that maximizes $R^e(u)$ in which each tree in $\underline{T_u}$ is attached to a single node u_i, for some $i = 1, 2, ..., k$.*

Proof Sketch. We denote the trees in $\underline{T_u}$ as $T_1, \cdots, T_s$. According to the definition of the external reward, it holds that

$$R^e(u) = B(\overline{T_u}, \underline{T_u}) = \sum_{i=1}^{s} B(\overline{T_u}, T_i).$$

Suppose that by attaching T_1 to u_t $(1 \leq t \leq k)$, $B(\overline{T_u}, T_1)$ can be maximized. The proof works by showing that by attaching each tree T_i $(i = 1, 2, ...s)$ to u_t, we can maximize $R^e(u)$. □

We now know that $R^e(u)$ can be maximized when each tree in $\underline{T_u}$ is attached to a single node in $\overline{T_u}$. For any given $\overline{T_u}$, in order to maximize $R^e(u)$, we thus only need to consider partition in which each tree in $\underline{T_u}$ is attached to some node u^* in $\overline{T_u}$. Then using this property, we show that an $\epsilon - chain$ is the best partition for maximizing u's external reward.

LEMMA 4.9. *If $R^e(u)$ is maximized, $\overline{T_u}$ must be an $\epsilon - chain$ and u^* is the leaf node of $\overline{T_u}$.*

Proof Sketch. The first step is to show that if $R^e(u)$ is maximized, $\overline{T_u}$ must be a chain and u^* is a leaf node in $\overline{T_u}$. We prove it by contradiction. Suppose $\overline{T_u}$ is not a chain or u^* is not a leaf node in $\overline{T_u}$. Then we find that there exists a leaf node u_L in $\overline{T_u}$ which is not u^*. As no tree in $\underline{T_u}$ is attached to u_L, it holds that $B(u_L, \underline{T_u}) = 0$. We delete u_L in $\overline{T_u}$ and relocate u_L to be the root of $\overline{T_u} \setminus u_L$. The external reward of u will increase due to this change. So if $R^e(u)$ is maximized, $\overline{T_u}$ must be a chain and u^* is a leaf node in $\overline{T_u}$.

Our next step is to show $\overline{T_u}$ is an $\epsilon - chain$. We also prove it by contradiction. Suppose $\overline{T_u}$ is a chain but not an $\epsilon - chain$ and u can get the maximum external reward. Then there exists a node x which is not the root node of $\overline{T_u}$ and has contribution $C(x) < \mu$. As x is not the root, we denote x's parent as y. Then we find that if we change $C(x)$ to $C(x) + \alpha$ and $C(y)$ to $C(y) - \alpha$, (The constraints are $\alpha < \mu - C(x)$ and $\alpha < C(y)$; we can take very small α.) u can get higher external reward. This establishes the contradiction. Thus, if u wants to maximize $R^e(u)$, he must join the referral tree in such a way that $\overline{T_u}$ results in an $\epsilon - chain$, and u^* is the leaf node of $\overline{T_u}$. □

With this, we are now in a position to complete the proof. By Lemmas 4.7 and 4.9, we know that the partition which makes $\overline{T_u}$ an $\epsilon - chain$, and in which all trees in $\underline{T_u}$ are attached to the tail node of $\overline{T_u}$, can maximize both $R^i(u)$ and $R^e(u)$. According to the definition that $R(u) = R^i(u) + R^e(u) + \phi C(u)$, we can infer that such a partition thus maximizes $R(u)$. However, if the participant u simply joins the referral tree as a single, non-Sybil node with its entire contribution, TDRM will automatically also transform u partition into the same $\epsilon - chain$ in the reward computation tree. Thus, u has no benefit from joining as multiple identities, which proves USA.

Example : To show that TDRM does indeed violate UGSA, consider the following counter-example. Let u be a participant with $C(u) = \frac{1}{2}\mu$ and let $v_1, \cdots, v_k$ be u's children with $C(v_1) = \cdots = C(v_k) = \mu$ $(k > \frac{1}{ab\lambda})$. The profit of u as computed by TDRM is $P(u) = \frac{1}{2}((ak+1)\lambda\mu b + \phi\mu - \mu)$. If we increase u's contribution to $C'(u) = \mu$, then we can show that the new profit of u is $P'(u) = R'(u) - C'(u) = (ak+1)\lambda\mu b + \phi\mu - \mu$, which is larger than $P(u)$. That is, by increasing his contribution u can increase his profit, which violates UGSA.

4.4 Satisfying All But URO: Contribution-Deterministic Reward Mechanisms

Given the impossibility results in Theorem 4.3, we cannot expect to achieve a mechanism that achieves all the desirable properties defined in this paper, in particular, we cannot hope to simultaneously achieve UGSA and URO. The TDRM mechanism in the previous section has achieved all, but UGSA. In this section, we show that we can also relax the other property, URO, and satisfy instead all the remaining properties. For this, however, entirely different algorithmic techniques are required.

The key idea is that whereas the previously discussed mechanisms are *topology-dependent* (i.e., the reward is among other things a function of the structural property of a node's descendant tree), we now consider mechanisms in which the reward of a participant u is independent of the topology of its subtree. In particular, we seek mechanisms in which the reward $R(u)$ is purely a function of u's own contribu-

tion and the *sum* $\sum_{v \in T_u} C(v)$ of the contributions in T_u. We show that this can yield a family of mechanisms that achieve UGSA, albeit at the cost of URO.

For ease of notation, define $x_p = C(p)$ and $y_p = C(T_p \setminus \{p\})$ for a participant $p \in T$. Then, we want that the reward function $R(p)$ is purely a function of x_p and y_p. What properties should this function $R(x_p, y_p)$ have in order to satisfy the desirable properties? The SL constraint is automatically satisfied by the definition of $R(x_p, y_p)$. The CCI property demands that $R(x_p, y_p)$ is increasing in x_p, i.e. $0 < \frac{dR(x_p, y_p)}{dx_p}$. In order to satisfy CSI, it should hold that an increase in y_p increases p's reward, hence $0 < \frac{dR(x_p, y_p)}{dy_p}$. If we want to globally ensure the budget constraint, one way to do this is to demand that $R(x_p, y_p) < \Phi x_p$, and similarly, the $\varphi - RPC$ property can be enforced by $\phi x_p < R(x_p, y_p)$. It is important to point out that demanding the budget constraint to be satisfied by means of $R(x_p, y_p) < \Phi x_p$ implies that we cannot achieve the unbounded reward property URO. The reason is that if URO were to be satisfied, $R(x_p, y_p)$ would need to be able to grow larger and larger as y_p increases, which would eventually violate this constraint. In order to also achieve USA, we need the condition that for any x_p', x_p'' such that $x_p' + x_p'' = x_p$, it holds that $R(x_p, y_p) \geq R(x_p', x_p'' + y_p) + R(x_p'', y_p)$, and, finally, in order to achieve UGSA (under the assumption that we already have USA satisfied), we only need $\frac{dR(x_p, y_p)}{dx_p} < 1$.

Combining these observations, we can demand that a function $R(x_p, y_p)$ satisfy four properties. If it satisfies all of them, we call the function *successfully contribution -deterministic*. The properties are, for any $x_p > 0$, y_p:

$$i) \ 0 < \frac{dR(x_p, y_p)}{dx_p} < 1, \quad ii) \ 0 < \frac{dR(x_p, y_p)}{dy_p},$$

$$iii) \ \phi x_p < R(x_p, y_p) < \Phi x_p,$$

$$iv) \ R(x_p, y_p) \geq R(x_p', x_p'' + y_p) + R(x_p'', y_p),$$

for any x_p', x_p'' such that $x_p' + x_p'' = x_p$.

THEOREM 4.10. *If $R(x_p, y_p)$ is a successfully contribution-deterministic function, then the reward mechanism that distributes rewards according to $R(x_p, y_p)$ achieves all properties, except URO.*

PROOF. The proof follows closely along the lines of how the properties are defined. The SL constraint is obviously satisfied. CCI is satisfied because $R(x_p, y_p)$ is increasing in x_p (Property i); CSI is satisfied because $R(x_p, y_p)$ is increasing in y_p (Property ii); and both $\phi - PPC$ and the budget constraint are clearly satisfied because of Property iii.

We prove that USA is satisfied by contradiction. Suppose there is a participant p that can maximize his reward by joining the system as $k \geq 2$ nodes, and assume that the cardinality k is minimal among all those maximal splits. Consider two of these Sybil nodes p_1 and p_2, and define $x_1 = C(p_1)$, $x_2 = C(p_2)$, $y_1 = C(T_{p_1}) - C(p_1)$ and $y_2 = C(T_{p_2}) - C(p_2)$. There are two cases:

a) p_1 is an ancestor of p_2 (or vice versa). Then we know that $y_1 \geq x_2 + y_2$, $0 < \frac{dR(x_p, y_p)}{dy_p}$, so for any x_p and y_p,

$$R(x_1, y_1) + R(x_2, y_2) \leq R(x_1, y_1) + R(x_2, y_1 - x_2).$$

According to Property iv defined above, we know that

$$R(x_1, y_1) + R(x_2, y_1 - x_2) \leq R(x_1 + x_2, y_1 - x_2).$$

238

Combining these two expressions implies that the following inequality holds:

$$R(x_1, y_1) + R(x_2, y_2) \leq R(x_1 + x_2, y_1 - x_2).$$

This means that p can get at least the same reward by merging p_1 and p_2 into one node, which contradicts our assumption.

b) p_1 is not an ancestor of p_2 (or vice versa). According to Property iv, it holds that

$$R(x_1 + x_2, y_1 + y_2) \geq R(x_1, y_1 + y_2 + x_2) + R(x_2, y_1 + y_2)$$

$$> R(x_1, y_1) + R(x_2, y_2).$$

Like in case a), this implies that p can get at least the same reward by merging p_1 and p_2 which contradicts our assumption. This concludes the proof that USA is satisfied.

Finally, we prove that UGSA is satisfied. Consider some participant p. We need to compare two cases. In the first case, p joins the system as k nodes, $p_1, ..., p_k$. In the second case, p joins the system as a single node. In order to prove UGSA, we need to show that for any k and any $\Sigma_{i=1}^{k} C(p_i)$ which is equal to or larger than $C(p)$, in the second case, p can get higher payoff, namely $\Sigma_{i=1}^{k}(C(p_i) - R(C(p_i), C(T_{p_i} \backslash p_i))) \geq C(p) - R(C(p), C(T_p \backslash p))$. According to the USA property, we know that any participant p with a fixed cost can get the highest reward by joining the system as single node. Therefore, we can assume that there is an optimal choice in the scenario in which $k = 1$.

It remains to prove that for any $\epsilon > 0$, it holds $x_p - R(x_p, y_p) < x_p + \epsilon - R(x_p + \epsilon, y_p)$. According to Property i, we know that for any x_p, y_p,

$$\frac{dR(x_p, y_p)}{dx_p} < 1.$$

Therefore, it follows that for any $\epsilon > 0$,

$$R(x_p + \epsilon, y_p) - R(x_p, y_p) < \epsilon$$

$$\Rightarrow x_p - R(x_p, y_p) < x_p + \epsilon - R(x_p + \epsilon, y_p).$$

As $\epsilon > 0$, the total profit decreases, which implies that UGSA is satisfied. $\square$

4.4.1 CDRM Mechanisms

The properties derived in the previous section imply a family of reward mechanisms all of which achieve all properties except URO. It remains to find specific, practical functions that belong to this family. In this section, we give two examples. First, we set $R(x_p, y_p) = f(x_p, y_p)x_p$, so that the reward function is proportional to x_p.

Algorithm 5: Two examples of a CDRM Mechanism

i) $R(p) = (\Phi - \frac{\theta}{1 + x_p + y_p})x_p$, for $\theta + \phi < \Phi$

ii) $R(p) = \Phi x_p + \theta \ln \frac{1 + y_p}{x_p + y_p + 1}$, for $\theta + \phi < \Phi$

In both cases, it is easy to verify that the reward function does satisfy all the properties stated in the theorem. Hence, both CDRM mechanisms satisfy all our desirable properties, except URO.

5. CONCLUSIONS

In this work, we have studied incentive tree mechanisms, thus formalizing and generalizing previous algorithmic work on referral trees, lottery trees [9, 6] and multi-level marketing mechanisms [10][11]. We design two families of incentive tree mechanisms, both of which achieve all but one among the set of axiomatic properties. Furthermore, our impossibility result suggests that this is optimal. We are encouraged that both of these mechanisms achieve the slightly weaker notion of unprofitable Sybil attack (USA). This shows that mechanisms can be designed that are provably resilient against basic forms of multi-identity attacks.

Any axiomatic approach based on a choice of desirable properties is questionable as different people may deem different properties to be more important. Indeed, as we point out, not all of the properties are equally relevant to the successful operation of an incentive tree scheme in practice. However, in ongoing work, we have been studying the effect of our mechanisms in practical deployments; and experience has strengthened our belief the properties defined in this paper are indeed of critical practical importance.

6. REFERENCES

[1] http:\\ www.gigwalk.com.

[2] http:\\ www.mturk.com.

[3] M. Tennenholtz. Convention Evolution in Organizations and Markets. *Computational and Mathematical Organization Theory*, 2, 1996.

[4] P. Domingos and M. Richardson. Mining the Network Value of Customers. In *Proc. of SIGKDD*, 2003.

[5] J. Kleinberg and P. Raghavan. Query Incentive Networks. In *Proc. of OCS*, 2005.

[6] G. Pickard, W. Pan, I. Rahwan, M. Cebrian, R. Crane, A. Madan, and A. Pentland. Time Critical Social Mobilization. *Science*, 2011.

[7] J. Douceur. The Sybil Attack. In *Proc. of IPTPS*, 2002.

[8] A. Cheng and E. Friedman. Sybilproof Reputation Mechanism. In *Proc. of SIGCOMM*, 2005.

[9] J. Douceur and T. Moscibroda. Lottery Trees: Motivational Deployment of Networked Systems. In *Proc. of SIGCOMM*, 2007.

[10] Y. Emek, R. Karidi, M. Tennenholtz, and A. Zohar. Mechanisms for Multi-Level Marketing. In *Proc. of 12th ACM Conference on Electronic Commerce (EC)*, 2011.

[11] F. Drucker and L. Fleischer. Simpler Sybil-Proof Mechanisms for Multi-Level Marketing. In *Proc. of 13th ACM Conference on Electronic Commerce (EC)*, 2012.

[12] M. Babaioff, S. Dobzinski, S. Oren, and A. Zohar. On Bitcoin and Red Balloons. In *Proc. of 13th ACM Conference on Electronic Commerce (EC)*, 2012.

[13] D. Yang, G. Xue, X. Fang, and J. Tang. Crowdsourcing to Smartphones: Incentive Mechanism Design for Mobile Phone Sensing. In *Proc. of Mobicom*, 2012.

[14] A. Rai, K. K. Chintalapudi, V. Padmanabhan, and R. Sen. Zee: Zero-Effort Crowdsourcing for Indoor Localization. In *Proc. of Mobicom*, 2012.

[15] H. Wang, S. Sen, A. Elgohary, M. Farid, M. Youssef, and R. R. Choudhury. No Need to War-Drive: Unsupervised Indoor Localization. In *Proc. of MobiSys*, 2012.

What's a Little Collusion Between Friends?

Edmund L. Wong and Lorenzo Alvisi
Department of Computer Science
The University of Texas at Austin
Austin, TX, USA
{elwong,lorenzo}@cs.utexas.edu

ABSTRACT

This paper proposes a fundamentally different approach to addressing the challenge posed by colluding nodes to the sustainability of cooperative services. Departing from previous work that tries to address the threat by disincentivizing collusion or by modeling colluding nodes as faulty, this paper describes two new notions of equilibrium, k-indistinguishability and k-stability, that allow coalitions to leverage their associations without harming the stability of the service.

Categories and Subject Descriptors

C.2.4 [**Computer-Communication Networks**]: Distributed Systems; H.1.1 [**Models and Principles**]: Systems and Information Theory—*General systems theory*; K.6.0 [**Management of Computing and Information Systems**]: General—*Economics*

Keywords

Game theory, collusion, cooperative services, P2P

1. INTRODUCTION

This paper proposes a new approach to address the challenge posed by collusion to the sustainability of peer-to-peer (P2P) cooperative services. These services rely on resources offered by their participants to implement popular applications, including content distribution (e.g., [1]), file backup (e.g., [5]), and BGP routing [38]. When resources are not under the control of a single administrative domain, the necessary cooperation cannot simply be achieved by diktat. Instead, the service must be structured so that participants have an incentive to help sustain it. Practitioners (e.g., [1]) and researchers (e.g., [2, 18]) alike have recognized that game theory can provide a rigorous basis for designing and analyzing the incentive mechanisms behind cooperative services (e.g., [5, 17, 20, 24, 25, 26, 28, 32, 35, 36, 42]). These mechanisms typically aim to ensure that a service's protocol is a best response for every individual so that no

individual can profitably deviate from the service, making such a protocol, or strategy, an equilibrium strategy.

Preventing *individual* deviations, however, is unlikely to be sufficient to build robust cooperative services. The social nature of these services suggests that participants will develop, or may have already established, a rich web of relationships (based, for instance, on friendship or on belonging to the same organization), which may cause *coalitions* of participants to collude and deviate together [29]. Participants may even be able to fabricate colluders by launching Sybil attacks [13]. We submit that cooperative services that ignore the possibility of collusion do so at their own peril. That most cooperative services still choose to do so is a testament to how hard it is to address the threat posed by collusion to the stability of an equilibrium.

The literature offers two approaches to address this threat. The first is to model collusion as a fault and colluding participants as Byzantine [5, 15, 32]. The limitations of this approach are obvious: since basic distributed computing primitives such as consensus and reliable broadcast cannot be implemented if more than one third of the participants are Byzantine [23], modeling colluding participants as Byzantine imposes a cap on the number and size of coalitions that is both artificial (since it lacks a game theoretic basis) and dangerously low.

The second approach is to deny any benefit to colluders. If the equilibrium is a best response not just to every individual, but also to every possible coalition, then collusion poses no harm to the equilibrium's stability, since participants gain no benefit by colluding. This is the aim of solution concepts such as strong Nash [7] and k-resilient equilibria [3, 4], which offer this guarantee, respectively, for all conceivable coalitions and for arbitrary coalitions of size at most k. Coalition-proof Nash equilibria [8] similarly ensure that participants cannot gain any benefit from colluding and deviating in a self-enforcing way (such that there cannot be further profitable deviations from sub-coalitions).

Our work is motivated by what we believe to be a critical flaw of the second approach: its inability to account for the role played by social factors that are impossible to completely capture a priori (such as friendships or shared participation in social groups) in determining whether a participant will consider a strategy to be a best response. Intuitively, participants in coalitions formed on the basis of social "side channels" are likely to know more about each other, trust each other more, and in general be able to hold stronger assumptions about one another than about non-coalition members. Since stronger assumptions typically lead to more efficient protocols, techniques that aim to deny benefits to coalitions face a fundamentally uphill battle: as we show in Section 3, identifying a single strategy that is a best response both inside and outside every possible coalition is very hard.

To overcome this impasse, this paper introduces and begins to explore a fundamentally different approach to dealing with coalitions. The key observation is that the fundamental property provided by an equilibrium is *stability*—in that participants do not want to deviate—and that while finding a single best response between all participants is sufficient to achieve stability, it is not *necessary*: insisting on this requirement as the means to providing stability puts the cart (i.e., best responding) before the horse (i.e., stability). As a first concrete step in this new direction, we introduce two new solution concepts that do not require fighting the strong headwinds of social relationships to guarantee stable cooperative services; instead, they explicitly model the advantages that coalition members have while ensuring that participants do not want to deviate from the specified equilibrium. Both solution concepts achieve stability through a simple observation: coalitions (including the trivial singleton coalition of one non-colluding participant) will not deviate from an equilibrium as long as the equilibrium specifies a best-response strategy for every *coalition*. Thus, the strategy a participant follows depends on whom the participant is colluding with, allowing the equilibrium to specify how participants can benefit from their coalitions.

The first solution concept, *k-indistinguishability*, achieves stability through a guarantee that, while stronger than necessary, is attractively simple. In a k-indistinguishable equilibrium, the actions performed by a participant within its coalition may depend on who belongs to the coalition, but the actions towards those with whom that participant is not colluding are unaffected. Thus, in a k-indistinguishable equilibrium, participants cannot tell whether another participant, with whom they are not colluding, is itself part of some other coalition (of at most k participants). The second solution concept, *k-stability*, instead adheres to the conditions necessary for stability: like k-indistinguishability, k-stable equilibria specify a strategy per coalition that is a best response to the strategies played by all other possible coalitions; unlike k-indistinguishability, the actions that a participant takes as a part of a k-stable equilibrium may be informative about whether it is colluding and with whom. Finally, because k-stability and k-indistinguishability allow participants to change their strategies depending on whom they are colluding with, strategy profiles—traditionally used by equilibria to specify a single best-response strategy per participant—cannot capture the range of strategies that a participant may play. Instead, we use *strategy functions*, a new construct that lets us express a participant's strategy as a function of the coalition the participant belongs to.

In summary, our contributions are as follows:

- We illustrate the limits of generalizing Nash equilibria that prevent colluding participants from receiving any benefit. Specifically, we show that requiring that a single strategy be a best response for every participant, regardless of whether it is colluding, does not admit an equilibrium in several scenarios that commonly arise in cooperative services.

- We decouple the fundamental property that defines an equilibrium—stability—from the requirement that

a single strategy be a best-response. This requirement, while sufficient, is not necessary when participants may collude. We take a first step at leveraging this separation by introducing (1) a new construct, strategy functions, that allows us to describe, for each participant and each possible coalition it may be part of, the strategies the participant will play, and (2) two new solution concepts, k-indistinguishability and k-stability, that admit a strategy function as an equilibrium if no coalition wants to deviate from its specified strategy.

- We demonstrate the applicability and utility of specifying a strategy per coalition by showing how our solution concepts admit useful equilibria in the same scenarios where traditional solution concepts could not.

We proceed as follows. We describe our model and setup in Section 2. In Section 3, we demonstrate the limits of generalizing traditional equilibria in the context of several common scenarios encountered in many cooperative services. In Section 4, we define two new solution concepts—k-indistinguishability and k-stability—and demonstrate how they overcome challenges faced by traditional approaches. Finally, we discuss related work and conclude in Sections 5 and 6.

2. SETUP

We model cooperative services as a game played by a set of n players $N = \{1, \ldots, n\}$ that represent the nodes participating in the service. Each node x follows some protocol or *strategy* σ_x, which specifies the actions x takes at any point in the game. A *strategy profile* σ assigns a single strategy σ_x per node $x \in N$. A *utility function* U defines every node's preferences by mapping a strategy profile σ to a per-node *payoff*. Rational nodes prefer and select strategies that increase their payoffs as specified by the utility function, which we instantiate when discussing specific games in subsequent sections. We denote "everyone but x" as $-x$; indicate the combination of multiple strategies into a strategy profile using parentheses, e.g., $\sigma = (\sigma_x, \sigma_{-x})$; and drop parentheses when the meaning is obvious, e.g., $U_x(\sigma'_x, \sigma_{-x})$ denotes x's payoff when x plays σ'_x and everyone else plays σ_{-x}. We use the same notation for sets of nodes as well, e.g., for some set of nodes K, $-K$ represents "everyone but nodes in K."

Our goal is to find an *equilibrium*, which typically consist of a set of strategies in which no node deviates from its assigned strategy. For example, the celebrated Nash equilibrium achieves this stability by ensuring that the strategy σ_x^* of any given node x is a *best response* (i.e., it maximizes x's payoff) to everyone else following σ_{-x}^*. Thus, no node has any incentive to unilaterally deviate.

DEFINITION 1. *A strategy profile σ^* is a Nash equilibrium if for all $x \in N$, there does not exist some strategy σ'_x such that*

$$U_x(\sigma'_x, \sigma_{-x}^*) > U_x(\sigma^*)$$

A *solution concept* defines a set of conditions (e.g., Definitions 1, 2, 3, 9, and 10) that describe when a set of strategies is considered an equilibrium.

3. DISINCENTIVIZING COALITIONS

Solution concepts such as strong Nash equilibria and k-resilience specify, for each node, a single best response in which a node's actions towards a peer do not depend on whether the two are colluding. However, if coalition members trust each other more than other nodes, the practical applicability of these solution concepts are fundamentally limited. To illustrate this point, we describe techniques and scenarios likely to occur in cooperative services where the stronger assumptions that insiders can rely on when dealing with one another hamper the ability to achieve k-resilience. These examples are by no means comprehensive; rather, our goal is to provide a taste of the larger challenges faced by solution concepts that aim to discourage coalition formation.

Before we proceed, we first formally define k-resilience [3, 4], which generalizes the Nash equilibrium by requiring that the strategy profile be a best response (i.e., admit no profitable deviations) not only for every individual node (as required by a Nash equilibrium) but also for any coalition of up to size k. As a Nash equilibrium is simply a 1-resilient equilibrium, we generally focus on k-resilient equilibria where $k \geq 2$. Note that a strong Nash equilibrium is a n-resilient equilibrium.

DEFINITION 2. *A strategy profile σ^* is a k-resilient equilibrium if, for all $K \subseteq N$ such that $|K| \leq k$, there does not exist some strategy σ'_K such that for all $x \in K$,*

$$U_x(\sigma'_K, \sigma^*_{-K}) > U_x(\sigma^*)$$

We use this version of k-resilience to prove our negative results; our results therefore apply to stronger notions of k-resilience that guarantee stability even if coalitions are willing to deviate for less [3, 4]. Our negative results also do not rely on coalition members being able to "cheap talk", i.e., communicate at no cost, during the game [12, 16].

When there is randomness in the game, a node's best response and expected payoff depend on its *beliefs*, which represent the likelihood, from this node's viewpoint, of said random events occurring. Given every node's beliefs, we can define a Bayesian notion of k-resilient and strong Nash equilibrium similar to a Bayes (Nash) equilibrium.

DEFINITION 3. *A strategy profile and set of beliefs (σ^*, μ^*) is a k-resilient Bayes equilibrium if for all $K \subseteq N$ such that $|K| \leq k$, there does not exist some strategy σ'_K such that for all $x \in K$,*

$$\mathrm{E}^{(\sigma'_K, \sigma^*_{-K}), \mu^*}[U_x] > \mathrm{E}^{\sigma^*, \mu^*}[U_x]$$

where $\mathrm{E}^{\sigma, \mu}[U_x]$ represents x's expected payoff from the strategy profile σ with belief μ_x, given that $x \in K$.

It is important to note that all the solution concepts and equilibria we discuss in this paper are notions from *non-cooperative* game theory. There has also been extensive work in *cooperative* game theory (see any game theory text, e.g., [33], for a survey of related work) that explicitly studies the formation of coalitions in games where players are trying to work together. Cooperative and non-cooperative game theory significantly differ in focus: cooperative game theory focuses on interactions *within* a coalition—how and which coalitions form (players join a coalition based on the benefit the coalition offers) and how payoffs are allocated among coalition members (based on each member's value to the coalition)—whereas non-cooperative game theory focuses instead on the interactions *between* competing players (which, in our case, consist of exogenously-determined coalitions and non-colluding nodes).

3.1 Can trusted third parties limit equilibria?

Cooperative services often rely on a trusted third party to incentivize cooperation among nodes. This type of trust, which in some cases is indispensable (e.g., to implement fair exchange [22, 34]), is unnecessary among coalition members; indeed, perhaps surprisingly, it can actually render k-resilient equilibria impossible to achieve.

We illustrate this point through the following game, which models the fundamental choice that each node makes in P2P cooperative services: should I contribute my fair share?

DEFINITION 4. *The mediated pairwise-exchange game is a R-repeated game where, in each round $r \in \{1, \ldots, R\}$, each node $x \in N$:*

1. *Decides (simultaneously) on some set of peers $M_x^r \subseteq N \setminus \{x\}$ to use a mediator with.*

2. *Observes which peers are using a mediator with x.*

3. *Decides on some set of peers $\Gamma_x^r \subseteq N \setminus \{x\}$ to contribute to; any other peer is snubbed.*

4. *Receives a contribution from a peer y if y contributed to x and either (a) y did not use a mediator with x, or (b) x contributed to y. Denote the set of all such y as C_x^r, i.e., $y \in C_x^r$ iff $x \in \Gamma_y^r \wedge (x \notin M_y^r \vee y \in \Gamma_x^r)$.*

x pays γ per peer that x contributes to and ϵ per peer that x uses a mediator with. x earns $b > 2\gamma + \epsilon$ per received contribution, for a round payoff of $v_x^r = |C_x^r|b - |\Gamma_x^r|\gamma - |M_x^r|\epsilon$. A node's total payoff is the sum of all round payoffs: $\sum_{r=1}^{R} v_x^r$.

While this game resembles a finitely-repeated prisoner's dilemma, the mediator, who can serve as a trusted third party and ensure a fair pairwise exchange, enables the existence of Nash equilibria in which contribution occurs (without the mediator, no such equilibrium exists).

THEOREM 1. *Let σ^* be a strategy profile in the mediated pairwise-exchange game in which a node x, following σ_x^*, contributes to a peer y, using a mediator only in round R, iff (1) x and y have never snubbed each other in the past and (2) x and y have not used a mediator in any round other than R; otherwise, x snubs y without a mediator. Then σ^* is a Nash equilibrium.*

PROOF. Same as the backwards-induction half of the proof of Theorem 5. □

The Nash equilibrium in Theorem 1 uses the mediator to ensure cooperation in the last round, which encourages cooperation in prior rounds without the mediator. We now prove that this same mediator precludes the existence of k-resilient equilibria. The reason, essentially, is that using the mediator, which incurs cost, is undesirable between colluding nodes (Lemma 2) but necessary to ensure cooperation between two non-colluding nodes (Lemma 1). This tension makes it impossible for a single strategy to be a node's best response regardless of how it colludes (Theorem 2).

LEMMA 1. *In any k-resilient equilibrium of the mediated pairwise-exchange game where some node contributes, the last time in the game that any node contributes with positive probability to a peer must always involve a mediator.*

PROOF. By contradiction. Fix some k-resilient equilibrium σ^*, where the last time that any node contributes with positive probability does not involve a mediator with positive probability (if there exist multiple such node/peer pairings, choose one arbitrarily). During this "last contribution," let x be the node that contributes, y be the receiving peer, and α be the probability that x contributes to y after deciding not to use a mediator with y. By assumption, $\alpha > 0$.

Since σ^* must be a best response regardless of who is colluding, suppose x and y are not colluding. Then it must be the case that, in σ^*, y snubs x during the last contribution if x does not use a mediator: y expects to earn, from x's contribution, αb without incurring the cost of contributing; moreover, since this is the last time a contribution occurs with positive probability, y's choice of whether to snub x does not negatively impact y's *continuation* (i.e., subsequent) payoff. It follows that x could profitably deviate from σ^* by always snubbing y during the last contribution if x does not use a mediator: doing so would save x an expected cost of $\alpha\gamma$ with no negative effect on x's continuation payoff. Contradiction. □

LEMMA 2. *In any k-resilient equilibrium of the mediated pairwise exchange game where some node contributes, the last time in the game that any node contributes with positive probability to a peer must never involve a mediator.*

PROOF. By contradiction. Fix some k-resilient equilibrium σ^* where the last time that any node contributes with positive probability also involves a mediator with positive probability (if there exist multiple such node/peer pairings, choose one arbitrarily). During this "last contribution," let x be the node that contributes; y be the peer; $\alpha > 0$ be the probability that x decides *to use* a mediator with y; and p_x (p_y) be the probability that y (x) observes a contribution from x (y) in expectation over all possible combinations of x and y's choices regarding using a mediator and contributing with one another.

Since σ^* must be a best response regardless of who is colluding, suppose x and y *are* colluding. Consider an alternate strategy profile σ' in which all nodes play the same actions with the same probabilities as in σ^*, except, during the last contribution, x and y do not use a mediator with one another, x (y) contributes to y (x) with probability p_x (p_y), and x and y subsequently play actions as if x and y had instead followed σ^*. It follows that the payoffs for x and y are exactly the same, with the exception of the payoffs that x and y receive from one another during the last contribution, where (1) x and y's expected benefit remains the same, (2) x's expected cost is strictly lower since x contributes with the same probability in expectation without the cost of a mediator ($\alpha\epsilon > 0$), and (3) y's expected cost is no higher (and is lower if y was using a mediator in σ^*). Thus, x is better off and y is no worse off. Contradiction. □

THEOREM 2. *There exists no k-resilient equilibrium in the mediated pairwise-exchange game.*

PROOF. Lemmas 1 and 2 imply that there exists no k-resilient equilibrium where nodes contribute. Further, a strategy profile σ in which all nodes snub and earn 0, while a Nash equilibrium, is not a k-resilient equilibrium. To see why, consider an alternate strategy profile σ' and some coalition K (such that $|K| \geq 2$) where no one uses mediators and only members of K contribute to one another. σ' earns K's

members payoffs of $(|K| - 1)R(b - \gamma) > 0$ each, making it a profitable deviation from σ. □

3.2 What if nodes may fail?

When nodes may fail, a node's best response will generally depend on the probability with which it expects other nodes may fail. Greater trust and access to more information (e.g., concerning the frequency with which fellow coalition nodes are patched) may allow nodes within a coalition to reasonably believe that fellow coalition members have a lower probability of failing than outsiders. Unfortunately, even a slightly lower failure probability can make k-resilience practically unachievable.

We illustrate this point using a simple single-shot simultaneous game that models a simplified version of secret-sharing [3, 39]. In this game, each node wants to reconstruct a secret that requires the node to request shares from its peers. These peers deliver the requested shares unless they fail (e.g., by crashing). Each node must then decide how many shares to request: requesting more shares incurs more cost, but requesting fewer shares may result in the node being unable to reconstruct the secret because of peer failures.

DEFINITION 5. *The simple secret-sharing game is a single-shot, simultaneous game in which every node $x \in N$:*

1. *Selects a set $\Gamma_x \subseteq N \setminus \{x\}$ of nodes to request shares from.*

2. *Pays $|\Gamma_x|\gamma$ for this request.*

3. *Receives shares from some set $C_x \subseteq \Gamma_x$.*

4. *Earns benefit $b > |N|\gamma$ iff $|C_x| \geq m$, where m is the number of shares that x must gather from its peers before being able to reconstruct the secret.*

The simple secret-sharing game is a decision theory problem: a node's choice does not affect its peers' outcomes.[1] This is intentional: our goal is to show that, despite the game's simplicity, it is often impossible to find k-resilient equilibria. To account for a node's beliefs regarding how likely its peers are to fail, we use k-resilient Bayes equilibria (Definition 3). In this game, a strategy profile Γ represents the peers that each node requests from. A set of beliefs μ represents the view of each node, given the set of peers it is colluding with, regarding the likelihood that any peer will successfully deliver its share if requested. In other words, μ represents each node x's view of the likelihood that a peer in Γ_x will also be in C_x. An equilibrium in the simple secret-sharing game is some (Γ^*, μ^*) where no node x, colluding with any $(k - 1)$ peers, could do any better in expectation requesting shares from some set $\Gamma'_x \neq \Gamma^*_x$. More formally, for all $K \subseteq N$ such that $|K| \leq k$, there is no Γ' such that for all $x \in K$,

$$H[|C'_x| - m]b - |\Gamma'_x|\gamma > H[|C^*_x| - m]b - |\Gamma^*_x|\gamma$$

where $H[i]$ is the discrete unit step function ($H[i] = 1$ if $i \geq 0$; otherwise $H[i] = 0$).

---

[1] If the game were sequential, the choice of some node x to request a share from some peer y could inform y of whether x has failed. However, finding k-resilient equilibria is no less challenging, since (1) there is at least one node (the first node to move) that will never have such a signal and (2) even if x successfully requests a share from y, x could subsequently fail before y's turn.

THEOREM 3. *Let* (Γ^*, μ^*) *be a* k-*resilient Bayes equilibrium of the simple secret-sharing game in which some node* $x \in N$ *believes that a peer* y *will fail with probability* μ_x^* *if* x *and* y *are not colluding and* $\mu_x^* - \epsilon$ *if* x *and* y *are, where* $\epsilon > 0$. *Then either* x *requests secrets from no one or everyone, i.e.,* $\Gamma_x^* \in \{\emptyset, N \setminus \{x\}\}$.

PROOF. Suppose $k = 2$ and $K = \{x, y\}$, i.e., x and y are colluding. If x incurs more cost requesting shares than it earns in expectation from reconstructing the secret (e.g., because of high rates of failure), then $\Gamma_x^* = \emptyset$. Otherwise, suppose x requests shares from peers in $\Gamma_x^* \neq \emptyset$. It is obvious that since x believes that y will fail with probability $\mu_x^* - \epsilon$, which is lower than the probability of any other peer $z \neq y$ failing (μ_x^*), x should always request shares from y, so any 2-resilient Γ_x^* must contain y. However, as y can be any peer, the only Γ_x^* that is guaranteed to contain all possible y is $\Gamma_x^* = \{y \mid y \in N \wedge y \neq x\} = N \setminus \{x\}$. Finally, as k-resilience implies 2-resilience, this result applies to k-resilience for $k \geq 2$. ☐

A node that wants to reconstruct the secret rarely wants to request shares from all of its peers, since the cost of these additional requests is not worth the slight insurance that redundant shares provide. However, in such cases, it follows from Theorem 3 that no k-resilient Bayes equilibrium exists. Therefore, the only scenarios in which a node wants to reconstruct the secret as a part of a k-resilient Bayes equilibrium are those in which the secret's value is sufficiently high to justify requesting shares from all peers to maximize the likelihood of success.

Figure 1 quantifies what this value must be, using example numbers based on a movie-streaming context: $n = 100$ nodes; each node expects that coalition members never fail[2] and that non-coalition members fail with independent probability β; m is set such that, given an independent failure probability of β, there is at least a 0.99999 chance that at least m peers, out of $n - 1$ possible peers, will not fail; and γ is set to (1500 Kbps) × (2 hours) × (\$1/GB)/($m + 1$). As k increases, the expected probability of a coalition member reconstructing the secret increases, thus making it more difficult to convince such a node to request shares from every other peer. Note that while Figure 1 implies that the minimum required benefit goes up as probability of failure goes up, this is an artifact of how we define m; in reality, the minimum required benefit goes up as the probability of failure goes down, as expected.

As Figure 1 shows, even with coalitions of at most two nodes and beliefs that non-coalition nodes fail with probability 0.01, a 2-resilient equilibrium exists only if a node values a two-hour movie, which incurs $\gamma(n - 1) > \$1.37$ in communication costs, at over \$268.95!

3.3 Do nodes want to punish one another?

Cooperative services often incentivize nodes not to deviate by relying on the threat of punishment. In this section, we show that punishments that hurt both the enforcing and receiving nodes are never used within a coalition, and other forms of punishment will be difficult, if not impossible, to

---

[2] While this may seem extreme, note that this is exactly what failure-aware k-resilient solution concepts, such as (k, t)-robustness [3, 4], require: nodes do not deviate assuming that the coalition and set of faulty nodes do not overlap.

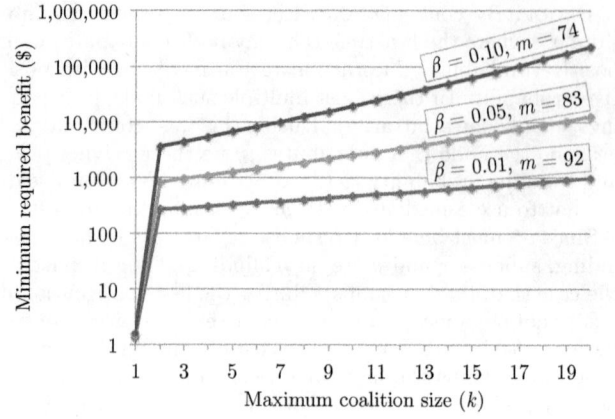

Figure 1: In the simple secret-sharing game (Definition 5), the minimum benefit needed for a k-resilient equilibrium where nodes attempt to reconstruct the secret.

achieve in real-world scenarios. We illustrate this through a simplified version of the mediated pairwise-exchange game.[3]

DEFINITION 6. *The simple pairwise-exchange game is an infinitely-repeated game where, in each round* $r \geq 0$, *every node* $x \in N$:

1. *Simultaneously decides on some set of nodes* $\Gamma_x^r \subseteq N \setminus \{x\}$ *that it will contribute to; any node not in* Γ_x^r *is snubbed.*

2. *Observes which peer* $y \neq x$ *contributed to it; let* C_x^r *denote the set of all such* y, *i.e.,* $y \in C_x^r$ *iff* $x \in \Gamma_y^r$.

x's *round payoff is* $v_x^r = |C_x^r| b - |\Gamma_x^r| \gamma$, *where* $b > \gamma$. x's *total payoff is the* δ-*weighted sum of the round payoffs:* $\sum_{r=0}^{\infty} \delta^r v_x^r$.

THEOREM 4. *Let* σ^* *be a* k-*resilient equilibrium in the simple pairwise-exchange game in which some contribution occurs. In other words,* σ^* *specifies that, at some point in the game, a node* y *contributes to some node* x, *who "rewards"* y *if* y *contributes and "punishes"* y *if* y *snubs* x. *Then either (1)* x *must prefer punishing to rewarding* y, *and/or (2)* x *punishing* y *is not a* k-*resilient best response (i.e.,* x *may threaten to punish* y, *but, given the opportunity,* x *and* y *can profitably deviate by not following through).*

PROOF. Fix some k-resilient equilibrium σ^* in which contribution occurs and, unlike condition (1) above, x is no worse off rewarding y. We prove that condition (2) follows: x punishing y is not a k-resilient best response. Let r be the round in which this contribution occurs, $U_x(\sigma^* | (\Gamma_x^r, C_x^r \cup \{y\}))$ denote x's continuation payoff from rewarding y, and $U_x(\sigma^* | (\Gamma_x^r, C_x^r \setminus \{y\}))$ denote x's continuation payoff for punishing y. We have:

$$U_x(\sigma^* | (\Gamma_x^r, C_x^r \cup \{y\})) \geq U_x(\sigma^* | (\Gamma_x^r, C_x^r \setminus \{y\})) \quad (1)$$

Denote y's continuation payoff from contributing to and snubbing x as $U_y(\sigma^* | (\Gamma_y^r \cup \{x\}, C_y^r))$ and $U_y(\sigma^* | (\Gamma_y^r \setminus \{x\}, C_y^r))$,

---

[3] While we could use the mediated pairwise-exchange game to illustrate this point, we instead use a game with an infinite horizon (which enables the existence of Nash equilibria where contribution occurs) and no mediator as the mediator already makes k-resilient equilibria impossible to achieve.

respectively. As y contributes to x as a part of a k-resilient equilibrium, y must be no worse off doing so:

$$|C_y^r|b - |\Gamma_y^r \cup \{x\}|\gamma + U_y(\sigma^*|(\Gamma_y^r \cup \{x\}, C_y^r)) \geq$$
$$|C_y^r|b - |\Gamma_y^r \setminus \{x\}|\gamma + U_y(\sigma^*|(\Gamma_y^r \setminus \{x\}, C_y^r))$$

Unsurprisingly, it follows that y, in continuation, is worse off being punished than being rewarded:

$$U_y(\sigma^*|(\Gamma_y^r \cup \{x\}, C_y^r)) \geq \gamma + U_y(\sigma^*|(\Gamma_y^r \setminus \{x\}, C_y^r))$$
$$> U_y(\sigma^*|(\Gamma_y^r \setminus \{x\}, C_y^r)) \quad (2)$$

Suppose $K = \{x, y\}$, and let σ'_K specify the same actions as in σ^*, except x and y play σ^* as if y contributed even if y snubbed x. We can see that by inequality (1),

$$U_x((\sigma'_K, \sigma^*_{-K})|(\Gamma_x^r, C_x^r \setminus \{y\})) = U_x(\sigma^*|(\Gamma_x^r, C_x^r \cup \{y\}))$$
$$\geq U_x(\sigma^*|(\Gamma_x^r, C_x^r \setminus \{y\}))$$

and, by inequality (2),

$$U_y((\sigma'_K, \sigma^*_{-K})|(\Gamma_y^r \setminus \{x\}, C_y^r)) = U_y(\sigma^*|(\Gamma_y^r \cup \{x\}, C_y^r))$$
$$> U_y(\sigma^*|(\Gamma_y^r \setminus \{x\}, C_y^r))$$

Thus, x punishing y is not a k-resilient best response. $\square$

Theorem 4 applies to many forms of punishment, including various flavors of grim trigger, forgiving trigger, and tit-for-tat (if $b/\gamma > 1/\delta$). A k-resilient equilibrium can still use these punishments as a non-credible threat and hope that such bluffs are not called in practice. Alternatively, any punishment in which nodes strictly prefer to punish than reward can be part of a k-resilient equilibrium. However, if network loss is a possibility (as in real-world environments), (1) behaviors that are not part of a k-resilient equilibrium (e.g., snubbing when only contribution is supposed to be played) may be observed, resulting in a node (rationally) reneging on its non-credible threat and the collapse of any k-resilient equilibrium that encourages contribution using such threats; and (2) the inability to observe what a node has observed (as in [42]) may result in nodes feigning being snubbed and frivolously punishing their peers under false pretenses.[4]

3.4 What other issues are there?

Finally, we briefly describe two commonly-used techniques that are often not k-resilient. *Digital signatures*, with their guarantee of non-repudiation, are useful in adversarial environments, but their bandwidth and computational costs are hard to justify within a coalition where members trust each other. Generally, digitally signing messages is part of a k-resilient protocol only if not signing may affect the protocol's outcome, e.g., if this message is passed around to more than k nodes that check the signature, and coalition members cannot sign for each other.

Junk, i.e., semantically meaningless data, has been used (e.g., [5, 28, 44]) as a form of payment to ensure that nodes contribute their fair share to the cooperative service. For instance, if a node is required to send data but has nothing useful to send, it may instead send protocol-specified "junk." By making junk more expensive to transfer than useful content, junk transfers discourage free-riding by incentivizing nodes to send real content whenever possible. However, junk transfers incur bandwidth costs on the sender and receiver

while providing no benefit to the receiver; nodes that trust each other have no incentive to perform them. It follows that no protocol that relies on junk transfers is k-resilient.

4. ACCEPTING COALITIONS

The scenarios in Section 3 suggest that it is difficult for a single strategy profile to specify strategies that a node, colluding with up to $(k-1)$ peers, prefers over all possible deviations, as required by k-resilience. Yet, we believe these scenarios are symptomatic of a more general problem: the ability for colluding nodes to hold stronger beliefs and assumptions about fellow coalition members (and potentially about the system as a whole) often results in more efficient protocols. As a result, we believe there are likely very few scenarios in which k-resilience will bear fruit.

In this section, we show that the insight to overcome this impasse is to recognize that denying benefits to nodes that belong to a coalition, while sufficient for stability, is not necessary. We propose a fundamentally different notion of equilibrium: instead of specifying a single best-response strategy to each node, our equilibria map each node to possibly multiple strategies, depending on whom it colludes with. By effectively mapping each possible coalition to a strategy, our equilibria can specify, as a part of the strategy, the efficiencies that a coalition can leverage among its members. Despite this flexibility, our equilibria guarantee that the strategies specified for every coalition is a best response to what other nodes play, despite how they collude.

Specifying coalitional strategies. Because our equilibria specify a strategy per coalition, the strategies that the nodes, within each coalition, follow may depend on whom they are colluding with. Our equilibria cannot use strategy profiles used by traditional equilibria because they specify only a single strategy per node. Our equilibria instead use a novel construct, a *strategy function*, to specify a node's strategy based on whom the node is colluding with. We formally represent how nodes collude by a partition P of N, in which two nodes x and y are colluding if there exists some element (a coalition) $K \in P$ such that $x, y \in K$. Intuitively, each partition represents one way that nodes can collude. We use $\mathbb{P}^k = \{P : \forall K \in P, |K| \leq k\}$ to denote the space of all partitions that contains no coalition larger than size k.

DEFINITION 7. *A strategy function $\mathcal{S}$ is a mapping from a partition (representing a particular way that nodes have chosen to collude) to a strategy profile (which specifies the strategies that these nodes will play as a result) such that if there exists some coalition K that is in P and P', $\mathcal{S}$ maps the same strategy to K in P and P', i.e., if $K \in P$ and $K \in P'$, $\mathcal{S}_K(P) = \mathcal{S}_K(P')$, where $\mathcal{S}_K(P)$ and $\mathcal{S}_K(P')$ denote the strategies deployed by K given partitions P and P'.*

Note that a node's strategy does not depend on how nodes outside of its coalition collude, which a node may not know. We define $\mathcal{M}$ as the membership function: $\mathcal{M}(x, P) = K$ if, in partition P, K is the coalition that x is a part of, i.e., $K \in P$ and $x \in K$. With respect to a node x in coalition K, all nodes in K are *insiders*, and all others are *outsiders*.

4.1 Coalition-indistinguishable equilibria

Where k-resilience makes coalitions futile, k-indistinguishability makes them invisible; where k-resilience fundamentally aims to deny coalitions any claim of exceptionalism

---

[4]We omit further discussion due to lack of space; see [41].

and sees a system as a collection of individual nodes, k-indistinguishability sees a system as a collection of coalitions, some of which may contain a single node; where k-resilience ensures that every node best responds to every other node, k-indistinguishability ensures that every coalition best responds to every other coalition: in both equilibria, nodes that belong to different coalitions interact with each other as if no coalition existed.

DEFINITION 8. *Two strategy profiles σ and σ' are indistinguishable with respect to some node x, denoted as $\sigma \overset{x}{=} \sigma'$, if all histories resulting from σ and σ', as observed by x, occur with equal probability and $U_x(\sigma) = U_x(\sigma')$.*

DEFINITION 9. $\mathcal{S}^*$ *is a k-indistinguishable equilibrium if:*

- *For any $P, P' \in \mathbb{P}^k$, any coalition K such that $K \in P$ and $K \in P'$, and any $x \in K$, $\mathcal{S}^*(P) \overset{x}{=} \mathcal{S}^*(P')$.*

- *For all $P \in \mathbb{P}^k$ and all $K \in P$, there does not exist a strategy σ'_K such that for all $x \in K$,*

$$U_x(\sigma'_K, \mathcal{S}^*_{-K}(P)) \geq U_x(\mathcal{S}^*(P))$$

and, for some $y \in K$, the inequality is strict.

The first condition (indistinguishability) requires that a node cannot distinguish whether an outsider is itself colluding with others; the second condition (best response) requires that in any partition, there exists some node in every coalition that prefers the equilibrium-specified strategy to any coalitional deviation. Note that while we defined best response to be consistent with the definition of k-resilience, weaker or stronger notions could have been used instead. Also, observe that the best-response condition of k-indistinguishable equilibria must hold for all possible partitions. Therefore, like k-resilient equilibria, a k-indistinguishable equilibrium consists of strategies that make up a best response for *all* possible coalitions of up to size k, not just one particular coalition or set of coalitions.

Every k-resilient and Nash equilibrium σ^* has an equivalent k-indistinguishable equilibrium $\mathcal{S}^*$ in which $\mathcal{S}^*(P) = \sigma^*$ for all P. However, by allowing nodes to base their strategies on whom they collude with, k-indistinguishable equilibria circumvent the challenges described in Section 3 while ensuring that no coalition will deviate from its specified strategy (Section 4.3). Moreover, similar to k-resilience, any service that uses a protocol which is the non-colluding strategy in a k-indistinguishable equilibrium is guaranteed to be supported and maintained by nodes, even if they may collude. Although k-indistinguishability cannot guarantee that the exact protocol will be followed to the letter by a node when interacting with a fellow insider, k-indistinguishability does guarantee that any actions that a node takes when interacting with an outsider is the same as those specified by the service's protocol. Thus, from the service's perspective, every node is effectively running the service's protocol and supporting the service.

4.2 From indistinguishability to stability

Although indistinguishability is an attractive guarantee, it may in practice prove too stringent for some applications. For example, a content-distribution service in which colluding nodes freely exchange content with one another may not be k-indistinguishable because non-colluding nodes may be able to detect the presence of a coalition simply by observing that colluding nodes statistically have more content at any given time than everyone else. k-stable equilibria do away with indistinguishability, focusing only on the conditions necessary for stability.

DEFINITION 10. $\mathcal{S}^*$ *is a k-stable equilibrium if for all $P \in \mathbb{P}^k$ and all $K \in P$, there does not exist a strategy σ'_K such that for all $x \in K$,*

$$U_x(\sigma'_K, \mathcal{S}^*_{-K}(P)) \geq U_x(\mathcal{S}^*(P))$$

and, for some $y \in K$, the inequality is strict.

As in k-indistinguishable equilibria, a k-stable equilibrium requires a best response for all possible coalitions of up to size k, and every k-resilient and Nash equilibrium has a k-stable equivalent. Moreover, every k-indistinguishable equilibrium is also k-stable. However, k-stable equilibria do not guarantee that a colluding node's strategy is indistinguishable from that of a non-colluding node. In other words, it is possible that the strategy of a colluding node x provides outsiders with information about whether x is colluding, with whom x is colluding, etc. In addition, if x chooses to collude, x's coalition may affect the payoffs of peers both inside and outside of x's coalition. Nevertheless, a k-stable equilibrium still guarantees that, for any coalition, the specified strategy is a best response to the strategies played by all outsiders, regardless of how these other nodes may collude.

Other k-stable solution concepts. k-stability is a very general notion that, we believe, provides a useful basis for developing new solution concepts that guarantee stability in the presence of collusion. k-indistinguishability is one such solution concept, the result of adding indistinguishability to k-stability. Another requirement that one may desire is some notion of self-enforcement (no profitable deviation by sub-coalitions), e.g., a solution concept could require that, in equilibrium, nodes prefer to be with their respective coalitions over working alone (k-stability and k-indistinguishability do not have any such requirement). Alternatively, one could devise a Bayesian version of k-stability that guarantees an expected best response for each coalition based on the likelihood that certain coalitions will form. Yet another interesting direction would be to devise a version of k-stability that bounds the "price of collusion," i.e., how much a node's payoff is affected when outsiders choose to collude (similar to the notion of a safety-net guarantee used in [44]). We leave exploring these and other notions of equilibrium to future work.

4.3 Examples of equilibria

In this section, we show the applicability of k-stability and k-indistinguishability by showing that such equilibria exist in the scenarios described in Section 3, where k-resilient equilibria did not exist before.

k-stability and k-indistinguishability in the mediated pairwise-exchange game. It is simple to prove that there exists a k-indistinguishable equilibrium in the mediated pairwise-exchange game (Definition 4). Because k-indistinguishable and k-stable equilibria allow nodes to base their play on whom they are colluding with, a node, as a part of a k-indistinguishable equilibrium, can use the mediator with outsiders (as in Theorem 1) and leverage the trust provided by the coalition with insiders.

THEOREM 5. *Let $\mathcal{S}^*$ be a strategy function such that, for any partition $P \in \mathbb{P}^k$ and any $x \in N$, $\mathcal{S}_x^*(P)$ specifies that*

- *For $y \in \mathcal{M}(x, P)$ such that $y \neq x$, x never uses a mediator and always contributes.*

- *For $y \notin \mathcal{M}(x, P)$, x contributes to y, using a mediator only in round R, iff (1) x and y have never snubbed each other in the past and (2) x and y have not used a mediator in any round other than R. Otherwise, x snubs y without a mediator.*

Then $\mathcal{S}^*$ is a k-indistinguishable equilibrium.

PROOF. Without loss of generality, fix some partition P,[5] and consider the interactions of some node x with some peer y.[6] Suppose that y is an insider, i.e., $y \in \mathcal{M}(x, P) = K$. Let R_s be the set of rounds in which x snubs y and R_m be the set of rounds in which x uses a mediator with y. In each round in R_s, x gains γ, but y loses b. In each round in R_m, x loses ϵ; y's payoff is unaffected. Any deviation in which $R_s \neq \emptyset$ or $R_m \neq \emptyset$ is then not in K's best interest.

Suppose instead that y is an outsider, i.e., $y \notin \mathcal{M}(x, P)$. We can show that by following $\mathcal{S}_x^*(P)$ with respect to y is x's best response by backwards induction.

Base case: round R (the last round). We first show that $\mathcal{S}_x^*(P)$ is a best response for x with respect to y by considering the following two cases:

- x and y have always contributed to one another. If x deviates by snubbing and/or not using a mediator, x saves at most $\gamma + \epsilon$. However, since y is using a mediator, x loses benefit b it would have received from y otherwise. Since $b > 2\gamma + \epsilon > \gamma + \epsilon$ by assumption (Definition 4), x is clearly worse off.

- x and/or y have snubbed one another in the past. If x deviates by contributing to y or using a mediator, x is obviously worse off: x must pay at least $\min(\gamma, \epsilon) > 0$ but receives no additional benefit.

Inductive step. Assume that for all rounds following some round $r_0 > 1$, $\mathcal{S}_x^*(P)$ is a best response for x with respect to y. We now prove the inductive step—$\mathcal{S}_x^*(P)$ is a best response for x with respect to y in round r_0—in a similar fashion by considering the following two cases:

- y has always contributed to x. If x deviates by using a mediator, x is at least ϵ worse off in round r_0. If x deviates by snubbing y, x saves γ in round r_0. Regardless, y will snub x in every subsequent round, resulting in x losing at least $b - (\gamma + \epsilon)$ per round. x is then worse off since the net change in x's payoff is at least $\gamma - (b - (\gamma + \epsilon)) = -b + 2\gamma + \epsilon < 0$.

- y has snubbed x. If x deviates by contributing or using a mediator, x is worse off, as argued in the base case.

---

[5] As our proof makes no assumptions about P, it follows that our proof holds for all possible partitions $P \in \mathbb{P}^k$.
[6] We can safely do this because each interaction between any two pairs of nodes in $\mathcal{S}^*$ is independent.

Thus, $\mathcal{S}_x^*(P)$ is a best response for x. □

The mediated pairwise-exchange game, as defined in Definition 4, involves every node x *privately* observing which peers use a mediator with or contribute to x; x does not know what other peers have chosen with respect to one another. If such choices were publicly observable (e.g., if the mediator published a list describing which pairs of nodes it would mediate for), $\mathcal{S}^*$ would no longer be a k-indistinguishable equilibrium, since non-colluding nodes would be able to observe that coalition members never use a mediator with one another. However, because nodes, regardless of whom they collude with, are still better off following the strategies specified in $\mathcal{S}^*$, $\mathcal{S}^*$ would remain a k-stable equilibrium.

k-stability in the simple secret-sharing game. Likewise, it is straightforward to show that the simple secret-sharing game (Definition 5) has a k-stable equilibrium. In particular, a node, depending on whom it is colluding with, can choose the exact set of peers to request secrets from that the node expects will maximize its payoff.

k-stability and k-indistinguishability in the simple pairwise-exchange game. We can incorporate the punishments in Section 3.3 into a protocol that is k-stable or k-indistinguishable in the simple pairwise-exchange game (Definition 6). As an example, we demonstrate how a local grim-trigger punishment can be used here.

THEOREM 6. *Let $\mathcal{S}^*$ be the following strategy function: for any partition $P \in \mathbb{P}^k$ and for any $x \in N$, $\mathcal{S}_x^*(P)$ specifies the following action for x:*

- *For $y \in \mathcal{M}(x, P)$ such that $y \neq x$, contribute to y.*

- *For $y \notin \mathcal{M}(x, P)$, contribute to y iff $r = 0$ or x and y have always contributed to one another.*

Then $\mathcal{S}^*$ is a subgame-perfect k-indistinguishable equilibrium (i.e., at every point in the game, nodes play a k-indistinguishable best response) if $b/\gamma \geq 1/\delta$.

PROOF. Without loss of generality, fix P. For any $K \in P$ in which $|K| > 1$, $\mathcal{S}_K^*(P)$ is a best response when interacting with fellow insiders. To see why, observe that following $\mathcal{S}_K^*(P)$ in each round earns a round payoff of $(n-1)(b-\gamma)$. Deviating by snubbing an insider improves one node's payoff by γ but causes a loss of $b > \gamma$ to another's; the coalition as a whole earns $(n-2)(b-\gamma) < (n-1)(b-\gamma)$ as a result in that round, so someone in the coalition must be worse off.

Now consider any two nodes x, y that are not colluding, i.e., $y \notin \mathcal{M}(x, P)$. If x and y have always contributed to each other and x snubs y, x gains γ in the current round but loses at least $(b-\gamma)$ in every subsequent round. This is profitable only if $\delta(b-\gamma)/(1-\delta) < \gamma$, which is never the case. Finally, if y has snubbed x and x deviates by contributing to (rather than snubbing) y, x incurs an additional cost of γ; this is clearly not in x's best interest. □

Similar to the previous example, $\mathcal{S}^*$ as defined in Theorem 6 would remain a k-stable equilibrium (but would not be indistinguishable at every point in the game) if a node's choices of whom to contribute to were publicly observable.

k-stability and k-indistinguishability with digital signatures and junk. Mechanisms such as digital signatures or junk transfers fit naturally within a k-stable or k-indistinguishable equilibrium. The equilibrium may specify that these mechanisms are used between outsiders and by-passed between insiders when unneeded.

5. RELATED WORK

We have seen how hard it is to achieve useful equilibria in cooperative services using strong Nash equilibrium [7], which requires a strategy profile be Pareto optimal, and k-resilience [3, 4], which has weaker but similar requirements. As previously mentioned, Bernheim et al. [8] describe coalition-proof Nash equilibria, which weaken strong Nash equilibria by requiring that the equilibrium be preferable only to self-enforcing deviations, i.e., a deviation by a coalition in which no subset of this coalition can further deviate and profit. Considering only self-enforcing deviations provides little benefit when coalitions have exogenous means to ensure that coalition members deviate together, which we argue is often the case in cooperative services. For instance, a set of Sybil nodes [13] controlled by a single entity will not deviate within their coalition, and friends may avoid hurting each other because of social repercussions (which can be formally modeled using notions of binding commitments or multimarket contact [9]). Finally, there has been work in defining correlated versions of strong Nash and coalition-proof equilibria (e.g., [10, 14, 31]); like their non-correlated counterparts, these equilibria require a best response despite how nodes collude and thus have similar shortcomings.

Along with [3, 4], there has been much work in providing incentives when some nodes may arbitrarily fail (e.g., [5, 15, 27, 28, 43]). Although collusion can be modeled as an arbitrary failure, these approaches typically only handle a bounded number of failures and thus a limited amount of collusion, which is further restricted if failure can occur. Moreover, failure and collusion are fundamentally separate concerns, and k-indistinguishability and k-stability can be augmented to require a best response despite failure.

In the context of mechanism design and auctions, Chen et al. [11] describe rationally-robust implementation, an interesting non-equilibrium-based solution concept that primarily aims to ensure that even if every individual or coalition is given no initial hint of what to play, the underlying mechanism induces individuals or coalitions to choose strategies that ultimately preserve some desired system property. As a result, players may play multiple strategies, as in our equilibria; unlike equilibrium-based approaches, rationally-robust implementation does not predict the exact strategies that will be used, which ultimately may be any undominated strategy. It is unclear whether rationally-robust implementation's notion of dominance can remove enough strategies in games based on cooperative services to enable the existence of useful properties that hold for all surviving strategies.

Another way to deal with collusion is by aiming for an approximate best response or ϵ-equilibrium (e.g., [25, 27]), which guarantees that deviations only provide minimum benefit. This approach could be used to disincentivize coalitions if colluding provides limited benefit (which, as seen in Section 3, may not be the case) and is largely complementary to our approach. Similarly, DCast [44] is an overlay multicast protocol that guarantees each node that follows the protocol some baseline payoff, even if others may collude. However, DCast does not aim to be an equilibrium and thus provides no guarantees that nodes will actually follow the protocol.

In some cases (e.g., in a multicast cost-sharing game [6]), mechanisms can be designed that are robust to coalitional deviations. However, since it is difficult to devise such mechanisms, many systems focus instead on detecting or reducing the effects of collusion. Several content distribution systems (e.g., [35, 36]) use incentives that attempt to reduce the benefits of collusion. Lian et al. [29] use a variety of techniques to detect collusion in a popular P2P service. Reiter et al. [37] design a reputation mechanism that require nodes to solve puzzles to prove they have the content in question. Tran et al. [40] develop a credit-based system in which a node's reputation is based on the number of distinct credit issuers it has received credit from and filters out those issuers that have issued excessive credits. EigenTrust [21] uses trusted peers to provide reputations that are robust against limited misbehavior (due to coalitions or failure). Similarly, Feldman et al. [19] and Marti et al. [30] describe reputation systems that place more trust and weight in certain peers' opinions. Finally, Zhang et al. [45] describe a heuristic for preventing colluding administrators from using links to increase the ranks of their pages in Google's PageRank algorithm. These systems can only ameliorate, not eliminate, the effects of collusion and provide no rigorous assurance that rational nodes will not deviate.

6. CONCLUSION

Trying to identify strategies that eliminate all incentives to collude, as traditional approaches attempt to do, is difficult, possibly futile, and fundamentally unnecessary. This paper introduces a new approach to handle the challenge posed by collusion: accept that coalitions will form, allow coalitions to benefit among themselves, and aim for stability by ensuring that the strategies or protocols specified for every *coalition*, not just every *node*, are best responses. While we are only beginning to explore the space of solution concepts and equilibria allowed by this new approach, we believe our initial results are encouraging: our proposed framework offers rigorous guarantees to both colluding and non-colluding nodes in cooperative services where traditional approaches are often provably unable to yield an equilibrium.

Acknowledgments. We are grateful to Tom Wiseman for many illuminating discussions. This material is based upon work supported by the National Science Foundation under grant 0905625.

7. REFERENCES

[1] BitTorrent. http://bittorrent.com.

[2] ABRAHAM, I., ALVISI, L., AND HALPERN, J. Y. Distributed computing meets game theory: Combining insights from two fields. *SIGACT News 42*, 2, 69–76.

[3] ABRAHAM, I., DOLEV, D., GONEN, R., AND HALPERN, J. Distributed computing meets game theory: Robust mechanisms for rational secret sharing and multiparty computation. In *PODC 2006*.

[4] ABRAHAM, I., DOLEV, D., AND HALPERN, J. Y. Lower bounds on implementing robust and resilient mediators. In *TCC 2008*.

[5] AIYER, A. S., ALVISI, L., CLEMENT, A., DAHLIN, M., MARTIN, J.-P., AND PORTH, C. BAR fault tolerance for cooperative services. In *SOSP 2005*.

[6] ARCHER, A., FEIGENBAUM, J., KRISHNAMURTHY, A., SAMI, R., AND SHENKER, S. Approximation and

collusion in multicast cost sharing. *Games and Economic Behavior 47*, 1, 36–71.

[7] AUMANN, R. J. Acceptable points in general cooperative *n*-person games. *Annals of Mathematics Study 40 4*, 287–324.

[8] BERNHEIM, B. D., PELEG, B., AND WHINSTON, M. D. Coalition-proof Nash equilibria, I. Concepts. *Journal of Economic Theory 42*, 1, 1–12.

[9] BERNHEIM, B. D., AND WHINSTON, M. D. Multimarket contact and collusive behavior. *The RAND Journal of Economics 21*, 1, 1–26.

[10] BLOCH, F., AND DUTTA, B. Correlated equilibria, incomplete information and coalitional deviations. *Games and Economic Behavior 66*, 2, 721–728.

[11] CHEN, J., MICALI, S., AND VALIANT, P. Robustly leveraging collusion in combinatorial auctions. In *ICS 2010*.

[12] CRAWFORD, V. P., AND SOBEL, J. Strategic information transmission. *Econometrica 50*, 6, 1431–1451.

[13] DOUCEUR, J. R. The Sybil attack. In *IPTPS 2002*.

[14] EINY, E., AND PELEG, B. Coalition-proof communication equilibria. In *Social Choice, Welfare, and Ethics: Proceedings of the Eighth International Symposium in Economic Theory and Econometrics*.

[15] ELIAZ, K. Fault tolerant implementation. *Review of Economic Studies 69*, 589–610.

[16] FARRELL, J., AND RABIN, M. Cheap talk. *Journal of Economic Perspectives 10*, 3, 103–118.

[17] FEIGENBAUM, J., RAMACHANDRAN, V., AND SCHAPIRA, M. Incentive-compatible interdomain routing. In *EC 2006*.

[18] FEIGENBAUM, J., AND SHENKER, S. Distributed algorithmic mechanism design: Recent results and future directions. In *DIAL-M 2002*.

[19] FELDMAN, M., LAI, K., STOICA, I., AND CHUANG, J. Robust incentive techniques for peer-to-peer networks. In *EC 2004*.

[20] GOLDBERG, S., HALEVI, S., JAGGARD, A. D., RAMACHANDRAN, V., AND WRIGHT, R. N. Rationality and traffic attraction: Incentives for honest path announcements in BGP. In *SIGCOMM 2008*.

[21] KAMVAR, S. D., SCHLOSSER, M. T., AND GARCIA-MOLINA, H. The EigenTrust algorithm for reputation management in P2P networks. In *WWW 2003*.

[22] KREMER, S., MARKOWITCH, O., AND ZHOU, J. An intensive survey of fair non-repudiation protocols. *Computer Communications 25*, 1606–1621.

[23] LAMPORT, L., SHOSTAK, R., AND PEASE, M. The Byzantine generals problem. *ACM TOPLAS 4*, 3, 382–401.

[24] LEVIN, D., LACURTS, K., SPRING, N., AND BHATTACHARJEE, B. BitTorrent is an auction: Analyzing and improving BitTorrent's incentives. In *SIGCOMM 2008*.

[25] LEVIN, D., SHERWOOD, R., AND BHATTACHARJEE, B. Fair file swarming with FOX. In *IPTPS 2006*.

[26] LEVIN, H., SCHAPIRA, M., AND ZOHAR, A. Interdomain routing and games. In *STOC 2008*.

[27] LI, H. C., CLEMENT, A., MARCHETTI, M., KAPRITSOS, M., ROBISON, L., ALVISI, L., AND DAHLIN, M. FlightPath: Obedience vs. choice in cooperative services. In *OSDI 2008*.

[28] LI, H. C., CLEMENT, A., WONG, E. L., NAPPER, J., ROY, I., ALVISI, L., AND DAHLIN, M. BAR Gossip. In *OSDI 2006*.

[29] LIAN, Q., ZHANG, Z., YANG, M., ZHAO, B. Y., DAI, Y., AND LI, X. An empirical study of collusion behavior in the Maze P2P file-sharing system. In *ICDCS 2007*.

[30] MARTI, S., AND GARCIA-MOLINA, H. Limited reputation sharing in P2P systems. In *EC 2004*.

[31] MORENO, D., AND WOODERS, J. Coalition-proof equilibrium. *Games and Economic Behavior 17*, 1, 80–112.

[32] MOSCIBRODA, T., SCHMID, S., AND WATTENHOFER, R. When selfish meets evil: Byzantine players in a virus inoculation game. In *PODC 2006*.

[33] MYERSON, R. B. *Game Theory: Analysis of Conflict*. Harvard University Press, Cambridge, MA.

[34] PAGNIA, H., AND GÄRTNER, F. C. On the impossibility of fair exchange without a trusted third party. Tech. Rep. TUD-BS-1999-02, Darmstadt University of Technology Department of Computer Science.

[35] PETERSON, R. S., AND SIRER, E. G. Antfarm: Efficient content distribution with managed swarms. In *NSDI 2009*.

[36] PIATEK, M., KRISHNAMURTHY, A., VENKATARAMANI, A., YANG, R., ZHANG, D., AND JAFFE, A. Contracts: Practical contribution incentives for P2P live streaming. In *NSDI 2010*.

[37] REITER, M. K., SEKAR, V., SPENSKY, C., AND ZHANG, Z. Making peer-assisted content distribution robust to collusion using bandwidth puzzles. In *ICISS 2009*.

[38] REKHTER, Y., LI, T., AND HARES, S. A Border Gateway Protocol 4 (BGP-4). http://www.ietf.org/rfc/rfc4271.txt.

[39] SHAMIR, A. How to share a secret. *CACM 22*, 11, 612–613.

[40] TRAN, N., LI, J., AND SUBRAMANIAN, L. Collusion-resilient credit-based reputations for peer-to-peer content distribution. In *NetEcon 2010*.

[41] WONG, E. L., AND ALVISI, L. What's a little collusion between friends? Tech. Rep. TR-12-03, The University of Texas at Austin Department of Computer Science.

[42] WONG, E. L., LENERS, J. B., AND ALVISI, L. It's on me! The benefit of altruism in BAR environments. In *DISC 2010*.

[43] WONG, E. L., LEVY, I., ALVISI, L., CLEMENT, A., AND DAHLIN, M. Regret freedom isn't free. In *OPODIS 2011*.

[44] YU, H., GIBBONS, P. B., AND SHI, C. DCast: Sustaining collaboration in overlay multicast despite rational collusion. In *CCS 2012*.

[45] ZHANG, H., GOEL, A., GOVINDAN, R., MASON, K., AND ROY, B. V. Making eigenvector-based reputation systems against collusions. In *WAW 2004*.

A Distributed Algorithm for Gathering Many Fat Mobile Robots in the Plane[*]

Chrysovalandis Agathangelou   Chryssis Georgiou   Marios Mavronicolas

Department of Computer Science
University of Cyprus
CY-1678 Nicosia, Cyprus
{cs06ac2, chryssis, mavronic}@cs.ucy.ac.cy

ABSTRACT

We revisit the problem of gathering autonomous robots in the plane. In particular, we consider non-transparent unit-disc robots (i.e., *fat*) in an asynchronous setting with vision as the only means of coordination and robots only make local decisions. We use a state-machine representation to formulate the gathering problem and develop a distributed algorithm that solves the problem for any number of fat robots. The main idea behind the algorithm is to enforce the robots to reach a configuration in which all the following hold:

(*i*) The robots' centers form a convex hull in which all robots are on the convex hull's boundary;

(*ii*) Each robot can see all other robots;

(*iii*) The configuration is *connected*: every robot touches another robot and all robots form together a connected formation.

We show that starting from any initial configuration, the fat robots eventually reach such a configuration and terminate yielding a solution to the gathering problem.

Categories and Subject Descriptors

I.2.9 [**Robotics**]: Autonomous vehicles; F.2.2 [**Nonnumerical Algorithms and Problems**]: Geometric problems and computations; C.2.4 [**Distributed Systems**]: Distributed applications

General Terms

Algorithms, Theory

Keywords

Gathering, Fat robots, Asynchrony, State-machines

1. INTRODUCTION

Motivation and Prior Work. There is an increasing number of applications that benefit from having a team of autonomous robots to cooperate and complete various tasks in a self-organizing manner. Such application tasks may require, for example, that robots

---

[*]This work is supported by research funds from the University of Cyprus.

work in dangerous and harsh environments (e.g., for space, underwater or military purposes) or achieve high accuracy or speed (e.g., in nanotechnology, scientific computing). It is usually desirable for the robots to be as simple as possible and have limited computing power, in order to be able to produce them fast in large numbers and cheap.

A fundamental problem that has drawn much attention recently is *gathering* [2, 3, 5, 12, 14, 15], where a team of autonomous mobile robots must gather to a certain point or region or form a certain formation (e.g., geometric shape) in the plane. The problem has been studied under various modeling assumptions; for example, *asynchronous*, *semi-synchronous* and *synchronous* settings have been considered. Robots may have a common coordination system, or have common sense of direction and use compasses to navigate in the plane; they may have stable memory or be history-oblivious. In all considered models, robots are equipped with a vision device (e.g., a camera) and their range of visibility is either limited or unlimited. Robots operate under the *Look-Compute-Move* cycle. Within a cycle, a robot takes a snapshot of the plane (*Look*), performs some local computation (*Compute*), and possibly decides to move to some other point in the plane (*Move*). We refer the reader to surveys [5, 15] and the recent monograph [11] for a more comprehensive exposition of works on the gathering problem.

Up until the work of Czyzowicz *et al.* [9], the gathering problem was considered only under the assumption that each robot is a point on the plane and transparent: a robot can "see" through another robot. This assumption does not reflect reality as real robots are not points but have a physical extent. This means that robots may collide with each other. Furthermore, robots are not transparent: they may block the view of other robots. To depart from such assumptions, Czyzowicz *et al.* [9] initiated the study of the gathering problem with *fat* robots: non-transparent, unit discs. As fat robots cannot occupy the same space on the plane, the gathering problem no longer requires robots to gather at the same point. Instead, per [9], *gathering fat robots means forming a configuration for which the union of all discs is connected*.

In the model considered in [9], robots operate in *Look-Compute-Move* cycles, they are identical, anonymous, history-oblivious, non-transparent, and fat. They do not share a common coordination system and vision is the only mean of coordination; robots have unlimited visibility unless their view is obstructed by another robot. An asynchronous setting is considered, where an adaptive adversary can stop a robot for finite time, control the "speed" of a robot, or cause robots moving into intersecting trajectories to collide. Under this model, the authors present solutions to the gathering problem for *three* and *four* robots. The proposed solutions rely on exhaustive consideration of all possible classes of configurations; a different gathering strategy corresponds to each possible case. As the number of cases may grow exponentially with the number of robots, this approach fails to generalize. The authors of [9] left open the question of whether it is possible to solve gathering for any collection of $n \geq 5$ fat robots.

Our Contribution. We provide a positive answer to the above question. In particular, we consider the model of [9] with the additional assumption of *chirality* [11]: robots agree on the orientation of the axes of their local coordination system. We present a distributed algorithm for the gathering problem for *any* number n of fat robots.

The key feature of our algorithm is to bring the robots into a configuration of *full visibility* where all robots can see all other robots. Given the power of the adversary and the fact that robots are non-transparent, this task becomes challenging; that was in fact, the main challenge of our work. The idea for settling the challenge is for the robots to aim in forming a *convex hull* in which all robots will be on the convex hull's boundary. During the computation, robots on the boundary do not move; robots inside the convex hull try to move towards the boundary. However, if robots that are on the hull's boundary realize that they obstruct other robots that are also on the boundary from seeing each other, then they move away from the convex hull so that they no longer cause any obstruction. If a robot on the boundary realizes that there is no "enough space" for robots inside the convex hull to be placed on the boundary, then it moves to a direction away from the convex hull to make space. Asynchrony only makes things harder as robots may have very different local views of the system. We show that eventually the convex hull will "expand" so that all robots will be on the boundary of the convex hull and *no three robots are on the same line*[1]; this leads to a configuration that all robots have full visibility. This is the first conceptual phase of the algorithm.

In the second conceptual phase, once all robots have full visibility and are aware of this, robots start to converge in a way that full visibility is not lost. To do so, robots exploit their knowledge of n and the common unit of distance (since all robots are unit-discs, this gives them "for free" a common measure of distance [9]). We show that eventually all robots form a connected configuration and terminate yielding a solution to the gathering problem. Note that robots must have full visibility to be aware that gathering is accomplished [9].

The key to successfully proving the correctness of the algorithm is the formulation of the model, the problem and the algorithm with a state-machine representation. This enables employing typical techniques for proving safety and liveness properties and argue on the state transitions of the robots, which, against asynchrony, becomes a very challenging task.

Other Works Considering Fat Robots. After the work in [9] some attempts were made to solving the gathering problem with $n \geq 5$ fat robots in different models [6, 7, 8, 10]. In [7], it is assumed that the fat robots are transparent. This assumption makes the problem significantly easier as robots have full visibility at all times. As discussed above, having the robots reach a configuration with full visibility was the main challenge in our work. In [8], fat robots are non-transparent and have limited visibility, but a synchronous setting is considered. Furthermore, the gathering point is predefined and given as an input to the robots; the goal is for the robots to gather in an area as close as possible to this point. Two versions of the problem are studied: in continuous space and time, and in discrete space (essentially $\mathbb{Z}^2$) and time. In the continuous case, a randomized solution is proposed; in the discrete case the

proposed solutions require additional modeling assumptions such as unique robot ids, or direct communication between robots. The work in [10] also considers fat robots with limited visibility, but in an asynchronous setting. In contrast with the model we consider, robots have a common coordination system: they agree both on a common origin and axes (called *Consistent Compass* in [11]). The objective of the robots is to gather to a circle with a center given as an input along with the radius of the circle. The common coordination system and the predefined knowledge of the circle to be formed enables the use of geometric techniques that cannot be used in our model. In [6], they consider fat robots with limited visibility and without a common coordination system, but in a synchronous setting. Furthermore the correctness of their proposed algorithm is not proven but rather demonstrated via simulations.

2. MODEL AND DEFINITIONS

Our model of computation is a formalization of the one presented in [9] with the additional assumption of *chirality*; the formalism follows the one from [4].

Robots. We assume n asynchronous, fault-free robots that can move along straight lines on the (infinite) plane. The robots are *fat* [9]: they are closed unit discs. They are identical and anonymous (i.e., they are indistinguishable). They do not have access to any global coordination system, but we assume *chirality* [11]: the robots agree on the orientation of the axes[2]. Robots are equipped with a 360-degree-angle vision device (e.g., camera) that enables the robots to take snapshots of the plane. The vision device has unlimited range and captures any point of the plane provided there is no obstacle (e.g., another robot). We assume that robots know n.

Geometric configuration. A *geometric configuration* is a vector $\mathcal{G} = (c_1, c_2, \ldots, c_n)$ where each c_i represents the center of the position of robot r_i on the plane. So, a configuration can be viewed as a snapshot of the robots on the plane. Note that the fact that robots are fat prohibits the formation of a configuration in which any two robots share more than a point in the plane. (Two robots share a point if the discs representing them touch each other.)

We say that a geometric configuration $\mathcal{G}$ is *connected* if between any two points of any two robots there is a polygonal line each of whose points belongs to some robot. Informally, a configuration is connected if every robot touches another robot and all robots form together a connected formation.

Visibility and fully visible configuration. We say that point p in the plane is *visible* by a robot r_i (or equivalently, r_i can see p) if there is a point p_i in the circle bounding robot r_i such that the straight segment (p_i, p) does not contain any point of any other robot. So, a robot r_i can see another robot r_j if there is at least one point on the bounding circle of r_j that is visible by r_i. Given a geometric configuration $\mathcal{G}$, robot r_i has *full visibility* in $\mathcal{G}$ if r_i can see all other $n-1$ robots. If *all* robots have full visibility in $\mathcal{G}$, then configuration $\mathcal{G}$ is *fully visible*.

Robots' states. Each robot r_i is modeled as a (possibly infinite) state machine with state set S_i; i is the index of robot r_i (used only for reference purposes). Each set S_i contains five states: **Wait**, **Look**, **Compute**, **Move**, and **Terminate**. Initially each robot is in state **Wait**. State **Terminate** is a terminal state: once a robot reaches this state it does not take any further steps. We now describe each state:

- In state **Wait**, robot r_i is idling. In addition, the robot has

---

[1] Note that there are cases where having all robots on the boundary does not necessarily imply that all robots can see each other.

[2] Note that this is a weaker assumption than having a common coordinate system or having a consistent compass [11, Section 2.7].

no memory of the steps occurred prior entering this state, i.e., robots are *history-oblivious*.

- In state **Look**, robot r_i takes a snapshot of the plane and identifies all robots that are visible to it. We denote by V_i the set of the centers of the robots that are visible to robot r_i when it takes a snapshot in configuration $\mathcal{G}$. So, $V_i \subseteq \mathcal{G}$ is the *local view* of robot r_i in configuration $\mathcal{G}$. This view does not change in subsequent configurations unless the robot takes a new snapshot. In a nutshell, in state **Look**, the robot takes as an input a configuration $\mathcal{G}$ and outputs the local view $V_i \subseteq \mathcal{G}$.

- In state **Compute**, robot r_i runs a local algorithm A_i that takes as an input the local view V_i (i.e., the output of the previous state **Look**) and outputs a point p in the plane. This point is specified from V_i, hence we will write $p = A_i(V_i)$. If A_i returns the special output $\bot$, then the robot's state changes into state **Terminate**. Otherwise it changes into state **Move**; intuitively, in this case p is the point that the center of the robot will move to. Note that it is possible for $p = c_i$ — the robot might decide not to move.

- In state **Move**, robot r_i, starting from its current position, called *start* point, moves on a straight line towards point $A_i(V_i)$ (as calculated in state **Compute**). We call $A_i(V_i)$ the *target* point of r_i. If during its motion the robot touches another robot (i.e., the circles representing these robots become tangent), then it stops and the robot's state changes into state **Wait**. As we discuss next, the adversary may also stop a robot at any point before reaching its target point. Again, in this case, the robot's state changes into state **Wait**. If the robot finds no obstacles or it is not stopped by the adversary, then it eventually reaches its target point (its center is placed on $A_i(V_i)$) and its state changes into state **Wait**.

State configuration. A *state configuration* is a vector $\mathcal{S} = (s_1, s_2, \ldots, s_n)$ where each s_i represents the state of robot r_i. An *initial* state configuration is a configuration $\mathcal{S}$ in which each s_i is an initial state of robot r_i (that is, $\forall i \in [1, n]$, $s_i = \textbf{Wait}$). Similarly, a *terminal* state configuration is a configuration $\mathcal{S}$ in which each s_i is a terminal state of robot r_i (that is, $\forall i \in [1, n]$, $s_i = \textbf{Terminate}$).

Robot configuration. A *robot configuration* is a vector $\mathcal{R} = (\langle s_1, c_1 \rangle, \ldots, \langle s_n, c_n \rangle)$ where each pair $\langle s_i, c_i \rangle$ represents the state of robot r_i and the position of its center on the plane. Informally, a robot configuration is the combination of a geometric configuration with the corresponding state configuration.

Adversary and events. We model asynchrony as a sequence of events caused by an online and omniscient adversary. The adversary can control the speeds of the robots, it can stop moving robots, and it may cause moving robots to collide, provided that their trajectories have an intersection point. Specifically, we consider the following events (state transitions — see Figure 1 for a pictorial):

Look(r_i): Causes robot r_i that is in state **Wait** to get into state **Look**.

Compute(r_i): Causes robot r_i that is in state **Look** to get into state **Compute**.

Done(r_i): Causes robot r_i that is in state **Compute** and its local algorithm A_i has returned the special point $\bot$, to get into the terminating state **Terminate**.

Move(r_i): Causes robot r_i that is in state **Compute** and its local algorithm A_i has returned a point other than $\bot$, to get into state **Move**.

Stop(r_i): Causes r_i that is in state **Move** to get into state **Wait**. Robot r_i is stopped at some point in the straight segment between

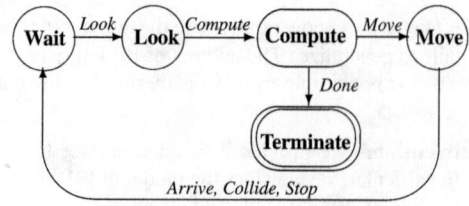

Figure 1: A cycle of the state transitions of robot r_i.

its start point and its target point $A_i(V_i)$ (under a constraint discussed next).

Collide(R): Causes a subset of the robots R that are in state **Move** and their trajectories have an intersecting point to collide (i.e., their circles become tangent). Note that $2 \leq |R| \leq n$ (two or more robots could collide between them but only one collusion occurs per a *Collide* event). Also, other robots that are in state **Move** could be stopped (without colluding with other robots). Then all affected robots enter in state **Wait**.

Arrive(r_i): Causes robot r_i that is in state **Move** to arrive at its target point and change its state into **Wait**.

Note that events *Look(r_i)*, *Move(r_i)*, *Stop(r_i)* and *Arrive(r_i)* may also cause robots other than r_i that are in state **Move** to remain in that state, but on a different position (along their trajectories, and closer to their destination).

Execution. A distributed algorithm is a collection of local algorithms, one per robot. An *execution fragment* α of a distributed algorithm is a (finite or infinite) alternating sequence $\mathcal{R}_0, e_1, \mathcal{R}_1, e_2, \ldots$, where each $\mathcal{R}_k$ is a robot configuration and each e_k is an event. If α is finite, then it ends in a configuration. An *execution* of an algorithm is an execution fragment where $\mathcal{R}_0$ is an initial configuration.

Liveness conditions. We impose the following liveness conditions (i.e., restrictions on the adversary):

1. In an infinite execution, each robot is allowed to take infinitely many steps.
2. During a **Move** event, each robot traverses at least a distance $\delta > 0$ unless its target point is closer than δ. Formally, each robot r_i traverses at least a distance $\min\{dist_i(start, target), \delta\}$, where $dist_i(start, target)$ is the distance between the start and target points of robot r_i. Parameter δ is not known to the robots.

Gathering problem. We now state the problem studied in this work:

DEFINITION 1 (GATHERING). *In any execution, there is a connected, fully visible, terminal robot configuration.*

3. GEOMETRIC FUNCTIONS

We list a collection of functions that perform geometric calculations. These functions are used by the robots' local algorithm as shown in Section 4. Here we present the problems these functions solve. Pseudocodes, their proofs of correctness and more details and insights can be found in the full paper [1].

Function `On-Convex-Hull`: We denote by $CH(c_1, c_2, \ldots, c_m)$ the *convex hull* formed by points $c_1, c_2, \ldots, c_m$, and by $\vartheta CH(c_1, c_2, \ldots, c_m) \subseteq \{c_1, c_2, \ldots, c_m\}$ the set of points that are *on the boundary* of the convex hull. Then, function `On-Convex-Hull` gets as *input* a set of m points $c_1, c_2, \ldots, c_m$ and another point c and *outputs* (i) $CH(c_1, c_2, \ldots, c_m)$ and (ii) whether $c \in \vartheta CH(c_1, c_2, \ldots, c_m)$ or not.

Figure 2: An example where point p is not valid and hence it will not be returned by Function Find-Points.

Function Move-to-Point: This function gets as **input** two points c_1 and c_2 and a positive integer m and **outputs** a point μ defined as follows: Consider the straight segment $\overline{c_1 c_2}$ and let $\overline{pc_2}$ be the straight segment which is vertical to $\overline{c_1 c_2}$ with p on the perimeter of the unit disc with center c_2, and with direction towards inside of the convex hull. Next consider the point c on segment $\overline{pc_2}$ which has distance $\frac{1}{2m} - \varepsilon$ from c_2. Then point μ is the intersection of the straight segment $\overline{c_1 c}$ and the perimeter of the unit disc with center c_2.

Function Find-Points: This function is significant for our algorithm. It gets as **input** a convex hull of n points, where $\vartheta CH(c_1, c_2, \ldots, c_m)$, $m \leq n$, and **outputs** a set of $k < m$ points $p_1, \ldots, p_k$ so that a unit disc with center p_i, $1 \leq i \leq k$, can be placed on the convex hull *without* causing the convex hull to change. (It is possible that $k = 0$.) The following claim is essential for our solution to gathering.

LEMMA 3.1. *Given a convex hull, let c_l and c_r be the centers of any two unit discs that are adjacent on the hull's boundary. Then there is a minimum distance between c_l and c_r for which Function Find-Points returns a point between them. We refer to this distance as* **safe**.

PROOF. Consider that given a number of points, a convex hull always exists. Consider four neighbor points on a convex hull, as shown on Figure 2, without loss of generality. In order for a unit disc with center p to be on the convex hull and not cause the current convex hull to change, the distance between μ, the middle point of $\overline{c_l c_r}$ and p must be at least $\frac{1}{n}$. Note that p is outside of the current convex hull. Additionally, consider q the point on the line segment $\overline{pc_{r+1}}$, where a vertical line to c_r starts from line segment $\overline{pc_{r+1}}$ with direction to the inside of the convex hull. Then $d(q, c_r)$ must be equal with at least $\frac{1}{n}$, where r is the point that $\overline{pc_{r+1}}$ is tangent with $\overline{\mu c_r}$. Angle $\widehat{pr\mu}$ is equal with angle $\widehat{c_r r q}$.

We need to calculate the distance between c_l and c_r which will give us the safe distance. The distance between c_l to μ must be equal with the distance between c_r to μ. We need to calculate both $d(\mu, c_r)$ and $d(\mu, c_l)$, find the biggest and double it, in order to find the safe distance. First we must calculate the necessary distance between μ and c_r. Observe that $d(\mu, c_r) = d(\mu, r) + d(r, c_r)$. We now have that $tan(\widehat{pr\mu}) = \frac{\frac{1}{n}}{d(\mu, r)}$, hence $d(\mu, r) = \frac{1}{n \cdot tan(\widehat{pr\mu})}$. We now calculate $d(r, c_r)$; we have that $sin(\widehat{c_r r q}) = \frac{\frac{1}{n}}{d(r, c_r)}$, hence $d(r, c_r) = \frac{1}{n \cdot sin((\widehat{c_r r q}))} = \frac{1}{n \cdot sin((\widehat{pr\mu}))}$. Finally, it follows that $d(\mu, c_r) = \frac{1}{n \cdot tan(\widehat{pr\mu})} + \frac{1}{n \cdot sin((\widehat{pr\mu}))}$.

This is the minimum distance that $\overline{\mu c_r}$ must be. We do the same as above with $\overline{\mu c_l}$ and choose the biggest distance between the two, double it and set it as the safe distance. ∎

Function Connected-Components: Consider a set of m unit discs on the plane. A *connected component* of this set is a collection of connected unit discs; in a connected component there can be up to two empty spaces of distance less or equal to $1/2m$ among the unit discs. Note that a given set of unit discs may contain many connected components and only one in the case that all unit discs are connected. Then, Function Connected-Components gets as **input** a set of m points $c_1, c_2, \ldots, c_m$ and an additional point c and **outputs** a set of pairs of the form $\langle (c_l, c_r), k \rangle$. Each pair (c_l, c_r) represents a connected component of unit discs, where c_l is the center of the leftmost (counter clock-wise) unit disc and c_r the center of the rightmost (clock-wise) unit disc in the component; k is the number of unit discs contained in this component (including those with centers c_l and c_r).

As this function plays an important role in forming the final, single connected component, we provide some additional insight: Function Connected-Components is called by a robot r with center c. The m points are the centers of the robots that robot r can see (its local view) in the current configuration. As we will see later, this function is called when the robot can see all other robots, i.e., $m = n$. The robot wishes to find the connected components formed in the current configuration. Intuitively, we can include two spaces of length $1/2n$ in a configuration, since if all the robots can see each other, then the robots can move taking steps of length $1/2n$ until they meet (see also the proof of Lemma 5.4).

Function In-Straight-Line-2: This function gets as **input** three points c_l, c_m and c_r and **outputs** YES, if the three points are on the same line, and NO otherwise.

The next three functions make use of Function Connected-Components.

Function How-Much-Distance: This function gets as **input** a set of m points $c_1, c_2, \ldots, c_m$ and an additional point c and **outputs** 1,2 or 3. Consider the connected components formed by the unit discs with centers $c_1, c_2, \ldots, c_m$. If the unit disc with center c is the rightmost (the straight direction is considered to be the inside of the convex hull) element of the component that has the smallest (space-wise) distance between the components, then the answer is 1. If all components have the same distance, then the answer is 2. Otherwise the answer is 3.

Function In-Largest-Component: This function gets as **input** a set of m points $c_1, c_2, \ldots, c_m$ and an additional point c and **outputs** 1,2 or 3. Consider the connected components formed by the unit discs with centers $c_1, c_2, \ldots, c_m$. If the unit disc with center c belongs in the largest component (wrt the number of discs), then the answer is 1; if all components are larger than the one it belongs, then the answer is 2. Otherwise the answer is 3.

Function In-Smallest-Component: This function gets as **input** a set of m points $c_1, c_2, \ldots, c_m$ and an additional point c and **outputs** 1,2 or 3. Consider the connected components formed by the unit discs with centers $c_1, c_2, \ldots, c_m$. If the unit disc with center c belongs in the smallest component (wrt the number of discs), then the answer is 1; if all components are smaller than the one it belongs, then the answer is 2. Otherwise the answer is 3.

4. LOCAL ALGORITHM FOR COMPUTE

We present the algorithm that each robot runs locally while in state **Compute**. It takes as input the view of the robot (obtained in state **Look**) and calculates the position the robot should move next (in state **Move**). In Section 4.1 we overview in verbose the states of the algorithm; in Section 4.2 we list the procedures that implement the transitions from one state to another. Full details are given in the full paper [1].

4.1 States of the Algorithm

Once a robot r_i is in state **Compute** it starts executing the local algorithm A_i. Recall that V_i denotes robot's r_i local view: the set of robots that are visible to r_i upon entering state **Compute**. The algorithm consists of 17 states; we refer to them using the notation **Compute**.$\langle$**algorithm-state-name**$\rangle$. Figure 3 describes these states and Figure 4 depicts all possible states and transitions of the algorithm run by robot r_i.

4.2 Description of the Algorithm

The algorithm consists of 17 procedures, each treating a corresponding algorithmic state. In particular, once the algorithm is in a state **Compute**.$\langle$**algorithm-state-name**$\rangle$ it runs the corresponding procedure algorithm-state-name that either implements a state transition or outputs a point the robot should move to (in the next state **Move**); it implements a state transition if it is in a nonterminal state and outputs a point otherwise. In a nutshell, the algorithm consists of conditional expressions:

LOCAL ALGORITHM
---

if state= **Compute**.$\langle$**algorithm-state-name**$\rangle$ **then** run procedure algorithm-state-name.

We now overview the procedures and their properties. The procedures are given with respect to a robot r_i and its center c_i. The robot takes action based on its local view V_i, which might be different from other robots' views. But as we show in Section 5, the local decisions made by each robot are designed in such a way that robots coordinate correctly in the face of asynchrony and eventually reach a solution to the gathering problem. Recall that $\vartheta CH(V_i)$ is the set of points that are on the boundary of the convex hull formed by the points in V_i. Detailed pseudocodes and omitted proofs can be found in the full paper [1].

1. Procedure Start: It calls Function On-Convex-Hull and if $c_i \in \vartheta CH(V_i)$, it changes the state from **Compute.Start** to **Compute.OnConvexHull**; otherwise it changes the state to **Compute.NotOnConvexHull**. The correctness of Function On-Convex-Hull (e.g., Graham's algorithm [13]) yields the following:

LEMMA 4.1. Start(**Compute**.$\langle$**Start**$\rangle$) = **Compute**.$\langle$**OnConvexHull**$\rangle$ iff $c_i \in \vartheta CH(V_i)$.

2. Procedure OnConvexHull: It changes the state from **Compute.OnConvexHull** to **Compute.AllOnConvexHull** if $|\vartheta CH(V_i)| = n$ and no three robots are on the same line; otherwise it changes the state to **Compute.NotAllOnConvexHull**. It checks whether three robots are on the same line, using Function In-Straight-Line-2. Then:

LEMMA 4.2. OnConvexHull(**Compute**.$\langle$**OnConvexHull**$\rangle$) = **Compute**.$\langle$**AllOnConvexHull**$\rangle$ iff $|V_i| = n$ and $|\vartheta CH(V_i)| = n$ and all robots have full visibility in V_i.

3. Procedure AllOnConvexHull: It changes the state from **Compute.AllOnConvexHull** to **Compute.Connected** if all robots form a *connected configuration*; otherwise it changes state to **Compute.NotConnected**. Then:

LEMMA 4.3. AllOnConvexHull(**Compute**.$\langle$**AllOnConvexHull**$\rangle$) = **Compute**.$\langle$**Connected**$\rangle$ iff V_i is a connected configuration.

4. Procedure Connected: It returns the special output $\bot$, which leads to the termination of the algorithm for robot r_i (it enters state **Terminate** in which r_i does not perform any further steps).

5. Procedure NotConnected: Its purpose is to eventually cause all robots to form a *connected* configuration. This procedure

gives first priority to components with the smallest size, and then to components that the distance to their neighboring component on the right is the smallest distance between any two components. The rightmost robot of the component with the highest priority moves to the left of its right neighbor component using Function Move-To-Point. If all components have equal priority (i.e., all components have the same size and the distance between any two components is the same), then, using Function Connected-Components, the robots start to converge. Of course, the procedure is run by each robot locally and individually, but as it is shown in Section 5, global convergence is eventually reached. Robots can start moving only if for any three neighboring robots of the component, say r_l, r_m and r_r, the vertical distance from line $\overline{r_l r_r}$ to r_m is equal or greater than $\frac{1}{n}$. Then:

LEMMA 4.4. *The point returned by* NotConnected(**Compute**.$\langle$**NotConnected**$\rangle$) *keeps* V_i *as a fully visible configuration and* $|\vartheta CH(V_i)| = n$.

6. Procedure NotAllOnConvexHull: It changes the state from **Compute.NotAllOnConvexHull** to **Compute.OnStraightLine** if r_i is on the same line with at least two other robots that are also on the boundary of the convex hull; otherwise it changes the state to **Compute.NotOnStraightLine**. Then:

LEMMA 4.5. NotAllOnConvexHull(**Compute**.$\langle$**NotAllOnConvexHull**$\rangle$) = **Compute**.$\langle$**OnStraightLine**$\rangle$ *iff* r_i *is on the same line with any two other robots that are also on the boundary of the convex hull.*

7. Procedure NotOnStraightLine: It changes the state from **Compute.NotOnStraightLine** to **Compute.SpaceForMore** if there is enough space for at least one robot on the boundary of the convex hull; otherwise it changes the state to **Compute.NoSpaceForMore**. Then:

LEMMA 4.6. NotOnStraightLine(**Compute**.$\langle$**NotOnStraightLine**$\rangle$) = **Compute**.$\langle$**SpaceForMore**$\rangle$ iff $|\vartheta CH(V_i)| = n$ *or there is enough space for at least one robot between any two adjacent robots that are on the boundary of the convex hull.*

8. Procedure SpaceForMore: It returns a point p outside the convex hull if r_i is touching with another robot on the convex hull's boundary that is not adjacent to r_i on the boundary. Otherwise, it returns c_i and the robot does not move.

LEMMA 4.7. SpaceForMore(**Compute**.$\langle$**SpaceForMore**$\rangle$) = c_i *iff* r_i *is not tangent with any robot* r_j, $r_j \in \vartheta CH(V_i)$ *that they are not adjacent on* $\vartheta CH(V_i)$, **else** SpaceForMore(**Compute**.$\langle$**SpaceForMore**$\rangle$) = p, *were* p *is at distance* $\frac{1}{2n} - \varepsilon$ *away from* $\vartheta CH(V_i)$.

The reason that p is outside of the convex hull by a distance $\frac{1}{2n} - \varepsilon$ is because if two robots are not adjacent on the boundary and are touching, then it would be possible to obstruct other robots from seeing each other.

9. Procedure NoSpaceForMore: It returns a point p with direction away from the convex hull such that:

LEMMA 4.8. NoSpaceForMore(**Compute**.$\langle$**NoSpaceForMore**$\rangle$) = p, *were* p *is at distance* $\frac{1}{2n} - \varepsilon$ *away from* $\vartheta CH(V_i)$.

10. Procedure OnStraightLine: It changes the state from **Compute.OnStraightLine** to **Compute.SeeOneRobot** if r_i is not in straight line with its left and right neighbors on the boundary of the convex hull; otherwise it changes the state to **Compute.SeeTwoRobot**.

1. **Compute.Start**:
   - The initial state of the algorithm run by robot r_i.

2. **Compute.OnConvexHull**:
   - Robot r_i is on the boundary of the convex hull formed by the robots in V_i: $c_i \in \vartheta CH(V_i)$.

3. **Compute.AllOnConvexHull**:
   - $c_i \in \vartheta CH(V_i)$
   - Robot r_i has full visibility.
   - $\forall k \in [1, n], k \neq i$, $c_k \in \vartheta CH(V_i)$ and V_i is a fully visible configuration.

4. **Compute.Connected**:
   - Same conditions as in state 3.
   - V_i is a connected component.

5. **Compute.NotConnected**:
   - Same conditions as in state 3.
   - V_i is not a connected component.

6. **Compute.NotAllOnConvexHull**:
   - $c_i \in \vartheta CH(V_i)$.
   - $|V_i| \neq n$ **or** $\exists r_k$ s.t. $c_k \notin \vartheta CH(V_i)$ **or** $|V_i| = n$, $\forall k \in [1, n]$, $c_k \in \vartheta CH(V_i)$, but $\exists r_j$ with no full visibility.

7. **Compute.NotOnStraightLine**:
   - Same conditions as in state 6.
   - There are no two other robots on the same line with robot r_i (on the boundary).

8. **Compute.SpaceForMore**:
   - Same conditions as in state 7.
   - According to V_i there is space on the boundary for another robot: there are two neighboring robots on the boundary with distance at least 2.

9. **Compute.NoSpaceForMore**:
   - Same conditions as in state 7.

   - According to V_i there is no space on the boundary for another robot.

10. **Compute.OnStraightLine**:
    - Same conditions as in state 6.
    - There are at least two other robots on the same line with robot r_i on the boundary.

11. **Compute.SeeOneRobot**:
    - Same conditions as in state 10.
    - Robot r_i can see only one robot on the line.

12. **Compute.SeeTwoRobot**:
    - Same conditions as in state 10.
    - Robot r_i can see two robots on the line; this implies that robot r_i is between these two robots.

13. **Compute.NotOnConvexHull**:
    - Robot r_i is *inside* the convex hull $CH(V_i)$.

14. **Compute.IsTouching**:
    - Same conditions as in state 13.
    - Robot r_i is touching another robot.

15. **Compute.NotTouching**:
    - Same conditions as in state 13.
    - Robot r_i does not touch another robot.

16. **Compute.ToChange**:
    - Same conditions as in state 15.
    - If robot r_i moves as calculated, then the convex hull will change, and this cannot be avoided.

17. **Compute.NotChange**:
    - Same conditions as in state 15.
    - If robot r_i moves as calculated, then there is a way to avoid a change to the convex hull.

Figure 3: The states of the local algorithm, given for a robot r_i, its center c_i and its local view V_i.

LEMMA 4.9. OnStraightLine(**Compute.$\langle$OnStraightLine$\rangle$**) = **Compute.$\langle$SeeTwoRobots$\rangle$** *iff r_i is on the same line with two robots on the boundary, its left neighbor r_l and its right neighbor r_r.*

11. Procedure SeeOneRobot: It returns c_i.

LEMMA 4.10. SeeOneRobot(**Compute.$\langle$SeeOneRobot$\rangle$**)= c_i.

12. Procedure SeeTwoRobot: It returns a point p with direction away from the convex hull such that:

LEMMA 4.11. *The point p returned by* SeeTwoRobot(**Compute.$\langle$SeeTwoRobot$\rangle$**) *is such that if robot r_i moves there (c_i is on p), then r_i will no longer be in a straight line with its two adjacent robots on the boundary of the convex hull.*

13. Procedure NotOnConvexHull: It changes the state from **Compute.NotOnConvexHull** to **Compute.IsTouching** if r_i is touching another robot; otherwise it changes the state to **Compute.NotTouching**.

LEMMA 4.12. NotOnConvexHull(**Compute.$\langle$NotOnConvexHull$\rangle$**) = **Compute.$\langle$IsTouching$\rangle$** *iff r_i's unit disc is tangent with a unit disc of another robot.*

14. Procedure IsTouching: Given a geometric configuration (e.g., a robot's local view), we consider that a robot has *higher proximity* compared to the other robots of the configuration if it is the closest to its closest point on the boundary of the convex hull or to the closest point that Function FindPoints returns (depending on the case). If more than one robots in the configuration have the same distance to the closest point, then the rightmost of these robots has the highest proximity (straight direction is considered to be towards the outside of the convex hull of the target point). If r_i has the highest proximity, then Procedure IsTouching returns a point on the boundary of the convex hull; otherwise it returns c_i.

LEMMA 4.13. IsTouching(**Compute.$\langle$IsTouching$\rangle$**) *will result robot r_i's unit disc to no longer be tangent with any other robot's unit disc (from the robots that r_i touches) if r_i has the highest proximity (among the robots that are touching). If there is no space of size at least 2 on the boundary of the convex hull, then r_i stays in the same position.*

LEMMA 4.14. IsTouching(**Compute.$\langle$IsTouching$\rangle$**) *will cause at least one of the robots touching each other to move towards the convex hull if there is space of size at least 2 on the boundary.*

15. Procedure NotTouching: It calls Function Find-Points. If it returns at least one point, then the state

255

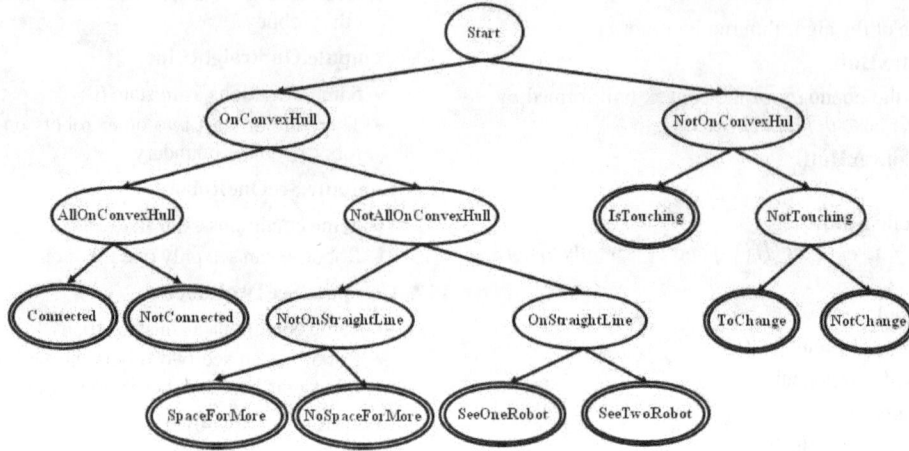

Figure 4: All possible states and transitions of the algorithm run by robot r_i. For better readability the prefix Compute is voided. States with no transition to another state are terminal, and they output the position that the robot will move next (and the robot exits state Compute and enters state Move). State Compute.Connected outputs the special point $\perp$ which causes robot r_i to exit state Compute and enter state Terminate, in which the robot takes no further steps.

changes from **Compute.NotTouching** to **Compute.NotChange**; else it changes to **Compute.ToChange**.

LEMMA 4.15. NotTouching(**Compute.⟨NotTouching⟩**) = **Compute.⟨NotChange⟩** *iff r_i can move on the boundary of the convex hull while maintaining the convex hull.*

16. Procedure ToChange: If there is space of size at least 2 on the convex hull's boundary, then it returns the closest space to r_i; else it returns c_i.

LEMMA 4.16. ToChange(**Compute.⟨ToChange⟩**) = p, *when $p \in \vartheta CH(V_i)$ if there is space of size at least 2 on the convex hull; else* ToChange(**Compute.⟨ToChange⟩**) = c_i.

17. Procedure NotChange: It returns the closest point to r_i among the points that Function Find-Points returns.

LEMMA 4.17. NotChange(**Compute.⟨NotChange⟩**) = p, *where $p \in \vartheta CH(V_i)$.*

5. THE DISTRIBUTED ALGORITHM

The high level idea of the algorithm is as follows: The objective is for the robots to form a convex hull and be able to see each other. In particular, all robots are intended to be on the boundary of the convex hull in such a way that no three robots are on the same line. Once this is achieved, then the robots start to converge (to get closer) while maintaining the convex hull formation, so that they form a connected component. It follows that when all robots are on the boundary of the convex hull, they can see each other, and are connected, then each robot terminates and the gathering problem has been solved. The **distributed algorithm** is essentially composed of the asynchronous execution of the robots' state transition cycles, including the local algorithm when in state **Compute**.

Before showing that the distributed algorithm correctly solves the gathering problem, we provide necessary definitions. Given a robot configuration $\mathcal{R}$, we denote by $\mathcal{G_R}$ the geometric configuration of $\mathcal{R}$. Recall that for a geometric configuration $\mathcal{G}$, we denote by $CH(\mathcal{G})$ the convex hull formed by the points in $\mathcal{G}$. Also, we denote by $\vartheta CH(\mathcal{G}) \subseteq \mathcal{G}$ the set of points in $\mathcal{G}$ that are *on the boundary* of the convex hull.

5.1 Bad and Safe Configurations

Our proof of correctness (presented in the next subsection) relies on the notions of *bad* and *safe* configurations, which we discuss here.

Bad Configurations. A robot configuration $\mathcal{R}_x$ is a *bad* configuration when one of the two following cases is true:

1. *Bad configuration of Type 1.* When all of the following hold:
   - Configuration $\mathcal{G}_{\mathcal{R}_x}$ is *fully visible* and $|\vartheta CH(\mathcal{G}_{\mathcal{R}_x})| = n$;
   - A robot r_i in this configuration has as local view V_i, a previous configuration $\mathcal{G}_{\mathcal{R}_y}$, $y < x$, such that $|\vartheta CH(\mathcal{G}_{\mathcal{R}_y})| < n$, $r_i \in \vartheta CH(\mathcal{R}_y)$ and r_i sees that there is not enough space for more robots to get on the boundary of the convex hull.

2. *Bad configuration of Type 2.* When all of the following hold:
   - Configuration $\mathcal{G}_{\mathcal{R}_x}$ is *fully visible* and $|\vartheta CH(\mathcal{G}_{\mathcal{R}_x})| = n$;
   - There is a preceding configuration $\mathcal{G}_{\mathcal{R}_y}$, $y < x$, in which at least four robots, call them r_l, r_{m1}, r_{m2} and r_r, are on a straight line and $r_l, r_{m1}, r_{m2}, r_r \in \vartheta CH(\mathcal{G}_{\mathcal{R}_y})$.

Both types are considered bad since they can potentially lead to a configuration following $\mathcal{R}_x$ that is no longer fully visible or all robots are on the boundary of the convex hull; these are properties that we would like, once holding, to hold for all succeeding configurations.

We now explain how the adversary can cause such bad configurations:

Type 1. According to the local algorithm, when robot r_i witnesses a view as described in the second bullet of Type 1 bad configuration, robot r_i must start moving with direction outside of the convex hull so to make space for more robots to get on the convex hull's boundary. This is also the case for all robots sharing the same or similar view with r_i. When r_i starts moving (it gets in state **move**), the adversary can impose the following strategy: It makes r_i to "move too slow" and lets the other robots move with such "a speed" that the robots reach configuration $\mathcal{R}_x$. Since r_i has not changed its state (it is still in state **move**), it continues to move outside of the convex hull. This may cause a neighboring robot of r_i not to be on the convex hull's boundary anymore or not be able to see all robots. Hence, while $\mathcal{G}_{\mathcal{R}_x}$ was a *fully visible* configuration and

$|\vartheta CH(\mathcal{G}_{\mathcal{R}_x})| = n$, it is possible for a succeeding configuration not to have one (or both) of the these properties anymore.

Type 2. According to the local algorithm, if robots r_l, r_{m1}, r_{m2}, r_r witness configuration $\mathcal{G}_{\mathcal{R}_y}$, then robots r_{m1} and r_{m2} must start moving with direction outside of the convex hull (the robots that realize they are in the middle of the straight line must move outside so to enable the "edge" robots to see each other; the "edge" robots do not move). When r_{m1} and r_{m2} start moving (they get in state **move**) the adversary can impose the following strategy: It lets robot r_{m1} to move slightly and then it stops it (with a $stop(r_{m1})$ event). It lets robot r_{m2} to move slightly and then the adversary makes it to move very slow (so robot r_{m2} is still in state **move**). The adversary could stop robot r_{m1} and delay r_{m2} in such a way that configuration $\mathcal{R}_x$ is reached (recall that $|\vartheta CH(\mathcal{G}_{\mathcal{R}_x})| = n$ and $\mathcal{G}_{\mathcal{R}_x}$ is a *fully visible* configuration). But since r_{m2} continues to move, it is possible to cause robot r_{m1} to no longer be in ϑCH or some other robot (including r_{m2}) not be able to see all other robots. Hence it is possible for a succeeding configuration of $\mathcal{G}_{\mathcal{R}_x}$ not to have one (or both) of the these properties anymore.

Safe Configurations. We say that a robot configuration $\mathcal{R}$ is a *safe* configuration, when the following is true:

$|\vartheta CH(\mathcal{G}_{\mathcal{R}})| = n$, $\mathcal{G}_{\mathcal{R}}$ is *fully visible* **and** $\forall r_i$, $|\vartheta CH(V_i)| = n$ **and** V_i is a *fully visible* configuration (i.e., all robots know that the configuration is fully visible).

The reason we consider such configurations as safe is that, as we will show in the next subsection, once an execution of the algorithm reaches a safe configuration, then no succeeding configuration can be a bad configuration.

We define a *bad execution fragment* (resp., bad execution) of the algorithm to be an execution fragment (resp., execution) that contains at least one bad robot configuration. Similarly, we define a *good execution fragment* (resp., good execution) to be an execution fragment (resp., execution) that contains only good configurations.

5.2 Proof of Correctness

The proof of correctness is broken into two parts. In the first part we prove safety and liveness properties considering only good executions. Then we show that the algorithm is correct for any execution, including ones containing bad configurations. *Omitted and full proofs can be found in the full paper [1].*

5.2.1 Correctness for Good Executions

We first prove safety and then liveness properties.

Safety Properties. The following lemma states that as long as not all robots are on the convex hull's boundary, or even if all robots are on the boundary but there is at least one robot that cannot see all other robots, then the convex hull can only "expand". (Note that this property holds *even* for bad execution fragments.)

LEMMA 5.1. *Given an execution fragment $\mathcal{R}_0, e_1, ..., \mathcal{R}_{m-1}$ such that for all $\mathcal{R}_k$, $0 \le k \le m-1$ holds that:*
c1: $|\vartheta CH(\mathcal{G}_{\mathcal{R}_k})| < n$, or
c2: $|\vartheta CH(\mathcal{G}_{\mathcal{R}_k})| = n$ and $\mathcal{G}_{\mathcal{R}_k}$ is not a fully visible configuration.
Then for any step $\langle \mathcal{R}_{m-1}, e_m, \mathcal{R}_m \rangle$, $CH(\mathcal{G}_{\mathcal{R}_{m-1}}) \subseteq CH(\mathcal{G}_{\mathcal{R}_m})$.

PROOF SKETCH: For each possible event e_m, we show that either the invariant is not affected or it is reestablished in configuration $\mathcal{R}_m$. The challenge lies to the fact that robots, due to asynchrony, might have different local views. The detailed case-by-case analysis can be found in [1]. ∎

The next lemma states that if in a non-connected configuration all robots are on the boundary of the convex hull and it is fully visible, then these properties are not lost and the convex hull can only "shrink".

LEMMA 5.2. *Given a good execution fragment $\mathcal{R}_x, e_x, ..., \mathcal{R}_{m-1}$ such that $\forall \mathcal{R}_k$, $x \le k \le m-1$ holds that*
*c1: $|\vartheta CH(\mathcal{G}_{\mathcal{R}_k})| = n$ and $\mathcal{G}_{\mathcal{R}_k}$ is a fully visible configuration, **and***
c2: $\mathcal{G}_{\mathcal{R}_k}$ is not a connected configuration.
Then, for any step $\langle \mathcal{R}_{m-1}, e_m, \mathcal{R}_m \rangle$, c1 holds for $\mathcal{G}_{\mathcal{R}_m}$ and $CH(\mathcal{G}_{\mathcal{R}_{m-1}}) \supseteq CH(\mathcal{G}_{\mathcal{R}_m})$.

As with the previous proof, all possible events e_m are examined.

Liveness Properties. The first liveness lemma states that a configuration where all robots are on the convex hull's boundary and it is fully visible is eventually reached.

LEMMA 5.3. *Given any good execution of the algorithm, there is a configuration $\mathcal{R}_m$ such that $|\vartheta CH(\mathcal{G}_{\mathcal{R}_m})| = n$ and $\mathcal{G}_{\mathcal{R}_m}$ is a fully visible configuration.*

PROOF SKETCH: If $\mathcal{R}_0$ has the stated properties we are done. So consider the case that $\mathcal{R}_0$ satisfies either c1: $|\vartheta CH(\mathcal{G}_{\mathcal{R}_0})| < n$ or c2: $|\vartheta CH(\mathcal{G}_{\mathcal{R}_0})| = n$ and $\mathcal{G}_{\mathcal{R}_0}$ is not a fully visible configuration. By Lemma 5.1, if c1 or c2 holds, then $\vartheta CH(\mathcal{G}_{\mathcal{R}_0})$ can only expand; hence, $\vartheta CH(\mathcal{G}_{\mathcal{R}_0})$ will not shrink unless c1 and c2 do not hold. Then several cases need to be examined, depending whether c1 or c2 is true. For example, if c1 is true, then based on the local algorithm, the robots that are on the boundary of the convex hull do not move (but the robots inside the convex hull do move towards the boundary), unless there is no space for more robots to get on the boundary; in such a case they move to the outside of the convex hull. From Lemma 3.1, and using chirality and the liveness conditions, we argue that eventually there is space for all robots to get on the convex hull's boundary. Then we consider the case of full visibility (i.e., c2 holds). In this case we investigate the cases of how robots might "block" the views of other robots and how the local algorithm arranges so that eventually all robots are able to see all other robots, while all robots keep being on the convex hull. The proof completes by examining various combinations of cases; see [1] for full details. ∎

The next lemma states that starting from any initial configuration, when the robots form a configuration where all robots are on the convex hull and they can see each other, they eventually form a connected configuration.

LEMMA 5.4. *Given any good execution of the algorithm, if $\mathcal{R}_l$ is such that $|\vartheta CH(\mathcal{G}_{\mathcal{R}_l})| = n$ and $\mathcal{G}_{\mathcal{R}_l}$ is a fully visible configuration and not a connected configuration, then $\exists \mathcal{R}_k$, $l \le k$ so that $\mathcal{R}_k$ is a connected configuration.*

PROOF. Based on Lemma 5.2, if a configuration $\mathcal{R}_m$ is such that $|\vartheta CH(\mathcal{G}_{\mathcal{R}_m})| = n$ and $\mathcal{G}_{\mathcal{R}_m}$ is a *fully visible* configuration, then $|\vartheta CH(\mathcal{G}_{\mathcal{R}_{m+1}})| = n$, $\mathcal{G}_{\mathcal{R}_{m+1}}$ is a *fully visible* configuration and $CH(\mathcal{G}_{\mathcal{R}_m}) \subseteq CH(\mathcal{G}_{\mathcal{R}_{m+1}})$.

Based on Procedure `NotConnected`, no robot will start moving unless: Between any three adjacent robots on the convex hull's boundary, say r_l, r_m and r_r left robot, middle robot and right robot respectively, the distance between line segment $\overline{r_l r_r}$ and r_m must be equal or more than $\frac{1}{n}$. This, along with Lemma 5.3 guarantee that no robot will move unless the distance of at least $\frac{1}{n}$ exists and that eventually all robots will be on the convex hull's boundary and have full visibility. Because no robot moves unless the distance of at least $\frac{1}{n}$ exists, all robots will eventually move to state

Look and see that the observed configuration is *fully visible* and $|\vartheta CH(V_i)| = n$. We get the three following cases:

1. There exists at least one component that is smaller than at least one other component, with respect to the number of the robots that consist each component (size).

   Function `NotConnected` results in all robots of the smallest component(s) to join another larger component. Given the liveness condition that whenever a robot decides to move, it moves at least a distance of δ, eventually the number of the components become smaller and eventually the convex hull shrinks. Also the robots of the components that are not the smallest, do not move.

2. All components are of the same size. The distance between two neighboring components is not the same for all the neighboring components.

   Function `NotConnected` results in all robots of the component that has the smallest distance to its neighbor component on the right, to join the component on its right (here chirality is needed). Given the liveness condition that whenever a robot decides to move, it moves at least a distance of δ, eventually the number of the components become smaller and eventually the convex hull shrinks. The robots of the other components do not move.

3. All components are of the same size, and the distance between any two neighboring components is the same.

   Function `NotConnected` results in all the components start moving with direction to the inside of the convex hull. First, the leftmost and rightmost robots need to move forward at distance $\frac{1}{2n-\varepsilon}$ (due to the required minimum distance of $\frac{1}{n}$, the small steps of $\frac{1}{2n-\varepsilon}$ cannot cause three robots to be on the same line). These robots will not move again until the component has no spaces (this is the reason that a component can have up to 2 spaces). After these robots, the second leftmost and second rightmost robots move to touch the first robots; these robots will not move again until there is a space between them and the first robots. The same happens for the remaining robots. Full visibility and the design of Function `NotConnected` results the component to converge with small steps each time. Given the liveness condition that whenever a robot decides to move, it moves at least a distance of δ, it follows that eventually all the components will touch, because the convex hull shrinks (while preserving its formation).

From the cases above, it follows that either all the robots of any component that has the smallest number of robots (first case) or of any component that has the smallest distance (second case) to its right neighbor will move to its right neighbor until the number of components become one, or the components will move to the inside of the convex hull until all the components touch (third case).

In every case, robot r_i runs the Procedure `NotConnected`. Hence, per Lemma 4.4, robot r_i moves in such a way that it does not cause $|\vartheta CH(\mathcal{G}_{\mathcal{R}_{m+1}})| < n$ or $\mathcal{G}_{\mathcal{R}_{m+1}}$ not to be a *fully visible* configuration. This completes the proof. ∎

From Lemmas 5.3 and 5.4 we get the following:

COROLLARY 5.5. *Given any good execution of the algorithm, there is a configuration $\mathcal{R}_m$ so that $\mathcal{G}_{\mathcal{R}_m}$ is a connected and fully visible configuration.*

5.2.2 Correctness for All Executions

We now consider any execution (including ones with bad configurations).

LEMMA 5.6. *Given any execution of the algorithm, if there is a bad execution fragment α_{bad}, then eventually a safe configuration $\mathcal{R}_{safe}$ is reached, after which there are no longer bad configurations.*

PROOF. There are 2 possible cases:
(a) The adversary deploys a strategy that aims in causing bad configurations as long as it can (i.e., indefinitely if possible).
(b) The adversary, at some point of the execution, stops causing bad configurations.

We focus on the first case and we show that any execution under this adversarial strategy will eventually reach a configuration in which the adversary will no longer be able to cause bad configurations. It is easy to see that this case covers also the second case.

Recall that both types of bad configurations involve configurations in which the robots are momentarily in a configuration in which all robots are on the convex hull and it is fully visible, but the adversary manages to break this property. The adversary, as explained, exploits the fact that some robots, due to asynchrony, are not aware that such a configuration has been reached. We now consider the two types of bad configurations.

(i) Bad configuration of type 1. Consider the case in which the first bad configuration, call it $\mathcal{R}_x$, that appears in the bad execution fragment α_{bad} is of type 1 (the other type is considered later). As explained, the adversary may deploy a strategy which can result into a configuration $\mathcal{R}_z$, $z > x$, so that $\mathcal{G}_{\mathcal{R}_z}$ is no longer fully visible or/and not all robots are on the convex hull. The adversary can do so, if there is at least one robot that according to its local view in configuration $\mathcal{R}_x$, not all robot are on the convex hull and there is no more space for an "internal" robot to get on the convex hull (per Function `NoSpaceForMore` this robot will move to a direction outside of the convex hull). It follows that $CH(\mathcal{G}_{\mathcal{R}_z}) \supseteq CH(\mathcal{G}_{\mathcal{R}_x})$. Furthermore, from Lemma 5.1 we get that for all successive configurations of $\mathcal{R}_z$ in which not all robots are on the convex hull or are fully visible, the convex hull can only expand (until a configuration in which these properties hold is reached). The adversary may repeat this strategy (e.g., involving other robots on the convex hull), every time causing the convex hull to expand. However, per Lemma 3.1, this cannot be repeated indefinitely, as the convex hull will expand that much, that the *safe* distance will be reached for all pairs of adjacent robots on the convex hull. From this and that the adversary must allow a robot to move by at least δ distance, it follows that a configuration is eventually reached after which no bad configuration of type 1 can exist (no robot will get into state **Compute.NoSpaceForMore**). Observe that when such a configuration is reached, it is still possible for a bad configuration of type 2 to be reached. This is covered by the next case we consider (with the difference that this bad configuration is not the first appearing in α_{bad}).

(ii) Bad configuration of type 2. Consider the case in which the first bad configuration, call it R_x, that appears in the bad execution fragment α_{bad} is of type 2. This is the situation where in a preceding configuration there are at least four robots on a straight line on the convex hull. As explained in Section 2, the adversary can yield a configuration in which not all robots are any longer on the convex hull, or there is no full visibility. However, per Function `SeeOneRobot` and Lemma 4.10 the robots on the straight line that are not in the middle (i.e., they see only one robot) do not move. In contrast, according to Function `SeeTwoRobot` and Lemma 4.11, each robot in the middle of the straight line moves in a direction outside of the convex hull, in such a way that it will no longer be in a straight line with its two adjacent robots (on the convex hull). It follows that if every time the adversary repeats the same strategy, and say initially there are x robots on straight line, then in every iteration the number of robots that are on the same line is $x - 2$. This may continue only until x is less than 3, hence it eventually stops. Observe that during these iterations, since robots in the middle move towards a direction outside of the convex hull and per Lemma 5.1, the convex hull can only expand. Hence a bad configuration of type 2 can no longer exist. Furthermore, note that if during this expansion, the robots involved have also reached the safe distance (per Lemma 3.1's definition), then as explained above, a bad configuration of type 1 also cannot exist. Otherwise, we are back in case (i) as discussed above. Note however that once robots reach the safe distance, and a bad configuration of type 2 is reached, a configuration of type 1 can no longer exist again: when a robot has already safe distance between its adjacent robots on the convex hull, then the middle robots by moving towards outside the convex hull can only increase the safe distance (and hence it will not be possible for a robot to get into state **Compute.NoSpaceForMore**).

From cases (i) and (ii) and Lemma 5.3 it follows that a fully visible configuration in which $|\vartheta CH| = n$ is reached. By a similar argument as in the proof of Lemma 5.4 we get that eventually a safe configuration is reached (all robots are on the convex and they are aware that the configuration is fully visible). From Function NotConnected and Lemma 4.4 it follows that any succeeding configuration maintains the property that all robots can see each other and that are on the convex hull. Hence, the algorithm is such that once a safe configuration is reached, it is no longer possible for a bad configuration to exist. This completes the proof. ■

Finally, we prove the correctness of our gathering algorithm.

THEOREM 5.7 (GATHERING). *In any execution of the algorithm, there is a configuration $\mathcal{R}_m$, so that $\mathcal{G}_{\mathcal{R}_m}$ is a connected, fully visible configuration and $\forall s_i \in \mathcal{S}_{\mathcal{R}_m}, s_i = $* **Terminate**.

PROOF. Consider the following two cases.

- If no bad configurations exist, based on Corollary 5.5, given any good execution of the algorithm, there exists $\mathcal{R}_m$ so that $\mathcal{G}_{\mathcal{R}_m}$ is a connected and fully visible configuration.

- If bad configurations exist, based on Lemma 5.6, given any execution of the algorithm, if there is a bad execution fragment α_{bad}, then eventually a $safe$ configuration $\mathcal{R}_{safe}$ is reached, and after a $safe$ configuration there are no longer any bad configurations in the execution until termination. Therefore, from this point onward, we get from Corollary 5.5 that there exists $\mathcal{R}_m$ so that $\mathcal{G}_{\mathcal{R}_m}$ is a connected and fully visible configuration.

When a *connected* and *fully visible* configuration is reached, it is easy to see that robots no longer move and eventually all robots get into state **Compute.Connected** and hence into state **Terminate**. ■

6. CONCLUSIONS

We have considered the problem of gathering non-transparent, fat robots in an asynchronous setting. We formulated the problem and the model with a state-machine representation and developed a distributed algorithm for any number of robots. The correctness of the algorithm exploits the assumption of *chirality* [11]: robots agree on the orientation of the axes of their local coordination system. This is the only assumption we needed to add to the model considered in [9]. We believe this is a very small price to pay,

while we feel it would not be manufacturally unrealistic to provide, in order to solve the gathering problem for any number of fat robots. Nevertheless, an intriguing open problem is to investigate whether it is possible to remove the assumption of chirality and still be able to solve the gathering problem for any number of fat robots, or whether chirality is necessary.

7. REFERENCES

[1] Ch. Agathangelou, Ch. Georgiou, and M. Mavronicolas. A distributed algorithm for gathering many fat robots in the plane. In arXiv:1209.3904, 2012.

[2] N. Agmon and D. Peleg. Fault-tolerant gathering algorithms for autonomous mobile robots. In *Proc. of the 15th ACM-SIAM Symposium on Discrete Algorithms (SODA 2004)*, pages 1070–1078.

[3] H. Ando, Y. Oasa, I. Suzuki, and M. Yamashita. Distributed memoryless point convergence algorithm for mobile robots with limited visibility. *IEEE Transactions on Robotics and Automation*, 15(5):818–828, 1999.

[4] H. Attiya and J. Welch. *Distributed Computing: Fundamentals, Simulations and Advanced Topics.* Second edition, Wiley & Sons, 2004.

[5] A. Bandettini, F. Luporini, G. Viglietta. A survey on open problems for mobile robots. In arXiv:1111.2259v1, 2011.

[6] K. Bolla, T. Kovacs, and G. Fazekas. Gathering of fat robots with limited visibility and without global navigation. In *Proc. of ICAISC/SIDE-EC 2012*, pages 30–38.

[7] S.G. Chaudhuri and K. Mukhopadhyaya. Gathering asynchronous transparent fat robots. In *Proc. of the 6th International Conference on Distributed Computing and Internet Technology (ICDCIT 2010)*, pages 170–175.

[8] A. Cord-Landwehr, B. Degener, M. Fischer, M. Hüllmann, B. Kempkes, A. Klaas, P. Kling, S. Kurras, M. Märtens, F.M.A Der Heide, C. Raupach, D. Swierkot, D. Warner, C. Weddemann, and D. Wonisch. Collisionless gathering of robots with an extent. In *Proc. of SOFSEM 2011*, pages 178–189.

[9] J. Czyzowicz, L. Gasieniec, and A. Pelc. Gathering few fat mobile robots in the plane. *Theoretical Computer Science*, 410(6–7):481–499, 2009.

[10] A. Dutta, S. G. Chaudhuri, S. Datta, and K. Mukhopadhyaya. Circle formation by asynchronous fat robots with limited visibility. In *Proc. of ICDCIT 2012*, pages 83–93.

[11] P. Flocchini, G. Prencipe, N. Santoro. *Distributed Computing by Oblivious Mobile Robots.* Synthesis Lectures on Distributed Computing Theory, Morgan & Claypool, 2012.

[12] P. Flocchini, G. Prencipe, N. Santoro, and P. Widmayer. Gathering of asynchronous robots with limited visibility. *Theoretical Computer Science*, 337(1–3):147–168, 2005.

[13] R.L. Graham. An efficient algorithm for determining the convex hull of a finite planar set. *Information Processing Letters*, 1(4):132–133, 1972.

[14] S. Kamei, A. Lamani, F. Ooshita, and S. Tixeuil. Gathering an even number of robots in an odd ring without global multiplicity detection. In *Proc. of the 37th International Symposium on Mathematical Foundations of Computer Science (MFCS 2012)*, pages 542–553.

[15] S. Souissi, T. Izumi, and K. Wada. Distributed algorithms for cooperative mobile robots: A survey. In *Proc. of the 2nd Second International Conference on Networking and Computing (ICNC 2011)*, pages 364–371.

Stable and Scalable Universal Swarms

Ji Zhu
University of Illinois
jizhu1@illinois.edu

Stratis Ioannidis,
Nidhi Hegde
Technicolor
stratis.ioannidis@technicolor.com,
nidhi.hegde@technicolor.com

Laurent Massoulié
MSR-Inria Joint Centre
laurent.massoulie@inria.fr

ABSTRACT

Hajek and Zhu recently showed that the BitTorrent protocol can become unstable when peers depart immediately after downloading all pieces of a file. In light of this result, Zhou *et al.* propose bundling swarms together, allowing peers to exchange pieces across different swarms, and claim that such "universal swarms" can increase BitTorrent's stability. In this work, we formally characterize the stability region of universal swarms and show that they indeed exhibit excellent properties. In particular, bundling allows a single seed with limited upload capacity to serve an arbitrary number of disjoint swarms if the arrival rate of peers in each swarm is lower than the seed upload capacity. Our result also shows that the stability region is insensitive to peers' upload capacity, piece selection policies and number of swarms.

Categories and Subject Descriptors: C.2.1 [**Computer-Communication Networks**]: Network Architecture and Design - distributed networks

Keywords: Missing Piece Syndrome; P2P; Stability

1. INTRODUCTION

BitTorrent is one of the most popular peer-to-peer protocols, used by millions of Internet users to share files online. In simple terms, peers interested in downloading a single file from a distinguished user, termed the *seed*, form a so-called *swarm*. Peers in a swarm exchange file *pieces* (or *chunks*) with each other. Each peer thereby acts as both a client and a server, contributing to the aggregate upload capacity of the swarm. A natural question about BitTorrent is what is its *stability region*: assuming the seed's upload capacity is U pieces per second, what is the largest arrival rate of peers λ that can be supported without the swarm growing to infinity? Intuitively, as every incoming peer increases the swarm's aggregate upload capacity, one would expect BitTorrent to support high arrival rates.

Determining the stability region of BitTorrent has been an open problem for more than ten years. It was resolved recently by Hajek and Zhu [3], who showed that the swarm remains stable if $\lambda < U$, and unstable if $\lambda > U$.

In light of this, a series of recent works have focused on extending the stability region of BitTorrent [11, 10, 8, 6, 4]. Zhou *et al.* [10] propose bundling multiple autonomous swarms together into a *universal swarm*: peers immediately depart upon retrieving the file they desire but, while in the system, they store and exchange pieces with peers belonging to *different swarms*. Intuitively, such inter-swarm exchanges utilize bandwidth that would otherwise remain idle. As such, Zhou *et al.* conjecture that a universal swarm with a single seed has an increased stability region compared to autonomous swarms. Sharing pieces with different swarms introduces a trade-off between stability and the average *sojourn time*, *i.e.*, the time peers stay in the system: by consuming bandwidth for pieces they are not interested in, peers may take longer to retrieve the file they desire.

In this paper, we establish that universal swarms have excellent stability properties. In addition, they can be designed so that peers *do not* experience increased delays. In particular, we make the following contributions: First, we formally characterize the stability region of universal swarms, proving necessary and sufficient conditions under which such swarms remain stable. Second, we show that bundling swarms together significantly increases BitTorrent's stability region, making it scale in the number of bundled swarms. We show that the capacity region under limited seed upload capacity *is insensitive to the number of swarms, as well as the peers' uploading capacity and piece selection policies.* Third, we show that the increased stability region of universal swarms comes at the cost of increased delays, that scale with the total number of bundled swarms. Finally, to address this, we propose a modified system design that provably extends the stability region *and* does not affect delays.

Our stability result (Theorem 2) is general: in contrast to previous work [3, 11, 7, 10], it covers all work-conserving piece selection policies, determining which pieces peers exchange upon contact with each other. As a consequence, our result has interesting implications for single swarms as well. Moreover, to the best of our knowledge, we are the first to observe and exploit the fact that swarms become *meta-stable* when the swarm seed and peers prioritize rare pieces.

The remainder of the paper is organized as follows. We review related work in the next section. Our model of universal swarm is introduced in Section 3. Earlier results and our new results on stability constitute Sections 4 and 5 respectively. We study sojourn time numerically in Section 6 and conclude in Section 7.

2. RELATED WORK

The stability of BitTorrent is determined by a phenomenon called the *missing piece syndrome*, described in detail in Section 4. This was first observed by Hajek and Zhu [3] and, independently, by Norros and Reittu [7] (in the context of a two-piece file sharing system). Hajek and Zhu observed that the phenomenon persists—and the stability region remains the same—when using source coding as well as when prioritizing the transmission of rare pieces.

One way to extend the stability region of BitTorrent is to require that peers remain in the system after they have downloaded all pieces, effectively turning from leechers to seeds. In follow-up work, Zhu and Hajek show that this indeed extends the stability region by a factor that depends on the mean additional time peers spend in the system [11]. By setting the latter to a high enough value, the system remains stable for arbitrary arrival rates. Requiring that peers spend additional time in the system assumes they are altruistic. Universal swarms also presume altruism, though of a different kind: though peers immediately leave upon retrieving a file, they contribute their storage and bandwidth resources to other swarms while in the system, by storing and uploading pieces of files they may not be interested in.

Oğuz *et al.* [8] propose an alternative approach to extending BitTorrent's stability region. The authors consider schemes where (a) newly arriving peers do not accept pieces unless they are sufficiently rare, and (b) peers missing a single piece do not download it before uploading a piece that is sufficiently rare. Crucially, the rarity of a piece is estimated in a distributed fashion, through sampling a small number of peers. The resulting system is stable under arbitrary arrival rates, and also assumes peers are altruistic, as they do not download useful pieces at all opportunities to do so.

Zhou *et al.* [10] propose universal swarms as a means of extending the stability region of BitTorrent. They study stability under a model in which (a) files consist of only one piece and (b) swarms are *seedless* [5]: no seed exists, and all peers arrive already endowed with certain pieces. The authors observe an extension of the stability region under these assumptions; in our work, we consider the more realistic setup of [3, 8, 11], in which files consist of multiple pieces and peers arrive empty, while pieces are injected by a seed.

Bundling across swarms has also been studied in other contexts. Menasche *et al.* [6] show that bundling swarms together improves file availability, while Wu *et al.* [9] show that bundling improves the performance of live streaming. In contrast, our work presents a rigorous analysis of the stability of universal swarms under various sharing policies. Finally, measurement studies [4] establish the prevalence of file bundling in BitTorrent: $50-80\%$ of swarms contain bundled files, with content such as movies, TV series and music being bundled more often than games. These real-world measurements attest to the relevance and practical significance of studying universal swarms.

3. SYSTEM DESCRIPTION

We consider a BitTorrent-like file-sharing system, consisting of multiple swarms. Suppose all files are divided into *pieces* of equal size. We denote by $\mathcal{F} = \{1, 2, \ldots, K\}$ the set of all pieces of all files. A distinguished peer, the seed, is always present and holds $\mathcal{F}$. Represent a *file* C to be a non-empty subset of $\mathcal{F}$: $\emptyset \neq C \subseteq \mathcal{F}$. We refer to the set of peers

interested in downloading file C as *Swarm C*. Assume peers in Swarm C arrive according to a Poisson process with rate λ_C, independent across swarms. We do *not* require different swarms to be disjoint subsets of $\mathcal{F}$, so our model captures a scenario where arriving peers are interested in multiple files.

Each peer maintains a cache to store pieces it downloads. We assume peers arrive with empty caches, and each peer's cache is large enough to hold $\mathcal{F}$. Peers in Swarm C depart *immediately* upon retrieving all pieces in C. We partition peers into *types* according to (a) the swarm they belong to and (b) the set of pieces in their cache. Hence, a peer in Swarm C holding $S \subseteq \mathcal{F}$ is denoted to be of type $\langle C, S \rangle$. Assume the seed is of type $\langle \{\bot\}, \mathcal{F} \rangle$ for some piece $\bot \notin \mathcal{F}$. Denote $n_{\langle C,S \rangle}$ to be the number of type $\langle C, S \rangle$ peers and $\mathbf{n} = (n_{\langle C,S \rangle})$ to be the vector of numbers of peers in all types. The seed uploads pieces at instants of a Poisson process of rate U. At each such instant, the seed contacts a peer selected uniformly at random among all peers across all swarms, and replicates a piece in $\mathcal{F}$ to this peer. Similarly, at instances that follow a Poisson process of rate $\mu > 0$, each peer contacts another peer (also selected uniformly among all peers) and replicates a piece from its cache.

The piece replicated when a source (either a peer or the seed) contacts a receiver is determined by the source's piece selection policy. We consider a broad class of work-conserving piece selection policies satisfying the following:

ASSUMPTION 1. *If a source in type $\langle C, S \rangle$ contacts a receiver in type $\langle C', S' \rangle$, no piece is replicated if $S \subseteq S'$. Otherwise exactly one piece in $S \setminus S'$ is replicated, with piece $i \in S \setminus S'$ replicated with probability $h_{\langle C,S \rangle}(i, \langle C', S' \rangle, \mathbf{n}) \in [0, 1]$, determined by the types of the source and the receiver, the piece id, and the current state $\mathbf{n}$. Function $h_{\langle C,S \rangle}$, also referred to as the policy, satisfies:*

$$\sum_{i \notin S \setminus S'} h_{\langle C,S \rangle}(i, \langle C', S' \rangle, \mathbf{n}) = 0,$$
$$\sum_{i \in S \setminus S'} h_{\langle C,S \rangle}(i, \langle C', S' \rangle, \mathbf{n}) = 1 \text{ if } S \nsubseteq S'.$$

Suppose a type $\langle C, S \rangle$ source contacts a type $\langle C', S' \rangle$ receiver. Examples of work-conserving policies considered are:
Random Novel [RN]: If $S \setminus S' \neq \emptyset$, the source replicates a piece chosen uniformly from $S \setminus S'$.
Rarest First [RF]: Define the *availability* of a piece $i \in \mathcal{F}$ to be the number of peers holding it. The source replicates the piece in $S \setminus S'$ that has the least availability, with ties broken randomly.
Priority Rarest First [PRF]: The source prioritizes pieces within the swarm of the receiver: if $(S \setminus S') \cap C' \neq \emptyset$, it replicates the piece in $(S \setminus S') \cap C'$ that has the least availability; if $(S \setminus S') \cap C'$ is empty but $S \setminus S'$ is not, the source reverts to RF. **Priority Random Novel [PRN]** is defined similarly.

Notice that sources of the same type apply the same policy. The piece selection policy of the system is denoted by a tuple of $h_{\langle C,S \rangle}$ indexed by each $\langle C, S \rangle$, where all sources in type $\langle C, S \rangle$ apply the policy $h_{\langle C,S \rangle}$ in the tuple. Different policies h can co-exist across types: *e.g.*, the seed may implement a random novel policy, while peers implement priority rarest first. Contrary to random novel, the RF and PRF policies depend on the system state $\mathbf{n}$, and require knowledge of a global property; as such, they are harder to implement in a distributed fashion. In a centralized setting, which includes most present BitTorrent implementations, the availability is monitored by a distinguished peer called the swarm tracker. Alternatively, distributed techniques such as gossiping or sampling can be used to estimate availability. Other definitions are as follows:

DEFINITION 1. *Define* $\lambda_{total} := \sum_{C:C\in\mathcal{C}} \lambda_C$ *to be the total arrival rate. Define* $n_S := \sum_{C:C\in\mathcal{C}} n_{\langle C,S\rangle}$ *to be the number of peers holding the set of pieces* S.

Let $\mathcal{C} := \{C : C \in 2^{\mathcal{F}} \setminus \{\emptyset\}, \lambda_C > 0\}$ *be the set of swarms. Define* $\mathcal{T} := \{\langle C,S\rangle : C \in \mathcal{C}, S \in 2^{\mathcal{F}} \setminus \{\mathcal{F}\}, C \nsubseteq S\}$ *to be the set containing all peer types for peers in the system, and* $\tilde{\mathcal{T}} = \mathcal{T} \cup \{\langle\{\bot\},\mathcal{F}\rangle\}$ *to be the extended set of peer types. Define* $\mathcal{D} = \mathbb{N}^{|\mathcal{T}|}$ *to be the set of all possible vectors* $\mathbf{n}$.

Our main stability result (Theorem 2) assumes that the seed applies RN, while peers apply piece selection policies satisfying Assumption 1.

3.1 Markov Process Description and Stability

The system evolution is described by a Markov process $\{\mathbf{n}(t)\}_{t\in\mathbb{R}_+}$ with state space $\mathcal{D}$. The transition rates of the process depend on how pieces are uploaded.

Assume that the seed implements RN, and peers apply policies as in Assumption 1. Given a state $\mathbf{n}$, let $T_C(\mathbf{n})$ be the new state resulting from the arrival of a new peer in swarm C. Given $\langle C,S\rangle \in \mathcal{T}$ such that $i \notin S$, and a state $\mathbf{n}$ such that $n_{\langle C,S\rangle} \geq 1$, let $T_{\langle C,S\rangle,i}(\mathbf{n})$ denote the new state resulting from a type $\langle C,S\rangle$ peer downloading piece i. The positive entries of the generator matrix $Q = (q(\mathbf{n},\mathbf{n}') : \mathbf{n},\mathbf{n}' \in \mathcal{D})$ are given by:

$$q(\mathbf{n}, T_C(\mathbf{n})) = \lambda_C$$

$$q(\mathbf{n}, T_{\langle C,S\rangle,i}(\mathbf{n})) = \frac{n_{\langle C,S\rangle}}{n}\left[\frac{U}{K-|S|} + \mu \sum_{v\in\mathcal{T}} n_v h_v(i,\langle C,S\rangle,\mathbf{n})\right]$$

We follow the usual definitions of stability and instability for Markov processes [2]:

DEFINITION 2. *The system is* unstable *if it is transient and the number of peers converges to infinity with probability one; and the system is* stable *if it is positive recurrent and it has a finite mean number of peers in equilibrium.*

4. SINGLE SWARM AND MISSING PIECE SYNDROME

Hajek and Zhu study the above system in the case of a single, autonomous swarm, *i.e.*, a system in which all peers are interested in downloading the file $C = \mathcal{F}$. They determine the stability region under the RN policy:

THEOREM 1 (HAJEK AND ZHU [3]). *Consider a single swarm of peers requesting all pieces in* $\mathcal{F}$, *in which both the seed and peers follow the random novel piece selection policy. The system is stable if* $\lambda_{\mathcal{F}} < U$, *and unstable if* $\lambda_{\mathcal{F}} > U$.

Hajek and Zhu further establish that the so-called missing piece syndrome [3, 7] is the reason of instability when $\lambda_{\mathcal{F}} > U$. This phenomenon arises when there is a large number of peers in the system that store all pieces in $\mathcal{F}$ except for one missing piece. When this set of peers, termed the *one-club*, is large enough, most of the contacts of new peers arriving in the system will be with such peers. The new peers thus quickly retrieve all pieces except the missing piece, thus joining the one-club set. Since peers holding the missing piece are few, departures from the one-club are mostly due to uploads by the seed; as a result, the departure rate of the one-club is close to the seed upload rate U.

Since $\lambda_{\mathcal{F}} > U$, the rate of growth of peers in the one-club is positive, causing the size of this set to increase to infinity and resulting to instability.

Theorem 1 has an immediate corollary in the case of multi-swarm systems. In particular, suppose that each swarm operates in an *autonomous mode*, independently and in isolation of other swarms. More specifically, peers in swarm $C \in \mathcal{C}$ contact and exchange pieces only with other peers in the same swarm. In addition, the seed divides its upload capacity across different swarms (possibly unevenly), serving each with an appropriate fraction of its total capacity. Finally, peers in swarm C store and exchange only pieces in set C. Theorem 1 directly applies to each such system and, thus, it is easy to verify the following:

COROLLARY 1. *Consider a multi-swarm system operating in autonomous mode. The seed can allocate its upload capacity so that the system is stable if* $\sum_{C\in\mathcal{C}} \lambda_C < U$; *the system is unstable for all allocations of the seed's upload capacity if* $\sum_{C\in\mathcal{C}} \lambda_C > U$.

Note that the corollary assumes a static allocation of a seed's rate to each swarm. Though formally studying the capacity of a dynamic allocation is beyond the scope of this work, we observe through simulations that an allocation that is proportional to the size of each swarm does not improve stability or prevent the missing piece syndrome (see Figure 1(a)).

In what follows, we study multi-swarm systems that operate as described formally in Section 3. To distinguish this system, we refer to it as a multi-swarm system in *universal mode* or, simply, a *universal swarm*.

5. STABILITY REGION OF A UNIVERSAL SWARM

The following is our main result regarding the stability region of the Markov process defined in Section 3.1:

THEOREM 2. *If the seed implements RN and peers implement work-conserving piece selection policies in Assumption 1, the system is*

    i) *unstable if* $\max_{i:i\in\mathcal{F}} \sum_{C:i\in C} \lambda_C > U$,

    ii) *stable if* $\max_{i:i\in\mathcal{F}} \sum_{C:i\in C} \lambda_C < U$.

Beyond considering universal swarms, Theorem 2 extends Theorem 1 to the case where peers implement arbitrary piece selection policies. In fact, an immediate corollary of Theorem 2, applied to the single swarm setup, is that the stability region of Theorem 1 extends to such policies as well. The theorem assumes that the seed uses the RN policy; our numerical evaluations in Section 7 suggest that other seed policies (*e.g.*, RF) also yield the same stability region.

Note that the theorem implies that bundling swarms together yields a significant increase in the stability region. Observe that, when the files $C \in \mathcal{C}$ are disjoint, Theorem 2(ii) becomes $\max_{C\in\mathcal{C}} \lambda_C < U$. This defines a larger stability region than the one of autonomous mode, given by Corollary 1. In particular, by bundling swarms together, the stability region scales extremely well as the number of swarms increases: a single seed can support an *unbounded number* of swarms with constant arrival rate, with no effect on the stability region! However, as discussed in Section 7, bundling swarms together comes at the cost of increased delays. Hence, the number of swarms cannot be arbitrarily large in practice. In Section 7.4, we address this by proposing a *hybrid system* that, by alternating between the universal and autonomous mode, maintains the same stability region as a universal swarm while also ensuring small delays for large numbers of swarms.

The stability region is insensitive to peer piece selection policies. However, policies can be quite different w.r.t. other performance metrics. For example, as we will see in Section 7, policies can differ drastically in how quickly they stabilize the system when operating within the stability region, as well as in how quickly the missing piece syndrome manifests under the condition of Theorem 2(ii).

6. LYAPUNOV FUNCTION FOR PROOF OF Theorem 2(ii)

We provide the detailed proof of Theorem 2(i) in Appendix A. In this section we describe the Lyapunov function applied for the proof of Theorem 2(ii). We establish the stability by Foster's criterion [1]. Specifically, we use the result below, itself a standard version of the criterion:

LEMMA 1. *The Markov process* $\mathbf{n}$ *is stable, if there exist a non-negative function* $W(\mathbf{n})$ *on space* $\mathcal{D}$*, with* $\{\mathbf{n} : W(\mathbf{n}) \leq c\}$ *a finite set for any* $c \geq 0$*, and constants* $n_o \geq 0, \xi > 0$*, such that* $\forall n \geq n_o$*,* $QW \leq -\xi n < 0$*, where* Q *denotes the infinitesimal generator of the process. We then say that* W *is a valid Lyapunov function.*

We devote the remainder of this section to the description of our Lyapunov function, and show in Appendix B that it satisfies the above Foster criterion.

DEFINITION 3. $\Delta := U - \max_{i:i \in \mathcal{F}} \sum_{C:i \in C} \lambda_C > 0$.

DEFINITION 4. $\mathcal{E}_C := \{\langle C', S' \rangle : C' \not\subseteq C, S' \subseteq C\}$ *is set of types of peers which may hold the set of pieces* C *in the future,* $E_C := \sum_{\langle C', S' \rangle \in \mathcal{E}_C} n_{\langle C', S' \rangle}$ *is the number of peers with types in* $\mathcal{E}_C$*:*

DEFINITION 5. $\mathcal{H}_C := \bigcup_{i \in \mathcal{F} \setminus C} \{\langle C', C \cup \{i\} \rangle : C' \not\subseteq C \cup \{i\}\}$ *is set of types of peers which hold one more piece than* C*,* $H_C := \sum_{\langle C', S' \rangle \in \mathcal{H}_C} n_{\langle C', S' \rangle}$ *is the number of peers with types in* $\mathcal{H}_C$*.*

DEFINITION 6. $r \in (0, \frac{1}{2}), d \in (1, \infty), \beta \in (0, \frac{1}{2}), \alpha := 8K(\lambda_{total} + \Delta/2)/U$ *are four constants, and*

$$\phi(x) := \begin{cases} (2d + \frac{1}{2\beta} - x) & 0 \leq x \leq 2d \\ \frac{\beta}{2}(x - 2d - \frac{1}{\beta})^2 & 2d < x \leq 2d + \frac{1}{\beta} \\ 0 & x > 2d + \frac{1}{\beta} \end{cases}$$

DEFINITION 7. *The Lyapunov function* W *is defined as* $W := \sum_C r^{|C|} T_C$*, where*

$$T_C := \begin{cases} \frac{1}{2}E_C^2 + \alpha E_C \phi(H_C), |C| \leq K - 2, \\ \frac{1}{2}E_C^2, |C| = K - 1 \end{cases}$$

Function ϕ is affine in the range $[0, 2d]$, and thus the Lyapunov function W is quadratic in the state variable $\mathbf{n}$ in a corresponding range. However, we need to go beyond quadratic functions in order to apply the Foster criterion. We show in Appendix B that for suitable choices of constants r, d, β the function W satisfies Foster's criterion.

7. EVALUATION

In this section, we evaluate the performance of universal swarms through simulations, studying swarm behavior for different piece selection policies, as well as the dependence of the sojourn time in swarm parameters. In what follows, we denote by RF, RN, PRN and PRF the piece selection policies rarest first, random novel, priority random novel and priority rarest first. Note that PRF and PRN reduce to RF and RN when the system operates in autonomous mode.

7.1 Autonomous vs. Universal Swarms

We begin by validating Theorems 1 and 2. We do so by studying the evolution of the system size n in autonomous and universal mode for a system comprising 3 swarms, each requesting a different 3-piece set. The seed rate is $U = 3.1$ and the arrival rate in each swarm is $\lambda = 3.0$; note that Theorems 1 and 2 imply that the autonomous mode is unstable while the universal system is stable, in this regime.

Figure 1(a) shows the evolution of the system size in autonomous mode, when the seed statically allocates $1/3$ of its upload rate to each swarm, for different combinations of policies at the seed and the peers. All simulations start from an empty system. Even though applying RF at both the seed and the peers leads to a slightly smaller system size, the missing piece syndrome manifests in all four cases. We repeat these experiments with the seed allocating its rate dynamically, so that each swarm receives pieces at a rate proportional to its size. The results (inset of Figure 1(a)) show that instability persists in this setup too.

We repeat these experiments in universal mode, starting the system from an initial state comprising 8500 peers forming a *one-club*: all peers belong to the same swarm, and store in their cache all nine pieces *except for one common piece they request*. Figure 1(b) shows the system evolution when the seed applies RN; indeed the system stabilizes after 10^5 time units, confirming Theorem 2. The system stabilizes faster (in the order of 10^4 time units) when the seed applies RF, as seen in Figure 1(c), with RF at both seed and peers stabilizing the system the fastest (in roughly $3 \cdot 10^4$ time units). Interestingly, prioritizing pieces at peers (through either PRN or PRF) leads to *slower* stabilization: this is precisely because these policies reduce piece diversity.

7.2 Instability and Meta-Stability in Universal Mode

We next consider the same experiments as above with $U = 2.9$. As the arrival rate at each swarm is $\lambda = 3$, Theorem 2 stipulates that when the seed applies RN the system is unstable. A question we wish to address here is how quickly the missing piece syndrome manifests in this case, depending on the piece selection policies.

To evaluate this, we conduct the following experiments. We start our simulations with initial system size n_0, where the initial state comprises all peers forming a one-club (*i.e.*, storing all pieces but one). We then terminate the simulation when either the system size increases to the threshold $\max(2000 + n_0, 2n_0)$ or the simulation time reaches 10^7, whichever occurs first. We first conduct this experiment with an empty initial state $n_0 = 0$; if the experiment does not reach the threshold in 10^7 units, we increase n_0 by 100 and repeat the experiment. This way, we identify the *critical one-club size*: if the system reaches a state with a one-club of that size, it becomes unstable.

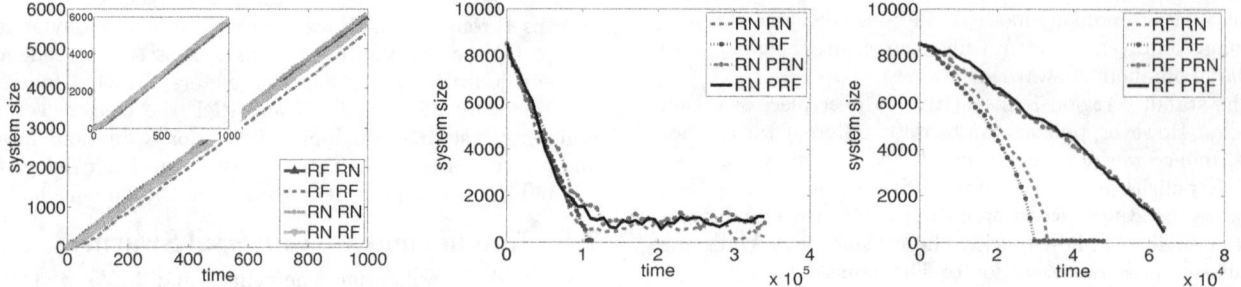

(a) Autonomous mode, static and dynamic (inset) allocation.

(b) Universal mode, RN at seed.

(c) Universal mode, RF at seed.

Figure 1: System size VS time. ("RN RF" means RN at seed and RF at peers, other legends follow similarly.)

Table 1: Critical One Club Size

Policy		Critical	Final	Final One	Sim.
Seed	Peer	n_0	Size	Club Ratio	Duration
RN	PRN	0	2000	95.6%	13181
	PRF	0	2000	95.4%	17211
	RN	0	2000	93.3%	13603
	RF	500	2500	94.7%	22655
RF	PRN	2100	4200	98.1%	74655
	PRF	2000	4000	98.0%	51415
	RN	8000	16000	99.4%	283197
	RF	8100	16200	99.4%	323738

Our simulation results for the case where the seed applies RN are summarized in the top half of Table 1. We see that the missing piece syndrome indeed manifests at the critical initial conditions, with the one-club comprising more than 90% of the peer population at termination time. When peers use any policy other than RF, the critical one-club size is 0. In contrast, when peers use RF, the syndrome manifests only when $n_0 = 500$; indeed, using RF improves the diversity of pieces in the system, which in turns makes reaching a critical one-club size more difficult. This behavior becomes even more striking when the seed uses RF: as shown in the bottom half of Table 1, piece diversity is so high that critical one-club sizes lie between 2 and 8 thousand peers.

Crucially, in all simulations starting from an initial size below the critical value, we observe interestingly that the system size actually *decreases* to a size below 200 and lingers around this value for the entire 10^7 time units! This implies that, though the system is clearly not stable in any of the cases in Table 1, applying RF at the seed or peers yields *meta-stability*: although there exists a critical one-club size, its value is so high that it is quite hard to reach from the "typical" size at which the system operates most of the time (~200 peers in our simulations). A natural question to ask is what is the critical value n_0, as well as what is the "typical" size at which a meta-stable system operates most of the time; we revisit these questions below, in Section 7.4.

7.3   Average Sojourn Time

We next turn our attention to the sojourn time. First we study a universal system comprising 3 swarms with 3 pieces each. The seed rate is fixed at $U = 3.0$ and the swarm arrival

rate varies as $\lambda = U(1 - \frac{1}{2^i})$, for $i = 1, \ldots, 10$, remaining within the stability region but approaching U from below. In Figure 2(a), we plot the average sojourn time for different piece selection policies as a function of $1/(U-\lambda)$. We observe that, as λ approaches U, the sojourn time under the RN policy at the seed increases considerably, with the exception of the RN-RF case, *i.e.*, when peers use RF. In all four cases for which the seed uses RF, the sojourn time remains practically constant as λ approaches U. This is consistent with the fact that, by meta-stability, when the seed uses RF the system size remains small most of the time even if $\lambda > U$; as such, there is no sharp increase in the sojourn time as λ approaches U from below.

We next study how the sojourn time scales with the number of swarms L. In Figure 2(b), we plot the average sojourn time vs L for the case where each swarm comprises peers requesting a k-piece file, for $k \in \{10, 30, 60\}$. The total number of pieces is $K = kL$. Across all values of k, the average sojourn time increases linearly as L increases. Similarly, the sojourn time also increases proportionally to k. Thus, the increased stability offered by bundling swarms together comes at the cost of increased delays; we address this in the next section by showing that delays can be suppressed for a wide range values of L by using a *hybrid* approach, alternating between universal and autonomous mode.

7.4   Stable, Low Sojourn Universal Swarms

Our simulations suggest that, in a meta-stable swarm, there are two important system sizes: the *operating* size n_{op}, which is the size around which the system stays most of the time, and the *critical size* n_0, which is the size of a one-club that, once attained, leads the system to instability. If the two sizes are sufficiently far apart from each other, the system will exhibit meta-stability: when $N \approx n_{op}$, it will take a long time for N to reach n_0, from which the missing piece syndrome manifests.

Calculating exactly n_{op} and n_0 is quite challenging, and is beyond the scope of this paper. Nevertheless, in Appendix C, we derive some simple estimates of n_{op} and n_0 when (a) the system comprises of a single swarm, (b) $\lambda > U$, and (c) both the seed and peers use RF. In particular, we show that in such a single swarm system:

$$n_{op} \approx \frac{\lambda K}{\mu}, \text{ and } n_0 \approx \frac{\lambda(K-1)}{\mu}[\frac{1}{2}\frac{U(K-1)}{\lambda - U} - 1]. \quad (1)$$

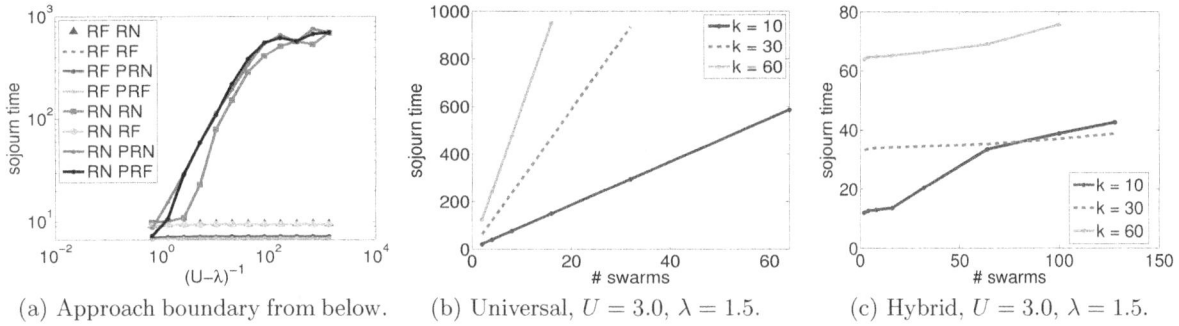

| (a) Approach boundary from below. | (b) Universal, $U = 3.0$, $\lambda = 1.5$. | (c) Hybrid, $U = 3.0$, $\lambda = 1.5$. |

Figure 2: Average sojourn time for universal swarms.

Using these two estimates, we propose a *hybrid system* that attains the increased stability region of the universal swarm, while also ensuring that the sojourn times remain small for a wide range values of L. The hybrid system alternates between the autonomous mode, whereby swarms operate in isolation while sharing a U/L portion of the seed's capacity, and the universal mode, where swarms are bundled together. In particular, consider a system with L swarms, each requesting a file of $k = K/L$ pieces. The system alternates between the two modes according to the following rules: (a) If in autonomous mode, the system switches to universal mode if any single swarm has size $\geq n_{op} + \max(n_0, 2n_{op})$; (b) if in universal mode, the system switches to autonomous mode if each piece requested by a swarm is held by at least $\max(n_{op}/10, 1)$ peers within the swarm. Values n_{op}, n_0 are computed by (1), assuming an upload rate U/L and a number of pieces k. Intuitively, the universal mode is applied when there is strong evidence that the missing piece syndrome is manifesting, as the swarm size becomes greater than $n_{op} + n_0$. The system reverts to an autonomous mode when there is enough diversity in each swarm—each piece is held by at least the one tenth of the peer population.

The hybrid system switches to the universal mode when the system size becomes large, so it exibits the increased stability region of universal swarms described in Theorem 2. Figure 2(c) shows the sojourn time of a hybrid system as L increases. In contrast to Figure 2(b), for $k = 30$ and $k = 60$, the sojourn time stays close to the value attained when $L = 1$ (~33 and ~64 time units, respectively). For $k = 10$, the sojourn time starts increasing linearly after $L = 12$.

These improved sojourn times appear precisely because of the meta-stability. Indeed, swarms operate fine most of the time without the intervention of other swarms, and this is why they experience the same delay as if $L = 1$. As $U/L < \lambda$, the autonomous mode is unstable; however, at the few (and rare) occasions when the missing piece syndrome manifests, bundling swarms together ensures the system quickly stabilizes and reverts to its operating size.

The knee observed for $k = 10$ suggests that this behavior cannot be sustained for arbitrarily large L. Equation (1) can help us give an approximate answer to how large L can be. Indeed, for the system to be meta-stable, the critical one-club size must be significantly larger than the operating size. Requiring that $n_0 > 2n_{op}$, so that the missing piece syndrome rarely manifests, and taking $K/(K-1) \approx 1$, gives the following heuristic for metastability when L=1: $K\frac{U}{\lambda - U} > 6$.

Considering now $L > 1$ swarms in autonomous mode, each requesting $k = K/L$ pieces. Each swarm gets a U/L upload rate in autonomous mode. Then, the above condition becomes $L < \frac{U}{6(\lambda - \frac{U}{L})}k \approx \frac{U}{6\lambda}k$. In other words, the hybrid system can support a number of swarms L with small delay so long as L is of the order of k, the number of pieces in each swarm. As the number of pieces in a file typically numbers in the thousands, this implies that the above system can sustain low sojourn times for a large number of swarms.

8. CONCLUSION

In this paper, we formally characterized the stability region of universal swarms. Our simulations reveal an interesting relationship between stability and piece selection policies. Though piece selection policies may share the same stability region they can differ in their ability to resist the missing piece syndrome. This intuition helps us design a hybrid system that achieves simultaneously a large stability region and low sojourn times; establishing its properties analytically, and investigating other hybrid designs, remains an open question.

9. ACKNOWLEDGMENTS

This work was supported by the National Science Foundation under Grant NSF CCF 10-16959, and was partially funded by the European Commission under the FIRE SCAMPI (FP7- IST-258414) project.

10. REFERENCES

[1] F. Foster. On the stochastic matrices associated with certain queuing processes. *The Annals of Mathematical Statistics*, 24(3):355–360, 1953.

[2] B. Hajek. An exploration of random processes for engineers. December 20, 2011.

[3] B. Hajek and J. Zhu. The missing piece syndrome in peer-to-peer communication. *Stochastic Systems*, 1(2):246–273, 2011.

[4] J. Han, T. Chung, S. Kim, T. T. Kwon, H.-c. Kim, and Y. Choi. How prevalent is content bundling in bittorrent. In *ACM SIGMETRICS*, 2011.

[5] L. Massoulié and M. Vojnović. Coupon replication systems. In *ACM SIGMETRICS*, 2005.

[6] D. S. Menasche, A. A. Rocha, B. Li, D. Towsley, and A. Venkataramani. Content availability and bundling in swarming systems. In *ACM CoNEXT*, 2009.

[7] I. Norros and H. Reitu. On the stability of two-chunk file sharing systems. *Queueing Systems*, 3, 2011.

[8] B. Oğuz, V. Anantharam, and I. Norros. Stable, distributed p2p protocols based on random peer sampling. In *IEEE Allerton*, pages 915–919, 2012.

[9] D. Wu, Y. Liu, and K. W. Ross. Queuing network models for multi-channel P2P live streaming systems. In *IEEE INFOCOM*, 2009.

[10] X. Zhou, S. Ioannidis, and L. Massoulié. On the stability and optimality of universal swarms. In *ACM SIGMETRICS*, 2011.

[11] J. Zhu and B. Hajek. Stability of a peer-to-peer communication system. *IEEE Transactions on Information Theory*, 2012.

APPENDIX

A. PROOF OF Theorem 2(i)

If $K = |\mathcal{F}| = 1$, Theorem 2 follows because $\mathbf{n}$ is an $M/M/1$ queue, with arrival rate $\lambda_{\mathcal{F}}$ and service rate U.

Assume that $K \geq 2$ and that, w.l.o.g., $\lambda_1 := \sum_{C:1\in C} \lambda_C > U$. Notice that $\mathbf{n}$ is irreducible; as such, to show it is transient, it suffices to show that there exists a transient state [2, Proposition 6.3.5]. We show that the initial state where many peers are missing piece one is a transient state: starting from this state, the number of peers converges to infinity with a positive probability. Transience directly implies that the number of peers converges to infinity with probability one, as (a) there is a finite number of states where the number of peers is bounded by a constant, and (b) the probability for $\mathbf{n}$ to stay in any finite set is zero. To construct a transient initial state, we assume:

ASSUMPTION 2. *Select positive values* $\epsilon, \xi, \rho, \epsilon_o, B, N_o$ *so that*

$$3\epsilon < \lambda_1 - U, \xi < 0.5, \epsilon > 4K\xi U, \quad (2)$$

$$\rho := 2\xi(K-1) < 0.5, \epsilon_o < \xi(\lambda_1 - U - 3\epsilon), \quad (3)$$

$$e^{\lambda_{total}[2(K-1)/\mu+1]} 2^{-B} \leq 0.1(1 - 2^{-\epsilon_o}), \quad (4)$$

$$64K^2 \xi U \leq 0.2B(\epsilon - 4K\xi U), \quad (5)$$

$$\lambda_{total} \leq 0.2B\epsilon, U \leq 0.2B\epsilon, \quad (6)$$

$$N_o > 6B, B + 1 < \xi(N_o - 3B - 1). \quad (7)$$

We partition the set of peers in two classes: *one-club peers*, which are the peers having all pieces in $\mathcal{F} \setminus \{1\}$, and *young peers*, which are peers missing at least one piece from $\mathcal{F}\setminus\{1\}$. We also refer to peers holding piece 1 as *infected peers*; note that infected peers are necessarily young.

DEFINITION 8. *Define the following random processes:*

- A_t : *cumulative number of arrivals of peers wanting to download piece one, up to time t*
- N_t : *number of peers at time t*
- Y_t : *number of young peers at time t*
- D_t : *cumulative number of uploads of piece one by infected peers, up to time t*
- Z_t : *cumulative number of uploads of piece one by the seed, up to time t*

We construct the following initial state:

ASSUMPTION 3. *At $t = 0$, $N = N_o$ and all N peers are one-club peers.*

Let τ be the extended stopping time defined by $\tau = \min\{t \geq 0 : Y_t \geq \xi N_t\}$, with the usual convention that $\tau = \infty$ if $Y_t < \xi N_t$ for all t.

LEMMA 2. *Under Assumption 2 and Assumption 3,*

$$P\{A_t > -B + (\lambda_1 - \epsilon)t \text{ for all } t \in [0, \tau)\} \geq 0.9, \quad (8)$$

$$P\{Z_t < B + (U + \epsilon)t \text{ for all } t \in [0, \tau)\} \geq 0.9, \quad (9)$$

$$P\{Y_t < B + \epsilon_o t \text{ for all } t \in [0, \tau)\} \geq 0.9, \quad (10)$$

$$P\{D_t < B + \epsilon t \text{ for all } t \in [0, \tau)\} \geq 0.9. \quad (11)$$

The proof of Lemma 2 is given after this section. Lemma 2 implies Lemma 3, thereby Theorem 2(i) follows because the state in Assumption 3 is a transient state.

LEMMA 3. $P\{\tau = \infty \text{ and } \lim_{t\to\infty} N_t = +\infty\} \geq 0.6$

PROOF. let $\mathscr{Z}$ be the intersection of the four events on the left sides of (8)-(11). We have $P(\mathscr{Z}) \geq 0.6$. Note that $N_0+A_t-D_t-Z_t$ is no larger than the number of peers wanting to download piece one at t. So, on $\mathscr{Z}$,

$$N_t \geq N_0 + A_t - D_t - Z_t > N_0 - 3B + (\lambda_1 - U - 3\epsilon)t$$

for all $t \in [0, \tau)$. We claim that τ cannot be finite on $\mathscr{Z}$. Otherwise, at time τ,

$$\xi \leq \frac{Y_\tau}{N_\tau} < \frac{B + 1 + \epsilon_o\tau}{N_0 - 3B - 1 + (\lambda_1 - U - 3\epsilon)\tau}$$

$$\leq \max\left\{\frac{B+1}{N_0 - 3B - 1}, \frac{\epsilon_o}{\lambda_1 - U - 3\epsilon}\right\} < \xi,$$

a contradiction. Thus, on $\mathscr{Z}$ we have $\tau = \infty$. So $N_t \to \infty$, and $\forall t$, $Y_t/N_t < \xi$. Thus, $\mathscr{Z}$ is a subset of the event on the left side of Lemma 3, and so Lemma 3 follows. □

A.1 Proof of Lemma 2

Define an alternative process to be a process the same as the original process $\mathbf{n}$, but it terminates at time $\tau = \min\{t \geq 0 : Y_t \geq \xi N_t\}$. It is sufficient to prove for the alternative process. In the alternative process, A is a Poisson process with rate λ_1, and Z is stochastically dominated by a Poisson process with rate U. Thus, both (8) and (9) follow from (6) and the consequence of Kingman's moment bound below.

PROPOSITION 1 (COROLLARY 6.1 IN [3]). *Let C be a compound Poisson process with $C_0 = 0$, with jump times given by a Poisson process of rate α, and jump sizes having mean m_1 and mean square value m_2. Then for all $B > 0$ and $\epsilon > \alpha m_1$, $P\{C_t < B + \epsilon t \text{ for all } t\} \geq 1 - \frac{\alpha m_2}{2B(\epsilon - \alpha m_1)}$.*

The inequality (10) follows from (4), Lemmas 4 and 5:

LEMMA 4 (LEMMA 6.2 IN [3]). *Let M denote the number of customers in an $M/GI/\infty$ queue, with arrival rate λ and mean service time m. Suppose that $M_0 = 0, B, \epsilon > 0$, then $P(M_t \leq B + \epsilon t \text{ for all } t) \geq 1 - \frac{e^{\lambda(m+1)}2^{-B}}{1 - 2^{-\epsilon}}$.*

LEMMA 5. *The process Y is stochastically dominated by the number of customers in one $M/GI/\infty$ queue initially empty, arrival rate λ_{total}, and service times $\sim Gamma(K - 1, 2/\mu)$.*

PROOF. We construct one $M/GI/\infty$ queue on the same probability space as the alternative system, so that $Y_t \leq$ the number of peers in the $M/GI/\infty$ queue. Let the $M/GI/\infty$ queue have the same arrival process as the alternative system—i.e., a Poisson process of rate λ_{total}. As $\xi < 0.5$, for any young peer, the intensity of downloads from the one-club is always greater than or equal to $\mu/2$ for the alternative system. Suppose thus that each young peer has an internal Poisson clock, which ticks at rate $\mu/2$, and is such that whenever the internal clock of a young peer ticks, that young peer downloads a piece from the one-club. We declare that a peer remains in the $M/GI/\infty$ system until its internal clock ticks $K-1$ times. This gives the desired service time distribution, and the service times of different peers in the $M/GI/\infty$ are independent. A young peer may leave the group of young

Table 2: Specification of comparison system

Alternative system	Comparison system
The seed creates infected peers at a rate $\leq \xi U_s$.	The seed creates infected peers at rate ξU_s.
An infected peer creates infected peers at rate $\leq \xi \mu$.	An infected peer creates infected peers at rate $\xi \mu$.
An infected peer uploads piece one to one-club at a rate $\leq \mu$.	An infected peer uploads piece one to one-club at rate μ.
Any infected peer needs at most $K-1$ additional pieces, at rate $\geq \mu/2$.	A new infected peer must get $K-1$ additional pieces, at rate $\mu/2$.

peers (depart or join the one-club) sooner than it leaves the $M/GI/\infty$ system, because a young peer in the alternative system can possibly download pieces at times when its internal clock doesn't tick. But if a peer is still a young peer in the alternative system, it is in the $M/GI/\infty$ system. $\square$

To prove (11), consider the stochastic system described in Table 2, which we call the *comparison system*. It should be clear to the reader that both the alternative system and the comparison system can be constructed on the same underlying probability space; in particular, such a construction can be done so that any infected peer in the alternative system at a given time is also in the comparison system. To enforce this, when a peer becomes infected in the alternative system, we require that (a) it also arrives to the comparison system, (b) it discards all pieces it may have downloaded before becoming infected, and (c) it subsequently ignores all opportunities to download except those occurring at the times its internal Poisson clock with ticking rate $\mu/2$ ticks. Because infected young peers may stay longer in the comparison system than in the alternative system, some of the peers in the comparison system correspond to peers that already departed from the alternative system. There can also be some infected peers in the comparison system that never existed in the alternative system because the higher arrival rate of infected peers in the comparison system.

In all cases, any infected peer in the alternative system is also in the comparison system. That is, any of the following events occurring in the alternative system also occurs in the comparison system: (a) the seed creates an infected peer, (b) an infected peer creates an infected peer, and (c) an infected peer replicates piece one to a one-club peer. Events of types (b) and (c) correspond to the two possible ways that infected peers can upload piece one. Therefore, this property implies the Lemma 6, where $\widehat{D}$ is the cumulative number of uploads of piece one by infected peers, up to time t, in the comparison system.

LEMMA 6. *The process $(D_t : t \geq 0)$ is stochastically dominated by $(\widehat{D}_t : t \geq 0)$.*

LEMMA 7. *$(\widehat{D}_t : t \geq 0)$ can be stochastically dominated by a compound Poisson process $(\widetilde{D}_t : t \geq 0)$, with arrival rate of batches $= \xi U$, and first and second moments of batch sizes bounded by $4K$ and $64K^2$, respectively*

PROOF. Identify two kinds of infected peers in the comparison system–the *root peers*, which are those created by the seed, and the infected peers created by other infected

peers. Assume each root peer signs uniquely on its piece one received from the seed, and the signature is inherited by all copies of piece one replicated from the root peer. Partition the uploads of piece one according to their signatures. Let $(\widetilde{D}_t : t \geq 0)$ denote a new process which results when all of the uploads of piece one signed by a root peer (in the comparison system) are counted at the arrival time of the root peer. Since $\widetilde{D}$ counts the same events as $\widehat{D}$, but does so earlier, $\widehat{D}_t \leq \widetilde{D}_t$ for all $t \geq 0$. It is sufficient to prove (11) with D replaced by $\widetilde{D}$.

The random process $\widetilde{D}$ is a compound Poisson process. Jumps occur at the arrival times of root peers, which form a Poisson process of rate ξU. Let J be the size of the jump of $\widetilde{D}$ associated with a typical root peer. Then $J = J_1 + J_2$, where (a) J_1 is the number of infected peers holding piece one signed by the root peer, not counting the root peer itself, and (b) J_2 is the number of uploads of piece one to the one club by the root peer and these J_1 peers. Consider one $M/GI/1$ queueing system with arrival rate $\xi \mu$ and service times following the distribution of a random variable $\widetilde{X} \sim Gamma(K-1, 2/\mu)$. Then the sum of all the times that the root peer and these J_1 peers are in the comparison system is the same as the duration, L, of a busy period of the $M/GI/1$ queue. And J_1 has the same distribution as the number of customers in a busy period of the $M/GI/1$ queue, not counting the customer who started the busy period. Note that ρ in (3) is the load factor for the $M/GI/1$ queue: $\rho = \xi \mu E[\widetilde{X}]$. Apply results on busy periods of $M/GI/1$ queueing system (see [3, Lemma 6.3]) and Assumption 2, follow a similar argument as in [3, Page 259], we have $E[J] = \frac{1+\mu E[\widetilde{X}]}{1-\rho} - 1 \leq 4K$, and $E[J^2] \leq 2\{E[J_1^2] + E[J_2^2]\} \leq 64K^2$. Lemma 7 follows. $\square$

Hence, (11) with D replaced by $\widetilde{D}$ follows from Proposition 1 and (5). Lemma 2 therefore follows.

B. PROOF OF LYAPUNOV FUNCTION VALIDITY

We show here that W in Definition 7 is a valid Lyapunov function. Define:

DEFINITION 9. $M_\phi := 3d + \frac{1}{\beta}$. Note $M_\phi > \max_x \phi(x)$ and $M_\phi > \min\{x : \phi(x) = 0\} + d > 1$.

DEFINITION 10. *Define $D_{\langle C, S \rangle}$ to be the transition rate for type $\langle C, S \rangle$ peers to download pieces.*
Define $D_S := \sum_{C:C \in \mathcal{C}, C \not\subseteq S} D_{\langle C, S \rangle}$.
Define $D_{total} := \sum_{S:S \subseteq \mathcal{F}} D_S$.
Note that $D_{\langle C, S \rangle}, D_S, D_{total}$ are functions of the state $\mathbf{n}$.

The following two lemmas obviously hold:

LEMMA 8. *Function ϕ verifies $\phi'(x) = -1$ for $0 \leq x \leq 2d$ and $\phi'(x) = 0$ for $x \geq 2d + 1/\beta$. And ϕ' increases linearly from -1 to 0 in $[2d, 2d + 1/\beta]$. $\forall x \geq 0, \phi'(x) \in [-1, 0]$.*

LEMMA 9. *$D_S \leq U + \mu \min\{n_S, n - n_S\}$, $D_{total} \leq U + n\mu$, $D_S \geq (U + H_S \mu) n_S / n$.*

In the proof, we consider the following two classes of states, where σ is to be selected within $\sigma \in (0, 1/2)$. The classes overlap and their union includes every non-zero state:

DEFINITION 11. *Class I is the set of states* $\mathbf{n}$ *such that there exists* $S \subsetneq \mathcal{F}$, *and* $n_S/n > 1 - \sigma$; *Class II is the set of states* $\mathbf{n}$ *such that there exist* $C_1, C_2 \subsetneq \mathcal{F}$, *so that,* $n_{C_1}/n > \sigma/2^K$ *and* $n_{C_2}/n > \sigma/2^K$.

For a specific σ, a state $\mathbf{n}$ can either be Class I or Class II, or both. The main idea of the proof is to show that W is a valid Lyapunov function for an appropriate choice of (r, d, β, σ). The given parameters of the network, $\lambda_C(C \in \mathcal{C}), U$ and μ, are treated as constants. Functions on the state space may or may not depend on the variables r, d, β and σ. It is convenient to adopt the big theta notation $\Theta(\cdot)$, with the understanding that it is uniform in these variables; this is summarized in the following definitions.

DEFINITION 12. *Given functions* f *and* g *on the state space* $\mathcal{D}$, *we say* $f = \Theta(g)$ *if there exist* $k_1, k_2, n_0 > 0$, *not dependent on* (r, d, β, σ), *such that* $k_1|g(\mathbf{n})| \leq |f(\mathbf{n})| \leq k_2|g(\mathbf{n})|$ *for all* $\mathbf{n}$ *such that* $n > n_0$.

For example, $2 = \Theta(1)$, $\lambda_{total} n = \Theta(n)$, $d = \Theta(d)$, $1 \leq \Theta(n)$ and $\Theta(n) - \Theta(n)/2 = \Theta(n)$. Notice that d and $\Theta(1)$ cannot be compared. Similarly, we adopt notions of "small enough" and "large enough" that are uniform in (r, d, β, σ):

DEFINITION 13. *We say that "condition* A *is true if* $x > 0$ *is small enough" if there exists a constant* $k > 0$, *not depending on* (r, d, β, σ), *such that* A *is true for any* $x \in (0, k)$. *Similarly, we say that "condition* A *is true if* $x > 0$ *is large enough" if there exists a constant* $k > 0$, *not depending on* (r, d, β, σ), *such that* A *is true for any* $x \in (k, \infty)$.

We identify an approximation to the drift of W. Notice that the infinitesimal generator Q is linear, so that $Q(W) = \sum_C r^{|C|}Q(T_C)$, with $Q(T_C) = \frac{1}{2}Q(E_C^2) + \alpha Q(E_C \phi(H_C))$.

DEFINITION 14. *Define* QW, *an approximation of* $Q(W)$, *as* $QW := \sum_C r^{|C|}QT_C$, *with*
$QT_C := E_C Q(E_C) + \alpha E_C Q(\phi(H_C))$ *if* $|C| \leq K - 2$,
$QT_C := E_C Q(E_C)$ *if* $|C| = K - 1$.

Our proof relies on Lemmas 10 to 13, which are conditioned on (r, d, β, σ), to bound terms in $Q(W)$ and QW. The proofs of these lemmas are provided after this section.

LEMMA 10. *Bound for the approximation error:*
$$|Q(W) - QW| \leq M_\phi(D_{total} + 1)\Theta(1). \qquad (12)$$

LEMMA 11. *If* d *is large enough,* $\forall C \subsetneq \mathcal{F}$, $Q(E_C) \leq \Theta(1)$, $Q(\phi(H_C)) \leq M_\phi \Theta(1)$, *and* $QT_C \leq M_\phi \Theta(E_C) \leq M_\phi \Theta(n)$.

LEMMA 12. *If* d *is large enough,* $\sigma M_\phi, \beta$ *are small enough, for any* $S \subsetneq \mathcal{F}$ *and any nonzero state* $\mathbf{n}$ *such that* $n_S/n > 1 - \sigma$, $QT_S \leq -\frac{1}{2}\Delta E_S$.

Lemmas 11 and 12 imply Lemma 13:

LEMMA 13. *If* d *is large enough,* $\beta, rM_\phi, \sigma M_\phi r^{-K}$ *are small enough, (a) on Class I,* $QW \leq -r^K\Theta(n)$; *(b) on Class II,* $QW \leq -r^K\sigma^3\Theta(n^2) + M_\phi\Theta(n)$.

Notice that the conditions of Lemmas 10 to 13 are consistent with each other, so we claim

LEMMA 14. *There exists* (r, d, β, σ) *satisfying all conditions of Lemmas 10 to 13, such that* W *is a valid Lyapunov function.*

PROOF. On Class I, $D_{total} = D_S + \sum_{C:C \neq S} D_C \leq 2U + 2(n - n_S)\mu \leq 2U + 2\sigma n\mu = \Theta(1) + 2\sigma\Theta(n)$ by Lemma 9. So Lemma 10 implies that on Class I, $|Q(W) - QW| \leq \sigma M_\phi \Theta(n) + M_\phi \Theta(1)$. Combined with Lemma 13(a), on Class I, $Q(W) \leq -r^K\Theta(n) + M_\phi\Theta(1)$ if $\sigma M_\phi r^{-K}$ is small enough. On Class II, $D_{total} \leq U + n\mu = \Theta(n)$, so Lemma 10 implies that $|Q(W) - QW| \leq M_\phi\Theta(n)$. On Class II, Combined with Lemma 13(b), $Q(W) \leq -r^K\sigma^3\Theta(n^2) + M_\phi\Theta(n)$. Thus, if (r, d, β, σ) satisfies conditions of Lemmas 10 to 13, and $\sigma M_\phi r^{-K}$ is small enough, $\exists \varsigma > 0$ such that $Q(W) \leq -\varsigma n$ whenever n is larger than some constant. Thus W is a Lyapunov function. $\square$

We provide proofs for Lemmas 10 to 13 below. Additional definitions are applied:

DEFINITION 15. *Define* Γ_{J_1, J_2} *for* $J_1, J_2 \in \mathcal{T}, J_1 \neq J_2$ *to be the transition rate for type* J_1 *peers to become type* J_2 *peers.*
Define $\Gamma_{\mathcal{X}_1, \mathcal{X}_2} := \sum_{J_1:J_1 \in \mathcal{X}_1} \sum_{J_2:J_2 \in \mathcal{X}_1} \Gamma_{J_1, J_2}$, *where* $\mathcal{X}_1 \cap \mathcal{X}_2 = \emptyset$.
Define $D_{\mathcal{H}_S} := \sum_{J:J \in \mathcal{H}_S} D_J$, *for* $\mathcal{H}_S$ *in Definition 5.*
Define $A_{\mathcal{H}_S}$ *to be the total transition rate for peers to join the group of peers with types in* $\mathcal{H}_S$.
Let $\mathcal{P}_S := \{\langle C, S \rangle : C \nsubseteq S, C \in \mathcal{C}\}$ *be the set of types of peers holding piece set* S.
Notice that Γ, D, A *are all functions of* $\mathbf{n}$.

B.1 Proof of Lemma 10

We compare $Q(W)$ and QW term by term. Consider terms $Q(T_C)$ and QT_C. First, assume $|C| \leq K - 2$. Because α is fixed, we have $|Q(T_C) - QT_C| \leq a_1 + \alpha(a_2 + a_3)$,

$$a_1 = \left| \frac{1}{2}Q(E_C^2) - E_C Q(E_C) \right| \leq \lambda_{total} + D_{total},$$

$$a_2 = |Q(E_C\phi(H_C)) - Q(E_C)\phi(H_C) - E_C Q(\phi(H_C))|,$$

$$a_3 = |Q(E_C)\phi(H_C)| \leq M_\phi(\lambda_{total} + D_{total}).$$

The only way E_C and $\phi(H_C)$ can simultaneously change is that some peer with type in $\mathcal{E}_C$ becomes a peer with type in $\mathcal{H}_C$, causing E_C to decrease by one, and $\phi(H_C)$ to decrease by at most one, so $a_2 \leq \Gamma_{\mathcal{E}_C, \mathcal{H}_C}$. Notice the fact that $\Gamma_{\mathcal{E}_C, \mathcal{H}_C} \leq D_{total}$, we have $\forall |C| \leq K - 2$, $|Q(T_C) - QT_C| \leq M_\phi(D_{total} + 1)\Theta(1)$. Secondly, assume $|C| = K - 1$. Then, $|Q(T_C) - QT_C| = a_1 \leq \lambda_{total} + D_{total} \leq M_\phi(D_{total} + 1)\Theta(1)$. There are only finitely many terms of T_C in W (2^K in total), and notice that $r < 1$, Lemma 10 follows. $\square$

B.2 Proof of Lemma 11

The upper bound for the drift of E_C is obvious: $Q(E_C) \leq \lambda_{total} = \Theta(1)$. Next consider $Q(\phi(H_C))$. Because ϕ is a decreasing function, only the rate for H_C to decrease contributes to the positive part in the drift of $\phi(H_C)$, so to consider an upper bound of $Q(\phi(H_C))$ it suffices to consider the rates of transitions which reduce H_C. There is only one way for H_C to decrease: peers with types in $\mathcal{H}_C$ to download a novel piece – with aggregate rate $D_{\mathcal{H}_C}$. Each peer with type in $\mathcal{H}_C$ downloading a novel piece can cause $\phi(H_C)$ to increase at most one. Thus, an upper bound for the drift of $\phi(H_C)$ is $Q(\phi(H_C)) \leq D_{\mathcal{H}_C} \leq U + H_C\mu = \Theta(1) + H_C\Theta(1)$.

We can choose d large enough, i.e. $d > 1$, so $M_\phi > 2d + 1/\beta + 1$. Thus $Q(\phi(H_C))$ vanishes when $H_C > M_\phi$, because $\phi(H_C)$ vanishes when $H_C > 2d + 1/\beta$ and the decreasing of H_C when state changes is bounded by $1 < d$. Hence $Q(\phi(H_C)) \leq M_\phi\Theta(1)$, because $M_\phi > 1$.

Finally, the bound on QT_C follows from the other two bounds already proved. □

B.3 Proof of Lemma 12

Assume that $n_S/n > 1 - \sigma$, where $0 < \sigma < \frac{1}{4}$ is to be specified. We consider two cases. Suppose first $|S| = K - 1$. Peers with cache S only miss one piece $i \in \mathcal{F} \setminus S$, and $QT_S = E_S Q(E_S) \le E_S \left[\sum_{C : i \in C} \lambda_C - U(1 - \sigma) \right] \le -\frac{1}{2}\Delta E_S$, if σ is set to be small enough: $\sigma < \Delta/(2U)$. Lemma 12 follows.

Suppose now that $|S| \le K - 2$, then by [11, Lemma 19],

$$
\begin{aligned}
Q(\phi(H_S)) &\le \phi'(H_S)Q(H_S) + \beta/2(A_{\mathcal{H}_S} + D_{\mathcal{H}_S}) \\
&= \phi'(H_S)(A_{\mathcal{H}_S} - D_{\mathcal{H}_S}) + \beta/2(A_{\mathcal{H}_S} + D_{\mathcal{H}_S}).
\end{aligned}
$$

Substitute the above inequality into $Q(E_S) + \alpha Q(\phi(H_S))$, which is one component in Definition 14, apply Lemma 9,

$$Q(E_S) + \alpha Q(\phi(H_S)) \le \bar{\varsigma} - \varpi, \text{ where} \tag{13}$$

$$
\begin{cases}
\bar{\varsigma} := \lambda_{total} - \frac{1}{2}D_S + \alpha\phi'(H_S)A_{\mathcal{H}_S} \\
\varpi := \frac{1}{2}D_S + \alpha\phi'(H_S)D_{\mathcal{H}_S} - \alpha\beta/2(A_{\mathcal{H}_S} + D_{\mathcal{H}_S})
\end{cases}
$$

We claim first that $\bar{\varsigma} \le -\Delta/2$. To prove, suppose first that $H_S < d$: Then, $\phi'(H_S) = -1$ and because the seed applies RN, $A_{\mathcal{H}_S} \ge \Gamma_{\mathcal{P}_S, \mathcal{H}_S} \ge U(1-\sigma)/K \ge U/(4K)$. So $\bar{\varsigma} \le \lambda_{total} - \alpha U/(4K) \le -\Delta/2$. Suppose secondly that $H_S \ge d$: Then, $D_S \ge d\mu(1 - \sigma) \ge \frac{1}{2}d\mu$. So $\bar{\varsigma} \le \lambda_{total} - \frac{1}{2}d\mu \le -\frac{1}{2}\Delta$, for d large enough: $d > 2(\lambda_{total} + \Delta/2)/\mu$.

We further claim that $\varpi \ge 0$. To prove, let ω_S be the number of peers holding pieces not in S. For $\sigma < \frac{1}{2}$, we have

$$D_S \ge (U + \omega_S \mu)(1 - \sigma) \ge \frac{1}{2}(U + \omega_S \mu). \tag{14}$$

Notice that pieces novel to peers with types in $\mathcal{H}_S$ are not contained in S. The number of peers that can upload pieces to peers with types in $\mathcal{H}_S$ is no larger than ω_S, so

$$D_{\mathcal{H}_S} \le (U + \omega_S \mu)\sigma \le 2\sigma D_S. \tag{15}$$

In addition, $A_{\mathcal{H}_S} = \Gamma_{\mathcal{P}_S, \mathcal{H}_S} + \Gamma_{I_S, \mathcal{H}_S}$, where $I_S := \{\langle C', S' \rangle : |S'| = |S|, S' \ne S\}$. The number of peers with types in I_S is no larger than ω_S. Therefore $\Gamma_{I_S, \mathcal{H}_S} \le U + \omega_S \mu \le 2D_S$ by (14). And notice $\Gamma_{\mathcal{P}_S, \mathcal{H}_S} \le D_S$, we have $A_{\mathcal{H}_S} \le 3D_S$. Combine it with Lemma 9, and (15), we have $\varpi \ge \frac{1}{2}D_S - 2\alpha D_{\mathcal{H}_S} - \frac{\alpha\beta}{2}A_{\mathcal{H}_S} \ge (\frac{1}{2} - 4\alpha\sigma - \frac{3}{2}\alpha\beta)D_S$. We can set $4\alpha\sigma < \frac{1}{4}, \frac{3}{2}\alpha\beta < \frac{1}{4}$ so that $\varpi \ge 0$ follows.

Therefore, $\bar{\varsigma} \le -\frac{1}{2}\Delta$ and $\varpi \ge 0$ imply that, when $n_S/n > 1 - \sigma$ and $|S| \le K - 2$, $QT_S = [Q(E_S) + \alpha Q(\phi(H_S))]E_S \le -\frac{1}{2}\Delta E_S$ and Lemma 12 follows. □

B.4 Proof of Lemma 13

First, consider Lemma 13(a). Since there are only finitely many types, we can fix a set $S \subsetneq \mathcal{F}$ and consider the set of Class I states $\mathbf{n}$ for which $n_S/n > 1 - \sigma$. Since $\sigma \in (0, \frac{1}{2})$, $E_S > \frac{1}{2}n$. By Definition 3, $\triangle > 0$. By Lemma 12,

$$QT_S \le -\frac{1}{4}\triangle n = -\Theta(n). \tag{16}$$

Consider two conditions: (a) for type C with $|C| > |S|$, E_C may be larger than E_S. Lemma 11 and (16) imply $r^{|C|}QT_C \le rM_\phi r^{|S|}\Theta(n) < 2^{-K-1}r^{|S|}|QT_S|$, if rM_ϕ is selected to be small enough; (b) for type C with $|C| \le |S|$ but $C \ne S$, $E_C \le \sigma n$. Note that $r^{|C|}r^K \le r^{|S|}$, Lemma 11 and (16) imply $r^{|C|}QT_C \le r^{|C|}M_\phi\Theta(E_C) \le \sigma M_\phi r^{-K}r^{|S|}\Theta(n) < 2^{-K-1}r^{|S|}|QT_S|$, if $\sigma M_\phi r^{-K}$ is selected to be small enough.

Notice that $E_S \ge n/2$, apply Lemma 12, we have $QW = r^{|S|}QT_S + \sum_{C : C \ne S} r^{|C|}QT_C \le r^{|S|}QT_S + \frac{1}{2}r^{|S|}|QT_S| \le -\frac{1}{8}r^{|S|}\triangle n \le -r^K\Theta(n)$, which proves Lemma 13(a).

Second, consider Lemma 13(b). Suppose $C_1 \not\subseteq C_2$ and consider the set of Class II states $\mathbf{n}$ such that $n_{C_1}/n > \eta, n_{C_2}/n > \eta$, where $\eta = \sigma/2^K$. In such states: $D_{C_2} \ge n_{C_2}n_{C_1}\mu/n \ge \mu\eta^2 n \in \sigma^2\Theta(n)$. Notice that $E_{C_2} \ge n_{C_2} \ge \eta n$, we have $E_{C_2}Q(E_{C_2}) \le E_{C_2}(\lambda_{\varepsilon_{C_2}} - D_{C_2}) \le -\sigma^3\Theta(n^2) + \Theta(n)$. Lemma 11 indicates $E_{C_2}Q(\phi(H_{C_2})) \le M_\phi\Theta(n)$, so

$$QT_{C_2} = E_{C_2}Q(E_{C_2}) + \alpha E_{C_2}Q(\phi(H_{C_2})) \le -\sigma^3\Theta(n^2) + M_\phi\Theta(n).$$

Obviously the above inequality works for the case $|C_2| = K - 1$ where the ϕ term does not exist too. Apply the above inequalities and the result $\forall C$, $QT_C \le M_\phi\Theta(n)$ from Lemma 11, we claim that, over the set of all Class II states, $QW \le r^{|C_2|}QT_{C_2} + \sum_{C : C \ne C_2} QT_C \le -r^K\sigma^3\Theta(n^2) + M_\phi\Theta(n)$, which proves Lemma 13(b).

C. OPERATING AND CRITICAL SIZE

Consider a single swarm, where peers arrive with rate λ and wish to download K pieces. Assume that the seed has upload rate $U < \lambda$, so that the system is unstable, and peers have upload rate μ. When the system is in the operating state, we expect that the diversity of pieces is high enough, so that every contact a peer makes leads to a piece download. Under this assumption, as a peer wishes to download K pieces, the expected sojourn time is K/μ. By Little's law, as the arrival rate is λ, an approximation of the operating size is therefore $n_{\text{op}} \approx \frac{\lambda K}{\mu}$.

Estimating the critical size of a one-club requires a more involved argument. Suppose that a one-club with size B has formed. For B large, peers outside the one club download pieces from the one club at a rate close to μ. As such, the expected time it takes a new peer to be converted to a one club peer is approximately $(K - 1)/\mu$; hence, the number of *young peers*, *i.e.*, peers outside the one-club, is approximately $\lambda(K - 1)/\mu$. Young peers can become *infected*, *i.e.*, obtain the piece the one-club peers are missing. As the seed uses the RF policy, the rate with which the seed infects young peers is $U\frac{\lambda(K-1)/\mu}{B+\lambda(K-1)/\mu}$. Ignoring the fact that young peers may also infect other young peers, and assuming that an infection occurs at an instant sampled uniformly at random within a young peer's lifetime, each infected peer stays for $(K - 1)/2\mu$ time units before it departs, in expectation. Then, the drift of the one club is roughly $\Delta B = \lambda - U - U\frac{\lambda(K-1)/\mu}{B+\lambda(K-1)/\mu}\frac{(K-1)}{2\mu}\mu$. Requiring the drift to be zero and solving for B, we obtain (1).

269

Early-Deciding Consensus is Expensive

Danny Dolev
Hebrew University of Jerusalem
Edmond Safra Campus
91904 Jerusalem, Israel
dolev@cs.huji.ac.il

Christoph Lenzen
Massachusetts Institute of Technology
32 Vassar Street
02139 Cambridge, USA
clenzen@csail.mit.edu

ABSTRACT

In consensus, the n nodes of a distributed system seek to take a consistent decision on some output, despite up to t of them *crashing* or even failing maliciously, i.e., behaving *"Byzantine"*. It is known that it is impossible to guarantee that synchronous, deterministic algorithms consistently decide on an output in fewer than $f + 1$ rounds in executions in which the *actual number of faults* is $f \le t$. This even holds if faults are crash-only, and in this case the bound can be matched precisely. However, the question of whether this can be done efficiently, i.e., with little communication, so far has not been addressed.

In this work, we show that algorithms tolerating Byzantine faults and deciding within $f + 2$ rounds must send $\Omega(nt + t^2 f)$ messages; as a byproduct, our analysis shows that decision within $f+1$ rounds is impossible in this setting (unless $f = t$). Moreover, we prove that any crash-resilient algorithm deciding in $f + 1$ rounds has worst-case message complexity $\Omega(n^2 f)$. Interestingly, this changes drastically if we restrict the fault model further. If crashes are *orderly*, i.e., in each round, each node picks an order in which its messages are sent, and crashing nodes successfully transmit a prefix of their sequence, deciding in $f + 1$ rounds can be guaranteed with $\mathcal{O}(nt)$ messages.

Categories and Subject Descriptors

C.4 [**Computer Systems Organization**]: Performance Of Systems—*Fault-Tolerance*; F.2.2 [**Analysis of Algorithms and Problem Complexity**]: Nonnumerical Algorithms and Problems

General Terms

Algorithms, Reliability, Theory

Keywords

lower bounds; cubic message complexity; Byzantine faults; crash faults; early-stopping

1. INTRODUCTION & RELATED WORK

In consensus, each node of a distributed system has an input value, and all nodes that do not fail need to decide on the same output value. To make this output meaningful, it is required that the output must be input of at least one node.[1] This easily stated task is very fundamental, as it captures the essence of exploiting redundancy to establish resilience to faults of (some of) the components of a system.

Consequently, consensus has been studied very deeply and extensively in the last three decades. There are scores of lower bounds on many aspects of the problem in a variety of models. In the current paper, we come back to the question of *early-deciding* and study its message complexity. Informally, an algorithm is early-deciding if, in each execution, it minimizes the number of rounds until all nodes have decided depending on the number of *actual* faults f, as opposed to t, the maximal number of faults it can tolerate, or the number of nodes n. This property is highly desirable, as in most scenarios it is reasonable to assume that most of the executions will experience few or no faults. It is closely related to the concept of *early-stopping* algorithms, where the requirement is to not only decide on the output, but also stop sending messages. Roughly speaking, early decision and termination go hand in hand; to the best of our knowledge, in all published early-deciding algorithms, after taking a decision nodes can stop communicating once they have shared their decision value with all other nodes, i.e., at most one round after taking a decision.

The question of early decision so far has not been considered for randomized algorithms. With randomization and/or asynchrony involved (and the resulting variety of adversarial models) the current understanding of both time and message complexity is much poorer than in the synchronous, deterministic case. For this reason, we consider synchronous, deterministic algorithms only, for which at the least one parameter—the time complexity—has been analyzed in great detail and precision. The basic time lower bound in this setting states that $\min(f + 2, t + 1)$ rounds are required for termination, even if we consider crash faults only [7, 8]; showing that $f + 1$ rounds are required for decision (in the worst case) follows from standard bivalency arguments in virtually any reasonable fault model [11]. A message complexity lower bound of $\Omega(nt)$ has been known for long [6]. The question whether stopping early is more

---

[1]The precise requirement depends on the considered model. The common theme is that pre-existing agreement must be maintained; in particular, the trivial algorithm always returning a default value is not a feasible solution.

costly in terms of communication was not considered up to the present date.

Contribution

In the current paper, we show a lower bound of $\Omega(t^2 f)$ on the number of messages sent, in the worst case, by any protocol that decides within $f + 2$ rounds and tolerates up to t Byzantine faults. Doing so, we also see that in the case of Byzantine faults, decision before round $f + 2$ is not always possible. Moreover, we establish a lower bound of $\Omega(n^2 f)$ on the worst-case message complexity of crash-resilient algorithms that decide within $f + 1$ rounds. In other words, there are executions in which, essentially, in each round all pairs of operational nodes need to exchange messages. In contrast, we provide a simple algorithm that decides in $f + 1$ rounds (and stops in $f + 2$) using $\mathcal{O}(nt)$ messages, provided that crashes are *orderly*. A crash is orderly if the crashing node succeeds in sending exactly the messages in some prefix of a priority list; this list is chosen by the algorithm.

Related Work

The message complexity of achieving consensus (without the constraint of deciding or stopping early) was studied extensively, with many efforts in matching and circumventing the known lower bounds. Reischuk looked at improving the efficiency by looking at average complexity [25]. Perry and Toueg [23] focused on marching the number of rounds in weaker fault models. This approach was later followed by Parvedy and Raynal [21] as well.

Fitzi and Martin [12] skirted the message complexity lower bound of $\Omega(nt)$ by introducing a small probability of error. King and Saia [16, 17] used randomization to simultaneously beat the time and message complexity lower bounds that hold for deterministic algorithms, with "practical and scalable protocols". Many sublinear-time randomized algorithms have been published before, but all of them are much more costly in terms of communication; we make no attempt to cover the related work on randomized algorithms here.

Researchers looked at the difference between early-decision and early-stopping mainly in the context of *uniform* consensus. In uniform consensus, the decision value needs to be the same for *all* nodes that decide, even those that fail after deciding. Keidar and Rajsbaum [15] proved a slightly stronger lower bound for crash-resilient algorithms for uniform consensus: deterministic protocols cannot always *decide* before round $\min\{f + 2, t\}$. We show essentially the same bound, but for Byzantine-tolerant algorithms without requiring uniformity. Charron-Bost and Schiper [2] proved that this bound does not hold for crash-tolerant consensus algorithms, where it is possible to decide by the end of round $f + 1$. Michel Raynal [24] presents a thorough study of early-deciding algorithms in a crash-fault model.

Matching the round complexity lower bound of $\min\{f + 2, t + 1\}$ for the general case of Byzantine faults was solved by Berman et al. [1].[2] *Omission* faults, where besides crashing nodes may also fail to send (or receive) messages non-faulty nodes would send (or receive), but continue executing the algorithm afterwards, strictly contain crash faults. Hence, in particular all lower bounds for crash faults apply. Parvedy and Raynal [21] give an algorithm for uniform consensus

that matches the decision and stopping time lower bounds of $\min\{f + 2, t + 1\}$. The algorithm has message complexity $\mathcal{O}(n^2 f)$, but its optimality is not immediate since our lower bound for crash faults requires decision in $f + 1$ rounds. We conjecture, however, that it is straightforward to adapt the techniques we introduce to establish a matching lower bound for uniform consensus.

Finally, the communication costs of early-deciding and early-terminating algorithms must be contrasted against the ones of algorithms that sacrifice these properties or incur suboptimal bounds in exchange for a smaller number of sent messages. Coan and Welch [4, 5] considered the special case of $n = 3t + 1$, achieving asymptotically optimal $\mathcal{O}(t^2)$ communicated bits. Hadzilacos and Halpern devised algorithms that ensure optimality of fault-free runs [14], for an entire spectrum of fault models. Dwork and Moses [9] and later Mizrahi and Moses [19, 20] considered continuous agreement, where one can exploit that over time faulty processes may be identified and ignored. Lately, Liang and Vaidya attained asymptotically optimal bit complexity for very long output (or a sequence of outputs) [18]; Patra [22] leverages randomization to obtain the same bound in a constant expected number of rounds. None of these algorithms are early-deciding or -stopping, in the sense that they may run for at least $t + 1$ rounds even if there are few faults. In contrast, Galil et al. [13] manage to achieve a strong combination of early-decision and message complexity: they present a crash-resilient algorithm that solves consensus in $\mathcal{O}((f + 1)8^{1/\epsilon})$ rounds with $\mathcal{O}(n + fn^\epsilon)$ messages, for arbitrary $\epsilon > 0$. Slightly better bounds are known if the requirement of early-stopping is dropped altogether: In $\mathcal{O}(t)$ rounds, consensus can be solved with up to $t \in n - \Omega(n)$ crash faults using $\mathcal{O}(n \log^2 t)$ messages [3]. The authors of [1] claim that a nearly round-optimal and Byzantine tolerant solution exists that is also asymptotically bit (and thus message) optimal, i.e., sends $\mathcal{O}(nt)$ bits.[3]

2. MODEL AND PROBLEM

We are given a fully connected system of n nodes, up to t of which may become faulty. In each synchronous round $1, 2, \ldots$, each node (i) performs deterministic local computations, (ii) sends (possibly different) messages to (a subset of) the other nodes, and (iii) receives the messages sent to it by other nodes. Since we are concerned with a worst-case lower bound on the number of messages sent by non-faulty nodes, we assume that nodes have unique identifiers $V = \{1, \ldots, n\}$, the recipient of a message can identify the source of a message (i.e., messages are authenticated), and we put no bound on the size of messages or the amount of local computations performed. Clearly, the derived lower bound then extends to any weaker system model. An algorithm can thus be interpreted as a collection of functions that, for each round $r \in \mathbb{N}$, maps the input of each node v and the history $H_v(r)$ of messages it received up to and including round $r - 1$ (including the information who sent which message) to (i) the messages it sends in round r and (ii) whether it decides on an output o_v. We do permit v to send messages also after deciding on o_v, but v may decide on an output only once, i.e., such a decision is final.

An *execution* $\mathcal{E}$ of a *binary consensus Algorithm* $\mathcal{A}$ is specified by (i) the input values $b_v^{\mathcal{E}} \in \{0, 1\}$, (ii) the sets of faulty

[2]The extended abstract contains a proof sketch; no full version is available.

[3]No proof of this result has been published.

nodes $F_1^{\mathcal{E}} \subseteq F_2^{\mathcal{E}} \subseteq \ldots$ in each round, where $|F_r^{\mathcal{E}}| \leq t \in \mathbb{N}$ for all rounds $r \in \mathbb{N}$, and (iii) the messages sent by faulty nodes in $F_r^{\mathcal{E}}$ to non-faulty nodes in $V \setminus F_r^{\mathcal{E}}$ in each round r. The faulty nodes may send arbitrary messages, whereas the messages sent by non-faulty nodes as well as when they decide on what output are determined by the algorithm. By $f^{\mathcal{E}} := \max_{r \in \mathbb{N}}\{|F_r|\} \leq t$ we denote the number of (actual) faults in execution $\mathcal{E}$. For ease of notation, we may omit the superscript $\mathcal{E}$ denoting the execution whenever it is clear from the context. We remark that considering the nodes in the sets F_r non-faulty until they actually fail merely serves to facilitate intuition; the same asymptotic lower bound on the number of messages sent by non-faulty nodes follows from our arguments if we consider the set $\bigcup_{r \in \mathbb{N}} F_r$ faulty for the entire execution. We may also talk of an r-round execution, which is the restriction of an execution to its first r rounds, and extensions, which add further rounds to a given execution.

We say that an execution $\mathcal{E}$ is indistinguishable at node v from an execution $\mathcal{E}'$ (before round $r+1$), if $b_v^{\mathcal{E}} = b_v^{\mathcal{E}'}$ and $H_v^{\mathcal{E}}(r') = H_v^{\mathcal{E}'}(r')$ for all $r' \in \mathbb{N}$ (for $r' = r$). Note that since the actions of node v until round r and the messages it sends in round $r+1$ are a function of b_v and $H_v(r)$ only, v will behave identically in $\mathcal{E}$ and $\mathcal{E}'$ until receiving messages in round $r+1$ of these executions if they are indistinguishable before round $r+1$.

For $\mathcal{A}$ to be a correct binary consensus algorithm, it must satisfy the following properties in all feasible executions $\mathcal{E}$.

Termination: Nodes v that remain non-faulty eventually output some $o_v \in \{0,1\}$.

Agreement: There is a value o such that $o_v = o$ for all non-faulty nodes v.

Validity: There is some node $v \in V$ so that $b_v = o$.

3. BYZANTINE FAULTS

As deterministic consensus is impossible if $n \leq 3t$ and faults are arbitrary (i.e., Byzantine), we assume that $n > 3t$ throughout this section. In the introduction we discussed that for all deterministic binary consensus algorithms and all $0 \leq f < t$, there are executions so that a non-faulty node stops sending messages in a round $r \geq f+2$ [7, 8]. This bound can be matched for any $t < n/3$, i.e., there is an early-stopping algorithm that guarantees that all non-faulty nodes stop by round $\min\{f+2, t+1\}$ [1]. We consider a weaker constraint in that we require that nodes decide quickly, but may continue to send messages in support of the yet undecided nodes.

DEFINITION 3.1 (EARLY-DECIDING AND -STOPPING). *A consensus algorithm is d-deciding if in each execution $\mathcal{E}$ of the algorithm with $f^{\mathcal{E}} = f$, each node $v \in V \setminus F_{d(f)}$ has decided in some round $r_v \leq d(f)$. It is called d-stopping, if it is d-deciding and non-faulty nodes do not send messages in rounds $r > d(f)$ of executions with f faults.*

As a byproduct of our analysis, we will show that also early-deciding algorithms must run for at least $f+2$ rounds for all nodes to decide on the output, for any $0 \leq f < t$. Our main result in this section, however, is the following lower bound on the number of messages sent by deterministic early-deciding consensus algorithms.

THEOREM 3.2. *For any $(f+2)$-deciding binary consensus algorithm and any $1 \leq f \leq t/2$, there is an execution $\mathcal{E}$ of the algorithm in which $f^{\mathcal{E}} = f$ and non-faulty nodes send at least $t^2 f / 44$ messages.*

In the remainder of this section we will prove Theorem 3.2. Let us start with an outline of the key ideas of the proof.

PROOF OUTLINE FOR THEOREM 3.2. Clearly, as possibly $t \in \Theta(n)$ and in any round $\mathcal{O}(n^2)$ messages are exchanged, we must construct executions that have $\Omega(f)$ rounds. In fact, it will be vital that in each round exactly one node fails, as this guarantees that if no further faults happen after round r, all nodes must decide by the end of round $r+2$. Similar to the classic lower bound [7, 8] of $f+2$ on the round complexity of deterministic consensus algorithms, we will achieve this by failing, in each round, a "pivotal" node that is decisive for whether the execution would result in output 0 or output 1, so that some of the nodes perceive an execution that would end up in output 0 and others one that would produce output 1 (without further faults and for a certain behavior of the faulty nodes).

However, the simple proof of existence of such nodes from [7, 8] is insufficient for our purposes, as we also need to make sure that in each round $\Omega(t^2)$ messages are sent. To this end, we leverage the argument from [6] yielding the well-known lower bound of $\Omega(t^2)$ on the message complexity of consensus algorithms. Essentially, we argue that not only $\Omega(t^2)$ messages need to be exchanged to achieve consensus, but (i) this has to happen in round $r+1$ if we fail no node in rounds r and $r+1$ (as the algorithm needs to verify the decision it must take by the end of round $r+1$), and (ii) this can be exploited to do the "pivoting" such that indeed also in the modified execution with more faults many messages are sent in round $r+1$. While in general it can not be guaranteed that many messages must be sent right away, $(f+1)$-deciding algorithms are forced to act quickly, as in each round r, each node must be able to prove that at least $r-1$ faults occurred or decide by the end of the round. This enables to repeat the argument inductively to show that indeed $\Omega(t^2)$ messages must be sent in each of f rounds of some execution with $f \leq t/2$ faults. Bounding $f \leq t/2$ here ensures that still potentially $\Omega(t)$ additional nodes may fail, which makes it expensive (in terms of messages) for the algorithm to, if necessary, prove to all nodes that there have been further faults. □

We need to capture the properties we require from executions in order to follow the approach outlined above. We call the node v_r that is "pivotal" in round r critical, since failing it can delay the decision process further. The definition is phrased such that v_r must act as the arbiter that suggests an output of the execution and therefore determines the output provided faulty nodes do not interfere further. For an $(f+1)$-deciding algorithm, this must happen exactly in round r, since round $r+1$ must be used to check whether v_r failed in round r and suggested different outputs to different subsets of nodes.

DEFINITION 3.3 (CRITICAL EXECUTIONS). *For $r \in \mathbb{N}$, a pair of executions $\mathcal{E}_0, \mathcal{E}_1$ of a binary consensus algorithm $\mathcal{A}$ is called r-critical if there is a critical node v_r such that the following properties are satisfied:*

send \ receive	F_r	W	$V \setminus (W \cup F_r)$
F_r	(faulty)	as in $\mathcal{E}_0^{(r)}$	as in $\mathcal{E}_1^{(r)}$
W	as in $\mathcal{E}_0^{(r)}$ and $\mathcal{E}_1^{(r)}$		
$V \setminus (W \cup F_r)$			

(a) Messages sent in round r of execution $\mathcal{E}(W)$.

send \ receive	F_r	W	$V \setminus (W \cup F_r)$
F_r	(faulty)	as in $\mathcal{E}_0^{(r)}$	as in $\mathcal{E}_1^{(r)}$
W	as in $\mathcal{E}_0^{(r)}$		
$V \setminus (W \cup F_r)$	as in $\mathcal{E}_1^{(r)}$		

(b) Messages sent in round $r + 1$ of execution $\mathcal{E}(W)$.

Figure 1: Rounds r and $r + 1$ of execution $\mathcal{E}(W)$. Nodes in $V \setminus F_r$ cannot distinguish $\mathcal{E}_0^{(r)}$, $\mathcal{E}_1^{(r)}$, and $\mathcal{E}(W)$ before round r and therefore send the same messages in round r of all three executions. If $W' = W \cup \{v_{r+1}\}$, the only non-faulty node that can distinguish $\mathcal{E}(W)$ and $\mathcal{E}(W')$ in round r is v_{r+1}, and only through its messages in round $r + 1$ other non-faulty nodes can distinguish these executions in round $r + 1$.

- v_r is non-faulty in both executions,

- the restrictions of $\mathcal{E}_0$ and $\mathcal{E}_1$ to the first $r - 1$ rounds differ only at $v_r \in V$,

- in round r, all pairs of nodes not involving v_r exchange the same messages in both executions,

- no nodes fail in round $r' \geq r$ of either execution,

- nodes in $F_{r-1}^{\mathcal{E}_0} = F_{r-1}^{\mathcal{E}_1}$ do not send messages in rounds $r' > r$,

- there are $r - 1$ faulty nodes in both executions,

- in $\mathcal{E}_0$ non-faulty nodes will output 0, and

- in $\mathcal{E}_1$ non-faulty nodes will output 1.

We are going to show that for such executions, an $(f + 1)$-deciding algorithm is forced to exchange many messages in round $r + 1$, as otherwise some nodes would have to decide on an output without being certain that there are no other nodes taking the opposite decision in some execution. At the same time, we will be able to fail the critical node in a way that maintains that many messages are sent, yet keeps the output of the execution uncertain.

The construction proceeds inductively. The induction anchor is given by the well-known fact that for any (binary) consensus algorithm, there is a way to assign the inputs such that flipping just one of them will change the output of the algorithm [10].

LEMMA 3.4. Let $\mathcal{A}$ be any binary consensus algorithm. Then there is a critical pair of 1-round executions of $\mathcal{A}$.

PROOF. A 1-round execution is fully specified by the set of non-faulty nodes and their inputs, plus the messages sent by faulty nodes in round 1. For each input assignment $B : V \to \{0, 1\}$ define $o(B)$ as the output in the unique execution without faults. By the validity property, $o(v \mapsto 0) = 0$ and $o(v \mapsto 1) = 1$. Hence there must be some inputs B and B' that differ only at a single node v_1, such that $o(B) = 0$ and $o(B') = 1$. Trivially, the corresponding pair of executions is indistinguishable before round 1 at all nodes except v_1, as $H_v(1)$ is, by definition, empty for all nodes $v \in V$ and $B(v) = B'(v)$ for all $V \setminus \{v_1\}$. By designating v_1 as the critical node, the definition of a critical pair is thus met by the two executions defined by B and B' (where we set $F_0 := \emptyset$ for both executions). $\square$

In the following, we fix an $(f + 1)$-deciding binary consensus algorithm $\mathcal{A}$ and denote by $\mathcal{E}_0^{(1)}$, $\mathcal{E}_1^{(1)}$ a critical pair of 1-round executions of $\mathcal{A}$. The hypothesis of the induction we want to perform is that, for some $r \in \{1, \ldots, f\}$ with $f \leq t/2$, a critical pair $\mathcal{E}_0^{(r)}$, $\mathcal{E}_1^{(r)}$ of r-round executions of $\mathcal{A}$ exists satisfying that $\Omega(t^2(r - 1))$ messages are sent by the non-faulty nodes in both executions. To complete the induction, it thus suffices to construct a critical pair of $(r + 1)$-round executions $\mathcal{E}_0^{(r+1)}$, $\mathcal{E}_1^{(r+1)}$ and show that in round $r + 1$ of these executions, $\Omega(t^2)$ messages are sent by non-faulty nodes.

The construction itself is fairly straightforward; the harder part will be to show the lower bound on the number of sent messages. We first show that we indeed can construct critical pairs of $(r + 1)$-round executions from critical pairs of r-round executions.

LEMMA 3.5. Suppose for $1 \leq r \leq t$ we are given an r-critical pair of executions $\mathcal{E}_0^{(r)}$, $\mathcal{E}_1^{(r)}$. Then an $(r + 1)$-critical pair of executions exists.

PROOF. The proof is similar in spirit to the reasoning for Lemma 3.4, where the messages sent by the critical node v_r of $\mathcal{E}_0^{(r)}$, $\mathcal{E}_1^{(r)}$ in round r take the role of the "inputs". Denote for each node $v \in V \setminus \{v_r\}$ by $m_0^{(r')}(v)$ and $m_1^{(r')}(v)$ the messages v_r sends to v in round $r' \in \mathbb{N}$ of $\mathcal{E}_0^{(r)}$ and $\mathcal{E}_1^{(r)}$, respectively.

Recall that $F_{r-1}^{\mathcal{E}_0^{(r)}} = F_{r-1}^{\mathcal{E}_1^{(r)}}$ for critical pairs; thus we may simply write F_{r-1}, F_r, etc. in the following. We set $F_r := F_{r-1} \cup \{v_r\}$, which is feasible since $|F_{r-1}| = r - 1 < t$. For any set $W \subseteq V \setminus F_r$, define $\mathcal{E}(W)$ as follows. Take an r-round execution that all non-faulty nodes can distinguish from neither $\mathcal{E}_0^{(r)}$ nor $\mathcal{E}_1^{(r)}$ except by the message v_r sends to them in round r (such an execution exists by the definition of r-critical pairs). We rule that this message is $m_0^{(r)}(v)$ in case $v \in W$ and $m_1^{(r)}(v)$ if $v \in V \setminus (F_r \cup W)$ (see Figure 1a). Likewise, in round $r + 1$ (see Figure 1b) it will send $m_0^{(r+1)}(v)$ respectively $m_1^{(r+1)}(v)$ to v;[4] it does not send any messages in rounds $r' > r + 1$. Other faulty nodes do not send messages in rounds $r' > r$. Observe that this fully specifies the messages sent from faulty nodes to non-faulty nodes; as non-faulty nodes follow the deterministic algorithm $\mathcal{A}$, we

---

[4]This ensures that it does not give away to non-faulty nodes in W (resp. $V \setminus (W \cup F_r)$) that the execution is different from $\mathcal{E}_0^{(r)}$ (resp. $\mathcal{E}_1^{(r)}$).

send \ receive	$F_r \cup S$	$V \setminus (F_r \cup S \cup \{v,w\})$	v	w
$F_r \cup S$	(faulty)		as in $\mathcal{E}_0^{(r)}$	as in $\mathcal{E}_1^{(r)}$
$V \setminus (F_r \cup S \cup \{v,w\})$		(irrelevant)	none	
v			(as in $\mathcal{E}_0^{(r)}$ and $\mathcal{E}_1^{(r)}$)	
w				

Figure 2: Round $r+1$ of the contradictive execution constructed in Lemma 3.7, which is indistinguishable from $\mathcal{E}_0^{(r)}$ and $\mathcal{E}_1^{(r)}$ before round $r+1$. If too few messages are sent in $\mathcal{E}_0^{(r)}$ and $\mathcal{E}_1^{(r)}$ in round $r+1$, we can find a small set S that might fail, permitting to construct the shown execution.

thus obtain $\mathcal{E}(W)$ as the unique extension of the r-round execution we started with in which no further nodes become faulty and faulty nodes send the messages we just specified.

Observe that, by construction, $\mathcal{E}(V \setminus F_r)$ and $\mathcal{E}(\emptyset)$ cannot be distinguished from $\mathcal{E}_0^{(r)}$ and $\mathcal{E}_1^{(r)}$, respectively, by non-faulty nodes before round $r+2$. Hence, non-faulty nodes must decide by the end of round $r+1$ in these executions since $|F_{r-1}| = r-1$ and $\mathcal{A}$ is $(f+1)$-deciding. Since the output value of $\mathcal{E}_0^{(r)}$ is 0, the same must hold true for $\mathcal{E}(V \setminus F_r)$; analogously, $\mathcal{E}(\emptyset)$ outputs 1. Consequently, there must be some $W \subset V \setminus F_r$ and $v_{r+1} \in V \setminus (W \cup F_r)$ such that $\mathcal{E}(W)$ and $\mathcal{E}(W \cup \{v_{r+1}\})$ have outputs 1 and 0, respectively. In both executions the set of faulty nodes is F_r, there are no new faults in rounds $r' \geq r+1$, and, since v_r is faulty, the only non-faulty node that can distinguish between the two executions in round r (or earlier) is v_{r+1}. Therefore, all non-faulty nodes except v_{r+1} send the same messages in round $r+1$ of both executions. The same is true for faulty nodes, with the exception of the message from v_r to v_{r+1}: all faulty nodes except v_r do not send messages, and we defined the executions such that v_r behaves identical in round $r+1$ towards all nodes but v_{r+1}. Finally, no faulty node sends any messages in rounds $r' > r+1$. Note that in the $(r+1)$-critical pair, v_{r+1} is (still) non-faulty. Overall, $\mathcal{E}(W \cup \{v_{r+1}\})$ and $\mathcal{E}(W)$ are an $(r+1)$-critical pair with critical node v_{r+1}, completing the proof. $\square$

An observation that can be derived immediately is that the time complexity lower bound of $\min\{f+2, t+1\}$ rounds also applies to $(f+1)$-deciding algorithms. This is stronger than the result from [7, 8] which only applies if nodes must also stop sending messages when deciding, but also requires more restrictive assumptions, as [7, 8] holds for crash faults (cf. Definition 4.1). This is of particular interest as with crash faults it is possible to achieve that all nodes decide within $f+1$ rounds [24].

THEOREM 3.6. *For any consensus protocol and any f, $0 \leq f \leq t-1$, there are executions where some non-faulty node decides in or after round $f+2$.*

PROOF. By inductive application of Lemma 3.5, anchored by Lemma 3.4, we obtain an $(f+1)$-critical pair of executions $\mathcal{E}_0^{(f+1)}$, $\mathcal{E}_1^{(f+1)}$. In both executions, the same set F_f of $f < t$ nodes fails. As in Lemma 3.5, failing v_{f+1} (in round $f+1$) permits to create an execution $\mathcal{E}(W)$ (for some $\emptyset \neq W \subset V \setminus (F_f \cup \{v_{f+1}\})$) that is indistinguishable before round $f+2$ from $\mathcal{E}_0^{(f+1)}$ by nodes in W and from $\mathcal{E}_1^{(f+1)}$ by nodes in $V \setminus (W \cup F_f \cup \{v_{f+1}\})$. Hence, assuming that both in $\mathcal{E}_0^{(f+1)}$

and $\mathcal{E}_1^{(f+1)}$ all non-faulty nodes decide in or before round $f+1$, the same would be true for $\mathcal{E}(W)$. However, nodes in $W \neq \emptyset$ would decide 0 (as in $\mathcal{E}_0^{(f+1)}$) and nodes in $V \setminus (W \cup F_f \cup \{v_{f+1}\}) \neq \emptyset$ would decide 1 (as in $\mathcal{E}_1^{(f+1)}$), violating the agreement property. Hence, in one of the executions $\mathcal{E}_0^{(f+1)}$ and $\mathcal{E}_1^{(f+1)}$, which both have f faults, there must be a non-faulty node that decides in round $f+2$ or later. $\square$

Note that a similar result was proven by Keidar and Rajsbaum [15] and Charron-Bost and Schiper [2] for uniform consensus.

The construction from Lemma 3.5 leaves some flexibility. Depending on the algorithm, there might be many choices of W and v_{r+1}. Our task is now to identify one that ensures a large number of messages exchanged. Our argument will proceed in two steps. First we will show that many messages are sent in round $r+1$ of at least one of the executions $\mathcal{E}_0^{(r)}$ and $\mathcal{E}_1^{(r)}$. Then we will use this information to identify a set W_0 of size $\lceil t/2 \rceil$ that sends many messages (say, in $\mathcal{E}_0^{(r)}$ and thus also $\mathcal{E}(V \setminus F_r)$) and show that $\mathcal{E}(W_0)$ cannot have output 0. A critical pair then can be obtained as in the proof of Lemma 3.5 by inductively adding nodes to W_0, since $\mathcal{E}(V \setminus F_r)$ outputs 0. The lower bound on the number of sent messages then follows since the nodes in W_0 must send the same messages in round $r+1$ as they do in $\mathcal{E}_0^{(r)}$, since they cannot distinguish these executions before round $r+2$.

The next lemma deals with showing that many messages are sent in $\mathcal{E}_0^{(r)}$ or $\mathcal{E}_1^{(r)}$.

LEMMA 3.7. *Suppose we are given a pair of r-critical executions $\mathcal{E}_0^{(r)}$, $\mathcal{E}_1^{(r)}$ for some $1 \leq r \leq t/2$. Then in at least one of the two executions, at least $nt/22$ messages are sent by non-faulty nodes in round $r+1$.*

PROOF. We use the notation from Lemma 3.5. Recall that whether some non-faulty node sends a message to some other node in round $r+1$ of execution $\mathcal{E}(W)$ for any $W \subseteq V \setminus F_r$ solely depends on the message it receives from node v_r in round r of $\mathcal{E}(W)$ (or the fact that it does not receive one). Hence, node $v \in V \setminus F_r$ behaves identically as in $\mathcal{E}_0^{(r)}$ (if $v \in W$) or in $\mathcal{E}_1^{(r)}$ (if $v \in V \setminus (W \cup F_r)$).

Assume for contradiction that fewer than $nt/11 < n^2/33$ messages are sent in total in both executions by non-faulty nodes. Since there are at least $|V \setminus F_r| \cdot (|V \setminus F_r| - 1)/2 > 2n^2/9$ pairs of non-faulty nodes, for more than $2n^2/9 - n^2/33 > 2n^2/11$ such pairs $\{v,w\}$ it holds that v and w exchange messages in neither $\mathcal{E}_0^{(r)}$ nor $\mathcal{E}_1^{(r)}$. Hence, they do not exchange messages in $\mathcal{E}(W)$ either, irrespectively of the

send \ receive	F_r	W_0	v	$V \setminus (F_r \cup W_0 \cup \{v\})$
F_r	(faulty)		as in $\mathcal{E}(W_0)$ and $\mathcal{E}_1^{(r)}$	
W_0	as in $\mathcal{E}(W_0)$			
v	as in $\mathcal{E}(W_0)$ and $\mathcal{E}_1^{(r)}$			
$V \setminus (F_r \cup W_0 \cup \{v\})$				

Figure 3: Round $r + 1$ of execution $\mathcal{E}_0$, which is identical to round $r + 1$ of $\mathcal{E}(W_0)$. See Lemma 3.5 and Figure 1 for the definition of $\mathcal{E}(W_0)$.

send \ receive	F_r	W_0	v	$V \setminus (F_r \cup W_0 \cup \{v\})$
F_r	(faulty)		as in $\mathcal{E}(W_0)$ and $\mathcal{E}_1^{(r)}$	
W_0			as in $\mathcal{E}_1^{(r)}$	as in $\mathcal{E}(W_0)$
v	as in $\mathcal{E}(W_0)$ and $\mathcal{E}_1^{(r)}$			
$V \setminus (F_r \cup W_0 \cup \{v\})$				

Figure 4: Round $r + 1$ of execution $\mathcal{E}_1$. Node v cannot distinguish $\mathcal{E}_1$ from $\mathcal{E}_1^{(r)}$ in round $r + 1$. Since $\mathcal{E}_1^{(r)}$ has $r - 1$ faults and outputs 1, v must thus decide on 1 at the end of round $r + 1$ of $\mathcal{E}_1$.

choice of W.

We claim among these pairs there are $v, w \in V \setminus F_r$ which, summed over both nodes and executions, receive at most $t/2$ messages from non-faulty nodes in $\mathcal{E}_0^{(r)}$ nor $\mathcal{E}_1^{(r)}$. Otherwise, summing over all pairs (that do not exchange messages) and both executions, we had at least $n^2 t/11$ received messages, where for each individual execution and node we have counted a message up to $|V \setminus F_r| - 1 < n$ times. This makes for a total of more than $nt/11$ messages, which by assumption is not reached. Consequently, the claim holds and we have a pair $\{v, w\}$ that is non-faulty, does not exchange messages in $\mathcal{E}(W)$, and receives at most $t/2$ messages from non-faulty nodes in $\mathcal{E}(W)$, independently of the specific choice of W.

We fix some W such that $v \in W$ and $w \notin W$. Denote by $S \subset V \setminus F_r$ the set of non-faulty nodes that sends messages to v or w in round $r + 1$ of $\mathcal{E}_0^{(r)}$ or $\mathcal{E}_1^{(r)}$. By the choice of v and w, we have that $|S| \leq t/2$. Since in $\mathcal{E}(W)$ the number of faulty nodes is $r \leq t/2$, we can construct an $(r+1)$-round execution that is identical to $\mathcal{E}(W)$ before round $r+1$, while in round $r+1$ (see Figure 2) all nodes in S fail. Faulty nodes send the same messages as in round $r + 1$ of $\mathcal{E}_0^{(r)}$ to v and the same messages as in round $r + 1$ of $\mathcal{E}_1^{(r)}$ to w (the remaining messages are chosen arbitrarily). By construction, v and w cannot distinguish this execution from $\mathcal{E}_0^{(r)}$ and $\mathcal{E}_1^{(r)}$, respectively, before round $r + 2$. Thus, as in $\mathcal{E}_0^{(r)}$ and $\mathcal{E}_1^{(r)}$ only $r - 1$ nodes fail and the algorithm is $(f + 1)$-deciding, v and w must decide on 0 and 1, respectively. This violates the agreement property, implying that the assumption that fewer than $nt/11$ messages are sent by non-faulty nodes in round $r + 1$ of $\mathcal{E}_0^{(r)}$ and $\mathcal{E}_1^{(r)}$ together must be wrong. We conclude that indeed in one of the executions, at least $nt/22$ messages are sent in round $r + 1$. $\square$

We now move on to the last step in the proof of Theorem 3.2, which consists of showing that in the construction from Lemma 3.5, we can choose a critical pair for which many messages are sent in round $r + 1$.

LEMMA 3.8. *Suppose for $1 \leq r \leq t/2$ we are given an r-critical pair of executions $\mathcal{E}_0^{(r)}, \mathcal{E}_1^{(r)}$. Then an $(r+1)$-critical pair of executions exists where the non-faulty nodes—excluding v_{r+1}—send at least $t^2/44$ messages in round $r+1$ of both executions.*

PROOF. Again, we use the notation from Lemma 3.5. By Lemma 3.7, in round $r + 1$ of at least one of the executions $\mathcal{E}_0^{(r)}$ and $\mathcal{E}_1^{(r)}$, $nt/22$ messages are sent by non-faulty nodes. Suppose w.l.o.g. that this holds for $\mathcal{E}_0^{(r)}$ (the other case is symmetrical). Order the nodes $V \setminus F_r$ in descending order according to the number of messages they send in round $r+1$ of $\mathcal{E}_0^{(r)}$, and label them by $v(1), \ldots, v(n-r)$ according to this order. Clearly, the nodes $v(1), \ldots, v(\lceil t/2 \rceil)$ will together send at least

$$\frac{t/2}{n-r} \cdot \frac{nt}{22} > \frac{t^2}{44} \qquad (1)$$

messages in round $r + 1$ of $\mathcal{E}_0^{(r)}$.

Denote $W_0 := \{v(1), \ldots, v(\lceil t/2 \rceil)\}$. We claim that $\mathcal{E}(W_0)$ has output 1. Assuming otherwise, in $\mathcal{E}(W_0)$ all non-faulty nodes decide 0 by the end of round $r + 2$. We will construct two executions $\mathcal{E}_0$ and $\mathcal{E}_1$ that cannot be distinguished by a node that is non-faulty in both executions, yet have conflicting outputs. Both executions are identical to $\mathcal{E}(W_0)$ before round $r + 1$. In round $r + 1$ of $\mathcal{E}_1$ (see Figure 4), all nodes in W_0 fail, which is feasible since $r \leq t/2$ and $|W_0| = \lceil t/2 \rceil$. In this round of $\mathcal{E}_1$, faulty nodes behave like in $\mathcal{E}(\emptyset)$ towards some fixed non-faulty node $v \in V \setminus (W_0 \cup F_r)$, but like in $\mathcal{E}(W_0)$ towards all remaining nodes. Hence, v cannot distinguish $\mathcal{E}_1$ from $\mathcal{E}(\emptyset)$ (and therefore also not from $\mathcal{E}_1^{(r)}$ with only $r - 1$ faults) before round $r + 2$, and must decide 1 by the end of round $r + 1$. We define round $r + 1$ of $\mathcal{E}_0$ to be identical to round $r + 1$ of $\mathcal{E}(W_0)$ (see Figure 3); in particular, we do not fail any additional nodes in this round of $\mathcal{E}_0$.

Observe that $\mathcal{E}_0$ and $\mathcal{E}_1$ are indistinguishable from each

receive \\ send	F_r	W_0	v	$V \setminus (F_r \cup W_0 \cup \{v\})$
F_r	(faulty)		(faulty)	
W_0		as in $\mathcal{E}(W_0)$		
v	(faulty)		(faulty)	as in $\mathcal{E}_1^{(r)}$
$V \setminus (F_r \cup W_0 \cup \{v\})$				

Figure 5: Round $r+2$ of execution $\mathcal{E}_0$. W_0 cannot distinguish this execution from $\mathcal{E}(W_0)$ in this round. Since $\mathcal{E}(W_0)$ has r faults, nodes in W_0 must thus decide on the same value in $\mathcal{E}_0$ and $\mathcal{E}(W_0)$ by the end of round $r+2$.

receive \\ send	F_r $\quad$ W_0	v	$V \setminus (F_r \cup W_0 \cup \{v\})$
F_r $\quad$ W_0	(faulty) $\quad$ (irrelevant)		as in $\mathcal{E}(W_0)$
v		as in $\mathcal{E}_1^{(r)}$	
$V \setminus (F_r \cup W_0 \cup \{v\})$		as in $\mathcal{E}(W_0)$	

Figure 6: Round $r+2$ of execution $\mathcal{E}_1$. Figures 3–6 show that nodes in $V \setminus (F_r \cup W_0 \cup \{v\})$ cannot distinguish $\mathcal{E}_0$ and $\mathcal{E}_1$ before round $r+3$.

other and from $\mathcal{E}(W_0)$ at all nodes in $V \setminus (W_0 \cup \{v\} \cup F_r)$ before round $r+2$ by construction. Consequently, these nodes send the same messages in round $r+2$ of all three executions. We let the nodes in F_r send no messages in rounds $r' \geq r+2$ of executions $\mathcal{E}_0$ and $\mathcal{E}_1$, just like in $\mathcal{E}(W_0)$. In round $r+2$ of $\mathcal{E}_0$ (see Figure 5), we fail node v, and make it send the same messages as in round $r+2$ of $\mathcal{E}(W_0)$ to the nodes in W_0. In $\mathcal{E}_0$, the (non-faulty) nodes in W_0 will send the same messages as in $\mathcal{E}(W_0)$ in this round as well, since $\mathcal{E}_0$ is identical to $\mathcal{E}(W_0)$ before round $r+2$. Consequently, the nodes in W_0 cannot distinguish $\mathcal{E}_0$ from $\mathcal{E}(W_0)$ (with r faults) before round $r+3$ and must decide 0 by the end of round $r+2$ in $\mathcal{E}_0$. Towards the nodes in $V \setminus (W_0 \cup F_r \cup \{v\})$, v mimics its behavior in round $r+2$ of $\mathcal{E}_1$ (where it is non-faulty and thus computes its messages according to the algorithm). In turn, in round $r+2$ of $\mathcal{E}_1$ (see Figure 6) the nodes in W_0 mimic their behavior in execution $\mathcal{E}_0$. Hence, nodes in $V \setminus (W_0 \cup \{v\} \cup F_r)$ receive the same messages from all other nodes in round $r+2$ of both $\mathcal{E}_0$ and $\mathcal{E}_1$.

In summary, at the end of round $r+2$, we have that (i) in $\mathcal{E}_0$ the non-faulty node v decided 0, (ii) in $\mathcal{E}_1$ the non-faulty nodes in W_0 decided 1, and (iii) no node in $V \setminus (W_0 \cup \{v\} \cup F_r)$ can distinguish between $\mathcal{E}_0$ and $\mathcal{E}_1$ before round $r+3$. Therefore, in order to force an erroneous decision by some non-faulty node (in one of the executions), it is sufficient to extend $\mathcal{E}_0$ and $\mathcal{E}_1$ without further faults so that nodes in $V \setminus (W_0 \cup \{v\} \cup F_r) \neq \emptyset$ cannot distinguish between the two executions. This is done by induction on $r' \geq r+3$, where the hypothesis is that nodes in $V \setminus (W_0 \cup \{v\} \cup F_r)$ cannot distinguish $\mathcal{E}_0$ and $\mathcal{E}_1$ before round r'. The statement holds for $r' = r+3$ by the previous observations. By the hypothesis, nodes in $V \setminus (W_0 \cup \{v\} \cup F_r)$ will send the same messages in round r' of both executions, as is true for F_r which sends no messages. With respect to W_0 and v, recall that these nodes are non-faulty in only one of the two executions. In the execution where they are faulty, we thus rule that they simply send the same messages as their non-faulty counterparts in the respective other execution. It follows that nodes in $V \setminus (W_0 \cup \{v\} \cup F_r)$ receive the same messages in round r' of both executions and thus cannot distinguish between them before round $r'+1$. This concludes the induction.

As non-faulty nodes eventually decide, each node in $V \setminus (W_0 \cup \{v\} \cup F_r)$, which must behave identically in executions $\mathcal{E}_0$ and $\mathcal{E}_1$, will violate the agreement property in at least one of the executions due to (i) and (ii). It follows that the assumption that $\mathcal{E}(W_0)$ outputs 0 must be wrong. From here, we proceed as in Lemma 3.5 by adding nodes to W_0 one by one until we finally end up with an $(r+1)$-critical pair of executions $\mathcal{E}(W \cup \{v_{r+1}\})$, $\mathcal{E}(W)$ satisfying that $W_0 \subseteq W$. Finally, because the nodes in W_0 will send the same messages in round $r+1$ of $\mathcal{E}(W \cup \{v_{r+1}\})$ and $\mathcal{E}(W)$ as in round $r+1$ of $\mathcal{E}(V \setminus F_r)$ and thus also $\mathcal{E}_0^{(r)}$, Inequality (1) shows that the constructed $(r+1)$-critical pair meets the requirements of the lemma. $\square$

Theorem 3.2 now follows by straightforward application of the derived results.

PROOF OF THEOREM 3.2. Fix any $(f+1)$-deciding binary consensus algorithm $\mathcal{A}$. By Lemma 3.4, there is a 1-critical pair of executions of $\mathcal{A}$. We inductively apply Lemma 3.8 $f \leq t/2$ times to obtain an $(f+1)$-critical pair of executions, where in all rounds $2, \ldots, f+1$, at least $t^2/44$ messages are sent by non-faulty nodes; here we make use of the fact that when applying Lemma 3.8, in both executions of the constructed $(r+1)$-critical pair, all non-faulty nodes behave identically in round $r+1$ as they do in the r-critical pair we started from. Since in the constructed executions f nodes fail, we obtain the desired worst-case lower bound of $t^2 f/44$ on the number of messages sent by non-faulty nodes in executions with f faults. $\square$

Taking into account the lower bound from [6], we arrive at the following result.

COROLLARY 3.9. *For any $(f+2)$-deciding consensus algorithm $\mathcal{A}$ that tolerates t faults and each $0 \leq f \leq t$, there are executions of $\mathcal{A}$ in which non-faulty nodes send $\Omega(t^2 f + nt)$ messages.*

4. CRASH FAULTS

In this section, we focus on the following restricted fault model.

DEFINITION 4.1 (CRASH FAULTS).
Node $v \in F_r^{\mathcal{E}} \setminus F_{r-1}^{\mathcal{E}}$ crashes in round r of execution $\mathcal{E}$, if there is a subset $W \setminus V$ of the nodes such that the following holds.

- *In round r, v sends the same message to each $w \in W$ as it would have if it was non-faulty.*

- *In round r, v sends no messages to nodes $w \in V \setminus W$.*

- *In rounds $r' > r$, v sends no messages.*

A consensus algorithm is resilient to t crash faults, *if it satisfies termination, agreement, and validity in all executions with at most t crashing nodes and no other faults.*

Crash faults are much easier to handle and permit $(f+1)$-deciding algorithms [2]. We will show now that $(f+1)$-deciding algorithms essentially require all non-faulty nodes to exchange messages in each round of the algorithm.

LEMMA 4.2. *Let $\mathcal{E}_0^{(r)}$, $\mathcal{E}_1^{(r)}$ be an r-critical pair of executions of an $(f+1)$-deciding algorithm $\mathcal{A}$ resilient to $t > r$ crash faults, where $t \le n - 2$. Then an $(r+1)$-critical pair of executions of $\mathcal{A}$ exists, satisfying that in both executions at least $(n-r-1)^2$ messages are sent in round $r+1$ by the nodes in $V \setminus (F_r \cup \{v_{r+1}\})$.*

PROOF. Set $F_r := F_{r-1} \cup \{v_r\}$. First, we are going to show that non-faulty nodes will have to send a lot of messages in round $r+1$, no matter when exactly v_r crashes. Afterwards it will be simple to construct an $(r+1)$-critical execution in which many messages are sent just as in Lemma 3.5.

Consider the execution $\mathcal{E}_1$ in which v_r crashes before sending any message in round r and no further faults occur. Suppose w.l.o.g. that $\mathcal{E}_1$ outputs 1 (the other case is symmetrical). No further faults happen in $\mathcal{E}_1$, so it is a valid execution as $r < t$. Moreover, all live nodes must decide 1 by the end of round $r + 1$.

For each $v \in V \setminus F_r$, we define an execution $\mathcal{E}_0(v)$ as follows. $\mathcal{E}_0(v)$ is identical to $\mathcal{E}_0^{(r)}$ before round r. In round r, v_r crashes, successfully sending only its message to v. No further faults happen in $\mathcal{E}_0(v)$, thus it is a valid execution. Observe that v cannot distinguish $\mathcal{E}_0(v)$ from $\mathcal{E}_0^{(r)}$, which has $r - 1$ faults, and thus must decide 0 at the end of round r of $\mathcal{E}_0(v)$. No further faults occur in $\mathcal{E}_0(v)$, implying that by the end of round $r + 1$, all live nodes must decide. Since v already decided 0 and does not crash, it follows that the output of all nodes must be 0.

We claim that in all these executions, each non-faulty node sends a message to each other non-faulty node. Assume for the sake of contradiction that there is a pair of nodes $v, w \in V \setminus F_r$ such that v does not send a message to w in $\mathcal{E}_0(v)$ or $\mathcal{E}_1$. We examine first the case where v does not send a message to w in $\mathcal{E}_1$. Consider the execution that is identical to $\mathcal{E}_0(v)$ before round $r + 1$, while in round $r + 1$ node v crashes, sending all its messages except for the one to w; this is feasible since $r + 1 \le t$. Clearly, no node but w can distinguish this execution from $\mathcal{E}_0(v)$ before round $r+2$. Hence, as $t \le n - 2$, it holds that $V \setminus (F_r \cup \{v, w\}) \ne \emptyset$, implying that there is some node that decides 0 by the end of round $r + 1$ of this execution. However, since w does not

receive a message from v, just like in $\mathcal{E}_1$, it must decide 1 by the end of round $r + 1$ of this execution, violating agreement. We conclude that indeed v must send a message to w in $\mathcal{E}_1$. Analogously, if v does not send a message to w in round $r+1$ of $\mathcal{E}_0(v)$, we can make it fail in round $r + 1$ of $\mathcal{E}_1$ to enforce violation of the agreement property.

From here we argue analogously to Lemma 3.5. We consider executions $\mathcal{E}(W)$ that are identical to $\mathcal{E}_0^{(r)}$ and $\mathcal{E}_1$ before round r, where v_r crashes in round r such that node $w \in V \setminus F_r$ receives the message from v_r exactly if $w \in W \subseteq V \setminus F_r$. Starting from the empty set, adding nodes to W one by one will eventually lead to a critical pair, since $\mathcal{E}(\emptyset) = \mathcal{E}_1$ outputs 1 and $\mathcal{E}(V \setminus F_r)$ outputs 0. Because in all these executions, each non-faulty node must send the same messages as in $\mathcal{E}_0^{(r)}$ or $\mathcal{E}_1$, we conclude that at least $|V \setminus F_r|(|V \setminus F_r| - 1) = (n - r)(n - r - 1)$ messages are sent in both executions of the critical pair. Not counting the messages sent by the critical node v_{r+1}, we have at least $(n - r - 1)^2$ messages. □

Applying this lemma inductively, we arrive at the following bound.

THEOREM 4.3. *Let $\mathcal{A}$ be an $(f+1)$-deciding algorithm resilient to $t > 1$ crash faults. Then for each $f < t$ there is an execution of $\mathcal{A}$ with f faults in which $nf(n-f) + f^3/3 - O(nf) \subset \Omega(n^2 f)$ messages are sent.*

PROOF. W.l.o.g. assume that $t \le n - 2$. By Lemma 3.4, there is a 1-critical pair of executions of $\mathcal{A}$ (since this execution has no faults, the lemma applies also to the restricted fault model). We inductively apply Lemma 4.2 f times, resulting in an execution with f faults in which at least

$$
\sum_{i=1}^{f} (n - i - 1)^2
$$
$$
= \frac{(n-2)(n-1)(2n-3)}{6}
$$
$$
- \frac{(n-f-3)(n-f-2)(2(n-f)-5)}{6}
$$
$$
\in \frac{6n^2 f - 6nf^2 + 2f^3 + 6n^2 - O(nf)}{6}
$$
$$
\subseteq nf(n-f) + \frac{f^3}{3} - O(nf)
$$

messages are sent.[5] □

Orderly Crash Faults

Interestingly, there is a straightforward algorithm that is much more efficient if the fault model is constrained further in that nodes may choose the order in which they (attempt to) send messages in a given round.

DEFINITION 4.4 (ORDERLY CRASHES). *Assume that an algorithm $\mathcal{A}$ specifies for each round and node also in which order the node sends its messages to other nodes. Denoting for some round and a crashing node v this sequence by $v_1, \ldots, v_{n-1}$, the crash is* orderly *if the subset W of nodes*

---

[5]Like in the proof of Theorem 3.2, we exploit here that applying Lemma 4.2 will, in round r, change only the behavior of node v_r in comparison to the previous critical pair, and therefore still many messages are sent in round r of the new pair.

receiving messages from v is a prefix of this sequence. An algorithm is resilient to t orderly crashes, *if termination, agreement, and validity hold in any execution where there are at most t faulty nodes, all of which crash orderly.*

It should be noted that the lower bound of $\min\{f+2, t+1\}$ on the number of rounds until all nodes stop applies even if crashes are orderly [26]. In this work it is also shown that $(f+1)$-stopping becomes feasible if one further allows that nodes may send multiple messages to the same recipient in one round, as confirmation messages may be used to prove that all other nodes have received a previously sent batch of messages.

The following variant of the simple (not early-stopping) crash-tolerant algorithm given in [24] that sends $\mathcal{O}(nt)$ messages is $(f+1)$-deciding and resilient to t orderly crashes.

1. If node $i \in V$ receives a message containing value b, it decides b.

2. If node $i \in \{1, \ldots, t+1\}$ does not receive a message before round i, it decides on its input value at the beginning of round i (i.e., before sending messages).

3. If node $\{1, \ldots, t+1\}$ decides on value b at the beginning of round r or at the end of round $r-1$, it sends b to all nodes $i+1, \ldots, n$ (in this order) in round r.

THEOREM 4.5. *The above algorithm is resilient to t orderly crash faults, is $(f+1)$-deciding and $(f+2)$-stopping, and sends at most $(n - t/2 - 1)(t+1) < n(t+1)$ messages.*

PROOF. **Decision and Stopping:** Denote by $i \leq f+1$ the node with smallest ID that does not fail. It will decide on and send some value b to all nodes $i' > i$ at the latest in round $f+1$. Hence all live nodes decide by the end of round $f+1$ and stop by the end of round $f+2$.

Correctness: If node $i \in V$ decides b before round i, it has received b from some other node $i' < i$ that already decided b. If node i decides in round i, it decides on its input and all nodes $i' < i$ must have crashed (otherwise i would have received a message before round i). Thus, there is a unique node i_0 deciding in round i_0 on its input, all nodes $i < i_0$ crash, and all nodes $i > i_0$ decide on the same value as i_0.

Message complexity: Nodes $i \in \{1, \ldots, t+1\}$ send up to $n - i$ messages, while nodes $i \in \{t+2, \ldots, n\}$ never send a message. □

5. OPEN PROBLEMS

We conclude with a brief list of open problems regarding the trade-offs between early decision and message complexity.

- Can we have $(f + \mathcal{O}(1))$-deciding algorithms that have optimal resilience and use $\mathcal{O}(nt)$ messages?

- Are $(f + \mathcal{O}(1))$-deciding algorithms possible that are resilient to crash or omission faults and send $o(nt)$ messages for all n and t?

- Can we show strong lower bounds beyond $(f+1)$- and $(f+2)$-decision in any of the models?

- Is the message complexity of the $(f+1)$-deciding algorithm resilient to orderly crashes that we present asymptotically optimal?

- Of what use is cryptography to early-deciding algorithms, in terms of the trade-off between round and message complexity?

- Can randomized algorithms be made more efficient in runs with few faults, in terms of the trade-off between round and message complexity?

Acknowledgements

This material is based upon work supported by the National Science Foundation under Grant Nos. CCF-AF-0937274, CNS-1035199, 0939370-CCF and CCF-1217506, the AFOSR under Contract No. AFOSR Award number FA9550-13-1-0042, the Swiss National Science Foundation (SNSF), the Swiss Society of Friends of the Weizmann Institute of Science, the German Research Foundation (DFG, reference number Le 3107/1-1), the Israeli Centers of Research Excellence (I-CORE) program, (Center No. 4/11), grant 3/9778 of the Israeli Ministry of Science and Technology, and the Google Inter-university center for "Electronic Markets and Auctions". Danny Dolev is incumbent of the Berthold Badler Chair.

6. REFERENCES

[1] P. Berman, J. Garay, and K. J. Perry. Optimal Early Stopping in Distributed Consensus. In *Proc. 6th Workshop on Distributed Algorithms (WDAG)*, pages 221–237, 1992.

[2] B. Charron-Bost and A. Schiper. Uniform Consensus is Harder than Consensus. *Journal of Algorithms*, 51(1):15–37, 2004.

[3] B. S. Chlebus and D. R. Kowalski. Robust Gossiping with an Application to Consensus. *Journal of Computer and System Sciences*, 72(8):1262–1281, 2006.

[4] B. A. Coan. A Communication-Efficient Canonical Form for Fault-tolerant Distributed Protocols. In *Proc. 5th Symposium on Principles of Distributed Computing (PODC)*, pages 63–72, 1986.

[5] B. A. Coan and J. L. Welch. Modular Construction of a Byzantine Agreement Protocol with Optimal Message bit Complexity. *Information and Computation*, 97(1):61–85, 1992.

[6] D. Dolev and R. Reischuk. Bounds on Information Exchange for Byzantine Agreement. *Journal of the ACM*, 32:191–204, 1985.

[7] D. Dolev, R. Reischuk, and H. R. Strong. 'Eventual' is Earlier than 'Immediate'. In *Proc. 23rd Symposium on Foundations of Computer Science (FOCS)*, pages 196–203, 1982.

[8] D. Dolev, R. Reischuk, and H. R. Strong. Early Stopping in Byzantine Agreement. *Journal of the ACM*, 37(4):720–741, 1990.

[9] C. Dwork and Y. Moses. Knowledge and Common Knowledge in a Byzantine Environment: Crash Failures. *Information and Computation*, 88(2):156–186, 1990.

[10] M. Fischer, N. Lynch, and M. Patterson. Impossibility of Distributed Consensus with one Faulty Process. *Journal of the ACM*, 32(2):374–382, 1985.

[11] M. J. Fischer and N. A. Lynch. A Lower Bound for the Time to Assure Interactive Consistency. *Information Processing Letters*, 14:183–186, 1982.

[12] M. Fitzi and M. Hirt. Optimally Efficient Multi-valued Byzantine Agreement. In *Proc. 25th Symposium on Principles of Distributed Computing (PODC)*, pages 163–168, 2006.

[13] Z. Galil, A. Mayer, and M. Yung. Resolving Message Complexity of Byzantine Agreement and Beyond. In *Proc. 36th Symposium on Foundations of Computer Science (FOCS)*, pages 724–733, 1995.

[14] V. Hadzilacos and J. Y. Halpern. Message-optimal Protocols for Byzantine Agreement. *Mathematical Systems Theory*, 26:41–102, 1993.

[15] I. Keidar and S. Rajsbaum. A Simple Proof of the Uniform Consensus Synchronous Lower Bound. *Information Processing Letters*, 85(1):47–52, 2003.

[16] V. King and J. Saia. Scalable Byzantine Computation. *SIGACT News*, 41(3):89–104, 2010.

[17] V. King and J. Saia. Breaking the $\mathcal{O}(n^2)$ Bit Barrier: Scalable Byzantine Agreement with an Adaptive Adversary. *Journal of the ACM*, 58:18:1–18:24, 2011.

[18] G. Liang and N. H. Vaidya. Complexity of Multi-Value Byzantine Agreement. *CoRR*, abs/1006.2422, 2010.

[19] T. Mizrahi and Y. Moses. Continuous Consensus via Common Knowledge. *Distributed Computing*, 20:305–321, 2008.

[20] T. Mizrahi and Y. Moses. Continuous Consensus with Failures and Recoveries. In *Proc. 22nd Symposium on Distributed Computing (DISC)*, pages 408–422, 2008.

[21] P. R. Parvédy and M. Raynal. Optimal Early Stopping Uniform Consensus in Synchronous Systems with Process Omission Failures. In *Proc. 16th Symposium on Parallelism in Algorithms and Architectures (SPAA)*, pages 302–310, 2004.

[22] A. Patra. Error-free Multi-valued Broadcast and Byzantine Agreement with Optimal Communication Complexity. In *Proc. 15th Conference on Principles of Distributed Systems (OPODIS)*, pages 34–49, 2011.

[23] K. Perry and S. Toueg. Distributed Agreement in the Presence of Processor and Communication Faults. *IEEE Transactions on Software Engineering*, SE-12(3):477–482, 1986.

[24] M. Raynal. *Fault-tolerant Agreement in Synchronous Message-passing Systems*. Synthesis Lectures on Distributed Computing Theory. Morgan & Claypool, 2010.

[25] R. Reischuk. A New Solution for the Byzantine Generals Problem. *Information and Control*, 64(1–3):23–42, 1985.

[26] R. Zhang, Y. M. Teo, Q. Chen, and X. Wang. Lower Bounds for Achieving Synchronous Consensus with Orderly Crash Failures. In *Proc. 27th Conference on Distributed Computing Systems Workshops (ICDCSW)*, pages 61–68, 2007.

On the Complexity of Asynchronous Agreement Against Powerful Adversaries

Allison Lewko
Microsoft Research New England
allew@microsoft.com

Mark Lewko[*]
University of California, Los Angeles
mlewko@math.ucla.edu

ABSTRACT

We introduce new techniques for proving lower bounds on the running time of randomized algorithms for asynchronous agreement against powerful adversaries. In particular, we define a *strongly adaptive adversary* that is computationally unbounded and has a limited ability to corrupt a dynamic subset of processors by erasing their memories. We demonstrate that the randomized agreement algorithms designed by Ben-Or and Bracha to tolerate crash or Byzantine failures in the asynchronous setting extend to defeat a strongly adaptive adversary. These algorithms have essentially perfect correctness and termination, but at the expense of exponential running time. In the case of the strongly adaptive adversary, we show that this dismally slow running time is *inherent*: we prove that any algorithm with essentially perfect correctness and termination against the strongly adaptive adversary must have exponential running time. We additionally interpret this result as yielding an enhanced understanding of the tools needed to simultaneously achieving perfect correctness and termination as well as fast running time for randomized algorithms tolerating crash or Byzantine failures.

Categories and Subject Descriptors

F.1.2 [**Computation by Abstract Devices**]: Modes of Computation—*parallelism and concurrency, probabilistic computation*

Keywords

consensus; randomized algorithms

1. INTRODUCTION

Achieving agreement in a distributed system despite failures is a central problem in distributed computing. We con-

[*]Supported by a NSF Postdoctoral Fellowship, DMS-1204206.

sider a complete network of n processors able to communicate with each other by passing messages. Initially, each processor has an input bit. The task is to design a failure-resilient protocol that allows all non-faulty processors to agree on an output value, with the restriction that it must be equal to at least one of their inputs (this rules out the trivial solution of having a constant decision value independent of the inputs). The difficulty of this problem depends heavily on several additional specifications that must be made. In particular, is communication synchronous or asynchronous? What kinds of failures should be tolerated? If the errors and/or scheduling are controlled by an adversary, what resources and information does the adversary have access to?

We will consider a very challenging setting of asynchronous communication where message scheduling is controlled by an adversary with unbounded computational power who is given unrestricted access to all message contents and internal states of all processors. The adversary will also be empowered to cause limited types and quantities of processor failures. In this work, we will consider two kinds of failures: crash failures, which cause a processor to quit without warning, as well as resetting failures, which we will define and motivate below.

In this setting, the elegant result of Fischer, Lynch, and Paterson [14] shows that it is already impossible to design a deterministic protocol for agreement that always terminates, even if the adversary is limited to causing at most *one* crash failure. A common approach for tolerating this obstacle in practice is to use an algorithm that terminates as long as worst-case scheduling does not occur indefinitely. This is a property achieved by the well-known Paxos algorithm constructed by Lamport [22]. Randomized algorithms provide a potential alternative. Quickly following the impossibility result, Ben-Or [7] and Bracha [10] presented randomized algorithms terminating with probability one, even against such strong adversaries. These algorithms were intuitively structured, and Bracha's algorithm tolerated an optimal number of failures, namely allowing for t processors to behave in an arbitrary malicious fashion, for any $t < \frac{n}{3}$. Also, Aguilera and Toueg [1] have provided a new correctness proof for Ben-Or's randomized consensus algorithm when there are $< \frac{n}{2}$ crash failures. However, for some settings of the initial input bits, the algorithms of [7, 10] run for time that is exponential in n (with high probability) when $t = \Omega(n)$.

The algorithms in [7, 10] seem to provide even stronger failure resilience than is captured by the adversarial model employed. In particular, the original proofs of correctness rely only on the fact that at most t processors are faulty *at one time*, where the notion of "time" must be defined in an appropriate (and perhaps subtle) way. This gives some hope for recovering from even more than $t < \frac{n}{3}$ failures over the course of long executions if individual processor faults are fleeting occurrences. In particular, one might suppose that faulty processors could be detected and fixed during the course of a protocol execution, thereby allowing for more total failures.

In order to more fully characterize the failure resilience provided by the basic algorithm underlying [7, 10], we define the notion of *resetting failures*. A resetting failure at a processor results in loss of internal state: a processor that is reset is assumed to lose the entire contents of its memory (except for its initial input bit and its output bit). A resetting failure can model a processor that is detected to be faulty and has its memory reset in order for it to rejoin the protocol as a non-faulty processor. We define a strongly adaptive adversary who can cause up to t resetting failures in a certain window of time, where our measure of time is appropriately linked to the events of the execution. (Some kind of linking is necessary to avoid allowing the adversary to always cause a failure at the processor currently taking a step in the execution, for example.)

We prove that a simple variant of the algorithms in [7, 10] is indeed successful against such a strongly adaptive adversary (with probability one). Of course, this retains the exponentially slow running time. We then show that exponential slowness for $t = \Omega(n)$ is inherent to any algorithm achieving success with probability one against this strongly adaptive adversary. This provides a rather complete understanding of what is achievable in the presence of adaptive resetting faults.

In contrast, the relatively recent algorithm of Kapron et. al. [16] runs very quickly (polylogarithmic time in n) and tolerates $t < \left(\frac{1}{3} - \epsilon\right)$ non-adaptive Byzantine failures, but incurs a non-zero probability of non-termination or termination with invalid outputs. It is an interesting question to study to what extent the sacrifices made here (non-adaptivity, non-zero probability of incorrect output) are necessary to achieve fast running time. The algorithm in [16] works by iteratively dividing the processors into small "committees" that can afford to run the slow algorithm of [10] to hold elections to select random smaller subsets of processors to continue into new committees. A single final committee is reached that, with $1 - o(1)$ probability, contains a suitably bounded percentage of faulty processors. This final committee runs the algorithm of [10] and informs the other processors of the result.

It is clear that this approach cannot be used against an adaptive adversary, who can simply wait for the final committee to be determined and then cause faults. This approach also seems to inherently incur non-zero probability of an invalid result, as there is always a nonzero chance that the final committee is composed entirely of faulty processors. With the goal of beginning a systematic study of what can be achieved without incurring these disadvantages, Lewko [24] previously proved that a class of algorithms generalizing Ben-Or and Bracha's algorithms in [7, 10] cannot achieve subexponential running time against an adversary causing $t = \Omega(n)$ non-adaptive Byzantine failures. The class of algorithms was restricted in several ways, including a constant bound on the support size of all message distributions sampled by processors and a requirement for received messages

from different processors to be treated symmetrically. (For a more detailed description of the algorithm class, see [24].)

The techniques we introduce to prove the lower bound against strongly adaptive adversaries can be applied in this setting to yield an exponential lower bound on running time for a new class of algorithms tolerating $t = \Omega(n)$ crash failures. This class is incomparable to the class considered in [24], and this result yields several new insights. Most notably, our lower bound technique can tolerate arbitrary use of randomness by the processors, allowing us to avoid requiring any restriction on the support size as in [24]. We also avoid any requirement of symmetry in how received messages are treated, and our class is more intuitively defined.

Concurrently with this work, King and Saia [19] have discovered a Las Vegas polynomial-time algorithm tolerating adaptive Byzantine faults that falls outside the classes of algorithms considered here and in [24]. This implies a separation between what can achieved against the classical adaptive Byzantine adversary and the strongly adaptive adversary.

Our Techniques.

To prove the exponential lower bound on running time, we rely crucially on a general probabilistic inequality of Talagrand [28], which roughly states that any product distribution $\Omega_1 \times \Omega_2 \times \ldots \times \Omega_n$ cannot put too much weight simultaneously on two sets A and B in n-dimensional space that are "far apart." For our purposes, "far apart" can be interpreted as having Hamming distance $\Omega(n)$. We also can interpolate this result: if some product distribution $\Omega_1 \times \ldots \times \Omega_n$ puts significant weight on A and some other product distribution $\Pi_1 \times \ldots \times \Pi_n$ puts significant weight on B, then there is some mixed product distribution $\Omega_1 \times \ldots \times \Omega_i \times \Pi_{i+1} \times \ldots \times \Pi_n$ that puts small weight on each of A and B.

To use these tools in order to prove a lower bound on running time, we define iterative pairs of sets in the joint state space of the n processors that represent different levels of progress towards a final decision. By leveraging the capabilities of the strongly adaptive adversary (or later by leveraging the defining properties of the algorithm class), we prove that each of these pairs of sets is sufficiently separated in Hamming distance. We then apply the probabilistic inequalities repeatedly as an execution travels through the state space of the n processors, showing that for some initial setting of the inputs, the adversary can prevent the algorithm from making much progress in a given window of time with high probability. This ultimately yields our lower bound.

Our approach of leveraging general properties of product distributions in this iterative fashion represents a meaningful expansion of the suite of available tools for proving lower bounds in a distributed setting. In particular, there are essentially only a few core tools for proving lower bounds for randomized algorithms, and previous approaches do not achieve exponential lower bounds on running time when arbitrary amounts of randomness can be used. We consider our new techniques to be the main contribution of this work. In the following subsection, we briefly survey prior lower bounds and other relevant work.

1.1 Related Work

The problem of reaching agreement despite faults was introduced by Pease, Shostak, and Lamport in [26], who also proposed the Byzantine failure model in [23]. Since its introduction, the problem of fault-tolerant agreement has been widely studied in a variety of models. Several works have considered computationally bounded adversaries, a setting in which cryptographic tools can be employed ([27, 29, 9, 12, 11, 25], for example). In the synchronous communication setting, polylogarithmic round randomized protocols for Byzantine agreement against non-adaptive adversaries were obtained in [20, 21, 8, 15]. Recent work has focused on reducing the communication overhead of synchronous protocols [17, 18].

Several lower bounds are also known. In addition to the impossibility of deterministic algorithms in the asynchronous setting mentioned above, there is a sharp lower bound of t rounds for deterministic algorithms in the synchronous setting [13]. This lower bound is proven by assembling a chain of executions where any two adjacent executions are indistinguishable to some non-faulty processor and the two ends of the chain represent different decision values. This basic strategy is adapted and expanded in [24] to yield a lower bound for a class of randomized algorithms, but this class inherently limits the amount of randomness used in choosing an individual message.

Polynomial lower bounds for randomized algorithms include the result of Bar-Joseph and Ben-Or [6], which proves a lower bound of $t/\sqrt{n \log n}$ on the number of expected rounds for a randomized synchronous protocol against an adversary who can adaptively choose to fail t processors. Interestingly, their proof employs Schectman's theorem to analyze one-round coin flipping games, similar to our core use of Talagrand's inequality. However, they employ different techniques to build their analysis of multiple rounds. Another lower bound is due to Attiya and Censor [4], who show that for any integer k, the probability that a randomized Byzantine agreement algorithm does not terminate in $k(n-t)$ steps is at least $1/c^k$ for some constant c. Their technique involves constructing a chain of indistinguishable executions and bounding the termination probability in terms of the length of the chain. Aspnes [3] proves a lower bound of $\Omega(t/\log^2 t)$ on the expected number of local coin flips for asynchronous algorithms against adaptive adversaries that holds in either the shared memory or message passing model. This result is proven by establishing an extension of the techniques in [14] to a randomized setting. In the shared memory model, there are polynomial time randomized algorithms tolerating crash failures, and tight bounds on their total step complexity are proven by Attiya and Censor in [5]. This work also uses an analysis of product probability spaces, similarly to the proof in [6].

2. MODELS AND DEFINITIONS

We let n denote the total number of processors, and consider each processor to be endowed with a unique identity between 1 and n. We let $0 < t < n$ be a fixed positive integer (we let t be arbitrary for the purposes of definition, but note that in our theorems below, we will take $t = cn$ for a suitably small positive constant c). We assume that each processor has its own source of random bits, and all of these sources are unbiased and independent. Each processor also has a fixed input bit, and a write-once output bit that is initially set to $\perp$. We work in a message-passing model, where any single processor can send a message to any other processor along a dedicated "message channel," meaning that the recipient of a message will always correctly identify the sender. We let $\mathcal{M}$ denote the space of all possible messages (this can be infinite). An element $m \in \mathcal{M}$ contains a sender identity, a receiver identity, and a string of bits interpreted as its contents.

We define the *state* of a processor to include the current contents of its memory (note that this holds its identity, its input bit, and its output bit with current value 0, 1, or $\perp$). We let Σ denote the set of possible processor states. An n-tuple of states, $\sigma \in \Sigma^n$ specifies a *configuration* for the n processors.

An *algorithm* $\mathcal{A}$ is a collection of probability distributions on $\Sigma \times \mathcal{M}^n$, parameterized by $\Sigma \times \mathcal{M}$. In other words, an algorithm specifies how a processor should sample a new state and outgoing messages, depending on the current state as well as a just received message. The new state may contain updated memory contents (the output bit may or may not change). The new sent messages can depend on the freshly received message, the current memory of the processor, and freshly sampled random bits. We include $\emptyset \in \mathcal{M}$ to allow a processor to choose not to send a message.

We will adopt the usual notion of asynchrony and imagine that message delivery is controlled by an adversary. We will allow our adversary complete access to the current states of all the processors and the contents of all messages. We also allow our adversary unbounded computational power.

It is typical to define an execution as a sequence of steps, where each step consists of a processor (potentially) receiving a message, performing some local computation, and then possibly placing some outgoing messages into a "message buffer." The adversary then controls the sequence of steps by deciding which processor will take the next step and what message (if any) that processor will receive.

To model an adversary able to crash up to t processors, one can insist that in any infinite execution, all but at most t processors take infinitely many steps and that every message sent to an infinitely stepping processor is eventually delivered. It is also common to consider a stronger Byzantine adversary, who instead has the power to corrupt the messages sent by up to t processors. In this setting, we may require all processors to take infinitely many steps - but note that corrupted processors may simulate crashed processors by maliciously choosing not to send messages (changing a non-empty message m to $\emptyset$ is considered a permissible corruption by the adversary). We note that corruption of messages allows an adversary to lie about the random coins sampled by a limited number of processors.

We will instead define a adversary who is able to "reset" a *changing* set of $\leq t$ processors. *Resetting* a processor will correspond to erasing the contents of its memory, except for its input bit, its output bit, its processor identity, and a special counter that will increment each time a reset occurs. We assume that a processor keeps a local copy of the counter's value in its state, and hence will detect a reset when the local copy is erased and the real counter is non-zero. This mechanism of detection is just a book-keeping device, the key point is that we are assuming resets are events processors can internally detect (note that this strengthens our lower bound result).

We now consider executions expressed as sequences of more fine-grained steps between configurations, where we allow three distinct types of steps. A *resetting step* will cause the memory of a specified processor to be reset. A *receiving step* will deliver a message from the message buffer to its intended recipient. The recipient will then perform a local computation (perhaps sampling from some fresh local randomness). This will be the only kind of step that involves randomization.

Finally, a *sending step* will allow a processor to place a set of new messages into the message buffer (this set may be empty if the processor chooses not to send anything). We assume that a single sending step represents a complete response to prior events, meaning that if a processor takes a sending step and then takes another sending step without taking any resetting or receiving steps in between, then the second sending step will have no effect - the state of the processor will remain unchanged and no new messages will be sent. The adversary will control the order and nature of the steps.

Given a partial execution expressed as a finite sequence of such steps, we define its probability (with respect to a fixed algorithm $\mathcal{A}$) to be the product of the probabilities of each state change induced by a step, under the distributions specified by the algorithm. (This is assuming the initial configuration is valid.) Note that this will be zero if deterministic transitions are not followed, or if a step indicates delivery of a message that was never sent, etc.

Naturally, it would be impossible to make progress against an adversary allowed to reset processors arbitrarily. In particular, we must design a model that rules out the trivial case of an adversary that resets the memory of the receiving processor after every message delivery, as no algorithm can make progress under such adverse circumstances. To ensure feasibility, we could limit the adversary to resetting at most t processors throughout an execution. However, we can achieve success against even stronger adversaries. To specify an interesting such adversary, we make one key definition:

DEFINITION 1. *An **acceptable window** is a consecutive segment of steps of the following form. First, all n processors take sending steps. Then, for sets $S_1, S_2, \ldots, S_n \subseteq [n]$ all of size $\geq n - t$, a sequence of receiving steps follows that delivers to each processor i the messages just sent to it from processors in the set S_i. Finally, a sequence of at most t resetting steps occurs.*

The notion of an acceptable window is a formal unit of "time" during an execution in which at most t processors are faulty, and hence the other processors may not receive any messages from them. One could imagine adding a requirement that $i \in S_i$ for each i, as a processor can always safely wait to receive a message from itself, but this is unnecessary, as no resets occur between sending and receiving. This means that any information the processor could pass to itself through a message can instead be stored directly in the processor's state. Thus, adding a requirement that $i \in S_i$ would be superfluous here.

We define the *Strongly Adaptive Adversary* to be an adversary allowed to reset processors and control message sending and receiving up to the constraint that any infinite execution is composed entirely of adjacent, disjoint acceptable windows. We observe that this adversary is incomparable to the usual Byzantine asynchronous adversary. Our strongly adaptive adversary has the additional power to erase processor memory, but it lacks the power to have corrupted processors "lie" about their local random bits.

Our use of the phrase "the strongly adaptive adversary" is a bit imprecise, since this technically constitutes a class of adversaries in the following sense. A single adversary should be thought of as a deterministic function that maps a partial execution to a next applicable step. Such a function need not be efficiently computable. We will consider the class of strongly adaptive adversaries to be the collection of individual adversaries that satisfy the requirement above to produce acceptable windows.

It may seem a bit unnatural to impose the constraint that an adversary should stick to acceptable windows, but we feel this captures the intuitive notion that the adversary should only corrupt t processors "at one time," as otherwise progress would be impossible. Furthermore, as our main result in this model is a lower bound, placing restrictions on the adversary strengthens our result.

We call a configuration *reachable* if it occurs as the consequence of some partial execution with non-zero probability that is decomposable as a concatenation of acceptable windows. Note that the notion of reachability depends on the algorithm employed.

DEFINITION 2. *We say an algorithm $\mathcal{A}$ achieves **measure one correctness** against all strongly adaptive adversaries if any reachable configuration contains only agreeing or $\perp$ output bits, (in other words, one output bit being 0 and another being 1 is disallowed, but any assortment of 0's and $\perp$'s or any assortment of 1's and $\perp$'s is allowed). We also require that when an output is not $\perp$, it must agree with one of the inputs. This means that if all processors have inputs equal to 0, the decision cannot be 1, and vice versa.*

DEFINITION 3. *We say an algorithm $\mathcal{A}$ achieves **measure one termination** if any infinite execution (composed of acceptable windows) in which some processor taking an infinite sequence of sending and receiving steps never sets its decision bit has probability zero (we define the probability of an infinite execution to be the limit of the probabilities of its finite partial executions).*

In an asynchronous setting, defining the running time of an execution can be a bit subtle. One typical measure is to consider the length of the longest message chain before a decision is reached, where a message chain includes messages $m_1, m_2, \ldots, m_k$ such that m_i is received by the sender of m_{i+1}, at some point prior to the sending of m_{i+1}. It is not immediately clear how a "message chain" should be defined in the presence of resetting faults: should a message sent after a reset be counted as continuing a chain of messages received before the reset? Since our strongly adaptive adversary is constrained to keep to schedules that are approximately synchronous, we will employ a more obvious measure, namely the number of acceptable windows that pass before the first processor decides. When we later reformulate our techniques to obtain a lower bound for a class of algorithms in the presence of crash failures, we will define the running time of an execution as the length of the longest message chain preceding a decision.

3. FEASIBILITY AGAINST THE STRONGLY ADAPTIVE ADVERSARY

Both Ben-Or [7] and Bracha [10] provide expected exponential time algorithms for Byzantine agreement against a full-information asynchronous adversary (terminating and succeeding with probability 1). Bracha's algorithm introduces a bit more complexity in order to achieve the optimal resilience of $t < \frac{n}{3}$ in the Byzantine setting.

Inspired by these algorithms, we provide a close variant that succeeds against the strongly adaptive adversary. We will not be concerned with obtaining the optimal resilience, and so will favor simplicity of presentation over possible improvements to the constant fraction of resets allowed per acceptable window. The algorithm is parameterized by several thresholds, $T_1 \geq T_2 \geq T_3$, and we will discuss appropriate settings of these below.

Throughout the algorithm, each processor p will store its input bit, its (write-once) output bit, and a few additional variables. The variable r_p will hold the current "round number" and is initialized to 1. The variable x_p is initialized to be equal to the input bit of processor p.

step 1:.
Send the message (r_p, x_p) to all processors.

step 2:.
Wait until T_1 messages of type (r_q, x_q) have arrived from other processors with values of $r_q = r_p$.

step 3:.
If at least T_2 of these T_1 messages have the same bit value v for the last entry, then write v to the output bit (assuming this bit is not yet written). If at least T_3 of these T_1 messages have the same bit v, then set $x_p = v$. Otherwise, set x_p to be a freshly sampled uniformly random bit.

step 4:.
Set $r_p = r_p + 1$ and return to step 1.

handling resets.
To address resets, a processor p also does the following. If p has just been reset (an event that is detectable), then processor p waits to receive at least T_1 messages (r_q, x_q) from other processors with a common value of r. It then sets its own r_p value to the match this and returns to step 3 above (note that a newly reset processor refrains from sending messages until it resumes normal operation).

We note that $2T_3 > T_1$ should hold in order for the behavior in step 3 to be clear. This is a constraint we will always impose.

THEOREM 4. *The above algorithm achieves measure one correctness and termination against the strongly adaptive adversary for $t < \frac{n}{6}$ when the thresholds T_1, T_2, T_3 are set to satisfy $n - 2t \geq T_1 \geq T_2 \geq T_3 + t$, and $2T_3 > n$.*

PROOF. We note that whenever $t < \frac{n}{6}$, the constraints on the thresholds T_1, T_2, T_3 specified above are achievable by setting $T_1 := n - 2t$, $T_2 = T_1$, $T_3 = n - 3t$. (Having a smaller value of t allows one to set T_2 smaller than T_1, which will lead to improvement in running time but is not relevant for measure one correctness and termination.)

We first establish measure one correctness. Suppose that σ is a reachable configuration in which some processor has decided. We consider a non-zero probability partial execution composed of acceptable windows leading to σ (such a partial execution must exist by definition of reachability). Now, we let w denote the earliest acceptable window in

which a decision is made, and we let p denote a processor deciding in window w. In order to decide on a bit v, p must have received $\geq T_2$ messages of the form (r, v) for its current value of r_p. Each other processor q must have received $\geq T_2 - t$ of these messages (r, v) during the receiving steps in window w.

We now consider how the internal round numbers r maintained by the processors evolve during a sequence of acceptable windows. Initially, all round numbers are 1. Assuming that $n - t \geq T_1$, all processors will increment r to be 2 during the first acceptable window. Thus, entering the second acceptable window, all processors that were *not reset* during the first window will have $r = 2$, and the reset processors will have blank r values (denoted by $\perp$). During the second acceptable window, each processor will receive at least $n - 2t$ messages from processors with r values equal to 2. Assuming that $T_1 \leq n - 2t$, every processor will then have $r = 3$ before the resetting steps.

Extending this reasoning inductively, we see that in window w, at least $n - t$ processors will enter the window with $r = w$ (with the rest having $r = \perp$). Again assuming that $T_1 \leq n - 2t$ and additionally assuming that $T_2 - t \geq T_3$, every processor will have $x_q = v$ and $r = w + 1$ just before the resetting steps that conclude window w. It follows that every processor who has not yet decided will decide v in window $w + 1$. We must also check that it is impossible for some processor to decide the opposite of v during window w. This is impossible as long as $2T_2 > n$.

We have thus shown that it is impossible to obtain contradicting decision values in a reachable configuration. To see that decision values conflicting with a unanimous setting of the inputs are also impossible, note that if all inputs are equal to a common value v, then all processors will decide v in the first acceptable window. This completes our proof of measure one correctness.

To establish measure one termination, we first argue that during any given acceptable window, no two processors p and q can fix x_p and x_q deterministically to conflicting values. If p deterministically sets x_p to v, this means it received $\geq T_3$ messages with the value v. Processor q could not have received $\geq T_3$ messages with the opposite value if we impose the constraint that $2T_3 > n$. Assuming this constraint, no two processors can deterministically set conflicting values. Thus, there is at least a 2^{-n} probability that all processors p set the same value for x_p during any given window. Thus, the probability of not deciding approaches 0 as the number of acceptable windows approaches infinity. This implies measure one termination. $\square$

We observe that for any constant $c < \frac{1}{6}$, setting $t = cn$ makes measure one correctness and termination attainable through the above algorithm, but the algorithm will incur exponential running time (with high probability) against an adversary that chooses initial inputs evenly split between 0 and 1. To see this, note that T_3 will always need to be $> \frac{1}{2}n$, and hence T_2 will always need to be $> (\frac{1}{2} + c)n$. Decision will then be contingent on obtaining a strong majority that occurs with probability that is exponentially small (depending on c). This is a consequence of the simple fact that with high probability, a sampling of n independent uniformly random bits will yield a deviation of only $\mathcal{O}(n^{\frac{1}{2} + \epsilon})$ from the mean (for any small $\epsilon > 0$). Hence, with high probability per round, the adversary can continually extend the execution to last one more round without deciding by showing every processor an approximate split between 0 and 1 messages, and then having all of them set their next bits randomly in step 3. We expect this to continue for an exponential number of rounds until a strong enough majority happens by chance to prevent the adversary from continuing in this fashion.

4. IMPOSSIBILITY OF EXPECTED POLYNOMIAL TIME AGAINST THE STRONGLY ADAPTIVE ADVERSARY

Here we establish our main result: an exponential lower bound on the running time for any algorithm achieving measure one correctness and termination against the strongly adaptive adversary.

THEOREM 5. *We set $t = cn$ where $c > 0$ is any fixed positive constant. Then there exist absolute positive constants C, α (depending only on c) such that, for any algorithm achieving measure one correctness and termination, there is a strongly adaptive adversary and a setting of the inputs bits such that with probability $\geq \frac{1}{2}$, the running time is $\geq Ce^{\alpha n}$.*

We first give a high-level outline of our proof. As a base case, we observe that the reachable configurations corresponding to a decision of 0 and the reachable configurations corresponding to a decision of 1 form two sets (denoted Z_0^0 and Z_1^0) that are significantly separated in Hamming distance. Intuitively, if conflicting decision states were too close, then the differing processors could be temporarily silenced, and the other processors could be forced to make a decision that could conflict. By interpolating over the input possibilities and applying Talagrand's inequality, we could use this base observation to prove that there is a setting of the inputs such that reaching a decision in just one "round" of communication is very unlikely.

To work up to analyzing many rounds, we inductively build pairs of sets Z_0^k and Z_1^k of configurations further out from decisions. These pairs of sets will remain Hamming-separated and will be designed so that if a configuration is *not* in Z_0^k, say, then the adversary will have a good chance of continuing the execution for k more rounds without a decision of 0 occurring. We define Z_0^k such that if we start from a configuration in Z_0^k and apply certain acceptable windows, then there is always a sufficient chance of landing in Z_0^{k-1}. We define Z_1^k analogously. To show that Z_0^k and Z_1^k are still significantly separated in Hamming distance, we argue that if they were too close, this would imply the existence of a single product distribution placing too much weight simultaneously on Z_0^{k-1} and Z_1^{k-1}. Since these are assumed to be Hamming-separated by the inductive hypothesis, this would contradict Talagrand's inequality.

We then show that as long as one avoids the union of the sets Z_0^k and Z_1^k, then there is an acceptable window that can be used to extend the execution to a state avoiding $Z_0^{k-1} \cup Z_1^{k-1}$ with high probability. This is essentially an interpolation argument: since we know there is a choice of window that avoids Z_0^{k-1} and another that avoids Z_1^{k-1}, we can interpolate to obtain a single choice of extending window that avoids the union. Finally, we show that if one begins outside of $Z_0^k \cup Z_1^k$, then one can extend the execution for k

steps without a decision occurring with constant probability for a value of k that is exponential in n.

To prove this theorem formally, we develop some key lemmas and definitions in the next subsections.

4.1 A Probabilistic Lemma

We will crucially rely on Talagrand's inequality, a very general tool for studying product measures. We will state a consequence of it here in the context of Hamming distance, as we will not need the additional generality provided by the full statement. A fuller statement and proof can be found in [2], for example.

We first develop some convenient notation. We let $\Omega = \prod_{i=1}^{n} \Omega_i$, where each Ω_i is a probability space and Ω is endowed with the product measure. We employ the usual notion of Hamming distance between points in Ω: for $x = (x_1, \ldots, x_n)$ and $y = (y_1, \ldots, y_n) \in \Omega$, we define $\Delta(x, y)$ to be the number of coordinates i such that $x_i \neq y_i$. Given a set $A \subseteq \Omega$ and a point $x = (x_1, \ldots, x_n) \in \Omega$, we define the Hamming distance $\Delta(x, A)$ between the point x and the set A to be the minimal Hamming distance attained between x and a point $a \in A$:

DEFINITION 6. *For $A \subseteq \Omega$ and $x \in \Omega$,*
$$\Delta(x, A) := \min\{\Delta(x, a) : a \in A\}.$$

Similarly, we define the Hamming distance between two sets $A, B \subseteq \Omega$ to be the minimal Hamming distance attained between a point $a \in A$ and a point $b \in B$:

DEFINITION 7. *For $A, B \subseteq \Omega$,*
$$\Delta(A, B) := \min\{\Delta(a, b) : a \in A, b \in B\}.$$

Finally, given a set $A \subseteq \Omega$ and a non-negative real number d, we define the set $\mathcal{B}(A, d)$ to be the subset of points in Ω which are at a Hamming distance of at most d from A:

DEFINITION 8. *For $A \subseteq \Omega$ and $d \geq 0$,*
$$\mathcal{B}(A, d) := \{x \in \Omega : \Delta(x, A) \leq d\}.$$

We are now prepared to state the required consequence of Talagrand's inequality (see [2], for example):

LEMMA 9. *For any $A \subseteq \Omega$ and any $d \geq 0$,*
$$\mathbb{P}[A](1 - \mathbb{P}[\mathcal{B}(A, d)]) \leq e^{-\frac{d^2}{4n}}.$$

4.2 The Building Blocks of the Proof

We now recursively define two sequences of subsets of Σ^n that will form the building blocks of our proof of Theorem 5. These definitions will be made with respect to a fixed algorithm $\mathcal{A}$ and a threshold parameter $\tau > 0$ that we will set later. Our base sets are defined as follows:

DEFINITION 10. *We let Z_0^0 denote the set of reachable configurations in Σ^n such that at least one processor has written 0 to its output bit. Similarly, we let Z_1^0 denote the set of reachable configurations in Σ^n such that at least one processor has written 1 to its output bit.*

LEMMA 11. *If the algorithm $\mathcal{A}$ satisfies measure one correctness and measure one termination, then $\Delta(Z_0^0, Z_1^0) > t$.*

PROOF. We suppose not. Then there exist reachable configurations $\sigma, \gamma \in \Sigma^n$ such that $\sigma \in Z_0^0$, $\gamma \in Z_1^0$, and $\Delta(\sigma, \gamma) \leq t$. Without loss of generality, we suppose that σ and γ only differ in the first t coordinates (i.e. only in the local states of processors 1 through t). Consider a nonzero probability partial execution composed of acceptable windows that results in configuration σ. The adversary can continue such an execution by always delivering the messages from the last $n - t$ processors. This will allow an arbitrarily long sequence of new acceptable windows.

Since the algorithm $\mathcal{A}$ satisfies measure one termination, if the adversary keeps extending this execution by appending new acceptable windows, with probability one a decision must eventually be reached, and since $\sigma \in Z_0^0$, this decision must be 0 (with probability one). However, we can apply the same argument to a partial execution reaching γ and then similarly delivering messages only from the last $n - t$ processors. Since the distribution of the states of the last $n - t$ processors is the same in both cases, it must be that their decision is also the same. Since $\gamma \in Z_1^0$, this contradicts measure one correctness. □

Given sets $R, S_1, \ldots, S_n \subseteq [n]$ satisfying $|R| \leq t$, $|S_i| \geq n - t \; \forall i$, we say the strongly adaptive adversary can *apply* this set to a reachable configuration $\sigma \in \Sigma^n$, meaning that the adversary can execute sending steps for all processors, deliver to each processor i the messages sent to it by senders in S_i, in some fixed order, and then reset the processors in R. Note that the application of sets $R, S_1, \ldots, S_n$ with the specified properties results in an acceptable window (by definition).

Once we have defined sets Z_0^{k-1} and Z_1^{k-1} for some positive integer k, we define the next sets Z_0^k and Z_1^k as follows:

DEFINITION 12. *We let Z_0^k denote the set of reachable configurations in Σ^n such that, for any sets R, S such that $|R| \leq t$, $|S| \geq n - t$, the adversary applying $R, S, S, \ldots, S$ to the configuration will result in a new configuration that belongs to Z_0^{k-1} with probability $> \tau$. Similarly, we let Z_1^k denote the set of reachable configurations in Σ^n such that, for such R and S, the adversary applying $R, S, S, \ldots, S$ to the configuration will result in a new configuration that belongs to Z_1^{k-1} with probability $> \tau$.*

LEMMA 13. *If the algorithm $\mathcal{A}$ satisfies measure one correctness and termination and $\tau \geq e^{-\frac{t^2}{8n}}$, then $\Delta\left(Z_0^k, Z_1^k\right) > t$ for all non-negative integers k.*

PROOF. We proceed by induction on k. The base case $k = 0$ is addressed above in Lemma 11. We assume the result holds for $k - 1 \geq 0$, and we suppose it is false for k. Then there exist reachable configurations $\sigma, \gamma \in \Sigma^n$ such that $\sigma \in Z_0^k$, $\gamma \in Z_1^k$, and $\Delta(\sigma, \gamma) \leq t$. Without loss of generality, we suppose that σ and γ only differ in the first t coordinates. We let R denote the set $\{1, 2, \ldots, t\}$ and S denote the set $\{t + 1, t + 2, \ldots, n\}$. By definition of Z_0^k, if the adversary applies $R, S, \ldots, S$ to σ, this will with probability $> \tau$ result in a new configuration belonging to Z_0^{k-1}. Similarly, if the adversary applies $R, S, \ldots, S$ to γ, this will with probability $> \tau$ result in a new configuration belonging to Z_1^{k-1}.

We first suppose that both σ and γ are configurations in which no decisions have occurred. In other words, no processors have yet written to their output bits. Assuming this, the resets will obliterate the differences between the first t

processor states. Hence the distribution of the resulting configuration is *identical* in these two cases, as it is independent of the prior contents of the memories of the reset processors, as these have been erased (and their messages went undelivered). Since local randomness is sampled independently by each processor only in response to the message receipts in the window, which occur *after* the deterministic sending steps, the distribution on the resulting configuration (which is reachable with probability one) is in fact a product distribution. This distribution places weight $> \tau$ on each of two sets, Z_0^{k-1} and Z_1^{k-1}, that are separated by a Hamming distance $> t$. Applying Lemma 9, we thus have that

$$\tau^2 < e^{-\frac{t^2}{4n}} \Leftrightarrow \tau < e^{-\frac{t^2}{8n}}.$$

This contradicts our stipulation on the value of τ.

We finally consider the case where some decision has already been made in σ. Since $\sigma \in Z_0^k$, this decision must be 0. However, repeatedly applying acceptable windows of $R, S, \ldots, S$ to σ must result in a decision of 1 with nonzero probability, since $\gamma \in Z_1^k$, and the distribution of the final $n - t$ states here is independent of the output bits of the first t processors, as their messages are never delivered. This contradicts measure one correctness. □

We now prove that if a reachable configuration is not in Z_0^k or Z_1^k, then the adversary can choose the next acceptable window in a way that will (with high probability) avoid landing in $Z_0^{k-1} \cup Z_1^{k-1}$. The intuition for this can be developed as follows. We know that there is a product distribution induced by an acceptable window that places low probability on Z_0^{k-1}, and we know there is a (potentially different) product distribution induced by an acceptable window that places low probability on Z_1^{k-1}. We will obtain a single product distribution that places low probability on both sets simultaneously by interpolating between these two distributions. We use the fact that Lemma 9 yields graceful degradation in the quality of the threshold for "low probability" as we perturb one coordinate of the product distribution at a time. If we interpolate carefully, we can also ensure that the interpolated distribution we obtain is itself induced by an acceptable window.

LEMMA 14. *Suppose the algorithm $\mathcal{A}$ satisfies measure one correctness and termination and $\tau := e^{-\frac{t^2}{8n}}$. Then, for any reachable configuration σ not in $Z_0^k \cup Z_1^k$, there exist sets $R, S_1, \ldots, S_n$ that can be applied to σ such that the resulting reachable configuration falls outside $Z_0^{k-1} \cup Z_1^{k-1}$ with probability $\geq 1 - 2e^{-\frac{(t-1)^2}{8n}}$.*

PROOF. Consider a reachable σ in the complement of $Z_0^k \cup Z_1^k$. By definition of Z_0^k, this means there is some choice of R, S such that applying $R, S, \ldots, S$ to σ will avoid Z_0^{k-1} with probability $\geq 1 - \tau$. Similarly, by definition of Z_1^k, there is some choice R', S' such that applying $R', S', \ldots, S'$ to σ will avoid Z_1^{k-1} with probability $\geq 1 - \tau$.

We assume without loss of generality that $R' = \{1, 2, \ldots, t'\}$ for some $t' \leq t$. For each j from 0 to n, we define the set R_j to be the union of $R \cap \{1, 2, \ldots, j\}$ and $R' \cap \{j + 1, \ldots, t'\}$. We observe that $|R_j| \leq t$ for each j. We also define $S_i^j := S$ for $i \leq j$ and $S_i^j := S'$ for $i > j$. Then, for each j, we can apply $R_j, S_1^j, \ldots, S_n^j$ to σ to produce a new reachable configuration. For each j, this induces a product distribution π_j on the set of reachable configurations.

286

By construction, the distribution π_0 places probability $\leq \tau$ on Z_1^{k-1} and the distribution π_n places probability $\leq \tau$ on Z_0^{k-1}. The first j coordinates of π_j have the same distributions as in π_n, will the remaining coordinates have the same distribution as in π_0. We define $\eta := e^{-\frac{(t-1)^2}{8n}}$. We let j^* denote the minimal value of j such that π_j places probability $\leq \eta$ on Z_0^{k-1}. (Such a j^* exists since $j = n$ satisfies this condition.) If $j^* = 0$, then π_0 then places probability $\leq \eta$ on *each of* Z_0^{k-1} and Z_1^{k-1}. Otherwise, we argue as follows.

We use $\mathbb{P}_{\pi_j}(A)$ for a set A to denote the probability that π_j places on a set A. We claim that:

$$\mathbb{P}_{\pi_{j^*}}\left[\mathcal{B}\left(Z_0^{k-1}, 1\right)\right] \geq \mathbb{P}_{\pi_{j^*-1}}\left[Z_0^{k-1}\right]. \quad (1)$$

To see this, consider that the product distributions π_{j^*} and π_{j^*-1} only differ in a single coordinate. Thus, if we sample a configuration according to π_{j^*-1} and obtain a result in Z_0^{k-1}, we can resample the differing coordinate to match π_{j^*} and we are guaranteed to obtain a result in $\mathcal{B}\left(Z_0^{k-1}, 1\right)$. The inequality (1) follows.

We observe that the set $\mathcal{B}(Z_1^{k-1}, t-1)$ is disjoint from the set $\mathcal{B}(Z_0^{k-1}, 1)$, since $\Delta(Z_0^{k-1}, Z_1^{k-1}) > t$. Hence,

$$1 - \mathbb{P}_{\pi_{j^*}}\left[\mathcal{B}\left(Z_1^{k-1}, t-1\right)\right] \geq \mathbb{P}_{\pi_{j^*}}\left[\mathcal{B}\left(Z_0^{k-1}, 1\right)\right]. \quad (2)$$

Combining (1) and (2), we see that

$$\mathbb{P}_{\pi_{j^*}}\left[Z_1^{k-1}\right]\left(1 - \mathbb{P}_{\pi_{j^*}}\left[\mathcal{B}\left(Z_1^{k-1}, t-1\right)\right]\right) \geq \eta \mathbb{P}_{\pi_{j^*}}\left[Z_1^{k-1}\right].$$

Applying Lemma 9 and recalling the definition of η, we have

$$\mathbb{P}_{\pi_{j^*}}\left[Z_1^{k-1}\right] \leq \frac{1}{\eta}e^{-\frac{(t-1)^2}{4n}} = \eta.$$

We now have a product distribution π_{j^*} induced by an acceptable window that places probability $\leq \eta$ on each set Z_0^{k-1}, Z_1^{k-1}, and hence $\mathbb{P}_{\pi_{j^*}}\left[Z_0^{k-1} \cup Z_1^{k-1}\right] \leq 2\eta$, as required. □

4.3 Proof of Theorem 5

We now employ the notation and lemmas of the previous subsections to prove Theorem 5. We define $\alpha := \frac{c^2}{9}$ and we define C sufficiently small such that

$$Ce^{\alpha n} \leq \frac{1}{4}e^{\frac{(cn-1)^2}{8n}} \quad (3)$$

holds for all positive integers n. For convenience of notation, we define $E := Ce^{\alpha n}$.

We consider the sets Z_0^E, Z_1^E. By Lemma 13, we know that $\Delta\left(Z_0^E, Z_1^E\right) > t$. We consider an initial configuration σ in which all input bits are set to 0. Then, it must be the case that $\sigma \notin Z_1^E$. Otherwise, there would be a non-zero probability partial execution beginning with σ and leading to a decision of 1, which contradicts measure one correctness. Similarly, an initial configuration γ in which all input bits are set to 1 cannot belong to Z_0^E. Hence, as we interpolate between σ and γ, changing the input bit of one processors at a time, we must discover an initial configuration δ such that $\delta \notin Z_0^E \cup Z_1^E$. We fix this setting of the inputs.

Our strongly adaptive adversary is now defined as follows. Confronted with a partial execution resulting in a configuration σ, the adversary determines the maximum value of $k \leq E$ such that $\sigma \notin Z_0^k \cup Z_1^k$. If no such k exists, it

continues arbitrarily within the constraint of producing acceptable windows. If such a k does exist, then it applies the sequence of sets guaranteed by Lemma 14 in order to yield a $\geq 1 - 2e^{-\frac{(cn-1)^2}{8n}}$ probability of reaching a new configuration at the end of the acceptable window that is not in $Z_0^{k-1} \cup Z_1^{k-1}$.

Since we begin with an initial configuration that is not in $Z_0^E \cup Z_1^E$, the probability that this strongly adaptive adversary will succeed in causing $\geq E$ acceptable windows to occur before any decision is made is at least:

$$1 - 2Ee^{-\frac{(cn-1)^2}{8n}} \geq \frac{1}{2},$$

recalling (3) and the definition of E. This completes our proof of Theorem 5.

5. CONSEQUENCE FOR RESILIENCE AGAINST CRASH FAILURES

The techniques developed to prove the exponential lower bound in the previous section have implications beyond the strongly adaptive adversary. In fact, we can use the same techniques (with a few minor modifications) to prove a lower bound for more traditional asynchronous adversaries that applies to a large, natural class of algorithms. In particular, we consider an asynchronous adversary (with unbounded computational power and knowledge of all messages and internal states) that can cause up to t crash failures during an execution as well as controlling the message scheduling. The only constraint on message delivery is that all messages sent must eventually be delivered, if the recipient has not crashed.

We now define the crucial properties of an algorithm that are needed to apply our lower bound techniques in this setting:

DEFINITION 15. *We say an algorithm $\mathcal{A}$ is forgetful if each message sent by a processor depends only on its input bit as well as messages received and local randomness sampled since the previous sending event.*

Intuitively, this means that processors do not "remember" prior events that are not reflected by the most recently received messages. We define one more property of an algorithm that we will require in conjunction with forgetfulness:

DEFINITION 16. *We say an algorithm $\mathcal{A}$ is fully communicative if whenever a processor receives the most recently sent messages from $n-t$ processors, it sends a new message to all n processors.*

These properties are both present in the algorithms in [7, 10], and seem natural in the context of crash failures, where one cannot wait for messages from t processors that may have crashed. We will prove that our exponential lower bound extends to forgetful, fully communicative algorithms against an adversary able to cause $\leq t$ crash failures, making only minor semantic modifications to the proof in Section 4. Intuitively, the combination of forgetfulness and full communication mimics the effect of the resetting failures we previously considered. Now processors are retaining old information forever in their state, but they are basing current actions only on "recent" information, thereby proceeding as if they have forgotten the outdated portions of their internal state.

In this context, we define a *reachable configuration* to be any configuration that occurs with non-zero probability with at most t crash failures (note that we have dropped the notion of acceptable windows). We analogously define measure one correctness and termination for algorithms by requiring that all reachable configurations display only valid combinations of input and output bits and that any infinite execution in which at most t crash failures occur and all other processors take infinitely many sending and receiving steps has probability zero.

We will prove:

THEOREM 17. *We set $t = cn$ where $c > 0$ is any fixed positive constant. Then there exist absolute positive constants C, α (depending only on c) such that, for any fully communicative and forgetful algorithm achieving measure one correctness and termination, there is an asynchronous adversary and a setting of the inputs bits such that with probability $\geq \frac{1}{2}$, the running time is $\geq C e^{\alpha n}$.*

5.1 Definitions and Lemmas

We first adjust our definitions to obtain suitable sets Z_0^k, Z_1^k for this setting. Since there are no longer any resets, we can assume without loss of generality that the local state of a processor includes a log of all messages the processor has received and sent throughout the execution so far. We will define all of our sets Z_0^k, Z_1^k to be subsets of reachable configurations containing no crashed processors. We will rely on the fully communicative nature of the algorithm to additionally restrict to reachable configurations in which all processors are ready to send to all other processors.

Given a reachable configuration σ and sets $S_1, \ldots, S_n$ all of size $\geq n - t$, we say the adversary *applies* these sets to σ to mean that the adversary executes the following sequence of steps. First, all processors taking sending steps. Then, each processor i receives the messages just sent to it from the processors in S_i (in some fixed order). Note that when the algorithm is fully communicative, beginning from an initial configuration and repeatedly applying such n-tuples of sets will result in every processor sending to every other processor in each sending step.

Now, analogously to the definitions in Section 4.2, we define:

DEFINITION 18. *We let Z_0^0 denote the set of reachable configurations in Σ^n such that at least one processor has written 0 to its output bit. Similarly, we let Z_1^0 denote the set of reachable configurations in Σ^n such that at least one processor has written 1 to its output bit.*

DEFINITION 19. *For $k \geq 1$, we let Z_0^k denote the set of reachable configurations in Σ^n where all processors are poised to send messages to all other processors and for any set $|S| \geq n - t$, the adversary applying $S, S, \ldots, S$ to the configuration will result in a new configuration that belongs to Z_0^{k-1} with probability $> \tau$. Similarly, we let Z_1^k denote the set of reachable configurations in Σ^n such that, for any $|S| \geq n - t$, the adversary applying $S, S, \ldots, S$ to the configuration will result in a new configuration that belongs to Z_1^{k-1} with probability $> \tau$.*

We then have:

LEMMA 20. *If a fully communicative and forgetful algorithm $\mathcal{A}$ satisfies measure one correctness and termination*

and $\tau \geq e^{-\frac{t^2}{8n}}$, then $\Delta\left(Z_0^k, Z_1^k\right) > t$ for all non-negative integers k.

PROOF. We first establish the base case, i.e. that

$$\Delta\left(Z_0^0, Z_1^0\right) > t.$$

This is similar to the proof of Lemma 11.

We suppose there exist reachable configurations $\sigma, \gamma \in \Sigma^n$ such that $\sigma \in Z_0^0$, $\gamma \in Z_1^0$, and $\Delta(\sigma, \gamma) \leq t$. Without loss of generality, we suppose that σ and γ only differ in the first t coordinates (i.e. only in the local states of processors 1 through t). We let S denote the set $\{t+1, \ldots, n\}$.

Consider a non-zero probability partial execution that results in configuration σ. We can define another non-zero probability partial execution by executing most of the same steps, but crashing each of the first t processors before they send any messages that are not sent in a partial execution resulting in γ. In other words, we reach a new configuration δ that agrees with σ, γ in the final $n - t$ coordinates, and the steps taken by the first t processors in δ are precisely the common steps taken by these processors in both σ, γ: at the point where the actions of these processors diverge in σ and γ, the processors are crashed.

Now δ is reachable, and the adversary can continue a partial execution from δ by continually executing sending and receiving steps among the final $n - t$ processors. Since the algorithm $\mathcal{A}$ satisfies measure one termination, if the adversary keeps extending this execution, with probability one a decision must eventually be reached. Let's suppose that this decision is 1 with non-zero probability. Then the same extension can be applied to a partial execution reaching σ and this will yield conflicting decisions with non-zero probability, contradicting measure one correctness. Similarly, if the decision reached from extending δ is 0 with probability 1, then a partial execution reaching γ can be extended to yield conflicting decisions. We may conclude that $\Delta(Z_0^0, Z_1^0) > t$.

We now proceed by induction on k (similarly to the proof of Lemma 13). We assume the result holds for $k - 1 \geq 0$, and we suppose it is false for k. Then there exist reachable configurations $\sigma, \gamma \in \Sigma^n$ such that $\sigma \in Z_0^k$, $\gamma \in Z_1^k$, and $\Delta(\sigma, \gamma) \leq t$. Without loss of generality, we suppose that σ and γ only differ in the first t coordinates. We let S denote the set $\{t+1, t+2, \ldots, n\}$. By definition of Z_0^k, if the adversary applies $S, \ldots, S$ to σ, this will with probability $> \tau$ result in a new configuration belonging to Z_0^{k-1}. If the adversary applies $S, \ldots, S$ to γ, this will with probability $> \tau$ result in a new configuration belonging to Z_1^{k-1}.

We first consider the case where no output bits have yet been written in σ or γ. By the forgetful and fully communicative properties of the algorithm, the distributions of the configurations resulting from applying $S, \ldots, S$ to σ and to γ only differ in portions of the local state that can no longer affect behavior of the processors going forward. This is because the new messages to be sent by all n processors will only depend on the input bits and the newly received $n - t$ messages, not the prior portions of the state that differed between γ and σ. Hence, the product distribution induced by applying $S, \ldots, S$ to γ places weight $> \tau$ of each of two sets, Z_0^{k-1} and Z_1^{k-1}, that are separated by a Hamming distance $> t$. Applying Lemma 9, we thus have that

$$\tau^2 < e^{-\frac{t^2}{4n}} \Leftrightarrow \tau < e^{-\frac{t^2}{8n}}.$$

This contradicts our stipulation on the value of τ.

In the case that an output bit has already been written as 0 in σ, say, then we reach a contradiction by repeatedly applying $S, \ldots, S$ to σ. Since $\gamma \in Z_1^k$, there is a nonzero probability that this results in a decision of 1 by processors outside of the first t, since these are unaffected by the first t processor states when these processors are no longer heard. $\square$

LEMMA 21. *Suppose a fully communicative and forgetful algorithm $\mathcal{A}$ satisfies measure one correctness and termination and $\tau := e^{-\frac{t^2}{8n}}$. Then, for any reachable configuration σ not in $Z_0^k \cup Z_1^k$, there exist sets $S_1, \ldots, S_n$ that can be applied to σ such that the resulting reachable configuration falls outside $Z_0^{k-1} \cup Z_1^{k-1}$ with probability $\geq 1 - 2e^{-\frac{(t-1)^2}{8n}}$.*

The proof of this lemma is essentially the same as the proof of Lemma 14. The proof of Theorem 17 then follows similarly to the proof of 5, and a complete treatment can be found in the full version.

6. REFERENCES

[1] M. K. Aguilera and S. Toueg. The correctness proof of ben-or's randomized consensus algorithm. *Distributed Computing*, 25(5):371–381, 2012.

[2] N. Alon and J. Spencer. *The Probabilistic Method*. John Wiley, 1992.

[3] J. Aspnes. Lower bounds for distributed coin-flipping and randomized consensus. In *STOC*, pages 559–568, 1997.

[4] H. Attiya and K. Censor. Lower bounds for randomized consensus under a weak adversary. In *PODC*, pages 315–324, 2008.

[5] H. Attiya and K. Censor. Tight bounds for asynchronous randomized consensus. *J. ACM*, 55(5), 2008.

[6] Z. Bar-Joseph and M. Ben-Or. A tight lower bound for randomized synchronous consensus. In *PODC*, pages 193–199, 1998.

[7] M. Ben-Or. Another advantage of free choice: Completely asynchronous agreement protocols. In *PODC*, pages 27–30, 1983.

[8] M. Ben-Or, E. Pavlov, and V. Vaikuntanathan. Byzantine agreement in the full-information model in o(log n) rounds. In *STOC*, pages 179–186, 2006.

[9] P. Berman and J. A. Garay. Randomized distributed agreement revisited. In *FTCS*, pages 412–419, 1993.

[10] G. Bracha. An asynchronous [(n-1)/3]-resilient consensus protocol. In *PODC*, pages 154–162, 1984.

[11] C. Cachin, K. Kursawe, and V. Shoup. Random oracles in constantinople: Practical asynchronous byzantine agreement using cryptography. *J. Cryptology*, 18(3):219–246, 2005.

[12] R. Canetti and T. Rabin. Fast asynchronous byzantine agreement with optimal resilience. In *STOC*, pages 42–51, 1993.

[13] D. Dolev and R. Strong. Polynomial algorithms for byzatine agreement. In *STOC*, pages 401–407, 1982.

[14] M. J. Fischer, N. A. Lynch, and M. Paterson. Impossibility of distributed consensus with one faulty process. In *PODS*, pages 1–7, 1983.

[15] S. Goldwasser, E. Pavlov, and V. Vaikuntanathan. Fault-tolerant distributed computing in full-information networks. In *FOCS*, pages 15–26, 2006.

[16] B. M. Kapron, D. Kempe, V. King, J. Saia, and V. Sanwalani. Fast asynchronous byzantine agreement and leader election with full information. In *SODA*, pages 1038–1047, 2008.

[17] V. King and J. Saia. From almost everywhere to everywhere: Byzantine agreement with $\tilde{O}(n^{3/2})$ bits. In *DISC*, pages 464–478, 2009.

[18] V. King and J. Saia. Breaking the $O(n^2)$ bit barrier: scalable byzantine agreement with an adaptive adversary. In *PODC*, pages 420–429, 2010.

[19] V. King and J. Saia. Byzantine agreement in polynomial expected time. In *STOC*, 2013.

[20] V. King, J. Saia, V. Sanwalani, and E. Vee. Scalable leader election. In *SODA*, pages 990–999, 2006.

[21] V. King, J. Saia, V. Sanwalani, and E. Vee. Towards secure and scalable computation in peer-to-peer networks. In *FOCS*, pages 87–98, 2006.

[22] L. Lamport. The part-time parliament. *ACM Trans. Comput. Syst.*, 16(2):133–169, 1998.

[23] L. Lamport, R. E. Shostak, and M. C. Pease. The byzantine generals problem. *ACM Trans. Program. Lang. Syst.*, 4(3):382–401, 1982.

[24] A. Lewko. The contest between simplicity and efficiency in asynchronous byzantine agreement. In *DISC*, pages 348–362, 2011.

[25] J. B. Nielson. A threshold pseudorandom function construction and its applications. In *CRYPTO*, pages 401–416, 2002.

[26] M. Pease, R. Shostak, and L. Lamport. Reaching agreement in the presence of faults. *Journal of the ACM*, 27(2):228–234, 1980.

[27] M. Rabin. Randomized byzantine generals. In *FOCS*, pages 403–409, 1983.

[28] M. Talagrand. Concentration of measure and isoperimetric inequalities in product spaces. *Inst. Hautes Études Sci. Publ. Math.*, (81):73–205, 1995.

[29] S. Toueg. Randomized byzantine agreements. In *PODC*, pages 163–178, 1984.

Introducing Speculation in Self-Stabilization

An Application to Mutual Exclusion

Swan Dubois
École Polytechnique Fédérale de Lausanne
LPD, Station 14
1015 Lausanne, Switzerland
swan.dubois@epfl.ch

Rachid Guerraoui
École Polytechnique Fédérale de Lausanne
LPD, Station 14
1015 Lausanne, Switzerland
rachid.guerraoui@epfl.ch

ABSTRACT

Self-stabilization ensures that, after any transient fault, the system recovers in a finite time and eventually exhibits correct behavior. Speculation consists in guaranteeing that the system satisfies its requirements for any execution but exhibits significantly better performances for a subset of executions that are more probable. A speculative protocol is in this sense supposed to be both robust and efficient in practice.

We introduce the notion of speculative stabilization which we illustrate through the mutual exclusion problem. We then present a novel speculatively stabilizing mutual exclusion protocol. Our protocol is self-stabilizing for any asynchronous execution. We prove that its stabilization time for synchronous executions is $\lceil diam(g)/2 \rceil$ steps (where $diam(g)$ denotes the diameter of the system).

This complexity result is of independent interest. The celebrated mutual exclusion protocol of Dijkstra stabilizes in n steps (where n is the number of processes) in synchronous executions and the question whether the stabilization time could be strictly smaller than the diameter has been open since then (almost 40 years). We show that this is indeed possible for any underlying topology. We also provide a lower bound proof that shows that our new stabilization time of $\lceil diam(g)/2 \rceil$ steps is optimal for synchronous executions, even if asynchronous stabilization is not required.

Categories and Subject Descriptors

D.1.3 [**Programming Techniques**]: Concurrent Programming—*Distributed programming*

General Terms

Algorithms

Keywords

Fault-tolerance, Speculation, Self-stabilization, Mutual exclusion

1. INTRODUCTION

The speculative approach to distributed computing [21, 23, 18, 13, 14] lies on the inherent trade-of between robustness and efficiency. Indeed, we typically require distributed applications to be safe and live under various hostile conditions such as asynchronism, faults, attacks, and contention. This typically leads to high consumption of system resources, *e.g.* time of computation, which is due to the need to perform synchronizations, redundancies or checking.

The speculative approach assumes that, even if degraded conditions are indeed possible, they are less probable than friendly conditions (for example, synchronous executions without faults). The underlying idea is to simultaneously ensure that the protocol is correct whatever the execution is (even in degraded conditions) but to optimize it for a subset of executions that are the most probable in practice. Even if this idea was applied in various contexts, it has never been applied to distributed systems tolerant to transient faults, *i.e.* self-stabilizing systems [8]. In fact, it was not clear whether self-stabilization and speculation could be even combined because of the specific nature of transient faults, for they could corrupt the state of the entire system. The objective of this paper is to explore this avenue.

Self-stabilization was introduced by Dijkstra [8]. Intuitively, a self-stabilizing system ensures that, after the end of any transient fault, the system reaches in a finite time, without any external help, a correct behavior. In other words, a self-stabilizing system repairs itself from any catastrophic state. Since the seminal work of Dijkstra, self-stabilizing protocols were largely studied (see *e.g.* [9, 24, 16]). The main objective has been to design self-stabilizing systems tolerating asynchronism while reducing the stabilization time, *i.e.*, the worst time needed by the protocol to recover a correct behavior over all executions of the system.

Our contribution is twofold. First, we define a new variation of self-stabilization in which the main measure of complexity, the stabilization time, is regarded as a function of the adversary and not as a single value. Indeed, we associate to each adversary (known as a *scheduler* or *daemon* in self-stabilization) the worst stabilization time of the protocol over the set of executions captured by this adversary. Then, we define a speculatively stabilizing protocol as a protocol that self-stabilizes under a given adversary but that exhibits a significantly better stabilization time under another (and weaker) adversary. In this way, we ensure that the protocol stabilizes in a large set of executions but guarantees efficiency only on a smaller set (the one we speculate more probable in practice). For the sake of simplicity, we present our notion of speculative stabilization for two adversaries. It could be easily extended to an arbitrary number of adversaries.

Although the idea of optimizing the stabilization time for some subclass of executions is new, some self-stabilizing protocols satisfy (somehow by accident) our definition of speculative stabilization. For example, the Dijkstra's mutual exclusion protocol stabilization time falls to n steps (the number of processes) in synchronous executions. The question whether one could do better has been open since then, *i.e.* during almost 40 years. We close the question in this paper through the second contribution of this paper.

Indeed, we present a novel speculatively stabilizing mutual exclusion protocol. We prove that its stabilization time for synchronous executions is $\lceil diam(g)/2 \rceil$ steps (where $diam(g)$ denotes the diameter of the system), which significantly improves the bound of Dijkstra's protocol. We prove that we cannot improve it. Indeed, we present a lower bound result on the stabilization time of mutual exclusion for synchronous executions. This result is of independent interest since it remains true beyond the scope of speculation and holds even for a protocol that does not need to stabilize in asynchronous executions.

Designing our protocol went through addressing two technical challenges. First, we require the stabilization of a global property (the uniqueness of critical section) in a time strictly smaller than the diameter of the system, which is counter-intuitive (even for synchronous executions). Second, the optimization of the stabilization time for synchronous executions must not prevent the stabilization for asynchronous ones.

The key to addressing both challenges was a "reduction" to clock synchronization: more specifically, leveraging the self-stabilizing asynchronous unison protocol of [2] within mutual exclusion. We show that it is sufficient to choose correctly the clock size and to grant the access to critical section upon some clock values to ensure (*i*) the self-stabilization of the protocol for any asynchronous execution as well as (*ii*) the optimality of its stabilization time for synchronous ones. This reduction was also, we believe, the key to the genericity of our protocol. Unlike Dijkstra's protocol which assumes an underlying ring shaped communication structure, our protocol runs over any communication structure.

We could derive our lower bound result for synchronous executions based on the observation that a process can gather information at most at distance d in d steps whatever protocol it executes. Hence, in the worst case, it is impossible to prevent two processes from simultaneously entering a critical section during the first $\lceil diam(g)/2 \rceil$ steps of all executions with a deterministic protocol.

The rest of this paper is organized as follows. Section 2 introduces the model and the definitions used through the paper. Section 3 presents our notion of speculative stabilization. Section 4 presents our mutual exclusion protocol. Section 5 provides our lower bound result. Section 6 ends the paper with some perspectives. Due to space limitations, some proofs are only given in the appendix.

2. MODEL AND DEFINITIONS

We consider the classical model of distributed systems introduced by Dijkstra [8]. Processes communicate by atomic reading of all neighbors' states and the (asynchronous) adversary of the system is captured by an abstraction called *daemon*.

Distributed protocol.

The distributed system consists of a set of processes that form a communication graph. The processes are vertices in this graph and the set of those vertices is denoted by V. The edges of this graph are pairs of processes that can communicate with each other. Such pairs are neighbors and the set of edges is denoted by E ($E \subseteq V^2$). Hence, $g = (V, E)$ is the communication graph of the distributed system. Each vertex of g has a set of variables, each of them ranges over a fixed domain of values. A state $\gamma(v)$ of a vertex v is the vector of values of all variables of v at a given time. An assignment of values to all variables of the graph is a configuration. The set of configurations of g is denoted by Γ. An action α of g transitions the graph from one configuration to another with the restriction that each process can only update its state based on locally available information. The set of actions of g is denoted by A ($A = \{(\gamma, \gamma') | \gamma \in \Gamma, \gamma' \in \Gamma, \gamma \neq \gamma'\}$). A *distributed protocol* π on g is defined as a subset of A that gathers all actions of g allowed by π. The set of distributed protocols on g is denoted by Π ($\Pi = P(A)$ where, for any set S, $P(S)$ denotes the powerset of S).

Execution.

Given a graph g, a distributed protocol π on g, an *execution* σ of π on g, starting from a given configuration γ_0, is a sequence of actions of π of the following form $\sigma = (\gamma_0, \gamma_1)(\gamma_1, \gamma_2)(\gamma_2, \gamma_3) \ldots$ that is either infinite or finite but its last configuration is terminal (*i.e.* there exists no actions of π starting from this configuration). The set of all executions of π on g, starting from all configurations of Γ, is denoted by Σ_π.

Adversary (daemon).

Intuitively, a daemon is a restriction on the executions of distributed protocols to be considered possible. For a distributed protocol π, at each configuration γ, a subset of vertices are *enabled*, that is there exists an action of π that modifies their state (formally, v is enabled if $\exists \gamma' \in \Gamma, (\gamma, \gamma') \in \pi, \gamma(v) \neq \gamma'(v)$). The daemon then chooses one of the possible action of π starting from γ (and hence, selects a subset of enabled vertices that are allowed to modify their state during this action). A formal definition follows.

DEFINITION 1 (DAEMON). *Given a graph g, a daemon d on g is a function that associates to each distributed protocol π on g a subset of executions of π, that is $d : \pi \in \Pi \longmapsto d(\pi) \in P(\Sigma_\pi)$.*

Given a graph g, a daemon d on g and a distributed protocol π on g, an execution σ of π ($\sigma \in \Sigma_\pi$) is *allowed* by d if and only if $\sigma \in d(\pi)$. Also, given a graph g, a daemon d on g and a distributed protocol π on g, we say that π *runs on* g under d if we consider that the only possible executions of π on g are those allowed by d.

Some classical examples of daemons follow. The unfair distributed daemon [19] (denoted by ud) is the less constrained one because we made no assumption on its choices (any execution of the distributed protocol is allowed). The synchronous daemon [15] (denoted by sd) is the one that selects all enabled vertices in each configuration. The centralized (*a.k.a.* central) daemon [8] (denoted by *cd*) selects only one enabled vertex in each configuration.

This way of viewing daemons as a set of possible executions (for a particular graph g) drives a natural partial order over the set of daemons. For a particular graph g, a daemon d is more powerful than another daemon d' if all executions allowed by d' are also allowed by d. Overall, d has more scheduling choices than d'. A more precise definition follows.

DEFINITION 2 (PARTIAL ORDER OVER DAEMONS). *For a given graph g, we define the following partial order $\preccurlyeq$ on $\mathcal{D}$: $\forall(d, d') \in \mathcal{D}, d \preccurlyeq d' \Leftrightarrow (\forall \pi \in \Pi, d(\pi) \subseteq d'(\pi))$. If two daemons d and d' satisfy $d \preccurlyeq d'$, we say that d' is more powerful than d.*

For example, the unfair distributed daemon is more powerful than any daemon (in particular the synchronous one). Note that some daemons (for example the synchronous and the central ones) are not comparable. For a more detailed discussion about daemons, the reader is referred to [10].

Further notations.

Given a graph g and a distributed protocol π on g, we introduce the following set of notations. First, n denotes the number of vertices of the graph whereas m denotes the number of its edges ($n = |V|$ and $m = |E|$). The set of neighbors of a vertex v is denoted by $neig(v)$. The distance between two vertices u and v (that is, the length of a shortest path between u and v in g) is denoted by $dist(g, u, v)$. The diameter of g (that is, the maximal distance between two vertices of g) is denoted by $diam(g)$. For any execution $e = (\gamma_0, \gamma_1)(\gamma_1, \gamma_2)\ldots$, we denote by e_i the prefix of e of length i (that is $e_i = (\gamma_0, \gamma_1)(\gamma_1, \gamma_2)\ldots(\gamma_{i-1}, \gamma_i)$).

Guarded representation of distributed protocols.

For the sake of clarity, we do not describe distributed protocols by enumerating all their actions. Instead, we represent distributed protocols using a local description of actions borrowed from [8]. Each vertex has a local protocol consisting of a set of guarded rules of the following form: $<label> :: <guard> \longrightarrow <action>$. $<label>$ is a name to refer to the rule in the text. $<guard>$ is a predicate that involves variables of the vertex and of its neighbors. This predicate is true if and only if the vertex is enabled in the current configuration. We say that a rule is enabled in a configuration when its guard is evaluated to true in this configuration. $<action>$ is a set of instructions modifying the state of the vertex. This set of instructions must describe the changes of the vertex state if this latter is activated by the daemon.

Self-stabilization.

To formally define self-stabilizing distributed protocols, we need first to introduce the notion of specification. The specification of a problem is the set of executions that satisfies the problem. We say that an execution satisfies the specification of a problem if it belongs to this specification.

Intuitively, to be self-stabilizing [8], a distributed protocol must satisfy the two following properties: (*i*) *closure*, that is there exists configurations such that any execution of the distributed protocol starting from them satisfies the specification; and (*ii*) *convergence*, that is starting from any arbitrary configuration, any execution of the distributed protocol reaches in a finite time a configuration that satisfies the closure property.

Self-stabilization induces fault-tolerance since the initial configuration of the system may be arbitrary because of a burst of transient faults. Then, a self-stabilizing distributed protocol ensures that after a finite time (called the convergence or stabilization time), the distributed protocol recovers on his own a correct behavior (by convergence property) and keeps this correct behavior as long as there is no faults (by closure property).

DEFINITION 3 (SELF-STABILIZATION [8]). *A distributed protocol π is self-stabilizing for specification spec under a daemon d if starting from any arbitrary configuration every execution of $d(\pi)$ contains a configuration from which every execution of $d(\pi)$ satisfies spec.*

For any self-stabilizing distributed protocol π under a daemon d for a specification *spec*, its convergence (or stabilization) time (denoted by $conv\_time(\pi, d)$) is the worst stabilization time (that is, the number of actions to reach a configuration from which any execution satisfies *spec*) of executions of π allowed by d. Note that, for any self-stabilizing distributed protocol π under a daemon d and for any daemon d' such that $d' \preccurlyeq d$, π is self-stabilizing under d' and $conv\_time(\pi, d') \leq conv\_time(\pi, d)$.

3. SPECULATIVE STABILIZATION

Intuitively, a speculative protocol ensures the correctness in a large set of executions but is optimized for some scenarios that are speculated to be more frequent (maybe at the price of worse performance in less frequent cases).

Regarding self-stabilization, the most common measure of complexity is the stabilization time. Accordingly, we choose to define a speculatively stabilizing protocol as a self-stabilizing protocol under a given daemon that exhibits a significantly better stabilization time under a weaker daemon (the latter gathers scenarios that are speculated to be more frequent). We can now define our notion of speculative stabilization.

DEFINITION 4 (SPECULATIVE STABILIZATION). *For two daemons d and d' satisfying $d' \prec d$, a distributed protocol π is (d, d', f, f')-speculatively stabilizing for specification spec if: (i) π is self-stabilizing for spec under d; and (ii) f and f' are two function on g satisfying $f' < f$, $conv\_time(\pi, d) \in \Theta(f)$, and $conv\_time(\pi, d') \in \Theta(f')$.*

We restrict ourselves for two daemons here for the sake of clarity. We can easily extend this definition to an arbitrary number of daemons (as long as they are comparable). For instance, we can say that a distributed protocol π is $(d, d_1, d_2, f, f_1, f_2)$-speculatively stabilizing (with $d_1 \prec d$ and $d_2 \prec d$) if it is both (d, d_1, f, f_1)-speculatively stabilizing and (d, d_2, f, f_2)-speculatively stabilizing.

Still for the sake of simplicity, we say in the following that a distributed protocol π is d-speculatively stabilizing for specification *spec* if there exists a daemon $d \neq ud$ such that π is (ud, d, f, f')-speculatively stabilizing for specification *spec*. In other words, a d-speculatively stabilizing distributed protocol is self-stabilizing under the unfair distributed daemon (and hence always guarantees convergence) but is optimized for a given subclass of executions described by d.

Examples.

Although the idea of speculative approach in self-stabilization has not been yet precisely defined, there exists some examples of self-stabilizing distributed protocols in the literature that turn out to be speculative. We survey some of them in the following.

The seminal work of Dijkstra [8] introduced self-stabilization in the context of mutual exclusion. His celebrated protocol operates only on rings. It is in fact $(ud, sd, g \mapsto n^2, g \mapsto n)$-speculatively stabilizing since it stabilizes upon $\Theta(n^2)$ steps under the unfair distributed daemon and it is easy to see that it needs only n steps to stabilize under the synchronous daemon. The well-known $min + 1$ protocol of [17] is $(ud, sd, g \mapsto n^2, g \mapsto diam(g))$-speculatively stabilizing for BFS spanning tree construction. Its stabilization time is in $\Theta(n^2)$ steps under the unfair distributed daemon while it is in $\Theta(diam(g))$ steps under the synchronous daemon. Another example is the self-stabilizing maximal matching protocol of [22]. This protocol is $(ud, sd, g \mapsto m, g \mapsto n)$-speculatively stabilizing: its stabilization time is 4n+2m (respectively 2n+1) steps under the unfair distributed (respectively synchronous) daemon.

4. MUTUAL EXCLUSION PROTOCOL

Mutual exclusion was classically adopted as a benchmark in self-stabilization under various settings [8, 20, 11, 5, 1]. Intuitively, it consists in ensuring that each vertex can enter infinitely often in critical section and there are never two vertices simultaneously in the critical section. Using such a distributed protocol, vertices can for example access shared resources without conflict.

Our contribution in this context is a novel self-stabilizing distributed protocol for mutual exclusion under the unfair distributed daemon that moreover exhibits optimal convergence time under the synchronous daemon. Contrary to the Dijkstra's protocol, our protocol supports any underlying communication structure (we do not assume that the communication graph is reduced to a ring). Thanks to speculation, our protocol is ideal for environment in which we speculate that most of the executions are synchronous.

We adopt the following specification of mutual exclusion. For each vertex v, we define a predicate $privileged_v$ (over variables of v and possibly of its neighbors). We say that a vertex v is privileged in a configuration γ if and only if $privileged_v = true$ in γ. If a vertex v is privileged in a configuration γ and v is activated during an action (γ, γ'), then v executes its critical section during this action. We can now specify the mutual exclusion problem as follows.

SPECIFICATION 1 (MUTUAL EXCLUSION $spec_{ME}$). *An execution e satisfies $spec_{ME}$ if at most one vertex is privileged in any configuration of e (safety) and any vertex infinitely often executes its critical section in e (liveness).*

The rest of this section is organized as follows. Section 4.1 overviews our protocol. Section 4.2 proves the correctness of our protocol under the unfair distributed daemon. Section 4.3 analyzes its stabilization time under the synchronous and the unfair distributed daemon.

4.1 Speculatively Stabilizing Mutual Exclusion

As we restrict ourselves to deterministic protocols, we know by [4] that, to ensure mutual exclusion, we must assume a system with identities (that is, each vertex has a

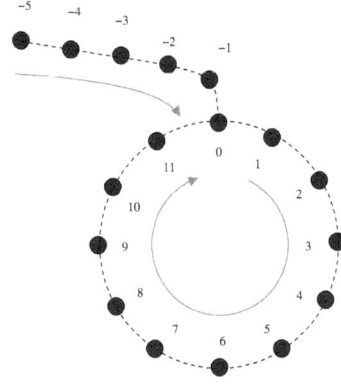

Figure 1: A bounded clock $\mathcal{X} = (cherry(\alpha, K), \phi)$ **with** $\alpha = 5$ **and** $K = 12$.

distinct identifier). Indeed, we know by [4] that the problem does not admit deterministic solution on anonymous (*i.e.* without identifiers) rings of composite size. Moreover, we assume the set of identities (denoted by ID) to be equal to $\{0, 1, \ldots, n-1\}$.

Our protocol is based upon an existing self-stabilizing distributed protocol for the asynchronous unison problem [12, 6]. This problem consists in ensuring, under the unfair distributed daemon, some synchronization guarantees on vertices' clocks. More precisely, each vertex has a register r_v that contains a clock value. A clock is a bounded set enhanced with an incrementation function. Intuitively, an asynchronous unison protocol ensures that the difference between neighbors' registers is bounded and that each register is infinitely often incremented.

In the following, we give the definition of this problem and the solution proposed in [2] from which we derive our mutual exclusion protocol.

Clock.

A bounded clock $\mathcal{X} = (C, \phi)$ is a bounded set $C = cherry(\alpha, K)$ (parametrized with two integers $\alpha \geq 1$ and $K \geq 2$) enhanced with an incrementation function ϕ defined as follows.

Let c be any integer. Denote by $\bar{c}$ the unique element in $[0, \ldots, K-1]$ such that $c = \bar{c} \bmod K$. We define the distance $d_K(c, c') = min\{\overline{c-c'}, \overline{c'-c}\}$ on $[0, \ldots, K-1]$. Two integers c and c' are said to be locally comparable if and only if $d_K(a, b) \leq 1$. We then define the local relation $\leq_l$ as follows: $c \leq_l c'$ if and only if $0 \leq \overline{c'-c} \leq 1$ (note that this relation is not an order). Let us define $cherry(\alpha, K) = \{-\alpha, \ldots, 0, \ldots, K-1\}$. Let ϕ be the function defined by:

$$\phi : c \in cherry(\alpha, K) \mapsto \begin{cases} (c+1) & \text{if } c < 0 \\ (c+1) \bmod K & \text{otherwise} \end{cases}$$

The pair $\mathcal{X} = (cherry(\alpha, K), \phi)$ is called a bounded clock of initial value α and of size K (see Figure 1). We say that a clock value $c \in cherry(\alpha, K)$ is incremented when this value is replaced by $\phi(c)$. A reset on $\mathcal{X}$ consists of an operation replacing any value of $cherry(\alpha, K) \setminus \{-\alpha\}$ by $-\alpha$. Let $init_{\mathcal{X}} = \{-\alpha, \ldots, 0\}$ and $stab_{\mathcal{X}} = \{0, \ldots, K-1\}$ be the set of initial values and correct values respectively. Let us denote $init_{\mathcal{X}}^* = init_{\mathcal{X}} \setminus \{0\}$, $stab_{\mathcal{X}}^* = stab_{\mathcal{X}} \setminus \{0\}$, and $\leq_{init}$ the usual total order on $init_{\mathcal{X}}$.

Asynchronous unison.

Given a distributed system in which each vertex v has a register r_v taken a value of a bounded clock $\mathcal{X} = (C, \phi)$ with $C = cherry(\alpha, K)$, we define a legitimate configuration for asynchronous unison as a configuration satisfying: $\forall v \in V, \forall u \in neig(v), (r_v \in stab_{\mathcal{X}}) \wedge (r_u \in stab_{\mathcal{X}}) \wedge (d_K(r_v, r_u) \leq 1)$. In other words, a legitimate configuration is a configuration in which each clock value is a correct one and the drift between neighbors' registers is bounded by 1. We denote by Γ_1 the set of legitimate configurations for asynchronous unison. Note that we have, for any configuration of Γ_1 and any pair of vertices, (u, v), $d_K(r_u, r_v) \leq diam(g)$ by definition. We can now specify the problem.

SPECIFICATION 2 (ASYNCHRONOUS UNISON $spec_{AU}$). *An execution e satisfies $spec_{AU}$ if every configuration of e belongs to Γ_1 (safety) and the clock value of each vertex is infinitely often incremented in e (liveness).*

In [2], the authors propose a self-stabilizing asynchronous unison distributed protocol in any anonymous distributed system under the unfair distributed daemon. The main idea of this protocol is to reset the clock value of each vertex that detects any local clock inconsistence (that is, whenever some neighbor that has a not locally comparable clock value). Otherwise, a vertex is allowed to increment its clock (of initial or of correct value) only if this latter has locally the smallest value. The choice of parameters α and K are crucial. In particular, to make the protocol self-stabilizing for any anonymous communication graph g under the unfair distributed daemon, the parameters must satisfy $\alpha \geq hole(g) - 2$ and $K > cyclo(g)$, where $hole(g)$ and $cyclo(g)$ are two constants related to the topology of g. Namely, $hole(g)$ is the length of a longest hole in g (*i.e.* the longest chordless cycle), if g contains a cycle, 2 otherwise. $cyclo(g)$ is the cyclomatic characteristic of g (*i.e.* the length of the maximal cycle of the shortest maximal cycle basis of g, see [2] for a formal definition), if g contains a cycle, 2 otherwise. Actually, [2] shows that taking $\alpha \geq hole(g) - 2$ ensures that the protocol recovers in finite time a configuration in Γ_1. Then, taking $K > cyclo(g)$ ensures that each vertex increments its local clock infinitely often. Note that, by definition, $hole(g)$ and $cyclo(g)$ are bounded by n.

The mutual exclusion protocol.

The main idea behind our protocol is to execute the asynchronous unison of [2], presented earlier, with a particular bounded clock and then to grant the privilege to a vertex only when its clock reaches some value. The clock size must be sufficiently large to ensure that at most one vertex is privileged in any configuration of Γ_1. If the definition of the predicate *privileged* guarantees this property, then the correctness of our mutual exclusion protocol follows from the one of the underlying asynchronous unison.

More specifically, we choose a bounded clock $\mathcal{X} = (cherry(\alpha, K), \phi)$ with $\alpha = n$ and $K = (2.n - 1)(diam(g) + 1) + 2$ and we define $privileged_v \equiv (r_v = 2.n + 2.diam(g).id_v)$. In particular, note that we have : $privileged_{v_0} \equiv (r_{v_0} = 2.n)$ and $privileged_{v_{n-1}} \equiv (r_{v_{n-1}} = (2.n - 2)(diam(g) + 1) + 2)$.

Our distributed protocol, called $\mathcal{SSME}$ (for $\mathcal{S}$peculatively $\mathcal{S}$tabilizing $\mathcal{M}$utual $\mathcal{E}$xclusion), is described in Algorithm 1.

Note that this protocol is identical to the one of [2] except for the size of the clock and the definition of the predicate *privileged* (that does not interfere with the protocol).

We prove in the following that this protocol is self-stabilizing for $spec_{ME}$ under the unfair distributed daemon and exhibits the optimal convergence time under the synchronous one. In other words, we will prove that this protocol is sd-speculatively stabilizing for $spec_{ME}$.

4.2 Correctness

We prove here the self-stabilization of $\mathcal{SSME}$ under the unfair distributed daemon.

THEOREM 1. *$\mathcal{SSME}$ is a self-stabilizing distributed protocol for $spec_{ME}$ under ud.*

PROOF. As we choose $\alpha = n \geq hole(g) - 2$ and $K = (2.n - 1)(diam(g) + 1) + 2 > n \geq cyclo(g)$, the main result of [2] allows us to deduce that $\mathcal{SSME}$ is a self-stabilizing distributed protocol for $spec_{AU}$ under ud (recall that the predicate *privileged* does not interfere with the protocol). By definition, this implies that there exists, for any execution e of $\mathcal{SSME}$ under ud, a suffix e' reached in a finite time that satisfies $spec_{AU}$.

Let γ be a configuration of e' such a vertex v is privileged in γ. Then, by definition, we have $r_v = 2.n + 2.diam(g).id_v$. As γ belongs to e', we can deduce that $\gamma \in \Gamma_1$. Hence, for any vertex $u \in V \setminus \{v\}$, we have $d_K(r_u, r_v) \leq diam(g)$. Then, by definition of the predicate $prvileged$, no other vertex than v can be privileged in γ. We can deduce that the safety of $spec_{ME}$ is satisfied on e'. The liveness of $spec_{ME}$ on e' follows from the one of $spec_{AU}$ and from the definition of the predicate *privileged*.

Hence, for any execution of $\mathcal{SSME}$ under ud, there exists a suffix reached in a finite time that satisfies $spec_{ME}$, that proves the theorem. $\square$

4.3 Time Complexities

This section analyses the time complexity of our self-stabilizing mutual exclusion protocol. In particular, we provide an upper bound of its stabilization time under the synchronous daemon (see Theorem 2) and under the unfair distributed daemon (see Theorem 3).

Synchronous daemon.

We first focus on the stabilization time of $\mathcal{SSME}$ under the synchronous daemon. We need to introduce some notations and definitions.

From now, $e = (\gamma_0, \gamma_1)(\gamma_1, \gamma_2) \ldots$ denotes a synchronous execution of $\mathcal{SSME}$ starting from an arbitrary configuration γ_0. For a configuration γ_i and a vertex v, r_v^i denotes the value of r_v in γ_i.

DEFINITION 5 (ISLAND). *In a configuration γ_i, an island I is a maximal (w.r.t. inclusion) set of vertices such that $I \subsetneq V$ and $\forall (u, v) \in I, u \in neig(v) \Rightarrow correct_v(u)$. A zero-island is an island such that $\exists v \in I, r_v^i = 0$. A non-zero-island is an island such that $\forall v \in I, r_v^i \neq 0$.*

Note that any vertex v that satisfies $r_v \in stab_{\mathcal{X}}$ in a configuration $\gamma \notin \Gamma_1$ belongs by definition to an island (either a zero-island or a non-zero-island) in γ.

DEFINITION 6 (BORDER AND DEPTH OF AN ISLAND). *In a configuration γ_i that contains an island $I \neq \emptyset$, the*

294

Algorithm 1 $\mathcal{SSME}$: Mutual exclusion protocol for vertex v.

Constants:

$id_v \in ID$	:	identity of v
$n \in \mathbb{N}$	:	number of vertices of the communication graph
$diam(g) \in \mathbb{N}$	:	diameter of the communication graph
$\mathcal{X} = (cherry(n, (2.n-1)(diam(g)+1)+2), \phi)$	:	clock of v

Variable:

$r_v \in \mathcal{X}$: register of v

Predicates:

$$
\begin{aligned}
privileged_v &\equiv (r_v = 2.n + 2.diam(g).id_v) \\
correct_v(u) &\equiv (r_v \in stab_\mathcal{X}) \wedge (r_u \in stab_\mathcal{X}) \wedge (d_K(r_v, r_u) \leq 1) \\
allCorrect_v &\equiv \forall u \in neig(v), correct_v(u) \\
normalStep_v &\equiv allCorrect_v \wedge (\forall u \in neig(v), r_v \leq_l r_u) \\
convergeStep_v &\equiv r_v \in init_\mathcal{X}^* \wedge \forall u \in neig(v), (r_u \in init_\mathcal{X} \wedge r_v \leq_{init} r_u) \\
resetInit_v &\equiv \neg allCorrect_v \wedge (r_v \notin init_\mathcal{X})
\end{aligned}
$$

Rules:

$$
\begin{aligned}
NA &:: normalStep_v &\longrightarrow& \quad r_v := \phi(r_v) \\
CA &:: convergeStep_v &\longrightarrow& \quad r_v := \phi(r_v) \\
RA &:: resetInit_v &\longrightarrow& \quad r_v := -n
\end{aligned}
$$

---

border of I (denoted by $border(I)$) is defined by $border(I) = \{v \in I | \exists u \in V \setminus I, u \in neig(v)\}$ and the depth of I (denoted by $depth(I)$) is defined by $depth(I) = max\{min\{dist(g,v,u) | u \in border(I)\} | v \in I\}$.

Then, we have to prove a set of preliminary lemmata before stating our main theorem.

LEMMA 1. *If a vertex v is privileged in a configuration γ_i (with $0 \leq i < diam(g)$), then v cannot execute rules CA and RA in e_i.*

PROOF. As the result is obvious for $i = 0$, let γ_i (with $0 < i < diam(g)$) be a configuration such that a vertex v is privileged in γ_i. Then, we have by definition that $r_v^i = 2.n + 2.diam(g).id_v$.

By contradiction, assume that v executes at least once rule CA or RA in e_i. Let j be the biggest integer such that v executes rule CA or RA during action (γ_j, γ_{j+1}) with $j < i$.

Assume that v executes rule RA during (γ_j, γ_{j+1}). Then, we have $r_v^{j+1} = -n$. From this point, only rule CA may be enabled at v but v does not execute it by construction of j. Then, we can deduce that $r_v^i = -n$ that is contradictory.

Hence, we know that v executes rule CA during (γ_j, γ_{j+1}). Consequently, we have $r_v^{j+1} \in init_\mathcal{X}$ by construction of the rule. As v can only execute rule NA between γ_{j+1} and γ_i by construction of j, we can deduce that $r_v^i \in init_\mathcal{X} \cup \{0, \ldots, 0 + i - (j+1)\}$. As $0 + i - (j+1) < diam(g)$, this contradiction proves the result. $\square$

LEMMA 2. *If a vertex v is privileged in a configuration γ_i (with $0 \leq i < diam(g)$), then v cannot belong to a zero-island in any configuration of e_i.*

PROOF. Let γ_i (with $0 \leq i < diam(g)$) be a configuration such that a vertex v is privileged in γ_i. Then, we have by definition that $r_v^i = 2.n + 2.diam(g).id_v$.

By contradiction, assume that there exists some configurations of e_i such that v belongs to a zero-island. Let j be the biggest integer such that v belongs to a zero-island I in γ_j with $j \leq i$.

By definition of a zero-island, we know that there exists a vertex u in I such that $r_u^j = 0$. As $dist(g, u, v) \leq diam(g)$ and u and v belongs to the same island in γ_j, we have

$d_K(r_u^j, r_v^j) \leq diam(g)$. By construction of the clock, we have so $r_v^j \in \{(2.n-2)(diam(g)+1)+3, \ldots, 0, \ldots, diam(g)\}$.

By Lemma 1, we know that v may execute only rule NA between γ_j and γ_i. Then, we have $r_v^i \in \{(2.n-2)(diam(g)+1)+3, \ldots, 0, \ldots, diam(g)+(i-j)\}$. As $diam(g)+(i-j) < 2.diam(g) < 2.n + 2.diam(g) < \ldots$, v cannot be privileged in γ_i (whatever is its identity). This contradiction proves the result. $\square$

LEMMA 3. *If a vertex v belongs to a non-zero-island of depth $k \geq 0$ in a configuration γ_i (with $0 < i < diam(g)$), then v belongs either to a non-zero-island of depth at least $k+1$ or to a zero-island in γ_{i-1}.*

PROOF. Let γ_i (with $0 < i < diam(g)$) be a configuration such that a vertex v belongs to a non-zero-island I of depth $k \geq 0$ in γ_i.

Assume that v does not belongs to any island in γ_{i-1}. In other words, we have $r_v^{i-1} \in init_\mathcal{X}^*$. Consequently, v may only execute rule CA during action (γ_{i-1}, γ_i) and we have $r_v^i \in init_\mathcal{X}$. This means that v either belongs to a zero-island or does not belong to any island in γ_i. This contradiction shows us that v belongs to an island in γ_{i-1}.

If v belongs to a zero-island in γ_{i-1}, we have the result. Otherwise, assume by contradiction that v belongs to a non-zero island I' such that $depth(I') \leq k$ in γ_{i-1}. By definition of a non-zero-island, all vertices of $border(I')$ are enabled by rule RA in γ_{i-1}. As we consider a synchronous execution, we obtain that I (the non-zero-island that contains v in γ_i) satisfies $depth(I) < k$. This contradiction shows the lemma. $\square$

LEMMA 4. *If $\gamma_0 \notin \Gamma_1$, then any vertex v satisfies $r_v^{diam(g)} \in init_\mathcal{X} \cup \{(2.n-2)(diam(g)+1)+3, \ldots, 0, \ldots, 2.diam(g)-1\}$.*

PROOF. Assume that $\gamma_0 \notin \Gamma_1$. Then, by definition of Γ_1 and by the construction of the protocol, we know that there exists a set $\emptyset \neq V' \subseteq V$ such that vertices of V' are enabled by rule RA in γ_0. Let v be an arbitrary vertex of V.

If v executes at least once the rule RA during $e_{diam(g)}$, let i be the biggest integer such that v executes rule RA during (γ_i, γ_{i+1}) with $i < diam(g)$. Then, we have $r_v^{i+1} = -n$. As $diam(g) - (i+1) < n$, we can deduce that v may execute only rule CA between γ_i and $\gamma_{diam(g)}$. Consequently, we have $r_v^{diam(g)} \in init_X$.

If v executes at least once the rule CA but never executes rule RA during $e_{diam(g)}$, let i be the biggest integer such that v executes rule CA during (γ_i, γ_{i+1}) with $i < diam(g)$. Then, we have $r_v^{i+1} \in init_X$. By construction of i, we can deduce that v may execute only rule NA between γ_i and $\gamma_{diam(g)}$. As $diam(g)-(i+1) < diam(g)$, we have $r_v^{diam(g)} \in init_X \cup \{0, \ldots, diam(g) - 1\}$.

Otherwise (v executes only rule NA during $e_{diam(g)}$), let i be the integer defined by $i = min\{dist(g, v, v')|v' \in V'\}$. Note that $0 < i \le diam(g)$ by construction (recall that $v \notin V'$). We can deduce that v belongs to a zero-island in γ_i (otherwise, v executes rule RA or CA during (γ_i, γ_{i+1})). By definition of a zero-island, we have then $r_v^i \in \{(2.n-2)(diam(g)+1)+3, \ldots, 0, \ldots diam(g)\}$. As v may execute only rule NA between γ_i and $\gamma_{diam(g)}$ and $diam(g) - i < diam(g)$, we can deduce that $r_v^{diam(g)} \in \{(2.n-2)(diam(g)+1)+3, \ldots, 0, \ldots, 2.diam(g) - 1\}$. $\square$

THEOREM 2. $conv\_time(SSME, sd) \le \left\lceil \frac{diam(g)}{2} \right\rceil$

PROOF. By contradiction, assume that $conv\_time(SSME, sd) > \left\lceil \frac{diam(g)}{2} \right\rceil$. This means that there exists a configuration γ_0 such that the synchronous execution $e = (\gamma_0, \gamma_1)(\gamma_1, \gamma_2)\ldots$ of $SSME$ satisfies: there exists an integer $i \ge \left\lceil \frac{diam(g)}{2} \right\rceil$ and two vertices u and v such that u and v are simultaneously privileged in γ_i. Let us study the following cases (note that they are exhaustive):

Case 1: $\left\lceil \frac{diam(g)}{2} \right\rceil \le i < diam(g)$

By Lemma 1, we know that u may execute only rule NA in e_i. This implies that $\forall j \le i, r_u^j \in stab_X$ and then $d_K(r_u^i, r_u^0) \le i$. By the same way, we can prove that $d_K(r_v^i, r_v^0) \le i$.

If u is privileged in γ_i, this means that $r_u^i \in stab_X$ and $d_K(r_u^i, 0) > diam(g)$. As u and v are simultaneously privileged in γ_i, we have by definition that $d_K(r_u^i, r_v^i) > diam(g)$. This implies that $\gamma_i \notin \Gamma_1$ and that u belongs to a non-zero-island I such that $depth(I) \ge 1$ in γ_i. By recursive application of Lemmas 2 and 3, we deduce that u belongs to a non-zero-island I' such that $depth(I') \ge i + 1 \ge \left\lceil \frac{diam(g)}{2} \right\rceil + 1$ in γ_0. The same property holds for v. As $dist(g, u, v) \le diam(g)$, we can deduce that u and v belongs to the same non-zero-island in γ_0, that allows us to state $d_K(r_u^0, r_v^0) \le diam(g)$.

Without loss of generality, assume that $id_u < id_v$. Let us now distinguish the following cases:

If $id_v - id_u \ge 2$, as u and v are simultaneously privileged in γ_i, we have $d_K(r_u^i, r_v^i) \ge 2.n + diam(g) + 1$ (if $id_u = n-1$ and $id_v = 0$) or $d_K(r_u^i, r_v^i) \ge 4.diam(g)$ (otherwise). Note that in both cases, we have $d_K(r_u^i, r_v^i) \ge 3.diam(g)$. Recall that d_K is a distance. In particular, it must satisfy the triangular inequality. Then, we have $d_K(r_u^i, r_v^i) \le d_K(r_u^i, r_u^0) + d_K(r_u^0, r_v^0) + d_K(r_u^0, r_v^i)$. By previous result, we obtain that $d_K(r_u^i, r_v^i) \le diam(g) + 2.i < 3.diam(g)$, that is contradictory.

If $id_v - id_u = 1$, by construction of γ_i, we have $r_u^i = 2.n + 2.diam(g).id_u > 0$ and $r_v^i = 2.n + 2.diam(g).(id_u + 1)$. Then, we obtain $r_v^i - r_u^i = 2.diam(g)$. Hence, we have $0 < r_u^0 \le r_u^i < r_v^0 \le r_v^i$. Then, we can deduce from $r_v^i - r_u^i = 2.diam(g)$ and $r_u^i - r_u^0 \ge 0$ that $r_v^i - r_u^0 \ge 2.diam(g)$. On the

other hand, previous results show us that $r_u^0 - r_u^0 \le diam(g)$ and $r_v^i - r_v^0 < diam(g)$. It follows $r_v^i - r_u^0 < 2.diam(g)$, that is contradictory.

Case 2: $diam(g) \le i < 2.n + diam(g)$

As u and v are simultaneously privileged in γ_i, we have by definition that $d_K(r_u^i, r_v^i) > diam(g)$. This implies that $\gamma_i \notin \Gamma_1$ and then $\gamma_0 \notin \Gamma_1$ (otherwise, we obtain a contradiction with the closure of $spec_{AU}$).

By Lemma 4, for any vertex w, $r_w^{diam(g)} \in init_X \cup \{(2.n-2)(diam(g)+1)+3, \ldots, 0, \ldots, 2.diam(g)-1\}$. As w may execute at most $i - diam(g) < 2.n$ actions between $\gamma_{diam(g)}$ and γ_i, we can deduce that $r_w^i \in init_X \cup \{(2.n-2)(diam(g)+1)+3, \ldots, 0, \ldots, 2.n + 2.diam(g) - 1\}$ for any vertex w.

By construction of the clock and the definition of the predicate $privileged$, we can conclude that there is at most one privileged vertex (the one with identity 0) in γ_i, that is contradictory.

Case 3: $i \ge 2.n + diam(g)$

By [3], we know that $SSME$ stabilizes to $spec_{AU}$ in at most $\alpha + lcp(g) + diam(g)$ steps under the synchronous daemon where $lcp(g)$ denotes the length of the longest elementary chordless path of g. As we have $\alpha = n$ by construction and $lcp(g) \le n$ by definition, we can deduce that $SSME$ stabilizes to $spec_{AU}$ in at most $2.n + diam(g)$ steps under the synchronous daemon.

In particular, this implies that $\gamma_i \in \Gamma_1$. Then, using proof of Theorem 1, we obtain a contradiction with the fact that u and v are simultaneously privileged in γ_i.

We thus obtain that $conv\_time(SSME, sd) \le \left\lceil \frac{diam(g)}{2} \right\rceil$. $\square$

Unfair distributed daemon.

We now interested in the stabilization time of our mutual exclusion protocol under the unfair distributed daemon. Using a previous result from [7], we have the following upper bound:

THEOREM 3. $conv\_time(SSME, ud) \in O(diam(g).n^3)$

PROOF. Remind that the stabilization time of $SSME$ for $spec_{AU}$ is an upper bound for the one for $spec_{ME}$ whatever the daemon is. The step complexity of this protocol is tricky to exactly compute. As the best of our knowledge, [7] provides the best known upper bound on this step complexity.

The main result of [7] is to prove that $SSME$ stabilizes in at most $2.diam(g).n^3 + (\alpha + 1).n^2 + (\alpha - 2.diam(g)).n$ steps under ud. Since we chose $\alpha = n$, we have the result. $\square$

5. SYNCHRONOUS LOWER BOUND

We prove here a lower bound on the stabilization time of mutual exclusion under a synchronous daemon, showing hereby that our speculatively stabilizing protocol presented in Section 4.1 is in this sense optimal. We introduce some definitions and a lemma.

DEFINITION 7 (LOCAL STATE). *Given a configuration γ, a vertex v and an integer $0 \le k \le diam(g)$, the k-local state of v in γ (denoted by $\gamma_{v,k}$) is the configuration of the communication subgraph $g' = (V', E')$ induced by $V' = \{v' \in V | dist(g, v, v') \le k\}$ defined by $\forall v' \in V', \gamma_{v,k}(v') = \gamma(v')$.*

Note that $\gamma_{v,0} = \gamma(v)$ by definition.

DEFINITION 8 (RESTRICTION OF AN EXECUTION).
Given an execution $e = (\gamma_0, \gamma_1)(\gamma_1, \gamma_2) \ldots$ and a vertex v, the restriction of e to v (denoted by e_v) is defined by $e_v = (\gamma_0(v), \gamma_1(v))(\gamma_1(v), \gamma_2(v)) \ldots$.

LEMMA 5. *For any self-stabilizing distributed protocol π for $spec_{ME}$ under the synchronous daemon and any pair of configuration (γ, γ') such that there exists a vertex v and an integer $1 \leq k \leq diam(g)$ satisfying $\gamma_{v,k} = \gamma'_{v,k}$, the restrictions to v of the prefixes of length k of executions of π starting respectively from γ and γ' are equals.*

PROOF. Let π be a self-stabilizing distributed protocol for $spec_{ME}$ under the synchronous daemon and (γ, γ') two configurations such that there exists a vertex v and an integer $1 \leq k \leq diam(g)$ satisfying $\gamma_{v,k} = \gamma'_{v,k}$. We denote by $e = (\gamma, \gamma_1)(\gamma_1, \gamma_2) \ldots$ (respectively $e' = (\gamma', \gamma'_1)(\gamma'_1, \gamma'_2) \ldots$) the synchronous execution of π starting from γ (respectively γ'). We are going to prove the lemma by induction on k.

For $k = 1$, we have $\gamma_{v,1} = \gamma'_{v,1}$, that is the state of v and of its neighbors are identical in γ and γ'. As the daemon is synchronous, we have $(e_1)_v = (e'_1)_v$, that implies the result.

For $k > 1$, assume that the lemma is true for $k - 1$. The induction assumption and the synchrony of the daemon allows us to deduce that $(e_{k-1})_v = (e'_{k-1})_v$ and $\forall u \in neig(v), (e_{k-1})_u = (e'_{k-1})_u$. Hence, we have $(\gamma_{k-1})_{v,1} = (\gamma'_{k-1})_{v,1}$. Then, by the same argument than in the case $k = 1$, we deduce that $(\gamma_k)_{v,0} = (\gamma'_k)_{v,0}$, that implies the result. $\square$

THEOREM 4. *Any self-stabilizing distributed protocol π for $spec_{ME}$ satisfies $conv\_time(\pi, sd) \geq \left\lceil \frac{diam(g)}{2} \right\rceil$.*

PROOF. By contradiction, assume that there exists a self-stabilizing distributed protocol π for $spec_{ME}$ such that $conv\_time(\pi, sd) < \left\lceil \frac{diam(g)}{2} \right\rceil$. For the sake of notation, let us denote $t = conv\_time(\pi, sd)$.

Given an arbitrary communication graph g, choose two vertices u and v such that $dist(g, u, v) = diam(g)$ and an arbitrary configuration γ_0. Denote by $e = (\gamma_0, \gamma_1)(\gamma_1, \gamma_2) \ldots$ the synchronous execution of π starting from γ_0.

By definition, e contains an infinite suffix in which u (respectively v) executes infinitely often its critical section. Hence, there exists a configuration γ_i (respectively γ_j) such that u (respectively v) is privileged in γ_i (respectively γ_j) and $i > t$ (respectively $j > t$).

As $t < \left\lceil \frac{diam(g)}{2} \right\rceil$ and $dist(g, u, v) = diam(g)$, there exists at least one configuration γ'_0 such that $(\gamma'_0)_{u,t} = (\gamma_{i-t})_{u,t}$ and $(\gamma'_0)_{v,t} = (\gamma_{j-t})_{v,t}$. Let $e' = (\gamma'_0, \gamma'_1)(\gamma'_1, \gamma'_2) \ldots$ be the synchronous execution of π starting from γ'_0.

By Lemma 5, we can deduce that the restriction to u of the prefix of length t of e' is the same as the one of the suffix of e starting from γ_{i-t}. In particular, u is privileged in γ'_t. By the same way, we know that v is privileged in γ'_t. This contradiction leads to the result. $\square$

6. CONCLUSION

This paper studies explicitly for the first time the notion of speculation in self-stabilization. As the main measure in this context is the stabilization time, we naturally consider that a speculatively stabilizing protocol is a self-stabilizing protocol for a given adversary that exhibits moreover a better stabilization time under another (and weaker) adversary.

This weaker adversary captures a subset of most probable executions for which the protocol is optimized.

To illustrate this approach, we consider the seminal problem of Dijkstra on self-stabilization: mutual exclusion. We provide a new self-stabilizing mutual exclusion protocol. We prove then that this protocol has an optimal stabilization time in synchronous executions.

Our paper opens a new path of research in self-stabilization by considering the stabilization time of a protocol as a function of the adversary and not as a single value. As a continuation, one could naturally apply our new notion of speculative stabilization to other classical problems of distributed computing and provide speculative protocols for other adversaries than the synchronous one. It may also be interesting to study a composition tool that automatically ensures speculative stabilization.

7. REFERENCES

[1] J. Beauquier and J. Burman. Self-stabilizing mutual exclusion and group mutual exclusion for population protocols with covering. In *OPODIS*, pages 235–250, 2011.

[2] C. Boulinier, F. Petit, and V. Villain. When graph theory helps self-stabilization. In *PODC*, pages 150–159, 2004.

[3] C. Boulinier, F. Petit, and V. Villain. Synchronous vs. asynchronous unison. *Algorithmica*, 51(1):61–80, 2008.

[4] J. E. Burns and J. K. Pachl. Uniform self-stabilizing rings. *ACM Trans. Program. Lang. Syst.*, 11(2):330–344, 1989.

[5] V. Chernoy, M. Shalom, and S. Zaks. A self-stabilizing algorithm with tight bounds for mutual exclusion on a ring. In *DISC*, pages 63–77, 2008.

[6] J.-M. Couvreur, N. Francez, and M. G. Gouda. Asynchronous unison. In *ICDCS*, pages 486–493, 1992.

[7] S. Devismes and F. Petit. On efficiency of unison. In *TADDS*, pages 20–25, 2012.

[8] E. W. Dijkstra. Self-stabilizing systems in spite of distributed control. *Communication of ACM*, 17(11):643–644, 1974.

[9] S. Dolev. *Self-stabilization*. MIT Press, 2000.

[10] S. Dubois and S. Tixeuil. A taxonomy of daemons in self-stabilization. *CoRR*, abs/1110.0334, 2011.

[11] P. Duchon, N. Hanusse, and S. Tixeuil. Optimal randomized self-stabilizing mutual exclusion on synchronous rings. In *DISC*, pages 216–229, 2004.

[12] M. G. Gouda and T. Herman. Stabilizing unison. *Information Processing Letters*, 35(4):171–175, 1990.

[13] R. Guerraoui, N. Knezevic, V. Quéma, and M. Vukolic. The next 700 bft protocols. In *EuroSys*, pages 363–376, 2010.

[14] R. Guerraoui, V. Kuncak, and G. Losa. Speculative linearizability. In *PLDI*, pages 55–66, 2012.

[15] T. Herman. Probabilistic self-stabilization. *Information Processing Letters*, 35(2):63–67, 1990.

[16] T. Herman. A comprehensive bibliography on self-stabilization. http://www.cs.uiowa.edu/ftp/selfstab/bibliography/, 2002.

[17] S.-T. Huang and N.-S. Chen. A self-stabilizing algorithm for constructing breadth-first trees. *Information Processing Letters*, 41(2):109–117, 1992.

[18] P. Jayanti. Adaptive and efficient abortable mutual exclusion. In *PODC*, pages 295–304, 2003.

[19] H. Kakugawa and M. Yamashita. Uniform and self-stabilizing token rings allowing unfair daemon. *IEEE Transactions on Parallel and Distributed Systems*, 8(2):154–162, 1997.

[20] H. Kakugawa and M. Yamashita. Uniform and self-stabilizing fair mutual exclusion on unidirectional rings under unfair distributed daemon. *J. Parallel Distrib. Comput.*, 62(5):885–898, 2002.

[21] B. W. Lampson. Lazy and speculative execution in computer systems. In *ICFP*, pages 1–2, 2008.

[22] F. Manne, M. Mjelde, L. Pilard, and S. Tixeuil. A new self-stabilizing maximal matching algorithm. *Theoretical Computer Science*, 410(14):1336–1345, 2009.

[23] F. Pedone. Boosting system performance with optimistic distributed protocols. *IEEE Computer*, 34(12):80–86, 2001.

[24] S. Tixeuil. *Algorithms and Theory of Computation Handbook, Second Edition*, chapter Self-stabilizing Algorithms, pages 26.1–26.45. Chapman & Hall/CRC Applied Algorithms and Data Structures. CRC Press, Taylor & Francis Group, November 2009.

Leaplist: Lessons Learned in Designing TM-Supported Range Queries

Hillel Avni
Tel-Aviv University
hillel.avni@gmail.com

Nir Shavit
MIT and Tel-Aviv University
shanir@csail.mit.edu

Adi Suissa
Ben-Gurion University
adisuis@cs.bgu.ac.il

ABSTRACT

We introduce *Leaplist*, a concurrent data-structure that is tailored to provide linearizable range queries. A lookup in *Leaplist* takes O(log n) and is comparable to a balanced binary search tree or to a Skiplist. However, in *Leaplist*, each node holds up-to K immutable key-value pairs, so collecting a linearizable range is K times faster than the same operation performed non-linearizably on a Skiplist.

We show how software transactional memory support in a commercial compiler helped us create an efficient lock-based implementation of *Leaplist*. We used this STM to implement short transactions which we call Locking Transactions (LT), to acquire locks, while verifying that the state of the data-structure is legal, and combine them with a transactional Consistency Oblivious Programming (COP) [2] mechanism to enhance data structure traversals.

We compare *Leaplist* to prior implementations of Skiplists, and show that while updates in the *Leaplist* are slower, lookups are somewhat faster, and for range-queries the *Leaplist* outperforms the Skiplist's non-linearizable range query operations by an order of magnitude. We believe that this data structure and its performance would have been impossible to obtain without the STM support.

Categories and Subject Descriptors

D.1.3 [**Software**]: Programming Techniques—*Concurrent Programming*

Keywords

Transactional-Memory, Data-Structures, Range-Queries

1. INTRODUCTION AND RELATED WORK

Consider linearizable concurrent implementations of an abstract dictionary data structure that stores key-value pairs and supports, in addition to the usual Update(key, value), Remove(key), and Find(key), a Range-Query(a, b) operation, where a ≤ b, which returns all pairs with keys in

the closed interval [a, b], where a and b may not be in the data structure. This type of data structure is useful for various database applications, in particular in-memory databases. This paper is interested in the design of high performance dictionaries with linearizable concurrent range queries. As such, the typically logarithmic search for the first item in the range is not the most important performance element. Rather, it is the coordination and synchronization around the sets of neighboring keys being collected in the sequence. This is a tricky new synchronization problem and our goal is to evaluate which transactional support paradigm, if any, can help in attaining improved performance for range queries.

1.1 Related Work

Perhaps the most straightforward way to implement a linearizable concurrent version of an abstract dictionary-with-range-queries, is to directly employ software transactional memory (STM) in implementing its methods.[1] An STM allows a programmer to specify that certain blocks of code should be executed atomically relative to one another. Recently, several fast concurrent binary search-tree algorithms using STM have been introduced by Afek et al. [2] and Bronson et al. [4]. Although they offer good performance for Updates, Removes and Finds, they achieve this performance, in part, by carefully limiting the amount of data protected by the transactions. However, as we show empirically in this paper, computing a range query means protecting all keys in the range from modification during a transaction, leading to poor performance using the direct STM approach.

Another simple approach is to lock the entire data structure and compute a range query while it is locked. One can refine this technique by using a more fine-grained locking scheme, so that only part of the data structure needs to be locked to perform an update or compute a range query. For instance, in leaf-oriented trees, where all key-value pairs in the set are stored in the leaves of the tree, updates to the tree can be performed by local modifications close to the leaves. Therefore, it is often sufficient to lock only the last couple of nodes on the path to a leaf, rather than the entire path from the root. However, as was the case for STM, a range query can only be computed if every key in the range is protected, so typically every node containing a key in the range must be locked.

Brown and Avni [5] introduced range queries in k-ary trees with immutable keys. The k-ary trees allow efficient range-

---

[1]STM is now in the mainline GCC compiler. Unfortunately, mature hardware TM is still unavailable.

queries by collecting nodes in a depth-first-search order, followed by a validation stage. The nodes are scanned, and if any node is outdated, the process is retried from the start. Although this is an efficient solution, it is not practical, as the k-ary search tree is not balanced.

Prokopec et al. [10] presented Ctrie which is a non-blocking concurrent hash trie that offers $O(1)$ time snapshot. Keys are hashed, and the bits of these hashes are used to navigate the trie. To facilitate the computation of fast snapshots, a sequence number is associated with each node in the data structure. Each time a snapshot is taken, the root is copied and its sequence number is incremented. An update or search in the trie reads this sequence number *seq* when it starts and, while traversing the trie, it duplicates each node whose sequence number is less than *seq*. The update then performs a variant of a double-compare-single-swap operation to atomically change a pointer while ensuring the root's current sequence number matches *seq*. Because keys are ordered by their hashes in the trie, it is hard to use Ctrie to efficiently implement range queries. To do so, one must iterate over all keys in the snapshot.

The B-Tree data structure can be used for range queries, however, when looking at the concurrent versions of B-Trees such as the lock-free one of Braginsky and Petrank [3], and the blocking, industry standard from [12], both do not support the range-query functionality. Both algorithms do not have leaf-chaining, forcing one to perform a sequence of lookups to collect the desired range. In [12] this would imply holding a lock on the root for a long time, and in [3] it seems difficult to get a linearizable result. In addition, the keys in both are mutable so one would have to copy each entry individually.

1.2 The Leaplist in a Nutshell

Leaplists are Skiplists [11] with "fat" nodes and an added shortcut access mechanism in the style of the String B-tree of Ferragina and Grossi [7]. They have the same probabilistic guarantee for balancing, and the same layered forward pointers as Skiplists. Each *Leaplist* node holds up to K immutable keys from a specific range, and an immutable bitwise trie is embedded in each node to facilitate fast lookups when K is large.

When considering large range queries, the logarithmic-time lookup for the start of the range accounts for only a small part of the operation's complexity. Especially when the whole structure resides in memory. The design complexity of a full k-ary structure (in which nodes at all levels have K elements), with $\log_k(n)$ lookup time is thus not justified. In our *Leaplist*, unlike full k-ary structures, an update implies at most one split or merge of a node, and only at the leaf level. This allows updates to lock only the specific leaf being changed and only for the duration of changing pointers from the old node to the new one.

For *Leaplist* synchronization, we checked the following options, sorted in an increasing order of required effort:

- **Pure STM:** We tried to put each *Leaplist* operation in a software transactional memory (STM) transaction. This option was especially attractive with the rising support for STM in mainstream compilers. Unfortunately, as we report, we discovered that this aproach introduced unacceptable overheads.

- **Read-write locks:** We explored read-write locks per

Leaplist. The read-locks were unscalable in NUMA executions, while the write locks serialized many workloads.

- **COP:** We employed consistency oblivious programming (COP) [2] to reduce the overhead of STM. In COP, the read-only prefix of the operation is executed without any synchronization, followed by an STM transaction that checks the correctness of the prefix execution and performs any necessary updates. The COP requires that an un-instrumented traversal of the structure will not crash, which implies strong isolation of transactions in the underlying STM. Otherwise the traversal encounters uncommitted data, and hitting uncommitted data inevitably leads to uninitialized pointers, unallocated buffers, and segmentation faults. The current GCC-TM compiler uses weakly isolated transactions [6], i.e., a non-transactional read operation may see the state of an incomplete transaction. Thus, we had to add transactions also in read-only regions of the code which hurt performance. As argued in [6], weak isolation TM implementations will likely have less overhead than a strong isolation TM implementation, and better performance.

- **Locking Transactions (LT):** With LT, transactions are used only to acquire locks, and not to write tentative data. Thus, a read which sees unlocked data knows it is committed. Another aspect of LT, is that using a short transaction anyone can lock any data and use it.

We use LT to improve the performance of the previous COP algorithm. In the COP, an updating operation performs its read-only prefix without synchronization, and then executes the verification and updates inside a transaction. In LT, the read-only part is checking for locks, and retries. These checks have negligible overhead compared to a transaction. Then the transaction atomically verifies validity and locks the written addresses. After the transaction commits, a postfix of the operation writes the data to the locked address locations and releases them.

- **Fine grained locks:** To generate the fine grained version of LT *Leaplist* we had to recreate mechanisms that exist in STM, and still, did not manage to create a correct and efficient implementation.

In case of a merge, where a remove replaces two old nodes by one new node, we need to lock all pointers to and from both nodes. Here, unlike the skiplist case [9], locking can fail at any point and force us to release all locks and retry to avoid deadlocks. This unrolling is "free" using an STM.

Once a set of nodes is locked, a thread needs to perform validations on the state of the data structure, such as checking live marks etc. With LT, using STM, these validations happen before acquiring the locks, and then when committing, an abort will happen if any check should fail. Thus the locks are taken for a shorter duration. To improve our performance we would need to execute a form of STM revalidation.

After executing the above sequence, we found that our fine grained implementation still suffered from live-locks; we did not manage to avoid them. These live-locks were eliminated with the STM based LT approach.

Our conclusion was that we were effectively reproducing the very mechanisms that are already given by an STM, and still did not get the stability of an STM. The LT *Leaplist* implementation has minimal overhead because lookups do not execute transactions and range-queries execute one instrumented access per K values in the range. The LT *Leaplist* is thus the most effective solution.

An added value for using TM based synchronization is that we can compose operations on multiple *Leaplists* into one atomic transaction. In Section 2, we discuss the design of operations that support atomic access of multiple *Leaplists*, and in Section 3, we evaluate their performance.

This paper is organized as follows. Section 2 gives a detailed description of the *Leaplist* design and operations' implementation. In Section 3 we show the LT technique is the best performer for *Leaplist* synchronization, and is scalable even when transactions encompass operations on multiple *Leaplists*. Finally, in Section 4 we summarize our work, and give some directions for future work.

2. LEAPLIST DESIGN

We now describe the detailed design of our *L-Leaplists* data structure. Note that the updating functions compose operations on multiple *Leaplists*. Our implementation supports the following operations:

- **Update**(*ll*, *k*, *v*, *s*) - Receives arrays of *Leaplists*, keys and values of size *s*, and updates the value of the key $k[i]$ to be $v[i]$ in *Leaplist* $ll[i]$. If the key $k[i]$ is not present in $ll[i]$, it is added to $ll[i]$ with the given value $v[i]$.

- **Remove**(*ll*, *k*, *s*) - Receives arrays of *Leaplists* and keys of size *s*, and removes the key-value pair of the given key $k[i]$ from $ll[i]$.

- **Lookup**(*l*, *k*) - Receives a single *Leaplist* and a key, and returns the value of the corresponding given key *k* in *l*. The operation returns an indication in case the key is not present in *l*.

- **Range-Query**(*l*, k_{from}, k_{to}) - Receives a single *Leaplist* and 2 keys, and returns the values of all keys in *l* which are in the range [k_{from}, k_{to}].

The *Update* and *Remove* operations are applied to *L Leaplists* which allows concurrent operations on multiple database table indexes. We do this to demonstrate that the implementation of *Leaplist* with TM allows composing its operations.

2.1 Leaplist Data-Structure

The *Leaplist* node holds a *live* mark, which is used in COP verification stage; *high*, which bounds its keys range; *count*, which is the number of key-value pairs present in the node, and *level* which is the same as a level in Skiplist. It also holds an array of forward pointers *next* each pointing to the next element in the corresponding level. A *trie* is used to quickly find the index of key *k* in the keys-values array, a

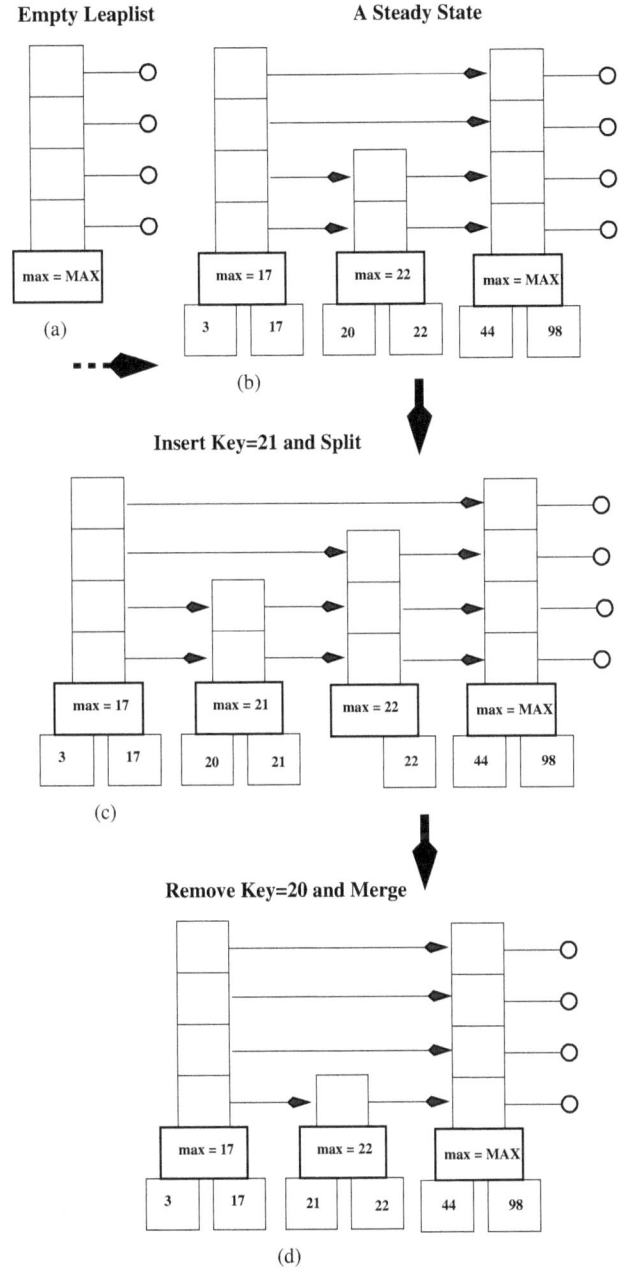

Figure 1: A single *Leaplist* with maximum height of 4 and node size of 2. Each node is composed of a column of up to 4 pointers, below it a square with the high key of that node, and in the bottom, the keys.
Initial state (a) is empty, with all pointers pointing to **null**. (b) is some arbitrary state of the *Leaplist*. In (c) an Insert causes a split and in (d) a Remove yields a merge.
State (b) is long after the initial state (a), but states (b), (c) and (d) are consecutive, i.e., separated by one operation.

301

Leaplist Search Predecessors

```
input  : Leaplist l, key k
output: Two node arrays of pointers - pa and na
1  node *x, *x_next;
2  int i;
3  retry:
4  x := l;
5  for i = max_level- 1; i ≥ 0; i = i - 1 do
6      while (true) do
7          x_next := x→next[i];
8          if MARKED(x_next) ∨ (¬x_next→live) then
               goto retry;
9          if x_next→high ≥ k then
10             break;
11         else
12             x := x_next
13         end
14     end
15     pa[i] := x;
16     na[i] := x_next;
17 end
18 return (pa, na);
```

Figure 2: *Leaplist* Search Predecessors

Leaplist Lookup

```
input  : Leaplist l, key k
output: Value or ⊥
19 node *na[max_level ];
20 (null, na)←PredecessorsSearch(l,k);
21 return (na[0]→values[get_index(na[0]→trie,k)].value);
```

Figure 3: *Leaplist* Lookup

technique introduced in the String B-tree of Ferragina and Grossi [7]. Note that unlike in a Skiplist, where each node represents a single key, in *Leaplist* each node represents a range of keys, i.e. all the keys from a certain range. The *keys-values* array of size *count* holds all the keys and their corresponding values in the node. The trie uses the minimal number of levels to represent all the keys in the node, where the lowest level is comprised of indexes of the keys' values in the *keys-values* array.

In *Leaplist*, a node's keys-values array is immutable, and never changes after an update. We do this to support consistent range-query operations.

When the key or value (and possibly the encompassed range) of a node is updated (due to an update or a remove operation), that node is replaced by a newer node with the modified keys-values array. If the node is full (i.e., the number of keys in the node reaches some predefined number), it is split into two consecutive nodes and the upper bound of the lower node is determined by the highest value in it. An example is Figure 1(c), where key 21, is inserted into a node that is already full in Figure 1(b), and the node is split.

In case the modified node and its subsequent node are sparse (the number of keys in both nodes is less than some predefined number), the nodes are merged into a single node. This scenario is demonstrated in Figure 1(d), where key 20 is deleted, and two consecutive nodes are merge.

In the rest of this section we describe the *Leaplist* functions.

2.1.1 Searching for Predecessors

The search predecessors function from Figure 2 receives a key k, and traverses the *Leaplist* until the node N (that encompasses the range where key k is included) is reached. The function returns two arrays of nodes, *pa* and *na*, each of size **max_level**. The *pa* array includes all the nodes that "immediately precede" node N. That is for each level i up to N's level, $pa[i]→next[i]$ points to N, and for levels higher than

N's level, the nodes that encompass keys that are smaller than k and their next pointer at level i points to a node with higher keys than k. The *na* array includes all the nodes that are adjacent to the *pa* nodes, and encompass keys that are greater-than-or-equal-to k (thus $na[i]→next[i]$ is N for all levels up to N's level). This function is used in the lookup and range-query operations, as well as in the beginning of the update and remove operations.

The traversal only compares the *high* key of the node in line 9 and decides if it should continue or stop at that node. When reading a pointer, the thread verifies that that pointer is not marked and that the node is still live in line 8, so it only traverses committed and valid nodes. (As previously noted, an alternative method would be replacing the mark by executing line 7 in a transaction. However, with the current GCC-TM implementation the overhead of starting a transaction is too high. We estimate that with HTM this would work much better, and will actually make the lookup wait-free, as a single-location read transaction must succeed.)

2.1.2 Lookups

The lookup operation is presented in Figure 3, and is using the predecessors search function. Note that the node returned in $na[0]$ is the node that has k in its range. We can prove the lookup is linearizable, as the predecessors search traverses only committed nodes. If a thread searches for the key k, it must traverse a node that k is in its range, and if such a live node is reached, then this node was present in the data-structure during the lookup execution.

In line 21, *Lookup* uses the node's trie to extract the index of the value of key k in the array values, and returns the value from that index.

2.1.3 Range Queries

The range query operation is presented in Figure 4, and starts with a predecessors search to find the node where the range starts from. Then, within a transaction, it first checks that the node is still live in line 30 and if not aborts, and retries the range-query operation in line 36. If the node is still marked as live, the transaction traverses the lowest level of the *Leaplist*'s pointers from the first node to the node which has a *high* value which is higher than the requested range high bound, and retrieves a snapshot range query. Note that in line 32 the algorithm ensures that even in the case of a partial update to the pointer to the next node (due to update or remove operations), it can still traverse through it.

2.1.4 Updates

Figure 5 describes the update function. As previously described, the function receives arrays of *Leaplists*, keys and values, and their size. The update operation either inserts a

```
Leaplist Range Query
   input  : Leaplist l, key low, key high
   output: Set S of nodes
22 node *na[max_level ], *n;
23 boolean committed ← false;
24 retry:
25 S← ∅;
26 (null, na)←Search(l,low);
27 n := na[0];
28 tx_start;
29 while n→high<high do
30    if ¬n→live then tx_abort;
31    add(S,na[0]);
32    n := unmark((n→next[0]));
33 end
34 committed := true;
35 tx_end;
36 if ¬committed then goto retry;
37 return S;
```

Figure 4: *Leaplist* Range Query

```
Leaplists Update
   input  : Leaplists ll, keys k, values v, and size s
38 node *pa[max_lists ][max_level ], *na[max_lists
   ][max_level ], *n[max_lists ];
39 node *new_node[max_lists ][2];
40 int max_height[max_lists ];
41 boolean committed := false, split[max_lists ];
42 foreach j<s do
43    new_node[j][0] := new node;
44    new_node[j][1] := new node;
45 end
46 retry:
47 Update_Setup(ll, k, v, s, pa, na, n, new_node,
   max_height, split);
48 tx_start ;
49 Update_LT(s, pa, na, n, new_node, max_height);
50 committed := true;
51 tx_end;
52 if ¬committed then goto retry;
53 Update_Release_and_Update(s, pa, na, n, new_node,
   split);
54 Deallocate unneeded nodes.
```

Figure 5: *Leaplist* Update

new key-value pair to each *Leaplist* if the key is not already present, or otherwise updates the key's value.

The function is divided into the following 3 parts: (1) setup (Figure 6), (2) LT (Figure 7), and (3) release and update (Figure 8). During the setup part, a thread iterates over each *Leaplist*, performs a predecessors search, and creates a new node with its key-value pairs (including the updated key-value pair). Note that in case the number of keys in the node is above some threshold, it *splits* that node. During a split it creates 2 nodes: one with a new random height that holds the first half of the key-value pairs, and another with the same height as the old node that holds the second half of the key-value pairs. The *max_level* is set to the maximum between the heights of the two nodes. The *CreateNewNodes* function updates the new node (nodes) with its (their) key-value pairs.

The LT part is executed in a single transaction. The algorithm again iterates over each *Leaplist* and first verifies that the updated node is still live (line 71), that all the predecessors' next pointers point to that node, and that the next pointers from that node are still valid (lines 72-80). (In case of a split, the algorithm also verifies this up to the *max_level* height.) In lines 81-87 it continues to verify and mark the pointers to the node and from the node, and in case of a split the nodes to and from the nodes up to *max_height*. Note that if one of the conditions does not hold, the transaction is aborted, and the whole operation restarts. It finishes the transaction by setting the old node's live bit to false (line 89), and attempting to commit the transaction. We note that in this part, the transaction does not observe partial modifications made by other transactions, and so a successful commit ensures a consistent view of the nodes that are affected by the operation.

Following a successful transaction commit, the third part releases and updates the pointers of the predecessor nodes to point to the new node (nodes). In lines 92-113 the algorithm sets the next pointer of the new node (nodes) to the previous nodes that were in the *Leaplist*. It continues by setting the next pointers of the predecessor nodes to the new node (nodes) in lines 115-121, and finishes by setting the live flags of the new node (nodes) to true.

2.1.5 Remove

The remove function is presented in Figure 9. The function receives arrays of Leaplists, keys and their size, and linearizably removes the key-value pair of each given key from its corresponding Leaplist. In case a key is not found in a Leaplist, that Leaplist is not modified.

Similarly to the update function, the remove function is also divided to the setup (Figure 10), LT (Figure 11) and release and update (Figure 12) parts. During the setup part, the thread again iterates over each Leaplist, performs a predecessors search, and searches for the key to be removed. If a Leaplist does not contain the corresponding key, it moves on to the next Leaplist. In case the key exists it keeps the node that holds the key and its successor node in the *old_node* variables (line 145-152). The node and its adjacent node are merged if the sum of the key-value pairs in both nodes is below some threshold. It then verifies that the node and the adjacent node (upon merge) are live, and if not, the retry of the last key removal from the current Leaplist is performed. The thread concludes this part by calling *RemoveAndMerge* which updates a new node with the key-value pairs from the node (and the adjacent node), without the removed key-value pair.

The second part, the LT, is performed in a single transaction. In this part the thread first verifies the nodes that were found in the setup part are still valid (i.e., they are still live), their successive nodes are still live, and the pointers from their predecessors point to them. If one of the conditions does not hold, the transaction is aborted, and the whole remove operation is restarted. It then continues to mark the next pointers of the nodes that are about to be removed, and the next pointers of their predecessors. The transaction concludes by setting the live bit of the nodes to false, and attempts to commit. In case the commit fails, the remove operation is retried from the beginning of the setup part.

However, if the transaction successfully commits, the third

```
Leaplist Update - Setup
   input : Leaplists ll, keys k, values v, size s, nodes pa,
           nodes na, nodes n, nodes new_node, integers
           max_height, booleans split
55 foreach j<s do
56    (pa[j],na[j])←PredecessorSearch(ll[j],k[j]);
57    n[j] := na[j][0];
58    if n[j]→count = node_size then
59       split[j] := true;
60       new_node[j][1]→level := n[j]→level;
61       new_node[j][0]→level := get_level();
62       max_height[j] := max(new_node[j][0]→level,
                              new_node[j][1]→level);
63    else
64       split[j] := false;
65       new_node[j][0]→level := n[j]→level;
66       max_height[j] := new_node[j][0]→level;
67    end
68    CreateNewNodes(new_node[j], n[j], k[j], v[j], split[j]);
69 end
```

Figure 6: *Leaplist* Update - Setup

part releases and updates each Leaplist to include its new node. It first sets the next pointers of the new node to point to the unmarked removed nodes next pointers in lines 208-218. Following this we set the next pointers of the old nodes pointers to the new node (lines 220-221). It concludes, in line 223, by setting the new nodes live bit.

3. EVALUATION

In this section we present the evaluation of our *Leaplist* implementation using COP and the LT technique and compare it to an STM-based *Leaplist*, an STM based *Leaplist* implementation that uses only COP, and a RW-Lock *Leaplist* implementation that uses a reader-writer lock. In Section 3.1 we compare to *Skiplist* implementations.

Experimental setup: We collected results on a machine powered by four Intel E7-4870. An Intel E7-4870 is a chip multithreading (CMT) processor, with 10 2.4 GHz cores each multiplexing 2 hardware threads, for a total of 20 hardware strands per chip. All implementations were compiled using GCC version 4.7 [1] which has built-in support for transactional memory. We used the linearizable memory allocation manager which was proposed in [8]. We compared the throughput (operations per second) of the following four algorithms:

1. **Leap-LT** - our proposed algorithm that uses COP and the LT technique as described in Section 2.

2. **Leap-tm** - a *Leaplist* implementation which wraps each operation within a transaction.

3. **Leap-COP** - an STM-based Leaplist implementation that uses COP (separating the search and update/remove operation).

4. **Leap-rwlock** - A Read-Write lock *Leaplist* implementation, in which the lookup and range-query operations acquire the read-lock, and the update and remove operations acquire the write-lock.

```
Leaplist Update - LT
   input : size s, nodes pa, nodes na, nodes n, nodes
           new_node, integers max_height
70 foreach j<s do
71    if ¬n[j]→live then tx_abort;
72    foreach i<n[j]→level do
73       if pa[j][i]→next[i]≠n[j] then tx_abort;
74       if ¬n[j]→next[i]→live then tx_abort;
75    end
76    foreach i<max_height[j] do
77       if pa[j][i]→next[j][i]≠na[j][i] then tx_abort;
78       if ¬pa[j][i]→live then tx_abort;
79       if ¬na[j][i]→live then tx_abort;
80    end
81    foreach i<n[j]→level do
82       if MARKED(n[j]→next[i]) then tx_abort;
83       n[j]→next[i] := MARK(n[j]→next[i]);
84    end
85    foreach i<max_height[j] do
86       if MARKED(pa[j][i]→next[i]) then tx_abort;
87       pa[j][i]→next[i] := MARK(pa[j][i]→next[i]);
88    end
89    n[j]→live := false ;
90 end
```

Figure 7: *Leaplist* Update - LT

Settings: We compared different mixtures of update, remove, lookup and range-query operations using the above algorithms on 4 *Leaplists* (i.e., the size of the arrays on update and remove operations is 4). Each *Leaplist* is configured with a node of size 300, and with a maximal level of 10. We experimentally found these values achieve good performance. Each experiment execution is set to 10 seconds, and is repeated three times. We show the average of the three results. We now present the throughput of the above algorithms using various workload configurations. The keys range between 0 to 100000, and a range-query operation range spans a random range between 1000 to 2000.

Figure 13 exhibits the throughput of the different algorithms when varying the number of threads from 1 to 80. In this scenario each *Leaplist* is initialized with 100,000 successive elements. The write-only case, 100% modifications (only updates and removes), is presented in Figure 13-(a). We observe that the throughput of the *Leap-LT* is better than all other algorithms, and scales well up to 32 threads. It achieves up to 220%, 355%, and 930% better throughput compared with the *Leap-COP*, *Leap-tm*, and *Leap-rwlock* algorithms respectively. This shows that even under an extreme write-dominated workload, our algorithm still performs well.

In Figure 13-(b) we present a read-dominated case with a mixture of 40% lookups, 40% range-queries and 20% modifications. *Leap-LT* scales up to 40 threads because there are less modifications. Compared with the *Leap-COP*, *Leap-tm*, and *Leap-rwlock* algorithms it achieves up to 200%, 330%, and 980% better throughput respectively. When comparing the absolute throughput values, one can see that the read-dominated workload has a higher throughput than the write-only workload. This is because a higher modifications rate incurs a high overhead of update and remove operations

```
      input : size s, nodes pa, nodes na, nodes n, nodes
              new_node, booleans split
91  foreach j<s do
92      if split[j] then
93          if new_node[j][1]→level > new_node[j][0]→level
            then
94              foreach i<new_node[j][0]→level do
95                  new_node[j][0]→next[i] := new_node[j][1];
96                  new_node[j][1]→next[i] :=
                        UNMARK(n[j]→next[i]);
97              end
98              foreach
                new_node[j][0]→level≤i<old_node[j][1]→level
                do
99                  new_node[j][1]→next[i] :=
                        UNMARK(n[j]→next[i]);
100             end
101         else
102             foreach i<new_node[j][1]→level do
103                 new_node[j][0]→next[i] := new_node[j][1];
104                 new_node[j][1]→next[i] :=
                        UNMARK(n[j]→next[i]);
105             end
106             foreach
                new_node[j][1]→level≤i<old_node[j][0]→level
                do
107                 new_node[j][0]→next[i] :=
                        UNMARK(na[j][i]);
108             end
109         end
110     else
111         foreach i<new_node[j][0]→level do
112             new_node[j][0]→next[i] :=
                    UNMARK(n[j]→next[i]);
113         end
114     end
115     foreach i<new_node[j][0]→level do
116         pa[j][i]→next[i] := new_node[j][0];
117     end
118     if split[j] ∧ (new_node[j][1]→level >
        new_node[j][0]→level) then
119         foreach
            new_node[j][0]→level≤i<old_node[j][1]→level do
120             pa[j][i]→next[i] := new_node[j][1];
121         end
122     end
123     new_node[j][0]→live := true;
124     if split[j] then new_node[j][1]→live := true;
125 end
```

Figure 8: *Leaplist* Update - Release and Update

```
      input : Leaplists ll, keys k, size s
126 node *pa[max_lists ][max_level ], *na[max_lists
    ][max_level ], *n[max_lists ];
127 node *old_node[max_lists ][2];
128 boolean committed := false, merge[max_lists ],
    changed[max_lists ];
129 foreach j<s do
130     n[j] := new node;
131 end
132 retry_all:
133 Remove_Setup(ll, k, v, s, pa, na, n, old_node, merge,
    changed);
134 tx_start;
135 Remove_LT(s, pa, na, n, old_node, merge, changed);
136 committed := true;
137 tx_end ;
138 if ¬committed then goto retry_all;
139 Remove_Release_and_Update(s, pa, na, n, old_node,
    merge, changed);
140 Deallocate unneeded nodes.
```

Figure 9: *Leaplist* Remove

```
      input : Leaplists ll, keys k, values v, size s, nodes pa,
              nodes na, nodes n, nodes old_node, booleans
              merge, booleans changed
141 foreach j<s do
142     int total;
143     retry_last: merge[j] := false;
144     (pa,na)←PredecessorSearch(ll[j],k[j]);
145     old_node[j][0] := na[j][0];
146     if get_index(old_node[j][0]→trie,k[j]) =
        NOT_FOUND then
147         changed[j] := false;
148         continue;
149     end
150     repeat
151         old_node[j][1] := old_node[j][0]→next[0];
152         if ¬ then goto retry_last;
153     until ¬is_marked(old_node[j][1]) ;
154     total := old_node[j][0]→count;
155     if old_node[j][1] then
156         total += old_node[j][1]→count;
157         if total≤node_size then merge[j] := true;
158     end
159     Set n[j] level, count, high and low;
160     if ¬old_node[j][0]→live then goto retry_last;
161     if merge[j] ∧ ¬old_node[j][1]→live then goto
        retry_last;
162     changed[j] := RemoveAndMerge(old_node[j], n[j],
        k[j], merge[j]);
163 end
```

Figure 10: *Leaplist* Remove - Setup

(compared to the lookup operations), and increased number of conflicts and retries.

Figure 14 shows the performance of the algorithms while varying the number of elements each *Leaplist* is initialized with, and setting the number of threads to 80. (The x-axis is log-scaled). We observe that when there are only update and remove operations (Figure 14-(a)), the highest throughput is achieved when a *Leaplist* is initialized with 1,000,000 elements. This is because there are less conflicts due to

the high number of nodes. Note that when the number of elements is higher, the overhead stems from the long predecessors search operation. In Figure 14-(b) we see that when there are only lookup operations, the highest throughput is achieved when the number of elements is 10,000. This is

```
input : size s, nodes pa, nodes na, nodes n, nodes
        old_node, booleans merge, booleans changed
164  foreach j<s do
165      if changed[j] then
166          if ¬old_node[j][0]→live then tx_abort;
167          if merge[j] ∧ ¬old_node[j][1]→live then
             tx_abort;
168          foreach i<old_node[j][0]→level do
169              if pa[j][i]→next[i]≠old_node[j][0] then
                 tx_abort;
170              if ¬pa[j][i]→live then tx_abort;
171              if ¬old_node[j][0]→next[i]→live then
                 tx_abort;
172          end
173          if merge[j] then
174              if old_node[j][0]→next[0]≠old_node[j][1] then
                 tx_abort;
175              if old_node[j][1]→level > old_node[j][0]→level
                 then
176                  foreach i<old_node[j][0]→level do
177                      if ¬old_node[j][1]→next[i]→live then
                         tx_abort;
178                  end
179                  foreach old_node[j][0]→level ≤ i <
                     old_node[j][1]→level do
180                      if pa[j][i]→next[i]≠old_node[j][1] then
                         tx_abort;
181                      if ¬pa[j][i]→live then tx_abort;
182                      if ¬old_node[j][1]→next[i]→live then
                         tx_abort;
183                  end
184              else
185                  foreach i<old_node[j][1]→level do
186                      if ¬old_node[j][1]→next[i]→live then
                         tx_abort;
187                  end
188              end
189              foreach i<old_node[j][1]→level do
190                  if MARKED(old_node[j][1]→next[i])
                     then tx_abort;
191                  old_node[j][1]→next[i] :=
                     MARK(old_node[j][1]→next[i]);
192              end
193          end
194          foreach i<old_node[j][0]→level do
195              if MARKED(old_node[j][0]→next[i]) then
                 tx_abort;
196              old_node[j][0]→next[i] :=
                 MARK(old_node[j][0]→next[i]);
197          end
198          foreach i<n[j]→level do
199              if MARKED(pa[j][i]→next[i]) then tx_abort;
200              pa[j][i]→next[i] := MARK(pa[j][i]→next[i]);
201          end
202          old_node[j][0]→live := false;
203          if merge[j] then old_node[j][1]→live := false;
204      end
205  end
```

Figure 11: *Leaplist* Remove - LT

```
input : size s, nodes pa, nodes na, nodes n, nodes
        old_node, booleans merge, booleans changed
206  foreach j<s do
207      if changed[j] then
208          if merge[j] then
209              foreach i<old_node[j][1]→level do
210                  n[j]→next[i] :=
                     UNMARK(old_node[j][1]→next[i]);
211              end
212              foreach
                 old_node[j][1]→level≤i<old_node[j][0]→level
                 do
213                  n[j]→next[i] :=
                     UNMARK(old_node[j][0]→next[i]);
214              end
215          else
216              foreach i<old_node[j][0]→level do
217                  n[j]→next[i] :=
                     UNMARK(old_node[j][0]→next[i]);
218              end
219          end
220          foreach i<n[j]→level do
221              pa[j][i]→next[i] := n[j];
222          end
223          n[j]→live := true ;
224      end
225  end
```

Figure 12: *Leaplist* Remove - Release and Update

again due to the long predecessors search operations when the number of nodes is larger.

Figure 15-(a) and Figure 15-(b) depict the throughput when using 80 threads, a *Leaplist* with 100,000 elements and varying the rate of lookup and range-query operations respectively between 0% to 90%. Both figures show that as the modifications rate is decreased, the throughput of all algorithms increases. In the case where no range-query operations occur (Figure 15-(a)) *Leap-LT* shows between 190% (0% lookup rate) to 260% (90% lookup rate) higher throughput compared with *Leap-COP*. The case where no lookup operations occur (Figure 15-(b)) exhibits similar results where *Leap-LT* shows between 240% (0% range-queries rate) to 200% (90% range-queries rate) higher throughput compared with *Leap-COP*. Note that in the case of 100% lookup and range-query operations rate (not shown here) the *Leap-LT* results are even better. *Leap-LT* is better by 650% and 320% compared to the second best *Leap-COP* in the 100% lookup and 100% range-query cases respectively.

3.1 Comparison to Skiplists

It is natural to compare our *Leap-LT* to the known *Skiplist* data-structure. We compare the throughput of various settings of a single *Leaplist* to: (1) *Skip-tm* - a Skiplist implementation that uses the GCC-TM to synchronize operations; (2) *Skip-cas* - a Skiplist implementation as described in [8]. These implementations store a single key-value pair in each node, and use mutable objects, thus having a lower modify operations overhead compared to our *Leap-LT*. Note that for this comparison we used a single Leaplist data-structure ($L = 1$), and that the range-query operation of the *Skip-*

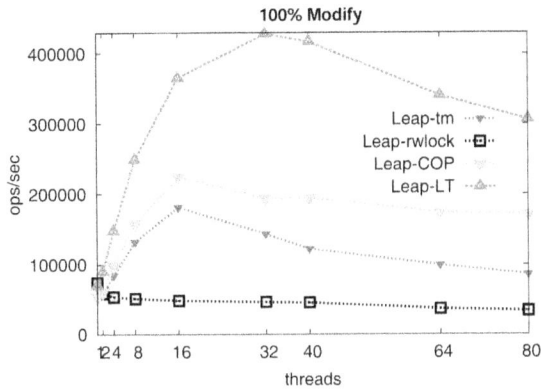

(a) various threads - 100% modify operations

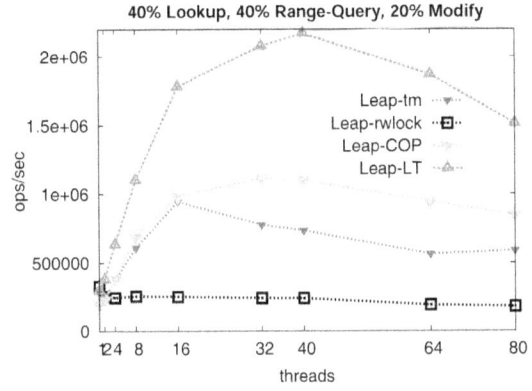

(b) various threads - 40% lookup, 40% range-query, 20% modify operations

Figure 13: Leaplist size 100K. Workload: different amount of modifications (updates and removes), lookups and range queries. (a) 100% modify operations, (b) 40% lookup, 40% range-query and 20% modify operations.

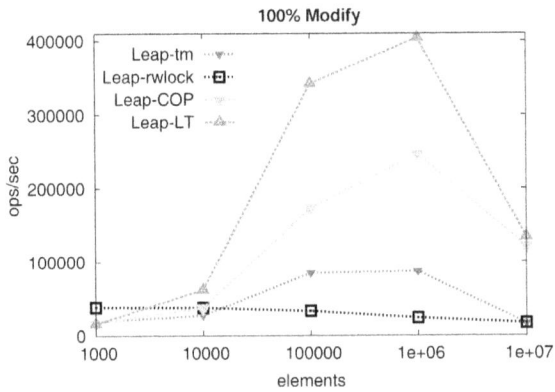

(a) various total elements - 100% modify operations

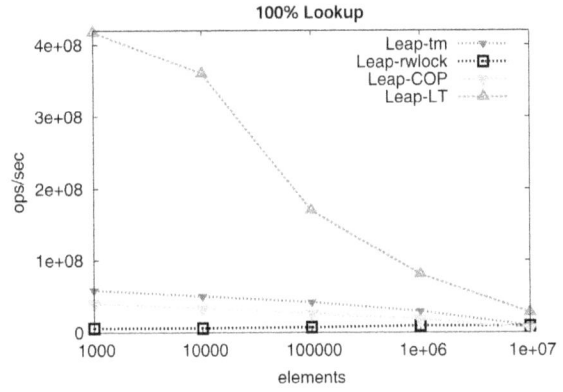

(b) various total elements - 100% lookup operations

Figure 14: Various total elements number. Workload: different amount of modifications (updates and removes) and lookups. (a) 100% modifications, (b) 100% lookups.

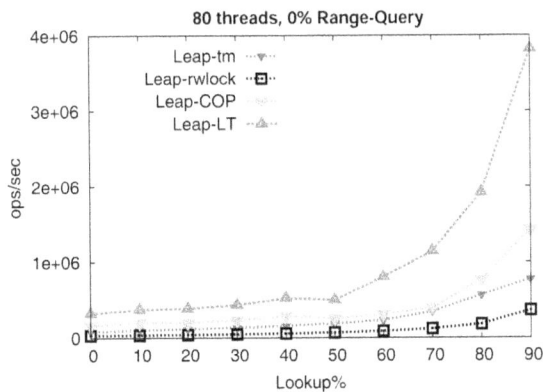

(a) No range-query

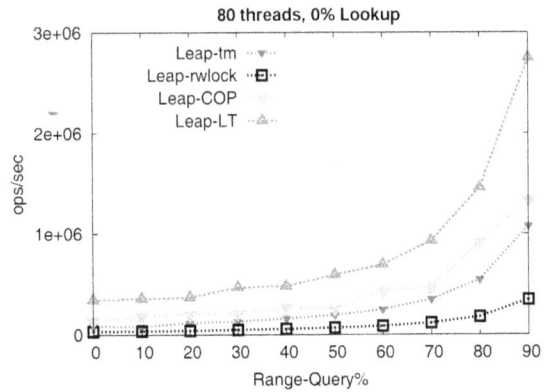

(b) No lookup

Figure 15: Leaplist size 100K, 80 threads. Workload: different rates of modifications. (a) 0%-90% lookup and modify operations (no range-query), (b) 0%-90% range-query and modify operations (no lookup).

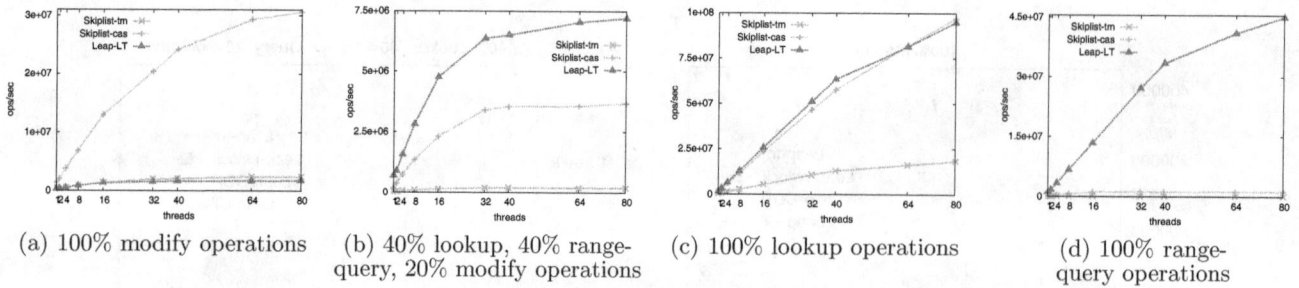

(a) 100% modify operations   (b) 40% lookup, 40% range-query, 20% modify operations   (c) 100% lookup operations   (d) 100% range-query operations

Figure 16: Leaplist comparison to Skiplists with 1M elements. Workload: different amount of modifications (updates and removes), lookups and range queries. (a) 100% modify operations, (b) 40% lookup, 40% range-query and 20% modify operations, (c) 100% lookup operations, (d) 100% range-query operations.

cas implementation does not return a consistent range-query (i.e., this operation is non-atomic and may return an inconsistent result).

Figures 16-(a), 16-(b), and 16-(c) show the throughput when using a data-structure with 1,000,000 elements, and varying the number of threads between 1 to 80. When there are only modify operations (Figure 16-(a)), we observe that both *Skip-cas* and *Skip-tm* are better than *Leap-LT*, and that *Skip-cas* is much better. This is due to the higher overhead of the update and remove operations in *Leap-LT*.

However, we see different results when there are more lookup and range-query operations, as can be seen in Figure 16-(b) where there are 40% lookups, 40% range-queries and 20% modifications. Here we see that *Leap-LT* is up to 2x and 38x better than *Skip-cas* and *Skip-tm* respectively. This is due to the overhead of the range-query operation that needs to iterate many nodes and to the large number of elements which reduces conflicts between concurrent modifying operations.

A workload which exhibits only lookup operations (Figure 16-(c)), shows that *Leap-LT* and *Skip-cas* are comparable and are much better than *Skip-tm*. This is because no contention occurs, and the reduced overhead of the former algorithms produces better throughput.

Figure 16-(d) shows the main strength of our *Leap-LT* implementation on a workload of only range-query operations. It achieves better scalability and up to 35x better throughput on this workload compared to the *Skip-cas* implementation. Moreover, we note that this is achieved while ensuring a consistent operation result (which is not ensured in *Skip-cas*).

4. SUMMARY

In this paper we presented a novel concurrent data-structure, *Leaplist*, that provides linearizable range queries. We implemented it using a technique called *Locking Transactions*, which reduces the executed transactions' lengths. We compared different *Leaplist* implementations, and also compared our technique to a *Skiplist* implementation.

We believe that the availability of hardware transactions will greatly enhance *Leaplist* performance because its implementation is based on short transactions. In the future we plan to test the Leaplist in an In-Memory Data-Base implementation, to replace the B-trees for indexes. We believe this can significantly improve the throughput of many Data-Base workloads.

5. ACKNOWLEDGEMENTS

The work of the first and second authors was supported in part by NSF grant CCF-1217921, ISF grant 1386/11, DoE ASCR grant ER26116/DE-SC0008923, and by grants from the Oracle and Intel corporations. The third author was partially supported by the Lynne and William Frankel Center for Computer Science, and by ISF grant 1227/10.

6. REFERENCES

[1] Gcc version 4.7.0, (http://gcc.gnu.org/gcc-4.7/), Apr. 2012.

[2] Y. Afek, H. Avni, and N. Shavit. Towards consistency oblivious programming. In *OPODIS*, pages 65–79, 2011.

[3] A. Braginsky and E. Petrank. A lock-free b+tree. In *SPAA*, pages 58–67, 2012.

[4] N. G. Bronson, J. Casper, H. Chafi, and K. Olukotun. Transactional predication: high-performance concurrent sets and maps for stm. In *PODC*, pages 6–15, 2010.

[5] T. Brown and H. Avni. Range queries in non-blocking k-ary search trees. In *OPODIS*, 2012.

[6] L. Dalessandro and M. L. Scott. Strong isolation is a weak idea. In *TRANSACT '09: 4th Workshop on Transactional Computing*, feb 2009.

[7] P. Ferragina and R. Grossi. The string b-tree: a new data structure for string search in external memory and its applications. *J. ACM*, pages 236–280, 1999.

[8] K. Fraser. *Practical lock freedom*. PhD thesis, Cambridge University Computer Laboratory, 2003.

[9] M. Herlihy, Y. Lev, V. Luchangco, and N. Shavit. A simple optimistic skiplist algorithm. In *Proceedings of the 14th international conference on Structural information and communication complexity*, pages 124–138, 2007.

[10] A. Prokopec, N. G. Bronson, P. Bagwell, and M. Odersky. Concurrent tries with efficient non-blocking snapshots. In *Proceedings of the 17th ACM SIGPLAN symposium on Principles and Practice of Parallel Programming*, PPoPP '12, pages 151–160, 2012.

[11] W. Pugh. Skip lists: A probabilistic alternative to balanced trees. In *WADS*, pages 437–449, 1989.

[12] O. Rodeh. B-trees, shadowing, and clones. *Trans. Storage*, 3(4):2:1–2:27, Feb. 2008.

A Programming Language Perspective on Transactional Memory Consistency

Hagit Attiya
Technion

Alexey Gotsman
IMDEA Software Institute

Sandeep Hans
Technion

Noam Rinetzky
Tel-Aviv University

ABSTRACT

Transactional memory (TM) has been hailed as a paradigm for simplifying concurrent programming. While several consistency conditions have been suggested for TM, they fall short of formalizing the intuitive semantics of atomic blocks, the interface through which a TM is used in a programming language.

To close this gap, we formalize the intuitive expectations of a programmer as *observational refinement* between TM implementations: a concrete TM observationally refines an abstract one if every user-observable behavior of a program using the former can be reproduced if the program uses the latter. This allows the programmer to reason about the behavior of a program using the intuitive semantics formalized by the abstract TM; the observational refinement relation implies that the conclusions will carry over to the case when the program uses the concrete TM. We show that, for a particular programming language and notions of observable behavior, a variant of the well-known consistency condition of opacity is sufficient for observational refinement, and its restriction to complete histories is furthermore necessary.

Our results suggest a new approach to evaluating and comparing TM consistency conditions. They can also reduce the effort of proving that a TM implements its programming language interface correctly, by only requiring its developer to show that it satisfies the corresponding consistency condition.

Categories and Subject Descriptors

D.1.3 [**Programming Techniques**]: Concurrent Programming;
D.2.4 [**Software Engineering**]: Software/Program Verification

Keywords

Transactional memory; atomic blocks; observational refinement

1. INTRODUCTION

Transactional memory (TM) eases the task of writing concurrent applications by letting the programmer designate certain code blocks as *atomic*. TM allows designing a program and reasoning about its correctness as if each atomic block executed as a

```
node := new(StackNode);
node.val := val;
result := abort;
while (result == abort) do {
    result := atomic {
        node.next = Top.read();
        Top = node;
    }
}
```

Figure 1: Example of transactional memory usage

transaction—in one step and without interleaving with others. As an example, Figure 1 shows how atomic blocks yield simple code for pushing an element onto a stack represented as a singly-linked list: in this case it is possible to read the top-of-the-stack pointer, point the new element to it, and change the top-of-the-stack pointer, all at once. Many TM implementations have been proposed [10], using a myriad of design approaches that, for efficiency, may execute transactions concurrently, yet aim to provide the programmer with an illusion that they are executed atomically. This illusion is not always perfect—for example, as evident from Figure 1, transactions can abort due to conflicts with concurrently running ones and need to be restarted.

How can we be sure that a TM indeed implements atomic blocks correctly? So far, researchers have tried to achieve this through a *consistency condition* that restricts the possible TM executions. Several such conditions have been proposed, including *opacity* [8, 9], *virtual world consistency* [16], *TMS* [5, 18] and *DU-opacity* [3]. Opacity is the best-known of them; roughly speaking, it requires that for any sequence of interactions between the program and the TM, dubbed a *history*, there exist another history where:

(i) the interactions of every separate thread are the same as in the original history;

(ii) the order of non-overlapping transactions present in the original history is preserved; and

(iii) each transaction executes atomically.

Unfortunately, this definition is given from the TM's point of view, as a restriction on the set of histories it can produce, and is not connected to the semantics of a programming language. The situation for other TM consistency conditions is the same and, in fact, it is not clear which of them provide the programmer with behaviors that correspond to the intuitive notion of atomic blocks, and which of them puts the minimal restrictions on TM implementations needed to achieve this.

In this paper, we aim to bridge this gap by formalizing the intuitive expectations of a programmer as *observational refinement* [13, 14] between TM implementations. Consider two TM implementations—a *concrete* one, such as an efficient TM, and an *abstract* one, such as a TM executing every atomic block atomically. Informally, the concrete TM observationally refines the abstract one if every behavior a user can observe of a program P linked with the concrete TM can also be observed when P is linked with the abstract TM instead. This allows the programmer to reason about the behavior of P using the intuitive semantics formalized by the abstract TM; the observational refinement relation implies that the conclusions will carry over to the case when P uses the concrete TM.

We show that one TM implementation observationally refines another if they are in an *opacity relation*. The relation requires that every history of the concrete TM have a matching history of the abstract TM satisfying the conditions (i) and (ii) above. By instantiating it with an abstract TM implementation that executes transactions atomically, we obtain the existing notion of opacity. However, our definition also allows comparing two TM implementations that execute transactions concurrently, such as a more and a less optimized one. Furthemore, we show that observational refinement between two TM implementations implies the opacity relation between thir restriction to *complete* histories, i.e., ones in which every transaction either commits or aborts.

We note that the formalization of observational refinement, and thus our results, depend on the particular choices of programming language and the notion of observations. In this first treatment of this topic, we consider a basic programming language and particular forms of observations. The features of the language are as follows:

- Threads can access shared global variables outside transactions, but not inside them. However, thread-local variables (such as node in Figure 1) can be accessed in both cases.

- An aborted transaction is not restarted automatically and modifications to thread-local variables that it may have performed are not rolled back.

- A program cannot explicitly ask the TM to abort a transaction.

- Nesting of atomic blocks is not allowed.

As observable behaviors of a program, our result allows one to take either the set of its reachable states or the set of all sequences of actions performed by its finite computations. This allows a programmer to reason about safety, but not about liveness properties.

It is likely that for other programming languages or notions of observations, other consistency criteria will be necessary or sufficient for observational refinement, resulting in different trade-offs between the efficiency of TM implementations and the flexibility of their programming interfaces (see Section 8 for discussion). We hope that the link between TM consistency conditions and programming language abstractions we establish in this paper will enable TM implementors and language designers to make informed decisions about such trade-offs. Our approach can also reduce the effort of proving that a TM implements its programming interface correctly, by only requiring its developer to show that it satisfies the corresponding consistency condition.

2. PROGRAMMING LANGUAGE

We develop our results for a simple concurrent programming language with programs consisting of a fixed, but arbitrary, number m of *threads*, identified by ThreadID $= \{1, \ldots, m\}$. Every thread $t \in$ ThreadID has a private set of *local variables* $\mathrm{LVar}_t = \{x, y, \ldots\}$, and all threads share access to a set of *global variables* GVar $= \{g, \ldots\}$. For simplicity, we assume that all variables are of type integer. Let Var $=$ GVar $\uplus \biguplus_{t=1}^{m} \mathrm{LVar}_t$ be the set of all program variables (where $\uplus$ denotes disjoint union). In addition to variables, threads can access software or hardware

transactional memory, which from now on we refer to as the *transactional system*. The system manages a fixed collection of *transactional objects* Obj $= \{o, \ldots\}$, each having a set of *methods* Method $= \{f, \ldots\}$ that threads can call. For simplicity, we assume that each method takes one integer parameter and returns an integer value, and that all objects have the same set of methods.

The syntax of the language is as follows:

$$
\begin{aligned}
C & ::= \quad c \mid C; C \mid \mathtt{if}\,(b)\,\mathtt{then}\,C\,\mathtt{else}\,C \mid \\
& \qquad \mathtt{while}\,(b)\,\mathtt{do}\,C \mid x := \mathtt{atomic}\,\{C\} \mid x := o.f(e) \\
P & ::= \quad C_1 \parallel \ldots \parallel C_m
\end{aligned}
$$

where b and e denote Boolean and integer expressions over local variables, left unspecified. A program P is a parallel composition of *sequential commands* $C_1, \ldots, C_m$, which can include *primitive commands* c from a set Pcomm, sequential compositions, conditionals, loops, atomic blocks and object method invocations.

Primitive commands are meant to execute atomically. We do not fix their set Pcomm, but assume that it at least includes assignments to local and global variables: e.g., $g := x$. We partition the set Pcomm into $2m$ classes: Pcomm $= \biguplus_{t=1}^{m}(\mathrm{LPcomm}_t \uplus \mathrm{GPcomm}_t)$. The intention is that commands from LPcomm_t can access only the local variables of thread t (LVar_t); commands from GPcomm_t can additionally access global variables ($\mathrm{LVar}_t \uplus \mathrm{GVar}$). We formalize these restriction in Section 4. We forbid a thread t from accessing local variables of other threads. Thus, the thread cannot mention such variables in the conditions of if and while commands and can only use primitive commands from $\mathrm{LPcomm}_t \uplus \mathrm{GPcomm}_t$.

An *atomic block* $x := \mathtt{atomic}\,\{C\}$ executes the command C as a *transaction*, which the transactional system can decide to *commit* or *abort*. The system's decision is returned in the local variable x, which gets assigned distinguished values committed or aborted. We forbid nested atomic blocks and, hence, nested transactions. Inside an atomic block (and only there), the program can invoke methods on transactional objects, as in $x := o.f(e)$. Here the expression e gives the value of the method parameter, and x gets assigned the return value after the method terminates. The transactional system may decide to abort a transaction initiated by $x := \mathtt{atomic}\,\{C\}$ not only upon reaching the end of the atomic block, but also during the execution of a method on a transactional object. Once this happens, the execution of C terminates. We do not allow programs in our language to abort a transaction explicitly. A typical pattern of using the transactional system is to execute a transaction repeatedly until it commits, as shown in Figure 1.

We forbid accessing global variables inside atomic blocks; thus, a thread t can use primitive commands from GPcomm_t only outside them. A transaction can use local variables of the current thread; if the transaction is aborted, these variables are not rolled back to their initial values, and the values written to them by the transaction can thus be observed by the following non-transactional code. We note that, whereas transactional objects are managed by the transactional system, global variables are not. Thus, threads can communicate via the transactional system inside atomic blocks, and directly via global variables outside them. We also note that the transactional system is not part of a program, but is a library used by it. Hence, the state of the transactional system is separate from the variables in Var to which the program has access.

A correct transactional system implementation has to ensure that the program behaves as though atomic blocks indeed execute atomically, i.e., without interleaving with actions of other threads, and that operations invoked on transactional objects in aborted transactions have no effect. This does not require the implementation to execute atomic blocks like this internally; it only has to provide the illusion of their atomicity to the rest of the program. In the rest of the paper, we prove that a variant of a well-known criterion of transactional system correctness, opacity, is sufficient and necessary to validate this illusion for our programming language.

3. THE OPACITY RELATION

Histories

In this section we formalize the notion of opacity in our setting, and along the way, show how to make it more flexible. To this end, we introduce the notion of a history, which records all the interactions a program in the language of Section 2 has with the transactional system in one of its executions. A **history**, ranged over by H and S, is a finite[1] sequence of interface actions, defined as follows.

DEFINITION 1. *An* **interface action** ψ *is an expression of one of the following forms:*

Request actions	*Response actions*
$(t, \text{txbegin})$	(t, OK)
$(t, \text{txcommit})$	$(t, \text{committed}) \mid (t, \text{aborted})$
$(t, \text{call } o.f(n))$	$(t, \text{ret}(n') \, o.f) \mid (t, \text{aborted})$

where $t \in \text{ThreadID}$, $o \in \text{Obj}$, $f \in \text{Method}$ *and* $n, n' \in \mathbb{Z}$.

Interface actions denote the control flow crossing the boundary between the program and the transactional system: request actions correspond to the control being transferred from the program to the transactional system, and response actions correspond to the control being transferred the other way around. A $(t, \text{txbegin})$ action denotes a thread t requesting the transactional system to start executing a transaction; this action is generated upon entering an `atomic` block. An OK action is the only possible response by the transactional system. A txcommit action is issued when a transaction tries to commit upon exiting an `atomic` block. The transactional system responds with a committed or aborted action, depending on the result. Actions call and ret denote a call to and a return from an invocation of a method on a transactional object; they are annotated with the parameter or the return value. As we noted in Section 2, the transactional system may also decide to abort a transaction while executing a method on a transactional object. In such cases, the corresponding call action is followed by an aborted action instead of a ret one.

We use the following notation: ε is the empty history; $H(i)$ is the i-th element of a history H; $H|_t$ is the projection of H onto actions of thread t; $H|_{\neg t}$ is the projection of H onto actions of threads other than t; $H|_o$ is the projection of H onto call and ret actions on object o; $|H|$ is the length of H; $H\downarrow_i$ is the prefix of H containing i actions; $H_1 H_2$ is the concatenation of H_1 and H_2. We denote by _ an expression that is irrelevant and implicitly existentially quantified.

The interactions of programs in the language of Section 2 with the transactional system are not arbitrary; they are recorded by histories that satisfy certain well-formedness properties, summarized in the following definition.

DEFINITION 2. *A history H is* **well-formed** *if*

- *request and response actions are properly matched: for every thread t, $H|_t$ consists of alternating request and corresponding response actions, starting from a request action;*

[1] We do not consider infinite computations in this paper; see Section 8 for a discussion.

- *actions denoting beginning and end of transactions are properly matched: for every thread t, in the projection of $H|_t$ to txbegin, committed and aborted actions, txbegin alternates with committed or aborted, starting from txbegin; and*

- call *and* ret *actions occur only inside transactions: for every thread t, if $H|_t = H_1 \, \psi \, H_2$ for a call or ret action ψ, then $H_1 = H_1' \, \psi' \, H_1''$ for some txbegin action ψ', and histories H_1' and H_1'' such that H_1'' does not contain txbegin, txcommit, committed or aborted actions.*

Program executions that run utill completion are described by *complete* histories, in which every transaction either aborts or commits. This class of histories is of a particular importance to us because our necessity result holds only for this class.

DEFINITION 3. *A well-formed history H is* **complete** *if all transactions in it have completed: if $H = H_1 \, (t, \text{txbegin}) \, H_2$, then H_2 contains a $(t, \text{committed})$ or $(t, \text{aborted})$ action.*

We specify the behavior of a transactional system implementation by the set of possible interactions it can have with its clients— its **history set** $\mathcal{H}$, which is a prefix-closed set of well-formed histories. For our purposes, this specifies the behaviour of a transactional system completely; thus, in the following, we often conflate the notion of a transactional system and its history set.

We denote the **complete subset** of a history set $\mathcal{H}$ by

$$\mathcal{H}|_{\text{complete}} = \{H \mid H \in \mathcal{H} \wedge (H \text{ is complete})\}.$$

The definition of the opacity relation

We define the notion of opacity in a slightly more flexible way than the original one [8, 9], inspired by the approach taken when defining the correctness of concurrent libraries via linearizability [15]. Namely, we define the correctness of a transactional system implementation by relating its history set to that of an **abstract** implementation, whose behavior it has to simulate; in this context, we call the original implementation **concrete**. The abstract implementation is typically one in which `atomic` blocks actually execute atomically and methods called by aborted transactions have no effect. As we show below, we can obtain the original definition of opacity by instantiating ours with such an abstract implementation; however, our definition can also be used to compare two arbitrary implementations. To disambiguate, in the following we refer to our notion as the *opacity relation*, instead of just opacity.

According to the following definition, a concrete transactional system $\mathcal{H}_C$ is in the opacity relation with an abstract transactional system $\mathcal{H}_A$, if every history H from $\mathcal{H}_C$ can be matched by a history S from $\mathcal{H}_A$ that "looks similar" to H from the perspective of the program. The similarity is formalized by a relation $H \sqsubseteq S$, which requires S to be a permutation of H preserving the order of actions within a thread and that of non-overlapping transactions (whether committed or aborted). Here the duration of a transaction is defined by the interval from its txbegin action to the corresponding committed or aborted action (or to the end of the history if there is none).

DEFINITION 4. *A well-formed history H is in the* **opacity relation** *with a well-formed history S, denoted $H \sqsubseteq S$, if there is a bijection $\theta : \{1, \ldots, |H|\} \to \{1, \ldots, |S|\}$ such that $\forall i.\, H(i) = S(\theta(i))$ and*

$$\forall i, j.\, i < j \wedge ((\exists t.\, H(i) = (t, \_) \wedge H(j) = (t, \_)) \vee$$
$$(H(i) \in \{(\_, \text{committed}), (\_, \text{aborted})\} \wedge$$
$$H(j) = (\_, \text{txbegin})))$$
$$\implies \theta(i) < \theta(j).$$

A transactional system $\mathcal{H}_C$ is in the **opacity relation** with a transactional system $\mathcal{H}_A$, denoted $\mathcal{H}_C \sqsubseteq \mathcal{H}_A$, if

$$\forall H \in \mathcal{H}_C . \exists S \in \mathcal{H}_A . H \sqsubseteq S.$$

In the following, for $i < j$ we say that the actions $H(i)$ and $H(j)$ are in the **per-thread order** in H when they are by the same thread and in the **real-time order** when $H(i) = (\_, \text{committed})$ or $H(i) = (\_, \text{aborted})$ and $H(j) = (\_, \text{txbegin})$. Thus, $H \sqsubseteq S$ requires that the per-thread and real-time orders between actions in H be preserved in S. We now make some comments concerning the choices taken in this definition.

- As we show in Section 7, preserving the real-time order in Definition 4 is necessary to validate observational refinement due to the fact that, in our programming language, threads can access global variables outside transactions and, hence, can notice the order of non-overlapping transactions.

- Definition 4 treats committed and aborted transactions uniformly. This is a characteristic feature of opacity: it ensures that the results returned by methods of transactional objects inside aborted transactions are as consistent as those returned inside committed transactions (we return to this point in Sections 7 and 8).

- The abstract history S in Definition 4 is not required to be sequential, i.e., it may have overlapping executions of transactions. This allows the definition to compare behaviors of two realistic transactional system implementations that actually execute transactions concurrently. We also allow H to contain uncompleted transactions (without a final committed or aborted action) arising, e.g., because the corresponding thread has been preempted. In this case, we require the same behavior to be reproduced in the matching history S, which is possible because the latter does not have to be sequential [7].

Comparison with the original opacity definition

We now show how the original notion of opacity [8, 9] can be obtained from ours by instantiating Definition 4 with an abstract transactional system $\mathcal{H}_{\text{atomic}}$ in which atomic blocks execute atomically and methods called by aborted transactions have no effect. We first introduce the ingredients needed to define this system. We start by defining a special class of *non-interleaved* histories.

DEFINITION 5. *A well-formed history H is **non-interleaved** if actions by any two transactions do not overlap: if $H = H_1 (t, \text{txbegin}) H_2 (t', \text{txbegin}) H_3$, where H_2 does not contain* txbegin *actions, then either H_2 contains a $(t, \text{committed})$ or a $(t, \text{aborted})$ action, or there are no actions by thread t in H_3.*

Note that a non-interleaved history does not have to be complete. In fact, the history set $\mathcal{H}_{\text{atomic}}$ we are about to define contains only non-interleaved histories, but some of them are incomplete. This is because a concrete transactional system may produce histories with incomplete transactions, and our opacity relation requires these transactions to stay incomplete in the matching history of the abstract system. To check whether an incomplete history should be included into $\mathcal{H}_{\text{atomic}}$, we first complete it with the aid of the operation defined below, which aborts every transaction that has not tried to commit yet and commits or aborts every transaction that has tried to commit (as witnessed by a txcommit action), but has not yet got a response.

DEFINITION 6. *A history H is a **completing history** for an interface action ψ, if the following holds:*

- *if $\psi = (t, \text{call } o.f(n))$, then $H = (t, \text{aborted})$;*

- *if $\psi = (t, \text{txbegin})$, then*
  $H = (t, \text{OK}) (t, \text{txcommit}) (t, \text{aborted})$;

- *if $\psi \in \{(t, \text{ret}(n) \ o.f), (t, \text{OK})\}$, then*
  $H = (t, \text{txcommit}) (t, \text{aborted})$;

- *if $\psi = (t, \text{txcommit})$, then*
  $H = (t, \text{committed})$ or $H = (t, \text{aborted})$;

- *otherwise, $H = \varepsilon$.*

DEFINITION 7. *A history H_c is a **non-interleaved completion** of a non-interleaved history H, if H_c is a non-interleaved complete history that can be constructed from H by adding a completing history for the last action of every thread right after this action. We denote the set of non-interleaved completions of H by* nicomp(H).

To define $\mathcal{H}_{\text{atomic}}$, we also need to know the intended semantics of operations on transactional objects. We describe the semantics for an object $o \in \text{Obj}$ by fixing all sequences of actions on o that are considered correct when executed by a sequential program. More precisely, a **sequential specification** of an object o is a set of histories $\llbracket o \rrbracket$ such that:

- $\llbracket o \rrbracket$ is prefix-closed;

- each $H \in \llbracket o \rrbracket$ consists of alternating call and ret actions on o, starting from a call action, where every ret is by the same thread as the preceding call; and

- $\llbracket o \rrbracket$ is insensitive to thread identifiers: for any $H \in \llbracket o \rrbracket$, changing the thread identifier in call-ret pair of adjacent actions in H yields a history in $\llbracket o \rrbracket$.

For example, $\llbracket o \rrbracket$ for a register object o would consist of histories where each read method invocation returns the value written by the latest preceding write method invocation (or the default value if there is none).

Using sequential specifications for all objects, we now define when a complete and non-interleaved history H respects the object semantics. Let $H(i)$ be a call or ret action on an object o. We say that $H(i)$ is **legal** in H if $H'|_o \in \llbracket o \rrbracket$, where H' is the history obtained from H by projecting $H\downarrow_i$ on all actions by committed transactions and the transaction containing $H(i)$. A complete and non-interleaved history H is **legal** if all call and ret actions in H are legal. We now let $\mathcal{H}_{\text{atomic}}$ to be the set of all non-interleaved histories that can be completed to a legal history:

$$\mathcal{H}_{\text{atomic}} = \{H \mid H \text{ is non-interleaved} \wedge \exists \text{ legal } H_c \in \text{nicomp}(H)\}.$$

Thus, we can say that a transactional system $\mathcal{H}_C$ establishes the illusion of atomicity for transactions if $\mathcal{H}_C \sqsubseteq \mathcal{H}_{\text{atomic}}$. Note that, since we require the history set of a transactional system to be prefix-closed, this criterion checks every prefix of any history produced by $\mathcal{H}_C$, just like opacity as formulated in [9]. However, in other aspects this definition is of a different form than opacity, which we can formulate in our setting as follows.

DEFINITION 8. *A history H_c is a **suffix completion** of a history H, if it is a complete history, H is a prefix of H_c, and H_c can be constructed from H by appending to it a completing history for the last action of every thread. We denote the set of suffix-completions of H by* scomp(H).

DEFINITION 9. *A transactional system $\mathcal{H}_C$ is **opaque** if for every history $H \in \mathcal{H}_C$, there exists a history $H_c \in \text{scomp}(H)$ and a complete, non-interleaved and legal history S_c such that $H_c \sqsubseteq S_c$.*

The main difference is that Definition 9 first completes a history from $\mathcal{H}_C$ and then finds its match according to the opacity relation;

our criterion $\mathcal{H}_C \sqsubseteq \mathcal{H}_{\text{atomic}}$ first finds the match and then completes the matching history. For technical reasons, Definition 9 also uses a slightly different completion, putting completing histories at the end to avoid creating new real-time orderings.

Fortunately, completion and matching commute, and thus the two formulations of opacity are equivalent.

PROPOSITION 10. *A transactional system $\mathcal{H}_C$ is opaque if and only if $\mathcal{H}_C \sqsubseteq \mathcal{H}_{\text{atomic}}$.*

We prove the proposition in [2, Appendix A]. The formulation $\mathcal{H}_C \sqsubseteq \mathcal{H}_{\text{atomic}}$ is more convenient for us, since the statement of observational refinement we give in Section 5 below requires us to leave the histories of the concrete transactional system intact. Stating transactional system consistency in this way also avoids the need to bake in completions (Definition 7) into the definition of the opacity relation (Definition 4): the treatment of incomplete transactions can be deferred to the choice of the abstract transactional system.

4. PROGRAMMING LANGUAGE SEMANTICS

Our goal is to establish a connection between conditions on transactional system implementations, such as the opacity relation from Section 3, and the behavior of programs that use these systems, such as those in the language of Section 2. To this end, in this section we define the *semantics* of our programming language, i.e., what kinds of computations can result when a program executes with a particular transactional system.

A program computation is captured by a *trace τ*, which is a finite sequence of *actions*, each describing a computation step.

DEFINITION 11. *An **action** φ is an expression of one of the following forms: $\varphi ::= \psi \mid (t, c)$, where $t \in \mathsf{ThreadID}$ and $c \in \mathsf{Pcomm}$. We denote that set of all actions by Action.*

In addition to interface actions, we have actions of the form (t, c), which denote the execution of a primitive command by thread t. To denote the evaluation of conditions in `if` and `while` statements, we assume that the sets LPcomm_t contain special primitive commands $\mathsf{assume}(b)$, where b is a Boolean expression over local variables of thread t, defining the condition. We state their semantics formally below; informally, $\mathsf{assume}(b)$ does nothing if b holds in the current program state, and stops the computation otherwise. Thus, it allows the computation to proceed only if b holds. The assume commands are only used in defining the semantics of the programming language; hence, we forbid threads from using them directly.

We denote by $\mathsf{history}(\tau)$ the history obtained by projecting a trace τ to interface actions. We use various operations on histories defined in Section 3 for traces as well. As is the case for histories, programs in the language of Section 2 do not generate arbitrary traces, but only those satisfying certain conditions summarized in the following definition.

DEFINITION 12. *A trace τ is **well-formed** if*

- *the history $\mathsf{history}(\tau)$ is well-formed;*
- *thread t does not access local variables of other threads: if $\tau = \tau_1 (t, c) \tau_2$, then $c \in \mathsf{LPcomm}_t \uplus \mathsf{GPcomm}_t$; and*
- *commands in τ do not access global variables inside a transaction: if $\tau = \tau_1 (t, c) \tau_2$ for $c \in \mathsf{GPcomm}_t$, then it is not the case that $\tau_1 = \tau_1' (t, \mathsf{txbegin}) \tau_1''$, where τ_1'' does not contain committed or aborted actions.*

We denote the set of well-formed traces by WTrace.

We use two additional operations on traces. For a trace τ, we define $\mathsf{trans}(\tau)$ and $\mathsf{nontrans}(\tau)$ as the subsequence of actions in τ executed inside transactions (including txbegin, committed and aborted actions), respectively, outside them (excluding txbegin, committed and aborted actions). Formally, we include an action $\varphi = (t, \_)$ such that $\tau|_t = \tau_1 \varphi \tau_2$ into $\mathsf{trans}(\tau)$ if:

- φ is a txbegin, committed or aborted action; or
- $\tau_1 = \tau_1' (t, \mathsf{txbegin}) \tau_1''$, where τ_1'' does not contain committed or aborted actions.

All other actions form $\mathsf{nontrans}(\tau)$. Actions in τ that are in $\mathsf{trans}(\tau)$ are **transactional** and all others are **non-transactional**.

A **state** of a program records the values of all its variables: $s \in \mathsf{State} = \mathsf{Var} \to \mathbb{Z}$. The semantics of a program $P = C_1 \parallel \cdots \parallel C_m$ is given by the set of traces $[\![P]\!](s, \mathcal{H}) \in \mathcal{P}(\mathsf{WTrace})$ it produces when run with a transactional system $\mathcal{H}$ from an initial state s. We define this set in two stages. First, we define the set $[\![P]\!](s) \in \mathcal{P}(\mathsf{WTrace})$ that a program produces when run from s with the behaviors of the transactional system unrestricted. We then compute the set of traces produced by P when run with a given transactional system $\mathcal{H}$ by selecting those traces that interact with the transactional system in a way consistent with $\mathcal{H}$:

$$[\![P]\!](s, \mathcal{H}) = \{\tau \mid \tau \in [\![P]\!](s) \wedge \mathsf{history}(\tau) \in \mathcal{H}\}. \quad (1)$$

The set $[\![P]\!](s)$ is itself computed in two stages[2]. First, we compute a trace set $A(P) \in \mathcal{P}(\mathsf{WTrace})$ that resolves all issues regarding sequential control flow and interleaving. Intuitively, if one thinks of each sequential command C_t in P as a control-flow graph, then $A(P)$ contains all possible interleavings of paths in the control-flow graph of all the commands C_t starting from their source nodes. The set $A(P)$ is a superset of all the traces that can actually be executed: e.g., if a thread executes the command

$$x := 1;\ \mathtt{if}\ (x = 1)\ y := 1\ \mathtt{else}\ y := 2 \quad (2)$$

where x is a local variable, then $A(P)$ will contain a trace where $y := 2$ is executed instead of $y := 1$. To filter out such nonsensical traces, we *evaluate* every trace to determine whether its control flow is consistent with the expected behavior of its actions. This is formalized by a function $\mathsf{eval} : \mathsf{State} \times \mathsf{WTrace} \to \mathcal{P}(\mathsf{State})$ that, given an initial state and a trace, produces the set of states resulting from executing the actions in the trace, or an empty set if the trace is infeasible. Then we let

$$[\![P]\!](s) = \{\tau \mid \tau \in A(P) \wedge \mathsf{eval}(s, \tau) \neq \emptyset\}. \quad (3)$$

The rest of this section defines the trace set $A(P)$ and the evaluation function eval formally. The definitions follow the intuitive semantics of our programming language and can be skipped on first reading (they are only used in the proofs of Lemmas 18 and 20 in Section 6 and in the detailed proof of Theorem 24 in [2, Appendix B]).

Trace set $A(P)$

The function $A(\cdot)$ in Figure 2 maps commands and programs to the set of their possible traces. $A(C)t$ gives the set of traces produced by a command C when it is executed by thread t. To define $A(P)$, we first compute the set of all the interleavings of traces produced by the threads constituting P. Formally, $\tau \in \mathsf{interleave}(\tau_1, \ldots, \tau_m)$ if and only if every action in τ is performed by some thread $t \in \{1, \ldots, m\}$, and $\tau|_t = \tau_t$ for every thread $t \in \{1, \ldots, m\}$. We then let $A(P)$ be the set of all prefixes of the resulting traces, as denoted by the prefix operator. We take prefix

---

[2]Here we define the set $[\![P]\!](s)$ in a denotational style; a definition using structural operational semantics would also be appropriate.

$$
\begin{aligned}
A(c)t &= \{(t,c)\} \\
A(C_1;C_2)t &= \{\tau_1\,\tau_2 \mid \tau_1 \in A(C_1)t \wedge \tau_2 \in A(C_2)t\} \\
A(\text{if }(b)\text{ then }C_1\text{ else }C_2)t &= \{(t,\mathsf{assume}(b))\,\tau_1 \mid \tau_1 \in A(C_1)t\} \cup \{(t,\mathsf{assume}(\neg b))\,\tau_2 \mid \tau_2 \in A(C_2)t\} \\
A(\text{while }(b)\text{ do }C)t &= \{((t,\mathsf{assume}(b))\,(A(C)t))^*\,(t,\mathsf{assume}(\neg b))\} \\
A(x := o.f(e))t &= \{(t,\mathsf{assume}(e=n))\,(t,\mathsf{call}\ o.f(n))\,(t,\mathsf{ret}(n')\ o.f)\,(t, x := n') \mid n, n' \in \mathbb{Z}\}\ \cup \\
&\quad \{(t,\mathsf{assume}(e=n))\,(t,\mathsf{call}\ o.f(n))\,(t,\mathsf{aborted}) \mid n \in \mathbb{Z}\} \\
A(x := \mathtt{atomic}\ \{C\})t &= \{(t,\mathsf{txbegin})\,(t,\mathsf{OK})\,\tau\,(t,\mathsf{aborted})\,(t, x := \mathsf{aborted}) \mid \tau\,(t,\mathsf{aborted}) \in A(C)t\}\ \cup \\
&\quad \{(t,\mathsf{txbegin})\,(t,\mathsf{OK})\,\tau\,(t,\mathsf{txcommit})\,(t,\mathsf{committed})\,(t, x := \mathsf{committed}) \mid \tau \in A(C)t \wedge \tau \neq \_\,(t,\mathsf{aborted})\}\ \cup \\
&\quad \{(t,\mathsf{txbegin})\,(t,\mathsf{OK})\,\tau\,(t,\mathsf{txcommit})\,(t,\mathsf{aborted})\,(t, x := \mathsf{aborted}) \mid \tau \in A(C)t \wedge \tau \neq \_\,(t,\mathsf{aborted})\} \\
A(C_1 \parallel \ldots \parallel C_m) &= \mathsf{prefix}(\textstyle\bigcup\{\mathsf{interleave}(\tau_1,\ldots,\tau_m) \mid \forall t.\,1 \le t \le m \implies \tau_t \in A(C_t)t\})
\end{aligned}
$$

Figure 2: The function $A(\cdot)$ mapping commands and programs to the set of all their possible traces

closure here to account for incomplete program computations as well as those in which the scheduler preempts a thread forever.

$A(c)t$ returns a singleton set with the action corresponding to the primitive command c (recall that primitive commands execute atomically). $A(C_1;C_2)t$ concatenates all possible traces corresponding to C_1 with those corresponding to C_2. The set of traces for a conditional considers cases where either branch is taken. We record the decision using an assume action; at the evaluation stage, this allows us to ensure that this decision is consistent with the program state. The trace set for a loop is defined using the Kleene closure operator * to produce all possible unfoldings of the loop body. Again, we record branching decisions using assume actions.

The trace set of a method invocation $x := f(e)$ includes both traces where the method executes successfully and where the current transaction is aborted. The former set is constructed by non-deterministically choosing two integers n and n' to describe the parameter n and the return value n' for the method call. To ensure that e indeed evaluates to n, we insert $\mathsf{assume}(e = n)$ before the call action, and to ensure that x gets the return value n', we add the assignment $x := n'$ after the ret action. Note that some of the choices here might not be feasible: the chosen n might not be the value of the parameter expression e when the method is invoked, or the method might never return n' when called with n. Such infeasible choices are filtered out at the following stages of the semantics definition: the former at the evaluation stage (3) by the semantics of assume, and the latter in (1) by selecting the traces from $[\![P]\!](s)$ that interact with the transactional system correctly.

The trace set of $x := \mathtt{atomic}\ \{C\}$ contains traces in which C is aborted in the middle of its execution (at an object operation) and those in which C executes until completion and then the transaction commits or aborts. From the restrictions on programs introduced in Section 2, we immediately get:

PROPOSITION 13. *For any program P, the set $A(P)$ contains only well-formed traces.*

Semantics of primitive commands

To define evaluation, we assume a semantics of every command $c \in \mathsf{Pcomm}$, given by a function $[\![c]\!]$ that defines how the program state is transformed by executing c. As we noted in Section 2, different classes of primitive commands are supposed to access only certain subsets of variables. To ensure that this is indeed the case, we define $[\![c]\!]$ as a function of only those variables that c is allowed to access. Namely, the semantics of $c \in \mathsf{LPcomm}_t$ is given by

$$[\![c]\!] : (\mathsf{LVar}_t \to \mathbb{Z}) \to \mathcal{P}(\mathsf{LVar}_t \to \mathbb{Z}),$$

and the semantics of $c \in \mathsf{GPcomm}_t$, by

$$[\![c]\!] : ((\mathsf{LVar}_t \uplus \mathsf{GVar}) \to \mathbb{Z}) \to \mathcal{P}((\mathsf{LVar}_t \uplus \mathsf{GVar}) \to \mathbb{Z}).$$

For a valuation q of variables that c is allowed to access, $[\![c]\!](q)$ yields the set of their valuations that can be obtained by executing c from a state with variable values q. Note that this allows c to be non-deterministic. For example, an assignment command $x := g$ has the following semantics:

$$[\![x := g]\!](q) = q[x \mapsto q(g)],$$

where $q[x \mapsto q(g)]$ is the function that has the same value as q everywhere, except for x, where it has the value $q(g)$. We define the semantics of assume commands following the informal explanation given at the beginning of this section: for example,

$$[\![\mathsf{assume}(x = n)]\!](q) = \begin{cases} \{q\}, & \text{if } q(x) = n; \\ \emptyset, & \text{otherwise.} \end{cases} \quad (4)$$

Thus, when the condition in assume does not hold of q, the command stops the computation by not producing any output states.

We lift functions $[\![c]\!]$ to full states by keeping the variables that c is not allowed to access unmodified. For example, if $c \in \mathsf{GPcomm}_t$, then for all $u \in \mathsf{Var}$ we let

$$[\![c]\!](s)(u) = \begin{cases} [\![c]\!](s|_{\mathsf{LVar}_t \uplus \mathsf{GVar}})(u), & \text{if } u \in \mathsf{LVar}_t \uplus \mathsf{GVar}; \\ s(u), & \text{otherwise.} \end{cases}$$

where $s|_{\mathsf{LVar}_t \uplus \mathsf{GVar}}$ is the restriction of s to variables in $\mathsf{LVar}_t \uplus \mathsf{GVar}$.

Trace evaluation

Using the semantics of primitive commands, we first define the evaluation of a single action on a given state:

$$\mathsf{eval} : \mathsf{State} \times \mathsf{Action} \to \mathcal{P}(\mathsf{State})$$
$$\mathsf{eval}(s, (t, c)) = [\![c]\!](s);$$
$$\mathsf{eval}(s, \varphi) = \{s\} \text{ for all other actions } \varphi.$$

Note that this does not change the state s as a result of interface actions, since their return values are assigned to local variables by separate actions introduced when generating $A(P)$. We then lift eval to traces as follows:

$$\mathsf{eval} : \mathsf{State} \times \mathsf{WTrace} \to \mathcal{P}(\mathsf{State})$$
$$\mathsf{eval}(s, \varepsilon) = \{s\};$$
$$\mathsf{eval}(s, \tau\varphi) = \{s'' \mid \exists s'.\, s' \in \mathsf{eval}(s, \tau) \wedge s'' \in \mathsf{eval}(s', \varphi)\}.$$

This allows us to define $[\![P]\!](s)$ as the set of those traces from $A(P)$ that can be evaluated from s without getting stuck, as formalized by (3). Note that this definition enables the semantics of `assume` defined by (4) to filter out traces that make branching decisions inconsistent with the program state. For example, consider the program (2). The set $A(P)$ includes traces where both branches are explored. However, due to the semantics of the `assume` actions added to the traces according to Figure 2, only the trace executing $y := 1$ will result in a non-empty set of final states after the evaluation and, therefore, only this trace will be included into $\llbracket P \rrbracket(s)$.

5. OBSERVATIONAL REFINEMENT

Informally, a concrete transactional system $\mathcal{H}_C$ observationally refines an abstract transactional system $\mathcal{H}_A$, if replacing $\mathcal{H}_C$ by $\mathcal{H}_A$ in a program leaves all its original user-observable behaviors reproducible. The formal definition depends on which aspects of program behavior we consider observable. One possibility is to allow the user to observe the values of all variables during the program execution. The corresponding notion of observational refinement is stated as follows.

DEFINITION 14. *A transactional system $\mathcal{H}_C$* **observationally refines** *a transactional system $\mathcal{H}_A$* **with respect to states**, *denoted by $\mathcal{H}_C \preceq_{\mathsf{state}} \mathcal{H}_A$, if*

$$\forall P. \forall s. \forall \tau \in \llbracket P \rrbracket(s, \mathcal{H}_C). \exists \tau' \in \llbracket P \rrbracket(s, \mathcal{H}_A).$$
$$\mathsf{eval}(s, \tau) = \mathsf{eval}(s, \tau').$$

Note that, since the semantics of a program P includes traces corresponding to its incomplete computations (see the use of prefix-closure in Figure 2), we allow observing intermediate program states as well as final ones. Definition 14 implies that, if a program using the abstract transactional system $\mathcal{H}_A$ satisfies a correctness property stated in terms of such states, then it will still satisfy the property if it uses the concrete system $\mathcal{H}_C$ instead.

In some situations, we may also be interested in observing separate program actions and the order between them, rather than the set of all reachable program states. In particular, this is desirable for checking the validity of linear-time temporal properties over program traces. We formulate the corresponding notion of observational refinement as follows.

DEFINITION 15. *Well-formed traces τ and τ' are* **observationally equivalent**, *written $\tau \sim \tau'$, if*

$$(\forall t \in \mathsf{ThreadID}. \tau|_t = \tau'|_t) \land (\mathsf{nontrans}(\tau) = \mathsf{nontrans}(\tau')).$$

A transactional system $\mathcal{H}_C$ **observationally refines** *a transactional system $\mathcal{H}_A$* **with respect to traces**, *denoted by $\mathcal{H}_C \preceq_{\mathsf{trace}} \mathcal{H}_A$, if*

$$\forall P. \forall s. \forall \tau \in \llbracket P \rrbracket(s, \mathcal{H}_C). \exists \tau' \in \llbracket P \rrbracket(s, \mathcal{H}_A). \tau \sim \tau'.$$

Traces related by $\sim$ are thus considered indistinguishable to the user, and, hence, the user can observe which equivalence class over $\sim$ the trace executed by the program belongs to.

We are now in a position to state our main result.

THEOREM 16.

$$\mathcal{H}_C \sqsubseteq \mathcal{H}_A \implies \mathcal{H}_C \preceq_{\mathsf{trace}} \mathcal{H}_A \implies$$
$$\mathcal{H}_C \preceq_{\mathsf{state}} \mathcal{H}_A \implies \mathcal{H}_C|_{\mathsf{complete}} \sqsubseteq \mathcal{H}_A|_{\mathsf{complete}}.$$

Thus, for our programming language, the opacity relation implies observational refinement with respect to traces or states, and either of these implies that the complete subsets of the transactional systems are in the opacity relation.

The first and the second implications from Theorem 16 are proved in Section 6, and the third one, in Section 7.

6. SUFFICIENCY OF THE OPACITY RELATION

Our goal in this section is to show that the opacity relation implies observational refinement with respect to traces. The next lemma (proved below) is key in establishing this: it shows that a trace τ_H with a history H can be transformed into an equivalent trace τ_S with a history S that is in the opacity relation with H.

LEMMA 17 (REARRANGEMENT). *For any well-formed histories H and S:*

$$H \sqsubseteq S \implies (\forall \text{well-formed } \tau_H. \mathsf{history}(\tau_H) = H \implies$$
$$\exists \text{well-formed } \tau_S. \mathsf{history}(\tau_S) = S \land \tau_H \sim \tau_S).$$

We also rely on the following lemma, which straightforwardly implies that observational refinement with respect to traces implies that with respect to states. The proof of the lemma (given below) relies on the restrictions on accesses to variables in Definition 12.

LEMMA 18. *For all well-formed traces τ_H and τ_S,*

$$\tau_H \sim \tau_S \land \mathsf{eval}(s, \tau_H) \neq \emptyset \implies \forall s. \mathsf{eval}(s, \tau_H) = \mathsf{eval}(s, \tau_S).$$

COROLLARY 19. $\mathcal{H}_C \preceq_{\mathsf{trace}} \mathcal{H}_A \implies \mathcal{H}_C \preceq_{\mathsf{state}} \mathcal{H}_A.$

Lemma 18 also allows us to conclude that the trace τ_S resulting from the transformation in Lemma 17 can be produced by a program P if so can the original trace τ_H.

LEMMA 20. *If $\tau_H \in \llbracket P \rrbracket(s)$ and $\tau_H \sim \tau_S$, then $\tau_S \in \llbracket P \rrbracket(s)$.*

PROOF. Let $P = C_1 \parallel \ldots \parallel C_m$. Consider s, τ_H and τ_S such that $\tau_H \in \llbracket P \rrbracket(s)$ and $\tau_H \sim \tau_S$. Then for some τ' we have $\tau_H \tau' \in A(P)$ and $\mathsf{eval}(s, \tau_H) \neq \emptyset$. This implies $(\tau_H \tau')|_t \in A(C_t)t$ for any thread t. Since $\tau_H \sim \tau_S$, we have that, $\tau_S|_t = \tau_H|_t$. Then $(\tau_S \tau')|_t \in A(C_t)t$ and by the definition of $A(P)$ in Figure 2 we get $\tau_S \in A(P)$. Furthermore, by Lemma 18, $\mathsf{eval}(s, \tau_S) \neq \emptyset$, so that $\tau_S \in \llbracket P \rrbracket(s)$. $\square$

THEOREM 21. $\mathcal{H}_C \sqsubseteq \mathcal{H}_A \implies \mathcal{H}_C \preceq_{\mathsf{trace}} \mathcal{H}_A.$

PROOF. Assume $\mathcal{H}_C \sqsubseteq \mathcal{H}_A$ and consider a program P, a state s and a trace $\tau_H \in \llbracket P \rrbracket(s, \mathcal{H}_C)$. Let $\mathsf{history}(\tau_H) = H$; then $\tau_H \in \llbracket P \rrbracket(s)$ and $H \in \mathcal{H}_C$. Since $\mathcal{H}_C \sqsubseteq \mathcal{H}_A$, there exists a history $S \in \mathcal{H}_A$ such that $H \sqsubseteq S$. Since H and S are well-formed, Lemma 17 implies that there is a well-formed trace τ_S such that $\tau_H \sim \tau_S$ and $\mathsf{history}(\tau_S) = S$. Then by Lemma 20 we have $\tau_S \in \llbracket P \rrbracket(s)$. Since $S \in \mathcal{H}_A$, this implies $\tau_S \in \llbracket P \rrbracket(s, \mathcal{H}_A)$. $\square$

Proof of Lemma 17 (Rearrangement)

Consider H, S and τ_H such that $H \sqsubseteq S$ and $\mathsf{history}(\tau_H) = H$. Note that $|H| = |S|$. To obtain the desired trace τ_S, we inductively construct a sequence of well-formed traces τ^i, $i = 0..|S|$ with well-formed histories $H^i = \mathsf{history}(\tau^i)$ such that

$$H^i|_i = S|_i; \quad H^i \sqsubseteq S; \quad \tau_H \sim \tau^i. \tag{5}$$

We then let $\tau_S = \tau^{|S|}$, so that $\tau_H \sim \tau^{|S|}$ and

$$\mathsf{history}(\tau^{|S|}) = H^{|S|} = H^{|S|}|_{|S|} = S|_{|S|} = S,$$

as required. Note that the condition $H^i \sqsubseteq S$ in (5) is not used to establish the required properties of τ_S; we add it so that the induction goes through.

We start the construction of the sequence of traces τ^i with $\tau^0 = \tau_H$, so that $H^0 = H$ and all the requirements in (5) hold trivially. Assume a trace τ^i satisfying (5) was constructed; we get τ^{i+1} from τ^i by applying the following lemma. Since $\sim$ is transitive, the conclusion of the lemma implies the desired properties of τ^{i+1}.

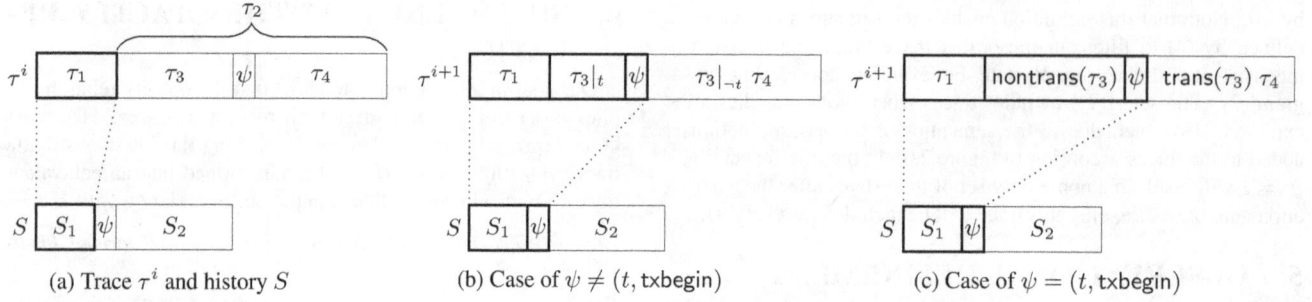

(a) Trace τ^i and history S (b) Case of $\psi \neq (t, \text{txbegin})$ (c) Case of $\psi = (t, \text{txbegin})$

Figure 3: An illustration of the transformations performed in the proof of Lemma 22

LEMMA 22. *Assume well-formed histories H^i and S and a well-formed trace τ^i such that*

$$\text{history}(\tau^i) = H^i; \quad H^i\!\downarrow_i = S\!\downarrow_i; \quad H^i \sqsubseteq S.$$

Then there exist some well-formed history H^{i+1} and a well-formed trace τ^{i+1} such that

$$\text{history}(\tau^{i+1}) = H^{i+1}; \quad H^{i+1}\!\downarrow_{i+1} = S\!\downarrow_{i+1};$$
$$H^{i+1} \sqsubseteq S; \quad \tau^i \sim \tau^{i+1}.$$

PROOF. Let $S = S_1\,\psi\,S_2$, where $|S_1| = i$. By assumption, $\text{history}(\tau^i)\!\downarrow_i = H^i\!\downarrow_i = S\!\downarrow_i = S_1$. Thus, for some traces τ_1 and τ_2, we have $\tau^i = \tau_1\,\tau_2$, where τ_1 is the minimal prefix of τ^i such that $\text{history}(\tau_1) = S_1$. We also have $H^i \sqsubseteq S$, and, hence, there exists a bijection $\theta : \{1, \ldots, |H^i|\} \to \{1, \ldots, |S|\}$ satisfying the conditions of Definition 4. Since θ preserves the per-thread order of actions and $\text{history}(\tau_1) = S_1$, we can assume that θ maps actions in $\text{history}(\tau_1)$ to the corresponding actions in S_1. Hence, for some traces τ_3 and τ_4, we have

$$\text{history}(\psi) = \psi, \quad \tau_2 = \tau_3\,\psi\,\tau_4, \quad \tau^i = \tau_1\,\tau_2 = \tau_1\,\tau_3\,\psi\,\tau_4,$$

and θ maps the ψ in $\text{history}(\tau^i)$ to ψ in S, i.e., $\theta(|\text{history}(\tau_1\,\tau_3)| + 1) = |S_1| + 1$; see Figure 3(a).

Let $\psi = (t, \_)$. We note that, since θ preserves the per-thread order of actions and $\text{history}(\tau_1) = S_1$, we have $\text{history}(\tau_3|_t) = \varepsilon$. We proceed by case analysis on the kind of ψ.

Case I: $\psi \neq (t, \text{txbegin})$. Let $\tau^{i+1} = \tau_1\,(\tau_3|_t)\,\psi\,(\tau_3|_{\neg t})\,\tau_4$ and $H^{i+1} = \text{history}(\tau^{i+1})$; see Figure 3(b). Intuitively, τ^{i+1} is obtained from $\tau^i = \tau_1\,\tau_3\,\psi\,\tau_4$ by moving all the actions in τ_3 performed by thread t, together with ψ, to the position right after τ_1.

Since $\text{history}(\tau_3|_t) = \varepsilon$, $\text{history}(\tau_1) = S_1$ and $|S_1| = i$, we get:

$$\begin{aligned} H^{i+1}\!\downarrow_{i+1} &= (\text{history}(\tau_1\,(\tau_3|_t)\,\psi\,(\tau_3|_{\neg t})\,\tau_4))\!\downarrow_{i+1} \\ &= S_1\,\psi = S\!\downarrow_{i+1}, \end{aligned}$$

as required. We also have:

$$\begin{aligned} \tau^{i+1}|_t &= (\tau_1\,(\tau_3|_t)\,\psi\,(\tau_3|_{\neg t})\,\tau_4)|_t \\ &= (\tau_1|_t)\,(\tau_3|_t)\,\psi\,(\tau_4|_t) \\ &= (\tau_1\,\tau_3\,\psi\,\tau_4)|_t \\ &= \tau^i|_t; \end{aligned}$$

$$\begin{aligned} \tau^{i+1}|_{\neg t} &= (\tau_1\,(\tau_3|_t)\,\psi\,(\tau_3|_{\neg t})\,\tau_4)|_{\neg t} \\ &= (\tau_1|_{\neg t})\,(\tau_3|_{\neg t})\,(\tau_4|_{\neg t}) \\ &= (\tau_1\,\tau_3\,\psi\,\tau_4)|_{\neg t} \\ &= \tau^i|_{\neg t}. \end{aligned}$$

Hence, for any thread t', we have $\tau^i|_{t'} = \tau^{i+1}|_{t'}$ and $H^{i+1}|_{t'} = H^i|_{t'} = S|_{t'}$. Any real-time order between two actions that ex-

ists in H^{i+1}, but not in H^i, also exists between the actions in S corresponding to them according to θ. Thus, $H^{i+1} \sqsubseteq S$.

Since $\psi \neq (t, \text{txbegin})$ and $\text{history}(\tau_3|_t) = \varepsilon$, all the actions performed by t in the subtrace τ_3 of τ^i are transactional. Hence,

$$\begin{aligned} \text{nontrans}(\tau^{i+1}) &= \text{nontrans}(\tau_1\,(\tau_3|_t)\,\psi\,(\tau_3|_{\neg t})\,\tau_4) \\ &= \text{nontrans}(\tau_1\,\tau_3\,\psi\,\tau_4) \\ &= \text{nontrans}(\tau^i) \end{aligned}$$

and therefore $\tau^i \sim \tau^{i+1}$.

Case II: $\psi = (t, \text{txbegin})$. Note that the subtrace τ_3 of τ^i does not contain any committed or aborted actions ψ'. Indeed, assume otherwise. Since $\text{history}(\tau_1) = S_1$, the action in S corresponding to ψ' according to θ would be in S_2. This would mean that the real-time order between ψ' and ψ in H^i is not preserved in S, contradicting our assumption that $H^i \sqsubseteq S$. Thus, for any thread $t' \neq t$, $\tau_3|_{t'}$ consists of some number of non-transactional actions followed by some number of transactional ones, and $\tau_3|_t$ does not contain any transactional actions. Motivated by these observations, we let

$$\tau^{i+1} = \tau_1\,\text{nontrans}(\tau_3)\,\psi\,\text{trans}(\tau_3)\,\tau_4$$

and $H^{i+1} = \text{history}(\tau^{i+1})$; see Figure 3(c).[3] Intuitively, τ^{i+1} is obtained from $\tau^i = \tau_1\,\tau_3\,\psi\,\tau_4$ by moving all transactional actions in τ_3 to the position right before τ_4.

Since $\text{history}(\text{nontrans}(\tau_3)) = \varepsilon$, $\text{history}(\tau_1) = S_1$ and $|S_1| = i$, we get:

$$\begin{aligned} H^{i+1}\!\downarrow_{i+1} &= (\text{history}(\tau_1\,\text{nontrans}(\tau_3)\,\psi\,\text{trans}(\tau_3)\,\tau_4)\!\downarrow_{i+1} \\ &= S_1\,\psi = S\!\downarrow_{i+1}, \end{aligned}$$

as required.

Since for every thread $t' \neq t$, $\tau_3|_{t'}$ consists of non-transactional actions followed by transactional ones,

$$(\text{nontrans}(\tau_3)\,\psi\,\text{trans}(\tau_3))|_{t'} = (\tau_3\,\psi)|_{t'}.$$

Since $\tau_3|_t$ does not contain any transactional actions, $\tau_3 = \text{nontrans}(\tau_3)$ and, hence,

$$(\text{nontrans}(\tau_3)\,\psi\,\text{trans}(\tau_3))|_t = (\tau_3\,\psi)|_t.$$

Thus, for any t'' we have

$$\begin{aligned} \tau^{i+1}|_{t''} &= (\tau_1\,\text{nontrans}(\tau_3)\,\psi\,\text{trans}(\tau_3)\,\tau_4)|_{t''} \\ &= (\tau_1\,\tau_3\,\psi\,\tau_4)|_{t''} = \tau^i|_{t''} \end{aligned}$$

---

[3] Here we are applying nontrans to a part τ_3 of a well-formed trace τ^i. Note that, in the absence of txbegin actions in τ_3, the definition of nontrans given in Section 4 considers all actions in τ_3 non-transactional.

316

and $H^{i+1}|_{t''} = H^i|_{t''} = S|_{t''}$. Any real-time order between actions in H^{i+1} also exists in H^i, and hence, $H^{i+1} \sqsubseteq S$. Finally,

$$
\begin{aligned}
\mathsf{nontrans}(\tau^{i+1}) &= \mathsf{nontrans}(\tau_1\,\mathsf{nontrans}(\tau_3)\,\psi\,\mathsf{trans}(\tau_3)\,\tau_4) \\
&= \mathsf{nontrans}(\tau_1\,\tau_3\,\psi\,\tau_4) \\
&= \mathsf{nontrans}(\tau^i),
\end{aligned}
$$

so that $\tau^i \sim \tau^{i+1}$. $\quad\square$

Proof of Lemma 18

Consider s, τ_H and τ_S such that $\tau_H \sim \tau_S$ and $\mathsf{eval}(s, \tau_H) \neq \emptyset$. We need to show that $\mathsf{eval}(s, \tau_S) \neq \emptyset$. The proof of this fact is similar in its structure to that of Lemma 17. We inductively construct a sequence of well-formed traces τ^i, $i = 0..|\tau_S|$ such that

$$
\tau^i|_i = \tau_S|_i; \quad \tau^i \sim \tau_S; \quad \mathsf{eval}(s, \tau^i) = \mathsf{eval}(s, \tau_H) \neq \emptyset. \quad (6)
$$

Then for $i = |\tau_S|$ we get $\tau^i = \tau_S$, which implies the required.

To construct the sequence of traces τ^i, we let $\tau^0 = \tau_H$, so that all the requirements in (6) hold trivially. Assume now that a trace τ^i satisfying (6) has been constructed. Let $\tau_S = \tau_1\,\varphi\,\tau_2$, where $|\tau_1| = i$, and $\varphi = (t, \_)$. By assumption, $\tau^i|_i = \tau_S|_i$ and, since $\tau^i \sim \tau_S$, we also have $\tau^i|_t = \tau_S|_t$. Hence, for some traces τ_2' and τ_2'', we get

$$
\tau^i = \tau_1\,\tau_2'\,\varphi\,\tau_2'',
$$

where τ_2' does not contain any actions by thread t. Let

$$
\tau^{i+1} = \tau_1\,\varphi\,\tau_2'\,\tau_2'';
$$

then $\tau^{i+1}|_{i+1} = \tau_S|_{i+1}$. We now show that $\tau^{i+1} \sim \tau^i$ and $\mathsf{eval}(s, \tau^{i+1}) = \mathsf{eval}(s, \tau^i)$, which implies the required.

First note that $\tau^i|_{t'} = \tau^{i+1}|_{t'}$ for any thread t' since τ_2' does not contain any actions by thread t. Next, consider the case when the action φ in τ^i is non-transactional. Since $\tau^i|_t = \tau_S|_t$, so is the corresponding action φ in τ_S. Assume that some action $\varphi' = (t', \_)$ in the subtrace τ_2' of τ^i is non-transactional as well, where $t' \neq t$. Let φ' be the j-th action by thread t' in τ^i. Since $\tau^i|_{t'} = \tau_S|_{t'}$, φ' is also the j-th action by thread t' in τ_S and is non-transactional in this trace. But then φ' has to be in the subtrace τ_2 of τ_S and thus follow φ, contradicting $\mathsf{nontrans}(\tau^i) = \mathsf{nontrans}(\tau_S)$. Hence, if the action φ in τ^i is non-transactional, then the subtrace τ_2' of τ^i does not contain any non-transactional actions. This implies $\mathsf{nontrans}(\tau^{i+1}) = \mathsf{nontrans}(\tau^i)$ and thus $\tau^{i+1} \sim \tau^i$.

The restrictions on accesses to variables by commands from LPcomm_t and GPcomm_t (stated in Section 2 and formalized in Section 4) imply

PROPOSITION 23. *Assume φ_1 and φ_2 are actions by different threads and, if $\varphi_1 = (t_1, c_1)$ and $\varphi_2 = (t_2, c_2)$, then*

$$
(c_1 \in \mathsf{LPcomm}_{t_1} \wedge c_2 \in \mathsf{LPcomm}_{t_2} \uplus \mathsf{GPcomm}_{t_2}) \vee
$$
$$
(c_1 \in \mathsf{LPcomm}_{t_1} \uplus \mathsf{GPcomm}_{t_1} \wedge c_2 \in \mathsf{LPcomm}_{t_2}).
$$

Then $\mathsf{eval}(s, \varphi_1\,\varphi_2) = \mathsf{eval}(s, \varphi_2\,\varphi_1)$ for any state s.

Since τ^i is well-formed, by Definition 12 for any action (t', c) in it we have that $c \in \mathsf{LPcomm}_t \uplus \mathsf{GPcomm}_t$ and, if $c \in \mathsf{GPcomm}_t$, then the action is non-transactional. Given this and the properties of τ_2' established above, by applying Proposition 23 repeatedly we get that $\mathsf{eval}(s', \varphi\,\tau_2') = \mathsf{eval}(s', \tau_2'\,\varphi)$ for any state s'. Hence,

$$
\mathsf{eval}(s, \tau^{i+1}) = \mathsf{eval}(s, \tau_1\,\varphi\,\tau_2'\,\tau_2'') =
$$
$$
\mathsf{eval}(s, \tau_1\,\tau_2'\,\varphi\,\tau_2'') = \mathsf{eval}(s, \tau^i). \quad \square
$$

7. NECESSITY OF THE OPACITY RELATION

In this section we prove that observational refinement with respect to states implies the opacity relation restricted to the complete subsets of the transactional systems. We only give a proof sketch here and defer the full proof to [2, Appendix B].

THEOREM 24. $\mathcal{H}_C \preceq_{\mathsf{state}} \mathcal{H}_A \implies \mathcal{H}_C|_{\mathsf{complete}} \sqsubseteq \mathcal{H}_A|_{\mathsf{complete}}$.

PROOF SKETCH. For every complete history $H \in \mathcal{H}_C$ we construct a program P_H where every thread performs the sequence of transactions specified by H, records the return values obtained from methods of transactional objects, and monitors whether the real-time order between actions includes that in H.

In more detail, given that the history H is well-formed, we construct the code of every thread t as a sequence of `atomic` blocks, corresponding to txbegin, committed and aborted actions in $H|_t$, which perform the sequence of method invocations determined by call and ret actions in $H|_t$. We record the return value for every method invocation in a dedicated variable local to the corresponding thread, which is never rewritten (this is possible because H is finite). The return status of every transaction is also recorded in a dedicated local variable. As a result, from the final state of an execution of P_H, we can reconstruct the interaction of each thread with the transactional system. (We rely here on the fact that the histories considered are complete; our notion of observation is not strong enough to distinguish between, e.g., histories $H\,\varphi\,H'$ and $H\,H'$ where φ is a call action that does not return.)

To check whether an execution of P_H complies with the real-time order in H, we exploit the ability of threads to communicate via global variables outside transactions. For each transaction in H, we introduce a global variable g, which is initially 0 and is set to 1 by the thread executing the transaction right after the transaction completes, by a command following the corresponding `atomic` block. Before starting a transaction, each thread checks whether all transactions preceding this one in the real-time order in H have finished by reading the corresponding g variables. The outcome is recorded in a dedicated local variable.

Let s be a state with all variables set to distinguished initial values. From the above it follows that, given any trace $\tau \in [\![P_H]\!](s)$, by observing the states in $\mathsf{eval}(s, \tau)$, we can unambiguously determine whether the per-thread projections of $\mathsf{history}(\tau)$ are equal to those of H and whether the real-time order in $\mathsf{history}(\tau)$ includes that in H.

Now given $H \in \mathcal{H}_C$, we construct a trace $\tau \in [\![P_H]\!](s, \mathcal{H}_C)$ such that $\mathsf{history}(\tau) = H$ and $\mathsf{eval}(s, \tau) = \{s'\}$, where the state s' signals the above correspondence of the trace to H. By Definition 14, there exists a trace $\tau' \in [\![P_H]\!](s, \mathcal{H}_A)$ such that $\mathsf{eval}(s, \tau') = \{s'\}$. But then the per-thread projections of $S = \mathsf{history}(\tau')$ are equal to those of H and the real-time order in H is preserved in S. By Definition 4, this implies $H \sqsubseteq S$. $\quad\square$

The proof highlights the features of our programming model that lead to the necessity result. First, the ability to access global variables outside transactions allows us to monitor the real-time order. Second, we use the ability of programs to observe values assigned to local variables during the execution of a transaction, even if the transaction aborts: P_H records the return values of method invocations by aborted transactions in special local variables, which can then be observed in final states. This necessitates treating aborted transactions in the same way as committed ones in the consistency definition.

8. RELATED WORK AND DISCUSSION

Previous work has studied transactional memory consistency by:

- investigating the semantics of different programming languages with atomic blocks and the feasibility of their efficient implementation [1, 11, 19]; or

- defining consistency conditions for TM [3,5,8,9,18] and proving that particular TM implementations validate them [4,9].

Thus, previous work has tended to address the issue from the perspective of either programming languages or TM implementations and has not tried to relate these two levels in a formal manner. An exception is the work by Harris et al. [12], which proved that a specific TM implementation, Bartok-STM, validates a particular semantics of atomic blocks in a programming language.

This paper tries to fill in the gap in existing studies by relating the semantics of a programming language with atomic blocks to that of a TM system implementing them. Our work is complementary to previous proofs that certain TM systems satisfy opacity [4], as it lifts such results to the language level. Our work is also more general than that of Harris et al. [12], since our results allow establishing observational refinement for *any* TM implementation satisfying opacity. However, some of the above-mentioned papers [1, 19] investigated advanced language interfaces that we do not consider, such as nested transactions and access to shared data both inside and outside transactions.

This paper employs a well-known technique from the theory of programming languages, observational refinement [13, 14], to explore the most appropriate way to specify TM consistency. Observational refinement has previously been used to characterize correctness criteria for libraries of concurrent data structures. Thus, Filipovic et al. [6] proved that, in this setting sequential consistency [17] is necessary and sufficient for observational refinement, and so is linearizability [15] when client programs can interact via shared global variables. Gotsman and Yang [7] adjusted linearizability to account for infinite computations and showed its sufficiency for observational refinement in the case when the client can observe the validity of liveness properties. Our work takes this approach from the simpler setting of concurrent libraries to the more elaborate setup of transactional memory. Since we allow the abstract transactional system to have incomplete transactions, we hope that in the future we can generalize our consistency condition to specify liveness properties, along the lines of [7].

Opacity requires the TM behavior observed by aborted transactions to be as consistent as that observed by committed ones. Other proposed consistency conditions tried to relax this requirement. For example, *virtual world consistency (VWC)* [16] requires the behavior observed by an individual aborted transaction to be consistent only with the committed transactions from which it reads and those previously committed by the same thread. Our necessity result implies that VWC does not imply observational refinement for our programming language. However, this does not rule out the viability of VWC and related notions as a consistency condition for TM. VWC may well imply observational refinement for a programming language in which aborted transactions do not affect the rest of the computation (in particular, their modifications to local variables are rolled back) and a weaker notion of observations. This paper establishes an approach for evaluating and comparing TM consistency conditions, and in future work, we hope to apply it to VWC and other conditions, such as TMS [5, 18] and DU-opacity [3]. We also intend to investigate the behaviour of incomplete histories with respect to observational refinement, whose treatment by the opacity relation causes our result to fall short of the strict equivalence between the relation and the observational refinement.

Acknowledgements

This work is supported by EU FP7 projects TRANSFORM (238639) and ADVENT (308830). We thank Victor Luchangco, Eran Yahav, Hongseok Yang and the reviewers for helpful comments.

9. REFERENCES

[1] M. Abadi, A. Birrell, T. Harris, and M. Isard. Semantics of transactional memory and automatic mutual exclusion. In *POPL*, pages 63–74, 2008.

[2] H. Attiya, A. Gotsman, S. Hans, and N. Rinetzky. A programming language perspective on transactional memory consistency. Technical Report CS-2013-04, Department of Computer Science, Technion, 2013.

[3] H. Attiya, S. Hans, P. Kuznetsov, and S. Ravi. Safety of deferred update in transactional memory. In *ICDCS*, 2013. To appear.

[4] A. Bieniusa and P. Thiemann. Proving isolation properties for software transactional memory. In *ESOP*, pages 38–56, 2011.

[5] S. Doherty, L. Groves, V. Luchangco, and M. Moir. Towards formally specifying and verifying transactional memory. *Formal Aspects of Computing*, pages 1–31, March 2012.

[6] I. Filipovic, P. W. O'Hearn, N. Rinetzky, and H. Yang. Abstraction for concurrent objects. In *ESOP*, pages 252–266, 2009.

[7] A. Gotsman and H. Yang. Liveness-preserving atomicity abstraction. In *ICALP (2)*, pages 453–465, 2011.

[8] R. Guerraoui and M. Kapalka. On the correctness of transactional memory. In *PPOPP*, pages 175–184, 2008.

[9] R. Guerraoui and M. Kapalka. *Principles of Transactional Memory*. Synthesis Lectures on Distributed Computing Theory. Morgan & Claypool, 2011.

[10] T. Harris, J. Larus, and R. Rajwar. *Transactional memory*. Synthesis Lectures on Computer Architecture. Morgan & Claypool Publishers, 2010.

[11] T. Harris, S. Marlow, S. L. P. Jones, and M. Herlihy. Composable memory transactions. In *PPOPP*, pages 48–60, 2005.

[12] T. Harris, M. Plesko, A. Shinnar, and D. Tarditi. Optimizing memory transactions. In *PLDI*, pages 14–25, 2006.

[13] J. He, C. Hoare, and J. Sanders. Data refinement refined. In *ESOP*, pages 187–196, 1986.

[14] J. He, C. Hoare, and J. Sanders. Prespecification in data refinement. *Information Processing Letters*, 25(2):71 – 76, 1987.

[15] M. Herlihy and J. M. Wing. Linearizability: a correctness condition for concurrent objects. *ACM Transactions on Programming Languages and Systems*, 12(3):463–492, 1990.

[16] D. Imbs, J. R. G. de Mendívil, and M. Raynal. Brief announcement: virtual world consistency: a new condition for STM systems. In *PODC*, pages 280–281, 2009.

[17] L. Lamport. How to make a multiprocessor computer that correctly executes multiprocess programs. *IEEE Transactions on Computers*, 28(9):690–691, 1979.

[18] M. Lesani, V. Luchangco, and M. Moir. Putting opacity in its place. In *WTTM*, 2012.

[19] K. F. Moore and D. Grossman. High-level small-step operational semantics for transactions. In *POPL*, pages 51–62, 2008.

Brief Announcement:
An Asymmetric Flat-Combining Based Queue Algorithm*

Michael Gorelik
Dept. of Computer-Science
Ben-Gurion Univ. of the Negev
smgorelik@gmail.com

Danny Hendler
Dept. of Computer-Science
Ben-Gurion Univ. of the Negev
hendlerd@cs.bgu.ac.il

ABSTRACT

We present *asymmetric flat-combining*, an extension of flat-combining in which the behavior of producers and consumers differs, and use it to implement a linearizable FIFO queue. Unlike a flat-combining queue where all queue operations are blocking, in our algorithm enqueue operations are wait-free. Moreover, non-combiner threads performing dequeue operations are able to share the computational load instead of just waiting. Our experimental evaluation shows that the new queue algorithm outperforms the flat combining queue and other state of the art queue implementations for most producer-consumer workloads while allowing producer threads to operate in a wait-free manner.

Categories and Subject Descriptors

D.1.3 [**Programming Techniques**]: Concurrent Programming—*Concurrent programming*

General Terms

Algorithms

Keywords

Shared memory, flat combining, FIFO queue

1. INTRODUCTION

Concurrent first-in-first-out (FIFO) queues are widely used in parallel applications, concurrent data-structure libraries and operating systems [3, 6, 7, 8, 10, 11]. A concurrent queue supports the enqueue and dequeue operations with linearizable FIFO semantics [4].

Hendler et al. introduced *flat combining* [3], a synchronization mechanism based on coarse-grained locking in which a single thread holding a lock performs the combined work

---

*This work was supported in part by the Israel Science Foundation (grant number 1227/10).

of other threads. Due to the very low synchronization overhead of flat-combining, it exhibits excellent performance in low and medium concurrency levels. However, since the combiner thread applies the combined operations of other threads to a central data-structure representing the object's state, the flat combining algorithm is essentially sequential, implying that its performance does not scale and even deteriorates when concurrency levels are high. Moreover, since other threads must wait for the combiner thread to apply their operations to the object, flat-combining is a blocking synchronization mechanism. In this work we show that, at least for some concurrent object implementations, these drawbacks of flat-combining can be mitigated while still maintaining its low synchronization overhead.

We present *asymmetric flat-combining* (henceforth AFC), an extension of flat combining (henceforth FC) in which the behavior of producers and consumers differs, and use it to implement a linearizable FIFO queue. Unlike an FC queue where all queue operations are blocking, in our AFC queue algorithm enqueue operations are wait-free; dequeue operations, on the other hand, are still blocking, as in the FC queue. Unlike flat combining where a single combiner thread applies operations on behalf of all other threads in a sequential manner, the AFC algorithm provides real parallelism: enqueue operations by different threads may proceed in parallel, and dequeue operations share work instead of simply waiting for the combiner thread. Our experimental evaluation shows that the AFC queue outperforms the FC queue and other state of the art queue implementations for most producer-consumer workloads even though it supports wait-free producers.

Recent work by Attiya et al. [1] proved that strong synchronization, in the form of either an atomic write-after-read (AWAR) or a read-after-write (RAW) access pattern, is unavoidable for concurrent implementations of many key data-structures. Specifically, for FIFO queues, their proofs imply that *dequeue* operations must apply either an AWAR or a RAW operation. However, it was open whether there exists any FIFO queue implementation whose *enqueue* operations avoid using both AWAR and RAW patterns. Our work also makes a theoretic contribution since, to the best of our knowledge, the AFC queue is the first FIFO queue algorithm where *enqueue* operations avoid using both these access patterns.

2. OVERVIEW OF THE AFC ALGORITHM

We now provide an overview of the algorithm. Pseudo-code and detailed descriptions may be found in the full version of this paper.[1] The key idea underlying the AFC queue is simple: each producer thread has a local queue of its own to which it can enqueue items in a wait-free manner without having to use strong synchronization operations. Thus, AFC **enqueue** operations are much faster than FC **enqueue** operations. In order to maintain FIFO order, a timestamp is associated with each enqueued item. Consumer threads use the FC protocol to synchronize their accesses to producer queues. A combiner thread must then serve consumer requests by providing them the least recent queued items. As FIFO order is only implicit in the timestamps associated with the items in multiple producer queues, these items must be "consolidated" to a single total order respecting the partial order of the corresponding **enqueue** operations. The new algorithm is therefore faced with the following two technical challenges. First, this consolidation process must not violate linearizability even when producers are adding new items to their local queues concurrently with **dequeue** operations by other threads. Second, consolidation must be done in an efficient manner.

The first challenge is solved by computing a *safe collect* - a collection of queue prefixes the items of which can be safely dequeued before all items in the corresponding queue suffixes. The second challenge is dealt with by having consumer threads other than the combiner thread share the computational task of queues consolidation rather than simply busy waiting.

Each active consumer owns a single node in a *consumers publication list*. The consumers publication list is protected by a lock manipulated by compare-and-swap (CAS) operations. Each publication list node contains a *request* field to which a consumer writes when it applies a **dequeue** operation and from which it reads the response written there after its operation was applied. Active producers own nodes in a separate *producers list*. Each node in the producers list contains a monotonically-increasing timestamp field, a pointer pq to a *producer queue* array owned by the producer and in and out indexes into this array. Each producer queue entry consists of an item and an associated timestamp. In order to maintain linearzaibility, queue items stored in producer queues must be totally ordered. Consolidation is implemented by computing what we call a *safe collect*, which we now define.

Let pq be a producer queue. A *queue prefix of pq* is a (possibly empty) sequence of consecutive items in pq, starting with the oldest item in pq (the one pointed at by its out index). Thus, a queue prefix of pq is defined by a pair of indexes $<pq.out,x>$, for some $x \in \{pq.out,\ldots,pq.in-1\}$, and contains all the items residing in the corresponding entries of pq. Let Op_1, Op_2 be two operations applied to the FIFO queue. We say that Op_1 precedes Op_2 if Op_1 terminates before Op_2 starts.

DEFINITION 1. *Let $C=<pq_1.out,x_1>\ldots<pq_k.out,x_k>$ be a sequence of (possibly empty) queue prefixes - one from each producer queue. We say that C is a* safe collect *if it satisfies the following requirements: 1) Let i_1 be an item in one of C's queue prefixes and let E_1 be the* **enqueue** *operation that added it. Also, let i_2 be an item, enqueued by some operation E_2 to entry $y > x_j$ of producer queue pq_j, for some $j \in \{1,\ldots,k\}$. Then E_2 does not precede E_1; 2) If all the*

prefixes of C are empty, then there was a point in time during C's computation in which all producer queues were empty.

To dequeue an item, a consumer thread t publishes its request to apply a dequeue operation by writing to the *request* field of its publication record. Thread t then busy-waits until its request is served or until it becomes a combiner thread. If t succeeds in acquiring the lock by performing a successful CAS then it becomes a combiner thread. It then proceeds by collecting pointers to publication records holding a request and by counting their number. Thread t then serves requests until either all requests are served or until the AFC queue becomes empty. If not all requests were served, then t proceeds to compute a new safe collect. If the new safe collect is empty, then all remaining requests receive an EMPTY indication and the combiner thread exits.

Parallel Consolidation.

The items in each producer queue are stored in increasing timestamp order, hence an item with a minimum timestamp can be found by comparing the timestamps of items in the safe collect's prefixes pointed at by the respective *out* indexes. If the safe collect consists of many prefixes, consolidation may be time-consuming and may slow-down **dequeue** operations considerably. The key mechanism that we use to mitigate this problem is *parallel consolidation*, in which multiple consumer threads may be deployed in parallel for accelerating the consolidation task. The parallel consolidation mechanism allows a combiner thread to deploy other consumer threads, which we call *helper threads*, to assist it in the consolidation process. Deploying exactly two helper threads yielded the best results in the architectures on which we conducted our experimental evaluation. Only consumer threads waiting for a response may be deployed.

3. EVALUATION

Here we provide results for evaluation we conducted on a Sun SPARC T5240 machine[2], comprising two UltraSPARC T2 plus (Niagara II) chips, running the Solaris operating system. Each chip contains 8 cores, each multiplexing 8 hardware threads, for a total of 64 hardware threads per chip. We ran our experiments on a single chip to avoid cross-chip communication. The algorithms we evaluated are implemented in C++ and compiled for SPARC using the cc compiler with the -O5 flag.

We compared the AFC algorithm with the H-Synch based queue [2], the flat-combining queue, the Baskets queue [5] and Michael and Scott's lock-free queue (MSQueue) [9]. To check the benefits of parallel consolidation, we also evaluated a variant of AFC that does not apply this mechanism, which we name *AFC_Ser*. For lack of space we report only on evaluation results for tests with equal numbers of producers and consumers.

In the N:N **throughput** benchmark, N producers and N consumers, for varying values of N, apply operations to the queue during a period of 3 seconds. Average throughput (for three runs) per millisecond is measured. As shown by Figure 2-(a), the Baskets queue hardly scales at all and has the worst performance. The MSQueue algorithm scales slowly with the level of concurrency. FC and H-Synch scale quickly

[1] http://www.cs.bgu.ac.il/~hendlerd/papers/AFC-full.pdf

[2] Our evaluation results on an Intel i7-2760QM machine can be found in the full paper.

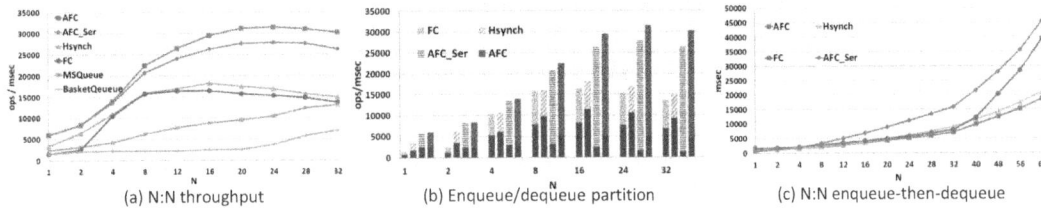

Figure 1: SPARC evaluation graphs.

up to 8-16 producer/consumer pairs and then their throughput slightly declines. The H-Synch queue provides somewhat better throughput. The best performers are AFC and AFR_Ser, both scaling up to 24 producer/consumer pairs. AFC provides up to 15% more throughput than AFC_Ser and outperforms H-Synch by a factor of approximately 2 for concurrency levels of 20 producer/consumer pairs or more.

Figure 2-(b) provides better understanding of the results of the four best-performing algorithms by showing the division to operation types. For every number of producer/consumer pairs, 4 bars are shown, one per each algorithm. The lower and upper parts of each bar respectively represent the number of dequeue and enqueue operations performed by the respective algorithm. It can be seen that there are very significant differences in the ratio between the numbers of enqueues and dequeues performed by different algorithms.

The FC algorithm is the most balanced, performing roughly equal numbers of enqueues and dequeues in all concurrency levels. This is because the FC combiner thread applies the operations of all waiting threads - both enqueues and dequeues - in each traversal of the publication list. The H-Synch algorithm performs significantly more dequeue operations than enqueue operations - up to 75% more for 16 producer/consumer pairs. AFC_Ser exhibits the greatest imbalance, reaching a ratio of more than 20 enqueues per a single dequeue operation for 32 producer/consumer pairs. The reason for this imbalance is clear: while AFC's enqueue operations are wait-free and quick, its dequeue operations are blocking. Moreover, with AFC_Ser, the task of consolidating producer local queues is performed sequentially by the combiner thread.

This imbalance is much smaller in the AFC algorithm, since multiple consumer threads perform the consolidation task in parallel. The numbers of enqueues performed by the AFC and AFC_Ser are more-or-less equal, but AFC performs much more dequeues than AFC_Ser, almost 4 times more for 32 producer/consumer pairs. Nevertheless, AFC still presents significant imbalance and performs almost 5.5 enqueue operations per each dequeue operation for 32 producer/consumer pairs.

Due to the significant differences in balance between enqueues and dequeues exhibited by different algorithm, we also evaluate the algorithms using a second benchmark that we name the N:N Enqueue-then-dequeue benchmark. In this benchmark, N threads, for varying values of N, first act as producers and perform 1M enqueue operations each. After completing these enqueues, each thread becomes a consumer and performs dequeue operations until the queue becomes empty. The N:N Enqueue-then-dequeue benchmark provides a more realistic view of AFC's relative performance than that provided by the N:N throughput bench-

mark, since at the end of the latter the queue may contain a large surplus of items that were not dequeued. Since the set of N threads first operate as producers and then as consumers, N can reach a maximum value of 64 for the SPARC machine.

Figure 2-(c) presents the results of the N:N Enqueue-then-dequeue benchmark on the SPARC machine. Baskets and MSQueue are the worst performers and are not shown since they are out-of-scale. The best performers are HSynch and AFC. AFC is faster than HSynch in almost all concurrency levels by about 10%-15%. AFC_Ser is consistently slower than AFC and the ratio keeps increasing with concurrency level. The bottom line for these tests is that AFC provides the best performance and H-Synch is second-best, even though AFC's producers are wait-free whereas H-Synch's producers are blocking.

4. REFERENCES

[1] H. Attiya, R. Guerraoui, D. Hendler, P. Kuznetsov, M. M. Michael, and M. T. Vechev. Laws of order: expensive synchronization in concurrent algorithms cannot be eliminated. In *POPL*, pages 487–498, 2011.

[2] P. Fatourou and N. D. Kallimanis. Revisiting the combining synchronization technique. In *PPOPP*, pages 257–266, 2012.

[3] D. Hendler, I. Incze, N. Shavit, and M. Tzafrir. Flat combining and the synchronization-parallelism tradeoff. In *SPAA*, pages 355–364, 2010.

[4] M. P. Herlihy and J. M. Wing. Linearizability: a correctness condition for concurrent objects. *TOPLAS*, 12(3):463–492, 1990.

[5] M. Hoffman, O. Shalev, and N. Shavit. The baskets queue. In *OPODIS*, pages 401–414, 2007.

[6] E. Ladan-Mozes and N. Shavit. An optimistic approach to lock-free fifo queues. *Distributed Computing*, 20(5):323–341, 2008.

[7] D. Lea. *The Java concurrency package (JSR-166)*.

[8] J. M. Mellor-Crummey. Concurrent queues: Practical fetch-and-ϕ algorithms. Technical Report 229, University of Rochester, 1987.

[9] M. M. Michael and M. L. Scott. Simple, fast, and practical non-blocking and blocking concurrent queue algorithms. In *PODC*, pages 267–275, 1996.

[10] S. Prakash, Y.-H. Lee, and T. Johnson. A non-blocking algorithm for shared queues using compare-and-swap. In *ICPP (2)*, pages 68–75, 1991.

[11] J. M. Stone. A simple and correct shared-queue algorithm using compare-and-swap. In *SC*, pages 495–504, 1990.

Brief Announcement: Resettable Objects and Efficient Memory Reclamation for Concurrent Algorithms

Zahra Aghazadeh
Dept. of Computer Science
University of Calgary
zaghazad@ucalgary.ca

Wojciech Golab
Dept. of Electrical and
Computer Engineering
University of Waterloo
wgolab@uwaterloo.ca

Philipp Woelfel
Dept. of Computer Science
University of Calgary
woelfel@ucalgary.ca

ABSTRACT

We present a new technique for reclaiming memory in concurrent shared memory algorithms with n asynchronous processes. Our methodology can be applied in the same settings as hazard pointers [10], but provides better worst-case guarantees: For the same tasks for which hazard pointers have *expected* constant *amortized* complexity, our technique guarantees constant time in the *worst-case*.

We use our technique to implement efficient randomized *long-lived* test-and-set (TAS) objects from registers, based on known constructions of randomized one-time TAS objects [2, 9]. One of our constructions uses $O(n)$ space (which is optimal), and the reset() and Test&Set() operations have expected step complexity $O(\log \log n)$ against the oblivious adversary.

We also present a general method of augmenting shared objects with a reset() operation which can be used to reset the object into its initial state at any time. In many cases the transformation is optimal with respect to the time complexity of the resulting object. E.g., an object implemented from m registers can be augmented with a reset() operation which has $O(1)$ time complexity and without affecting the asymptotic time complexity of other operations; the resulting object uses $O(n^2 \cdot m)$ unbounded registers.

Categories and Subject Descriptors

E.1 [**Data Structures**]: Distributed data structures; F.2.2 [**Analysis of Algorithms and Problem Complexity**]: Nonnumerical Algorithms and Problems

Keywords

Memory reclamation; test-and-set; long-lived test-and-set; resettable objects; shared memory; memory management;

1. INTRODUCTION

Many synchronization primitives, such as renaming, timestamp, leader election, mutex or test-and-set objects

PODC'13, July 22–24, 2013, Montréal, Québec, Canada.
ACM 978-1-4503-2065-8/13/07.

have *one-shot* and *long-lived* variants. In one-shot algorithms, each process participates at most once, for example when electing a leader. In contrast, in long-lived algorithms, processes may participate repeatedly. Internally, such algorithms tend to solve smaller synchronization tasks repeatedly. An interesting case occurs when a long-lived algorithm internally solves these smaller tasks using one-shot base objects. In a practical implementation, the pool of one-shot objects is finite, and so eventually enough of the one-shot objects are "spent" so that reclamation becomes necessary.

One example is that of a test-and-set (TAS) object in a shared memory system. The one-shot version allows only the operation Test&Set(), which sets a bit (that is initially 0) to 1, and returns the previous value of that bit. A long-lived TAS object also provides a reset() operation, which resets the bit to 0 (and has no return value). Only the process which *wins* a Test&Set() operation (i.e., the operation returns 0) is allowed to subsequently reset it [1].

TAS objects are standard synchronization primitives that can, for example, be used to protect a critical section in a mutual exclusion algorithm. Recently, there has been significant progress on implementing randomized one-shot TAS objects from registers [2, 3, 9]. The fastest implementations have expected step complexity $O(\log \log n)$ or even $O(\log^* n)$ against an oblivious adversary. But for many applications we need long-lived TAS objects. Previous randomized long-lived TAS implementations from registers, e.g. those by Afek, Gafni, Tromp and Vitányi [1], have an expected step complexity that is at least logarithmic in n and thus exponentially larger than that of the recent one-shot TAS implementations. As pointed out by Alistarh and Aspnes [2], it is easy to implement a long-lived TAS object from an infinite array of one-shot ones without sacrificing time complexity, but this scheme requires unbounded space.

Space complexity in the above scenario can be bounded using garbage collection (GC). Compared to manual memory management, where the lifetime of an object is annotated explicitly in the algorithm, in GC the decision to reclaim an object is automated, leading to a performance overhead [4]. This overhead can be unpredictable and application-dependent, making effective GC difficult in real-time environments. Furthermore, lock-free garbage collectors rely on atomic read-modify-write primitives for synchronization (e.g., see [8]).

Results. We design a wait-free memory reclamation algorithm that uses only atomic registers of sufficient size to hold process IDs and memory locations. (We are not aware of any existing reclamation techniques that have the same optimal time performance as ours and bounded memory at the same time, even in the case when stronger primitives, such as compare-and-swap or load-linked/store-conditional, are available.) Our technique achieves strong worst-case guarantees and usually increases the time complexity of operations only by a constant additive term. Our technique can be applied in the same settings as Michael's hazard pointers [10]. However, Michael's algorithm reclaims memory in batches, and achieves only amortized complexity bounds. An overview of our memory reclamation technique and a more careful comparison to hazard pointers will be provided in Section 2.

Our memory reclamation technique can be combined with other algorithmic techniques to obtain long-lived resettable TAS objects and to augment a wide class of objects with reset() operations. An overview of these results is presented in Sections 3 and 4, respectively.

2. MEMORY RECLAMATION

We assume that processes access a concurrent data structure through shared *objects*, such as nodes in a linked list or tree. To simplify the description of our technique, we assume that processes can allocate and deallocate such objects in shared memory. In our applications, this is usually done by assigning each process a pool of objects in advance; then allocation amounts to taking objects from the pool, and deallocation returns objects back into the pool. For technical reasons explained later on, we also assume that two shared $(\log n)$-bit registers Ctr_x and $Owner_x$ are associated with every object x, and are initialized to 1 and $\bot$, respectively. The data structure may grow and shrink dynamically, and thus references to shared objects may be added to and removed from the data structure. We say that an object gets *retired* when a process removes the last reference of it from the data structure. We assume that a process knows when it retires an object and the same object cannot be retired by multiple processes at the same time. (In our applications this is not always the case, and then we have to use a slightly modified approach.)

At its core, our memory reclamation technique solves the same problem as Michael's hazard pointers [10]; However, our method provides better worst-case guarantees: for each object that gets retired from the data structure only a constant time overhead is incurred in the worst-case. Michael's randomized solution has *expected* constant *amortized* time overhead, i.e., the time devoted to reclaiming a sequence of R retired objects is $O(R)$ in expectation. Both techniques, Michael's and ours, guarantee that at any point $O(n^2)$ objects which are not referenced by a data structure anymore have not yet been deallocated.

Our technique requires that processes use a shared *announce array* $A[0 \ldots n-1]$ with one entry per process. (The announce array plays a similar role as hazard pointers in Michael's technique.) Before a process p accesses an object from the data structure it has to *announce* this by writing a reference to the object in $A[p]$. We say object x is *announced by process* p whenever $A[p] = x$. The algorithm that uses our technique has to guarantee the following:

If a process accesses a retired object x at some point t_a and that object was retired at point $t_r < t_a$, then there is an index p such that $A[p] = x$ throughout $[t_r, t_a]$. $\qquad$ (∗)

Given property (∗), our memory reclamation scheme ensures that no process will try to access a retired object which has been deallocated. (Sometimes it is necessary that a process can announce $k > 1$ objects in order to ensure that (∗) is satisfied, but usually k is a small constant. It is easy to accommodate our algorithms for this case, but the space requirements increase by a factor of k.)

The memory reclamation algorithm works as follows. Every process p has two private n-element queues, $retired_p$ and $announced_p$, containing references to objects and $\bot$-values. They each initially contain n $\bot$-values. Finally, each process p has a private modulo n counter d_p.

The register $Owner_x$ associated with object x is used to indicate which process retired object x. Register Ctr_x has value 1 as long as object x is not retired. Once x gets retired, Ctr_x is the number of occurrences of x in the queues $retired_p$ and $announced_p$. If $Ctr_x = 0$, then this means that x is retired and in no queue and our algorithm guarantees that x can safely be deallocated.

Each time a process p retires an object x, it performs the following steps: First it writes p to $Owner_x$ and adds x to queue $retired_p$. This is done without updating Ctr_x, as the object is now retired and occurs once in $retired_p$. Then p increments d_p modulo n and reads a value y from $A[d_p]$. If $y \neq \bot$ and if $Owner_y = p$, then p adds y to $announced_p$ and increments the value of Ctr_y; otherwise p adds $\bot$ to $announced_p$. Next the process removes a value x_0 from $retired_p$ and a value x_1 from $announced_p$, and for $i \in \{0, 1\}$ the processes decrements the value of Ctr_{x_i} unless $x_i = \bot$. (After that, both queues contain exactly n elements again.) Finally, for $i \in \{0, 1\}$, if $x_i \neq \bot$ and $Ctr_{x_i} = 0$ the process deallocates object x_i.

The idea underlying this algorithm is the following: When process p retires object x, other processes may still try to access x. Property (∗) ensures that if a process may still access x, then x must be announced. Process p could now simply scan through the entire announce array and deallocate x only if it doesn't find a reference to x there. In order to achieve constant worst-case time for the memory reclamation, the process instead scans through A lazily, i.e., each time it retires an object it reads the next entry of A.

Suppose some process q tries to access a retired object x at some point. We argue that no process p will deallocate x before that point: Property (∗) ensures that x must have been announced continuously by some process q' since x got retired. Before p can deallocate object x, it must have retired it (at a point when x was already announced), then added x to $retired_p$, and then p retired another n objects (and thus scanned through the entire announce array) before it removed object x from the queue $retired_p$ again. Hence, p must have seen the announcement by q'. Thus, p cannot deallocate object x as long as q is still trying to access it.

The technique described above or variants of it can be applied to bound the space required by some recent algorithms without sacrificing their performance. E.g., Ellen and Woelfel [7] give an optimal implementation of Fetch-and-Increment from load-linked/store-conditional objects. Each time a process executes a Fetch&Inc() operation it has to allocate a new node and add it to a tree, where each node has a pointer to its parent. Each such node will eventually become a leaf whose parent is the root, and then it will not be accessed anymore. Ellen and Woelfel argue that using our technique one can easily reclaim such old nodes and thus bound the space of their algorithm without increasing the asymptotic time complexity of the algorithm. Brown, Ellen, and Ruppert [5] present an implementation of generalizations of load-linked/store-conditional objects that relies on garbage collection, which our memory reclamation technique can avoid.

3. RESETTABLE TEST-AND-SET

Our memory reclamation technique can be used to construct long-lived TAS objects where Test&Set() and reset() operations have sub-logarithmic (in fact, close to constant) time complexity. In order to facilitate those constructions, we define *weakly resettable* objects, which support a weak_reset() operation to reset an object to its initial state. However, no two weak_reset() operations are allowed to overlap, and if a non-weak_reset() operation overlaps with a weak_reset() operation, then it must either complete and be correct (in terms of linearizability), or it must *fail*. A failed operation must return a special return value, and may not "corrupt" the object. This is (almost) what we need for long-lived TAS objects: A failed Test&Set() operation can return 1, as it must overlap with a reset().

We show how to transform an object $\mathcal{O}$, which is implemented from m registers, into a weakly resettable one that uses $O(n + m)$ registers. Each reset() operation needs to execute $O(m)$ shared register operations, and every other operation has asymptotically the same time complexity as the corresponding operation on $\mathcal{O}$.

Employing this transformation and other techniques we obtain constructions of long-lived TAS objects. In particular, we can transform any one-shot TAS object implemented from registers (e.g., a randomized implementation) into a long-lived TAS, preserving the time complexity of Test&Set() operations, and increasing the space complexity by a factor of $O(n)$, such that a reset() operation takes only constant time. Applying our techniques to two recent randomized implementations of one-shot TAS objects [2,9], we obtain two randomized long-lived TAS implementations from registers which perform well against the oblivious adversary. The first one uses $O(n^2)$ space, each reset() operation takes $O(1)$ steps, and the Test&Set() operation has $O(\log^* k)$ expected individual step complexity, where k is the maximal point contention. (The expected individual step complexity is the expectation of the maximum number of steps any process needs for its Test&Set() operation which is linearized between two consecutive reset() operations.) Our second implementation uses $O(n)$ space, and each reset() operation takes $O(\log \log n)$ steps in expectation, and the Test&Set() operation has $O(\log \log n)$ expected individual step complexity. Note that the space complexity of this construction is asymptotically optimal for long-lived TAS objects, due to a matching lower bound for mutual exclusion [6].

4. GENERAL RESETTABLE OBJECTS

We develop a general technique to augment an object with a wait-free and efficient reset() operation, which resets the object to its initial state. Our technique applies to every object $\mathcal{O}$ that is *sequentially resettable*, meaning that it provides an operation sq_reset() which resets the object but may not be executed concurrently with any other operation. (I.e., any execution on $\mathcal{O}$ has to be linearizable only if no sq_reset() operation overlaps with any other opera-

tion.) Note that many of the standard primitives can easily be made sequentially resettable, as can any object implemented from sequentially resettable base objects. (There is a slight complication if processes use information from previous method calls during future ones, e.g., stored in local static variables; but those problems we can deal with.) E.g., a compare-and-swap object can be augmented with a sq_reset() operation in which the calling process reads the object value into *old* and then executes a CAS($old, \perp$), where $\perp$ is the initial value of the object.

Our construction allows us to augment any sequentially resettable object $\mathcal{O}$ with a reset() operation and preserve linearizability even if reset() operations are executed concurrently with other operations. The construction requires $O(n^2)$ instances of object $\mathcal{O}$ and $O(n^2)$ unbounded registers. The time complexity of a reset() operation is asymptotically the same as that of a sq_reset() operation on an instance of $\mathcal{O}$, and the asymptotic time complexity of other operations on $\mathcal{O}$ is not affected by our transformation. In the special case that $\mathcal{O}$ is implemented only from atomic registers, we can even implement the reset() operation in such a way that it has $O(1)$ worst-case time complexity.

Acknowledgments

The authors thank Faith Ellen for helpful comments on an earlier draft of the full version of this paper. This research was undertaken, in part, thanks to funding from the Canada Research Chairs program, the NSERC Discovery Grant and the HP Labs Innovation Research Program.

5. REFERENCES

[1] Y. Afek, E. Gafni, J. Tromp, and P. M. B. Vitányi. Wait-free test-and-set. In *Proc. of 6th WDAG*, pages 85–94, 1992.

[2] D. Alistarh and J. Aspnes. Sub-logarithmic test-and-set against a weak adversary. In *Proc. of 25th DISC*, pages 97–109, 2011.

[3] D. Alistarh, H. Attiya, S. Gilbert, A. Giurgiu, and R. Guerraoui. Fast randomized test-and-set and renaming. In *Proc. of 24th DISC*, pages 94–108, 2010.

[4] S. M. Blackburn, P. Cheng, and K. S. McKinley. Myths and realities: the performance impact of garbage collection. *SIGMETRICS Perform. Eval. Rev.*, 32(1):25–36, June 2004.

[5] T. Brown, F. Ellen, and E. Ruppert. Pragmatic primitives for non-blocking data structures. In *Proc. of 32th PODC*, 2013. To appear.

[6] J. E. Burns and N. A. Lynch. Bounds on shared memory for mutual exclusion. *Information and Computation*, 107(2):171–184, 1993.

[7] F. Ellen and P. Woelfel. An optimal implementation of fetch-and-increment. Manuscript, 2013.

[8] H. Gao, J. F. Groote, and W. H. Hesselink. Lock-free parallel and concurrent garbage collection by mark&sweep. *Sci. Comput. Program.*, 64(3):341–374, Feb. 2007.

[9] G. Giakkoupis and P. Woelfel. On the time and space complexity of randomized test-and-set. In *Proc. of 31th PODC*, pages 19–28, 2012.

[10] M. M. Michael. Hazard pointers: Safe memory reclamation for lock-free objects. *IEEE Trans. Parallel Distrib. Syst.*, 15(6):491–504, 2004.

Randomized Broadcast in Radio Networks with Collision Detection

Mohsen Ghaffari
MIT
ghaffari@mit.edu

Bernhard Haeupler
MIT
haeupler@mit.edu

Majid Khabbazian
University of Alberta
mkhabbazian@ualberta.ca

ABSTRACT

We present a randomized distributed algorithm that in radio networks with collision detection broadcasts a single message in $O(D + \log^6 n)$ rounds, with high probability. This time complexity is most interesting because of its optimal additive dependence on the network diameter D. It improves over the currently best known $O(D \log \frac{n}{D} + \log^2 n)$ algorithms, due to Czumaj and Rytter [FOCS 2003], and Kowalski and Pelc [PODC 2003]. These algorithms where designed for the model without collision detection and are optimal in that model. However, as explicitly stated by Peleg in his 2007 survey on broadcast in radio networks, it had remained an open question whether the bound can be improved with collision detection.

We also study distributed algorithms for broadcasting k messages from a single source to all nodes. This problem is a natural and important generalization of the single-message broadcast problem, but is in fact considerably more challenging and less understood. We show the following results: If the network topology is known to all nodes, then a k-message broadcast can be performed in $O(D + k \log n + \log^2 n)$ rounds, with high probability. If the topology is not known, but collision detection is available, then a k-message broadcast can be performed in $O(D + k \log n + \log^6 n)$ rounds, with high probability. The first bound is optimal and the second is optimal modulo the additive $O(\log^6 n)$ term.

Categories and Subject Descriptors

F.2.2 [**Analysis of Algorithms and Problem Complexity**]: Non-numerical Algorithms and Problems—*Computations on Discrete Structures*; G.2.2 [**Discrete Mathematics**]: Graph Theory—*Network Problems*

Keywords

Wireless networks, Radio Networks, Broadcast, Collision Detection, Random Linear Network Coding

1. INTRODUCTION

The classical information dissemination problem in radio networks is the problem of broadcasting a single message to all nodes of the network (single-message broadcast). This problem and its generalizations have received extensive attention.

A characteristic of radio networks is that multiple messages that arrive at a node simultaneously interfere (collide) with one another and none of them is received successfully. Regarding whether nodes can distinguish such a collision from complete silence, the model is usually divided into two categories of with and without collision detection. Throughout studies of problems in radio networks, it has been observed that many problems can be solved faster in the model with collision detection [20]. Despite this trend, it had remained unclear whether this is also the case for broadcast or not [19]. We show that single-message broadcast can be indeed solved faster, in simply diameter plus poly-logarithmic time, if collision detection is available. Even though our work is theoretical, we remark that most practical radio networks can detect collisions.

Broadcasting k messages from one node to all nodes is a natural and important generalization of the single-message broadcast problem. Usually, this generalization involves new and significantly different challenges, mainly because the dissemination of different messages can interfere with each other. We show how to overcome these challenges and obtain an (almost) optimal k-message broadcast algorithm.

1.1 Model and Problem Statements

We work in the *radio network model with collision detection* [4]: a synchronous network $G = (V, E)$ where in each round, each node either transmits a packet with B bits or listens. As a standard assumption, to ensure that each packet can contain a constant number of ids, we assume that $B = \Omega(\log n)$. Each node v receives a packet from its neighbors only if it listens in that round and exactly one of its neighbors is transmitting. If two or more neighbors of v transmit, then v only detects the collision, which is modeled as v receiving a special symbol $\top$ indicating a collision. We explain that some of our results hold even in the model *without collision detection*, where if two or more neighbors of v transmit, then v does not receive anything.

---

*The research in this paper was supported by AFOSR award No. FA9550-13-1-0042, NSF grant Nos. CCF-AF-0937274, CNS-1035199, 0937370-CCF, CCF-1217506, and NSF-PURDUE-STC award 0937370-CCF.

The single-message broadcast problem is defined as follows: A single *source* node has a single message of length at most $\Theta(B)$ bits and the goal is to deliver this message to all nodes in the network. The k-message single-source broadcast problem is defined similarly, with the difference that the source has k messages which need to be delivered to all other nodes. We focus on randomized solutions to these problems where we require that the message(s) are delivered to all nodes with high probability[1]. In the unknown topology setting (which is our default setting), we assume[2] that nodes know a polynomial upper bound on n and a constant factor upper bound on diameter D. In the known topology setting, similar to [7], we assume that nodes know the whole graph.

1.2 Our Results

Our main results are as follows:

Theorem 1.1. *In radio networks with unknown topology and with collision detection, there is a randomized distributed algorithm that broadcasts a single message in $O(D + \log^6 n)$ rounds, with high probability.*

Theorem 1.2. *In radio networks with known topology (even without collision detection), there is a randomized distributed algorithm that broadcasts k messages in $O(D + k \log n + \log^2 n)$ rounds, with high probability.*

Theorem 1.3. *In radio networks with unknown topology and with collision detection, there is a randomized distributed algorithm that broadcasts k messages in $O(D + k \log n + \log^6 n)$ rounds, with high probability.*

About Theorem 1.1, we remark that prior to this work, the best known solution for single-message broadcast was the $O(D \log n/D + \log^2 n)$ algorithms presented independently by Czumaj and Rytter [6], and Kowalski and Pelc [15], for the model without collision detection. In that model, these bounds are optimal [1,17]. As Peleg points out in [19], prior to this work, it was unclear whether these upper bounds can be improved in the model with collision detection. Theorem 1.1 answers this question by showing that a better upper bound is indeed achievable. We remark that the bound of Theorem 1.1 is within an additive poly-log of the $\Omega(D + \log^2 n)$ lower bound, that follows from the $\Omega(\log^2 n)$ lower bound of [1] and the obvious lower bound of $\Omega(D)$.

About Theorems 1.2 and 1.3, we remark that these two results use random linear network coding (RLNC). Moreover, we note that even in the strong model of centralized algorithms with full topology knowledge, with collision detection, and with network coding, k-message broadcast has a lower bound of $\Omega(D + k \log n + \log^2 n)$ rounds. This lower bound follows from the $\Omega(k \log n)$ throughput-based lower bound of [10] for a k-message broadcast, the $\Omega(\log^2 n)$ lower bound of [1] for a single message broadcast, and the trivial $\Omega(D)$ lower bound. Thus, the complexity of Theorem 1.2 is optimal and the complexity of Theorem 1.3 is optimal modulo the additive $O(\log^6 n)$ term.

---

[1] We use the phrase "high probability" to indicate a probability at least $1 - \frac{1}{n^c}$, for a constant $c \geq 1$, and where n is the network size.

[2] It is easy to see that the latter assumption can be removed without any change is our time-bounds, by finding a 2-approximation of D in time $O(D)$, using the beep waves tool of [9].

When looking at the issue from a practical angle, Theorem 1.1 and Theorem 1.3 have an interesting message: they show that one can replace the (expensive and not-completely-reasonable) assumption of all nodes knowing the full topology of the network, with (the considerably more reasonable and usually-available) collision detection, and still perform single or multiple broadcast tasks almost in the same time.

To achieve the above three results, we present three new technical elements, which each can be interesting on their own:

(A) The first element is a distributed construction of a Gathering-Spanning-Tree (GST) with round complexity of $O(D \log^4 n)$. GSTs were first introduced by [7] to obtain broadcast algorithms with an additive $O(D)$ diameter dependence in the known topology setting [7, 8, 18]. The only known construction of GST prior to this work was the centralized algorithm of Gasieniec et al. [7], which has step-complexity of $O(n^2)$ operations and requires the full knowledge of the graph. We use our new GST construction to prove Theorem 1.1. For this we first decompose the graph appropriately, then we construct a GST for every part in parallel and lastly we use this setup to broadcast the (single) message efficiently.

(B) The second element is a novel transmission schedule atop GST for solving multiple message broadcast problems. We contend this schedule to be the right generalization of [7] for multiple messages. Such a generalization was also attempted in [18] but its correctness was disproved [21].

(C) The third element is *backwards analysis*, an new way to analyze the progress of messages during a multi-message radio network broadcast. Backward analysis shows that a message spreads quickly even when other messages that are spread at the same time cause collisions. A priori it is not clear that information dissemination remains efficient in the presence of these collisions, which only arise in the mutli-message setting. Insights from the backwards analysis were crucial in the design of our multi-message transmission schedule and also enable us to apply the projection analysis of Haeupler [11] for analyzing random linear network coding to proof Theorem 1.2 and Theorem 1.3.

1.3 Related Work

Designing distributed broadcast algorithms for radio networks has received extensive attention, starting with the pioneering work of Bar-Yehuda, Goldreich and Itai (BGI) [2]. Here, we present a brief review of the results that directly relate to this paper.

Single-Message Broadcast: Peleg [19] provides a comprehensive survey of the known results about single-message broadcast. BGI [2] present the Decay protocol which broadcasts a single message in $O(D \log n + \log^2 n)$ rounds. The best known distributed algorithms for single-message broadcast in for the setting where the topology is unknown are the $O(D \log \frac{n}{D} + \log^2 n)$ algorithms presented independently by Czumaj and Rytter [6], and Kowalski and Pelc [15]. These algorithms can be viewed as clever optimizations of the Decay protocol [2]. Moreover, similar to the Decay protocol,

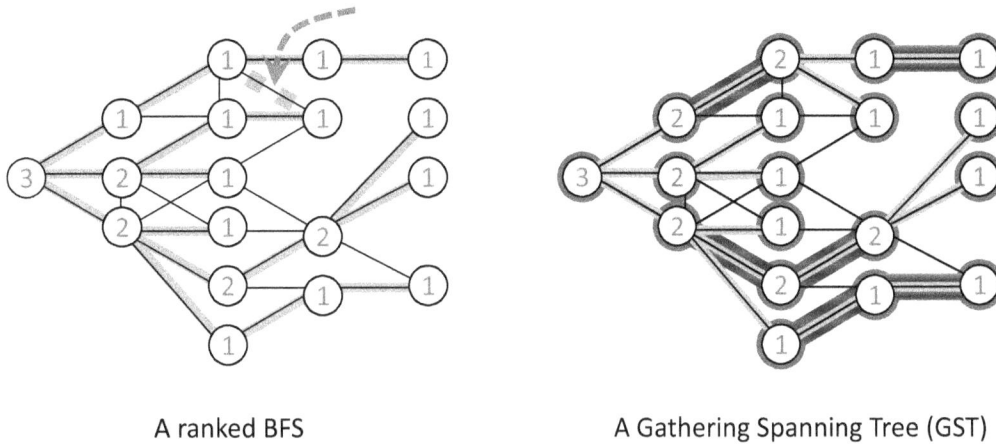

A ranked BFS   A Gathering Spanning Tree (GST)

Figure 1: Gathering Spanning Tree

these two algorithms are presented for the model without collision detection and are optimal in that model [1, 17]. Prior to this work, no better algorithm was known for the model with collision detection. If the topology of the network is known, then the algorithm of Gasieniec, Peleg and Xin [7] achieves the optimal $O(D + \log^2 n)$ time complexity. Kowlaski and Pelc [16] gave an explicit deterministic broadcast protocol which achieves the same time complexity.

Multi-Message Broadcast: The complexity of multi-message broadcast (with bounded packet size) is less understood. In the model without collision detection, the following results are known. The earliest work on multi-message broadcast problem is by BarYehuda et al. [3], which broadcasts k messages in $O((n + (k + D) \log n) \log \Delta)$ rounds, where Δ is the maximum node degree. Chlebus et al. [5] present a deterministic algorithm that broadcasts k messages in $O(k \log^3 n + n \log^4 n)$ rounds. The best known algorithm for multi-message broadcast is by Khabbazian and Kowalski that broadcast k messages using network coding in $O(k \log \Delta + (D + \log n) \log n \log \Delta)$ rounds [14]. Again, prior to this work, no better algorithm was known for the model with collision detection. Ghaffari et al. [10] showed a lower bound of $\Omega(k \log n)$ rounds.

2. SINGLE-MESSAGE BROADCAST

We first recall the definition of a Gathering-Spanning-Tree (GST) [7], in Section 2.1. Then, in Section 2.2, we present a distributed algorithm with time complexity $O(D \log^4 n)$ for constructing a GST, in radio networks with unknown topology (even without collision detection). In Section 2.3, we then show that this algorithm can be used to broadcast a single message in $O(D + \log^6 n)$ rounds, in radio network with unknown topology but with collision detection.

2.1 Gathering Spanning Trees (GST)

Ranked BFS: Consider a BFS tree $\mathcal{T}$ in graph G, rooted at source node s. Also, suppose that in this tree, we have assigned to each node v a level number $\ell(v)$, which is equal to the distance of v from s. We *rank* the nodes of $\mathcal{T}$ using the following inductive *ranking rule*: Each leaf of $\mathcal{T}$ gets rank 1. Then, consider node v and suppose that all children of v in $\mathcal{T}$ are already ranked. Let r be the maximum rank of these

children. If v has exactly one child with rank r, then node v gets rank r. If v has two or more children with rank r, then v gets rank $r + 1$. As shown in [7], one can easily see that in each *ranked BFS*, the largest rank is at most $\lceil \log_2 n \rceil$.

Gathering Spanning Tree (GST) [7]: A ranked BFS-tree $\mathcal{T}$ is called a GST of graph G if and only if the following *collision-freeness property* is satisfied:

> In graph G, any node of rank r on level l of $\mathcal{T}$ is adjacent to *at most one* node of rank r at level $l-1$ of $\mathcal{T}$. In other words, if there are two nodes u_1 and u_2 with rank r on level l of $\mathcal{T}$, and their parents in $\mathcal{T}$ are respectively v_1 and $v_2 \neq v_1$ (on level $l-1$ of $\mathcal{T}$), and v_1 and v_2 have rank r as well, then there is no edge between v_1 and u_2 or between v_2 and u_1.

Fast Stretches in a GST: In a GST $\mathcal{T}$, for each path in $\mathcal{T}$ from a node v to a node u that is a descendant of v in $\mathcal{T}$, we call this path a *fast stretch* if all the nodes on the path have the same rank. Note that a fast stretch might be just a single node.

Distributed GST: In a distributed construction of a GST, each node u must learn the following four items[3]: (1) its level $\ell(u)$, (2) its own rank $r(u)$, (3) the id of its parent v, and (4) the rank of its parent $r(v)$.

Figure 1 presents an example of a GST. The black edges present the graph G and the thicker green edges present a rank labeled BFS tree $\mathcal{T}$ of G. On the left side, we see a rank-labeled BFS tree, but this tree is not a GST because of the violation of the collision-freeness property indicated by the red dashed arrow. On the right side, we see another rank-labeled BFS of the same graph G, which is a GST. In this GST, the green edges that are coated with wide blue lines indicate the fast stretches. Each node that is not incident on any of these blue-coated edges forms a trivial fast-stretch made of just a single node.

Broadcast Atop GST: In [7] Gasieniec et al. presented an algorithm to broadcast a single message in $O(D + \log^2 n)$ rounds, atop a GST. A high-level explanation is as follows:

---

[3]From (2) and (4), any node u can easily infers whether it is the first node in a fast stretch and whether its parent is in that stretch as well.

with a careful timing, the message can be sent through the fast stretches without any collision. That is, we can (almost simultaneously) send the message through different stretches such that in each fast stretch, the message gets broadcast from the start of the stretch to the end of the stretch in a time asymptotically equivalent to the length of the stretch. On the other hand, since the largest rank in the tree $\mathcal{T}$ is at most $\lceil \log_2 n \rceil$ and because on each path from the source to any node v, the ranks are non-increasing, we get that the path from the source to each node v is made of at most $\lceil \log_2 n \rceil$ distinct fast stretches. By using the *decay protocol*[4] [2] on each of the (at most) $\lceil \log_2 n \rceil$ connections between the fast stretches, we get a broadcast algorithm with time complexity $O(D + \log^2 n)$. We refer the reader to [7] for the details of this broadcast algorithm. We remark that we will use [7] simply as a black-box that broadcasts a single-message in time $O(D + \log^2 n)$ on top of the GSTs we construct.

2.2 Distributed GST Construction

In this subsection, we present the following result:

Theorem 2.1. *In the radio networks (even without collision detection), there exists a distributed GST construction algorithm with time complexity $O(D \log^4 n)$ rounds.*

We show a GST construction with round-complexity of $O(D \log^5 n)$ in Sections 2.2.1 to 2.2.3. We later improve this to $O(D \log^4 n)$ rounds, in Section 2.2.4.

2.2.1 Black-Box Tools

Before starting the construction, we first present two black-box tools which we use in our construction.

Decay Protocol [2]: Rounds are divided into phases of $\log n$ rounds, and in the ith round of each phase, each node v transmits with probability 2^{-i} (if it has a message for transmission).

Lemma 2.2. *(Bar-Yehuda et al. [2]) For each node v, if at least one neighbor of v has a message for transmission, then in each phase of decay, node v receives at least one message with probability at least $\frac{1}{8}$. Moreover, in $\Theta(\log n)$ such phases, v receives at least one message, with high probability.*

Recruiting Protocol: This tool can be abstracted by the guarantees that it provides, which we present in Lemma 2.3.

Lemma 2.3. *Consider a bipartite graph $\mathcal{H}$ where nodes on one side are called* red *and nodes on the other side are called* blue. *The recruiting protocol achieves the following three properties, w.h.p., in $\Theta(\log^3 n)$ rounds:* **(a)** *for each blue node u, we assign an adjacent red node of v to u. In this case, we say u is* recruited *by v (then called parent of u),* **(b)** *each red node v knows whether it recruited zero, one, or at least two blue nodes,* **(c)** *each recruited blue node u knows whether its parent v recruited zero, one, or at least two blue nodes.*

Next, we present the *recruiting protocol*. We defer the proof of Lemma 2.3 to the full version.

---

[4]Decay is a standard technique for coping with collisions in radio networks. We present a short recap on it in Section 2.2.1.

Recruiting Protocol: The protocol consists of $\Theta(\log^2 n)$ recruiting iterations, each having $2 + \Theta(\log n)$ rounds as follows:

- In the first round of the jth recruiting iteration, each red node transmits its id with probability $2^{-\lceil \frac{j}{\Theta(\log n)} \rceil}$.

- Then, we run a phase of Decay protocol, consisting of $\Theta(\log n)$ rounds, from the side of blue node. In this phase, each not-recruited blue node u that received a message of a red node v tries to transmit $u.id$ and $v.id$ (together in one packet).

- After that, the red nodes repeat the exact transmissions of the first round of this iteration, with new contents as follows: (1) if in the previous Decay phase, a red node v received its own id from exactly one blue node u, then v broadcasts $v.id$, (2) if the red node v received its own id from two or more blue nodes, then v broadcasts a special message Σ. (3) Otherwise, v transmits an empty message.

- Next, if a blue node u received its own id or the special message Σ in the last round, then we say u is recruited by red node v, where v is the red node such that u received $v.id$ in the first round. Note that each red node v knows whether it recruited zero, one or at least two blue nodes.

2.2.2 GST Construction Outline

We first construct a BFS-tree of G and assign to each node v a level $\ell(v)$ that is equal to the distance of v from the source. This can be done in $O(D \log^2 n)$ rounds, as follows: Rounds are divided into D epochs each consisting of $\Theta(\log n)$ phases of decay (thus, each epoch has $\Theta(\log^2 n)$ rounds). In each epoch, a node v participates in the decays iff it is the source or it has received a message by the end of the last epoch. During these rounds, each node relays the first message it received. The epoch in which a node v receives a message for the first time determines the BFS level $\ell(v)$ of node v.

Now that we have a BFS-tree, we build the GST on top of this BFS layering, level by level, and from the largest level towards the source. For this, the problem boils down to the following scenario: Consider level l of layering and assume that the GST is already built for levels $j \geq l$. Consider the bipartite graph H induced on the nodes of level $l-1$ and level l, ignoring the (possible) edges inside each level. The core of the problem is to design an algorithm to construct the part of GST between levels $l-1$ and l, i.e., the part that is H.

Let us call the nodes on level $l-1$ *red nodes*, and the nodes on level l *blue nodes*. To construct the part of GST that is in H, we assign a red *parent* v to each blue node u, from amongst the red neighbors of u in H. In this case, v is known as u's *parent* and u is a *child* of v. This assignment, along with the rankings of blue nodes, leads to a ranking for the red nodes. More precisely, let v be a red node and let i be the maximum rank of blue node children of v in the assignment. Node v gets rank i if it has only one child with rank i, and v gets rank $i + 1$ if it has more than one child with rank i.

To have a GST, these assignments should be *collision-free*. That is, if there exist blue nodes u_1 and u_2 and their respective parents v_1 and v_2, all four with rank i, then H must have no edge between v_1 and u_2, or between v_2 and u_1. We refer to the problem of finding such an assignment as the *Bipartite Assignment Problem*.

More precisely, in the *Bipartite Assignment Problem*, we should achieve the following 6 properties: (1) For each blue node u, we should assign a red neighbor v as its parent, (2) we should rank the red nodes as follows: for each red node v, suppose i is the maximum rank of the children of v. Then, v should get rank i if v has exactly one blue child of rank i, and v should receive rank of $i+1$ if v has two or more blue children of rank i, (3) the assignment should be *collision-free*, (4) each red node must know its rank and (5) each blue node u should know the id of its parent and (6) each blue node u should know the rank of its parent.

The *Bipartite Assignment Problem* is the core of the GST construction and once we have a solution for it, repeating the solution level by level from the largest level to source constructs a GST. In the next subsection, we explain how to solve this problem in $O(\log^5 n)$ rounds.

2.2.3 The Bipartite Assignment Algortihm

Consider bipartite graph H as explained. We solve the bipartite assignment problem (defined above) in H in a rank by rank basis, starting with the largest possible rank $\lceil \log n \rceil$ (of blue nodes), and going down in ranks until reaching rank 1. We spend $\Theta(\log^4 n)$ rounds on each rank. Let us consider the case of a bipartite assignment for blue nodes of rank i in graph H, assuming that ranks greater than i are already solved.

We first identify the red neighbors of the blue nodes with rank i. This is done by using $\Theta(\log n)$ phases of Decay where blue nodes of rank i transmit. This identifies the desired red nodes as every such red node receives at least one message with high probability and no other red node receives any message. From now on, throughout the procedure for rank i, only these red nodes are active. Now the algorithm is divided into $\Theta(\log n)$ epochs. Each epoch consists of three stages as follows:

Stage I: Call a blue node u of rank i a *loner* if u has exactly one active red neighbor. We first detect the loner blue nodes. For this, in one round, each active red node transmits a message. Only loner blue nodes receive a message and each other blue node receives a collision. We then use $\Theta(\log n)$ phases of Decay, where each blue loner tries transmitting. This with high probability informs all red nodes that are connected to at least one loner blue node. We call these red nodes *loner-parents*.

Stage II: This stage is divided into three parts, and each red node is active in only one of the parts. Loner-parents, which we identified in the stage I, are active only in part 1. Each other active red node randomly and uniformly decides to be either *brisk* or *lazy*, which respectively mean it is active in part 2 or in part 3. These parts are as follows:

> **Part 1.** Loner-parents use a *recruiting protocol*. During this recruiting protocol, each blue neighbor of each red loner-parent get recruited with high probability. These assignments are *permanent*.

All the blue nodes that are recruited become inactive for the rest of the assignment problem.

> **Part 2.** Brisk red nodes run a Recruiting protocol. Then, each blue node that is not the only recruited child of its parent considers its parent as its *permanent* GST parent and becomes inactive permanently (for the GST construction). The other recruited blue nodes become inactive only for the remainder of this epoch, but these assignments are *temporary* and the related nodes restart in the next epoch, ignoring their temporary assignments.

> **Part 3.** We repeat the procedure of part 2, but this time with lazy red nodes and with the active blue nodes that did not get recruited in parts 1 or 2.

Stage III: Let us say that a red node is *marked* if it was a loner-parent or if it recruited zero or strictly more than one blue nodes in parts 2 or 3. Each marked red node becomes inactive after this epoch. Thus, the only red nodes that remain active after this epoch are those that do not have any loner neighbor and recruited exactly one child in part 2 or 3 of the stage II. Each marked red node knows whether it recruited zero, one, or at least two children (in stage II). We use this knowledge to rank these marked red nodes giving them rank of i if they recruited exactly one blue child and rank of $i+1$ if they recruited more than one blue child. Blue children of marked red nodes also know that their parents of marked and they can also compute the rank of their parents (refer to property (c) of Lemma 2.3).

Before inactivating the marked red nodes, we do one simple thing: marked red nodes run $\Theta(\log n)$ phases of Decay sending their id and rank. Each blue node of any rank strictly lower than i that receives a red node id considers the first red node that it heard from as its permanent GST parent, records the id and rank of that red parent, and then, becomes inactive for the rest of the assignment problem.

After running the bipartite assignment algorithm for all the ranks, if a red node v has no child, then v is a leaf and in the GST, v gets rank 1.

Figure 2 shows an example of assignments during an epoch (the first epoch). The green arrows in the leftmost part indicate the loner blue nodes at the start of the epoch. The loner parent red nodes are indicated by a number 1 next to them, meaning they are active in part 1. Brisk and lazy red nodes are respectively indicated by numbers 2 and 3, next to them. The smaller nodes present the (temporarily or permanently) deactivated nodes. The green dashed lines show the permanent assignments and the (thicker) orange dashed lines show the temporary assignments. After the end of epoch, nodes with temporary assignment are re-activated. The graph remaining after the first epoch is presented on the right side of the Figure 2, by solid blue lines.

Analysis: In Lemma 2.4, we prove that in each of the $\Theta(\log n)$ epochs except the first one, we reduce the size of the assignment problem for rank i by at least a constant factor, with at least a positive constant probability. Here,

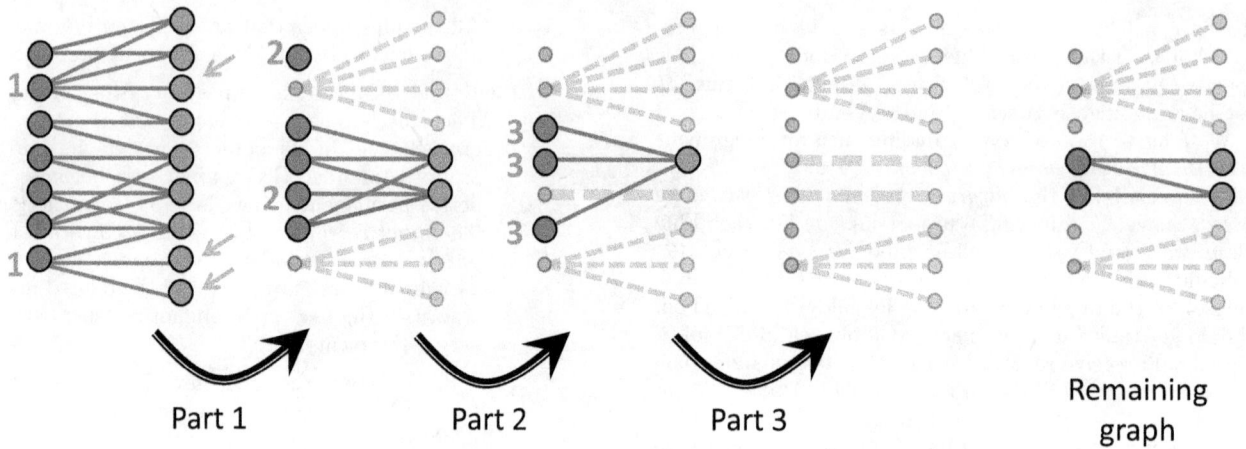

Figure 2: Parts 1, 2, and 3 of the stage II of the first epoch of the assignment algorithm, and the graph remaining after the first epoch

by size of the assignment problem, we mean the number of the active red nodes with a blue neighbor of rank i. A standard Chernoff bound then shows that in $\Theta(\log n)$ epochs, each blue node of rank i has a parent. It is clear that the parents are ranked according to the ranking rules of GST and nodes know their own rank, the id of their parents, and the rank of their parents. We show in Lemma 2.5 that with high probability, the assignment is collision-free.

Lemma 2.4. *In each epoch $j' \leq 2$, with a probability at least $1/7$, the number of remaining active red nodes for the next epoch goes down with a factor at least $8/7$.*

Proof. Consider epoch $j' \geq 2$ and let η be the number of active red nodes at the start of this epoch. We show that the expected number of red nodes that remain active at the end of this epoch is at most $\frac{3\eta}{4}$. This is enough for the proof because with this, and by Markov's inequality, we get that with probability at least $1/7$, the number of active remaining red nodes at the end of this epoch is at most $\frac{7\eta}{8}$.

Each red node remains active after epoch j' only if it gets a temporary assignment, i.e., if it is not a loner-parent and it recruits exactly one child during parts 2 and 3 of Stage II. Thus, the expected number of red nodes that remain active is at most equal to the expected of number of brisk red nodes (those that act in part 2) plus the number of blue nodes that are active in part 3. The expected number of brisk red nodes is at most $\frac{\eta}{2}$. To complete the proof, we show that the expected number of blue nodes that remain active for part 3 (after the assignments of part 2) is at most $\frac{\eta}{4}$.

After each epoch, the only red nodes that remain active are those that have a temporary assignment, i.e., those that each have recruited exactly one child and that child is not a loner. Moreover, the only active remaining blue nodes are those blue nodes temporarily matched to the remaining red nodes. Thus, after each epoch, the number of remaining active red nodes and the number of remaining active blue nodes are equal. From this, we can conclude that since $j' \geq 2$, at the start of epoch j', the number of active blue nodes is at most η.

Using Lemma 2.3, we infer that in part 1 of stage II, each blue neighbor of a loner-parent is w.h.p. recruited by a red

loner-parent. Thus, in particular, each loner is recruited with high probability. Hence, at the start of part 2 of stage II, each remaining active blue node has at least 2 red node neighbors. Since each non-loner-parent red node is active in part 2 of stage II with probability $1/2$, and because in part 2 of stage II each active blue node that has an active red node neighbor gets recruited with high probability (by Lemma 2.3), each blue node remains active after part 2 of stage II with probability at most $1/4$. We know that because of the previous paragraph, the number of active remaining blue nodes at the start of part 2 of stage II is at most η. Hence, the expected number of blue nodes remaining active after part 2 is at most $\frac{\eta}{4}$. This completes the proof of the lemma. □

Lemma 2.5. *With high probability, the bipartite assignment algorithm creates a collision-free assignment.*

Proof. We show that if there exist blue nodes u_1 and u_2 ($u_1 \neq u_2$) and their respective red parents v_1 and v_2 ($v_1 \neq v_2$), all four with rank i, then with high probability, H must not have any edge between u_2 and v_1, or between u_1 and v_2. For the sake of contradiction, and without loss of generality, suppose that there is an edge between u_2 and v_1. Since v_2 and u_2 have rank i, blue node u_2 must have been a loner when v_2 recruited it. Thus, v_2 recruited u_2 after v_1 became inactive. Hence, in the epoch that v_1 recruited u_1, u_2 was active. Therefore, using Lemma 2.3 we get that in the part 1 of the epoch in which v_1 recruited u_1, u_2 must have been w.h.p. recruited by either v_1 or some other loner-parent. Since $v_2 \neq v_1$ recruited u_2, we get that v_2 must have been that other loner parent. This means that at that time, v_2 had a loner child ($\neq u_2$) and thus, v_2 has recruited more than one child of rank i. This means that v_2 must have had rank $i + 1$ which contradicts with the assumption that v_2 has rank i. □

2.2.4 Pipelining the GST Construction

Note that in the above algorithm, and in assignment problem between levels $l - 1$ and l, once we are done with the assignment problem of ranks i and $i - 1$, nodes of level $l - 1$ that receive rank i are already determined, i.e., no other node in level $l - 1$ will receive rank i. Thus, we can solve the two problems of rank $i-2$ assignment between levels $l-1$ and l and rank i assignments between levels $l-2$ and $l-1$, essentially simultaneously, by interleaving them in even and odd rounds. Using the same idea, it is easy to see that one can pipe-line the assignment problems of different ranks between different levels. Then, the assignment problem between levels $l-1$ and l starts after $\Theta((D-l)\log^4 n)$ rounds. Thus, the assignment problem of largest possible rank between levels 0 and 1 starts after $\Theta(D\log^4 n)$ rounds. The largest rank is at most $\lceil \log n \rceil$. Since each rank takes $\Theta(\log^4 n)$ rounds, the whole GST construction problem finishes after $\Theta(D\log^4 n)$ rounds.

2.3 Unknown Topology Single-Message Broadcast in $O(D+\log^6 n)$ Rounds

Theorem 1.1. *(restated) In radio networks with unknown topology and with collision detection, there is a randomized distributed algorithm that broadcasts a single message in $O(D+\log^6 n)$ rounds, with high probability.*

Proof. We first use a wave of collisions to get a BFS layering in time D. That is, the source transmits in all rounds $[1, D]$, and each node v transmits in all rounds $[r, D]$ where r is such that v receives a message or a collision in round $r-1$. For each node v, the round $r-1$ in which v receives the first message or collision determines distance of v from the source.

Having this BFS layering, we decompose the graph into $O(\log^4 n)$ rings, each consisting of $D' = D/\log^4 n$ consecutive layers of the BFS layering.

Then, we compute a gathering spanning tree for each of the rings in $O(D'\log^4 n) = O(D)$ rounds. Note that computation of a GST for each ring only depends on D' which is the number of BFS layers that the ring contains, and that given the BFS-layering, the computation of the GSTs of all rings is performed in parallel.

Having these GSTs, broadcasting the message inside each ring takes $O(D' + \log^2 n)$ rounds, using [7]. Finally, we use $O(\log^2 n)$ rounds of decay protocol [2] to propagate the message from the outer boundary of one ring to the inner boundary of the next ring. Since there are $O(\log^4 n)$ rings, the whole broadcast takes $\left(O(D' + \log^2 n) + O(\log^2 n)\right) \cdot O(\log^4 n) = O(D + \log^6 n)$ rounds. $\square$

3. MUTLI-MESSAGE BROADCAST

While broadcasting one message in the known topology setting is well understood, having a tight bound $\Theta(D + \log^2 n)$ [7], achieving the optimal broadcast time for multiple messages is non-trivial even for networks with known topology. We show the following:

Theorem 1.2. *(restated) In radio network with known topology (even without collision detection), there is a randomized distributed algorithm that broadcasts k messages in $O(D + k\log n + \log^2 n)$ rounds, with high probability.*

We remark that this bound is optimal, given the $\Omega(k \log n)$ lower bound of [10] for k-message broadcast, the $\Omega(\log^2 n)$ lower bound of [1] for single message broadcast, and the trivial $\Omega(D)$ lower bound.

Furthermore, it is easy to combine the known topology algorithm of Theorem 1.2 with the ideas of the proof of Theorem 1.1 (i.e., breaking the graph into rings of radius $\lceil \frac{D}{\log^4 n} \rceil$)

and the standard technique of grouping messages and pipelining the groups, to prove Theorem 1.3. We defer the details to the full version.

3.1 Challenges in Broadcasting Multiple Messages

Given the known transmission schedules for broadcasting a single message in optimal $O(D + \log^2 n)$ time on top of a GST, it is intriguing to try to use the same transmission schedule to solve the multi-message broadcast problem. However, since we cannot disjoin the spreading process of different messages this approach faces two challenges:

Firstly, when a node v has already learned multiple messages and is triggered by the schedule to transmit, v needs to decide which message to forward. Choosing one message over the others can slow down the progress of those other messages.

Fortunately, random linear network coding (RLNC) [13] provides a general technique for making such decisions: Instead of deciding on one specific message whenever a node is triggered to send it, node v transmits a random linear combination of all packets it has received. It has been shown that this is the universal optimal strategy, that is, this succeeds with high probability as soon as it was possible (in hindsight) to send k messages to each of the receivers [12]. We think that network coding might be in fact necessary for obtaining the optimal throughput performance that we achieve. Our multi message broadcast utilizes RLNC and uses recent advances in analyzing RLNC performance [11] for the proofs. Even though RLNC and its analysis need to be carefully tailored to broadcast in radio networks, this gives us a good plan to remedy the first issue.

The second issue is subtle but turns out to be more problematic: When proving progress of messages all known single-message schedules and their analysis (e.g., those of [7]) rely crucially on nodes that do not have the (single) message to remain silent and cause no collisions. In a multi-message setting it becomes a necessity that we make progress for a message while allowing other nodes that do not have this message to transmit to make progress on other messages.

Trying to understand this problem prompted us to define the property *multi-message viable (MMV)*: We say a transmission schedule broadcasts one message in a MMV way if it broadcasts one message while nodes that do not have the message but are scheduled to transmit are allowed to send noise. Intuitively, this captures the viewpoint where we focus on one message and the transmissions of other messages are regarded as noise, possibly harming the progress of the message in consideration. We later see that a property very close to MMV is exactly what is enough to prove that a schedule works well with RLNC.

Unfortunately proving that a schedule is MMV is not straightforward and it is a priori not clear whether the already existing schedules are MMV. The easiest example to see this is the simple Decay algorithm of [2]: in Decay, if a node is scheduled to transmit but it does not have the message, then this node remain silent. Decay broadcasts a single message in $O(D\log n + \log^2 n)$ rounds [2]. This follows almost directly from a simple progress lemma which shows that in $O(\log n)$ rounds of Decay a node gets informed (receives the single message) with constant probability if at least one of its neighbors is informed. However, if the nodes that do not have the message are allowed to send noise when the schedule prompts them to transmit, then the key progress lemma of [2] does not hold anymore. Surprisingly, even though this lemma breaks, it is still true that one message is spread quickly in this case (when uninformed nodes are noising), meaning that Decay broadcasts in time $O(D \log n + \log^2 n)$ rounds in a MMV way:

Lemma 3.1. *Consider the transmission schedule of Decay: for each round r, for each node v at distance l_v from source, if $r \equiv l_v + 1 \mod 3$, then v is prompted to transmit with probability $2^{-((r-l_v-1)/3 \mod \lceil \log n \rceil)}$. Also, suppose that each node that is prompted to transmit but does not have the message sends "noise". Then, all nodes receive the message by round $O(D \log n + \log^2 n)$, with high probability.*

To prove this lemma, we need to go away from the analysis approach in [2] that chooses a shortest path from source s to node v and shows that the broadcast message makes fast progresses along this path when moving forwards in time. Instead we use what we call *backwards analysis*: in a nutshell, we move backwards in time and find a sequence of collision-free transmissions from s to v, where hops of this sequence are unraveled backwards (from v to s). Meanwhile unraveling this sequence, each of these transmission can be the broadcast message or just "noise", depending on whether the sender has received the broadcast message or not. Once we reach s, it means the transmissions in the sequence indeed where the broadcast message. We defer the details of the proof to the proof of Lemma 3.1 in the full version.

Unfortunately, in contrast to the simple Decay schedule, the schedule of [7] appears to be not MMV. In Section 3.2, we present a new transmission schedule for GSTs that is MMV. In the proof of Theorem 1.2, we again use our backwards analysis to show that this new schedule is in fact MMV, while also proving that our multi-message algorithm which combines RLNC with this schedule broadcasts k messages in optimal time $O(D + k \log n + \log^2 n)$.

3.2 A Multi-Message Transmission Schedule Atop GST

In this section, we present our transmission schedule for GSTs. Later we use this schedule along with random linear network coding to achieve our optimal multi-message algorithm.

Suppose we have a GST T for graph G. For each node u, let l_u be the distance of u from source s in graph G (that is, the BFS level of u). Also, let r_u be the rank of u in GST T. We first construct a virtual directed graph G', from graph G, as follows: we add a directed edge from every node u with rank r that is the first node of a fast stretch to every descendant of u in T that has rank r (thus, to all nodes in that fast stretch). We call this a *fast* edge. We use the notation d_u to denote the length of the shortest (directed) path from s to u in G', and we call this *virtual-distance*. Given graph G, GST T, and the respective virtual graph G' (and the related virtual-distances), our schedule is defined as follows:

Multi-Message Viable GST Schedule: In round t, each node u at BFS-level l of G with rank r in GST T and virtual-distance d in the virtual graph G' does as follows: (a) if $t \equiv 2(l+3r) \pmod{6\lceil \log_2 n \rceil}$, then u transmits; (b) if $t \equiv 1 + 2d \pmod 6$), then u transmits with probability $2^{-((t-1-2d)/6 \mod \lceil \log_2 n \rceil)}$; otherwise, u listens.

Note that the case (a) only happens in even rounds and case (b) happens only in odd rounds. As in [7], we call the transmissions triggered by case (a) *fast transmissions* and the transmissions triggered by case (b) *slow transmissions*.

We remark that this schedule uses fast transmissions exactly as in [7, 18] to pipeline the messages along the fast stretches of GST. We see in Lemma 3.3 that these fast transmissions are collision-free. The crucial difference with the schedule in [7,18] lies in defining the slow transmissions with respect to the virtual-distance in graph G' (instead of levels in G). This change results in slow transmissions not trying to push messages away from the source themselves, but instead trying to push messages towards entry points of the fast stretches (even if this leads to the message going back towards the source). While this modification seems minor, it is crucial for allowing the *backwards analysis* technique to show that the new schedule is efficient and MMV.

Lemma 3.2. *In virtual graph G', for each node u, we have $d_u \le 2\lceil \log_2 n \rceil$.*

Lemma 3.3. *There are no collisions between any two fast transmissions.*

Proposition 3.4. *If node u with level l is the beginning of a fast stretch in GST T and u sends a message at time t in a fast transmission round, then any node v with level $l' > l$ on the same fast stretch receives this message by time $t' = t + 2(l' - l)$.*

Lemma 3.5. *For any node u with virtual-distance d_u, if there is at least one node v connected to u in G with virtual-distance $d_v = d_u - 1$, then during each interval of $6\lceil \log_2 n \rceil$ rounds, with probability at least $\frac{1}{8}$, node u receives a message from one node with virtual-distance $d_u - 1$.*

3.3 Optimal Multi-Message Broadcast Algorithm

We achieve our optimal multi-message broadcast algorithm by combining random linear network coding (RLNC) with the Multi-Message GST Schedule that we presented in Section 3.2. We first recall on the exact working of RLNC [12, 13] and then present our multi-message broadcast algorithm.

In RLNC, the k messages are regarded as bit-vectors $\vec{m}_1$, ..., $\vec{m}_k \in \mathbb{F}_2^l$ over $\mathbb{F}_2$, the finite field of order two. Each network coded packet p consists of a linear combination of messages, that is, the vector $\sum_{i=1}^k \alpha_i \vec{m}_i \in \mathbb{F}_2^l$. We remark that the standard implementation of RLNC requires that the coefficient vector $\vec{\alpha} = (\alpha_1, \ldots, \alpha_k) \in \mathbb{F}_2^k$ is transmitted with each message. Doing this would increase the packet size to k bits which could be too large. We note that in the known topology setting there is no need for actually including the coefficient vectors in the packets because using the topology knowledge, all nodes can compute the coefficients offline in a consistent manner. In the unknown topology scenario, using generations, that is, dividing messages into groups of size $\log n$ and then doing network coding only inside each group keeps the coefficient overhead to $O(\log n)$ bits. We defer the details for this to the full version.

Because of linearity, a node that has a number of these packets can create a packet of this form for any coefficient combination that is spanned by the coefficient vectors of the packets that it has received by that time. Also, if a node has a set of k packets with linearly independent coefficient vectors, then this node can reconstruct all the k messages using Gaussian elimination. In RLNC, every node u stores all its received packets to maintain the subspace that is spanned by them. Whenever u decides to generate a *new coded packet*, it chooses a random coefficient vector from this subspace by taking a random linear combination of the packets stored. Once the subspace spanned by the coefficient vectors in packets received by u is the full space $\mathbb{F}_2^k$, then u decodes and reconstructs all the messages.

Multi-Message Broadcast Algorithm: Whenever in MMV schedule of Section 3.2, a node u is prompted to transmit, u transmits a packet determined as follows: (a) if this is a slow transmission, or if this is a fast transmission and u is the first node on a fast stretch, then u transmits a new coded packet, that is, a packet that is created using network coding by combining the messages u has received earlier, (b) if this is a fast transmission but node u is an intermediate node in a fast stretch, then u simply relays the packet it received in the previous fast transmission round (if any).

3.4 Analysis of the Multi-Message Broadcast Algorithm

In the analysis of our Multi-Message Broadcast Algorithm we combine our new backwards analysis with a carefully designed potential function and the projection analysis from [11] to show that using the schedule from Section 3.2 together with random linear network coding achieves an optimal multi-message broadcast.

The following definition and proposition are taken from [11] and form a simple and clean platform for analyzing random linear network coding:

Definition 3.6 ([11, Definition 4.1]). *A node v is* infected *by a coefficient vector $\vec{\mu} \in \mathbb{F}_2^k$ if v has received a packet with a coefficient vector $\vec{c} \in \mathbb{F}_2^k$ that is not orthogonal to μ, that is, $\langle \vec{\mu}, \vec{c} \rangle \neq 0$.*

Proposition 3.7 ([11, Lemma 4.2]). *If a node v is infected by a coefficient vector $\vec{\mu}$ and after that, a node u receives a packet from node v, then u gets infected by $\vec{\mu}$ with probability at least $1/2$. Furthermore, if a node v is infected by all the 2^k coefficient vectors in $\mathbb{F}_2^k$, then v can decode all the k messages.*

We now present our analysis for the *multi-message broadcast algorithm* presented in Section 3.3.

Proof of Theorem 1.2. For a large enough constant λ let $T = \lambda(D + k\lceil \log_2 n \rceil + 2\lceil \log_2 n \rceil^2)$. We claim that for any node v and any fixed non-zero vector $\vec{\mu} \in \mathbb{F}_2^k$, the probability that node v is not infected by $\vec{\mu}$ in T rounds is at most $2^{-(k+2 \log n)}$. Using this claim, we conclude via a union bound over all the 2^k coefficient vectors in $\mathbb{F}_2^k$ that by round T, with high probability, v is infected by all the coefficient vectors in $\mathbb{F}_2^k$. That is, by round T, v can decode all the k messages. Using another union bound over all the choices of node v then shows that by round T, with high probability, all nodes have received all the messages.

Fix a node v and a non-zero vector $\vec{\mu} \in \mathbb{F}_2^k$. To prove the claim, we use *backwards analysis* to view the process of infection spreading of vector $\vec{\mu}$. In this method, we go back in time, from round T to round 1, and we find a sequence of collision-free transmissions from source node s to node v such that all the transmissions in this chain are successful *with respect to* vector $\vec{\mu}$. Since we are moving back in time, we find this sequence starting from v and going backwards till reaching s.

For each t, we say node u is *transmission-connected* to v by backwards time t" if there is a sequence of transmissions $u = w_1, w_2, \ldots w_\ell = v$ where for each $i \in [1, \ell - 1]$, w_i transmits in a round $r_i \in [T - t, T]$, we have $r_i < r_{i+1}$, and in round r_i, w_{i+1} receives a message from w_i. Let S_t be the set of all nodes that are transmission-connected to v by backwards time t. Moreover, we then define the potential of v with respect to vector $\vec{\mu}$ at backwards time t to be $\Phi_{\vec{\mu}}(t) = \min_{u \in S_t} d_u \lceil \log_2 n \rceil + l_u$. Note that $\Phi_{\vec{\mu}}(0) \leq 2\lceil \log_2 n \rceil^2 + D$. To prove the claim, we show that with probability at least $1 - 2^{-(k+2 \log n)}$, we have $\Phi_{\vec{\mu}}(T) = 0$. For this, moving backwards in time, we show that in every $8\lceil \log_2 n \rceil$ interval of consecutive rounds, this potential decreases with probability at least $\frac{1}{16}$ by at least $\lceil \log_2 n \rceil - 1$. For a backwards time t, let node u be the node in S_t that minimizes the potential of v. The proof is now divided into two cases as follows:

Case (A): Suppose u has at least one G-neighbor that has a lower virtual-distance. In this case, Lemma 3.5 guarantees that with probability at least $\frac{1}{8}$ during the rounds in $[T - t - 6\lceil \log_2 n \rceil, T - t]$, there is a collision-free transmission from a node u' with $d_{u'} = d_u - 1$ to u, and is successful with respect to $\vec{\mu}$, with probability $1/2$. Since u' and u are neighbors their levels l_u and $l_{u'}$ differ at most by one, thus a successful transmission decreases the potential by at least $(d_u \lceil \log_2 n \rceil + l_u) - (d_{u'} \lceil \log_2 n \rceil + l_{u'}) = (d_u - d_{u'})\lceil \log_2 n \rceil - (l_u - l_{u'}) \geq \lceil \log_2 n \rceil - 1$. Thus, if u has a neighbor with a virtual-distance lower than d_u then with probability at least $\frac{1}{16}$ the potential decreases by at least $\lceil \log_2 n \rceil - 1$ within any $8\lceil \log_2 n \rceil$ rounds when moving backwards in time.

Case (B): Suppose u does not have a G-neighbor with a lower virtual-distance. Note that this can only happen if $u = s$ or if there is one directed edge in G' representing a fast stretch, originating from a node u' one level below u in G' and going into u. First observe that the starting node of any fast stretch initiates a "transmission wave" every $6\lceil \log_2 n \rceil$ rounds by creating a new coded packet and sending it as a fast transmission. This packet gets then pipe-lined through the fast stretch with one progress every fast transmission round (that is, once in every two rounds) until it reaches the end of the stretch. Thus, for any node on a fast stretch, there is a new wave arriving every $6\lceil \log_2 n \rceil$ rounds. Moreover, each of these waves is successful with respect to $\vec{\mu}$ with probability at least $1/2$. Thus, at a time $t' \in [T - t - 6\lceil \log_2 n \rceil, T - t]$, a fast transmission wave arrives in u, and with probability $1/2$ leads to an extended sequence of collision-free transmissions that are successful with respect to $\vec{\mu}$. In particular, if the wave originated from u' during the rounds $[T - t' - 2\lceil \log_2 n \rceil, T - t']$, then there is a sequence of transmission from u' to v in round interval $[T - t - 8\lceil \log_2 n \rceil, T - t]$, and otherwise the wave propagated for $\lceil \log_2 n \rceil$ steps and there is a node u'' between u' and u on the fast stretch with a sequence of transmission to v starting at time $T - t - 8\lceil \log_2 n \rceil$. Thus, in both cases, the potential drops by at least $\lceil \log_2 n \rceil - 1$. In the first case the potential drop comes from the fact that $d_{u'} = d_u - 1$ and $l_{u'} < l_u$, while in the second case we have $d_{u''} \leq d_{u'} + 1 = d_u$ and $l_{u''} \leq l_u - \lceil \log_2 n \rceil$.

The above argument shows that when moving backwards in time, in every $8\lceil \log_2 n \rceil$ consecutive rounds, with probability at least $\frac{1}{16}$, the potential of v decreases by at least $\lceil \log_2 n \rceil - 1 > \lceil \log_2 n \rceil / 2$, until reaching zero. When the potential reaches zero, it means that there is a sequence of successful and collision-free transmission from s to v. Hence, the expected time for such a sequence to appear is thus a constant times the initial potential of v, $\Phi_{\vec{\mu}}(0) \leq 2\lceil \log_2 n \rceil^2 + D$. A Chernoff bound furthermore shows that the probability of not finding such a sequence is exponentially concentrated around this mean. In particular, after $T = \lambda(D + k\lceil \log_2 n \rceil + 2\lceil \log_2 n \rceil)$ rounds, we expect at least $\lambda'(2D/\lceil \log_2 n \rceil + 4\lceil \log_2 n \rceil + k)$ sets of $8\lceil \log_2 n \rceil$ consecutive rounds in which the potential of v drops at least by $\lceil \log_2 n \rceil / 2$, for a constant λ'. Furthermore, the probability that there are less than $(2D/\lceil \log_2 n \rceil + 4\lceil \log_2 n \rceil$ such rounds is exponentially small in the expectation, that is, at most $2^{-(2\lceil \log_2 n \rceil + k)}$. This completes the proof of Theorem 1.2 $\qquad\square$

4. REFERENCES

[1] ALON, N., BAR-NOY, A., LINIAL, N., AND PELEG, D. A lower bound for radio broadcast. *Journal of Computer and System Sciences 43*, 2 (1991), 290–298.

[2] BAR-YEHUDA, R., GOLDREICH, O., AND ITAI, A. On the time-complexity of broadcast in multi-hop radio networks: An exponential gap between determinism and randomization. *Journal of Computer and System Sciences 45*, 1 (1992), 104–126.

[3] BAR-YEHUDA, R., ISRAELI, A., AND ITAI, A. Multiple communication in multi-hop radio networks. *SIAM Journal on Computing 22*, 4 (1993), 875–887.

[4] CHLAMTAC, I., AND KUTTEN., S. On broadcasting in radio networks: Problem analysis and protocol design. *IEEE Transactions on Communications 33*, 12 (1985), 1240–1246.

[5] CHLEBUS, B. S., KOWALSKI, D. R., PELC, A., AND ROKICKI, M. A. Efficient distributed communication in ad-hoc radio networks. In *Proceedings of the International Conference on Automata, Languages and Programming* (2011), pp. 613–624.

[6] CZUMAJ, A., AND RYTTER, W. Broadcasting algorithms in radio networks with unknown topology. In *Proceedings of the Symposium on Foundations of Computer Science* (2003), pp. 492–501.

[7] GASIENIEC, L., PELEG, D., AND XIN, Q. Faster communication in known topology radio networks. In *Proceedings of the ACM SIGACT-SIGOPS Symposium on Principles of Distributed Computing* (2005), pp. 129–137.

[8] GASIENIEC, L., AND POTAPOV, I. Gossiping with unit messages in known radio networks. In *IFIP TCS* (2002), pp. 193–205.

[9] GHAFFARI, M., AND HAEUPLER, B. Near optimal leader election in multi-hop radio networks. In *Proceedings of the ACM-SIAM Symposium on Discrete Algorithms* (2013), pp. 748–766.

[10] GHAFFARI, M., HAEUPLER, B., AND KHABBAZIAN, M. A Bound on the Throughput of Radio Networks. *arXiv http://arxiv.org/abs/1302.0264* (2013).

[11] HAEUPLER, B. Analyzing network coding gossip made easy. In *Proceedings of the Symposium on Theory of Computing* (2011), STOC '11, pp. 293–302.

[12] HAEUPLER, B., KIM, M., AND MEDARD, M. Optimality of network coding with buffers. In *Proceedings of the IEEE Information Theory Workshop* (2011), pp. 533–537.

[13] HO, T., KOETTER, R., MEDARD, M., KARGER, D. R., AND EFFROS, M. The benefits of coding over routing in a randomized setting. In *Proceedings of IEEE International Symposium on Information Theory* (2003).

[14] KHABBAZIAN, M., AND KOWALSKI, D. Time-efficient randomized multiple-message broadcast in radio networks. In *Proceedings of the ACM SIGACT-SIGOPS Symposium on Principles of Distributed Computing* (2011), pp. 373–380.

[15] KOWALSKI, D., AND PELC, A. Broadcasting in undirected ad hoc radio networks. In *Proceedings of the ACM SIGACT-SIGOPS Symposium on Principles of Distributed Computing* (2003), pp. 73–82.

[16] KOWALSKI, D. R., AND PELC, A. Optimal deterministic broadcasting in known topology radio networks. *Distributed Computing 19*, 3 (2007), 185–195.

[17] KUSHILEVITZ, E., AND MANSOUR, Y. An $\Omega(D \log(N/D))$ lower bound for broadcast in radio networks. In *Proceedings of the ACM SIGACT-SIGOPS Symposium on Principles of Distributed Computing* (1993), pp. 65–74.

[18] MANNE, F., AND XIN, Q. Optimal gossiping with unit size messages in known topology radio networks. In *Proceedings of the Workshop on Combinatorial and Algorithmic Aspects of Networking* (2006), pp. 125–134.

[19] PELEG, D. Time-efficient broadcasting in radio networks: A review. In *Proceedings of The International Conference on Distributed Computing and Internet Technologies* (2007), pp. 1–18.

[20] SCHNEIDER, J., AND WATTENHOFER, R. What is the use of collision detection (in wireless networks)? *Distributed Computing* (2010), 133–147.

[21] XIN, Q. personal communication, May, 2012.

Maximal Independent Sets in Multichannel Radio Networks

Sebastian Daum
University of Freiburg
Freiburg, Germany
sdaum@cs.uni-freiburg.de

Mohsen Ghaffari
MIT
Cambridge, MA, USA
ghaffari@csail.mit.edu

Seth Gilbert
National Univ. of Singapore
Singapore, Singapore
seth.gilbert@comp.nus.edu.sg

Fabian Kuhn
University of Freiburg
Freiburg, Germany
kuhn@cs.uni-freiburg.de

Calvin Newport
Georgetown University
Washington D.C., USA
cnewport@cs.georgetown.edu

ABSTRACT

We present new upper bounds for fundamental problems in multichannel wireless networks. These bounds address the benefits of dynamic spectrum access, i.e., to what extent multiple communication channels can be used to improve performance. In more detail, we study a multichannel generalization of the standard graph-based wireless model without collision detection, and assume the network topology satisfies polynomially bounded independence.

Our core technical result is an algorithm that constructs a maximal independent set (MIS) in $O\left(\frac{\log^2 n}{\mathcal{F}}\right) + \tilde{O}(\log n)$ rounds, in networks of size n with $\mathcal{F}$ channels, where the $\tilde{O}$-notation hides polynomial factors in $\log \log n$.

Moreover, we use this MIS algorithm as a subroutine to build a constant-degree connected dominating set in the same asymptotic time. Leveraging this structure, we are able to solve global broadcast and leader election within $O\left(D + \frac{\log^2 n}{\mathcal{F}}\right) + \tilde{O}(\log n)$ rounds, where D is the diameter of the graph, and k-message multi-message broadcast in $O\left(D + k + \frac{\log^2 n}{\mathcal{F}}\right) + \tilde{O}(\log n)$ rounds for unrestricted message size (with a slow down of only a log factor on the k term under the assumption of restricted message size).

In all five cases above, we prove: (a) our results hold with high probability (i.e., at least $1 - 1/n$); (b) our results are within polyloglog factors of the relevant lower bounds for multichannel networks; and (c) our results beat the relevant lower bounds for single channel networks. These new (near) optimal algorithms significantly expand the number of problems now known to be solvable faster in multichannel versus single channel wireless networks.

Categories and Subject Descriptors

C.2.1 [**Network Architecture and Design**]: Wireless Communication; F.2.2 [**Analysis of Algorithms and Problem Complexity**]: Non-numerical Algorithms and Problems *computations on discrete structures*

General Terms

Algorithms, Theory

Keywords

wireless networks, shared spectrum, multichannel, maximal independent set, connected dominating set

1. INTRODUCTION

Modern wireless devices rarely operate on a fixed communication channel. It is more common for them to use a wide swath of spectrum that has been subdivided into multiple independent channels (e.g., [1,6]). This reality inspires a compelling question: When and how can we leverage the availability of multiple channels to improve the performance of wireless algorithms?

One might hope that using $\mathcal{F}$ channels you can always achieve an $\mathcal{F}$-times speed-up. For distributed algorithms, however, this goal is complicated by two factors: (a) each device can only use a single channel at a time; and (b) the size and density of the network is often unknown *a priori*. (In fact, some well-known problems, such as multihop wake-up, provably derive *no* benefit from multiple channels [11].) In this paper, we overcome these challenges to significantly increase the corpus of algorithms known to solve problems faster in multichannel versus single channel wireless networks. In more detail, we prove new randomized upper bounds for the following fundamental problems in graphs satisfying polynomial bounded independence (defined below): (i) establishing a maximal independent set

*The research in this paper was supported by NUS FRC grant R-252-000-443-133; the Swiss National Science Foundation under grant n. 200021-135160; Ford Motor Company University Research Program; AFOSR Contract No. FA9550-13-1-0042; NSF Award No. CCF-1217506; NSF Award No. 0939370-CCF; NSF Award No. CCF-AF-0937274; AFOSR Contract No. FA9550-08-1-0159; and NSF Award No. CCF-0726514.

(MIS); (ii) establishing a constant-degree connected dominating set (CDS); (iii) broadcasting one message — or a set of messages — to every device in a network; and (iv) electing a leader in a network. For each of these problems, we give solutions that are within polyloglog factors of optimal in the multichannel setting, and that are faster than their corresponding lower bounds in single channel networks.

We argue that these results provide a powerful argument for wireless algorithm designers to more aggressively embrace the availability of multiple channels to gain performance.

Results. We assume a multichannel generalization of the standard graph-based wireless model [4,8]. In each round, each node can choose a single channel to participate on from among $\mathcal{F} \geq 1$ available channels. We further assume that the graph representing our network topology satisfies polynomial bounded independence (the independence number of a radius r neighborhood is bounded by $f(r)$ for some polynomial f) [22,26]. This assumption generalizes a variety of attempts to model the topology of wireless networks, including the widely used unit-disk graphs, quasi-unit-disk graphs, or, more generally, unit-ball graphs where the underlying metric has bounded doubling dimension [26].

The primary technical result of the paper is an algorithm that constructs an MIS in $O\left(\frac{\log^2 n}{\mathcal{F}}\right) + \tilde{O}(\log n)$ rounds where $\tilde{O}$ hides polynomial factors in $\log \log n$ — with high probability[1]. This algorithm consists of two main pieces: a "decay filter" that reduces the number of nodes competing in each "area" to $O(\text{polylog } n)$, and a "herald filter" that leverages multiple channels to efficiently further reduce the nodes down to a constant number per area.

Much of the complexity resides in the herald filter, where we reduce the number of contenders to join the MIS from $O(\text{polylog } n)$ to $O(1)$. Part of the complexity comes from asynchrony: new arrivals and neighboring regions can force existing nodes to "restart," preventing progress toward the MIS. Part of the complexity comes from the fact that randomized symmetry breaking works well over large populations, but less predictably as the number of participants gets small.

To put this result in context, in the single channel model, building an MIS requires $\Theta(\log^2 n)$ time [11,18,20,24]. Based on the lower bound techniques developed in [10,11,13,20], we show in [9] that in bounded independence graphs (and even in unit-disk graphs) any MIS algorithm requires at least $\Omega\left(\frac{\log^2 n}{\mathcal{F}} + \log n\right)$ rounds in a network with $\mathcal{F}$ channels. Our algorithm matches this multichannel lower bound up to polyloglog factors and beats the single channel lower bound. The lower bound also implies that even if the number of channels is arbitrarily large, solving the MIS problem still requires at least $\Omega(\log n)$ rounds, and our upper bound achieves almost the same time with just $\Theta(\log n)$ many channels.

Having developed an MIS algorithm, we use it as a subroutine to build a constant-degree CDS, with high probability, also in $O\left(\frac{\log^2 n}{\mathcal{F}}\right) + \tilde{O}(\log n)$ rounds. The key challenge here is to efficiently — i.e., in $o(\log^2 n)$ time — identify short paths between nearby MIS nodes, even while the MIS subroutine is ongoing. We then leverage the overlay provided by our

CDS algorithm to solve global broadcast and leader election (with synchronous starts) in $O\left(D + \frac{\log^2 n}{\mathcal{F}}\right) + \tilde{O}(\log n)$ rounds, and k-message multi-message broadcast in $O\left(D + k + \frac{\log^2 n}{\mathcal{F}}\right) + \tilde{O}(\log n)$ rounds for unrestricted message size (with a slow down of only a log factor on the k term under the assumption of restricted message size). These bounds (nearly) match the relevant $\Omega\left(D + \frac{\log^2 n}{\mathcal{F}}\right)$ bound for multichannel networks [16], and beat the relevant $\Omega(D + \log^2 n)$ lower bound for single channel networks [3].

Related Work. There has been much research on algorithms for graph-based *single channel* wireless network models, beginning with Chlamtac and Kutten [8] in the centralized setting and Bar-Yehuda et al. [4] in the distributed setting. The problem of finding an MIS in a distributed fashion has been studied extensively for a standard message passing model (i.e., *without* collisions). On general network topologies, an MIS can be built in $O\left(\min\left\{\log n, \sqrt{\log n} \log \Delta\right\}\right)$, where Δ is the largest degree of the network graph [2, 5, 23]. For bounded independence graphs, this is improved to $O(\log^* n)$ [27]. For single-channel radio networks (i.e., *with* collisions), without collision detection that satisfy the unit disk graph property, it has been shown that $O(\log^2 n)$ rounds are sufficient [24]. Using a reduction from the single-hop wake-up problem, this bound was shown tight [11,18,20,24].

To our knowledge, the use of a connected dominating set (CDS) as a wireless network backbone was first described in [17]. It is well-known (and already described in [17] for the case of unit disk graphs) that a CDS can be constructed by first computing a small dominating set (in the case of bounded independence graphs, an MIS provides such a small dominating set), and then connecting the nodes of the dominating set through 2 and 3 hop paths. In a bounded independence graph, connecting all MIS nodes at distance at most 3 by a short path leads to a CDS where the graph induced by the CDS is connected and has bounded degree. The MIS algorithm of [24] combined with the CDS algorithm of [7] (which assumes an MIS as a precondition) provides a constant-degree CDS in $O(\log^2 n)$ rounds in the radio network model with synchronous starts (i.e., where all nodes start during the same round).[2]

The study of algorithms for multichannel wireless networks is more recent. Initially, much of the focus in multichannel networks was providing increased fault-tolerance: even if some of the channels were faulty, the computation would proceed. This basic model of unreliable multichannel wireless communication, often called *t-disrupted*, was introduced in [14], and has since been well-studied; e.g., [12–15, 19,25,28,29].

We previously tackled the problem of leader election in single-hop networks (i.e., the diameter is 1) [10], where we solved the problem in $O\left(\frac{\log^2 n}{\mathcal{F}} + \log n\right)$ rounds. These techniques did not directly translate to multihop networks. We also have studied the problem of broadcast in multihop networks [16]. In this case, we assumed that nodes had access to collision detection, showing how to leverage this information to solve broadcast in $O\left((D + \log n)\left(\log \mathcal{F} + \frac{\log n}{\mathcal{F}}\right)\right)$. For $\mathcal{F} = \log n$, this yields results similar to this paper, i.e., $O(D) + \tilde{O}(\log n)$. The results are hard to compare, however,

---

[1] We use the phrase *high probability* to indicate a probability at least $1 - \frac{1}{n^c}$, for some arbitrary constant $c \geq 1$.

[2] The MIS result of [24] does not require the synchronous start property, but the CDS piece from [7] does.

as [16] assumes collision detection (which we do not), but we assume bounded independence (which [16] does not).

Finally, we have studied the problem of wake-up and approximating a minimum dominating set (MDS) in a multi-hop network with a topology that satisfies a clique decomposition assumption [11]. For the MDS problem, we achieved a constant-factor approximation of an MDS, in expectation, requiring $O\left(\frac{\log^2 n}{\mathcal{F}}\right) + \tilde{O}(\log n)$ rounds. We found the technique could not easily be extended to achieve the strict independence of an MIS (with high probability) or tolerate the more general bounded independence assumption (instead of a clique decomposition assumption).

2. PRELIMINARIES

Radio Network Model. We consider a multichannel variant of the standard graph-based radio network model [4]. The network is modeled as an n-node graph $G = (V, E)$. Each node knows n or a polynomial upper bound on n. There are $\mathcal{F}$ communication channels. Time is divided into synchronized slots, i.e., rounds. For the purpose of analysis, we imagine a global round numbering, but nodes do not have access to this global time. In each round, each node can choose one of the $\mathcal{F}$ channels to operate on; it can either transmit or listen on the channel. A node u that listens on a channel C receives a message from a neighbor v if and only if node v is transmitting on C and no other neighbor of u is transmitting on C. If two or more neighbors of u transmit on C, or if no neighbor of u transmits on C, then u receives silence. That is, we assume there is no collision detection available. A node that transmits does not receive anything. Notably, a node that operates on channel C in a given round learns nothing about events on channels other than C in that round.

Notation. For a subset of nodes $S \subseteq G$, we use $N_G^d(S)$ to denote the set $\{u \mid \exists v \in S, \; dist_G(u, v) \leq d\}$, where $dist_G(u, v)$ is the shortest distance between u and v in graph G. When $|S| = 1$, e.g., $S = \{v\}$, we use $N_G^d(v)$ to mean $N_G^d(\{v\})$. We use $N_G(v)$ to denote the neighbors of v, i.e., $N_G(v) = N_G^1(v) \backslash \{v\}$. When clear from the context, we omit the subscript G. In later sections, we describe algorithms in which nodes can be in various states, e.g.: $\mathbb{A}$, $\mathbb{H}'$, $\mathbb{H}$, $\mathbb{L}'$, $\mathbb{L}$, $\mathbb{M}$, $\mathbb{E}$. Where appropriate, we slightly abuse notation and use the state names to denote the set of nodes in a given state, e.g., $\mathbb{A}$ to denote the set $\{v \in V : v \text{ is in state } \mathbb{A}\}$. We sometimes study $N^d(u) \cap \mathbb{A}$ and write $N_{\mathbb{A}}^d(u)$. When referring to a local variable X of a node u, we write $X(u)$. If the round number is not clear from the context, we denote $X(u)$ in round r as $X(u, r)$.

Bounded Independence. We assume that the network graph G is a bounded independence graph as introduced and described in [22, 26]. Formally, any independent set $S \subseteq N_G^d(v)$ for any node v has size at most $\alpha(d)$, where $\alpha(d)$ is a polynomial function in d and (in particular) independent of n. Hence, any subgraph induced by a subset of a neighborhood $N_G^d(v)$ for $d = O(1)$ has only constant size independent sets.

Probability Notation. Consider an event A, a constant c, and a variable k. If $\mathbf{P}(A) \geq 1 - e^{-ck}$, then we say that A happens with very high probability with regard to k (w.v.h.p.(k)). If $\mathbf{P}(A) \geq 1 - k^{-c}$, then we say A happens with high probability with regard to k (w.h.p.(k)), and if A happens w.h.p.(n), then we simply say A happens with

high probability (w.h.p.). Finally, w.c.p. abbreviates *'with constant probability'*.

Number of Channels. We assume $\omega(1)$ channels are available; otherwise there are existing algorithms that solve the problem in the same asymptotic time frame. If $\omega(\log n)$ channels are available, we restrict the usage to $\Theta(\log n)$, as there is no benefit from using more   in [9] we show that computing an MIS requires $\Omega\left(\frac{\log^2 n}{\mathcal{F}} + \log n\right)$ rounds. Solely for ease of exposition, we assume a minimum number of $\Omega(\log \log n)$ channels for all descriptions and proofs in this paper; this is not a requirement for the algorithm to work. We explain in [9] how to adapt our algorithms to work in a setting with $o(\log \log n)$ channels.

3. PROBLEM STATEMENT

We study randomized algorithms for the following problems, with high probability:

Maximal Independent Set. We say that an algorithm solves MIS in time T, if the following three properties hold: *(P1)* Each node v that wakes up in round r declares itself as either *dominating* or *dominated* by round $r' \in [r, r + T]$ and this decision is permanent. *(P2)* For each round r and node v, if v is *dominated* in round r, then v has at least one *dominating* neighbor in that round. *(P3)* For each round r and node v, if v is *dominating* in round r, then v does not have any neighboring *dominating* node in that round.

Connected Dominating Set. We say that an algorithm solves (constant-degree) CDS in time T, if the following four properties hold: *(P1)* Each node v that wakes up in round r declares itself as either *dominating* or *dominated* by round $r' \in [r, r + T]$ and this decision is permanent. *(P2)* For each round r and node v, if v is *dominated* in round r, then v has at least one *dominating* neighbor in round r. *(P3)* For each round r and node v, if v is *dominating* in round r, then v has at most $O(1)$ *dominating* neighbors in that round. *(P4)* For each round r and each *connected component* C in the graph induced by nodes awake in round $r - T$, the *dominating* nodes in C form a connected subgraph within C.

Other Problems. We also consider **global broadcast**, where a node starts with a message, and **multi-message broadcast**, where k nodes start with a message; in both cases the algorithm succeeds when every node in the network has received the message(s). Finally, we consider leader election, which terminates when exactly one node has declared itself the leader (and no future nodes declare themselves the leader).

4. OVERVIEW OF MIS ALGORITHM

In this section, we provide an overview of the MIS algorithm.

Algorithm Outline. Our algorithm consists of two main building blocks: the *decay filter* and the *herald filter*. The decay filter is used to reduce the maximum degree of the communication graph to $O(\text{polylog } n)$. The herald filter assumes that the maximum degree is bounded accordingly and establishes an MIS in this setting.

The flow of the algorithm is as follows. Each node, on activation, starts in the decay filter. As time passes, some of the nodes move from the decay filter to the herald filter. Nodes exit the herald filter when either they have joined the MIS and have status *dominating*, or when they have an MIS neighbor and are thus *dominated*. In order to analyze the time complexity of our algorithm, we bound the time each node spends in each of the filters.

We note that nodes do not move backward in this flow. The dominating and dominated statuses are permanent; a node that is in the herald filter does not go back to the decay filter. However, a node u that is in the decay filter might skip the herald filter and directly become *dominated* if u receives a message from a *dominating* neighbor node v. Also, a node that has made progress in one of the filters can be forced to restart at the beginning of its current filter.

A node halts as soon as it discovers that it is dominated. On the other hand, a dominating node v cannot halt: it continues transmitting its status to its neighbors every so often, ensuring that each neighbor w that awakes at a later time becomes *dominated*.

Filter Guarantees. We now present the guarantees of both filters. We later discuss how the filters are implemented and prove the specified guarantees. The first property holds for all components of the algorithm, and acts in parallel with the other filter guarantees. It plays an important role in combining the filters.

(G1) For each node u, if u is awake in round r and it has a *dominating* neighbor v in that round, then w.h.p. node u becomes *dominated* by round $r' = r + O(\log n)$.

Implementation is straightforward: each node u that does not have its final status listens to one of a constant number of channels, w.c.p., every $O(1)$ rounds. Each node that is *dominating* periodically transmits on those channels, w.c.p., every $O(1)$ rounds. If u receives a message from a *dominating* neighbor, then u becomes *dominated*. Since each node can have at most $\alpha(1)$ *MIS* neighbors, applying Chernoff bound gives us guarantee (G1). We show later that both filters satisfy this guarantee.

The guarantees that we get from the decay filter are as follows:

(G2) W.h.p., for each node v and each round r, at most $O(\log n)$ nodes in $N_G^1(v)$ exit the decay filter in round r to enter the herald filter. Each node v that enters the herald filter has spent $\Omega(\log n)$ rounds in the decay filter, long enough to become dominated if v already had a dominating neighbor after waking up.

(G3) W.h.p., for each node v that is in the decay filter in round r, by round $r' = r + O\left(\frac{\log^2 n}{\mathcal{F}} + \log n\right)$, either v is *dominated*, in which case it has a dominating neighbor, or at least one node in $N_G^1(v)$ exits the decay filter and enters the herald filter between rounds r and r'.

The guarantees that we get from herald filter are as follows:

(G4) W.h.p., for each node v that is in the herald filter in round r, by round $r' = r + \tilde{O}(\log n)$, v is *dominating* or *dominated*. In the latter case, v has a dominating neighbor.

(G5) W.h.p., in any round r, the set of dominating nodes is an independent set.

Note that (G2) and (G4) together provide that, w.h.p., the maximum degree in the graph induced by undecided nodes in the herald filter is bounded by some $\Delta_H = O(\text{polylog } n)$.

We will describe the algorithm and prove guarantees (G1)–(G5) in the following two sections. Before doing so, we state our main theorem (for a detailed proof we refer to [9]).

THEOREM 4.1. *W.h.p., an algorithm satisfying (G1)–(G5) solves the MIS problem in time* $O\left(\frac{\log^2 n}{\mathcal{F}}\right) + \tilde{O}(\log n)$.

PROOF SKETCH. Property (G5) implies that the set of dominating nodes is independent. It remains only to show that within $O(\log^2(n)/\mathcal{F}) + \tilde{O}(\log n)$ time, every node is either dominating or dominated. We claim that for each node v that is awake in round r, there is a round $r' = r + O(\log^2(n)/\mathcal{F}) + \tilde{O}(\log n)$ such that, by the end of round r', either v is dominating or dominated, or at least one 'new' node $w \in N_G^2(v)$ that was not dominating in round r has become *dominating*. Since the MIS can contain at most $O(1)$ dominating nodes in $N_G^2(v)$, the result follows from this claim. The claim follows from the fact that, by (G3), within $O(\log^2(n)/\mathcal{F}) + \tilde{O}(\log n)$ rounds, either v is dominated or it has a neighbor u that has entered the herald filter; by (G4), within $\tilde{O}(\log n)$ rounds, either u itself or a neighbor of u is dominating. □

5. DECAY FILTER

The decay filter is a slightly modified version of the active state of the active wake-up algorithm in [11]. In essence, the decay filter is a backoff style protocol in which nodes broadcast with exponentially increasing probabilities; whenever a node receives a message from another node, it is knocked out and restarts the filter. To reduce contention, the broadcasts are distributed uniformly over the $\mathcal{F}$ channels.

Algorithm description. For pseudo-code and detailed proofs we refer to [9]. The decay filter uses $\Theta(\mathcal{F})$ channels, divided into two sets: (i) the *decay channels* $\mathcal{D}_1, \ldots, \mathcal{D}_F$, where $F = \Theta(\mathcal{F})$; and (ii) the *report channels* $\mathcal{R}_1, \ldots, \mathcal{R}_{3\alpha(1)}$.

A node v in the decay filter proceeds as follows. First, v spends $\Theta(\log n)$ rounds listening to one of the report channels, chosen at random in each round. If it hears from an MIS node, it halts and becomes dominated.

Otherwise, node v proceeds through $\log n$ phases. In these phases, the nodes use a subset of $F = \Theta(\mathcal{F})$ out of the total $\mathcal{F}$ channels, the "decay channels." Each phase consists of $\Theta\left(\frac{\log n}{F}\right) = \Theta\left(\frac{\log n}{\mathcal{F}}\right)$ rounds, except for the last phase, which consists of $\Theta(\log n)$ rounds.

In each round of each phase, each node listens to one of the report channels with probability $1/2$. If node u is not listening to a report channel and it is in phase j, then u chooses uniformly at random one of the $F = \Theta(\mathcal{F})$ channels $\mathcal{D}_1, \ldots, \mathcal{D}_F$. Then, with probability $\frac{2^j}{4n}$, u transmits on this selected channel and otherwise u listens to this selected channel. Thus, transmission probabilities are exponentially increasing over the phases, going from $\frac{1}{2n}$ to $\frac{1}{4}$.

If a node u transmits in a round, then u immediately exits the decay filter. Moreover, if a node u receives a message on some channel $\mathcal{D}_m$, then u gets knocked out and it restarts the decay filter. If u passes through all the phases without ever transmitting, then u moves to the herald filter.

Analysis. The main difference between the decay filter here and the version in [11] is that the graph model of the present paper is more general. Based on the following weighted version of Turán's theorem it is possible to generalize the analysis from bounded-degree clique partition assumption to general bounded independence graphs.

338

LEMMA 5.1. *Let $G = (V, E)$ be a graph with independence number $\alpha(G)$ and assume that every node $u \in V$ has a positive edge weight $w_u > 0$. Define $W := \sum_{v \in V} w_v$ and for each $u \in V$, $W_u := \sum_{v \in N_G^+(u)} w_v$. urther, let $V_{heavy} \subseteq V$ be the set of nodes v for which $W_v \geq \frac{W}{2\alpha(G)}$. Then,*

$$\sum_{v \in V} \frac{w_v}{W_v} \leq \alpha(G), \qquad \sum_{v \in V} w_v \cdot W_v \geq \frac{W^2}{\alpha(G)}$$

$$and \qquad \sum_{v \in V_{heavy}} w_v > \frac{W}{2\alpha(G)}.$$

LEMMA 5.2. *W.h.p., for all rounds $r \geq 1$ and for all nodes $u \in V$, we have $P_u(r) = O(F) = O(\log n)$.*

PROOF SKETCH. For a round r, let $p_u(r)$ be the transmission probability of node u in round r. Moreover, let $P_u(r) := \sum_{v \in N^1(u)} p_v(r)$. For the sake of contradiction, suppose that $P_u(r)$ exceeds threshold $3cF$ for the first time in round r. It is easy to see that in all rounds $r' \geq r - T$, $P_u(r') \in [cF, 3cF]$, where $T = \Theta(\log n/F)$ is the length of one phase. This is because, in each phase the transmission probability of each node can at most double, and the newly awakened nodes can contribute at most cF. In each such round r', w.v.h.p.(F), for $\Theta(F)$ channels, each of these channels are chosen by a set of nodes from $N^1(u)$ that contribute a probability mass that is on the order of $\Theta(c)$. Similarly, we see that on at least half of these channels, there is no parge probability mass within distance 2. Thus, for each such channel, w.c.p., a single node $v \in N^1(u)$ transmits and no node in $N^2(u)$ interferes. Lemma 5.1 says that the transmitting node itself has a constant chance to be part of a set $S \subseteq N^1(u)$ of nodes, which together contribute a constant fraction to the probability mass on that channel, in which case a constant fraction of the probability mass in $N^1(u)$ on that channel is knocked out. This happens w.c.p. on each of the aforementioned channels, and w.v.h.p.(F) there are $\Theta(F)$ of them. Thus, assuming that the constants in $T = \Theta(\log n/F)$ are sufficiently large, we get that, w.h.p., the probability mass is reduced by at least $1/3$ over the course of T rounds, contradicting our initial assumption. □

It is then easy to show that property (G2) holds:

LEMMA 5.3. *(G2): With high probability, for each node v and each round r, at most $O(\log n)$ nodes in $N_G^1(v)$ come out of the decay filter in round r to enter the herald filter. Each node that enters herald filter has spent $\Omega(\log n)$ rounds in decay filter.*

Property (G3) follows from the structure of the protocol:

LEMMA 5.4. *(G3): W.h.p., for each node u that is in decay filter in round r, by round $r' = r + O\left(\frac{\log^2 n}{F}\right) + \tilde{O}(\log n)$, either u is dominated, in which case it has a dominating neighbor, or at least one node in $N^1(u)$ gets out of decay filter and enters herald filter.*

6. HERALD FILTER ALGORITHM

In this section, we present the herald filter. Detailed pseudo-code can be found in [9]. Recall that, to simplify explanations and ease understanding, we assume $\Omega(\log \log n)$ channels to be available.

The herald filter assumes that in the subgraph induced on the nodes in the filter the degree of each node is always bounded by $\Delta_H = O(\text{polylog } n)$. Given this assumption, the objective of the filter is to find an MIS.

6.1 Algorithm Outline

During the algorithm, each node is in one of 7 states: the *active state* $\mathbb{A}$, the *handshake states* $\mathbb{H}'$ and $\mathbb{L}'$, the *red-blue game* states $\mathbb{H}$ and $\mathbb{L}$, the MIS state $\mathbb{M}$ or the exclusion state $\mathbb{E}$. State $\mathbb{A}$ (*active*) indicates the initial state; state $\mathbb{M}$ indicates that the node is in the MIS (permanently); and $\mathbb{E}$ (*eliminated*) indicates nodes that know of a neighboring MIS node. States $\mathbb{L}'$ (*leader candidate*) and $\mathbb{L}$ (*leader*) are temporary states through which a node v passes to get to state $\mathbb{M}$, while states $\mathbb{H}'$ (*herald candidate*) and $\mathbb{H}$ (*herald*) are accompanying temporary states through which a node u passes to help a neighboring node v to pass through states $\mathbb{L}'$ and $\mathbb{L}$ to get to state $\mathbb{M}$.

In general, a node v can go to state $\mathbb{M}$ (i.e., join the MIS) in two ways: (1) either v does not receive any message for a long time and it joins the MIS assuming it is alone, or (2) v joins the MIS with the help of one of its neighbors u. In the latter case, in order to get to state $\mathbb{M}$, node v goes through states $\mathbb{L}'$ and $\mathbb{L}$, while u goes through states $\mathbb{H}'$ and $\mathbb{H}$ simultaneously. During these states, u helps node v to make sure that no other neighbor of v is trying to join MIS.

Until the state of a node v in herald filter is determined (i.e., until it moves to $\mathbb{M}$ or $\mathbb{E}$), it maintains a counter $lonely(v)$ that measures for how long v has not heard from any neighbors; in addition, it maintains a parameter $\gamma(v)$, called the *activity level*, which is always in $\left[\frac{1}{4\Delta_H}, \frac{1}{2}\right]$ and governs the behavior of v in state $\mathbb{A}$. By definition, we assume that for nodes v in states $\mathbb{M}$ and $\mathbb{E}$ and for nodes v that are not presently in the herald filter, we have $\gamma(v) = 0$.

We divide the filter into 4 parts, depending on whether:

(i) the node is in the active state $\mathbb{A}$ (Section 6.2),
(ii) the handshake states $\mathbb{H}'$ and $\mathbb{L}'$ (Section 6.3),
(iii) the red-blue game states $\mathbb{H}$ and $\mathbb{L}$ (Section 6.4), or
(iv) the MIS state $\mathbb{M}$ (Section 6.5).

6.2 Active State

Consider a node w that is in state $\mathbb{A}$ in round r. In the active state, we use $O(\log \log n)$ channels, divided into three sets:

(i) the *active channels* $\{\mathcal{A}_1, \ldots, \mathcal{A}_{n_\mathcal{A}}\}$, (ii) the *lonely channels* $\{\mathcal{S}_1, \ldots, \mathcal{S}_{n_\mathcal{S}}\}$, and (iii) the *report channels* (see Section 5), where $n_\mathcal{A}, n_\mathcal{S} = O(\log \Delta_H) = O(\log \log n)$. In round r, node w does one of the following three things, with probability $\gamma(w)$ for (a), probability $0.9 - \gamma(w)$ for (b), and probability 0.1 for (c):

(a) Node w picks an active channel using an exponential distribution, choosing channel $\mathcal{A}_j$ with probability 2^{-j}. Then, with a fixed constant probability π_ℓ (chosen in the analysis), w listens to that channel, and with probability $1 - \pi_\ell$, w transmits its *ID* on that channel.

(b) Node w listens to one of the $3\alpha(1)$ report channels chosen uniformly at random.

(c) Node w runs a protocol that we call the *loneliness support block*, and explain later in this subsection.

In (a), if w transmits on a channel $\mathcal{A}_i$ in state $\mathbb{A}$, then w goes to state $\mathbb{L}'$, attempting to become a leader. On the other hand, if w listens and receives a message from a node v, then

w goes to state $\mathbb{H}'$ (while v moves to state $\mathbb{L}'$). Node w will try to help v to become a leader and join the MIS. In (b), if w hears an *ID* with status $\mathbb{M}$ on a report channel, then w is dominated by an MIS node and enters state $\mathbb{E}$ (*eliminated*).

Loneliness Support Block. Each node w maintains a counter *lonely*, to keep track of how long it has been in the herald filter without receiving any messages. Whenever w receives a message from a neighbor (anywhere in the herald filter), it resets the *lonely* counter. If *lonely* exceeds a threshold $\tau_{lonely} = \Theta(\log n \log \log n)$, then node w 'assumes' that it is isolated (i.e., that it does not have any neighbor in the herald filter). In this case, w joins the MIS and moves to state $\mathbb{M}$. Node w may in fact *not* be isolated, since a neighbor can show up later. However, we show in Theorem 7.10 that this is in fact safe.

Every time w executes the loneliness support block, it picks a channel $\mathcal{S}_j$ uniformly at random from the lonely channels. Then w transmits on channel $\mathcal{S}_j$ with probability 2^{-j}; otherwise, it listens to channel $\mathcal{S}_j$. If w receives a message, it resets its *lonely* counter to zero.

Activity Level Adjustment. Now we explain the adjustment of $\gamma(w)$. When w enters the herald filter, $\gamma(w)$ is $\frac{1}{4\Delta_H}$. The value of $\gamma(w)$ is gradually increased by a small constant factor every round, until it reaches the maximal possible value of $1/2$ after $O(\log \log n)$ rounds. The intuitive idea behind this activity level is as follows. Because of nodes waking up asynchronously and the fact that nodes exit the decay filter and enter the herald filter in an asynchronous manner, we need to deal with an undesirable fact: the transmission of the new nodes that enter the herald filter might affect the MIS election process which is going on among the nodes that entered the herald filter a while before that. With the gradual change in the activity level $\gamma(w)$, we can control this undesired effect and keep it below a tolerable level.

Thus, on first entering the herald filter, a node listens most of the time, but eventually, after some $O(\log \log n)$ steps, it spends a constant fraction of its time using the active channels to try to become a leader or a herald.

6.3 The Handshake

Consider a node h that just moved from state $\mathbb{A}$ to state $\mathbb{H}'$ when it received a message from a node ℓ, that has also just entered state $\mathbb{L}'$. Then, h and ℓ perform a 6-round *handshake* on a designated handshake channel $\mathcal{H}$. If this handshake succeeds, then node h moves to state $\mathbb{H}$ and ℓ moves to state $\mathbb{L}$. Otherwise, both return to state $\mathbb{A}$.

The handshake proceeds as follows: In rounds 1 and 2, h transmits the *ID* of ℓ on $\mathcal{H}$, and ℓ listens. If ℓ receives both of these messages successfully, then in rounds 3 and 4, ℓ transmits its *ID* on $\mathcal{H}$, and h listens. In addition, ℓ transmits a *meeting channel*, i.e., a randomly chosen report channel, which is used in the red-blue game (see Section 6.4). Finally, assuming that these messages are received successfully by h, then in rounds 5 and 6, h again transmits the *ID* of ℓ on $\mathcal{H}$ and ℓ listens. If in any of these rounds, either of these nodes does not receive the message that it was supposed to receive, then it considers the handshake failed and returns to state $\mathbb{A}$.

Each of the 3 transmissions in the handshake is repeated twice in order to synchronize properly with the red-blue game and the nodes in the MIS. Nodes in these later states broadcast in every other round. By requiring two consecutive successful rounds of the handshake, we can be sure that there is no concurrent red-blue game or neighboring MIS node.

Note that it is possible for ℓ to consider the handshake failed due to not receiving a message in round 5 or 6, while h assumes that the handshake was performed successfully. This situation is detected in the first 6 rounds of the red-blue game.

It is easy to see that one of the necessary conditions for a handshake between some $v \in \mathbb{L}'$ and $u \in \mathbb{H}'$ to be successful is that h must be the only herald candidate trying to perform a handshake with ℓ at that time. Hence, the nodes that enter states $\mathbb{H}$ and $\mathbb{L}$ can be viewed as *leader-herald pairs*.

6.4 The Red-Blue Game

Ideally, we would like the leaders to form an independent set (and to also be independent of nodes in $\mathbb{M}$). This would allow us to send the leaders directly to the MIS. However, this is not always the case as multiple leaders can be adjacent. The goal of the red-blue game is to detect such bad leaders (i.e., adjacent leaders) and *knock them out*, back to state $\mathbb{A}$, along with their heralds.

For this purpose, we use a simple algorithm which we call the *red-blue game*. The red-blue game uses a designated channel $\mathcal{G}$, along with the handshake channel $\mathcal{H}$ and the report channels.

A single red-blue game is a 6-round protocol that is executed by a leader-herald pair (ℓ, h). During each game, it is possible that the pair is *knocked out*, meaning that both nodes go back to state $\mathbb{A}$. If the pair finishes $\Theta(\log n)$ red-blue games without getting knocked out, then ℓ assumes that it does not have an adjacent leader and joins the MIS.

The 6 rounds of a red-blue game are as follows: In rounds 1, 3 and 5 of the game, both ℓ and h transmit on the handshake channel $\mathcal{H}$. These transmissions block channel $\mathcal{H}$ so that adjacent nodes cannot perform a successful handshake and thus, no new adjacent leader-herald pair can be created until either ℓ joins the MIS or the pair is knocked out.

The main rounds of the game are rounds 2 and 4. In both rounds, h broadcasts ℓ's *ID* on channel $\mathcal{G}$. ℓ picks a random color in the set $\{red, blue\}$ at the beginning of the 6-round protocol. In round 2, if ℓ chose *red*, then it transmits its *ID* on channel $\mathcal{G}$, and if it chose *blue*, it listens to $\mathcal{G}$. In round 4, the behavior is reversed: ℓ listens if it chose *red* and it transmits if it chose *blue*.

Each time ℓ is listening to channel $\mathcal{G}$, by default, it should receive the message of h. If ℓ does not receive that message, it means that another node is also transmitting on channel $\mathcal{G}$ — either a leader, another herald or an MIS node. If this happens, ℓ gets knocked out.

In round 6, ℓ transmits on the meeting channel, while h listens on it. The content of the sent message is whether the red-blue game succeeded (i.e., whether ℓ detected any collisions) and the meeting channel for the next red-blue game chosen uniformly at random among the report channels (for the first red-blue game, the meeting channel is fixed during the handshake). If h does not receive a message from ℓ indicating that the game succeeded, then h gets knocked out. (Notice that h may not receive such a message due to a collision, in which case ℓ gets knocked out in the next red-blue game when it fails to receive a message from h.) Note that the nodes that are knocked out go back to state $\mathbb{A}$ only after they have finished the 6 rounds of their red-blue game.

The objective of the even rounds is that if two leaders are adjacent and act synchronously (round-wise), then with probability $1/2$, *both* leaders get knocked out. This is because if both leaders choose different colors *red* and *blue*, then they fail to receive the message from their respective heralds in rounds 2 and 4. Thus, if a leader-herald pair passes the red-blue game $O(\log n)$ times, then,w.h.p., there is no synchronized neighboring leader.

In the analysis, we show that because of the handshake rules, there are only very few configurations for two leader-herald pairs to be adjacent. Basically either the two leaders or the two heralds neighbor each other and operate synchronously, or if the leader of one and the herald of another pair are neighboring, then their starts of the red-blue games are shifted by exactly 2 rounds. When combined with the properties of the red-blue game, this ensures that only one leader moves on to the MIS.

6.5 The MIS State

Nodes in the MIS state need to continue to broadcast to prevent neighboring nodes from joining the MIS. This is accomplished by broadcasting with constant probability on $\mathcal{H}$, $\mathcal{G}$ and the report channels. More specifically, each node v that is in state $\mathbb{M}$ (i.e., that has joined MIS) performs one of the following two steps: (i) If v did not broadcast its *ID* on channel $\mathcal{H}$ in the previous round, then it does so in the current round. (ii) If v did broadcast on channel $\mathcal{H}$ in the previous round, then with probability:

a. $1/2$ it broadcasts its *ID* and status on channel $\mathcal{H}$,
b. $1/4$ it broadcasts its *ID* and status on channel $\mathcal{G}$,
c. $1/4$ it broadcasts its *ID* and status on channel $\mathcal{R}_k$, with k chosen uniformly at random in $\{1, \ldots, 3\alpha(1)\}$.

Case (a) blocks any ongoing handshakes. Case (b) knocks back neighboring leaders to state $\mathbb{A}$, preventing the red-blue game from succeeding. Case (c) knocks back neighboring heralds to state $\mathbb{A}$, and also eliminates neighboring nodes in state $\mathbb{A}$, causing them to move to $\mathbb{E}$. These ongoing broadcasts ensure that we satisfy guarantee (G1) introduced in Section 4.

Note that channel $\mathcal{H}$ is blocked at least once every two rounds. Thus, after v has been in state $\mathbb{M}$ for 6 rounds, no new neighbors of v can switch to state $\mathbb{L}$. On the other hand, note that in every period of two rounds, with constant probability, v transmits once on channel $\mathcal{G}$. The transmissions on channel $\mathcal{G}$ knock back adjacent leaders that might have been created when (or immediately after) v switched to state $\mathbb{M}$ due to the *lonely* counter. Finally, the transmissions on the report channels let the neighboring nodes of v know that they are dominated by v, causing them to halt. Note that those transmissions can also knock back neighboring heralds to state $\mathbb{A}$.

7. HERALD ANALYSIS

Here, we present and overview of the analysis of the herald filter. For detailed proofs we refer to [9].

7.1 The Analysis of the Active State

We first present some facts about the transitions of nodes from state $\mathbb{A}$ to states $\mathbb{L}'$ and $\mathbb{H}'$. We show that for the k-neighborhood of some node u, the probability that no node in $N^k(u)$ is being elected as a herald candidate (switching from state $\mathbb{A}$ to $\mathbb{H}'$) is constant, and, by adjusting π_ℓ, arbitrarily close to 1. We then give some conditions under which

the creation of a single herald candidate happens with constant probability.

DEFINITION 7.1. *(**Activity Sum**) or a node u we define $\Gamma(u) := \sum_{v \in N^1(u)} \gamma(v)$. We call this the activity sum or activity mass of node u.*

LEMMA 7.2. *ix a constant positive integer k. or any round t and node u, with probability $1 - O(\pi_\ell \alpha(k))$, no node $v \in N^k(u)$ switches from state $\mathbb{A}$ to state $\mathbb{H}'$ in round t.*

PROOF SKETCH. For the proof we solely focus on non-isolated nodes in the graph $G_{\mathbb{A}}$ induced by nodes in state $\mathbb{A}$. For a node v to become a herald candidate it has to receive a message from one of its neighbors w (event $B^{v,w}$). Careful analysis of those events gives us that the probability that v receives a message from *any* neighbor on channel $\mathcal{A}_m$ is at most $\pi_\ell 2^{-2m+2} \gamma(v) \Gamma(v) e^{-2^{-m-1}\Gamma(v)}$. This probability is maximized on channel $\mathcal{A}_\lambda$ for $\lambda :\approx \log \Gamma(v)$ (or $\lambda := 1$ if $\Gamma(v) < 1$) where the probability is $O\left(\pi_\ell \frac{\gamma(v)}{\Gamma(v)}\right)$. The probability falls rapidly as we move away from channel $\mathcal{A}_\lambda$. A union bound over all $v \in N^k(u)$, combined with Lemma 5.1, gives the desired result. $\square$

DEFINITION 7.3. *(**Fatness**) We call a node u (or respectively its neighborhood $N(u)$) η-fat for some value $\eta > 0$, if it holds that $\Gamma(u) \geq \eta \cdot \max_{v \in N(u)}\{\Gamma(v)\}$.*

LEMMA 7.4. *Let t be a round in which for a node u in state $\mathbb{A}$ in the herald filter it holds that there is no herald, leader, or herald candidate in $N^2(u)$. urthermore, all neighbors of MIS nodes in $N^2(u)$ are in state $\mathbb{E}$, $\Gamma(u) \geq 1$, and either*

(a) $\Gamma(u) < 3\alpha(1)$, u is $\frac{1}{3\alpha(1)}$-fat, and $\gamma(u) = \frac{1}{2}$, or

(b) u is $\frac{1}{2}$-fat and $\Gamma(u) \geq 3\alpha(1)$.

Then by round $t' \in [t, t + 7]$, with probability $\Omega(\pi_\ell)$ either a node in $N^2(u)$ joins the MIS or a pair $(l, h) \in \mathbb{L} \times \mathbb{H}$ is created in $N^1(u)$ such that $(N(\{l, h\}) \setminus \{l, h\}) \cap (\mathbb{H} \cup \mathbb{H} \cup \mathbb{L}) = \emptyset$.

PROOF SKETCH. The proof is much more delicate, but partially follows the lines of the proof of Lemma 7.2. First we make sure that w.c.p. either in round t or $t + 1$ in $N^1(u)$ nodes contributing a constant fraction to $\Gamma(u)$ are in state $\mathbb{A}$, including u itself. Then we first lower bound the probability that some nodes $v, w \in N_{\mathbb{A}}^1(u)$ in that round meet alone on some channel and no other nodes nearby receive a message there. For case (a) we analyze the probability that this event happens for channel $\mathcal{A}_1$ and manage to lower bound it by $\Omega(1)$. For case (b) we use Lemma 5.1 to ensure the existence of neighbors v of u with high activity levels in u's and v's joint neighborhoods. Here we choose channel $\mathcal{A}_\lambda$ with $\lambda :\approx \log \Gamma(u)$ and show that for the previously mentioned neighbors the probability of meeting someone from $N^1(u)$ is in $\Omega\left(\frac{\gamma(v)}{\Gamma(u)}\right)$. Lemma 5.1 also gives us a lower bound of how much activity levels such neighbors provide and in total we can prove that exactly one of u's neighbors v meets another node w on $\mathcal{A}_\lambda$ is in $\Omega(1)$. Lemma 7.2 gives us a $1 - O(\pi_\ell)$ probability that no herald candidate is created at all. Lower bounding the probability that no herald candidate is created on a different channel than $\mathcal{A}_\lambda$ and combining this with the previous results gives the creation of a single herald candidate in round t resp. $t + 1$. Lemma 7.2 applied to the remaining rounds in $[t, t + 7]$ finishes the proof. $\square$

7.2 The Analysis of the Handshake

In the following lemma, we study the circumstances under which two adjacent leader-herald pairs can coexist.

LEMMA 7.5. *In round r consider two leader-herald pairs (l_1, h_1) and (l_2, h_2) and suppose that the pairs started their most recent handshakes in rounds r_1 and r_2, $r_1 \leq r_2$, respectively. Say that edge e is* crossing *if one of its endpoints is in $\{l_1, h_1\}$ and its other endpoint is in $\{l_2, h_2\}$. Then, either no crossing edge exists or exactly one of the following conditions is satisfied: (1) $r_1 = r_2$ and crossing edges are $\{l_1, l_2\}$ and/or $\{h_1, h_2\}$, (2) $r_2 = r_1 + 2$ and the only crossing edge is $\{l_1, h_2\}$.*

7.3 The Analysis of the Red-Blue Game

We next study the exact guarantees of when and how pairs get knocked out in the red-blue games.

DEFINITION 7.6. *(Maturity) We say that candidate v is* mature *in round t, if v is in round 5 or 6 of its respective handshake.*

DEFINITION 7.7. *(Good Pair, Bad Pair) Consider a leader-herald pair (l, h) in round t. We say pair (l, h) is a* good pair *if in round t none of the neighbors of l (other than h) is in state $\mathbb{L}$, $\mathbb{H}$ or is a mature candidate. Otherwise we say that (l, h) is a* bad pair.

LEMMA 7.8. *If a pair (l, h) is good in round t and they started their first red-blue game in round r, then, w.h.p., either*

- *the related leader l joins the MIS by the end of round $r + \tau_{red-blue} = r + O(\log N)$, or*
- *a node $v \in N(l) \cup N(h)$ joins the MIS before round $r + \tau_{red-blue} = r + O(\log N)$ by increasing its lonely counter above τ_{lonely}.*

LEMMA 7.9. *Consider a node v and suppose that in an arbitrary round t, there is a leader or herald of a bad pair in $N^3(v)$. Then, with constant probability, in round $t + 12$, no node in $N^3(v)$ is in state $\mathbb{H}'$ and all leaders and heralds are part of a good pair.*

PROOF SKETCH. First we look at the leaders (or leaders-to-be) that are *not* neighboring other leaders. The pairs related to these leaders either become good or the leaders neighbor heralds of other pairs. Those leaders form an independent set, thus, their amount is limited. W.c.p., all of them choose the wrong color in their respective red-blue game which causes them to be kicked out by those heralds. Second we look at leaders that have other leaders nearby, which by Lemma 7.5 have to by completely synchronized. If we just look at the graph induced by these leaders (synced to one specific round), then we can find two disjoint independent sets S and T, and by adding at most $O(1)$ further nodes to T we get that each such leader either is in S or T and neighbors at least one node of the other, or it has each a neighbor in each of those sets. If all nodes in S choose blue and all nodes in T choose red, which happens w.c.p., then all nodes get kicked out in their red-blue game. $\square$

7.4 The Analysis of the MIS State

Here we present the main safety guarantee of our MIS algorithm.

LEMMA 7.10. *W.h.p., the nodes in state $\mathbb{M}$ always form an independent set. Moreover, if a node v enters state $\mathbb{M}$ in round t and a node $w \in N(v)$ is awake in round t, then in round $t' = t + O(\log n)$, w.h.p., w is in state $\mathbb{E}$.*

7.5 Putting the Pieces Together

In this section, we wrap everything up to show that guarantees (G1), (G4) and (G5) hold. Together with the guarantees (G2) and (G3) handled in Section 5 we finalize the proof of Theorem 4.1.

Lemma 7.10 immediately proves (G1) for all nodes currently in the herald filter. All nodes in the decay filter, both at the beginning as well as during the main body part, listen to the report channels w.c.p. in every round. Thus, either they learn of a neighboring MIS node within $O(\log n)$ rounds, or they move forward to the herald filter in that time bound. In the latter case, after that transition, Lemma 7.10 takes care of those nodes.

Lemma 7.10 also immediately gives us (G5). The only thing that remains to be shown is the progress guaranteed by (G4). To do so, we use the following lemma.

LEMMA 7.11. *Consider two neighboring nodes u and v such that both are in the herald filter at time t and assume that no node in $N(u) \cup N(v)$ has joined the MIS by time t. Then, w.h.p., some node u' in the $O(\log \log N)$-neighborhood of u joins the MIS between times t and $t + O(\log N)$.*

We now sketch how to obtain guarantee (G4). A node u in the herald filter in round r does not leave the herald filter before becoming dominating or dominated. If u has no neighboring nodes in the herald filter for $O(\log n \log \log n)$ consecutive rounds, u joins the MIS. Also, u can only have $\alpha(2)$ periods in which it is alone and where MIS nodes in $N^2(u)$ have already eliminated their neighbors. Each such period starts when some neighbor in the herald filter gets eliminated by a new MIS node in distance 2 from u. Whenever u has a neighbor in the herald filter Theorem 7.11 implies that within $O(\log n)$ rounds, w.h.p., a new MIS node is created in the $O(\log \log n)$-neighborhood of u. Clearly this can only happen $O(\alpha(\log \log n)) = O(\text{polyloglog } n)$ times and thus after $O(\log(n)\alpha(\log \log n))$ rounds, either u or one of its neighbors is dominating and thus guarantee (G4) is satisfied.

8. OTHER PROBLEMS

In this section, we use our MIS algorithm solution as a building block in solving other problems efficiently in the multichannel environment. Our main technical result is a new algorithm that uses the MIS solution as a subroutine to build a constant-degree connected dominating set (CDS) in $O\left(\frac{\log^2 n}{\mathcal{F}}\right) + \tilde{O}(\log n)$ rounds. We then use this structure as an overlay to derive solutions to broadcast and leader election that run in $O\left(D + \frac{\log^2 n}{\mathcal{F}}\right) + \tilde{O}(\log n)$ rounds, and to k-message multi-broadcast that runs in $O\left(D + k + \frac{\log^2 n}{\mathcal{F}}\right) + \tilde{O}(\log n)$ and $O\left(D + k \log n + \frac{\log^2 n}{\mathcal{F}}\right) + \tilde{O}(\log n)$ rounds for unrestricted and restricted message sizes, respectively.

Connected Dominating Set. First, we show how to construct a constant-degree CDS in $O\left(\frac{\log^2 n}{\mathcal{F}}\right) + \tilde{O}(\log n)$ rounds. At a high-level: our solution builds an MIS then connects every pair of MIS nodes that are within 3 hops using a constant-length path. The result is a constant-degree

CDS (see [7]). We provide a brief description of the algorithm here. See [9] for further details.

Special care must be taken to deal with two factors related to the transition of nodes from the MIS stage to the CDS stage: (1) MIS nodes must keep revisiting the MIS algorithm to prevent newly activated nodes from joining the MIS; (2) since nodes might end the MIS stage at different rounds, they might also start the CDS stage at different rounds, causing synchronization issues (the CDS stage cycles through fixed-length phases). In [9], we detail our strategy for addressing these issues. For concision, in the summary below, assume that nodes start the CDS stage in the same round and MIS nodes do not revisit the MIS algorithms.

The CDS stage consists of repeatedly iterating four phases made of six total rounds. During the first phase, an MIS node broadcasts on a designated *CDS channel* with constant probability. This announcement notifies nearby neighbors of its existence, informs them that a new iteration is beginning, and sends out a random sequence of bits, the *coin sequence*, that is used to synchronize neighbors in the remaining rounds of the iteration. It also includes a list of nearby MIS nodes (that it knows about so far) and (short) paths to these nodes. Any node that learns that it is on such a path adds itself to the CDS. Also during this phase, any non-MIS node that is already in the CDS broadcasts a message with constant probability in the announcement phase on the CDS channel, propagating its information about the currently selected paths. (Once an MIS node selects a path, this allows the information to propagate down the path.)

Rounds 2 and 3 are the *search phase*. To reduce contention, a non-MIS node u broadcasts in this phase only if there is a single MIS neighbor w that has a 1 in its coin sequence for this round. Otherwise it will only receive. In round 2, which handles sparse regions, a node broadcasts the *ID* of MIS node w on the CDS channel: in each iteration, it cycles through the $\log \log n$ probabilities $\{\frac{1}{2}, \frac{1}{4}, \ldots, \frac{1}{\log n}\}$. In round 3, which handles dense regions, a node chooses a channel $c \in [\log n]$ with probability 2^{-c} (i.e., as in the herald protocol from the MIS algorithm), and then broadcasts MIS node w with constant probability. In both search rounds, a non-broadcaster listens on the CDS channel (round 2), or a channel chosen uniformly from $[\log n]$ (round 3). If a node learns about a new MIS node, it adds it to the set of *discovered* MIS nodes.

The remaining rounds 4–6 are the *report phase*. If a non-MIS node u has discovered a new MIS node (and a path to this node), and if u has a single MIS neighbor w with a 1 in its coin sequence for this round, then u will report to w. In round 3, it broadcasts its new knowledge on the CDS channel with constant probability. In round 5, it chooses channel $c \in [\log n]$ with probability 2^{-c} and then broadcasts its new information with constant probability. If u decides to listen and it receives a message it then acts as a herald for this message, rebroadcasting it on the CDS channel with constant probability in the next round.

The basic argument is as follows: imagine two MIS nodes u and z are connected by a two-hop path. in this case they have a neighbor in common, and will learn about each other in a subsequent report phase. Assume, on the other hand, they are connected by a three-hop path. Let V be the neighbors of u and let W be the neighbors of z. If some node $w \in W$ has only a few neighbors in V (i.e., $< \log n$), then w receives a message from V during the sparse search phase

rounds within $O(\log \log n)$ rounds, with constant probability. The same holds symmetrically if some node $v \in V$ has only a few neighbors in W. Otherwise, if every node $w \in W$ has at least $\log n$ neighbors in V, and every node $v \in V$ has at least $\log n$ neighbors in W, then, with constant probability, during the dense search phase rounds where W nodes are broadcasting but not V nodes, there will be a single broadcaster from W on some channel with at least one listener from V. This information will be relayed to u in subsequent report phases. This leads to the following conclusion:

THEOREM 8.1. *We can construct a constant-degree CDS in $O\left(\frac{\log^2 n}{\mathcal{F}}\right) + \tilde{O}(\log n)$ rounds, w.h.p.*

The problems below use a CDS as an overlay network. To best match the typical assumptions for these problems, we will assume synchronous starts i.e., the CDS algorithm starts and ends at the same rounds for all nodes. Our algorithms all work without this assumption as well, requiring in this case only that the theorem statements be rewritten to guarantee their running time holds *after the first round in which a complete CDS is constructed.*

Broadcast. First, build a constant-degree CDS using the above algorithm. Then, the source delivers the message to its CDS neighbors. On receiving the message, a CDS node re-broadcasts it with constant probability in each round. Because the CDS nodes have constant degree, a standard Chernoff analysis shows the message will reach every CDS node in $O(D + \log n)$ rounds (and therefore every node within $O(\log n)$ more rounds), w.h.p. Combined with the running time of the CDS algorithm, the total running time is $O\left(D + \frac{\log^2 n}{\mathcal{F}}\right) + \tilde{O}(\log n)$ rounds, nearly reaching the $\Omega\left(D + \frac{\log^2 n}{\mathcal{F}}\right)$ centralized lower bound for the multi-channel setting [16]. Formally:

THEOREM 8.2. *We can solve the problem of global broadcast in $O\left(D + \frac{\log^2 n}{\mathcal{F}}\right) + \tilde{O}(\log n)$ rounds, w.h.p.*

Multi-Message Broadcast. The multi-message broadcast problem assumes k messages must be propagated to the entire network. As before, first build a constant-degree CDS. We then use the same logic as the report phase of the CDS algorithm to propagate the k messages from their sources to nearby CDS nodes. This routine uses $\log n$ channels and can deliver all k messages to nearby nodes in $O(k + \log n)$ rounds, w.h.p. Once the messages are in the CDS, how we propagate depends on our assumption on message size. For unrestricted message size, we can run the above simple broadcast algorithm, simply combining all messages a node has received into a single message, in each round. This requires $O(D + \log n)$ rounds to propagate all k once we have our CDS. If we assume restricted message size (i.e., $O(\text{poly}(\log n))$ bits), we can use the algorithm and analysis of [21]. As established in [21], this will require $O(D + k \log n)$ rounds (formally, F_{prog} in the relevant theorem is $O(1)$ while F_{ack} is $O(\log n)$). From this we conclude:

THEOREM 8.3. *It is possible to solve k-multi-broadcast in time $O\left(D + k + \frac{\log^2 n}{\mathcal{F}}\right) + \tilde{O}(\log n)$ with unrestricted messages sizes, and in $O\left(D + k \log n + \frac{\log^2 n}{\mathcal{F}}\right) + \tilde{O}(\log n)$ rounds with restricted message sizes, w.h.p.*

Leader Election. To elect a leader, run the broadcast algorithm with *all* nodes initiating broadcast with a message containing their own *ID*, and having each node update its broadcast message in each round to include the largest *ID* it has received so far. Using a standard Chernoff analysis, we can show that the largest *ID* will propagate to all nodes within $O(D + \log n)$ rounds. Formally:

THEOREM 8.4. *W.h.p., leader election can be solved in* $O\left(D + \frac{\log^2 n}{F}\right) + \tilde{O}(\log n)$ *rounds.*

9. REFERENCES

[1] I. 802.11. Wireless LAN MAC and Physical Layer Specifications, June 1999.

[2] N. Alon, L. Babai, and A. Itai. A Fast and Simple Randomized Parallel Algorithm for the Maximal Independent Set Problem. *Journal of Algorithms*, 1986.

[3] N. Alon, A. Bar-Noy, N. Linial, and D. Peleg. A Lower Bound for Radio Broadcast. *Journal of Computer and System Sciences*, 43(2):290–298, 1991.

[4] R. Bar-Yehuda, O. Goldreich, and A. Itai. On the Time-Complexity of Broadcast in Multi-Hop Radio Networks: An Exponential Gap Between Determinism and Randomization. *J. Computer and System Sciences*, 45(1):104–126, 1992.

[5] L. Barenboim, M. Elkin, S. Pettie, and J. Schneider. The Locality of Distributed Symmetry Breaking. In *Proc. 53rd Symp. on oundations of Computer Science (OCS)*, pages 321–330, 2012.

[6] Bluetooth Consortium. *Bluetooth Specification Version 2.1*, July 2007.

[7] K. Censor-Hillel, S. Gilbert, F. Kuhn, N. Lynch, and C. Newport. Structuring Unreliable Radio Networks. In *Proc. 30th Symp. on Principles of Distributed Computing (PODC)*, pages 79–88, 2011.

[8] I. Chlamtac and S. Kutten. On Broadcasting in Radio Networks–Problem Analysis and Protocol Design. *IEEE Transactions on Communications*, 33(12):1240–1246, 1985.

[9] S. Daum, M. Ghaffari, S. Gilbert, F. Kuhn, and C. Newport. Maximal independent sets in multichannel radio networks. Technical Report 275, University of Freiburg, Department of Computer Science, 2013.

[10] S. Daum, S. Gilbert, F. Kuhn, and C. Newport. Leader Election in Shared Spectrum Networks. In *Proc. Symp. on Principles of Distributed Computing (PODC)*, pages 215–224, 2012.

[11] S. Daum, F. Kuhn, and C. Newport. Efficient Symmetry Breaking in Multi-Channel Radio Networks. In *Proc. 26th International Symposium on Distributed Computing (DISC)*, pages 238–252, 2012.

[12] S. Dolev, S. Gilbert, R. Guerraoui, D. R. Kowalski, C. Newport, F. Kuhn, and N. Lynch. Reliable Distributed Computing on Unreliable Radio Channels. In *the Proceedings of the 2009 Mobi oc S³ Workshop*, 2009.

[13] S. Dolev, S. Gilbert, R. Guerraoui, F. Kuhn, and C. Newport. The Wireless Synchronization Problem. In *Proceedings of the Principles of Distributed Computing*, pages 190–199, 2009.

[14] S. Dolev, S. Gilbert, R. Guerraoui, and C. Newport. Gossiping in a Multi-Channel Radio Network: An Oblivious Approach to Coping with Malicious Interference. In *Proc. Symp. on Distributed Computing (DISC)*, 2007.

[15] S. Dolev, S. Gilbert, R. Guerraoui, and C. Newport. Secure Communication Over Radio Channels. In *Proc. Symp. on Principles of Distributed Computing (PODC)*, 2008.

[16] S. Dolev, S. Gilbert, M. Khabbazian, and C. Newport. Leveraging Channel Diversity to Gain Efficiency and Robustness for Wireless Broadcast. In *Proc. Symp. on Distributed Computing (DISC)*, 2011.

[17] A. Ephremides, J. E. Wieselthier, and D. J. Baker. A Design Concept for Reliable Mobile Radio Networks With Frequency Hopping Signaling. *Proc. of the IEEE*, 75(56–73), 1987.

[18] M. Farach-Colton, R. J. Fernandes, and M. A. Mosteiro. Lower Bounds for Clear Transmissions in Radio Networks. In *Proc. Latin American Symposium on Theoretical Informatics*, 2006.

[19] S. Gilbert, R. Guerraoui, D. Kowalski, and C. Newport. Interference-Resilient Information Exchange. In *Proc. Conf. on Computer Communication (IN OCOM)*, 2009.

[20] T. Jurdzinski and G. Stachowiak. Probabilistic Algorithms for the Wakeup Problem in Single-Hop Radio Networks. In *Proc. Int. Symp. on Algorithms and Computation*, pages 535–549, 2002.

[21] F. Kuhn, N. Lynch, and C. Newport. The Abstract MAC Layer. In *Proc. Symp. on Distributed Computing (DISC)*, 2009.

[22] F. Kuhn, T. Moscibroda, T. Nieberg, and R. Wattenhofer. Fast Deterministic Distributed Maximal Independent Set Computation on Growth-Bounded Graphs. In *Proc. 19th International Symposium on Distributed Computing (DISC)*, 2005.

[23] M. Luby. A Simple Parallel Algorithm for the Maximal Independent Set Problem. *SIAM Journal on Computing*, 15(4):1036–1053, 1986.

[24] T. Moscibroda and R. Wattenhofer. Maximal Independent Sets In Radio Networks. In *Proc. 24th Symp. on Principles of Distributed Computing (PODC)*, pages 148–157, 2005.

[25] C. Newport. *Distributed Computation on Unreliable Radio Channels*. PhD thesis, MIT, 2009.

[26] S. Schmid and R. Wattenhofer. Algorithmic Models for Sensor Networks. In *Proc. 14th Int. Workshop on Parallel and Distributed Real-Time Systmes*, pages 1–11, 2006.

[27] J. Schneider and R. Wattenhofer. A Log-Star Distributed Maximal Independent Set Algorithm for Growth-Bounded Graphs. In *Proc. Symp. on Principles of Distributed Computing (PODC)*, pages 35–44, 2008.

[28] M. Strasser, C. Pöpper, and S. Capkun. Efficient Uncoordinated FHSS Anti-jamming Communication. In *Proc. Symp. on Mobile Ad oc Networking and Computing (MOBI OC)*, 2009.

[29] M. Strasser, C. Pöpper, S. Capkun, and M. Cagalj. Jamming-resistant Key Establishment using Uncoordinated Frequency Hopping. In *the Proceedings of the IEEE Symposium on Security and Privacy*, 2008.

The Cost of Radio Network Broadcast for Different Models of Unreliable Links*

Mohsen Ghaffari
MIT CSAIL
Cambridge, MA
ghaffari@csail.mit.edu

Nancy Lynch
MIT CSAIL
Cambridge, MA
lynch@csail.mit.edu

Calvin Newport
Georgetown University
Washington, DC
cnewport@cs.georgetown.edu

ABSTRACT

We study upper and lower bounds for the global and local broadcast problems in the dual graph model combined
with different strength adversaries. The dual graph model
is a generalization of the standard graph-based radio network model that includes unreliable links controlled by an
adversary. It is motivated by the ubiquity of unreliable links
in real wireless networks. Existing results in this model [11,
12, 3, 8] assume an *offline adaptive* adversary—the strongest
type of adversary considered in standard randomized analysis. In this paper, we study the two other standard types
of adversaries: *online adaptive* and *oblivious*. Our goal is
to find a model that captures the unpredictable behavior
of real networks while still allowing for efficient broadcast
solutions.

For the online adaptive dual graph model, we prove a
lower bound that shows the existence of constant-diameter
graphs in which both types of broadcast require $\Omega(n/\log n)$
rounds, for network size n. This result is within log-factors
of the (near) tight upper bound for the offline adaptive
setting. For the oblivious dual graph model, we describe
a global broadcast algorithm that solves the problem in
$O(D \log n + \log^2 n)$ rounds for network diameter D, but
prove a lower bound of $\Omega(\sqrt{n}/\log n)$ rounds for local broadcast in this same setting. Finally, under the assumption of
geographic constraints on the network graph, we describe a
local broadcast algorithm that requires only $O(\log^2 n \log \Delta)$
rounds in the oblivious model, for maximum degree Δ. In
addition to the theoretical interest of these results, we argue
that the oblivious model (with geographic constraints) captures enough behavior of real networks to render our efficient
algorithms useful for real deployments.

*Research supported in part by: Ford Motor Company Uni-
versity Research Program; AFOSR Contract No. FA9550-
13-1-0042; NSF Award No. CCF-1217506; NSF Award No.
0939370-CCF; NSF Award No. CCF-AF-0937274; AFOSR
Contract No. FA9550-08-1-0159; NSF Award No. CCF-
0726514.

Categories and Subject Descriptors

C.2.1 [**Network Architecture and Design**]: Wireless Communication; G.2.2 [**Discrete Mathematics**]: Graph Theory—*network problems*

Keywords

radio network; broadcast; dual graph; unreliability

1. INTRODUCTION

Most models used to study algorithms for wireless networks assume *static* links between devices; i.e., the strength
of each link remains fixed throughout an execution. This assumption is captured by these models' use of deterministic
rules for determining when a message is received. Given a
set of transmitters, the receive behavior is fixed. This property is true, for example, of the graph-based *protocol* model
(e.g., [4, 2]) and SINR-based *physical* model (e.g., [16]).[1] In
real wireless networks, by contrast, links are rarely static.
Changes to the environment, interference from unrelated
protocols on overlapping spectrum, and even shifting weather
conditions can all cause links to exhibit *dynamic* fluctuations
in strength (e.g., [18]).

To succeed in establishing a mathematical foundation for
the design and analysis of practical wireless network algorithms, the theory community needs to consider wireless
models that include dynamic links. A recent series of papers
takes up this challenge by studying global broadcast [11, 12],
local broadcast [8], and graph algorithms [3] in the context
of the *dual graph* model—a generalization of the graph-based
protocol model that includes both static and dynamic links.

A defining feature of the dual graph model is that an adversary controls the behavior of the dynamic links (as previously argued [11, 12, 3, 8], simpler assumptions, such as
independent loss probabilities, do a poor job of capturing
the unpredictable and sometimes highly-correlated nature of
dynamic behavior in real networks). Applying the standard
terminology from randomized analysis, this existing work
on the dual graph model assumes an *offline adaptive adversary*. This adversary type—sometimes also called *strongly
adaptive*—can use the execution history and the nodes' random choices for a given round before fixing the link behavior.
This definition is strong and therefore, perhaps not surprisingly, most existing radio network results proved with re-

[1]SINR-based models include a *noise parameter*, N,
which in theory could be determined on a per-link basis and potentially change over time. In practice, however, it is almost
always treated as a fixed constant.

spect to this adversary type are negative. They show, for example, that both global and local broadcast (defined below) require $\Omega(n)$ rounds [11, 12] in constant-diameter graphs of size n. This is exponentially worse than the $\Theta(\log^2 n)$ round solution of the static protocol model [2, 8]. These lower bounds are not entirely satisfying as they leverage adversary behavior—such as basing link behavior on the outcome of private random choices—that is unrealistically pessimistic.

In this paper, we take the natural next step and derive new upper and lower bounds for global and local broadcast in the dual graph model combined with the two successively weaker adversary types typically considered in randomized analysis: *online adaptive* and *oblivious*. Motivated by the importance of these broadcast problems, our goal is to find a model that can capture the unpredictable behavior of real networks, yet still allow efficient broadcast solutions.

In more detail, the online adaptive adversary—sometimes also called *weakly adaptive*—can use the execution history when deciding the link behavior for a given round, but does not know the nodes' random choices for the round. The oblivious adversary must make all decisions at the beginning of the execution.

The global broadcast problem requires a designated source node to disseminate a message to the entire network. This is arguably the most studied problem in the radio model (see [17]) due to its importance to both theory (it isolates the fundamental difficulty of this setting—multihop contention) and practice (solutions provide key synchronization and search capabilities in real networks). Local broadcast assumes a subset of nodes are provided broadcast messages to deliver to their neighbors in the network graph. In this paper, we focus only on the time for each receiver (i.e., node neighboring a broadcaster) to receive *some* message.[2] This property proves crucial when analyzing local broadcast as a subroutine (e.g., [9]). In addition, this form of the problem reduces to most nontrivial problems in the radio setting as most problems require some communication between nearby nodes to break symmetry. Therefore, lower bounds on local broadcast can extend to many other problems.

Results for the Online Adaptive Dual Graph Model: We begin by proving that there exists a constant-diameter graph of size n such that both global and local broadcast required $\Omega(n/\log n)$ rounds in this graph in the online adaptive dual graph model. Our lower bound uses a simulation-based reduction from an abstract game that leverages the adversary's knowledge of expected behavior.[3]

Results for the Oblivious Dual Graph Model: For the oblivious setting, we first describe a global broadcast algorithm that runs in $O(D \log n + \log^2 n)$ rounds, for network diameter D, which essentially matches the best known results in the static protocol model [2, 10, 7]. The core insight driving this algorithm is that the source can generate a set of random bits after the execution begins (e.g., bits unknown to the adversary) and then include them in the source mes-

sage. Nodes that have received the message can use the bits to coordinate their probabilistic broadcast behavior. For local broadcast, however, we establish a $\Omega(\sqrt{n}/\log n)$ lower bound. This bound counters the coordination strategy of global broadcast by using the graph topology to isolate key nodes.

Results for the Oblivious Dual Graph Model with Geographic Constraints: Under the assumption of a geographic constraint that generalizes the unit disk graph model (a natural assumption for wireless settings), we describe an algorithm that solves local broadcast in $O(\log^2 n \log \Delta)$ rounds, for maximum degree Δ. This result is only a log-factor slower than the optimal $\Theta(\log n \log \Delta)$ result in the static protocol model [2, 8]. The algorithm use a more involved version of the coordination strategy from our global broadcast bound that leverages the geographic constraint to achieve local coordination. In Figure 1, we summarize all the above results and compare them to existing work.

Contributions.

From a theory perspective, these results provide a complete characterization of broadcast in unreliable radio networks with respect to the classic adversary types—identifying the key relationships between adversary power and the efficiency of these important primitives. From a practical perspective, we argue that our efficient upper bounds for the oblivious adversary are well-suited for real world deployment. The oblivious model can capture the unpredictable behavior observed in real networks. At the same time, its obliviousness to the algorithm's ongoing execution is a tolerable concession, as the adversary is playing the role of environmental forces that are independent of the protocols running in the network. Our best algorithms, therefore, can provide practitioners significantly more robustness without sacrificing efficiency.

Related Work.

The static graph-based radio network model was introduced by Chlamtac et al. [4], and has since been extensively studied (see [17] for examples). In this paper, following recent naming conventions, we call it the *protocol* model. Bar-Yehuda et al. [2] described a randomized distributed broadcast solution that runs in $O(D \log (n) + \log^2 n)$ rounds in the protocol model. This result was later slightly improved to $O(D \log (n/D) + \log^2 n)$ rounds [10, 7], which is optimal [1, 15]. For local broadcast, a slight tweak to the strategy of [2] provides a local broadcast solution the runs in $O(\log n \log \Delta)$ rounds [8]. The dual graph model was introduced by Clementi et al. [5], where it was called the *dynamic fault* model. We independently reintroduced the model in [11] with the *dual graph* name. In this model combined with an offline adaptive adversary, global and local broadcast now require $\Omega(n)$ rounds, even in constant diameter graphs [11]. The closest matching upper bounds require $O(n \log^2 n)$ rounds for global broadcast [12], $O(n)$ rounds for local broadcast.[4] See Figure 1 for a summary of these results and how they compare to the new results in this paper. Other problems, including building graph structures [3] and deterministic broadcast [13] have also been studied in the dual graph model with this strong adversary. A related lit-

---

[2] The other property studied with respect to these algorithms is the time for a sender to successfully deliver its message to all its receivers. We do not study that property here because we recently proved a strong lower bound in the static protocol model, leaving us no gap to close in our dual graph variants [8].

[3] We note that a similar bound was independently discovered, using a different method, by Cornejo, Ghaffari, and Haeupler. Their version is unpublished.

---

[4] Local broadcast can always be solved in $O(n)$ rounds using round robin broadcasting on the n node ids.

	Global Broadcast	Local Broadcast
DG + Offline Adaptive	$\Omega(n)$ [11] / $O(n\log^2 n)$ [13]	$\Omega(n)$ [11] / $O(n\log n)$ [8]
DG + Online Adaptive	$\Omega(n/\log n)$	$\Omega(n/\log n)$
DG + Oblivious	$O(D\log n + \log^2 n)$	General Graphs: $\Omega(\sqrt{n}/\log n)$ Geo. Graphs: $O(\log^2 n \log \Delta)$
No Dynamic Links	$\Theta(D\log\left(\frac{n}{D}\right) + \log^2 n)$ [10, 1, 15]	$\Theta(\log n \log \Delta)$ [2, 8]

Figure 1: All results in the second and third rows are new results proved in this paper. Existing results are described in the first and last rows along with the relevant citations.

erature studies distributed algorithms in the *dynamic network* model, in which the entire communication topology can change from round to round under different constraints (see [14] for a good survey). These results, however, assume reliable communication among neighbors in each round. The dynamic model studied in this paper, by contrast, assumes concurrent communication yields collisions—making it well-suited for describing radio networks. The exception is the work of Clementi et al. [6], which studies a dynamic network model that preserves the standard radio network collision rules. In this model, they show a tight bound of $\Theta(n^2/\log n)$ rounds for solving broadcast with a strong adversary constrained only to keep the graph connected in a useful manner in each round.

2. MODEL AND PROBLEMS

We define the *dual graph* model, which describes randomized algorithms executing in a synchronous multihop radio network with both static and dynamic links. The model describes the network topology with two graphs on the same vertex set: $G = (V, E)$ and $G' = (V, E')$, where $E \subseteq E'$, and the $n = |V|$ nodes in V correspond to the wireless devices. An *algorithm* in this model consists of n randomized *processes*. An execution of an algorithm in a given network (G, G') begins with an adversary assigning each process to a node in the graph. This assignment is unknown to the processes. To simplify notation, we use the terminology *node u*, with respect to an execution, to refer to the process assigned to node u in the graph in a given execution. Executions then proceed in synchronous rounds. In each round r, each node decides whether to transmit a message or receive based on its randomized process definition. The communication topology in r consists of the edges in E plus *some subset* of the edges in $E' \setminus E$. This subset, which can change from round to round, is determined by an adversary that we call a *link process* (see below). Once a topology is fixed for a given round, we use the following communication rules: a node u receives a message m from v in r, if and only if: (1) u is receiving; (2) v is transmitting m; and (3) v is the only node transmitting among the neighbors of u in the communication topology *fixed by the link process for* r. Notice, the dual graph model is a strict generalization of the static protocol model. In more detail: for $G = G'$, the model is the same as the protocol model described with respect to topology G.

For a given $G' = (V, E')$ and $u \in V$, we use $N_{G'}(u)$ to describe the neighbors of u in E', and define $\Delta = \max\{|N_{G'}(u)| : u \in V\}$. We assume n and Δ are known to processes in advance. Some of our bounds require a geographic constraint on the G and G'. In these cases, we assume the same constraint introduced in [3], which itself is a generalization of

the *unit disk graph* property. In more detail, our constraint assumes the existence of a constant $r \geq 1$, such that we can embed the nodes in our graph in a Euclidean plane with distance function d, and, $\forall u, v, u \neq v$: if $d(u, v) \leq 1$ then (u, v) is in G, and if $d(u, v) > r$, (u, v) is not in G'. This constraint says that close nodes can communicate, far away nodes cannot, and for nodes in the *grey zone* in between, the behavior is dynamic and unpredictable. We call a dual graph network topology that satisfies this property a *geographic graph*.

Adversary Types.

In our model, the choice of which edges from $E' \setminus E$ to include in the communication topology each round is determined by an adversary called a link process. In this paper, we study the three classical definitions of such adversaries from the randomized analysis literature: offline adaptive, online adaptive, and oblivious. In more detail, the *offline adaptive* link process, when making a decision on which links to include in a given round r, can use knowledge of: the network topology; the algorithm being executed; the execution history through round $r - 1$; and the nodes' random choices for round r. The *online adaptive* link process weakens this definition such that it no longer learns the nodes' random choices in r before it makes its link decisions for r. The *oblivious adversary*, by contrast, must make all of its link decisions at the beginning of the execution—though it can still make use of the network topology and algorithm description in generating this behavior.

In this paper, when we refer to the "⟨*adversary type*⟩ *dual graph model*", we mean the dual graph model combined with link processes that satisfy the ⟨*adversary type*⟩ constraints.

Global and Local Broadcast.

We study the global and local broadcast problems. The global broadcast problem assumes a designated source node is provided a message. The problem is solved when it has disseminated the message to the entire network. The local broadcast problem assumes some subset of nodes $B \subseteq V$ are provided a message. Let R be the set of nodes with at least one neighbor in B by G. The problem is solved when every node in R has received at least one message from a neighbor in B. Both problems assume G is connected. When we say a randomized algorithm solves one of these problems, we require that it solves it with high probability (i.e., probability at least $1 - 1/n$).

3. ONLINE ADAPTIVE DUAL GRAPH MODEL

Previous work proved the existence of constant-diameter graphs where both global and local broadcast require $\Omega(n)$ rounds in the offline adaptive dual graph model [11]. Here we prove a similar bound holds when we weaken the adversary to the online adaptive model. This result demonstrates that the difficulty of broadcasting in an adaptive dual graph model is not dependent on the strong assumption that the link process knows random choices in advance. Formally:

THEOREM 3.1. *There exists a constant-diameter dual graph network such that every algorithm requires $\Omega(n/\log n)$ rounds to solve global and local broadcast in this network in the on-line adaptive dual graph model.*

The proof of our theorem reduces an abstract game, called *β-hitting*, to broadcast. We show that an efficient broadcast solution allows a player to efficiently win the *β*-hitting game by simulating the solution in a specific type of constant-diameter network we call *dual clique*. We then leverage an existing bound on *β*-hitting to bound broadcast in the dual clique network.

The β-Hitting Game: The game is defined for integer $\beta > 0$. There is a player represented by a probabilistic automaton $\mathcal{P}$. At the beginning of the game, an adversary chooses a *target* value, $t \in [\beta]$, which it keeps secret from the player. The $\mathcal{P}$ automaton executes in rounds. In each round, it can output a guess from $[\beta]$. The player wins the game when $\mathcal{P}$ outputs t. The only information it learns in other rounds is that it has not yet won the game. In previous work [11], we bound this game as follows:

LEMMA 3.2 (ADAPTED FROM [11]). *Fix some $\beta > 3$ and $k, 1 \le k \le \beta - 2$. There does not exist a player that solves β-hitting in k rounds with probability greater than $k/(\beta - 1)$.*

The Dual Clique Network: Partition the n nodes in V into two equal sized sets, A and B. Connect the nodes in A (resp. B) to form a clique in G. Connect a single node $t_A \in A$ to a single node $t_B \in B$, forming a *bridge* between the two cliques. Let G' be the complete graph over all nodes. Notice, this graph has constant diameter. It is also a geographic graph (which strengthens our lower bound).

We now proceed with the proof of our main theorem:

PROOF OF THEOREM 3.1. Fix some broadcast algorithm $\mathcal{A}$. The bulk of our proof is dedicated to proving the following claim: if $\mathcal{A}$ solves either global or local broadcast in $f(n)$ rounds, then we can construct a player $\mathcal{P}_\mathcal{A}$ that solves the β-hitting game in $O(f(2\beta)\log\beta)$ rounds, with probability at least $1 - 1/\beta$. Once established, our theorem statement follows directly from this claim and Lemma 3.2: if $f(n) = o(n/\log n)$, then $\mathcal{P}_\mathcal{A}$ would solve β-hitting in $o(\beta)$ rounds with probability at least $1 - 1/\beta$—violating Lemma 3.2 which established the necessity of $\Omega(\beta)$ rounds to achieve this success probability.

We proceed argue the following claim. Our strategy is to have $\mathcal{P}_\mathcal{A}$ simulate a collection of 2β nodes in a dual clique network of size $n = 2\beta$. The player uses the behavior of the simulated nodes to specify its guesses for the hitting game. Below, we begin by describing the network it simulates, then its rules for determining guesses, and finally we prove these rules solve the game with the needed time complexity.

Simulated Network: To simulate nodes in the dual clique network the player must assign the processes to nodes in the graph. In more detail, let $\{1, ..., 2\beta\}$ be the ids of the $n = 2\beta$ nodes we simulate. The player places nodes 1 to β in clique A and $\beta + 1$ to 2β in clique B. Let t be the target for this instance of the hitting game. The network the player will

simulate assigns node t to t_A and $t + \beta$ to t_B. That is, the nodes on either side of the bridge have their ids correspond to the target for the hitting game. Of course, *the player does not know t in advance*, but we will prove that its simulation remains consistent with this particular instantiation of the dual clique network. For the remainder of the proof, we call this assignment of ids to the dual clique network our *target* network.

Guess Generation Rules: We now describe how to connect the player's simulation of the target network with its guesses or the β-hitting game. Fix some simulated round. The player begins by simulating the broadcast behavior of its simulated nodes in this round. If $\mathcal{A}$ is a global broadcast algorithm, it assumes that node $1 \in A$ is the global broadcast message source; if it is local broadcast, it puts all nodes in A in the broadcast set. Based on this broadcast behavior, the player will generate a series of guesses for the hitting game. If none of these guesses solve the game, it will then finish its simulation of the round by simulating the receive behavior, and then moving on to the next simulated round. Therefore, every simulated round generates a variable number of hitting game guesses. Here we describe how it uses the simulated broadcast behavior to generate its guesses. In the next piece of the proof we will describe how it simulates the receive behavior if its guesses fail.

Let X_A be the nodes from A that broadcast in our simulated round, and let X_B be the nodes from B that broadcast in the round. Let $X = X_A \cup X_B$. Finally, let S be the state of the nodes at the *beginning* of this round. This state includes the execution history through $r - 1$, but does not include the random bits the nodes will use in round r. It captures the information an online adaptive link process can use to make link decisions in this round. We have our player calculate the expected value of $|X|$ given S. If $\mathbb{E}[|X| \mid S] > c\log\beta$, for a constant $c \ge 1$ which we will fix later, then the player labels the round *dense*, otherwise it labels the round *sparse*.

Now we are ready to generate our guesses. If the round is dense and, once the player simulates the broadcast behavior, $X = \{i\}$: then the player guesses, one by one, all values from 1 to β (guaranteeing that it will win the hitting game). If the round is dense and $|X| \ne 1$: then the player makes no guesses. If the round is sparse: the player guesses the ids in X, one by one, subtracting β from the ids in $X \cap X_B$ to transform them into values in $[\beta]$. In other words, the player's guesses are a combination of the *expected* and *actual* broadcast behavior in the simulated round.

Simulating Receive Behavior: If none of the guesses generated with the above process win the hitting game, the player must now conclude its simulated round by simulating the receive behavior in a manner that is valid for our target network and the online adaptive link process constraints. To do so, the player must first decide which edges from $G' \setminus G$ to include in the communication topology (that is, it plays the role of the link process). In our simulation, the player uses the rule to determine this decision: if the rounds in dense, it includes all G' edges in the topology; if the round is sparse, it includes no G' edges between A and B. At this point, we must be careful to confirm that these link process decision made by the player satisfy the constraints of an online adaptive link process. If, for example, the player used more information than is allowed by an online adaptive link process, it would be simulating a network more difficult than what is expected by $\mathcal{A}$ and therefore $\mathcal{A}$ is not required to work correctly. As mentioned above, however, an online adaptive link process *is* able to determine if a round is dense or sparse as this requires only the state at the beginning of the round, not the random choices made during the round.

After fixing the G' topology, the link process has almost enough information to simulate the receive behavior. The only piece of the graph topology it is missing is the edge between in G between t and $t+\beta$ (as it does not know t, it does not know the endpoints of this edge). Our approach is to have the player simulate receive behavior under the assumption that there is *no* edge in G between A and B. We will later argue that the behavior it simulates in this incomplete network is consistent with what would occur in our target network that includes this edge between the cliques.

Proving the Validity of the Simulation: We now argue by induction on the simulated round number that this simulation remains a valid simulation of $\mathcal{A}$ in our target network until the player wins the hitting game. For our hypothesis, assume that the first $r > 0$ rounds of the simulation are valid, and the player has not yet won the hitting game. For our step, we will show that in simulated round $r + 1$, either the player wins the hitting game or this round is also valid.

By our inductive hypothesis, we know the broadcast behavior simulated at the beginning of round $r + 1$ is valid. If the corresponding guesses win the hitting game, we are done. Assume, therefore, that the guesses do not win. We consider the possible cases for the simulated receive behavior and argue all case are valid for our target network.

If the round is dense, then we know $|X| \neq 1$ (if $|X| = 1$ then the player would have guesses all values and won the game in the preceding guess phase). In this case, the player would simulate no messages being received, as the G' edges included in the topology make it a complete graph (if multiple messages broadcast, all receive a collision). The fact that the player did not know the edge between t and $t + \beta$ does not matter here.

If the round is sparse, then the player simulates receive behavior as if the two cliques are isolated in the communication topology. This receive behavior will be the same as in our target network (which includes an edge between t and $t + \beta$) if neither t nor $t + \beta$ broadcast. On the other hand, if t or $t + \beta$ *do* broadcast, our simulated receive behavior would no longer necessarily be valid. However, in this case, we would have guessed t during the preceding guesses and won the hitting game.

Proving that a Valid Simulation Wins the Hitting Game: Having established that our simulation is valid, we must now argue that a valid simulation of our broadcast algorithm will lead our player to eventually win the game. By assumption, $\mathcal{A}$ solves either local or global broadcast in the dual clique network with any online adaptive link process. Because we argued that our simulation of $\mathcal{A}$ is valid, it too will eventually solve broadcast (or win the hitting game before it gets a chance to finish). Notice, if $\mathcal{A}$ solves broadcast, it follows that at least one message must pass between A and B. (Recall from above: for global broadcast, we put the source in A, and for local broadcast, we placed all nodes in A, including the endpoint of the bridge, in the broadcast set.) Given the link process behavior used in our simulation, there are only two cases where this is possible: (1) a round in which just a single node broadcasts; or (2) a sparse round in which t or $t + \beta$ broadcast. In both cases, when we get to such a round, we will guess t and win the game.

Bounding the Number of Guesses Per Simulated Round: Because $\mathcal{A}$ solves broadcast with high probability, we have established that our player simulating $\mathcal{A}$ will also solve the game with high probability. In particular, with probability at least $1 - 1/(2\beta)$ (we are substituting 2β for n in the definition of high probability). Our final step is to bound *how long* this takes. We know that $\mathcal{A}$ finishes in $f(2\beta)$ rounds. But because we can have multiple guesses per simulated round, the number of rounds required by our player to win the hitting game might be much longer. We will show that with sufficient probability the player never need more than $O(\log \beta)$ guesses per simulated round.

Returning to the guessing rules, we see that there are two cases where the player might have to guess multiple values for a given simulated round. The first case is occurs when only a single node broadcasts during a dense round. If this occurs, then the player guesses all β values. Recall, however, that if a round is dense, then $\mathbb{E}[|X| \mid S] > c \log \beta$. For a sufficiently large constant c, we can apply a Chernoff bound to prove that the probability that there is 1 node broadcasting is less than $1/(2\beta)^4$.

The second case with multiple guesses occurs when the round is sparse. In this instance, all broadcasters are guessed. For a sparse round, however, the expected number of broadcasters is low; i.e., $\mathbb{E}[|X| \mid S] \leq c \log \beta$. Plugging in the c we used for case 1, there exists some other smaller constant c' such that the probability there are more than $c' \log \beta$ broadcasters in a sparse round is also less than $1/(2\beta)^4$. By a union bound, the probability we have to guess more than $c' \log \beta$ values in a given round is less than $1/(2\beta)^3$. We can assume w.l.o.g. that our broadcast algorithm requires no more than $(2\beta)^2$ rounds,[5] so by another union bound, the probability that we have too many broadcasters in *any* simulated round is bounded by $1/(2\beta)$.

We can now piece together our two failure probabilities. We know that $\mathcal{A}$ solves global broadcast in $f(n)$ rounds with probability at least $1 - 1/n$. Therefore, it will solve broadcast in our target network in $f(2\beta)$ rounds with probability at least $1 - 1/(2\beta)$. It follows that it fails to solve broadcast with probability no more than $1/(2\beta)$. As shown above, it fails to bound its guesses per round to $O(\log \beta)$ also with probability no more than $1/(2\beta)$. Therefore, the probability that it solves the game in $O(f(2\beta) \log \beta)$ rounds, is at least $1 - 1/(2\beta) + 1/(2\beta) = 1 - 1/\beta$, as required by our claim. $\qquad\square$

4. OBLIVIOUS DUAL GRAPH MODEL

Having just proved that broadcast cannot be solved efficiently in the online adaptive setting, we turn our attention to the oblivious dual graph model. As argued in the introduction, this model is important because the adversary is powerful enough to replicate the unpredictable behavior of real radio networks. Upper bounds proved in this model, therefore, should still hold in real deployment.

4.1 Global Broadcast Upper Bound

We begin by describing an algorithm that solves global broadcast in $O(D \log n + \log^2 n)$ rounds in the oblivious dual graph model. Notice, this bound matches the well-known solution of Bar-Yehuda et al. [2] in the protocol model. In fact, our new upper bound is based on the classic result

---

[5]We can always solve broadcast among 2β nodes in $(2\beta)^2$ rounds by doing round robin broadcast 2β times.

of [2]. This existing global broadcast algorithm is based on a *decay* subroutine that has nodes with the message cycle (in a coordinated manner) through the $\log n$ probabilities: $\{1/2, 1/4, ..., 2/n, 1/n\}$. For each potential receiver, one of these probabilities is appropriate for the number of broadcasters it neighbors. This strategy works well for advancing the message in the protocol model, but it can be attacked by an oblivious adversary because the fixed schedule of broadcast probabilities allows it to calculate in advance the expected broadcast behavior, and choose dynamic link behavior accordingly (as the online adaptive adversary did in our bound from Section 3). In our new protocol, we sidestep this attack by having the source generate random bits at the beginning of the execution, and then append them to the broadcast message. Nodes that have received the message can use these bits to permute the order in which they visit the decay probabilities. From the perspective of the adversary, these permutations are random, thwarting his attack. The formal description follows (to simplify notation, we assume that log is base-2 and n is a power of 2):

Permuted Decay Subroutine.

The *permuted decay* subroutine, used by our global broadcast algorithm, is called with a broadcast message m, a string S of $\gamma \log n \log \log n$ *permutation bits*, and an integer parameter $\gamma \geq 1$. The routine runs for $\gamma \log n$ rounds. During each round, it selects a value $i \in [\log n]$ using $\log \log n$ new bits from S. It then broadcasts m with probability 2^{-i}.

Global Broadcast Algorithm.

Our global broadcast algorithm works as follows. The source, provided message m', creates a new message $m = \langle m', S \rangle$, where S is a collection of $32 \log^2 n \log \log n$ bits generated with uniform and independent randomness *after* the execution begins. In the first round, the source broadcasts m to its neighbors. At this point, the source's role in the broadcast is finished. For every other node u, on first receiving a message $\langle m', S \rangle$ in round r, it waits until the first round $r' \geq r$, where r' mode $16 \log n = 0$, and then calls *permuted-decay*$(m, 16, s)$, $2 \log n$ times in a row, where each time s includes $16 \log n \log \log n$ new bits from S.

THEOREM 4.1. *The algorithm described above solves global broadcast in $O(D \log n + \log^2 n)$ rounds in the oblivious dual graph model.*

To prove our theorem, we note that our global broadcast algorithm is the same as the algorithm in [2] with the exception that we replaced decay with permuted decay. Fortunately, the existing proof from [2] treats the decay subroutine as a black box, requiring only that a node receives a message from some broadcasting neighbor with probability greater than 1/2 after each call to the subroutine. To prove our above theorem, therefore, it is sufficient to prove that the same property holds for permuted decay. We accomplish this with the below lemma (which, technically, replaces part *ii* of Theorem 1 of [2]):

LEMMA 4.2. *Fix some node u, constant $\gamma \geq 16$, message m, string s of $16 \log n \log \log n$ bits generated with uniform and independent randomness after the execution begins, and sets I_G and $I_{G'}$, where I_G is a non-empty subset of u's G neighbors and $I_{G'}$ is a subset of u's G' neighbors. Assume the nodes in $I = I_G \cup I_{G'}$ call* permuted-decay(m, γ, s) *during*

the same round and all other neighbors of u remains silent. Node u will receive m from a node in I during this instance of permuted-decay *with probability greater than 1/2.*

PROOF. Fix some round r during the decay instance. Let $I_r \subseteq I$ be the subset of nodes in I connected to u in the topology selected by the oblivious link process for this round. Notice, by definition $I_G \subseteq I_r$, so $I_r \neq \emptyset$. If $|I_r| > 1$, then let our *target* $i' = \lfloor \log |I_r| \rfloor$. Otherwise, let $i' = 1$. All nodes that called decay will select the same i as they all use the same permutation bits from m to select i. By assumption, the choice of i is random and, because the bits were generated after the execution begins, independent of I. Therefore, with probability at least $1/\log n$, $i = i'$.

In a round where $i = i'$, we can bound the probability p_u that u receives a message from I, as follows: $p_u = \sum_{v \in I_r} \frac{1}{2^{i'}} (1 - \frac{1}{2^{i'}})^{|I_r \setminus \{v\}|} > \frac{|I_r|}{2^{i'}} (\frac{1}{4})^{\frac{|I_r|}{2^{i'}}} \geq \frac{1}{16}$.

For the final step of the reduction, we note that $i' \in (\log |I_r|/2, \log |I_r|]$, and used the largest possible value for i' for the first term and the smallest for the second, to ensure we end up with a lower bound.

Combining our two observations, we see that u receives the message in any given round with probability greater than $1/(16 \log n)$ Therefore, the probability that it fails for γ consecutive rounds of the subroutine is bounded as $(1 - \frac{1}{16 \log n})^{\gamma \log n} < e^{-\gamma/16} < 1/2$ as required by our lemma. □

4.2 Local Broadcast Lower Bound

The strategy used by our global broadcast upper bound in Section 4.1 does not directly apply to the local broadcast setting, as we can no longer assume that all nodes needing to broadcast are coordinated by a common broadcast message. Here we show that *no* strategy can achieve efficient local broadcast in the oblivious model, by proving a $\Omega(\sqrt{n}/\log n)$ lower bound. This result establishes a strict separation between these two problems in this model:

THEOREM 4.3. *There exists a dual graph network such that every algorithm requires $\Omega(\sqrt{n}/\log n)$ to solve local broadcast in this network in the oblivious dual graph model.*

We use the same proof structure (and much of the proof argument) from our lower bound for the online adaptive model in Section 3. That is, we reduce the β-hitting game to solving local broadcast in a particular type of dual graph network, by showing how solve β-hitting by simulating a local broadcast algorithm in this network. Because we have a weaker adversary, however, our task is complicated. We are now required to use a different network type and more involved simulation strategy.

The Bracelet Network: Select from among the n nodes two non-intersecting subsets of $\sqrt{n/2}$ nodes each: $A = \{a_1, a_2, .., a_{\sqrt{n/2}}\}$ and $B = \{b_1, b_2, .., b_{\sqrt{n/2}}\}$. As in the dual clique network, connect some $a_t \in A$ to some $b_t \in B$ in G. For each $a_i \in A$, construct a line of length $\sqrt{n/2}$ that contains a_i, labeling the nodes as $a_i, a_{i,2}, a_{i,3}, ..., a_{i,\sqrt{n/2}}$. Connect each consecutive pair in the line in G. Do the same for each b_i in B (now labeling the nodes $b_i, b_{i,2}, b_{i,3}$, and so on). We call each such line a *band*. Because we require our graphs to be connected in G, also connect the endpoints of these bands (i.e., each node labelled $a_{i,\sqrt{n/2}}$ or $b_{i,\sqrt{n/2}}$) into a clique in G. Finally, add G' edges between every pair

$(a_i, b_j), a_i \in A, b_j \in B$. Notice, this yields $2(\sqrt{n/2})^2 = n$ total nodes. We call this network a *bracelet* network, as it is defined by $\sqrt{n/2}$ bands in G edge, which are connected at one end by a single G edge (between a_t and b_t), forming a clasp.

Isolated Broadcast Functions: Our reduction argument leverages the following insight: nodes in A and B must behave independently of each other until common information can reach both. Due to the length of their bands, this takes a while. During this time, therefore, an oblivious adversary can do a good job of estimating their broadcast behavior. To formalize this strategy, we define a *support sequence* to be a bit sequence of sufficient size to contain all the bits needed for the nodes in a band in the bracelet network to resolve their random choices for $\sqrt{n/2}$ rounds. We can represent this information as a bit string of length $(\delta n)/2$, where δ is the maximum number of random bits needed by a node in a single round (δ bits per round for $\sqrt{n/2}$ rounds for $\sqrt{n/2}$ nodes in a band yields $(\delta n)/2$ total bits). We also say an execution of an algorithm in the bracelet network is *isolated* with respect to a node $u \in A \cup B$ through round $r > 0$, if node u only receives messages from its neighbor in the band through the first r rounds.

Leveraging these definitions, we prove the existence of a useful formalism:

LEMMA 4.4. *Fix some algorithm $\mathcal{A}$ and node $u \in A \cup B$ from the bracelet network. We can construct an isolated broadcast function $f_{\mathcal{A},u} : \{0,1\}^{(\delta n)/2} \times \{1, ..., \sqrt{n/2}\} \to \{0,1\}$ that satisfies the following property: for any support sequence γ and round $r \leq \sqrt{n/2}$: $f_{\mathcal{A},u}(\gamma, r) = 1$ if and only if node u would broadcast in round r of an isolated execution where u's band uses the random bits described by γ.*

PROOF. We can construct $f_{\mathcal{A},u}$ by simulating node u in the bracelet network as follows: For a given γ and r, we can calculate $f_{\mathcal{A},u}(\gamma, r)$ by running an r round simulation of nodes in u's band, where: in the first round of the simulation, initialize all nodes in u's band with the first round bits from γ; in the second round, simulate nodes $u, u_2, u_3, ..., u_{\sqrt{n/2}-1}$; in the third, $u, u_2, u_3, ..., u_{\sqrt{n/2}-2}$; and so on, until round r. The simulated behavior of u in round r determines the output of the broadcast function for that round. This approach drops each node from the simulation right before its externally observable behavior (e.g., messages sent) could possibly be influenced by a node from outside the band (recall that the definition of our network connects the endpoints of the bands together in a clique). We can only maintain the simulation for $\sqrt{n/2}$ rounds, because, at that point, information from outside u's band could have made it u, affecting its behavior in a way we cannot capture in a simulation that know only about the behavior of the band. $\square$

The key property regarding isolated broadcast functions is that they are independent. That is, the behavior of one function provided a randomly generated support sequence is independent of the behavior of another function provided a different randomly generated support sequence. This independence is a direct consequence of the graph topology (and would be impossible to achieve if we had to satisfy a geographic constraint). The following lemma proves, therefore, that calling these functions multiple times with different random bits should generate similar outcomes:

LEMMA 4.5. *Fix a constant $x \geq 1$ and an array F of $k \geq 1$ isolated broadcast functions. Construct two arrays S_1 and S_2, each consisting of k support sequences generated with uniform and independent randomness. For $r \in [\sqrt{n/2}]$, let $Y_r^1 = \sum_i^k F[i](S_1[i], r)$ and $Y_r^2 = \sum_i^k F[i](S_2[i], r)$. The following two properties hold with probability at least $1 - n^{-x}$: For every $r \in [\sqrt{n/2}]$: (1) if $Y_r^1 > 16(x+1)\ln n$ then $Y_r^2 \geq 2$; and (2) if $Y_r^1 \leq 16(x+1)\ln n$ then $Y_r^2 \leq 64(x+1)\ln n$.*

PROOF. Consider some isolated broadcast function $F[i]$ and round r, $i \in [k], r \in [\sqrt{n/2}]$. Notice that for a randomly generated support sequence γ, $F[i](\gamma, r)$ behaves as an indicator variable X_i where $Pr[X_i = 1] = p_i$ and $Pr[X_i = 0] = 1 - p_i$, for some probability p_i we can determine based on the definition of the broadcast function. Crucially, we note that X_i and X_j, for $i \neq j$, defined with independent support sequences, are independent. Let $Y = \sum_i^k X_i$; i.e., the outcome of a trial where we call each function in F with a randomly generated support seqeuence. Notice that Y_r^1 and Y_r^2 describe the value of Y for two different trials. To prove our theorem statement, therefore, it is sufficient to show that it is unlikely that Y will differ by too much between any pair of trials. We turn to Chernoff to aid in this effort. To simplify notation, in the following, let $c = 16(x+1)$.

We begin by bounding the probability that property 1 fails to hold. Let $\mu = \mathbb{E}[Y]$. There are two cases to consider. In the first case, μ is closer to Y_r^1 then Y_r^2. It follows that $\mu > (c/2)\ln n$ and Y_r^2 is less than half the expectation. A Chernoff Bound tells us that: $Pr[Y_r^2 < (1/2)\mu] \leq e^{(-\mu)/8} < e^{(-c/16)\ln n} = n^{-(x+1)}$.

The second case is where μ is closer to Y_r^2 then Y_r^1. Here, we know $\mu \leq (c/2)\ln n$ and Y_r^1 is at least a factor of 2 greater than the expectation. Applying a Chernoff Bound to this direction tells us that: $Pr[Y_r^1 \geq 2\mu] \leq e^{(-\mu)/3} < e^{(-c/6)\ln n} < n^{-(x+1)}$.

In other words, for any given round r, the probability that we violate property 1 is no more than $n^{-(x+1)}$. A union bound over $\sqrt{n/2}$ rounds gives us a final probability of failure in at least one round that is less than n^{-x}, as needed.

The argument for property 2 proceeds symmetrically, except now our μ is bounded around $2c\ln n$ in our argument. This only decreases the probability of violating the properties, so the final probability upper bound of n^{-x} still holds. $\square$

Now we are ready to prove our main theorem:

PROOF OF THEOREM 4.3. At a high-level, we apply the same argument as in Theorem 3.1. If $\mathcal{A}$ terminates quickly in the bracelet network, then we can create a player $\mathcal{P}_{\mathcal{A}}$ that simulates $\mathcal{A}$ in this network, to solve the β-hitting game quickly. The bound on β-hitting from Lemma 3.2 provides our bound for $\mathcal{A}$. Instead of recreating the entire proof from Theorem 3.1, we will focus here only where things differ.

In more detail, the player simulates in $\mathcal{A}$ in the bracelet network with a_t and b_t corresponding to the hitting game guess. It will use the behavior of nodes in its simulation to determine guesses for the hitting game. The player does not know a_t and b_t, but, as in the previous proof, we will show that this lack of knowledge does not matter, as the player will win the hitting game before this piece of the topology can affect its simulation.

In simulating each round of $\mathcal{A}$, the player must simulate the oblivious link process. To do so, it first constructs the isolated broadcast functions corresponding to all $2\sqrt{n/2}$

351

nodes in $A \cup B$ (as in Lemma 4.4). Let F be an array of these functions. It then generates, with uniform and independent randomness, a support sequence for each function. Let S be the array consisting of these $2\sqrt{n/2}$ support sequences, one for each function in F. Using F and S, the player then labels each of the first $\sqrt{n/2}$ rounds as *dense* or *sparse* as follows: if the number of functions in F that output 1 in the round, when called with the sequences in S, is greater than $c \ln n$ (for some constant c we will define later), then the round is dense, otherwise it is sparse.

Once these labels are determined the player chooses the topology and generates as in the proof of Theorem 3.1. Notice, the simulation of the link process here satisfies the constraints of an oblivious adversary, as the isolated support functions can be constructed and simulated for all rounds before the execution begins. We are arguing, in other words, that the behavior of these functions (which capture the broadcast behavior of nodes in $A \cup B$) cannot change much based on the random bits supplied as input (which correspond to the random choices of nodes in a particular execution). This allows an oblivious adversary to simulate the behavior of these specific nodes, for a constrained number of rounds, before the execution begins.

Applying Lemma 4.5, we can show that, with high probability, that for the first $\sqrt{n/2}$ rounds: if multiple nodes in $A \cup B$ broadcast if the round was dense, and $O(\log n)$ broadcast if the round was sparse. These are the key properties needed by the argument in Theorem 3.1 to prove that: (a) the player never needs more than $O(\log n)$ hitting game guesses per simulated round; and (b) the player's lack of knowledge of a_t and b_t will not affect the validity of is simulation in any round before it has won the hitting game. We conclude the proof by selecting our constants carefully such that, after the needed union bounds, we end up with sufficiently high probability as success (see the full version of the proof of Theorem 3.1 for an example of working through these values). □

4.3 Local Broadcast Upper Bound

In Section 4.2, we proved a negative result: $\Omega(\sqrt{n}/\log n)$ rounds are necessary to solve local broadcast in the oblivious model. Notice, however, that this proof argument relied on local neighborhoods with large independence numbers—a property that is unlikely to occur in topologies generated by omnidirectional wireless broadcast. With this in mind, we assume in this section the geographic constraint defined in Section 2. Under this constraint, we describe an algorithm that solves the problem in $O(\log^2 n \log \Delta)$ rounds, which is within a log-factor of the optimal solution in the static protocol model.

Local Broadcast Algorithm.

Our algorithm executes in two stages: *initialization* and *broadcast*. The initialization stage locally disseminates shared randomness to coordinate nearby nodes. The broadcast stage uses these shared bits to efficiently solve local broadcast.

In more detail, the initialization stage divides rounds into $\log \Delta$ *phases*, each consisting of $O(\log^2 n)$ rounds. All nodes begin the stage *active*. During the first round of a given phase $i \in [\log \Delta]$, each node that is still active elect itself a *leader* with probability $2^{-(\log \Delta - i + 1)}$ (i.e., we use the probabilities: $1/\Delta, 2/\Delta, ..., 1/4, 1/2$, as the phases advance). Each

leader then generates a *seed* consisting of $O(\log^3 n(\log \log n)^2)$ bits, selected with uniform and independent randomness. It then *commits* to this seed. During the remaining $O(\log n)$ rounds of the phase, each leader broadcasts its seed in each round with probability $1/\log n$. At the end of the phase, the leaders become *inactive*. Any node that was active but *not* a leader during the phase, and that received at least one seed, will commit to the first seed it received and become inactive as well. The only nodes remaining for the next phase, therefore, are those that were active, not a leader, and did not receive a seed message. If a node ends the initialization stage still active, it generates its own seed and commits to it. Therefore, at the end of this stage, all nodes have committed.

The broadcast stage has each node in B (e.g., node with a message to broadcast to its neighbors) execute the permuted decay subroutine from Section 4.1, $O(\log^2 n)$ times in a row. We call each call to decay an *iteration*. For each iteration, each node in B (i.e., node with a local broadcast message) decides to participate in the iteration with probability $1/\log n$. It use $\log \log n$ bits from its seed to make this random choice, so all nodes with the same seed make the same participation decision for each iteration. If a node decides to participate, it runs permuted decay providing it the needed $\Theta(\log n \log \log n)$ bits also from its seed. Therefore, all nodes with same seed will run permuted decay with the same permutation bits. If a node decides not to participate in an iteration, it does nothing until the next iteration begins.

THEOREM 4.6. *The algorithm described above solves local broadcast in $O(\log^2 n \log \Delta)$ rounds in geographic graphs in the oblivious dual graph model.*

To prove our theorem, we first highlight a property of the geographic graphs first established in [3]. Given such a geographic dual graph, we can partition the nodes into *regions* $\mathcal{R} = \{R_1, R_2, ..., R_n\}$, such that all nodes in the same region are connected in G, and for any given region R_i, the number of *neighboring* regions (i.e, regions that contain a G'-neighbor of a node in R_i) is bounded by some constant γ_r, dependent on the value of r. We will use this region decomposition in the remainder of our analysis.

We begin our analysis by focusing on the initialization stage. In the following, for a given phase j and region $R_i \in \mathcal{R}$, let $a_i(j)$ describe the number of active nodes in R_i at the beginning of phase j, and $\ell_i(j)$ describe the number of leaders elected in R_i in the first round of j. We say R_i is *active* in phase j if $\ell_i(j) > 0$. We say a given phase j is *good* if for all $R_i \in \mathcal{R}$, $\ell_i(j) < c \log n$, where c is some constant we fix later. We use p_j, for phase j, to describe the leader election probability associated with this phase. We use $P_{i,j} = a_i(j) p_j$ to describe the leader election probability sum for R_i in j.

The following three lemmas establish that the initialization phase provides the needed density of seeds.

LEMMA 4.7. *With probability at least $1 - 1/n^7$, the following holds for every good phase j and region $R_i \in \mathcal{R}$ that is active in j: At the end of phase j, every node in R_i has committed to a seed and is inactive.*

PROOF. By assumption, the phase is good. It follows that there are no more than $\gamma_r c \log n = O(\log n)$ leaders in this phase within range of nodes in R_i. We also assume that R_i is active in this phase, so we know it includes at least one node, $u \in R_i$, this is a leader. In each round, u broadcasts with probability $1/\log n$. In each such round, it succeeds in delivering its message to all nodes that are still active in R_i with probability p, bounded as: $p \geq 1/\log n(1 - 1/\log n)^{\gamma_r c \log n} > 1/(4^{\gamma_r c} \log n) = \Omega(1/\log n)$.

The phase lasts for $c' \log^2 n$ rounds. Therefore, the probability that u fails in every round of the phase is bounded as $(1 - p)^{c' \log^2 n} < e^{-\frac{c'}{4 \gamma_r c} \log n}$, which, for sufficiently large constant c', is less than $1/n^9$. A union bound over all regions (of which there can be no more than n) and all good phases, provides us with a result that holds with probability $1/n^7$, as required by the lemma. $\square$

Next, we leverage this property to prove that good phases are ubiquitous. The intuition behind the following result is that before the leader election probabilities can get large enough to elect more than $c \log n$ leaders in a region (eliminating goodness in the network), that region passes through a phase where the probability is *just right* for us to apply the previous lemma and render all nodes inactive.

LEMMA 4.8. *With probability at least $1 - 1/n^3$, every initialization stage phase is good.*

PROOF. Fix some phase j. Let region R_i be the region that maximizes $P_{i,j}$. Recall that $c \geq 1$ is the constant used in the definition of good. We begin the proof by establishing the following claim: there exists a constant $c', 1 \leq c' < c$, such that if $P_{i,j} \leq c' \log n$, then phase j is good.

To establish this claim, we first note that region i has the largest expected value of ℓ for this phase. To bound this expectation, let A_i be the active nodes in R_i at the beginning of j, and let X_u, for each $u \in A_i$ be the indicator variable that is 1 if u elects itself leader in this phase, and is otherwise 0. It follows:

$$\mathbb{E}[\ell_i(j)] = \mathbb{E}[\sum_{u \in A_i} X_u] = \sum_{u \in A_i} \mathbb{E}[X_u] = P_{i,j} \leq c' \log n.$$

Chernoff tells us that if we fix constant c to be appropriately large compared to c', then the probability that $\ell_i(j) > c \log n$ is less than n^{-6}. Notice, the expectation for the other regions is no larger than the expectation for region i, therefore this same bound applies for any region during this phase. Finally, a union bound tells us that this holds for every region and every phase, with probability at least $1 - n^{-4}$. Moving forward, assume this property holds.

We are left to prove that the probability a leader election sum ever exceeds $c' \log n$ is small. To do so, let us consider the first region to exceed this sum. Say, region R_i in phase $j + 1$. Notice, the leader election sum in R_i can at most double between j and $j+1$ (the election probability doubles between phases but the number of active nodes can never increase). For R_i to exceed $c' \log n$ in some phase $j + 1$, therefore, it must first spend phase j with $c'/2 \log n < P_{i,j} \leq c' \log n$. We will now show that the probability R_i survives phase j without having all nodes become inactive is small.

In more detail, by our above assumption, we know j is a good phase (as $j + 1$ would be the first phase where a leader election sum exceeded $c' \log n$). Given that $P_{i,j} > c'/2 \log n$, for a sufficiently large constant c', a Chernoff bound tells us that the probability $\ell_i(j) < 1$ is small—say less than

n^{-7}. (It is here that we can fix our constant value c' which allows us to fix constant c which we use in our definition of goodness.) This implies that the region is active in this phase. Our above assumption tells us that the phase is also good. We can, therefore, apply Lemma 4.7, which tells us that if the phase is active and good then all nodes in R_i will become inactive during j with probability also at least $1 - n^{-7}$. If this event occurs, of course, then the leader election sum is 0 for all future phases. By a union bound, the probability that the sum exceeds $c' \log n$ in $j + 1$ is less than n^{-6}. A union bound over all regions and phases tells us that the probability that any region ever exceeds $c' \log n$ is bounded as n^{-4}.

We are left to combine, with a union bound, two failure probabilities: (1) that our first claim—if the election sums are small the phase is good—fails; (2) that our second claim—the election sums are always small—fail. Both these failure probabilities are less than n^{-4}, so the probability that at least one fails is less than n^{-3}. It follows that the probability that all phases are good is at least $1 - 1/n^3$, as required. $\square$

If all phases are good, we can conclude by arguing that we never generate more than $O(\log n)$ seeds per region, which, in turn, restricts the total number of unique seeds neighboring any given node to be $\leq \gamma_r \cdot O(\log n) = O(\log n)$:

LEMMA 4.9. *With probability at least $1 - 1/n^2$, at the end of the initialization phase, every node has committed to a seed, and no node neighbors more than $O(\log n)$ unique seeds in G'.*

PROOF. By the definition of the algorithm, every node ends up with a unique seed (as it will generate its own seed if it gets to the end of the stage without having committed). We turn our attention, therefore, to the bound on the number of nearby seeds. Let us first consider the seeds generated during the stage (as oppose to the seeds generated at the end of the stage). Lemma 4.8 tells us that every phase is good, with probability at least $1 - 1/n^3$. It follows that no more than $c \log n$ leaders are ever elected in a single region in a single phase, with this same probability. Lemma 4.7, however, tells us that the if a region is active during a good phase, all nodes in this region are inactive for the remainder of the stage, with probability at least $1 - 1/n^6$. Combining these two observations (and, with a union bound, their respective probabilities), it follows that with probability at least $1 - 1/n^2$, the total number of leaders ever elected in a region is bounded by $c \log n$.

Now we consider the seeds generated by uncommitted nodes at the end of the stage. Let R_i be a region that contains one such uncommitted node. there cannot be more than $2c' \log n$ nodes left uncommitted in R_i at the end of the stage, where $1 \leq c' < c$ is the constant we defined in the proof of Lemma 4.8. If there were *more* nodes left in R_i, then the leader election sum in the final phase would have been strictly more than $c' \log n$. If we dive into the proof of Lemma 4.8, however, we see that it works, in part, by establishing that the the leader election sum never exceeds $c' \log n$. Therefore, if we assume this lemma holds, we can assume no election sum ever exceeds this bound

Because each node can neighbor at most $\gamma_r = O(1)$ regions, and each region has $\max\{c \log n, 2c' \log n\} = O(\log n)$ nodes, the needed bound on nearby unique seeds holds probability $1 - 1/n^2$, as needed. $\square$

We conclude by proving our main theorem:

PROOF OF THEOREM 4.6. The time complexity follows from the definition of the algorithm, as both the initialization and broadcast stages require $O(\log^2 n \log \Delta)$ rounds. Lemma 4.9 tells us that every node ends the initialization stage with a seed, and no node neighbors more than $O(\log n)$ unique seeds in G' (with probability at least $1 - 1/n^2$). Assume this lemma holds. Next, consider some node $u \in R$. It follows that u has a neighbor $v \in B$ in G such that v has a broadcast message. Let $\mathcal{S} = \{S_1, S_2, ..., S_k\}$ be a partition of the nodes in $N_{G'}(u) \cap B$ such that all nodes in S_i have the same seed from the initialization stage. Notice, by our above assumption, $k = O(\log n)$.

Let $S_i \in \mathcal{S}$ be the partition that includes v. Consider a particular decay iteration. The probability that u receives a message from S_i during this iteration is $p_{solo} p_{succ}$, where p_{solo} is the probability that S_i is the only partition from $\mathcal{S}$ to participate in this iteration, and p_{succ} is the probability that u gets a message during an iteration preconditioned on the assumption that only S_i participates . We can bound this quantity as: $p_{solo} p_{succ} > (1/\log n)(1-1/\log n)^k \cdot (1/2) > 1/(2\log n) 4^{-O(\log n)/\log n} = \Omega(1/\log n)$, where we get $p_{succ} > 1/2$ from Lemma 4.2 in Section 4.1.

The broadcast stage consists of $O(\log^2 n) = c'' \log^2 n$ iterations of decay, for some constant c''. We note that for a sufficiently large constant c'', the probability that u fails to receive a message in all k iterations is less than n^{-3}. A union bound tells us that the probability that at least one node in R fails to receive a message is less than n^{-2}. Finally, using another union bound, we combine this probability with the probability that Lemma 4.9 fails to hold, which tells us that local broadcast fails with probability less than $1/n$. □

5. CONCLUSION

In this paper, we proved upper and lower bounds for global and local broadcast in unreliable radio networks where the link behavior is controlled by either an online adaptive or oblivious adversary. Existing results were proved with respect to an offline adaptive adversary. This paper fills in the gaps for these weaker adversary types—finding the thresholds at which efficiency becomes possible. In terms of future work, it remains an interesting open question to explore other problems—such as rumor spreading, leader election, or graph algorithms—under these weaker dual graph variants. It is also interesting to explore the impact of this style of unreliable behavior in SINR-style radio network models.

6. REFERENCES

[1] N. Alon, A. Bar-Noy, N. Linial, and D. Pelegi. A Lower Bound for Radio Broadcast. *Journal of Computer and System Sciences*, 43(2):290–298, 1991.

[2] R. Bar-Yehuda, O. Goldreigch, and A. Itai. On the Time-Complexity of Broadcast in Multi-Hop Radio Networks: An Exponential Gap between Determinism and Randomization. *Journal of Computer and System Sciences*, 45(1):104–126, 1992.

[3] K. Censor-Hillel, S. Gilbert, F. Kuhn, N. Lynch, and C. Newport. Structuring Unreliable Radio Networks. In *Proceedings of the ACM Conference on Distributed Computing*, 2011.

[4] I. Chlamtac and S. Kutten. On Broadcasting in Radio Networks–Problem Analysis and Protocol Design. *IEEE Transactions on Communications*, 33(12):1240–1246, 1985.

[5] A. Clementi, A. Monti, and R. Silvestri. Round Robin is Optimal for Fault-Tolerant Broadcasting on Wireless Networks. *Journal of Parallel and Distributed Computing*, 64(1):89–96, 2004.

[6] A. E. Clementi, A. Monti, F. Pasquale, and R. Silvestri. Broadcasting in Dynamic Radio Networks. In *Proceedings of the ACM Conference on Distributed Computing*, 2007.

[7] A. Czumaj and W. Rytter. Broadcasting algorithms in radio networks with unknown topology. *Journal of Algorithms*, 60:115–143, 2006.

[8] M. Ghaffari, B. Haeupler, N. Lynch, and C. Newport. Bounds on Contention Management in Radio Networks. In *Proceedings of the International Conference on Distributed Computing*, 2012.

[9] M. Khabbazian, D. Kowalski, F. Kuhn, and N. Lynch. Decomposing Broadcast Algorithms using Abstract MAC Layers. In *Proceedings of the International Workshop on the Foundations of Mobile Computing*, 2010.

[10] D. Kowalski and A. Pelc. Broadcasting in Undirected Ad Hoc Radio Networks. *Distributed Computing*, 18(1):43–57, 2005.

[11] F. Kuhn, N. Lynch, and C. Newport. Brief Announcement: Hardness of Broadcasting in Wireless Networks with Unreliable Communication. In *Proceedings of the ACM Conference on Distributed Computing*, 2009.

[12] F. Kuhn, N. Lynch, C. Newport, R. Oshman, and A. Richa. Broadcasting in Unreliable Radio Networks. In *Proceedings of the ACM Conference on Distributed Computing*, 2010.

[13] F. Kuhn, N. Lynch, and R. Oshman. Distributed Computation in Dynamic Networks. In *Proceedings of the Symposium on Theory of Computing*, 2010.

[14] F. Kuhn and R. Oshman. Dynamic Networks: Models and Algorithms. *ACM SIGACT News*, 42(1):82–96, 2011.

[15] E. Kushilevitz and Y. Mansour. An $\Omega(D\backslash\log(N/D))$ Lower Bound for Broadcast in Radio Networks. *SIAM Journal on Computing*, 27(3):702–712, 1998.

[16] T. Moscibroda and R. Wattenhofer. The Complexity of Connectivity in Wireless Networks. In *Proceedings of the IEEE International Conference on Computer Communications*, 2006.

[17] D. Peleg. Time-Efficient Broadcasting in Radio Networks: a Review. *Distributed Computing and Internet Technology*, pages 1–18, 2007.

[18] K. Srinivasan, M. Kazandjieva, S. Agarwal, and P. Levis. The β-Factor: Measuring Wireless Link Burstiness. In *Proceedings of the Conference on Embedded Networked Sensor System*, 2008.

Connectivity and Aggregation in Multihop Wireless Networks

Marijke H.L. Bodlaender
ICE-TCS
School of Computer Science
Reykjavik University, Iceland.
mbodlaender@gmail.com

Magnús M. Halldórsson
ICE-TCS
School of Computer Science
Reykjavik University, Iceland.
magnusmh@gmail.com

Pradipta Mitra
ICE-TCS
School of Computer Science
Reykjavik University, Iceland.
ppmitra@gmail.com

ABSTRACT

We present randomized distributed algorithms for connectivity and aggregation in multi-hop wireless networks under the SINR model. The connectivity problem asks for a set of links that strongly connect a given set of wireless nodes, along with an efficient schedule. Aggregation asks for a spanning in-arborescence (converge-cast tree), along with a schedule that additionally obeys the partial order defined by the tree. Here we treat the multi-hop case, where nodes have limited power that restricts the links they can potentially form. We show that connectivity is possible for any set of n nodes in $O(\log n)$ slots, which matches the best centralized bound known, and that aggregation is possible in $O(D + \log n)$ time (D being the maximum hop-distance), which is optimal.

Categories and Subject Descriptors

C.2.1 [**Computer-Communication Networks**]: Network Architecture and Design—*Wireless communication*; F.1.2 [**Computation by Abstract Devices**]: Modes of Computation—*Probabilistic computation*

General Terms

Algorithms, Design, Theory

Keywords

Wireless Networks, SINR, Multihop, Connectivity, Aggregation, Distributed Algorithms

1. INTRODUCTION

We deal in this paper with two fundamental and related problems in wireless algorithmics: connectivity and aggregation. Given a set of n wireless nodes in the Euclidean plane, the *connectivity* problem asks for a set of links (i.e. directed edges) that strongly connect the nodes along with an efficient schedule for those links. The *aggregation* problem is

similar: find both a set of links forming a tree directed toward a root and a schedule that obeys the aggregation order, with links entering a node scheduled before the link leaving it. The limiting factor in both cases is interference: all of the communication goes through a single wireless channel (divided into time slots), thus links cannot be arbitrarily scheduled together. The algorithms and the results necessarily depend crucially on the adopted model of interference.

While wireless interference is notoriously difficult to model, the physical or *SINR model* has garnered reputation as a relatively close fit to reality [15, 19], and has recently received increased attention in the algorithms community. Connectivity (and aggregation) actually received the first worst-case algorithm analysis in the SINR model by Moscibroda and Wattenhofer [18]. Their result — that any set of n points can be connected in $O(\log^4 n)$ slots — has been improved over the years to $O(\log n)$ [6], and more recently that bound has been obtained with a distributed algorithm [5]. All of these results assume, however, either that power is unlimited or that the environmental noise is negligible, so that any pair of nodes could communicate, no matter how far apart.

We consider here the full multi-hop picture, where noise affects reachability and power limits restrict the way power control can overcome interference. We find that excellent connectivity and aggregation is possible in the power limited setting. Assuming connectivity is possible at all (with a little bit of slack), $O(\log n)$ slots suffice to connect any set of points, matching the bound for unbounded power. For aggregation we show that $O(D + \log n)$ slots suffice, where D is the appropriately defined diameter. This is asymptotically optimal for any input and implies therefore constant-factor approximation. Moreover, we show that these results are achievable using a distributed algorithm, where nodes begin with minimal information about the network. These are the first such results that do not depend on local density or similar structural properties of the input.

For distributed algorithms, it is important to distinguish between the initial running time of the algorithm on one hand, and the quality of the final schedule (which can then be repeatedly reused) on the other hand. The latter has already been mentioned. The initial running time of our distributed algorithm is $O(D + \log \Delta \log^2 n)$ or $O(D + g^2 \log^2 n)$ depending on one of two variations, where both Δ and g are length diversity measures discussed later.

We also take one of the first steps to relax the inherent determinism of the basic SINR model. Whereas the basic model states that reception is successful iff the measured

SINR is above a certain threshold, experimental results generally suggest an intermediate gray area, where transmissions succeed largely randomly. Motivated by these observations, we adopt a graded version of the SINR model, and show that our results hold equally well in this extended model.

In the process, we also obtain several more subtle technical contributions. We show that those results can be obtained without making strong assumptions about the environment. In particular, we do without location or neighborhood information, which would greatly simplify the task of distributed algorithms, and we make do with absolutely minimal assumptions about connectivity. We also obtain some improvements for the single-hop case, both regarding the time complexity and a new method for power assignment.

2. MODEL

Given are n wireless nodes located at points on the plane. The nodes have synchronized clocks, and start running the distributed algorithm simultaneously using slotted time. Each node has a globally unique ID.

A *link* is a directed edge between two nodes, indicating a transmission from the first node (the sender) to the second (the receiver). A link between u and v is denoted by (u, v) or by the generic ℓ. The Euclidean *distance* between two nodes u and v is denoted by $d(u, v)$ (which is the *length* of the link (u, v)). If clear from the context ℓ is also used to denote the length. We say that a link $\ell = (u, v)$ transmits to mean that the sender u transmits with v as the intended receiver. We will use, for two links $\ell = (u, v)$ and $\ell' = (u', v')$, the asymmetric distance $d_{\ell\ell'} = d(u, v')$, for the distance between the sender of ℓ and the receiver of ℓ'.

In the SINR (*signal-to-interference-and-noise ratio*) model of interference, a link ℓ is successful if,

$$SINR(\ell, L) \equiv \frac{p_\ell/\ell^\alpha}{N + \sum_{\ell' \in L \setminus \{\ell\}} p_{\ell'}/d_{\ell'\ell}^\alpha} \geq \beta , \quad (1)$$

where N is the ambient *noise*, β is the required SINR level, $\alpha > 2$ is the so-called path loss constant, p_ℓ is the *power* used by the sender of link ℓ, and L is the set of links transmitting simultaneously. A set of links is said to be *feasible* if it is possible to assign power to the senders to satisfy (1) for each receiver simultaneously.

We enhance this model, by allowing an intermediate region: if $SINR \in [\beta_1, \beta)$ (for some $\beta_1 < \beta$), then the transmission succeeds with probability $0 < \kappa < 1$ (for lower levels of SINR, the transmission fails with probability 1). This version of the SINR model is similar to some previous graded versions of the SINR model (e.g., [21]). In adopting this, we are motivated by experimental results that demonstrate such transitional regions where transmission is spotty, and a smaller region (corresponding to $SINR \geq \beta$) where transmissions are reliable [3, 24].

Both of our problems (aggregation and connectivity) ask for a set of links along with a schedule meeting the required conditions. If a number of links transmit in the same slot, the successes of individual links are defined by the SINR constraints, measured at the receivers. The set L in this case is the set of senders from all concurrent links. For a set of links, we say that we have a schedule of *cost* C if there is an algorithm that succeeds with high probability to successfully schedule the links in C slots. This "algorithm"

could in principle be anything, but in practice will either be an assignment of each link to a fixed slot in $\{1, 2 \ldots C\}$, or a simple probabilistic algorithm. We will say that a link set is scheduled "in the aggregation order" to mean that links into a node (i.e., links for which it is the receiver) are scheduled before the link leaving it (the link for which it is the sender).

The minimum distance between nodes is 1 (which is a matter of choosing a unit). It is assumed that nodes are restricted in their use of power by a maximum power P. The SINR constraint implies that the maximum distance a node can possibly transmit is $\Delta \equiv \left(\frac{P}{N\beta_1}\right)^{1/\alpha} > 1$. For any fixed constant $\epsilon < 1$, let $G = G_\epsilon$ be the undirected graph on the nodes with edges between nodes of distance at most $(1-\epsilon)\Delta$. We assume that G is connected, for some given value ϵ; we then say that the set of nodes is ϵ-*connected*. Let D be the diameter of G. Set the constant $\epsilon' = \min(\epsilon, \left(\frac{\beta}{2\beta_1}\right)^{1/\alpha}, \frac{1}{2}\alpha)$

A *length class* is a set of (potential) links with lengths within a factor 2. We define g as the number of non-empty length classes, or:

$$g = |\{i \leq \log \Delta + 1 : \exists \, x, y \text{ such that } d(x, y) \in [2^i, 2^{i-1}]\}|$$

While $\log \Delta + 1$ is an obvious upper bound on the number of length classes into which the links can be partitioned, g provides a tighter bound by counting only non-empty classes.

We shall use "time" to refer to the the initial number of slots required for algorithm to form the required aggregation or connectivity network, and "cost" to refer to the number of slots in the final schedule. When clear from the context, we may drop the qualification "with high probability".

We shall use the following particular Chernoff bound (see Chapter 4 in [16]): Let $\{X_i\}$ be independent Poisson trials such that $X = \sum_i X_i$ and $\mathbb{E}(X) = C \ln n$, for some $C > 0$. Then,

$$\mathbb{P}(X \leq (1 - \delta)\mathbb{E}(X)) \leq n^{-C\delta^2/2} . \quad (2)$$

Assumptions

Recall that we assumed that it suffices to use links of length at most $(1 - \epsilon)$-fraction of maximum possible. This assumption is unavoidable, since arbitrarily weak links can require arbitrarily bad schedules. We assume the nodes know (a lower bound on) ϵ.

We assume that nodes know the signal transmission parameters $N, \alpha, \beta, \beta_1$. These values can be arbitrary, except necessarily $\alpha > 2$ (as otherwise limited interference integrated over the whole plane goes to infinity). Also, that they know a polynomial approximation to n (i.e., the value of $\log n$, up to constant factors), without which there is a $\Omega(n/\log n)$-lower bound [9]. In the Δ-based algorithms, the nodes need a polynomial approximation of Δ, while the g-based algorithms do not assume prior knowledge of g.

We assume that nodes can measure the SINR (in case of a successful reception), or total received power (in other cases). This power reception feature is comparable to the RSSI function of real wireless motes. Nodes can use this feature to measure distances from the sender of a received message. In some parts of our algorithm, only measuring whether or not the SINR crosses a threshold is needed. We clarify this usage in the respective sections.

We do not assume nodes have knowledge of their locations in space, the diameter D, nor anything about their neighborhood.

Implications of the graded model

Note that the graph G is defined in terms of β_1, not β. Thus the algorithm is forced, at least on occasion, to use links that succeed only probabilistically. Note that by repeating the same transmission $\approx \log n$ times, links with $SINR \in [\beta_1, \beta)$ can be converted to a link succeeding with high probability. We are interested in bounds better than those that incur this obvious multiplicative $O(\log n)$ factor. Indeed, the bounds we derive are optimal even if links succeeded with probability 1 in the $[\beta_1, \beta)$ range.

3. RESULT AND RELATED WORK

THEOREM 1. *There is a distributed algorithm that runs in time $O(D + \log \Delta \log^2 n)$ (alternatively, $O(D + g^2 \log^2 n)$) that produces an aggregation network of cost $O(D + \log n)$ and connectivity network of cost $O(\log n)$ on any given ϵ-connected set of n nodes, for any fixed ϵ.*

The SINR model was first proposed in an influential paper of Gupta and Kumar [4], who showed that $O(\log n)$-slots suffice to connect a set of n uniformly distributed nodes. Moscibroda and Wattenhofer were the first to formalize the connectivity problem from a worst case perspective in the SINR model in [18]. They proposed a centralized algorithm that connects an arbitrary set of n nodes in $O(\log^4 n)$ slots. This was improved to $O(\log^3 n)$ [20], $O(\log^2 n)$ [17], and $O(\log n)$ [6].

Distributed algorithms for aggregation in the SINR model include [14], [7] and [1]. These works have network costs that are polynomials in $O(\log \Delta)$ or $O(d)$ (where d is the max-degree, i.e., the number of nodes within a radius of $\approx \Delta$). Dependence on degrees or $\log \Delta$ make these works closer to disk graph models, and the power of the SINR model in handling density (as seen by the works cited in the previous paragraph) is not fully utilized.

In [5] a distributed algorithm for finding a tree that connects an arbitrary set of n nodes in $O(\log n)$ slots was given, matching the best centralized result known [6]. Our work builds upon this work, and we extensively use, modify or improve techniques from this paper. It was also shown there that such results require the use of arbitrary power control; namely, algorithms using power assignments that are functions of link length alone are forced to use $\Omega(n)$ slots in worst case.

Another set of related results involves finding dominating sets and/or a broadcast network in a multi-hop scenario. The work we directly use is that of [22], where an algorithm is provided to find dominating sets in the SINR model in $O(\log n)$ time. Also relevant is [13], where a dominating set is constructed using a distributed algorithm in a quasi unit disk model, which can be converted to the SINR model (see [23]). These works do not attempt to construct a network among dominators. Broadcast or aggregation networks among dominators are formed in some works [23, 8] (as well as the works in the previous paragraph), but none give quite what we need. They either need a large ϵ (at least 2/3) to work [23, 7], use precise location information [8], and/or do not form an aggregation network [8, 23].

4. ALGORITHM OUTLINE

Our algorithm has two major parts. In the first part, we select a small set of dominators such that all (other) nodes are within a small distance of a dominator. We then construct a low-cost aggregation or connectivity network between the dominators. This network can be thought of as the backbone of the combined network. To achieve this, we use existing work to find a dominating set, and then show to how form the network among them. For this part, the initial running time (as well as the cost of the final schedule) is $O(D + \log n)$ for aggregation and $O(\log n)$ for connectivity. This is detailed in Section 5.

The second part deals with clusters (i.e. a dominator and nodes dominated by it). Each cluster is a single-hop environment, so we can apply ideas from [5], with technical changes needed to take care of power limits and the fact we are computing networks for different clusters simultaneously. We also improve the running time. After these conversions, we compute an aggregation (or connectivity) network. The initial running time is either $O(\log \Delta \log^2 n)$ or $O(g^2 \log^2 n)$, depending on which algorithm is used, and the final schedule cost is $O(\log n)$. These bounds apply both for connectivity and aggregation. This is detailed in Section 6.

Each part is divided into multiple sub-parts, which are described in the appropriate subsections. Several proofs are omitted and deferred to the full version of this paper.

5. DOMINATING NETWORK

5.1 Finding a dominating set

An *R-dominating set* is a subset of nodes such that each input node is within a distance R from a dominator (possibly itself). A *clustering* is a function f assigning each node a valid dominator (i.e., within distance R).

An *R-ball* is a disk in the plane of radius R. The *density* of an R-dominating set is the maximum number of dominators in an R-ball (over all balls in the plane). Let

$$\eta = \epsilon' \Delta / 4 .$$

By running the dominating-set algorithm of Scheideler et al. [22] with adjusted power settings, their Theorem 2.1 can be rephrased as:

THEOREM 2. *There is a distributed algorithm running in time $O(\log n)$ that produces, with high probability, a η-dominating set of constant density, along with the corresponding clustering function.*

Note that this result does not hold immediately in the graded SINR region of $[\beta_1, \beta)$, but since $\epsilon' \leq \left(\frac{1}{\beta_1} \beta \right)^{1/\alpha}$, by definition, no communication uses the graded SINR region.

5.2 Network Formation

We next seek an efficient network on top of the η-dominating set. Note that dominators can be far enough apart that the use of the transitional region is unavoidable. This is the only section where we use such links.

THEOREM 3. *There is a distributed algorithm that runs in time $O(D + \log n)$ and forms an aggregation network with cost $O(D + \log n)$ on any given η-dominating set of constant density.*

In proving this, we focus on forming an aggregation network, with a connectivity network achieved along the way.

Note that we only deal with dominators in this section. Thus when we talk about properties of the node set (like the minimum ID, or number of neighbors) we mean the set of dominators, not the original set.

Since we have an η-dominating set, the graph G' formed by connecting nodes at distance at most $\Delta(1 - \epsilon' + 2\frac{\epsilon'}{4}) = \Delta(1 - \frac{1}{2}\epsilon')$ is connected. In this section, graph terminology such as "neighbors" refers to G'.

We shall use the following two simple primitives:

com A COM consist of a slot in which each nodes transmits with a (low enough) fixed probability q.

ncomm An NCOMM (neighborhood communication) consists of $O(\log n)$ COM slots (with a sufficiently large implicit constant).

We shall say that a node u *informs* a neighbor v if it successfully transmitted to v in a given step. The following lemma encapsulates our requirements of the interference model. The results of this section will apply to any model for which this lemma holds.

LEMMA 4. *During* COM, *any given node u informs any given neighbor v with probability at least $\zeta \doteq \frac{1}{2}\kappa q(1 - q)$.*

The omitted proof of this lemma uses the now standard technique of bounding interference within concentric circles. A straightforward application of the Chernoff bound (2) gives that each node successfully transmits to each of its neighbors $\Omega(\log n)$ times (details omitted).

LEMMA 5. *During* NCOMM, *each node informs each of its neighbors ($\Omega(\log n)$ times), w.h.p.*

For simplicity, in what follows, we will consider communication with neighbors during an NCOMM as a deterministic event.

Note that COM and NCOMM apply in the transitional region – and of course in the safe region of $SINR \geq \beta$. These lemmas abstract away this particular issue, which then needs no further consideration.

Using these primitives as building blocks, the algorithm can be outlined as follows: The eventual root of the network will be the node with the minimum ID. All nodes start a flooding process to find out the minimum node (assuming initially that the node itself is the minimum). Eventually the global minimum wins and the edges involved in the flooding initiated by the root form the final tree.

An initial NCOMM informs all nodes of the IDs of their neighbors. Node u maintains the following state:

$r(u)$ the smallest ID currently known by u. Initially $r(u) = u$.

$p(u)$ the "parent" of u, or the node that *first* informed u about $r(u)$. Initially $p(u) = u$.

We use the term "child" (and children) of a node u to mean a node v such that $p(v) = u$.

In each slot, a node transmits a message using COM. There are two types of messages — M and A. Intuitively, an M-message is a broadcast message intended to inform neighbors about a node's current state (especially $r(u)$), while an A-message acts as an acknowledgment intended for the node's parent (and ultimately the root). They both contain the same information (along with the message type) — the sender u, and the current values of $p(u)$ and $r(u)$. The conditions for sending these messages and the behavior upon receiving them for a node u are as follows:

1. For each neighbor v, let $m(v)$ be the last message received by u from v. Condition SameRoot holds if the $r(v)$ value contained in $m(v)$ is the same as the current $r(u)$. Condition ChildAck holds true for $m(v)$ if the $p(v)$ value in the message is equal to u. Node u will decide on an A-message in slot $t + 1$ if u has received at least one message from each of its neighbors v by the end of slot t, and for each message: Condition SameRoot holds, and either ChildAck is false, or ChildAck holds and the message is an A-message. If the conditions hold but $p(u) = u$, the node decides to become the root instead of sending an A-message.

2. If the conditions of the previous paragraph do not apply, u decides on an M-message with the current values of $r(u)$ and $p(u)$.

The node transmits the message it has decided on with probability q, and listens for messages otherwise.

At the end of every step, node u will update its state as follows: If u has not received a message in the slot, nothing happens. Otherwise, suppose u received a message from v. If $r(u) > r(v)$ ($r(v)$ as included in the message), then u sets $r(u) \leftarrow r(v)$ and $p(u) \leftarrow v$.

The following lemma claims a time bound on how quickly nodes learn about the global minimum.

LEMMA 6. *Let $u_{\min}$ be the node with the globally minimum ID. Then, for each node u, $r(u) = u_{\min}$ by $O(D+\log n)$ slots, w.h.p.*

PROOF. It is clear that once $r(v) = u_{\min}$ for a node v, it remains that way. Let us call a node for which this is true *communicated*. The message type does not matter since $r(u)$ is updated regardless (if it has not already been communicated).

Let R_t be the set of nodes communicated after t slots with the convention $R_0 = \{u_{\min}\}$. Now fix a node u and define d_t be the distance from u to the nearest node in R_t. Note that $d_0 \leq D$. Define $\delta_t = d_{t-1} - d_t$ as the progress made at time t. Now, δ_t is a Bernoulli random variable with $\mathbb{E}[\delta_t] \geq \zeta$ for all t, as long as $d_t > 0$; $\delta_t = 0$ after that. Let $\tilde{\delta}_t$ be Bernoulli random variable where $\tilde{\delta}_t$ has the distribution of δ_t as long as $d_t > 0$ (equivalently $\sum_{i=1}^{t} \delta_i < d_0$), and an i.i.d. Bernoulli random variable with expectation ζ after that. Let $\tilde{\Delta}_t = \sum_{i=1}^{t} \tilde{\delta}_t$. It is clear that for any t, $\mathbb{P}\left(\sum_{i=1}^{t} \delta_i < d_0\right) = \mathbb{P}\left(\tilde{\Delta}_t < d_0\right)$, thus we can focus on $\tilde{\delta}_i$ exclusively.

Define $Z_t = \tilde{\Delta}_t - \zeta t$. Now, $\mathbb{E}(Z_t|\delta_1, \delta_2 \ldots \delta_{t-1}) = \tilde{\Delta}_{t-1} - \zeta(t-1) + \mathbb{E}(\tilde{\delta}_t) - \zeta \geq Z_{t-1}$. Thus, Z_t is a sub-martingale. If $t \geq 5c_1\frac{1}{\zeta}(D + \log n)$ for a large enough constant c_1, then the event that $\tilde{\Delta}_t < d_0$ implies that $Z_t < d_0 - \zeta t \leq D - 5c_1(D + \log n) \leq -4c_1(D + \log n)$. We can now upper bound $\mathbb{P}(Z_t \leq -4c_1(D+\log n))$ using the Azuma-Hoeffding inequality (see, e.g., [16, Thm. 12.4]). The Azuma-Hoeffding inequality for sub-martingale Z_t with $|Z_t - Z_{t-1}| \leq c_t$ looks as follows

$$P(|Z_t - Z_0| \leq -x) \leq \exp\left(\frac{-x^2}{2 \cdot \sum_{k=1}^{x} c_t{}^2}\right) .$$

Filling in the value for t, $c_t \leq 1$, and $x = 4c_1\frac{1}{\zeta}(D + \log n)$ yields

$$
\begin{aligned}
P(Z_t \leq -4c_1(D + \log n)) &\leq \exp\left(\frac{-(4c_1(D + \log n))^2}{2 \cdot \sum_{k=1}^{(5c_1(D+\log n))} 1}\right) \\
&\leq \exp(-2c_1(D + \log n)/5) .
\end{aligned}
$$

A union-bound over all nodes u then yields the lemma. □

Lemma 6 describes dissemination of root information to other nodes, but we also need to ensure that $u_{\min}$ realizes this fact quickly.

LEMMA 7. *Let $u_{\min}$ be the node with the globally minimum ID. Then by $O(D + \log n)$ slots, $u_{\min}$ decides to become the root.*

PROOF. Assume that the process described in Lemma 6 has communicated everyone. The passing of messages continues, and we are now interested in tracking the progress of the A-messages. A node starts to transmit A-messages once it has received the same from all of its children. Our goal will be to claim that $u_{\min}$ will fulfill the requirements of sending an A-message in $O(D + \log n)$ steps, and, according to the algorithm description, decide to become the root.

Consider a modified process, where within the M-messages that a node transmits, it forwards the A-messages from its descendants. Thus, an A-message will not be stopped by waiting for a child, but will travel up the tree independent of what happens in subtrees outside that path. This modified process completes once A-messages from all nodes in the tree have been forwarded to the root. It should be clear that this occurs at exactly the same time as when the root receives the last A-message from its children in the original process.

In the modified process, we can track the progress of each path $\langle u_0, u_1, \ldots, u_{k-1}, u_{\min}\rangle$ from a leaf u_0 to the root. The process will remove nodes from this path in the order $u_0, u_1 \ldots$. The current node u_i is removed with a probability $\mathbb{P}(u_i)$, and this probability is set to the probability of a message being successfully transmitted from u_i to u_{i+1}, which can be lower bounded by ζ (as described in Lemma 6). The process can be modeled as a sub-martingale essentially identically the process in Lemma 6 and given a similar concentration bound. A union bound over all leaf-to-root paths then yields the lemma. □

We also need to make sure of the following.

LEMMA 8. *No node other than the global minimum decides to become the root.*

PROOF. By contradiction, assume $v > u_{\min}$ did decide to become the root. As before, consider the tree between nodes with $r(u) = v$ with directed links from nodes to their parents. All nodes with $p(u) = v$ must clearly be part of v. Also, to become the root, v needs to receive an A-message from its children in the tree, and this recursively is true for all nodes in the tree. Thus the links in the tree represent A-messages as well.

Consider any simple path from a node in the tree to $u_{\min}$. This path will not be empty since $u_{\min}$ will never be part of the tree. Let x be the first node on this path and y be a neighbor of x in the tree. If $r(x) = v$ then x has to be part of the tree, a contradiction. On the other hand, if $r(x) \neq v$ then y will never fulfill the requirement needed for an A-message and will not be part of the tree. □

5.3 Stopping criterion and Schedule construction

The algorithm as described does not have a stopping criterion. This issue is easily dealt with. Once deciding to become a root, $u_{\min}$ can flood a high priority termination message that will force out other messages and inform all nodes in $O(D + \log n)$ rounds that a root has been found.

Since links used in this section can have $SINR \in [\beta_1, \beta)$, we cannot compute a fixed schedule that is guaranteed to work (since, links can fail even without any interference). However, the following scheme will, with high probability, schedule all links in $O(D + \log n)$ time in the aggregation order. The links are simply the tree of A-messages ending up in $u_{\min}$. Nodes can identify these links by one use of NCOMM. When scheduling these links in future, a node transmits its outgoing link in each slot with probability q once it has received messages from its children. This is essentially a repetition of the process described in Lemma 7 and will have the same running time.

5.4 Carrier sense assumption

For the algorithms of this section to work, we do not need the full SINR or received power primitive assumed in Section 2. It is enough to know whether or not the received power has exceeded a certain threshold. This applies both to the result from [22] to form the dominating set, and the network formation part. In the later part, nodes need to make sure that they accept messages only from neighbors. For this, it is enough to know if the distance from a sender has crossed a certain threshold, equivalent to the crossing a received power threshold, as mentioned.

6. CONNECTIVITY IN A CLUSTER

Our goal in this section is to form a network among nodes in a cluster, for all clusters simultaneously. In this part, links will only form between nodes in a cluster, ending up with an aggregation tree with the dominator as the root. As the previous section provides aggregation among the dominators, these two structures, combined, provide the total aggregation tree. Connectivity is achieved similarly. Since links will only form between nodes in a cluster, which have small radii, we need not worry about the transitional SINR phase for this section: all established links in this section will have $SINR \geq \beta$ and thus will succeed with probability 1.

We use the following definition:

DEFINITION 9. *A set of clusters is* well-separated *if nodes in different clusters are of distance at least*

$$\hat{R} \doteq \Upsilon \cdot \epsilon' \cdot \Delta \,,$$

for a sufficiently large constant Υ.

Claiming the following:

CLAIM 6.1. *The clusters are well-separated.*

To achieve this, we run a a simple coloring scheme using $O(1)$ colors, running in time $O(\log^2 n)$ (which is subsumed by the overall runtime of this section). Details are given in the full version. The final aggregation schedule contains the schedule for each color in order, followed by the schedule for the dominators.

Since nodes can measure distances from message senders, they can easily filter out stray communication from nodes of different clusters via Claim 6.1.

We provide two methods to form connectivity or aggregation in a cluster. Both algorithms are based on the single-hop algorithm from [5]. The first is identical to it except for the power assignment part (where we improve the running time), and the second is a modification to achieve a potentially faster g-based run-time. We will address aggregation in the following; identical results apply for connectivity in all cases.

6.1 $O(\log \Delta)$-based runtime

THEOREM 10. *There is a distributed algorithm running in time $O(\log \Delta \log^2 n)$ that computes, simultaneously for all clusters, an aggregation network with the dominator as the root, and a schedule of length $O(\log n)$.*

We prove this by following closely arguments from [5], with repeated use of an algorithm finding a large feasible subset according to the following lemma:

LEMMA 11. *There is a distributed algorithm running in time $O(\log \Delta \log n)$ that, given a set of m nodes divided into b disjoint clusters, finds a feasible set L of intra-cluster links with $\mathbb{E}(|L|) = \delta \cdot (m - b)$, for some fixed constant δ.*

We call a node v a *top node* with respect to a link set L if v is not a sender of a link in L. We use the following algorithmic framework (defined for a single cluster):

Algorithm 1 ClusterTree

Set $i = 0$ and $M_i = M$ (the original input set)
for $i = 0, 1, 2 \ldots$ **until** $|M_i| = 1$ **do**
    Construct feasible set L on M_i using alg. from Lem. 11
    Let M_{i+1} be the set of top nodes w.r.t. L
end for
Construct a link ℓ between $\{M_i\}$ and the cluster dominator.

We output the schedule where the nodes in set M_i send in slot i. We claim that this process takes $O(\log n)$ steps to complete.

LEMMA 12. *Algorithm 1 ends after $O(\log n)$ iterations, w.h.p., producing a spanning aggregation tree.*

PROOF. Note that by Lemma 11, $\mathbb{E}(|M_{i+1}|) \leq |M_i| - \mathbb{E}(|L|) \leq (1 - \frac{1}{2}\delta)|M_i|$. We use this to argue termination.

CLAIM 6.2. $\mathbb{P}(|M_t| > 1) \leq n^{-4}$, *for* $t = 6\frac{1}{\delta} \ln n$.

PROOF. Since M_i is non-increasing in i, for contradiction, condition on all $M_i \geq 2$ for $i \leq t$. Then by Lemma 11

$$\mathbb{E}(|M_t|) \leq \left(1 - \frac{1}{2}\delta\right)^{6\frac{1}{\delta}\ln n} \frac{1}{n} \leq e^{-3\ln n}\frac{1}{n} = n^{-4} ,$$

from which the claim follows by Markov's inequality. $\square$

For any i, each node in $M_{i+1} \setminus M_i$ is connected by a link to a node in M_i. Thus, every node is connected to a root, and thus the structure is an aggregation tree. Note that by the way the algorithm proceeds, the scheduling order of the links follows the direction of the links in the tree. Also, note that since each iteration uses a single slot, the bound on iterations implies the bound on the number of slots in the schedule, thus proving the theorem.

In the remainder of Sec 6.1, we will prove Lemma 11.

6.1.1 Choosing a feasible set

First, a few definitions. Given ν, define a ν-*class-partition* to be a partition of a link set L into ν length classes $L_1 \ldots L_\nu$ sorted in descending order (with links in L_i longer than those in L_{i+1}), along with the assumption that all links (i.e. nodes involved in the links) *know* the index i of the length class they belong to. Given a class-partition and a link ℓ in class i, define $S_\ell^- = \cup_{j \leq i} L_j \setminus \{\ell\}$ (i.e., the set of links in the same or longer length classes), and similarly, $S_\ell^+ = \cup_{j \geq i} L_j \setminus \{\ell\}$.

The following was essentially shown in [5]:

THEOREM 13. *Consider a set of n nodes partitioned into well-separated clusters. Then, there is an algorithm running in time $O(\log \Delta \log n)$ that finds a set L of links of expected $\Omega(n)$ size, along with a $\log \Delta$-class-partition, with the property that for each link ℓ in L,*

$$\sum_{\ell' \in S_\ell^+} \left(\frac{\ell'^\alpha}{d_{\ell\ell'}^\alpha} + \frac{\ell'^\alpha}{d_{\ell'\ell}^\alpha} \right) \leq \tau, \text{ with } \tau = \frac{1}{2\beta(1 + 4 \cdot 3^\alpha)} . \quad (3)$$

In [5] (Sections 6, 7 and 8), this result was proven for one cluster. But given well-separated clusters (Claim 6.1), the arguments go through easily (details omitted). From this, the following lemma follows easily (proof omitted):

LEMMA 14. *The link set L found by the algorithm of Thm. 13 satisfies*

$$\sum_{\ell' \in S_\ell^-} \frac{\ell^\alpha}{d_{\ell'\ell}^\alpha} = O(1) , \quad (4)$$

for each link $\ell \in L$.

To find a feasible power assignment we need to tighten property in Lemma 14. The proof of the following lemma is omitted.

LEMMA 15. *Let L' be a set of n links, along with a ν-class-partition, satisfying Eqn. 4, such that for each link ℓ in L',*

$$\sum_{\ell' \in S_\ell^-} \frac{\ell^\alpha}{d_{\ell'\ell}^\alpha} \leq C ,$$

for some constant C. Then, there is a distributed algorithm to find in $O(\nu)$ time a subset L of $\Omega(n)$ links, each satisfying

$$\sum_{\ell' \in L} \frac{\ell^\alpha}{d_{\ell'\ell}^\alpha} \leq \frac{1}{4\beta} . \quad (5)$$

6.1.2 Finding a feasible power assignment.

With these results in hand we give a distributed algorithm computing a feasible power assignment respecting the power limit. Assume we are given a set L of links satisfying Eqn. 5 along with a class-partition $L_1, \ldots L_\nu$.

The algorithm runs in ν rounds, with links in L_i computing their powers simultaneously in round i in two steps. First, all links ℓ' in $\cup_{j < i} L_j$ (which have already received their power) transmit with their assigned power $p_{\ell'}$. Each link ℓ in L_i measures the interference I_ℓ^- at its receiver:

$$I_\ell^- = N + \sum_{\ell' \in \cup_{j < i} L_i} p_{\ell'} / d_{\ell'\ell}^\alpha .$$

Then, ℓ computes its power as

$$p_\ell = 2\beta\ell^\alpha I_\ell^- \ . \tag{6}$$

To show feasibility with limited power we need to show that: a) power limits are not exceeded, and b) the SINR constraints are fulfilled.

LEMMA 16. *All powers assigned by the algorithm above are at most the maximum power P.*

PROOF. The proof is by induction, closely resembling the proof of Thm. 2.22 from [11]. Note that since we only have intra-cluster links, we have that $\ell \le \frac{1}{2}\epsilon'\Delta \le \frac{1}{2}\left(\frac{P}{2N\beta}\right)^{1/\alpha}$, by definition of ℓ, ϵ' and Δ, which implies that $P \ge 4\beta N\ell^\alpha$.

Links $\ell \in L_1$ compute $p_\ell = 2\beta\ell^\alpha N$, which is clearly less than P. For $i > 1$, all links ℓ' in length classes $L_j, j < i$, have $p_{\ell'} \le P$, by the inductive hypothesis. Thus, the power p_ℓ of link ℓ in L_i satisfies

$$
\begin{aligned}
p_\ell &= 2\beta N\ell^\alpha + 2\beta \sum_{\ell' \in \cup_{j<i} L_j} \frac{p_{\ell'}}{d_{\ell'\ell}^\alpha}\ell^\alpha \\
&\le 2\beta N\ell^\alpha + 2\beta P \sum_{\ell' \in S_\ell^-} \frac{\ell^\alpha}{d_{\ell'\ell}^\alpha} \\
&\le 2\beta N\ell^\alpha + 2\beta P \frac{1}{4\beta} \\
&\le P \ ,
\end{aligned}
$$

using the inductive hypothesis, Eqn. 5, and the bound $4\beta N\ell^\alpha \le P$, respectively. □

THEOREM 17. *The power assignment computed on set L is feasible.*

PROOF. As mentioned, the algorithm is a parallel version of an algorithm presented in [11, 12]. We show that this is not a problem, and proof ideas from those papers carry through.

We can bound the final interference received by a link ℓ as $I_\ell^+ + I_\ell^-$, where $I_\ell^+ = \sum_{\ell' \in S_\ell^+} p_{\ell'}/d_{\ell'\ell}^\alpha$ and $I_\ell^- = N + \sum_{\ell' \in S\setminus(S_\ell^+ \cup \{\ell\})} p_{\ell'}/d_{\ell'\ell}^\alpha$. Note that $I_\ell^- = \frac{1}{2\beta}p_\ell/\ell^\alpha$.

We first expand I_ℓ^+ using the powers assigned:

$$I_\ell^+ = \sum_{\ell' \in S_\ell^+} p_{\ell'} \frac{1}{d_{\ell'\ell}^\alpha} \tag{7}$$

$$= \sum_{\ell' \in S_\ell^+} \left(2\beta N\ell'^\alpha \frac{1}{d_{\ell'\ell}^\alpha} + 2\beta \sum_{\ell'' \in S_{\ell'}^-} \frac{1}{d_{\ell'\ell}^\alpha} \left(p_{\ell''} \frac{\ell'^\alpha}{d_{\ell''\ell'}^\alpha} \right) \right) \ . \tag{8}$$

The first term is bounded by $2\beta N \sum_{\ell' \in S_\ell^+} \ell'^\alpha / d_{\ell'\ell}^\alpha \le 2\beta N\tau$, by Eqn. 3. By rearranging indices, the second term is bounded by

$$
\sum_{\ell' \in S_\ell^+} 2\beta \sum_{\ell'' \in S_{\ell'}^-} \frac{1}{d_{\ell'\ell}^\alpha} \left(p_{\ell''} \frac{\ell'^\alpha}{d_{\ell''\ell'}^\alpha} \right)
$$

$$
\le 2\beta \left(\sum_{\ell'' \in S_\ell^-} \sum_{\ell' \in S_\ell^+} \frac{p_{\ell''} \cdot \ell'^\alpha}{d_{\ell'\ell}^\alpha \cdot d_{\ell''\ell'}^\alpha} + \sum_{\ell' \in S_\ell^+} \sum_{\ell' \in S_\ell^+} \frac{p_{\ell''} \cdot \ell'^\alpha}{d_{\ell'\ell}^\alpha d_{\ell''\ell'}^\alpha} \right) \ .
$$

The internal sum $\sum_{\ell' \in S_\ell^+} \frac{p_{\ell''} \cdot \ell'^\alpha}{d_{\ell'\ell}^\alpha d_{\ell''\ell'}^\alpha}$ can be bounded in both cases by $2 \cdot 3^\alpha \cdot \tau \cdot \frac{p_{\ell''}}{d_{\ell''\ell}^\alpha}$, following the precise arguments in Observation 4 of [10]. The first sum becomes

$$2\beta \sum_{\ell'' \in S_\ell^-} 2 \cdot 3^\alpha \cdot \tau \cdot \frac{p_{\ell''}}{d_{\ell''\ell}^\alpha} \le 2 \cdot 3^\alpha \cdot \tau \cdot p_\ell/\ell^\alpha \ ,$$

by the definition of p_ℓ. Using (7), the second sum is smaller than $4\beta \cdot 3^\alpha \cdot \tau \cdot I_\ell^+$. Thus,

$$I_\ell^+ \le 2\beta N\tau + 2 \cdot 3^\alpha \cdot \tau \cdot p_\ell/\ell^\alpha + 4\beta \cdot 3^\alpha \cdot \tau \cdot I_\ell^+ \ ,$$

which we can solve for I_ℓ^+, obtaining:

$$I_\ell^+ \le \frac{2\beta N + 2 \cdot 3^\alpha \cdot p_\ell/\ell^\alpha}{1/\tau - \beta \cdot 3^\alpha} \ . \tag{9}$$

Using the bound $2\beta N \le p\ell/\ell^\alpha$ in (9) and plugging in the value for τ gives $I_\ell^+ \le \frac{1}{2\beta}p_\ell/\ell^\alpha$ and thus $I_\ell^+ + I_\ell^- \le \frac{1}{\beta}p_\ell/\ell^\alpha$, implying the required SINR. This together with the proof for Lemma 16 concludes the proof. □

6.2 g-based run-time

To remove dependence on $\log\Delta$, we need to allow links to form without careful round-by-round control. Indeed, this is not too difficult, a $O(g\log n)$ algorithm that connects a set of n nodes is easy to demonstrate (and has been done recently in the unpublished [2]). However, for us, merely forming a network is not enough. It has to have the structure allowing extraction of a large feasible subset with Eqn. 5 holding. To do this, we must exert control over link length without the stringent conditions of the $O(\log\Delta)$-based algorithm.

We prove the following theorem:

THEOREM 18. *There is an algorithm running in time $O(g^2 \log^2 n)$ that forms an aggregation network for all clusters with cost $O(\log n)$.*

We need to prove the following counterpart of Lemma 11:

LEMMA 19. *There is a distributed algorithm running in time $O(g^2 \log n)$ that, given a set of m nodes divided into b disjoint clusters, finds a feasible set L of intra-cluster links with $\mathbb{E}(|L|) = \delta \cdot (m - b)$, for some fixed constant δ.*

Once this lemma is proven, the overall performance of the algorithm from Thm. 18 follows from the same argumentation for the $\log\Delta$ based algorithm.

We first provide an algorithm to form a set in $O(g\log n)$ time that connects the nodes (without a cost guarantee at this point):

LEMMA 20. *There is an algorithm that connects the nodes (and finds an aggregation and a complementary broadcasting network) in each cluster in time $O(g\log n)$.*

Once we prove this, we will relate it to feasibility and power assignments in Section 6.2.1 to achieve Lemma 19.

The algorithm proceeds in rounds running in $O(\log n)$ time and continues until there is only one active node in each cluster. When this happens the dominators of the clusters will terminate the algorithm. We will prove in the analysis that the latter will happen within g rounds, thus explaining the running time.

Each round contains three phases. The first two phases run in $O(\log n)$ time. In the first phase active nodes decide whether to participate and in the second phase links are formed. The last phase only takes a constant number of slots for the dominator to decide whether to proceed to the next round or to terminate the algorithm. All nodes start out active.

Participation Decision (PD): During this phase, an active node u transmits with probability q for $\frac{48}{q(1-q)}\ln n$ slots. When not transmitting, it listens for messages. If, at the end of this phase, u has heard from *some* node more than $12\ln n$ times, it sets $\delta_u = d(u, z)$, where z is the nearest node from which it has heard in this phase. Otherwise it sets $\delta_u = 0$.

Link Formation (LF): This phase contains $\frac{48}{q(1-q)}\ln n$ slot pairs (a slot pair is simply two consecutive slots). In the first slot still active nodes transmit with probability q. If a non-transmitting (but active and participating) node u receives such a message from v such that $d(u, v) \leq 4\min\{\delta_u, \delta_v\}$ (where δ_v is encoded in the message from v), then u acknowledges the message with probability q. If v receives the acknowledgment, the link $\ell = (v, u)$ is created and v becomes inactive.

Termination Decision: In the first slot all active nodes transmit and the dominators listen. If a dominator received no message, the algorithm proceeds to the next round. If the dominator did receive a message from a node x, then the dominator broadcasts in the following slot telling all active nodes except x to retransmit in the next slot. If in this next slot the dominator receives a message, the algorithm proceeds to the next round. If the dominator doesn't receive a message, it measures the received power. If the received power is $> 2P/(\epsilon'\Delta)^\alpha$ the algorithm proceeds to the next round (note that this is the lower bound on the received power from a node in the same cluster). Otherwise the dominator decides that x is the only active node in the cluster and the cluster stops trying to form new nodes. In the last slot of the phase the dominators broadcast their decisions.

We claim that this algorithm connects the set (with an aggregation and a complementary broadcasting network) in time $O(g\log n)$.

We prove the following:

THEOREM 21. *Within the first g rounds, the above algorithm finds a set of links that connects each cluster.*

To prove this we first show the following:

LEMMA 22. *Consider the execution of any round of the algorithm, and assume that the minimum distance among active nodes is d. Let $\phi(u)$ be the distance from active node u to the nearest active node. Then:*

1. *If $\phi(u) \in [d, 2d)$, then $\delta_u = \phi(u)$.*

2. *If $\delta_u > 0$, then $\delta_u = \phi(u)$.*

PROOF. The first part says that nodes that have the closest possible neighbors (up to a factor of 2), hear from them $\Omega(\log n)$ times, thus setting $\phi(u)$ as claimed in the Lemma. We prove this using a technique very similar to Lemma 4 (also known from [5] – Lemmas 5 and 6) and the use of a Chernoff bound.

CLAIM 6.3. *The probability of node u hearing from a given node v with $d(u, v) \leq 2d$ in a given time slot of the*

PD or LF-phases is at least $\frac{1}{2}q(1-q)$, when q is sufficiently small.

PROOF. The proof of this claim is almost identical to that of Lemma 4. We set $\kappa = 1$, since the graded SINR region does not play a role. Furthermore, instead of a given density we use a minimal distance of d between active nodes but this does not influence the proof. $\square$

CLAIM 6.4. *If $\phi(u) \in [d, 2d)$, then $\delta_u = \phi(u)$.*

PROOF. Let v be the closest neighbor of u, in which case $d(u, v) \leq 2d$. By Claim 6.3, the probability that u receives a message from v in any given time slot is at least $\frac{1}{2}q(1-q)$. Letting X be the number of successful (u, v) transmission in the PD-phase, we get that $\mathbb{E}(X) \geq 24\ln n$. Using the Chernoff bound (2) with $\delta = 1/2$, it follows that $P(X \leq 12\ln n) \leq n^{-3}$. $\square$

The second claim from the lemma is a bit different. Note that this claim places no restriction on $\phi(u)$. What the claim says is that if u does hear from *some* node $\geq 12\ln n$ times, it will be able to compute $\phi(u)$ correctly.

In the following definition we capture the case where a node y would receive a message from a node x if the latter was transmitting and the former was not. The definition specifies no behavior for the two nodes, beyond the fact that such a transmission would succeed were it to occur.

DEFINITION 23. *Consider two nodes x and y forming the (potential) link $\ell = (x, y)$. The event $ps(x, y)$ is said to occur in a slot if $SINR(\ell, T) \geq \beta$, where T is the set of nodes transmitting in the slot.*

CLAIM 6.5. *Consider any three points u, x and y such that $d(u, x) \leq d(u, y)$. Then, $\mathbb{P}(ps(x, u)) \geq \mathbb{P}(ps(y, u))$.*

PROOF. Since interference is computed at the receiver, the interference from any point z received at u is identical for (x, u) and (y, u). The signal is at least as strong for (x, u) since x is the closer node. Thus, for any configuration for which (y, u) succeeds, so will (x, u). The claim follows. $\square$

CLAIM 6.6. *Let u be a node and v be a node from which u received at least $12\ln n$ messages during the PD-phase. Then, during each slot of the PD-phase, $\mathbb{P}(ps(v, u)) \geq \frac{1}{12}$.*

PROOF. Let $\mathbb{P}(ps(v, u)) = \rho$. The probability that v successfully transmits to u in any given slot is $q(1-q)\cdot\rho$, so the expected number over the whole phase is $\mathbb{E}(X) = q(1-q)\cdot\rho\cdot\frac{48}{q(1-q)}\ln n = 48\rho\ln n$. Suppose for contradiction that $\rho < \frac{1}{12}$. Let X be the number of successful (v, u) transmissions in the phase. Noting that success is i.i.d. across slots, we employ the following Chernoff-type bound [16]: $\mathbb{P}(X \geq (1+\delta)\mathbb{E}(X)) < \left(\frac{e^\delta}{(1+\delta)^{(1+\delta)}}\right)^{\mathbb{E}(X)}$. Using $\delta = 2$ it gives that $\mathbb{P}(X \geq 12\ln n) \leq \left(\frac{e^2}{27}\right)^{4\ln n} \leq n^{-4}$, implying that with high probability the message (u, v) will not succeed the required $12\ln n$ times. $\square$

Now we can prove the second claim in Lemma 22. If $\delta_u > 0$, there was a v from which u received at least $12\ln n$ messages in the PD-phase From Claim 6.6, $ps(v, u) \geq \frac{1}{12}$. Let z be the node closest to u (thus $d(z, u) = \phi(u)$). Then by Claim 6.5, $ps(z, u) \geq \frac{1}{12}$. Now the probability that u has never heard from z is at most $\left(1 - \frac{1}{12}q(1-q)\right)^{\frac{48}{q(1-q)}\ln n} \leq e^{-4\ln n} = n^{-4}$.

Which proves Lemma 22 and leads to the following:

LEMMA 24. *After each round, the minimum distance among active nodes increases by a factor of 2.*

PROOF. Let d be the minimum distance at the beginning of the round. Consider any two active nodes u, v with $d(u, v) \leq 2d$. Now by the first part of Lemma 22, $\delta_u > 0$ and $\delta_v > 0$ (i.e. both of them actively participate in the link formation phase). By Claim 6.3 there is a constant probability of the link (u, v) forming in each slot pair of the link formation phase. An application of the Chernoff bound over the $\Omega(\log n)$ slot pairs proves the Lemma. □

The proof of Thm. 21 now follows automatically, since each of the g non-empty length classes are exhausted in $O(\log n)$ slots.

To prove the actual runtime and correctness of the algorithm we now need to show that dominators terminate at the correct moment.

THEOREM 25. *Every dominator correctly determines within g rounds that there is at most one active node in its cluster and succeeds to subsequently terminate the algorithm for his cluster.*

PROOF. We need to prove:

CLAIM 6.7. *A dominator does not mistakenly decide that there is only one active node in the cluster.*

PROOF. If a message was not received in the slot, the dominator decides correctly. If a message was received from x, let y be another active node in the cluster. Since it transmits in the second slot, from the cluster radius it can be verified that the received power at the dominator will be larger than the threshold and thus the dominator will decide correctly to enter the next round. □

Moreover,

CLAIM 6.8. *Within g rounds, a dominator decides that there is only one active node in the cluster.*

PROOF. After g rounds there will be exactly one active node in each cluster. In the first slot, each dominatee will hear from this node (proof omitted). Thus, we enter the case of second slot, where no one transmits. The noise level is not enough to break the received power threshold and thus the dominators will correctly decide the existence of only one active node. □

If each dominator broadcasts a message, all nodes in the respective clusters will receive the relevant message (details omitted). And thus every dominator succeeds to inform their cluster of their decision. A union bound over all nodes completes the proof of the Theorem.

6.2.1 Link selection and power control

We now show how to select a feasible set from the link set constructed above. We need a crucial definition from [5]:

DEFINITION 26. *A set L of links is ψ-sparse if, for every closed ball B in the plane,*

$$B \cap L(8 \cdot rad(B)) \leq \psi \ ,$$

where $rad(B)$ is the radius of B, $L(d)$ is the set of links in L of length at least d, and $B \cap Q$ denotes the links in a set Q with at least one endpoint in ball B.

LEMMA 27. *For the link set constructed in the previous section, consider the nodes with degree bounded by some (large constant) C. The link set induced by these nodes is $O(C)$-sparse and has expected size $\Omega(n)$.*

PROOF. Every time a node forms a link, it has probability $\frac{1}{2}$ of becoming inactive (and thus forming no more links). Thus, the probability of a node having more than C incident links falls exponentially. The statement about the expected size being $\Omega(n)$ follows from this (also see Thm. 8, [5]).

For sparsity, consider any disc B of radius ρ in the plane. Let L be the set of links induced by the node considered in the statement of the Lemma. We claim that at most one node in B has a node incident to a link in $L(8 \cdot \rho) \cap B$, from which C-sparsity follows since the node has degree at most C.

For contradiction, assume that there are two such nodes u and v. Assume without loss of generality that v is active in the slot pair when u forms the first link in $L(8 \cdot \rho) \cap B$ (call this link ℓ). Then $\phi(u) \leq d(u, v) \leq 2\rho < \ell$. But then, by Lemma 22 and the description of the link formation phase, the link ℓ cannot be formed. This is a contradiction. □

It is known that $O(1)$-sparsity implies Eqn. 4 [6]. It would appear that the link selection and power control algorithm of Section 6.1 applies at this point. Specifically, one could invoke Lemma 13 and the algorithm for power assignment from Section 6.1.2 setting $\nu = g$ (instead of $\nu = \log \Delta$), achieving a $O(g)$ running time. However, in this case, the assumption that link ℓ **knows** the L_i it belongs to is missing. In the g-based algorithm, links can form out of order, thus the round i in which it was formed is not indicative of the L_i it belongs to.

To this end, links of length in the range $[\frac{\hat{R}}{n^{10/\alpha}}, \Delta]$ and links of smaller lengths are considered separately. The larger of the two feasible sets extracted from these two sets enter the solution. For the longer set, link $\ell \in [\frac{\Delta}{2^{i-1}}, \frac{\Delta}{2^{i-2}})$ gets the index i, for a total of $O(\log n)$ indices. This is precisely the same type of partition employed in the $O(\log \Delta)$ based algorithm, thus a $O(\log^2 n)$ time algorithm suffices to choose and assign powers to a constant factor feasible set, in the same way described for the $O(\log \Delta)$ based algorithm. This runtime is subsumed by the runtime of other parts of the algorithm.

Let us assume now that all links are shorter than $\frac{\hat{R}}{n^{10/\alpha}}$. For these links the index i can be learned with some extra cost:

LEMMA 28. *Assume all links have length shorter than $\frac{\hat{R}}{n^{10/\alpha}}$. All links can learn the L_i ($i \leq g$) to which they belong in $O(g^2 \log n)$ time.*

PROOF. Let us limit ourselves to a single cluster first. Let M be the maximum length of a link in L. We simply aggregate this value up to the root. Aggregating from nodes up to a dominator takes time $O(g \log n)$ (since the connected set formed in time $O(g \log n)$ includes an aggregation tree). This value can be transmitted back from the root to each node in a single broadcast, and links with length in $[M, M/2)$ set $i = 1$. Now the maximum link length smaller than $M/2$ is aggregated in a similar way, and recursively until all links are exhausted. This process takes g rounds of aggregation for a total cost of $O(g^2 \log n)$.

As mentioned, the above ignores the possibility that links from different clusters of widely varying lengths may be assigned the same i. We argue that since inter-cluster separation is much larger than the lengths of the links, this does not matter. We shall demonstrate this using the case of Eqn. 3, the case of others are similar. The equation is as follows:

$$\sum_{\ell' \in S_\ell^+} \frac{\ell'^\alpha}{d_{\ell\ell'}^\alpha} + \frac{\ell'^\alpha}{d_{\ell'\ell}^\alpha} \leq \tau \ .$$

Note that by Claim 6.1, if ℓ and ℓ' are in different clusters, $d_{\ell'\ell} \geq \hat{R}$. On the other hand, ℓ and ℓ' are both upper bounded by $\frac{\hat{R}}{n^{10/\alpha}}$. Thus, $\frac{\ell'^\alpha}{d_{\ell\ell'}^\alpha} + \frac{\ell'^\alpha}{d_{\ell'\ell}^\alpha}$ is bounded by $\frac{2}{n^{10}}$, which even summed over at most n possible links is a minuscule value which does not asymptotically affect the bound. $\square$

With this lemma in hand, the arguments of Lemma 13 and Section 6.1.2 now apply directly, with $\nu = g$, thus achieving the claimed results from Lemma 19 and consequently Thm. 18.

7. REFERENCES

[1] M. K. An, N. X. Lam, D. T. Huynh, and T. N. Nguyen. Minimum latency data aggregation in the physical interference model. *Computer Communications*, 35(18):2175–2186, 2012.

[2] E. I. Ásgeirsson, J. T. Foley, H. Gudmundsdottir, A. Gudmundsson, M. M. Halldórsson, S. F. Kristjansson, P. Mitra, H. Ulfarsson, and Y. Vigfusson. A clean-slate design of a low-latency wireless aggregation network. Submitted, Dec 2012.

[3] N. Baccour, A. Koubâa, L. Mottola, M. A. Zúñiga, H. Youssef, C. A. Boano, and M. Alves. Radio link quality estimation in wireless sensor networks: A survey. *TOSN*, 8(4):34:1–34:33, 2012.

[4] P. Gupta and P. R. Kumar. The Capacity of Wireless Networks. *IEEE Trans. Information Theory*, 46(2):388–404, 2000.

[5] M. M. Halldórsson and P. Mitra. Distributed connectivity of wireless networks. In *PODC*, pages 205–214, 2012.

[6] M. M. Halldórsson and P. Mitra. Wireless Connectivity and Capacity. In *SODA*, pages 516–526, 2012.

[7] N. Hobbs, Y. Wang, Q.-S. Hua, D. Yu, and F. C. M. Lau. Deterministic distributed data aggregation under the SINR model. In *TAMC*, pages 385–399, 2012.

[8] T. Jurdzinski, D. R. Kowalski, T. Maciejewski, and G. Stachowiak. Distributed broadcasting in wireless networks under the SINR model. *CoRR*, abs/1207.6732, 2012.

[9] T. Jurdzinski and G. Stachowiak. Probabilistic algorithms for the wakeup problem in single-hop radio networks. In *ISAAC*, pages 535–549, 2002.

[10] T. Kesselheim. A Constant-Factor Approximation for Wireless Capacity Maximization with Power Control in the SINR Model. In *SODA*, pages 1549–1559, 2011.

[11] T. Kesselheim. *Approximation Algorithms for Spectrum Allocation and Power Control in Wireless Networks*. PhD thesis, RWTH Aachen, 2012.

[12] T. Kesselheim. Approximation algorithms for wireless link scheduling with flexible data rates. In *ESA*, pages 659–670, 2012.

[13] F. Kuhn, T. Moscibroda, and R. Wattenhofer. Initializing Newly Deployed Ad Hoc and Sensor Networks. In *MOBICOM*, pages 260–274, 2004.

[14] H. Li, Q. S. Hua, C. Wu, and F. C. M. Lau. Minimum-latency aggregation scheduling in wireless sensor networks under physical interference model. In *MSWIM*, pages 360–367, 2010.

[15] R. Maheshwari, S. Jain, and S. R. Das. A measurement study of interference modeling and scheduling in low-power wireless networks. In *SenSys*, pages 141–154, 2008.

[16] M. Mitzenmacher and E. Upfal. *Probability and computing - Randomized algorithms and probabilistic analysis*. Cambridge University Press, 2005.

[17] T. Moscibroda. The worst-case capacity of wireless sensor networks. In *IPSN*, pages 1–10, 2007.

[18] T. Moscibroda and R. Wattenhofer. The Complexity of Connectivity in Wireless Networks. In *INFOCOM*, 2006.

[19] T. Moscibroda, R. Wattenhofer, and Y. Weber. Protocol Design Beyond Graph-based Models. In *HotNets*, 2006.

[20] T. Moscibroda, R. Wattenhofer, and A. Zollinger. Topology control meets SINR: The scheduling complexity of arbitrary topologies. In *MOBIHOC*, pages 310–321, 2006.

[21] P. Santi, R. Maheshwari, G. Resta, S. Das, and D. Blough. Wireless link scheduling under a graded SINR interference model. In *FOWANC '09*, pages 3–12, 2009.

[22] C. Scheideler, A. W. Richa, and P. Santi. An $O(\log n)$ dominating set protocol for wireless ad-hoc networks under the physical interference model. In *MobiHoc*, pages 91–100, 2008.

[23] D. Yu, Q.-S. Hua, Y. Wang, H. Tan, and F. C. Lau. Distributed multiple-message broadcast in wireless ad-hoc networks under the SINR model. In *SIROCCO*, pages 111–122, 2012.

[24] M. Z. Zamalloa and B. Krishnamachari. An analysis of unreliability and asymmetry in low-power wireless links. *TOSN*, 3(2), 2007.

The Multi-Agent Rotor-Router on the Ring[*]

A Deterministic Alternative to Parallel Random Walks

Ralf Klasing
CNRS / University of Bordeaux
LaBRI, Talence, France
ralf.klasing@labri.fr

Adrian Kosowski
Inria Bordeaux Sud-Ouest
LaBRI, Talence, France
adrian.kosowski@inria.fr

Dominik Pająk
Inria Bordeaux Sud-Ouest
LaBRI, Talence, France
dominik.pajak@inria.fr

Thomas Sauerwald
MPI für Informatik
Saarbrücken, Germany
sauerwal@mpi-inf.mpg.de

ABSTRACT

The *rotor-router mechanism* was introduced as a deterministic alternative to the random walk in undirected graphs. In this model, an agent is initially placed at one of the nodes of the graph. Each node maintains a cyclic ordering of its outgoing arcs, and during successive visits of the agent, propagates it along arcs chosen according to this ordering in round-robin fashion. In this work we consider the setting in which multiple, indistinguishable agents are deployed in parallel in the nodes of the graph, and move around the graph in synchronous rounds, interacting with a single rotor-router system. We propose new techniques which allow us to perform a theoretical analysis of the multi-agent rotor-router model, and to compare it to the scenario of parallel independent random walks in a graph. Our main results concern the n-node ring, and suggest a strong similarity between the performance characteristics of this deterministic model and random walks.

We show that on the ring the rotor-router with k agents admits a cover time of between $\Theta(n^2/k^2)$ in the best case and $\Theta(n^2/\log k)$ in the worst case, depending on the initial locations of the agents, and that both these bounds are tight. The corresponding expected value of cover time for k random walks, depending on the initial locations of the walkers, is proven to belong to a similar range, namely between $\Theta(n^2/(k^2/\log^2 k))$ and $\Theta(n^2/\log k)$.

Finally, we study the limit behavior of the rotor-router system. We show that, once the rotor-router system has stabilized, all the nodes of the ring are always visited by some agent every $\Theta(n/k)$ steps, regardless of how the system

[*]Supported by ANR project DISPLEXITY and by NCN under contract DEC-2011/02/A/ST6/00201. The full version of this paper is available online at: http://hal.inria.fr/hal-00735113.

was initialized. This asymptotic bound corresponds to the expected time between successive visits to a node in the case of k random walks. All our results hold up to a polynomially large number of agents ($1 \leq k < n^{1/11}$).

Categories and Subject Descriptors

C.2.4 [**Computer-Communication Networks**]: Distributed Systems

Keywords

graph exploration, parallel exploration, rotor walk, Propp machine, random walk, ring

1. INTRODUCTION

The study of deterministic exploration strategies in agent-based models of computation is largely inspired by considerations of random walk processes. For an undirected graph $G = (V, E)$, exploration with the random walk has many advantageous properties: the expected arrival time of the agent at the last unvisited node of the graph, known as the *cover time* $C(G)$, can in general be bounded as, e.g., $C(G) \in O(D|E| \log |V|)$, where D is the diameter of the graph. The random walk also has the property that in the limit it visits all of the edges of the graph with the same frequency, on average, traversing each once every $|E|$ rounds. The rotor-router model, introduced by Priezzhev *et al.* [12] and further popularised by James Propp, provides a mechanism for the environment to control the movement of the agent deterministically, whilst retaining similar properties of exploration as the random walk.

In the rotor-router model, the agent has no operational memory and the whole routing mechanism is provided within the environment. The edges outgoing from each node v are arranged in a fixed cyclic order known as a *port ordering*, which does not change during the exploration. Each node v maintains a *pointer* which indicates the edge to be traversed by the agent during its next visit to v. If the agent has not visited node v yet, then the pointer points to an arbitrary edge adjacent to v. The next time when the agent enters node v, it is directed along the edge indicated by the pointer, which is then advanced to the next edge in the cyclic order of the edges adjacent to v.

The behavior of the rotor-router for a single agent is well understood. Yanovski *et al.* [15] showed that, regardless of the initialization of the system, the agent stabilizes to a traversal of a directed Eulerian cycle (containing all of the edges of the graph) within $2D|E|$ steps. A complementary lower bound was provided by Bampas *et al.* [3], who showed that for any graph there exists an initialization of the system for which covering all the nodes of the graph and entering the Eulerian cycle takes $\Theta(D|E|)$ steps.

Our work deals with the problem of exploring a graph with the *multi-agent rotor-router*, i.e., a rotor-router system in which more than one agent are deployed in the same environment. Due to the interaction of the agents, which move the same set of pointers at nodes, this can be seen as an example of a deterministic interacting particle system. We compare our results with the so-called *parallel random walk*, achieved by deploying independent agents performing random walks in a graph independently and without any form of coordination. Recent work on the area of parallel random walks [2, 10, 9, 13] contains a characterization of the improvement of the cover time due to the deployment of k independent random walkers with respect to the case with a single walker. It is shown in these works that the achieved speed-up depends on different parameters, such as the mixing time [10] and edge expansion [13] of the graph. The speed-up may sometimes be as low as $\Theta(\log k)$ [2], and sometimes as high as exponential in terms of k [9]. For many classes of graphs the speed-up is linear in terms of k (especially when k is small, $k \in O(\log n)$).

1.1 Our results and organization of the paper

In this work, we perform a comparative case study of two seemingly different scenarios: deterministic exploration with interacting particles in the rotor-router model vs. randomized exploration with non-interacting particles in the random walk, showing certain similarities between them.

We focus on two parameters of exploration. The first is the *cover time*, understood as the time before each node of the graph is covered by at least one agent. The second is the *return time*, i.e., the longest time during which some node remains unvisited in the limit, disregarding the initialization phase of the rotor-router. (Note that the rotor-router, as a deterministic finite-state system, has to stabilize to a cyclic traversal of some set of configurations on the graph.) We present our results taking into account different initial locations of the set of agents.

In Section 2, we formally describe the model of the rotor-router system, and introduce the techniques used in the analysis of the multi-agent rotor-router system. The basic tool is applicable to general graphs and gives us an algorithmic perspective for analysis of the rotor-router through *delayed deployments* (Subsection 2.1), allowing the occasional stopping of some of the agents without affecting asymptotic cover time. For the specific case of the rotor-router on the ring (cycle), we describe states in the evolution of the system in which particular agents cover nearly disjoint, dynamically changing parts of the graph, known as *agent domains* (Subsection 2.2). We also introduce a *continuous time approximation* of the evolution of the system on the ring (Subsection 2.3), which allows us to postulate an asymptotic description of the behavior of the agents on the ring. Formal proofs of correctness are obtained through an analysis of

the motion of agents within their domains in delayed deployments of the rotor-router.

Our main results for the case when the explored graph is a ring are presented in Section 3 (cf. Table 1 for an overview). We show that for a k-agent rotor-router system, the cover time is between $\Theta(n^2/k^2)$ and $\Theta(n^2/\log k)$, depending on the initial placement of the agents in the rotor-router. The first bound is achieved, in particular, for agents distributed uniformly on the ring, while the latter for agents initially located on the same node of the ring. The return times for the ring of the k-agent rotor-router is determined in Section 4 as $\Theta(n/k)$.

We remark that for a single agent, the rotor-router on the ring deterministically achieves a cover time of $\Theta(n^2)$, which matches that of the random walk. As the number of agents k increases, the speed-up of the rotor-router with respect to a single-agent system is seen from our results as between $\Theta(\log k)$ and $\Theta(k^2)$, depending on the initialization. These results are comparable with the corresponding speed-up of the random walk, which is between $\Theta(\log k)$ and $\Theta(k^2/\log^2 k)$. The speed-up in terms of return time is $\Theta(k)$, in both cases.

1.2 Related work

Studies of the rotor-router started with works of Wagner *et al.* [14] who showed that in this model, starting from an arbitrary configuration (arbitrary cyclic orders of edges, arbitrary initial values of the port pointers and an arbitrary starting node) the agent covers all edges of the graph within $O(|V||E|)$ steps. Bhatt *et al.* [5] showed later that within $O(|V||E|)$ steps the agent not only covers all edges but *enters (establishes) an Eulerian cycle*. More precisely, after the initial *stabilisation period* of $O(|V||E|)$ steps, the agent keeps repeating the same Eulerian cycle of the directed symmetric version $\vec{G}$ of graph $\vec{G}$ (see the model description for a definition). Subsequently, Yanovski *et al.* [15] and Bampas *et al.* [3] showed that the Eulerian cycle is in the worst case entered within $\Theta(D|E|)$ steps in a graph of diameter D. Considerations of specific graph classes were performed in [11]. Robustness properties of the rotor-router were further studied in [4], who considered the time required for the rotor-router to stabilize to a (new) Eulerian cycle after an edge is added or removed from the graph. Regarding the terminology, we note that the rotor-router model has also been referred to as the *Propp machine* [3] or *Edge Ant Walk algorithm* [14, 15], and has also been described in [5] in terms of traversing a maze and marking edges with pebbles.

In the context of graph exploration, before this work, the only study of the multi-agent rotor-router was performed by Yanovski *et al.* [15], who showed that adding a new agent to the system cannot slow down exploration, and provided some experimental evidence showing a nearly-linear speed-up of cover time with respect to the number of agents in practical scenarios. They also show that the multi-agent rotor-router eventually visits all edges of the graph a similar number of times. Beyond this, a characterization of the behavior of the k-agent rotor-router in general graphs remains an open question.

A variant of the multi-agent rotor-router mechanism has been extensively studied in a different setting, in the context of balancing the workload in a network. The single agent is replaced with a number of agents, referred to as *tokens*. Cooper and Spencer [7] study d-dimensional grid graphs and

Model	Cover time		Return time
	for worst placement	*for best placement*	
k-agent rotor-router	$\Theta(n^2/\log k)$	$\Theta(n^2/k^2)$	$\Theta(n/k)$
	Thm 3.2, 3.4	Thm 3.5, 3.7	Thm 4.1
k random walks (expectations)	$\Theta(n^2/\log k)$	$\Theta\left(n^2\Big/\frac{k^2}{\log^2 k}\right)$	$\Theta(n/k)$
	[2]	Thm 3.11	e.g. [1]

Table 1: The cover time of the multi-agent roter-router on the ring compared to multiple random walks (for $k < n^{1/11}$).

show a constant bound on the difference between the number of tokens at a given node v in the rotor-router model and the expected number of tokens at v in the random-walk model. Subsequently Doerr and Friedrich [8] analyse in more detail the distribution of tokens in the rotor-router mechanism on the 2-dimensional grid.

Finally, a related line of research on deterministic graph exploration is devoted to *equitable strategies*, in which the environment attempts to mimic the fairness properties of the random walk with respect to the use of edges. Two such strategies, in which the agent is always directed to the least often used, or the longest unused, from among the edges adjacent to the current node were studied in [6].

1.3 Model definition

Let $G = (V, E)$ be an undirected connected graph with n nodes, m edges and diameter D. We denote the neighborhood of a node $v \in V$ by $\Gamma(v)$. The directed graph $\vec{G} = (V, \vec{E})$ is the directed symmetric version of G, where the set of arcs $\vec{E} = \{(v, u), (u, v) : \{v, u\} \in E\}$.

We consider the rotor-router model (on graph G) with $k \geq 1$ indistinguishable agents, which run in rounds, synchronized by a global clock. In each round, each agent moves in discrete steps from node to node along the arcs of graph $\vec{G}$. A *configuration* at the current step is defined as a triple $((\rho_v)_{v \in V}, (\pi_v)_{v \in V}, \{r_1, \ldots, r_k\})$, where ρ_v is a cyclic order of the arcs (in graph $\vec{G}$) outgoing from node v, π_v is an arc outgoing from node v, which is referred to as *the (current) port pointer at node v*, and $\{r_1, \ldots, r_k\}$ is the (multi-)set of nodes currently containing an agent. For each node $v \in V$, the cyclic order ρ_v of the arcs outgoing from v is fixed at the beginning of exploration and does not change in any way from step to step (unless an edge is dynamically added or deleted as discussed in the previous section). For an arc (v, u), let $next(v, u)$ denote the arc next after arc (v, u) in the cyclic order ρ_v.

The exploration starts from some initial configuration and then keeps running in all future rounds, without ever terminating. During the current round, first each agent i is moved from node r_i traversing the arc π_{r_i}, and then the port pointer π_{r_i} at node r_i is advanced to the next arc outgoing from r_i (that is, π_{r_i} becomes $next(\pi_{r_i})$). This is performed sequentially for all k agents. Note that the order in which agents are released within the same round is irrelevant from the perspective of the system, since agents are indistinguishable. For example, if a node v contained two agents at the start of a round, then it will send one of the agents along the arc π_v, and the other along the arc $(v, next(\pi_v))$. In some considerations, we will also assign explicit labels $\{0, 1, \ldots, \deg(v) - 1\}$

to the ports adjacent to v, in such a way that initially $\pi_v = 0$, and $next(v, i) = (v, (i + 1) \mod \deg v)$. Then, at the completion of any round, the total number of traversals of agents along an arc (v, u) is equal to $\left\lceil \frac{e_v - port_v(u)}{\deg(v)} \right\rceil$, where e_v is the total number of times agents exited node v until the completion of the round and $port_u(v)$ denotes the label of the port leading from v to u.

In all our considerations, we will assume that the initialization of ports and pointers in the system is performed by an adversary. In particular, when studying a best-case scenario of initial agent locations, we assume that the ports and pointers have been set by the adversary so as to maximize the studied parameter (e.g., cover time). For the case of the ring, there exists only one cyclic permutation of the two neighbors of each node, hence only the initial pointer arrangement (and not the configuration of ports) is relevant.

2. TECHNIQUES FOR THE MULTI-AGENT ROTOR-ROUTER

2.1 Delayed deployments

In our work we will consider both the unmodified k-agent rotor-router system $R[k]$ and its *delayed deployments*, in which some agents may be stopped at a node, skipping their move for some number of rounds. A delayed deployment D of k agents is formally defined as a function $D : V \times \mathbb{N} \to \mathbb{N}$, where $D(v, t) \geq 0$ represents the number of agents which are stopped in vertex v in round t of the execution of the system. (The rotor-router system $R[k]$ corresponds to the deployment $R[k](v, t) = 0$, for all v and t). Delayed deployments may be conveniently viewed as algorithmic procedures for delaying agents, and are introduced for purposes of analysis, only.

We will say that a node is *visited* by an agent in round t if the agent is located at this node at the start of round $t+1$. Let $n_v^D(t)$ denote the total number of visits of agents to node v during the interval of rounds $[1, t]$ for agents following some (possibly delayed) deployment D, and let $C(D)$ be the cover time of this deployment. The notation $n_v^D(0)$ refers to the number of agents at a node directly after initialization (at the start of round 1).

We start by showing that by delaying more agents in a deployment, one cannot increase the number of visits to nodes at any time. We assume that all considered deployments start from the same (arbitrarily chosen) initial configuration.

LEMMA 2.1. *Let D_1 and D_2 be two delayed deployments of the k-agent rotor-router system, such that for all vertices*

$v \in V$ and rounds t, $D_1(v,t) \geq D_2(v,t)$. Then, for all vertices $v \in V$ and rounds t, we have $n_v^{D_1}(t) \leq n_v^{D_2}(t)$.

(Some proofs are omitted from this extended abstract.)

We remark that the above lemma immediately implies that $n_v^{R[k-1]}(t) \leq n_v^{R[k]}(t)$, since the $(k-1)$-agent rotor-router $R[k-1]$ is equivalent to a deployment of the k-agent rotor-router with one agent permanently stopped. (This observation is due to [15].)

LEMMA 2.2. *Let D be a delayed deployment of the k-agent rotor-router system. Let T be any fixed time round, and let τ be the number of rounds in the interval $[1,T]$ such that all the agents are active in D, i.e., $\tau = |\{t \in [1,T] : \forall_{v \in V} \; D(v,t) = 0\}|$. Then, for all vertices v, we have: $n_v^{R[k]}(\tau) \leq n_v^D(T) \leq n_v^{R[k]}(T)$.*

Observe that by the above lemma, we have that if node v is visited for the first time after T rounds in a delayed deployment D, i.e., $n_v^D(T) = 0$ and $n_v^D(T+1) = 1$, then $n_v^{R[k]}(\tau) = 0$ and $n_v^{R[k]}(T+1) \geq 1$. From this, we directly obtain the key lemma for the approach we use to analysing the cover time of k-rotor-router systems in this paper.

LEMMA 2.3. (**the slow-down lemma**). *Let $R[k]$ be a k-rotor router system with an arbitrarily chosen initialization, and let D be any delayed deployment of $R[k]$. Suppose that deployment D covers all the vertices of the graph after $T = C(D)$ rounds, and in at least τ of these rounds, all agents were active in D. Then, the cover time $C(R[k])$ of the system can be bounded by: $\tau \leq C(R[k]) \leq T$.* $\square$

If the deployment D is defined so that agents in D are delayed in at most a constant proportion of the first $C(D)$ rounds, then the above inequalities lead to an asymptotic bound on the value of the undelayed rotor-router, $C(R[k]) = \Theta(C(D))$. This is the case, e.g., in the proof of Theorem 3.2.

2.2 Agent domains on the ring

For a given (possibly delayed) deployment of the k-rotor-router system such that no two agents ever occupy the same node at the same time, and a fixed round t, we consider the partition of the node set into so called *domains*. We set $V(t) = V_0(t) \cup V_1(t) \cup \ldots \cup V_k(t)$, where $V_0(t)$ denotes the set of nodes which have not yet been visited until round t, and $V_i(t)$, $1 \leq i \leq k$, is the set of all nodes such that the i-th agent was the last agent visiting the node until round t, inclusive. When the considered graph is a ring, we have the following simple characterization of the structure of the domains of particular agents in deployments in which agents never meet. We state the following simple properties without proof.

LEMMA 2.4. *Consider a deployment in which no two agents ever meet at a node, and let $v_i(t) \in V_i(t)$ be the location of the i-th agent at a given round t, $1 \leq i \leq k$. The following properties hold:*

- *$V_i(t)$ induces a sub-path of the ring.*

- *The pointers of all nodes $u \in V_i(t)$ point away from $v_i(t)$, i.e., not along the arc on the path leading from u to $v_i(t)$ in $V_i(t)$. In particular, if $v_i(t)$ is an end-point of the path induced by $V_i(t)$, then all the pointers of $V_i(t) \setminus \{v_i(t)\}$ point in the same direction.*

- *In each round, $V_i(t)$ loses or gains at most one node at each end of the path. In particular, $|V_i(t+1) \oplus V_i(t)| \leq 2$.* $\square$

The following three lemmas provide a partial characterization of the changes of size of domains during the runtime of a deployment. We first define the borders and interiors of the domains. Suppose that at some time t the domain of each agent is of size at least 3. For time t, we define the *border* between these two domains as the two adjacent nodes from these two domains. The *interior* of a domain at this time t is defined as the domain without its border nodes. For $t' > t$, borders and interiors are defined recursively based on borders from previous step and positions of agents. We will denote the interior of the domain of agent i in any step $t' \geq t$ by $I_i(t')$. Let j be an agent with a domain neighboring with that of i. If in step t', $I_i(t'-1) \cap V_j(t') \neq \emptyset$ (i.e., if j captured some node belonging to the interior of the domain of agent i in step t') then the border between the domains of i and j moves by two nodes towards the domain of agent i. Thus, the interior of the domain of agent j grows by two nodes. Note that in order to move the border, agent j has to make two visits to the border, in between which there is no visit to this border by agent i.

We will say that agent a makes a full cycle starting at some node v when it visits every node of its domain and returns to v. Note that in order to make a full cycle agent a has to visit every node of its domain twice, except extremal nodes from both sides of the domain.

Let a,b,c any three agents with consecutive domains. Let t be the time step, when borders were defined. We first show that if the interiors of the domains are sufficiently large at some point, then the will never decrease below a threshold size of $11k$.

LEMMA 2.5. *If $k \geq 5$ and initially the interior of every domain has size at least $22k$, then for any $t' \geq t$:*

(1) if $|I_a(t')| - 7 > |I_b(t')|$ and $|I_b(t')| \leq 2|I_c(t')|$, then in step $t' + 1$ the border between a and b will not move towards b,

(2) the size of the interior of any domain is at least $11k$.

We now show two auxiliary lemmas which allow us to conclude that the sizes of all domains will eventually even out in time.

LEMMA 2.6. *If $k \geq 5$ and initially the interior of every domain has size at least $22k$ and $|I_a(t')| > 1.3|I_b(t')|$, then in step $t' + 1$ the border between a and b will not move towards b.*

LEMMA 2.7. *If $|I_a(t^*)| - 4 > |I_b(t^*)|$ holds for $2n^2$ consecutive time steps $t^* = t', t'+1, t'+2, \ldots, t'+n^2-1$ for some $t' \geq t$, then border between a and b will move towards a.*

From our considerations, we obtain the lemma which will prove crucial in characterizing the limit behavior of the rotor-router on the ring.

LEMMA 2.8. (**agent domains**). *If at some time step t every domain has size at least $22k + 2$ and $k \geq 5$, then after a sufficiently large number of steps the interiors of adjacent domains will differ by at most 7.*

2.3 Continuous-time approximation

To provide an asymptotic description of the behavior of agent domains in time, we introduce the continuous-time approximation of the agents' behavior. This is useful under the assumption that the sizes of all the domains are sufficiently large, i.e., that the change of size of $V_i(t)$ in the number of rounds of the order $|V_i(t)|$ is negligible with respect to $|V_i(t)|$.

Suppose that the domains of the agents are ordered along the ring as $V_0(t), V_1(t), \ldots, V_k(t)$. Assuming that only the i-th agent is moving, the agent will reach each of the endpoints of its domain every $1/(2|V_i(t)|)$ rounds. Consequently, within T rounds, the agent enlarges its domain by approximately $T/(2|V_i(t)|)$ to the left, and $T/(2|V_i(t)|)$ to the right, thus by about $T/|V_i(t)|$ in total. This movement is counteracted by the moves of the adjacent agents occupying domains V_{i-1} and V_{i+1}. Consequently, we define the *continuous-time approximation* of the rotor-router through the set of differential equations:

$$\frac{d\nu_i(t)}{dt} = \frac{1}{\nu_i(t)} - \frac{1}{2\nu_{i-1}(t)} - \frac{1}{2\nu_{i+1}(t)}, \quad \text{for } 1 \leq i \leq k,$$

where $\nu_i(t) = |V_i(t)|$, for all $1 \leq i \leq k$. The interpretation of $\nu_0(t)$ and $\nu_{k+1}(t)$ depends on whether the whole ring has already been covered: if so, then $\nu_{k+1}(t) \equiv \nu_1(t)$ and $\nu_0(t) \equiv \nu_k(t)$; if not, i.e., if $|V_0(t)| > 0$, then we put $\nu_0(t) = \nu_{k+1}(t) = +\infty$.

Whereas the above differential model provides the basic intuition for many of the proofs, the main difficulty lies in taking into account the differences between the continuous-time model and the real rotor-router. In particular, we have to consider the position of the agent within its domain, the discrete changes of the domain size in time, and the initial pointer arrangement in the unvisited part of the ring.

3. COVER TIME OF THE MULTI-AGENT ROTOR ROUTER ON THE RING

3.1 Worst-case initial placement

The following lemma introduces a sequence $\{a_i\}_{i=0}^{k+1}$, useful in analyzing initial placements in which all agents start from the same point of the ring. It corresponds to a normalized solution to the continuous-time model of the rotor-router (i.e., $a_i(t) = \nu_i(t)/\sum_j \nu_j(t)$), subject to the constraint that the proportions of domain sizes do not change in time (i.e., $\frac{da_i(t)}{dt} = 0$), and specific boundary conditions.

LEMMA 3.1. *For any $k > 3$ there exists a sequence of positive numbers $(a_0, a_1, \ldots, a_k, a_{k+1})$ which satisfies the following properties:*

(1) $a_0 = +\infty$,

(2) $a_{k+1} = a_k < a_{k-1} < \ldots < a_1$,

(3) $\sum_{i=1}^{k} a_i = 1$,

(4) $a_i \cdot a_1 = \frac{2}{a_i} - \frac{1}{a_{i-1}} - \frac{1}{a_{i+1}}$, *for all* $1 \leq i \leq k$,

(5) $\frac{1}{4(H_k+1)} \leq a_1 \leq \frac{1}{H_k}$, *where* $H_k = 1 + \frac{1}{2} + \ldots + \frac{1}{k}$ *denotes the k-th harmonic number,*

(6) $\frac{1}{4i(H_k+1)} \leq a_i$, *for all* $1 \leq i \leq k$.

We are now ready to analyse a specific initialization, for which the k-agent rotor-router covers the ring particularly slowly.

THEOREM 3.2. *In the case when all the agents are initially placed at the same node v, a group of k agents explores the ring of size n in time $\Theta(\frac{n^2}{\log k})$ when $k < n^{1/11}$, when all pointers are initialized along the shortest path to v.*

PROOF. Consider a scenario with K agents on an N-node ring. Since $C(R[K-1]) \geq C(R[K]) \geq C(R[K+1])$, and the cover time is also monotonous with respect to the size of the ring, without affecting asymptotic bounds we can assume that K is even an N is odd, i.e., $K = 2k$ and $N = 2n-1$. By induction, we can show that the number of agents at node v will be even at all times, and the arrangement of pointers on the ring (except for node v) is symmetric with respect to the axis of symmetry passing through v. Consequently, the cover time for the N-node ring with K agents is asymptotically the same as the cover time of a n-node path with k agents, starting from an initial placement of all agents on one of the end-points v of the path.

Let $R[k]$ be this deployment on the path P_n. We now propose a delayed deployment D of $R[k]$ in which, starting from a certain moment in time, the domains of all agents are separate. Let the domains be ordered along the path according to decreasing numbers, i.e., the agent with domain V_k is the one located closest to the starting point v, while the agent with domain V_1 is the furthest from v, i.e., it is the only agent to explore previously unvisited nodes of the path. The goal of the formalization below is to define the delayed deployment so that the ratios of domain sizes satisfy $|V_i| \sim a_i$, for $k \geq i \geq 1$, throughout time.

We will identify the path P_n with the integer interval $[1, n]$ (with $v = 1$), and domains with subsets of this interval. For $k \geq i \geq 1$, let $p_i = \sum_{j=i}^{k} a_j$. For a given value S, $n \geq S > 0$, we will call a configuration of agents and pointers on the path a *desirable configuration of length S* if it has the following properties:

- The position of the i-th agent on the path is $v_i = \lfloor p_i S \rfloor$.

- Each agent is at the right endpoint of its domain, i.e., $V_k = [1, v_k]$ and $V_i = [v_{i+1} + 1, v_i]$ for $k - 1 \geq i \geq 1$.

- For all the nodes on the path (including those containing agents), except for node 1, the pointer points to the left (towards node 1).

The evolution of the delayed deployment D is defined in two phases, as follows:

- *Phase A.* Form a desirable configuration with $S_0 = \frac{n}{\sqrt{k \log k}}$. To achieve this, release the agents one-by-one, starting from agent 1 to agent k, and perform exactly $(\lfloor p_i S_0 \rfloor - 1)^2$ moves with each agent, so that each agent i occupies position $\lfloor p_i S_0 \rfloor$ and all pointers on the path point to the left.

- *Phase B.* For successive $j = 0, 1, \ldots$, iterate the following procedure, until the path has been covered. Starting from an initial desirable configuration of some length S_j, form a new desirable configuration of length $S_{j+1} = S_j + \lceil k^4 a_1 a_k \rceil + 12k$ as follows:

B1. Starting from the current desirable configuration, release all agents simultaneously for $\lceil 2k^4 a_k S_j \rceil$ rounds.

B2. Adjust the positions of the agents, so as to reach the desirable configuration of length S_{j+1}. To achieve this, release the agents one-by-one, starting from agent 1 to agent k, allowing each agent i to move until it has reached position $\lfloor p_i S_{j+1} \rfloor$.

We denote by T the cover time of deployment D, by A, the total number of rounds of Phase A, by B_1, the total total number of rounds of Phase B1, and by B_2, the total number of rounds of Phase B2. We also remark that during Phase B1 none of the agents is delayed, hence, by Lemma 2.3 we have: $B_1 \leq C(R[k]) \leq T = A + B_1 + B_2$.

We begin by bounding time A. The agents are released sequentially in Phase A. The number of rounds required for each agent to reach its position is less than $\frac{n^2}{k \log k}$. Thus, $A < \frac{n^2}{\log k}$.

We now proceed to Phase B (see Fig. 1 for an illustration). The size of the smallest domain in configuration S_0 is:

$$\left\lfloor \frac{n}{\sqrt{k \log k}} a_k \right\rfloor \geq \left\lfloor \frac{n}{\sqrt{k \log k}} \frac{1}{4(H_k+1)k} \right\rfloor \geq$$
$$\geq \left\lfloor \frac{k^{11}}{k^{3/2} \log k \, (4 \log k + 8)} \right\rfloor \geq k^9,$$

where the last inequality holds for $k \geq 10^6$. Consider now the j-th step of the phase, starting from length $S = S_j$, and the change of the configuration within part B1 of this step. The number of rounds used in part B1 of the step is $2a_k S k^4$. Let $|V_i|_j = \lfloor p_i S \rfloor - \lfloor p_{i+1} S \rfloor \geq a_i S - 1$ be the size of the domain of the i-th agent at the beginning of the j-th step, and let $|V_i|_j + g_i$ be its size after completion of part B1 of this step. In order to increase the size of its domain, the i-th agent needs to perform at least g_i traversals of its domain (such that during these traversals the size of this domain is at least $|V_i|_j$), where a traversal is understood as starting and ending at the right endpoint of the domain. These traversals require more than $a_i S g_i$ rounds, whereas the total duration of part B1 of the j-th step is $\lceil 2a_k S k^4 \rceil$, hence we obtain $g_i < 2k^4$. Since the total size of all domains is non-decreasing in time, it follows that $\sum_{i=1}^{k} g_i \geq 0$, and so:

$$-2k^5 \leq g_i < 2k^4.$$

We now proceed to refine this bound on g_i. Initially, the size of the i-th domain is between $a_i S - 1$ and $a_i S + 1$. Thus, for the i-th agent, the number of completed traversals c_i of its domain during the considered part B1 is:

$$\frac{2a_k S k^4}{a_i S + 1 + 2k^4} \leq c_i \leq \frac{2a_k S k^4 + 1}{a_i S - 1 - 2k^5}.$$

If the i-th node performed c_i complete traversals, then it reached each of the boundaries of its domain at lest c_i times and one boundary could be reached $c_i + 1$ times. Thus, considering the change in size of domain g_i during the traversals of agents i, $i-1$ and $i+1$, we have:

$$2c_i - c_{i-1} - c_{i+1} - 2 \leq g_i \leq 2c_i + 1 - c_{i-1} - c_{i+1}$$

and introducing the bounds on c_i, c_{i-1}, c_{i+1} to the above we obtain (details of the calculations are omitted in this extended abstract):

$$2a_i a_k k^4 a_1 - 11 - \frac{8}{k} \leq g_i \leq 2a_i a_k k^4 a_1 + 11 + \frac{8}{k}$$

We obtain bounds on the position of the i-th agent after Phase B1:

$$\lfloor p_i S \rfloor + \sum_{l=i}^{k} g_l < \lfloor p_i S \rfloor + \sum_{l=i}^{k} (a_l a_1 a_k k^4 + 11 + 8/k) \leq$$
$$\leq p_i S + p_i a_1 a_k k^4 + 11k + 8 <$$
$$< \lfloor p_i S_{j+1} \rfloor.$$

$$\lfloor p_i S \rfloor + \sum_{l=i}^{k} g_l \geq \lfloor p_i S \rfloor + \sum_{l=i}^{k} (a_l a_1 a_k k^4 - 11 - 8/k) \geq$$
$$\geq p_i S + p_i a_1 a_k k^4 a_1 - 11k - 9 >$$
$$> \lfloor p_i S_{j+1} \rfloor - 24k.$$

Next, we obtain that the duration of Phase B2 is bounded by $24Sk^2 + 48k^7 + 1152k^5$. (Details of the analysis are omitted.)

Observe that the duration of part B1 of the step was $2a_k S k^4 \geq \frac{2}{4k(H_k+1)} S k^4 > 24Sk^2$ for $k > 10^3$, because $a_k \geq \frac{1}{4k(H_k+1)}$ from Lemma 3.1. Thus, overall we have that the execution of B1 dominates the complexity of the algorithm, $B_1 \in \Omega(B_2)$ and $B_1 \in \Omega(A)$. It follows that $C(R[k]) = \Theta(B_1)$. Now, in order to bound time B_1, observe that the j-th step of Phase B results in the increase of S_j, the number of already covered nodes, by $\Theta(k^4 a_1 a_k)$, which means that Phase B consists of $\Theta\left(\frac{n}{k^4 a_1 a_k}\right)$ steps. Since more than half of these steps are performed for $n/2 < S_j < n$, we obtain a tight bound on the cover time $B_1 \in \Theta(\frac{n^2}{a_1})$. Noting that $a_1 = \Theta(\frac{1}{H_k})$ by Lemma 3.1, we eventually obtain $B_1 \in \Theta(\frac{n^2}{\log k})$. Thus, $C(R[k]) \in \Theta(\frac{n^2}{\log k})$. $\square$

We now show that the initialization considered above, with all agents starting from one node and all ports pointing to the left, is indeed asymptotically the worst possible. The proof of this theorem proceeds in two steps, first by considering agents starting from one node with an arbitrary placement of pointers on the ring, and then by extending this result to the general case through the application of delayed deployments.

LEMMA 3.3. *In the case when all the agents are initially placed at the same node v, a group of k agents explores the ring of size n in time $O(\frac{n^2}{\log k})$ when $k < n^{1/11}$, regardless of the initial placement of pointers.*

PROOF. We extend the proof of the upper bound from Theorem 3.2 to different initializations of pointers. We consider the case of the rotor-router deployment $R[k]$ on the n-node path with all agents initially positioned at the left endpoint of the path (but with arbitrary pointer initialization along the path). As in the proof of Theorem 3.2, we consider a delayed deployment with similarly defined Phases A and B, using the same set of desirable configurations of length S_j. Note that in a desirable configuration, all the pointers along the path point to the left for all nodes which have already been visited by an agent at least once. In Phase A, agents are released one-by-one, until the i-th agent reaches position $\lfloor p_i S_0 \rfloor$, after which the agent is stopped (this may happen after a smaller number of steps than in

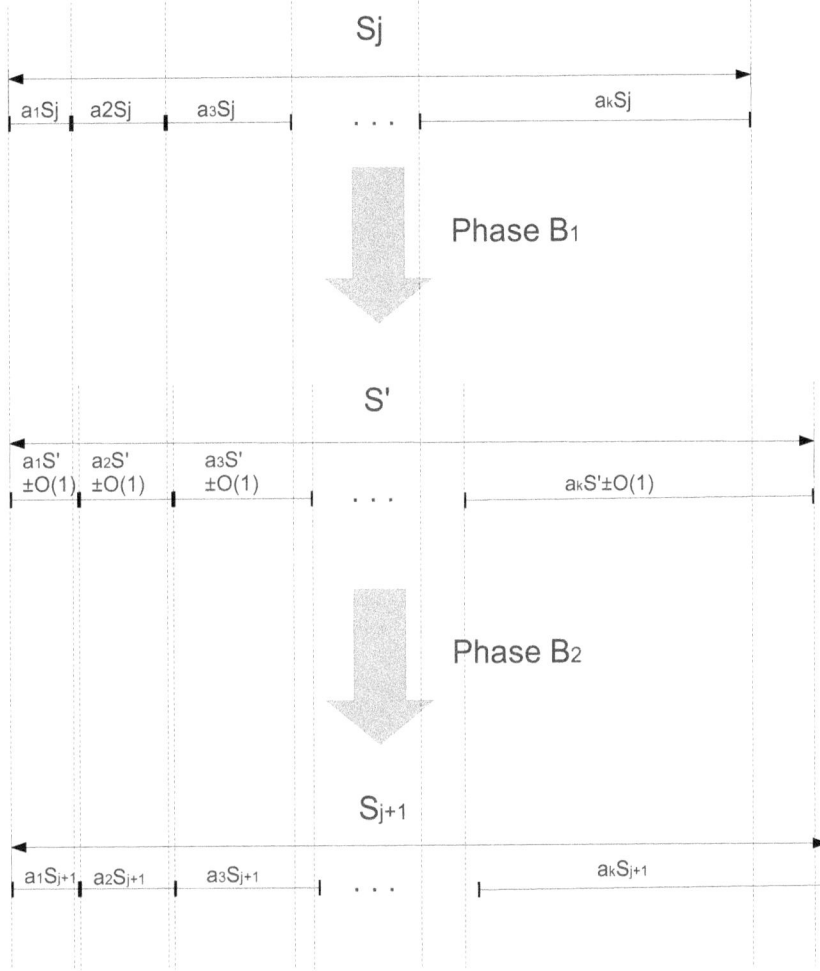

Figure 1: An iteration of Phase B of delayed deployment D (proof of Theorem 3.2)

the proof of Theorem 3.2). In the j-th step of Phase B, the only difference concerns the definition of part B1, where we add the condition that, upon reaching position $\lfloor p_i S_{j+1} \rfloor$ for the first time, the i-th agent stops and waits for the other agents to complete part B1 of the step. By induction, one can show that for $i > 1$, agent i will only stop moving in part B1 after agent $i - 1$ has stopped moving, and consequently, it may never happen that a moving agent meets a stationary agent. The analysis of the time spent within parts A, B1 and B2 is performed as before, and we obtain $C(R[k]) = A + B_1 + B_2 = O(\frac{n^2}{\log k})$.

The analysis on the ring proceeds by a modification of the argument for a path, treating the ring as two sub-paths connected at the common node 1. In Phase B, the deployments on both sub-paths are synchronized so that the agents a_k of the respective deployments arrive at node 1 simultaneously. If agent a_k of one of the sub-paths, say the left one, arrives before the agent a_k of the right sub-path, then all the agents of the left sub-path are stopped at their current locations until the other agent a_k arrives at node 1. (Note that the two sub-paths do not have to be performing the same step j of Phase B at the same time.) This transformation

of the deployment on the path does not affect asymptotic analysis, hence the cover time of the deployment on the ring is also $O(\frac{n^2}{\log k})$. $\square$

THEOREM 3.4. *For any initialization of the k-agent rotor-router system on the ring, the cover time is $O(\frac{n^2}{\log k})$, for $k < n^{1/11}$.*

PROOF. Let $R[k]$ be a deployment of the rotor-router on the ring. Fix a subset $P \subset V$ of $P = k^{2/3}$ points on the ring which are evenly spaced, i.e., $G[V \setminus P]$ is a set of disjoint paths of length at most $n/k^{2/3}$. Consider a delayed deployment of $R[k]$, which begins with a Phase in which the agents of $R[k]$ are activated and moved one by one, stopping each agent as soon as it has reached a node from P. Since the cover time of a path of length $O(n/k^{2/3})$ for a single agent is $O(n^2/k^{4/3})$, the duration of this Phase is at most $O(n^2/k^{1/3})$. After this initial phase, by the pigeonhole principle, there must exist a node $v \in P$ which contains $k' \geq k^{1/3}$ agents. We now continue the delayed deployment by releasing $k'' = \min\{k^{1/3}, n^{1/11}\}$ agents which are located at v, and permanently stopping (removing) all other agents. By Theorem 3.2, the path will be covered by the delayed deployment within $O\left(\frac{n^2}{\log k''}\right)$ rounds. By summing the duration of the two phases and using the slow-down lemma, we obtain the claim: $C(R[k]) \in O\left(\frac{n^2}{k^{1/3}} + \frac{n^2}{\log k''}\right) = O(\frac{n^2}{\log k})$, for $k < n^{1/11}$. □

3.2 Best-case initial placement

We start by proposing the initialization with agents equally spaced along the path as a candidate for (asymptotically) best-case initial placement with $O\left((\frac{n}{k})^2\right)$ cover time. The proof is straightforward in the case if we assume that the adversary initially directs all pointers towards the nearest agent, so as to block it. However, the adversary may apply a different strategy, and there do indeed exist port arrangements which deflect agents from some section of the ring, leading to a larger value of cover time. In our proof we show such actions of the adversary do not affect the asymptotics of the cover time.

THEOREM 3.5. *Consider an initialization of the rotor-router system on the ring with agents starting on a set of points $P = \{p_1, p_2, \ldots, p_k\}$, such that $G[V \setminus P]$ is a set of paths of length at most n/k. Then, the system covers all of the nodes of the ring in time $O\left((\frac{n}{k})^2\right)$, regardless of the initial pointer arrangement.*

PROOF. W.l.o.g, let $1 \le p_1 < p_2 < \ldots < p_k \le n$. Given a fixed initial pointer arrangement, let $x \in [1, n]$ be the node which is visited last by the rotor-router. To prove the claim, by the slow-down lemma, it suffices to construct a delayed deployment D of the rotor-router such that point x is visited by some agent within $O\left((\frac{n}{k})^2\right)$ rounds. We define deployment D as follows. Initially, we release all agents simultaneously, so that each agent moves left while the pointer of its current node points to the left, and stops as soon as it encounters a node whose pointer points to the right. Let q_i denote the position of the agent starting from p_i after this phase is complete; we have $p_i - n/k \le q_i \le p_i$, hence the duration of this phase is at most n/k. We also have $|q_{i+1} - q_i| \le 2\lceil n/k \rceil$. After this initialization phase, the deployment proceeds in steps of duration $4\lceil n/k \rceil$. The deployment is defined so that at the start of each step, agent i is located at point q_i. We describe the deployment through the following procedure, performed simultaneously by each agent i. The agent moves (to the right), stopping when it has either reached point q_{i+1}, or a node whose pointer points to the left. It then waits until the end of the $2\lceil n/k \rceil$-th round of the step to synchronize with other agents, and then returns to node q_i, where it waits until the end of the step.

We observe that in each step such that agent i does not reach q_{i+1}, it reaches a node on the path $[q_i, q_{i+1}]$ which has not previously been visited by any agent. Suppose that i is such that $q_i < x < q_{i+1}$. It follows that node x will be visited by agent i within $|q_{i+1} - q_i| \le 2\lceil n/k \rceil$ steps. Since the duration of each step is $4\lceil n/k \rceil$, the second phase of the delayed deployment takes at most $8\lceil n/k \rceil^2$ round. Overall, point x is covered within $O\left((\frac{n}{k})^2\right)$ rounds from the start of the process, and the claim follows. □

To prove that the equally-spaced initialization is the best possible, we provide a general case lower-bound of $\Omega\left((\frac{n}{k})^2\right)$ on cover time for all initializations. To do this, we introduce an auxiliary notion of a *good vertex* for an initialization of

the rotor-router. Such vertices are shown to always exist (in fact, to be in the majority in the vertex set) and take a long time to cover, regardless of the initial placement of agents.

DEFINITION 3.1. *For any placement of the k agents let $S = \{s_1, s_2, \ldots, s_k\}$ be the k not necessarily distinct starting vertices. We will consider the subset of good vertices of the cycle, defined as all nodes v which satisfy the following two constraints:*

1. *For all $1 \le r \le k$, $\left|[v, v + r\frac{n}{10k}] \cap S\right| \le r$.*

2. *For all $1 \le r \le k$, $\left|[v, v - r\frac{n}{10k}] \cap S\right| \le r$.*

The following lemma concerning the relation between good vertices and the starting positions of the agents, and proves useful in the analysis of the k-agent rotor-router, as well as the k-agent random walk.

LEMMA 3.6. *For any initial placement $S = \{s_1, s_2, \ldots, s_k\}$ of the k agents, there are at least $0.8n - o(n)$ good vertices.*

THEOREM 3.7. *If $n \ge 440k^2$, then for any set of initial locations of k agents, there exists an initial arrangement of pointers on the ring such that the cover time of the rotor-router system is $\Omega\left((\frac{n}{k})^2\right)$.*

3.3 Comparison with the Random Walk

The question of the cover time of random walks starting from a worst-case initial placement has already been resolved in the literature. On the one hand, it is known that the speed-up of cover time for a k-agent random walk with respect to the single agent case is $\Omega(\log k)$ for any graph whose cover time is asymptotically equal to the maximum hitting time [2], regardless of the initial placement of agents. Since this is clearly the case for the ring [1], we have that the cover time of the k-agent random walk is $O(n^2/\log(k))$. On the other hand, the adversary may choose to place all agents at one node of the ring. Such an all-one-one initialization has a cover time of precisely $\Theta(n^2/\log(k))$ [2]. Thus, the cover time for k random walks on the ring with worst-case initialization is $\Theta(n^2/\log(k))$.

To establish an upper bound for the best-case scenario, we consider k random walks with initial positions given with equal spacing, i.e., with offsets $0, n/k, 2(n/k), \ldots, (k-1)(n/k)$ relative to some node. (For simplicity, we assume here that k divides n.) The following lemma implies that in this case the cover time is $O((n/k)^2)$.

LEMMA 3.8. *Let $\alpha \ge 20$, $k \ge 2$ and let $t := \alpha^2 \cdot (n/k)^2 \cdot \log^2(k)$. Then, with probability at least $1 - k^{1-\alpha/20}$, k random walks starting from initial positions with equal spacing cover all the vertices of the ring within t steps.*

We now prove a corresponding lower bound on the cover time in the best-case scenario, showing that the position with equal spacing is asymptotically the best possible. We first prove an auxiliary result which relies on the notion of good vertices introduced in the previous subsection.

LEMMA 3.9. *Let $t = 10^{-4} \cdot (n/k)^2 \cdot \log^2(k)$, $k = \omega(1)$, and let u be any good vertex at distance at least $\frac{n}{10k}$ from the starting points of all random walks. Then, with probability at least $k^{-1/2}$, u is not covered after t steps by any of the k random walks.*

PROOF. First we will consider a random walk with distance $(n/k)/10 \le d \le 4 \cdot \sqrt{t}$ to u (recall that $t = 10^{-4} \cdot (n/k)^2 \cdot \log^2(k)$). We are interested in the probability that the random walk reaches a point with distance at least $4 \cdot \sqrt{t}$ to u before visiting u. Using the Gambler's ruin problem, this probability is equal to

$$\frac{d}{4 \cdot \sqrt{t}}.$$

Once the random walk has distance $4 \cdot \sqrt{t}$ to u, the probability that it does not visit u within t steps is at least $1/2$ (this follows by using a standard Chernoff bound). Combining these insights, we obtain that a random walk with distance $d \le 4 \cdot \sqrt{t}$ does not visit the vertex u within t steps with probability at least

$$\frac{d}{4 \cdot \sqrt{t}} \cdot \frac{1}{2}.$$

Consider now *all* random walks with distance less than $4 \cdot \sqrt{t}$. The number of these random walks is $4 \cdot \sqrt{t}/(n/k) = (1/25) \log k$. The probability that none of these random walks visits u is at least

$$\prod_{j=0}^{(1/25)\log(k)-1} \frac{\frac{n}{10k} + j \cdot \frac{n}{10k}}{4 \cdot \sqrt{t}} \cdot \frac{1}{2} \ge$$

$$\ge 4^{-(1/25)\log(k)} \prod_{j=1}^{(1/25)\log(k)} \frac{j \cdot \frac{n}{10k}}{\sqrt{t}}$$

$$= 4^{-(1/25)\log(k)} \cdot \prod_{j=1}^{(1/25)\log(k)} \frac{j}{(1/10)\log(k)}$$

$$= 10^{-(1/25)\log(k)} \cdot \prod_{j=1}^{(1/25)\log(k)} \frac{j}{(1/25)\log(k)}$$

$$\ge 10^{-(1/25)\log(k)} \cdot \frac{((1/25)\log(k))!}{((1/25)\log(k))^{(1/25)\log(k)}}$$

$$\ge 10^{-(1/25)\log(k)} \cdot e^{-(1/25)\log(k)},$$

where the last line follows from Stirling's approximation, i.e., for any sufficiently large integer $m \in \mathbb{N}$, $m! \ge (m/e)^m$.

For a random walk with distance $d = c \cdot \sqrt{t}$, $c \ge 4$ to u, the probability to visit u is at most $e^{-c/2}$ by a Chernoff bound. Hence the probability that u is visited by none of the random walks with distance at least $4 \cdot \sqrt{t}$ is lower bounded by

$$\prod_{j=(1/25)\log(k)}^{k} \left(1 - e^{-\frac{j \cdot \frac{n}{k}}{\sqrt{t}} \cdot \frac{1}{2}}\right) =$$

$$= \prod_{j=(1/25)\log(k)}^{k} \left(1 - e^{-\frac{1}{100} \frac{j}{\log(k)} \cdot \frac{1}{2}}\right)$$

$$= \prod_{j=(1/25)\log(k)}^{k} \left(1 - e^{-\frac{50j}{\log(k)}}\right)^{e^{\frac{50j}{\log(k)}} \cdot e^{-\frac{50j}{\log(k)}}}$$

$$\ge 4^{-\sum_{j=(1/25)\log(k)}^{\infty} e^{-\frac{50j}{\log(k)}}}$$

$$\ge 4^{-\frac{\log(k)}{25} \cdot \sum_{j=1}^{\infty} e^{-2j}} \ge 4^{-\frac{\log(k)}{25}},$$

where the third line used the fact that $(1-x)^{1/x} \ge \frac{1}{4}$ for $x \le 1/2$. Hence none of the k random walks will visit u with probability at least

$$10^{-(1/25)\log(k)} \cdot e^{-(1/25)\log(k)} \cdot 4^{-\frac{\log(k)}{25}} \ge k^{-1/2}.$$

$\square$

The lower bound on cover time is completed when we prove the existence of a good vertex satisfying the conditions of Lemma 3.9. We do this taking into account Lemma 3.6.

LEMMA 3.10. *For arbitrary starting positions of k random walks, we need at least $\Omega((n/k)^2 \log^2 k)$ steps to visit all n vertices with probability at least $1/2$.*

PROOF. Let $S = \{s_1, s_2, \ldots, s_k\}$ be the k not necessarily distinct starting vertices. Fix $t = 10^{-4} \cdot (n/k)^2 \cdot \log^2(k)$. and 3.9. We define intervals $I_i, 0 \le i < k/\log^2 k$, of the form $I_i = [(i-1)(n/k)\log^2 k, i(n/k)\log^2 k)$. The length of the union of all intervals with even indices is equal to $I = \bigcup_{0 \le j < k/2\log^2 k} I_{2j}$, and $|I| = 0.5n - o(n)$.

If F is the set of good vertices, then by Lemma 3.6, $|F| \ge 0.8n - o(n)$. Let H be the set of all nodes at distance at least $(n/k)/10$ to node from S; we have $|H| \ge 0.8n$. Thus $|I \cap F \cap H| \ge 0.1n - o(n)$ and $|I \cap F \cap H| \ge 0.09n$ for sufficiently large n. Since each interval I_i is of length $(n/k)\log^2 k$, at least $0.09k/\log^2 k$ intervals with even indices must contain a good vertex satisfying assumptions of lemma 3.9. We pick one such vertex from each interval. In this way, we obtain set S of $0.09k/\log^2 k$ vertices, at pairwise distances of at least $(n/k)\log^2 k$ from each other.

We denote by Y the event that none of random walks reached a distance more than $40 \cdot \sqrt{t} \log k$ to its origin. We note that $\mathbf{Pr}[Y] \ge 1 - k^{-40}$. We also denote by X the event, that every vertex in S is explored in time t by k random walks. Note, that $\mathbf{Pr}[X|Y] \le \left(1 - k^{-1/2}\right)^{\frac{k}{10} \frac{1}{\log^2(k)}}$ because if event Y happened, then each vertex $s \in S$ remains uncovered with probability at least $k^{-1/2}$ and these events are independent for different vertices in S. Hence

$$\mathbf{Pr}[X] \le \mathbf{Pr}[Y]\mathbf{Pr}[X|Y] + 1 - \mathbf{Pr}[Y] \le$$

$$\le \left(1 - k^{-1/2}\right)^{\frac{k}{100} \frac{9}{\log^2(k)}} + k^{-40} \le 1/2$$

The last inequality holds for $k > 1$. $\square$

Now, the characterization of the cover time of k random walks in the best-case scenario follows directly from Lemmas 3.8 and 3.10.

THEOREM 3.11. *The cover time of k random walks on the ring for best-case initial placement is $\Theta((n/k)^2 \log^2 k)$.* $\square$

4. RETURN TIME OF THE MULTI-AGENT ROTOR ROUTER ON THE RING

The considerations of the rotor-router in the previous section concerned the time required to cover all nodes in the initialization phase. As a deterministic system with a finite number of states, the rotor-router eventually reaches its limit behavior, cycling through a finite number of configurations. In this section, we characterize this limit behavior of the rotor-router using the concept of *return time*, i.e. the maximum over $v \in V$ of the length of the longest time interval during which v is not visited by any agent of the rotor-router system in its limit behavior. We show that this performance parameter of the rotor-router on the ring achieves the best possible value of $\Theta(\frac{n}{k})$, regardless of the initial placement of the agents.

THEOREM 4.1. *If $k \in O\left(n^{1/6}\right)$ then after a sufficiently large number of time steps, the k-agent rotor-router system will visit every node of the n vertex ring once every $\Theta(\frac{n}{k})$ time steps.*

No strong analogue of the above theorem holds for a system with k random walks. The only property which can be bounded is the expected time between two successive visits to a node, which is precisely equal to n/k on the ring (since the stationary distribution of each of the k walks is uniform with probability $1/n$ on each node). However, the random variable which describes the expected time between successive visits to a node has high variance.

5. CONCLUSIONS

We have shown that the muliti-agent rotor-router and the parallel random walk have similar speed-up characteristics w.r.t. the number of deployed agents, at least in terms of cover time and return time on the ring. It is interesting to note that the worst-case speed-up on the ring is $\Theta(\log k)$ for both the k-agent random walk and the k-agent rotor-router, even though this speed up has a different explanation in both cases. For the random walk, it is a consequence of the properties of probability distributions of independent Markovian processes, while for the rotor-router, it results directly from the interactions between different agents and the pointers in the graph.

Our work may also be seen as a step in the direction of understanding and characterizing the behavior of the multi-agent rotor-router in graphs different from the ring. Some of the techniques developed in this paper, in particular analysis based on delayed deployments, are also applicable in the general case.

Acknowledgement

A. Kosowski and R. Klasing thank Leszek Gąsieniec and Tomasz Radzik for inspiring discussions.

6. REFERENCES

[1] D. Aldous and J. A. Fill. Reversible Markov Chains and Random Walks on Graphs, 1995. http://stat-www.berkeley.edu/users/aldous/RWG/book.html.

[2] N. Alon, C. Avin, M. Koucký, G. Kozma, Z. Lotker, and M. R. Tuttle. Many random walks are faster than one. In *SPAA*, pages 119–128. ACM, 2008.

[3] E. Bampas, L. Gasieniec, N. Hanusse, D. Ilcinkas, R. Klasing, and A. Kosowski. Euler tour lock-in problem in the rotor-router model. In *DISC*, volume 5805 of *LNCS*, pages 423–435, 2009.

[4] E. Bampas, L. Gasieniec, R. Klasing, A. Kosowski, and T. Radzik. Robustness of the rotor-router mechanism. In *OPODIS*, volume 5923 of *LNCS*, pages 345–358, 2009.

[5] S. N. Bhatt, S. Even, D. S. Greenberg, and R. Tayar. Traversing directed eulerian mazes. *J. Graph Algorithms Appl.*, 6(2):157–173, 2002.

[6] C. Cooper, D. Ilcinkas, R. Klasing, and A. Kosowski. Derandomizing random walks in undirected graphs using locally fair exploration strategies. *Dist. Comp.*, 24(2):91–99, 2011.

[7] J. N. Cooper and J. Spencer. Simulating a random walk with constant error. *Combinatorics, Probability & Computing*, 15(6):815–822, 2006.

[8] B. Doerr and T. Friedrich. Deterministic random walks on the two-dimensional grid. *Combinatorics, Probability & Computing*, 18(1-2):123–144, 2009.

[9] K. Efremenko and O. Reingold. How well do random walks parallelize? In *APPROX-RANDOM*, volume 5687 of *LNCS*, pages 476–489, 2009.

[10] R. Elsässer and T. Sauerwald. Tight bounds for the cover time of multiple random walks. In *ICALP (1)*, volume 5555 of *LNCS*, pages 415–426, 2009.

[11] T. Friedrich and T. Sauerwald. The cover time of deterministic random walks. In *COCOON*, volume 6196 of *LNCS*, pages 130–139, 2010.

[12] V. Priezzhev, D. Dhar, A. Dhar, and S. Krishnamurthy. Eulerian walkers as a model of self-organized criticality. *Phys. Rev. Lett.*, 77(25):5079–5082, Dec 1996.

[13] T. Sauerwald. Expansion and the cover time of parallel random walks. In *PODC*, pages 315–324. ACM, 2010.

[14] I. A. Wagner, M. Lindenbaum, and A. M. Bruckstein. Distributed covering by ant-robots using evaporating traces. *IEEE Trans. Robotics and Automation*, 15:918–933, 1999.

[15] V. Yanovski, I. A. Wagner, and A. M. Bruckstein. A distributed ant algorithm for efficiently patrolling a network. *Algorithmica*, 37(3):165–186, 2003.

Efficient Distributed Source Detection
with Limited Bandwidth

Christoph Lenzen
Massachusetts Institute of Technology
32 Vassar Street
02139 Cambridge, USA
clenzen@csail.mit.edu

David Peleg
Dept. of Computer Science and Applied Math.
Weizmann Institute of Science
76100 Rehovot, Israel
david.peleg@weizmann.ac.il

ABSTRACT

Given a simple graph $G = (V, E)$ and a set of sources $S \subseteq V$, denote for each node $v \in V$ by $\mathcal{L}_v^{(\infty)}$ the lexicographically ordered list of distance/source pairs $(d(s, v), s)$, where $s \in S$. For integers $d, k \in \mathbb{N} \cup \{\infty\}$, we consider the *source detection*, or (S, d, k)-*detection* task, requiring each node v to learn the first k entries of $\mathcal{L}_v^{(\infty)}$ (if for all of them $d(s, v) \leq d$) or all entries $(d(s, v), s) \in \mathcal{L}_v^{(\infty)}$ satisfying that $d(s, v) \leq d$ (otherwise). Solutions to this problem provide natural generalizations of concurrent breadth-first search (BFS) tree constructions. For example, the special case of $k = \infty$ requires each source $s \in S$ to build a complete BFS tree rooted at s, whereas the special case of $d = \infty$ and $S = V$ requires constructing a partial BFS tree comprising at least k nodes from every node in V.

In this work, we give a simple, near-optimal solution for the source detection task in the CONGEST model, where messages contain at most $\mathcal{O}(\log n)$ bits, running in $d + k$ rounds. We demonstrate its utility for various routing problems, exact and approximate diameter computation, and spanner construction. For those problems, we obtain algorithms in the CONGEST model that are faster and in some cases much simpler than previous solutions.

Categories and Subject Descriptors

G.2.2 [**Discrete Mathematics**]: Graph Theory—*Graph algorithms, Path and circuit problems*; C.2.4 [**Computer-Communication Networks**]: Distributed Systems

Keywords

concurrent incomplete breadth-first search; distance and diameter computation; all-to-all shortest paths; compact routing; additive spanners; Bellmann-Ford

1. INTRODUCTION

This work concerns a basic network-algorithmic task hereafter referred to as the *source detection* or (S, d, k)-*detection* task. Given a subset $S \subseteq V$ of source nodes and a node $v \in V$, let $\mathcal{L}_v^{(\infty)}$ denote the (ascending) lexicographically ordered list of pairs $(d(v, s), s)$, where $s \in S$ and $d(v, s)$ is the length of a shortest path from v to s. The (S, d, k)-detection problem requires that each node $v \in V$ learns the first $\min\{k, \lambda_v^d\}$ entries of $\mathcal{L}_v^\infty$, where λ_v^d is the number of sources $s \in S$ satisfying that $d(s, v) \leq d$. The paper develops a time efficient algorithm for this task in the CONGEST model, and illustrates its usefulness by discussing some of its applications.

To motivate the source detection task, and illustrate its scope of applicability, let us discuss two application domains where this task can be utilized. The first is the construction of shortest-path spanning trees, which is one of the most fundamental problems in algorithmic graph theory. Shortest-path spanning trees, and breadth-first search (BFS) trees in the special case of unweighted graphs, play a key role in a wide variety of applications in graph algorithms, communication networks, distributed and parallel computing, and many other areas of computer science. In many cases one is interested in but one complete shortest path (or BFS) spanning tree. Nevertheless, frequently some other variant is in demand. In particular, for certain applications one is interested in finding *all* shortest path trees (or BFS trees) of the given graph, one for each source node. In other applications, one is interested in a *partial* shortest path tree (or BFS tree), e.g., one spanning all nodes at distance up to d from the source. A basic task encompassing all of the above variants of the problem is the *multiple source partial BFS trees* problem. This problem is characterized by two parameters: a subset $S \subseteq V$ of source nodes, and an integer d. The problem is to construct, for each source node $s \in S$, a partial BFS tree T_s^d spanning all the nodes at distance at most d from s. Clearly, this problem can be cast as a special case of the source detection task.

A second application domain concerns *fault-tolerant centers* and *facility location* problems. Consider a setting where it is necessary to place some *service centers*, or *production facilities*, in some of the nodes of the graph at hand. Those centers are planned to provide certain crucial services to some other nodes of the network, acting as *clients*. A client $v \in V$ selects the nearest server, $\varphi(v)$, and gets served by that server. Hence the relevant efficiency measure is the distance $d(v, \varphi(v))$ from v to its designated server (or sometimes the product of that distance times the *demand* issued by v). Hence it is important to optimize the spread of servers in the network. The problem of selecting locations for centers or facilities is typically NP-hard, and is not considered here. Rather, we are concerned with the situation *after* a set S of service centers has already been fixed. Let us further concentrate on a scenario where service centers might occasionally *fail*, forcing their clients to re-compute their choice of a temporary designated server. In network settings, where such failures occur frequently, it may be important to devise an efficient distributed algorithm for re-computing the assignment of centers to clients. In particular, one solution approach would be to prepare to the eventuality of (up to f) failures of centers by requiring each client node to learn in advance a list of the $f + 1$ service centers closest to it, so that in case some of its closest centers fail, it may switch without delay to using the next closest center. (Here we assume that failures make a center incapable of providing service, but the associated network node can still be used for communiation.) This fault-tolerant centers problem maps to $(S, \infty, f + 1)$-detection. If, in addition, clients refuse using very distant centers, then a threshold d, which is smaller than the diameter D of the network (namely, the maximum distance between network nodes) may be imposed on the maximum allowed service distance, yielding an instance of the $(S, d, f + 1)$-detection problem.

The complexity of the source detection task clearly depends on the model at hand. Here we focus on the CONGEST model (cf. [19]), formally defined in Section 3, which takes bandwidth limitations into account. The source detection task has a straightforward optimal algorithm in a distributed model with no bandwidth limitations, such as the LOCAL model (which is identical to the CONGEST model except that it imposes no restrictions on the size of messages). Our main goal in this paper is to develop a time-efficient distributed algorithm for the (S, d, k)-detection task, and in turn, for the multiple source partial BFS trees problem, in the CONGEST model, where bandwidth is limited. It is noteworthy that as a byproduct of our technique, one may also compute for every node v the next hop on the shortest paths to its sources. This makes our algorithm a powerful tool for computing or approximating the network diameter, routing, and many other related tasks.

Contributions

Our main contribution is the introduction of the basic paradigm of (S, d, k)-detection in networks and an efficient distributed algorithm for solving it in the CONGEST model in time $\min\{d, D\} + \min\{k, |S|\}$ (Section 4). In contrast, solving (S, d, k)-detection using existing techniques results in time complexity $\Omega(|S|)$. Hence, we obtain improvements of $\Theta(n)$ for extreme cases (where n is the number of nodes in the network). Note that the time complexity of our solution is not asymptotic, and the dependency on d and k is optimal due to a trivial lower bound. (With respect to k this bound requires that only one identifier fits into a message; otherwise the lower bound, as well as the upper bound of the algorithm, decrease by the respective factor in the k-summand.) Even for the special case of (S, ∞, ∞)-detection (or, equivalently, (S, D, n)-detection), the appealing simplicity of our approach therefore results in $(1 + o(1))$-optimal solutions for several tasks granted that $\log D \in o(\log n)$.[1] While this is a

mere constant-factor improvement over the results from [15, 20], we consider it valuable because it affects the complexity of some fundamental tasks.

We further motivate this result by leveraging it for applications in Section 5:

- **All-to-all shortest paths and diameter:** Each node needs to learn the distance and next routing hop to each other node. From this information one can also compute the diameter in $\mathcal{O}(D)$ time. Variations of this problem result from considering different wake-up mechanisms. In all cases, we obtain a deterministic $(n + \mathcal{O}(D))$-round solution.

- **3/2-approximation of the diameter:** The task is to compute an estimate $\tilde{D}$ of the diameter in the range $[2D/3, D]$. Utilizing our solution for (S, d, k)-detection, this can be done by a randomized algorithm within $\mathcal{O}(\sqrt{n} \log n + D)$ rounds.

- **Approximation of all-to-all shortest paths:** Here it is required to construct a mechanism allowing all nodes to determine the next routing hop on a path that is at most by some multiplicative *stretch* factor longer than a shortest path to the destination. Furthermore, we allow assigning (new) labels to the nodes, replacing their identifiers, as otherwise nodes cannot learn the entire namespace quickly. For any $\gamma \in \{1, \dots, \log n\}$, it is possible to construct such a mechanism ensuring stretch $\mathcal{O}(\gamma)$ by a randomized preprocessing algorithm requiring $\tilde{\mathcal{O}}(n^{1/2+1/\gamma} + D)$ rounds.[2]

- **Compact Routing:** The task is the same as in the previous case, but we now also ask for low memory requirements by the routing tables. We can construct such compact routing tables achieving stretch $\mathcal{O}(\gamma^2)$ and using $\mathcal{O}(n^{1/\gamma} \log^{\mathcal{O}(1)} n)$ memory by a randomized preprocessing algorithm requiring $\tilde{\mathcal{O}}(n^{1/2+1/(2\gamma)} + D)$ rounds.

- **Constructing 2-additive spanners:** We seek to select a small subset of the edges so that in the resulting graph, distances do not increase by more than 2. We obtain a randomized construction of running time $\mathcal{O}(\sqrt{n} \log n + D)$ that produces 2-additive spanners with $\mathcal{O}(n^{3/2} \log n)$ edges.

For all the listed tasks, previous solutions exist, but are slower than the ones we provide. In addition, in many cases our approach simplifies the resulting algorithms. All randomized constructions succeed with high probability.

Before presenting our algorithm for (S, d, k)-detection, we discuss related work in the following section and introduce the system model in Section 3.

2. RELATED WORK

The all-pairs shortest path (APSP) problem has been studied extensively in the sequential setting, and was also given several solutions in the distributed setting [3, 8, 14, 16, 23]. The algorithm of [16] is fast ($O(n)$ time) but involves using large messages, hence does not apply in the CONGEST model. The algorithm of [3] uses short ($O(\log n)$

---

[1] Otherwise the size of distance counters is not negligible, and we can conclude asymptotic optimality only.

[2] Here, the $\tilde{\mathcal{O}}(x)$ notation hides any polylogarithmic factors in x.

bits) messages, hence it can be executed in the CONGEST model, but it requires time $O(n \log n)$, and moreover, it applies only to the special family of BHC graphs, which are graphs structured as a balanced hierarchy of clusters. Most of the distributed algorithms for the APSP problem aim at minimizing the message complexity, rather than the time. The algorithm of [14] requires time $O(n^2)$.

In the CONGEST model, a trivial lower bound of $\Omega(n)$ applies, which has independently been asymptotically matched by two algorithms [15, 20]. Our solution improves on these works in that we achieve an optimal multiplicative constant with respect to n.

Note that the network diameter can easily be computed exactly by first solving the APSP problem. It was shown in [12] that, in the CONGEST model, computing the exact diameter requires time $\tilde{\Omega}(n)$; this nontrivial lower bound holds even for networks of constant diameter. Hence these results also imply near-optimal algorithms for computing the exact diameter in the CONGEST model. In the LOCAL model, computing the diameter exactly trivially requires exactly D rounds (using large messages). An efficient algorithm for doing this in $\mathcal{O}(D)$ rounds (using $O(n \log n)$ bit messages) is found in [2].

Similar to the exact setting, an approximation of the diameter can be obtained by any algorithm that computes an approximation of APSP (see for example [4, 9, 10]). A sequential algorithm that approximates the diameter in weighted directed graphs in $\tilde{O}(n^2 + |E|\sqrt{n})$ steps was presented in [1]. This algorithm returns an acyclic path of length at least $2D/3$. It has been leveraged for computing a distributed $3/2$-approximation in the CONGEST model in $\tilde{O}(\sqrt{n}D)$ randomized rounds [20]. An algorithm that computes a $(1 + \epsilon)$-approximation of the diameter in time $O(n/D + D)$ was presented in [15], and combining these two algorithms yielded a randomized $3/2$-approximation within time $\mathcal{O}(n^{3/4} + D)$. This running time was very recently improved to $\tilde{\mathcal{O}}(\sqrt{n} + D)$ by the authors of [15, 20], relying also on a new result of [22]. The same result follows from our technique, solely relying on the original algorithm from [1], and with a smaller leading constant factor. These results are tight up to a factor of $\mathcal{O}(\log^2 n)$, as is shown in [12]: even approximating the diameter by a factor of $3/2 - \epsilon$ may sometimes require $\tilde{\Omega}(\sqrt{n})$ time, for any constant $\epsilon > 0$. (In contrast, a 2-approximation for D is easily computed in time $\mathcal{O}(D)$ by constructing one BFS tree and measuring its depth.)

Our results with respect to approximation of all-to-all shortest paths build on recent results for this problem in weighted graphs [18]. Specialized to the unweighted case, our solution to (S, d, k)-detection can replace a subroutine from [18] in order to achieve a stretch of $\mathcal{O}(\gamma)$ within time $\tilde{\mathcal{O}}(n^{1/2+1/\gamma} + D)$. This notably improves the trade-off between stretch and running time; for the same running time bound, the stretch guarantee is $\mathcal{O}(\gamma \log \gamma)$ for the algorithm from [18]. In contrast to the results discussed above, this non-constant improvement of the running time cannot be achieved by previous algorithms for building multiple BFS trees concurrently. The latter is due to the fact that the algorithm from [18] requires to build partial trees only, i.e., $k \ll n$ in the corresponding instances of (S, d, k)-detection. The same holds for our statement on compact routing, where we also build on [18]; however, [18] itself does not pro-

vide a result regarding compact routing, as we need to exploit that distances are unweighted in order to store routing paths efficiently in a distributed manner. Both the shortest paths and the compact routing problems have been studied extensively (cf. [4, 6, 13, 17, 19, 21, 24] and references). However, most previous work on these problems either focused on efficient performance (stretch, memory) and ignored the time-efficiency of the preprocessing stage, provided time-efficient seqential (centralized) preprocessing algorithms, or gave time-efficient distributed algorithms in the LOCAL model (which allows unbounded message size).

There are essentially three known constructions for additive spanners. Constructions for 2-additive spanners with $\mathcal{O}(n^{3/2})$ edges were presented and expanded in [1, 9, 11, 21, 25]. An efficient construction for 6-additive spanners with $\mathcal{O}(n^{4/3})$ edges was later presented in [5]. Recently, a construction for 4-additive spanners with $\mathcal{O}(n^{7/5})$ edges was presented in [7]. In the distributed case, the construction for 2-additive spanners requires to concurrently build $\tilde{\mathcal{O}}(\sqrt{n})$ complete BFS trees. Hence, it can be implemented in the CONGEST model utilizing the results from [15] in $\tilde{\mathcal{O}}(\sqrt{n} + D)$ randomized rounds. Again, employing our routine yields the same result, but with a smaller multiplicative constant in the dominating term of the running time.

3. MODEL

We follow the CONGEST model as described in [19]. The distributed system is represented by a simple, connected graph $G = (V, E)$ of $n = |V|$ nodes. Each node $v \in V$ has a unique identifier of $\mathcal{O}(\log n)$ bits that we identify with the node, i.e., v denotes both the node and its identifier. Communication is synchronous; in each round, each node $v \in V$ can send a (possibly distinct) message comprising $\mathcal{O}(\log n)$ bits to each of its neighbors $\mathcal{N}_v = \{w \in V \mid \{v, w\} \in E\}$. Initially, node $v \in V$ is aware of $\mathcal{N}_v$ only. In the case of randomized algorithms, each node has access to an independent, infinite, and unbiased source of random bits.

We use the following additional notation. A path p of length d is a sequence of nodes $(v_0, \ldots, v_d)$ satisfying that $\{v_{i-1}, v_i\} \in E$ for all $i \in \{1, \ldots, d\}$. For $v, w \in V$, let $d(v, w)$ denote the minimal length of any path from v to w. The diameter of the graph is then $D = \max_{v, w \in V}\{d(v, w)\}$, the maximum distance between nodes in the graph.

We consider a setting where a subset $S \subseteq V$ of the nodes in the graph is marked as *source* nodes. In the distributed context, each node v maintains a variable s_v set to $s_v = v$ if $v \in S$ and $s_v = \bot$ otherwise. Given a node $v \in V$, the *S-proximity-list* (or simply *S-list*) of v, denoted $\mathcal{L}_v^{(\infty)}$, is the (ascending) lexicographically ordered list of pairs $(d(v, s), s)$, for every $s \in S$. Here, by ascending lexicographical order we mean that $(d(v, s), s) < (d(w, s'), s')$ iff $d(v, s) < d(w, s')$ or $d(v, s) = d(w, s')$ and $s < s'$ (where the latter is determined by an order on the node identifiers). For an integer $d > 0$, denote the prefix of v's S-proximity-list consisting of the sources at distance at most d from v by $\mathcal{L}_v^{(d)} = \{s \in S \mid d(v, s) \leq d\}$, and let $\lambda_v^d = |\mathcal{L}_v^{(d)}|$.

4. DETECTING NEARBY SOURCES

In this section, we present an efficient deterministic algorithm for the *source detection* task. The (S, d, k)-detection problem requires that each node $v \in V$ learns the first

$\min\{k, \lambda_v^d\}$ entries of $\mathcal{L}_v^{(\infty)}$ (i.e., either all sources up to distance d or just the k closest ones, if there are too many).

In absence of restrictions on bandwidth, the straightforward distributed implementation of the classical Bellmann-Ford algorithm matches the requirements of this problem perfectly. Each node v maintains a list L_v of the distance/source pairs that it knows about. The list is initially empty if $s_v = \perp$ and contains $(0, s_v)$ otherwise. In each round, each node v broadcasts L_v. Upon reception of such a message, for each received pair (d_s, s) for which there is no own pair $(d_s', s) \in L_v$, it adds (d_s+1, s) to L_v. After d rounds, v knows the sources within distance d from itself, and their correct distance; thus it is able to order the source/distance pairs correctly. This approach results in concurrently constructing BFS trees for all sources $s \in S$ up to depth d. (Note that the algorithm as presented does not store the parent of each node, but the respective modification is trivial.)

The situation gets more involved if nodes may only send $\mathcal{O}(\log n)$ bits in each round, as this implies that they can communicate only a constant number of entries out of each list per round. Trivially, one can simply dedicate $|S|$ rounds to the simulation of a single round of the unconstrained algorithm. This results in a running time of $\mathcal{O}(|S|d)$ for an algorithm solving (S, d, k)-detection for arbitrary k. More generally, sending only the $k \in \mathbb{N}$ smallest distance/source pairs (according to the lexicographical order) solves (S, d, k)-detection in kd rounds (cf. [18]).

Observe, however, that a trivial lower bound of $d + k - 1$ holds if one can send only one identifier per round. To see this, consider a chain of nodes of length $d - 1$ and append k sources to one of its endpoints; since the other endpoint needs to receive the k source identifiers sequentially and the first one arrives no earlier than round d, the lower bound follows.

In light of this lower bound, the question arises whether one can solve the task in $\mathcal{O}(d+k)$ rounds in the CONGEST model. Clearly, such an improved time bound requires a more sophisticated strategy, as resending the entire list L_v is wasteful if there are no relevant updates. In [15, 20], n BFS constructions are started in a staggered fashion, essentially ensuring that on each round, at most one update needs to be sent on every edge. In [15], a second algorithm resolves this issue slightly differently, by giving the updates preference according to the (total) order of source identifiers and requiring that in each iteration only one update is transmitted over each edge, i.e., for nodes v and $w \in \mathcal{N}_v$ either v sends an update to w or vice versa, not both. It is shown that this ensures that each node will receive accurate distance information for each source with the first update it receives regarding the respective source. Neither of these strategies is sufficient to achieve a complexity bound of $\mathcal{O}(d + k)$ for the (S, d, k)-problem for the entire range of parameters, though, as they use the *identifiers* as the primary means of ordering, rather than the *distances*.

Consequently, in this paper we use the arguably even simpler mechanism that assigns priorities according to distance: In each round, each node v just sends to all neighbors the smallest pair in L_v that it has not transmitted yet. Note that this entails that a node might possibly send multiple updates regarding the same source, each notifying its neighbors that it learned that the respective source is in fact closer to it than previously announced. The pseudo-code of this approach is given by Algorithm 1.

We first establish correctness of the algorithm, by arguing that eventually the lists L_v do not change any more, and this final state must satisfy that all source/distance pairs reflect actual distances in G. In order to formalize this statement, denote by $L_v^{(r)}$ the state of L_v at the beginning of round $r \in \mathbb{N}$ of the algorithm.

LEMMA 4.1. *For any graph and any $S \subseteq V$, there is some round $r_0 \in \mathbb{N}$ such that no node $v \in V$ sends messages or modifies L_v in rounds $r \geq r_0$. Moreover, $L_v^{(r_0)} = \mathcal{L}_v^{(\infty)}$, i.e., $d_s = d(v, s)$ for every $(d_s, s) \in L_v^{(r_0)}$.*

PROOF. Each list is initially empty or contains some pair $(0, s)$. For a source $s \in S$ and round $r \in \mathbb{N}$, define

$$d_{\max}(s, r) = \max\{d_s \in \mathbb{N} \mid \exists v \in V : (d_s, s) \in L_v^{(r)}\}.$$

Clearly, $d_{\max}(s, r+1) \leq d_{\max}(s, r) + 1$, and in case of equality, some node v that did not have any pair $(d_s, s) \in L_v^{(r)}$ added such a pair to L_v in round r. Hence, $d_{\max}(s, r)$ is uniformly bounded by $n - 1$ for all s and r. It follows that each node $v \in V$ modifies its variables only finitely often: For each $s \in S$, it can add at most $n - 1$ pairs (d_s, s) to L_v during the course of the algorithm, and for each pair, it will initialize $\text{sent}_v(d_s, s)$ to FALSE and set it to TRUE at most once.

Now consider a round r in which no node modifies the contents of its variables; we just showed that such a round exists. In particular, no node sends a message (as this results in modifying the respective sent variable), implying that the same must hold for the next round (because no node v had an unsent entry in L_v, and contents of variables did not change). Consequently, no node v adds an entry to L_v in round $r + 1$, implying that no variables are changed in this round either. Repeating this argument inductively, we see that for the minimal round r_0 in which no variables change, it holds that the algorithm has reached a steady state in which all local variables, in particular the lists L_v, become invariant.

It remains to show that for all $s \in S$ and $v \in V$ it holds that $(d(v, s), s) \in L_v^{(r_0)}$ (this is sufficient because $(\cdot, s)$ is deleted from L_v before adding such an entry). We first prove that we have $(d_s, s) \in L_v^{(r_0)}$ with $d_s \leq d(v, s)$. To see this, consider a shortest path $(v_0 = s, v_1, \ldots, v_{d(v,s)} = v)$ from s to v. Since s initializes L_s to $(0, s)$ and $\text{sent}(0, s)$ to FALSE, it will send $(0, s)$ in the first round. We claim that each node v_i, $i \in \{1, \ldots, d(v, s)\}$, will eventually receive a message (d_{i-1}, s) with $d_{i-1} \leq i - 1$. This follows by induction anchored at $i = 1$, where the step consists of observing that if v_i receives (d_{i-1}, s), it must have already sent or will eventually send a message (d_i, s) with $d_i \leq d_{i-1} + 1$.

To complete the proof, we now show that also $d_s \geq d(v, s)$. At initialization, the contents of all lists satisfy that they represent accurate distance information, i.e., for the pairs $(0, s) \in L_s$, $s \in S$, it holds that $0 = d(s, s)$. Hence, assume for contradiction that the claim is false and suppose that v is a node that adds (d_s, s) with $d_s < d(v, s)$ to L_v in a minimal round $r \geq 1$. It follows that v received a message $(d_s - 1, s)$ from some neighbor $w \in \mathcal{N}_v$. Thus, this neighbor added $(d_s - 1, s)$ to L_w in an earlier round (or at initialization). However, since $d(w, s) \geq d(v, s) - 1$, it follows that there is an earlier violation of the claim, contradicting the assumption that r is minimal (or the observation that at initialization the claim holds). Thus indeed $d_s = d(v, s)$ for all $(d_s, s) \in L_v^{(r_0)}$, $v \in V$, concluding the proof. $\square$

Algorithm 1: DBF(S): Distributed Bellmann-Ford at node $v \in V$. Each node initially only needs to know whether it is in S itself. As stated, the algorithm does not terminate. The local termination condition depends on the application and is discussed later on.

1 $L_v := ()$ // list of distance/source pairs $(d_s, s) \in \mathbb{N}_0 \times S$, lexicographically ordered
2 $\text{sent}_v : L_v \to \{\text{TRUE}, \text{FALSE}\}$ // whether a pair in L_v has already been sent by v
3 if $v \in S$ **then**
4 $\quad L_v := ((0, v))$
5 $\quad \text{sent}_v(0, v) := \text{FALSE}$
6 // each iteration of the loop takes one round
7 while TRUE **do**
8 $\quad$ **if** $\exists (d_s, s) \in L_v : \text{sent}(d_s, s) = \text{FALSE}$ **then**
9 $\quad\quad (d_s, s) := \operatorname{argmin}\{(d'_s, s') \in L_v \mid \text{sent}_v(d'_s, s') = \text{FALSE}\}$
10 $\quad\quad$ send (d_s, s) to all neighbors
11 $\quad\quad \text{sent}_v(d_s, s) := \text{TRUE}$
12 $\quad$ **for** *received (d_s, s) from some neighbor* **do**
13 $\quad\quad$ **if** $\nexists (d'_s, s) : d'_s \le d_s + 1$ **then**
14 $\quad\quad\quad L_v := L_v \setminus \{(\cdot, s)\}$ // remove outdated entry, if there is one
15 $\quad\quad\quad L_v := L_v \cup \{(d_s + 1, s)\}$
16 $\quad\quad\quad \text{sent}_v(d_s + 1, s) := \text{FALSE}$

Since the algorithm accepts that we might "waste" messages by sending updates that contain incorrect distance information, we need to show that there are not too many such wasted messages. As the previous lemma shows that eventually the algorithm determines correct values, this can be rephrased in terms of bounding the number of rounds for which the k smallest entries of L_v might change. To this end, for an entry $(d_s, s) \in L_v^{(r)}$, let $\ell_v^{(r)}(d_s, s)$ denote its index in the (lexicographically ordered) list $L_v^{(r)}$.

LEMMA 4.2. *For every node $v \in V$ and round $r \in \mathbb{N}$ of Algorithm 1,*

(i) v does not send a message (d_s, s) with

$$(d_s, s) + \ell_v^{(r)}(d_s, s) < r$$

in round r,

(ii) v does not add a pair (d_s, s) to L_v with

$$(d_s, s) + \ell_v^{(r)}(d_s, s) \le r$$

in round r.

PROOF. Clearly, if (i) holds in round $r \in \mathbb{N}$, then (ii) also holds in round r because nodes increase d_s by 1 upon adding pairs to L_v. Moreover, (i) is trivially satisfied in round 1, as $\ell_v^{(r)}(d_s, s) \ge 1$ for all v, d_s, r, and s. Hence, in order to prove the claim, assume for contradiction that there is a minimal round $r > 1$ such that (i) is violated, while (ii) holds for all rounds $r' < r$.

Thus, some node $v \in V$ sends a message (d_s, s) with

$$d_s + \ell_v^{(r)}(d_s, s) < r$$

in round r. Note that $d_s \ne 0$, i.e., (d_s, s) is not one of the entries of L_v at initialization since these are all sent in the first round. This implies that v has added (d_s, s) to L_v in some round $1 \le r' < r$. Because $\ell_v^{(r)}(d_s, s)$ is non-decreasing with r, we have that

$$\ell_v^{(r)}(d_s, s) \ge \ell_v^{(r')}(d_s, s).$$

By Statement (ii) for round r', this entails that

$$r > d_s + \ell_v^{(r)}(d_s, s) \ge d_s + \ell_v^{(r')}(d_s, s) > r',$$

yielding that in fact $r' \le r - 2$ as the involved values are all integer. Therefore, considering that v did not send (d_s, s) in round $r - 1$ but in round r, it must have sent a different pair $(d_{s'}, s')$ in round $r - 1$. By Statement (i) for round $r - 1$, it holds that

$$d_{s'} + \ell_v^{(r-1)}(d_{s'}, s') \ge r - 1.$$

However, since $(d_{s'}, s')$ must be lexicographically smaller than (d_s, s), we have that

$$d_{s'} + \ell_v^{(r-1)}(d_{s'}, s') < d_s + \ell_v^{(r-1)}(d_s, s).$$

Overall, we arrive at the contradiction that

$$
\begin{aligned}
d_s + \ell_v^{(r-1)}(d_s, s) &> d_{s'} + \ell_v^{(r-1)}(d_{s'}, s') \\
&\ge r - 1 \\
&\ge d_s + \ell_v^{(r)}(d_s, s) \\
&\ge d_s + \ell_v^{(r-1)}(d_s, s),
\end{aligned}
$$

where the last step once more applies the fact that $\ell_v^{(r)}(d_s, s)$ is non-decreasing with r. $\quad\square$

Together, both lemmas show that the algorithm is a near-optimal solution to the (S, d, k)-detection problem.

LEMMA 4.3. *Given an instance of the (S, d, k)-detection problem, for every $v \in V$ and for any round r of an execution of Algorithm 1 with*

$$r \ge r(S, d, k) = \min\{d, D\} + \min\{k, |S|\},$$

$L_v^{(r)}$ truncated to the (up to) k first entries $(d_s, s) \in L_v^{(r)}$ with $d_s \le d$ solves (S, d, k)-detection.

PROOF. Without loss of generality, $d \le D$ (no source can be further away) and $k \le |S|$ (for any $k \ge |S|$ all nodes need to learn about all sources). By Lemma 4.1, there is a round $r_0 \in \mathbb{N}$ such that for all $v \in V$ and $r' \ge r_0$, $L_v^{(r')} = L_v^{(r_0)} = \mathcal{L}_v^{(\infty)}$. By definition, the first (up to) k entries $(d_s, s) \in L_v^{(r_0)}$

with $d_s \leq d$ thus solve (S, d, k)-detection. By Lemma 4.2, these entries do not change in any round $r' \geq d + k = r(S, d, k)$, completing the proof. □

THEOREM 4.4. *Algorithm 1 solves (S, d, k)-detection in time $\min\{d, D\} + \min\{k, |S|\}$.*

We conclude this section with two remarks. First, the proof of Lemma 4.2 can be generalized to show that if up to $\alpha \in \mathbb{N}$ list entries are sent in each round, then node v will not add pairs with $(d_s, s) + \lceil \ell_v^{(r)}(d_s, s)/\alpha \rceil \leq r$ to L_v in round r. Therefore, if α list entries may be sent, then (S, d, k)-detection can be solved within $\min\{d, D\} + \lceil \min\{k, |S|\}/\alpha \rceil$ rounds. Likewise, we have a trivial lower bound of $d + \lceil k/\alpha \rceil$ for (S, d, k)-detection in this setting. Our technique is thus, up to the bits encoding the distance information d_s for an entry (d_s, s), optimal for the entire parameter range. In particular, if $\log D \in o(\log n)$, then it is $(1 + o(1))$-optimal for arbitrary message size.

Secondly, the algorithm can be generalized to permit that subsets of nodes are identified into a single "source cluster" $s \in S$. This is done simply by passing all nodes v in cluster s the input $s_v = s$. The feasibility of this modification follows from a simple simulation argument given in [18] that also applies in the unweighted case.

5. APPLICATIONS

In this section, we present applications of our solution to the generic (S, d, k)-detection problem.

Exact All-to-all Shortest Paths and Diameter

In the distributed version of the all-to-all shortest paths problem, we require that each node v learns for each other node w the next routing hop on a shortest path to w. This is equivalent to constructing for each node v a BFS tree rooted at it. The diameter then can be determined as the maximum of the depths of the trees. These tasks can be solved efficiently by means of Algorithm 1.

COROLLARY 5.1. *All-to-all shortest paths routing tables can be constructed in $n + \mathcal{O}(D)$ time by a uniform algorithm (i.e., n and D are initially unknown to the nodes).*

PROOF. With a slight modification of Algorithm 1, constructing BFS trees rooted at the sources comes for free: Instead of adding pairs (d_s, s) to the list L_v, node v stores triples (d_s, s, p), where the sender p of the message $(d_s - 1, s)$ causing the triple to be stored becomes the parent of v in the BFS tree rooted at s; p then is the next routing hop from v to s.

To solve the problem, we first construct a single BFS tree rooted at some node r (e.g., the one with smallest identifier), determine its depth (i.e., a 2-approximation of D) and count the number of nodes, and finally distribute these values to all nodes. This can be done by standard techniques in $\mathcal{O}(D)$ rounds (even with asynchronous wake-up). Subsequently r initiates a run of (the modified version of) Algorithm 1 (another D rounds) with $S = V$ that is stopped at all nodes after $n + \tilde{D}$ rounds, where $D \leq \tilde{D} \leq 2D$ is twice the depth of the BFS tree rooted at r. By Theorem 4.4, all nodes will have accurate distance information on all other nodes, i.e., all constructed trees are indeed complete BFS trees. □

COROLLARY 5.2. *All nodes can learn the diameter D in $n + \mathcal{O}(D)$ rounds, without any prior knowledge on n or D.*

PROOF. We construct for each node a BFS trees as in the previous corollary. Note that along with their parent with respect to each root, nodes store the distance to this parent. We collect $D = \max_{v \in V}\{\max_{s \in V}\{d(v, s)\}\}$ over the BFS tree rooted at r and distribute it to all nodes. As this takes at most $2D$ rounds, by the previous corollary the overall running time is $n + \mathcal{O}(D)$. □

3/2-Approximation of the Diameter

A deterministic centralized algorithm computing a $3/2$-approximation to the diameter is given in [1]. A randomized distributed implementation of this algorithm in the CONGEST model that runs in $\tilde{\mathcal{O}}(\sqrt{n}D)$ rounds with high probability[3] (w.h.p.) is presented in [20]. This running time was very recently improved to $\tilde{\mathcal{O}}(\sqrt{n} + D)$ by the authors of [15, 20], relying also on a new result of [22]. The same result follows from Algorithm 1 in a simpler way and with a smaller leading constant factor.

COROLLARY 5.3. *An estimate $\tilde{D}$ of the diameter D satisfying that $D \leq \tilde{D} \leq 3D/2$ can be computed by a uniform randomized algorithm in $\mathcal{O}(\sqrt{n \log n} + D)$ rounds w.h.p.*

PROOF. For a parameter $\sigma \in \{1, \ldots, n\}$, the algorithm of [1] operates as follows.

1. For each node $v \in V$, compute the partial BFS tree consisting of the σ nodes closest to v.

2. Select a vertex v_0 whose partial BFS tree is deepest.

3. For each node in the partial BFS tree of v_0, construct a complete BFS tree.

4. Select a subset $W \subseteq V$ such that each node has a node from W among its σ closest nodes.

5. For each node $w \in W$, construct the complete BFS tree rooted at w.

6. Output $3/2$ times the maximal depth of all constructed partial and complete BFS trees.

As explained before, nodes can obtain n and a 2-approximation of D in $\mathcal{O}(D)$ rounds. Thus, each node can compute the choice $\sigma = \lceil \sqrt{n \log n} \rceil$. By Theorem 4.4, running Algorithm 1 with $S = V$ for 2σ rounds (with the modification from Corollary 5.1) is sufficient to determine, at each node, the distances to the closest σ nodes; we will see that there is no need to explicitly construct all partial BFS trees. Taking the maximum such distance over all nodes, we can select and publish v_0 (using a convergecast over the distinguished BFS tree we already used to determine n and a 2-approximation $\tilde{D}$ of D). Since v_0 already knows its closest σ nodes and the next hop on a shortest path to them, informing all σ nodes in its partial subtree of their membership can be performed within another 2σ rounds (the depth of the tree is at most σ and at most σ messages need to be sent over each edge). Completing the third step of the algorithm thus can be done by calling Algorithm 1 with the nodes in the partial BFS tree of v_0 as source set S and terminating the instance after $\sigma + \tilde{D}$ rounds.

For the fourth step, we simply select each node with uniform and independent probability $\mathcal{O}(\log n/\sigma)$. As each node

---

[3] That is, with probability at least $1 - 1/n^c$ for an arbitrary predefined constant $c > 0$.

could be covered by $\sigma + 1$ nodes, by Chernoff's bound all nodes are covered and $|W| \in \Theta(n \log n/\sigma)$ w.h.p. Consequently, Theorem 4.4 shows that running Algorithm 1 a third time with source set W for $\mathcal{O}(n \log n/\sigma) + \tilde{D}$ rounds will, w.h.p., for each $w \in W$ correctly construct the complete BFS tree rooted at w. Finally, the last step of the algorithm is done by a convergecast and flooding on the initially constructed distinguished BFS tree.

Overall, we obtain a running time of $\mathcal{O}(\sigma + n \log n/\sigma + \tilde{D}) = \mathcal{O}(\sqrt{n \log n} + D)$ w.h.p. Since, w.h.p., our algorithm performs the same steps as a correct execution of the centralized algorithm of [1], the approximation ratio follows from the analysis of [1]. $\square$

Approximation of All-to-All Shortest Paths

In [18], it is shown how to distributedly construct routing tables for approximate all-to-all shortest path, where the actual routing path may be longer than an optimal one by a multiplicative stretch. The bounds in [18] hold for the weighted case, i.e., there is a non-negative cost incurred by each traversed edge. A central subroutine employed in this work is a solution to (S, d, k)-detection with certain parameters, and the utilized subroutine is the aforementioned trivial translation of the Bellmann-Ford algorithm to the CONGEST model of running time $\mathcal{O}(dk)$. As a result, [18] needs to overcome the obstacle of the multiplicative running time by a fairly involved construction. This comes at a cost: For an overall running time bound of $\tilde{\mathcal{O}}(n^{1/2+1/\gamma} + D)$, the algorithm incurs a stretch of $\mathcal{O}(\gamma \log \gamma)$ and has the disadvantage that the destination's label must be known in order to find a routing path of bounded stretch;[4] the latter issue can be resolved, however only by suffering a much larger stretch of $\mathcal{O}(\gamma^3)$. For the unweighted case, the improved performance of Algorithm 1 permits to construct the required structure, ensuring a stretch of $\mathcal{O}(\gamma)$, in $\tilde{\mathcal{O}}(n^{1/2+1/\gamma} + D)$ rounds.

COROLLARY 5.4. *In $\tilde{\mathcal{O}}(n^{1/2+1/\gamma} + D)$ rounds, one can assign a unique label $\psi(v)$ of size $\mathcal{O}(\log n)$ to every node v and construct routing tables, so that for each label ψ, w.h.p. the routing tables indicate a routing path to the node w with $\psi(w) = \psi$ that is at most a factor $\mathcal{O}(\gamma)$ longer than the shortest path between v and w. Moreover, the set of labels is $\{1, \ldots, n\}$.*

PROOF. The construction in [18] combines a *short-range* and a *long-range* scheme. Using Algorithm 1 one can reduce the number of levels in the hierarchical short-range scheme to one as follows. The goal of the short-range construction is to provide a (small) top-level set of skeleton nodes $\mathcal{S}$ and, for each pair of nodes $v, w \in V$ that are not sufficiently far apart to suffer only a constant stretch when routing via the closest nodes in $\mathcal{S}$, to provide appropriate routing paths.

The set $\mathcal{S}$ is a uniformly random subset of V and therefore, if each node knows how to route to the $\mathcal{O}(n \log n/|\mathcal{S}|)$ nodes closest to it, there will be a node from $\mathcal{S}$ among these w.h.p. With Algorithm 1 at hand, we can achieve this in $\mathcal{O}(n \log n/|\mathcal{S}|)$ rounds using source set V (as already used in the proof of Corollary 5.3). If node v now cannot route to some node w using this information, it follows that its closest node $s_v \in \mathcal{S}$ is closer than w. Moreover, the closest node $s_w \in \mathcal{S}$ to w satisfies that $d(w, s_w) \leq d(w, s_v) \leq$

$d(v, w) + d(v, s_v) \leq 2d(v, w)$; another application of the triangle inequality shows that $d(s_v, s_w) \leq 4d(v, w)$. Therefore, routing via s_v and s_w incurs a constant stretch.

The remaining ingredients to the routing scheme (relabeling of the nodes and constructing the routing paths from v to s_v, s_v to s_w, and s_w to w) can be taken from [18] without modification (where we use the variant that assigns labels $1, \ldots, n$ from Theorem 5.9). In particular, the issues regarding the constructed labels that arise from the use of multiple levels in the short-range scheme are trivially resolved. $\square$

Compact Routing Tables

In [18], a variant of the routing scheme is used to compute *distance sketches* of size $\mathcal{O}(n^{1/\gamma} \log^{\mathcal{O}(1)} n)$, computing labels such that each node v, given the label $\psi(w)$ of another node w, is capable of computing an $\mathcal{O}(\gamma^2)$ approximation of the distance $d(v, w)$. Because [18] considers weighted distances, the approach does not yield full-fleged, memory-efficient routing tables. The main obstacle preventing this is that in the weighted case, if a shortest path from v to a node w that is one of its k closest sources within d hops goes via $u \in \mathcal{N}_v$, this does not imply that w is among the k closest sources within d hops of u as well: Since edge weights are arbitrary, there could be a lot of sources that are exactly d and $d + 1$ hops away from u and v, respectively, but are among the sources closest to u in terms of weighted distance. This requires storing routing pointers for each iteration of the used variant of the Bellman-Ford algorithm, resulting in memory requirements of $\tilde{\Theta}(dk)$.

This is not true for the unweighted case: If u is the next hop on a shortest path from v to w, and $(d(u, w'), w') < (d(u, w), w)$ (i.e., w' is closer to u than w), then it follows that $(d(v, w'), w') \leq (d(u, w') + 1, w') < (d(u, w) + 1, w) = (d(v, w), w)$. Thus, if w is among the k sources closest to v and u is the next routing hop according to (the modified version of) Algorithm 1, then w is also among the k sources closest to v. Hence, storing routing pointers for the k first entries of the final lists L_v when calling (the modified version of) Algorithm 1 is sufficient for routing purposes.

COROLLARY 5.5. *For any integer $\gamma \in \{1, \ldots, \log n\}$, in $\tilde{\mathcal{O}}(n^{1/2+1/(2\gamma)} + D)$ rounds it is possible to compute labels of size $\mathcal{O}(\gamma \log n)$ for each node and routing tables of size $\mathcal{O}(n^{1/\gamma} \log^{\mathcal{O}(1)} n)$ with respect to these labels at each node v that enable routing with stretch $\mathcal{O}(\gamma^2)$ w.h.p.*

PROOF. We follow the strategy of Theorem 5.1 from [18], augmenting the distance sketches by the required routing information (cf. Corollary 4.20 in [18]). For routing, one needs to store the next routing hop for each node detected by a call to (the modified) Algorithm 1, which by the above reasoning requires up to $\mathcal{O}(n^{1/\gamma} \log^{\mathcal{O}(1)} n)$ memory bits for each of the $\gamma \leq \log n$ calls, and $\mathcal{O}(\gamma \log^{\mathcal{O}(1)} n)$ bits in order to permit routing from the nodes that are higher in the hierarchy to the nodes for which they serve as landmarks (see [18] for details; this component remains unchanged). $\square$

2-Additive Spanners

A spanner for a given network is a (sparse) spanning subgraph enjoying certain useful properties. Spanner constructions are often based on building (complete or partial) BFS trees in the network. As a concrete example, consider additive spanners. An α-additive spanner H for the graph G is

---

[4]The algorithm needs to assign new labels to the nodes, as otherwise it is infeasible to achieve a running time that is sublinear in n on all graphs of $D \in o(n)$ [18].

a spanning subgraph with the property that for every two nodes v and w the distance between v and w in H is at most α greater than their distance in G.

The well-known construction for 2-additive spanners [1, 9] is based on two main components. The first involves including in the spanner H all edges incident to nodes of degree at most $\sqrt{n}$. This is a local step requiring no communication. The second component requires selecting (say, uniformly at random) a set of nodes M in the graph, of size $|M| = \mathcal{O}(\sqrt{n}\log n)$, and constructing a (complete) BFS tree from every source $s \in M$. This part of the distributed construction dominates the total cost. A naive distributed implementation for this construction in the CONGEST model might cost $\mathcal{O}(D\sqrt{n}\log n)$ time in an n-node network of diameter D. Using the techniques of [15], the distributed time complexity of 2-additive spanner construction can be reduced to $\mathcal{O}(\sqrt{n}\log n + D)$. The same time bound (with a better leading constant) can be achieved using our efficient procedure for multiple source partial BFS tree construction.

COROLLARY 5.6. *For any graph G, an additive 2-spanner of G can be constructed in the CONGEST model within $\mathcal{O}(\sqrt{n}\log n + D)$ rounds w.h.p.*

Acknowledgements

This material is based upon work supported by the National Science Foundation under Grant Nos. CCF-AF-0937274, CNS-1035199, 0939370-CCF and CCF-1217506, the AFOSR under Contract No. AFOSR Award number FA9550-13-1-0042, the Swiss National Science Foundation (SNSF), the German Research Foundation (DFG, reference number Le 3107/1-1), the Israel Science Foundation (grant 894/09), the United States-Israel Binational Science Foundation (grant 2008348), the Israel Ministry of Science and Technology (infrastructures grant), and the Citi Foundation.

6. REFERENCES

[1] D. Aingworth, C. Chekuri, P. Indyk, and R. Motwani. Fast estimation of diameter and shortest paths (without matrix multiplication). *SIAM Journal on Computing*, 28(4):1167–1181, 1999.

[2] P. Almeida, C. Baquero, and A. Cunha. Fast distributed computation of distances in networks. In *Proc. 51st Conf. on Decision and Control (CDC)*, pages 5215–5220, 2012.

[3] J. Antonio, G. Huang, and W. Tsai. A fast distributed shortest path algorithm for a class of hierarchically clustered data networks. *IEEE Transactions on Computers*, 41:710–724, 1992.

[4] S. Baswana and T. Kavitha. Faster algorithms for approximate distance oracles and all-pairs small stretch paths. In *Proc. 47th Symp. on Foundations of Computer Science (FOCS)*, pages 591–602, 2006.

[5] S. Baswana, T. Kavitha, K. Mehlhorn, , and S. Pettie. Additive spanners and (α, β)-spanners. *ACM Transactions on Algorithms*, 7(1), 2010. Article No. 5.

[6] S. Baswana and S. Sen. Approximate distance oracles for unweighted graphs in expected $O(n^2)$ time. *ACM Transactions on Algorithms*, 2:557–577, 2006.

[7] S. Chechik. New additive spanners. In *Proc. 24th Symp. on Discrete Algorithms (SODA)*, 2013.

[8] S. Cicerone, G. D'Angelo, G. Di Stefano, D. Frigioni, and A. Petricola. Partially dynamic algorithms for distributed shortest paths and their experimental evaluation. *Journal on Computers*, 2:16–26, 2007.

[9] D. Dor, S. Halperin, and U. Zwick. All-pairs almost shortest paths. *SIAM Journal on Computing*, 29(5):1740–1759, 2000.

[10] M. Elkin. Computing almost shortest paths. *ACM Transactions on Algorithms*, 1:283–323, 2005.

[11] M. Elkin and D. Peleg. $(1 + \epsilon, \beta)$-spanner constructions for general graphs. *SIAM Journal on Computing*, 33(3):608–631, 2004.

[12] S. Frischknecht, S. Holzer, and R. Wattenhofer. Networks cannot compute their diameter in sublinear time. In *Proc. 23rd Symp. on Discrete Algorithms (SODA)*, pages 1150–1162, 2007.

[13] C. Gavoille and D. Peleg. Compact and localized distributed data structures. *Distributed Computing*, 16:111–120, 2003.

[14] S. Haldar. An 'all pairs shortest paths' distributed algorithm using $2n^2$ messages. *Journal of Algorithms*, 24(1):20–36, 1997.

[15] S. Holzer and R. Wattenhofer. Optimal distributed all pairs shortest paths and applications. In *Proc. 31st Symp. on the Principles of Distributed Computing (PODC)*, pages 355–364, 2012.

[16] S. Kanchi and D. Vineyard. An optimal distributed algorithm for all-pairs shortest-path. *International Journal Information Theories and Applications*, 11(2):141–146, 2004.

[17] T. Kavitha. Faster algorithms for all-pairs small stretch distances in weighted graphs. In *Proc. 27th Conf. on Foundations of Software Technology and Theoretical Computer Science (FSTTCS)*, pages 328–339, 2007.

[18] B. Patt-Shamir and C. Lenzen. Fast Routing Table Construction Using Small Messages [Extended Abstract]. In *Proc. 45th Symposium on the Theory of Computing (STOC)*, 2013. Full version at http://arxiv.org/abs/1210.5774.

[19] D. Peleg. *Distributed Computing: A Locality-Sensitive Approach.* Society for Industrial and Applied Mathematics, Philadelphia, PA, USA, 2000.

[20] D. Peleg, L. Roditty, and E. Tal. Distributed algorithms for network diameter and girth. In *Proc. 39th Colloquium on Automata, Languages, and Programming (ICALP)*, pages 660–672, 2012.

[21] L. Roditty, M. Thorup, and U. Zwick. Deterministic constructions of approximate distance oracles and spanners. In *Proc. 32nd Colloquium on Automata, Languages, and Programming (ICALP)*, pages 261–272, 2005.

[22] L. Roditty and V. Williams. Approximating the diameter of a graph. *CoRR*, abs/1207.3622, 2012.

[23] A. Segall. Distributed network protocols. *IEEE Transactions on Information Theory*, 29:23–35, 1983.

[24] M. Thorup and U. Zwick. Approximate distance oracles. *Journal of the ACM*, 52:1–24, 2005.

[25] M. Thorup and U. Zwick. Spanners and emulators with sublinear distance errors. In *Proc. 17th Symp. on Discrete Algorithms (SODA)*, pages 802–809, 2006.

Distributed Algorithms for Barrier Coverage Using Relocatable Sensors

Mohsen Eftekhari
Dept. Comp. Sci. & Soft. Eng.
Concordia University
Montreal, Canada
m_eftek@cs.concordia.ca

Evangelos Kranakis
School of Comp. Sci.
Carleton University
Ottawa, Canada
kranakis@scs.carleton.ca

Danny Krizanc
Dept. of Math. and Comp. Sci.
Wesleyan University
Middletown, USA
dkrizanc@wesleyan.edu

Oscar Morales-Ponce
Dept. of Comp. Science
Chalmers U. of Tech.
Gothenburg, Sweden
mooscar@chalmers.se

Lata Narayanan
Dept. Comp. Sci. & Soft. Eng.
Concordia University
Montreal, Canada
lata@cs.concordia.ca

Jaroslav Opatrny
Dept. Comp. Sci. & Soft. Eng.
Concordia University
Montreal, Canada
opatrny@cs.concordia.ca

ABSTRACT

We study the barrier coverage problem using relocatable sensor nodes. We assume each sensor can sense an intruder or event inside its sensing range. Sensors are initially located at arbitrary positions on the barrier and can move along the barrier. The goal is to find final positions for sensors so that the entire barrier is covered. In recent years, the problem has been studied extensively in the centralized setting. In this paper, we study the problem in the distributed setting. We assume each sensor repeatedly executes a Look-Compute-Move cycle: based on what it sees in its vicinity, it makes a decision on where to move, and moves to its next position. We make two strong but realistic restrictions on the capabilities of sensors: they have a *constant visibility range* and can move only a *constant distance* in every cycle. In this model, we give the first two distributed algorithms that achieve barrier coverage for a line segment barrier when there are enough nodes in the network to cover the entire barrier. Our algorithms are synchronous, and local in the sense that sensors make their decisions independently based only on what they see within their constant visibility range. One of our algorithms is oblivious whereas the other uses two bits of memory at each sensor to store the type of move made in the previous step. We show that our oblivious algorithm terminates within $\Theta(n^2)$ steps with the barrier fully covered, while the constant-memory algorithm is shown to take $\Theta(n)$ steps to terminate in the worst case. Since any algorithm that can only move a constant distance in one step requires $\Omega(n)$ steps on some inputs, our second algorithm is asymptotically optimal. Finally, both our algorithms are self-stabilizing, and can be easily extended to the case of non-homogeneous sensors, and for the case when the barrier is a circle.

Categories and Subject Descriptors

F.2.2 [**Analysis of Algorithms and Problem Complexity**]: Nonnumerical Algorithms and Problems

Keywords

Barrier coverage, wireless mobile sensors, autonomous mobile robots, optimal algorithms, distributed algorithms

1. INTRODUCTION

Intrusion detection is one of the main applications of wireless sensor networks. A wireless sensor network consists of several sensor nodes. Each node is equipped with a sensing module and can detect intruders within its sensing range. Nodes also have a communication module that enables them to send or receive information to or from other nodes or a base station. Finally, nodes may have a mobility module that enables them to change their location after initial deployment. The literature on intrusion detection using wireless sensors can be classified into two major categories: *area monitoring* and *barrier coverage*. The goal of the former is the monitoring of an entire region [12, 14, 16], on the assumption that the intruder might appear at any point in the region and must be detected within a fixed time delay. In contrast to area monitoring, the focus of barrier coverage is on the boundary of a given region [2, 3, 7, 8, 13]. Assuming that an intruder cannot enter a region without crossing its boundary, monitoring the boundary of the region is sufficient to detect all intruders with possibly fewer nodes.

There are three major node deployment policies: *deterministic* deployment, *multi-round random* deployment, and *ad hoc* deployment using relocatable sensor nodes. In deterministic deployment, nodes are positioned in predetermined locations. In multi-round random deployment, in each round, nodes are dispersed randomly on the barrier. More rounds of deployment are necessitated if the barrier is not fully covered in the previous round [21]. Finally, in ad hoc deployment using mobile sensors, nodes are initially located at arbitrary positions. But some of the nodes may relocate to new positions so that the entire barrier is covered [19, 7, 8, 4]. With deterministic deployment or using mobile sensor nodes, one can possibly use fewer nodes. However, deterministic deployment may not be feasible in some situations (e.g. hazardous areas).

Our focus in this paper is on the barrier coverage problem using ad hoc deployment of relocatable sensor nodes. A barrier can be modeled with a line segment or a collection of line segments. Given initial positions of the nodes, the goal is to determine how the nodes should move to new positions such that the entire barrier is covered. The centralized version of the problem has been studied with respect to different constraints: minimizing the maximum distance traveled by every node (MinMax), minimizing the sum of the distances traveled by all nodes (MinSum), or minimizing the number of nodes that moved (MinNum). In [7], an $O(n^2)$ centralized algorithm is introduced to address the MinMax problem on a single line segment barrier when all nodes have the same sensing range. It is also shown that if the barrier consists of more than one line segment, the problem becomes NP-complete. A polynomial time algorithm for the same problem when nodes have different sensing ranges was recently given in [4]. In [8], the authors addressed the MinSum problem when the barrier contains a single line segment. It is shown that the problem is NP-complete when sensor nodes have different sensing ranges and an $O(n^2)$ algorithm is presented for the case when sensor nodes have identical sensing ranges. The MinNum problem on a single line segment is studied in [17]. The results are similar to the MinMax and the MinSum problems: the problem is NP-complete when sensor nodes have different sensing ranges and an $O(n^2)$ algorithm is introduced for the case when sensor nodes have the same sensing range.

All the previous papers on barrier coverage with relocatable sensor nodes consider only centralized algorithms; given the initial positions of all sensors, the algorithm determines their final positions. But in the context of sensor networking, and relocatable sensor nodes deployed in an ad hoc manner, a very realistic assumption is there is *no centralized authority*. Moreover, a node has no knowledge of the locations of the other nodes, and in fact may not even know the number of nodes or the length of the barrier. Every node must make decisions on whether and where to move, based only on *local* information, that is, the information the node gains by sensing or possibly communicating with nodes within its range. In other words, a practical algorithm for barrier coverage used by the sensor nodes should be *distributed and local*.

1.1 Related work

In this paper we study distributed local algorithms for barrier coverage of a line segment barrier with relocatable sensor nodes. While this specific problem has not been studied to our knowledge in the distributed setting, there is a large body of recent work on the capabilities of *autonomous mobile robots* that is related to our work; see for example [10, 15, 18, 20]. Initially the robots are assumed to be at arbitrary positions on the plane. Their goal is to collectively solve a given task; a typically studied task is the formation of some kind of pattern in the plane. Each robot repeatedly performs a *Look-Compute-Move* cycle. First it looks at the positions of the other robots, then it computes its own next position, and finally it moves to this new position. The robots are anonymous and identical, have no centralized coordination, nor do they communicate with each other; their decisions are made solely based on their observations of their surroundings. Different variations of the model exist based on whether or not the robots are synchronized, have agreement on a coordinate system, and have a local memory.

The computation model we use in this paper falls into the same general framework. Indeed, our sensors follow a Look-Compute-Move cycle, are synchronized, and have partial agreement on a coordinate system. However, our sensors have two important restrictions compared to the standard model of autonomous mobile robots. The sensors in our model have a *constant visibility range*, and in each step, they move a *constant distance*. Both these restrictions are quite realistic for sensor nodes. There are two other differences between our sensors and the typical autonomous mobile robot. First, the sensors may not be identical; for example, their sensing ranges could be different. Second, the sensors are not points on the plane; indeed they are similar to the *fat robots* studied in [6, 9], in the sense that they can detect each other's presence when their sensing ranges overlap.

Limited visibility is indeed an important restriction, and some papers have studied the impact of this restriction. As mentioned in [1], there is no deterministic algorithm for the *point formation* or *gathering* problem, even for two robots under limited visibility, if they don't see each other at first. The authors give a synchronous algorithm that solves point formation for nodes in the same visibility graph, even if they don't share a coordinate system. In [11], an asynchronous algorithm for the same problem is given under limited visibility and a common coordinate system. In terms of movement capabilities, in the autonomous mobile robot literature, while the distance a robot can move in one cycle is assumed to be finite, there is no fixed bound on this distance.

The two problems that are closest to the barrier coverage problem and have been studied in the context of autonomous robots are the *line or circle formation problem* and the *spreading problem*. In the line formation problem, n robots are initially placed at arbitrary positions on the plane, and they must move to place themselves on a line, which is not specified in advance. The problem can be solved with total or partial agreement on the coordinate system and unlimited visibility. Our problem differs in that the sensors are already on the same line; they must move to achieve complete coverage of the barrier. In the spreading problem [5], n robots are initially placed on a line, and must move to equidistant positions between the leftmost and rightmost robots. Clearly in a fully synchronized model, where each robot can see all the other robots, the problem can be solved in one step, and is similar to the line formation problem. However, the authors of [5] make an assumption of a particular type of limited visibility: a robot can only see the robots that are closest to it. They show that the simple strategy of moving to the midpoint of the two neighbours converges in $n - 2$ steps. Our problem has the same input as the spreading problem, but it differs in that the final positions are not required to be equidistant; instead they are required to achieve coverage. Equidistant positions are neither necessary nor sufficient for barrier coverage in general, though in the situation where the number and range of identical sensor nodes is exactly enough to cover the barrier (which can be assumed to be the line segment between the leftmost and rightmost sensors), the final positions of sensors would have to be equidistant. It is important to point out that in contrast to [5], in our model, a sensor node only sees nodes in its visibility range, and therefore may not even see the sensor node that is closest to it. Additionally, it cannot move an arbitrary distance in one step as in [5], it can move only a fixed distance independent of the distance between any two sensors.

1.2 Our results

We present two synchronous local distributed algorithms for the barrier coverage problem with identical sensors that have constant visibility range and constant movement per time step. The first algorithm is an oblivious $\Theta(n^2)$ algorithm that achieves barrier coverage on a line segment barrier when nodes have identical sensing ranges and there are enough nodes to cover the entire barrier. In contrast to the first algorithm, our second algorithm uses two bits of memory for each node to store its state. It improves the running time of the first algorithm to $\Theta(n)$. Note that any algorithm that can move only a constant distance in one step requires $\Omega(n)$ time in the worst case, and so our second algorithm is asymptotically optimal. Our algorithms are self-stabilizing: if any sensors were to be removed after coverage has been achieved, the remaining sensors can re-establish coverage. Finally, our algorithms can be easily extended to the case of non-homogeneous sensors, and for the case when the barrier is a circle.

The rest of this paper is organized as follows: In Section 2 we present our model of the network and barrier, and introduce some terminology and basic facts. In Sections 3 and 4, we present our algorithms and prove their correctness and running times. Finally in Section 5 we conclude our paper and discuss some open problems.

2. COMPUTATIONAL MODEL AND PRELIMINARIES

We model the barrier with a line segment of length $b \in Z$ covering the interval $[0, b]$ on the x-axis. A sensor network consists of a set of n nodes $S = \{s_1, s_2, \ldots, s_n\}$. Each node in the network is a mobile device equipped with a sensing module. We assume a node can sense an intruder or event if and only if it lies within the sensor's sensing range. Every node also has a communication module that can send and receive information within its communication range, and a movement module that enables the node to move along the barrier. Let $s_i^t = (x_i^t, y_i^t, r_i, R_i)$ denote a sensor node s_i located at (x_i^t, y_i^t) at time t with sensing range r_i and communication range R_i. In this paper, we assume that all nodes have the same sensing range r, and let $L = 2r$ denote the coverage length of a node. We assume that for every sensor $r \le x_i^0 \le b - r$, and that for $i \ne j$, we have $x_i^0 \ne x_j^0$. For convenience, we assume that $x_1^0 \le x_2^0 \cdots \le x_n^0$. We emphasize that while these names and positions of sensor nodes facilitate our proofs, they are not known to any of the sensors, which are completely anonymous.

We assume a synchronized model where time is divided into globally agreed time steps. In each step, every node executes a look-compute-move cycle. We assume *limited visibility*: the visibility radius of the node is twice the sensing range (range in which the sensor node can sense intruders). More precisely, node s_i^t is able to see all other nodes located in $[x_i^t - 2r, x_i^t + 2r]$. We say s_i^t sees s_j^t on its right if and only if $0 < x_j^t - x_i^t \le 2r$ and s_i^t sees s_k^t on its left if and only if $0 < x_i^t - x_k^t \le 2r$. Note that each node has its own conception of left and right, but there is no necessity for global

agreement on this. Observe that a node is able to detect when its sensing area overlaps with another node's sensing area. This could be the case for example for light sensors that cover a barrier by illuminating it. Another example is barrier coverage with humanoid robots with outstretched hands, where a robot can see/feel another robot if the tips of their fingers touch. For networked sensor nodes, visibility could be achieved by exchanging *hello* messages so long as the communication range is twice the sensing range. An important additional assumption is that a sensor node can sense an endpoint of the barrier if it lies within its sensing range. Finally, we also assume *limited movement*: in a single time step, a node can move at most one unit of distance.

We study a discrete version of the problem where the coverage length L of every node is an integer greater than 1 ($L \in \mathbb{N}_{>1}$). Note that an input with sufficient nodes to cover the border and nodes at distinct initial positions would necessarily already cover the border for $L = 1$. Initially every node's coverage area starts and ends on integer points in the interval $[0, b]$. In other words, at time $t = 0$ every node's position is in the form $x_i^0 = L/2 + m$ for $0 \le m \le b - L$, and $m \in Z$. We say an algorithm A for barrier coverage *terminates* on input S at time t if and only if when running A on S, no node in S moves at any time $t' \ge t$.

We start with some terminology and simple facts about the behaviour of algorithms in our model. We define a *gap* as a maximal interval on $(0, b)$, where no point in this interval is within the sensing range of any node in the network. A *pile* is a subset of nodes that contains all nodes between two consecutive gaps, or between a gap and a barrier endpoint.

DEFINITION 1 (PILE). *A pile at time t is a maximal set of $k \ge 1$ consecutive nodes $P^t = \{s_j \in S | i \le j \le i+k-1\}^t$, with $x_{j+1}^t - x_j^t \le L$ for all $i \le j < i+k-1$.*

Observe that there is no gap between x_i^t and x_{i+k-1}^t in a pile. In Figure 2 at time $t = 2$, the piles in the network are $\{s_1\}^2$, $\{s_2, s_3\}^2$, $\{s_4, s_5, s_6, s_7\}^2$, and $\{s_8\}^2$. In the figures, a sensor node's coverage length is represented as a rectangle of length $L = 2r$. For convenience, two nodes whose coverage lengths overlap are placed at different levels in the illustration; however all nodes are initially placed on the barrier in our assumption and can only move on the barrier. Clearly, at any time, nodes in the network are partitioned into piles that are collectively exhaustive and mutually exclusive.

For any pile $P^t = \{s_i, s_{i+1}, \ldots, s_{i+k-1}\}^t$, we call s_i^t the *leftmost* node, s_{i+k-1}^t the *rightmost* node, the set $\{s_{i+1}, s_{i+2}, \ldots, s_{i+k-2}\}^t$ the *middle* nodes and $|P^t| = k$ the *size* of P^t. Also we define $g_l(P^t) = x_i^t - r$ and $g_r(P^t) = x_{i+k-1}^t + r$ as the leftmost and rightmost points on $[0, b]$ that are covered by nodes in P^t respectively. The *length* of P^t can be calculated as $g_r(P^t) - g_l(P^t)$. See Figure 1 for an example of a pile.

Let $U^t = \{s_i, s_{i+1}, \ldots, s_j\}^t$ denote a subset of P^t. Then there is no gap between every two consecutive nodes in U^t. We define *excess* of U^t denoted $e(U^t)$ as the difference between the maximum length of the barrier that can be covered by nodes in U^t and the actual length of the barrier that is covered by nodes in U^t, that is, $e(U^t) = L*(j-i) - (x_j^t - x_i^t)$.

FACT 1. *For any pile $P^t = \{s_i, s_{i+1}, \ldots, s_j\}^t$ and integer k if $i \le k \le j$ then:*

$$e(P^t) = e(\{s_i, s_{i+1}, \ldots, s_k\}^t) + e(\{s_k, s_{k+1}, \ldots, s_j\}^t)$$

PROOF. Using the definition of excess of P^t:

$$
\begin{aligned}
e(P^t) &= L*(j-i) - (x_j^t - x_i^t) \\
&= L*(j-k+k-i) - (x_j^t - x_k^t + x_k^t - x_i^t) \\
&= L*(j-k) - (x_j^t - x_k^t) + L*(k-i) - (x_k^t - x_i^t) \\
&= e(\{s_k, \ldots, s_j\}^t) + e(\{s_i, \ldots, s_k\}^t)
\end{aligned}
$$

□

Based on their excess and length, we distinguish two special types of piles below.

DEFINITION 2 (HEAVY PILE). *A pile* $P^t = \{s_i, s_{i+1}, \ldots, s_{i+k-1}\}^t$ *is called a* heavy pile *if it has the following properties:*

$$
\begin{cases}
e(P^t) \geq 2 & \text{if } g_l(P^t) > 0 \text{ and } g_r(P^t) < b \\
e(P^t) \geq 1 & \text{if } g_l(P^t) = 0 \text{ xor } g_r(P^t) = b \\
e(P^t) \geq 0 & \text{if } g_l(P^t) = 0 \text{ and } g_r(P^t) = b
\end{cases}
$$

DEFINITION 3 (MEDIUM PILE). *A pile* $P^t = \{s_i, s_{i+1}, \ldots, s_{i+k-1}\}^t$ *is called a* medium pile *if* $e(P^t) = 1$ *and* $|P^t| \geq 3$ *and* $g_l(P^t) > 0$ *and* $g_r(P^t) < b$.

In Figure 2, the piles $\{s_4, s_5, s_6, s_7, s_8\}^0$ and $\{s_5, s_6, s_7, s_8\}^3$ are heavy piles, while $\{s_1, s_2, s_3\}^0$ is a medium pile. For a heavy or medium pile P^t, we define $o_l(P^t)$ and $o_r(P^t)$ as the leftmost and rightmost points on the barrier that are covered by more than one node from P^t:

$$
\begin{aligned}
o_l(P^t) &= \min\{x : 0 \leq x \leq b \text{ and } \exists s_i^t, s_j^t \in P^t \text{ and } \\
& \quad x \text{ is covered by both } s_i^t \text{ and } s_j^t\}
\end{aligned}
$$

$$
\begin{aligned}
o_r(P^t) &= \max\{x : 0 \leq x \leq b \text{ and } \exists s_i^t, s_j^t \in P^t \text{ and } \\
& \quad x \text{ is covered by both } s_i^t \text{ and } s_j^t\}
\end{aligned}
$$

Figure 1 shows the values o_l, o_r, g_l, and g_r on a heavy pile. The following lemma shows that there exists at least one heavy pile in the network at any time, if there are enough nodes to cover the entire barrier.

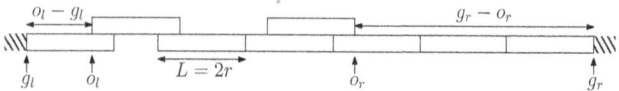

Figure 1: An example of a (heavy) pile. The shaded areas are gaps.

LEMMA 1. *If there are enough nodes to cover the entire barrier, the network contains at least one heavy pile .*

PROOF. Assume at any time t the set of the nodes in the network S is partitioned into m piles $U_1^t, U_2^t, \ldots, U_m^t$. Since the number of nodes is enough to cover the entire barrier, it is easy to see that $\sum_{i=1}^m e(U_i^t)$ is at least equal to the number of gaps on the barrier. We also know that there is a gap between the covered areas of every two consecutive piles. Therefore there are at least $m-1$ gaps on the barrier between the piles. Consider the left and right endpoints of the barrier:

Both points are covered by nodes.
If both endpoints are covered by the same pile, we have a single pile in the network which is heavy. Without

loss of generality assume U_1^t and U_m^t are two piles covering the endpoints. If $e(U_1^t) > 0$ ($e(U_m^t) > 0$), then U_1^t (U_m^t) is a heavy pile. If $e(U_1^t) = e(U_m^t) = 0$, since there are $m-1$ gaps on the barrier, $\sum_{i=2}^{m-1} e(U_i^t) \geq m-1$. Therefore there is at least one pile U_i^t, with $1 < i < m$ where $e(U_i^t) > 1$ and hence U_i^t is a heavy pile.

Only one of the points is covered by a node.
Without loss of generality let U_1^t be the heavy pile covering the endpoint of the barrier. If $e(U_1^t) > 0$, then U_1^t is a heavy pile. Otherwise $e(U_1^t) = 0$ and since there are m gaps on the barrier, $\sum_{i=2}^m e(U_i^t) \geq m$. Therefore there is at least one pile U_i^t, and $1 < i \leq m$ where $e(U_i^t) > 1$ and hence U_i^t is a heavy pile.

Neither of the points is covered by any node.
There are $m+1$ gaps on the barrier and therefore $\sum_{i=1}^m e(U_i^t) \geq m+1$. Therefore, we know there is at least one pile U_i^t and $1 \leq i \leq m$ where $e(U_i^t) > 1$ and hence U_i^t is a heavy pile.

□

3. AN OBLIVIOUS DISTRIBUTED ALGORITHM FOR BARRIER COVERAGE

In this section, we describe a simple oblivious distributed algorithm for barrier coverage and prove that it terminates in $\Theta(n^2)$ steps. As shown in Algorithm 1, in each step, every node that senses another node on one side and a gap on the other side moves one unit toward the gap. An example of this algorithm is shown in Figure 2.

Algorithm 1 Oblivious algorithm for barrier coverage

Every node $s_i \in S$ at the beginning of every step does the following:

if s_i sees another node on one side and there is a gap on its other side **then**

s_i moves one unit toward the gap during this step

end if

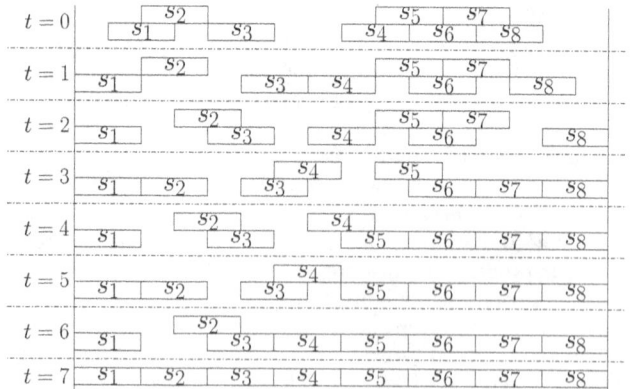

Figure 2: Algorithm 1 example, $L = 2$

Next we prove the correctness of Algorithm 1. We start with some lemmas that show the behavior of heavy and medium piles. First we establish a relationship between piles in consecutive steps.

DEFINITION 4 (PARENT PILE). *We call U_1^{t-1} the parent of U_2^t (and U_2^t is a child of U_1^{t-1}) if and only if*

$$\begin{cases} U_2^t \text{ contains all nodes in } U_1^{t-1} & \text{if } |U_1^{t-1}| \leq 2 \\ U_2^t \text{ contains all middle nodes in } U_1^{t-1} & \text{if } |U_1^{t-1}| > 2 \end{cases}$$

In Figure 2, the pile $\{s_5, s_6, s_7, s_8\}^3$ is a child of the pile $\{s_4, s_5, s_6, s_7\}^2$. Observe that a heavy or medium pile at time t can be the child of two or more heavy piles at time $t-1$. The following technical lemmas show that heavy and medium piles cannot appear *out of nowhere*, they must always have one or more parents in the previous step.

LEMMA 2. *Let P^{t+1} be a heavy or medium pile at time $t+1$ and U^t be a pile at time t. If P^{t+1} contains at least two nodes from U^t then U^t is a heavy or medium pile and a parent of P^{t+1}.*

PROOF. Let s_i and s_j be the leftmost and rightmost nodes in $U^t \cap P^{t+1}$ respectively. First we show that U^t is a parent of P^{t+1}. If $\{s_i, s_j\}$ are the leftmost and rightmost nodes of U^t then P^{t+1} contains all nodes of U^t. Otherwise one of $\{s_i, s_j\}$ is a middle node of U^t, and since middle nodes of a pile do not move P^{t+1} contains all middle nodes of U^t. In both cases, U^t is a parent of P^{t+1}.

Second we show U^t is either a heavy or medium pile. We consider the possibilities for movement of s_i^t and s_j^t. Since s_i^t and s_j^t are both are in the same pile U^t, either s_i^t moves to the left or it does not move. Similarly either s_j^t moves to the right or does not move at all. Therefore all possible cases are as follows:

s_i^t and s_j^t move to the left and right respectively:
Therefore $e(U^t) = e(\{s_k^t | i \leq k \leq j\}) = 2 + e(\{s_k^{t+1} | i \leq k \leq j\}) \geq 2$ and hence U^t is a heavy pile.

s_i^t moves to the left and s_j^t does not move:
Since s_i^t moves to the left $e(U^t) \geq e(\{s_k^t | i \leq k \leq j\}) = 1 + e(\{s_k^{t+1} | i \leq k \leq j\}) \geq 1$. Also since s_j^t does not move either $j = n$ (it is the rightmost node in the network and reached the right end of the barrier) or s_j^t is a middle node of U^t. If $j = n$ then U^t is a heavy pile. If not, then s_j^t is a middle node of U^t, and $|U^t| \geq 3$ and is a medium pile. Thus U^t is a heavy pile or a medium pile.

s_j^t moves to the right and s_i^t does not move:
This case is similar to the previous case and either U^t is either a heavy pile or a medium pile.

neither s_i^t nor s_j^t move:
Since s_i^t does not move, either it is the leftmost node in the network and reached the left end of the barrier or it is the leftmost middle node of U^t. In both cases it is the leftmost node of P^{t+1}. Similarly s_j^{t+1} is the rightmost node of P^{t+1}. Therefore $P^{t+1} \subseteq U^t$ and U^t is either a heavy or medium pile.

We have shown that in all cases U^t is either a heavy or a medium pile and a parent of P^{t+1}. □

LEMMA 3. *Any heavy or medium pile P^{t+1} at time $t \geq 0$ is a child of one or more heavy or medium piles at time t.*

PROOF. First consider the case where $g_l(P^{t+1}) > 0$ or $g_r(P^{t+1}) < b$. Since P^{t+1} is a heavy or medium pile, we

have $|P^{t+1}| \geq 2$. Let s_i^{t+1} and s_{i+1}^{t+1} denote two consecutive nodes of P^{t+1} such that $e(\{s_i, s_{i+1}\}^{t+1}) \geq 1$. The existence of such two nodes is guaranteed since P^{t+1} is either a heavy or medium pile with $g_l(P^{t+1}) > 0$ or $g_r(P^{t+1}) < b$. Let U_1^t and U_2^t denote the piles containing s_i^t and s_{i+1}^t. One of the following two cases holds:

$U_1^t = U_2^t$ Therefore $\{s_i, s_{i+1}\} \subseteq P^{t+1} \cap U_1^t$ and by Lemma 2, U_1^t is a heavy or medium pile and a parent of P^{t+1}.

$U_1^t \neq U_2^t$ Since $e(\{s_i, s_{i+1}\}^{t+1}) \geq 1$, nodes s_i^t and s_{i+1}^t move to the right and left respectively and $e(\{s_i, s_{i+1}\}^{t+1}) = 1$. Since P^{t+1} is a heavy or medium pile, it must contain at least one other node. Without loss of generality assume $s_{i+2}^{t+1} \in P^{t+1}$. Since s_{i+1}^t moves to the left therefore s_{i+1}^t and s_{i+2}^t belong to the same pile U_2^t. By Lemma 2, U_2^t is a heavy or medium pile and a parent of P^{t+1}.

Second consider the case where $g_l(P^{t+1}) = 0$ and $g_r(P^{t+1}) = b$. In this case P^{t+1} contains all nodes in the network. Take any heavy pile U^t (Lemma 1 guarantees the existence of such a pile); clearly U^t is a parent of P^{t+1}. □

Additionally, it follows from the definition of a parent pile that a pile can be a parent to at most one pile in the next step. Thus, the number of heavy and medium piles in the network can never increase. We now proceed to show that the total excess in the heavy and medium piles is guaranteed to decrease within $2n - 1$ steps. The following technical lemma is useful in some of the proofs below.

LEMMA 4. *Let U^t be a heavy or medium pile with a heavy or medium pile child P^{t+1}, and let s_i^t and s_k^{t+1} be the rightmost node of U^t and P^{t+1} respectively. If P^{t+1} is not a child of V^t, the next medium or heavy pile, if any, to the right of U^t, then:*

$$e(\{s_{i-1}, \ldots, s_k\}^{t+1}) \leq e(\{s_{i-1}, s_i\}^t)$$

PROOF. First note that node s_{i-1}^t does not move to the right. We consider the possibilities for k (see Figure 3):

$k = i - 1$: Then node s_i^t was dropped from the pile, and $e(\{s_{i-1}, s_i\}^t) \geq e(\{s_{i-1}\}^{t+1}) = 0$.

$k = i$: Since s_i^t does not move to the left $e(\{s_{i-1}, s_i\}^{t+1}) \leq e(\{s_{i-1}, s_i\}^t)$

$k = i + 1$: Then either the next pile after U^t was of size one and s_{i+1}^t does not move, in which case $e(\{s_{i-1}, s_i, s_{i+1}\}^{t+1}) \leq e(\{s_{i-1}, s_i\}^t) - 1$ or the next pile was of size at least two, and s_{i+1}^t separated from it and moved left to join P^{t+1}. If it did not create an overlap with s_i^{t+1} (recalling that s_i^t moved right), then $e(\{s_{i-1}, s_i, s_{i+1}\}^{t+1}) \leq e(\{s_{i-1}, s_i\}^t) - 1$. If instead it created an overlap with s_i^{t+1} then $e(\{s_{i-1}, s_i, s_{i+1}\}^{t+1}) \leq e(\{s_{i-1}, s_i\}^t)$.

$k = i + 2$: In this case, since P^{t+1} is not a child of the next heavy or medium pile to the right of U^t, it must be that s_{i+1} is a singleton pile, followed by a gap of size one and s_{i+2}^t separates from its pile to move left to join P^{t+1}. In this case, $e(\{s_{i-1}, \ldots, s_{i+2}\}^{t+1}) \leq e(\{s_{i-1}, s_i\}^t) - 1$.

$k > i + 2$: Then P^{t+1} contains two nodes from V^t and by Lemma 2, is a child of V^t, a contradiction.

□

Clearly the same arguments hold for nodes at the left endpoint of U^t:

COROLLARY 1. *Let U^t be a heavy or medium pile with a heavy or medium pile child P^{t+1}, and let s_i^t and s_k^{t+1} be the leftmost node of U^t and P^{t+1} respectively. If P^{t+1} is not a child of V^t, the next medium or heavy pile, if any, to the left of U^t, then:*

$$e(\{s_k, \ldots, s_{i+1}\}^{t+1}) \leq e(\{s_i, s_{i+1}\}^t)$$

Next we show that if two or more heavy or medium piles *merge* into one child, the excess of the child is strictly less than the combined excess of the parents, while if a heavy or medium pile has a single parent, its excess cannot be more than that of its parent.

LEMMA 5. *Let P^{t+1} be a heavy or medium pile. If P^{t+1} has $k \geq 1$ heavy or medium pile parents $\{U_1^t, \ldots, U_k^t\}$, then $e(P^{t+1}) \leq \Sigma_{j=1}^k e(U_k^t) - (k-1)$.*

PROOF. Let s_i^t and s_j^t be the leftmost and rightmost nodes of U_1^t and U_k^t respectively. Lemma 4 and Corollary 1 imply that movements of nodes to the left of s_{i+1}^t and s_{j-1}^t do not add to the excess of P^{t+1} relative to its parents. Thus, we consider only the difference in excess between $\{s_{i+1}, \ldots, s_{j-1}\}^{t+1}$ and $\{s_{i+1}, \ldots, s_{j-1}\}^t$. Recall that the excess of a set of nodes is the difference between capacity of the pile and the length of barrier covered by the set. The two sets contain the same nodes, therefore their capacities are the same. However, the length of the barrier covered by $\{s_{i+1}, \ldots, s_{j-1}\}^{t+1}$ is at least $k-1$ more than the length of barrier covered by $\{s_{i+1}, \ldots, s_{j-1}\}^t$, since the total lengths of gaps between the parents is at least $k-1$. The lemma follows. □

We claim that a heavy pile with a single parent cannot have a medium pile parent. For heavy piles with excess ≥ 2, this follows immediately from Lemma 5. A heavy pile with excess 0 contains all nodes in S and must have a heavy pile parent, since by Lemma 1, there exists a heavy pile in the previous step. Consider a heavy pile P^{t+1}, with excess 1 and a single parent that is a medium pile U^t. Assume without loss of generality that $g_r(P^{t+1}) = b$, and let s_i^t be the rightmost node of U^t. Using a case analysis similar to the proof of Lemma 4, it is easy to see that $g_r(P^{t+1}) = b$ implies that the rightmost node of P^{t+1} must be either s_i^{t+1} or s_{i+1}^t with s_{i+1}^t being a singleton node. In both these cases, it is easy to see that $e(P^{t+1}) = e(U^t) - 1 = 0$, which contradicts the fact that P^{t+1} is a heavy pile with excess one. We conclude that the single parent of a heavy pile must be a heavy pile itself.

We proceed to show that while the excess of a heavy pile with a single parent is not necessarily smaller than its parent, some notion of progress in terms of the excess is in fact achieved.

LEMMA 6. *Let P^t be a heavy pile that does not cover the entire barrier. If P^t is the only heavy pile parent of heavy pile P^{t+1}, then one of the following must hold:*

(i) t is an excess-reducing step: $e(P^{t+1}) < e(P^t)$

(ii) t is a pile-maintaining step: $e(P^{t+1}) = e(P^t)$ and one of the following is true:

(a) $o_l(P^{t+1}) = o_l(P^t) < o_r(P^t) < o_r(P^{t+1}) = g_r(P^{t+1}) - L + 1$

(b) $g_l(P^{t+1}) + L - 1 = o_l(P^{t+1}) < o_l(P^t) < o_r(P^t) = o_r(P^{t+1})$

(c) $g_l(P^{t+1}) + L - 1 = o_l(P^{t+1}) < o_l(P^t) < o_r(P^t) < o_r(P^{t+1}) = g_r(P^{t+1}) - L + 1$

(iii) t is a pile-shortening step: $e(P^{t+1}) = e(P^t)$ and $o_r(P^{t+1}) = o_r(P^t)$ and $o_l(P^{t+1}) = o_l(P^t)$ and $|P^{t+1}| < |P^t|$

PROOF. Let s_i^t and s_j^t be the leftmost and rightmost nodes of P^t respectively, and let s_p^{t+1} and s_q^{t+1} be the leftmost and rightmost nodes of P^{t+1} respectively. Assume that $e(P^{t+1}) = e(P^t)$, that is, t is not an excess-reducing step. Then from the proof of Lemma 4, it can be seen that only one of two cases is possible for the rightmost node of P^{t+1}. Either $q = j - 1$, that is, s_j^t is dropped from the pile in which case $o_r(P^{t+1}) = o_r(P^t)$, or $q = j + 1$ and s_{j+1}^t is added to the pile so that there is an overlap between s_j^{t+1} and s_{j+1}^{t+1}, and $o_r(P^t) < o_r(P^{t+1}) = g_r(P^{t+1}) - L + 1$. Similarly at the left end of the pile, either $p = i + 1$, that is, s_i^t is dropped from the pile in which case $o_l(P^{t+1}) = o_l(P^t)$, or $p = i - 1$ and s_{i-1}^t is added to the pile so that there is an overlap between s_{i-1}^{t+1} and s_i^{t+1} with $g_l(P^{t+1}) + L - 1 = o_l(P^{t+1}) < o_l(P^t)$. It is now easy to see that if a node is dropped at one endpoint, and not added at another, then t is a pile-shortening step, while if a node is added at either endpoint, then t is a pile-maintaining step. □

THEOREM 1. *Given any input of n nodes with enough nodes to cover the barrier ($n \geq b/L$), Algorithm 1 terminates in $O(Ln^2)$ steps with the whole barrier fully covered.*

PROOF. Let $X(t)$ be the *total heavy and medium pile excess* at time t. Then it follows from Lemma 5 that $X(t+1) \leq X(t)$. We prove that as long as the barrier is not completely covered, this quantity must in fact decrease within at most $2n - 1$ steps. Assume for the purpose of contradiction that t is a step when the barrier is not completely covered and $X(t + 2n - 1) = X(t)$. Then Lemma 5 implies that the number of heavy and medium piles at time $t + 2n - 1$ is the same as the number of heavy and medium piles at time t. Additionally, every medium or heavy pile at time $t + 2n - 1$ has a unique ancestor at every step in the time interval $[t, t + 2n - 2]$. Let P^{t+2n-1} be a heavy pile; we denote its unique heavy pile ancestor at time i as P^i for $t \leq i \leq t + 2n - 2$. Since $X(t + 2n - 1) = X(t)$, it follows from Lemma 5 that $e(P^t) = e(P^{t+i})$ for $0 \leq i \leq 2n - 1$. Lemma 6 implies that for every t' such that $t \leq t' < t + 2n - 1$, step t' is either a pile-maintaining step or a pile-reducing step. Since $|P^t| \leq n$, there must exist at least one pile-maintaining step; let T be the first pile-maintaining step in the time interval $[t, t + 2n - 2]$.

Without loss of generality assume $o_r(P^{T+1}) > o_r(P^T)$. Then by Lemma 6, $o_r(P^{T+1}) = g_r(P^{T+1}) - L + 1$. Then $T + 1$ cannot be a pile-reducing step, and by assumption, it cannot be an excess-reducing step. Therefore $T + 1$ is also a pile-maintaining step. The same argument can be repeated for every step from T to $t + 2n - 2$, proving that they must be all be pile-maintaining steps. However, in each such pile-maintaining step t', $P^{t'}$ acquires a new rightmost node, and this can happen at most $n - 2$ times. We conclude that

388

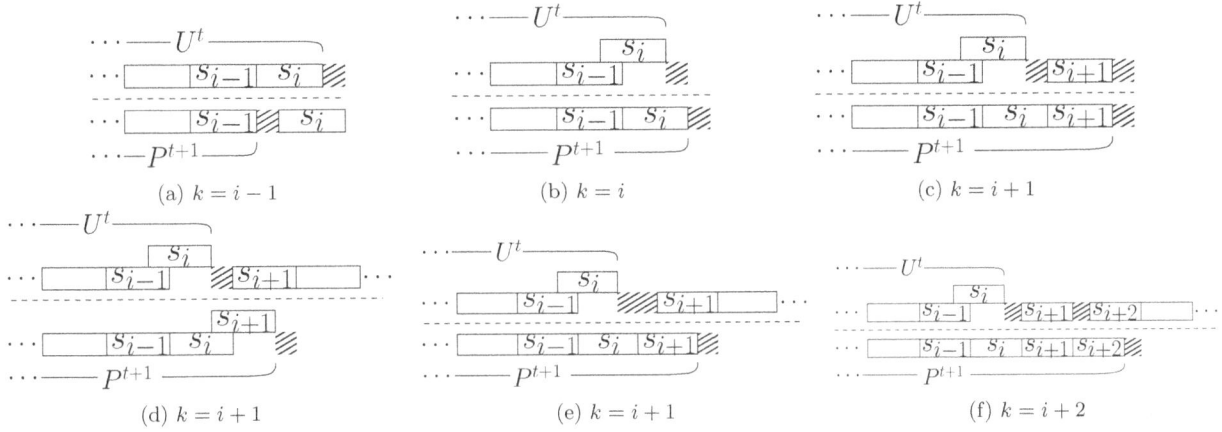

(a) $k = i - 1$ (b) $k = i$ (c) $k = i + 1$

(d) $k = i + 1$ (e) $k = i + 1$ (f) $k = i + 2$

Figure 3: The different possibilities for the rightmost node s_k^{t+1}.

$T \geq t + n + 1$. Since T was the first pile-maintaining step in the time interval $[t, t + 2n - 2]$, it must be that every t' such that $t \leq t' < T$ was a pile-shortening step. However, since $|P^t| \leq n$, there can be at most n consecutive pile shortening steps. Thus, $T \leq t + n$, a contradiction. We have proved that $X(t + 2n - 1) < X(t)$ for any time t that the barrier is not completely covered.

Therefore, either the barrier is completely covered at time $2ni$ or $X(2ni) \leq X(0) - i$. On any input of n nodes, $X(0)$ is $O(Ln)$. It follows that the barrier must be completely covered in $O(Ln^2)$ steps. □

THEOREM 2. *There exist inputs of n nodes with $n \geq \frac{b}{L}$ where the running time of Algorithm 1 is $\Omega(n^2)$.*

PROOF. (Sketch.) We claim that Algorithm 1 takes $\Omega(n^2)$ time on the input shown in Figure 4.

Figure 4: A worst case input for Algorithm 1

Call S_i the configuration of $4n$ nodes defined as follows:

- Start with a heavy pile of $2n - i$ nodes with their left ends starting at consecutive positions 0 to $2n - i - 1$.

- then a gap of size 1 followed by i piles of two nodes of excess 1 separated by gaps of size 1.

- then a gap of 1 followed by (a) $n - i/2$ piles of two nodes and zero excess, separated by gaps of size 2, if i is even and (b) $n - (i - 1)/2$ piles of two nodes and zero excess, separated by gaps of size 2, and finally a single node if i is odd.

The configuration S_0 is shown in Figure 4. We consider the time taken by Algorithm 1 on input S_0. It is easy to see that the final configuration must be a pile of $4n$ nodes of excess 0, and the node initially at position 1 (the second leftmost node) must move in any solution. However, we claim that in Algorithm 1, this node cannot move until time $8n^2 - 10n + 2$, thus giving a $\Omega(n^2)$ lower bound for Algorithm 1. For convenience we number the nodes in the heavy pile thus: the leftmost node is labelled $2n - 1$, the next node is labelled

$2n - 2$ and so forth, until the rightmost node in the heavy pile is labelled 0. We prove by induction that node i in the heavy pile moves for the first time at time $t_i = 2i^2 + 3i$ and the configuration at this time is S_i. The basis is clearly true since node 0 moves at step 0 and the initial configuration is S_0. For the inductive step, after node i moves at time t_i, observe that there will be $2i + 1$ pile-maintaining steps, followed by an excess-reducing step, followed by $2i + 3$ pile-reducing steps to reach configuration S_{i+1}, thus $t_{i+1} = t_i + 4i + 5 = 2(i + 1)^2 + 3(i + 1)$ as desired. □

4. A CONSTANT-MEMORY ALGORITHM FOR BARRIER COVERAGE

In this section, we describe Algorithm 2, a non-oblivious algorithm for barrier coverage and prove its correctness and complexity. In Algorithm 2, each node remembers whether it moved and the direction of the move in the previous step. Initially, or if not moving in the previous step, a node behaves like in Algorithm 1: if it senses a gap on one side and a node on the other it moves in the direction of the gap. However, the key difference is that once a node makes a move in one direction, it keeps moving in that direction in the subsequent steps as long as there is a gap next to it in that direction. Once it is "blocked" by a node in that direction, it stops and waits for one time step, before making a new decision as in Algorithm 1 again.

Thus, two bits of memory are needed in Algorithm 2 to remember the type of the previous move, however, it achieves full barrier coverage in linear time. Note that in Algorithm 2, although every node needs to distinguish between its own left and right sides, no global agreement among nodes on the concept of left and right is assumed.

In the proofs below we use the following concept of a *collection* of nodes.

DEFINITION 5 (COLLECTION). *For every heavy pile $P = U^0$ at time 0, let $C^t(P)$ denote the collection of P at time t. $C^t(P)$ is defined recursively as follows:*

$$\begin{cases} C^0(P) = P & \text{if } t = 0 \\ C^t(P) = C^{t-1}(P) \cup A_l^t(P) \cup A_r^t(P) & \text{if } t > 0 \end{cases}$$

where $A_l^t(P)$ and $A_r^t(P)$ are the piles at time t that contains the leftmost and rightmost nodes of $C^{t-1}(P)$ respectively.

Algorithm 2

Every node $s_i \in S$ initially does the following:

    $s_i.STATE =$ NO-MOVE

Every node $s_i \in S$ at the beginning of every time step does the following:

switch $s_i.STATE$

    case RIGHT-MOVE:

        if s_i senses a gap on its right **then**

            s_i moves one unit to the right during this step

        else

            $s_i.STATE=$ NO-MOVE

    case LEFT-MOVE:

        if s_i senses a gap on its left **then**

            s_i moves one unit to the left during this step

        else

            $s_i.STATE=$ NO-MOVE

    case NO-MOVE:

        if s_i senses a node on its left and a gap on its right **then**

            s_i moves one unit to the right during this step

            $s_i.STATE=$ RIGHT-MOVE

        else

            if s_i senses a node on its right and a gap on its left **then**

                s_i moves one unit to the left during this step

                $s_i.STATE=$ LEFT-MOVE

end switch

See Figure 5 for an illustration of a collection. Observe that while there are no gaps between the nodes of a pile, there can be gaps between the nodes of a collection.

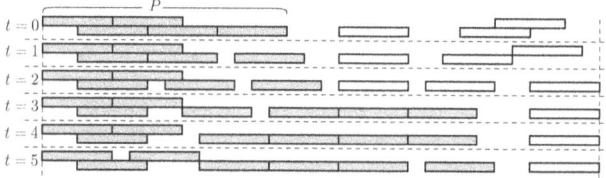

Figure 5: The shaded areas show the collections of the pile P at consecutive steps, $L = 4$.

LEMMA 7. *Let $P = U^0$ and P^t be two heavy piles at time 0 and $t \geq 0$ respectively. If P^t is a descendant of P, then $P^t \subseteq C^t(P)$.*

PROOF. We present an inductive proof. The basis follows directly from the definition of $C^0(P)$. Assume $P^t \subseteq C^t(P)$ for some $t \geq 0$. Let P^{t+1} denote a descendant of P at time $t+1$, then it is the only child of P^t. We show that $P^{t+1} \subseteq C^{t+1}(P)$. Let s_i and s_j be the leftmost and rightmost nodes of $C^t(P)$. If $s_i \in P^{t+1}$, then $P^{t+1} = A_l^{t+1}(P) \subset C^{t+1}(P)$. Similarly if $s_j \in P^{t+1}$, then $P^{t+1} = A_r^{t+1}(P) \subset C^{t+1}(P)$. If neither s_i nor s_j is in P^{t+1}, then $P^{t+1} \subset C^t(P) \subseteq C^{t+1}(P)$. □

LEMMA 8. *Let $P = U^0$ and P^t denote two heavy piles at time 0 and $t \geq 0$ respectively. If P^t is a descendant of P then $C^t(P)$ has the following properties:*

(i) *Either $C^t(P)$ is a pile (no gap between its leftmost and rightmost nodes), or*

(ii) *Between the leftmost and the rightmost node of $C^t(P)$ there are only gaps of length one and for each such gap between $s_i^t \in C^t(P)$ and $s_{i+1}^t \in C^t(P)$ we have:*

    - *if s_{i+1}^t is to the right of the rightmost node of P^t, then node s_i^t moves one unit to the right and s_{i+1}^t does not move to the left.*

    - *if s_i^t is to the left of the leftmost node of P^t, then s_{i+1}^t moves one unit to the left and s_i^t does not move to the right.*

PROOF. We present an inductive proof. It is clear that $C^0(P) = P$ and therefore it is a pile. Assume the argument is true for $C^t(P)$. We show that it is also true for $C^{t+1}(P)$. We assume $C^{t+1}(P)$ is not a pile and show that all gaps in $C^{t+1}(P)$ have unit length and all nodes on both sides of the gaps behave as stated.

Take any gap between $s_i^{t+1}, s_{i+1}^{t+1} \in C^{t+1}(P)$ to the right of the rightmost node of P^{t+1}. Observe that $s_{i+1}^t \in C^t(P)$; if not, $s_{i+1}^{t+1} \notin C^{t+1}(P)$ either, since there is a gap between s_i^{t+1} and s_{i+1}^{t+1}. Since s_i^t is to the left of s_{i+1}^t, clearly $s_i^t \in C_t(P)$ as well. Since s_i^t and s_{i+1}^t are both in $C^t(P)$, one of the following cases holds at time t:

There is no gap between s_i^t and s_{i+1}^t:

    Therefore s_i^t cannot move to the right, and even if there is a gap between s_{i-1}^t and s_i^t, by the inductive hypothesis, s_i^t does not move to the left. We conclude that s_i^t does not move. However, since there *is* a gap between s_i^{t+1} and s_{i+1}^{t+1}, it must be that s_{i+1}^t moved one unit to the right, thereby creating the gap. Observe that this gap must be of length one, as needed for the induction. Since s_{i+1}^t moved to the right, s_{i+1}^{t+1} cannot move to the left, as needed. We now show that s_i^{t+1} moves to the right. If there is a gap between s_{i-1}^t and s_i^t, by the inductive hypothesis, s_{i-1}^t moves right and as already observed s_i^t does not move, so there is no gap between s_{i-1}^{t+1} and s_i^{t+1}. If there is no gap between s_{i-1}^t and s_i^t, by the inductive hypothesis, s_{i-1}^t does not move to the left and as already observed s_i^t does not move, so there is no gap between s_{i-1}^{t+1} and s_i^{t+1}. Since (a) there is no gap between s_{i-1}^{t+1} and $s_i t + 1$, (b) there is a gap between s_i^{t+1} and s_{i+1}^{t+1}, and (c) s_i^t does not move, according to the algorithm, s_i^{t+1} moves to the right as needed.

There is a gap of unit length between s_i^t and s_{i+1}^t:

    By the inductive hypothesis, s_i^t moves one unit to the right and s_{i+1}^t does not move to the left. Since there is a gap between s_i^{t+1} and s_{i+1}^{t+1}, we conclude that both s_i^t and s_{i+1}^t move one unit to the right and the gap between s_i^{t+1} and s_{i+1}^{t+1} is of size one, as needed. Furthermore, since s_{i+1}^t moved to the right, s_{i+1}^{t+1} cannot move to the left, and since s_i^t moved to the right, and s_i^{t+1} has a gap on its right, s_i^{t+1} moves to the right, as needed.

We have shown that the gap between s_i^{t+1} and s_{i+1}^{t+1} is of length one, and the two nodes behave as stated. The proof of the case where s_i^{t+1} and s_{i+1}^{t+1} are to the left of the leftmost node of P^{t+1} is similar. This completes the proof by induction. □

THEOREM 3. *Given any input of n nodes with enough nodes to cover the barrier ($n \geq b/L$), Algorithm 2 terminates in at most $(2L+1)n$ steps with the whole barrier fully covered.*

PROOF. Let P denote the heavy pile ancestor of a heavy pile that exists at time $(2L+1)n$ (Lemma 1 guarantees the existence of at least one heavy pile at all times). We denote the heavy pile descendant of P at time t by P^t. First we show that the right endpoint of $C^{t+2}(P)$ is to the right of the right endpoint of $C^t(P)$. Let s_j^t be the rightmost node of $C^t(P)$ and assume it does not touch the endpoint of the barrier. Observe that even if there is a gap to the left of s_j^t, by Lemma 8, s_j^t cannot move to the left. We claim that if s_j^t does not move, then there is no gap between s_{j-1}^{t+1} and s_j^{t+1}. If there is no gap between s_{j-1}^t and s_j^t, and s_j^t does not move, then since by Lemma 8, s_{j-1}^t cannot move to the left, there is no gap between s_{j-1}^{t+1} and s_j^{t+1}. If instead there is a gap between s_{j-1}^t and s_j^t then by Lemma 8, this gap is of length one, and s_{j-1}^t moves to the right and closes the gap so that there is no gap between s_{j-1}^{t+1} and s_j^{t+1}. This proves the claim. Therefore either s_j^t does not move and there is no gap between s_{j-1}^{t+1} and s_j^{t+1} or s_j^t moves to the right. Now consider s_j^{t+1}: if there is gap to its right, it moves to the right, and if not, s_j^{t+1} does not move, but clearly the rightmost node of $C^{t+1}(P)$ is a node s_k with $k > j$. In both cases, the right endpoint of $C^{t+2}(P)$ is at least one unit further to the right than that of $C^t(P)$. A similar argument can be made about the left endpoint of $C^{t+1}(P)$. We conclude that $C^{2Ln}(P)$ must span the entire barrier.

If there is no gap in $C^{2Ln}(P)$, then $C^{2Ln}(P)$ is a pile and the algorithm terminates leaving the entire barrier covered. Assume instead that $C^{2Ln}(P)$ contains some gaps. Let s_i^{2Ln} and s_{i+1}^{2Ln} be the nodes that surround the rightmost gap in $C^{2Ln}(P)$ to the right of P^{2Ln}. As shown in Lemma 8, s_i^{2Ln} moves to the right while s_{i+1}^{2Ln} does not move to the left. Furthermore, no node to the right of s_{i+1}^{2Ln} can move since there are no gaps to the right of s_{i+1}^{2Ln}. Thus the rightmost gap in $C^{2Ln}(P)$ is consumed in step $2Ln$ and the rightmost gap in $C^{2Ln+1}(P)$ is between s_k and s_{k+1} where $k \leq i-1$. A similar argument holds for the leftmost gap in $C^{2Ln}(P)$ to the left of P^{2Ln}. Thus the distance between the rightmost and leftmost gap reduces by at least one node in every step, and after n steps, the algorithm terminates with the barrier completely covered. □

THEOREM 4. *There exist inputs of n nodes with $n \geq \frac{b}{L}$ where the running time of any algorithm that can only move constant distance in a step, including Algorithm 2, is $\Omega(n)$.*

PROOF. Take for example an input where all the nodes are piled up at distinct positions at the left end of the barrier and there is a gap of size $\Omega(n)$. □

As shown in the next theorem, when the number of given nodes is insufficient to cover the barrier, there are cases for which both Algorithm 1 and Algorithm 2 never terminate.

THEOREM 5. *Given any input of n nodes with $\frac{b+1}{L+1} < n < \frac{b}{L}$, neither Algorithm 1 nor Algorithm 2 terminates.*

PROOF. First we show that at any time $t \geq 0$ there exists a pile P^t such that $|P^t| \geq 2$. Assume to the contrary that

at some time t every pile contains exactly one node. Let s_1^t and s_n^t be the leftmost and rightmost nodes. Since there is a gap between any two nodes, the distance between the leftmost end of s_1^t and the rightmost end of s_n^t is at least $Ln + n - 1 > \frac{L(b+1)}{L+1} + \frac{b+1}{L+1} - 1 = b$. Thus, at least one node must cover a space outside the barrier, which cannot happen in either of our algorithms, a contradiction.

If there is a pile P^t of size ≥ 2 at time t, we show that some nodes in the network must move at time $t' \geq t$. Clearly, since $n < b/L$, there must be a gap either to the right or to the left of P^t. Let s_i^t be the node of P^t with a gap to the right or left to it. Thus, in Algorithm 1, node s_i^t must move. In Algorithm 2 either a neighboring node of P^t moves at time t, eliminating the gap next to s_i^t, or a neighbor of s_i^t in P^t moves at time t, otherwise node s_i moves at time t or $t+1$. In all cases, some node moves at time $t' \geq t$. Thus, neither Algorithm 1 nor Algorithm 2 terminates at time t. □

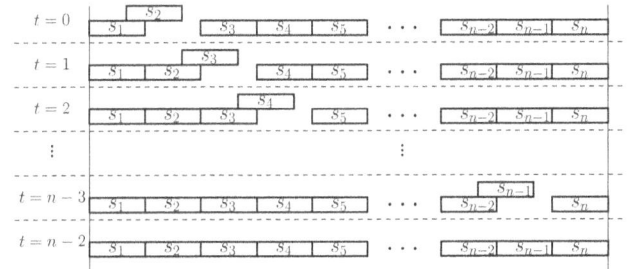

Figure 6: An example where Algorithm 1 takes $\Omega(n)$ time to terminate while an optimal algorithm terminates in one step.

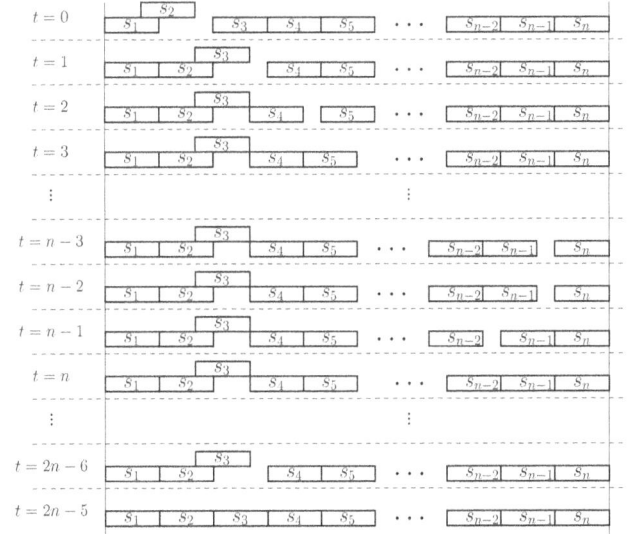

Figure 7: An example where Algorithm 2 takes $\Omega(n)$ time to terminate while an optimal algorithm terminates in one step.

There exist input configurations where both Algorithms 1 and 2 take $\Omega(n)$ steps to terminate while clearly an optimal algorithm needs only 1 step; see Figures 6 and 7.

5. CONCLUSION

In this paper we studied the barrier coverage problem when the barrier consists of a single line segment, mobile nodes are located on the barrier and the sensing range of all nodes are the same. We presented two local distributed algorithms that achieve barrier coverage when there are enough nodes to cover the entire barrier. Our first algorithm is oblivious and the worst case running time of this algorithm is $O(n^2)$. Our second algorithm uses two bits of memory to store the state of a node. We showed that our second distributed algorithm terminates after $O(n)$ steps and is asymptotically optimal. Our results can be extended to the case when sensors don't have identical range, as well as when the barrier is a circle.

Many open questions remain. Does there exist a linear-time oblivious algorithm for barrier coverage in our model? Would some generalization of our model, such as a larger visibility range, help? Is there an asynchronous algorithm for barrier coverage with our model's restrictions of constant visibility and constant movement per unit step?

6. ADDITIONAL AUTHORS

Additional authors: Sunil Shende (Dept. of Comp. Sci., Rutgers U., Camden, NJ, USA), email: shende@crab.rutgers.edu.

7. REFERENCES

[1] H. Ando, I. Suzuki, and M. Yamashita. Formation and agreement problems for synchronous mobile robots with limited visibility. In *Proceedings of IEEE International Symposium on Intelligent Control*, pages 453–460, 1995.

[2] P. Balister, B. Bollobas, A. Sarkar, and S. Kumar. Reliable density estimates for coverage and connectivity in thin strips of finite length. In *Proceedings of MobiCom'07*, pages 75–86, 2007.

[3] B. Bhattacharya, M. Burmester, Y. Hu, E. Kranakis, Q. Shi, and A. Wiese. Optimal movement of mobile sensors for barrier coverage of a planar region. *Theoretical Computer Science*, 410(52):5515 – 5528, 2009.

[4] D. Z. Chen, Y. Gu, J. Li, and H. Wang. Algorithms on minimizing the maximum sensor movement for barrier coverage of a linear domain. In *Proceedings of SWAT'12*, pages 177–188, 2012.

[5] R. Cohen and D. Peleg. Local algorithms for autonomous robots systems. In *Proceedings of SIROCCO'06, LNCS v. 4056*, pages 29–43, 2006.

[6] J. Czyzowicz, L. Gasieniec, and A. Pelc. Gathering few fat mobile robots in the plane. *Theoretical Computer Science*, 410(6-7):481–499, 2009.

[7] J. Czyzowicz, E. Kranakis, D. Krizanc, I. Lambadaris, L. Narayanan, J. Opatrny, L. Stacho, J. Urrutia, and M. Yazdani. On minimizing the maximum sensor movement for barrier coverage of a line segment. In *Proceedings of ADHOC-NOW, LNCS v. 5793*, pages 194–212, 2009.

[8] J. Czyzowicz, E. Kranakis, D. Krizanc, I. Lambadaris, L. Narayanan, J. Opatrny, L. Stacho, J. Urrutia, and M. Yazdani. On minimizing the sum of sensor movements for barrier coverage of a line segment. In *Proceedings of ADHOC-NOW, LNCS v. 6288*, pages 29–42, 2010.

[9] S. Datta, A. Dutta, S. C. Chaudhuri, and K. Mukhopadhyaya. Circle formation by asynchronous transparent fat robots. In *Proceedings of ICDCIT'13*, pages 195–207, 2013.

[10] P. Flocchini, G. Prencipe, and N. Santoro. *Distributed Computing by Oblivious Mobile Robots: Synthesis Lectures on Distributed Computing Theory*. Morgan and Claypool Publishers, 2012.

[11] P. Flocchini, G. Prencipe, N. Santoro, and P. Widmayer. Gathering of asynchronous mobile robots with limited visibility. In *Proceedings of STACS'01, LNCS v. 2010*, pages 247–258, 2001.

[12] C. F. Huang and Y. C. Tseng. The coverage problem in a wireless sensor network. In *Proceedings of WSNA'03*, pages 115–121, 2003.

[13] S. Kumar, T. H. Lai, and A. Arora. Barrier coverage with wireless sensors. In *Proceedings of MobiCom'05*, pages 284–298, 2005.

[14] S. Kumar, T. H. Lai, and J. Balogh. On k-coverage in a mostly sleeping sensor network. In *Proceedings of MobiCom'04*, pages 144–158, 2004.

[15] M. Matarić. *Interaction and Intelligent Behavior*. PhD thesis, MIT, 1994.

[16] S. Meguerdichian, F. Koushanfar, M. Potkonjak, and M. B. Srivastava. Coverage problems in wireless ad-hoc sensor networks. In *Proceedings of IEEE INFOCOM'01*, pages 1380–1387, 2001.

[17] M. Mehrandish, L. Narayanan, and J. Opatrny. Minimizing the number of sensors moved on line barriers. In *Proceedings of IEEE WCNC'11*, pages 1464–1469, 2011.

[18] G. Prencipe and N. Santoro. Distributed algorithms for autonomous mobile robots. In *Proc. 5th IFIP Int. Conf. on Theoretical Computer Science (TCS'06)*, volume 209, pages 47–62, 2006.

[19] C. Shen, W. Cheng, X. Liao, and S. Peng. Barrier coverage with mobile sensors. In *Proceedings of I-SPAN'08*, pages 99 –104, 2008.

[20] I. Suzuki and M. Yamashita. Distributed anonymous mobile robots: Formation of geometric patterns. *SIAM Journal on Computing*, 28(4):1347 – 1363, 1999.

[21] G. Yan and D. Qiao. Multi-round sensor deployment for guaranteed barrier coverage. In *Proceedings of IEEE INFOCOM'10*, pages 2462–2470, 2010.

Delegation of Computation with Verification Outsourcing: Curious Verifiers

Gang Xu
Department of Electrical and
Computer Engineering
Iowa State University
Ames, Iowa 50011
gxu@iastate.edu

George Amariucai
Department of Electrical and
Computer Engineering
Iowa State University
Ames, Iowa 50011
gamari@iastate.edu

Yong Guan
Department of Electrical and
Computer Engineering
Iowa State University
Ames, Iowa 50011
guan@iastate.edu

ABSTRACT

In the Cloud Computing paradigm, a user often reduces financial, personnel, and computational burdens by outsourcing computation and other IT services to a professional service provider. However, to be able to assure the correctness of the result, the user still needs to perform the verification himself. Such verification may be tedious and expensive. Consequently, users are likely to outsource (again) the verification workload to a third party. Other scenarios such as auditing and arbitrating may also require the use of third-party verification. Outsourcing verification will introduce new security challenges. One such challenge is to protect the computational task and the results from the untrusted third party verifier. In this work, we address this problem by proposing an efficient verification outsourcing scheme. To our knowledge, this is the first solution to the verification outsourcing problem. We show that, without using expensive fully-homomorphic encryption, an honest-but-curious third party can help to verify the result of an outsourced computational task without having to learn either the computational task or the result thereof. We have implemented our design by combining a novel commitment protocol and an additive-homomorphic encryption in the argument system model. The total cost of the verification in our design is less than the verifier's cost in the state-of-the-art argument systems that rely only on standard cryptographic assumptions.

Categories and Subject Descriptors

F.1.2 [**Theory of Computation**]: Modes of Computation; F.2.0 [**Theory of Computation**]: Analysis of Algorithms and Problem Complexity *General*; K.6.5 [**Management of Computing and Information Systems**]: Security and Protection

General Terms

Algorithms, Security, Theory

Keywords

Delegation of verification, argument systems, PCPs, cloud computing, delegating computation, privacy

1. INTRODUCTION

Cloud Computing represents a new trend in modern computing. Since computation can be purchased as a service, companies and individual users can cut down their computing assets and outsource any burdensome computational workload. In addition to savings in computing infrastructure, the Cloud may also provide expert technical consulting. But while outsourcing computation provides appealing benefits, one must fully consider a critical security issue: there is no guarantee on the correctness of the results. That is, the Cloud servers should be considered error-prone and may or may not be fully trustable. Thus an immediate need for *result assurance* naturally arises.

This need motivates a growing body of research on verification of outsourced computation. Some recent works focus on specific problems and exploit properties of these problems for efficient verification [11] [13] [22] [31] [33] [44] [45] [46] [47] [4] [24] [40]. Others strive for verifying the result of general computation, not limited to a specific computational task. Extending classical proof systems, interactive proof (IP) systems [30] and probabilistically checkable proof (PCP) systems [3] [5] provide basic theoretical models and meaningful tools for applications. In these models, the server plays the role of a *prover*, trying to convince the client who plays the role of a *verifier* that the result is correct. Based on probabilistic proof systems, many solutions have been proposed, which are efficient in terms of asymptotic complexity. Motivated by the delegation of computation [28], IP systems have been used to assure the client that an untrusted prover has actually performed the correct computation [28] [16] [17]. One notable variant of the PCP model is the idea of *argument systems* [14], which hold a more practical assumption that, in addition to the verifier being polynomial-time probabilistic, the prover is also computationally bounded. Recent breakthroughs in argument systems [32] [41] [42] [43] have made PCP-based approaches more practical.

The ultimate goal of all these methods is to ensure that the amount of verification workload performed by the client is less than the workload of performing the same computation from scratch. Although recent solutions show encouraging results, making verification closer to practicality than ever, the workload of verification remains quite expensive, especially for those cases requiring large-scale verification (such as when large amounts of computation need to be outsourced, and then the results verified). But the average users may not be willing to spend their valuable time and resources on verification work, even though this new computational task is much less demanding than the original one, and neglect verification altogether. We can hardly imagine a hand-held device user devote CPU time and wireless bandwidth to verification.

In the spirit of outsourcing computation, a natural idea is to also outsource the verification. For this purpose, the client may delegate the verification to a third party – *the verifier*. The verifier does not need to be as powerful as the server doing the original computation. In the pay-per-use paradigm, the client should pay the verifier far less than the prover.

In addition to this novel verification-outsourcing paradigm, third-party verification may benefit other, equally-important applications. For example, disputes between the server and the client can be solved by an arbitrator who plays the role of the third-party verifier. Similar verifications may be required by government agencies, nonprofit organizations, and consumer organization, for the purpose of quality evaluation, project management, etc.

However, outsourcing verification is not trivial to implement. Several challenges emerge when outsourcing verification to untrusted verifiers. One of these, and the main focus of this paper, is the confidentiality concern. The results of computing are often confidential. Moreover, in many instances, even the details of the computation task itself may constitute sensitive material.

To the best of our knowledge, there is no feasible solution to these challenges. The two-party verification schemes cannot be directly adopted, either. Recomputing requires the verifier to have the same resources as the prover. If the prover provides a traditional NP-proof, the verifier is able to verify the result with fewer resources than required to recompute. But he still needs to read the entire proof, which costs polynomial time in the size of the computational task. Apart from the high cost, recomputing or checking NP-proofs provides little defense against curious verifiers.

In IP-based or PCP-based two-party verification schemes, it is necessary for the verifier to have perfect knowledge of the computation task and the result (in the context of computational complexity, the verifier needs to know the instance of the problem). If the third party simply runs the verifier's algorithms according to these two-party designs, the computation task and the result cannot be protected unless an expensive fully-homomorphic encryption system (e.g. [26]) is deployed.

The challenge here is how a third party can verify the correctness of the result *without* knowing the computation task and the result and without using expensive fully-homomorphic encryption [26]. In this paper, we describe a secure third-party confidentiality-preserving verification scheme.

Our work is related to, but different from delegation of computation to two or more servers [15] [7] [23] [16], where multiple servers with the same computational power compute individually and compete to convince the client to accept their results. In our design, without performing the same computation as the prover, the third party only needs fewer resources to verify the result from the prover.

The rest of this paper is structured as follows. We formally present the problem in Section 2. We start our demonstration with a brief exposition of current argument systems as the preliminaries in Section 3, since our protocols are related to the works of [32] [42] [43]. In Section 4, we propose our basic scheme, which enables the third party to verify the computational result without knowing the computational task. Then, in Section 5, we apply the additive homomorphic encryption technique to the basic scheme and describe the full solution to outsource the verification to an honest-but-curious verifier while protecting the secrecy of both the computation task and the input/output of corresponding circuit. In Section 6, we demonstrate the practical usage, and analyze the complexity of our design. Analysis shows the efficiency of our design. Section 7 concludes our findings and directs our future work.

2. PROBLEM STATEMENT

2.1 System Model

In the context of cloud computing, we propose a computation architecture involving three different parties: the client $\mathcal{C}$, who is computationally weak, has computation tasks to be delegated to the cloud; the cloud server $\mathcal{P}$, who is computationally powerful, provides computing services to the client; the verifier $\mathcal{V}$, who is not required to be computationally powerful, provides verification services, helping $\mathcal{C}$ to check the results computed by $\mathcal{P}$. $\mathcal{P}$ also plays the role of the prover that attempts to convince $\mathcal{C}$ (through $\mathcal{V}$) that the result is correct.

The computation tasks are formalized into the *arithmetic circuit satisfiability problem* – i.e., the *Circuit-SAT* problem over an arithmetic circuit. This problem is NP-complete, hence any other NP problem can be deterministically and efficiently reduced to it. The reason we choose this arithmetic circuit version instead of the original Boolean Circuit-SAT is that most real-world computation tasks can be easily mapped to arithmetic circuits. Let x be a single-output, n-gate arithmetic circuit (n includes the input gates and the output gate). In the language of computational complexity, we can consider x as an instance of the *arithmetic circuit satisfiability problem*. Formally, $x \in L$ where L is the language of the arithmetic circuit satisfiability problem. If x is satisfiable for a given output value $E \in \mathbb{F}$, then there exists an input y of length $|y| = m$ to the circuit x, which results in the circuit outputting E. This translates into a *correct assignment z* of the set of the outputs of all the gates in x. The assignment z can be in fact the concatenation of the input y with all the intermediate results inside the circuit, and has length $|z| = n$.

$\mathcal{C}$ is providing $\mathcal{P}$ with an output $E \in \mathbb{F}$, and expects $\mathcal{P}$ to return the input y which makes the circuit output E.

2.2 Threat Model

The threats faced by a client in our outsourced verification scenario come from malicious behaviors of both the prover $\mathcal{P}$ and the verifier $\mathcal{V}$. We assume $\mathcal{P}$ and $\mathcal{V}$ do not collude. This assumption is commonly used in multi-prover scenarios [15] [7] [23] [16]. Similar to previous proof systems, $\mathcal{P}$ can provide wrong responses to any queries, trying to cheat $\mathcal{C}$. In this paper, we only address the problem caused by an "honest-but-curious" $\mathcal{V}$ – one that is interested in learning the computation task and/or the result, but performs the protocol faithfully. Different attack models such as dishonest $\mathcal{V}$ will be addressed in future work.

We need to point out that in all of our schemes we omit the authentication part, since authentication is a mature technology and it is not within the scope of our paper. In our context, we assume that all parties are appropriately authenticated.

2.3 Design Goals

First of all, our proposed scheme should provide defense against the curious verifier $\mathcal{V}$ under the aforementioned model. To enable correct and efficient outsourcing of verification, the proposed scheme should satisfy the following requirements:

- *Correctness:* If y is the correct result, $\mathcal{P}$ can always construct a proof and convince the client $\mathcal{C}$ and the verifier $\mathcal{V}$ of the correctness of y.

- *Soundness:* If y is not the correct result, then for any proofs provided by a malicious $\mathcal{P}^*$, the probability that $\mathcal{V}$ wrongly accepts is negligibly small.

- *Efficiency:* The overall workload for the client $\mathcal{C}$ should be less – in an *amortized* sense (we will detail it later in Section 6) – than performing the verification himself. The workload for the verifier $\mathcal{V}$ should be comparable to that for verification in current two-parties designs [32, 42, 43]. Naturally, the workload for $\mathcal{V}$ should be far less than recomputing the result from scratch.

3. PRELIMINARIES

3.1 Probabilistically Checkable Proofs (PCPs)

In the PCP model, the verifier, a probabilistic polynomial-time (PPT) algorithm $\mathcal{V}$ can be convinced by a prover $\mathcal{P}$ that a string x belongs to a language L in an interactive way: $\mathcal{V}$ has random access to the proof π which is constructed by $\mathcal{P}$. By querying π (accessing the proof and reading several values), $\mathcal{V}$ will either accept or reject. *Correctness:* If $x \in L$, $\mathcal{P}$ can always construct a proof π such that $\mathcal{V}$ will accept that $x \in L$. We call π the *correct proof* for x. *Soundness:* If $x \notin L$ then for any π, the probability that $\mathcal{V}$ wrongly accepts is less than a constant ϵ. Let L be any language. The PCP theorem [6] [5] [3] [2] [18] guarantees that, if $L \in NP$, then with only a constant number of queries, $\mathcal{V}$ can verify $x \in L$ with negligible error probability (soundness).

Early results of PCP [2] [3] [5] [7] [12] [12] [34] [35] [37] were viewed as important discoveries only in the theory of computational complexity. Recent research focuses on the efficiency [9] [36], length [9] [8] [10] [18] [39] or soundness error [19] [38] [20] [21] of PCPs.

3.2 Homomorphic Encryption

The commitment protocols of existing efficient argument systems are all based on homomorphic encryption. This homomorphic encryption does not refer to fully-homomorphic encryption [26]. Only additive homomorphism is used in current argument systems: that is, the ciphertext of the result of adding two plaintexts can be efficiently computed from the ciphertexts of the two plaintexts. Formally, for any valid ciphertexts $c_1 = \texttt{Enc}(pk, m_1)$ and $c_2 = \texttt{Enc}(pk, m_2)$, there is an efficient algorithm $\mathcal{H}$ such that $\mathcal{H}(c_1, c_2) = \texttt{Enc}(pk, m_1 + m_2)$, where pk is the public key and m_1, m_2 are plaintexts. In this paper, the underlying homomorphic encryption is assumed to be semantically secure [29].

3.3 Efficient Arguments without Short PCPs

Arguments [14] are interactive proof systems, consisting of two PPT algorithms: the prover $\mathcal{P}$ and the verifier $\mathcal{V}$. For an NP language L with soundness error $\epsilon(\cdot)$, an argument is both *complete* and *sound* if it satisfies the following conditions: (a) Completeness: for any $x \in L$ and corresponding NP witness w, the interaction between $\mathcal{V}(x)$ and $\mathcal{P}(x, w)$ leads $\mathcal{V}$ to accept the proof as true. (b) Soundness: for any $x \notin L$, and any efficient prover $\mathcal{P}^*$, the interaction between $\mathcal{V}(x)$ and $\mathcal{P}^*(x)$ leads $\mathcal{V}$ to accept the proof with probability less than $\epsilon(|x|)$.

To make argument systems efficient, current implementations rely on PCPs. However, PCP algorithms assume that the proof is computed by the prover, and fixed before the interaction with the verifier begins. The same assumption cannot be made in the context of argument systems. To bridge the gap between arguments and PCPs, an additional protocol is required, in which the prover commits to the proof before starting the PCP protocol with the verifier. Consequently, an argument is generally formed by joining together two protocols: a *PCP* and a *commitment*. Since the commitment protocol should maintain the efficiency of the argument, it is generally not feasible to require $\mathcal{P}$ to send the entire PCP proof to $\mathcal{V}$ due to the length of the proof. Two solutions can be implemented to overcome this obstacle: (1) make the PCP proof short, and (2) use cryptographic techniques to enable even shorter commitments to these short proofs. One of the first efforts in the latter direction is that of [37], which proposed to use a Merkle hash-tree construction to enable the prover to efficiently commit to the proof. Implicitly, the security of the protocol is bound to the security of the underlying hash function. To avoid the need for convoluted short PCP proofs, as well as the uncertain security of practical hashing primitives, [32] takes a new approach to argument systems: maintain a large (exponential-size) proof, and base the commitment on (computationally) provably-secure encryption primitives – public-key primitives.

The protocols of [32] are restricted to linear PCPs ([2], Section6). It is shown how SAT problems, formulated in the context of a boolean circuit, can be readily addressed by a simple linear PCP [32]. To form the argument system, [32] complemented the linear PCP with the notion of *commitment with linear decommitment*, which is instantiated with a simple public-key-based protocol. Since our work is closely related to that of [32], we will provide both the definition of *commitment with linear decommitment*, and a brief sketch of its instantiation in this section.

DEFINITION 1. *Commitment with Linear Decommitment ([32]) A commitment with linear decommitment (in the context of argument systems) is a protocol between the prover $\mathcal{P}$ and verifier $\mathcal{V}$ – both modeled as interactive PPT algorithms – consisting of a commitment phase, and a decommitment phase, and aiming to securely commit the prover to a linear function $f_d : \mathbb{F}^n \to \mathbb{F}$ expressed as $f_d(z) = \langle d, z \rangle$, where $d, z \in \mathbb{F}^n$, and $\langle d, z \rangle$ is the natural inner (dot) product over vector spaces. In the commitment phase, an environment $\mathcal{E}$ gives $\mathcal{P}$ inputs d and $\mathbb{F}$, and gives $\mathcal{V}$ inputs $\mathbb{F}$ and the arity n. The interaction between $\mathcal{P}$ and $\mathcal{V}$ results in decommitment information z_P and z_V, respectively. In the decommitment phase, $\mathcal{E}$ gives $\mathcal{P}$ a decommitment query $q \in \mathbb{F}^n$. After further interaction between $\mathcal{P}$ and $\mathcal{V}$, the verifier $\mathcal{V}$ outputs either a value $a \in \mathbb{F}$, or the symbol $\bot$ (reject).*

A commitment with linear decommitment has the following properties. (a) Correctness: for any n and $\mathcal{E}$ generating d, q, at the end of the decommitment phase, the verifier outputs $a = f_d(q)$. (b) Binding: for the same decommitment information z_P, z_V (obtained after the commitment phase) and environment inputs q in the decommitment phase, the probability that at the end of the protocol the verifier outputs two different values (a_1, a_2) is negligible in n.

Ishai et al. [32] took L as the satisfiability problem over an arithmetic circuit to show how to construct a correct proof for any arithmetic circuit and how to verify this circuit is satisfiable. Since this problem is NP-complete, every other NP problems can be deterministically and efficiently reduced to it. The PCP theorem guarantees that, if $L \in NP$ then with only constant number of queries, $\mathcal{V}$ can verify $x \in L$ with negligible error probability (soundness).

The instance x is an arithmetic circuit in this problem. For $x \in L$, there is a correct assignment z of the inputs to all gates in x. z can be also viewed as values of both the input of x and intermediate results. The correct proof is an exponential size PCP, which consists of two substrings. Each of the substrings can be viewed as a linear function: $\pi^{(1)} : \mathbb{F}^n \mapsto \mathbb{F}$ and $\pi^{(2)} : \mathbb{F}^{n^2} \mapsto \mathbb{F}$ where n is the length of a correct assignment z, $\pi^{(1)}(\cdot) = \langle z, \cdot \rangle$ and $\pi^{(2)}(\cdot) = \langle z \otimes z, \cdot \rangle$. Here, $\langle u, v \rangle$ denotes the inner product of two vectors u and v, and $u \otimes v$ denotes the outer product of two vectors u and v. The outer product is equivalent to a matrix multiplication uv^T, provided that u and v are both represented as a column vector. The whole proof string can be viewed as one single linear function $\pi : \mathbb{F}^{n^2+n} \mapsto \mathbb{F}$ such that $\pi(\cdot) = \langle z || z \otimes z, \cdot \rangle$ where $z || z \otimes z$ is the concatenation of the two vectors z and $z \otimes z$. When $\mathcal{V}$ sends the query q to π, he will get back $\pi(q)$. For $q \in \mathbb{F}^n$, $\pi(q) = \langle z || z \otimes z, q || 0^{n^2} \rangle = \langle z, q \rangle$. For $q \in \mathbb{F}^{n^2}$, $\pi(q) = \langle z || z \otimes z, 0^n || q \rangle = \langle z \otimes z, q \rangle$. For $q \in \mathbb{F}^{n^2+n}$, $\pi(q) = \langle z || z \otimes z, q \rangle$.

As in the first column of Table 1, the commitment protocol was designed in [32], where a commitment to a proof is constructed and $\mathcal{V}$ can verify that the proof he queries is committed to a linear function.

Once the proof is committed, $\mathcal{V}$ will check the proof in the linear PCP fashion. The verification consists of three kinds of tests. The first is the linearity test. $\mathcal{V}$ picks at random $q_1, q_2 \in \mathbb{F}^n$ and verifies $\pi(q_1) + \pi(q_2) = \pi(q_1 + q_2)$. The second is the quadratic consistency test. $\mathcal{V}$ picks at random $q_3, q_4 \in \mathbb{F}^n$ and verifies $\pi(q_3) \cdot \pi(q_4) = \pi(q_3 \otimes q_4)$. The third is the circuit correctness test. Each gate implies a constraint. For each constraint f_u, $(u = 1, 2, \cdots n)$, $\mathcal{V}$ picks at random a weight δ_u and constructs the weighted sum $\sum_{u=1}^{n} \delta_u f_u$. The sum can be rewritten as $\pi(q_5) + c = 0$, $c \in \mathbb{F}$. If each constraint is satisfied, the weighted sum of the constraints $\pi(q_5) + c = 0$ is also satisfied. If there are some constrains not satisfied, the probability that the $\pi(q_5) + c = 0$ is $1/|\mathbb{F}|$. All these tests can be performed several times to drive the error probability down.

3.4 Two Recent Efficient Arguments: PEPPER and GINGER

Several recent works build upon the ideas developed in [32]. Of these, [42] and [43] are the most relevant to our work. To bring the protocol of [32] closer to practicality, [42] introduces a new protocol called PEPPER. It first shows that large savings in both computation and communication

overhead can be achieved by expressing the SAT problem in the format of arithmetic circuits with *concise gates* [42] instead of the boolean circuits of [32]. In addition, by batching together multiple queries (to the same committed function), [42] can decommit all of them in a single commit-decommit round, rather than providing separate decommitments for each query.

In Ishai et al.'s original commitment design [32], one query is accompanied by an auxiliary query which is associated to a commitment. This requires many commitments, therefore increases the overhead. In [42], one auxiliary query is made, which is a random linear combination of all the PCP queries and the secret information that is associated to the commitment. In this design, one decommitment can guarantee many PCP queries are bound to the committed function. This sharply reduced the computational cost of generating the commitment information (although remaining cost is still very high.). The Single-Commit-Multi-Decommit design is demonstrated in the second column of Table 1.

Finally, by batching together multiple computations, [42] only requires a single random commitment query r for all computations involved (rather than a different r for each computation), hence achieving great savings in the encryption process – recall that the query r is transmitted to the prover after it has been encrypted by the homomorphic encryption algorithm.

Building on top of [42], additional improvements are provided in [43], in the context of a more efficient protocol called GINGER. A thorough analysis of PEPPER pointed out that the linearity tests are superfluous [43], and that in fact the commitment protocol alone guarantee the linearity of the proof. In addition, several queries of the quadratic correction test may be omitted [43] from the $\mathcal{V}$-to-$\mathcal{P}$ transmission, as they can be easily computed by the prover from the remaining quadratic correction queries.

DEFINITION 2. *A commitment to a function with multiple decommitments (CFMD)(from [42]) A commitment to a function with multiple decommitments (C MD) is defined by a pair of PPT algorithms $(\mathcal{P}, \mathcal{V})$ (a sender and receiver, which correspond to our prover and verifier) anticipating the following experiment with an environment $\mathcal{E}$. $\mathcal{E}$ generates $\mathbb{F}, w$ and $Q = (q_1, \cdots, q_\mu)$. The two phases are:*

- *Commitment phase: $\mathcal{P}$ has w, and $\mathcal{P}$ and $\mathcal{V}$ interact, based on their random inputs.*

- *Decommitment phase: $\mathcal{E}$ gives Q to $\mathcal{V}$, and $\mathcal{P}$ and $\mathcal{V}$ interact again, based on further random inputs. At the end, $\mathcal{V}$ outputs $A = (a_1, \cdots, a_\mu) \in \mathbb{F}^\mu$ or $\perp$.*

A commitment to a function with multiple decommitments (CFMD) should satisfy the following properties:

- ***Correctness:*** *at the end of the decommitment phase, $\mathcal{V}$ outputs $\pi(q_i) = \langle w, q_i \rangle$, (for all i), if $\mathcal{P}$ is honest.*

- *ϵ_B-**Binding:***. *Consider the following experiment. The environment $\mathcal{E}$ produces two (possibly distinct) μ-tuples of queries: $Q = (q_1, \cdots, q_\mu)$ and $\hat{Q} = (\hat{q}_1, \cdots, \hat{q}_\mu)$. $\mathcal{V}$ and a cheating $\mathcal{P}^*$ run the commitment phase once and two independent instances of the decommitment phase. In the two instances $\mathcal{V}$ presents the queries as Q and $\hat{Q}$, respectively. We say that $\mathcal{P}^*$ wins if $\mathcal{V}$'s outputs at the end of the respective decommit phases are*

$A = (a_1, \cdots, a_\mu)$ and $\hat{A} = (\hat{a_1}, \cdots, \hat{a_\mu})$, and for some i, j, we have $q_i = \hat{q}_j$ but $a_i \neq \hat{a}_j$. The protocol holds the ϵ_B-Binding property if for all $\mathcal{E}$ and for all efficient $\mathcal{P}^*$, the probability of $\mathcal{P}^*$ winning is at most ϵ_B. The probability is taken over three sets of independent randomness: the commitment phase and the two runnings of the decommitment phase.

4. BASIC SCHEME: VERIFICATION WITHOUT CIRCUIT INFORMATION

We present a basic version of our protocol in this section. We then bootstrap the process to develop the full solution in next section. In this basic scheme, the client $\mathcal{C}$ delegates the verification task to the verifier $\mathcal{V}$ and $\mathcal{V}$ can verify the proof without knowing the computational task, i.e., the underlying arithmetic circuit x. Our basic scheme is designed by joining together two protocols: a novel linear PCP and a new commitment protocol. Recall that PCP systems assume the proof is computed by $\mathcal{P}$, and fixed before the interaction with the $\mathcal{V}$ begins. The same assumption cannot be made in Cloud Computing. For efficiency reasons, it is also not feasible to require $\mathcal{P}$ to send the entire PCP proof to $\mathcal{V}$. It is the commitment protocol that guarantees $\mathcal{P}$ commits to the proof before starting the PCP protocol with $\mathcal{V}$.

4.1 A Building Block: A New Commitment Protocol

In the context of Circuit-SAT problem over an arithmetic circuit, we propose the following new commitment protocol for linear PCP system. It is a two-party protocol between the prover $\mathcal{P}$ and another party denoted by $\mathcal{C}/\mathcal{V}$ (as in "client/verifier"). We do not differentiate between the client $\mathcal{C}$ and the verifier $\mathcal{V}$ in this subsection. This separation will be done in next subsection. Recall that the Circuit-SAT problem is to find an input $y = (y_1, y_2, \cdots, y_m)$ which makes the circuit x output a given value E. The arithmetic circuit x consists of $n = |x|$ arithmetic gates. Each gate implies a constraint $f_u, 1 \leq u \leq n$ as follows:

- $f_u(z_u) = z_u$ for $1 \leq u \leq m$. These are the constraints for the input gates.

- $f_u(z_i, z_j, z_k) = 0$ for $m + 1 \leq u \leq n - 1$, where f_u is a linear or quadratic polynomial of z_i, z_j, z_k. Here z_i, z_j, z_k are the two inputs and one output of a certain gate of x.

- $f_n(z_n) = E$. This is the constraint for the output gate.

Our commitment protocol rearranges the argument system to put the circuit-dependent portions inside the commitment phase (the offline stage). This approach not only simplifies the client/verifier's operation on the verification side, but also provides circuit-secrecy against the verifiers while outsourcing the verification tasks.

Our commitment protocol is demonstrated in the third column of Table 1. This protocol eventually includes two decommitment processes, one is from Step 4 to Step 7, the other is from Step 8 to Step 11.

We will prove that after the commitment construction phase, all of $\mathcal{P}$'s answers to later queries that pass both the decommitment checks are guaranteed to be bound to one single function (from queries to answers) with high probability. That is, having committed, $\mathcal{P}$ is very likely incapable

of cheating the verifiers with fake answers. Moreover, this function is guaranteed to be linear with high probability.

THEOREM 1. (Main Theorem) or our commitment protocol, the following holds. or any environment $\mathcal{E}$, for any query q in either of the decommitment phases, the corresponding answer accepted by $\mathcal{V}$ at the end of the protocol is guaranteed to be the function value $\tilde{\pi}(q)$ except with probability less than $\frac{1}{|\mathbb{F}|} + neg(n)$, where $\tilde{\pi}(q)$ is a linear function, $neg(n)$ is a negligible function, and the probability is over all randomness of $\mathcal{P}^*$ and $\mathcal{V}$ in all phases.

We prove this theorem in Appendix of the full version [1].

4.2 A Delegation-of-Verification Scheme with Partial Circuit Confidentiality

As in the context of cloud computing, $\mathcal{C}$ sends the circuit description x to $\mathcal{P}$. After finding out the solution y with his powerful computation ability, $\mathcal{P}$ returns y to $\mathcal{C}$. Before outsourcing the verification task, $\mathcal{C}$ constructs the commitment according to our basic commitment scheme. $\mathcal{C}$ plays the role of $\mathcal{C}/\mathcal{V}$ in that commitment construction protocol and gets: $w_0, r_1, R_1, r_0, R_0, s_1, S_1, s_0 S_0$. The decommitment phases are a little bit different from our basic commitment scheme. $\mathcal{C}$ generates a random value $\alpha_0 \in \mathbb{F}$ and computes $(r_1 || R_1) + \alpha_0(r_0 || R_0)$. Then, $\mathcal{C}$ outsources the verification task to a third party $\mathcal{V}$. $\mathcal{C}$ sends w_0, $(r_1 || R_1) + \alpha_0(r_0 || R_0)$, s_1, S_1, $s_1 + S_1 + \alpha_0(s_0 + S_0)$, E, and y_i's ($i = 1, \cdots m$) to $\mathcal{V}$. Later, $\mathcal{V}$ will perform the decommitment.

Since our commitment protocol has inherently provided the linearity test, (see the full version for details [1]) it is sufficient to conduct only circuit and quadratic consistency tests. For the circuit test, $\mathcal{V}$ generates w_1 and w_2 as in Step 4 and Step 5 of our basic commitment scheme. As in Step 5 and Step 6, $\mathcal{V}$ queries $\mathcal{P}$ with w_1 and w_2, receives back A_1, a_1, B_1 and b_1. Then $\mathcal{V}$ checks the equations as in Step 7. $\mathcal{V}$ will also check the circuit correctness, i.e., whether

$$A_1 + a_1 = \sum_{u=1}^{m} y_u w_{1u} + w_{1n} E. \qquad (4.1)$$

For the quadratic consistency tests, $\mathcal{V}$ first conducts the second decommitment according to Steps 8, 9, 10, 11. Here, $\mathcal{V}$ uses only three testing queries (that is, $\mu = 3$) and the decommit query t. $\mathcal{V}$ randomly generates queries q_2, q_3 both from $\mathbb{F}^n$. He randomly generates $\alpha_2, \alpha_3, \alpha_4$, all from $\mathbb{F}$. He constructs the following queries: $q_4 = q_2 \otimes q_3$, and $t = (r_1 || R_1 + \alpha_0(r_0 || R_0)) + \sum_{i=2}^{3}(q_i || 0^{n^2}) + \alpha_4(0^n || q_4)$, where 0^u is the u-dimension zero vector. $\mathcal{V}$ queries $\mathcal{P}$ with (q_2, q_3, q_4, t). $\mathcal{P}$ returns (a_2, a_3, a_4, b_2) where $a_2 = \langle q_2, z \rangle$, $a_3 = \langle q_3, z \rangle$, $a_4 = \langle q_4, z \otimes z \rangle$, $b_2 = \langle t, z \otimes z \rangle$. At the second decommitment, $\mathcal{V}$ checks whether $b_2 = (s_1 + S_1 + \alpha_0(s_0 + S_0)) + \sum_{i=2}^{4} \alpha_i a_i$. For quadratic consistency, $\mathcal{V}$ checks whether $a_4 = a_2 a_3$.

If all the checks pass, $\mathcal{V}$ will instruct $\mathcal{C}$ to accept. Otherwise, $\mathcal{V}$ instructs $\mathcal{C}$ to reject.

4.3 Theoretical Analysis: Correctness and Soundness

It is easy to see that without knowing the circuit x, $\mathcal{V}$ conducts all the PCP checks (except the linearity tests, since the commitment has provided linearity tests already) for $\mathcal{C}$. The correctness and soundness of this scheme follows directly from the linear PCP scheme. However, it should be noted that $\mathcal{V}$ has access to the pair $((r_1 || R_1) + \alpha_0(r_0 || R_0), s_1 +$

Table 1: Comparison of Commitment Protocols

Ishai et al. [32]	GINGER [43]	Our Basic Commitment Scheme
Commitment Phase	**Commitment Phase**	**Commitment Phase**
Prover's Input: a vector $d \in \mathbb{F}^{n^2+n}$, a linear function $\pi : \mathbb{F}^{n^2+n} \to \mathbb{F}$ where $\pi(q) = \langle q, d \rangle$.	**Prover's Input:** $z \in \mathbb{F}^n$, a linear function $\pi : \mathbb{F}^{n^2+n} \mapsto \mathbb{F}$ where $\pi(\cdot) = \langle z \| z \otimes z, \cdot \rangle$.	**Prover's Input:** a vector $z \in \mathbb{F}^n$, a linear function $\pi : \mathbb{F}^{n^2+n} \mapsto \mathbb{F}$ where $\pi(\cdot) = \langle z \| z \otimes z, \cdot \rangle$, n is the length of a correct assignment z.
Verifier's Input: arity $n^2 + n$, security parameter k for the homomorphic encryption.	**Verifier's Input:** arity n, security parameter k of the encryption.	**Verifier's Input:** arity n, security parameter k of the encryption, the circuit x, the circuit's input $y = (y_1, \cdots, y_m)$ and output E.
Step 1: $\mathcal{V}$ generates the key pair $(pk, sk) \leftarrow \mathbf{Gen}(1^k)$ and $r = (r_1, \cdots, r_{n^2+n}) \in_R \mathbb{F}^{n^2+n}$, $r_i \in \mathbb{F}$, $i = 1, \cdots, n^2 + n$. $\mathcal{V}$ encrypts each entry of r and sends $\mathbf{Enc}(pk, r_1), \cdots, \mathbf{Enc}(pk, r_{n^2+n})$ to $\mathcal{P}$.	**Step 1:** $\mathcal{V}$ generates the key pair $(pk, sk) \leftarrow \mathbf{Gen}(1^k)$ and $r = (r_1, \cdots, r_{n^2+n}) \in_R \mathbb{F}^{n^2+n}$, $r_i \in \mathbb{F}$, $i = 1, \cdots, n^2 + n$. $\mathcal{V}$ encrypts each entry of r and sends $\mathbf{Enc}(pk, r_1), \cdots, \mathbf{Enc}(pk, r_{n^2+n})$ to $\mathcal{P}$.	**Step 1:** $\mathcal{C}/\mathcal{V}$ randomly picks $r_0 \in \mathbb{F}^n$ and $R_0 \in \mathbb{F}^{n^2}$ and constructs the corresponding commitments (s_0, S_0) according to Ishai et al.'s commitment protocol [32].
Step 2: $\mathcal{P}$ makes use of the homomorphism of $\mathbf{Enc}$ and gets $e = \mathbf{Enc}(pk, \langle r, d \rangle)$. $\mathcal{P}$ sends e to $\mathcal{V}$.	**Step 2:** Using the homomorphism, $\mathcal{P}$ gets: $e = \mathbf{Enc}(pk, \langle r, z \rangle)$ and sends it to $\mathcal{V}$.	**Step 2:** $\mathcal{C}/\mathcal{V}$ randomly generates an n-dimension weight vector $w_0 = (w_{01}, w_{02}, \ldots, w_{0n}) \in \mathbb{F}^n$, where each entry corresponds to a constraint f_u ($u = 1, \cdots, n$) of the arithmetic circuit x. $\mathcal{C}/\mathcal{V}$ multiplies each constraint f_u of the circuit by w_{0u}, $u = 1, \cdots, n$ and constructs their summation as $\sum_{u=1}^{n} w_{0u} f_u = \sum_{u=1}^{m} w_{0u} y_u + w_{0n} E$. The summation of all these weighted constraints can be rewritten as $\langle R_1, z \otimes z \rangle + \langle r_1, z \rangle = c_0$, where $c_0 = \sum_{u=1}^{m} y_u w_{0u} + w_{0n} E$.
Step 3: $\mathcal{V}$ decrypts e and gets $s = \langle r, d \rangle = \mathbf{Dec}(sk, e)$. (s, r) will be kept for decommitment.	**Step 3:** $\mathcal{V}$ receives e. He gets $s = \langle r, z \rangle = \mathbf{Dec}(sk, e)$. (s, r) will be kept for decommitment.	**Step 3:** Using R_1 and r_1, $\mathcal{C}/\mathcal{V}$ constructs the corresponding commitments (s_1, S_1) according to Ishai's commitment protocol [32].
Decommitment Phase	**Decommitment Phase**	**Decommitment Phase**
Prover's Input: d, π	**Prover's Input:** z, π, n	**Prover's Input:** x, z including y and E, π, n.
Verifier's Input: arity $n^2 + n$, a PCP query q, decommitment information (r, s).	**Verifier's Input:** arity n, μ PCP queries $q_1, \cdots, q_\mu$, decommitment information (r, s).	**Verifier's Input:** n, μ PCP queries $q_1, \cdots, q_\mu$, decommitment information $(w_0, r_0, R_0, r_1, R_1, s_0, S_0, s_1, S_1)$.
Step 4: $\mathcal{V}$ picks at random a secret $\alpha \in_R \mathbb{F}$.	**Step 4:** $\mathcal{V}$ picks μ secrets $\alpha_1, \cdots, \alpha_\mu \in \mathbb{F}$	**Step 4:** $\mathcal{C}/\mathcal{V}$ generates randomly an n-dimension weight vector $w_1 = (w_{11}, \ldots, w_{1n}) \in \mathbb{F}^n$ and a secret $\alpha_1 \in \mathbb{F}$.
Step 5: $\mathcal{V}$ sends $q, r + \alpha q$ to the prover.	**Step 5:** $\mathcal{V}$ queries $\mathcal{P}$ with $q_1, \cdots, q_\mu$ and $t = r + \sum_{i=1}^{\mu} \alpha_i q_i$.	**Step 5:** $\mathcal{C}/\mathcal{V}$ queries $\mathcal{P}$ with vector w_1 and $w_2 = w_0 + \alpha_1 w_1$.
Step 6: $\mathcal{P}$ responds with 2 values that are in $\mathbb{F}$: (a, b) where a is supposed to be $\pi(q)$ and b is supposed to be $\pi(r + \alpha q)$.	**Step 6:** $\mathcal{P}$ returns $\mu + 1$ values: $(a_1, \cdots, a_\mu, b)$ where $a_i = \pi(q_i)$ for $i = 1, \cdots, \mu$ and $b = \pi(t)$	**Step 6:** From w_1, $\mathcal{P}$ constructs the weighted summation of all constraints just like what $\mathcal{C}/\mathcal{V}$ does in Step 2 and gets $\langle Q_0, z \otimes z \rangle + \langle q_0, z \rangle = \sum_{u=1}^{m} y_u w_{1u} + w_{1n} E$. From it, $\mathcal{P}$ learns Q_0 and q_0 and returns: $A_1 = \langle Q_0, z \otimes z \rangle$ and $a_1 = \langle q_0, z \rangle$. Similarly, from w_2, $\mathcal{P}$ constructs the weighted summation $\langle T_1, z \otimes z \rangle + \langle t_1, z \rangle = \sum_{u=1}^{m} y_u w_{2u} + w_{2n} E$ and learns T_1 and t_1. $\mathcal{P}$ returns: $B_1 = \langle T_1, z \otimes z \rangle$ and $b_1 = \langle t_1, z \rangle$.
Step 7: $\mathcal{V}$ will determine whether $b = s + \alpha a$. If it holds, the $\mathcal{V}$ will accept and output a; otherwise it will reject and output $\perp$.	**Step 7:** $\mathcal{V}$ checks whether $b = s + \alpha_1 a_1 + \cdots \alpha_\mu a_\mu$ holds. If so, $\mathcal{V}$ outputs $a_1, \cdots, a_\mu$. Otherwise, he rejects and output $\perp$.	**Step 7:** $\mathcal{C}/\mathcal{V}$ checks whether $b_1 = s_1 + \alpha_1 a_1$ and $B_1 = S_1 + \alpha_1 A_1$. If both hold, $\mathcal{C}/\mathcal{V}$ goes on to Step 8. Otherwise, $\mathcal{C}/\mathcal{V}$ rejects the proof.
		Step 8: $\mathcal{C}/\mathcal{V}$ randomly generates $\alpha_0, \alpha_1, \cdots, \alpha_\mu$ from $\mathbb{F}$. $\mathcal{C}/\mathcal{V}$ constructs $t = (r_1 \| R_1) + \alpha_0(r_0 \| R_0) + \sum_{k=1}^{\mu} \alpha_k q_k$.
		Step 9: $\mathcal{C}/\mathcal{V}$ queries $\mathcal{P}$ with $q_1, \cdots, q_\mu$ and t.
		Step 10: $\mathcal{P}$ returns $\mu + 1$ corresponding answers $(a_1, \cdots, a_\mu, b_2)$ where for $k = 1, 2, \cdots \mu$, $a_k = \langle q_k, z \| z \otimes z \rangle$ and $b_2 = \langle t, z \| z \otimes z \rangle$.
		Step 11: $\mathcal{C}/\mathcal{V}$ checks whether $b_2 = (s_1 + S_1 + \alpha_0(s_0 + S_0)) + \sum_{k=1}^{\mu} \alpha_k a_k$ holds. If so, $\mathcal{C}/\mathcal{V}$ accepts. Otherwise $\mathcal{C}/\mathcal{V}$ rejects.

$S_1 + \alpha_0(s_0 + S_0))$, which leaks information about the circuit. Hence the *partial circuit confidentiality* is afforded by this scheme. Nevertheless, building upon this scheme, full circuit confidentiality is achieved by the full solution outlined in the next section. Our basic scheme is also a distinct improvement over existing argument systems. During the verification procedure, the verifier does not need to read the circuit. He can generate all the queries with the cost of merely generating random numbers. By comparison, to generate a query, current argument systems need to both generate random numbers, and to calculate weighted summations of all circuit's constraints.

5. THE FULL SOLUTION TO DELEGATING VERIFICATION TO A CURIOUS VERIFIER

In certain scenarios, both the computation circuit and input/output of this circuit are sensitive. A curious verifier may be interested in information regarding the computation task (the circuit) and/or the circuit's input and output. In this section, we use the previously described basic scheme to develop the full solution against the curious verifier. The full version of the protocol consists of four phases, detailed in the following subsections: outsourcing computation, constructing commitments, outsourcing verification, and making a decision.

5.1 Outsourcing Computation Phase

C possesses an additive homomorphic cryptosystem. He generates a key pair (SK, PK). C sends the arithmetic circuit description x along with the public key PK to P. After finding out the solution y with his powerful computation ability, P returns y to C. After this computation, P obtains a correct assignment z of all the input of each gate in x. z can be viewed as the values of both y (the input of x) and intermediate results. P possesses a corresponding linear function: $\pi : \mathbb{F}^{n^2+n} \mapsto \mathbb{F}$ (remember $n = |x| = |z|$) such that, $\pi(\cdot) = \langle z || z \otimes z, \cdot \rangle$.

5.2 Constructing Commitments

Before outsourcing the verification task to a third party, C constructs the commitment according to the protocol described in Table 1. At the end of the construction, C possesses: w_0, r_1, R_1, r_0, R_0, and s_1, S_1, s_0, S_0. C generates a random value $\alpha_0 \in \mathbb{F}$ and computes $(r_1||R_1) + \alpha_0(r_0||R_0)$. After constructing the commitment, C randomly picks $w_{11}, w_{12}, \cdots, w_{1m}$ and w_{1n}, all in $\mathbb{F}$. Let w_1' be $((w_{11}, w_{12}, \cdots, w_{1m})||0^{n-m-1}||w_{1n})$. With these numbers, C computes $c_0 = \sum_{u=1}^{m} w_{1u} y_u + w_{1n} E$, then randomly generates α_1 and sends α_1, s_1, S_1, c_0, $w_0 + \alpha_1 w_1'$, $(r_1||R_1) + \alpha_0(r_0||R_0)$, $\text{Enc}(PK, (s_1 + S_1 + \alpha_0(s_0 + S_0)))$, and the public key PK to V. Meanwhile, C sends $w_{11}, \cdots, w_{1m}$, w_{1n} and PK to P.

5.3 Outsourcing Verification Phase

In this phase, V will verify the result without knowing the circuit and any of the assignments z (including y) in a PCP fashion. Given that the commit/decommit protocol has inherently provided the linearity test, it is sufficient to conduct only circuit tests and quadratic consistency tests.

The first step is the circuit satisfiability test. As in Section 4, V generates randomly two weight vectors. However, the vectors are a little bit different here: he gener-

ates $(w_{1(m+1)}, w_{1(m+2)}, \cdots, w_{1(n-1)})$, all from $\mathbb{F}$. Let w_1'' be $(0^m||(w_{1(m+1)}, w_{1(m+2)}, \cdots, w_{1(n-1)})||0)$. He generates w_2 as $w_2 = (w_0 + \alpha_1 w_1') + \alpha_1 w_1''$, and queries P with w_1'' and w_2. This time, he will receive back $\text{Enc}(PK, A_1)$, $\text{Enc}(PK, a_1)$, $\text{Enc}(PK, B_1)$, $\text{Enc}(PK, b_1)$. Using PK, V computes $\text{Enc}(PK, (s_1 + \alpha_1 c_0))$ from s_1, α_1 and c_0. Using the additive homomorphism of underlying encryption, V can compute $\text{Enc}(PK, (b_1 - ((s_1 + \alpha_1 c_0) + \alpha_1 a_1)))$ from $\text{Enc}(PK, (s_1 + \alpha_1 c_0))$, $\text{Enc}(PK, a_1)$, and $\text{Enc}(PK, b_1)$. $\text{Enc}(PK, (b_1 - ((s_1 + \alpha_1 c_0) + \alpha_1 a_1)))$ is denoted by $\text{Enc}(PK, plain_1)$. Similarly, he gets $\text{Enc}(PK, B_1 - (S_1 + \alpha_1 A_1))$, denoted by $\text{Enc}(PK, plain_2)$. Using the additive homomorphism of underlying encryption, from $\text{Enc}(PK, A_1)$ and from $\text{Enc}(PK, a_1)$, V computes $\text{Enc}(PK, A_1 + a_1)$, denoted by $\text{Enc}(PK, plain_3)$.

The second step is the quadratic consistency test. V randomly generates $\alpha_2, \alpha_3, \alpha_4$ all from $\mathbb{F}$. He randomly generates queries q_2, q_3 and constructs following queries: $q_4 = q_2 \otimes q_3$, $t = r_1||R_1 + \alpha_0(r_0||R_0) + \sum_{i=2}^{3} \alpha_i(q_i||0^{n^2}) + \alpha_4(0^n||q_4)$. V queries P with (q_2, q_3, q_4, t) and gets back $\text{Enc}(PK, a_2)$, $\text{Enc}(PK, a_3)$, $\text{Enc}(PK, a_4)$, and $\text{Enc}(PK, b_2)$ where $a_2 = \langle q_2, z \rangle$, $a_3 = \langle q_3, z \rangle$, $a_4 = \langle q_4, z \otimes z \rangle$, $b_2 = \langle t, z||z \otimes z \rangle$. We denote $\text{Enc}(PK, (b_2 - ((s_1 + S_1 + \alpha_0(s_0 + S_0)) + \sum_{i=2}^{4} \alpha_i a_i)))$ by $\text{Enc}(PK, plain_4)$, which can be computed from $\text{Enc}(PK, (s_1 + S_1 + \alpha_0(s_0 + S_0)))$, $\text{Enc}(PK, a_i)$'s $(i = 2, 3, 4)$ and $\text{Enc}(PK, b_2)$ using the homomorphism of the underlying cryptosystem. Then, V randomly generates four random numbers from $\mathbb{F}$: $\theta_1, \cdots, \theta_4$, and constructs $\text{Enc}(PK, \sum_{i=1}^{4} plain_i \cdot \theta_i)$ from $\text{Enc}(PK, plain_i)$'s using the homomorphism. V sends $\text{Enc}(PK, \sum_{i=1}^{4} plain_i \cdot \theta_i)$ to C with $\text{Enc}(PK, a_4)$, $\text{Enc}(PK, a_3)$, and $\text{Enc}(PK, a_2)$ to C.

5.4 Making A Decision

C first decrypts $\text{Enc}(PK, \sum_{i=1}^{4} plain_i \cdot \theta_i)$ and determines whether the plaintext is 0. If not, C will reject. Otherwise C decrypts $\text{Enc}(PK, a_2)$, $\text{Enc}(PK, a_3)$ and $\text{Enc}(PK, a_2)$. Then, C determines whether $a_2 a_3 = a_4$. If so, he will accept that y is the correct solution of his computational task.

5.5 Security Analysis

THEOREM 2. *(Correctness) If the arithmetic circuit x is satisfiable, then a prover P with the knowledge of the correct input y is able to make the client C accept y by performing our protocol.*

PROOF. It is easy for a prover P who has found out the correct result y of the computation task to find out the correct assignment $z = (z_1, z_2, \cdots, z_n)$ including the correct result y and all the intermediate results of the circuit. That is, z satisfies all the constraints $f_u, u = 1, \cdots, n$. If P responds with correct values as in the protocol, all corresponding test equations (unencrypted version) will hold. Given the encryption used in this section is additive homomorphic, the ciphertexts of all the corresponding linear combinations are ciphertexts of 0. The conclusion follows. $\square$

DEFINITION 3. *We say that a verification protocol for the arithmetic circuit satisfiability problem x wins λ-confidentiality if the following properties are satisfied. In the context of computational complexity, x can be represented as a binary string, and so can the correct assignment z. Let $P_x, P_z : \{0,1\}^* \rightarrow \{0,1\}$ be arbitrarily-defined predicates, extracting one bit of information about binary strings of arbitrary length. or every probabilistic polynomial-time algorithm A,* for every possible transmitted messages $m = (m_1, \cdots, m_k)$ with $k = |m| = poly(\lambda)$, for every positive polynomial $p(\cdot)$, for every P_x, P_z, we have:

$$Pr[A(1^\lambda, m, 1^{|z|}, commt) = P_x(x))] - \frac{1}{2} < \frac{1}{p(\lambda)} \quad (5.1)$$

$$Pr[A(1^\lambda, m, 1^{|z|}, commt) = P_z(z))] - \frac{1}{2} < \frac{1}{p(\lambda)} \quad (5.2)$$

where commt is the commitment information provided by C before verification. (The probability is over z as well as over the internal coin tosses of either algorithms.)

THEOREM 3. (Confidentiality) If the underlying homomorphic encryption in our protocol has the security parameter λ, then our verification protocol for the arithmetic circuit satisfiability problem wins λ-confidentiality.

PROOF. Recall that the commitment is $commt = (\alpha_1, s_1, S_1, c_0, w_0 + \alpha_1 w_1', (r_1 || R_1) + \alpha_0 (r_0 || R_0), \text{Enc}(PK, (s_1 + S_1 + \alpha_0(s_0 + S_0))))$. Given that all transmitted messages $m = (m_1, m_2, \cdots, m_k)$ are encrypted in our protocol, for every probabilistic polynomial-time algorithm A there exists a probabilistic polynomial-time algorithm A^* such that

$$Pr[A(1^\lambda, m, 1^{|z|}, commt) = x_i)]$$
$$< Pr[A^*(1^\lambda, 1^{|z|}, H) = x_i] + \frac{1}{p(\lambda)} \quad (5.3)$$

where $H = (\alpha_1, s_1, S_1, c_0, w_0 + \alpha_1 w_1', (r_1 || R_1) + \alpha_0 (r_0 || R_0))$. This follows directly from an appropriate formulation of semantic security ([27], Def. 5.2.1) of the underlying homomorphic encryption. Now since $(r_0 || R_0)$ is uniformly random, $(r_1 || R_1) + \alpha_0 (r_0 || R_0))$ is random and independent of $(r_1 || R_1)$ by the crypto lemma. Therefore, s_1, S_1 is the response of the prover to a query (on z) which is random and independent of $(\alpha_1, c_0, w_0 + \alpha_1 w_1', (r_1 || R_1) + \alpha_0 (r_0 || R_0))$. This implies that the entire H is independent of x and z, and hence for any algorithm A^*, $Pr[A^*(1^\lambda, 1^{|z|}, H) = x_i] \leq \frac{1}{2} + \frac{1}{p(\lambda)}$ The inequalities in (5.1) and (5.2) follow. $\square$

Theorem 3 implies that for sufficiently large λ, the advantage of an adversary finds out the circuit and the results in the execution of the protocol is negligible.

THEOREM 4. (soundness) The client will accept a wrong answer with probability less than $\leq \frac{4}{|\mathbb{F}|} - \frac{1}{|\mathbb{F}|^2} + (3\delta - 6\delta^2)$ where the tests guarantee the proof is δ-close to linear.

The proof is in Appendix of the full version paper [1].

6. PRACTICAL USE AND COMPLEXITY ANALYSIS

6.1 Amortized query costs

Our proposed schemes can amortize query costs. That is, our designs are able to use the same commitment/decommitment queries and PCP queries across many instances of the same circuit (with different input/output). The same commitment/decommitment queries and PCP queries make sure that it is still infeasible for P to know the secret commit query and provide uncommitted responses. (It is known that if we fix a given instance, the probability of wrongly accepting will not be influenced by other instances [42].)

The amortizing usage is as follows.

1. There is an off-line stage. In this stage, C reads the circuit and constructs the commitment queries and sends to P. This is done only once.

2. P possesses β proofs (linear functions) $\tilde{\pi}_1, \cdots, \tilde{\pi}_\beta$, one for each instance. For commitment construction, P will return β tuples of commitments, each of which is as in the previous section.

3. For each instance, P computes the results.

4. In the verification phase, for the *same* query tuple $q_1, \cdots, q_4, t$ from V, P will response β tuples of answers, each for one instance. For each instance, V verifies results as in the previous section. Totally, V runs β decommitments, β circuit tests, and β quadratic consistency tests, one for each instance.

We give a practical use example here. Suppose C has a large number of computational tasks. All these tasks can be reduced to an instance of the Circuit-SAT problem with the same circuit. Before using the Cloud server to do computing, C will generate the commitment queries: w_0, r_1, R_1, r_0, R_0. This is an off-line stage and it runs only once for all instances. The on-line stage is as in Section 5. First, C gives the computing tasks to P. Secondly, P computes the tasks and gives back the results and the commitments to C. After choosing a verifier V, C outsources the verification to V. V advises C to accept or reject.

6.2 Complexity Analysis

Our design meets the efficiency goal outlined in Section 2.3. As in [25], we are ignoring the time of the offline stage, since the cost of generating the commit/decommit queries can be amortized over many instances. We compare the computational cost and the communication cost of C between our protocol and other related work in Table 2. In this table, *Mult* and *Add* are the cost of multiplication and addition in $\mathbb{F}$. *RNG* is the cost of generating a random number in $\mathbb{F}$. *Oper* is the cost of the additive homomorphic operation. In our design, the computational and communication complexity of C for each instance is $O(m)$, (m is the length of results y) and is not dependent on the circuit size n. This is much more efficient than all current two-party verification schemes. We observe that V is also very efficient. *Even the cost of both C and V combined is less than the verifier's cost in the state-of-the-art argument systems that rely only on standard cryptographic assumptions.*

7. CONCLUSIONS AND FUTURE DIRECTIONS

In Cloud Computing, a client outsources computation to a more powerful server – the prover. To ensure the correctness of the results returned by the prover, the client has to perform a verification stage that is often tedious and expensive. In this work, we introduce the idea of delegation of verification in Cloud Computing. This natural approach relieves the client from performing the verification of the outsourced-computation results by outsourcing it to a third party – the verifier. We propose the first scheme that provides efficient outsourcing of the verification, while at the same time preserving the confidentiality of both the computational task and its result from untrusted verifiers. Given that the computational tasks are not limited to a specific

		Computation	Communication
Our Basic Scheme	$\mathcal{C}$'s cost	0	$m + O(1)$
	$\mathcal{V}$'s cost	$m \cdot Mult + m \cdot Add + \frac{1}{\beta}[n^2 \cdot Mult + (4n) \cdot RNG]$	$\frac{1}{\beta}O(n^2)$
Our Full Solution	$\mathcal{C}$'s cost	$(m+1) \cdot Mult + m \cdot Add + Enc + 3Dec$	$m + O(1)$
	$\mathcal{V}$'s cost	$poly(\lambda) \cdot Oper + O(1) \cdot Mult + O(1) \cdot Add + \frac{1}{\beta}[n^2 \cdot Mult + (4n) \cdot RNG]$	$\frac{1}{\beta}O(n^2)$
Re-computing		$\geq [poly(n) \cdot Mult + poly(n) \cdot Add]$	0
NP-proof		$poly(n) \cdot Mult + poly(n) \cdot Add$	n
Linear PCP (Ishai et al.)		$poly(n) \cdot Mult + poly(n) \cdot Add$	$O(n^2)$
GINGER		$[(m+1)\cdot Mult+m\cdot Add]+\frac{1}{\beta}[poly(n)\cdot Mult+poly(n)\cdot Add+(n^2+2n)\cdot RNG]$	$\frac{1}{\beta}O((n+m)^2)$

computational problem, it appears at a first glance that the fully-homomorphic encryption is necessary for hiding the computational task. However, by means of combining a novel commitment protocol and the linear PCP system with only additive homomorphic encryption, our design enables a honest-but-curious third party to perform the bulk of the verification procedure, without gaining access to information about the original computational task or its result. We are currently investigating delegation of verification with a verifier who does not perform the protocol faithfully – a *curious and lazy verifier.*

8. ACKNOWLEDGMENTS

This work was partially supported by NSF under grants No. CNS-0644238 and CNS-0831470. We appreciate anonymous reviewers for valuable suggestions and comments.

9. REFERENCES

[1] http://www.eng.iastate.edu/~guan/paper/delegation_of_verification.pdf.

[2] S. Arora, C. Lund, R. Motwani, M. Sudan, and M. Szegedy. Proof verification and the hardness of approximation problems. *J. ACM*, 45(3):501–555, May 1998.

[3] S. Arora and S. Safra. Probabilistic checking of proofs; a new characterization of NP. In *Proceedings of the 33rd Annual Symposium on oundations of Computer Science*, SFCS '92, pages 2–13, Washington, DC, USA, 1992. IEEE Computer Society.

[4] M. J. Atallah and K. B. Frikken. Securely outsourcing linear algebra computations. In *Proceedings of the 5th ACM Symposium on Information, Computer and Communications Security*, ASIACCS '10, pages 48–59, New York, NY, USA, 2010. ACM.

[5] L. Babai, L. Fortnow, L. A. Levin, and M. Szegedy. Checking computations in polylogarithmic time. In *Proceedings of the twenty-third annual ACM symposium on Theory of computing*, STOC '91, pages 21–32, New York, NY, USA, 1991. ACM.

[6] L. Babai, L. Fortnow, and C. Lund. Nondeterministic exponential time has two-prover interactive protocols. In *Proceedings of the 31st Annual Symposium on oundations of Computer Science*, SFCS '90, pages 16–25 vol.1, Washington, DC, USA, 1990. IEEE.

[7] M. Ben-Or, S. Goldwasser, J. Kilian, and A. Wigderson. Multi-prover interactive proofs: how to remove intractability assumptions. In *Proceedings of the twentieth annual ACM symposium on Theory of computing*, STOC '88, pages 113–131, New York, NY, USA, 1988. ACM.

[8] E. Ben-Sasson, O. Goldreich, P. Harsha, M. Sudan, and S. Vadhan. Robust PCPs of proximity, shorter PCPs and applications to coding. In *Proceedings of the thirty-sixth annual ACM symposium on Theory of computing*, STOC '04, pages 1–10, New York, NY, USA, 2004. ACM.

[9] E. Ben-Sasson, O. Goldreich, P. Harsha, M. Sudan, and S. Vadhan. Short PCPs verifiable in polylogarithmic time. In *Proceedings of the 20th Annual IEEE Conference on Computational Complexity*, CCC '05, pages 120–134, Washington, DC, USA, 2005. IEEE Computer Society.

[10] E. Ben-Sasson and M. Sudan. Short PCPs with polylog query complexity. *SIAM J. Comput.*, 38(2):551–607, May 2008.

[11] S. Benabbas, R. Gennaro, and Y. Vahlis. Verifiable delegation of computation over large datasets. In *Proceedings of the 31st annual conference on Advances in cryptology*, CRYPTO'11, pages 111–131, Berlin, Heidelberg, 2011. Springer-Verlag.

[12] M. Blum and S. Kannan. Designing programs that check their work. *J. ACM*, 42(1):269–291, Jan. 1995.

[13] D. Boneh and D. M. Freeman. Homomorphic signatures for polynomial functions. In *Proceedings of the 30th Annual international conference on Theory and applications of cryptographic techniques: advances in cryptology*, EUROCRYPT'11, pages 149–168, Berlin, Heidelberg, 2011. Springer-Verlag.

[14] G. Brassard, D. Chaum, and C. Crépeau. Minimum disclosure proofs of knowledge. *J. Comput. Syst. Sci.*, 37(2):156–189, 1988.

[15] R. Canetti, B. Riva, and G. N. Rothblum. Practical delegation of computation using multiple servers. In *Proceedings of the 18th ACM conference on Computer and communications security*, CCS '11, pages 445–454, New York, NY, USA, 2011. ACM.

[16] R. Canetti, B. Riva, and G. N. Rothblum. Two 1-round protocols for delegation of computation. Cryptology ePrint Archive, Report 2011/518, 2011. http://eprint.iacr.org/.

[17] G. Cormode, M. Mitzenmacher, and J. Thaler. Practical verified computation with streaming interactive proofs. In *Proceedings of the 3rd Innovations in Theoretical Computer Science Conference*, ITCS '12, pages 90–112, New York, NY, USA, 2012. ACM.

[18] I. Dinur. The PCP theorem by gap amplification. *J. ACM*, 54(3), June 2007.

[19] I. Dinur, E. Fischer, G. Kindler, R. Raz, and S. Safra.

PCP characterizations of NP: Towards a polynomially small error probability. In *Proc. 31st ACM Symp. on Theory of Computing*, pages 29–40, 1999.

[20] I. Dinur and P. Harsha. Composition of low-error 2-query PCPs using decodable PCPs. In *50th Annual IEEE Symposium on oundations of Computer Science, OCS 2009, October 25-27, 2009, Atlanta, Georgia, USA*. IEEE Computer Society, 2009.

[21] I. Dinur and O. Meir. Derandomized parallel repetition of structured PCPs. In *IEEE Conference on Computational Complexity*. IEEE Computer Society, 2010.

[22] F. Ergun and S. R. Kumar. Approximate checking of polynomials and functional equations. In *Proceedings of the 37th Annual Symposium on oundations of Computer Science*, FOCS '96, pages 592–, Washington, DC, USA, 1996. IEEE Computer Society.

[23] U. Feige and J. Kilian. Making games short (extended abstract). In *STOC*, pages 506–516, 1997.

[24] M. Garofalakis. Proof sketches: Verifiable in-network aggregation. In *IEEE Internation Conference on Data Engineering (ICDE)*, 2007.

[25] R. Gennaro, C. Gentry, and B. Parno. Non-interactive verifiable computing: outsourcing computation to untrusted workers. In *Proceedings of the 30th annual conference on Advances in cryptology*, CRYPTO'10, pages 465–482, Berlin, Heidelberg, 2010. Springer-Verlag.

[26] C. Gentry. Fully homomorphic encryption using ideal lattices. In *STOC*, pages 169–178, 2009.

[27] O. Goldreich. *oundations of Cryptography: Basic Applications*, page 381. Cambridge University Press, 2004.

[28] S. Goldwasser, Y. T. Kalai, and G. N. Rothblum. Delegating computation: interactive proofs for muggles. In *Proceedings of the 40th annual ACM symposium on Theory of computing*, STOC '08, pages 113–122, New York, NY, USA, 2008. ACM.

[29] S. Goldwasser and S. Micali. Probabilistic encryption how to play mental poker keeping secret all partial information. In *Proceedings of the fourteenth annual ACM symposium on Theory of computing*, STOC '82, pages 365–377, New York, NY, USA, 1982. ACM.

[30] S. Goldwasser, S. Micali, and C. Rackoff. The knowledge complexity of interactive proof systems. *SIAM J. Comput.*, 18(1):186–208, Feb. 1989.

[31] P. Golle and I. Mironov. Uncheatable distributed computations. In *Proceedings of the 2001 Conference on Topics in Cryptology: The Cryptographer's Track at RSA*, CT-RSA 2001, pages 425–440, London, UK, UK, 2001. Springer-Verlag.

[32] Y. Ishai, E. Kushilevitz, and R. Ostrovsky. Efficient arguments without short PCPs. In *Proceedings of the Twenty-Second Annual IEEE Conference on Computational Complexity*, CCC '07, pages 278–291, Washington, DC, USA, 2007. IEEE Computer Society.

[33] G. O. Karame, M. Strasser, and S. Čapkun. Secure remote execution of sequential computations. In *Proceedings of the 11th international conference on Information and Communications Security*, ICICS'09, pages 181–197, Berlin, Heidelberg, 2009. Springer-Verlag.

[34] J. Kilian. A note on efficient zero-knowledge proofs and arguments (extended abstract). In *Proceedings of the twenty-fourth annual ACM symposium on Theory of computing*, STOC '92, pages 723–732, New York, NY, USA, 1992. ACM.

[35] J. Kilian. Improved efficient arguments (preliminary version). In *Proceedings of the 15th Annual International Cryptology Conference on Advances in Cryptology*, CRYPTO '95, pages 311–324, London, UK, UK, 1995. Springer-Verlag.

[36] O. Meir. Combinatorial PCPs with efficient verifiers. In *Proceedings of the 2009 50th Annual IEEE Symposium on oundations of Computer Science*, FOCS '09, pages 463–471, Washington, DC, USA, 2009. IEEE Computer Society.

[37] S. Micali. Computationally sound proofs. *SIAM J. Comput.*, 30(4):1253–1298, Oct. 2000.

[38] D. Moshkovitz and R. Raz. Two-query PCP with subconstant error. *J. ACM*, 57(5):29:1–29:29, June 2008.

[39] A. Polishchuk and D. A. Spielman. Nearly-linear size holographic proofs. In *Proceedings of the twenty-sixth annual ACM symposium on Theory of computing*, STOC '94, pages 194–203, New York, NY, USA, 1994. ACM.

[40] B. Przydatek, D. Song, and A. Perrig. Sia: secure information aggregation in sensor networks. In *Proceedings of the 1st international conference on Embedded networked sensor systems*, SenSys '03, pages 255–265, New York, NY, USA, 2003. ACM.

[41] S. Setty, A. J. Blumberg, and M. Walfish. Toward practical and unconditional verification of remote computations. In *Proceedings of the 13th USENIX conference on ot topics in operating systems*, HotOS'13, pages 29–29, Berkeley, CA, USA, 2011. USENIX Association.

[42] S. Setty, R. McPherson, A. J. Blumberg, and M. Walfish. Making argument systems for outsourced computation practical (sometimes). In *NDSS*, 2012.

[43] S. Setty, V. Vu, N. Panpalia, B. Braun, A. J. Blumberg, and M. Walfish. Taking proof-based verified computation a few steps closer to practicality. In *USENIX Security*, 2012.

[44] R. Sion. Query execution assurance for outsourced databases. In *Proceedings of the 31st international conference on Very large data bases*, VLDB '05, pages 601–612. VLDB Endowment, 2005.

[45] B. Thompson, S. Haber, W. G. Horne, T. Sander, and D. Yao. Privacy-preserving computation and verification of aggregate queries on outsourced databases. In *Proceedings of the 9th International Symposium on Privacy Enhancing Technologies*, pages 185–201, Berlin, Heidelberg, 2009. Springer-Verlag.

[46] C. Wang, K. Ren, and J. Wang. Secure and practical outsourcing of linear programming in cloud computing. In *IN OCOM*, pages 820–828. IEEE, 2011.

[47] C. Wang, K. Ren, J. Wang, K. Mahendra, and R. Urs. Harnessing the cloud for securely solving large-scale systems of linear equations. In *ICDCS*, pages 549–558. IEEE, 2011.

Brief Announcement: A Shorter and Stronger Proof of an $\Omega(D\log(n/D))$ Lower Bound for Broadcast in Radio Networks

Calvin Newport[*]
Georgetown University, Washington DC
cnewport@cs.georgetown.edu

ABSTRACT

A seminal 1998 paper by Kushilevitz and Mansour [10] proved that for any randomized radio network broadcast algorithm, there exists a network in which the algorithm requires an expected time of $\Omega(D\log(n/D))$ rounds, for network size n and diameter D. In this study, we apply a new technique to generate a shorter and stronger version of this proof. In more detail, our new version fits in two pages, and it strictly strengthens the existing result by now allowing for active collision detection and an unlimited number of communication channels—assumptions which break the proof argument of [10].

Categories and Subject Descriptors

C.2.1 [**Network Architecture and Design**]: Wireless Communication

Keywords

Broadcast; Algorithms; Wireless; Theory

1. INTRODUCTION

Broadcast in radio networks has been studied from an algorithmic perspective for over 25 years (e.g., since [3]). Work on randomized distributed solutions to this problem build on three seminal papers written between 1987 and 1998: (1) the $O(D\log n + \log^2 n)$ randomized broadcast algorithm of Bar-Yehuda et al. [2], for network size n and network diameter D (a result which was later optimized slightly to $O(D\log(n/D) + \log^2 n)$ [9, 4]); (2) the $\Omega(\log^2 n)$ lower bound of Alon et al. [1], which proves the Bar-Yehuda bound tight for small D; and the (3) $\Omega(D\log(n/D))$ lower bound of Kushilevitz and Mansour [10], which proves (optimized) Bar-Yehuda optimal for larger D. Of these three important bounds, the proof argument by Kushilevitz and

Mansour is the longest and arguably the most complicated (which perhaps explains the long gap between this bound and the $\Omega(\log^2 n)$ bound of [1] that preceded it).

In this (purposefully) brief paper, we demonstrate a surprising reality: the core technical argument of Alon et al. [1] can be used to prove a strengthened and much simplified version of the Kushilevitz and Mansour bound. (That is, the authors of [1] had, probably without knowing it, all the pieces necessary to prove the *full* Bar-Yehuda result optimal.) To support this claim, we leverage a core result of [1] to prove $\Omega(D\log(n/D))$ rounds are necessary to solve distributed broadcast. Our proof, which uses a different approach than [10], requires *only two pages* (including discussion). Furthermore, the result is *strictly* stronger than the original, as it now holds even if we assume active collision detection (i.e., active nodes can use collision detection) and provide the nodes access to an unlimited number of orthogonal communication channels. Both of these additional assumptions break the proof argument in [10]. In fact, before this paper, it was an open question whether $D\log(n/D)$ rounds are needed for broadcast in the presence of collision detection or multiple channels: both these assumptions, for example, have been shown to speed up leader election in radio networks [7, 5], so it stands to reason they would do the same for multihop broadcast.[1] We prove here—perhaps surprisingly—they do not.

Related Work.

We are not the first to simplify the complex bound of Kushilevitz and Mansour. This effort was previously undertaken by Liu and Prabhakaran [11], who simplified the result of [10] by first bounding a key deterministic behavior, then translating the result to the randomized setting using Yao's minimax principle. Though this approach differs from ours in its specifics, it shares the same general attack: finding a way to bound the progress of the message through a layered network without having to argue directly about the behavior of the randomized algorithm (the main source of complexity in the original proof). Whereas Liu and Prabhakaran leverage a connection to determinism in this effort, we instead work by reducing randomized broadcast to an easily bounded combinatorial game. We also note that their solution assumes a graph structure that does not satisfy ge-

---

[*]The author was supported in part by a Ford Motor Company University Research Program grant.

---

[1]In fairness, the leader election algorithms of [7, 5] assume all nodes start the execution active, whereas the broadcast problem requires nodes to remain inactive before receiving the message, so these strategies do not directly translate to the broadcast setting.

ographic constraints such as the unit disk graph property, while our bound, as in the original bound of Kushilevitz and Mansour, still holds under such restrictions.

Model.

We model a multihop radio network as an undirected connected graph $G = (V, E)$, where the $n = |V|$ nodes in V correspond to the wireless devices, the edges in E indicate which devices are within communication range, and we use D to describe the graph diameter. An *algorithm* consists of n randomized processes. An execution begins with an adversary assigning the processes to nodes in V. It then proceeds in synchronous rounds. In each round, each node decides whether to transmit or receive, based on its corresponding process definition. A node u receives a message m in a given round r, if and only if : (a) u decides to receive in r; and (b) exactly one neighbor of u transmits in r and it transmits m. In the standard version of this model, a node cannot distinguish between silence and collision. Below, we define a type of *collision detection* for which our lower bound still holds.

We study the *broadcast* problem, which requires a designated *source* node to propagate a message to every node in the network. In this problem, a node is *inactive* until it first receives the broadcast message; at which point it becomes *active* and can participate in the algorithm. We say a graph satisfies the *unit disk graph* property if there is a way to assign nodes locations in a 2-dimensional cartesian plane such that $E = \{(u, v) \mid d(u, v) \leq 1\}$, for distance metric d. We say nodes have *active collision detection* if they can distinguish between silence and collisions once they become active (i.e., after they have received their first message). We say nodes have *access to multiple channels* to describe a generalization of the model where each node can choose a channel from a set of multiple orthogonal communication channels in each round, such that the message receive rules apply to each channel individually (e.g., u receives a message on channel i if and only if u chooses to receive on i and exactly one neighbor of u broadcasts on i). *Inactive* nodes can receive on some predetermined default channel.

2. LOWER BOUND

Alon et al. [1] proved the existence of a bipartite radio network (V_1, V_2) of size N, with $|V_1| = n$ and $|V_2| \approx n^c$, for some constant $c > 1$, where delivering a message from V_1 to every node in V_2 requires $\Omega(\log^2 n) = \Omega(\log^2 N)$ rounds. Their proof argument divided the nodes in V_2 into $\Theta(\log n)$ different *groups*, each corresponding to a different number of neighbors in V_1. Intuitively, each set of broadcasts $B \subset V_1$ can only help deliver messages to nodes in a small number of these groups. This observation is the starting point for their eventual argument that $\Omega(\log^2 N)$ rounds are necessary to get a message to every node in V_2. For our purposes, however, we do not need to follow this proof to its conclusion. We are instead content to make use of the following intermediate result (recently isolated and proved in [8]), which follows in a straightforward manner from the proof in [1]:

LEMMA 2.1 (ADAPTED FROM [8, 1]). *Fix any $n > 0$. There exists a constant $\alpha > 0$ and bipartite radio network $H = (V_1, V_2)$, with $|V_1| = n$ and $|V_2| > n$, such that in each round, regardless of which nodes in V_1 transmit, at most an $\alpha/\log n$ fraction of nodes in V_2 receive a packet.*

The above lemma provides the core technical result upon which we will now build our lower bound. At a high-level, our strategy will proceed as follows: (1) we will use Lemma 2.1 to bound an abstract game called *set isolation* (which we previously introduced in [6] to derive a shorter and stronger version of the $\Omega(\log^2 n)$ lower bound on the single-hop *wake-up* problem); (2) we will reduce set isolation to distributed broadcast, applying our bound from the preceding step to achieve a bound for distributed broadcast. The set isolation game, in other words, is the technical glue that connects the result of Alon et al. to the result of Kushilevitz and Mansour.

The Set Isolation Game.

The *k-set isolation game*, defined for some $k > 1$, has a *player* face off against an adversarial *referee*. At the beginning of the game, the referee secretly selects a *target set* $T \subseteq \{1, ..., k\}$. In each round, the player generates a *proposal* $P \subseteq \{1, ..., k\}$. If $|P \cap T| = 1$, then the player wins the game. Otherwise, the player moves on to the next round learning no information other than the fact that its proposal failed. We leverage Lemma 2.1 to prove a lower bound on the expected time to win this game:

LEMMA 2.2. *Fix some $k > 1$. There exists a referee strategy for the k-set isolation game, such that for every player strategy, the expected time to win the game is $\Omega(\log k)$ rounds.*

PROOF. We begin by discussing broadcast. Using $n = k$, fix the constant α and bipartite graph $H = (V_1, V_2)$ provided by Lemma 2.1. A consequence of Lemma 2.1 is that $\Omega(\log n)$ rounds of broadcasting in V_1 are needed before half or more of the nodes in V_2 have received the message. This follows because at most $(|V_2|\alpha)/\log n$ nodes in V_2 receive the message in each round, regardless of how we choose broadcasters (by Lemma 2.1). It takes, therefore, a minimum of $\beta = \lfloor \log n/(2\alpha) \rfloor$ rounds before at least half the nodes in V_2 can receive the message.

Now we connect this observation to set isolation. By construction, $k = |V_1|$. For use in the remainder of the proof, assign each node in V_1 a unique label from $\{1, ..., k\}$. When playing the k-set isolation game, we can interpret each proposal P from the player as the nodes $P \subseteq V_1$ broadcasting in H. Consider the referee strategy that chooses a node from $u \in V_2$ with uniform randomness, and then sets $T = N_H(u)$, where N_H is the neighbor function on H. It follows that the player wins the game during the first round when u receives a message in the corresponding broadcast simulation on H. By our above argument, the player's simulation will have delivered the message to less than half the nodes in V_2 by the end of round $\beta - 1$. Because the referee chooses u at random (without revealing this choice to the player), the probability that the player has won the game in $\beta - 1 = O(\log n)$ rounds is less than $1/2$. Therefore, regardless of the player strategy, this specific referee strategy yields an expected time of $\Omega(\log n)$ rounds to win the isolation game. □

Reducing Set Isolation to Distributed Broadcast.

We have used a lower bound regarding the existence of slow broadcast graphs to generate a lower bound for our abstract set isolation game. We will now use our set isolation game bound to generate a lower bound for the expected time for distributed broadcast. The following theorem statement is strictly stronger than the statement from [10]:

THEOREM 2.3. *For every broadcast algorithm $\mathcal{A}$, number of processors $n > 1$, and diameter $D > 0$: there exists a network in which the expected time to complete broadcast is $\Omega(D \log(n/D))$ rounds. This holds even if we restrict ourselves to network topologies that satisfy the unit disk graph property, and assume unique ids, active collision detection, and any number of available communication channels.*

PROOF. We proceed by reduction from a variant of set isolation. In more detail, let (k, k')-*multi-set isolation*, for $1 \leq k' \leq k$, be a variation of set isolation in which we run k' consecutive instances of $(\lfloor k/k' \rfloor)$-set isolation, requiring the player to win instance $i \in \{1, ..., k' - 1\}$ before proceeding to instance $i + 1$. Two technical points that aid the below argument: assume the referee selects all k' targets at the beginning of the game, and that the referee reveals the target for instance i in the round when the player wins that instance. For a given execution of a player and referee strategy for (k, k')-multi-set isolation, let X_i, for $i \in \{1, ..., k'\}$, be the time required to win instance i of the game, and let $Y = X_1 + X_2 + ... + X_{k'}$ be the time required to win the full multi-set game. By linearity of expectation and our result from Lemma 2.2, we note there is a referee strategy that allows us to bound $\mathbb{E}[Y]$ as follows: $\mathbb{E}[Y] = \mathbb{E}\left[\sum_i^{k'} X_i\right] = \sum_i^{k'} \mathbb{E}[X_i] = \Omega(k' \log(k/k'))$.

Assume that $\mathcal{A}$ solves broadcast in $f(n, D)$ rounds, in expectation, in networks of size n and diameter D. We now devise a (n, D)-multi-set isolation player strategy that simulates $\mathcal{A}$ to win the game in expected time $f(n, D)$ as well. In more detail, the player simulates $\mathcal{A}$ on a network consisting of $D + 1$ layers, $L_1, L_2, ..., L_D, L_{D+1}$, where the first D layers each include $\lfloor n/D \rfloor$ nodes, and the last layer includes at least 1 node (if D divides n evenly, then we can add an extra node to the system to populate L_{D+1}, without affecting the asymptotic bounds below; otherwise we add the leftover nodes from the smaller layers). For the sake of construction, for each L_i, assign unique ids from $\{1, ..., k\}$ to the nodes in L_i. Let T_i be the target chosen by the referee for instance i. In our construction, we connect L_i and L_{i+1} by including an edge from every node in L_i corresponding to a value in T_i to every node in L_{i+1}. Notice, the player simulating this network does not know these T_i values, but we will now show this does not matter. Finally, the nodes within each layer are connected as a clique. (Notice that this graph clearly satisfies the unit disk graph property.)

The simulation begins with the player choosing some node in L_1 as the source. In each round r of the simulation, let $\hat{i}$ be the largest value of i such that the nodes in L_i are active (i.e., have the message). Let $B_{\hat{i}}^r$ be the nodes in $L_{\hat{i}}$ that broadcast in r, if any. If we are assuming multiple channels, let $B_{\hat{i}}^r$ be the nodes in $L_{\hat{i}}$ that broadcast on the default channel where inactive nodes listen. The player uses $B_{\hat{i}}^r$ as its proposal in this round of the multi-set isolation game. The key insight of this reduction is that the player only needs to simulate communication between $L_{\hat{i}}$ and $L_{\hat{i}+1}$ if exactly one node connecting $L_{\hat{i}}$ to $L_{\hat{i}+1}$ is in $B_{\hat{i}}^r$. When this occurs, the player will learn of this fact, because its corresponding guess in the set isolation game will win this instance of the game (and once it wins instance i for the first time, it learns T_i, so it can, moving forward, successfully simulate all future communication between these two layers). Collision detection and multiple channels break the original proof of [10] because their argument requires that nodes in the same layer receive silence in all rounds before they advance the mes-

sage. If the active nodes in a layer had collision detection, for example, they could quickly achieve some communication using collisions, at which point the argument of [10] fails. Our argument can tolerate such intra-layer communication as it focuses only on the externally observable behavior of the layer: i.e., which nodes broadcast and whether or not they help advance the message.

We conclude by noting that the player using this strategy will win the multi-set isolation game when the message arrives at L_{D+1}. By assumption, this occurs in expected time of $f(n, D)$ rounds. By our above bound on $\mathbb{E}[Y]$, it must follow: $f(n, D) = \Omega(D \log(n/D))$, as needed. $\square$

3. ACKNOWLEDGEMENTS

The author thanks Mohsen Ghaffari for his helpful discussions regarding the arguments of Alon et al. [1].

4. REFERENCES

[1] N. Alon, A. Bar-Noy, N. Linial, and D. Peleg. A Lower Bound for Radio Broadcast. *Journal of Computer and System Sciences*, 43(2):290–298, 1991.

[2] R. Bar-Yehuda, O. Goldreigch, and A. Itai. On the Time-Complexity of Broadcast in Multi-Hop Radio Networks: An Exponential Gap between Determinism and Randomization. In *Proceedings of the ACM Conference on Distributed Computing*, 1987.

[3] I. Chlamtac and S. Kutten. On Broadcasting in Radio Networks–Problem Analysis and Protocol Design. *IEEE Transactions on Communications*, 33(12):1240–1246, 1985.

[4] A. Czumaj and W. Rytter. Broadcasting algorithms in radio networks with unknown topology. *Journal of Algorithms*, 60:115–143, 2006.

[5] S. Daum, S. Gilbert, F. Kuhn, and C. Newport. Leader Election in Shared Spectrum Radio Networks. In *Proceedings of the ACM Conference on Distributed Computing*. ACM, 2012.

[6] S. Daum, F. Kuhn, and C. Newport. Efficient Symmetry Breaking in Multi-Channel Radio Networks. In *Proceedings of the International Conference on Distributed Computing*, 2012.

[7] M. Ghaffari and B. Haeupler. Near Optimal Leader Election in Multi-Hop Radio Networks. 2013.

[8] M. Ghaffari, B. Haeupler, and M. Khabbazian. A Bound on the Throughput of Radio Networks. *Pre-print*, February 2013. ArXiv preprint arXiv:1302.0264.

[9] D. Kowalski and A. Pelc. Broadcasting in Undirected Ad Hoc Radio Networks. *Distributed Computing*, 18(1):43–57, 2005.

[10] E. Kushilevitz and Y. Mansour. An $\Omega(D\backslash\log(N/D))$ Lower Bound for Broadcast in Radio Networks. *SIAM Journal on Computing*, 27(3):702–712, 1998.

[11] D. Liu and M. Prabhakaran. On Randomized Broadcasting and Gossiping in Radio Networks. In *Proceedings the International Computing and Combinatorics Conference*, 2002.

Brief Announcement: A Local Approximation Algorithm for MDS Problem in Anonymous Planar Networks

Wojciech Wawrzyniak[*]
Faculty of Mathematics and Computer Science
Adam Mickiewicz University
Poznań, Poland
wwawrzy@amu.edu.pl

ABSTRACT

In research on distributed local algorithms it is commonly assumed that each vertex has a unique identifier in the entire graph. However, it turns out that in the case of certain classes of graphs (for example not lift-closed bounded degree graphs) identifiers are unnecessary and only a port ordering is needed [4]. One of the open issues was whether identifiers are essential in planar graphs. In this paper, we partially answer this question and we propose an algorithm which returns constant approximation of the MDS problem in the $\mathcal{CONGEST}$ model. The algorithm does not use any additional information about the structure of the graph and the nodes do not have unique identifiers. We hope that this paper will be helpful as a hint for further comparisons of the unique identifier model and the model with only a port numbering in other classes of graphs.

Categories and Subject Descriptors

F.2.2 [**Analysis of Algorithms and Problem Complexity**]: Nonnumerical Algorithms and Problems—*computations on discrete structures*; G.2.2 [**Discrete Mathematics**]: Graph Theory—*graph algorithms*; G.2.2 [**Discrete Mathematics**]: Graph Theory—*network problems*

Keywords

Local algorithm, Dominating set, Planar graph

1. INTRODUCTION AND MODEL

A distributed algorithm is called a *local algorithm* if it completes in a constant number of synchronised communication rounds. In recent years, there has been a growing interest in designing distributed local algorithms. It might come out of the easiness of applying these algorithms in reality. They run very fast (in constant time) and are tolerant to the network structure changes and node failures.

[*]The research supported by grant N N206 565740.

PODC'13, July 22–24, 2013, Montréal, Québec, Canada.
ACM 978-1-4503-2065-8/13/07.

It turns out the running time of these algorithms is completely decoupled from the size of the network and each node takes its decision based only on the knowledge about its k-neighbourhoods. This fact is very important for the scalability of an algorithm in large networks. If the structure of the network changes (i.e. a vertex is removed), then an algorithm must be re-called to repair a solution only for a small surrounding of the removed vertex. It is a significantly faster solution than in case of standard algorithms requirements, which require re-execution of the algorithm on the entire network.

In this paper we work in a synchronous communication model and as a representation of the network we use a planar graph $G = (V, E)$. Edges in the graph will correspond to communication links and vertices will correspond to processors. Moreover, we consider algorithm, that does not need any additional information about the structure of the graph and does not have unique identifiers on vertices.

In order to facilitate the reader to understand this paper, we use the same notations as in [7]. For vertices $A \subseteq V$ we define the set of inclusive neighbourhood of A as $N_A^+ := \{v : v \in A \vee \exists_{e=uv \in E} u \in A\}$. We also denote the neighbors of A not in A as $N_A := N_A^+ \setminus A$. To simplify the notation in cases where $A = \{a\}$ we may omit the braces, e.g. N_a instead of $N_{\{a\}}$.

2. RELATED WORK

Recently, several deterministic distributed local algorithms have been proposed. They return solutions that are good approximations of various problems (e.g. minimum edge cover, minimal dominating set[7], semi-matching[1]), in constant time in different classes of graphs (e.g. bounded degree graphs, planar graphs). However, these algorithms very often assume that vertices have unique identifiers. This assumption could be very important if we consider a more "real" model, in which in a single communication round, each vertex can send a message which contains at most $O(\log n)$ bits, where $n = |V(G)|$ is the number of vertices in the graph. This limitation makes it impossible to e.g. detect small cycles in the network, gather knowledge of all vertices in distance at most two (2-hop neighbourhood). Lately, Göös et al. in a paper [4] have shown that for lift-closed bounded degree graphs, the model with unique identifiers (known as $\mathcal{LOCAL}$ [8]) and the model with port numbering only(known as PO model[4]), are practically equivalent. However, the techniques used in their work do not allow us to consider the equivalence of these models for Minimum Dominating Set(MDS) problem in planar graphs.

There are now more than one hundred works referring, more or less closely, to the topic of local algorithms. Thus, it is not possible to briefly describe all of these publications. The best way to study this topic is to read excellent survey[9] written by Suomela. That article describes all the important results obtained so far by all the researchers.

Kuhn and Wattenhofer in [6], presented the first local but randomised algorithm for bounded degree graphs. Their algorithm does not require long messages. Then in [5] the algorithm has been improved by Kuhn et al. The first deterministic local algorithm for MDS problem for planar graphs was proposed by Lenzen et al. in [7], but their algorithm requires long messages and unique IDs on vertices.

There is also a lower bound for possible approximation factor of an algorithm. In [3] it has been shown that there is no algorithm which in a constant number of communication rounds returns an $(5-\epsilon)$ approximation of the MDS in planar graphs.

3. ALGORITHM

Execution of the algorithm is similar to the algorithm from article [7]. In the first phase, the algorithm perform some kind of preprocessing (function *Hop2Dominate* is called). Afterwards, each not yet dominated vertex $v \in V \setminus N_{D_1}^+$ add a vertex $w(v) \in (N_v \cap N_{D_1})$ to D_2. A set $D := D_1 \cup D_2$ is a resulting dominating set.

Algorithm 1 PortNumberingMds

1: $D_1' := Hop2Dominate(G, \emptyset)$
2: $D_1'' := Hop2Dominate(G, D_1')$, $D_1 := D_1' \cup D_1''$
3: **for** $v \in V$ in parallel **do**
4: $\quad \delta_v^{V \setminus N_{D_1}^+} := |N_v^+ \setminus N_{D_1}^+|$
5: $\quad$ **if** $v \notin N_{D_1}^+$ **then**
6: $\qquad W_v = \arg\max_{w \in (N_v^+ \cap N_{D_1})} \delta_w^{V \setminus N_{D_1}^+}$
7: $\qquad$ choose any $w(v) \in W_v$
8: $D_2 := \{w(v) : v \notin N_{D_1}^+\}$
9: **return** $D := D_1 \cup D_2$

Notice that we cannot easily remove first phase, because then $|D_2|$ can be much greater than the size of an optimal set M (see Figure 4). We can think about *Hop2Dominate* as a function, which add to the set D_1 vertices with quite high degree in the graph G (e.g. in Figure 4 it firstly dominates all black vertices). Note that *Hop2Dominate* is called twice because of the proof requirements. In the second phase each not yet dominated vertex add to D_2 one already dominated vertex with the largest residual degree (i.e. node that dominates the most not dominated yet vertices).

In order to prove that both sets D_1, and D_2 are small, we need divide our plane graph into special disjoint regions in such way that the number of these regions are proportional to the size of the set D, and moreover in each region there is at least one vertex from the set M.

As can be easily seen, the algorithm can be performed in twelve of communication rounds and returns a dominating set due to last round. Therefore, in our analysis we only need to show that the numbers of vertices added to the dominating set D in steps 2, 8 are small enough that our algorithm returns solutions which are a constant approximation of an optimal MDS.

Function 2 Hop2Dominate(G, D')

1: **for** $v \in V$ in parallel **do** $\delta_v^V := |N_v^+ \setminus N_{D'}^+|$
2: **for** $v \in V \setminus N_{D'}^+$ in parallel **do**
3: $\quad W_v = \arg\max_{w \in N_v^+} \delta_w^V$
4: $\quad$ choose any $x(v) \in W_v$
5: $X := \{x(v) : v \in V\}$
6: **for** $v \in V$ in parallel **do**
7: $\quad \delta_v^X := |N_v^+ \cap X|$
8: $\quad$ **if** $v \in X$ **then**
9: $\qquad W_v' = \arg\max_{w \in N_v^+} \delta_w^X$
10: $\qquad$ choose any $d(v) \in W_v'$
11: $D_{new} := \{d(v) : v \in X\}$
12: **return** D_{new}

---

4. BUNCHES

The main technique used in this paper is a partition the graph G into special subgraphs called *bunches*. They will be used to split the graph into disjoint regions in R^2, containing many vertices of the set M. We start by defining what we mean by a term *bunch*, which was first introduced in [2].

DEFINITION 1. *Let $G = (V, E)$ be a planar graph, $S \subseteq V$, $T \subseteq V$ and $W \subseteq V$. A v_i-v_j-path is called* **S-T-W-special** *if it has the form $v_i u v_j$, where $v_i \in S$, $u \in T$ and $v_j \in W$.*

Although our algorithm works in planar graphs, in the analysis we assume that the given graph G is plane. We assume that the reader is familiar with the basic concepts of planar graph. Let P, Q be two special v_i-v_j-paths. In any plane drawing, graph $P \cup Q$ contains exactly one bounded face. (We will assume here that the face is empty if $P = Q$.) Now we set $Reg(P \cup Q) := f$ and $Reg[P \cup Q] := (P \cup Q) \cup f$ where f is the bounded face in the drawing of $P \cup Q$.

DEFINITION 2. *Let $G = (V, E)$ be a plane graph and let $v_i \in S, v_j \in W$, $T \subset V$ where $i \neq j$. A maximal set B of S-T-W-special paths between v_i and v_j is called a* **S-T-W-bunch** *between v_i and v_j if there exist two distinct paths $P, Q \in B$ such that all paths from B are contained in $Reg[P \cup Q]$ and no vertex from $S \cup W$ is contained in $Reg(P \cup Q)$. In addition, the paths P, Q will be called* **the boundary paths** *of B.*

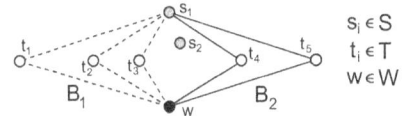

Figure 1: An example of graph G with two S-T-W-bunches. The graph $G \setminus \{s_2\}$ contains only one bunch.

A number of the A-B-C-bunches can be upper bounded by the size of $|A|, |B|, |C|$. The statement was formulated in the following lemma below.

LEMMA 1. *Let $G = (V, E)$ be a planar graph and $S, T, W \subseteq V$ be subsets of vertices such that the sets are pairwise disjoint and each vertex from B is adjacent to at least one vertex from each sets S and W. Then graph G contains at most $4(|S| + |W|) + \omega(V)$ S-T-W-bunches, where $\omega(V)$ denote the number of connected components in graph G.*

5. SKETCH OF PROOF

Our aim is to upper bound the sets D_1 and D_2. For this purpose we divide $D_1 \setminus M$ (vertices added in step 2) to the following disjoint sets $D_1^M := \{v \in D_1 : u \in M \wedge d(u) = v\}$, $D_1^S := \{v \in D_1 : u \notin M \wedge d(u) = v \wedge |N(v) \cap X| \leq q\}$, $D_1^L := D_1 \setminus (D_1^M \cup D_1^S)$. We also define $X_M := \{v \in (V \setminus N_{D_1}^+) : d(v) \in D_1^M\}$ and sets X_S, X_L analogously.

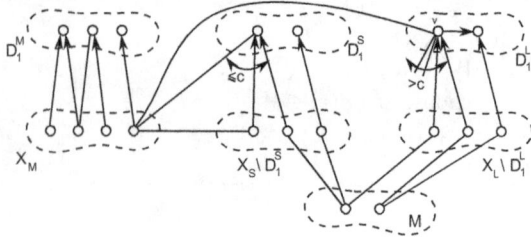

Figure 2: An example of a partition a graph G. If $d(v) = u$ then edge $e = vu$ is marked by an arrowhead.

Estimations of D_1^M and D_1^S are almost obvious. However, estimation of D_1^L requires a lot of more effort (e.g. using a bunch technique). Since the set D_1^L has many neighbors, the graph G contains many D_1^L-$(X^L \setminus D_1^L)$-M-bunches with at least five special paths (see Figure 3). Using a Lemma 1 and additional statements it can be shown that inside a bunch there are many vertices from M. Hence $|D_1^L| = O(|M|)$.

Using a similar technique with other kind of bunches it can be shown that also $|D_2| = O(|M|)$.

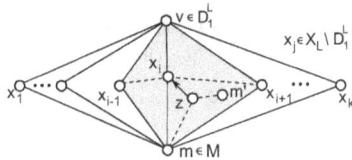

Figure 3: An example of a bunch in a graph G.

The reasoning above allow us to state the main theorem of the article.

THEOREM 1. *Let $G = (V, E)$ be a planar graph and D be a set returned by the algorithm PortNumberingMds and M be an optimal solution of the Minimum Dominating Set for a given graph G. Then $|D| \leq 636|M|$.*

6. CONCLUSION

In this paper we presented a constant approximation algorithm for the MDS problem in planar graphs. The algorithm is deterministic and strictly local. So nodes do not need any additional information about the structure of the graph and don't have unique identifiers. In our algorithm we use only short messages with at most $O(\log n)$ bits ($\mathcal{CONGEST}$ model). Recently in paper "Lower Bounds for Local Approximation"[4] Mika Göös et al. have shown that for lift-closed bounded degree graphs models PO and ID are practically equivalent. In this paper we show that it is true for planar graphs and MDS problem. We hope that this work will be very helpful as a hint for further comparisons of these models in other classes of graphs.

Moreover the approximation factor is 636, so there is a large gap to the known lower bound $(5 - \epsilon)$ from paper [3]

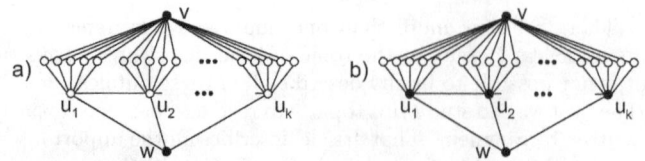

Figure 4: An example of possible results for a) an optimal algorithm b) algorithm in which each vertex chooses one the neighbor of the largest degree. The vertices from the resulting DS are marked(black).

and approximation factor 130 from paper [7]. An interesting issue might be a reduction of this gap in a PO or ID model.

7. ACKNOWLEDGEMENTS

We would like to thank anonymous reviewers and Edyta Szymańska for providing us with constructive comments and suggestions.

8. REFERENCES

[1] A. Czygrinow, M. Hanćkowiak, E. Szymańska, and W. Wawrzyniak. Distributed 2-approximation algorithm for the semi-matching problem. In *Proceedings of the 26th international conference on Distributed Computing*, DISC'12, pages 210–222, Berlin, Heidelberg, 2012. Springer-Verlag.

[2] A. Czygrinow, M. Hanćkowiak, and W. Wawrzyniak. Distributed packing in planar graphs. In *Proceedings of the twentieth annual symposium on Parallelism in algorithms and architectures*, SPAA '08, pages 55–61, New York, NY, USA, 2008. ACM.

[3] A. Czygrinow, M. Hanćkowiak, and W. Wawrzyniak. Fast distributed approximations in planar graphs. In *Proceedings of the 22nd international symposium on Distributed Computing*, DISC '08, pages 78–92, Berlin, Heidelberg, 2008. Springer-Verlag.

[4] M. Göös, J. Hirvonen, and J. Suomela. Lower bounds for local approximation. In *Proceedings of the 2012 ACM Symposium on Principles of Distributed Computing*, PODC '12, pages 175–184, New York, NY, USA, 2012. ACM.

[5] F. Kuhn, T. Moscibroda, and R. Wattenhofer. The price of being near-sighted. In *Proceedings of the seventeenth annual ACM-SIAM symposium on Discrete algorithm*, SODA '06, pages 980–989, New York, NY, USA, 2006. ACM.

[6] F. Kuhn and R. Wattenhofer. Constant-time distributed dominating set approximation. In *Proceedings of the twenty-second annual symposium on Principles of distributed computing*, PODC '03, pages 25–32, New York, NY, USA, 2003. ACM.

[7] C. Lenzen, Y.-A. Pignolet, and R. Wattenhofer. Distributed minimum dominating set approximations in restricted families of graphs. *Distributed Computing*, 26(2):119–137, 2013.

[8] N. Linial. Locality in distributed graph algorithms. *SIAM J. Comput.*, 21(1):193–201, Feb. 1992.

[9] J. Suomela. Survey of local algorithms. *ACM Comput. Surv.*, 45(2):24:1–24:40, Mar. 2013.

Author Index

www.ingramcontent.com/pod-product-compliance
Lightning Source LLC
Chambersburg PA
CBHW080651220326
41598CB00033B/5167

* 9 7 8 1 4 5 0 3 2 0 6 5 8 *